THE
ABC-CLIO
COMPANION TO

Transportation in America

This 1870 cartoon of Cornelius Vanderbilt and Jim Fisk portrays the great race for the west.

THE
ABC-CLIO
COMPANION TO

Transportation in America

William L. Richter

ABC-CLIO

All photographs were provided by the Library of Congress, except the following: NASA, pp. 51, 59; National Archives, pp. 98, 162, 199, 241, 442; AP/Wide World, pp. 396, 477, 523.

Library of Congress Cataloging-in-Publication Data

Richter, William L. (William Lee), 1942–
    The ABC-CLIO companion to transportation in America by William L. Richter.
        p.   cm. — (ABC-CLIO companions to key issues in American history and life)
    Includes bibliographical references and index.
    1. Transportation —United States—History.
I. Title. II. Series.
HE203.R54   1995   388'.0973—dc20   95-13170

ISBN 0-87436-789-1 (alk. paper)

02 01 00 99 98 97 96 95   10 9 8 7 6 5 4 3 2 1 (hc)

ABC-CLIO, Inc.
130 Cremona Drive, P.O. Box 1911
Santa Barbara, California 93116-1911

This book is printed on acid-free paper ∞.
Manufactured in the United States of America

*To Lynne
for everything over the long haul*

ABC-CLIO Companions to Key Issues in American History and Life

The ABC-CLIO Companion to the American Labor Movement
Paul F. Taylor

The ABC-CLIO Companion to the American Peace Movement in the 20th Century
Christine A. Lunardini

The ABC-CLIO Companion to the Civil Rights Movement
Mark Grossman

The ABC-CLIO Companion to the Environmental Movement
Mark Grossman

The ABC-CLIO Companion to the Media in America
Daniel W. Hollis

The ABC-CLIO Companion to Transportation in America
William L. Richter

The ABC-CLIO Companion to Women in the Workplace
Dorothy Schneider and Carl J. Schneider

The ABC-CLIO Companion to Women's Progress in America
Elizabeth Frost-Knappman

Forthcoming

The ABC-CLIO Companion to the Native American Rights Movement
Mark Grossman

The ABC-CLIO Companion to Reconstruction
William L. Richter

Contents

Acknowledgments, ix

Introduction, xi

Transportation in America, 3

Chronology, 565

Bibliography, 585

Index, 633

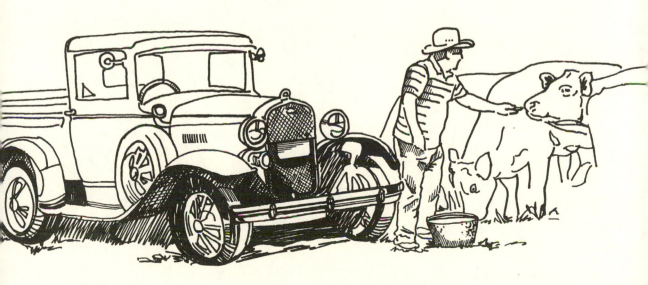

Acknowledgments

In writing this study I received much help from many wonderful people who endured my constant pestering and listened to my endless tales of American transportation history trivia and research problems. The professionals at the libraries at the University of Arizona were ever ready to assist and further my inquiry with cooperation, good humor, and much insight. Others who made suggestions and acted, sometimes unwittingly, as unofficial research assistants include Yvette M. Frutiger, James A. Rybski, and Gerald M. Dzara, good friends and students of history. Todd Hallman at ABC-CLIO suggested the topic, got me started, and kept me on the straight and narrow. Finally, I appreciate the constant, loving support of my wife, Lynne, who encouraged me to enter upon this project in the first place and provided much-needed moral backing when the going got rough. To these people belongs whatever merit this work possesses. The rest is all mine.

Introduction

A MULTIDISCIPLINARY MODEL FOR NATIONAL TRANSPORTATION GROWTH Transportation is the movement of goods, services, and people from place to place. It is a network of exchange. It is the individual components that make up that network. It can be local, national, and worldwide. Transportation is continuous. It takes place in light or dark, rain or shine, heat or cold, day after day, all year long, year after year. It is the lifeline that helps create our so-called standard of living. Its collapse would send any modern society back into the Stone Age. It brings the freedom to travel. Transportation not only liberates, it also makes for social, economic, and political interdependence. It brings nations and the world together in a unity that both solves problems and creates new ones that threaten to drive peoples apart once again.

Transportation, for example, helps the United States gain by sharing the world's economic wealth and creating its own through the General Agreement on Tariffs and Trade (GATT, 1994). But at the same time, the nation loses some of the traditional barriers that have protected its sovereignty and existence for over 200 years. In one context, the result is that people invent the ships, trains, motor vehicles, and planes to exchange products, ideas, and peoples easily; and in another context, they create the impetus for the Strategic Defense Initiative (SDI) or "Star Wars," as it is popularly char-

acterized, to keep the adverse effects (actual or imagined) of those transportation systems at bay. Any way one looks at it, transportation and mobility bring change.[1]

The technology of modern transportation is awesome. The movement of freight, for example, is now down to an exact science. A recent nationally broadcast video followed 30 tons of Toyota automobile engines from their manufacture in Nagoya, Japan, to their placement in automotive chassis at Georgetown, Kentucky. The whole load was packed in containers at the port of origin and never touched by hand the rest of the way. Indeed, nothing is "handled" anymore in the world of freight. It is all containerized and transferred by machines—cranes, intermodal ships, trains, and trucks. Computerization allows the exact minute-to-minute tracking of any particular cargo, be it a simple letter or 30 tons of engines. The Toyota cargo arrived at Georgetown after two weeks of travel by land and sea (air travel is by and large passenger oriented, most freight being too bulky to be flown economically) within 15 minutes of its predicted time. The engines were immediately placed in the ready chassis and no storage was necessary. The concept is called "just in time" inventory and reduces the space and costs needed to manufacture anything, and the whole network is global in scope.[2]

Geographers, economists, and historians who write and theorize about transportation have described the internal accessibility of a select country as the key to its evolution toward modernity. To help in describing this development scholars have envisioned transportation as a continuous process of spatial diffusion—an irregular, sporadic ebb and flow influenced by economic, social, and political forces. Like all social scientists, these investigators have created descriptive generalizations of an ideal-typical sequence of transportation development.

Geographers, for example, see the process of transportation development as one of steps. First, there is a scattering of small settlements along the sea coast. Then some of these ports begin to extend their influence into the hinterland, seeking supplies and markets. Each of the interior centers of trade extends its own influence farther inland. Next, the more vigorous coastal and interior towns initiate a sort of "piracy," creating interconnecting routes through the hinterland hoping to attract or intercept trade going elsewhere, even to neighboring ports. This process continues with the interconnections becoming more and more sophisticated until all of the interior suppliers and markets are tapped. Finally, certain select routes become primary, high-priority trunk lines that connect the bigger centers of trade together.[3]

Like geographers, economists agree with the process concept, tending to emphasize phases of development. First, they describe a traditional society of limited production functions in which the potentialities flowing from modern science and technology are either unavailable or not regularly applied. Such societies devote a large portion of their time and effort to subsistence agriculture. Family and clan are the bases of social organization. People have little expectation that future generations will be more "worldly" than their ancestors. Indeed there is a ceiling to all economic activity, although it is possible to advance moderately within the established norm. This stage is followed by a predevelopment period that is a transitional time in which science and technology are learned, the shock of change is absorbed and conquered, and economic development

becomes a goal of individual, family, town, and nation as a matter of collective pride. Education becomes the vehicle of change as new enterprising people come forward who are willing and able to risk all on a different approach to problem solving. Banks and other institutions able to mobilize capital appear. Manufacturing takes on a modern look, and the scope of commerce and political organization throughout the nation-state increases.

After the predevelopment period, economists envision an economic takeoff stage with savings rising, investment booming, new industries being born, and revolutionary changes in agriculture permitting more time to be devoted to other pursuits. As this growth becomes sustainable, a drive toward economic maturity and modernization occurs, and the economic efforts expand beyond the heavy industries and technologies that gave them birth to machine tools, chemicals, and electrical equipment. The country in question now develops the entrepreneurial and technological skills to produce everything it might choose, regardless of the resources available locally, as import and export become crucial to the national life. Finally, there is the stage of high mass consumption in which the shift is toward durable consumer goods and services. Real income rises to where most can afford more than the basics of life. Jobs are concentrated in offices and skilled factory positions. The extension of technology becomes an overriding objective of the society. The welfare state, or some version of it, appears. Historically, much of this prosperity is connected with the cheap family car and the glorification of consumerism, discretionary income, and leisure activities.[4]

Historians differ from geographers and economists only as to emphasis on individual transportation modes and systems, often referring to specific everyday events, personages, and ideas.[5] The idea of evolving process, however, remains the same. If you will, one can stand at the Cumberland Gap with the premier American historian, Frederick Jackson Turner, and watch the cultural evolution of the frontier—feral animal, Native American, fur-trader, hunter, cattle raiser, farmer, city dweller—and see not only the passage of peoples and a society becoming more removed from its origins overseas and Americanized, but also something Turner did not emphasize: a change in the means of their locomotion.[6]

As Turner implied in his idea of continual Americanization, the transportation process that aids in transforming immigrant into American is also a circular and never-ending pattern: The discovery of a new market or a means of production, such as farmland or minerals for exploitation, leads to an opportunistic increase of population and the creation of goods and services, which in turn cause the need for more transportation. Like Turner, we can stand in the Appalachians in the eighteenth century and in the Rocky Mountains at South Pass 100 years later and see a similar procession, not only of peoples and cultures, but of innovative new styles of transport.

Theoretically, we can repeat the process again in 1980 at Dallas–Fort Worth International Airport and perhaps a new next century at some yet-to-be-built space port. Animal power gives way to steam, steam to gasoline, canals to railroads, trains to motor vehicles, ground transport to airplanes, and terrestrial vehicles to the extraterrestrial. The society in question can be either relatively primitive or modern. More recent societies have the advantage of employing all of the means of transport developed up to now in a preplanned fashion, but also the disadvantage of having to catch up. The older developed nations get to tack any new means of transportation onto their existing networks. This can be advantageous on the cost spectrum, unless the new disrupts the old excessively. Generally, however, already developed nations can raise the capital to build new networks that developing countries can only dream of.[7]

The evolution of the United States' present-day transportation network, then, occurred in a series of "waves." The nation had passed through a colonial or traditional society before the American Revolution, a preindustrial development period from the Revolution to the War of 1812, an era of economic takeoff lasting from 1815 to the Civil War, and a modern epoch of intense industrial growth eventuating in an industrialized nation emphasizing mass consumption. The approximate dividing line between the latter two events can be set at 1890—a watershed that saw the end of "free" land on the American frontier, the beginning of government regulation of business, the disfranchisement of the African American and the Native American and the institutionalization of Jim Crow (social segregation), and the transformation from agrarianism to industrialism, although one could argue (as many have) for any date between 1880 and 1928.[8]

Although each form of transportation went through its own cycles of birth, development, and maturity, the process took place synonymously in the several types of transportation and the country as a whole. But because of the capital necessary to advance a particular form of transportation, one form usually dominated the others in public awareness and discussion at any particular moment. Superimposed over American transportation history was not only the development of the industrial revolution and the growth of cities and suburbs, but the phenomenal growth of the national population through immigration, the expansion of the national territory through treaty and conquest, and a prolonged constitutional argument over whether the private sector or the government (and if the latter, which governmental level—local, state, or federal) was responsible for financing and building the overall network.

TRANSPORTATION AND COLONIAL AMERICA, 1607–1781

Initially, what became the United States was a part of the traditional social and mercantile system of the first British Empire, which was destroyed by the American Revolution.[9] The colonies were established as part of an integrated economic order that saw them as resources of raw materials for the British homeland and a place to dump the unwanted poor, habitual criminals, and religious dissenters. It was also potentially a land of great opportunity, where a person might start once more to become a productive part of society. With the emphasis on coastal settlement and the exploitation of raw materials, it was no wonder that America became the source for much of the British merchant marine. Hardwoods for shipbuilding grew abundantly along the coast, tall and straight, easily taken advantage of. Besides providing the raw materials and skills to build ships, Americans manned the vast British merchant fleet, holding a vast empire together.

Protected by the Navigation Acts, which restricted trade to citizens of the British Empire, Americans developed a coastal trade between cities that specialized in various raw materials—rum and lumber in New England, furs and foodstuffs in the Middle Colonies, and sea island cotton, indigo, and tobacco in the South. The colonists also traded with the vast Caribbean sugar holdings of the empire, sending foodstuffs to the slave-dependent plantations and integrating the whole thing together in a very profitable triangular Atlantic trade route. One sea lane involved rum taken to Africa and exchanged for slaves that were transported to the New World where sugar from the Caribbean was taken to New England to make the rum that was exported back to Africa. Another involved taking American raw materials to England for manufacture (although primitive manufacture took place in New England and the Middle Colonies in violation of pure mercantile theory) and feeding finished goods into the slave trade. Engaging in this traffic, the American element of the British imperial merchant marine reached one of its historical high points.

Inland travel in the new American continent was quite primitive when compared to the more sophisticated movement on the high seas. Trade with Native Americans involved finished goods produced in England exchanged for furs and land. As war, disease, and increased immigration (ensured by the fact that the British American colonies, alone among European New World

holdings, accepted settlers from any ethnicity who would take a simple loyalty oath to the king) destroyed the coastal tribes, the need for interior transportation to supply the advancing white settlers grew. Initial transportation was via the time-honored use of rivers. Various craft, especially the indigenous peoples' canoes and dugouts, plied the western waters. As the trade possibilities grew, bigger rafts and flatboats entered the traffic, but most had a problem in traveling against the current. This led to trading canoes and keelboats that could buck the currents and go upstream by hugging the banks and shallows.

The limited carrying capacity of the river craft and their general east-west direction of travel demanded that different transportation applications be employed to connect the northern and southern colonies by land. The most advanced land carriage of the time was by coach and wagon. This necessitated the construction of roads. Now the great east-west rivers became obstacles to be crossed by fords and ferries (there were no major bridges until after the Revolution). When it came to roads, the native peoples again showed the way. The American wilderness was a nearly impenetrable mass of forest and mountains east of the Mississippi River, which is why early travel was by the streams that wended their ways through the hinterland. But there were select trails made popular by game, hunters, and warriors that indigenous peoples had used since time immemorial. Widened and improved, these became the beginnings of the first road system in America.[10]

Unfortunately for the English, the main water transportation network in interior North America, the St. Lawrence–Great Lakes–Ohio–Mississippi system, was under the control of their French and Spanish enemies. These Latin powers, particularly the French, moved to cut the British off from the fur regions and the numerous tribes beyond the Appalachian Mountains, and direct the trade instead to their ports in Canada and the Gulf of Mexico. Some Native Americans helped in this effort because they preferred the French and Spanish over the English (if, indeed, they were to have contact with any Europeans). The Latin powers merely traded needed manufactured goods and kept their actual settlements to a minimum. The British, on the other hand, were known for their insatiable land hunger whereby intensive farming methods and settling instincts had displaced every indigenous tribe unfortunate enough to be in their way. Only a British alliance with the powerful Iroquois Confederacy, which dominated the Mohawk Valley in New York, had prevented a disastrous Indian war until the British were well entrenched in their coast-hugging colonies.[11] To compromise the French control of the desirable interior, England and her colonies fought a series of wars to dominate North America. As the French had the waterways secured, the English had to rely on roads to support their westward advance. This was especially true in regions where few rivers ran westward into the backcountry.

By 1755, most of these road-building efforts pointed toward the French post at Fort Duquesne, where the Monongahela and Allegheny Rivers joined to form the Ohio River, the key gateway to the West from the Middle Colonies. The first attempt to gain the West from the French resulted in Braddock's Road, named after the British officer who constructed it. This was an old route paralleling the Potomac River first marked by a Delaware Indian, Nemacolin, later expanded by George Washington and, after his failure to penetrate the wilderness and repel the French, by Colonel Edward Braddock. The defeat of Braddock's Virginia column at the beginning of the French and Indian War (1756) led to the road's abandonment and, unmaintained, it soon disappeared under new growth timber. A second British campaign against Fort Duquesne out of Philadelphia resulted in Forbes' Road (sometimes referred to as the Old Glade Road), named after Braddock's replacement, Colonel John Forbes. It was more successful and his advancing column forced the French to abandon their fort, which the English renamed Pittsburgh. Forbes' Road gave Philadelphia one of the few real roads

to the West and a real economic advantage. After many battles, a final victory at Québec in 1759 secured most of North America for the British Empire.[12]

Meanwhile other colonial cities sought to keep abreast of Pennsylvania and solve the transportation problems they faced. Boston, for example, began to construct a post road to New York City. Now that the French had been ejected from North America, New York relied on the Hudson–Mohawk River system to open up the Great Lakes, the only practicable waterway across the mountains. Philadelphia countered by improving and expanding Forbes' Road into the German grain region near Lancaster and the Cumberland Valley beyond. Charleston constructed many roads into the Piedmont region above the fall line that marked the end of tidewater navigation. When the South Carolina roads reached Augusta, they joined the Great Wagon Road that extended up the Shenandoah into the Cumberland. By the time of the Revolution the American colonies had a road system that paralleled the coast and was far enough inland to be safe from seaward attack. The interruption of this vital supply route that ferried men and munitions to the colonial forces would be one of the objectives that lured the British army inland so deeply in the South during the War for American Independence.[13]

It was also off the Great Wagon Road that Daniel Boone marked the first real path for westward advance through the Cumberland Gap into Kentucky (a neutral hunting ground not permanently occupied by Native Americans) and Tennessee, the Wilderness Road. After the defeat of the French in 1760, their Native American allies had revolted against the victorious, land-greedy British colonists in Pontiac's Rebellion. Finally crushing Pontiac's assemblage of tribes at Bushy Run, the British government sought to meet Native American complaints against land-hungry Americans and reduce colonial military requirements (and the overextended British budget, which led to the taxes that spurred the American Revolution) by announcing the Proclamation of 1763, which created a "permanent" Indian frontier and prohibited the colonists from crossing the Appalachian Mountains.[14]

But Britain's colonial subjects were not about to be denied what they saw as the fruits of victory—millions of acres of exploitable new western lands. Known only to local settlers like Boone was a Native American path, the Warrior's Trail, which wound through the Cumberland Gap. Boone widened it into a real road. Drawn by tales of the lush prairies and forests to the west, and often by a desire to avoid the coming Revolutionary War, settlers from all over the South and Pennsylvania poured down the Great Wagon Road and over the Cumberland Gap, the king's law be damned. That Boone's Wilderness Road became a primary route westward can be seen from the fact that Kentucky and Tennessee were the first new states to join the Union after the Revolution. Not far behind came Ohio, filled by settlers using Forbes' Road and Zane's Trace, an extension of the road west of Pittsburgh.[15]

TRANSPORTATION AND
PREINDUSTRIAL CONSOLIDATION

From its triumph in the Revolutionary War until the time of the Civil War, the United States experienced a leisurely era of economic consolidation before 1815 and pell-mell development thereafter. Both periods involved important political, industrial, and transportation innovations. Most momentous was the writing of the Constitution of 1789. Critics often contend that the Constitution was a well-concealed conservative counterrevolution designed to snatch power from the people and the states guaranteed under the 1781 Articles of Confederation. They also maintain that the Articles' alleged economic pitfalls could have been corrected by mere amendment rather than a whole new fundamental law. But in economic terms important to the future of transportation development, the Constitution improved over the Articles of Confederation by creating a colonial free-trade era unmatched anywhere (except perhaps by the nineteenth-century British Second Empire

in Asia and Africa) until the formation of the post–World War II European Common Market.[16]

On the other hand, the Constitution had problems of its own that would affect the coming transportation revolution. Short on investment capital, the private sector and many of the states lacked the ability to finance large public works projects like the roads, canals, and railroads that would mark this era. Until the nationalism stimulated by the victory of the War of 1812, the United States passed through an interwar period marked by the characteristics preliminary to real economic takeoff. First, there was the absorption of change brought about by the new national government. With the creation of essential institutions of finance like the Bank of the United States, the funding of the Revolutionary War debt, and the assumption of the states' internal debts, the new government inadvertently created political parties—permanent divisive factions not desired by the Founding Fathers. The main question became how far could the fundamental contract be stretched to accommodate public need and greed. Those who believed that it could be innovative and freely construed under the "necessary and proper" and "general welfare" clauses were called "loose constructionists." Their leader became Alexander Hamilton, the first secretary of the treasury, backed by President George Washington. Opponents, who believed the Constitution should mean what it literally said, were called "strict constructionists." Their leader was James Madison, one of the writers of the original document, backed by Thomas Jefferson.[17]

In 1801, the government was peacefully transferred from the Federalists, who supported the innovative reading (Washington and John Adams) to the Democratic Republicans who did not (Jefferson), giving the new political party system, which was institutionalized in the Twelfth Amendment to the Constitution, its current viability. Jefferson immediately found that he could govern more to his advantage by copying the tactics of the Federalists. He bought Louisiana, instituted an undeclared war against Mediterranean pirates, endorsed the Yazoo land frauds in the Old Southwest, set up an embargo on American ships headed for Europe in a vain effort to stay out of the Napoleonic Wars, and sought ways to finance building a permanent Cumberland Road (Braddock's old trail) out of Washington, D.C., and plan other comprehensive internal improvements. None of this had the specific endorsement of the Constitution, which Jefferson had promised to follow strictly before his election. Meanwhile, Americans conquered the cis-Mississippi West through massive migration and the War of 1812. The war was technically a draw, but it drove the British from select border forts they had held in violation of the Peace of Paris (1783) in retaliation for the U.S. seizing of Tory lands after the Revolution, and broke the Native American cultural and political resistance led by the Shawnee twin brothers Tecumseh and Tenskwatawa, the Shawnee Prophet.[18]

TRANSPORTATION AND THE EARLY INDUSTRIAL ECONOMY, 1815–1860

The nationalism produced by the war, especially from General Andrew Jackson's one-sided victory at New Orleans, led to a new pride in being American. This resulted in economic development becoming a goal of the individual, family, town, and nation as a matter of collective exultation. Politicians who had made their careers by opposing federal power reconsidered and passed measures reestablishing the Bank of the United States (its original charter had expired in 1812) and applying its rechartering bonus to the building of roads. President James Madison signed the first, but vetoed the latter as too manipulative of the Constitution. But the National Road was financed in other ways endorsed by Madison's successor, James Monroe. Earlier inventions, particularly related to the employment of steam and the building of the Erie Canal, which led to new engineering techniques and the creation of technical schools, resulted in a massive new western migration and the entrance of six new states to the Union. It was, in the words of participants and historians, "The Era of Good Feelings."[19]

But the pre–Civil War period started off slowly for a merchant marine that had once thrived under the protection of the British fleet and its Navigation Acts. In the Peace of Paris that separated the United States from British control, Americans had suddenly been excluded from the profitable British West Indies trade that had been their mainstay under the empire. But the Napoleonic Wars led to both sides in Europe relying on the neutral Americans for their overseas export and import shipping. Although both sides tried to intercept American-flagged ships going to the other's ports, the traditional U.S. hatred of Britain, with its more effective navy and its policy of impressment of American seamen, led Americans to fight a second war with England from 1812 to 1815. Besides, British Canada (long remembered by Americans as the "Fourteenth Colony" that failed to gain independence in 1783) was the only place the United States could hit Europe in the New World. After the War of 1812, the British made it a point to go out of their way not to antagonize Americans. They even reopened their old West Indies trade routes to Americans and demilitarized the Great Lakes. With the combination of Great Britain's commitment to free trade in the 1840s and America's creative new clipper ships, the U.S. merchant marine reached its most vital form in history right before the Civil War.[20]

Just as the merchant marine thrived, the pre–Civil War era marked the high point of water travel on interior waterways. The rivers became dominated by the steamboat. The Robert Fulton–style craft was a deep-bottomed boat designed for the eastern tidewater rivers. It was of little use on the shallow Mississippi system until Henry Shreve developed the flat-bottomed steamboats that Americans associate with the Cotton Kingdom of the prewar South. At first using a stern-wheeler, Shreve went on to perfect the bigger side-wheeler as the more efficient and maneuverable boat. Thereafter, the smaller stern-wheelers were limited to shallow rivers like the Missouri and the Red or any body of water with floating objects where the keel protected the paddle wheel from damage.[21]

The natural rivers were interconnected by man-made canals. Beginning with the Erie Canal in 1826, Americans went canal crazy for two decades. As New York demonstrated, canals could be built with state funds and thus avoid the federal aid question. But unfortunately, the only really profitable route was the Erie. With the exception of some canals that thrived off the Erie's connection to the Great Lakes and New York City, and the anthracite-hauling ditches across Pennsylvania and New Jersey, few canals did much but drain local treasuries. Indeed, with the Panic of 1837, several state canal systems literally went broke, Indiana's Wabash and Erie and Pennsylvania's Main Line being two prominent examples.[22]

Meanwhile debate raged nationally over another early-nineteenth-century American mania—the building of roads. The early history of the nation was pockmarked with transportation challenges that manifested themselves in the form of rebellions or secession movements. The Whiskey Rebellion involved the lack of transportation available to market western-grown crops in the East as much as it did the taxing of corn. The Willie Blount Conspiracy, an abortive and misbegotten attempt to take the mouth of the Mississippi by force, which led to Blout's removal from the U.S. Senate (preventing full disclosure of evidence that a threatened impeachment would have necessitated), dealt as much with the fear that loss of Americans' use of the port city of New Orleans (controlled by the Spanish and then the French) would damage agricultural exports as it did with the grandiose visions that possessed the senator and his cohorts.[23]

President Thomas Jefferson put an end to these fears when he bought New Orleans (and the whole of the Great Plains as a bonus) from France in the Louisiana Purchase, although his former and now-disgraced vice-president, Aaron Burr, and Philip Nolan, one of Burr's adherents, made other attempts to separate the West from the rest of the nation for personal empires.

But Jefferson's action led to a great debate on the constitutionality of such a land purchase—an eventuality not foreseen by the Founding Fathers and not specifically sanctioned by the fundamental law of the land. Like so many presidents, Jefferson had come into power promising less federal interference with the states and a literal reading of the Constitution. And like the rest, he astutely refused to be limited in his power if he could do something for the good (or what he saw as the good) of the nation. This led to a party split, with the opposition quaintly known as the Tertium Quids, and to more finagling with the Constitution, especially when it came to road building.[24]

As with most transportation projects, local governments lacked the tax base to finance capital-intensive projects like properly built roads. Jefferson turned to his secretary of the treasury, Albert Gallatin, for a legal solution. Author of an extensive internal-improvements plan that would connect all parts of the West with the rest of the country through a system of canals and roads, Gallatin theorized that roads could be financed constitutionally with a percentage of monies obtained from the sale of public lands. The result was America's first publicly financed highway, the National Road. Initially running from Baltimore through Washington, D.C., to Cumberland, Maryland (hence its early popular name, the Cumberland Road), the National Road eventually crossed the Ohio River at Wheeling and passed through the capitals of all the states in the Old Northwest (Columbus, Indianapolis, and Vandalia, the first capital of Illinois), eventually winding up in St. Louis. John Quincy Adams and Henry Clay, with the latter's American System of planned national economic development, gave Gallatin's vision real currency in the 1820s.

But the arrival of Andrew Jackson and his states' rights advocate, Martin Van Buren, on the scene put a long-standing end to the federal financing of highways. Van Buren had multiple motives in his strict reading of the Constitution, not the least of which was to keep other states from doing with federal money what New York had done with its own in constructing the Erie Canal. Jackson, worried more about tariffs and southern nullification schemes, took a traditional, strict constructionist stand for and gave his endorsement to Van Buren's philosophy by issuing the Maysville Road Veto in 1830, which by and large pulled the national government out of supporting internal improvements and caused a realignment of political parties based on Jackson's presidency. The Era of Good Feelings was over.[25]

By 1838 no more money was available for the National Road. Its maintenance and further construction were turned over to the states. How much of this retrenchment was Jacksonian-Democrat political theory and how much was economic reaction to the Panic of 1837 is open to interpretation. The government did continue building military roads (specifically endorsed in the Constitution) in the territories, ringing Detroit with such roads and constructing a vast road system along the ninety-fourth meridian between various forts lying along the western edges of Minnesota, Iowa, Missouri, and Arkansas (or the Permanent Indian Frontier, as it was naïvely and erroneously labeled). It also provided occasional military escorts down the Santa Fe Trail and onto the plains, which resulted in the creation of the first permanent cavalry regiments to cope with the mobile Plains Indian warriors of the Lakota (Sioux), Comanche, Cheyenne, and other mounted tribes.[26]

The federal government went on to create a Pacific Wagon Roads Office to supervise several surveys and minor improvements along western trails after the Mexican War of 1846–1848, the most extensive of which was probably the Mullan Road in present-day Washington State. But most of the famous trails were originally marked by mountain men who followed old Native American routes or blazed new paths of their own. They became roads only when large parties of immigrants moved to Oregon, California, and Utah seeking new farmland, gold, or religious freedom. The freighting firm of Russell, Majors, & Waddell did much to popularize various trails as it supplied western army posts after the Mexican

Cession. Possible troubles with individual tribes of Native Americans (like the Blackfeet along the Canadian border or the Lakota further south and west) and the British Hudson's Bay Company in Oregon led to more trails being blazed (Montana Trail, Applegate Road, Siskiyou Trail, and Sawyer's Wagon Road), as did the perennial desire for shortcuts (Hastings Cutoff and Sublette Cutoff), new routes to gold and silver deposits (the Smoky Hill Trail, Gila Trail, and Bozeman Trail), and less arduous routes (the Barlow Road around the dangerous Dalles in Oregon).[27]

After the Oregon Treaty of 1845, the Mexican Cession in 1848, and the California gold rush in 1849, the United States once again had the same problem that faced it during Jefferson's time—disconnected western settlements (this time along the Pacific Coast) that needed to be brought closer to the rest of the nation. The distances were so vast, the rivers so shallow, the Rocky Mountains so high, and the roads and sea lanes so slow that some other technology had to be devised to meet the challenge. The answer already was at hand in the railroads that were being introduced in the East. Indeed, the nature of the American West—the enormous land mass of the continent—would in time make the United States the primary railroad nation in the world.

Begun about the time of the completion of the Erie Canal, railroads offered an oftentimes cheaper, and definitely more flexible, all-weather approach to the nation's transportation needs. By the 1830s short lines began to appear, carrying passengers as well as freight. Within a decade they had replaced canals as the main carriers of goods and people. By the 1840s, it was possible to travel from Washington, D.C., to New York and Chicago on a northerly route or south through the Appalachians to New Orleans. But many station changes had to be made as the rails did not connect directly through major cities. By the Civil War's end, however, railroads would surmount the competition of the steamboats and highways and become, through a series of standardized car interchange policies, a universal track gauge, and standard time zones, the dominant mode of transportation nationwide.[28]

Once again the problems of financial resources and constitutionality raised their heads, this time made more volatile by the addition of a new element to the argument—the slavery question. Although railroads were cheap to construct (made more so by the shoddy building standards of corrupt entrepreneurs), the distance to be covered to the Pacific Coast meant that only one line could be built, even if federal support could be had. Naturally, every town along the Mississippi River worth its salt wanted to be the city of origin. Congress delayed the problem as long as possible, no doubt hoping that something would develop to solve the sectional divisiveness. Survey parties were sent out along probable routes to mark possible rights-of-way. To the horror of northerners, who comprised a majority of the voting white population of the nation, many of the arguments, from a purely analytical point of view, favored a route through the South, especially after the Gadsden Purchase in 1854. The South had the best all-weather routes, the fewest mountains, and the most settlers (customers) living farther west in Texas than elsewhere. To counter this development, the freighting firm of Russell, Majors, & Waddell pioneered the Pony Express along the Central Overland Route, not to deliver the mail in the shortest time possible (although it did that), but to demonstrate that a more northerly passage of the Plains was possible year-round.[29]

But more needed to be done to preserve the northern route. Senator Stephen A. Douglas of Illinois tinkered with the idea of new territories in Kansas and Nebraska to entice settlers out along the Central Overland Route. To keep southerners happy with this development, Douglas proposed a scheme to repeal the 1820 Missouri Compromise and open the western Great Plains to settlement by slaveholders through a process known as "popular sovereignty." Now, Douglas had no intention of assisting the spread of human bondage. He knew that slavery would not prosper in the colder plains climate where staple crops common to the South would not grow. He also realized that antislave farmers moved west faster than southerners encumbered by slaves.

Douglas hoped that whenever any Plains territory applied for statehood, the predominately northern settlers already there would vote for a free state. He just never made this clear to the South. It was this fact, the hidden antislavery quirk in popular sovereignty, that Abraham Lincoln forced Douglas to admit to during the Lincoln-Douglas debates in 1858. The result was the reelection of Douglas as senator from Illinois, but the split-up of the southern-dominated Democratic Party in 1860 and the election of Lincoln as president with a purely northern vote, realigning American political parties under the familiar Republican and Democratic labels. Meanwhile, as northern and southern agitators flooded into Kansas, the new territory became engulfed in civil war five years before the rest of the nation joined in.[30]

TRANSPORTATION AND THE DEVELOPMENT OF ECONOMIC MATURITY, 1861–1890

The Civil War, and the Reconstruction Era that followed, saw the Republican Party shift its goals from idealism (public agricultural colleges, abolition of slavery, and black civil rights) to a more cynical, pro–big business attitude (national banks, railroads, and hard money), and transportation was the biggest of the big businesses. Abandoning the small businessmen, miners, and farmers who brought it to power, the party sustained its position by emphasizing the victory against the Southern Rebellion. Voters were cautioned to "vote as you shot," and to beware of Southern attempts to join with the dwindling remnants of the Northern Democratic Party to control the nation as they had before the war in a demagogic appeal called "waving the bloody shirt." Some historians claim that even the idealism of supporting the black vote was a ploy to keep the white Democratic South controlled by black voters and that the Enforcement Acts, designed on their face to suppress the Ku Klux Klan, were really employed mostly against Democratic political machines in big Northern industrial cities to control the often-Catholic, immigrant white vote there.

In any case, when southern conservatives agreed to support northern industrial goals in the Compromise of 1876 (and some would question just how far and how long this lasted), the Republicans abandoned the blacks to their fate as second-class citizens. Democrats were dismissed as the party of "Rum, Romanism, and Rebellion." The only Democratic president of the period was Grover Cleveland who, mercifully for the powers that be, turned out to be as fully committed to the transportation and business communities as the Republicans who preceded and followed him. Lack of difference on real issues led to vicious personal campaigns (that of 1884 was reputedly the dirtiest in American history), the trademark of an essentially one-party state.[31]

The decades that ensued were marked by tremendous growth in business, in general, and transportation, in particular. Fueled by rising savings and the monetary policies of the 1862 national banking system, investment boomed. New industries were born and old ones enlarged as iron and steel, oil, manufacturing, and especially railroad support products boomed. Revolutionary changes in agriculture (steam tractors, more machines) permitted more time to be devoted to other pursuits and necessitated fewer people to manage a farm. Postwar corruption, a process that has intrigued and repelled many historians, ran rampant. But closer analyses posit that not all business was corrupt and exploitative. There were actually at least two types of businessmen during this "Gilded Age": the evil "Robber Barons" who took the nation and their industries for all they were worth in the "Great Barbecue," and the more constructive "Market Entrepreneurs" who actually funded and built the industrial foundation of the nation and the transportation systems that connected it together. The latter provided jobs for the numerous native-born and immigrants and gave America a sound industrial base for the next century.[32]

As this growth became sustainable, that is, after the national rail strike of 1877 and the end of Reconstruction, the nation turned to industrialization full time. A drive toward economic maturity and modernization occurred in the East, while emigration filled the Plains, killed off the buffalo, and subdued the Indians in the West. Along with the agricultural products of the South and Great Plains, the exploitable raw materials of the West created a continental version of the old British colonial empire for the finished products of the industrial East (and that still endures somewhat in the Rocky Mountain states today in industries such as mining, cattle, and farm products). The railroads linked it all together. As 1890 approached, American economic efforts expanded beyond the heavy industries (iron and steel) and technologies (railroads) that gave them birth to machine tools, chemicals, and electrical equipment. The Panic of 1893 witnessed the "re-Morganization" of the railroads, as J. P. Morgan and others bought up and merged vast rail empires from individual lines that had grown fat and lazy through overbuilding on government land grants. By the decade of the nineties, the country had developed the entrepreneurial and technological skills to produce everything it might choose, regardless of the resources available locally (even though the U.S. had most of them), and imports and exports become crucial to national existence, although overseas trade was accomplished increasingly in foreign "bottoms" (cargo ships).[33]

The Civil War had driven the prosperous American merchant marine fleeing to the flags of other nations to escape Confederate commerce raiders—a change that U.S. shipping never really recovered from. After the war, American ship technology remained dedicated to wooden ships moved by sail. It was as if the revolutionary steam-powered, ironclad ships of the war had never existed. While the rest of the world graduated to steel bottoms and the screw propeller,

Americans still relied on wood and paddle-wheelers. Eventually, this oversight cost American shippers much trade. By the time of the Spanish-American War in 1898, there was great doubt as to whether sufficient American bottoms existed to support the troops abroad in taking over what remained of the old Spanish Empire. Canal and river trade also fell off, as did the road infrastructure. Their evolution interrupted by the Civil War, these methods of transportation faced the unbeatable competition of railroads during the period that followed. Indeed, all of American energy and capital seemed to flow into the conquest of the Plains and intermountain regions and criss-crossing the nation by rail.[34]

Much of the railroad building in the East was marked by a consolidation of smaller lines into bigger networks. Tragically, as in the West, too much of the consolidation had a corrupt flavor to it. Little was thought of public interest ("The public be damned," intoned railroad mogul William Vanderbilt in a statement often erroneously attributed to his father). Often the financial manipulations appeared to their authors as games in which they "took" their opponents. Perhaps the worst example was that of the Erie Railroad, which was so thoroughly looted in the 1860s that it really never recovered until it was absorbed by Conrail 110 years later. Freight rates were marked with pools and rebates that the average shipper never knew of. Sweetheart deals were common. Often the railroads could not afford to ignore them, as when John D. Rockefeller demanded favoritism lest he ship his oil through a competitor. By the 1890s, such a public reaction had set in that the railroads' own best advocates in Congress instituted the Interstate Commerce Commission, reasoning that controlled but gutless regulation by the advocates of railroads was better than rampant reprisals by angry customers.[35]

In the West, the main rail problem was assuring liberal governmental financial support. The method settled on was the land grant, by which the rail investors would receive lands along the right-of-way that could be sold to potential agricultural and industrial customers for the railroad. First instituted as a sectional deal in 1850, with the initial grants going to the Illinois Central up North and the Gulf & Ohio in the Deep South, the land-grant system became tangled up in the slavery problem when it became evident that only one line would be built to the Pacific. Each section wanted the transcontinental route to emanate from a city in their orbit, and the individual cities quarreled in a lesser manner as did the nation at large.[36]

The secession of the Democratic South, however, allowed the remaining Republicans to pass programs held up by the sectional controversy for years. They established land-grant colleges, a new national banking system, and created a transcontinental railroad route across the Plains out of Omaha, Nebraska. In the style of the day, the Union Pacific company milked the government for all it was worth, setting up a fake construction subsidiary, the Crédit Mobilier of America, that overcharged the railroad with kickbacks to the investors and both houses of Congress. Nonetheless, the transcontinental railroad became a reality in 1869. But it would take until well into the 1880s before capital to complete other similar routes was available. Indeed, the full transcontinental system was not complete until the opening of the Santa Fe's Belen Cutoff east of Albuquerque, the Western Pacific's mainline through Feather River Canyon, and the Milwaukee Road's branch into the Pacific Northwest around the beginning of World War I.[37]

TRANSPORTATION AND THE ERA OF
MASS CONSUMPTION,
1891 TO THE PRESENT

By 1890, then, America was ready to become the society of high mass consumption that has marked its imprint on the twentieth century. Big-business philosophy dominated all political parties. There was little difference between Democrat Grover Cleveland and Republicans Benjamin Harrison or William McKinley, leading to the one-time aberration where a sitting American president (Cleveland) was replaced by his opponent (Harrison) only to take back the White House four years later for a split double-term. Conservatives initiated reforms like the Interstate Commerce Commission as much to protect business from radical changes at the state level as to recast them in a new mold, and went off the bimetalism standard (money backed by gold and silver) to the straight gold standard. [38]

The disgust of reformers with the existing parties manifested itself with the organization of the People's Party (the Populist Revolt), whose candidates took over the Democrats with the slogan of "free silver" coinage only to fall prey to "Gold-bug" McKinley, "the Advance Agent of Prosperity," in 1896. The Populist's defeat marked the swan song of agrarian America and the notion that the hard–soft money issue could solve all social ills. The next wave of political innovators would be the city-bound Progressives, a bipartisan phenomenon involving Republicans Theodore Roosevelt and William Howard Taft (to a lesser degree) and Democrat Woodrow Wilson. It would be these men who would bust the trusts and put teeth into the Interstate Commerce and Sherman Antitrust Acts. [39]

Arriving with the twentieth-century stage of high mass consumption was a shift toward durable consumer goods and services. Real income rose as Henry Ford offered employment at an unheard-of $5 a day. The Progressives initiated minimum wages, the 8-hour workday, child labor laws, the 40-hour workweek, workers' compensation, and paid vacations that allowed most Americans to afford more than the basics of life. Jobs were concentrated in offices and skilled factory positions. Urbanization became the watchword of social change. The extension of technology became an overriding objective of society. Inventions and tinkering were accepted to such a degree that the Dodge Brothers' automobile firm, for example, set up a "playroom" to encourage such activity among its retired workers and current employees on their times off. Historically, much of this urbanized prosperity was connected with the cheap family car and the glorification of consumerism, discretionary income, and leisure activities. [40]

Beginning at the turn of the twentieth century, expanding during the Great Depression, and culminating in the 1960s was the appearance of the welfare state or a watered-down American version of socialism. Its beginnings were in the revulsion of the Populists in the countryside and Social Gospel advocates in the cities against the dog-eat-dog world of Social Darwinism. Politically, it had numerous names; practically, it affected transportation, by and large, for the good. The Square Deal (Theodore Roosevelt) took on the allegedly monopolistic railroads in the Northern Securities case. Roosevelt's handpicked successor, William Howard Taft, reduced antitrust business confrontations (he saw good and bad trusts differently than "TR"), causing Roosevelt to run against him in the Bull Moose Party. This split of the Republicans permitted a Democratic victory in 1912 with the first southern-born president since before the Civil War. Woodrow Wilson's New Freedom brought transportation regulation to a new high point with the passage of the Clayton Act that prevented corporation mergers that would limit competition. He also instituted a new banking system (the Federal Reserve) and the beginnings of government financing of modern highways, and ended most constitutional arguments against federal aid. [41]

Compromised but not ended by the Republican administrations of the Roaring Twenties (Warren G. Harding, Calvin Coolidge, and Herbert Hoover)—highways received a big boost during the decade—governmental interference with transportation took on a new comprehensiveness during the New Deal (Franklin D. Roosevelt and Harry Truman) and World War II. Road construction was a way to spend the nation out of depression and into worldwide victory against fascism. Government-guaranteed cartels of limited competition in the public interest (whatever that was) dominated transportation industries. The welfare-state philosophy became so pervasive that after the war "accommodationist" Republicans

Dwight D. Eisenhower, Richard Nixon, and Nelson Rockefeller declined to attack the basic idea of the welfare state. They merely claimed that they could do the job cheaper and better than the spendthrift Democrats. Under this banner (and that of his military victory over the Nazis) Eisenhower defeated the more conservative Senator Robert Taft of Ohio (son of the former president) for the 1952 Republican presidential nomination. The result was more government aid to the airlines and the beginnings of the interstate highway system, although Eisenhower's administration also witnessed the first rumblings in favor of transportation deregulation, particularly for railroads, during the 1958 recession. [42]

But the respite was brief. After welfarism was repromoted in the New Frontier by John F. Kennedy, conservative Barry Goldwater questioned its veracity and the "me-too-ism" of fellow Republican Nelson Rockefeller, as had Robert Taft earlier. Although Goldwater captured the Republican nomination, he lost out in the election, unfairly branded as a warmonger in the first throes of the Vietnam conflict. Under the aegis of the Great Society of Lyndon B. Johnson came the final act of the New Deal. Once again, opponents Nixon and Gerald R. Ford claimed that Republicans could do it better. But the American transportation system began to fail, pushed into the doldrums by poorly run, overregulated trucking companies, railroads, and airlines, and a Middle East oil embargo that revealed all the cracks that the system had lived with for years. Doubts as to the whole economic veneer of the country reached their crescendo during the administration of President Jimmy Carter, who began the earnest deregulation of transportation. Government transportation regulation was largely destroyed altogether by Goldwater disciple Ronald Reagan and his "Laffer curve" or supply-side economics. Reagan's decimation of the Professional Air Traffic Controllers Organization also pointed out the fate of unions under the new order. [43]

Reagan's successor, George H. W. Bush, having once accused the actor-turned-president of operating economically under a guise of "smoke and mirrors," returned to compromise with the Democrats. The change caused him to lose out to "New Democrat" William J. Clinton in 1992. But "Clintonomics" (as of this writing) has turned out to be more of the same high-cost, tax-and-spend welfarism that had plagued his Democratic predecessors, and its precepts were rechallenged once again in 1995 by House Speaker Newt Gingrich and his Contract with (some critics prefer "on") America.

Through all of the twists and turns of twentieth-century U.S. domestic policy, transportation has received much federal largesse, although it was somewhat selective and limited to canals (the Panama Canal, Sault Ste. Marie, the Intercoastal and Gulf Waterways, Mississippi flood control facilities, and the St. Lawrence Seaway), roads, and aircraft support at the expense of maritime shipping and, particularly, railroads. As deregulation of rates came into being, governmental controls over transportation shifted to environmental and antidrug monitoring, company and industrywide bailouts, and other peripheral areas. [44]

During the era of the welfare state in America, the merchant marine suffered greatly with the exception of the periods during the world wars and the Korean and Vietnam conflicts. American seamen first gained their constitutional rights in the LaFollette Seamen's Act in 1915, but other federal measures to increase the numbers of ships built and registered under the American flag failed miserably, especially as the "flags of convenience" (British through World War I, and Nigerian, Panamanian, and Liberian afterward) allowed ships to operate at lower costs and tax rates. Traditional American response has been to require that the vast supplies needed by its worldwide posted armed forces be hauled in American bottoms, but this has done little to solve the problem. On the inland waters, however, barge traffic has actually improved with powerful tugboats and sophisticated tows hauling bulk products that ply the Mississippi system and special, extra long cargo ships on the Great Lakes, augmented by modern rebuilt and extended canal and lock systems like those on the Lakes, the Upper Mississippi and the Ohio Rivers, and the construction of new facilities like the Panama Canal, the Intercoastal Waterway, the Gulf Waterway, the Tennessee-Tombigbee (Tenn-Tom), the Chicago-Illinois River, and the St. Lawrence Seaway. On the Mississippi and its eastern tributaries, tour boats, built to resemble the old steamboats of 100 years ago, have increased their appeal as tourist diversions, as have old-style gambling boats moored in or traveling on the rivers outside the scope of restrictive land laws. [45]

As the inland waterways have become more profitable, the railroads have approached the merchant marine in the seriousness of their problems. The railroads, which were the original form of land transportation that federal regulations, pushed by the Populists and Progressives, were designed to control, are today a far cry from their early days of massive government subsidy. Kickbacks, rebates, pools, and holding companies all came under the watchful eye of the regulators. At first, unfavorable court decisions forced the federal government to modify the original Sherman Antitrust Act and Interstate Commerce Commission regulatory laws. The Congress finally got an effective combination under the Clayton Act in 1914. But the railroads had already been regulated too much or too unwisely, depending on whom one wishes to believe, and collapsed under the increased traffic generated during World War I. The government had little time for the argument about who was to blame at that moment. Caught up in the Great War, the Woodrow Wilson administration simply nationalized the whole industry under the U.S. Railroad Administration as a part of the war effort. By the time of the Treaty of Versailles, however, the desire for full government control had lessened and the rails were returned to private ownership. [46]

Throughout the 1920s, government regulators, business theorists, and railroad managers jockeyed for preeminence. The railroads were happy to accept government programs that allowed them to merge, so long as the railroads themselves determined who joined with whom. Indeed, merger mania became the watchword of the decade. But it all had to be accomplished by somehow skirting the strictures of the Clayton Act. Ironically, much of the rail problem was temporarily alleviated by New Deal government controls, which established cartel arrangements (a violation of the Clayton Act) to mitigate the throes of the Great Depression. By World War II, the rails functioned well enough to avoid a repeat of government takeover. Along with labor agreements, these measures began to permit more and more merger schemes and less passenger service, prompted by the failures of the once great eastern roads like the New York Central, the Pennsylvania, and the several anthracite and "bridge" lines—the big coal haulers and their connecting routes to the Midwest.[47]

The rail crisis prompted the Congress to form several quasigovernmental cartels like Amtrak for passenger service (which has not, as of 1994, shown a profit) and Conrail (which not only became profitable but completely private when the government sold its stock holdings) to straighten out the eastern rail mess. Other lines nationwide merged under loosened regulatory commission rules. One of the mergers involved the enjoinment of the Chicago, Burlington & Quincy with the Great Northern and the Northern Pacific to form the Burlington Northern, the largest system in the country. This merger actually negated one of Theodore Roosevelt's more celebrated "trust-busting" measures in the Northern Securities case (1904).[48]

Since the passage of the Staggers Rail Act of 1980, some railroads have merged wholesale while abandoning unprofitable lines and services, and others have gone broke. The mighty transcontinental lines, always in better shape than their eastern cousins because the length of the haul allowed them to compete favorably with trucking, have found a bonanza in container shipping (as has the eastern giant, Conrail). The intercostal sea-land routes across the United

States are today cheaper and faster than the old Panama Canal sea lane. Railroading has become so profitable in the late twentieth century that very efficient, independent short lines are opening and operating routes that were previously shut down. [49]

The two biggest advances in transportation during the twentieth century involved the motor vehicle and its concomitant highways and the airplane. By 1890, the road system so laboriously built across the nation earlier in the century had collapsed into ruin. The rails were far too efficient to permit horse-drawn vehicles to compete except in places the rails could not or would not go. But the popularity of bicycling changed everything. Cyclists began to come out of the paved city streets into the countryside and were dismayed with rural roads conditions. Through the Good Roads Movement at the turn of the century, they began to lobby for improvements. They also led the way in building early autos and airplanes.

With the advent of the automobile the clamor grew for a paved, cross-country highway system. At first, the same problem that had daunted early roads raised its head—the constitutionality of road building subsidized by the federal government. It had been a state function since Andrew Jackson's Maysville Road veto. But Congress rose to the occasion, helped by the interventionist government philosophy that marked the Progressive and New Deal periods. In 1914, Congress declared all roads to be "post roads," which the Constitution openly permitted the federal government to administer. Later, the even more compelling rationale of military defense and the job necessities of the Great Depression would clinch federal control of the national road system.

As Ransom Olds and Henry Ford began to build the affordable family car, which displaced the horse and buggy by the end of World War I, the federal government passed numerous federally aided highway projects. At first, the government acted merely as a storehouse for information and built short demonstration roads to let the public see what could be done. The destruction of the highways by the heavy traffic generated dur-

ing World War I, however, led to massive federal investment in a national highway system that could respond to military as well as civil demands. Federal control of the construction money meant federal standards had to be upheld to receive it. Highways were numbered and interconnected at state lines to form a national road network.[50]

In one of the more important serendipitous events of the century, the failure of the railroads in World War I led to the advent of the trucking industry. Without sufficient trains, trucks for the American Expeditionary Force in France had to be driven to coastal ports for shipment overseas. The War Department sent them fully loaded, and a new, more flexible, door-to-door means of transferring freight was born. After the war, hundreds of men entered the trucking business with a half dozen vehicles or less, until New Deal controls forced new companies to meet certain capital standards. As in the Great War, World War II traffic demands resulted in the ignoring of weight limits, once again sacrificing the roadways to the necessities of war. With the advent of the interstate highway system in 1956, the national government established numerous vehicle length and width limits, types of loads, and weight requirements until they became standardized nationwide. With the deregulation of trucking in the 1980s, the independent trucker, "the Last American Cowboy," again came to the fore as big unionized companies became less important.[51]

In the noncommercial world of the family car, Americans hit the road with the curved-dash Oldsmobile at the beginning of the century and never looked back. The Ford Model T became the desire of every family, and Henry Ford saw to it that his operation was the epitome of efficiency and simplicity. Prices dropped until everyone could afford to buy an automobile. Ford raised his wages to a new height to make sure that no one could afford not to buy. Other grumbling industrialists had to follow suit as workers fled to the auto plants for work. After the Great War, Ford fell behind because he kept the same old, black-painted design first sold in 1908. New companies like General Motors and Chrysler emphasized pastel colors, annual style changes, planned obsolescence, gadgets of convenience (like electric starters), and engineering advances.

By World War II, the many smaller firms were going out of business and the market became dominated by the Big Three. By the mid-sixties, little competition existed for American car makers and, as a result, their standards dropped precipitously. With the Arab oil embargoes of the 1970s and the entrance of the Japanese into the market with more fuel-efficient, environmentally correct vehicles, American car makers had to struggle to survive. Chrysler's bailout by the federal government, Ford's aggressive campaign to make quality "job one," GM's new Saturn line, and the Japanese movement of assembly plants to the United States, along with a corresponding shift to the luxury car market, helped to stabilize the business by the 1990s.[52]

If the United States has led the world in any phase of twentieth-century transportation, it has been in the business of aircraft. Beginning with the Wright brothers in 1903 and culminating in the wide-body and jumbo jets of today, American aircraft designers, builders, and airline executives have been in the forefront of aviation's cutting edge—except for the supersonic transports. The pre–World War I era was the day of the "birdmen," stunt flyers who risked all when flying was a very risky business. The use of aircraft for intelligence observation, the fight for control of the skies, and air bombing during the Great War opened the eyes of the world to the future possibilities of the airplane, not only in the realm of military applications but also in commercial applications as well. In the 1920s, Americans took a great interest in air mail flights, and by the end of the decade enough adventurous people wanted to use the machines for business and pleasure travel. Aircraft developers met the challenge with the Boeing 277, the DC (Douglas Commerical) 3, and the various "flying boats" lumped under the name of Pan American Clippers. By the end of the decade, radio communication, improved navigation, new runways, pressurized cabins,

and four-engine models were on the way.[53]

Nothing spurred on the development of the airplane like World War II. Numerous improvements in design and avionics were necessary to best the Japanese Zeros and German Messerschmitts and Focke-Wulfs and bomb enemy homelands. Most important for later commercial applications were the American multiengine medium and heavy bombers. The innovations of radar, blind flying, accurate navigation, high-altitude flying, polar-circle routes, and long-distance flying came out of military necessity. By 1950, the airlines had surpassed the railroads in hauling passengers. Less than five years later they had also bested the transoceanic liners. By the end of the fifties the jet engine had become the predominant means of propulsion, replacing noisy propeller-driven planes. Within a decade, commercial airlines had advanced to the jumbo jets and wide-bodies, planes that could haul hundreds of passengers safely and quickly to their destinations across the nation and around the world. The Arab oil embargoes and the deregulation of the airline industry (the first of the transportation undertakings to be freed from government supervision) led to a reshuffling of companies, more efficient aircraft, and emergence of an entrepreneur who would rather gut the company than fight the unions. The struggle between unions and management is a problem that still plagues the industry today.[54]

Although all forms of transportation underwent modernization, nothing stirred the modern soul as much as the use of air transport to explore space. Beginning in the late 1950s with small satellites, the U.S. space program advanced to larger craft that hauled small animals, and then men, into the near heavens. The first manned flights were short, suborbital jaunts that were followed by orbital expeditions. After several successful one-person flights, the National Aeronautics and Space Administration (NASA), which coordinates the whole American space program, graduated from two-astronaut flights around Earth to three-man flights to and around the Moon, finally resulting in several landings on that eternal satellite. Given the later decline in overt public interest in the space program, it is quite possible that without the cold war and Soviet competition the United States might never have appropriated the vast sums of capital needed to complete such flights and their attendant technological developments. While the space shuttle of 1995 is really nothing more than a truck that flies—a massive cargo plane that hauls goods, services, and people into the nearby cosmos—it is but a part of a larger goal to build a space station that would serve as a launching pad for further space exploration and research. Current visions include a vast international project of a manned trip to Mars and perhaps a return to the Moon, using the Earth-orbiting space station as a base. Whether the building of a space station or further exploratory flights to Mars, or even back to the Moon, are made feasible seems a matter more dependent on domestic and international politics and humankind's self-vision than on current and evolving transportation technology.[55]

TRANSPORTATION, SOCIETY, AND THE FUTURE

Transportation has done much to shape the world we live in. One theorist views the development of cities as a function of transportation. Jerusalem, for instance, was built for donkeys and other beasts of burden, hence its narrow streets, often winding and up-and-down in nature. Boston was originally constructed to accommodate ships and wagons. Hence it is more spread out, with wider thoroughfares and ports fronting the sea. Chicago was a railroad town, with everything oriented to the massive, multiple rail terminals and commuter short lines that still dot the city. Los Angeles is an automobile town. It is a sprawling metropolis connected by suburban speedways that nowadays become vast, crawling parking lots during rush hour.

Transportation is what had allowed the construction of suburbs in the first place. They have grown bigger and become located farther and farther away from their central municipal source; some suburbs have become autonomous cities in their own right. The denizens of the old downtowns and their industrial facilities, which were the original cities' reason for existence, have frequently packed up and moved to the outskirts, too, leaving behind those who either could not afford to make the trip or were still fond of city ambience. The suburbs themselves then became interconnected by the automobile, and one could work, shop, and live without entering the city at all by skirting its edges. Public transportation became an anomaly because it went nowhere. Few wanted or needed to enter the city anymore. Those people left behind, often minorities and ethnic groups that had no cars, lost work because they could not utilize the edge highways. The automobile has in effect segregated people by their ability to own an automobile. It is a far different world from just 50 years ago when one commuted to the city to work, shop, and play—and many even lived there. It takes a big, old, eastern city like New York to outlast this transportation influence that is both negative and positive at the same time. Suburbanization is also why so many urban renewal projects were doomed from the outset—they emphasized a bygone era, not realities of late-twentieth-century urban life.[56]

The ignored immobility of nonmotorists (the old, the poor, minorities, and people who simply do not want to own a car) has prompted adverse comment from many observers, based on the concept that public works should benefit all of the community, not just motor vehicle owners. Some critics believe that highway building ought to be halted until some forms of growth control, traffic control, and public transportation allow nonmotorists to catch up. They gain some support from futurists who predict that the new world will be dominated by high-tech versions of the city-states that dominated the late Middle Ages, typified by the ports of the Hanseatic League, until the industrial era demanded mass production and centralized systems of communication that led to the nation-state.[57]

Yet all of this flies in the face of present-day political and economic reality. Analysts decry the lack of public works projects (roads, bridges, dams, and such) and point out that the declining middle class, after being "downsized" out of traditional industrial jobs, is taking an unfair lowering of expectations by having to resort to either flipping hamburgers for a living or gaining the computer skills to participate in the "information superhighway." In the cogent words of Texas newspaper columnist Molly Ivins, "Bubba Junior Bob is not going to become a computer nerd." But others point out that the government will not finance a massive rebuilding of the national transportation infrastructure under the prevalent "balanced budget" concepts of a less-intrusive federal presence in American life. [58]

America's current transportation system is impressive. It includes roughly 200,000 miles of railroad track, almost 15,000 airports, and well over 4 million miles of hard-surface roads. Transportation costs make up 15 percent of the average American's personal expenditures and over half of the nation's use of petroleum. It is a modern system—most of it has been created in the last half century, almost all of it in the twentieth century. But the real problem in transportation's future, as with all technology, will be accommodating social, economic, and political realities. [59] In the end, transportation futurists may still find hope in the words of rocket scientist Robert H. Goddard, who wrote in 1918 that the "only barrier to human development, or advancement, is ignorance, and this is not insurmountable." [60]

Notes

1. Several good videos exist on the relationship between transportation and modern life. See, for instance, *Wheels of Change* (American Filmworks, 1992); *Coming and Going* (Greater Washington Educational Telecommunications Association, Inc., 1994); and *Locomotion* (BBC-TV in cooperation with the Arts & Entertainment Network, 1993). See also the comments of Ben Wattenberg in *Busy Waterways: The Story of America's Inland Water Transportation* (New York: John Day Company, 1964), 123–124; Bob Greene, "Another Look at Highway Freedom," *Chicago Tribune*, reprinted in the *Tucson Citizen* (12 December 1994), 8A, 2.

2. *Coming and Going.* See also the dated but still valuable account by Hal Hellman in *Transportation in the World of the Future* (New York: M. Evans and Company, 1974), as to future transportation potentialities, many of which have already been implemented.

3. Edward J. Taaffe, Richard Morrill, and Peter R. Gould, "Transport Expansion in Underdeveloped Countries: A Comparative Analysis," *Geographical Review* 53 (1963), 503–529.

4. Walt W. Rostow, *The Stages of Economic Growth: A Non-Communist Manifesto*, 3d ed.

(New York: Cambridge University Press, 1990). Rostow's general pattern forms the outline of this essay.

5. Caroline E. MacGill et al., *History of Transportation in the United States before 1860* (Washington, DC: Carnegie Institution of Washington, 1917); George Rogers Taylor, *The Transportation Revolution, 1815–1860* (New York: Rinehart and Company, 1951).

6. Frederick Jackson Turner, "The Significance of the Frontier in American History," in his *The Frontier in American History* (New York: Henry Holt and Company, 1920), chapter 1. The essay was first expounded before the American Historical Association at the World's Columbian Exposition in Chicago in 1893.

7. Taaffe, Morrill, and Gould, "Transport Expansion in Underdeveloped Countries: A Comparative Analysis," 503–529, especially 528–529; D. Robert Altschul, "Transportation in African Development," *Journal of Geography* 79 (1980), 44–56.

8. Turner, "The Significance of the Frontier in American History"; Glenn Porter, *The Rise of Big Business, 1860–1910* (New York: Thomas Y. Crowell, 1973); Harold U. Faulkner, *Politics, Reform and Expansion,*

1890–1900 (New York: Harper and Row, 1959); Samuel P. Hayes, *The Response to Industrialism, 1885–1914* (Chicago: University of Chicago Press, 1957); H. Wayne Morgan, *From Hayes to McKinley: National Party Politics, 1877–1896* (Syracuse, NY: Syracuse University Press, 1969); C. Vann Woodward, *The Strange Career of Jim Crow* (New York: Oxford University Press, 1966); W. E. Burghardt DuBois, *Black Reconstruction in America: An Essay Toward a History of the Part Which Black Folk Played in the Attempt to Reconstruct Democracy in America, 1860–1888* (New York: Russell and Russell, 1935); John D. Hicks, *The Populist Revolt: A History of the Farmers' Alliance and the People's Party* (Minneapolis: University of Minnesota Press, 1931).

9. Lawrence Henry Gipson, *The British Empire before the American Revolution*, 12 vols. (New York: Alfred A. Knopf, 1936–1965); Charles M. Andrews, *The Colonial Period of American History*, 4 vols. (New Haven, CT: Yale University Press, 1934–1938); I. R. Christie, *Crisis of Empire: Great Britain and the American Colonies, 1754–1783* (New York: W. W. Norton, 1966); J. R. Pole, *Foundations of American Independence, 1763–1815* (Indianapolis: Bobbs-Merrill, 1972); Russell Kirk, *America's British Culture* (New Brunswick, NJ: Transaction Publishers, 1993); Stuart Bruchey, *The Roots of American Economic Growth, 1607–1861* (New York: Harper and Row, 1965), 16–73.

10. MacGill et al., *History of Transportation*, 3–64; Archer Butler Hulbert, *Paths of the Mound-Building Indians and Great Game Animals* and *Indian Thoroughfares*, vols. 1 and 2 of his *Historic Highways of America*, 16 vols. (Cleveland: Arthur H. Clark Co., 1902–1906).

11. George T. Hunt, *The Wars of the Iroquois: A Study in Intertribal Trade Relations* (Madison: University of Wisconsin Press, 1967).

12. Francis Parkman, *France and England in North America*, 7 vols. in 2 vols. (New York: The Library of America, 1983); Gregory Evans Dowd, *A Spirited Resistance: The North American Indian Struggle for Unity, 1745–1815* (Baltimore: The Johns Hopkins University Press, 1992), xii, 23–47, 60, 90–91, 100, 115, 141, 143, 191.

13. MacGill et al., *History of Transportation*, 65–131, 249–279, 299–305; Hulbert, *Washington's Road (Nemacolin's Path), Braddock's Road, Old Glade (Forbes') Road*, and *Boone's Wilderness Road*, vols 3, 4, 5, and 6 of his *Historic Highways of America*; Robert L. Kincaid, *The Wilderness Road* (Indianapolis: Bobbs-Merrill, 1947); Bruce H. Addington, *Daniel Boone and the Wilderness Road* (New York: Macmillan, 1922); Don Higginbotham, *The War of American Independence: Military Attitudes, Policies and Practice, 1963–1789* (New York: Macmillan, 1971), 352–388.

14. John Bakeless, *Daniel Boone* (New York: W. Morrow and Company, 1939), 35–36, 89–109; Jack M. Sosin, *The Revolutionary Frontier, 1763–1783* (New York: Holt, Reinhart, and Winston, 1967); Christie, *Crisis of Empire*, 23–45; Pole, *Foundations of American Independence*, 25–26.

15. U.S. Department of Transportation, Federal Highway Administration, *America's Highways* (Washington, DC: Government Printing Office, 1976), 2–8; Hulbert, *Old Glade (Forbes') Road* and *Boone's Wilderness Road*, vols. 5 and 6 of his *Historic Highways of America*.

16. Secondary accounts include Crane Brinton, *The Anatomy of Revolution* (New York: Vintage Books, 1965); R. R. Palmer, *The Age of Democratic Revolution: A Political History of Europe and America, 1760–1800* (Princeton, NJ: Princeton University Press, 1959); Jackson Turner Main, *The Sovereign States, 1775–1783* (New York: Franklin Watts, Inc., 1973), *The Anti-Federalists: Critics of the Constitution, 1781–1788* (Chapel Hill: University of North Carolina Press, 1961), and *Political Parties before the Constitution* (Chapel Hill: University of North Carolina Press, 1973); Merrill Jensen, *The New Nation: A History of the United States during the Confederation, 1781–1789* (New York: Alfred A. Knopf, 1950); Gordon S. Wood, *The Creation of the American Republic, 1776–1787* (Chapel Hill: University of North Carolina Press, 1969); Forrest MacDonald, *We the People: The Economic Origins of the*

Constitution (Chicago: University of Chicago Press, 1958), E Pluribus Unum: The Formation of the American Republic, 1776–1790 (Boston: Houghton Mifflin, 1965), and Novus Ordo Seclorum: The Intellectual Origins of the Constitution (Lawrence: University Press of Kansas, 1985); M. E. Bradford, Original Intentions: On the Making and Ratification of the United States Constitution (Athens: University of Georgia Press, 1993). A good collection of primary materials is Bernard Bailyn (ed.), The Debate on the Constitution: Federalist and Antifederalist Speeches, Articles, and Letters during the Struggle over Ratification (New York: Library of America, 1993).

17. Frederick K. Henrich, "The Development of American Laissez Faire: A General View of the Age of Washington," Journal of Economic History (Supplement) 3 (1943), 51–54; Bruchey, The Roots of American Economic Growth, 92–123; Joseph Charles, The Origins of the American Party System (New York: Harper and Row, 1961); William Nisbet Chambers, Political Parties in a New Nation: The American Experience, 1776–1809 (New York: Oxford University Press, 1963); Noble E. Cunningham, Jr., The Jeffersonian Republicans: The Formation of Party Organization, 1789–1801 (Chapel Hill: University of North Carolina Press, 1957); Manning J. Dauer, The Adams Federalists (Baltimore: The Johns Hopkins University Press, 1953); Bray Hammond, Banks and Politics in Early America from the Revolution to the Civil War (Princeton, NJ: Princeton University Press, 1957), 89–114; Pole, Foundations of American Independence, 183–232.

18. Dowd, A Spirited Resistance, 116–201; John Dos Passos, The Shackles of Power: Three Jeffersonian Decades (Garden City, NY: Doubleday and Co., Inc., 1966); Marshall Smelser, The Democratic Republic, 1801–1815 (New York: Harper and Row, 1968); George Dangerfield, The Era of Good Feelings (New York: Harcourt, Brace and World, 1952), 105–121; Frederick Paxton, History of the American Frontier (Boston: Houghton Mifflin, 1924), 86–226; John Anthony Caruso, The Southern Frontier (Indianapolis: Bobbs-Merrill, 1963); R. Carlyle

Buley, The Old Northwest: Pioneer Period, 1815–1840, 2 vols. (Bloomington: Indiana University Press, 1950), I: 1–57, 395–564.

19. Dangerfield, The Era of Good Feelings, 95–196; Guy S. Callender, "The Early Transportation and Banking Enterprises of the States in Relation to the Growth of Corporations," Quarterly Journal of Economics 17 (1902–1903), 111–162.

20. Taylor, The Transportation Revolution, 104–132. The vigor of the American merchant marine within the British Empire at this period gives some validity to the recently expressed misgivings on free trade in Pat Buchanan, "Free Trade and the Rise in Poverty," Washington Times (National Weekly Edition, 24–30 October, 1994), 34.

21. Taylor, The Transportation Revolution, 56–73; Louis C. Hunter, "The Invention of the Western Steamboat," Journal of Economic History 3 (1943), 202–220; Grant Foreman, "River Navigation in the Early Southwest," Mississippi Valley Historical Review 15 (1928), 34–55; William J. Petersen, "Steamboating on the Missouri River," Iowa Journal of History 53 (1955), 97–120.

22. Alvin F. Harlow, Old Towpaths: The Story of the American Canal Era (New York: D. Appleton and Company, 1926); Harry S. Drago, Canal Days in America (New York: Clarkson-Potter, 1972); Ronald E. Shaw, Canals for a Nation: The Canal Era in the United States, 1790–1860 (Lexington: University of Kentucky Press, 1990); Carter Goodrich (ed.), Canals and American Development (New York: Columbia University Press, 1961), and Government Promotion of Canals and Railroads, 1800–1890 (New York: Columbia University Press, 1961), 3–168; Taylor, The Transportation Revolution, 32–55; Alfred D. Chandler, Jr., "Anthracite Coal and the Beginnings of the Industrial Revolution," Business History Review 46 (1972), 143–181.

23. Leland D. Baldwin, Whiskey Rebels: The Story of a Frontier Uprising (Pittsburgh: University of Pittsburgh Press, 1939); Dale Van Every, Ark of Empire: The American Frontier, 1784–1803 (New York: William Morrow, 1963), 307–315, 342–343; Thomas P. Abernethy, The South in the New

Nation, 1789–1819 (Baton Rouge: Louisiana State University Press, 1961), 169–191.

24. Thomas P. Abernethy, *The Burr Conspiracy* (New York: Oxford University Press, 1954); Russell Kirk, *John Randolph of Roanoke: A Study in American Politics* (Indianapolis: Liberty Press, 1978), is the classic study on Jefferson's most outspoken opponent within the party.

25. Robert A. Lively, "The American System: A Review Article," *Business History Review* 29 (1955), 81–96; Taylor, *The Transportation Revolution*, 15–31; Philip D. Jordan, *The National Road* (Indianapolis: Bobbs-Merrill Company, 1948); U.S. Department of Transportation, Federal Highway Administration, *America's Highways*, 16–27; Bruchey, *The Roots of American Economic Growth*, 124–140. On the reintroduction of the two-party system, missing since the end of the War of 1812, see Robert V. Remini, *Martin Van Buren and the Making of the Democratic Party* (New York: W. W. Norton, 1970); Richard P. McCormick, *The Second American Party System: Party Formation in the Jacksonian Era* (Chapel Hill: University of North Carolina Press, 1966); Glyndon G. Van Deusen, *The Jacksonian Era, 1828–1848* (New York: Harper and Row, 1959).

26. Carter Goodrich, "The Revulsion against Internal Improvements," *Journal of Economic History* 10 (1950), 145–169; Francis Paul Prucha, *Broadax and Bayonet: The Role of the United States Army in the Development of the Northwest, 1815–1860* (Lincoln: University of Nebraska Press, 1967), 131–148; Otis E. Young, *The First Military Escort on the Santa Fe Trail, 1829...* (Glendale, CA: Arthur H. Clark, 1952), and *The West of Philip St. George Cooke, 1809–1895* (Glendale, CA: Arthur H. Clark, 1955); Bruchey, *The Roots of American Economic Growth*, 141–177.

27. Robert R. Russell, *Improvement of Communication with the Pacific Coast as an Issue in American Politics, 1783–1864* (Cedar Rapids, IA: Torch Press, 1948); W. Turrentine Jackson, *Wagon Roads West* (Berkeley: University of California Press, 1953); Oscar Osburn Winther, *The Trans-*

portation Frontier: Trans-Mississippi West, 1865–1890 (New York: Holt, Reinhart and Winston, 1964), 1–14.

28. Taylor, *The Transportation Revolution*, 74–103; Robert E. Riegel, "Trans-Mississippi Railroads during the Fifties," *Mississippi Valley Historical Review* X (1923–1924), 153–172.

29. Russell, *Improvement of Communication with the Pacific Coast as an Issue in American Politics, 1783–1864*; Lewis Henry Haney, *A Congressional History of Railways in the United States* (Madison: University of Wisconsin Press, 1910), 49–75; Goodrich, *Government Promotion of Canals and Railroads*, 169–297.

30. Robert W. Johannsen, *Stephen A. Douglas* (New York: Oxford University Press, 1973), 374–434; Arthur Bestor, "State Sovereignty and Slavery: A Reinterpretation of the Proslavery Constitutional Doctrine, 1846–1860," *Illinois State Historical Society Journal* 54 (1960), 117–180; James A. Rawley, *Race and Politics: "Bleeding" Kansas and the Coming of the Civil War* (Philadelphia: J. B. Lippincott Company, 1969). On the rise of the Republicans and the demise of the Democrats, see Alan Nevins, *The Emergence of Lincoln: Douglas, Buchanan and Party Chaos, 1857–1859* (New York: Charles Scribner's Sons, 1950); Roy Nichols, *The Disruption of American Democracy* (New York: Macmillan, 1948); George H. Mayer, *The Republican Party, 1854–1966* (New York: Oxford University Press, 1967), 23–48.

31. C. Vann Woodward, *Reunion and Reaction: The Compromise of 1877 and the End of Reconstruction* (New York: Doubleday and Co., Inc., 1951); Terry L. Seip, *The South Returns to Congress: Men, Economic Measures, and Intersectional Relationships* (Baton Rouge: Louisiana State University Press, 1983), 162–164, 178–187; Harold M. Hyman, *A More Perfect Union: The Impact of the Civil War and Reconstruction on the Constitution* (New York: Alfred A. Knopf, 1975), 526–532; Matthew Josephson, *The Politicos, 1865–1896* (New York: Harcourt Brace and World, 1938), 341–373; V. O. Key, Jr., *Southern Politics in State and Nation* (New York: Alfred A. Knopf, 1949), 3–12, for the premiere

study of politicians using personality and demagoguery to substitute for real issues.

32. The criticism of the era is in Matthew Josephson, *The Robber Barons: The Great American Capitalists, 1861–1901* (New York: Harcourt, Brace, 1934), 3–32, 315–351; the praise in Burton W. Folsom, Jr., *The Myth of the Robber Barons* (Herndon, VA: Young America's Foundation, 1991), 121–134; a middle ground is ably staked out in David J. Rothman, *Politics and Power: The United States Senate, 1869–1901* (Cambridge: Harvard University Press, 1966).

33. Peter Lyon, *To Hell in a Day Coach: An Exasperated Look at American Railroads* (Philadelphia: J. B. Lippincott Company, 1968); Carl Abbott, *The Metropolitan Frontier* (Tucson: University of Arizona Press, 1993); Winther, *The Transportation Frontier: Trans-Mississippi West*, 25–134; Robert A. Kilmark (ed.), *America's Maritime Legacy: A History of the U.S. Merchant Marine and Shipping Industry since Colonial Times* (Boulder, CO: Westview Press, 1979).

34. Winther, *The Transportation Frontier: Trans-Mississippi West*, 92–134; Kilmark, *America's Maritime Legacy*; Haney, *A Congressional History of Railways*, 76–154; Julius Grodinsky, *Transcontinental Railroad Strategy, 1869–1893: A Story of Businessmen* (Philadelphia: University of Pennsylvania Press, 1962), 1–55, 312–337, 365–387, 412–431; Glenn C. Quiett, *They Built the West* (New York: Appleton-Century, 1934).

35. Josephson, *The Robber Barons*, 100–177; Folsom, *The Myth of the Robber Barons*, 121–134; James A. Ward, *Railroads and the Character of America, 1820–1887* (Knoxville: University of Tennessee Press, 1986), 151–170.

36. Lloyd J. Mercer, *Railroads and Land Grant Policy: A Study in Government Intervention* (New York: Academic Press, 1982); Haney, *A Congressional History of Railways*, 13–23.

37. Grodinsky, *Transcontinental Railroad Strategy*, 56–311, 338–364, 388–400; Albro Martin, *James J. Hill and the Opening of the Northwest* (New York: Oxford University Press, 1976); Robert W. Fogel, *The Union Pacific Railroad: A Case Study in Premature Enterprise* (Baltimore: The Johns Hopkins University Press, 1960); David Lavender, *The Great Persuader* [Collis P. Huntington] (Garden City, NY: Doubleday and Co., Inc., 1970); James B. Hedges, *Henry Villard and the Railways of the Northwest* (New Haven, CT: Yale University Press, 1930); William S. Greever, *Arid Domain: The Santa Fe Railroad and Its Western Land Grant* (Palo Alto, CA: Stanford University Press, 1954).

38. John M. Dobson, *Politics in the Gilded Age: A New Perspective on Reform* (New York: Praeger, 1972); Robert D. Marcus, *Grand Old Party: Political Structure in the Gilded Age, 1880–1896* (New York: Oxford University Press, 1971); Horace Samuel Merrill, *Bourbon Leader: Grover Cleveland and the Democratic Party* (Boston: Little, Brown and Company, 1957); Ward, *Railroads and the Character of America*, 151–170; Faulkner, *Politics, Reform and Expansion*, 140, 187–211; Gabriel Kolko, *Railroads and Regulation, 1877–1916* (New York: W. W. Norton, 1965), 5, 26–27, 29, 35, 77–78, 120, 146–147, 202–207, 216, 218, 221–222, 231; George H. Miller, *Railroads and the Granger Laws* (Madison: University of Wisconsin Press, 1971), 161–200.

39. Robert P. Sharkey, *Money, Class, and Party: An Economic Study of Civil War and Reconstruction* (Baltimore: The Johns Hopkins University Press, 1959); Walter T. K. Nugent, *The Money Question during Reconstruction* (New York: W. W. Norton, 1967); Urwin Unger, *The Greenback Era: A Social and Political History of American Finance, 1865–1879* (Princeton, NJ: Princeton University Press, 1964); Solon Buck, *The Granger Movement: A Study of Agricultural Organization and Its Political, Economic, and Social Manifestations, 1870–1880* (Cambridge: Harvard University Press, 1913); Allen Weinstein, *Prelude to Populism: Origins of the Silver Issue, 1867–1878* (New Haven, CT: Yale University Press, 1970); Norman Pollack (ed.), *The Populist Mind* (Indianapolis: Bobbs-Merrill, 1967), xix–xlviii; Paul W. Glad, *The Trumpet Soundeth: William Jennings Bryan and His Democracy, 1896–1912* (Lincoln: University of Nebraska Press, 1960); Hicks, *The Populist Revolt*; Theodore

Saloutos, *Farmer Movements in the South, 1865–1933* (Berkeley: University of California Press, 1960), 1–153; John A. Garraty, *The New Commonwealth* (New York: Harper and Row, 1968), 306–308; Morgan, *From Hayes to McKinley*, 365–527; Hayes, *Response to Industrialism*, 137–139, 188–193; Faulkner, *Politics, Reform and Expansion*, 1–93, 187–211.

40. George E. Mowry, *The Era of Theodore Roosevelt and the Birth of Modern America, 1900–1912* (New York: Harper and Row, 1958), 1–105; John B. Rae, *American Automobile Manufacturers* (Philadelphia: Chilton, 1959); J. J. Flink, *The Car Culture* (Cambridge: Massachusetts Institute of Technology, 1975).

41. Thomas K. McCraw, "Regulation in America: A Review Article," *Business History Review* 49 (1975), 159–183; Richard Hofstadter, *The Age of Reform: Bryan to F.D.R.* (New York: Vintage, 1955), 23–271; Eric Goldman, *Rendezvous with Destiny* (New York: Vintage, 1956), 3–202; Mowry, *The Era of Theodore Roosevelt*, 106–295; Arthur S. Link, *Woodrow Wilson and the Progressive Era, 1910–1917* (New York: Harper and Row, 1954); John Morton Blum, *Woodrow Wilson and the Politics of Morality* (Boston: Little, Brown and Company, 1956); Milton Friedman and Anna Jacobson Schwartz, *A Monetary History of the United States, 1867–1960* (New Brunswick, NJ: Princeton University Press, 1963), 189–298; Robert Higgs, *Crisis and Leviathan: Critical Episodes in the Growth of American Government* (New York: Oxford University Press, 1987), 158.

42. Hofstadter, *The Age of Reform*, 272–328; Goldman, *Rendezvous with Destiny*, 203–347; Frederick Lewis Allen, *Only Yesterday: An Informal History of the 1920s* (New York: Harper and Brothers, 1931); William E. Leuchtenburg, *The Perils of Prosperity, 1914–1932* (Chicago: University of Chicago Press, 1958), *Franklin D. Roosevelt and the New Deal, 1932–1940* (New York: Harper and Row, 1963), and *In the Shadow of FDR: From Truman to Ronald Reagan* (Ithaca, NY: Cornell University Press, 1983), 1–62; Dexter Perkins, *The New Age of Franklin D. Roosevelt, 1932–1845* (Chicago: University

of Chicago Press, 1957); David McCullough, *Truman* (New York: Simon and Schuster, 1992); Herbert Parmet, *Eisenhower and the American Crusades* (New York: Macmillan, 1972); William Manchester, *The Glory and the Dream: A Narrative History of America, 1932–1972* (New York: Bantam, 1975), 31–886; Higgs, *Crisis and Leviathan*, 159–236; Michael Barone, *Our Country: The Shaping of America from Roosevelt to Reagan* (New York: Free Press, 1990), 3–306.

43. Leuchtenburg, *In the Shadow of FDR: From Truman to Ronald Reagan*, 63–246; Manchester, *The Glory and the Dream*, 889–1303; Higgs, *Crisis and Leviathan*, 237–262; Barone, *Our Country*, 307–670; Allen J. Matusow, *The Unraveling of America: A History of Liberalism in the 1960s* (New York: Harper and Row, 1984).

44. John Podhoretz, *Hell of a Ride: Backstage at the White House Follies, 1989–1993* (New York: Simon and Schuster, 1993); Charles Kolb, *White House Daze: The Unmaking of Domestic Policy in the Bush Years* (New York: Free Press, 1994); Bob Woodward, *The Agenda: Inside the Clinton White House* (New York: Simon and Schuster, 1994); John Brummett, *Highwire. From the Backroads to the Beltway: The Clinton Presidency* (New York: Hyperion, 1994); Elizabeth Drew, *On the Edge: The Clinton Presidency* (New York: Simon and Schuster, 1994).

45. René de la Pedraja, *The Rise and Decline of U.S. Merchant Shipping in the Twentieth Century* (New York: Twayne, 1992); David McCullough, *The Path between the Seas: The Creation of the Panama Canal* (New York: Simon and Schuster, 1977); Ben Wattenburg, *Busy Waterways* (New York: The John Day Company, 1964); Edward M. Brady, *Tugs, Towboats and Towing* (Cambridge, MD: Cornell Maritime Press, 1967); T. H. Hills, *The St. Lawrence Seaway* (New York: Praeger, 1960).

46. Porter, *The Rise of Big Business*; Kolko, *Railroads and Regulation*; Albro Martin, *Enterprise Denied: Origins of the Decline of American Railroads, 1897–1917* (New York: Columbia University Press, 1971); K. Austin Kerr, *American Railroad Politics, 1914–*

1920: Rates, Wages, and Efficiency (Pittsburgh: University of Pittsburgh Press, 1968); Aaron Austin Godfrey, *Government Operation of the Railroads* (Austin, TX: Jenkins, 1974).

47. William Norris Leonard, *Railroad Consolidation under the Transportation Act of 1920* (New York: AMS Press, 1968); Earl Latham, *The Politics of Railroad Coordination, 1933–1936* (Cambridge: Harvard University Press, 1959); Richard Saunders, *The Railroad Mergers and the Coming of Conrail* (Westport, CT: Greenwood Press, 1978).

48. Saunders, *The Railroad Mergers*, 236–245; Fred W. Frailey, *Zephyrs, Chiefs & Other Orphans: The First Five Years of Amtrak* (Godfrey, IL: RPC Publications, 1977); Jeffrey Orenstein, *United States Railroad Policy: Uncle Sam at the Throttle* (Chicago: Nelson-Hall, 1990).

49. Theodore E. Keeler, *Railroads, Freight and Public Policy* (Washington, DC: The Brookings Institution, 1983); Clifford Winston et al., *The Economic Effects of Surface Freight Deregulation* (Washington, DC: The Brookings Institution, 1990); David J. DeBoer, *Piggyback and Containers: A History of Intermodal Rail on America's Steel Highway* (San Marino, CA: Golden West Books, 1992); Transportation Research Board, *Intermodal Marine Container Transportation: Impediments and Opportunities* (Washington, DC: National Research Council, 1992).

50. U.S. Department of Transportation, Federal Highway Administration, *America's Highways*, 54–64.

51. U.S., Department of Transportation, Federal Highway Administration, *America's Highways*, 90–100; Michael H. Agar, *Independents Declared: The Dilemmas of Independent Trucking* (Washington, DC: The Smithsonian Institution Press, 1986); J. Peter Rothe, *The Trucker's World: Risk, Safety, and Mobility* (New Brunswick, NJ: Transaction Publishers, 1991); Jane Stern, *Trucker: A Portrait of the Last American Cowboy* (New York: McGraw-Hill, 1975); Charles Taff, *Commercial Motor Transportation* (Cambridge, MD: Cornell Maritime Press, 1975); James H. Thomas, *Long Haul: Truckers, Truck Stops, and Trucking* (Memphis, TN:

Memphis State University Press, 1979).

52. Arthur J. Kuhn, *GM Passes Ford* (University Park: The Pennsylvania State University Press, 1986); Brock Yates, *The Decline and Fall of the American Automobile Industry* (New York: Empire Books, 1983); David Halberstam, *Reckoning* (New York: William Morrow and Company, Inc., 1986); Robert Sobel, *Car Wars: The Untold Story* (New York: E. P. Dutton, 1984); Robert L. Shook, *Turnaround: The New Ford Motor Company* (New York: Prentice-Hall, 1990).

53. Roger E. Bilstein, *Flight in America: From the Wrights to the Astronauts* (Baltimore: The Johns Hopkins University Press, 1994), 3–124; Richard P. Hallion, "Commercial Aviation, 1919–1976," in Eugene M. Emme (ed.), *Two Hundred Years of Flight in America* (San Diego: Univelt, 1977), 155–180.

54. Bilstein, *Flight in America*, 125–204, 327–358; Hallion, "Commercial Aviation, 1919–1976," 155–180; J. W. R. Taylor, *Combat Aircraft of the World from 1909 to the Present* (New York: G. P. Putnam's Sons, 1969); George Williams, *The Airline Industry and the Impact of Deregulation* (Brookfield, VT: Ashgate, 1993).

55. Bilstein, *Flight in America*, 205–326; Charles Murray and Catherine Bly Cox, *Apollo: The Race to the Moon* (New York: Simon and Schuster, 1989); Tom Wolfe, *The Right Stuff* (New York: Farrar, Strauss and Giroux, 1979); Alan B. Shepard and Donald K. Slayton, *Moon Shot: The Inside Story of America's Race to the Moon* (Atlanta: Turner Publications, 1992); Gregg Easterbrook, "Why the Space Station Doesn't Fly," *Newsweek* 123 (11 April 1994), 30–33; Gerald J. Karaska and Judith B. Gertler (eds.), *Transportation, Technology, and Society* (Worcester, MA: Clark University Press, 1978), 3, 65; Carl Sagan, *Pale Blue Dot: A Vision of the Human Future in Space* (New York: Random House, 1994), xi–xviii, 367–377.

56. Joel Garreau, *Edge City: Life on the New Frontier* (Garden City, NY: Doubleday and Co., Inc., 1991), 4–15, 55–56, 69–97, 145, 152, 169, 269–301, 425–438. See also the good synopsis of his arguments in

Coming and Going (Greater Washington Educational Telecommunications Association, Inc., 1994).

57. Art Weber, "Transportation—Who Has a Right to What?" *Trains* 54 (January 1994), 80; Walter Truett Anderson, *Reality Isn't What It Used To Be* (New York: Harper and Row, 1990), 19–26, 256–258.

58. Molly Ivins, "Let's Get Busy on Roads and Dams, and Give Workers Jobs to Work On," *Fort Worth Star-Telegram*, reprinted in *The Arizona Daily Star*, 7 February 1994, 12A; George F. Will, "Spending Restraints May Cripple Government," reprinted in *The Arizona Daily Star*, 10 February 1994, 15A.

59. Karaska and Gertler (eds.), *Transportation, Technology, and Society*, 1–4.

60. Quoted in Karaska and Gertler (eds.), *Transportation, Technology, and Society*, 1.

THE
ABC-CLIO
COMPANION TO

Transportation in America

Adams Express Company

Born in 1804, Alvin Adams was a Vermonter who had gone to Boston as a young man, where he worked in the hotel trade. His hotel was a headquarters for several stage lines, and Adams developed an interest in transportation. Ruined in the Panic of 1837, Adams decided 2 years later to enter the express field. Within 15 years Adams would be a millionaire. By 1841, he had extended his service from rural Massachusetts to New York City, where his employees, William B. Dinsmore and John Hoey, would become expressmen in their own right—Dinsmore as Adams' partner and Hoey in his own company some years later. The unexpected death of William Harnden in 1845, Adams' biggest competitor, allowed the latter to absorb the dead man's company and launch a giant express enterprise.

In direct competition with the U.S. Post Office, which deeply resented Adams' (and other expressmen's) cost-cutting practices, Adams expanded service into Ohio, Indiana, and Illinois. He took over the New York–Philadelphia–Washington run by buying out several smaller companies, and by 1850 he had exclusive use of the New York, New Haven & Hartford Railroad to haul his shipments. That he could afford to pay $1,700 for this privilege gives some idea as to his profits. He also utilized canal companies and extended his rail service to the Baltimore & Ohio (B&O) and the Pennsylvania Railroads (PRR). He had all of his wagons painted a dark green, and moved into a five-story headquarters building in Philadelphia across from the U.S. Mint (which used Adams Express for its shipments). Needless to say, Adams had the important political connections that flowed from federal business, and his offices in Washington, D.C., were an informal meeting place for politicians from all over the nation.

By 1848, Adams was one of the largest concerns of its kind in the East. A young clerk, D. H. Haskell, recommended that the company send him to set up shop in California to service the goldfields. Adams, Dinsmore, and Haskell organized a new company, Adams and Company of California, and Haskell opened its first office in San Francisco. With its eastern connections, permitting sight drafts and bills of exchange nationwide, Adams soon assumed a commanding position on the Pacific Coast. Lesser companies were bought out and service extended until by 1852, Adams was *the* express in California. But there was trouble on the horizon. In the middle 1850s banks in California, including Adams and other express companies, found themselves unable to meet the demands for withdrawals. A panic resulted, which forced them to close their doors. Adams alone had a demand for over $200,000 and assets on hand of only $10,000. Its biggest competitor, Wells Fargo & Company, weathered the storm and grabbed a reputation that ended Adams' dominance in the West.

Although the failure of its West Coast subsidiary did not shake its upper hand in the East, Alvin Adams felt obliged to resign as company president in 1855 in favor of Dinsmore. Some say that he shrewdly had sold out his interest in the California operation ahead of time, but records are sketchy. In any case, he was still a major force in its operations as the biggest stockholder. But a new crisis loomed—the Civil War. Adams knew that the Southerners would not allow Yankees to run express companies in the new Confederacy, and Adams had much business in the Atlantic Coast South. Although again pertinent records do not exist, Adams' offices changed their name to Southern Express all on one day in 1861. The new company was headed by Adams' southern director, Henry B. Plant. It was the only sure legal way to send mail and express shipments between the lines during the war. Meanwhile, Adams' key position as the largest shipper out of Washington, D.C., made it a prime transporter of federal needs during the war. All express companies did a big business between the soldiers and the civilians back home.

At the end of the war, stockholders in

Adams Express expected to see the Southern Express name dropped and the old one restored. When this failed to occur, several sued Alvin Adams, suspecting him, Plant, and other directors of directly pocketing the Southern's profits. The suit failed but the suspicions remained. Unlike other express companies formed from the same original directors (Wells Fargo, American, United States), Adams and Southern never quarreled. When Plant died his estate still received stock interest of 8 percent per year. The war evidently had not hurt express shipments at all.

Until 1913, when the U.S. Post Office created parcel post to help regulate fees through government competition, the only way to ship small packages and valuables was by express. Hence Adams and the others did not have to advertise to get a profitable share of the business. They did their best to keep the federal government out of the express business through lobbying influential congressmen. By 1886, Adams was paying railroads over $2 million annually for use of trains to ship their packages. By the turn of the century, Adams and other companies were listed among the smug malefactors of great wealth that stifled the free flow of goods through excessive charges.

With the advent of American entry into World War I, the government nationalized many transportation facilities, including the express companies. The four major companies in operation then were Adams, Southern, American, and Wells Fargo. The government consolidated them under the name American Railway Express Company, with each firm subscribing to a quarter of the stock. The government guaranteed them against loss, but they had to share profits, getting only 49.75 percent as their group share. At the end of the war, none of the three companies desired to set up independently, so Railway Express continued in operation, this time as a private corporation. The days of the old express companies had come to an end.

See also American Express Company; American Railway Express Company; Central Overland California & Pike's Peak Express Company; Harnden & Company Express; Leavenworth & Pike's Peak Express Company; Pacific Union Express Company; Russell, Majors & Waddell Company; United States Express Company; Wells Fargo & Company.

Reference Harlow, Alvin F., *Old Waybills* (1934).

Aeronautics

Defined as the science of flight and operation of atmospheric aircraft by men and women referred to as pilots, aeronautics has a 200-year history in America. As in Europe, the first flyers were balloonists. But soon people began to look into *real* flying—like the birds, with maneuverability on demand. The first to achieve this were those who flew gliders. Most of the early work was carried on in Europe by the Englishman George Cayley and the German Otto Lilienthal. The latter's 1896 death in a glider crash graphically demonstrated the pitfalls of flying.

In the United States the first glider builder of note was Octave Chanute. He also published the first accurate observations on flight in 1894. Chanute was soon joined by James Means, an industrialist who set forth three outstanding collections of aeronautical data between 1895 and 1897. But the premier researcher of his day was Samuel Pierpont Langley, a distinguished astronomer at the Smithsonian Institution. With a $50,000 grant obtained through the graces of the assistant secretary of the navy, Theodore Roosevelt, Langley experimented with gliders and steam-powered aircraft. He then went over to lighter gasoline engines and built the plane, *Aerodrome*. Piloted by his mechanic, Charles Manly, the *Aerodrome* was catapulted off the deck of a houseboat in the Potomac in 1903. But it crashed each time. Nonetheless, Langley claimed the invention of the first airplane, a claim recognized by the Smithsonian for decades.

The problem was that it was hard to believe that the *Aerodrome* flew under its own power and not through the boost from the catapult. But that was not the case of an aircraft invented by two brothers, bicycle mechanics from Dayton, Ohio, flown a few days after Langley's last attempt. Wilbur and Orville Wright not only took off under the power of their twin engines, they flew 120 feet for 12 seconds and landed safely, to boot. Lacking the connections of a man like Langley, the feat, although recorded at the time (in a magazine on bee culture!), was virtually ignored for five years.

But during the hiatus, the Wrights improved their plane and made it the first operational aircraft in the world. The interest of the military arms of several European nations woke up the Americans, and the Wrights went public in 1908 with a series of air shows. The daring idiots who flew these early airplanes were called "Birdmen." They looked somewhat more sane after former President Theodore Roosevelt went up in 1910 and pronounced the new form of transport to be "bully." The Wrights were soon joined by another inventor of successful aircraft, Glenn Curtiss. Then, in 1910, two woman took to the air in France. They were followed a year later by American aviatrix Harriet Quimby, who flew the English Channel in 1912. She joined a majority of her male and female barnstorming compatriots when she died in a crash at Boston shortly thereafter. All risks aside, however, with the coming of the Great War the whole world was ready to take a serious look at the potential of the new aerial machine, which came to manifest itself in three basic applications: military, general (private), and commercial.

MILITARY AVIATION

One source estimates that between 1914 and 1969 the United States originated and put into service over 160 basic airframe designs, some of which had as many as a dozen variants, if one counts only those aircraft that carried armaments. In addition, twice that number were rejected by one service or another, and another 300 types of civilian aircraft wore the military star insignia on their wings and fuselages. Over 50 manufacturers produced these aircraft, and their technology improvements extended beyond airframes to engines, armament, and avionics. Dozens of volumes have appeared,

each dedicated to the history of a particular airframe, some of which have advanced civilian transportation efforts, and all of which have made some contribution to the overall modern air transportation picture indirectly.

The first American military aircraft was the Wright Flyer biplane, first flown in 1903 and improved many times before its acceptance by the army Signal Corps. The army fought long and hard to avoid this new air technology of the twentieth century. But finally it accepted the inevitable and enlisted the new invention as a noncombatant reconnaissance device. Up until the U.S. entrance into World War I, the American armed forces had tested 381 different types and designs of aircraft, only 55 of which (mostly trainers) were airworthy in 1917. No wonder that American military experience in the air was of dubious quality. The first use of airplanes had been the U.S. Navy's employment of a half dozen Curtiss flying boats against the Mexicans at Veracruz in 1914. The Army followed two years later, when the First Aero Squadron accompanied General John Pershing into northern Mexico in pursuit of the infamous Francisco "Pancho" Villa. The exercise provided little useful reconnaissance, but it did show that American aircraft lacked logistical support for the air campaign that was compounded by inexperience and faulty tactical doctrine.

Even though the European conflict had already demonstrated the essential nature of the third dimension to warfare (opposing pilots had long abandoned the friendly hand wave as they observed ground actions for murderous combat to clear the air), the United States did not produce its first single–seat fighter plane until 1919. It had to fight the Great War with machines donated by its allies, France and Great Britain. If there were any bright spots in the American war effort, it was General Billy Mitchell's coordinated 1,500–plane air offensive in the Meuse-Argonne, and the development of the in-line, liquid-cooled Liberty engine, prompted by a $640 million congressional appropriation. Although built too late to contribute to the war effort, the Liberty engine would place the Americans briefly in the forefront of airplane development during the next decade. But it was soon to be eclipsed by German and British advances, which left the United States and Japan employing air–cooled radial engines for the next war—one in which traditional geographical boundaries would play a lesser protective role, having been breached by the new concept of air power.

Military budgets and doctrine being what they were between the wars (i.e., meager), the development of aircraft was essentially left to the civilian entrepreneur. But under the Army Reorganization Act of 1920, aircraft were left in a subordinate role under ground commanders. This occurred despite the vociferous objections of General Mitchell, who held out for an independent air force with its own strategic and tactical doctrine. He demonstrated the potential of airplanes when he sunk the ex-German battleship, *Ostfriesland*, in less than 22 minutes, employing a flight of seven Martin MB-2 bombers, each with a specially designed one-ton bomb. Even without antiaircraft protection, navy strategists had maintained that a ship of such size, with its watertight compartments locked down, was unsinkable. Mitchell was soundly condemned for his success, and soon drummed out of the service by more conservative officers. But Congress organized the army Air Corps in 1926, giving flyers a more autonomous role in the command system, expanding the service over a five-year period, and creating the post of assistant secretary of war for air.

The navy flight programs were as halting as the army's. The same command quarrel broke out—whether aircraft were solely for patrols, as in World War I, or whether they had a combat role at sea. Navy flyers set several trans-Atlantic records, crossing in Curtiss flying boats. These lumbering craft were the ancestors of a whole fleet of reconnaissance craft built by Martin (PBM), Boeing (PB2B), and Consolidated (PBY) that did essential pedestrian service in World War II. When experiments revealed that small "floatplanes" launched by capital ships could direct gunfire with astounding accuracy, the navy accepted models from Curtiss-Wright (SO3C Seagull and SC Seahawk) and Vought-Sikorsky (OS2U Kingfisher).

But if U.S. ships could profit from directed fire, so could an enemy's. And if bombers could sink battleships, they would have to be stopped by fast fighters. Because of the vastness of the sea and the shortness of aircraft flying ranges, the airfields would have to be seaborne. The result was the aircraft carrier, developed by the British and soon adopted by all the bigger world naval powers. The United States converted the fleet collier *Jupiter* into the experimental aircraft carrier, USS *Langley*, in 1919. Throughout the 1920s the navy perfected flying tactics and planes until it laid down the keels of the first two attack carriers, the *Lexington* and the *Saratoga*. Originally built to be heavy cruisers, the ships were converted within the limits of the Washington Disarmament Conference of 1922. One of their first training exercises was a surprise dawn attack on the Panama Canal. (Japanese observers especially noted that it worked to perfection.) During the Great Depression, the Public Works Administration provided jobs for the unemployed by constructing more naval ships, including the carriers *Yorktown* and *Enterprise*.

Although advances were made in delivering the air army to the battlefield, in fighter aircraft the Americans remained behind most of the world. The United States abandoned the biplane only in 1937 (Army, P-26 Boeing Peashooter) and 1940 (Navy, F2A Brewster Buffalo), contemporaneously with the Japanese commitment to the monoplane fighter (Mitsubishi Zero Zen), but several years after the British (Hawker Hurricane, Supermarine Spitfire) and Germans (Messerschmitt Bf-109) had changed over. It is true that later biplanes were better aircraft than early monoplanes, but the technology for the World War II fighter was already available by 1932, including retractable landing gear, cantilevered wings, variable-pitch propellers, efficient air-cooled engines, wing flaps to produce airworthiness at low speeds, diving breaks, and enclosed cockpits. All of these items had already appeared on civilian aircraft, but conservative military leaders worried about fluttering wings and preferred open cockpits until the Europeans and Japanese moved beyond them for increased speed and maneuverability. Meanwhile, military flyers gained experience by flying in air shows, delivering the U.S. mail (recording a disastrous 12 dead pilots and 66 crashes in the process), and setting long–distance flight records.

No matter what their prewar flight experience, American flyers went into World War II with grossly underpowered fighters whenever they relied on in-line, liquid-cooled engines like the Allison. The Curtiss-Wright Warhawk P-40 was typical. Serving with the legendary Flying Tigers—a voluntary group of pilots who flew in China before the war—the P-40 proved slow and a poor performer at higher altitudes. The same was true of the Bell P-39 Airacobra, whose rear engine transferred its power to a front propeller, leaving room for a 37-mm canon in the nose. The American power defect was corrected in a revolutionary fighter produced by Clarence "Kelley" Johnson at Lockheed—the twin-boomed, double-engine P-38 Lightning. Two supercharged Allisons gave this craft the speed and agility that a single motor failed to deliver. Coupled with its long range, the Lightning was the plane of choice to penetrate deep into Japanese-held territory to assassinate Admiral Isoroku Yamamoto in 1943. The Germans also feared this Fork-tailed Devil, as they called it. So did American pilots until an ejection seat escape gave flyers the ability to clear safely the connected tail spars that might cut them in half as they bailed out of a crippled plane. The North American P-51 Mustang, arguably the best single fighter of the war, employing a new laminar wing design, was woefully underpowered until Packard Motors received a license to equip it with British Rolls-Royce Merlins that put the American Allison to shame.

But radial-powered fighters (Grumman F4F Wildcat, Vought F4U Corsair, and Grumman F6F Hellcat), dive bombers (Northrop/Douglas SBD Dauntless, Vought SB2U Vindicator, and Curtiss-Wright SB2C Helldiver), and torpedo bombers (Douglas TBD-1 Devastator and Grumman TBF Avenger) did well in the Pacific against the Japanese. Their speed was less than that of the Japanese Zero, but their construction was sturdier (armored and with self-sealing gas tanks), which meant they could take a bad hit and survive. The best example of a flying armored weapons platform, however, was the multipurpose Republic P-47 Thunderbolt. Powered by a double bank of radial cylinders, a supercharger, and a water injection system, the extra-heavy fighter-bomber maneuvered at a competitive 450 mph. Eight .50-caliber machine guns and a fantastic bomb load made it the most feared ground attack plane of the war.

In bombers, however, the Americans emerged ahead of the competition. Led by men like Glenn Martin, who developed his MB-1 bomber two years before the government-financed fighter, and Glenn Curtiss, who built massive flying boats like the H-12 (the first airplane to shoot down a Zeppelin and to sink a submarine), the United States moved reluctantly beyond the pedestrian development of big planes as envisioned by the armed forces. Martin developed a two-engine plane (the B-10) with enclosed crew positions that added 15 mph to its speed. The army air force reluctantly accepted the design (it preferred open cockpits and gun positions), which served well into World War II. One of the best examples of the designers' acumen was Boeing's Model 299 bomber. Developed in 1934 in answer to army specifications for a two-engine bomber, the M-299 was built with four radial engines and enclosed crew positions that provided for up to 13 machine guns. It was designed to break through antiaircraft fire and hostile interceptors in broad daylight to make use of the precision Norden bombsight. It was so well constructed and defended that it became known as the Flying Fortress, the famous B-17 that bombed Germany into smithereens by 1945.

Similar advances came from Consolidated (B-24 Liberator), Martin (B-26 Marauder), North American (B-25 Billy Mitchell), and Douglas (A-26 Invader). Not until after the war began did the government enter the picture to help develop the Boeing B-29 Superfortress, a giant plane with pressurized cabin and remote-controlled, radar-guided machine gun emplacements, which was used against the Japanese home islands; the Consolidated B-32 Dominator, a massive shoulder-winged, four-engine bomber that had so many developmental problems that only 15 of them ever saw combat; and the Consolidated-Vultee (Convair) B-36 Peacemaker, even bigger yet with six pusher-prop engines supplemented by a pair of jet engines under each wing ("six turnin' and four burnin'," in the parlance of the airmen who flew it), that served after the war and bridged the gap between piston and jet-powered flight. Finally, preceded by the smaller Boeing B-47, America's first jet bomber, the venerable Boeing B-52 became a 30-year veteran of the Strategic Air Command by constantly updating the same old airframe with modern electronics into the 1980s.

After World War II, spurred by the developing cold war, U.S. aircraft development changed. Rather than the private ventures that advanced well beyond military requirements and were marked by the outstanding contributions of a few select individuals, American military aircraft have been created at government behest with an official willingness to take risks in design (recently tempered by rapid technological advances that make aircraft obsolete before they can be built) and to abandon the system of incremental design improvement. New aircraft incorporated such totally unique avionics concepts that they forced other nations to meet them at once, merely to survive in combat. Americans have depended on a qualitative use of electronic technology over mere numbers, the exact reverse of the philosophy that won World War II.

The first change was in the power plant of aircraft from piston-propellers to jets, giving the pilot a more stable fighting platform. At high speeds the propeller becomes a significant factor in drag, actually hindering the forward motion of flight. In World War II, the Germans had developed the first really efficient jet airplane. After the war everyone else began to catch up, the first U.S. contribution being the Lockheed F-80 (the new independent air force had changed the operational prefix letter from the army's "P" for "pursuit" to "F" for "fighter") Shooting Star, a project that began in 1944. It was soon joined by the Republic F-84 Thunderjet and the North American F-86 Sabre, America's first sweptwing plane. These aircraft, along with the navy's carrier-based Grumman F9F Panther and McDonnell F2H Banshee, soon cleared the skies of Communist MiG aircraft as American and United Nations troops steadied the hold of the Republic of Korea over the southern half of the peninsula. But when it came to the ground support role of aircraft, Americans found that the World War II prop-driven planes (like the old Corsair and the newer Douglas AD-1 Skyraider) had the control and slow speeds necessary to penetrate mountainous valleys and deliver an accurate bomb load.

Next came the sweptwing solutions to fighting Soviet MiGs, learned in the Korean conflict. The navy went first with the Chance Vought F-8 Crusader. This airplane had a number of new concepts, like pinching the fuselage at its waist, which reduced transonic drag, and a shoulder-mounted, variable-incident wing whose leading edge could lift for low-speed landing, leaving the fuselage and cockpit perfectly level for visibility in landing on a carrier deck. It was the first fighter to reach 1,000 mph (accomplished first by a then-unknown marine pilot, John Glenn). Although the Crusader equipped half of all navy and marine squadrons, it was soon replaced with the McDonnell F-4 Phantom. It had improved sweptwing design and a tail assembly with elevators that sloped downward for control. It could carry a bomb load that rivaled the old B-29 and possessed a Mach 2.5 speed (two-and-a-half times the speed of sound). All flew off the new *Forrestal* class carriers, based on British designs, which were equipped with angled flight decks, steam catapults that could launch four aircraft a minute, and mirror landing systems. Later, some of these ships would be nuclear powered.

The air force went into the Century series with the North American F-100 Super Sabre, early crashes of which lead to a redesigned tail assembly. The Republic F-104 Starfighter wound up as a ground support aircraft instead of an interceptor as designed, capable of carrying 4,000 different combinations of weapons. And the delta-winged Convair F-102 Delta Dagger and F-106 Delta Dart, which could swoop up in an arc to 70,000 feet in a "zoom climb," were the first American aircraft that relied solely upon missiles for attack and defense. As costs and weaponry abounded, the air force joined the navy and adopted the F-4 Phantom as its primary fighter-bomber. But in Vietnam, the air force and the navy found once again that the prop-driven relics of the past like the Skyraider and Douglas B-26 Invader delivered the most accurate and frightening bomb loads on enemy ground targets.

As the decade of the 1960s opened, the big development in aviation was "varible geometry." This process is best seen in the changing of wing sweep in flight to present the best attack angle (ranging between 16 and 70 degrees) in the leading edge to assure the correct speed and maneuverability for the task to be carried out (interception, dogfighting, ground bombing, takeoff and landing). This solved a key problem for the faster supersonic fighters that had way too fast a takeoff and landing speed because of their permanent, drastic wing sweep. The leading plane in this technology was the General Dynamics F-111 fighter-bomber. As the Americans worked out the bugs in this new, difficult advance, the Soviets followed suit with late-model MiGs and SUs, and the Americans retaliated with the development of the Grumman F-14 Tomcat. Similar technology involving a movable nose structure as well as wings made the civilian Supersonic Transport (SST) possible.

Next came the advanced electronics that make individual American military aircraft so complex and expensive. Electronic Counter Measures (ECM) jammed enemy radars so that their antiaircraft missiles missed their targets. Ground sensors located enemy traffic and guided bombers to active targets obscured in the jungle. Early "smart bombs" homed in on their targets guided by television cameras and laser beams. The recent Gulf War (Operation Desert Storm) was the first real test and justification of this technology, most of which came after the American experience in Vietnam.

The exceptions to this rule of constant totally new designs have been continued incremental changes in the French-designed Dessault Mirage and the American Grumman A-6 Intruder, the Boeing B-52 Stratofortress, and the General Dynamics F-111 and the F-4 Phantom. But in general, aircraft employed in Korea cost ten times more than those flown in World War II, and today's planes (the air force's McDonnell-Douglas F-15 Eagle, General Dynamics F-16 Fighting Falcon, Lockheed F-117 Stealth Fighter, and the navy's Grumman F-14 Tomcat and Northrop/McDonnell-Douglas F/A-18 Hornet) cost ten times more again. In addition, the diverse armaments available today involving a wide variety of fixed-wing and rotary-wing aircraft, and the use of all the possible configurations of missiles, make the proper mix of fighting designs complex, expensive, and difficult to maintain.

GENERAL AVIATION

Aircraft manufacturers have sold their products in three areas—military aircraft, commercial aircraft, and all others. The latter category, called "general aviation" as a sort of aeronautical catchall (and to avoid the country-club image that the term "private aviation" implied), includes everything from crop-dusters to business users to pleasure flying, and amounts to as much as 97 percent of all aircraft registered with the Federal Aviation Administration. Three-quarters of the private aircraft are used in business, particularly for agricultural planting and spraying. Most of the rest of business aircraft are employed as fast transports for executives. The importance of such aircraft to American aviation can be seen in the fact that 90 percent of all general aircraft are constructed in the United States, with one company, Piper Aircraft Corporation, claiming at one time to have built 25 percent of all planes in the air.

General aviation is often overlooked for the more obvious commercial and military planes known to the public at large, but it is actually the largest part of aviation production. Most of these private planes are built with a job in mind to attract potential customers. Initially, after the boom in aviation that came out of World War I, the general-aviation market was limited to nonscheduled flying services of one or two passengers, small air freight deliveries, and flying schools. In 1920, there were 87 of these firms in existence. By the middle of the decade their number had increased to 357.

Besides the obvious carrying of passengers and freight, flying companies also offered skywriting, payroll transport, carrying perishables, herding of livestock, border and forest fire prevention patrols, police assistance, lifesaving and emergency medical services, real estate surveys, and archeology (where aerial surveys made fantastic discoveries hitherto unknown, particularly the line figures on the Nazca Plain in Peru). The pilots who popularized general aviation were known variously as "flying gypsies" or "barnstormers," and their plane of choice was the two-seated army surplus trainer, the Curtiss JN-4 (the redoubtable "Jenny"), a $5,000 prototype that sold used for a few hundred dollars. These daredevils, performing at county fairs and air shows, made flying a national rage. It was also a good way to carry illicit liquor and skirt national Prohibition restrictions.

But nothing beat the airplane's use in agriculture. In 1921 army Lieutenant John Macready dusted a field near Troy, Ohio, effectively demonstrating the ability of the plane to cover large planted fields to control common agricultural pests. Further tests by the Department of Agriculture at Tallulah, Louisiana, in spraying a cotton crop over a period of six weeks were more than promising. Both army worm and boll weevil infestations were successfully controlled. Joint military-civilian projects against the gypsy moth in New England and locusts in the Philippines followed. After the army and the Department of Agriculture planted several fields from the air and produced a 2,000-foot motion picture, *Fighting Insects from Airplanes*, private firms immediately entered the arena. Huff-Daland Manufacturing of Ogdensburg, New York, developed a specifically designed crop-duster in 1924. Operating from nine airfields in the Deep South, Huff-Daland dusted crops at $7 per acre for five applications. Insurance companies were impressed and began to offer crop insurance to farmers whose fields were being dusted from the air. The idea soon spread to other sections of the country.

Copying crop-dusting and other ideas for using planes came to the fore. Aerial photography, particularly for mapping and surveying rough backcountry areas, developed in the 1920s. Early experiments such as the mapping of Atlantic City, New Jersey, and Middletown, Connecticut, and town planning by aerial survey in Schoolcraft, Michigan, were highly successful. In less than two months at a cost of $4,000, the mapping of a town that ordinarily took four years and $48,000 could be completed. The Fairchild Aerial Camera Corporation first began by making equipment for photographing from planes. Then they expanded to provide the service itself. Soon the Fairchild Aircraft Corporation came into existence to design and build proper planes to give a steady base from which to take aerial photographs. Cities found that regular aerial photos could be used to make tax assessments without the usual hassles of entering a property. By 1925, Fairchild and other similar firms were a part of a million-dollar annual business.

As aircraft became more sophisticated, business leaders began to look into the efficiency of their own air travel by private plane. As regularly scheduled airlines were still a thing of the future in the 1920s, businesses purchased small multipassenger planes to send their sales staff and executives out of town. By 1930, over 300 companies had their own aircraft. Oil companies dominated the field, but were soon joined by large-volume sales organizations and lumber, paper, power, and mining companies. To increase their sales, aircraft manufacturers emphasized safety, comfort, and speed. Fairchild, Stinson, Mahoney-Ryan, Travel Air, Stearman, and Advance Aircraft were among industry leaders. Dealerships and distributorships spread throughout the nation.

After Charles Lindbergh's spectacular crossing of the Atlantic, general aviation began to spread beyond business applications, air racing, and exhibition flying into pleasure and personal flying. Although the market was severely limited by the Great Depression, advances were made nonetheless. The airplane was seen as the ultimate adventure, a sort of liberating of the human form from the confines of gravity. Feminists encouraged women to fly as a part of their rising above the restrictive environment of their day. Amelia Earhart became their idol. Aeronautical Corporation of America put out the Aeronca C-2, a single-seat, ultralight craft that developed around 30 horsepower and was priced under $2,000. Its success (164 planes by 1931) encouraged others to enter the field, including American Eagle, Alexander, Beech, Cessna, Curtiss-Wright, Welch, Rearwin, Fairchild, Porterfield, Waco, and Piper. By 1939, there were 7,412 airplanes of five-seat capacity or less (80 percent were two-seaters) being flown in the United States made by 13 companies. Most were of a wingspan of 35 feet, weighed 1,000 to 1,300 pounds, had an average speed of 80 miles per hour and a ceiling of 16,000 feet, and cost around $2,000.

By 1939, the Piper Aircraft Corporation of Lock Haven, Pennsylvania, had pulled way ahead of the competition with the J-3 Cub, fated to be the most popular airplane ever made. William Piper claimed to have built 31 percent of all private planes in 1937 alone. By 1941, the company had built over 8,000 aircraft, many now being used to train military pilots. At the beginning of World War II, private-plane ownership was still a luxury of the rich. It commonly cost $8 an hour to maintain a Piper Cub, and most owners had to sell their expensive toys within two years of original purchase. The plane cost only $1,500 to buy, but still was more expensive than a yacht. Such figures caused many advocates of light aircraft to criticize the producers. The critics hoped that small planes would soon reach a potential that matched the automobile through the same mass-production techniques. Most vocal was Eugene L. Vidal of the Aeronautics Branch of the Department of Commerce. He made a survey of private-plane owners and called for a "new deal" for aircraft production. He believed that if backed by government financing, producers could manufacture a $700 airplane that would reach at least 10,000 future flyers. Although the government did produce several experimental models, Vidal's plan broke down because of the industry's skepticism and the complex skills needed to fly the type of slow-moving aircraft his idea advocated.

The advent of World War II saw the creation of the Civil Air Patrol, which consisted of private pilots who volunteered their time to look for enemy submarines and aircraft. The light planes, like the Piper Cub, became a training device for bomber and fighter pilots, and thousands were used as liaison and communications aircraft, artillery spotters, and as special transportation for staff officers. Painted olive drab, they became known as "grasshoppers," and could land and take off where larger and more bulky planes could not.

With the close of World War II, many believed that the light airplane would replace the family car and permit great flexibility in location of home and place of business. Initial production jumped to 35,000 units in 1946, but that level of production could not be sustained. Within a year the sales plummeted and production fell off to match demand. Piper's Cub soon faced new competition from the Cessna 150 and 170

("Texas won't be much larger than Rhode Island," bragged its ad campaign) and the V-tailed Beechcraft Bonanza (popularized in the radio-television series, *Sky King*—sort of an aerial western). All companies faced the dilemma of competing with the used-aircraft market, which has limited their ability to expand to the present day. The single-engine companies have also had to contend with a high-liability problem brought on by aircraft that have passed through the hands of several owners. The failure of federally restricted liability legislation has driven most manufacturers to emphasize the production of safer, more-expensive, multi-engined planes.

Unlike the private-plane owner, however, business corporations have been able to afford the price tag that accompanied turboprop and turbojet engines and advanced airframes. Pressurized cabins, better ground-to-air communications, radar transponders, all-weather flying capabilities, and the ability to hold in-air business conferences en route to a destination have increased the appeal of aircraft to corporations. Newer sales have emphasized airplanes that seat four or more persons and the old two-seaters have fallen to represent only 23 percent of the total. Gates Learjet, Beech, Fairchild-Hiller, North American Rockwell, Grumman, Piper, and Cessna have all made contributions to this market of increased speed and carrying capacity with more safety and comfort. All of the top-ten companies in the *Fortune* 500 maintained their own air fleets by 1970, a trend that has continued to the present. Although general aviation has not been as spectacular as military and commercial applications, it still provides an important adjunct role to modern air transportation.

COMMERCIAL AVIATION

It only took a half century after the Wright Brothers' first flight before airliners were carrying more passengers than the nation's railroads. Although a Columbus, Ohio, department store had flown a bolt of silk in from the Wright brothers' home of Dayton as a stunt (it beat all current railroad express-freight times), American commercial aviation began on New Year's Day 1914 when pilot Tony Jannus flew passenger A. C. Thiel in a Benoit XIV flying boat from St. Petersburg to Tampa. This service flew over 1,200 persons in the next three months, but never turned a profit and went out of business. Similar experiments took place at San Francisco Bay (which local tradition claims were actually the first). But before World War I there were not enough means or demand to sustain air service. Moreover, the Wright and Curtiss companies (with Martin being the largest of over 50 producers of aircraft) litigated over patent rights until 1917.

Meanwhile, many were interested in moving the mails by air. Such an experiment had been conducted in New York State in 1911, but Congress refused to endorse it until 1916. Through the erstwhile efforts of Assistant Postmaster General Otto Praeger, the first official airmail service between Washington, D.C., and New York, with a stop in Philadelphia, began in 1918. In 1920, the Post Office inaugurated transcontinental airmail service from New York to San Francisco by way of Cleveland, Chicago, and Omaha. Nighttime flights followed a system of bonfires, later replaced by a series of flashing beacons. Pilots subscribed to the Post Office's *Book of Directions* and kept their own updated "black books" of select geographical information to fly by. This led to gems like the classic report of pilot Dean Smith: "On trip 4 westbound. Flying low. Engine quit. Only place to land on cow. Killed cow. Wrecked plane. Scared me."

Smith was lucky. Such early mail flights were known as "suicide runs." No wonder Charles Lindbergh was the only known tee-totaler among early pilots. Flight conditions and the notion that the mail had to go through led to the formation of the National Air Pilots Association in 1928, which became the Air Line Pilots Association by 1931. This created professional flyers who demanded proper, safe flight conditions and equipment. But meanwhile, airmail had knocked 22 hours off of transcontinental railroad service. Especially interested in the new service were American banks. They had huge amounts of money tied up in checks and other collectibles (called "float") that lay idle until presented at the parent institution for collection. The air facilities would speed up this process considerably. The airmail routes were well enough organized that the Post Office eliminated all rail contribution to airmail in 1924.

The first real passenger lines were those between Key West, Florida, and Havana, Cuba, using flying boats, and between the national capital and Milwaukee, the latter based on the efforts of Alfred Lawson to develop an actual passenger-carrying plane. When Lawson's newest-designed plane crashed through pilot error, he had to retire from the business, financially ruined. By the end of the decade, names now familiar to modern Americans, like Trans-World, United, American, Delta, Eastern, and Northwest, began to appear. There were 61 passenger lines, 47 mail lines, and 32 express lines in competition with what would become the major airlines. Most carriers, by the way, had passengers sign a waiver that allowed the company to drop them anywhere along the trip should a more lucrative cargo be in the offing. United Airlines' "The Friendly Skies" were a long way in the future.

The trimotor was the dominant multi-engined mail and passenger carrier of the 1920s because, with the weak engines of the time, two motors gave little advantage over one. Three not only offered power but a margin of safety should one quit functioning. Developed by the Dutch designer, Anthony Fokker, working off British and German prototypes, the trimotor became the basis of Hugo Junker's German company and even a division of Henry Ford's massive auto empire. The trimotor lost its appeal when a Fokker model crashed in 1931, killing Knute Rockne, the famous football

Blanche Stuart Scott prepares for takeoff in this undated photograph.

coach. An ensuing investigation found the fabric-covered wings too weak for the load. Airline operators had already complained of its cost of operation, noise, and lack of creature comforts. The way was open for technological advances that would lead to the modern airliner.

Chief among the new technologies was the radial engine, like the Wright Whirlwind or the Pratt & Whitney Wasp, which would dominate commercial aviation until the appearance of the jet. It was light and powerful when compared to the in-line motors, but its bulky, flat nose was anathema to the advocates of streamlining. The National Advisory Committee for Aeronautics' (NACA) development of cowls solved this problem (increasing the speed of the Lockheed Vega from 135 to 155 miles per hour, a graphic demonstration of the effects of streamlining). Also important for the future of aircraft construction were the single cantilevered wing and all-metal stretched aluminum monocoque construction (a design process in which the skin of the plane is melded with the body chassis to carry most of the stresses). Along with the controllable-pitch propeller, the radial engines were mounted in the wing with the nacelles (engine housings) extending well forward of the leading edge to increase propeller efficiency and engine power. Wing flaps allowed more lift, lower landing speeds, and increased payload. Then the landing gear was retracted into the trailing section of the radial-engine nacelle. Finally, a soundproof cabin kept noise at acceptable levels.

The first plane to incorporate these advances was the Lockheed Vega of 1927. But in 1933, Boeing introduced the 247, a twin-engine transport that began the modern commercial airline industry. With all-metal stretched skin, two cowled engines mounted forward on the wing, retractable landing gear hidden in the rear of the nacelle, and soundproof fuselage, it literally knocked the trimotors out of the sky. No one in the world could match it. Unfortunately for the competition, all of the 247 production was reserved for United Airlines, part of a parent holding company that included Boeing. Trans World asked for a consideration but Boeing refused. But Douglas Aircraft offered to better the 247 for TWA and all the other airlines. It threw out TWA's proposed improved trimotor (it feared the Rockne tragedy would put off passengers) and mounted a cutaway mockup of the 247 in its plant with the challenge: "Don't copy it! Do it better!" The result was the 12-passenger DC-1, with variable-pitch propellers and improved flaps that allowed it to operate from almost any airport in the country, and rendered the 10-passenger 247 obsolete. DC-1 passengers did not have to step over the central wing spar that ran through the 247's cabin, either. Special wind-tunnel tests allowed them to stop wing buffeting with a special faring at the cabin and swept-back leading wing edges.

But Douglas refused to place its new plane in production. Instead, it went on to improve it with the DC-2, the first commercial airliner that could turn a profit with passenger service. The airlines liked it, especially after it came in second in the 1934 England-to-Australia air race (a specially built, two-seat DeHavilland racer won, and a Boeing 247 came in third), but asked for a bigger model that could allow passengers to sleep during flight. Douglas then produced the DC-3 in 1936, with a range of 1,500 miles and carrying capacity of up to 21 passengers at only $1.27 per seat-mile. Not to be left behind, Lockheed introduced the twin-tailed L-10 Electra. It hauled 10 passengers faster than any other comparable aircraft with all of the technological advances of the larger craft, and appealed to the shorter-hop, smaller markets. But by 1938, Douglas carried 95 percent of all American air traffic, and American airplanes of all kinds led the world in commercial applications.

The 1930s also saw a rise in the professionalism and bureaucracy of the airlines. Early pilots were mostly barnstormers, individualistic men who knew how to survive the myriad challenges brought on by different aircraft, few instruments, changing weather, failed engines, and sudden crashes. As the airlines began to standardize equipment and the older pilots retired, the slack had to be made up by a different breed. Airlines began to train their new pilots in ground schools and on special planes that had instruments for navigation and radios for constant communication with ground controllers. There were so many instruments that functions were combined on one dial and flight engineers employed to fly along in the cockpit to regulate them. Automatic pilot came in mid-decade, as did de-icing equipment. No longer did the pilot have the right to fly when and where as he saw best. The skies were too crowded. In 1932, the federal government instituted a licensing program for commercial pilots that emphasized skills and physical and mental fitness. The new pilot was the "super careful, monosyllabic antithesis of a grandstand flyer," according to *Time* magazine. In 1938 the licensing requirements were extended to tower personnel, the ground controllers who directed traffic in and out of airports.

As the control of aircraft changed in the cockpit so did the atmosphere in the passenger cabin. Each airline sought to make flying their routes a pleasure, because as flights grew longer the passengers became hungry and often disgruntled. Usually it was the copilot's lot to handle serving meals, dole out aspirin, and clean up the unpleasant results of airsickness (a real possibility when planes flew at low altitudes and could suddenly rise or fall hundreds of feet in a storm). At the end of a particularly rough trip it was not unusual to hose out the inside of the whole plane. In 1928, Western Air Express hired the first stewards, 28 men supervised by a railroad restaurateur. Box lunches, hot coffee, and tea appeared. Next came china settings, fancy colored napkins, and gold or silver flatware.

Then United made the key move when, in 1930, it hired eight beautiful young women, all registered nurses, to serve its passengers. These women were expected to be well-bred types, not showgirls or floozies, and were expected to represent everything good and fine in the American woman. "By taking our home-making in-

stincts into the cabins of the commercial airlines we can lend familiar aspects to which passengers can cling," went the propaganda that United issued. It did not mention that the ladies helped load baggage and move the aircraft into and out of hangars, too. The hostesses were rigidly screened on the basis of health, character, and intelligence. Some had passed pilot's examinations and one even flew as copilot, although airline executives usually reserved that role for men. But the high standards caused one popular magazine to speculate about the possibility of stewardesses and the equally well-screened pilots eventually joining in marriage to "produce a race of superior Americans."

The service in the passenger cabin was not the only marketing device employed by airlines to attract customers. Immediately, discount rates came into use (the predecessors to today's various frequent-flyer programs). American Airlines offered an Air Travel Card that allowed the patron, for a $425 deposit, to be billed for flights at 15 percent off. Soon airlines agreed to allow each other's cards to be used on competing connecting flights at the lower rate. There were also installment billing plans to lure more travelers into the air. Advertising played on the public's supposed hesitancy to fly, with catch phrases like "catch up with other modern folks," or "I wonder if I've been missing something." One ad showed a businessman relaxing in comfort with his favorite cigarette and a book with the caption, "Here I am—the fellow who said he would never fly!" The rest of the ad urged the doubter to "try it and see" what it felt like to be among "the discoverers of a new world!" Evidently the new market approaches worked; flight increased threefold from 1932 to 1936, and was up sevenfold for the entire decade.

As the 1930s drew to a close, aviation expanded into four-engine models. At first, large planes were flying boats, as much of the potential market for four-engine planes involved transoceanic travel. Among the first to exploit this market was Juan Trippe and Pan American Airways. Beginning in the Caribbean in 1928, Trippe used a variety of S-42 flying boats made by Sikorsky. He soon expanded his service into the Pacific using the Martin M-130, the famous *China Clipper*. In the late 1930s, Trippe inaugurated service to Europe from Long Island through Marseilles via the Azores and Lisbon. To achieve this, Trippe asked Boeing to create a new flying boat, the four-engine 314 *Yankee Clipper*. Although flying boats could utilize existing harbor facilities, they were not cheap to operate because of the high wing, boatlike hull, and drag-producing floats. They cost about 5 cents per seat-mile to fly, while the DC-3 was one-third less. But the nearest real overseas flying competitors were the giant German airships at 29 cents per seat-mile, so Trippe was able to make serious inroads on the transoceanic trade. All offered first-class service that rivaled the finest steamships. But the winter of 1940 showed just how inflexible the flying boat was compared to conventional aircraft—Pan Am had to transfer its operations from Long Island to Baltimore, then further south to Norfolk, Charleston, and finally Miami to avoid iced-up harbors.

The four-engine land plane was harder to come by. Boeing was the first American firm to enter the race, but its 299 was created to answer the army's need for a long-range bomber, not for the civilian market. Douglas soon followed Boeing, but concentrated on the passenger-carrying trade. The DC-4E had many revolutionary features such as tricycle landing gear, power-boosted controls, slotted flaps, and a flush-riveted skin. But it was too costly, complex, and ambitious to win airline approval. So Douglas went back to the drawing boards and came out with the DC-4, a smaller, less-complex plane. It was an instant success. Boeing combined the technology of the B-17 and *Yankee Clipper* to field the 307 Stratoliner. It was the first civil airliner with a pressurized cabin, although Lockheed had experimented with pressurization earlier. The 307 had disadvantages—it still used the tail wheel undercarriage, and the Boeing emphasis on wartime bomber needs limited

the type to just ten production models. Perhaps the greatest aid to the new, bigger planes was the lowering of the cost for 100-octane aviation fuel brought on by increased wartime production. Before that, 90-octane fuel cost half that of the superior fuel and had been the affordable commercial aviation standard. The higher octane allowed higher compression ratios and more efficient operation.

Boeing's military emphasis left Douglas supreme in the airline field once again. The DC-4 type became the culmination of the piston-driven commercial aircraft the world over. The DC-4 was improved on through several successive model changes: the DC-6, DC-6A, DC-6B, DC-7, DC-7B, and DC-7C, nicknamed the Seven Seas, giving some indication of its range. But all were essentially the same plane. Lockheed came into competition with its own unique design, the triple-tailed L-104G Constellation, or Connie for short. It was much thinner in body and more cramped in passenger comfort. Boeing used its vast military experience to develop the 377 Stratoliner, based on the B-29/B-50 aerodynamics and the C-97 military transport. Convair introduced new two-engine planes (240/340/440) with loading/unloading stairs built into their doors and modern avionics that took the short-haul market away from the old DC-3. These aircraft reigned supreme over the post–World War II civilian airline market. By 1951, 80 percent of the world's aircraft were American-made, and 56 percent of these came from Douglas. Since the days of the trimotor, costs of operation had dropped three times (to 1.5 cents per seat-mile) while airliner speeds had gone up by 150 percent. Attempts to introduce large-capacity civilian planes (the Republic RC-2 Rainbow, Convair XC-99, and Lockheed Constitution) failed, because the market was not yet big enough to support them.

But the airline market was expanding. The major difference was an outgrowth of the war—international travel. There were many interests in the international market. Most nations had their own international airline, usually government supported. Pan

Am, in the overseas market from the start, hoped to convince the U.S. government to back it as America's international representative in the air. The United States, however, had numerous airlines that wanted a piece of the international pie. The Roosevelt and Truman administrations objected to the idea of a government-supported monopoly. They much preferred an "open skies" approach with a minimum amount of regulation. The result was that Pan Am wound up sharing its overseas trade with TWA (in Europe), Braniff (in Latin America), and Northwest (in the Far East).

With the advent of longer trips as promised by international agreement, larger planes, and a flood of passengers who acclimated to flight during the war (air miles surpassed railroad passenger miles by 1951), the airlines really had to work on the convenience aspect of commercial flying. Reservations and baggage handling grew in complexity as trips crossed numerous airline routes and international boundaries. The advent of the computer eventually solved these logistical problems. The meal problem was something else. Originally, airlines had encouraged patrons to eat before or after travel. But now mealtime would probably have to be in the air. Airlines opened their own catering services, transporting already prepared meals aboard to be reheated in flight. But the meals tended to be soggy, of small portions, tasteless, and often cold. Snacklike cold meals did not help, as the railroads and steamship lines did better. But with the advent of deep freezing, the meals could be prepared ahead of time, frozen, and thawed out aboard the plane as needed. To prevent an airline war over food, the International Air Transport Association (IATA) set up guidelines for menus, as well as legroom and headroom in economy class. The more expensive first class was exempted and the airlines were allowed to proceed as they pleased.

The popularity of domestic air travel was assured when President Dwight D. Eisenhower reported favorably on Air Force One, the new presidential jet. Other political figures followed suit, from the lowliest diplo-

mat to the highest king. Sports teams eschewed rail and bus transport for the airways. Vacations lengthened in number of days available at one's destination, and grew farther afield in distance. Those of the wealthy who worked on one coast and lived on the other, or took weekends abroad, came to be called "jet setters." The result was fantastic congestion at air terminals that needed more and more modern facilities to cope with the demand of jet travel. Chicago began the move with the construction of O'Hare Field by 1955. It introduced parallel and simultaneous landing and takeoff runways, special flexible loading ramps that took one directly into the buildings, and seemingly interminable concourses. It looked as if construction would never stop at most facilities as airports modernized their terminals, improved servicing facilities, and deepened the concrete on the runways to handle the big jets.

To smooth out the increased congestion of boarding and deplaning, the handicapped and children were loaded or unloaded first. Frequent flyers could purchase club memberships that allowed them to use special lounges, often equipped with bars, comfortable chairs, and conveniences for business representatives like phones and copiers. Smoking and nonsmoking sections cropped up, eventually resulting in most domestic flights being limited to no smoking at all. Special dietetic meals were available, and the small liquor bottles served on airliners became collectors items. Movies and radio, reading lights, and adjustable air flow devices made the contoured seats more comfortable. The increased altitudes made possible by pressurized cabins meant that most storms and air turbulence could be avoided. But now, with increased trip length, one suffered "jet lag"—unusual exhaustion and difficulty in thinking at one's new destination, especially on east-west routes. Secretary of State John Foster Dulles, the most conspicuous air traveler of the 1950s (and the butt of many jokes because of it), actually came to believe that his controversial decision to cancel American aid to build the Aswan High Dam project in Egypt (which led to the Suez Crisis of 1956, Soviet primacy in influence there, and strained relations between the United States, France, and Great Britain) came about in part because of his own frustrations compounded by pronounced jet lag.

The major technological change in the airline industry after World War II was the introduction of jet propulsion, which promised greater speed, better power, and smoother, more economical operation. Originally developed by DeHavilland in England, the jet commercial airliner threatened the American market supremacy immediately. The closest thing to the DeHavilland Comet in the United States was the Convair 240 turboprop. Then, suddenly, the Comets began to drop from the sky. Analysts theorized that the mysterious crashes were the result of metal fatigue that resulted in an explosive decompression of the cabin. The crashes nearly bankrupted DeHavilland and gave the American companies a respite in which to catch up. The new power plant was a natural for Boeing, which had been building strategic jet bombers (B-47, B-52) for the air force. Boeing had just developed a four-engine swept wing model that would become the KC-135 tanker. With modifications, this design produced the 707, the first American jet-powered civil airliner. Douglas soon came out with the DC-8 and Convair developed the 880 and 990. All had a similar outward appearance: swept main wings and tail surfaces and four podded jets under the wings. Although the Convair models were not up to the standards set by Boeing and Douglas, they all outperformed the revitalized Comet in speed and range.

The new Pratt & Whitney J-57 jet engines offered much-reduced costs of operation. Fuel costs dropped 25 percent, and time between overhauls lengthened from every 2,000 operating hours to every 8,000 hours. The DC-8 and Boeing 707 proved to be the most successful moneymakers in airline history. This led the American airlines to take a new look into longer "stretch" jets (Douglas DC-8) and wide-body planes (the giant 375-passenger Boeing 747, and the smaller Douglas DC-10 and Lockheed L1011). The new jets had a special set of economic problems. If they operated with full-capacity seating they were quite economical to run. But if they ran half full, their cost of operation soared, often quadrupling at 45 percent capacity. Combined with a sluggish American economy that inhibited air travel, and the oil crisis in the Middle East, this economy of operation was critical. Boeing, for example, had to rely on the sales of its smaller jets (707, 727 [a very popular three-engine version with one in the tail], 737, and 757) to offset the decline in demand for the jumbo 747.

More controversial than the jumbo jets and wide-bodies was the Supersonic Transport (SST). The Soviets and a British/French consortium both placed SSTs into the air in the mid-1970s. But the United States deliberately refused to go along. American SST thinking was influenced by the development of the Convair B-58 supersonic bomber and the proposed XB-70 as early as 1959. The FAA set up an SST advisory committee in 1961 and it recommended the SST as a top priority in 1963. The National Aeronautics and Space Administration (NASA) provided convincing wind-tunnel tests, and Boeing, Lockheed, and North American all submitted proposals. By the end of 1966, Boeing's 2707 was declared the winner. It had variable swept-back wings and was the outgrowth of the company's TFX fighter plane. Indeed, all of the top designs had a military design background. Lockheed had submitted a double delta-winged model and North American, one based on the XB-70.

But other considerations entered the picture. There was little doubt that the United States would never recover the money put into the program if a prototype were built. The Vietnam conflict had called all federal programs into question—and the nation was overextended financially. Environmental concerns on the "greenhouse effect" produced by exhaust from high-altitude flying had some effect. This left national pride and thousands of jobs in the Seattle-area Boeing plant as the major impetuses for proceeding with an SST. It was not enough. The Senate rejected continuing with the SST by one vote on 24 March 1971. The British/French Concorde and the Russian Tupolev TU-144 both went into operation, but the costs per seat-mile were three times the predicted four cents. The Concorde can outturn an air force Phantom jet at 60,000 feet and Mach 2 speed, but its fuel costs per passenger are nearly prohibitive at two-and-a-half times the amount used by a 747. The development of a hypersonic transport is presently envisioned—possible from a technological point of view but perhaps prohibitive from a political-economic perspective.

As the decade of the 1970s closed, airline travel had grown spectacularly since the 1930s. In 1932, for example, flights per day numbered 700. By 1978 that was the number *per hour*. But in reality the airline industry was in a slump. Fuel costs and a sluggish economy caused reduction of all business activity nationwide. President Jimmy Carter put forth airline deregulation as a solution. This permitted the 29 major national and international carriers to reshuffle their schedules and trim marginal cities as they sought to concentrate their activity around the key "hub" cities that each one had. The industry was also hit by a strike of the ground controllers, represented by the Professional Air Traffic Controllers Organization (PATCO). The controllers sought fewer working hours and higher salaries, arguing that high stress factors justified their claims. Incoming President Ronald Reagan warned the controllers that it was illegal for government employees to strike and ordered them back to work. When the controllers refused, Reagan fired all striking employees. It took two years to approach the efficiency of earlier years as new employees were hired and trained. The members of PATCO became the first to learn the ill-effects that deregulation would have on labor in all the transportation industries.

At the same time, the aircraft received more sophisticated navigation and landing systems, including reception of satellite information and on-plane weather radar. For landing, the runways are marked with spe-

cial lights (standardized worldwide) and the instrument landing system (ILS) was implemented. Each runway approach today has a stepped-down array of lights that gives the pilot a slope of attack for landing in unfavorable weather. Automatic controls can guide an airliner down in dense fog. A newer microwave landing system makes the signals to incoming planes even more clear. More accurate equipment has allowed newer planes like the Boeing 767 to eliminate the need for the on-board flight engineer.

Meanwhile, the airline industry has suffered from a campaign of terrorism that began innocently enough with simple skyjacking for money or political asylum to outright terrorism, most of which grew out of American support for Israel in the Arab-Jewish Middle East conflict. But as shocking as individual incidents were, the world was too committed to fast travel to allow more than a brief decline in air usage. The rise in the numbers of travelers seemed destined to overwhelm the system. The last major, fully functioning airport built was the Dallas–Fort Worth complex in 1974. The newest major airport, Denver International Airport, plagued by a malfunctioning computerized luggage retrieval system, was more than a year behind schedule when it finally opened in 1995. The "hub and spoke" system, whereby each airline takes it passengers through a central airport within its air routes, has become a "hub and choke" system as passengers crowd together at inadequate facilities all at the same time. Key hours see planes land and take off every 30 seconds at major fields such as those at Atlanta, New York City, or St. Louis. Hubs are nonetheless necessary as the major airlines are no longer required to provide service to marginal markets, leaving these up to small, independent providers who interconnect at the hubs.

Deregulation brought problems for the larger carriers, too. Beginning with Braniff in 1980, they began to go broke as competition grew lean and mean. No longer were there any protected routes or rates. Many of the original airlines fared the worst, but none exemplified the new trend better than

Continental and Eastern. Bought out by an entrepreneur in the aircraft leasing business, Frank Lorenzo, Continental went through a seesaw process that saw it merge with Lorenzo's Texas International, move its headquarters from Los Angeles to Houston, sell many of its aircraft to satisfy Lorenzo's need to raise operating capital, lay off 15 percent of its employees to cut operating costs, then close down altogether as Lorenzo filed a Chapter 11 bankruptcy reorganization, under which only one-third of its labor force kept their jobs at half pay and fewer benefits, and one-third of its cities kept their service. Lorenzo beat back union strikes against his policies with the aid of favorable federal court rulings. In the end, Continental emerged as a much leaner competitor, but Lorenzo earned a less-than-decent reputation for dealing with his employees. When Lorenzo moved to acquire TWA, the airline unions balked at the deal. A similar response occurred at Frontier. In both cases, Lorenzo walked out without control but with a sizable war chest of cash as opponents bought him off. Then he took over Eastern and instituted many of the same practices as he had at Continental. The high price of fuel resulting from the Gulf War did in Eastern in 1991, but Lorenzo managed to avoid the collapse and retire from the airline business with a $40 million profit in the process.

Pan Am soon followed Eastern out of business, for many of the same reasons, selling most of its overseas operations to domestic giants United and Delta. TWA soon moved to reorganize under Chapter 11. Overextended, United had to sell its hotel and car rental chains to survive. The 1990s saw the first decline in airline service as revenues from passengers fell off $6.5 billion by 1992. Half of all the U.S. market was in the hands of American, Delta, and United. The remaining second tier of the business turned to foreign investors to maintain their market share. Continental allied with Scandinavian Airlines System (SAS), and Northwest joined with KLM, the Royal Dutch company. USAir tried to merge with British Airways, but the plan came unglued at the last minute, as other American airline companies complained that British Air would gain entrance to U.S. markets without reciprocity. But USAir had succumbed to the rule of modern American airline companies: "Eat or be eaten." It had large debts as it expanded into West Coast operations from its northeastern base. Finally, in 1993, a revised British Air merger was concluded, coordinating schedules but denying British Air an actual entry into the U.S. domestic market.

Meanwhile, smaller companies went the way of Southwest Airlines and cut frills and prices to survive, while inproving their images through increased productivity and friendly service that sought "to amuse, surprise, and entertain." Part of that involved giving cut-rate prices, or awarding regular fares a "free" bottle of champagne. America West, once the old Howard Hughes airline that went broke, came back as a "no frills" company that overexpanded and had to cut back once more because of recession and the Persian Gulf War's effect on costs, particularly fuel. In spite of numerous trials and tribulations, the airways have done for nations what the railroads did 100 years ago—reduced traditional geographic barriers and united cultures. But the future of air travel remains an enigma as yet unsolved, putting them today in the same precarious position that the railroads were in 100 years ago.

See also Aerostatics; Air Commerce Act; Air Line Pilots Association; Airline Deregulation Act; American Airlines; Astronautics; Bermuda Agreement; Black-McKellar Act; Borman, Frank Frederick, II; Civil Aeronautics Act of 1938; Continental Airlines; Crandall, Robert L.; Delta Airlines; Earhart, Amelia; Eastern Air Lines; Federal Airport Act; Federal Aviation Act; Guggenheim Fund for the Promotion of Aeronautics; Helicopters; Hughes, Howard Robard, Jr.; Kelly Air Mail Act; Langley, Samuel Pierpont; Lindbergh, Charles A.; Lorenzo, Frank; McNary-Watres Air Mail Act; Military Air Transport Service; Mitchell, William "Billy"; National Advisory Committee for Aeronautics; National Transportation Safety Board; Northwest Airlines; Organization of Petroleum Exporting Countries; Pan American Airways; Professional Air Traffic Controllers Organization; Tire and Rubber Industry; Trans World Airlines; United Airlines; USAir; Wright, Orville and Wilbur.

References Allen, Oliver, *The Airline Builders*

(1981); Bilstein, Roger E., *Flight Patterns* (1983); Bilstein, Roger E., *Flight in America* (1994); Brooks, Peter W., *The Modern Airliner* (1961); Crouch, Tom D., "General Aviation, 1919–1976," in Eugene M. Emme (ed.), *Two Hundred Years of Flight in America* (1977), 111–136; Davies, R. E. G., *Airlines of the United States since 1914* (1982); Dwiggins, Don, *The Barnstormers* (1968); Freudenthal, Elsbeth E., *The Aviation Business* (1940); Hallion, Richard P., "Commercial Aviation, 1919–1976," in Eugene M. Emme (ed.), *Two Hundred Years of Flight in America* (1977), 155–180; Higham, Robin, *Airpower* (1972); Hudson, Kenneth, *Air Travel* (1972); Hudson, Kenneth, and Julian Pettifer, *Diamonds in the Sky* (1979); Ingells, Douglas J., *The Plane That Changed the World* (1966); Labich, Kenneth, "How Airlines Will Look in the 1990s," *Fortune* (1 January 1990) 121: 50–51, 54–56; Leary, William M. (ed.), *EABHB: The Airline Industry* (1992); Lewis, W. David, and William F. Trimble, *The Airway to Everywhere* (1988); Miller, Ronald, and David Sawers, *The Technological Development of Modern Aviation* (1970); Perry, Robert E., "Military Aviation, 1908–1976," in Eugene M. Emme (ed.), *Two Hundred Years of Flight in America* (1977), 137–154; Serling, Robert, *The Jet Age* (1982); Smith, Henry Ladd, *Airways* (1942); Taylor, J. W. R., *Combat Aircraft of the World from 1909 to the Present* (1969).

Aerostatics

The science that deals with atmospheric aircraft that gain their flight characteristics from one or more containers filled with gasses that are lighter than air, aerostatics includes flexible balloons (unpowered) and dirigibles (powered) and rigid-frame, powered airships.

BALLOONS

The two basic elements for human flight had been known for much of recorded history—fire and nonporous material. But it was not until 1783 that Joseph Michel Montgolfier and his brother Etienne combined them to achieve man-induced flight. Capitalizing on laboratory experiments that showed that heated air inside a nonporous globe of cloth would rise and carry weight with it, and then sending animals up to test whether the air at certain altitudes would support life, the Montgolfiers fired up one of their balloons, stepped aside to permit Jean Pilatre de Rozier and the Marquis d'Arlandes to get into the basket, and watched two men rise in the air for 25 minutes, traveling 5 miles on the air currents above Paris, France. Within days, the feat was duplicated by another independent researcher, Jacques Alexandre Caesar Charles, working with hydrogen-filled balloons, as he and an assistant took their own 2-hour, 27-mile trip through the heavens. In a second trip that day, Charles took the craft up to 10,000 feet, suffered from the extreme cold, got an earache, and saw two sunsets in one day. Man had flown at last. But Charles had had enough. He never went up again.

One of the observers of a Montgolfier flight (ballooning quickly became an international craze led by the French) was Benjamin Franklin, the U.S. minister to France and no mean scientist in his own right. Franklin immediately saw the great possibilities of flight and wrote extensively on it. George Washington and Thomas Jefferson agreed with Franklin, foreseeing ocean crossings, military applications, and scientific and commercial advantages. In 1784, Englishman Peter Carnes flew an unoccupied, tethered hot-air balloon north of Bladensburg, Maryland. After several of these flights, a 13-year-old, Edward Warren, volunteered to fly in the balloon at Baltimore, becoming the first American to go up. Nothing more was ever heard of little Ed Warren—evidently, he was satisfied with his brief part in the history of flight and lived a normal, forgotten life thereafter. A later flight at Philadelphia, with Carnes in the basket, ended in tragedy as the balloon hit a nearby wall, dumped Carnes out, and flew off on its own, only to burst into flames and crash at the end of its tether. Carnes never flew again.

One of the more enthusiastic early American flyers was Dr. John Jefferies, a loyalist during the Revolution who had fled to London. Jefferies became the first American to make a free flight, paying French aeronaut Jean-Pierre Blanchard for the privilege. Later the two flew across the English Channel, carrying the first airmail letters. Blanchard continued his exploits throughout Europe, finally coming to the United

States in 1792. He flew out of Philadelphia in a hydrogen-filled balloon 15 miles into the farmlands of New Jersey. Fortunately, the non-English-speaking Blanchard had a letter from George Washington in his pocket (the president and his cabinet had witnessed the ascent), as incredulous locals quickly covered this unexpected extraterrestrial with their rifles and pitchforks. Converted to the cause, the farmers transported Blanchard and his craft back to the city and a tumultuous welcome.

Blanchard toured the United States for a time, but soon went broke. Not until 20 years later did another flyer, the Frenchman Eugene Robertson, make an ascent from American soil, this one at Battery Park in New York City. He also trained the first real American balloonist, Charles F. Durant. Studying in France for a few years, Durant was interested in upper-air currents. He ascended from Boston, flew out to sea, and returned on a different wind at another altitude in 1834. He saw the use of balloons for upper-air studies, mapping, and as a military device to escape from besieged cities. After Durant's demonstrations, ballooning in the United States boomed. All sorts of stunts abounded. When men rode into the heavens astride horses in balloons in France, Americans did it astride alligators. "The alligators, it is supposed, were never so high before," reported a local New Orleans newspaper, tongue-in-cheek (hopefully), "but Messrs. [Alexander] Morat and [S. S.] Smith have been high often."

Smith went up again (without alligators or other companions) for the Washington's birthday celebration in the Crescent City and observed the cannonade honoring the country's first chief executive. He descended and reported that his view was excellent and recommended the balloon as a military reconnaissance vehicle. It was not a new idea, but the outbreak of the American Civil War gave Smith's report new credence and applicability. John Wise had already demonstrated that balloons could travel hundreds of miles as he went from St. Louis to New York State in less than 24 hours. On another trip, he even carried the first official

airmail letter between two Indiana towns. Wise used common muslin for his balloons, which brought the hobby within the monetary means of many. He also invented a rip cord that emptied the balloon of gas when landing to prevent its being dragged by surface winds, a common hazard. He also planned to cross the Atlantic, but failed to ascend when his financial backers pulled out.

Dr. John Jefferies and French aeronaut Jean-Pierre Blanchard were first to cross the English Channel by hot-air balloon in 1785.

Thaddeus S. C. Lowe hoped to cross the Atlantic in a balloon, but was prevented by a lack of gas and the bursting of his balloon during filling. He later undertook an experiment to test prevailing winds for the Smithsonian Institution. Lowe ascended at Cincinnati and drifted to Unionville, South Carolina. It was not a notable trip except that the date was 19 April 1861. Fortunately, a local hotel owner knew Lowe and prevented his being hanged as a Yankee spy. Going back up north, Lowe found that the war had brought on much interest in aerial reconnaissance. James Allen had already put up a balloon at Washington to prevent a surprise attack on the nation's capital. John Wise took an inflated balloon out of Washington to the battlefield of First Manassas, tethered to the back of a wagon. Unfortunately, it snagged a tree and the bag broke. A later Wise balloon got away from its crew and was shot down by infantrymen to prevent its falling into Confederate hands.

Balloonists were not always received with enthusiasm by tradition-bound government bureaucrats, civil or military. John La-Mountain volunteered his hydrogen balloon for the war effort but was ignored until the controversial and corrupt politico General Benjamin Butler at Fortress Monroe expressed interest. A Democrat-turned-Republican who was not beyond a little confiscatory larceny in the name of the Union, Butler liked anything that the powers-that-be did not. Hence LaMountain was given his chance. LaMountain's ascents were the first real military use of aerial observation. He worked both tethered from the fantail of a ship in the James River and in free flight over the rebel lines. When his balloon ran out of gas, so did his employment. He got into a quarrel with Lowe, now returned to head the government's official balloon corps, and never served again. Despite his courage and talent, most dismissed LaMountain's flights back and forth over the enemy lines as showboating. Or maybe the critics were simply jealous. In any case, future flights were tethered events.

Lowe became the chief federal balloonist, and (unlike LaMountain) cultivated the proper political contacts, including President Abraham Lincoln. Under Lincoln's tutelage, Lowe assembled a corps of 7 balloons and 12 hydrogen generators. He could inflate a balloon in three hours and, under normal weather conditions, each inflation lasted two weeks. Communication with the ground was by means of a telegraph key. His corps served with the Union Army

of the Potomac during its 1862 Peninsular Campaign and was instrumental in saving federal forces under Confederate attack at Fair Oaks and later at Gaines Mill. But Lowe's service was seen as a novelty with results not commensurate with the time spent, and it did not last out 1862.

The Confederates were a little more impressed. Their efforts, however, were not as successful as the Yankees'. One Confederate balloon, flown by Captain John R. Bryan, had its tether cut when a soldier's foot got caught in the line. The balloon floated across Union lines and came under fire. After a dunking in the James River the craft wound up in Confederate territory again, its pilot a little worse for wear, but safe. A second Confederate balloon went up at Gaines Mill and reported seeing Lowe's craft four miles away. A subsequent trip had the usual adverse results, only this time the balloon fell into Union hands. A later balloon was sent aloft at Charleston piloted by Charles Cevor, but broke loose and was carried away to sea and lost. Fortunately no one was aboard at the time. Many of the Confederate efforts were "silk dress" balloons, allegedly being made of patriotic clothing contributed by female devotees of the Southern cause. In reality, Captain Langdon Cheves built them from bolts of dress silk that had never graced the form of a southern belle. Covered with a rubbery naphtha varnish, they made a perfect gas orb. One is still in the hands of the Smithsonian Institution.

After the war, ballooning went back on the entertainment circuit, appearing at fairs, festivals, and circuses. P. T. Barnum featured balloon ascents at his Hippodrome. The thrills of ballooning were still dangerous. Washington H. Donaldson, a leading aeronaut, was killed with a companion at Chicago when a sudden lake storm smashed the craft to the ground. The premier aeronaut of the late nineteenth century was Samuel A. King, with 450 ascents to his credit. He invented the drag rope that automatically adjusted the ballast to keep the craft at a constant altitude. Women got into the act with Mary H. Myers ("Carlota, the lady aeronaut," as she was known in show circles). Indeed, female interest in ballooning has held to the present, with Connie Wolf, Vera Simmons, and the Reverend Dr. Jeanette Piccard. Dr. Piccard always carries a piece of angel food cake in her high altitude flights, "because one never knows who one might meet up there."

Although balloons whetted human interest in flight, they never rose above the level of practicality except in the realm of scientific research. The death of balloonists in the late nineteenth century has popularized the use of unmanned flights, often to great heights of over 30 miles. Typical in this aspect of balloon science has been the use of weather balloons by the National Weather Service since 1937. Astronaut space suits were tested in balloon flights into near space. One New Zealand effort circled the globe for over a year. Balloons are still used in military applications from observation to breaking up the paths of bombers (barrage balloons). Early balloons had been used to bomb enemy positions as early as the 1840s, often with adverse results as the missiles fell on friendly positions. In World War II, the Japanese sent incendiary balloons across the Pacific jet stream to fall in the American Northwest, with little effect. Balloons are still employed as cheap reconnaissance vehicles in the timber and fishing industries, and hot-air ballooning is growing yearly as a sport, with a spectacular annual festival at Albuquerque, New Mexico. As Jean-Pierre Blanchard inscribed on his balloon almost two centuries ago, *Sic Itur Ad Astra*—"This Way to the Stars." The balloon was the first step.

AIRSHIPS AND DIRIGIBLES

Between the two world wars, no other aircraft seemed to hold greater promise for carrying passengers and freight than airships and dirigibles. The difference between the two craft was in their gas bags. A dirigible is a flexible bag that obtains its form from the shape of the bag when extended by the lighter-than-air gas (helium or hydrogen) that gives it lift. The most obvious example for an American are the Goodyear blimps that hover over sporting events. The airship, on the other hand, is a rigid-frame craft that suspends its airbags inside a skin that is forever taught and shaped. The best examples were the several Zeppelins built by the Germans after World War I, as typified by the grandest of them all, the *Hindenburg*.

Regardless of form, Americans lagged behind their counterparts in Europe in building and exploiting the market for these flying machines. Early airships were mainly publicity stunts for such public gatherings as state and county fairs. The army bought the first airship for the government in 1912. It was sent on a public relations tour and then junked. The service had no other craft until 1921, when the navy turned several outmoded blimps over to it. Indeed, whatever advances that America had made in the field of dirigible machines came from the navy. Interested in crossing the vast oceans to support its surface vessels, the navy had experimented with flying boats—aircraft that took off from water—but found them woefully inadequate in payload carried and distance traveled. Its first airship was built by a contractor who lacked experience and turned out to be a great disaster (optimistic as usual before congressional oversight committees, the navy preferred to see it as a "learning experience"). The advent of U.S. entry into World War I allowed the navy to utilize British designs and by the end of the conflict, it had some 36 blimps, none of which saw war service.

After the war, a British airship, the R-34, flew the Atlantic nonstop from Scotland to Long Island, the first such crossing ever. It was not hard to envision a vast fleet of airships patrolling the oceans, and the navy received the job to perfect a type and make it available to the other services. Although General Billy Mitchell was not about to allow the navy to take the lead, his agent in Europe, trying to procure one of Count Ferdinand von Zeppelin's designs, was charged with trading with the enemy, the United States having never signed the Treaty of Versailles. But meanwhile the

Germans had wrecked their Zeppelin fleet to prevent its falling into Allied hands. Giving the army its blimps, the navy went with its own rigid-frame design. It produced three airships domestically and received one from Britain and another from Germany.

The real problem was the lifting gas used. The best lift came from hydrogen. It was also the cheapest to produce. But it had one great fault—its volatility. Helium did not have this fault. A fairly recent discovery, helium was first found on the sun through spectrum analysis in 1868. Americans soon realized that the gas could be manufactured through a complex process. Better yet, oil discoveries on the Texas panhandle proved rich in helium. But the process of separation remained complex and expensive. So did the flying characteristics of helium when compared to hydrogen. The latter gas could fill the airships' cells at 100 percent capacity. As the ship rose, the less-dense atmosphere caused the hydrogen to expand. An automatic bleeding system funneled the excess hydrogen into the atmosphere to maintain constant altitude. Landing was accomplished by emptying the gas bags until the craft sank to its mooring post. Helium was different.

A helium airship's cells could be filled only three-quarters full to allow for expansion. There would be no bleeding of the expensive helium. Instead, constant dirigibility was maintained by generating ballast during flight. This was accomplished by condensing the water vapor produced by its engines to replace the weight lost by the consumption of gasoline. Thus helium had less lift to start with, was expensive and could not be wasted through venting, and had to have a complicated condensation system that cost it more buoyancy and drag, limiting its applicability. But it was safe. Its availability was further limited in the 1920s when the oil fields began to lose pressure from overpumping. The result was a cutback in the American airship program until another helium-rich oil field could be opened up. The 1925 crash of the *Shenandoah* airship, with the loss of 14 of her crew of 43 in a summer thunderstorm, not only made the navy airship program look bad, but cost the service much of its available supply of helium.

Nonetheless the navy plowed on. It contracted for two of its post–World War I airships with the Goodyear Tire and Rubber Company of Akron, Ohio. The company had acquired the American rights to build Zeppelin-like airships from the German manufacturer. The navy asked that Goodyear build two airships at a cost of $5.4 million for the first and $2.5 million for the second. (The difference came from the need of Goodyear to build the plant to construct the ships.) The result was the delivery of two airships of similar design, the *Akron* and the *Macon*, the largest airships in the world to that time. Their most unusual feature was that they carried four airplanes that could be launched and recovered while the airship was in flight. These scout planes trebled the area of search and also flew flank guard on the slower mother ship. Both airships were lost at sea, the *Akron* only 18 months after launch in the Atlantic, and the *Macon* after a career of 3 years in the Pacific. They were the last rigid-frame military craft ever built, worldwide.

Meanwhile, the commercial aspect of airships burgeoned. But the cost of such rigid airframes was phenomenal, and government subsidy was needed. A bill to grant the airships an airmail contract hustled through Congress until an adjournment resulted in its being lost in the shuffle, through no lack of merit on its own. Then the *Akron* crashed and everyone was suddenly rethinking the airship equation. A government report concluded that because normal airplanes were so much cheaper and more flexible, building the big cargo-passenger airships like the Germans were doing was not cost effective or really a safe form of travel. The tragic explosion and crash of the *Hindenburg* at Lakehurst, New Jersey, in 1937 only reconfirmed this point. A Martin flying boat, popularized by Pan American Airways, cost less than a half million dollars. The Boeing 314 flying boat cost a half million dollars exactly. An airship ran close to $5 million— one could purchase 20 airplanes for the cost of one airship. Soon the Germans reached the same conclusion and junked what remained of their Zeppelin fleet.

As the rigid airship lost favor, the nonrigid blimp slowly advanced. The army soon decided to go with the fixed-wing, four-engine bomber. The navy would also make the same decision in favor of fixed-wing aircraft, but not until after World War II. During the war, the navy expanded its fleet of blimps to almost 200 machines of four types varying by size and weight. Their slow, steady speed was just the thing for antisubmarine patrols. About 50 of the craft were lost, all but one to collision or weather. The blimp K-74 fell to German antiaircraft fire from the submarine U-134 when the American ship's bombs failed to release. In 1944 the first blimps to cross the Atlantic flew from the United States to French Morocco. These six ships remained in the Mediterranean to protect Allied surface operations from German submarine attack. Although historians claimed that the deployment of navy blimps did much to restrict the German's Atlantic submarine campaign, more modern assessments favor the new, small escort aircraft carriers as the decisive weapon. The navy's penchant for the aircraft carrier after the war lends some verity to this latter view.

As the army's abandonment of the blimp program in the 1930s had shown, the real enemy of the dirigible has been the existence of cheaper, speedier, more reliable fixed-winged aircraft. As the cold war threat against Allied nations assumed more the form of ballistic missiles than of bombers, the blimp became a nullity in the early warning system. It was all up to radar now. The navy's blimp program ended in 1960. The final blimps were decommissioned two years later. In the private sector, the Goodyear Company considered whether it ought not divert its advertising dollar to the new medium, television, and get rid of its last blimp, the *Mayflower*. But careful research showed that the American public saw the terms "blimp" and "Goodyear" as synonymous. The more the ship flew over sporting events the more free air time Goodyear got.

Finally, as television improved its technology, the blimp became a fine platform to view games from a different perspective. The result was a new fleet of three blimps, with one stationed in Houston, another at Miami, and the last at Los Angeles. Each is equipped with 3,780 light bulbs and a computer tape that allows the ship to send crawling messages and pictures to the largely nighttime viewing crowds. The airship or dirigible that had begun as an advertising medium in 1904 has returned to that role today, except for a brief foray by unmanned blimps along the nation's southern borders in a vain effort to stem the booming drug trade.

See also Aeronautics; Astronautics; Lowe, Thaddeus S. C.

References Baldwin, Munson, *With Brass and Gas* (1967); Botting, Douglas, *The Giant Airships* (1980); Crouch, Tom D., "The Gasbag Era," *Aviation Quarterly* (1977) 3: 291–301; Haydon, Frederick S., *Aeronautics in the Union and Confederate Armies* (1941); Jackson, Donald D., *The Aeronauts* (1980); Millbank, Jeremiah, Jr., *The First Century of Flight in America* (1943); Pineau, Roger, "Ballooning in the United States from Straw to Propane," in Eugene M. Emme (ed.), *Two Hundred Years of Flight in America* (1977), 41–67; Robinson, Douglas H., *Giants in the Sky* (1973); Seibel, Clifford W., *Helium* (1969); Smith, Richard K., "The Airship in America, 1904–1976," in Eugene M. Emme (ed.), *Two Hundred Years of Flight in America* (1977), 69–108; Turnbull, Archibald, and Clifford L. Lord, *A History of United States Naval Aviation* (1949).

Agricultural Appropriation Acts

Many early highway provisions were hidden in the Department of Agriculture's appropriations, as it had initial responsibility for road projects. Four acts have important highway considerations.

AGRICULTURAL APPROPRIATION ACT OF 1893

As the culmination of a yearlong debate over the formation of a National Highway Commission brought on by the "good roads" movement, this measure appropriated $10,000 for the secretary to make inquiries into possible systems of road management throughout the nation, the best method of road making, and to dispense such information through the Agricultural and Mechanical College network utilizing the agricultural extension programs. The result was the formation of the Office of Road Inquiry under General Roy Stone. It marked a reinstitution of interest by the federal government in roads, which had been absorbed by the railroads since the Civil War.

AGRICULTURAL APPROPRIATION ACT OF 1905

In response to requests by Director Martin Dodge, Congress established the Office of Public Road Inquiry on a permanent basis and merged it with the Division of Tests from the Bureau of Chemistry. Also provided for was a chief of records, an instrument maker, and six clerks. The new entity was labeled the Office of Public Roads and was to be headed by a "scientifically" trained road director, which put Dodge out of a job. He was replaced by Logan Waller Page. It marked a change in the federal government's outlook on roads from a mere bureau to one that had a lot more technical expertise.

AGRICULTURAL APPROPRIATION ACT OF 1928

This measure authorized the secretary to perform engineering and road-building services for other governmental agencies, such as the Forest Service and the National Park Service, on a reimbursable basis. The act allowed the expansion of federal properties for recreational purposes and illustrated the impact of increased travel on the federal system.

AGRICULTURAL APPROPRIATION ACT OF 1936

Under the Hayden-Cartwright Act of 1934 the federal government could assist the states with money for plans, surveys, and engineering on future highway projects. This mandate was reinforced and buttressed in this 1936 legislation by including economic studies as well. States were permitted to expend up to 1.5 per-

cent of their federal matching funds for such investigations.

See also Dodge, Martin; Good Roads Movement; Hayden-Cartwright Act; Office of Road Inquiry; Page, Logan Waller; Roads and Highways, Colonial Times to World War I; Roads and Highways since World War I; Stone, Roy.

Reference U.S. Department of Transportation, Federal Highway Administration, *America's Highways* (1976).

Air Commerce Act (1926)

The haphazard development of civil aircraft standards after World War I caused Congress to get into the act once again. In 1926, the Air Commerce Act established the federal regulation of the new industry. It set up the Aeronautics Branch of the Department of Commerce (predecessor to the Federal Aviation Agency) to promote and regulate air commerce, register pilots and planes, establish standard air routes, and establish aids to aerial navigation. Some of these functions, like research and airways, were doled out to existing sections (Bureau of Standards and Bureau of Lighthouses, respectively) of the Department of Commerce, a dispersion that was not ended until the Civil Aeronautics Act of 1938 unified all aeronautical branches as one service.

See also Aeronautics; Civil Aeronautics Act of 1938; Kelly Air Mail Act.

References Bilstein, Roger E., *Flight in America* (1994); Komons, Nick, *Bonfires to Beacons* (1978).

Air Line Pilots Association (ALPA)

The Air Line Pilots Association had its birth in the hectic and dangerous open-cockpit days of flying the first airmail in the mid-1920s. It was glamorous but dangerous work—pilots had a one-in-four chance of being killed. With the advent of the Kelly Air Mail Act, the pilots had to go to work for independent contractors, as opposed to the Post Office Department as they had earlier. Pilots now had hours, working conditions, and wages that they hoped to protect from their new employers' desire to cut costs. David L. Behncke of Chicago began a campaign among pilots, whose ranks now included passenger-carrying flyers, and asked that interested persons contribute $50 to an "escrow" fund along with undated letters of resignation. This was to give the association clout to be used at the proper moment against the airline owners. He also affiliated the group with the American Federation of Labor, although the pilots have always considered themselves a notch above the average American laborer and not union workers in the ordinary sense. Initially the ALPA was formed a bit differently than a normal labor organization—the pilots wished to protect what they had rather than demand betterment of working conditions. The ALPA has tended to avoid collective bargaining. Rather, it tried to lobby the federal government for laws to protect jobs through roundabout safety legislation.

But at the same time, the ALPA was not averse to a normal strike, should all other methods fail. In the early 1930s, they struck Century Airline when its owner, E. L. Cord, tried to undercut other carriers by cutting costs, primary among them being pilot wages. But they also went to the Franklin D. Roosevelt administration and presented their case to government regulators, who eventually canceled Cord's mail contract. Their support of Roosevelt and Congress in the airmail frauds under the 1930 McNary-Watres Air Mail Act led them to receive bonuses. These were made available under a special grievance procedure, a rider to the Railroad Labor Act of 1936 and Decision 83 of the National Labor Relations Board, that exempted the ALPA from the regulations of the National Recovery Act's industry code requirements. This exemption from traditional government regulation was also ensconced in the Civil Aeronautics Act of 1938. Indeed, the ALPA was not an ordinary labor union.

When strikes were used against airline management, the ALPA applied the tactic of working at one airline at a time to gain concessions. These included actions in 1948 against National Airlines to gain acceptable conditions and rules for operating four-engine aircraft, and in the mid-1950s against Eastern to destroy the concept and union of the flight engineers by making

pilot training a condition of their employment (an advancement opportunity that the "third men" on the flight deck could hardly refuse). Traditional attitudes continued, such as the APLA lobbying against lax laws on air piracy in the 1970s and de-emphasizing their connection to the rest of organized labor by refusing to stand by the more militant Machinists Union during the deregulation fights in the 1980s, when the ALPA was among the first of unions to realize that the deregulation rules and actual or threatened airline bankruptcy had seriously changed the concept of collective bargaining.

See also Aeronautics; Professional Air Traffic Controllers Association.

References Hopkins, George H., *Flying the Line* (1982); Hopkins, George H., "Air Line Pilots Association," in William H. Leary (ed.), *Encyclopedia of American Business History and Biography* (1992), 17–19.

Airline Deregulation Act (ADA) of 1978

Regulation of the airline industry began in the 1920s when the government began to issue contracts for the carrying of mail and passengers. At first the Post Office and then the Interstate Commerce Commission handled the government supervision, but in 1938 Congress established the Civil Aeronautics Board (CAB) to monitor the airlines exclusively. The CAB operated under the assumptions of the New Deal—that the free-market system had essentially failed and needed to be watched to make business effective. The 16 existing airlines, now known as "trunks," were grandfathered into the system. All others had to make application and be reviewed by the CAB. Of 79 applicants for new airline licenses, not one was approved until the deregulation process began in 1978. Existing interstate airlines were allowed to expand to fill new public transportation needs, but only after a lengthy case-by-case process that generally took two years to complete.

At the same time, small airlines could enter the market, provided they restricted themselves to intrastate business. As the regulation process went along, a noticeable dichotomy in rates became evident. All economic factors considered, the regulated rates stayed relatively the same as the demand expanded, actually dropping, in effect, over the long run. But the unregulated intrastate rates were considerably lower, responding to free-market forces. Since regulation meant that interstate carriers could not compete in price, they offered other amenities like better meals, more service by stewardesses and stewards, and more frequent times of departure. Cut rates were allowed, but they were restricted to a certain percentage of seats and had to meet other restrictions, such as the age of the passenger, the length of stay at a destination, and family members traveling together. By 1970, the airlines had completed their conversion to jet-powered aircraft and petitioned the CAB for a rate increase to pay for the capital outlay, even though the jets were cheaper to operate and profits were up as much as 14 percent per year from 1949 to 1969.

Under public and congressional pressure to investigate, the CAB studied the rate problem and came to the conclusion that some deregulation would materially lower fares. The result was discounted "super saver" prices, most of which an airline could enact without government supervision. But these were still limited programs. Next, the CAB allowed carriers to abandon short hauls that were time consuming and more costly to serve. By now the public clamor for more deregulation had grown, primarily because of increased ridership. Congress responded with the Airline Deregulation Act of 1978, making the airlines (over their vociferous protests) the first transportation element to lose government supervision. The airlines came first as they had the most detailed records that demonstrated that the free market might work in interstate as well as intrastate routes. The ADA modified the CAB's authority over a period of years, ending its jurisdiction over routes in 1981, fares in 1983, and ending the independent board itself by 1984 (all responsibilities went to branches of the Department of Transportation). A so-called Essential Service Program was to end the existing subsidy to small markets within ten years, replacing it with a low-bid system.

The years since deregulation have been tumultuous, to say the least. Petroleum prices skyrocketed in 1979. Recession hit the American economy and travel declined. With it fell the customary airline profits. Worse yet, the established airline companies were bloated from the years of regulated competition and overloaded with expensive labor contracts and wide-body jets of large passenger capacity. When new companies entered the now-unregulated market with smaller planes and nonunion labor, the bottom fell out of the old companies. The first to fall was Braniff, which ceased operations in 1982. A new airline would reopen, then disappear, using the old Braniff name, but essentially the airline, one of the originals from the 1920s, was dead. The most dramatic incident of change came at Continental, which declared bankruptcy but continued to operate amid strikes, employee layoffs, reduced wages, reduced service, shifting schedules, and a poor public image that transferred to its boss, Frank Lorenzo. But Continental managed to survive, at least unto the time of this writing.

Gradually, all of the "trunks" experienced a scenario akin to Continental's. By the middle of the 1980s, they began to change their air fleets over to smaller aircraft (that needed fewer crew members to operate) to better compete with the new companies. Labor contracts were renegotiated, and many employees went on part time or accepted reduced benefits, often paid for by profit-sharing plans. Mistakes in marketing became deadly if unsuccessful. Most airlines completely rerouted their flights and initiated the "hub and spoke" system of operations. Under this concept, the one-time trunks operated between a central point of their choice and extended their tentacles into select cities. The smaller markets connected with the majors at their hubs. This led to many anomalies, such as a flight from St. Louis to Baton Rouge, Louisiana, that went by way of Atlanta. The idea was to keep the passenger on the same airline as long as possible.

The real problem today is that all airlines want to land during a select few hours to make their connections, which has led to an auctioning of the landing slots available at those popular hours to the highest bidders. Another trend has been to offer cheap rates with little service in the cabin, "no frills" to the Madison Avenue people, by small airlines that utilize older vacant airports like those at Newark, Chicago's Midway, or Dallas' Love Field. To most passengers, money talks. The cheaper line will likely be chosen unless the former trunks also meet that price. Then established reputation is the key. To meet the competition, the old trunk lines offer such things as frequent-flyer miles, cheap standby seats, and a score of incentive plans. The offers are often so complicated that the public has had to rely on computerized travel services to book their flights, experts who know how the programs work. Of course, the airlines offer travel agents incentives to book people on their flights, too. The net effect of deregulation has been a drop in fares of about 15 percent, making the free-market advocates accurate foreseers. The problem is that this has been achieved at the cost of much destabilization of the industry, the complete reordering of the labor structure, and many assertions (and some proof) that overall safety has been potentially compromised.

See also Aeronautics; Air Commerce Act; Civil Aeronautics Act of 1938; International Brotherhood of Teamsters; Motor Carrier Acts, Motor Carrier Act of 1980; Organization of Petroleum Exporting Countries; Professional Air Traffic Controllers Organization; Staggers Rail Act of 1980.

References Kaplan, Daniel P., "The Changing Airline Industry," in Leonard W. Weiss and Michael W. Klass (eds.), *Regulatory Reform* (1986), 40–77; Pickerell, Donald, "The Regulation and Deregulation of U.S. Airlines," in Kenneth Button (ed.), *Airline Deregulation* (1991), 5–47; Williams, George, *The Airline Industry and the Impact of Deregulation* (1993).

Alaska Highway (Alcan)

In 1867, Secretary of State William H. Seward, on behalf of the people of the United States, bought Alaska from Tsar Alexander II, emperor of all the Russias, for a cool $7 million. With the exception of the Klondike gold rush in 1898 (more men went to Cuba as a part of the army than here), not much had been done with "Seward's Folly," as the popular mind viewed the land to the north. But Pearl Harbor changed all that. By that time it was well known that the shortest route between the United States and Japan was the Great Circle—not directly across the Pacific, but in an arc from Seattle to Tokyo through Fairbanks, Alaska. Prior to the war nobody much cared. There was no one to make service to Alaska profitable. But now Alaska was the northernmost outpost of the United States against what lurid journalists once called the "Yellow Peril"—the attack from Asia.

On 16 January 1942, President Franklin D. Roosevelt appointed a committee to consider the feasibility of building a road to contribute to the defense of Alaska. By March of 1942, the army was ready to build a road to Alaska from the United States through Canada. This Alaska-Canada (hence Alcan), or Alaska Highway as it is officially named today, was to stretch 1,523 miles from Dawson Creek, in Canada's Northwest Territories, to Fairbanks in American Alaska. The idea was to provide communication with the far north independent of the sea, so recently the domain of the feared Imperial Japanese Navy. Both U.S. and Canadian government officials had made such suggestions before the war, the most important of which was British Columbia Premier Thomas "Duff" Pattullo's suggestion that such a public works project would alleviate effects of the depression. But inactivity, the whims of domestic politics, and international jealousies had prevented action. Some short-sighted political hacks even suggested that such a project would stimulate the Japanese to declare war. It took off with little delay after Pearl Harbor was attacked, however, spirited by a visit north by Canada's British High Commissioner Malcolm MacDonald, who feared an American takeover if Canada did not move to assert its interests in the area.

Although a Japanese invasion of Alaska

Through bushland, across muskeg and rivers, the Alaska Highway was constructed to serve as a main artery in North America's defense network against the Imperial Japanese Navy during World War II.

was not really in the cards except as a diversion from other assaults in the Pacific, no one knew that in 1942. But it seems in retrospect that the Alaska Highway was constructed during the war because it could be justified as a defense project. This rationalization knocked all prior objections aside, be they Canadian or American. As it was, the highway was not finished until the defeat of Japan and hardly any supplies or men went across it for the war effort. Indeed one could argue that the Alaska Highway project was an unnecessary drain on war matériel and men that could have been better used elsewhere. The manpower shortage was so severe that the army broke its racist policy of not employing black soldiers in northern climes. Ultimately, over a third of the army's road builders were black. But the time had come to take advantage of opportunity and the road was built ostensibly for wartime necessity, but in reality with an eye for postwar civilian use.

The construction was an American project from the first, especially when it came to money (wartime defense funds), construction machinery (old Civilian Conservation Corps retreads), and manpower (U.S. Army engineers). Work went on 24 hours a day, in 10-hour shifts, 7 days a week, as the Canadian summer when the ground was thawed was short. When it rained the bulldozers sank to their seats. The mud holes were corduroyed with cut logs, just as men had built roads 100 years earlier. Initial surveys were run in the air. Worse, some of the highway was located over permafrost, an ice barrier that bled into the highway after construction. It too had to be corduroyed. The ground surveyors were often only 30 miles ahead of the actual construction teams. The mosquitoes became rampant in drier weather, their hum so loud they interfered with voice communication. Every stream had to be bridged, the road right-of-way cleared for 30 feet to each side of the roadbed, which was to be 18 feet wide. The army engineers had a cleared section all the way to Fairbanks by October 1942. The civilian contractors who built the actual highway took until 1954 to get the surface laid. In

1946, the Canadian portion of the highway was turned over to them for administration and maintenance.

The military effort on the road was under the command of Colonel (later General) William M. Hoge. He was an experienced road builder in the Philippines and a professional military engineer who had supervised numerous troops in combat and noncombat assignments. After reconnaissance by dog sled and mule pack trains, he decided to construct the road in segments so that as many men from his 35th Combat Engineers as possible might be employed at once. Despite working a breakneck speed and doing a good job, Hoge's methods were often improvised, communication was poor, and the whole operation was not neat and orderly. This caused a desk-bound inspector general to have Hoge relieved before the project could be finished, and he received little credit for his leadership.

The real final work was not an army assignment but was done under the Public Roads Administration (PRA) crews that followed the military engineers. The Alaska Highway was its biggest operation to date. Using equipment left over from the Works Progress Administration (WPA) and the Civilian Conservation Corps (CCC), the PRA selected five civilian construction firms to build the road, four (one Canadian with Canadian employees only) to work on the roadbed and one to manage the housekeeping facilities. The companies were to turn the army's preliminary road into one with a paved asphalt two-lane surface over 2 feet of crushed stone that was 24 feet wide with a 36-foot easement on each side. It was the standard New Deal road that proliferated the byways of America. Often standards on grades forced the contractors to completely relocate the roadbed (much to the army's disgust). Things were not helped any when the summer of 1943 turned out to be a year of record rain. Work kept up by diverting men and equipment from project to project as determined by local weather. The highway was finished in 1943 but for the bridges, which were completed by the end of 1944. Over 20,000 men had worked on the road.

The Alaska Highway has been rebuilt and resurfaced many times since the war. Other stretches have been relocated a third time. Its impact on the region has been quite diverse. Recent studies hold that the Native Americans of the area suffered much from the introduction of disease from the workforce. The result was a heightened infant mortality rate and increased consumption of alcohol. Economic conditions have changed little since the days of the gold rush, because the effect of the road has been limited more to its exact corridor than the whole area, and to the period of construction rather than the era since. The one perennial thing was the arrival of more hunters looking for game trophies, who competed with the locals for food hunting. This has led to more reliance on government services for local inhabitants. The town of Dawson City, center of the region during and since the gold rush, has lost population and influence to White Horse, farther to the north, and closer to "civilization" through its connection to the Alaskan coast at Haines.

See also Roads and Highways since World War I.

References Coates, Kenneth (ed.), *The Alaska Highway* (1985); Coll, D. B., et al., *The Corps of Engineers* (1958); Creighton, Donald, *The Forked Road* (1976); Dziuban, Stanley W., *Military Relations between the United States and Canada* (1959); Hart, Val, *The Story of American Roads* (1950); Huntley, Theodore A., and R. E. Royall, *Construction of the Alaska Highway* (1945); Lee, Ulysses, *The Employment of Negro Troops* (1966); Rainey, Froelich, "Alaska Highway: An Engineering Epic," *National Geographic* (February 1943) 83: 143–168; Remley, David, *Crooked Road* (1976); U.S. Department of Transportation, Federal Highway Administration, *America's Highways* (1976).

Alaska Railroad (ARR)

Run by the U.S. Department of Transportation (and currently in line to be sold to the state of Alaska), the Alaska Railroad runs from Seward and Whittier through Anchorage, Denali National Park, and Fairbanks to Eielson Air Force Base. Trainmen on the Alaska Railroad work in what they call the "Ice Box State." Temperatures drop

The first car of the Alaska Railroad is loaded on a steamer in Seattle in this undated photograph.

as low as 70° F below zero and can fluctuate 60° to 70° F in a 24-hour period. Snowfall can run 15 to 20 feet and maintenance crews have to plow the track constantly to keep it open. Any warm spell can cause the snow to melt and form avalanches, burying hundreds of feet of track. Precipitation averages near 200 inches a year. Yet oddly enough, the Alaska Railroad crosses the Rocky Mountains at Broad Pass, the elevation of which, at 2,363 feet, makes it the lowest pass in the whole mountain chain as it wends it way through North America.

Congress chartered the Alaska Railroad in 1912, but actual construction began in 1915. Essentially, it was a connection between the existing Tanana Valley Railroad and the Alaska Central Railroad, all of which were combined into one line and renamed the Alaska Railroad. It was finished in 1923 and the line opened by President Warren G. Harding, who died suddenly thereafter on the return trip at San Francisco. The line was built to test the possibilities of rail operations in such an extreme climate, to promote national defense, and to open the interior to the outside world. The whole line was rehabilitated in the late 1940s, with the wooden bridges replaced by steel, sharp curves made more gradual, and heavier rail laid. The stations and maintenance buildings were also modernized.

Despite the weather problems in keeping the Alaska Railroad open, which rarely delay traffic more than three hours, one of its real hazards is the large moose population living along the right-of-way. Many a train has reached a standoff with an angry animal blocking the track and threatening to take on all comers. One suspects that the noisier steam locomotives had less problem with this than the quieter diesels. Usually, however, moose retreat in the face of the superior weight of the engine. Another unique problem faced less frequently, but eminently more disastrous, is earthquakes. The 1964 Kodiak quake, among the most powerful ever recorded, completely wrecked the yard at Seward. Frenzied work opened the Seward facility within a week and the second port at Whittier within a month. Naturally,

the scenic possibilities offered by the route of the Alaska Railroad are among the best in the world. When Union Pacific closed its passenger service in favor of Amtrak, the Alaska Railroad purchased its fleet of dome cars and ran the passenger train AuRoRa (ARR is the acronym for Alaska Railroad). Besides the wildlife, forests, and mountains, the road has two of the more spectacular rail bridges in the world across the Tanana River and Hurricane Gulch.

See also White Pass & Yukon Railroad.

References Drury, George H., *The Historical Guide to North American Railroads* (1985); Drury, George H., *The Train-Watcher's Guide* (1990); Fitch, Edwin M., *The Alaska Railroad* (1967); Hubbard, Freeman, *Encyclopedia of North American Railroading* (1981); Wilson, William H., *Railroad in the Clouds* (1977).

American Airlines (AA)

Originally a loose confederation of companies under the name of Aviation Corporation (AVCO), American Airlines' predecessor was designed by the Fairchild and Curtiss-Wright companies to exploit their planes through federal airmail contracts. Soon, like all early mail carriers, passengers became part of the business and AA merged with nine smaller airlines in the northeast and Canada and expanded its routes from New York City to Chicago. But the process put it into debt that seemed insurmountable. Worse yet, AA lost out in the airmail shuffle of 1930 and lost its contract routes. Led by Frank G. Coburn and then Cyrus R. Smith, AA tried to standardize its aircraft for low-cost maintenance purposes and establish profitable schedules coordinated with each other. The company was assisted by the new 1934 airmail laws that allowed it to regain the federal subsidy necessary to survival. But more was needed. The salvation was the Douglas DC-3, which AA converted to en masse in the late 1930s. Using the "sleeper models," AA flew transcontinental flights that made 1938 its first profitable year.

Profit led AA to move its corporate headquarters from New York to Chicago in 1939. The Midwest city was fast becoming an air hub much as it had attracted the railroads a century earlier. To meet compe-

In the 1940s, American Airlines' DC-4 was one of the first commercial aircrafts to fly from New York to Los Angeles.

tition, the company instituted the Admiral's Club, an exclusive home away from home at the terminals for weary travelers. Next came in-flight kitchens and the extension of its service into Mexico. During World War II, AA flew transport for the United States Army Air Force. This gave its pilots and administrative crews experience overseas, which the airline turned to practical advantage by merging with American Export Airlines in 1946 to fly commercial routes to Europe. AA used new equipment, particularly the advanced Douglas models—the DC-4 to fly to Los Angeles with a stop in Chicago in competition with United, and the DC-7 to fly the nonstop coast-to-coast routes in competition with Trans World Airlines. AA also paired up with select competitors (Delta and Continental) to share

routes, flying alternating runs, that they could not win outright from the Civil Aeronautics Administration.

Most important for AA's move ahead of its competition was the development of computer reservation systems. The story goes that company president Cyrus R. Smith was flying next to a businessman who appeared quite interested in Smith's complaints of how airlines suffered from not having a better reservation method. The interested listener turned out to be an IBM computer salesman. He promised Smith the problem could be solved and Smith put up $40 million for the development of Semi-Automated Business Research Development (SABRE), which gave AA an advantage over other airlines for a decade. The system was redesigned by American's own information systems division in the 1970s so that travel agents could tap into it, and it allowed the flexibility for SuperSaver fares, full planes, and frequent-flyer programs (to guarantee brand loyalty). The use of computers has been taken up by other airlines and has led to consumer groups charging that they tip each other off secretly as to price changes through coded entries. But inquiries by the Department of Justice have proven nothing.

With the arrival of the jet age, AA jumped into the lead with the Boeing 707 on its longer routes and the British Air Corporation's 111 to compete against Eastern in the New England commuter runs. The end of the 1960s saw AA extend its influence into the Pacific, routes later exchanged with Pan American to gain the latter's Caribbean runs. The introduction of the wide-bodied DC-10 was followed by deregulation, a move that AA countered with computerized passenger services that allowed it to avoid the embarrassing debt that plagued less fortunate companies. Under the able leadership of Robert L. Crandall, AA moved to cut its fixed costs further by selling its gas-guzzling older planes for more fuel-efficient models and renegotiated labor contracts to guarantee jobs for more production at lower wages, which has made it one of America's top airlines. Recently, however, American has proved it is not immune to modern economic reality. The line has announced that it will reduce its fleet by 18 planes and cut 3,600 more jobs. Moreover, its commuter flights, under American Eagle, have run afoul of recent FAA directives that limit the use of many of its turboprop aircraft under "icing conditions," forcing a cancellation of some flights and a rerouting of different planes into the northern U.S. airports that American services.

See also Aeronautics; Crandall, Robert L.

References Cornett, Lloyd H., Jr., "American Airlines," in William M. Leary (ed.), *Encyclopedia of American Business History and Biography* (1992), 36–43; Davies, R. E. G., *History of the World's Airlines* (1964); Davies, R. E. G., *Airlines of the United States since 1914* (1982); Davis, L. J., "And Now, Can Bob Crandall Have It All?" *New York Times Magazine* (23 September 1990): 25, 42, 44, 46; Serling, Robert, *Eagle* (1985).

American Association of State Highway Officials (AASHO)

Created in 1914 as an outgrowth of the "good roads" movement, the American Association of State Highway Officials sprang from the American Association of Highway Improvement (also known as the American Highway Association). Along with the American Automobile Association, it had sponsored several road congresses (1911–1914) that set up motoring and highway standards designed to promote safe and increased use of motor vehicles. The state professional road men believed that they needed a more technical organization tailored to the needs of employees of the new state highway departments springing up across the nation. The AASHO was to facilitate the exchange of information and cooperation between the various states and the states and the federal government. It also became an important lobbying body for highway legislation, and set standards for highway construction and maintenance with the approval of the federal government.

During World War I, the AASHO helped designate so-called war roads that would provide priority routes from factories to the ports along the East Coast. After the war, they sponsored various pieces of federal highway aid legislation that led up to the Federal Highway Act of 1921. The organization backed the National Highway Research program, designed to better standards to keep up with increased traffic, speeds, and vehicle weights. They also performed able assistance in World War II, selecting highways to haul war materials, setting standards of weight and speed, and planning the interstate highway system. They called for increased federal assistance to the states after the war, and helped the Lucius D. Clay Committee promote the interstate system. With the creation of the federal Department of Transportation in 1968, which altered many of the existing relationships between the states and the federal bureaus, AASHO changed its name to the American Association of State Highway and Transportation Officials. But much of the heretofore cordial relationship between the states, Washington, and AASHO was lost to bureaucratic wrangling.

See also Roads and Highways, Colonial Times to World War I; Roads and Highways since World War I.

Reference U.S. Department of Transportation, Federal Highway Administration, *America's Highways* (1976).

American Automobile Association (AAA)

The "Triple A," as it is commonly known, was founded in 1902 to serve as the national representative of the nine local auto clubs then in existence. By World War II, the number of affiliates had grown to 725, and had 1 million members. The organization has two functions: to work for the improvement of motoring conditions as an active participant in the Good Roads Movement, and to render personal assistance to members having motoring difficulties, such as towing stranded vehicles or changing blown tires. The AAA is interested in highway safety, and in guaranteeing that any highway fees are applied directly to solving road problems, rather than being sidetracked to other projects. Over the years the AAA has attacked any obstacle to crossing state borders; fought for the elimination of abuses in the sale and financing of cars, the creation of adequate parking facilities, the elimination of speed traps, and automobile education; and assisted thousands of stranded motorists. The association has been instrumental in mapping public highways and designing tourist jaunts for its members through its guidebook series on roadside services and trip planning. It also sponsors many experimental developments to improve motoring, including monitoring many automobile contests and keeping records. Its publicity efforts include its own publications and the writing of "public interest" articles for newspapers and magazines.

See also Roads and Highways, Colonial Times to World War I; Roads and Highways since World War I.

Reference U.S. Department of Transportation, Federal Highway Administration, *America's Highways* (1976).

American Express Company

American Express was a joint-stock company organized in 1850 by three competing firms that dominated the express business in northern and western New York State: Wells and Company; Butterfield Wasson and Company; and Livingston Fargo and Company. Generally, the two major express firms of the era, American and Adams, were northern and southern in scope. Although they jointly competed for New England's trade, American spread out across western New York, into Canada, along the Great Lakes, and into the Old Northwest. Adams went south along the Atlantic coast and west out to the Ohio River.

American initially made a big coup by using exclusive contracts with rail lines like the emerging New York Central (and its eventual subsidiary line, the Michigan Central), the Illinois Central, and the Chicago, Burlington & Quincy to spread its trade. Absorbing dozens of smaller companies as it went westward, the most important being United States Express, American Express popularized settlement in Michigan by promising merchants that the new territory would not be isolated from the normal transportation advantages of the East because of their services. They also provided cash on delivery (COD), which allowed merchants to get an easy line of credit independent of banks. The company sought out markets and crop improvements that allowed Michigan to become the first vegetable and fruit center of the United States—closer to the big-city markets than California and Florida competitors in those days. If American had a disadvantage over its main competitor, Adams, it was that the winters up north were more intense, which sometimes affected their ability to get shipments through.

Unlike Adams, which got into the California trade right after the gold strike, American waited three years to move. It was a more conservative company that liked to see a market so far-flung develop a little before taking action. In 1852, American created Wells Fargo Company as its western subsidiary, dividing the United States between them at the Mississippi and Missouri Rivers, American taking the eastern half. The new Wells Fargo was the first company that could fight on a one-to-one basis with Adams in California, which changed the free hand the latter had had in cornering the gold rush trade and dominating the hordes of smaller firms that could not compete effectively.

Unlike Adams and Southern Express, which grew into separate companies and remained allies, American feuded with its offspring, Wells Fargo Company and United States Express, which argued for a division of the spoils, usually in territory and rail lines exclusive to each. By the turn of the century, various express rates were so convoluted that one investigator was quoted three different prices in the same day for the same theoretical shipment. And the companies were so interconnected that few knew who really controlled what company: American was owned by the Chase Manhattan Bank, but Wells Fargo was owned by American Express, and so on.

Until 1913, when the U.S. Post Office created parcel post to help regulate fees through government competition, the only way to ship small packages and valuables was by express. Hence, American and the others did not have to advertise to get a profitable share of the business. They did their best, but failed to keep the federal government's idea of parcel post out of the express business through lobbying influential congressmen and were listed among the smug malefactors of great wealth that stifled the free flow of goods through excessive charges.

With the advent of American entry into World War I, the government nationalized many transportation facilities, including the express companies. The four major companies in operation then were American, Adams, Southern, and Wells Fargo. The government consolidated them under the name American Railway Express Company, with each firm subscribing to a proportion of the stock. The government guaranteed them against loss, but they had to share profits with the feds, getting only 49.75 percent as their collective share. At the end

of the war, none of the three companies desired to set up independently, so Railway Express continued in operation, this time as a private corporation. The days of the old express companies had come to an end, and the new one of travelers' checks and credit cards was about to begin.

See also Adams Express Company; American Railway Express Company; Central Overland California & Pike's Peak Express Company; Harnden & Company Express; Leavenworth & Pike's Peak Express Company; Pacific Union Express Company; Russell, Majors & Waddell Company; United States Express Company; Wells Fargo & Company.

References Friedman, Jon, and John Meehan, *House of Cards* (1992); Grossman, Peter Z., *American Express* (1987); Harlow, Alvin F., *Old Waybills* (1934).

American Freedom Train (1976)

A special train that toured the United States in 1975, 1976, and 1977 to celebrate the American Bicentennial, the American Freedom Train consisted of two dozen cars painted red, white, and blue, displaying over 400 originals and copies of artifacts ranging from the Declaration of Independence to historic materials from all walks of life. The train was often pulled by steam power in the form of a 4-8-4 Southern Pacific streamlined northern-type locomotive (restored at a cost of $100,000) and was sponsored by the American Freedom Train Foundation through private contributions. Among the sponsors were General Motors (which insisted that the consist be pulled occasionally by its red, white, and blue Electro-Motive Division diesels), PepsiCo, Prudential, and Kraft Foods. The train was introduced by a four-car abbreviated version called the Preamble in 1974, which toured all the continental 48 states to drum up support for the big project. As a part of the celebration, many railroads painted one or more of their regular road engines in the bicentennial red, white, and blue colors during 1976 and for some years afterward.

See also Locomotives, Steam Locomotives; Presidential Trains.

Reference Hubbard, Freeman, *Encyclopedia of North American Railroading* (1981).

American Railway Express Company

During World War I, when an organized effort of all American resources was deemed indispensable to curb German militarism, and as part of the culmination of the Progressive political movement, which saw government regulation as a necessary evil to curb business excesses, the United States government established a director general of railroads, William G. McAdoo. One of the numerous railroad-related functions that fell under McAdoo's domain was express delivery. At the time, four major companies dominated the field: American Express, Wells Fargo, Adams Express, and Southern Express (which some claimed was a secret adjunct to Adams). The government consolidated them under the name American Railway Express Company, with each firm subscribing to the stock in proportion to their business volume. The government guaranteed them against loss, but they had to share profits, getting only 49.75 percent as their collective share. At the end of the war, none of the three companies desired to set up independently, so American Railway Express continued in operation, this time as a private corporation, under the Transportation Act of 1920. This entity operated its 25,000 offices until 1929, when the various railroads created the Railway Express Agency (REA), which replaced it. The REA covered the nation with 50,000 miles of lines, exclusive of the Southeastern Express Company, an Alabama corporation, which handled traffic on the Southern Railway and the Mobile and Ohio Railroad. Contrary to the implications of its name, Railway Express Agency sent many of its shipments by air almost from the beginning, which marked the trend away from rail to truck and air shipments that continues today.

See also Adams Express Company; American Express Company; Central Overland California & Pike's Peak Express Company; Harnden & Company Express; Leavenworth & Pike's Peak Express Company; Pacific Union Express Company; Russell, Majors & Waddell Company; United States Express Company; Wells Fargo & Company.

Reference Harlow, Alvin F., *Old Waybills* (1934).

American System

A cleverly named political philosophy (what does one oppose it with, the "un-American System"?) developed by congressman, later senator, secretary of state, and perennial presidential candidate, Henry Clay of Kentucky, the American System expressed the nationalistic sentiments that swept America after the narrowly "won" War of 1812 in the so-called Era of Good Feelings. Americans were moved by the vastness of the West and desired to exploit and unite it readily with the rest of the nation. Clay leapt onto the bandwagon and put forth his ideas as a part of an organized federal policy proposal.

The concepts were not new. They had been put forth under different guises by Alexander Hamilton and economists Matthew Carey (whose son was not surprisingly named Henry Clay Carey) and Friedrich List. These men spoke against the laissez-faire doctrines of the English economic philosopher Adam Smith and his concept of natural forces (supply and demand) affecting a national economy. Clay stated that, contrary to Smith's assertions, a government could control its future growth by the laws it passed, and that a population suffered only because existing products could not reach them. Clay maintained that it was the duty of government to create new jobs, protect existing jobs, diversify national production, and prevent unnecessary foreign competition.

Clay's American System was based on four concepts: (1) a high protective tariff to protect U.S. industry and secure the domestic market against foreign competition, (2) a federal bank to regulate the economy and domestic currency, (3) the creation of internal improvements (any form of transportation) to distribute goods among the American people freely, and (4) the distribution of the sales proceeds of the vast western lands among the states on the basis of population for each state to use on its own internal improvements, or for the repatriation of African-American slaves back to the African homes from which they and their ancestors had been stolen. Clay's philosophy helped create the National Republican and Whig political parties for which he was presidential candidate and spokesman. It was the basis of the John Quincy Adams' administration in the mid-1820s. Clay's program was opposed by Martin Van Buren, who created the Democratic Party and used the popular war hero Andrew Jackson as his stalking horse.

See also Clay, Henry; Van Buren, Martin.

References Carroll, E. Malcolm, *Origins of the Whig Party* (1925); Dangerfield, George, *The Era of Good Feelings* (1952); Eaton, Clement, *Henry Clay and the Art of American Politics* (1957); Lively, Robert A., "The American System: A Review Article," *Business History Review* (1955) 29: 81–96; Poage, George Rawlings, *Henry Clay and the Whig Party* (1936); Van Deusen, Glyndon, *The Life of Henry Clay* (1937).

Amtrak

Officially the National Railroad Passenger Corporation, with headquarters in Washington, D.C., Amtrak was created by the Rail Passenger Service Act in 1970 and actuated the following year, as it likes to say, "with $40 million appropriation from Congress, cast-off passenger cars from the private railroads, and no track or facilities of its own." Although it was to be a two-year experiment, successive acts of Congress have made the entity pretty much permanent. The purpose of Amtrak was to rescue American rail passenger service from the doldrums brought on by lack of public use, because of the advent of the automobile and increased air service. It was hoped that rail passenger use would alleviate the necessity of building more highways and air facilities that tended to be noisy, congested, pollution oriented, and excessive in land use. Existing rail facilities were seen as underutilized and readily available.

Amtrak had just two years to do the job; it would not be easy. The drop in rail passenger interest was dramatic. In 1929, for example, there were 20,000 passenger trains operating on the nation's rail lines, carrying 77 percent of all travelers using mass transportation. Buses carried the second-highest amount, 15.5 percent. By 1970, this had changed drastically. The railroads had 450

intercity passenger trains and all but 100 were doomed to a quick extinction. Rail passenger service hauled just over 7 percent of all travelers. Buses now carried 16 percent. Airlines had 73 percent of all intercity travelers using mass transportation. Since 1949, the private rail owners had lost from a fifth to a half of their freight income subsidizing their passenger service, depending on whose figures one uses. The goal of Amtrak was to save mass rail transportation, modernize it to compete with other forms of transportation, and manage it as in the days of old when it was the pride of America. Hopefully, it would also turn a profit, something the private railroads had been unable to achieve for decades. If technology had killed passenger trains, technology could save them was the reasoning.

What really killed passenger trains? Technology played a part, with the advent of airplanes, automobiles, and superhighways. But there was more to it than that. Some of the blame must go to the government policy of great federal aid to motor vehicles through the federal highways and interstates. The railroads themselves sort of committed suicide in the passenger department. They were especially lax in promotional efforts. Even those who preferred trains did not easily ascertain their presence or schedules. Some lines were unsupportive of the draining passenger trains, opting instead for the more profitable freight business. They drove their own passengers away; they encouraged Amtrak to relieve them of a seemingly insoluble problem. Others, especially the western rail lines with their great transcontinental scenic streamliners, fought to keep passengers to the end. It was no accident that a lot of early Amtrak equipment came from these lines. Removal of U.S. Postal Service mail contracts was a mixed bag—it killed a lot of trains, but the railroads themselves did in even more of them before the mails went by air.

Amtrak began with a fleet of 1,300 old passenger cars, but by 1977 three out of four had been replaced with new equipment. By 1979, the shorter eastern corridor between Boston and the nation's capital were using fast turbo-trains. Other longer transcontinental runs were running new Superliner double-decked cars with great views of the passing scenery. Locomotives were modernized and then replaced with new powerful units. Over $650 million had been spent to make train travel worthwhile to the public. And the travelers responded with increased use, double the amount by 1980 to over 20 million riders. Reservations were computerized, new facilities built, others renovated, and different routes experimented with to improve public interest. By 1986, Amtrak ranked seventh in passenger traffic when compared to the top ten airlines. Package excursions, some with detraining rights several times along the way, became popular. In 1986, Amtrak Express came into being and necessitated the purchase of a new series of insulated boxcars called "merchandise-handling cars." Built with passenger trucks and all necessary electrical and brake connections, they were painted to match passenger-carrying cars. Today, they carry sealed U.S. mail bags (once again) and large packages, generally in one full car to one destination, but no baggage—that still being hauled in actual baggage cars.

Amtrak's greatest weakness continues to be its dependence on the whims of politics felt through government financing, some of which was felt early on by congressional demands that certain unprofitable areas in their districts be served. Many of these problems have been ironed out through more responsible congressional legislation, and the passage of time bringing new faces into the legislative committee system. Particularly important are the "403(b) trains," normally unprofitable runs that a state can request Amtrak to operate if they subsidize any losses. President Ronald Reagan's administration sought unsuccessfully to return Amtrak to private hands or simply cut it off. Whether any system of public transportation can interrupt America's love affair with the speed and independence of the automobile on the interstate, however, still remains to be seen. One historian believes that only fare reductions and frequent scheduling can keep Amtrak running, but cutbacks and lack of profit still haunt the venture.

See also Auto Train; Commuter Trains; Pell Plan; Trains in Cities; VIA Rail Canada, Incorporated.

References Brandes, Ely M., and Alan E. Lazar, *Rail Passenger Traffic in the West* (1966); Dorin, Patrick, *Amtrak Trains and Travel* (1979); Drury, George H., *The Historical Guide to North American Railroads* (1985); Drury, George H., *The Train-Watcher's Guide* (1990); Edmondson, Harold A., ed., *Journey to Amtrak* (1972); Frailey, Fred W., *Zephyrs, Chiefs & Other Orphans* (1977); Friedman, George H., "Rail Travel: Using Trains for Business Travel," *Passenger Train Journal* (October 1994) 25: 36–41; Hilton, George W., *Amtrak* (1980); Hubbard, Freeman, *Encyclopedia of North American Railroading* (1981); Itzkoff, Donald M., *Off the Track* (1985); Johnston, Bob, "The Train They Call Number One," *Trains* (December 1994) 54: 82–90; Lloyd, Arthur C., "Amtrak," in Keith L. Bryant, Jr. (ed.), *EABHB: Railroads in the Age of Regulation* (1988), 7–8; Lyon, Peter, *To Hell in a Day Coach* (1968); Musolf, Lloyd, *Uncle Sam's Private, Profit-seeking Corporations* (1983); Nock, O. S., *Railways of the USA* (1979); Orenstein, Jeffrey, *United States Railroad Policy* (1990); Roberts, Robert, "Amtrak Goal: Reduce Costs, Improve Service," *Modern Railways* (May 1983) 39: 30–37.

Amtrak Improvement Act of 1978

A tacit recognition by Congress that Amtrak might never be profitable, the Amtrak Improvement Act of 1978 made Amtrak a ward of federal largess, which continues to the present time. It makes federal subsidies a permanent part of Amtrak financing that was reemphasized in the Omnibus Reconciliation Act of 1981.

See also National Rail Passenger Act of 1971; Omnibus Reconciliation Act of 1981.

References Hilton, George W., *Amtrak* (1980); Musolf, Lloyd, *Uncle Sam's Private, Profitseeking Corporations* (1983); Orenstein, Jeffrey, *United States Railroad Policy* (1990).

Anthracite and Bridge Line Railroads

Before the era of oil and gas, fossil fuels meant coal, and along the upper Atlantic Coast, coal meant anthracite. Unlike the more common bituminous variety, the eastern foothills of the Appalachians were underlain with veins of hard coal, and the anthracite trade to the major cities above Baltimore was a lucrative one, at first made possible by the canals that spanned the area, then increased and sped up by the construction of railroads. By the twentieth century, numerous minor railroads and six major lines crisscrossed the coastal plains between the port cities and the bustling mines of the interior of Pennsylvania. Most are now a part of Conrail. One of the oddities of the anthracite railways was a locomotive with its cab over the center of the boiler housing instead of at its rear, an innovation caused by the Wooten extra-wide firebox designed to burn the hard anthracite coal. The fireman stood on a small platform behind the boiler, sheltered by an inadequate porch roof, while the engineer rode in the middle. Their peculiar appearance inspired the nicknames "Camelbacks" for the engineer's central cab, and "Mother Hubbards" for the little hood that covered the firing station.

One of the major routes was that of the Central of New Jersey (CNJ), which took coal into eastern New Jersey and New York City. First begun in 1852 between Elizabeth and Phillipsburg, the line was extended to Jersey City by the end of the Civil War, and then into the Pennsylvania mining region. Further expansion into the southern New Jersey resort area provided major passenger traffic for its all-coach Blue Comet, until the independence and convenience of the automobile put a stop to such trade. The CNJ was controlled by the Reading Company, and together they provided joint passenger service between Jersey City and Philadelphia. Both lines are now in the Conrail system.

Probably more famous nationally than the CNJ because of its inclusion in the popular 1930s board game, Monopoly ("Take a ride on the Reading Railroad," went the orange Chance card's spiel, "if you pass GO collect $200," which the forlorn player probably needed to pay the exorbitant fare), the Philadelphia & Reading hauled coal south to the City of Brotherly Love. Originally chartered in 1833, the Reading ran successfully until 1888 when hard times nationally drove it into receivership. The company then went into the coal business and prospered until a 1913 Su-

preme Court decision forced it to divest itself of subsidiary rail lines. Its major dock traffic fell to the competition of truck companies after World War II, a particular problem of shorter eastern lines in an area of numerous highways and even shorter cargo hauls. It became a part of Conrail in 1976.

More successful in the long run than its siblings, the Delaware & Hudson (D&H) carried the "black diamonds," as railroaders referred to coal, north into New England and Canada. Dating from 1823 as a canal company (which it sold in 1899), the D&H expanded its coal holdings and access to northern markets markedly. The mainline was an X-shaped figure that shared a common leg between Binghamton, New York, and Scranton, Pennsylvania. One branch ran from Newark and Philadelphia to Buffalo, while the other went from Washington, D.C., to Montreal. Among other things, the railroad ran tour boats on Lake Champlain. Although the D&H was to be a part of the Norfolk Southern System in 1964, the full merger never went through. The D&H instead formed an independent company, purchased several defunct rail properties when Conrail came into being, and obtained rights to use Conrail's tracks at Buffalo, Newark, and Washington. Its colorful diesels, once painted two-tone blue and silver separated by yellow piping, still run on its own lines, now owned by Guilford Transportation Industries and colored gray and orange with white lettering.

Like the D&H, the Lehigh Valley (LV) and the neighboring Delaware, Lackawanna & Western took the precious fuel north and west to Buffalo, where it was transshipped into Canada and the American Midwest. The LV began in 1846 as a coal hauler, reaching Buffalo in 1876 on a track-sharing plan with the Erie. As the Erie had a wider 6-foot gauge (such things not being standardized yet), the LV had to lay a third rail to move its trains gauged at 4 feet 8.5 inches. In 1896, it had built its own roadbed and track. Eastern branches went into Perth Amboy and New York City. Once renowned for its well-run passenger trains, the Black Diamond, the Maple Leaf (to Canada), and the John Wilkes (the first with fluorescent lighting), the LV was one of the first railroads to discontinue all passenger service in 1961. The Lackawanna reached New York City first in 1856 from Scranton. Then it built its line toward Buffalo, which it reached in 1882. Known for one of the best-maintained roadbeds in America, the Lackawanna ran its speedy Phoebe Snow from New York City to Buffalo. According to the tale, the line was christened by a model of her day, alias Phoebe Snow, and the LV's hard, dustless anthracite coal allowed her to travel the line in luxurious comfort without worrying about the soot common to bituminous roads. The LV and the Lackawanna are a part of Conrail today.

Instrumental in filling out the routes of the comparatively short mainlines of the anthracite roads were the so-called bridge lines that met the coal haulers at Buffalo and took over the carriage to St. Louis, Chicago, and points in between. The major ones of these were the Wabash and the Nickel Plate, both of which had longer and flatter distances to traverse. But much of their profit depended upon the coal trade, and when it began to decline, especially after World War II, the anthracite and bridge lines began to come into major trouble. This made them susceptible to the merger fever that swept American railroading beginning in the late 1950s and extending into the present time. Both Wabash and the Nickel Plate (New York, Chicago & St. Louis Railroad) would wind up in the modern Norfolk Southern conglomerate. Another shorter bridge line was the Lehigh & Hudson River that connected the old New Haven line with Central of New Jersey, Pennsylvania Railroad, and the Lehigh Valley at Easton, Pennsylvania. It transferred coal into New England on the New Haven. But it fell by the way with the others and eventually wound up as a part of Conrail.

See also Bessemer & Lake Erie Railroad; Boston & Maine Railroad; Conrail; Erie Lackawanna.

References Archer, Robert F., *A History of the Lehigh Valley Railroad* (1977); Bogen, Jules, *The Anthracite Railroads* (1927); Casey, Robert J., and W. A. S. Douglass, *The Lackawanna Story* (1951);

Chandler, Alfred D., Jr., "Anthracite Coal and the Beginnings of the Industrial Revolution," *Business History Review* (1972) 46: 143–181; Drury, George H., *The Historical Guide to North American Railroads* (1985); Drury, George H., *The Train-Watcher's Guide* (1990); Fisher, Joseph A., *The Reading's Heritage* (1958); Frey, Robert L., "Philadelphia & Reading Railroad," in Robert L. Frey (ed.), *EABHB: Railroads in the Nineteenth Century* (1988), 322–323; Grow, Lawrence, *On the 8:02* (1979); Harwood, Herbert H., Jr., "Oris Paxton Van Sweringen and Mantis James Van Sweringen," in Keith L. Bryant, Jr. (ed.), *EABHB: Railroads in the Age of Regulation* (1988), 450–458; Henwood, James N. J., "Central Railroad of New Jersey," in Keith L. Bryant, Jr. (ed.), *EABHB: Railroads in the Age of Regulation* (1988), 63–64; Henwood, James N. J., "Reading Company," in Keith L. Bryant, Jr. (ed.), *EABHB: Railroads in the Age of Regulation* (1988), 364–365; Hipp, James W., "Delaware, Lackawanna & Western," in Robert L. Frey (ed.), *EABHB: Railroads in the Nineteenth Century* (1988), 85–86; Hubbard, Freeman, *Encyclopedia of North American Railroading* (1981); Larkin, Katherine, "Delaware & Hudson Railroad," in Robert L. Frey (ed.), *EABHB: Railroads in the Nineteenth Century* (1988), 83–85; Lyon, Peter, *To Hell in a Day Coach* (1968); Nock, O. S., *Railways of the USA* (1979); Rehor, John A., *The Nickel Plate Story* (1965); Saunders, Richard, *The Railroad Mergers and the Coming of Conrail* (1978); Saunders, Richard, "Delaware & Hudson Railway," in Keith L. Bryant, Jr. (ed.), *EABHB: Railroads in the Age of Regulation* (1988), 110–111; Saunders, Richard, "Lehigh Valley Railroad," in Keith L. Bryant, Jr. (ed.), *EABHB: Railroads in the Age of Regulation* (1988), 256–258; Saunders, Richard, "New York, Chicago & St. Louis Railroad," in Keith L. Bryant, Jr. (ed.), *EABHB: Railroads in the Age of Regulation* (1988), 320–321; Shaughnessy, Jim, *Delaware & Hudson* (1967).

Applegate Road

After the American trek to Oregon (comprising the modern states of Oregon, Washington, and the Canadian province of British Columbia) became a flood in 1843, and British hospitality locally and internationally began to suffer from the "54° 40' or Fight" attitude of Americans (they wanted it all, including British Columbia), it became obvious that a war over Oregon would necessitate a more southerly route to the Willamette Valley than the old Oregon Trail. Led by Levi Scott, Jesse and Lindsay Applegate, and a scout, Moses "Black" Harris, a dozen men set off up the Willamette in

1846 and headed to the Klamath River to find a gap in the mountains for this emergency trail. They were unaware of the recent Oregon Treaty that willed present-day Oregon and Washington to the United States and British Columbia to Canada. As they reached the head of the valley, they captured an old Calapooya Indian who showed them the start of a trail that his people used to cross the mountains, following the twisted-off tops of brush along the way. The path led through Umpqua Canyon into the Rogue River country, finally reaching the Klamath some days later.

As they cut through to Lower Klamath Lake, they came upon the remnants of a white man's camp. It was that of the John C. Frémont party, which had departed for the Mexican War just a few days before, after a skirmish with the Indians in which two soldiers had been killed. The Applegates were much luckier. A friendly Native American showed them a spot on the Lost River where the water flowed 15 inches deep over a solid rock shelf. This became the crossing for decades. Circling around Goose Lake, the Applegates pushed on, headed up into Fandango Pass, and crossed into Surprise Valley, so named because it was an unexpected fertile spot in the midst of desolation. Nearby, in 1865, Fort Bidwell would be built to protect the road and friendly Indians from hostiles. Skirting Black Rock Desert, where a sudden storm could create a boggy morass, the trail was marked into High Rock Canyon. Then they crossed desert and mountain, coming upon the Humboldt River and the California Trail. Although it had merely been marked, 150 wagons used the trail in 1846. The following year, Scott improved the rough spots and 70 wagons followed. By 1848, the Applegate Road had become a popular if difficult route into Oregon from the southeast.

After gold was discovered in California, many argonauts in their "prairie schooners" followed the Applegate Road into Goose Lake, where they turned and took the Lassen Road to the Sacramento River from the north. Travelers on both trails were bothered by local Indians and had to keep their guard up. Peter Lassen led the first party over the route in 1848. Temporarily lost, Lassen's group was joined by a large party under Peter H. Burnett, later the first governor of California. The reinforcements had veteran Hudson's Bay Company mountain man Thomas McKay with them. McKay managed to lead the combined wagon train out of the Pitt River Valley into the Sacramento Valley beyond. There Lassen had set up Benton City, a town that virtually disappeared in the gold rush as everyone headed south to get rich. Lassen himself prospected back along his trail, where Indians ambushed his party and he was killed in 1849.

All that remained was for someone to establish a cutoff between the point the Applegate Road left the California Trail and the northern Sacramento River. In 1852, William H. Nobles had stumbled on the route to be given his name and realized that it was a direct way to the settlement in northern California. He managed to get the town of Shasta to put up $2,000 to mark his route and to turn wagon parties toward their settlements. Several townsmen went east with him to keep an eye on their investment. They soon returned and reported that Nobles Road had all of the advantages promised. Nobles himself went back east to publicize the new route, which included a speech before Congress. He was helped in his efforts by the recurring Indian attacks along the Applegate-Lassen Road and the fate of the Donner party in the High Sierras in 1846. And although the Nobles Road became a popular route into northern California, the town of Shasta never realized its $2,000 investment. The traffic moved on farther south, and the nascent city that hoped to boom became a ghost town, another victim of the hunt for gold.

See also California Trail; Oregon Trail.

Reference Dunlop, Richard, *Great Trails of the West* (1971).

Arago Decision
See Robertson v. Baldwin.

Association of American Railroads (AAR)

Formed in 1934 in response to the Emergency Transportation Act of 1933 as part of the National Recovery Administration (NRA) Blue Eagle recovery program, the Association of American Railroads was a cartel-like organization established to coordinate pro-railroad lobbying activities in Washington, D.C. Its first report stated that no more government coordination of railroads was necessary. Its belief that coordination and consolidation ought to be voluntary was written into the Transportation Act of 1940. In the 1960s the AAR came out for an end to government rate regulation, particularly government aid to airlines and a charge for government-related services like flight control and waterway control. In 1970 there was great fear that the AAR would be dominated by the Penn Central Railroad, but PC's quick bankruptcy negated that feeling.

A consolidation of the American Railway Association, the Association of Railway Executives, the Railway Accounting Officers Association, the Railway Treasury Officers Association, and the Bureau of Railway Economics, the AAR's functions can be deduced by noting the various divisions that make up the organization. These include law; patents and claims; legislative relations; research; finance and accounting; public relations; economics; the office of the vice-president with branches of purchases and stores, competitive transportation, and mail transportation; operations and maintenance; engineering; freight claims; car services; and data systems. Its Washington, D.C., headquarters also has the largest rail library in the world. The AAR is concerned with ongoing research and has a laboratory on the campus of the Illinois Institute of Technology in Chicago. It works in conjunction with other universities, railroads, and private manufacturers who supply railroads with equipment.

See also National Industrial Recovery Act of 1933; Transportation Acts.

References Abbey, Wallace W., "Association of American Railroads," in Keith L. Bryant, Jr. (ed.), *EABHB: Railroads in the Age of Regulation* (1988), 9–10; Hubbard, Freeman, *Encyclopedia of North American Railroading* (1981); Saunders, Richard, *The Railroad Mergers and the Coming of Conrail* (1978); Wilner, Frank N., "Predecessors to the Association of American Railroads," in Robert L. Frey (ed.), *EABHB: Railroads in the Nineteenth Century* (1988), 333–334.

Astronautics

Construed as the science of construction and operation of vehicles for travel in interplanetary or interstellar space, astronautics involves the unmanned and manned exploration of space by pilots called astronauts.

UNMANNED SPACE PROBES

As adventurers sought to fly in the atmospheric space surrounding Earth, other individuals began to probe into deeper space beyond Earth's gaseous envelope. At first these probes were quite unsophisticated, even the work of amateurs, but as time progressed the attempts grew more technical and more far-reaching. Modern astronautics eventually sprang from three sources: military (how can it contribute to or detract from national security?), scientific (what is out there and how does it relate to life on Earth?), and commercial interests (how can it be exploited?).

In 1955, three branches of the U.S. Armed Forces (Army, Navy, and Air Force) contributed individual proposals to send a satellite into near space. President Dwight D. Eisenhower organized a committee to examine the proposals and it picked the navy's Vanguard rocket program as the basis of the first space satellite. Eisenhower endorsed the committee's action and made the launching of a scientific satellite a part of America's contribution to the International Geophysical Year (1957–1958). But the program fell victim to a series of launch failures. Finally, directed by James Van Allen, the American satellite *Explorer I* discovered that Earth was surrounded by a belt of trapped radiation. This project was advanced two years before the race for space mastery with the Soviet Union and independently of military rocket applications. Both projects were being accomplished in slow, steady moves, well within budgetary restraints.

But in 1957, the Soviet Union began its launching of unmanned (and later manned) rockets, and beat the Explorer series into space. The result was that the American public felt cheated despite assurances from the Eisenhower administration that there was no reason for alarm or shame in the state of America's rocketry programs. But Congress was more responsive to the perceived failure and public sense of humiliation (whether manufactured by spin doctors and interest groups, or real as the world laughed at American intellectual softness) and put large sums of money into the space programs and much emphasis on scientific training into the schools, both civilian and military. National pride and international prestige seemed threatened if America "fell behind." Different branches of the military and scientific communities diffused these tremendous resources by direct competition, so Congress created the National Aeronautics and Space Administration (NASA) to coordinate U.S. space activities and give them direction. Allegedly, the whole program was being run to expand human knowledge of deep space for scientific reasons, but the concepts of ballistic-missile defense and attack were never far from consideration.

The American program emphasized two basic approaches: planetary science and sky science. The first was interested in the origin, composition, and evolution of the moon, the outlying planets, and the solar system. The second emphasized meteoric activity, solar and cosmic rays, plasma dynamics, and the interaction of solar and terrestrial electromagnetic fields. In 1958, the sky scientists were well organized, fairly well publicized, and active on many governmental, educational, and industrial commissions. They were the ones who managed the International Geophysical Year projects, determining who got space on which rocket for which experiment. They automatically went into NASA ad-

ministration, giving the administration a sky science emphasis. The planetary scientists were relatively isolated, unorganized, and dependent upon a program of deep space probes (manned and unmanned) that had yet to be fully envisioned.

The sky scientists proceeded to launch small rockets with instrument payloads, often complemented with television cameras to study space. The *Atlas-Able, Pioneer,* and *Mariner* missions took preliminary measurements of the moon, and the space between Mars, Venus, and Earth. But these important missions paled in comparison to the Soviet's advances in manned projects. The Soviets' *Luna I* became the first man-made object to escape from Earth's gravitational pull. Because of the prestige and political importance attached to these ventures, the planetary scientists got their break as NASA's programs turned to the glories of manned space flight and, after President John F. Kennedy's pledge (in response to information supplied to him by NASA administrators), particularly to a moon landing. The result was the delay of probes of other planets like Mars and a concentration on the problems of a moon landing. But unmanned space vehicles like *Ranger* (hard landing on the moon), *Surveyor* (soft landings), and *Prospector* (unmanned lunar exploration and "mining" of moon rocks and soils) were an important part of the preliminary moon project.

Driven by Soviet successes in putting men and a woman in space while Americans were still working with animals, NASA had to subrogate its unmanned scientific planetary projects to the one main goal—landing a human being on the moon. Preceded by the *Mercury* (putting an astronaut in orbit) and *Gemini* (placing a team in space to perform actual tasks), the *Apollo* (landing on the moon) absorbed most of the unmanned efforts into itself. The shrinking effect of *Apollo* on the satellite exploration of space was felt even further by the failure of the *Ranger* project to get a rocket up. In 1963, canceling the *Prospector*, a lunar orbiter project sent *Ranger* rockets up to photograph the moon's surface in preparation for a landing. The planetary exploration continued with the funds and rockets left over. Despite such restraints, the scientists managed to explore all of the inner planets (Mercury, Venus, and Mars) and one outer planet (Jupiter) by 1976, all through satellite probes like *Explorer* (deep space) and *Pioneer* (near space). Three small astronomical satellites and an equal number of larger Orbiting Astronomical Observatories made observations of space resources on nonvisual wavelengths, took ultraviolet pictures of stars, and photographed the sun and its corona in detail. Other satellite experiments sent back data on the results of weightlessness on plants and organisms sent into space for the Apollo project.

Meanwhile, the armed forces were interested in intelligence applications for satellites. For years the United States had been interested in getting information about affairs from behind the Iron Curtain. After World War II, American intelligence agencies had tried to recruit and drop native-born agents (many of whom had prior Nazi connections, which would lead to eventual embarrassment over their official protection from war crimes prosecution) into Soviet territory to relay information to the West. The project failed dismally. The next attempt was to fly over the Soviet Union at great heights in gliderlike planes called U-2s. A narrow, pencillike fuselage with long, tapered, high-aspect wings to permit the craft to glide at high altitudes, the Lockheed U-2 had a tremendous range. Although it revealed Soviet missile advances and their set-up in Cuba, it also could be shot down over the surveilled territory (the hard way to find out about Soviet surface-to-air missile advances), causing diplomatic controversy and embarrassment, as when Francis Gary Powers was shot down and captured in 1960, ruining an entire East–West summit negotiation at Paris. The U-2's vulnerability led to the development of the Lockheed SR-71 Blackbird, a two-man, two-engine reconnaissance aircraft with new aerodynamic design and structural features influenced by the "X-planes," which would affect subsequent generations of military aircraft.

The fear of renewed international tension should another manned aircraft be shot down caused much interest in the use of unmanned spy satellites. These were orbiting platforms of various sizes that could conduct strategic reconnaissance, relay radio and television messages, analyze terrestrial weather conditions, detect violations of various nuclear test-ban treaties (called *Vela* after the Spanish word for "watchman") or missile launchings, and serve as beacons for atmospheric air and sea navigation. By the mid-1960s, these projects were already well advanced. They have been incrementally improved and older satellites replaced until it is alleged that military spy cameras can read a license plate on a given vehicle anywhere on Earth. The truth about military application satellites is still classified.

Unlike the military space vehicles, the civilian space agency applications satellites are more fully known. Their purpose is to investigate meteorology (inherited from the armed forces' beginnings), communications (likewise an inheritance), Earth resources, and geodetic conditions. The earliest of these programs, beginning in 1951, was called the Television and Infrared Observation Satellite (TIROS), a project run jointly by Radio Corporation of America and the government. It revealed a perennial problem in civilian applications—the project had to meet NASA's technical requirements and the customer's special requirements. In 1964, the Department of Commerce and NASA agreed that the government would develop the satellites, launch them, and create ground monitoring stations. The U.S. Weather Bureau (now organized as part of the National Oceanic and Atmospheric Administration) would pay for the services, monitor the work, maneuver the satellites in orbit, and distribute the information obtained.

Like the weather satellites, communications orbiters were an early (1958) applications civilian development with military overtones. The first program placed *Echo*, a metalized balloon, in orbit, off which radio signals could be bounced to distant Earth stations. By 1962, NASA and American

Telephone and Telegraph combined to launch an active communications satellite named *Telstar*. Positioned over the Atlantic, *Telstar* amplified and transmitted radio, telephone, wire photos, and television signals between the United States and Western Europe. Radio Corporation of America followed with *Relay* and later *SatCom* for television, Western Union with *Westar*, and Hughes with *Galaxy*. Other satellites, like the *Syncom* series, were turned over to the armed forces for worldwide instant communication. In 1962, Congress acted to place all private communication satellites under the Communications Satellite Corporation (Comsat). NASA was to provide technical and launching information on a reimbursable basis and continue its own research in this field. In 1965, an international equivalent, Intelsat, began to place into orbit civilian communications satellites that now encircle the globe. Satellite Business Systems (SBS) organized in 1982 to provide launchers for civilian projects.

Satellites also play a role in other services as well. In the 1970s, the *Landsat* series provided imaging technology to survey worldwide agriculture, forestry, geology, hydrology, oceanography, and urban growth information for interested researchers. *Landsat* information is offered for public sale in the same manner as the U.S. Geological Survey sells maps and aerial photographs. These maps are made more accurate by their own satellite system, *Geos*. By bouncing laser beams off the *Geos* satellites, exact measurements of altitude and distance can be made, creating more accurate maps. Other researchers have used such satellites to chart the rotation of Earth and movements in Earth's crust to assist investigations of earthquakes and plate tectonics. The human risk and monetary expense of launching the American space shuttle has led to new calls for an expanded use of unmanned space vehicles to further scientific research in space, and on Earth from space, as a better utilization of scarce resources.

Although there have been numerous explorations of deep space and nearly all of the sun's known planets by unmanned satellites in the *Voyager*, *Galileo*, *Magellan*, *Viking*, and *Mariner* series, one of the most dramatic experiments has been the launching of the Hubble Telescope in 1990. As large as a long city bus, the space telescope can be maneuvered with fine precision at an altitude of 375 miles in perpetual Earth orbit, circling the globe once every 90 minutes. The launch was by space shuttle and entailed the largest single satellite taken up by rocket-powered transport. Proposed by Lyman Spitzer, Jr., in 1946, the space telescope would allow scientists to examine the far reaches of the solar system in its own ultraviolet light without the blurring of images brought on by the constantly changing atmosphere of Earth (which is why stars twinkle). It also demonstrated a cheap, safe way to explore space without the problems of manned flight.

Named after Edwin Hubble, an astronomer at the Mount Wilson 100-inch telescope in California who was interested in estimating distances to other galaxies and postulated Hubble's Law (all galaxies are receding from each other in direct proportion to their distances to each other), the space telescope was launched and deployed without a hitch, but then problems began. The mirror (designed like a honeycomb and "welded" together to save weight) had to be ground on Earth, where gravity tends to distort the glass. Such distortion had to be figured in, but no one could know if the calculations were correct until after deployment—"at first light," as the phrase goes. From the beginning, observation was not up to par. The images were blurred. Then the gyros and control systems began to fail and the telescope started to fall, very slowly. Eventually, it would enter Earth's atmosphere and burn up. So in late 1993 a new shuttle mission went up to repair the control package and clear up the blurring by installing a correction module, COSTAR. In the end, the Hubble telescope remains a better platform for observing deep space than anything here on Earth, but is still performing less well than expected.

The space telescope's partial success was an important failure for what analysts now label as "Big Science," a concept that describes the type of megaprojects that mark modern scientific activity—so big that they require government participation to manage the finances and scope of the experiment. The great worry is that Big Science will eventually absorb the intellect and financing of all other projects into itself and actually reduce the amount of investigation taking place. The cost of such projects have social and political implications beyond ordinary scientific research. This means that the decisions to engage in these big projects are not based solely on scientific need, but on political realities far removed from the scientific world. Hence their very bigness brings in government and puts science at the mercy of self-seeking politicians while more important earthly needs like domestic welfare, universal medical and health care, and national defense go un- or underfunded. Science is no longer "pure," if it ever really was. It also leads to poor decision making, as when the *Challenger* spacecraft was launched at temperatures below which its infamous O-rings were designed to function, resulting in unforgettable tragedy. The error of course was laid at the feet of the contractor, who had actually followed specifications completely only to be excoriated by the politicians who applied the pressure and the bureaucrats who refused to assume responsibility for the launch decision.

Bringing the government into science policy also leads to decisions as to which projects are more important, peaceful science or national defense. The epitome of this dilemma can be seen in the on-again/off-again development of the Strategic Defense Initiative (SDI), or "Star Wars," as it is known popularly, after the Hollywood film that widely featured such futuristic defense measures. Begun with a 1983 speech by President Ronald Reagan, SDI was soon criticized as too expensive, too theoretical, and downright impractical.

SDI critics also pointed out a possible "Dreadnought Syndrome," implying that any new advance in weapons technology actually helps the underdog nations by permitting them to shortcut to the new system without bearing the risks and expenses of its development. As with the British navy before World War I, a new battleship (the *Dreadnought*) actually helped the lesser-equipped Germans to catch up immediately by turning to the new technology and avoiding costly intermediary development through now-outmoded equipment. The Soviets, however, lacked the economic base to pull off the catch-up in the SDI case, which helped end the cold war in favor of the western Allies. Basically, SDI is a technological system still in the development stages (from which it may never emerge) that is designed to permit the United States to defend itself against missile attack without having to resort to all-out nuclear attack in response. There are various types of SDI approaches, from launching antimissile missiles that hit or explode to disable their targets, to ground- or space-mounted laser, particle-beam, or X-ray "guns."

SDI's goals were to change American nuclear defense from the traditional Mutually Assured Destruction (MAD) to one of Mutually Assured Survival (MAS) without relying on the easily violated international treaty process; to stimulate the economy through research and development grants that ran into the billions (but would divert talent and money from other, perhaps more valuable and definitely more diverse, civilian scientific projects, giving much credence to President Dwight D. Eisenhower's caveat against the military-industrial complex in 1961); and to carry the cold war forward to victory out of the stalemate that had lasted for decades by upping the ante to where the economically overextended Soviets could not compete. Hopefully, this would all take place before the weakening American economy fell victim, too. Of all the purposes of the program, the last proved to be the most effective, causing in part the foundering of the Soviet Union and its replacement with the Commonwealth of Independent States in the early 1990s. Advocates of the Reagan administration claim credit for this, while critics claim that the United States was plain lucky or that the collapse of the Soviet empire came from other factors.

SDI is Big Science's monetary drain writ large on the face of the American military-industrial economy as it struggles to come to grips with the end of the cold war and a return to peaceful civilian pursuits, on Earth or in space, scientific or otherwise. A first step in this direction is the reopening of Vandenburg Air Force Base as a satellite launch complex under the Commercial Space Launch Act of 1985 (private corporations can use government facilities on a cost-only basis), and the Dual Use Program that reserves one-third of the Air Force's Delta launch vehicles and three-fourths of the Atlas launchers for civilian use.

Already, a Canadian blind man, Charles La Pierre, has developed a portable position-locating system for the sightless using space technology. Begun as a class project when La Pierre was an electrical engineering student in Toronto, the first model weighed 33 pounds and was unwieldy and costly. La Pierre figures that in time he can reduce the size and weight to those of a portable cassette player, and the cost to under $1,000. His method works off of the Global Positioning System satellite positioned 12,000 miles above Earth for U.S. military use. It is hoped that such projects can be spirited forward through the "information superhighway." Seen as an aid to information dispersal in business, education, and transportation by most, scientists envision this system as an instant access route to powerful and expensive technology through computer networking.

MANNED SPACE TRAVEL

The idea of human space travel was not new in the 1950s. Among others, Russian Konstatine Tsolkovsky postulated that rockets could permit humans to travel to and colonize other worlds, a concept that led the French novelist Jules Verne to write *From the Earth to the Moon,* as he entitled his enchanting piece of nineteenth-century fiction. American Robert Goddard experimented with primitive liquid-fueled rockets, the first to do so. The Germans used rocketry principles as a part of their Vengeance

program (V-1, V-2) against Britain in late World War II. By 1954, Frederick C. Durant III, president of the International Astronautical Federation, had told delegates that the whole matter of human space travel was a matter of time and money—but that its era was close. The following year, he showed delegates the Walt Disney Productions film *Man in Space,* a 33-minute update and speculation on the future. Impressed delegates from the Soviet Union, attending the meeting for the first time, anxiously inquired as to the possibility of borrowing the film "for private demonstration." It appeared to them, especially in light of American pledges to launch a scientific satellite as a part of the International Geophysical Year (1957–1958), that the movie was a warning as well as an encouragement.

Within seven years both the United States and the U.S.S.R. would have sent men into space to orbit Earth. The quick development was possible because both nations had amassed a wealth of basic scientific and engineering data, much of it from captured German rocket scientists and their work. This marked one of the dilemmas facing the space program—it was highly duplicative. Both sides shrouded their efforts under a cloud of national security. Yet without this competition engendered by the cold war, neither program might have succeeded so soon, if at all. Indeed, until the 1957 flight of *Sputnik I,* rockets were still pretty much of a joke. The worldwide political realities made moneys and resources available that would have never been forthcoming if not for the guise of national security and international prestige. But as events would show, regardless of effort put forth, space flight was never to be easy, safe, or routine.

The first attempts to enter space came shortly after World War II. Government and industrial engineers realized that propeller planes had reached the extent of their speed. The jet engines of that time were too primitive to be of much help. So in cooperation with Bell Aircraft, the army and navy developed a rocket-propelled plane to probe transonic and supersonic speeds.

Liftoff for the 363-foot tall Apollo XI occurred 16 July 1969. Apollo XI marked the first U.S. lunar landing mission, and Commander Neil A. Armstrong's first steps on the moon marked a "giant leap for mankind."

Based at Edwards Air Force Base in California's Mojave Desert, the "X-projects" investigated thermal problems at high speed, air loads in near space, control problems, and protective clothing that equipped the first astronauts, and established new design parameters in shape and metals that played a big part in future military and civilian aircraft. They also whetted everyone's appetite to probe farther into space.

The first spacecraft to penetrate deep space were the Soviets' *Vostok* and the Americans' *Mercury*. Their purpose was to see if a human could be sent up beyond atmospheric space and recovered with impunity—alive. The first major problems were the g(ravity)-forces, vibrations, and noise that accompanied launch. Both sides solved the problems by custom-building their astronauts contour seats, molded to their individual bodies for maximum support in which they rode in semisupine modes. The next problem was the encounter with weightlessness—the notion of gravity balanced by centrifugal force. It was feared that zero-g(ravity) would adversely affect the astronaut's bodily and mental performance. But no one really knew what to expect. The Americans sent up rodents and primates, and the Russians sent dogs. The Soviets' dog Laika, sent up in *Sputnik II* (thereafter called *Mutnik* by the more irreverent of the American press), barked and moved about for days before dying in orbit from a lack of nourishment. The conclusion was that humans could enter space and return with no ill effects.

The two competitors next solved the problem of artificial environment. People breathe a 20–80 mixture of oxygen and nitrogen. They exhale carbon dioxide and water vapor. Both sides solved the problem of exhaling with lithium hydroxide canisters, which absorbed the carbon dioxide and water vapor, but they approached the need of inhalation differently. The Soviets supplied their cosmonauts with an Earth-like atmosphere. This reduced the danger of fire and was rather simple to do. The Americans decided to use a cabin atmosphere of one-third that of Earth and pure oxygen. The

advantage was that in an emergency, the space suit and helmet had the same conditions. The Soviet cosmonauts had to worry about decompression "bends" should they have to don their full space suits quickly. To prepare their astronauts for this environment, the Americans removed the nitrogen from their blood before flight to prevent airsickness. But they also had to fireproof the whole cabin interior. The Americans believed that their system, although more complicated to develop, was more reliable. The oxygen was stored in high-pressure bottles and released constantly. The Soviets preferred a "chemical bed" of alkali metal superoxides. This released oxygen as it absorbed carbon dioxide. It was simple and effective.

The key problem was not putting an astronaut into space—that was the easy part—but retrieving the space flyer alive. As an unprotected space adventurer reentered Earth's atmosphere, the spacecraft would generate heat and burn up like a meteor. Again, the Soviets and Americans approached the problem differently. As an essentially landlocked nation, the Soviets used a spherical capsule that entered Earth's atmosphere like a bullet. An ablative coating protected the sphere from heat. The sphere was weighted so that it automatically went right-side-up at about 21,000 feet. The cosmonaut was then ejected like a pilot in distress and parachuted to the ground separately from the remains of the spacecraft to be picked up by land-based units trained in this mission. Americans, on the other hand, used research from their incipient ballistic missile program that showed that a semiballistic shape (sort of like an old wooden child's top) would survive reentry well. As a nation with an expansive navy, the American craft would turn around (using pitch, yaw, and roll jets to control pilot attitude to Earth) and present its blunt side to the atmosphere, thus absorbing the intense reentry temperatures on a specially designed heat shield. The whole craft with astronaut inside would then land in the ocean and be picked up by a naval task force deployed for this reason. In either case, reentry had to be at a precise angle to minimize burnup.

From 1958 to 1961, both the Russians and the Americans worked feverishly to get someone into space. The Americans knew that the Soviets were ready to launch. The Americans were ready too—except in the eyes of rocket expert Werner von Braun. The last test rocket had developed an undiscovered glitch and shot too high. Von Braun wanted one more test, in spite of astronaut Alan B. Shepard's willingness to chance it and beat the opposition. Von Braun refused. Unlike the Soviet space shots, the Americans were going live on television where the mistakes would be magnified in the eyes of world public opinion. Of course the glory would be bigger, too, on successes.

So after five *Sputnik*-type flights, the Soviets sent up Yuri Gagarin on 12 April 1961, the first man in space. The Soviet manned capsules were the *Vostok* series, of which there were six, each staying up for more and more orbits (with one pair nearly touching in space in a mock docking), the final one being the flight of Valentina Tereshkova, the first woman in space. The Soviets were especially interested in the medical effects of weightlessness on the human body. All of the flights were orbital in nature.

Led by von Braun, the Americans took a more conservative tack. Their initial flights were ballistic rather than orbital. Their first two flights (Shepard in *Freedom* 7, Gus Grissom in *Liberty Bell* 7) went up on old Redstone rockets to check out capsule controls. Then Atlas took over as the booster craft. Both missions had minor flaws. Shepard found that he had drunk too much coffee. As the ground crew rechecked the systems, he had an uncontrollable urge to urinate. No, he could not get out of the capsule, said the monitors. Could he do it on the ship? He might short out the electrical systems, came the reply. Finally, Shepard said it was an event that could no longer be postponed. The power was shut off, he urinated, and all waited until the magic diapers dried, and the power went on. The flight was perfect. Grissom got off the ground and made his flight without a hitch. But when he landed

in the sea, the hatch blew off, and he and the capsule just managed to stay afloat until rescue.

Plagued by constant fuel leaks, bad weather, and an occasional blowup on the pad, the Atlas rocket was redesigned and John Glenn took the first orbital ride on 20 February 1962 in *Friendship* 7. Unlike the other American astronauts, Glenn was hero material. He had panache—a way of talking the public could understand and relate to, and evoked the all-American-boy, Marine-tough image. His craft had hit a lot of small particles that glowed and came to be called "luminescence." His heat shield came loose and it was feared that he might burn up on reentry. Reentry always blocked the astronauts' radio signals, so when Glenn came back on the air the nation heaved a collective sigh and the cheers began. It came as no surprise when he left the program to go into national politics.

Glenn's three orbits were followed by the last *Mercury* flights. Donald K. Slayton was next, but he had a flutter in his heart and NASA doctors panicked, even though they had known of it for years, and grounded him. Walter M. Schirra, Jr., was the backup pilot, but he was bypassed and M. Scott Carpenter (in *Aurora* 7) went up instead. Carpenter was a man who wanted to feel the effects of space and relate it to the ground. He discovered that the luminescence was actually waste water (urine) from the capsule. He spent a lot of fuel looking at the wonders before him and fired his reentry rockets late, coming in at the wrong angle and overshooting the drop zone by 200 miles. NASA never flew him again. Walter M. Schirra, Jr. (in *Sigma* 7), went six orbits and tested drifting in flight to save fuel for longer journeys like the moon shot. But Schirra flew during the Cuban Missile Crisis and his epic was lost on the back pages of America's newspapers.

The final Mercury astronaut was L. Gordon Cooper (in *Faith* 7), who stayed up a day and a half. He was a gutsy pilot who liked to buzz NASA headquarters just to prod the stuffy bureaucrats. NASA wanted to bypass him, but Slayton, now in charge of the astronauts, refused to let it happen.

Cooper was the first to actually fly his spacecraft, and he did it perfectly. Indeed, the major difference in the American and Soviet programs came to be control—the Russians generally were shot up and retrieved while being controlled on the ground. The American astronauts were actually pilots who controlled their spaceships and acted as engineers and experimenters, beyond their ground assistance.

The next step was to get more than one flyer up and to perform the complex tasks needed if a person were to land on the moon. By now, both sides had bad cases of "moon fever." The Americans tried to redesign the *Mercury* craft and wound up junking it and starting from scratch. Everything would have to be retested, but it would be the most advanced equipment to date, most of it simplified versions of the Mercury project, with no retreads. The result was a two-seat craft named *Gemini*. Twelve flights were planned, and the first two were to be unmanned tests of the new system—both were unqualified successes. To fill the available places in the new program came nine new astronauts. At first the originals made it tough for the rookies to find acceptance, but time healed the rift. The Russians, meanwhile, fearing to lose their lead on the Americans, merely redesigned their *Vostok* to hold three crew members (the historical Russian concept of troika) and went on from there. The new spaceship was called *Voskhod*. Their goal was to emerge from their program with fully proven, tested designs. To save space and weight, the ejection seat was eliminated. The *Voskhod* would land like a plane. The crew would work in shirt-sleeves for comfort. Their first test flight (October 1964) was a three-man affair (another first) that went off without a hitch, the new landing system functioning perfectly.

The Soviets led the way again with a second *Voskhod* flight, one in which the automatic landing systems failed, forcing the two-man crew to land manually. They overshot the runway and wound up in the woods of the Ural Mountains. A lengthy search found them safe and dropped supplies. But the two cosmonauts spent a night

in the snow until a dawn rescue party arrived. The Americans responded with their first *Gemini* flight (actually numbered *Gemini III*), in which Grissom and John W. Young flew the *Unsinkable Molly Brown* (a not-too-sly reference to NASA criticisms of Grissom's first flight, which almost sank) and maneuvered the craft in orbit. The next *Gemini* expedition, piloted by James A. McDivitt, featured a walk in space (something the Soviets had already done) by Glenn's replacement, Edward H. White, tethered to the spacecraft for safety. But *Gemini V*, with Cooper and Charles "Pete" Conrad, Jr., failed to rendezvous with a evaluation pod because of an internal power problem.

NASA still proposed to dock with a target vehicle on *Gemini VI* (Schirra, Thomas P. Stafford), but the target vehicle misfired on the launching pad. Coolly, Schirra and Stafford walked off the rocket, even though it was a potential bomb. NASA quickly decided to jump a step and send up *Gemini VII* (Frank Borman, James A. Lovell), followed by a rebuilt *Gemini VI*. The two craft would dock without a trial run. Schirra spent three revolutions of Earth in close proximity, precision flying (distances between the ships varying from an inch to 100 feet), before both craft returned to Earth (December 1965). *Gemini VII* had been up two weeks—the estimated time to get to the moon.

The Americans rolled on to success after success. *Gemini VIII* (Neil A. Armstrong, David R. Scott) actually docked with a target vehicle. But when they backed off, one of their thruster rockets stuck open, sending them for an unscheduled tumble. They managed to restore control by firing a retrorocket, normally used for landing. The next flight (Stafford, Eugene A. Cernan) experienced a nonfunctioning docking adapter, but all of the other experiments (including a two-hour space walk by Cernan in which he actually worked at tasks) went off well. The final three *Gemini* flights (Young and Michael Collins, Conrad and Richard F. Gordon, and Lovell and Edwin E. "Buzz" Aldrin, Jr.) docked and performed a pair of EVAs (NASA-talk for "extra vehicular activities" or space walks) each. Aldrin was typical of the new astronauts, a Ph.D., calculating, and dedicated to problem solving. No more hot-dog test pilots for NASA.

Both Russians and Americans were now ready for the next stage of space activity—the voyage to the moon. Things began as they always had—with bad luck. Sitting in their *Apollo* module, atop the Saturn I-B rocket, astronauts White, Griffin, and Roger Chaffee had been giving their craft a dry run when the vehicle burst into flames, killing all three. The setback was of great magnitude, blamed on overconfidence and sloppy methods, compounded by poor, often-flammable materials. The Americans decided to step back and redesign and rethink everything. The refit took 21 months.

The Soviets now had a clear chance to make the moon shot first. But suddenly the luck that had pushed the Soviet space effort forward seemed to leave their program. Premiere Nikita Khrushchev, an ardent supporter, was forced out of office by the party. Two top rocket designers died shortly thereafter. This caused a slowdown in the Soviet program, now called Soyuz, marked by a new booster rocket and a heavier, improved maneuver capsule. Later the Soviets would claim that Soyuz was merely intended to send up a space station (which it did). But others believed that it represented a Russian moon shot that went awry. *Soyuz I* had trouble from the beginning. It began to tumble in orbit. Automatic systems failed to respond. Finally bringing his ship under control, cosmonaut Vladimir Komarov attempted to land manually. But when he reached the correct altitude, the module began to spin again. His parachute lines became twisted and he fell to his death at 800 miles per hour.

As both nations retooled for the run to the moon, the Americans produced a completely rebuilt spacecraft for its Apollo program. The craft had two parts, a command module (CM) and a service module (SM). The conical CM was an office, cockpit, laboratory, communications center, galley, sleeping quarters, and personal hygiene center, all in one. The SM had the main propulsion system, reaction control system, and most of the spacecraft's consumables. Three unmanned flights in 1967 and 1968 tested the new system before a crew was sent up again. The Soviets also sent up a *Soyuz* in five unmanned flights, performing an automatic docking maneuver twice. Then they sent up *Soyuz III*, but it failed to dock after a rendezvous with *Soyuz II*, already in orbit. No one ever knew why.

The Americans meanwhile launched the *Apollo I* with a full three-man crew (Schirra, Donn F. Eisele, R. Walter Cunningham), who performed a ten-day test flight. Schirra had a head cold during the flight and got into a running fight with ground control over the amount of television coverage (Schirra said "none" and meant it), a new improvised flight plan (Schirra called it "junk"), and whether Schirra could come into reentry with his helmet off (he did). It was the only crew to fight with ground control. When they had landed Schirra and Slayton had it out again. NASA refused to use any of the three men again. Schirra retired to advertise a nationally known cold remedy developed by NASA doctors and used by him on the flight.

Then *Apollo VIII* (Borman, Lovell, William A. Anders) went up to circumnavigate the moon. Shot up by the new, powerful Saturn V rocket, they arrived on Christmas Eve, 1968, and shared their impressions with the world, reading verses from the Bible. One of their pictures, "Earth Rise," depicting Earth coming out from behind the moon, became popular as a postage stamp. Their trip showed that one could fly to the moon (it was the first time a human being had gone out of Earth's influence), go into orbit there, break back out of orbit, and survive for two weeks in space, returning safely. It was the pivotal moment in the American drive for the moon, and marked the first time that the Americans had pulled ahead of the Soviets. Indeed, the head of the Soviet space program praised the three American astronauts and indicated that the Soviets would concentrate on unmanned moon exploration. Many wondered if the

Soviets had ever really intended to land a man on the moon in the first place.

The American program went on without a hitch. *Apollo IX* (McDivitt, Scott, Russell L. Schweikart) tested all of the systems of lunar landing and takeoff while in Earth orbit. *Apollo X* (Stafford, Cernan, Young) repeated the same procedure from lunar orbit, approaching the moon to within 47,000 feet. *Apollo XI* (Armstrong, Aldrin, Collins) made the first manned lunar landing on 20 July 1969, with Collins staying behind in the CM as Armstrong and Aldrin landed on the moon in the lunar module (LM) "Eagle." Disembarking, they made the "giant leap for mankind." The lunar module made it down with scant fuel to spare—"on fumes," so to speak—after the autopilot failed and the designated landing spot proved too rocky, so they had to land by hand. They returned safely with moon rocks after making several scientific experiments on the lunar surface. President John F. Kennedy's announced goal (1961) of a man on the moon at the end of the decade had been met.

The flights continued on schedule. *Apollo XII* (Conrad, Gordon, Alan L. Bean) landed on the lunar surface to pick up pieces of the earlier *Surveyor III* unmanned flight. *Apollo XIII* (Lovell, John L. Sweigert, Jr., Fred W. Haise, Jr.) lived up to the notion of "unlucky 13" when an oxygen tank explosion in the SM forced the crew to move to the LM and use it as a lifeboat as they performed a slingshot maneuver around the moon to reenter Earth's atmosphere safely. The risk captured a lagging public interest as nothing else as dramatic had been done since the original moon walk. They never knew if the damaged heat shield would work until after they had landed. It did. *Apollo XIV* (Shepard, Stuart A. Roosa, Edgar D. Mitchell) was noteworthy in that Shepard had been grounded with an inner-ear problem since his Mercury flight and had been unable to go up. Now, he and his crew were to restore faith in the NASA programs.

As Shepard and Roosa began to land on the moon, the landing radar went blank. They would have to fix the problem by 13,000 feet or abort the mission. But Shepard was not about to miss his chance to walk on the moon, the only one of the original seven to get one. Finally, with ground control realizing that Shepard was not going to abort, someone discovered that the radar had been mistakenly set at "infinity." The device was restarted and the picture restored. The rest of the mission came off without further problems, with Aldrin even taking a few golf shots before returning to the CM. The next three *Apollo*s managed the lunar landing perfectly, using a lunar rover (a sort of battery-powered Jeep) to explore. The final three flights were canceled as public money and interest waned and domestic issues came to the fore on Earth. Left behind were the footprints of 12 astronauts, their special moon boots, and $517 million worth of junked equipment, including six lunar mobile launch pads, three battery-powered moon rovers, five scientific laboratories, a horde of television and camera gear, six American flags, a plaque honoring 14 dead U.S. and Soviet spacemen, a piece of the Wright brothers' original biplane, and a pair of Shepard's golf balls.

One of the oddest accounts of the *Mercury*, *Gemini*, and *Apollo* flights came from the pen of Maurice Chatelain, a French expert on navigation, communications, data processing, and radar. Holder of a patent for an automatic retrorocket firing device that allowed several soft landings of unmanned satellites on the moon, Chatelain worked for NASA as a communications scientist. According to his account, the astronauts did not merely experience technical difficulties. They also reported being followed by unidentified flying objects (UFOs). On the several times they communicated such concerns to the ground, they were told to keep quiet as the flights were all on television. Leave it to Wally Schirra to ignore this, transmitting to the ground in code that "Santa Claus" existed, on his Mercury flight. The viewing public ignored this bit of seeming irreverency (the Cuban Missile Crisis grabbed most of the attention from this flight, anyway), but the NASA program directors did not.

Similar UFO incidents occurred during the flights of *Gemini 4* (along with a photograph), *5* (Cooper, one of the best pilots of the astronauts, never flew again, having seen too much, according to Chatelain), *7* (more photos of trailing UFOs), and *12* (observations from a one-half mile distance). The process continued during *Apollo 8* (with Lovell referring to Santa Claus existing as his craft appeared from the dark side of the moon), *10* (UFOs on ground control's radar), and *11* (Aldrin photographed them overhead as he stepped on the moon and the pictures inadvertently appeared in the popular *Modern People* magazine without comment). Worse yet, Chatelain posits that the explosion aboard *Apollo 13* was actually an attack on the craft to prevent its discharging a nuclear seismic device on the moon's surface, the results to be monitored on Earth.

Regardless of Chatelain's bizarre tales of UFOs, Americans and Soviets continued their exploration of space from Earth orbit. The American effort was based on the Skylab program, a use of the old Apollo equipment to run scientific experiments on zero gravity; oceanography, pollution, and terrestrial mineral exploration from the sky; and a number of aspects of the solar system with the traditional three-man crews. The results caused some to posit that the new crystals and purer alloys developed in the zero gravity of space will eventuate another Industrial Revolution, a project currently in place on the more modern Space Lab aboard the space shuttle. The crews left behind performed experiments in weightlessness and the effects of living in space over a long period of time. The Soviets put up their *Salyut* space station and periodically resupplied it through *Soyuz* expeditions. But the proposed new American space station, *Freedom*, has fallen to bad economic times and a declining interest in space exploration at home.

In 1975, with the advent of cold war détente on Earth, the Americans and the Soviets sent up the first international flight, an Apollo (Stafford, Slayton [whose heart fibrillation had stopped as mysteriously as it began], and Vance D. Brand) and a Soyuz that docked, exchanged crews, and conducted joint experiments before returning to Earth. It was also the last U.S. manned flight before the launching of the space shuttle, America's reusable spacecraft. The Soviets managed to put up an expanded space station, *Mir*, but the breakup of the Soviet Union into component republics has limited its space efforts in favor of more important terrestrial issues.

The Americans have gone on using the space shuttle. About the size of a DC-9 jet, the American space shuttle (officially the Space Transportation System or STS in NASA-speak) was designed to bring about economical, routine, and reliable space flight. It has three basic elements: an orbiter (the spacecraft), an external booster, and solid-fuel strap-on boosters. With a delta-wingspan of 78 feet and a length of 12 feet, it weights 105 tons and can haul 27.5 tons of cargo. It has a payload bay that is 15 feet wide and 60 feet long, large enough to hold satellites that it can spin-launch into orbit and a crew of three. It also has a Canadian-built crane that permits it to capture and retrieve damaged satellites for repair in the payload bay or back on Earth. There is room in the cabin for up to six scientific personnel and their equipment. It carries cargoes from other nations, and the scientists often include other nationals. Projected to fly as often as 60 times a year, the shuttle has never lived up to that expectation. It quickly fell victim to the requirements of unmanned satellite programs like the Hubble Space Telescope and earthly cold war necessities, such as the costly, time-consuming research and planning of the Strategic Defense Initiative or "Star Wars" (which by then had drained the more vibrant American economy almost as much as it had ruined the more stagnant Soviet one).

Despite its limited cargo carrying capacity, the space shuttle has had its moments since its first launch in 1981. From more mundane matters like sending the first American woman (Sally Ride) and the first male and female African Americans into space (Guion S. Bluford, Jr., and Mae C. Jemison) and inviting visiting astronauts from other countries like Japan, Saudi Arabia, and Germany to accompany select missions, to more important scientific matters like on-board experiments in weightlessness and astrophysics in the on-board Space Lab in the cargo bay, the repair of communications satellites (some of which were taken back to Earth and later relaunched from the shuttle or other rockets), and the refocusing of the faulty Hubble Telescope, the shuttle has performed a multitude of interesting and challenging tasks. Originally, the experimental shuttle *Enterprise* (named for the spaceship in the popular television series *Star Trek*) performed all of the atmospheric tests of the shuttle's systems, being launched by a special piggyback 747. There were four actual space shuttles, *Atlantis, Challenger, Discovery,* and *Columbia,* used on a rotating basis after *Enterprise* was retired to the Smithsonian never having penetrated space. The tragic takeoff explosion of the *Challenger* and the shocking death of its crew (including New Hampshire school teacher and mother S. Christa McAuliffe) led to the building of a replacement, *Endeavor,* in 1991, but also to the cancellation of the conversion of the old Vandenburg Air Force Base into a shuttle complex and the end to NASA's passenger-in-space program, initiated the year before with the flight of U.S. Senator Jake Garn (R-Utah).

Since the end of the Apollo program, the long-term goal of NASA has been to send an expedition to Mars. Much planning has been done on this expedition, often envisioned as a joint Russian-American project because of its cost. But each nation has had its problems. The breakup of the Soviet Union has left its Russian Republic with an operating space station (with one crew stranded while the issues of ethnicity were sorted out on Earth) but little further capability beyond the rotation of crew members on a regular basis. The United States, meanwhile, has developed a plan that relies on the space shuttle hauling enough materials up to build an operating space station in Earth orbit, called *Freedom,* that can serve as a base for the Mars trip and as a scientific experimentation center.

The idea is to make a joint U.S.-Russian mission to Mars. Each nation would send up a spacecraft to its own space station, provision and make ready for the journey, blast off from orbit independently and dock all modules in deep space, circle Venus to gain a slingshot effect from its gravitational pull, and head for Mars. The return trip would be the reverse, minus the swing past Venus. The Mars expedition is envisioned in two scenarios—one of just 15 months, the Sprint Mission, that would require more fuel, and the other, a more leisurely effort, that would conserve fuel and include a year-long scientific stay on the Red Planet until Earth approached closer for the trip back.

Even though the George W. Bush administration was the friendliest in years to the notion of resumed manned flight (Vice President Dan Quayle heading the National Space Council), economic recession and the competition for funds from terrestrial projects, a possible relanding on the moon, unmanned satellite programs including the space shield aspect of "Star Wars," the space station, developing a new booster rocket to propel the increased loads, and modernizing the now-ancient shuttle (called the DC-X) have caused much adverse criticism from scientific sources, political circles, and the tax-paying general public. And so the U.S. space program stumbles along, held back by a lack of need (no cold war), declining interest (domestic issues like universal medical care), and a slow economy, receiving an occasional stimulus from a spectacular feat like the recent untethered space walk. This lack of interest has caused NASA head Daniel S. Goldin and scientist-writer-space guru Carl Sagan to posit that Americans are ignoring the essential answers to how to improve life here on Earth by refusing to accept the age-old need of humans to wander, once on Earth, now through the cosmos, after a brief rest called civilization.

See also Aeronautics; Aerostatics; Borman, Frank Frederick, II; National Aeronautics and Space Administration; Ride, Sally Kristen; Slayton, Donald K.; X-Planes.

References Armstrong, Neil, et. al., *First on the Moon* (1970); Atkinson, Joseph D., and Jay M.

Anchored on the end of the Remote Manipulator System arm, astronaut F. Story Musgrave works on the Hubble Space Telescope on 9 December 1993.

Shafritz, et al., *The Real Stuff* (1985); Baucom, Donald R., *The Origins of SDI* (1993); Bilstein, Roger E., *Flight in America* (1994); Brooks, Courtney, et al., *Chariots for Apollo* (1979); Chaisson, Eric J., *The Hubble Wars* (1994); Chatelain, Maurice, *Our Ancestors Came from Outer Space* (1978); Collins, Michael, *Mission to Mars* (1990); Dethloff, Henry C., *Suddenly Tomorrow Came* (1992); Dyson, John, "The Big Fix," *Reader's Digest* (February 1995) 146: 85–91; Easterbrook, Gregg, "Why the Space Station Doesn't Fly," *Newsweek* (11 April 1994) 123: 30–33; Ezell, Edward C., "The Heroic Era of Manned Space Flight," in Eugene M. Emme (ed.), *Two Hundred Years of Flight in America* (1977), 231–253; Field, George, and Donald Goldsmith, *The Space Telescope* (1989); Gatland, Kenneth (ed.), *Space Technology* (1981); Gray, Colin S., "The Transition from Offense to Defense," *Washington Quarterly* (1986) 9 (no. 3): 59–72; Green, Constance M., and Milton Lomask, *Vanguard* (1971); Hacker, Barton C., and James M. Grimwood, *On the Shoulders of Titans* (1977); Hall, R. Cargill, "Origins and Development of the Vanguard and Explorer Satellite Programs, *The Airpower Historian* (1964) 11 (no. 4): 101–112; Hall, R. Cargill, "Instrumented Exploration and Utilization of Space: The American Experience," in Eugene M. Emme (ed.), *Two Hundred Years of Flight in America* (1977), 183–212; Hall, R. Cargill, *Lunar Impact* (1977); Jastrow, Robert, "Reagan vs. the Scientists: Why the President Is Right about Missile Defense," *Commentary* (January 1984) 77: 23–32; King, Elliot, "Science and the Information Superhighway," *Scientific Computing & Automation* (July 1994) 10: 6–8; Lakoff, Sanford, and Herbert York, *A Shield in Space?* (1989); Lewis, Richard S., *The Voyages of Apollo* (1974); Logsdon, John M., *The Decision To Go to the Moon* (1970); Magill, Frank (ed.), *Space Exploration Series* (1989); Manchester, William, *The Glory and the Dream* (1974); Murray, Charles, and Catherine Bly Cox, *The Race to the Moon* (1989); Ordway, Frederick I., and Mitchell R. Sharpe, *The Rocket Team* (1979); Otto, Dixon P., *On Orbit* (1986); Paul, Günter, *The Satellite Spin-off* (1975); Payne, Keith B., "The Soviet Union and Strategic Defense: The Failure and Future of Arms Control," *Orbis* (1986) 29: 673–689; Phelps, J. Alfred, *They Had a Dream* (1994); Riabchikov, Evgeny, *Russians in Space* (1971); Robinson, David Z., *The Strategic Defense Initiative* (1987); Sagan, Carl, *Pale Blue Dot* (1994); Sagan, Carl, "Wanderers," *Parade* (18 September 1994): 14–17; Shayler, David, *Shuttle Challenger* (1987); Shepard, Alan B., and Donald K. Slayton, *Moon Shot* (1992); Smith, Robert W., *The Space Telescope* (1989); Stine, G. Harry, *The Third Industrial Revolution* (1975); Swenson, Lloyd S., et al., *This New Ocean* (1966); Taylor, Stuart Ross, *Lunar Science* (1975); Torres, George, *Space Shuttle* (1986); Van Dyke, Vernon, *Pride and Power* (1964); Vladimirov, Leonid, *The Russian Space Bluff* (1973); Wolfe, Tom, *The Right Stuff* (1979); York, Herbert F., *Race to Oblivion* (1970).

Atchison, Topeka & Santa Fe Railway (AT&SF)

Named for the Kansas cities of its origin and the southwestern city of its destination, this railroad paralleled roughly the mountain route of the old Santa Fe Trail over Ratón Pass (ultimately extending itself into Chicago in the east and across northern Arizona and the Mojave Desert to Los Angeles in the west) with other lines paralleling the Pacific coast from San Diego to Oakland via the San Joaquín Valley.

See also Santa Fe Railway.

Atlantic Coast Line (ACL)

A conglomerate of southeastern Atlantic coastal railroads organized in 1871, the Atlantic Coast Line had its beginnings in the Richmond & Petersburg Railroad in 1836. The road eventually extended from Richmond to Tampa, and each participating railroad was allowed to keep its own logo

and name, which was displayed along with the ACL saw-toothed circle until 1900, when everyone assumed the corporate name and logo alone. By 1902, the ACL had taken in all of the smaller rail systems in the Carolinas, which gave it its form for the next 50 years. In the 1920s it acquired an interest in Pan American Airways and began to operate its pre–World War II passenger and airmail services. In 1957, it merged with the Seaboard Airline Railroad to form the Seaboard Coast Line Railroad.

See also CSX Corporation; Family Lines System; Louisville & Nashville Railroad; Seaboard Air Line Railroad; Seaboard Coast Line Railroad.

References Dozier, Howard A., *A History of the Atlantic Coast Line Railroad* (1920); Drury, George H., *The Historical Guide to North American Railroads* (1985); Drury, George H., *The Train-Watcher's Guide* (1990); Hubbard, Freeman, *Encyclopedia of North American Railroading* (1981); Prince, Richard E., *Atlantic Coast Line Railroad* (1966); Stover, John F., *Railroads of the South* (1955); Ward, James A., "Atlantic Coast Line," in Keith L. Bryant, Jr. (ed.), *EABHB: Railroads in the Age of Regulation* (1988), 13–15.

Atlantic Highway

One of the "named highways" popular in the teens and twenties of the twentieth century, the Atlantic Highway was used by local chambers of commerce and tourism and the American Automobile Association to stimulate travel on the "good roads" and increase income in the towns and states through which they passed. The Atlantic Highway ran parallel to the Atlantic Ocean from Fort Kent, Maine, to the tip of Florida and, with the exception of the stretch from Augusta, Georgia, to Jacksonville, Florida, is presently listed as U.S. Highway 1. In Georgia it is now U.S. Highway 25, inland, and U.S. Highway 17, roughly the route of Interstate 95, along the coast.

See also Roads and Highways, Colonial Times to World War I; Roads and Highways since World War I.

Reference Hart, Val, *The Story of American Roads* (1950).

Auto Train

Begun in December of 1971, the Auto Train is a daily, fast passenger service from Lorton, Virginia (suburban Washington, D.C.), to Sanford, Florida (in the Orlando area). At one time, a second run from Louisville, Kentucky, to Sanford was in operation, but it no longer is. The thing that makes Auto Train unique is that the passengers take their cars along for the trip and have them available when they detrain. Emphasizing the unique motif is the train's purple, red, and white colors, inside and out. Originally designed by Carolyn Settles, an interior-design expert, the train gives a racy, extra-clean image that is enhanced by the reflective coating of its car lettering. The whole operation is a governmentally organized corporation funded by private investment, much like Amtrak was supposed to be but never quite made it. Original financing came from the sale of 70,000 shares of stock that sold for $7 million.

When passengers arrive at either terminal, they check in and have their automobiles inspected for existing damage and loaded onto special auto carriers. The full auto carriers are then coupled ahead of the passenger cars directly behind the engines. These special cars are equipped with dampening devices and shock absorbers so as not to damage the autos in transit. Then, passengers are assigned dining cars that are located in the middle of the consist to lessen the need for passing through the whole train to eat. Meals are served airline style, but are usually more varied as to menu. When the eating cars are not serving food, they are turned into miniature movie theaters that show feature-length films. Passengers are also assigned sleeping quarters and seats in the dome coaches—all seats are in domes for scenic views. The original equipment came from two of the West's noted passenger carriers, Union Pacific and Santa Fe, so it had the best railroad cars in America when it was inaugurated. It also made these purchases at the same time Amtrak was scouring the market, so it beat Amtrak to the punch from the start.

The train crews are regular employees of the railroad companies over whose tracks Auto Train operates, the CSX Corporation. Train crew members traveling in the passenger area usually wear civilian suits rather than train uniforms to remain as inconspicuous as possible. Public service is handled by specially trained passenger service assistants (PSAs) outfitted in clothes of Auto Train colors with name tags and supervised by a service director and a senior hostess. The PSAs work eight-and-a-half-hour shifts and sleep in a dorm car when off duty. A skeleton crew is available at night. They take a bus to a dorm at the end of the run for a four-hour rest before they take the train back again. The PSAs work two nights and have three nights off, as a rule. The train is kept clean by an hourly coach patrol. The car windows are cleaned at each stop and the whole exterior washed at the end of each trip.

Upon arrival at the end of the journey, the automobiles are unloaded at the rate of about three a minute. Early figures showed that 99 percent who ride the Auto Train would not use the rails if they could not take their own autos along. The train expends about 25 gallons of fuel per auto hauled. Although figures have changed with the increased popularity of compact autos, it would take about 90 gallons of gas to drive oneself. Early figures estimated saving over 11 million gallons of fuel a year, plus the attendant decrease in pollutants. The current figures are probably about the same. As autos have become more fuel efficient, so have the now-computerized diesels that haul them. But Auto Train is still a good way to travel the lower East Coast with one's auto and arrive at one's destination refreshed and ready to go—no motels or gas stations needed.

See also Amtrak.

Reference Hediger, Jim, "This Highway Is Not on Your Oil Company Map," *Trains* (December 1974) 35: 22–32.

Automobiles from Domestics to Imports

The idea of replacing the horse as a means of propulsion is an old one that got a real boost in the nineteenth century. Self-propulsion through levers or pedals, like on a bicycle, had been tried in 1645, by the Frenchman Jean Théson. Other similar machines turned up in various German states. But they were a bit tiring to operate all day, and old Dobbin again took his rightful place at the head end of carriages. Some tried to use wind and sail to power a land vehicle, but the wind rarely cooperated. George Pocock of England had such a device, named the Flying Chariot. Not much came of it, but he did receive the satisfaction of passing the Duke of Gloucester's fancy four-in-hand carriage once. Even Americans got into the act. Oliver Evans invented a combination paddle wheel boat–four-wheel amphibian steam vehicle that wheezed through Philadelphia in 1804. Steam carriages even ran on fixed schedules in England and France. All eventually disappeared, although Onésiphore Pecqueur developed a model that had modern two-wheel steering and a differential for rear-wheel drive.

By the middle of the nineteenth century, Joseph E. Lenoir developed the first practicable internal combustion engine. His idea was seized upon by others who developed methods of compressing a mist of the fuel in a cylinder. Nikolaus Otto made a machine that had four strokes (intake, compression, firing, and exhaust) that was called an Otto Silent, which led directly to the automobile engine 30 years later. One of Otto's assistants, Gottlieb Daimler, hit on using gasoline for power, as did Karl Benz. They used such modern items as a differential, electric ignition, and a water-cooled radiator. Daimler sold his patent to the French, which expanded the technology into a nation full of men like Renault, Citroën, and Peugeot.

In the United States, Charles Duryea invented the first practical American automobile in 1892. It looked like a carriage but he used the term "automobile." It weighed 750 pounds, and had two gears forward and one in reverse. He could produce 12 a year. By 1902, Ransom Olds had a mass assembly line going and his Oldsmobile sold 2,500 vehicles a year. Henry M. Leland, with his

Cadillac, quickly introduced interchangeable parts. In 1908, Henry Ford capitalized on all that had gone before him and introduced the Model T, nicknamed the Flivver or Tin Lizzie. It had a steering wheel on the left side (which took it out of the horse and early car era where the driver sat on the right) and a foot-operated gearshift, and was priced at $950. By 1912, the price had dropped to $550. Ford could make thousands a day on his Dearborn, Michigan, assembly line, which he streamlined into the most efficient workplace of his day. He paid his workers well enough so they could buy what they made. By 1928, he had sold over 15 million units. Over in England, Rudyard Kipling dismissed the auto as a "petropiddling monster." No matter. The automobile revolution was on its way. By 1920, there were as many cars and trucks on the road as horse-drawn vehicles. The gas buggies were sold as "pollution free," and their smooth rubber tires did not tear up the asphalt in hot weather like horses' iron shoes. From an industry that ranked one hundred fiftieth in the 1900 census, automobiles grew to first place among all American industries by 1925.

Auto manufacturing was a hot business in the early days before present-day Americans wound up with the Big Three (Ford, Chrysler, and General Motors). Some early entrepreneurs (and the date of their start-up) were: Stanley (1890, makers of a steam-powered car that lasted well into the twentieth century), Winton (1897), Olds (1897), Buick (1901), Pierce-Arrow (1901), Packard (1902), Cadillac (1902), Ford (1903), Reo (1904), General Motors (1907), Hudson (1909), and Hupp (1910). All of these makers had something in common. They used the Otto "silent" principle in their engines. In the United States, that patent was held by George B. Selden of Rochester, New York, and licensed through a front organization, the Association of Licensed Automobile Manufacturers, which got a percentage on all early autos produced—except for Ford's.

Others had tried to break the Selden monopoly but had failed. After an eight-year trial that produced 36 volumes of testimony,

Ford and his dealers won a reprieve. Ford claimed that his motors used a similar yet different process, the two-stroke Brayton cycle. This was an ably argued piece of legal fiction—all autos ran on the Otto principle. But the New York State Appeals Court bought it. The decision (Ford had lost in the trial court) was very important, however, because it broke up the monopoly in 1911. The rights would have expired the following year anyway—but it made Ford look like the hero of the common man, which did not hurt his sales. Now anyone could build an engine without paying a royalty, and car prices dropped precipitously. The gasoline engine was important because "electrics" had heavy, bulky batteries and a short range, and the steamers had a disconcerting habit of blowing up if not properly managed. Gasoline motors had reliability, range, and performance (especially the latter). The application of the Society of Automobile Engineers (SAE) standards to auto parts in 1911 made them (especially screws, bolts, washers, and nuts) interchangeable industry-wide. Now a smaller machinist company could earn a profit supplying off-the-shelf parts to someone else who made cars, reducing overall costs.

Although there were hundreds of producers over the years, the market soon boiled down to Ford, General Motors, Chrysler, and a few independents like Packard (a car of style until the 1960s), Hudson (among the first to use stamped, curved parts and a fully enclosed body in the 1920s), Willys-Overland (famous for the Jeep of World War II), Studebaker (from the old wagon-making days), and Nash (later to merge with others to become American Motors under George Romney in the 1950s, which would merge with Chrysler under Lee Iacocca in the 1980s).

The first big auto maker, Ford made his reputation on pure cussedness and the notion that one ought to do one thing and do it well. The result was the Model T, based on advanced French concepts (like a multi-cylinder engine in front, steering wheel instead of a stick, drive shaft and rear differential, multigear transmission, and steel frame), which knocked the original Oldsmobile out of the cheap-car business and earned Ford over 60 percent of the whole American market by 1921. Through moving assembly-line techniques, Ford cut costs almost annually (finally reaching $440 per unit); yet he kept his profit at 100 percent. He kept the same body ("you can have any color as long as it's black," was the saying) but added on new developments like electric starters, new tire styles, and a windshield with wipers. The result was that by 1927, when he announced a new type, the Model A, Ford was still selling a 1908 car with options.

Ford's myopic outlook (not easy to say about a man who made millions from his production philosophy) opened the field to others. The most important was General Motors, formed in 1908 from a series of smaller companies who were mostly bankrupt. The guiding light behind GM was William C. Durant, later run off by Pierre DuPont. The mainstays of the company were Buick and Cadillac, with support from Oldsmobile and Oakland (which became Pontiac in 1928), but other gems included Carter, Elmore, Ewing, Marquette, Ranier, Reliance, and Welch. Durant also bought support groups like Champion (spark plugs), Northway (engines), Weston-Mott (axles), and Heany (headlights).

GM had a different production policy than Ford's. The idea was to increase quality and sell at a few hundred dollars above Ford. They also made Ford's options standard equipment, decentralized their production plants throughout the nation to reduce shipping costs, and used a variety of colorful paints. Through a newly acquired subsidiary started by racing-car driver Louis Chevrolet, and under the leadership of William S. Knudsen (an ex-Ford executive run-off to assure Ford's ascendancy over his own destiny), GM managed to surpass Ford in sales by the Great Depression. GM and the independents were the first to realize that the "virgin" car market (new buyers) was depleted. They accepted trade-ins, began long-term financing through General Motors Acceptance Corporation—GMAC (although

Willys-Overland first did this in 1915 and Ford would follow in 1959), and set up a test track and laboratory to research new materials and methods. Under Alfred P. Sloan, Jr.—first a vice-president, then president after DuPont—the whole firm was reorganized to share information between divisions and respond to real market conditions.

Like GM, Chrysler was the result of the merging of several smaller companies, but came later in the 1920s. Much of Chrsyler's success came from its distribution network, something it obtained by merging with Dodge Brothers. John and Horace Dodge had been chassis makers for Henry Ford, but who had gone into business for themselves in 1914. Walter P. Chrysler was a GM executive who had been brought out of retirement to save Willys-Overland in 1919. When John Willys managed to regain the company, Chrysler went over to Maxwell to bring it out of the postwar recession, hiring several Studebaker executives to help out. He decided to modernize the whole operation and introduce a new model bearing his own name. It would be a high-performance, expensive-looking, but not overpriced enclosed car (a new innovation).

In so doing, Chrysler found the solution to the disappearance of the first-time car buyer that Ford relied on so much. Chrysler introduced the idea of annual model changes on vehicles that were highly engineered four- and six-cylinder models with new gadgets. It was GM with a difference, and it would keep the American car industry going for the next 50 years. By 1928, Chrysler had a new model, the Plymouth, to compete with Ford and Chevy, as well as the Dodge to compete with Pontiac, the DeSoto to compete with Oldsmobile (a competition to which Ford added the Mercury in 1938), Chrysler to compete with Buick, and Imperial to compete with Cadillac (and Ford's Lincoln, an independent company brought into the Ford company in 1922 and made a luxury car in 1939). That is where the business stood when World War II temporarily put an end to civilian car production.

After the war, with Ford, GM, and Chrysler now known as the Big Three, the independents began to decline. Although there were over a dozen and a half independents, the real producers were Packard, Nash, Studebaker (which bought up Pierce-Arrow), Hudson, and Willys-Overland. All would last in some form or another until the late 1950s or early 1960s. After World War II, at least two dozen companies tried to enter the auto market, but not one of them made it. Two of the most noteworthy were Crosley (one of the first compacts) and Kaiser-Frazer, which absorbed Willys and then went broke. Hudson and Nash combined to form American Motors Corporation (jettisoning the Hudson line in the process), while Studebaker and Packard merged in a hyphenated form (eventually dropping Packard). Both of these firms introduced the first "compact cars." There was the Rambler, then the American, and finally the really small Metropolitan at American Motors. Studebaker followed suit with the Lark. As all of these models hit the market at the time of the 1958 recession, it made both these companies and their presidents look like marketing geniuses, especially George Romney at American Motors.

In the early 1950s Chevrolet came out with the fiberglass-body Corvette, America's first true sports car. But sales never ran over 10,000 units a year (by choice, as it was something of a "limited edition" concept). Ford countered with the Thunderbird, a jazzy little two-seater that soon developed into a full-sized car in the middle price range. The up-sizing so common in the fifties occurred because the manufacturers wanted to grab the potential buyer while young and keep his business after he got married and had a family. (In those days women were not thought of much when it came to purchases like autos, unless it was to perk up an ad.) But the coup of the "baroque age" of auto manufacturing came in the mid-1960s when, under the leadership of Lee Iacocca, Ford presented the Mustang. Like the Corvette, it kept its two-seat capacity and an appeal to the young. But unlike the Corvette, the Mustang was affordable to a young person without much money.

All of this occurred at a time when the small-car market was dominated by a German import, the Volkswagen (VW) Bug. It had taken real courage to sell Volkswagen to Americans. The car had originally been developed by Ferdinand Porsche for Adolph Hitler in the 1930s as a car for the German *volk* (hence its name). Condemned as "Hitler's car," Volkswagen worked long and hard to emphasize its quality, simplicity, and economy. By the late 1950s, it had a set of dealers who specialized in the VW, which put them ahead of all other European imports, while Japanese cars were still an international joke ("not worth a plugged yen," went the analysis). It is ironic that the "pregnant roller skate" envisioned by *the* fascist ogre of the twentieth century endured to become the darling of left-wing American ecological ideologues of the 1960s. It was built on the old Henry Ford principle—the same old body plus successive mechanical improvements.

But Volkswagen was seen as an aberration. During the Age of Detroit Baroque, the idea was to have a cheap car that looked expensive. Yearly model changes, miles of chrome trim or "woody sided" (it was usually a plastic stick-on) station wagons, useless tail fins that began with Cadillac (and worked their way down the GM line and converted all of Chrysler), and powerful eight-cylinder engines (only Ford had them before in the cheaper classes) were all the rage. At first, Ford countered with recessed steering columns and seat belts, "selling safety instead of cars," sniffed the critics. Then it met the competition with a whole new model, the Edsel, shooting itself through the foot in the process.

One of the biggest busts in the auto business, Edsel fell flat on its face and was phased out within three years. The failure has been analyzed (either it came out as the economic recession of 1958 occurred and everyone had to cut back purchases, or it fell victim to the Soviet Union's *Sputnik* as yet another silly, effete bauble that revealed the hollowness of American society) and psychoanalyzed (the "horse collar" grill supposedly put off buyers who unconsciously compared it to a woman's vagina). But what could one expect from a vehicle that seemed a pure "lemon" from day one, with brakes that did not work, trunks and hoods and doors that would not open or stuck open, paint that peeled, batteries that died, oil pans that dropped off on the road, hubcaps that fell off, and transmissions that froze? Even the auto thieves wouldn't touch it, a unique commentary—until the advent of the imported Yugo in the 1980s. The independents countered with gadgets, but the growing problem of quality control that nearly killed the whole industry off by 1980 struck them first two decades earlier and soon infected Chrysler, too, with near-fatal results.

Because American Motors and Studebaker had weathered the 1958 recession with their domestic compacts, the Big Three joined them. At first they imported small cars from their European subsidiaries, but soon produced their own. The result was generally not pretty. The Ford Pinto allegedly blew up like Mount Vesuvius when hit by another car from the rear. The snappy little Chevy Corvair was so poorly designed that it sent critic Ralph Nader (author of *Unsafe at Any Speed*, 1965) into a lifelong career as a consumer advocate. Then there was a humorous story that summed up much of American's attitude about little cars—Ford and Chrysler combined their Comet and Valiant to produce a new compact called the Vomit that had bucket seats, a throw-up hood, and a horn that went "ble-e-e-a-a-ah!" That was the real crux of the issue—American cars simply were not well made. And GM and Chrysler forgot the vibrant "sloanism" that got them where they were and began to slump into "Fordism"—one boring product regardless of price range. Then came the Arab oil embargo of 1973–1974, and gasoline prices shot up through the ceiling—not good news for the owners of gas-guzzling American junk, made more so by increasing environmental requirements.

Into this void stepped the Japanese. They offered Americans small, fairly well-made, fuel-efficient automobiles. Toyota, Nissan

(Datsun), and Mazda were the Big Three of Japan's imports, but they all paled in comparison with Honda. The little CVCC ("compound vortex controlled combustion") Civic, with an engine mounted crossways between the direct-drive front wheels, sold only 39,000 cars in 1973. But they got 40 miles per gallon. By the end of the oil crisis, Honda had sold twice this annually, and by 1980, the sales had jumped sixfold from 1973. The Japanese accomplished their feat by a combination of industrial efficiency, intelligent marketing, good fortune, government aid and protection, and the offering of a superior product at low prices. In 1975, Congress passed the Energy Policy and Conservation Act. It required auto manufacturers to meet a corporate automobile fuel efficiency (CAFE) standard—a combination of all of its models made that year combined—of 20 miles per gallon by 1980 and nearly 30 miles per gallon by 1985. Now everyone would have to go small and efficient, because the Japanese were the only ones who could meet CAFE standards under current conditions.

The American's first efforts at downsizing were not good (Ford's Mustang II, Chrysler's Volaré, GM's Chevette), but they were designed as stopgap measures to hold the market until research, rethinking, and retooling caught up. A new urgency came in the form of the 1980 Iranian crisis, which saw one of the Arabian Gulf's largest producers of petroleum products isolated from the world. With quality control problems and continual recalls of defective products, the Americans slipped even further into the doldrums. The federal government enacted the Environmental Protection Act (1975) that restricted the output of hydrocarbons, nitrogen oxides, and carbon dioxide. As luck would have it, the engine that could best meet these standards was the rotary Wankel (used by Mazda in its RX-7 sports car), but it used more gas than a normal internal-combustion engine—not good in a world suffering from embargoed oil.

Under the twin pressures of economy and cleanliness, the triumph of the era was Honda's new Accord, a heavier vehicle than the Civic that carried four adults in relative comfort and got around 30 miles per gallon. By now Honda was fourth in sales in the United States behind the American Big Three. It also became obvious that as prices for cars went into five figures, Americans would want a vehicle that would last a while. With this in mind, the Japanese began to bring in bigger, luxury models challenging the position of Oldsmobile, Pontiac, Mercury, and even Lincoln and Cadillac. Even during the worst oil embargo days, Americans had preferred bigger vehicles. When the embargo stopped, they went back to the big cars en masse, leaving the smaller cars in such excess inventory that producers instituted a series of rebates to clear the storage lots, and V-8 engines had to be rationed in the factories.

At the same time, the U.S. government affected the picture in a big way on two levels. The first was the bailing out of Chrysler in 1980. Chrysler President Lee Iacocca, a Ford transplant and developer of the original Mustang, sold Congress on the need to maintain competition (although if Ford had bought Chrysler, which was under consideration, it might have made it a more viable company compared to GM) and reiterated the fact that Chrysler was the only manufacturer of military tanks for the army. Then Iacocca came out with the K-Cars, which sported front-wheel drive and were fairly roomy and efficient. They were an instant success, prompted by Iacocca's clever, patriotic-sounding ads and folksy demeanor, and Chrysler became viable again, causing some to tout Iacocca for president of the United States (he was smart enough to decline, probably not being able to stand the reduction in power and influence). GM, meanwhile, had trouble with its X-Cars (like the Chevy Citation), production being uncompetitive, which were then followed by the underpowered J-Cars (Chevy Cavalier). Ford responded with the Escort/Lynx, which did well but not well enough. They had the same quality problems as the other American-mades. Cynics maintained that FORD, for example, stood for "Found On Road Dead," or "Fix Or Repair Daily."

Ford was also dubbed Chrysler II, in reference to its shaky financial position.

To keep more competitive, the Big Three had to go to the unions and together work out a modernization of plants and a downsizing of labor forces. It was not easy to do. Labor and management hated each other. Also, one in five American jobs depended directly or indirectly on automobiles. Although Americans have not put together a team quite like the ever-cooperative Japanese, labor-management relations have been smoother than before—both realizing that their industry's survival is on the line. Meanwhile, to counter increasing criticism over "flooding the American market," the Japanese began to accept "voluntary" import quotas or transfer of their production sites to the United States to get around them—producing, in effect, American-made cars. This was a real public-relations coup, because one of the plants was located in Kentucky and employed people whose fathers had suffered and died in the Bataan Death March in World War II as part of the National Guard.

As the American company in the worst financial position by the mid-1980s, Ford launched a vigorous, well-planned campaign to improve its image and product. Ads emphasized that things were changing for the better. They used the popular black TV spokesman, Bill Cosby, and the slogan, "Quality Is Job One." The result of their design team was the Ford Taurus/Mercury Sable, *Motor Trend* magazine's Car of the Year in 1986. Since then, Ford took the award every year until 1990, the Lincoln Town Car being the last, marking the first time a luxury car had been chosen in 38 years. Ford now led the industry. But the others were not far behind. At Chrysler the new, roomy minivan replaced the station wagon as the family vehicle and was an instant success, prompting copies even among the Japanese.

Meanwhile Chrysler absorbed American Motors in 1987, which had been kept afloat that long only by its production of the Jeep. And GM came out with the A-Cars (Celebrity, Pontiac 6000) and a new division, Saturn, which struck the subcompact market dominated by the Japanese. Like the Japanese dealers in the United States, Saturn dealers did not haggle about price, which made them look good to Americans, many of whom saw price negotiation as the dealer's way to take customers for all they were worth. The next biggest trend seemed to be one that Henry Ford started back in 1908 (opening subsidiaries worldwide). Usually these take the form nowadays of combining with one of the Japanese, French, English, or German automobile companies; for example, Ford with Mazda, GM with Toyota, and Chrysler with Mitsubishi.

By 1989, market share in the American auto industry for the decade had shifted. Imports, which had 20.4 percent of the market in 1981, now took 25.4 percent of the total. Of the domestic producers, only Ford realized a gain, up from 16.6 in 1981 to 22.3 percent. Chrysler lost some ground, down from 11.9 to 10.4 percent. But the big loser was mighty GM. Its market share dropped from 44.6 in 1981 to 35.1 percent. The rest of the share went to other imports, rising from 6.5 to 6.8 percent, with Europeans losing some ground to the new entries from Korea. Now there are new technologies, like Ford's Duratec V-6 and Cadillac's Northstar system, that allow automakers to tout engines that can go 100,000 miles without a tune-up and run 50 miles without coolant in an emergency. Truly, transportation has been America's most important contribution to the twentieth century and the automobile continues to be its principal product.

See also Organization of Petroleum Exporting Countries; Roads and Highways, Colonial Times to World War I; Roads and Highways since World War I; Tire and Rubber Industry; Trucking.

References Arnold, Horace Lucien, and Fay Leone Faurote, *Ford Methods and the Ford Shops* (1915); Baranson, Jack, *The Japanese Challenge to U.S. Industry* (1981); Clymer, Floyd, *A Treasury of Early American Automobiles* (1950); Cray, E., *Chrome Colossus* (1980); Cusumano, Michael A., *The Japanese Automobile* (1985); Dawson, D. G., "Short History of Human-Powered Vehicles," *American Scientist* (1986) 74: 350–357; Derr, Thomas S., *The Modern Steam Car* (1945); Duncan, William, *U.S.-Japan Automobile Diplomacy* (1973); Halberstam,

David, *Reckoning* (1986); Kuhn, Arthur J., *GM Passes Ford* (1986); McLaughlin, Charles L., "The Stanley Steamer: A Study in Unsuccessful Innovation," *Explorations in Entrepreneurial History* (1954–1955) 7: 37–47; Manchester, William, *The Glory and the Dream* (1974); Maxcy, George, *The Multinational Automobile Industry* (1981); May, George S., *Encyclopedia of American Business History and Biography: The Automobile Industry, 1920–1989* (1989); May, George S. (ed.), *Encyclopedia of American Business History and Biography: The Automobile Industry, 1896–1920* (1990); Nader, Ralph, *Unsafe at Any Speed* (1965); Rader, James, *Penetrating the U.S. Auto Market* (1980); Rae, John B., *American Automobile Manufacturers* (1959); Shook, Robert L., *Turnaround* (1990); Sobel, Robert, *Car Wars* (1984); Stuart, Reginald, *Bailout* (1980); U.S. Department of Transportation, Federal Highway Administration, *America's Highways* (1976); Woodbury, George, *The Story of a Stanley Steamer* (1950); Yates, Brock, *The Decline and Fall of the American Automobile Industry* (1983).

Automobiles in American Society

It is not surprising that the automobile affected twentieth-century society greatly. Early drivers were an arrogant lot—and recent ones have not been much better. The first auto owners tended to be better educated, urbane types, who drove their horseless carriages, in the words of one popular author of the day, Englishman Kenneth Grahame (*Wind in the Willows*), "as if in a dream, all sense of right and wrong, all fear of obvious consequences, seemed suspended." And they were quite disgusted with the hicks they encountered in the countryside, slowly plodding along behind a team of horses. The hayseeds paid them back in their spite—after all, they still controlled the state legislatures and most public debate. And it was the farmer and his steeds who would have to pull most of the dudes out of the inevitable mudhole.

Outfits like the American Automobile Association realized this. Motoring clubs gave numerous suggestions for a good trip: Don't wait until the gas tank is empty to fill up, as the next place might have no fuel; keep your water can full—one never knows when a hose might burst; don't buy oil in bulk, use one-gallon cartons; don't forget your goggles; don't drive over 25 mph. But the most popular adjunct and incitement to auto driving was racing. William K. Vanderbilt built the Long Island Speedway in 1906, and Carl G. Fisher the Indianapolis Speedway in 1909. The hero of the decade was cigar-chomping Barney Oldfield, the first man to go a mile a minute. He was also billed as the savior of the white race after he beat prizefighter Jack Johnson in a racially promoted 1910 match race that set the trend for modern sports promotions. Of course, the whole cheap affair ignored the fact that Johnson was still king of the ring.

Early on, the Farmers' Anti-Automobile Association published the following rules: The auto driver at night must send up a rocket every mile, wait ten minutes and then proceed, with caution, blowing his horn; if a driver sees a team approaching, he must stop, pulling over to one side, and cover the machine with a blanket, camouflaged to match the scenery; if a horse was unwilling to pass a motor vehicle after the above procedure, the driver must dismantle the machine and conceal the parts in the bushes. It was a rough life. The average driver had a tool kit that he did not know how to use ("get out and get under" was a veteran driver's motto), a tire patch kit, a shovel, a shank of rope, a piece of two-by-four lumber for footing if stuck, and a galvanized pail to fill the radiator, which overheated all the time. Pennsylvania, ahead of the country as usual, even provided barrels of water on hilltops to help out. By now motorists cared little for constitutional arguments that blocked government-funded road construction. What they wanted was good roads that went somewhere, the legalities be damned.

In 1923, one out of six persons owned a car. Speed limits were low but the vehicles could do 50 mph, and the daring did. Speed traps and motorcycle officers abounded. Accidents soared. Hell, any fool could drive, and most did. Drivers' licenses were considered a violation of the rights of an individual. Sarcastic comics proposed a few license examiner's questions of their own: What do you use to keep a radiator from freezing, antifreeze or gin? What brand of gin? What is your recipe? Or, What language is spoken in Mexico? What language is used when you run out of gas nine miles from the pump? Compare each with an eye to picturesqueness and wealth of metaphor.

The automobile had a big effect on society. There was more traffic congestion, not less, as more optimistic and less unrealistic prognosticators expected. Traffic signals first appeared in 1912 in Salt Lake City and soon spread to other places, along with policemen who specialized in traffic control, but mostly wrote tickets—and inspired Hollywood's Keystone Kops. Roads had to be signed, at first haphazardly then methodically, and synchronized nationally (now internationally, with the diagonal hack mark through a circle prohibiting various motorist choices). Most important was the idea of traffic lanes being painted on the pavement, first used on New York City's Brooklyn Bridge in 1883, a nice touch nationally to prevent the unyielding from head-on "chicken" collisions. Stop lines followed in 1907 in Portsmouth, Virginia, and center lines on curves and bridges in 1912 in Wayne County, Michigan.

But there was more. The idea of a perpetual centerline occurred by accident when a repair crew sealed a crack that appeared in the road in 1920 Maryland. The slick, black oil mark kept the cars so much better organized, and with fewer accidents, that intentional white and yellow lines soon followed. Road maps, an idea from the ancient Greeks and Romans, kept drivers aware of the way to their destinations. Speeding was another ancient offense, but the power of the gasoline engine was a more serious matter than that of the racing horse. Driving on the right came from the habit that Conestoga-wagon drivers, and later army mule skinners, had of sitting on the near-wheel animal, and the swampers' left-side seat on following wagons in a caravan. The custom was enshrined in early road laws on the Lancaster Pike and in New York State, which flowed over to other pikes. Peasants in Europe had traditionally kept to the right

An A & W employee serves dinner to motorists in 1942.

as a matter of deference—the French Revolution sanctified this "democratic rule" and Napoleon I spread it to the rest of Europe. Of course, his sworn enemies in England did the opposite (which probably clinched the use of the right lane among doubters in still-anti-British middle America).

Early registration was expensive, keeping with the notion that only rich fools could afford a motorcar. New York led the way in registrations and developed reciprocity arrangements with 15 other states—they recognized the validity of New York's registration, New York honored theirs. But Massachusetts and New Jersey refused to go along with the reciprocity idea, causing their citizens to have to register in all of the states they wished to drive in. It was not much of problem in going to New York (the trains were plentiful), but for New Yorkers who had summer vacation homes along the New Jersey coast and Cape Cod, it was a nuisance. Some states licensed vehicles, as did some counties and cities. Other governmental entities also taxed the auto as personal property. It could be an expensive necessity or a classy luxury.

Burgeoning sales and tax relief during the Great Depression sorted most of these problems out. Auto sales hit the 1.6 million mark for 1921; by 1929 the number of annual sales was at 5.3 million units valued at $3.4 billion. Because of the Great Depression, World War II, and the Korean "police action," this mark would not be surpassed for over 20 years. In 1940, half of all car-owning families had a weekly income of $30 or less, three-fourths earned $40 or less, and 90 percent earned less than $60. The auto was fast becoming everyone's transportation of choice.

And why not? With "the forward look" that entailed "directional stabilizer" fins, "fall away" fenders, and "twin tower" tail lamps, no one wanted to be left out. Automakers bragged of "red ram" V-8 engines that soon became "super red ram" and "super-powered red ram" as the advertising hyperbole increased by model year. Others marketed "Blue Flame Six" or "TurboFire V-8" motors. Transmissions were given neat monikers like "TorqueFlight," "DynaFlo," "FlightPitch," "Merc-O-Matic," "Fluid Drive," "Hydra-matic," "Powerglide," "Turboglide," or "Mile-O-Matic." There were "sweepspar" side moldings, "fashion-aire" engine grills, and who could forget Buick's Ventiports along the side of the hood, patterned after the exhaust ports of renowned World War II fighters like the P-51 Mustang. One company touted a car with 160 chrome parts, each having "four facets for maximum sparkle." Often, it seemed that everything was named after airplanes. With the advance into deep space, it was a mighty short step to the "Rocket Olds."

With the mass ownership of autos came the move to the suburbs. Why put up with cramped, noisy, crime-ridden, dirty city housing when, for the price of a short drive, one's family could live in planned, clean neighborhoods with shopping centers (another auto-inspired idea), schools, and manicured lawns? Houses were redesigned around the new member of the family, the car's room—a garage or carport, that substitute for a garage that lacks walls or doors prevalent in the milder weather of southern California—being the center of attraction and function. The result was an urban traffic congestion problem that swamped the nation after World War II and remains today. The panacea was the parkway, now called a freeway, or even toll highways that ran from cities into the hinterland. But better roads only attracted more drivers and suburb dwellers. It was a never-ending problem. Besides, then as now, most trips were short ones to work or shopping of ten miles or less.

Downtowns began to disappear to urban blight. The automobile society revolved first around the shopping strip and then the shopping center or mall, surrounded by massive parking lots for the consumer's car. Who wanted to take the bus downtown? Not enough parking there. Romance also centered around the car. No teenaged boy dared face a date without wheels. Cruisin' was the sport of choice, a sort of mobile foreplay. Throaty comedienne Rusty Warren did raunchy shticks on lovemaking in the back seat.

The appearance of the van was a godsend to part-time lovers and professionals alike. Until Lee Iacocca made them substitutes for the station wagon (i.e., before they sprouted side windows), the enclosed vehicles hid a multitude of sins. The van came complete with provocative scenes painted on the sides and risqué slogans on the rear bumpers ("if this van's a rockin' don't come a knockin'," "Ford [or whatever] drivers make better lovers," and "Sin Bin"). The idea of one's child on a date with a van owner became a terrifying thought to many a mother or father. To a prostitute, it was a mobile bedroom that could not be searched without a warrant. Connected to her pimp by citizens' band radio or cellular phone, it was a wonder if law enforcers found her at all. The interior redecorating of vans, usually with plush, wall-to-wall carpeting, made President Bill Clinton's coy statement about Astroturf in the open-bed of the pickup truck of his youth almost naively innocent.

The drive-in window became the shopping place of choice, whether it was eating, film-watching, film-developing, boozing, banking, or saving souls. Speed was of the essence in doing anything. There were so many places to go, so many things to see or do. The idea of confined space (in 1900 most people had never been 10 miles from home or seen a federal official) was shot to smithereens. Nobody thought much of going 60 miles or more for a dinner, movie, or sporting event (Colorado Rockies baseball fans regularly come hundreds of miles from surrounding states to see a Denver game, for instance). Not satisfied with the idea of paved roads, Americans have gone into the backcountry, "4-wheelin'." They have also tired of the dirt roads and have taken to driving all over the pristine terrain of the once-virgin countryside.

The real victims of mass auto ownership were public transportation and the downtowns they served—commuter railroads, city buses, trolleys—many of which ceased to exist in some cities. Many families became two-vehicle owners (the Ford F-150 half-ton pickup truck is still the single best-selling model in the nation), but mileage and fuel consumption actually leveled off. Before World War II, as each family bought its first vehicle, purchases, mileage, and fuel consumption had a direct relationship. After the war, as families bought their second vehicle—"mom's car" (often a station wagon), or dad's pickup truck, or junior's hot rod—mileage and fuel consumption only went up 50 percent per new vehicle, as families split their driving among the vehicles owned. And God save the poor or the elderly who could not drive. Whether a ride to a job or to see the doctor, their very standard of living was at stake in the new self-mobile society.

But were there also other victims of the auto? In the 1930s the auto was seen as a force of liberation and social well-being. Stories like John Steinbeck's *Grapes of Wrath* portray the auto as the salvation of a people in limbo from forces beyond their control. But by 1977, the movie *The Car* portrayed the automobile as a menace of the machine age gone awry. It had a mind of its own, evil and vengeful. But the real embodiment of the automobile as Satan himself comes in Stephen King's horror novel, *Christine* (1983). A beautiful female wrapped up in the body of a sexy, blood red, 1957 Plymouth Fury, a model full of the chrome and tail fins that made for looks and little else, King's personified seductress roams the world with a mind of her own. She becomes the devil-woman of song, possessive of her male owner, vengeful to those who harm her or interfere with her man, the transmogrification of the female in steel— the allure of the automobile for men of all ages. She is a female portrayal of unlimited power, something former U.S. Secretary of State Henry Kissinger once called the "ultimate aphrodisiac." But then Detroit stylists, image makers, and bean counters had known this for decades.

See also Buses; Greyhound Corporation; Roads and Highways, Colonial Times to World War I; Roads and Highways since World War I; Trucking.

References Anderson, Rudolph E., *The Story of the American Automobile* (1950); Bayley, Stephen, *Sex, Drink and Fast Cars* (1986); Beasley, D. R., *The Suppression of the Automobile* (1988); Fabre, Maurice, *A History of Land Transportation* (1963); Flink, J. J.,

Automobiles in American Society

America Adopts the Automobile (1970); Flink, J. J., *The Car Culture* (1975); Flink, J. J., *The Automobile Age* (1988); Jordan, Philip D., *The National Road* (1948); Karolevitz, Robert F., *This Was Pioneer Motoring* (1968); Laux, James M., et al., *The Automobile Revolution* (1982); Lay, M. G., *Ways of the World* (1992); Lewis, David L., and Laurence Golstein (eds.), *The Automobile and American Culture* (1983); Rothschild, Emma, *Paradise Lost* (1973); Sears, Stephen W., *The American Heritage History of the Automobile in America* (1977); Sessions, G. M., *Traffic Devices* (1976).

Baltimore & Ohio Railroad (B&O)

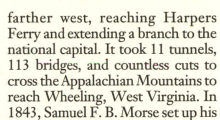

As the first common carrier railroad chartered in the United States, the Baltimore & Ohio was created in 1827 by a group of Baltimore investors, two of whom, Philip E. Thomas and George Brown, had investigated British rail companies as a possible solution to Baltimore's declining trade business. The result was the B&O Railroad, subscribed to by businessmen, the city of Baltimore, and the state of Maryland. Charles Carroll of Carrollton, the only living signer of the Declaration of Independence, laid the road's cornerstone. By 1830, 13 miles of track extended to Ellicott's Mills. The original rails were strap iron—a piece of iron rolled thin like a strap of leather—that laid on top of wooden rails that were affixed to wooden crossties or stone blocks.

The B&O's first train was the *Flying Dutchman*, a four-wheeled open car pulled by a horse. It had the first rail accident when the contraption hit a cow and rolled down an embankment—no one was hurt. The B&O also experimented with sail-driven rail carts before going back to a stagecoach-type car pulled by a team of horses. But longer distances made some type of mechanical motive power essential. Peter Cooper, a Baltimore merchant with mechanical knowledge and later founder of the Cooper's Union trade school in New York City, built the *Tom Thumb* and demonstrated that steam power would work. Even though the *Tom Thumb* lost in a race with a horse (because of mechanical failure), the railroad offered a prize for the best design of a larger, coal-burning locomotive. Three of the four entrants came from watchmakers. One by Phineas Davis won. Named the *York*, it pulled the B&O's first regularly scheduled steam passenger train.

By 1832, the line had reached Point of Rocks on the Potomac. Here it met the Chesapeake & Ohio Canal (which had been diverting Baltimore's trade to Alexandria, Virginia, in the first place), which had tried to stop the railroad in the state legislature and the courts, but failed. The line headed farther west, reaching Harpers Ferry and extending a branch to the national capital. It took 11 tunnels, 113 bridges, and countless cuts to cross the Appalachian Mountains to reach Wheeling, West Virginia. In 1843, Samuel F. B. Morse set up his experimental telegraph between Washington and Baltimore and sent his first message, "What hath God wrought?" and the railroads and the telegraph have been closely linked ever since. By the time of the Civil War, the B&O was open to the Middle West and became a critical link in the Union war effort, necessitating blockhouses at each bridge and a volunteer regiment, the Sixth West Virginia Infantry, whose sole purpose was to man these fortifications. Several parts of the line were destroyed by Confederate cavalry raiders, but the railroad served the Northern war effort well.

Peace saw the extension of the B&O to Chicago, Pittsburgh, and Sandusky. Like all aggressive rail companies, the B&O invested in grain elevators, steamships, and vacation hotels, all of which generated more rail traffic. It was among the first to create a nationally recognizable corporate emblem, a rendition of the capitol dome surrounded by the road's name and slogan: "All Trains via Washington with Stopover Privilege." Later, when it absorbed the Jersey Central and the Reading lines, the slogan was dropped for their names. In the 1930s noted designer, Otto Kuhler, simplified it to the dome and "B&O," which is how it stayed until the name disappeared forever in the early 1970s. Meanwhile the B&O and the Pennsylvania Railroad engaged in costly rate wars, each line buying out smaller roads in an effort to block the other from lucrative markets. An attempt by E. H. Harriman and the Pennsy to control B&O stock met opposition in the federal courts as a violation of the Sherman Antitrust Act, and by 1913, the B&O was independent again. With the Jersey Central and Philadelphia & Reading Railroad purchases, it finally reached New York City.

The next several decades before World War II were the years of Daniel Willard's management. He double-tracked all the main lines, added new cars and engines, and upgraded all of the road's maintenance infrastructure. Willard got the Columbia Broadcasting Company to make its first nationwide radio broadcast from a B&O train. It was the last in a long line of firsts by the B&O, which included: passenger revenue; door-to-door freight deliveries; car wheels that revolved with their axles; interior, conical flanges that worked on curves; published timetables; eight-wheeled passenger coach trucks; use of iron wheels (instead of pressed paper and wood); iron box cars; electric locomotives; streamlined passenger trains (most trains were named after past presidents of the United States); air-conditioned passenger cars; and all-air-conditioned passenger trains. In 1972, the financially strapped B&O ceased to exist in its own right as it merged with the Chesapeake & Ohio Railroad to form the Chessie System.

See also Chesapeake & Ohio Canal; Chesapeake & Ohio Railway; Chessie System; CSX Corporation.

References Bateman, Carrol, *The Baltimore & Ohio* (1951); Drury, George H., *The Historical Guide to North American Railroads* (1985); Drury, George H., *The Train-Watcher's Guide* (1990); Harwood, Herbert H., Jr., *Impossible Challenge* (1979); Hubbard, Freeman, *Encyclopedia of North American Railroading* (1981); Hungerford, Edward, *The Story of the Baltimore & Ohio* (1928); Lyon, Peter, *To Hell in a Day Coach* (1968); Nock, O. S., *Railways of the USA* (1979); Stover, John F., *History of the Baltimore & Ohio Railroad* (1987); Stover, John F., "Baltimore and Ohio Railroad," in Keith L. Bryant, Jr. (ed.), *EABHB: Railroads in the Age of Regulation* (1988), 23–25, and in Robert L. Frey (ed.), *EABHB: Railroads in the Nineteenth Century* (1988), 20–22.

Bangor & Aroostook Railroad (BAR)

Referred to as the BAR, this Maine line is famous for its sly handling of the potato season, which demanded that it keep large numbers of locomotives and refrigerated cars (reefers) available for that part of the year. To hold such assets in limbo for the rest of the year would tax any corporate structure. So the BAR leased its diesels to the old Pennsylvania Railroad and its reefers to the Union Pacific/Southern Pacific's Pacific Fruit Express Company. These cars were painted in three stripes, red, white, and blue, and marked in white lettering with "State of Maine Products." Originally created in 1891, the BAR has never been in receivership, a tribute to its corporate management's dealings and diversification to other industries in running this small railroad. It was among the first to cut passenger service in 1961, substituting a fleet of buses, and improvised a series of charcoal-heated boxcars before the insulated reefers kept the potato crop warm in Maine and the California vegetables and citrus cool during the rest of the year.

See also Boston & Maine Railroad; Maine Central Railroad; Vermont Railway.

References Baker, George P., *The Formation of the New England Railroad Systems* (1937); Drury, George H., *The Historical Guide to North American Railroads* (1985); Drury, George H., *The Train-Watcher's Guide* (1990); Harlow, Alvin F., *Steelways of New England* (1946); Hickcox, David H., "Bangor & Aroostook Railroad," in Keith L. Bryant, Jr. (ed.), *EABHB: Railroads in the Age of Regulation* (1988), 25–26; Hubbard, Freeman, *Encyclopedia of North American Railroading* (1981); Lindahl, Martin L., *The New England Railroads* (1965).

Barlow Road

Running south from the Dalles along the Deschutes River, the Barlow Road turned west at Tygh Valley, crossed Barlow Pass and entered the Willamette Valley at Oregon City. (The Dalles was a jumping-off spot for the last leg of the trip into the Willamette Valley settlements, where the pioneers shifted from land to water and traveled this rough-water section of the Columbia River that runs through a very steep canyon—very dangerous to pass through on the rafts used in those days.) As he started out on his journey to mark a new route into the Willamette Valley settlements, Samuel K. Barlow told the Oregon territorial legislature that "God never made a mountain that he had not made a place for some man to go over it or under it." He vowed, "I am going to hunt for that place." Barlow planned to scout the Cascade Range south of Mount Hood, build a road, and charge tolls to defray costs. He started out in late September 1845 with seven wagons and a party of 19. He crossed the Cascades on horseback and then proposed to go back after his wagons and complete the job, passing between Mounts Hood and Wilson. That very same year of 1846, 145 wagons and 1,600 head of livestock crossed on the Barlow Road. By using U.S. Highway 197 and Oregon State Highway 35, the Barlow extension of the Oregon Trail can still be followed today, a road that permitted settlers to avoid the perilous journey by raft through the Dalles to Portland, the most hazardous part of the trek to the Pacific Northwest

See also Oregon Trail.

Reference Dunlop, Richard, *Great Trails of the West* (1971).

BC Rail

A 1972 name given to British Columbia Railway, formerly the Pacific Great Eastern Railway, that extended into the Canadian hinterland in a "Y" shape from North Vancouver to Fort Nelson on the east and toward Dease Lake on the west.

See also British Columbia Railway.

Beale's Wagon Road

Government-surveyed and government-built wagon roads before the Civil War were, in a sense, the first stage in a continuing process that culminated in the construction of the transcontinental railroads. Various commercial conventions suggested that roads be located so as to facilitate rail projects later. So when Congress authorized six railroad surveys to the Pacific in 1853, it was the acceleration of a process already in place. Unfortunately, as with most measures pending before Congress in the 1850s, the surveys got embroiled in the slavery issue. This meant that the railroad to the Pacific would be delayed, but that the surveys and roads along those survey paths would be built immediately, each route seeking to be

the one chosen for the great Iron Horse.

Because the secretary of war, Jefferson Davis, was from Mississippi, it was logical that he would publicize the routes traversing the South. There were two possibilities: the thirty-second parallel out of New Orleans across the Gadsden Purchase to San Diego, and the thirty-fifth parallel out of Fort Smith to Santa Fe. With Davis' approval, Edward F. Beale, who had made several previous explorations in the Southwest, got the job to extend the survey from Santa Fe to the Colorado River and Los Angeles. Beale's trip was most noteworthy because he took along 76 camels as an experiment to determine their usefulness in supplying the West.

Beale left San Antonio in 1857 and traveled westward to the Rio Grande at El Paso. Turning north, he followed the river to Albuquerque. Then he surveyed a route directly west past the New Mexico pueblos and across northern Arizona, following the route of the Amiel Whipple party of some years before. Briefly lost in the San Francisco Mountains, he found his way and crossed the Colorado, coming into Los Angeles by way of Tejón Pass. Beale declared that his route could be easily improved, and that the camels had done well along it. He later used the camels in snow to show their adaptability to western environments. He then recrossed the route from west to east in midwinter to test its year-round capabilities, which he pronounced as good.

Using Beale's report, the army got $150,000 to construct roads and bridges from Fort Smith, Arkansas, to the Colorado River. Beale spent the next nine months improving the route, and then asked that Congress appropriate more money to continue the project (a common ploy then as now). He also believed that a railroad could be built from Fort Smith to Santa Fe for $21 million. The approach of the Civil War delayed any action and Beale retired to his California ranch. But his work laid the basis for the chartering of the Atlantic and Pacific Railroad in 1866, later absorbed as the main line of the Atchison, Topeka, and Santa Fe Railroad, and Beale's Wagon Road is still roughly followed by U.S. Highway 66 and Interstate 40.

See also Camels in the West.

Reference Jackson, W. Turrentine, *Wagon Roads West* (1952).

Bermuda Agreement (1946)

After World War II, it was evident that air travel would expand into a global system, imitating wartime efforts in this field. The Americans hoped for the airways to be as open as the oceans, but when it came to the rest of the world, the United States' "open skies" idea met much resistance, especially from the British. During the war the British had concentrated on producing fighters and bombers to win the conflict with Germany. This had left the Allied air transport networks for the Americans, who developed many large transport planes that now had immediate civilian application. The Americans wanted to continue to fly everywhere, but the English wanted their prewar spheres of influence back.

Initial negotiations on global airways took place at Havana, Cuba, in the context of the International Air Transport Association. Here in 1945, the United States and Great Britain agreed on preliminary rate and route structures. But the British did not want open skies—they preferred a complicated quota system for traffic distribution, regulation of fares, frequency of flights, and government subsidies. An earlier meeting at Chicago, the International Convention on Civil Aviation, solved all key issues except for fares and flight schedules. These included uniform international rules and procedures on communications, traffic control, licensing, aerology, and navigation. Eventually, the International Civil Aviation Organization would become part of the United Nations (1947). But before that occurred, the Americans and the British worked out fares and flight schedules and the problem of cabotage (whether an international flight could carry domestic passengers between cities of a foreign country—it could not) in the 1946 Bermuda Agreements. These became standard for international air agreements even where the United States and Great Britain were not involved.

See also Aeronautics.

References Bilstein, Roger E., *Flight in America* (1994); Schorr, Eugene, *The Politics of International Aviation* (1991); Smith, Henry Ladd, *Airways Abroad* (1950).

Bessemer & Lake Erie Railroad (B&LE)

With 13 major predecessors dating back to 1865, the Bessemer & Lake Erie was formed in 1900 as a subsidiary of U. S. Steel Corporation. The purpose of the line was twofold: to transport Appalachian coal to the Great Lakes for American and Canadian utilities, and to carry limestone and iron ore to Pittsburgh for the steel mills. It was a perfect arrangement, one that kept the B&LE in operation as long as the steel mills lasted. The B&LE was among the first railroads to install all-welded steel rail, testimony to its links to the steel industry and the heavy nature of its carriage. It also pioneered the use of radio communication between the caboose and engine, and between trains. This was used as a safety measure to spot hotboxes (overheated bearings) and other car problems. It acquired its first diesel unit in 1936, unusual for a railroad so connected with coal, and completed its dieselization just in time for the 1952 ice storm that put all engines in storage for months. The steamers never survived the hiatus. Although the coal mines are still booming, the steel industry around Pittsburgh is but a shadow of its former self, which may speak ill as to B&LE's future.

See also Anthracite and Bridge Line Railroads.

References Beaver, Roy C., *The Bessemer & Lake Erie Railroad* (1969); Bezilla, Michael, "Bessemer & Lake Erie Railroad, in Keith L. Bryant, Jr. (ed.), *EABHB: Railroads in the Age of Regulation* (1988), 31–32; Drury, George H., *The Historical Guide to North American Railroads* (1985); Drury, George H., *The Train-Watcher's Guide* (1990); Hubbard, Freeman, *Encyclopedia of North American Railroading* (1981).

Bicycles and Motorcycles

One of mankind's cheaper modes of transportation has been the bicycle. It is a highly adaptable vehicle, as demonstrated in the Asian modifications—the pedal rickshaw and the military supply-mover that did so much to defeat the American effort in Vietnam by ferrying enormous loads down the fabled Ho Chi Minh Trail. The two-wheeler really began in Paris about 1790 when a vehicle known as the *célérifere* appeared. It was a wooden frame with fixed wheels operated by pushing against the ground with one's feet. It had no steering mechanism or brakes, but it became an instant success, especially with city folk. Thirty years later, Drais von Sauerbronn of the German state of Baden Baden put in a sprung seat and handlebar to the front wheel. His modified bike, called a Draisine, also swept the young blades of the continent. It also crossed the Atlantic to larger American seaports. A Scot, Kirkpatrick MacMillan, added hand levers to power the Draisine, but ran down a young child with his bike and abandoned it in disgust. Too bad, because he had also developed the friction brake. This left it to Pierre Michaux across the Channel to invent the pedal in 1861. By the end of the decade, bike races were common. They were known as "velocipedes" or "bone shakers."

Modifications continued to follow the bicycle. The wooden wheel became metal, then spokes made it lighter, and by 1875, Jules Truffaut invented the inward curl of the rim so that a solid rubber tire could be fitted. The two-wheeler was king of the road until the advent of the automobile. When it was discovered that the bigger the front wheel (to which the pedals were attached) the greater the speed, big wheels became the rage. But the resulting bike was very difficult to mount and ride, which restricted it to young, daring men of little common sense. By 1880, Harry Lawson, back in Britain, figured out that placing the pedals on a reducing gear between the wheels with a chain drive to the rear one made for a safer ride. With wheels reduced to a practical size, bike riding became popular once again. Although Robert Thomson had invented the pneumatic tire in 1845, John Boyd Dunlop, of Northern Ireland, applied the balloon tire to the bicycle. Unfortunately, it had to be glued to the rim, so a puncture was a disaster. It took the Michelin brothers in France to make the tire interchangeable in 1891. The bicycle did not shake one's bones so much now, and it was faster.

Following an American bicycle-spending spree in 1896, March-Davis Cycle Manufacturing Company had good reason to advertise "Admirals" in 1897.

Bicycling was as popular in the United States as in Europe. In 1878 the first American bicycle club was founded in Boston. Other clubs followed and by 1890, they combined into a national organization, the League of American Wheelmen, whose interests in good roads for their cycling excursions led to an important change in American attitudes toward government assistance. The first bike path was dedicated in Brooklyn in 1895. Many early Americans of note in twentieth-century transportation were bicycle mechanics and racers—Wilbur and Orville Wright, Charles and Frank Duryea, and William Knudsen, the organizer of General Motors, for example. Early bicycle companies were numerous (over 500 by the 1890s) and included such manufacturing luminaries as Albert A. Pope, A. H. Overman, and Albert G. Spaulding. Gadgets helped novice riders take to the road and their machines—riding schools were common in bigger cities—including training wheels to make the bicycle stand up regardless of the talents of the student, and a patented harness that would hold one in the seat through thick and thin. Some machines even had brakes. Well, they had curved iron bars that rubbed against the wheel tread, sort of a mandatory option, one would think, for a device that was the fastest machine outside a locomotive at that time.

Trade shows popularized the bicycle. High-pressure advertising campaigns caused Americans to spend over $300,000 on bicycles in May 1896 alone. Repairs and gadgets to customize the basic machine cost $200,000 more during the same month. It was a booming business, but the economic competitors and guardians of American social mores were not impressed. Both groups thought that the bike was carrying Americans to the devil in short order—but for different reasons. Saloon keepers (it was hard to tie one on and ride home when walking was a problem), livery stable owners (no one wanted to risk a rental horse when a bike was handier and less temperamental), buggy and carriage makers (if they could have only seen what the automobile had in store for them), theater owners (people had become fresh-air nuts), candy makers and cigar dealers (one could not ride and chew or smoke with safety, thought these naive Americans of simpler and more proper times), hat dealers (cyclists wore caps instead), and even publishers (Americans stopped reading to

hit the road) all condemned bicycles, claiming that $113 million was lost to other trades by bicycle mania.

Worse yet, preachers called it a machine invented by Old Nick, and imagined that many young men used them for less than honorable intentions in sparking the young ladies into the lonely, lovely, romantic countryside. One nonsense statistic stated that 30 percent of all "fallen women" (Victorians eschewed direct terms like "prostitute") were or had been bicycle riders. One church voted to expel outright any member who rode the demon's device to worship. But the real problem was that many parishioners were taking to the streets rather than the pews on the Sabbath—surely evidence of the diabolical nature of the machine and its users. Of course, the automobile would bear the same accusations of defiling the Lord's Day shortly. One enterprising pastor took the opposite tack—he praised the bicycle for curing his congregation of dyspepsia, which he took as the source of agnosticism. Hence, he encouraged his flock to ride, ride, ride, and let the Lord into their hearts.

Others far and wide defended the morals and economic attraction of the bicycle. Clothing manufacturers could not praise the new device enough. New styles of riding clothes, which became next season's ordinary dress, came out on a monthly basis. Clothiers maintained that they could outfit man, woman, or child in a fashionable manner with outer and under garments that would protect the body from any ill effect that the naysayers claimed would befall one whose insides were shaken so regularly. Doubters were especially worried about the effects of bicycle riding upon the "weaker sex," as women were called then. It was feared that constant riding might develop the sensitive female form in a manner not designed by Mother Nature (more leg and hip, less breast). One group called for women to divest themselves of their corsets, to become free and let their muscles flex and breathe, while another (mostly corset-makers) brought out a line of undergarments that would protect the inner organs from excessive jarring. Most feared that the "new woman" of the era would upset established dress and social mores and even pursue such "manly" things as the vote. This equality thing could get out of hand! But the young swain courting his lady on a bike was too involved to worry about the fears of his elders until it was too late and fear became fact.

Worse were the ills that had no gender, like "bicycle walk" (where the afflicted promenaded as though they were still on the bike), "bicycle heart" (where the organ would be enlarged and weakened), "bicycle hump" (a pronounced curvature of the spine), "bicycle hands" (numbness caused by holding the handlebars too long, rendering them useless for any other task), "bicycle gums" (the result of riding with the mouth ajar and permitting cold air to strike the warm gums, resulting in the loss of teeth to a congestion of the blood), and the dreaded "bicycle face" (a malady divided into three terrifying symptoms—a strained eye from looking up from leaning over the handlebars, followed by wrinkles and strain lines around the mouth, resulting finally in a general implosion of the whole face). The result gave the rider the visage of a fish hawk looking for prey.

The alleged bad effects of bicycling never really came about, unless one wishes to count the daredevils and racers, both of whom abounded at the turn of the century. The army took one look at the two-wheeler and equipped whole battalions with it. A double-bike was envisioned that carried a machine gun mounted between the riders. The mechanical American army soon abandoned such notions for the gasoline engine, as did the civilian public, relegating the bike to a child's toy—until its revival in the 1980s. It was cars and trucks for the nation's adults, barring some disaster like the Great Depression, war, or an oil embargo. Today bicycling has again become a sport and health fad, often dismissed as the domain of nuts who lobby for bike paths and traffic rights. But we often forget that the German blitzkriegs of World War II were hastened by mounting entire units on bicycles.

Then the next step was taken. It had to be tried. The bike had to be motorized. It was a great test frame for the internal-combustion engine, and positions were tested for the engine's most advantageous location—above the front wheel, to the rear of the rear wheel, above the rear wheel, and various positions below the seat between the rider's legs. The result was a fairly dangerous, noisy, and uncomfortable device, but it was cheap, simple, and offered the rider the ultimate in freedom. And it sold. There was something almost mystical to riding a motorized bicycle, of being detached from the world in an antisocial way, yet being that much more a part of it, not isolated as in the cab of an automobile.

The first American motorcycles were quite light—much different than the current heavier machines. The first producers were bicycle manufacturers who added motors to their two-wheelers and then went on to design special frames and actual motorcycles. George Hendee of Springfield, Massachusetts, met a fellow named Oscar Hedström and in 1901 produced the first American motorcycle, the Indian. It had no gearshift levers or gas pedals—they were located in the handle grips. The first cycles were small one-cylinder jobs that soon gave way to larger engines, the epitome of which were the four-cylinder Henderson and Ace cycles. The Henderson brothers, William and Tom, had sold their company to Ignaz Schwinn, a bicycle manufacturer whose name and product became an American standard. Schwinn kept the Hendersons on to manage the motorcycle division, but they soon tired of being directed and left Schwinn's employ. William then founded Ace, but the finances never worked out. Indian soon bought up Ace and turned its design department over to Charlie Gustavson, who invented the side valve and the 7-horsepower, 998-cc Power Plus. Indian kept producing bikes until 1959, when it was taken over by an English conglomerate. All they retained was the Indian name on all of their products sold in the States.

Indeed, by the end of World War I the automobile had caused the downfall of many an erstwhile motorcycle company like

Henderson and Ace, as America's love affair with Tin Lizzie and her four-wheeled sisters began. But with the development of the Twin Vee—two cylinders working in juxtaposition to each other—the survivors went on. Probably no other company more typified the American motorcycle than Harley-Davidson. Formed in Milwaukee in 1903, Harley had small one-cylinder bikes but soon graduated into the Twin Vee design to keep up with Indian. Motorcycles were adapted to military requirements, mostly as quick transport for dispatch riders. But the Germans went to the extreme and equipped the reconnaissance battalions of their famed panzer divisions with several varieties of motorized bikes and sidecars, carrying machine guns and other light weapons. As Allied armies rolled across Europe, the common soldier got a new look at and respect for the motorcycle that would help expand its popularity later.

By the end of World War II, Harley had become the standard heavy bike, often approaching a quarter-ton in weight. Harley featured solid rear-wheel attachment to the frame, high, wide handlebars, footboards, the pan seat, and a powerful Twin Vee engine. The Hydra-Glide featured twin telescopic front-fork suspension that became an industry norm in a couple of years. The ensuing Duo-Glide introduced a flexible rear suspension and the Electra-Glide model featured an electric starter, a Japanese standard that had been put on the Indian as early as 1916. Known for its roadability and weight, the Harley has an engine capable of putting out 70 ft/lbs of torque at 4,000 rpm. For all of its luxury, it has a record of speed, particularly during the interwar period when it went head-to-head with Indian.

The motorcycle and its advocates have always had a sort of rogue image. Motorcyclists have been seen as "outlaws," "lone riders," and "cool," a little rebellious, independent, and free. But a lot of this changed with the entry of the Japanese bike into the American market. "You meet the nicest people on a Honda," went the new slogan. In 1957 Honda exported all of five machines; by 1967, the number was 600,000. The whole thing was accomplished by an aggressive advertising campaign that changed the concept of the rogue cyclist to the fashionable rider. Honda, Yamaha, and Suzuki approached Americans everywhere—in car magazines, sport magazines, women's magazines, glamour journals, college and university publications, on television, and even on programs for small children. Motorcycles had become the toy of the suave and sophisticated—except among Harley-Davidson advocates who still see much in buying a rugged American legend over a zippy, imported, stylish convenience.

See also Good Roads Movement; League of American Wheelmen.

References Fabre, Maurice, *A History of Land Transportation* (1963); Hough, Richard, and L. J. K. Streight, *A History of the World's Motorcycles* (1973); Lay, M. G., *Ways of the World* (1992); Nicholi, A., "The Motorcycle Syndrome," *American Journal of Psychiatry* (1970) 126 (no. 11): 1588–1595; Pirsig, Robert M., *Zen and the Art of Motorcycle Maintenance* (1975); Rothe, J. Peter, and Peter J. Cooper (eds.), *Motorcyclists* (1987); Schwinn, Frank W., *Fifty Years of Schwinn-Built Bicycles* (1945); Smith, Robert A., *A Social History of the Bicycle* (1972); Tragatsch, Erwin (ed.), *The Illustrated History of Motorcycles* (1979).

Big Medicine Trail

This was the name Native Americans on the Great Plains gave to the Central Overland Route, the road that carried so many whites across their ancestral hunting grounds from East to Far West toward some "big medicine" or good thing only the gods could explain.

See also Central Overland Route; Mormon Trail; Oregon Trail.

Black-McKellar Act (1934)

In the midst of the New Deal and the Great Depression, Congress applied the same solution to the airlines that it used in other industries—regulation. In the Black-McKellar Act of 1934, Congress changed the name of the Aeronautics Branch to the Bureau of Air Commerce, transferred all airmail regulatory functions to the Interstate Commerce Commission, forced the divestment of companies in production of aircraft from air transportation, and emphasized competitive bidding for airway access by a multitude of flying companies, a practice that critics called "cutthroat bidding." But Congress was not through with the airline industry yet, and would respond to criticism with the Civil Aeronautics Act in 1938.

See also Aeronautics; Civil Aeronautics Act of 1938; McNary-Watres Air Mail Act.

References Bilstein, Roger E., *Flight in America* (1994); Komons, Nick, *Bonfires to Beacons* (1978); Whitnah, Donald R., *Safer Skyways* (1966).

Blomberg, Martin (1888–1966)

A native of Ostervala, Sweden, Martin Blomberg was educated at the Technical Institute at Orebro and the University of Uppsala. A top-notch athlete, Blomberg was slated for the Swedish national Olympic team in 1912—instead, he emigrated to Canada. Continuing his technical education, the Swedish immigrant contracted typhoid fever and had several relapses, a commentary on his always restless mind and body. He seemed never to slow down. He moved across the border to the United States in 1916, joined the U.S. Army for World War I, and came home to marry Laura Van Buskirk.

In the United States, Blomberg went to work for the Pullman Company, where he specialized in truck and car body design. He was involved with the then-new idea of lightweight passenger cars and was instrumental in the design of the Denver Zephyr. In 1935 he transferred to what became the Electromotive Division of General Motors (GM). His job was the same as at Pullman, car body and truck design. He worked on the A-1-A diesel locomotive truck (two outside axles powered, with the center one an idler) and invented the outside "swing hanger" to provide lateral stability and excellent ride characteristics. The A-1-A truck powered the GM E-series of passenger locomotives for years.

But Blomberg's greatest contribution to American transportation was the four-wheel diesel engine truck that still bears his name. Possessing outside swing hangers, "journal box" springs, and "elliptic bolster springs," the Blomberg was the key to the propulsion of America's first successful freight diesel, the FT. It would go on to power over 15,000 locomotives of various cab and engine styles, and remains the major GM power truck today with only minor changes, despite the increased weight, power, and size of modern motive power. He also experimented widely and held over 100 patents.

A stern man outwardly, Blomberg was characterized by many as "Prussian." He was not a team man. When someone else came up with another way of doing things, Blomberg would demur politely, but firmly, in his heavy Swedish-accented English, "Ve do it my vay." He seldom had to say it twice. Not only was he well educated, he had an intuitive manner in approaching the solution to technical design problems. He liked to vacation in the northern woods, and went into gold mining upon retirement at a site he had discovered when he first came to the New World. An uncompromising man who hoped to imbue the younger generation with his high standards through engineering training programs, Blomberg died at his home in Florida in 1966.

See also Locomotives.

Reference Ephraim, Max, Jr., "Martin Blomberg, Designer Extraordinaire," *Trains* (October 1994) 54: 46–49.

Boeing, William Edward (1881–1956)

Born in Detroit, Boeing attended the Sheffield Scientific School at Yale, but failed to graduate. He became interested in flying and took lessons from Glenn Martin. Boeing founded the Pacific Aero Products Company in 1916, and served as a navy flyer during World War I. He and Martin tried to convince the government not to dump surplus aircraft on the open market after the war, but did not achieve their goal. Both men turned to air transport until the passage of the Kelley Air Mail Act in 1925. Then they returned independently to aircraft manufacture, seeking to develop safer, better-powered, and larger planes than the World War I trainers. Boeing created the B-40, a biplane with a Pratt and Whitney engine. The two companies merged to form United Aircraft Transportation Corporation, with Frederick Rentschler of Pratt and Whitney as president. Boeing became chairman of the board. Shortly thereafter, Hamilton and Standard, leading manufacturers of propellers, and Sikorsky, an important source of flying boats, were added. In 1934, when Congress mandated the separation of flying companies and manufacturers, Boeing reformed Boeing Aircraft and left Rentschler with United Aircraft Corporation. He won the Guggenheim medal for development of new planes that same year and left the field soon afterward. Boeing Aircraft, headquartered in Seattle, went on to become one of the giants in airplane production. Boeing himself continued to reside in Seattle until his death in the mid-1950s.

See also Aeronautics; Curtiss, Glenn Hammond; Douglas, Donald W.; Martin, Glenn Luther.

References Biddle, Wayne, *Barons of the Sky* (1991); Ingham, John H. (ed.), *Biographical Dictionary of American Business Leaders* (1983), 80–81; Mansfield, Henry C., *Vision: A Story of the Sky* (1956).

Bonus Bill

The Bonus Bill (not to be confused with the effort to pay veterans of World War I during the Great Depression) was a measure drawn up by Secretary of War John C. Calhoun in 1817 to finance the building of roads and canals. Calhoun's role in American history has been colored by the Union victory in the Civil War, a conflict for which many blame him because of his theories of nullification and secession. But as his biographers point out, the South Carolinian was actually a moderate who sought to prevent the breakup of the Union by outlining a complicated set of procedures designed to delay action and promote compromise. It is instructive that the secessionists in 1861 junked Calhoun's process and went straight to secession, fearing the result of a pro-

longed debate. Calhoun was ever the nationalist, based on his concept of what was necessary to prevent another war fiasco like that fought in 1812. It is in this light that his role in transportation must be viewed.

Calhoun saw the construction of roads, canals, and later, railroads (he was an active sponsor of one of the first rail lines into the South Carolina backcountry) as a coincidental combination of military, commercial, and postal purposes. As secretary of war in 1819, he presented an overall plan of internal improvements designed to achieve these purposes. He called for a major north–south road from Maine to Louisiana, and the realization of Albert Gallatin's plans from 1808. This included roads and canals from Albany to the Great Lakes; from Washington, Baltimore, Richmond, and Philadelphia to the Ohio; and from Augusta and Charleston to the Tennessee River Valley. He hoped to finance such a program under the Bonus Bill.

The Bonus Bill idea came about when Congress chartered the Second Bank of the United States after the War of 1812. Designed as the monitor of a sort of central banking system, the bank was to pay the federal government $1.5 million for the privilege of incorporation, the so-called bonus. Calhoun proposed that the principle and dividends be used to create a permanent fund for internal improvements. He justified the measure under the "general welfare" clause and the need for promoting national defense, so lacking in the recently terminated war. After a hot debate during which "old" Republicans decried Calhoun's use of methods reminiscent of the hated Alexander Hamilton, and "new" Republicans promoted the pride of the country in its narrow victory over the British, Congress passed Calhoun's plan. But President James Madison vetoed the measure on his last day in office (3 March 1817) because he felt it needed to be in the form of a constitutional amendment.

See also American System; Calhoun, John Caldwell; Gallatin Report.

References Capers, Gerald M., *John C. Calhoun* (1960); Freehling, William W., *Prelude to Civil War*

(1968); White, Leonard D., *The Jeffersonians* (1951); Wiltse, Charles M., *John C. Calhoun* (1944–1951).

Borman, Frank Frederick, II (b. 1928)

A Gary, Indiana, native, Frank Borman grew up in Tucson, Arizona. The Bormans went to Arizona because Frank (an only child) had respiratory problems. Evidently the desert air was good for him. He was active in school sports and led his high school football team to the state championships as quarterback. Borman always liked airplanes. He flew in the 1940s and received an appointment to the U.S. Military Academy, graduating from West Point as eighth in a class of 670. He chose the air force as his branch of service and became a fighter pilot.

In the service, Borman unhappily served in the Philippines, missing the Korean conflict and combat experience. He became a flight instructor and earned a master's degree at California Institute of Technology in 1957, which allowed him to become an instructor at West Point, teaching fluid mechanics and thermodynamics. Borman then became a test pilot at Edwards Air Force Base, which led him into the ranks of the second group of astronauts. He flew on *Gemini 7* with James Lovell, and was one of the investigators when the *Apollo* control module burned up on the launch pad during tests. He flew in *Apollo 8*, the first module to ride the big Saturn 5 rocket up. In 1969, Borman toured U.S. college campuses and was appalled at the inability of the administrators and faculty to maintain order in the face of student demonstrations against the war and other "anarchy," as he saw it. He also went to the Soviet Union and laid the groundwork for what became the joint *Apollo-Soyuz* flight. Borman never flew again, but he served for a number of years as an administrative officer at NASA before his resignation in 1970.

After his return to civilian life, Borman became a senior vice-president at Eastern Airlines (EAL). At Eastern he was responsible for engineering, maintenance, flight operations, and the coordination of company divisions. He took a cram course at Harvard Business School to learn management procedures. Borman's first task at EAL was to negotiate a new labor contract with pilots. Erroneously seeing them as fellow flyers, Borman got taken to the cleaners, resulting in a contract that Eastern could ill-afford. Unions would continue to see him as a chicken to be plucked and it led to many problems as Borman matured on the job. Borman was disturbed by what he found at Eastern. Executives had too many expensive, nonproductive perks. It was more important to beat fellow employees to the punch than it was to better the competition. Everyone from the baggage handlers to the vice-presidents made passing the buck and corporate throat cutting a fine art. There was no identification or loyalty to the company, a fact that galled the military man to the core. Everyone was out for number one, the company or public be damned. Eastern was saddled by many bad corporate decisions left over from previous administrations: too many unprofitable short hauls, not enough profitable long hauls, too many first-generation, gas-guzzling jets, and not enough fuel-efficient modern aircraft. Borman registered his protests but stayed loyal to the previous leaders.

By 1974, Borman had added day-to-day operations and sales to his repertoire. He received an appointment to Eastern's board of directors in 1975, and the following year became chief executive officer. He also served as chairman of the board until 1986. His loyalty had paid off. Once in power, however, Borman moved to correct what he perceived as EAL's major problems. He replaced the older planes with new Boeing 757s and European-made Airbus 300s. He centralized the corporate chain of command at Miami. Borman also installed a military-style discipline—anyone not prepared at meetings was cut short. He banned drinking at lunch, put executives to work loading baggage to see what made the company tick (he did the same and skipped lunch as he worked), fired 24 vice-presidents, and cut 3,000 lower-echelon employees. "If you don't like what I'm doing, just get out of the way because it has to be done," Borman proclaimed. Angered employees, used to the sloppy policies of the past, dismissed Borman as "the Moon Man" with a "Boy Scout mentality." But Borman slogged on.

The next problem turned out to be Borman's worst. He had to renegotiate labor contracts to reduce the fixed costs that threatened to swamp EAL in the wake of federal deregulation. Too many lean and mean nonunion companies were operating cheaper than Eastern. But here his purchase of new planes hurt him. Even *Fortune* magazine criticized his spending money there and asking the common worker to take it out of his salary. Borman set up wage freezes and substituted profit sharing. This worked fine for the four profitable years at the end of the 1970s. But EAL could not meet the 1980s without more sacrifice at all levels. Borman tried to merge with several other airlines, but no one would take on EAL's vast debt and fixed costs. He asked the unions, angry at profit sharing as there were no more profits to share, to cut back their demands. They threatened to strike. Borman had refused to get loans to build up a fund to counter such a move. Instead, he gave in to union demands regardless of costs, figuring to get it all back at a more propitious time. He also gave the unions four seats on EAL's board of directors.

In the middle of the whole mess, Frank Lorenzo came over and said that he would bail Eastern out. Borman hated what Lorenzo had done to Continental, but he agreed to the deal if the board and the unions would accept Lorenzo. Incredibly, in Borman's eyes, they hated him more than the strike-breaking Lorenzo. Unable to stop Eastern's economic decline (and vindicated when Lorenzo destroyed EAL and the jobs of all those who opposed him), Borman left the company in 1986 to go into other aerospace endeavors. He also served as special presidential ambassador in Europe and the Far East, and has taken a particular interest in the Prisoners of War/Missing in Action issue left over from the Vietnam conflict.

See also Aeronautics; Astronautics; Eastern Air Lines.

References Cassutt, Michael, *Who's Who in Space* (1987); Hawthorne, Douglas B., *Men and Women of Space* (1992); Lewis, W. David, "Frank Borman," in William M. Leary (ed.), *Encyclopedia of American Business History and Biography* (1992), 62–73; Murphy, Charles E., *The Airline That Pride Almost Bought* (1986); Serling, Robert J., *From the Captain to the Colonel* (1980); Shepard, Alan B., and Donald K. Slayton, *Moon Shot* (1994).

Boston & Maine Railroad (B&M)

Begun in 1833, the original purpose of the Boston & Maine was to connect Portland, Maine, to Boston. Absorbing other small lines throughout the nineteenth century, the B&M came to serve all of New England except Rhode Island. Although it managed to survive most of the twentieth century, the B&M succumbed to bankruptcy in 1970. Typically New England in its independence, the B&M sought to go its own way and refused to join Conrail. It cut back much of its service in eastern Massachusetts and got rid of its commuter cars, selling them to the Boston Metropolitan Transit Authority. It now operates these cars for the Transport Authority there and has bought several former New Haven Railroad divisions in Connecticut. The B&M still runs trains through the Hoosac Tunnel, a five-mile bore built in 1877 by the former general in charge of supplying the Union army in Virginia, Herman Haupt. The tunnel now has steel, welded rail and has been lowered and widened to permit passage of modern equipment. The B&M was purchased in 1982 by Guilford Transportation Industries, which also runs the Maine Central and the old Delaware and Hudson.

See also Anthracite and Bridge Line Railroads; Maine Central Railroad; Vermont Railway.

References Baker, George P., *The Formation of the New England Railroad Systems* (1937); Drury, George H., *The Historical Guide to North American Railroads* (1985); Drury, George H., *The Train-Watcher's Guide* (1990); Grow, Lawrence, *On the 8:02* (1979); Harlow, Alvin F., *The Steelways of New England* (1946); Hickcox, David H., "Boston & Maine Railroad," in Keith L. Bryant, Jr. (ed.), *EABHB: Railroads in the Age of Regulation* (1988), 35–36; Hubbard, Freeman, *Encyclopedia of North American Railroading* (1981); Kennedy, Charles J., "Boston & Maine Railroad," in Robert L. Frey (ed.), *EABHB: Railroads in the Nineteenth Century*

(1988), 25–26; Lindahl, Martin L., *The New England Railroads* (1965); Nelligan, Tom, and Scott Hartley, *The Route of the Minuteman* (1980); Ward, James A., *That Man Haupt!* (1973).

Boston Post Road

As with all of early America, the New England settlements were initially coast- and river-bound. Gradually the white settlers began to branch out into the interior, using Native American trails, which they often widened and improved for wagon use. In 1639, the Massachusetts colonial government passed a law providing for a road to be built between Boston and Plymouth. Thus began one of the earliest roads in America, the Boston Post Road (much of which today is U.S. Highway 1). Gradually, the road extended through New England to New York City as 250 miles of improved hard surface, along which, after 1673, rode mail and dispatch riders on the three-week trip. The mail was disrupted in the early 1680s when Indian troubles and disputes with the Dutch in New Amsterdam threatened, but all of this passed and service was reinstituted without interruption until the Revolutionary War. A system emerged where two riders would start from each end of the road and ride toward Saybrook, Connecticut, where they exchanged mailbags at a tavern and returned to their starting points.

Through extensions of the mail routes into the South (Virginia had regular mail by 1730), it was possible to communicate all the way to Charleston, South Carolina. In 1763, Benjamin Franklin, as colonial deputy postmaster (the other one was William Hunter of Virginia), made an inspection of this mail route and the following year so regularized the service that it ran night and day, and a letter from Boston could reach Charleston in the same three weeks it used to take to get to New York City. Freighting companies soon sprang up, but it took until 1772 before the first regular passenger coach service began. The Revolution soon

This 1885 Harper's Weekly *drawing depicts the relay method of delivering mail, whereby two riders, starting from opposite ends of the Boston Post Road, met halfway, exchanged mailbags, and returned to their original posts.*

stopped this. After the Revolution, traffic was slow to pick up, and by the time of George Washington's inauguration, 12 horses and 2 stagecoaches could handle the passenger demand between Boston and New York City.

See also Roads and Highways, Colonial Times to World War I.

References Hart, Val, *The Story of American Roads* (1950); Holbrook, Stewart H., *The Old Post Road* (1962); Jenkins, Stephen, *The Old Boston Post Road* (1913).

Bozeman Trail

Beginning with the California gold rush, prospectors flooded the West looking for places with similar geographic and geologic tendencies, hoping to find another strike. These searches took place on both sides of the Rocky Mountain chain, and in some cases, like on the Fraser River (British Columbia), Cherry Creek (near Denver), and the Washoe (near Carson City), success was had. In 1852, a man by the name of Francois Findlay discovered gold at Deer Lodge, Montana, on the eastern face of the Rockies. His strike caused others to come in a search for more. As the Civil War broke out in the East, miners hit big pay dirt at Deer Lodge, Grasshopper, and White's Bar, Bannack, Alder Gulch, and Last Chance Gulch. The rush was on.

During the American Civil War, Montana was relatively isolated. Although steamboats could reach Fort Benton if the water was high, few roads went into the gold country. Overland shipment of supplies was critical, as constant mining activity and the climate combined to make local agriculture minimal. The safest routes came out of Salt Lake and California, but many resented giving the Mormons and their price-gouging Gentile business allies in California an economic advantage in trade. The Overland Route out of Missouri and Iowa was a logical choice, but it would entail traveling all the way to Salt Lake City before turning north, a lengthy trip. The solution was provided by miners-turned-entrepreneurs John M. Bozeman (for whom the Montana

town was named) and John M. Jacobs, who created and popularized the Bozeman Cutoff or Bozeman Tail in 1863, coming out of the goldfields and winding along the east side of the Big Horn Mountains to join the emigrant trails at Fort Laramie, Wyoming.

From the beginning, the trail was controversial among the various Lakota (Sioux) bands that treasured the area as their prized buffalo hunting grounds. Angry with the whites over several incidents of the 1850s, such as the Mormon Cow War, which led to the Grattan Massacre, the Lakota were anxious that any of the numerous white using the Big Medicine Trail, as they styled the Overland Route, might turn north out of Laramie and disturb their game. Already the buffalo were separating into northern and southern herds, as determined by the white man's roads, and further incursions could become an ecological disaster to the tribe's food supply and nomadic way of life.

For these reasons, many whites preferred to use the Bridger Trail, a route that paralleled the Bozeman route, but on the west side of the Big Horn Mountains. There was less chance of meeting Lakota hunting or war parties here. This route had been pioneered by the legendary Jim Bridger in the early 1850s, when he guided a hunting party of European nobility in the Powder River country. Both trails joined at the north end of the Big Horns, crossed the Yellowstone, and turned west into Montana at Gallatin Pass to reach Bozeman. At the town, the road bore southwestward to Virginia City and the diggings. In 1865, the Montana Territorial legislature established the Broad Gauge Company to exploit the Bozeman and Bridger trails by improving them with ferries and recouping their cost and a profit through toll charges. Of course these contracts were let to the usual friends of the legislators, with ferry boatmen sent out that summer. It proved to be a hazardous job.

The boatmen soon noticed that no one was coming up either trail from Fort Laramie. They would soon discover that the army had decided to stop all traffic and send a punitive expedition up the Powder River to subdue the Lakota. Unfortunately no one had bothered to inform the boatmen, who operated out of isolated Montana. Realizing their exposed position, the ferry operators scattered as the Lakota moved first, attacking any whites with the temerity to stay. The army column moved out in July, under General Patrick E. Connor, and stayed in the field until October, but achieved little but to increase the Lakota's ire.

The following spring, heavy traffic appeared on the Bozeman Trail, having been delayed a year, and the Broad Gauge Company reopened its ferries. The Lakota had been scattered away from their usual food sources by the Connor Expedition, and appeared more interested in trading for provisions as a fee for safe passage than in war. The whites, particularly soldiers, had come to a similar conclusion on their own, and decided to treat with the tribes peacefully at Fort Laramie. All through the winter, spring, and summer, various bands of Native Americans came in to hear what the whites would offer. It was not much. The white peace delegation asked the Lakota and others (mostly Arapaho and Cheyenne) to observe a lasting peace but to allow the Bozeman and Bridger trails to operate, for which the federal government would pay liberally. Or, from the Indians' point of view, the whites, who could not defeat them in the field, were asking the Lakota to permit the destruction of their last hunting ground.

Then something stupid happened. Up the Oregon Trail into Fort Laramie came the Eighteenth Infantry, reinforcements for the frontier, specifically ordered to open up the Bozeman Trail by constructing three forts along its route. Fort Reno would be constructed at the Powder River crossing, Fort Phil Kearny at Big Piney Creek, and Fort C. F. Smith at the Big Horn crossing. Under Colonel Henry B. Carrington, the infantrymen's arrival was the last straw for the Lakota. Led by Red Cloud, they walked out of the talks. Now the whites had not only failed to gain rights to use the Bozeman Trail but had an inadequate force available to guard it. Carrington went out on the trail and built his forts anyhow, after the peace

commission got chiefs with no interest in the trail country to bargain it away. It all looked nice and legal.

Carrington and his men felt the sting of Red Cloud's attack immediately. The Indians began by running off most of the army's livestock. Pursuit led to ambush and soldier casualties. After the forts went up, Lakota warriors harassed stock-tending and wood- and hay-gathering parties. But by winter everyone was safe and snug. One problem, however, was that the forts were too far apart to be mutually supportive. To help out somewhat, the army sent a couple of companies of cavalry (mounted infantry, to be exact) to help out. Their commander was Captain William J. Fetterman. He was quite contemptuous of Carrington's lack of dash. The captain bragged that he could clean out the whole Sioux nation with his 80 mounted men. And in December 1866, he got his chance. A Lakota scouting party lunged at the fort and Fetterman and exactly 80 men went after them, much to the protests of everyone who knew anything about Indian fighting. It was all over in a matter of 30 minutes. The scouts lured Fetterman into an ambush, and not one of the 80 got out alive. The know-it-all captain and his second-in-command shot each other dead during the fray to escape a fate they feared might be worse than death.

Still, enterprising men like John Bozeman traveled the trail in search of lucrative army supply contracts. In the spring of 1867, Bozeman (who had been stripped naked years before and let go with a warning to stay out of Lakota land) was off trading with friendly Crows and got suckered in by some Blackfeet posing as Crows, who shot him dead and wounded his partner. The partner escaped to tell the tale. The Montana miners panicked at the news and organized a militia to go out and guard the passes into the goldfields. Ignoring the fact that Blackfeet had killed Bozeman, everyone expected a Lakota attack—which never came.

That summer of 1867 the hit-and-run attacks continued, but the result was not always one-sided. In August, a hay-gathering party at Fort C. F. Smith was hit by the

Lakota's Cheyenne allies. The gatherers' habit was to corral their numerous mules in a stout log pen while the work in the field was going on. About 25 soldiers and civilian contractors fled to the corral, encircled by an estimated 500 warriors. But the hayfield workers had a surprise for the attackers. About a week earlier the army had supplied the Bozeman Trail garrisons with breech-loading rifles. The Indians had habitually charged military parties to draw fire from the muzzle-loading weapons, then closed in to fight hand-to-hand, an endeavor at which they excelled. Now as they closed, the whites delivered volley after volley, dropping many Cheyenne from their saddles. After a few hours, the warriors retreated, unable to lure either the soldiers out of the corral or reinforcements from the fort (probably their main desire).

The very next day, Red Cloud and his Lakota attacked a wood-gathering party near Fort Phil Kearny. The party had dropped all of the numerous tool and supply boxes wagons carried in those days to haul more wood. The boxes had been set out in a circle and all harnesses and extra ammunition placed inside. It was a very wise move. At the first shot, the woodcutters retreated into their makeshift stockade. Lying down behind this miniature fort (a great advantage to breech-loading when compared to muzzle-loading), the soldiers gave Red Cloud's men the same reception reserved for their Cheyenne brethren a day earlier. Red Cloud took council and tried a dismounted attack. The wagon-box fort proved stout and small enough that the soldiers could shift about its perimeter and concentrate fire at will. Neither this Wagon Box Fight nor the Hayfield Fight could be called real victories, but they raised the morale of the troops significantly and caused the Native Americans second thoughts.

By 1867, Congress too had changed its mind about the West and decided to try another shot at peace talks. Over 100 men had died and countless dollars had been spent to open the route to no avail. Besides, with the advent of the Union Pacific Railroad, the whole question of the need for the Bozeman Trail and a planned eastward extension into Nebraska (the Sawyers Wagon Road) was moot. The treaty document, agreed to ahead of time by the white civilian and military members of the delegation, set aside all of present-day South Dakota west of the Missouri River as a permanent Lakota reservation. No part of this land could be ceded in the future without consent of three-fourths of all adult male residents. It was a provision that forced the whites to launch a war eight years later to open up the Black Hills gold strike and culminated in General George Custer's Last Stand.

In addition, the treaty had the usual denial-of-reality clauses, as one historian aptly called them. The government was to feed the Lakota for four years while they learned to become dry farmers. Since this type of farming was considered "women's work" in the most derogatory way possible, there was little chance that these clauses would do more than turn Lakota men into beggars or drive them from the reservation. It was the latter eventuality that occurred and permitted the government to cancel the treaty in 1876 and label them all as hostile. Two contradictory clauses promised the Lakota hunting rights in the Powder River area, and at the same time denied them the right to "trespass" off the reservation. The former phrase was the one translated and publicized among the Lakota negotiators.

In exchange for all this, the U.S. government would abandon the Bozeman Trail and its forts. After all, the transcontinental railroad was much more important than the Bozeman Trail, and the Montana Trail could supply the gold diggings from Utah after the rails reached there. And Philip H. Sheridan and William T. Sherman, in charge of the army's effort in the West, already saw the real vulnerability of the mounted Indian warriors—the culling of the buffalo by white hide hunters, already in progress on the southern plains. Many Lakota, including Red Cloud, had doubt about this treaty. Few signed at Fort Laramie, but Red Cloud agreed to come in after he saw the hated three forts abandoned. With cries of triumph, the Lakota burned the stockades to the ground even before the troops had marched out of sight and sound.

This Fort Laramie treaty of 1868 made Red Cloud one of the few Native Americans to win a war with the whites. But his victory proved somewhat illusive. He got rid of the Bozeman Trail, but his tribe was placed under U.S. government control. Most of the 15,000 Lakota followed him onto the reservation. But a splinter group of about 3,500 Cheyenne and Lakota followed Sitting Bull and refused to surrender. He roamed the Powder River region, the no-man's land reserved for hunting, until the destruction of the buffalo and the 1876 Battle of the Little Big Horn put an end to independent Lakota existence. Yet Red Cloud's legacy endures. It was under his Treaty of 1868 that the modern Lakota have sued the federal government (in the Unites States' own courts) to regain all of the territory lost without the consent of three-fourths of the males living there. They have refused all monetary settlement—they want the sacred Black Hills returned and the treaty honored. So the Bozeman Trail may have a bigger legacy than to be modern U.S. Highway 87 or Interstate Highways 25 and 90. It may be the issue that gives the Native Americans their ultimate victory in a war that has never ended.

See also Central Overland Route; Montana Trail.

References Burlingame, Merrill G., *John M. Bozeman, Montana Trail Maker* (1983); Drago, Harry S., *Roads to Empire* (1968); Dunlop, Richard, *Great Trails of the West* (1971); Gray, John S., "Blazing the Bridger and Bozeman Trails," *Annals of Wyoming* (1977) 49: 23–51; Gray, John S., *Custer's Last Campaign* (1991); Hebard, Grace R., and E. A. Brininstool, *The Bozeman Trail* (1922); Marshall, S. L. A., *Crimsoned Prairie* (1972); Utley, Robert M., *Cavalier in Buckskin* (1988); White, Lonnie J. (ed.), "Hugh Kirkendall's Wagon Train on the Bozeman Trail, 1866: Letters of C. M. S. Miller," *Annals of Wyoming* (1975) 37: 45–58.

Braddock's Road

Originally, Braddock's Road was a path blazed in 1751 by a friendly Delaware Indian and named for him as Nemacolin's Trail. It was no more than 2 feet wide, an Indian trail in all but the blaze marks of the trees it passed. In 1755, General Edward Braddock arrived in the New World to fight the French and Indian War. George Washington had gone out the previous year to demand that the French withdraw from Ohio lands claimed by Virginia and the British crown. In the process, he widened the trail with about 60 axemen, a task so arduous that Washington pretty much gave up the idea of wagons going west. He also found out that he was not much of a military man, being caught at Great Meadows, where he had constructed the aptly named Fort Necessity, which he soon surrendered to the besieging French.

Contemptuous of colonial "backwardness," as demonstrated by Washington's botched campaign, Braddock determined to carry the wisdom and luxuries of a European war machine into the American wilderness by widening and improving Nemacolin's Trail to accept the guns and wagons of his army. Braddock employed over six hundred men with axes, ten times Washington's effort. The resulting road was 12 feet wide, a virtual swath through the forest. But it had a lot of ups and downs. The horses could be double-teamed to get uphill, but primitive brakes could not hold the loads going down. So Braddock took a naval company with him; men with blocks and tackle and a knowledge of how to slow the guns and heavy wagons on the downgrades. It took ages to get near France's Fort Duquesne, as the modern city of Pittsburgh was called then, and in the battle that followed, Braddock's army was defeated, and he was killed and buried in the road of which he was so proud.

See also Cumberland Road; National Road; Washington's Road.

Reference Hulbert, Archer Butler, *Historic Highways of America* (1902–1906).

Bridger Trail

Running from Fort Laramie, parallel to the Bozeman Trail but on the west side of the Big Horn Mountains as opposed to the

Bozeman's use of the eastern side, northward to the Montana goldfields in the early 1860s, the Bridger Trail had been marked ten years earlier during a hunting expedition of European nobility led by the famous scout, Jim Bridger. It was preferred to the Bozeman Trail by many because it put the Big Horn Mountains between them and the Lakota tribal hunting grounds.

See also Bozeman Trail.

Bridges, Harry (1901–1990)

One of the most controversial American labor leaders of the twentieth century, Harry Bridges was born and raised in Australia. He read a lot of Jack London stories as a boy and shipped out as a sailor. He became disgusted with the way in which seamen were treated and wound up in San Francisco in time for the 1921 seamen's strike as a picket leader. The strike failed and angered Bridges with the more conservative tactics of local labor leader Andrew Furuseth. Bridges was blacklisted and jumped from dock to dock, working until the managers discovered who he really was. Although not a Communist, Bridges was not above combining with anyone to oppose management policies. By the 1930s, the New Deal promised a new day in labor's right to organize, and Bridges was there to capitalize on it. Bridges was well known among seamen and dock workers because of his itinerant work habits and the blacklist. He also had a knack for putting the average laborer's feelings into words. He tried to work with existing unions, but after the Big Strike of 1934 had been crushed by violence, he applied successfully to the Congress of Industrial Organizations to form a new union, the International Longshoremen's Association (later the International Longshoremen and Warehousemen's Union). Bridges, of course, was its first president.

As a labor leader, Bridges never lost touch with the masses. He was not a suit-and-tie man surrounded by thugs. He worked as one of the people he represented, which proved to be the source of his great power. He antagonized dock and steamship managers and the old union leaders alike. Because of his foreign birth and assertive role in labor conflicts, many efforts were made to deport him as an undesirable alien in 1934 (in an Immigration Service hearing, which failed), 1936 (a Labor Department hearing, which failed), 1940 (an act of Congress, which did not pass), 1941 (by court order under a new act of Congress), 1945 (the U.S. Supreme Court reversed a lower-court decision and granted Bridges citizenship), 1949 (his citizenship was revoked under an assertion that he lied about denying his Communist past), 1953 (the U.S. Supreme Court reversed another lower-court ruling), and 1955 (in lower courts a judge dismissed another case on his alleged perjury, ending the legal battles for all time).

After World War II, Bridges actually came to gain management's respect as they realized that he was the one man who could keep the dock workers in line. Bridges also mellowed and changed his party registration from Democrat to Republican. In 1960, he negotiated the Mechanization and Modernization (M&M) Agreement that allowed the docks to be modernized and container cargoes received and shipped. In exchange, the shippers paid into a fund that encouraged early retirement and increased pensions and benefits. This was a crucial step in the modern conversion to containerized shipping. Bridges opposed the Vietnam conflict but refused to close the docks to prevent supplies from reaching American soldiers overseas. He led a strike for more wages and benefits in 1972 but never threatened the M&M Agreement. He retired from the union in 1977 and died 13 years later, still haunted by the false "Communist" charges that linger even today.

See also Merchant Marine.

References Larrowe, Charles P., *Harry Bridges* (1972); Pedraja, René de la, *A Historical Dictionary of the U.S. Merchant Marine and Shipping Industry* (1994).

Bridges

Bridges represent beauty, power, and rational accomplishment. They are such a universal statement that one need not be an engineer to admire them. They are made of almost all building materials: stone, brick, wood, iron, steel, and concrete. At the time of the American Revolution, not one major stream was crossed by a bridge, although numerous small spans existed as a part of the colonial highway system. Today the United States is the home to uncounted bridges made of all these materials. Tragically, many of the nation's spans, up to half of them, are so outdated or ill-maintained that investigators fear that the bridge infrastructure is at a crisis point. Many call for a massive public works program to put them back in order and to provide jobs for many of the skilled trades left unemployed by the shift of the domestic economy from an industrial to a service base.

Among the first materials used for bridge construction was wood. In America, the existence of the vast forests from the sea to the plains, reinforced by the additional forests of the Rocky Mountains and the Pacific coastal ranges, provided more than adequate resources of timber for bridge construction. Indeed, the United States probably has more wood bridges than most countries. The wooden bridge is not a practical structure for long life. Barring catastrophe like flood or fire, a wooden span can be expected to be rebuilt every 30 years or so. They are easily constructed with a minimum of engineering talent, if small enough. But most rivers were of such a swift current, or possessed such sandy and soft bottoms, that to bridge them was a real engineering problem. Allegedly, the first major bridge in the American colonies was the Great Bridge across the Charles River at Boston in 1662. It was a structure of wooden piles covered with rough-hewn planks that endured over a century before a real bridge was constructed in its place.

After the colonies won their independence from England, they began to construct roads and other internal improvements to connect themselves together. One of the most popular structures was the trestle, a modified high-pile-and-beam bridge. This method was especially liked by the railroads. One of the more modern such structures was the Southern Pacific's Lucin Cutoff across the Great Salt Lake, erected in 1903. Although the trestle was later replaced by fill, at the time of its construction it was the longest trestle in the world. Another long span was the Lake Ponchartrain Bridge of the Southern Railway in Louisiana. It too has been replaced by fill until it is but a skeleton of its former self.

More complicated, but also crossing the gap with a true span, are truss-and-arch bridges. The first major builder to use this type of construction was Theodore Burr. He once built five different bridges across the Susquehanna River at the same time by juggling crews between them. One had a span of just over 360 feet, the longest span of its time. But like all builders of the early nineteenth century, Burr built by intuition and feel—he had no formal training or engineering knowledge. Ithiel Town did have such education, and his Town Truss was widely copied but lacked posts to prevent warping and twisting over longer spans. His truss was easily built and required less wood than other types. Many of his trusses still exist in covered bridges. Elias Howe, inventor of the sewing machine, also developed a truss named after him that was the basis of the first bridge across the Mississippi at Davenport, Iowa, in the 1850s. The spans were never completed, catching fire after being hit accidentally by a steamboat, whose owners sued, claiming that bridges were unnatural river obstructions. The bridge company and the railroad that was to use it won the case, represented among others by lawyer Abraham Lincoln. Other trusses came along after Howe's, including the McCallum Inflexible Arch Truss and the first truly scientific wooden truss, designed by Thomas Pratt, that later came into its own when iron became the material of choice about the time of the Civil War.

Other early materials used in bridges were stone and brick. These materials were especially important in building the piers and abutments connected by trusses of wood, iron, and steel. But early bridges across smaller streams were often made of quarried stone. These had the advantage of permanency, but took a long time to construct. One of the major uses for stone was in building aqueducts for water systems and particularly for early canals like the Erie and the Pennsylvania Main Line. The Baltimore & Ohio Railroad built its first bridges out of stone, too. Its Thomas Viaduct was the first multiple-span masonry bridge in the New World.

But nothing in masonry construction beat the massive Starrucca Viaduct on the Erie Railroad in upper Pennsylvania, built in one year (money was no problem, as with most such projects) and finished in 1848. It was 100 feet high, had 17 arches, and covered over 1,000 linear feet in length. It was designed to carry locomotives of 50 tons, but continued in use throughout most of the twentieth century with heavier and longer trains, demonstrating the strength of masonry. The famous Great Stone Bridge on the Great Northern just below St. Anthony's Falls on the Mississippi at Minneapolis was made of masonry with a 817-foot arch on a 6-degree curve. It is still in service. Brick was also used in the eastern United States, but infrequently, as it took longer to

finish a brick bridge than even a stone one. Americans tended to be in a hurry for everything, even 150 years ago.

Of all materials used in bridge building (stone, brick, wood, iron, steel, and concrete), iron was used for the shortest time and its relics are nearly all gone, replaced as they rusted out. Iron first came into use in England at the end of the eighteenth century. Oddly, the first American to experiment with the material was Thomas Paine, author of the American Revolution tract, *Common Sense*. His effort was interrupted by the builder's interest in the French Revolution and never completed. The first all-metal bridge in America was part of the Cumberland Road and was finished in 1836. The iron fittings are still under the present-day structure at Brownsville, Pennsylvania, on Dunlap's Creek. But the extended use of iron was held up by the inadequacies of early American foundries.

One of the early iron bridge builders was James Finley, who built the suspension bridge across the Potomac above Georgetown, called the Chain Bridge, in 1807. Finley was the first person to build a suspension bridge with a rigid roadway that could carry

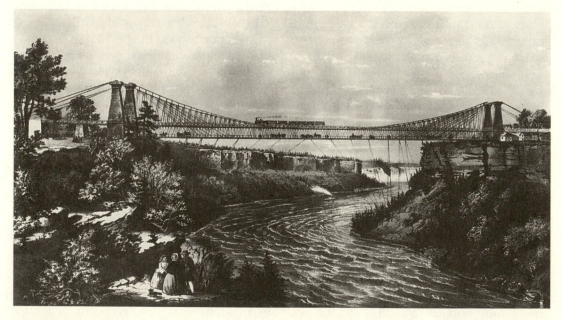

John A. Roebling, one of the most famous iron bridge builders, constructed this railroad suspension bridge near Niagara Falls in the mid-nineteenth century.

traffic safely. But it took until 1845 before an iron railroad bridge carried the Reading Railroad into Philadelphia from the west. The key to the extended use of iron was Squire Whipple's invention of a metal truss, based on an earlier design pioneered by Robert Fulton, of steamboat fame. Others also took up the idea of an iron truss, generally called a bowstring truss because of its suspension cables that dropped to the deck from a superior iron tubular arch. Both Whipple and Herman Haupt, a professional engineer to win fame during the Civil War for railroad building, wrote and published important treatises on bridge construction. Shortly afterward, Wendel Bollman, the last of the self-taught engineers, patented another truss in which the cables ran under the length of the span and drew it up, much like truss rods on an old-time railroad car.

But nothing became more common than the Pratt "through truss," reinforced with the overhead diagonal girder-work that makes up most of America's metal-truss bridges of all sizes. Indeed, the Pratt design is the only truss to appear in wood, iron, and steel. Other forms of trusses, particularly curved parabolic styles like the Whipple, and viaducts, which differed from trestles in that their spans were supported by towers rather than having each "bent" touch the ground, also were common. But the most famous iron bridge builders were James B. Eads, Charles Ellet, Jr., and John A. Roebling. Eads built the first iron bridge across the Mississippi at St. Louis in the late 1860s, and Ellet was the first to suggest the use of concrete piers for metal bridges. Both he and Roebling advanced the idea of suspension bridges, their most noted being Ellet's Schuylkill River Bridge in Philadelphia and his Wheeling Bridge over the Ohio (which later collapsed in a high wind), and Roebling's Niagara Bridge, the Cincinnati Bridge over the Ohio, and the Brooklyn Bridge (completed by his son, Washington).

Beginning in the last quarter of the nineteenth century, the material of choice for bridges became steel. Known about for centuries, steel was difficult and expensive to make, which limited its applications in large projects like bridges. But the development of the Bessemer process to remove impurities with a blast of hot air and the open-hearth Siemens-Martin method made steel more common, and its strength immediately challenged the users of iron. Steel was at first used in critical places (like suspension cables) for its strength, while the rest of the structural members were still made of iron. This method was followed in Eads' St. Louis Bridge and the Roeblings' Brooklyn Bridge. The first all-steel bridge was William Sooy Smith's spanning of the Missouri River at Glasgow, Missouri, in the mid-1870s. It was followed by a series of major Midwest railroad bridges all made of steel. In the East, one of the more spectacular structures was the two-span, lenticular truss bridge across the Monongahela at Pittsburgh. Its lithe, waving trusses looked almost like a modern infinity sign: ∞.

The strength and flexibility of steel led it to be the material of early twentieth-century bridges. Spans got longer, supports became more spidery, and designs more complex. Suspension bridges, viaducts, lattice-ribbed arches, parabolic arches, deck trusses, Pratt through trusses, and graceful cantilevered trusses abounded. In the early part of the century, massive vertical-lift, swing, and bascule bridges offered a way to cross busy waterways and still allow "removal" of the bridge for busy shipping routes. Later in the century, spindly, fixed bridges like the Huey P. Long Bridge in New Orleans, the Earl K. Long Bridge in Lake Charles, Louisiana, or the various San Francisco Bay bridges (Golden Gate, Transbay, Richmond-San Rafael) simply lifted vehicular traffic high enough into the air to clear shipping. As the century progressed, the designers and engineers borrowed a trick from the old Civil War military railroad men and began to standardize parts for ease and rapidity of construction.

Running neck and neck with steel in the modern era is concrete. Reinforced and prestressed to gain tinsel strength and flexibility, concrete can be poured into various functional and design-sensitive forms, besides the naturally compressed arch, that bring real beauty to bridge building. Early wire mesh reinforcement followed the pattern created by an Austrian engineer, Joseph Melan, although American W. E. Ward had proposed the use of iron rods some time earlier. The first place to use concrete bridges to create a design motif, as well as functional structures, was in Minnesota's Twin Cities during the teens and twenties. Although reinforced concrete has been used nationwide, the most spectacular examples occur the farther west one goes, with the Pacific Coast highways taking the prize. Concrete is often used in conjunction with other materials, especially steel, to create a viaduct-bridge combination, or, in the case of the 18-mile-long Chesapeake Bay Bridge Tunnel, a viaduct-bridge-tube combination. Precast, prestressed concrete members offer great flexibility in design and construction and predominate the numerous crossovers and flying interchanges in the recently completed interstate highway system.

See also Roads and Highways, Colonial Times to World War I; Roads and Highways since World War I.

References Beckett, Derrick, *Great Buildings of the World: Bridges* (1969); Cook, Richard J., *The Beauty of Railroad Bridges in North America* (1987); Gies, Joseph, *Bridges and Men* (1963); Hopkins, H. J., *A Span of Bridges* (1970); Plowden, David, *Bridges* (1974); Seely, Bruce E., *Building the American Highway System* (1987); Steinman, David B., and Sara Ruth Watson, *Bridges and Their Builders* (1941); U.S. Department of Transportation, Federal Highway Administration, *America's Highways* (1976).

Briscoe, Benjamin (1867–1945)

In the early twentieth century, Benjamin Briscoe had built up the Maxwell-Briscoe Company into one of the bigger competitors in the mid-price-range car market, and was pushing Buick for the lead. Along with the head of Buick, William C. Durant, Briscoe believed that the day of a single car line was limited. They deemed it much better to have several models in several price ranges so as to absorb the shock and fickleness of the buyers and the general economic fluctuations that regularly occurred, driving so many others (about 20 percent of early entrepreneurs each year) from the industry.

Briscoe believed that about four different models would assure the continued success of each other—no more than one would go bad at any given time. In addition, he believed that bigness had a production advantage in that all of the divisions could share plant space and marketing ventures. Finally, it would create a near-monopoly situation, which, as any businessman knows, is safer and more profitable to the participants.

Briscoe and Durant tried first to unify Buick, Maxwell, Reo, and Ford. They hoped to buy the others by issuing stock in the new firm in lieu of cash. Such a combination would gain about half of the existing auto market. Durant especially was interested in bringing in others, too. Henry Ford was willing to sell, but only for cold cash. Reo also agreed, but was unable to raise actual money and the deal went sour. Then Briscoe, on the advice of banker J. P. Morgan, withdrew Maxwell from the stock merger and said he wanted cash. The result was that Briscoe and Durant parted company. When Durant organized General Motors (GM) in 1908, Briscoe and his brother Frank (1875–1954) decided to try their own combination. With the aid of Electric Vehicle Corporation, Briscoe organized United States Motor Corporation, an imposing paper empire of nine auto and parts manufacturers. He even opened negotiations with Durant to join a second time, but they fell off.

It turned out that Briscoe's group had defects that Durant's did not. He had no luxury line like Durant's Cadillac, and no reputation leaders like Oldsmobile. One of the firms he bought had a large debt that Briscoe did not find out about until after the sale. The result was that Maxwell could not hold up the others and the whole scheme went into bankruptcy in 1912. The firm was reorganized by dropping all of the component partners except Maxwell. It was the last major merger on the scale of GM since, although smaller mergers have taken place and the more recent Chrysler-American Motors merger comes close. But nothing was ever as big as GM and Briscoe's United States Motors.

See also Automobiles from Domestics to Imports; Automobiles in American Society; Durant, William C.

References May, George S., *A Most Unique Machine* (1975); May, George S., "Benjamin Briscoe," in George S. May (ed.), *Encyclopedia of American Business History and Biography: The Automobile Industry* (1990), 48–53; Motor Vehicle Manufacturers Association of the United States, *Automobiles of America* (1974); Rae, John B., "The Electrical Vehicle Corporation: A Monopoly That Missed," *Business History Review* (1955) 22: 298–311; Thomas, Robert Paul, *An Analysis of the Pattern of Growth of the Automobile Industry* (1977).

British Columbia Railway (BC Rail)

Owned and operated by the provincial government, the British Columbia Railway, now known as BC Rail, was originally envisioned as a line that would stretch from Alaska to Mexico along the Pacific coast. It was chartered as the Pacific Great Eastern (PGE) in 1912. The name came from the fact that the investors were from the British Great Eastern Railroad. The initial line was to run north out of the Vancouver area to the Pearce River and encourage colonization of that valley. Construction was arduous, to say the least. One section of 30 miles had five tunnels, and much of the roadbed had to be blasted out of granite cliffs. The company soon went broke. But after World War I, the U.S. government finished work on the Alaska Railroad and the British Columbia government decided to acquire the stock and continue the run northward. But the task proved too daunting and work was suspended until 1949. Then work was resumed and the line connected to the Canadian National near Quesnel. Today, extensive forest and mineral development and interchanges with several Canadian and American lines has made BC Rail fairly profitable. Some passenger service is also available on alternate days.

See also Canadian National Railways; Canadian Pacific Railway.

References Drury, George H., *The Historical Guide to North American Railroads* (1985); Drury, George H., *The Train-Watcher's Guide* (1990); Hubbard, Freeman, *Encyclopedia of North American Railroading* (1981); Phillips, R. A. J., *Canada's Railways* (1968); Ramsay, Bruce, *PGE: Railway to the North* (1962).

Bureau of Public Roads (BPR)

From 1918 to 1939 the Bureau of Public Roads was the primary agency administering federal highway assistance to the states. Its chief was Thomas M. MacDonald, who expanded it from a minor advice-giving agency into a real power in the federal highway movement, responsible for research and development, dispensing of funds to the states, auditing the use of these funds, setting standards of construction, education of technical personnel, planning the interstate system, setting up highway safety programs, working in foreign affairs through road aid, and lobbying Congress. Under the New Deal, the BPR was responsible for "priming the pump" by providing jobs in the flat economy. The BPR became a section of the Public Roads Administration in a 1939 governmental reorganization, and a key part of the Department of Transportation (DOT) until 1970, when it was abolished in favor of its component parts being made independent agencies within the DOT.

See also Roads and Highways since World War I.

Reference U.S. Department of Transportation, Federal Highway Administration, *America's Highways* (1976).

Burlington Northern Incorporated (BN)

The Burlington Northern Corporation is a gigantic railroad conglomerate comprising the Great Northern Railroad, the Northern Pacific Railroad, the Chicago, Burlington & Quincy Railroad, and the Spokane, Portland & Seattle Railroad, that was formed in 1970. The BN has since that time added to its holdings the St. Louis-San Francisco Railroad in 1981. The passenger service on all of these lines had been in the hands of Amtrak since 1971. The BN's main carriage is grain, coal, forest products, chemicals, primary metals, pulpwood, and paper. The BN empire stretches from the Pacific Northwest to Chicago, and from Canada to the Gulf of Mexico.

Talks were under way in 1994 to merge the Atchison, Topeka & Santa Fe Railway (AT&SF) with BN, which would make BN, already the largest railroad combination in the United States, even larger. The Santa Fe merger would add a vast intermodal empire to the line and a direct route from Los Angeles to Chicago, although BN already has its own trucking company and an air freight operation. The BN refines about 10 percent of its own diesel fuel and holds vast untapped forest reserves and oil reserves in its own name. With the Santa Fe merger, BN-SF would have a key position to take advantage of the North American Free Trade Agreement, given BN's contacts in Canada and SF's with Mexico. But the Union Pacific (UP) has instituted what is seen by observers as a more unfriendly merger offer to Santa Fe, because unlike BN, which is a commodity hauler, UP is an intermodal railroad as is Santa Fe. Although UP and Santa Fe parallel each other in Midwest markets, a merger would give UP a shorter route into Los Angeles. But unlike BN-SF, a UP-SF merger would not tap the border areas as effectively, and some think it would hinder rather than aid competitiveness among western rail lines. In early 1995, the BN offer went before the Interstate Commerce Commission for approval amid speculation that UP drove up the price merely to load up BN-SF with excessive debt.

See also Chicago, Burlington & Quincy Railroad; Great Northern Railroad; Klitenic Plan; Northern Pacific Railway; St. Louis-San Francisco Railway; Santa Fe Railway.

References Drury, George H., *The Historical Guide to North American Railroads* (1985); Drury, George H., *The Train-Watcher's Guide* (1990); Hubbard, Freeman, *Encyclopedia of North American Railroading* (1981); Rush, Elson, "BNSF: Biggest Merger of All," *Pacific RAILNews* (September 1994) (no. 370): 16 –21; Schneider, Paul, *Burlington Northern Diesel Locomotives* (1993).

Buses

Buses and taxis have provided most of the public transit services inside American cities in the twentieth century. But the use of these services has been spotty, to say the least. Early in the century, commuter trains and trolley cars tapped much of the potential of bus travel. This pre–World War I period was marked by experimentation with different fuels, gasoline and electricity (batteries) being among the most frequently used. Just as the truck and auto designs were primitive, so were the buses. New York City was among the first to use buses, commonly double-decker models that lasted until the late 1940s when they were replaced with the single-floor arrangement. One of the earliest manufacturers was Fifth Avenue, which took its name from the transit services that its vehicles provided. Chicago Motor Bus Company did the same. Both of these city-named companies became a part of Yellow Coach, a premier manufacturer by the 1920s.

The World War I era and the Roaring Twenties marked the high point in bus usage. Figures for annual passengers hovered around the 20 billion level (each person's ride is considered a new "passenger"). Bus development strove to keep up with the demand. Most bus makers were also heavily involved with truck manufacture, Fageol and White being the leaders. Often the frame was built by one company and the body by another. The engine was still in front of the vehicle until 1927. An innovative design came from Mack, which introduced its AB model with a drop frame that allowed the floor to be placed below the height of the wheels. Another development was the use of pneumatic tires. Because innovation costs money, bus companies tend to stick with the tried and true, especially if it is cost effective. When Goodyear suggested that pneumatic tires would cushion the ride and allow greater load capacity, transit authorities ignored it. So Goodyear developed and built its own bus line to demonstrate the effectiveness of its new product. It even put out six- and eight-wheel versions and added four-wheel trailer cars behind.

With the advent of the Great Depression, bus ridership began to decline by one-third. Probably as important as economics was the widespread ownership of automobiles. In bus design, the thirties actually began in 1927 with the advent of Twin Coach's Model 40. This was a rear-engine vehicle that would become an industry standard. In addition to the various 1920s innovations incorporated into the design came new ones that would appear common to a bus user today. The front doors were ahead of the wheel housing, corner windows were of rounded glass, and the windshield wiper had a vertical position and horizontal sweep. At the same time, as capacity increased, buses began to use larger engines, most upgrading to 6-cylinder models, and the larger ones to 12. Positive chassis lubrication made maintenance necessary less often, fewer shakes and rattles occurred from the uni-body construction, and the wheels were of a smaller diameter, decreasing the interior space consumed and providing a lower silhouette. For the first time, a pull cord signaled the driver to stop. In the bigger cities buses began to burn propane/butane-fueled motors for cleanliness. The rest began to move away from gasoline to diesel.

The biggest advances in 1930s construction came from Yellow Coach, which introduced a new 35-foot-long bus that became standard, and General Motors (GM), which adapted its line to the newest in monocoque construction (blending the body and frame to save on weight with increased strength) invented for the airliners. Modified once again by Yellow Coach in 1940, this style of bus became known as the "old look" bus. It had front and rear doors to facilitate passenger traffic flow at stops, windows that raised like a double-hung sash house window, a windshield that slanted inward at the top to minimize nighttime reflections, and 28-, 30-, 34-, 35-, and 40-foot lengths. This basic design was produced until the 1960s, when the "new look" bus arrived. Over 38,000 vehicles of the old look were produced by all companies combined.

The rationing of World War II saw bus ridership climb to nearly 25 billion individual trips per year. The war caused bus production, however, to be sidetracked in favor of military vehicles. This later turned out to be an advantage as the armed services produced several vehicular developments that helped out motor vehicle industries after the war, like better diesel power plants, better

hydraulic control systems, automatic transmissions, and air-conditioning. The following decade was one of consolidation for bus companies. Many of the older manufacturers went out of the bus-building business or merged with other companies, a process that put GM at the top of bus makers. Propane disappeared as its costs relative to diesel and gasoline skyrocketed. It would make a comeback during the various Arab oil embargoes and increased environmental concerns two decades later. In 1959, GM brought out the "new look" bus, the model TDH-4561. It became the bus to beat for the next 20 years. It incorporated several new developments like increased use of anodized aluminum, air suspension, rivet construction, larger windows and doors, a push-to-open rear door, fluorescent lighting, adjustable air brakes, seats bolted to a track that allowed flexible seating patterns, and increased coach lengths and widths. By the end of the sixties, only GM and Flxible (the first "e" was dropped to distinguish it from its first effort as a maker of motorcycle sidecars 40 years before) continued to produce buses in the United States.

As bus technology improved in the ensuing decades, little was changed outwardly in coach design. The most important new change was the entrance of the federal government into the mass-transit picture with new laws and investigations into better transportation delivery to the public. A 1964 Urban Mass Transit Act put $375 million into the advance of public transportation systems. The Urban Mass Transportation Administration became a part of the Department of Transportation and was given a specific mandate to develop new public transportation technologies in an effort to alleviate smog conditions and massive overcrowding of urban highways. GM signed a consent decree in which it promised to make its buses and parts available to all comers without payment of royalties. This gave Flxible an aid to stay in business. Under federal support, the National Academy of Engineering made several studies of the "new look" bus and recommended the altering of step height, a lower main floor,

A grandmother amuses her companion at the New York City Greyhound Bus station in 1947.

more accessible seats, and a redesigned transmission and drive train. The goal of the government study was to make buses more accessible to the public and thus increase the likelihood of use.

The 1970s began with a new Urban Mass Transportation Act that procured another $10 billion over ten years for advanced designs and markets. The government sponsored several Advanced Design Buses (ADB) that were supposed to improve on the "new look" buses being produced. The new vehicle was called the Transbus. It provided for increased passenger safety, comfort, and convenience. Wider doors and windows, lower floors, increased "dwell time" (time spent at each stop), speeds up to 70 miles per hour, and a better esthetic look inside and out marked the project. One of the more unique aspects was the demand of the Rehabilitation Act of 1973 requiring each bus to "kneel," that is, hydraulically drop the front stairwell so that it is even with the ground—

usually accomplished by collapsing the shock absorbers in the front-right wheel housing—to assist older and physically challenged customers to mount, and the installation of a wheelchair lift that has more recently been declared unsafe. But in 1976, the federal government backed off and refused to order the new developments into production, preferring to rely on private companies to make the effort in a free-market environment. Grumman and GM have led the way. But the creation of new standards has led many other companies to attempt to crack a market once almost exclusively held by GM.

Then in 1979, the government reversed its prior position and required that all buses bought with the assistance of federal money be up to ADB standards. This was much like the Dreadnought decision of the British navy before World War I. It gave the new technology to GM's potential competitors and all started anew from the same level, much like the new battleship allowed the German Imperial Navy to catch up with the Royal Navy in one step. All products would now be ADBs. The result has been the entry into the market of nearly two dozen companies, where only GM and Flxible had been before. More emphasis was given to fuel economy and the use of cleaner alternative fuels. New bus designs look much like tractor trailers, with a power unit pulling an elongated passenger-carrying trailer called a Super Bus. Some European companies have introduced articulated buses of double length that hinge in the center and flex on a vestibule, much like passenger train cars. New products like fiberglass and various composite materials (carbon, aramide, and glass fibers) have been utilized to cut weight and increase cleanliness and efficiency. But although bus ridership is up for the past decades, it is but a little above the rate present at the beginning of the century—about 13 billion individual trips a year.

See also Automobiles from Domestics to Imports; Automobiles in American Society; Commuter Trains; Greyhound Corporation; Stagecoaches and Other Horse-Drawn Conveyances; Trucking.

Reference Mandell, Susan Meikle, et al., *A Historical Survey of Transit Buses in the United States* (1990).

Bush, George W., and Sons v. Maloy 267 US 317 (1925)

The Bush case presents different facts from the Duke and Buck cases that preceded it. In *Bush*, the state of Maryland had denied Bush a permit to engage in interstate commerce over roads built solely with Maryland moneys (without federal aid). But the Court agreed with Bush and found that the Maryland legislature had granted too broad a mandate to the state regulatory commission. The commission had thus proceeded to violate the interstate commerce clause of the federal Constitution. The Court admonished Maryland, and by extension all the states, to draw regulatory commission guidelines in the future narrowly and specifically to prevent such excesses.

Like concurrent federal cases of a more general nature on business regulation, the Court's decision restricting state regulatory commissions drew political flak. States complained that the Court ignored prior cases like *Munn v. Illinois* that granted the states a near blank check in regulatory prerogatives in the public interest. Various state's attorneys general pointed out that the cases only handled states interfering with interstate commerce and did not threaten such things as size and weight restrictions or anything else regulated for other reasons than the public good. And in the absence of any federal action, an earlier decision (*Hendrick v. Maryland* 235 US 619 [1934]) confirmed the right of states to act in any area, regardless of constitutional provision, where the federal government had not acted and thus abdicated its mandate.

See also Michigan Public Utilities Commission et al. v. Duke Cartage Company; Tyson and Brothers–United Theater Ticket Offices, Inc. v. Blanton.

Reference Childs, William R., *Trucking and the Public Interest* (1985).

Butterfield Trail

Established in 1857, the Butterfield Overland Stage Lines ran from St. Louis, Missouri, and Memphis, Tennessee, to Fort Smith, Arkansas, south to present-day Dennison, Sherman, Gainsville, and Jacksboro, Texas, to San Angelo, continuing past Fort Stockton on the high plains to Fort Davis on the mountains, and turning north through Fort Quitman and El Paso to end up in Fort Fillmore, New Mexico. There the stage ran west through Apache Pass and turned up the Santa Cruz River at Tucson to the Gila and down the Gila to Fort Yuma. All it had to do then was get to San Francisco "through the best passes and along the best valleys for staging." Butterfield chose Fort Tejón and the San Joaquín Valley route. Each stage was planned to carry six to nine passengers with 50 pounds of luggage, and 500 pounds of U.S. mail—the real reason for its being. John Butterfield was a friend of President James Buchanan (hence cries of "foul" when the contract was let), a former stagecoach driver in the East, and one of the founders of the American Express Company, a merging of several eastern lines.

This 1866 Harper's Weekly *wood engraving of the Butterfield Overland Dispatch depicts the dangers of traveling in the West.*

Butterfield invested over $1 million in facilities and equipment. He hired 750 employees and built relay stations and corrals for his 700 horses. They were never fully tamed and ran hell-bent-for-leather up the road for 2 miles after each team change before becoming manageable. His slogan— "Nothing on God's earth must stop the United States Mail"—reckoned without the Civil War or the Apaches. Six horses pulled the coach—especially designed by Abbott and Downing of Concord, New Hampshire. They cost $1,050 each. They were tough and fast for their day, averaging over 100 miles in 24 hours through the Ozarks, and faster on the flats. It could be a tough trip. The roads were not the best and, according to the old saw, "There [was] no

Sunday west of St. Louis and no God west of Fort Smith." As one Texan put it, "If you want to obtain distinction in this country, kill somebody." A lot of people tried to live up to that exhortation. To those who survived the dangers and discomforts, it took just under 24 days to make the trip. "Had I not just come out over the route," insisted one addle-brained traveler who survived the initial journey, "I would be perfectly willing to go back." Ignorance of the journey's travail was true bliss.

See also Gila Trail.

References Conkling, Roscoe P., and Mary P. Conkling, *The Butterfield Overland Mail* (1926); Dunlop, Richard, *The Great Trails of the West* (1971); Faulk, Odie B., *Destiny Trail* (1973).

Calhoun, John Caldwell (1782–1850)

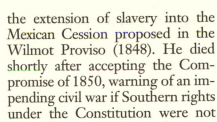

Born in Abbeville District, South Carolina, John C. Calhoun represented the nouveau riche planters made prosperous by the cultivation of upland cotton after the invention of the cotton gin. Educated at a local academy, Yale College, and the Litchfield Law School, he was extremely legalistic in his approach to politics and life in general. Indeed, one apocryphal story has him attempting to write a romantic poem to his future wife. The first word he wrote was "whereas." Since the only other one he could come up with was "therefore," Calhoun wisely abandoned the misguided effort. He was a tall, handsome, wiry man with a shock of coal black hair and a prominent forehead, which, with his shaggy eyebrows and aquiline nose, made his fiery eyes seem to be staring out of two caves. Hard to get to know, his nickname, "the cast iron man," was truly apropos.

After serving a term in the state legislature (1808–1809), Calhoun came to Congress (1811–1817) as a nationalist and War Hawk who wanted to fight the British in the War of 1812. He was secretary of war under James Monroe (1817–1825), famed for his construction of coastal fortifications, his concept of the "expansible" army, and his promotion of internal improvements; a candidate for president (1824); and twice vice-president, under both John Q. Adams (1825–1829) and Andrew Jackson (1829–1832). He was the first of two vice-presidents to resign the office (Spiro Agnew was the other), and the only one to do so under honorable circumstances. Always ambitious, ever-seeking the presidency, he was addressed by one sarcastic critic in the Senate as "Mr. Vice President and would-be President of the United States."

After his resignation from the Jackson administration, Calhoun served as a senator (1832–1843) promoting state rights and as secretary of state under John Tyler (1844–1845), where he supported Texas annexation. Again returned to the Senate (1845–1850), he fought against the limitation on the extension of slavery into the Mexican Cession proposed in the Wilmot Proviso (1848). He died shortly after accepting the Compromise of 1850, warning of an impending civil war if Southern rights under the Constitution were not fully protected.

See also Bonus Bill.

References Capers, Gerald M., *John C. Calhoun* (1960); Coit, Margaret L., *John C. Calhoun* (1950); Freehling, William W., *Prelude to Civil War* (1968); Sydnor, Charles, *The Development of Southern Sectionalism* (1948); Wiltse, Charles M., *John C. Calhoun* (1944–1951).

California Trail

The central road to the California goldfields was an offshoot of the Oregon Trail, beginning at Fort Hall. The route dropped southwestward into modern Nevada to the headwaters of the Humboldt River and followed its often slight and brackish course until it disappeared into the sands of the Humboldt Sink. Continuing to the southwest, the trail then hit the Walker River, crossed the Sierra Nevada at several places (Sonora, Carson, Truckee, or Donner Passes, being among the most noted), and descended into the central valley areas.

The whole Great Basin—interior Nevada and Utah—had been explored by fur trappers seeking new beaver streams in the 1820s and 1830s. In 1824, the John H. Weber party dropped down the Bear River and took hundreds of pelts. During this expedition, one of the trappers, Jim Bridger, received credit for discovering Great Salt Lake. Later, Jedediah Smith traveled along the north, east, and south sides of the inland salt sea on his journeys to and from California. In 1833, Joseph Walker and his men crossed over the north edge of the Great Salt Lake and reached the Humboldt, a geographic entity previously noted by the Hudson's Bay *engagé*, Peter Skene Ogden. Ogden had hoped to trap out the whole region, creating a "fur desert," to prevent the spread of United States influence, but the active, independent American trappers beat him to it and pushed the British back above the Columbia River with their own desecration of the fur supply.

Walker followed the Humboldt to its point of disappearance and crossed down to the Walker River, establishing the western end of what became the California Trail. Arrested by the Mexican government in California and invited to leave by the shortest route possible, Walker took this injunction somewhat liberally and dropped south down the San Joaquín Valley to present-day Bakersfield before turning north, recrossing the Sierra Nevada, and striking his old trail to return to his base. His military commander, Captain Benjamin L. E. Bonneville, reported the success of the expedition, received credit for much of Walker's sightings, and even grabbed credit from Bridger for the finding of the Great Salt Lake. Actually, it was not so much that Bonneville took the fame but that it was handed to him by his widely read biographer, Washington Irving. In addition, the great inland Precambrian sea that left its remnants as Great Salt Lake was named Lake Bonneville, as were the salt flats to the west, where modern land speed records are set by jet-powered automobiles.

Walker's trip was followed up by another under Kit Carson. In 1834, he came out of Fort Hall and headed southwestward to the head of the Humboldt, following it to the Sink before turning back. By now both ends and the middle of the trail had been blazed. All that was wanting was the arrival of settlers bent on going to California. They were not long in coming. Washington Irving's *Adventure of Captain Bonneville* had created instant interest in the Far West. California and Oregon societies sprang up in the eastern United States, promoting American colonization of both areas. One of those so inspired was John Bidwell, who organized a settlement party in 1841 bound for California. The members elected a man much older than the 26-year-old Bidwell as captain. He was John Bartleson, quarrelsome and quick-tempered, but they also had the luck to fall in with Thomas Fitzpatrick, an experienced mountain man, as guide and headed west. The party began to quarrel, a common occurrence among independent-minded Americans of the nineteenth century, and at South Pass, they split, half going on to Oregon with Bartleson, the other half heading for California under Bidwell.

Bidwell's group headed directly west looking for the Humboldt. They crossed over the desert just north of the Great Salt Lake, were forced to abandon their wagons as thirst ravaged the column, and lived off horseflesh as they proceeded down the brackish Humboldt. With little knowledge of the trail, they duplicated the feat of Walker and arrived in the Bay Area down the Stanislaus River route. They were extremely lucky.

That summer of 1843 saw the first wagons cross the Sierra Nevada. Joseph Walker guided a party into the Owens Valley, but they had to abandon their wheeled vehicle there and proceed on horseback. That same year, the Elisha Steven's party took three wagons across the California Trail, following it from its start in Fort Hall, down the Humboldt, and crossing the Sierras at Truckee Pass (the first time it had been used), arriving at Sutter's Fort via the American River. They were assisted by the fact that it was a wet spring and the water was up and sweeter than usual. They were also lucky. They had been caught by a sudden storm in the High Sierras, but managed to get themselves out. Three years later the Donner party would not be so fortunate.

The Donner party disaster came about through the agency of one Lansford Hastings. A propagandist, and full of the typical chicanery of a nineteenth-century American publicist—stretching the truth in favor of a good story—Hastings came to Oregon by sea in the early 1840s. Not liking the area (perhaps no one listened to him there), he journeyed overland with a party of malcontents to California. He observed the weakness of the Mexican government and decided to stimulate American immigration, so much of which was going to Oregon and so little to California. His pamphlet, *Emigrant's Guide to Oregon and California*, was full of all sorts of geographical falsehoods as he had never seen the land that he so thoroughly described. But it was widely distributed, read, and believed. He invented a new route to California—the Hastings Cutoff—that would shorten the traditional route by having the emigrants turn south at Fort Bridger, bear southwest to Great Salt Lake, and head due west across the desert to San Francisco. It left a lot out, but that hardly mattered to those wanting to head west.

Soon, however, even Hastings had come to realize that he had left a lot out of his book. In a noble fit of guilt, he traveled east to fill it in, crossing his cutoff in reverse. It turned out to be 80 miles of the cruelest desert he and his companions, a couple of hardy mountain men, had seen. And they had no wagons to pull. Although the mountain men were against advising emigrants to use the new route, Hastings ignored warnings. The Harlan-Young party tried it first. There is a legend that the blue haze of Utah's hills is made up of the remnants of their cursing Hastings as they struggled west across the desert. They made it, but had abandoned much of their belongings in the process. At least the cutoff was now well marked.

Jacob and George Donner were not so fortunate. Warned by mountain men to stick to the traditional route, some of their party did and made it to California without incident. The others went by Hastings' route. They waited 8 days at the head of Weber Canyon. Hastings had left a note saying he knew a better route and would return. He never did. But a messenger steered them to another canyon that proved nearly impassable and took 30 days to traverse. It took another 64 hours to cross the desert, and they were now out of supplies. They sent men on ahead for food and struggled on. New supplies arrived in October. They then got caught in the High Sierras by a vicious storm that came along a month earlier than usual. Snowbound, they sent out a group, the "forlorn hope," to reach California on foot. By the time they got through and returned, cannibalism reigned rampant not only in their party but among those left behind. Only half of the original 89 who left Fort Bridger ever saw California, but Donner Pass became the main route there nonetheless.

The next group to take Hastings' route were the Mormons, who came in 1847. When they reached the head of the canyons leading to the Great Salt Lake, they were amazed to find the results of the blind hacking of the Donners. Brigham Young was not that kind of man. He sent out numerous scouting parties, one of which discovered the route through Emigration Canyon that is Route 30-S today. Everyone set to work and within a week a safe passage had been cleared. Although Young picked a site that he thought was habitable, yet far from other Americans, he reckoned without knowledge of the California gold rush. As the Hasting's Cutoff was the shortest route, the argonauts took it through to the new city of 5,000, named after the Great Salt Lake nearby.

Like all Americans, the Mormons sought congressional aid in improving their connections with the Central Overland Route, within the Great Basin, and to California through the Old Spanish Trail to the southwest. But because of antagonisms with the territorial officials sent by Washington, Utah received much less money than any other western territory for roads. The improvement of the Old Spanish Trail got sidetracked with the investigation of the murder of Lieutenant John W. Gunnison by Indians. He had died earlier while surveying the thirty-ninth-parallel route. A Mormon jury found the accused innocent, much to Gunnison's subordinate's disgust. The Mormon War of 1857–1858, however, changed all that. As the army occupied the Great Basin, it began an extensive program of exploration. Captain J. H. Simpson took charge of the old Hastings Cutoff route and straightened it out considerably into an easier-traveled section that turned west at Utah Lake, passed through current Austin, Nevada, and followed the same route as modern U.S. Highway 50. This was known as the Central Overland Route and became the main freight road, and the route of the Pony Express in 1860, until the transcontinental railroad took a more northerly tack around Great Salt Lake after the Civil War and ended the importance of the California Trail.

See also Mormon Trail; Oregon Trail; Roads and Highways since World War I.

References Altrocchi, Julia, *Old California Trail* (1945); Bell, James C., *Opening a Highway to the Pacific* (1921); Coy, Owen C., *The Great Trek* (1931); Drago, Harry S., *Roads to Empire* (1968); Dunlop, Richard, *Great Trails of the West* (1971); Hartman, Amos W., "The California and Oregon Trail, 1849–1860," *Oregon Historical Quarterly* (1924) 25: 1–35; Jackson, W. Turrentine, *Wagon Roads West* (1952); Kroll, Helen B., "Books That Enlightened the Emigrants," *Oregon Historical Quarterly* (1944) 45: 103–120; Monaghan, Jaym, *Overland Trail* (1947); Moody, Ralph, *The Old Trails West* (1963); Schallenburger, Moses, *The Opening of the California Trail* (1953).

Camels in the West

Although distant cousins of the camel, the alpaca and the llama, inhabit the Andes, the camel (like the horse) was reintroduced into America by settlers and explorers of European ancestry. The horse came with the conquistadors; they also suggested the camel be brought over as a beast of burden. They knew of its merits from their contact with the Moors, and it seems that some were imported to the Hispanic New World as early as the late 1500s. They were even tried by the English in Virginia in the 1700s, but none of these experiments caught on— probably because the climate was not favorable for the camel's survival.

After the Mexican-American War and the acquisition of the great southwestern deserts by the United States, the idea of camels came up anew. The origin of the use of camels to supply army outposts was a suggestion by Major George H. Crossman, a quartermaster in the Seminole War. Crossman found few takers, but in 1848 one of his advocates, Major Henry C. Wayne, met and talked with an important man who did like the notion—Senator Jefferson Davis of Mississippi, a member of the Military Affairs Committee. Wayne believed that camels could be used in the deserts of the Mexican Cession and Davis agreed. In 1853, Davis became secretary of war in the administration of President Franklin Pierce, and went to work on the camel project, making it one of his first priorities. After much discussion and the initial refusal of Congress to act, a camel experiment was funded in 1855.

In 1855 Congress funded the transporting of nearly 70 camels from the Near East to Indianola, Texas, with the intent of using them in the deserts of the Mexican Cession.

Major Wayne and navy Lieutenant David Dixon Porter went to the Near East to purchase the camels. The Americans secured about three dozen of the beasts and brought them to Indianola, Texas, in 1856. The camels were dromedaries for riding and packing, Bactrians for packing alone as the double hump made riding difficult, and several mixed breeds that had the same sure-footed stamina but the same sterile reproductive qualities attributed to the native American mule. Further imports created a herd of around 70 head. A team of four Americans, three Arabs, and two Turks took charge of their care. The Arabs soon returned home, but the Turks, Greek George and Hi-Jolly (American corruptions of their Arabic names), remained in America until their deaths in the early twentieth century.

The excitement aroused among the public by the camels' arrival was high and led several private parties to emulate the government and try out camels as pack animals and mail carriers throughout the West. Some believe that but for the Civil War and the railroads the camels would have done quite well. Others claimed that the hard deserts of the American West caused them to go lame quite suddenly. It may be that the introduction of the camels to the American mule skinner and bullwhacker was more than either man or beast could stand. The hard-swearing drivers hated the ill-tempered camels; horses and mules would stampede at their mere sight or smell. Nonetheless, camels could pack a load of 600 to 800 pounds 35 miles a day. Lighter loads sped their march to as much as 75 miles a day. They were reputed to be able to go a week without water and subsist on the desert brush that no horse or mule would touch.

The army spread the camels in small herds from Texas to California. With the coming of the Civil War most were turned loose to fend for themselves as the soldiers went east to fight. Little effort was made to use them during the war by either Confederate or Union armies. The beasts roamed wild and some were sold to circuses. Edward F. Beale raised a small herd on his California ranch that he began to sell off after the war.

In the postwar era, surviving camels were used as pack animals in the mining regions of the Rockies all the way to Montana and British Columbia. But the hatred of teamsters at the competition and the propensity of horses and mules to panic when camels approached made them unpopular. Old-timers claimed it was easier to stop a blizzard or an avalanche than to corral a string of horses or mules spooked by camels. By the 1880s most had been turned loose in the wild where they survived for decades afterward. Indeed, shooting feral camels was considered a public service and indulged in quite often by angry prospectors whose burros had run off in fright.

See also Beale's Wagon Road; Freighting and Teamsters.

References Carroll, Charles G., *The Government's Importation of Camels* (1904); Faulk, Odie B., *The U. S. Camel Corps* (1976); Greenly, Albert Harry, *Camels in America* (1952); Lesley, Lewis Burt, *The Purchase and Importation of Camels by the U.S. Government* (1929); Lewis, William S., "The Camel Pack Trains in the Mining Camps of the West," *Washington Historical Quarterly* (1928) 19: 271–284; Murray, Edward P., *Camels to the Colorado* (1980); Stacey, May H., *Uncle Sam's Camels* (1929).

Camino Real (California)

All over the American Southwest ran a series of trails. During the days of the Spanish, these roads were known locally as *los caminos reales*, the "royal roads." The viceroys in Mexico City built these dirt highways to service the mines, presidios (forts), and missions that ringed New Spain, today's Republic of Mexico. One of the more important ran up the coast of California from San Diego to San Francisco, connecting the provincial capital at Monterey with Spain's far-flung outposts on the Pacific.

California was invented in 1510 by the Spanish author, Ordoñez de Montalvo, as a piece of fiction. It was a land of Amazon women that lay somewhere west of the Caribbean. Most important in the mind of the conquistador, it was a land of no metal but gold. It rivaled the Seven Cities of Cíbola in wealth. By 1553, explorers had discovered what is now known as Baja California, a peninsula lying across the Sea of Cortés, that appeared at the time to be the fabled island, except there was no gold—or Amazon women. But the Spanish had another myth, shared by the English and the French. The northern Europeans called it the Northwest Passage, the waterway through the New World that would allow ships to sail straight to the Orient, as Christopher Columbus theorized years before. The Spanish called it the Strait of Anián. Could the sea between California and Mexico be the strait? English sailors like Sir Francis Drake made a habit of raiding Spain's colonial Pacific coast during the sixteenth century. The English seemed to appear and disappear as if by magic. Perhaps the hated English had found the way to the Orient. Spain had to know.

The search for the passage to the Orient, the one around California, fell to Sebastián Vizcaíno. In 1602, he explored the California Pacific coast to find the strait and chart fortification sites. Vizcaíno did not find any new landforms not known before, but he did discover a beautiful bay he called Monterey. For over 150 years nothing else was done. Then the Jesuit order fell out of favor with the Spanish king, and the Russians showed an interest in moving their domain south from Alaska, setting up Fort Ross north of San Francisco. Replacing the Jesuits with the Franciscans, Spain moved to strengthen its hold on all of California. To set up missions, the priests would need livestock. Previous experience taught the Spanish that livestock traveled poorly by ship. To prevent great losses, it was decided to send them overland. The trail used was unique in the West—it followed neither known Native American trails nor waterways. It was made up as it went and was marked as the Camino Real, starting at La Paz and stretching northward, final destination as yet unknown.

When the land expedition reached San Diego Bay, they found a sea caravan awaiting them, but filled with scurvy. Most of the sailors were already dead. After founding San Diego, California Governor Juan Portolá left the new community in charge of Father Junípero Serra and went north to continue the occupation and find Monterey Bay. He also sought a bay to the north, named San Francisco by a shipwrecked sailor, Sebastián Rodríguez de Cermeñon, in 1595. Portolá failed to recognize Monterey from the land side, as it is a rather open harbor, and continued northward until he found San Francisco Bay. Portolá was actually the first European to see San Francisco, as it now appears that Rodríguez had been at Point Reyes instead. All others had missed it because the mouth of the Golden Gate is hard to spot from the sea. Portolá easily found it from the land side, however.

Although Portolá did not recognize Monterey from the land side, his description triggered Serra to realize that the soldier had been there. Under Serra's urging, the two men returned the following year (1770) and set up a new presidio and mission. Then they returned to Mexico City, leaving the new settlements functioning under a subordinate. There, Father Serra persuaded the government not to give up the fledgling California missions, but rather to strengthen them. To guarantee their livelihood, Viceroy António María Bucareli sent Juan Bautista de Anza by land to reprovision them via the Gila Trail and establish new missions and presidios. These missions were set up about one day's travel (40 miles) apart. Eventually there were 21 missions all connected by the Camino Real, from San Diego to beyond San Francisco Bay at Sonoma.

Connected to the rest of the United States after the Mexican Cession of 1848 by the Gila Trail, the Camino Real brought miners north from the southern states to the gold diggings. Most attempts to improve the road or get mail service organized in a methodical manner failed in the decade of the 1850s. Everyone was too interested in gold prospecting to the exclusion of normal commercial activities. The few men who made their riches off the miners had their establishments at San Francisco or in the goldfields proper. By the time of the Civil War, however, gold mining was shifting into the hands of the large operators, which returned the people's attention to the ignored parts of the state. Roads were abominable—not only in disrepair but dominated by road agents who robbed and murdered at will. The first mail contractor in the state, John Caldwell, disappeared, never to be seen again. Most mail went by sea, coming overland at the Panamanian Isthmus and then being carried by the Pacific Mail Steamship Company to California and points north.

In 1858, a new mail contractor appeared on the scene—John Butterfield and his Overland Mail Company. This event marked the return of mails and passengers to the Gila Trail through its feeder points in Memphis and St. Louis. The three-week trip was considered something of a miracle in speed, since much mail had been arriving a year late. It is still debatable whether the mail coaches actually went through Los Angeles—they were required only to get to San Francisco after leaving Fort Yuma. The route was variable. Eventually, the promise of an increase in business did cause the route to go into the City of Angels and up the old Camino Real. Because speed and a modicum of comfort and safety required better roads, the passes north of Los Angeles were leveled and graded. Smaller private lines called on the coastal communities as soon as the nearly nonexistent road to San Luis Obispo was rebuilt. It took until 1875 before this was done—the intervening time was spent in political and legal entanglements between various county commissioners and road contractors. The Civil War interrupted the transcontinental stage anyway, as did the Apache wars in Arizona, lasting until 1872.

At the same time, mail contracts went to the Southern Pacific, pushing its way south inland along the old Butterfield route. It did not take long for the trains to become the chosen mode of transportation. This left the stagecoaches to work the small communities bypassed by the rails or farther west along the Camino Real. At the turn of the century, the arrival of the automobile began to change California's love affair with trains; the flexibility and independence of the newer form of transportation became irresistible.

Between 1895 and 1912, Americans purchased 1 million cars, and Californians bought more than their fair share. Good roads had to follow, and in 1909, Governor James N. Gillette created the California Highway Commission. One of the first beneficiaries of highway building was the Camino Real. By 1911, the Progressive governor, Hiram Johnson, had two routes running the length of the state, one of which is today's U.S. Highway 101 along the Camino Real and the other, State Highway 99, which is paralleled by today's Interstate 5.

See also California Trail; Camino Real (Texas); Gila Trail; Roads and Highways since World War I.

References Berger, John A., *The Franciscan Missions of California* (1948); Bolton, Herbert E., *Outpost of Empire* (1931); Corle, Edwin, *The Royal Highway* (1949); Dunlop, Richard, *Great Trails of the West* (1971); Hague, Harlan, *The Road to California* (1978); Maynard, Theodore, *The Long Road of Father Serra* (1954); Moody, Ralph, *The Old Trails West* (1963); Outland, Charles F., *Stagecoaching on El Camino Real* (1973); Reisenberg, Felix, Jr., *The Golden Road* (1962); Weber, David J., *The Spanish Frontier in North America* (1992).

Camino Real (Texas)

From Saltillo in sun-parched Coahuila to Nachitoches on the humid banks of the Red River, the Camino Real ran through the Spanish province of Texas, later a part of Mexico, then an independent republic, and finally part of the United States, interrupted by a brief four years with the Confederate States of America. Like all early roads in North America, the Camino Real was a series of trails, some used one year, some another, depending on the course of rivers, how much rain fell, and how much traffic wore ruts in the surface that could not be repaired. It was a party of refugees from the failed Hernando de Soto expedition who first crossed the plains where the road would go. Led by Alvar Nuñez Cabeza de Vaca, they wandered for years seeking the outposts of Spanish rule and eventual salvation in Mexico. In 1575, a group of settlers founded Saltillo, and the first leg of the Camino Real had been laid.

Ten years later, Viceroy Alvaro Manrique de Zuñiga created a new concept on how the Indians of New Spain were to be brought under Spanish rule. He emphasized peaceful conversion—a far cry from the policy of conquest by fire and bloodshed of earlier administrations. Priests and a handful of soldiers would go into an area and offer technological assistance and protection to local tribesmen. It was agriculture and religion, not gold and the sword. Education centered on how to survive this life and the next, and it became an unquestioned (if unequivocal) success. And as the friars moved north, they built the road that became the lifeline for the missions. But across the Rio Grande, hostiles kept the system at bay. It was not until the visit to Texas in the 1680s by the Frenchman René Robert Cavelier, the Sieur de la Salle, looking for the mouth of the Mississippi River (he missed it) that the Spanish made their final move to the east to protect their interests in Texas.

Although he was killed by mutinous subordinates after the expedition proved a fiasco, La Salle's expedition stimulated the extension of Spanish power across the Great River. Again, Spanish purposes were twofold: the salvation of souls and the protection of the silver mines in northern Mexico, the wealth of the empire. After two minor expeditions failed to locate the French presence, the first *entrada* under Father Damián Massanet and Captain Alonso de León, Jr., crossed the river into Texas in 1689 and advanced to La Salle's old fort near Lavaca Bay. Finding evidence of the French after four years of searching, León returned to Mexico to report. The following year, the soldier and priest returned to the site of the French fort and proceeded to the Neches River where they set up San Francisco de los Tejas Mission. Returning in 1691, Massanet and Captain Domingo Terán de los Ríos, first governor of the Province of Texas, were to create eight missions. But they found that the men left behind had been decimated by hostile Indians and disease. Terán took an expedition up to the Red River, but the attempt to establish two more missions failed from Indian hostilities. Shortly afterward, Terán returned to Mexico after a quarrel with Massanet, and the priest followed when the mission was

flooded out and the increasingly hostile Indians made staying unsafe.

The problem with the Texas missions was that they were too far away from proper communication and support in northern Mexico. To be successful, a road into Texas needed to be built. But it took two decades before the money and interest could be found, stimulated once again by permanent French settlement at New Orleans, Louisiana. With the French in possession of the Mississippi from origin to mouth, the Spanish had to fortify Texas to maintain their claim. This was especially evident after the Spanish friar, Francisco Hidalgo, had the nerve to ask the French for support to establish Texas missions, since the Spanish crown refused. The French sent Louis Juchereau de St. Denis, a native-born American fluent in the ways of the frontier and with powerful political connections in Paris, to feel out the situation in Texas. He traveled by way of today's Natchitoches, Louisiana, where he set up an outpost (1713), and on across Texas past what is now San Antonio to the new outpost at San Juan Bautista de Rio Grande, the Spanish gateway to Texas on the Camino Real until the founding of Laredo in 1755 absorbed much of the traffic.

St. Denis' appearance on the Rio Grande and Father Hidalgo's letter were enough to trigger action in Mexico City. Captain Diego Ramón was put in charge of a massive expedition into east Texas. A very flexible St. Denis agreed to be his guide. The expedition was unusual as it contained four women. In 1716, the Spanish arrived among the Tejas Indians on the Neches and began setting up what would eventually be ten missions. It was hoped that the Tejas, as the most friendly and organized of the local inhabitants, would give the Spanish a sufficient base to christianize others and firmly establish Spanish power in the region. To back up the missions, soldiers created four presidios at San Antonio de Bexar, La Bahía (Goliad), Dolores on the Neches, and Nuestra Señora de Pilar at the most advanced mission at San Miguel de los Adaes (Robeline, Louisiana, today). The whole system of missions and forts was connected with San Juan Bautista on the Rio Grande by the royal highway, *el camino real*, with Bexar as the halfway point and supply station for the east.

This became the first and main road network in Texas for years. From Laredo the road split, a northern branch going through San Antonio and a southern section through Goliad. Although the Spanish lost Los Adaes to a French military expedition briefly in 1719, the area was retaken two years later. The new settlement was declared the capital of the Province of Texas and remained so for the next 56 years. The actual boundaries of Texas remained vague throughout the era. On the south, the Spanish initially used the Trinity River in the late 1600s, but it was soon moved to the Medina River (early 1700s) and finally to the Nueces (late 1700s). Only the adverse result of the Mexican-American War (1848) recognized the U.S. claim of the Rio Grande, first asserted by the Texas revolutionaries in the 1830s. On the north, the Spanish claimed land nearly to the Red River in Louisiana, with the French claiming the Sabine River. The French position became valid only after Louisiana was sold to the Americans, who received Spanish recognition in the Adams-Onís Treaty of 1919.

But the boundaries of Texas changed in more important ways. Because of various European wars during the eighteenth century, the French lost their foothold in the Gulf region to the Spanish. This changed Texas from a frontier state to one of the interior provinces of New Spain (Mexico). But the biggest change came in 1783, when Spain profited from its alliance with the victorious Americans during the Revolutionary War. The elimination of Britain meant that the new vigorous, grasping American nation was on Spain's northern colonial boundary. Immediately, Americans penetrated the boundary, ostensibly for trading purposes.

But under Philip Nolan, a military expedition of *filibusteros* (mercenaries) came down the Camino Real, capturing Nacogdoches, Texas, and Goliad before being routed (1801). With Nolan dying in the fight, his compatriots rolled dice to see who would hang for firing upon soldiers of the king. One Ephraim Blackburn lost, but the others rotted in Spanish jails for years. Nolan's connections with the American general, James Wilkinson, secretly on the Spanish payroll, and Aaron Burr and his pretensions to an independent empire in the Southwest, can only be speculated upon. Similar expeditions had similar fates, especially the filibuster on behalf of the Mexican Revolution, defeated at the Battle of the Medina River (1813). After Mexican independence in 1821, the Camino Real was the route by which General António López de Santa Anna marched to crush the American revolutionaries in 1836, leading to the massacres at Goliad and the Alamo.

After the American takeover of Texas following the successful 1836 Revolution, settlement prospered, and the Camino Real was lost in a mass of roads built by the republic and the United States. In the early twentieth century, state Senator Louis J. Wortham won permission of the state legislature to survey the old road and erect 123 monuments between the Rio Grande and the Sabine. But Mrs. Lipscomb Norvell of the Texas Old Roads and Trails Committee of the Daughters of the American Revolution would not stop there. She kept at it until in 1921 Texas built State Highway 21 from San Antonio to the Sabine, as much of it as possible on the path of the Camino Real. It was the first such road sponsored by a state for purely historical purposes. Across the Sabine, Louisiana Highway 6 extends the route to Natchitoches (Los Adaes). West of San Antonio, Interstate 35 follows the old Camino Real to Laredo, the royal road down which so much of Texas history has passed.

See also Camino Real (California); Gila Trail; Roads and Highways since World War I.

References Carter, Hodding, *Doomed Road of Empire* (1963); Chipman, Donald E., *Spanish Texas* (1992); Cruz, Gilbert R., *Let There Be Towns* (1988); Dunlop, Richard, *Great Trails of the West* (1971); Faulk, Odie B., *The Last Years of Spanish Texas* (1964); Vigness, David M., *Spanish Texas* (1983); Weber, David J., *The Spanish Frontier in North America* (1992).

Canadian National Railways (CN)

Not only Canada's largest rail system, the Canadian National is also a telecommunications network, a chain of hotels, a dockyard, and a ferry, coastal-shipping, trucking, and bus line. On top of all that, it also provides business-consulting services on an international basis. Canada has had two major railways, the Canadian National, which is publicly owned, and the Canadian Pacific, which is private. The Canadian National was an outgrowth of World War I when Canada's railways came close to bankruptcy with the end of massive immigration. The rail lines had been built to capitalize on the influx of immigrants, not to make money on freight per se. To save the major eastern railways of Canada, parliament passed a law in 1919 that set up the publicly owned Canadian National Railway Corporation. It combined the National Transcontinental, the Canadian Northern, the Intercolonial (Prince Edward Island), and the Grand Trunk into one company. It also had a telegraph firm and the nucleus of what became Canadian Broadcasting Corporation.

The creator of the CN was Sir Henry W. Thornton. He brought all of the modern components together and created special immigrant services to settle new arrivals near possible jobs and help them adjust to the New World. Each year the CN would take men from the East and bring them west to help harvest Canada's vast grain crops. It was company policy to permit migrants and hobos to ride the trains so long as they were looking for work. The end of World War II found the CN with much old, worn-out equipment that had to be replaced. It also faced competition from truckers and airlines. Under the leadership of Donald Gordon, the CN undertook a vast modernization project converting to cheaper-to-run (one-third the cost of steam) diesels. It also absorbed the narrow gauge lines in Newfoundland and the ferries that connected them to the mainland. New rails, such as the Great Slave Lake Railroad, were extended into the northland as minerals were discovered and exploited. To better compete, the CN pioneered container and piggyback freight, unit trains, and specialized cars. Passenger travel was enhanced by new lightweight turbo-trains, and a new CN logo, called the "spaghetti" logo, was adopted to bring a modern look to trains.

See also Canadian Pacific Railway; Grand Trunk Railway; VIA Rail Canada, Incorporated.

References Dorin, Patrick C., *The Canadian National Railways' Story* (1975); Drury, George H., *The Historical Guide to North American Railroads* (1985); Drury, George H., *The Train-Watcher's Guide* (1990); Hubbard, Freeman, *Encyclopedia of North American Railroading* (1981); Stevens, G. R., *History of the Canadian National Railways* (1973).

Canadian Pacific Railway (CP Rail)

Legally referred to as Canadian Pacific Limited, although its rail operations and the whole company are best known as CP Rail, the old Canadian Pacific Railway, like its government-owned sister, the Canadian National, has branched out into a multibillion-dollar diversified company involved in land, sea, and air transportation, as well as exploiting natural resources, running a hotel chain, and managing real estate and manufacturing and financial services. The railroad aspect is marked by unit trains (particularly of coal and sulfur), made up of cars painted red with one end adorned with the modern logo: a black isosceles triangle, with each even side being the radius of a white circle that surrounds it, with the third side paralleling the car end.

The CP had its birth in the act that annexed British Columbia (a Hudson's Bay Company province) to the rest of the Dominion in 1871. The measure provided for a railway to link British Columbia with the eastern provinces. In 1881, the Canadian Pacific Company was chartered under Duncan McIntyre and James J. Hill (who resigned when the line stayed in Canada rather than using his lines in the United States around the south shore of Lake Superior), with the construction supervised by William C. Van Horne, an American railroader. Essentially, Van Horne linked together several independent routes and finished the rails across the Rockies and along the swampy banks of Lake Superior, establishing a new city, Vancouver, as his Pacific terminus. It was truly an "impossible railroad," as it was nicknamed, but the discovery of silver along the Kootenay River kept interest up. Van Horne refused to have the CP give away the service industries in the American fashion, and the CP kept its own food services, mail express, sleeping cars, and hotels in order to earn the maximum profit. So much money was pledged to the construction that had Van Horne failed he could have brought the whole Canadian national economy down with him. But he did not. He became director in 1885 and announced that he would retire when the stock reached $1,000 per share. It did so in 1899 and he left the firm to build another railroad in Cuba.

As with all successful enterprises, CP continued to grow and diversify. It ran a Pacific steamship line, bought into hotels, and increased the scope of its rail services. Fine passenger trains, the *Imperial Limited* (various types of coaches and sleepers), the *Trans Canada Limited* (all sleepers and diners), the *Atlantic Express* (eastbound daily), and the *Pacific Express* (westbound daily) were among the finest trains of their day. New lines were absorbed, giving the CP control of rails on Vancouver Island and in northern areas of several plains provinces. CP trains held passenger speed records that were continued later under the VIA contracts. In 1942, CP Air Lines took over extensive brush routes in the Far North. CP has emphasized the notion of keeping itself modern. The first lightweight aluminum cars and the first double-decker passenger trains, all with air-conditioning, were introduced on the CP in the 1950s. CP also led the way into computerized yards and freight consists. In the 1970s CP gave its passenger service and equipment to VIA. By the 1980s, Union Pacific and CP agreed to share motive power rather than make up new trains when consists crossed the international border to save time and costs.

See also Canadian National Railways; Milwaukee Road; Soo Line; VIA Rail Canada, Incorporated.

References Berton, Pierre, *The Impossible Railway* (1972); Drury, George H., *The Historical Guide to* North American Railroads (1985); Drury, George H., *The Train-Watcher's Guide* (1990); Hubbard, Freeman, *Encyclopedia of North American Railroading* (1981); Lamb, W. K., *The History of the Canadian Pacific Railway* (1977); LaValle, Omer, *Van Horne's Road* (1975); MacBeth, Roderick G., *The Romance of the Canadian Pacific Railway* (1934); Mercer, Lloyd J., *Railroads and Land Grant Policy* (1982); Vaughn, Walter, *The Life and Work of Sir William Van Horne* (1920).

Canals

Canals are wholly or partially artificial waterways that convey carriage or, in the case of irrigation, water, from point to point. Up to the mid-nineteenth century, canals provided the surest and most consistent all-weather overland route for transportation, and generally were built with mostly artificial channels, the modern practice now tending to favor alteration of rivers. Like railroads, canal courses tended to be massive engineering projects with much land movement designed to guarantee a more or less level route. In the early days, power to move the canal vessels was supplied by men or animals moving along the sides of the canal on specially constructed towpaths yoked to the boats by long towropes. The scientific principle of canals was simple—one horse can haul 2 tons on a macadam road, but the same horse can tow 50 tons if the load floats on water in a specially designed towboat known as a "canawler."

The most important feature of the canal is the lock, a device that raises and lowers water levels, which gives the canal its ability to traverse terrain of varying elevations. The lock is a rectangular structure, the measurements of which determine more than any other the size of the barge that can utilize its functions. The lock has a gate at each end that allows water to flow into or out of the structure, thus raising or lowering the boat to the next canal level. The most common gate is a miter gate—two leaves of wood, iron, or steel that swing from the lock sides and meet at the center in a slight angle that generally points toward the higher level. Ten feet was considered the maximum lift achievable in the early nineteenth century, but modern structures are so improved as to be able to achieve a lift of over 40 feet.

The level of water was guaranteed by the use of wickets in the gates, which when opened allowed water to fill or drain the lock, depending on whether this was done on the upstream or downstream side. More modern locks use massive culverts, those of the Panama Canal, for example, being the size of a railway tunnel. Gates are generally so well balanced that they can be opened or closed by a single man or a small electric motor. In the nineteenth century, it was not unusual to use an inclined plane to move boats from one level to another, but the process greatly lessened the size and weight of the canal boat used. It was New York's ability to utilize simple locks for its Erie Canal that gave it the initial advantage over Pennsylvania's route across the Appalachian Mountains, which had to rely on inclined planes. Other routes would have to await the engineering innovations of railroads and tunnels.

American canals were largely based on their English predecessors, who built upon earlier French examples. In England such excavations were called "navigations," and the men who built them, "navigators," or "navvies" for short, which became a common term for a day laborer. In the United States the first canals were built at South Hadley, Massachusetts, and Richmond, Virginia. Most of these early structures merely bypassed waterfalls along the rivers, and those in Massachusetts made extensive use of inclined planes, until the completion of the Middlesex Canal in 1804. Running from Lowell to Charleston, the latter canal was 31 miles long and fed by the Concord River. In Virginia, interest in canal building preceded the American Revolution. But it took until the 1780s before the James River Company and the Potomac River Company (George Washington was one of its original investors) were organized. They became the nuclei of the James River & Kanawha and the Chesapeake & Ohio (C&O) canals.

Despite these earlier attempts, there were only 100 miles of canal in the United States as of 1816. There had been nothing yet to rival the canal era that had swept Europe during the preceding century. The main reason nothing was done was the great expense, which required amounts of capital not available before then. Besides, few of the earlier efforts had proved to be financial successes. Neither Middlesex Canal near Boston, the Dismal Swamp Canal between Norfolk and Albemarle Sound, nor the Santee Canal above Charleston were profitable. Worse, they required a constant influx of capital from new and original investors. Finally, canal engineering was almost unknown in the New World. To men in the know, all of this bespoke the need for some kind of governmental coordination and monetary assistance.

The big question in the United States after the War of 1812 was how to develop the West and consolidate it with the East. The lack of transportation over the Appalachian Mountains had led to continued questioning of the validity of the American Union in the early National Period, ranging from the Whiskey Rebellion to the Burr Conspiracy. By the War of 1812, the economic character of America was changing, and the Middle States emerged with a new, expanding base of industrialism. The key ports destined to benefit from this growth were New York City, Philadelphia, and Baltimore. After the war, the federal government responded to this economic expansion with a binge of national activity, prompted by America's alleged second victory (it was more like a tie, but nobody cared) over Great Britain. The Congress passed a series of nationalistic bills that were designed to promote the nation as a whole, but which seemed to assist the growth of New York's competitors in Pennsylvania (the Second Bank of the United States) and Maryland (the National Road—currently U.S. Highway 40).

But Philadelphia and Baltimore both had geographic disadvantages compared to New York City. It was no accident that the Baltimore & Ohio Railroad was one of America's earliest rail trunk lines, or that the Pennsylvania Railroad would become one of the finest-managed lines in the nation.

But all that would have to wait. Now smart politics and geography were about to make New York City the gateway to the West and New York the Empire State.

In the 1820s, New York's population growth was half again as big as all of New England's, and most of it occurred in the western part of the state. Moreover, the use of gypsum fertilizer increased the value and productive capabilities of western farmlands during this period. The key was that only New York had a more or less level route across the Appalachians to the Great Lakes and the Middle West: the Mohawk River Valley. As the fall line on the Mohawk is at Rome, New York, the earliest idea was a canal from Rome to Oswego on Lake Ontario along a centuries-old Indian route. But the shallowness of the rivers would necessitate much dredging, and the idea of a larger canal built from scratch was soon in vogue. A cross-country canal would require only three unloadings from western New York to New York City: from lake boats to canal boats at Buffalo, from canal boats to river boats at Albany, and from river boats to ocean vessels at the port city. The Lake Ontario route, however, would entail two more: to canal boats around Niagara Falls and from lake boats to river boats at Oswego. Also, the lake route was open to easy British interdiction from Canada. According to Robert Fulton of steamboat fame, this had to be a decisive factor after the recent War of 1812. (The treaty of 1819, which demilitarized the Great Lakes, was not yet a reality.) And the Middlesex canal in Massachusetts had demonstrated that a canal must tap deep into the Middle West for trade to be profitable.

New York now moved to develop a grand plan to exploit the West with the Erie Canal. Its goals were to develop western New York and to draw business from the Old Northwest (Ohio, Indiana, Illinois, Michigan, Wisconsin, and Minnesota) to New York City, trade that normally went to Canada down the St. Lawrence River. New York's canal system would also intercept trade destined for New Orleans. As Montréal had already proved that grain goods stored better in northern ports, a closer American alternative promised great economic opportunity.

The instantaneous success of the Erie Canal set off a craze nationwide for canal building east of the Mississippi. But in most locales the Appalachian Mountains proved too great a barrier to conquer until the advent of the railroad. In Virginia, the James River & Kanawha was not really begun until the 1830s and extended only to Buchanan, where it connected to a turnpike that led to the Kanawha Valley and the Ohio River. The C&O Canal took over the Potomac Company in 1824 and pushed its waterway from Georgetown in the District of Columbia to Cumberland, Maryland, at the foot of the Appalachians. Its designers intended to extend this route to Pittsburgh and compete with the Erie Canal, but projected costs of $22 million proved prohibitive, especially as the original investment had already exceeded that of the Erie Canal without the Erie's profitability. As it was, the C&O had had to tunnel and build 74 locks and an extensive aqueduct to reach Cumberland.

The C&O Canal's coal-hauling function was absorbed by the Chesapeake & Ohio Railroad by 1888, and it fell into disuse by 1924, ravaged by nature. Both the C&O and the James River Canals played a major transportation role during the Civil War, which also limited their further construction, as did the advent of railways. Virginians also opened up another canal between Portsmouth and Albemarle Sound in North Carolina. Designed to haul lumber through the swamps to the cities, the Dismal Swamp Company was created in 1787, but the canal was not completed until 1828. It continued to provide an alternate route behind Cape Henry until it was taken over by the federal government in 1929 and replaced by the Intracoastal Waterway.

Pennsylvania tried to keep up with her neighbors, but to no avail. Against much opposition from those who would not benefit from the canal's passage elsewhere (wagoneers who disliked the idea of competition and those supposedly crazed visionaries who pointed out that the mountains were too high and that railroads would do the job better later), the state plunged onward into the canal business in 1826. The proposed route was to run from Philadelphia to Pittsburgh and was dubbed the Pennsylvania Main Line Canal. At a cost of over $10 million, with 174 locks crossing 2,200-foot passes and using a combination of railroads, canals, and inclined planes, it was an engineering triumph and a first-class economic and political boondoggle. The locks and inclined planes delayed traffic; they were time consuming and costly. Like New York, Pennsylvania felt compelled to build branches to each outpost of opposition, but unlike her neighbor to the north, Pennsylvania built the whole system at once, at great cost and no income. By 1860, the state had spent $65.8 million on canals and had little to show for it but an empty treasury. It had had to compete for limited capital made more scarce by the Panic of 1837 and the increasing interest in railroads. It also had the terrain least suitable for canal building beyond the tidewater flats on its eastern border.

Pennsylvania and the other Middle Atlantic states did have an extensive and profitable system of "tidewater" canals that provided the Pennsylvania coalfields with connections to Chesapeake Bay, Philadelphia, and across New Jersey to New York City. The Union Canal connected the Schuylkill and the Susquehanna basins, the Schuylkill was canalled it its own right to the Delaware River, and another connection farther south, the Chesapeake and Delaware Canal, connected the two bays for which it was named. The Delaware and Raritan Canal crossed the New Jersey marshes to New Brunswick. The Morris Canal crossed New Jersey bringing Pennsylvania coal in from the Lehigh Valley, as did the Delaware and Hudson Canal, running from Honesdale, Pennsylvania, to Port Jervis, New York, on the Delaware, and then to Kingston on the Hudson. Indeed, the ability of nineteenth-century barges to go from the North Carolina sounds to New York City without ocean travel neatly previewed the whole concept of the Intracoas-

tal Canal of the twentieth century. Most of their carriage was absorbed by the "anthracite railroads" after the Civil War.

In the area west of the mountains and north of the Ohio River, the canal boom became a process of latching onto the prosperity of the Erie Canal by becoming a part of its system. Ohio was one of the first to accomplish this, linking the Ohio River with Lake Erie. Begun in 1825 in anticipation of the Erie Canal's success, Ohio constructed two state canals and numerous smaller ones. The Ohio and Erie Canal connected the Great Lakes with the Ohio between Cleveland and Portsmouth. The Miami and Erie Canal ran from Cincinnati to Toledo, and was completed by 1845. Both canals were well planned and constructed by engineers imported from New York. Most of the branches and smaller canals did not do well, but the canal fever was so strong that even private companies sprang up in a vain attempt to ride the crest to wealth. Often, local traffic was stronger than the cross-state business, but the whole boom fell to the advance of the rails in the 1850s, of which Ohio had the most mileage of any state by 1860.

Unlike Ohio, Indiana had a disastrous experience with canal building. Her most profitable project was a short route around the Falls of the Ohio across from Louisville, Kentucky. In 1836, the state voted in an extensive internal improvements program, the most important segment of which was the Wabash and Erie Canal. But before the undertaking could begin, the massive depression of 1837 set in and in no time at all Indiana was saddled with a large public debt of $13 million, most of it from incomplete transportation projects. But the state sold much of its debt, reserving all of its effort for the Wabash and Erie, which was finally completed in 1853. At 450 miles, it was the longest canal in the nation in its day. But it had died from neglect and rail competition by 1872.

Illinois did much better than its neighbor to the east. The first undertaking was to construct the Illinois and Michigan Canal along the old portage route between the

Chicago and Des Plaines Rivers, which would connect the Mississippi system with the Great Lakes. The result was a business boom for Chicago, which transshipped goods from the interior to the Erie Canal via the lake route. Intrigued by this profit, Illinois moved immediately into building the Illinois Central Railroad to tap areas untouched by the canal, like the central prairies. Another project that fell to rail competition in the end was the Hennepin Canal between Rock Island on the Mississippi inland to the Illinois River at Great Bend. It was built very late in the century (1892–1907) and soon became relegated to a drainage canal for flood waters. Utilizing the river system, the old canals, and the Chicago sanitary canals, the state eventually completed the Illinois Waterway, a modern shipping channel that is 327 miles long and still a direct route between the Windy City and the Deep South today.

All that remained was to connect Lake Superior to the rest of the Great Lakes System by the Sault Ste. Marie Canal at its opening into Lake Huron. The route was part of an old Native American portage used by the French. Only a mile in length, it traversed St. Mary's Falls. It had two deepwater locks 350 feet long and some 70 feet wide, and was financed by a land grant that helped open northern Michigan to settlement and speculation. Begun in 1853 and completed as the St. Mary's Falls Canal in 1855, the Sault Ste. Marie Canal would eventually be rebuilt several times, winding up with locks 1,200 feet long, 110 feet wide, and 32 feet deep. From the beginning, the "Soo" (as it was called) carried more traffic than any other of its sisters, even the fabled Erie. Indeed, it has carried more total traffic than any other canal in the world, surpassing the combined annual tonnages of the Panama, Kiel, and Suez Canals today.

The success and failure of canals are illuminating. Canals cost a lot to build. A good paved road cost $5,000 to $10,000 per mile. Canals usually came in at around $30,000 a mile. But before one dismisses them as expensive fads, one should remember that railroad costs ran more than that, unless they were built without drainage and right-of-way improvement, which lessened their costs and reliability accordingly. Canals also suffered by being built during a time of expensive money, brought on by the disastrous Panic of 1837, America's first really big economic depression, which lasted until the early 1840s. Finally, canals had the misfortune of becoming obsolete before they were even built, shelved for the often more expensive, but infinitely more flexible, railroads. Nonetheless, the canals played a decisive role in opening the cis-Mississippi West, particularly the Old Northwest, to settlement and commerce.

See also Chesapeake & Ohio Canal; Erie Canal; Great Lakes Freighters; Intracoastal Waterway; James River & Kanawha Canal; Panama Canal; Pennsylvania Main Line Canal; St. Lawrence Seaway.

References Baer, Christopher T., *Canals and Railroads of the Mid-Atlantic States, 1800–1860* (1981); Bourne, Russell, *Floating West* (1992); Chandler, Alfred D., Jr., "Anthracite Coal and the Beginnings of the Industrial Revolution," *Business History Review* (1972) 46: 143–181; Clarke, Mary S., *The Old Middlesex Canal* (1974); Dickinson, John, *To Build a Canal: Sault Ste. Marie, 1853–1854 and After* (1981); Drago, Harry S., *Canal Days in America* (1972); Dunaway, Wayland Fuller, *History of the James River and Kanawha Company* (1922); Goodrich, Carter, *Government Promotion of American Canals and Railroads, 1800–1890* (1960); Goodrich, Carter (ed.), *Canals and American Development* (1961); Gray, Ralph D., *The National Waterway: A History of the Chesapeake and Delaware Canal, 1769–1965* (1989); Harlow, Alvin F., *Old Towpaths: The Story of the American Canal Era* (1926); Hartz, Louis, *Economic Policy and Democratic Thought: Pennsylvania, 1776–1860* (1948); Hinshaw, Clifford Reginald, "North Carolina Canals before 1860," *North Carolina Historical Review* (1948) 25: 1–56; Hulbert, Archer Butler, *Historic Highways of America* (1902–1906); Johnson, Emory R., *Elements of Transportation* (1914); Kalata, Barbara N., *A Hundred Years, A Hundred Miles: New Jersey's Morris Canal* (1983); Kirkland, Edward C., *Men, Cities, and Transportation: A Study in New England History, 1820–1900* (1948); Lanati, Edward E., *A Brief Account of the Windsor Locks Canal* (1976); MacGill, Caroline E., et al., *History of Transportation in the United States before 1860* (1917); Phillips, U. B., *A History of Transportation in the Eastern Cotton Belt to 1860* (1908); Roberts, Christopher, *The Middlesex Canal* (1938); Sanderlin, Walter S., *The Great National Project: A History of the Chesapeake and Ohio Canal* (1946); Scheiber, Harry N., *Ohio Canal Era: A Case Study of Government and the Economy, 1820–*

1861 (1969); Shank, William H., *The Best from American Canals* (1972–1986); Shaw, Ronald E., *Canals for a Nation: The Canal Era in the United States, 1790–1860* (1990); Stapleton, Darwin H., *The Transfer of Early Industrial Technologies to America* (1987); Taylor, George Rogers, *The Transportation Revolution, 1815–1860* (1951); Wattenburg, Ben, *Busy Waterways* (1964).

Capper-Cramton Act (1930)

This congressional measure authorized the construction of the Mount Vernon Memorial Parkway that runs from the nation's capital to George Washington's house, now a national monument. The first part of the project had been let in 1928, for $4.5 million, to be built as a landscaped, four-lane, undivided highway on the pattern of the Westchester Parkway in New York. No expense was to be spared in making it the most beautiful road in the country, with its completion scheduled in time for Washington's three-hundredth birthday celebration. The timetable was adhered to and the project finished on time, but at a cost overrun. The project was such an improvement in highway construction and design that measures like the Capper-Cramton Act were passed to provide work for the many unemployed in the District of Columbia during the Great Depression.

See also Roads and Highways since World War I.

Reference U.S. Department of Transportation, Federal Highway Administration, *America's Highways* (1976).

Cargo Preference Act of 1954

A congressional measure to subsidize the American merchant marine, the Cargo Preference Act requires that 50 percent of governmentally owned cargoes be shipped on privately owned U.S.-flagged ships. It does not interfere with the Military Transportation Act of 1904, which limited such cargos to U.S. Navy cargo ships. The 1954 act has been strongly opposed by the military services as it increases their costs under already-tight budgets. The law has saved many shipping companies from bankruptcy, but has also kept in business many firms that could not make it in an open-

market environment. An amendment to the 1954 act in 1958 required certain agricultural producers to have 75 percent of their exports carried on U.S.-registered vessels, but neither the 1954 act nor the 1958 amendments have been strictly enforced, as agricultural representatives claim that the measures would price American farm exports out of the world market.

See also Merchant Marine; Military Transportation Act of 1904.

References Frankel, Ernst, *Regulation and Policies of American Shipping* (1982); Pedraja, René de la, *A Historical Dictionary of the U.S. Merchant Marine and Shipping Industry* (1994).

Central Overland California & Pike's Peak Express Company

A subsidiary of the famous freighting firm, Russell, Majors & Waddell, the Central Overland California & Pike's Peak Express Company was organized by William H. Russell and John S. Jones in 1860 to run mail, passengers, and express cargo via stagecoach between the Missouri River and Salt Lake City. Shortly thereafter, with the absorption of George Chorpenning's stage company (cut from its mail contract for poor service, a charge Chorpenning denied), the line operated all the way to California. The main purpose of the line was to show the feasibility of the Central Overland Route, in competition with other more southerly lines, to run all year around. Later, Russell instituted the Pony Express, delivering the mail from St. Joseph, Missouri, to Sacramento in ten days or less. Both the stage line and the Pony Express were great publicity stunts that provided a much-appreciated service and efforts by northerners to attract a nascent bid for the transcontinental railroad route, but neither business could return enough on the investment that went into setting them up. The result was the bankruptcy of Russell, Majors & Waddell by the end of 1861, and the melding of their operations into those of Ben Holladay's Overland Stage Company.

See also Adams Express Company; American Express Company; American Railway Express Company; Harnden & Company Express; Leavenworth & Pike's Peak Express Company; Pacific Union Express Company; Russell, Majors & Waddell Company; United States Express Company; Wells Fargo & Company.

References Harlow, Alvin F., *Old Waybills* (1934); Settle, Raymond W., and Mary L. Settle, *War Drums and Wagon Wheels* (1966).

Central Overland Route

The Central Overland Route was a combination of the Oregon Trail, the Mormon Trail, and the California Trail that led from St. Louis to San Francisco, particularly in the pre–Civil War West. It had its beginnings in events surrounding the Rocky Mountain fur trade. After news of the Lewis and Clark Expedition swept the East Coast, New Yorker John Jacob Astor decided to launch a fur-trading enterprise to exploit the Columbia River region. He sent a ship full of trade goods, the *Tonquin*, around Cape Horn to establish Fort Astoria at the mouth of the Columbia. A land party, under Wilson Hunt, was to duplicate the Lewis and Clark feat by going overland, trapping as they went. Hunt encountered one of Lewis' men, John Colter, on the Upper Missouri. Naked and destitute, Colter told a harrowing tale of escaping from the Blackfeet Indians by running for his life after his companions had been killed.

Heeding Colter's advice, which was backed up by others who had also been attacked, Hunt cut across the plains to the south, got lost but kept heading toward the mountains, crossed the Bighorn Mountains and the Grand Tetons, and wound up on the headwaters of the Snake River at an old cabin called Henry's Fort. Leaving part of his men there to trap, Hunt and the rest of the party floated down toward the Pacific in dugout canoes. Having run out of supplies, they abandoned their canoes to strike overland and made it to the coast in February 1812, but only through the generosity of Native Americans they met along the way. Once there, he found that local Indians, angered by slippery white trading methods, had attacked the *Tonquin* and killed most of the crew, leaving the rest, trapped in the hold, to blow themselves, their enemies, and the ship to pieces. Seeking to inform Astor

of the disaster, Hunt sent Robert Stuart back along the trail to St. Louis.

Picking up the men left at Fort Henry (they had made two fortunes in trapping only to have both stolen by Crow Indian bands), Stuart followed the advice of the friendly Shoshones and looped southward below the Tetons. There he became the first white man to find South Pass ("south" of Lewis and Clark's route), an opening through the mountains between the headwaters of the Green and Sweetwater Rivers. Here he forted up for the winter, and continued down the Platte River to the Missouri and St. Louis in the spring of 1813. For all practical purposes, Stuart had opened up what would later be the Oregon Trail. But the War of 1812, Astor's selling out to his St. Louis rivals, and the closing of the Oregon country to all Americans prevented him from gaining the fame that should have been his. That honor would go to the "free trappers" employed by Missourian William Ashley after the war.

The free trappers were the mountain men who explored the West and made travel by others possible before the Civil War. Ashley did not hire men like other fur companies did. Instead, he met these independent trappers in the Rocky Mountains each summer at a prearranged "rendezvous" with supplies and gewgaws, which he traded for their winter's fur catch. Then Ashley transshipped the furs down to St. Louis and sold them at a profit. Naturally, the free trappers considered themselves to be independent businessmen and superior to the engaged employees of men like Astor. Their names are legend: Jim Bridger, Hugh Glass, Tom Fitzpatrick, Jedediah Smith, William and Milton Sublette, and Kit Carson were just a few. In 1823, Smith and Fitzpatrick trapped up the Big Horn River to its headwaters. Loaded with furs, they knew that it would be dangerous to return in midwinter. In their search for a place to hole up, they crossed South Pass from the east, the same place that Stuart had found, and trapped the headwaters of the Green River all winter.

In the spring of 1824, they reasoned that the Sweetwater River would lead them back to the Missouri, and Fitzpatrick took it and the Platte back to St. Louis to sell their catch. It was an easy journey by canoe, and it avoided any interference by the feared Blackfeet far to the north. Meanwhile, Smith went to the rendezvous and told everyone of the beaver-rich country they had seen through South Pass. Everyone had forgotten about Stuart by then, and Smith and Fitzpatrick received credit for the discovery of the key to the central route to the Far West. More importantly, Fitzpatrick informed Ashley that the whole route was negotiable by wagon. This meant that the rendezvous could be bigger and richer than ever before. All that remained was for Smith to open up the rest of the route to Oregon in 1826, and the Oregon Trail was complete. When "Oregon fever" swept the East in the 1840s, thousands of emigrants began to use the road along the south bank of the Platte River, coming up from Independence, Missouri. This traffic was compounded by the creation of the Mormon Trail on the north bank, coming out of Council Bluffs in 1847, and the gold seekers who came after 1849.

As part of the program to improve wagon traffic on the Plains in the 1850s, Secretary of War Jefferson Davis proposed that the Mormon Trail be improved from Council Bluffs to Fort Kearny. The idea was to supply army posts out of the shorter trail through Omaha, relying more on riverboats than overland wagons. At the same time, various other routes across the Plains to the Pike's Peak and Denver areas still had to rely on Fort Leavenworth as a supply base. Of prime importance in this scheme was Fort Riley, on the Kansas River at the mouth of the Republican. In 1855, Congress appropriated $100,000 to be divided equally between two roads heading west from Fort Riley, one going to the Arkansas River and Bent's Fort, and the other headed out along the Republican River to Bridger's Pass. Lieutenant Francis Bryan supervised both routes, recommending that a series of bridges be constructed on the run to Bent's Fort and that a new branch of the Oregon Trail be laid out up Lodgepole Creek, south

of the traditional route. The main problem was that the route ended in Bridger's Pass in southern Wyoming. It needed to be attached to the Overland Route somewhere to the west. Again, small bridges were constructed to assist the passage of wagons.

The most ambitious project along the Central Overland Route in the 1850s came with the improvement of the trail from Fort Kearny to Honey Lake, Nevada, through South Pass. The work began under Frederick W. Lander, a civil engineer. Lander found two routes from South Pass to City Rocks, north of the Great Salt Lake. Both routes straightened out the Oregon and California Trails better than the existing Sublette Cutoff. The survey got caught up in the Mormon War and in an excessive expenditure of funds that derailed the project and brought on a series of accusations and recriminations among the army, Washington, and Lander. In the end, the engineer won out and spent the next three years supervising adjustments to the old California Trail along the Humboldt River and concluding a truce with Chief Winnemucca of the Paiutes, who was angry with whites trespassing over his land. Lander then improved water sources, constructing water tanks and wells. He finished his service by publishing an emigrant's guide outlining the changes and their advantages to the public.

By the time of the Civil War, the Central Overland Route had seen its heyday. Pioneered by the mountain men, utilized by the fur barons and freighters, followed by settlers, and improved by the government, it eventually became the path of the Union Pacific Railroad, U.S. Highways 26 and 30, and Interstates 80 and 84. The Big Medicine Trail, as it was known to Native Americans amazed by the hordes of whites who used it, became the main route between St. Louis and the Pacific—all because the Blackfeet had closed the Lewis and Clark Trail. It also meant that the way west would be by wheels, not water, because the Platte (an inch deep and a mile wide, according to the old saw) was virtually unnavigable.

See also California Trail; Lewis and Clark Trail; Mormon Trail; Oregon Trail.

References Drago, Harry S., *Roads to Empire* (1968); Dunlop, Richard, *Great Trails of the West* (1971); Eggenhofer, Nick, *Wagons, Mules, and Men* (1961); Gregg, Josiah, *Commerce of the Prairies* (1884); Hafen, LeRoy R., *The Overland Mail, 1849–1869* (1926); Jackson, W. Turrentine, *Wagon Roads West* (1952); Laut, Agnes, *Overland Trail* (1929); Majors, Alexander, *Seventy Years on the Frontier* (1893); Monaghan, Jay, *The Overland Trail* (1947); Moody, Ralph, *Old Trails West* (1963); Paden, Irene, *Wake of the Prairie Schooner* (1943); Settle, Raymond W., and Mary L. Settle, *Empire on Wheels* (1949); Settle, Raymond W., and Mary L. Settle, *Saddles and Spurs* (1955); Settle, Raymond W., and Mary L. Settle, *War Drums and Wagon Wheels* (1966).

Charles River Bridge Company v. Warren Bridge Company 11 Peters 240 (1837)

A U.S. Supreme Court decision announced by Chief Justice Roger B. Taney for the majority, *Charles River Bridge Company v. Warren* ruled that a contract could be construed as narrowly as possible by the state or federal government in the public interest, modifying the sanctity of contract doctrine and its broader implied rights as announced by Chief Justice John Marshal for the Court in the earlier case of *Dartmouth College v. Woodward* (1819). The Charles River Bridge Company had been granted a nonexclusive right to erect a toll bridge across the Charles River at Cambridge, Massachusetts. Over the years the bridge became rundown, rickety, too narrow for modern commerce, and a traffic hazard and bottleneck. The company refused to improve the old structure, so the city government let another contract to a new, competing company, the Warren Bridge Company, to build another structure. The Charles River Bridge Company cried foul and the court case ensued, with the above results. The ruling revealed a more flexible economic policy that typified Jacksonian democracy of which Chief Justice Taney was an exemplar, which emphasized competition over exclusivity. Such a policy gave impetus to transportation projects and improvements by opening the field to competitive ideas and inventions.

See also *Gibbons v. Ogden.*
References Kelly, Alfred H., and Winfred A. Harbison, *The American Constitution: Its Origins and Development* (1948); Swisher, Carl B., *The Taney Period* (1974); Warren, Charles, *The Supreme Court* (1922); White, G. Edward, and Gerald Gunther, *The Marshall Court, 1815–1825* (1988).

Chesapeake & Ohio Canal (C&O)

The Chesapeake & Ohio Canal had as it purpose to develop the Potomac River basin as the gateway to the West. In this endeavor, the two cities of importance on the eastern seaboard were Washington and Baltimore. The canal's origin lay in the Potomac Company, an entity that had the backing of George Washington and other Federalist politicians. These men saw the financial support of the federal government as essential to the success of their transportation projects, an idea put forth by Washington's secretary of the treasury, Alexander Hamilton, in his *Report on Manufactures* in 1791. Even staunch Republicans like James Madison and Albert Gallatin saw that federal financing for internal improvements benefited the nation at large. They differed mainly in how the financing ought to be effected: by appropriation or by reserving a percentage from the sale of public lands.

Washington's original Potomac Company was organized to extend navigation from Georgetown to Harpers Ferry and onward to the Monongahela River. He wanted to turn western trade to Virginia while the Erie Canal was still a dream far in the future. To achieve this, Washington appealed to Baltimore merchants, as the greater part of any Potomac project would be in their state. He gained their backing at the 1785 Mount Vernon Conference, and the company was chartered. The first parts of the canal were built in five sections around the five rapids above Georgetown, beginning at the Great Falls. These projects strained the company's finances to the maximum and increased the company's desire for federal aid. But this was an era of state power at the expense of federal influence.

In 1825, however, John Quincy Adams became president and the notion of Henry

Clay's American System waxed strong for the next four years. Under this influence a new company was chartered to replace the old Potomac Company and called the Chesapeake & Ohio Canal Company, under the leadership of Charles Fenton Mercer. Members of Congress bought much of its original stock offering, and President Adams turned the first spadeful of dirt. Mercer was not above using the canal's location to influence Washington politicians. His main problem was where to locate the eastern terminus of the ditch. Baltimore, Bladensburg, Georgetown, and Alexandria all wanted the terminal, and in the end Alexandria won, as it was the largest and closest harbor to the old diggings. An imposing aqueduct carried the canal across the Potomac. But in the long run, the failure to obtain a Chesapeake outlet fatally doomed the canal even before the Civil War. The railroads did the rest.

Construction of the C&O began with a flourish. The engineers were led by Benjamin Wright and Nathan Roberts of Erie Canal fame. Also present was Charles Ellet who, in league with John Roebling, would become one of the best American engineers in the antebellum years. The problems were much the same as with the Erie Canal, and the labor consisted largely of Irishmen, many of whom were recruited abroad. The canal company also hired many German immigrants, and in 1838 there was a demand by veteran laborers for a closed shop to guarantee jobs to the already-employed. The company refused and federal troops had to be called in on two occasions to preserve the peace.

The canal reached the coal mines at Cumberland in 1850, the farthest west it would go. The C&O's greatest engineering achievement was the Paw Paw Tunnel, a bore 3,118 feet long, complete with towpaths and two ventilation shafts. The canal was 185 miles long and had 74 locks and a rise of 609 feet. The channel was 50 feet wide above Harpers Ferry, but narrowed to 17 feet in the tunnel. But it suffered the problem that faced most canals except the fabled Erie—it did not produce enough

revenue to pay its debts. Moreover, the competing Baltimore & Ohio Railroad ran a parallel route and always offered lower freight rates and service directly to Chesapeake Bay. Finally, the company also suffered several natural disasters that threatened its existence, resulting in the whole project being sold in 1899 at a loss.

See also Canals.

References Johnston, Jay, "Waterway to Washington, The C&O Canal," *National Geographic* (March 1960) 117: 419–439; Sanderlin, Walter S., *The Great National Project: A History of the Chesapeake and Ohio Canal* (1946).

Chesapeake & Ohio Railway (C&O)

The Virginia legislature chartered the company that became the beginnings of the Chesapeake & Ohio Railway in 1836. First called the Louisa Railroad because it ran from the Hanover Junction of the Richmond, Fredericksburg & Potomac to Louisa Courthouse, the line soon became known as the Virginia Central. During the Civil War, it was the prime supply line for Robert E. Lee's Army of Northern Virginia in 1862 and 1863 and the target of continued Yankee cavalry raids in several unsuccessful attempts to close it. After the war, the remnants of the Virginia Central and the Covington & Ohio Railroad were reorganized as the Chesapeake & Ohio Railroad, a name changed to Railway during a subsequent reorganization in 1878. Its original roadbed used 197 miles of the old James River & Kanawah Canal towpath.

Both Virginia and West Virginia agreed to continue the expansion of the C&O after the Civil War. Through building and purchase, the line extended from Newport News to Cincinnati by 1888, and to Louisville four years later. Further expansion carried the line to Washington, D.C., in the East and into Indiana, Illinois, Michigan, Ontario Province (Canada), and Buffalo, New York, in the Middle West. Its primary cargo was coal, auto parts and automobiles, grain, and steel. Its passenger trains were among the finest of their time, and the "name train," the *George Washington*, bragged of its overnight service to Chicago with the slogan, "Sleep like a Kitten." The cat, nicknamed "Chessie," became the mascot and logo of the C&O System (1933), and in 1961 provided the new appellation for the combined C&O and Baltimore & Ohio (B&O) railroads.

The C&O was a big coal hauler, running as many as 70,000 hoppers, which meant that it needed big motive power. During the steam era this meant big 2-10-4's and compound Mallets like the 2-6-6-6 and the first noncompound (simple) 2-6-6-2. "Coal drags," as railroaders aptly call these trains, could have almost 12,000 tons behind them on the rails. In 1947, the C&O took delivery of a steam turbine locomotive that was 90 feet long without the tender and had a wheel arrangement of 4-8-0+4-8-4. Named the *Jawn Henry*, it had a coal bunker in front, then the boiler, and the turbine and generators in the rear. The tender came last with 25,000 gallons of water. At a speed of 40 miles per hour it could pull 21 tons. On a level run, it was able to reach speeds of up to 100 miles per hour. But it came way too late in the steam era to reach its potential, and like all of Chessie's steam engines, eventually gave way to diesels.

See also Baltimore & Ohio Railway; Chessie System; CSX Corporation; Locomotives, Steam Locomotives.

References Drury, George H., *The Historical Guide to North American Railroads* (1985); Drury, George H., *The Train-Watcher's Guide* (1990); Hubbard, Freeman, *Encyclopedia of North American Railroading* (1981); Lyon, Peter, *To Hell in a Day Coach* (1968); Nock, O. S., *Railways of the USA* (1979); Stover, John F., "Chesapeake & Ohio Railroad," in Keith L. Bryant, Jr. (ed.), *EABHB: Railroads in the Age of Regulation* (1988), 65–67, and in Robert L. Frey (ed.), *EABHB: Railroads in the Nineteenth Century* (1988), 41–43; Turner, Charles W., *Chessie's Road* (1956).

Chessie System

A combination of the Chesapeake & Ohio (C&O) Railway and the Baltimore & Ohio (B&O) Railroad, the Chessie System received its corporate name from the kitten once used to advertise C&O's crack passenger service between Chicago and Washington under the slogan, "Sleep like a Kitten." Appropriately, it is swiping chestnuts out of a fire in its modern depiction, because that

is what the Chessie System was designed to do. With the addition of the Western Maryland, a Pennsylvania–Maryland–West Virginia coal hauler, in 1972, the Chessie became the largest coal carrier (40 percent of its business) in the United States, possessing 78,000 hopper cars. The combined routes greatly complemented each other, flushing out areas the other could not conquer before, and making a circular route through 14 states, the District of Columbia, and one Canadian province. It also carried auto parts, automobiles, grain, and steel, and possessed a group of nonrailroad assets including forestlands, coal properties (over 500 mines), and investments. Along with the Norfolk Southern, the Chessie restructured railroading from the Atlantic to the Mississippi and forced the union of the Pennsylvania Railroad and the New York Central System, all of which eventually led to the creation of the northeastern conglomerate, Conrail. Chessie matched these developments by creating its own mega-railroad system, CSX Corporation.

See also Baltimore & Ohio Railroad; Chesapeake & Ohio Railway; CSX Corporation.

References Drury, George H., *The Historical Guide to North American Railroads* (1985); Drury, George H., *The Train-Watcher's Guide* (1990); Hubbard, Freeman, *Encyclopedia of North American Railroading* (1981); Nock, O. S., *Railways of the USA* (1979); Saunders, Richard, *The Railroad Mergers and the Coming of Conrail* (1978).

Chicago & North Western Railroad (C&NW)

Originally granted an Illinois state charter in 1836 to build a railroad from Chicago to the lead mines at Galena, the Chicago & North Western had a hard time getting from planning stage to reality. By 1855, the rails finally reached west to Fulton on the Mississippi. But the delay was crucial to the goal of the early road; the Illinois Central Railroad had beat them to the lead mines. But there were more lead lodes in the Old Northwest, and the railroad decided to head for them in Wisconsin. In 1859, the Chicago & North Western began using its modern name. By the end of the Civil War, it had linked Chicago and Milwaukee and fairly well covered the state of Wisconsin. Other extensions and purchases of existing lines (some of which operated as separate corporate structures within the C&NW system) expanded the C&NW to Omaha, Duluth, St. Louis, Kansas City, Rapid City, South Dakota, and Lander, Wyoming. From the beginning, it was the preferred route to connect the Southern (Central) Pacific and Union Pacific to Chicago, and joint passenger trains like the City of San Francisco were common until 1955 when they went to the Milwaukee Road. The C&NW had one peculiarity—it ran its trains left-handed in the English fashion as its early civil engineers had been from the British Isles.

The twentieth century brought slow, steady progress to the C&NW. The gigantic Proviso yard at Chicago was the biggest in the United States, so large that it had to operate as nine separate divisions. The C&NW was essentially a Granger railroad (i.e., one that bought from and sold to farmers across Iowa and the eastern Plains). But it also hauled a lot of iron ore, and its exploitation of the Powder River coalfields in Wyoming probably has much to do with its continued prosperity today. The Great Depression of the 1930s hit the C&NW hard. It lost about 75 percent of its business. Reorganization took until 1943, being delayed for years by waiting for the necessary Interstate Commerce Commission approval.

By that time, the C&NW's critical central position in the Middle West made it a natural carrier of wartime goods and passengers, a position that it kept in the years of peace that followed. Its speedy passenger trains between Chicago and the Twin Cities, the daylight 400 (its slogan was "400 miles in 400 minutes") and the North West Limited (a night run), were legendary for on-time arrival and comfort. At a time when the train world was abuzz about Burlington's Pioneer Zephyr and Union Pacific's M-10000, the C&NW was achieving better times with old standard steam engines and heavyweight, six-axle, steel passenger cars. This was the true beginning of modern, high-speed, American passenger service.

To compete with Burlington's silver Twin Zephyr and Milwaukee Road's yellow-orange Hiawatha in looks as well as speed, the C&NW came up with a flashy green-and-yellow paint scheme and streamlined, shrouded locomotives, and began referring to all of its fleet as "400s." There was Minnesota 400, the Twin Cities 400, the Dakota 400, the Rochester 400, the Flambeau 400 (to Wisconsin's resort country), the Peninsula 400 (to Michigan's Upper Peninsula), and the Kate Shelley 400 (into the Iowa plains), named after a 15-year-old heroine who saved the lives of an engine crew when their train collapsed a bridge weakened by floods near her home. A large commuter service into Chicago and between the Windy City, Milwaukee, and Madison (of course, there was a Capitol 400, a City of Milwaukee 400, and a Commuter 400) kept the railroad running double-decked cars into the 1970s. After World War II, steam was gradually phased out in favor of six-axle diesels.

But as profits rose, expenses graduated geometrically. The automobile hit the C&NW's passenger service as it did most railroads. The Union Pacific transferred its overland service to the Milwaukee Road. Bankruptcy loomed on the horizon again. In 1956, Ben W. Heineman took over, determined to save the aging railroad. He cut all steam locomotives and went over to diesel to save operating costs. Existing diesels were made to haul the tonnage; previous orders placed for new motive power were canceled. Passenger service was pruned and spiffed up, as were the commuter lines, the only profitable trains of their class in the whole country. Several smaller lines were incorporated into the C&NW system, including the Chicago & Great Western Railway.

By 1968, the C&NW was at the largest size in its history. But that would not last long as unprofitable sections of the road were closed down or sold off. In the early 1970s, the managers negotiated a sale of the railroad to its employees, and the C&NW logo now boasted the proud slogan, "Employee Owned," on all its engines. The paint on the motive power was standardized into one pattern, the familiar green and safety yellow, once used on the passenger service. The more subdued freight livery was dropped. C&NW also dropped its Falcon piggyback service as unprofitable, and shifted its interest to container freight (from American President Lines through Union Pacific), coal, and grain, using "unit trains" (one train of the same cars and cargo). A decline in the grain market has caused coal to surge to the top as the single biggest freight revenue producer. Although the employees sold out to the Blackstone Capital Partners in 1989, which proceeded to downsize the line even more than in the past, its coal-hauling unit trains from Wyoming, and trackage agreements with Union Pacific for the latter to come into Chicago once again on C&NW rails (1991), have kept the C&NW still among those modern mid-sized railroads that can make a profit; so much so, in fact, that Union Pacific announced its intention of merging with C&NW outright—a process still pending before the Interstate Commerce Commission (as of 1994).

See also Klitenic Plan; Milwaukee Road; Union Pacific Railroad.

References Bee, Roger, et al., *The Chicago Great Western in Minnesota* (1984); Casey, Robert J., and W. A. S. Douglas, *Pioneer Railroad* (1948); Dorin, Patrick C., *Chicago and North Western Power* (1972); Drury, George H., *The Historical Guide to North American Railroads* (1985); Drury, George H., *The Train-Watcher's Guide* (1990); Grant, H. Roger, *The Cornbelt Route* (1984); Grant, H. Roger, "Chicago & North Western Railroad," in Keith L. Bryant, Jr. (ed.), *EABHB: Railroads in the Age of Regulation* (1988) 69–71, and in Robert L. Frey (ed.), *EABHB: Railroads in the Nineteenth Century* (1988), 43–44; Grow, Lawrence, *On the 8:02* (1979); Hastings, Philip R., *Chicago Great Western Railway* (1981); Lyon, Peter, *To Hell in a Day Coach* (1968); Olmstead, Robert P., *Prairie Rails* (1979); Scribbins, Jim, *The 400 Story* (1982).

Chicago, Burlington & Quincy Railroad (CB&Q)

Chartered in 1848, the Illinois-based Chicago, Burlington & Quincy, often called simply "the Q," was one of the oldest rail companies in the Midwest. Its first rails were made of secondhand iron spiked to the top of 12 miles of wooden rails. Bought by a Boston, Massachusetts, investment firm, the company had adopted the name, which indicated its actual destinations. In 1865, the CB&Q was the first railroad to run trains into what would become Chicago's stockyards. It also managed a few other firsts over the years: It had one of the first bridges across the Mississippi River; it had the railway post office to sort mail while the train was running; it begot Kansas City's claim to fame as a rail center; it ran the first dining cars; it tested George Westinghouse's airbrake system that made him rich; and it built the first vista-dome car in its own shops. And more commonplace, it was robbed by the Jesse James gang in 1881, with the conductor being murdered. In the 1880s, the Q extended its mainline out to Denver. But throughout it all, it remained essentially a Granger railroad, supplying farmers on the Plains and buying their crop surpluses.

Because of this relationship, which the managers knew to be essential to its prosperity, the Q brought many European immigrants over, settled them on the Plains, and saw to it that they learned to survive and use the rails for their own (and the railroad's) good. Its slogans early on were "the Cheapest, Best and Quickest" and "the Original Dining Car Route." It had some of the best passenger service in American railroading. It ran the nation's first diesel-powered train, the *Pioneer Zephyr* (an articulated train, where the cars shared the tracks of those that preceded and followed them), also the subject of a Hollywood adventure film, and it ran many other trains of note, such as the *Twin Zephyr*, the *Denver Zephyr*, the *Texas Zephyr*, and, in conjunction with Western Pacific and the Rio Grande, the *California Zephyr*, arguably the single finest passenger train ever run. As the stock was owned 50-50 by the Great Northern and the Northern Pacific, who shared the same office building as headquarters, it was but a small step to create the Burlington Northern Incorporated in 1970. Its greatest handicap was not the Interstate Commerce Commission, but the unwieldy name proposed for the massive rail conglomerate: the

Great Northern Pacific & Burlington Lines. No wonder the name Burlington Northern won out.

See also Burlington Northern Incorporated; Forbes, John Murray.

References Drury, George H., *The Historical Guide to North American Railroads* (1985); Drury, George H., "The Chicago, Burlington & Qunicy Railroad," in Keith L. Bryant, Jr. (ed.), *EABHB: Railroads in the Age of Regulation* (1988), 71–73; Drury, George H., *The Train-Watcher's Guide* (1990); Grow, Lawrence, *On the 8:02* (1979); Hubbard, Freeman, *Encyclopedia of North American Railroading* (1981); Larson, John Lauritz, "Chicago, Burlington & Quincy Railroad," in Robert L. Frey (ed.), *EABHB: Railroads in the Nineteenth Century* (1988), 47–48; Lyon, Peter, *To Hell in a Day Coach* (1968); MacGregor, Bruce A., and Ted Benson, *Portrait of a Silver Lady* (1977); Overton, Richard C., *Burlington Route* (1965).

Chicago, Milwaukee, St. Paul & Pacific Railroad (CMSt P&P)
See Milwaukee Road.

Chicago, Rock Island & Pacific Railroad (CRI&P)
See Rock Island Lines.

Chilkoot Trail

In 1898, Canadian Mounties counted more than 60,000 people crossing the Chilkoot Pass in the Coast Range at the head of the Inside Passage of the Alaskan Sounds. There were so many of them that they had to stand in line, day after day. The problem was Canadian customs officials. No one was allowed across the international border without a ton of supplies to subsist on in the Klondike goldfields. No exceptions. Canada did not want to have a bunch of starving miners, come winter.

It took several trips for such a load to be hauled up and pass inspection. Lucky ones hired Native American packers, beefy men from the coastal tribes, to help carry the packs. They were hard bargainers and firm Presbyterian converts, who refused to work on Sundays. Up the narrow canyon they trudged, passable only by foot, 3,500 feet up, 28 miles each time. At the summit the trail rose at a rate of 1,800 feet in 3 miles, then 1,000 feet in a half mile. It was no place

for the weak. One had to pay someone to hold his space in line if he had to drop out for any reason. It rained constantly every day, and blizzards were possible at the summit even in July. An avalanche killed 60 in one swath. In later years, the railroads would use gentler White Pass to the south, some 600 feet lower; but this was gold fever, and the shortest route, no matter how difficult, was the one the miners would take. Over the summit, past the inspection station, it was another 548 miles to Dawson City and the gold.

It all began in 1897 when the *Excelsior* (aptly named) brought down a gang of prospectors from Alaska to Seattle, headquarters of the Alaskan trade. They filed off the steamer, each carrying bags of gold worth $500,000 to $750,000, in all—one man had a suitcase loaded with 200 pounds of nuggets worth nearly $55,000. The crowd went berserk. So did the rest of the United States and the world. Never mind that the early ones made all the good strikes. Every ship that could float (and a few that could not very well) was pressed into service. Beds were so full of those waiting to book passage that people slept wedged together like books. The ships were loaded to the point of capsizing. Of course, everyone paid full price for everything, full price plus a special miner's rate tacked on to maximize profits. Seattle was not a town run by greenhorns.

Through Haines, Skagway, and Dyea (a city of 20,000 that no longer exists but for one house) the throng moved onto the trail. There they moved forward single file in a peculiar shuffle, known as the "Chilkoot Lock-Step." Woe unto him who fell off the trail. He might lose his place in line. If lucky, he might pay to get it back or to cut into line where he was. Everything cost money on the road to the Klondike. They would follow up a trail so steep that footholds had to be cut out of the rock to proceed—the "Golden Stairs," they were called, in anticipation of what lay ahead. A couple of men stayed up all night to clean the stairs out, for which they received donations from the grateful miners. Everyone had drawn lots as their ship docked to see who would get to disembark first, person and gear. An elected beachmaster took charge of the process. No one was to leave the beach until the appointed hour, but the incoming tide had a way of quickening the evacuation. Teamsters charged $20 an hour when the tide was ebbing, $50 an hour when the greedy waves began to roll landward. But they only went to the trailhead, not beyond.

Once the prospectors reached Alaska, the odds of getting to the trail were slim. Gamblers, con men (well organized in gangs of over 100), and other temptations awaited the naive "cheechakos," as the dudes were labeled (the veteran miners were "sourdoughs," after the bread they baked). It was a dangerous job to run a con, especially if it involved the stealing of one's grubstake. Miners' courts prescribed quick hangings for malefactors. But the real money came from providing supplies to the newcomers. The cheechakos never brought the right stuff, or they brought too much. One could make a good business buying out the disheartened who had turned back and reselling their gear to new suckers, eager to cross the toughest climb in the Americas.

The Canadians had collected $150,000 in customs duties at the summit in 1898. The problem, for government and miner alike, was how to get the money back East, past the crooks, murders, and con men. Finally, Zachary Taylor Wood, a distant relative of the one-time American president, volunteered. Disguised as a Mountie, he hauled the cash down to Dyea and by skiff to Skagway. The gangs had tipsters all along the way and were waiting. Wood held them off at gunpoint. Just about the time he figured that he would have to surrender, a British ship nosed into the harbor, its crew armed with rifles. Wood slipped out to the Jacob's ladder and climbed aboard, safe at last. Returning miners did not have such luxuries.

From the summit the prospectors had to run the rivers to Dawson Creek. In the spring they ran dangerously full. Many turned back rather than risk the turbulent waters. It was not much easier by land, because sooner or later one had to reckon with crossing the flooded streams. Dysentery was common from the unsanitary conditions and abominable food of the trip. But everything went over the Chilkoot Trail by men's backs. Included were pianos for the saloons and bordellos (the girls had to walk, too), lumber, steamboats (knocked down and reassembled later), fine glassware (there were standards to uphold in the "hurdy-gurdy" houses), and every drop of food and drink. One tough Native American hauled a 350-pound barrel to the summit. Like all others, he dropped his load at the top and jumped over the side to toboggan to the bottom in a matter of minutes on mud and snow. There was no place to stay at the summit, and firewood was $1 a pound. Later a tramway was built in an effort to bring technology (and lucrative free enterprise) into the movement.

By 1899 it was all over. The White Pass & Yukon Railroad had come to the Klondike, pushing its way through White Pass out of Skagway. And a modicum of sanity returned to the process as the busted miners went home. Most of them had never struck it rich, had blown it all in the saloons and fancy parlors, or had fallen prey to some con game or outright robbery. But those who did make it found riches that lasted a lifetime and beyond. But few profited more than the wise merchants of Seattle, who stayed home and made a bundle on the going and returning argonauts. After the initial emptying of the city (mostly of expendable riff-raff and idealists), the city fathers set about to guarantee their place in business acumen. They organized the Alaska Steamship Company to get the cheechakos to their destinations (gold was found right on the sandy beaches of Nome after the Klondike) and sold them everything they needed and a lot more; they provided assay facilities for those returning, and hotels and other less reputable places boomed, coming and going—all at premium prices. The gold might have been panned in Alaska, but it was refined in Seattle—the true head of the Chilkoot Trail.

See also Bozeman Trail; California Trail; Gila Trail.

References Berton, Pierre, *Klondike Fever* (1958); Dunlop, Richard, *Great Trails of the West* (1971); Speidel, William C., *Sons of the Profits* (1967).

Chisholm Trail

After the Civil War, returning Texans found that, while spared the worst ravages of war, their state had gone to seed with the rest of the Confederacy. It was not so much that Texas was torn up; it was that everything had fallen into disrepair. Deep in the southwestern part of the state, this chaos manifested itself in the form of thousands of unbranded longhorn cattle (called "mavericks" in the trade), breeding and running wild on the prairies and bottomlands. Then came unbelievable news. The worthless wild bovines were worth big money back East, their hides needed to furnish the leather belts of the Industrial Revolution, their meat to feed the workers, and the fancy cuts in demand in the top hotels in New York and Philadelphia. All one had to do was get the cattle to a buyer. And the buyers, led by Joseph G. McCoy, let it be known that they were ready, cash in hand, to receive cattle at the railheads in Kansas. The result was the greatest movement of domestic animals in world history, up the cattle trails from Texas to the markets in Kansas. It became such a lucrative deal that, when the buffalo had been hunted into oblivion and the Native Americans defeated on the Plains, the cattlemen spread their enterprise northward into Colorado and Montana. The Cattle Kingdom was born.

The cattle trails are all gone today. The eastern and western sections of Interstate Highway 35—running from Laredo and Houston, through San Antonio, Dallas, Fort Worth, Oklahoma City, and Wichita—and I-135 to Salina and Abilene approximate the route the cattle took. But then there were numerous trails: the Sedalia on the Missouri Pacific Railroad; the Chisholm (probably the best known and named for Indian trader Jesse Chisholm, who pioneered it as a trade route) to Newton on the Santa Fe Railroad line or to Ellsworth and Abilene on the Kansas Pacific Railroad; the Western to Dodge City, again on the Santa Fe; and the Goodnight-Loving in the West, curving through Colorado up to Cheyenne on the Union Pacific. All of the railroads sent the beef to Chicago, whose one-mile-square stockyards became the standard for the whole butchering and meatpacking business.

Moving a thousand cattle to a railhead with a dozen cowhands took real organization. Each trail herd had a trail boss, a man with near-dictatorial powers; his assistant, the ramrod; a cook in charge of the chuck (food) wagon; a wrangler, responsible for the horse herd (each cowboy had several horses and changed them three or four times a day); a scout, who rode on ahead and kept an eye out for water, competing herds, Native Americans (who usually let herds pass with the ransom of a few head), and worst of all, outlaws; and the cowhands, who rode point (giving the herd direction), flank (keeping the herd in a tight column), or drag (bringing up the rear, pushing stragglers, and eating the dust of everyone else). Cowboys usually rotated jobs, so no one got stuck with drag all the time. After soaking rains, freezing sleet, and a dozen or more stampedes (one outfit suffered 18 in one run to Abilene), no wonder the cowboys raised pluperfect hell at the trail's end. It was the cattle trail that gave America its western heroes like Wild Bill Hickok, Bat Masterson, and Wyatt Earp. They were the subjects of Ned Buntline's dime novels and made Hollywood a bundle a century later.

The drives tended to move westward year by year, following the progress of the railroads. But the real push west came from settlers and Native Americans who protested the chewing up of their lands by the cloven hoofs of the steers. And the Texas wild cattle brought tick fever and other diseases that could wreak havoc on a farmer's bloodlined herd. Kansas state law soon restricted the driving of cattle up from the south. Besides, the length of the trail wore off valuable poundage, especially the farther west the herds went, where the grass was minimal. The solution was to establish permanent ranches on the Plains, a process that

The Chisholm Trail was one of the most popular trails following the Civil War, as cowboys moved thousands of Texas cattle to railheads in Kansas for transport to other markets.

took the cattlemen up into Montana by the 1880s. Syndicates of easterners and European nobility all invested in the cattle industry. Barbed wire (invented in 1874) not only closed the open Plains to cattle drives, but it permitted cattlemen to fence off their ranches. Eventually the saturation point was reached and the Plains could take no more. Bovine grazing was destroying the ecology of the grasslands. The climax came in the Great Blizzards of 1885, 1886, and 1887, which left thousands of frozen carcasses in their wakes.

The cattle trails gave the United States a uniquely rich heritage known the world over. Picking up on Spanish words—after all, they were the people who brought the ancestors of the longhorns to America and became the first cowboys (*vaqueros*)— American English obtained a singular vernacular. The roundup became the *rodeo*, saddlebags and horsepacks were *aparejos*, stirrups were covered by pointed pieces of leather to protect a rider's boots called *tapaderos* or taps, the leather coverings that protected a cowboy's legs were *chaparreras*

or chaps, and the rope he threw was a *lariata* or lariat. His whole rig was a takeoff on the Spanish stock saddle—heavy wood covered in leather, with a high cantle and swells and horn—rugged enough to hold up under the weight of throwing a ton of wild beef. And the clothes that the cowboys used for practical reasons are still stylish and worn by a new genre of drugstore cowboy amateurs and rodeo professionals. The cattle trails are gone but the romance that they gave birth to endures.

See also Camino Real (Texas); Railroads from Appomattox to Deregulation.

References Atherton, Lewis, *The Cattle Kings* (1961); Dale, Edward Everette, *The Range Cattle Industry* (1930); Drago, Henry Sinclair, *Great American Cattle Trails* (1965); Dunlop, Richard, *Great Trails of the West* (1971); Dykstra, Robert R., *The Cattle Towns* (1968); Frantz, Joe B., and Julian E. Choate, Jr., *The American Cowboy* (1955); Gard, Wayne, *The Chisholm Trail* (1954); Jordan, Terry G., *Trails to Texas* (1981).

Chorpenning, George (1820–1894)

A Sommerset, Pennsylvania, man, George Chorpenning was an innkeeper when the gold strike in California lured him westward. He and two others wended their way to the goldfields on riverboats and by wagon. In 1851, with Absolam Woodward, Chorpenning secured the first mail contract between Sacramento and Salt Lake City. Delivery was to be made once a month. Using mule packs, they managed to cross the Sierra Nevada and reach the Mormon capital in 53 days, having been delayed by late snows. They continued the run, with Woodward being killed by Paiutes at the Malad River. Further delay in delivery by heavy snow in 1852 caused the federal government to cancel his contract and give it to W. L. Blanchard.

But Chorpenning went to Washington and got the contract reinstated and kept it until 1860. Chorpenning returned to California and increased his service, adding stagecoach runs and delivering on a weekly basis. The contract was again canceled on the assertion that he failed to fulfill it, but it may have been more political than anything else as it went to Russell, Majors & Waddell's Central Overland California & Pike's Peak Line. He went east again during the Civil War, helped raise two regiments of infantry, and served briefly as major in the First Maryland Volunteers. He filed a claim for nearly $500,000 against the government for services rendered delivering the mail. The government, however, stopped payment on the warrant issued to him and he never received the money. He died in poverty in 1894.

See also Central Overland & Pike's Peak Express Company; Russell, Majors & Waddell Company.

References Settle, Raymond W., and Mary L. Settle, *Saddles and Spurs* (1955); Settle, Raymond W., and Mary L. Settle, *War Drums and Wagon Wheels* (1966).

Chrysler, Walter P. (1875–1940)

Originally connected with American Locomotive Company (ALCO), Walter P. Chrysler left trains for automobiles in 1911 to become president of Buick. Retired, but with a reputation for getting things done, Chrysler was brought in to restructure Willys-

Overland by bankers working on that company's debt in 1920. Chrysler sold off its subsidiary nonauto divisions and cut John Willys' salary in half (although Chrysler himself made a cool million a year by prior agreement). He also brought over several engineers from Studebaker to design and produce a new six-cylinder car, but the company could not be saved. Willys went under in 1921, although Willys himself managed to buy it back within the year.

Auto industry leader Walter P. Chrysler

Chrysler really did not do Willys justice. He was also involved at Maxwell and put most of his effort in there. Maxwell was the remnant of Benjamin Briscoe's old empire and in big trouble in the post–World War I recession. Maxwell had a good reputation but had been poorly engineered of late. Chrysler changed all that. He reengineered the drive train and sold off outdated inventory. The reorganized company put out new models, one of which bore the Chrysler name and was an enclosed vehicle, the latest innovation in modern cars. The use of new machinery allowed the enclosed car to be built at a similar price to the open cars, a problem that had limited its sales before. Chrysler competed in the middle-range market with Buick (which Chrysler knew well from his association with GM) and had a high-performance, high-compression, six-cylinder engine and an expensive appearance. This success made him an instant industry leader that the others had to catch up with. The Chrysler became known as the "engineer's car." Bankers were impressed and the money rolled in (one loan was $50 million). This allowed Chrysler to replace the Maxwell with a four-cylinder Chrysler.

Chrysler still kept an eye on GM. What he wanted to do was introduce "Sloanism" to his revitalized firm, which was the notion of having a model in every price range. What he needed were a low-priced model to take on Ford and Chevy and production and distribution facilities. All of this would be expensive and time consuming to create from scratch. But Dodge Brothers was up for sale, and it had the facilities and distributorships. So Chrysler bought Dodge in 1927. Overnight, he had become the third biggest car manufacturer in the United States. He immediately announced a new vehicle, the Plymouth. The first Plymouths were modified Chryslers, but in the matter of a year a new model was out, competing with Ford and Chevrolet on the GM principle: giving more value per dollar. He soon had the Plymouth (to compete with Ford and Chevy), the Dodge (with Pontiac), the DeSoto (with Oldsmobile), the Chrysler (with Buick), and the Imperial (which challenged Cadillac) all in production. The appearance of Chrysler as a miniature GM forced Ford to reassess its position and to come out with Mercury and purchase Lincoln within a decade to compete.

See also Automobiles from Domestics to Imports; Automobiles in American Society.

References Chrysler, Walter P., *Life of an American Workman* (1950); Halberstam, David, *The Reckoning* (1986); Langworth, Richard M., and Jan P. Norbye, *The Complete History of the Chrysler Corporation* (1985); Moritz, Michael, and Barret Seaman, *Going for Broke* (1981); Motor Vehicle Manufacturers Association of the United States, *Automobiles of America* (1974); Scharchburg, Richard P., "Walter P. Chrysler," in George S. May (ed.), *Encyclopedia of American Business History and Biography: The Automobile Industry* (1990), 52–64; Shook, Robert L., *Turnaround* (1990); Thomas, Robert Paul, *An Analysis of the Pattern of Growth of the Automobile Industry* (1977).

Civil Aeronautics Act of 1938

After a series of fatal airline crashes were laid at the feet of the Department of Commerce and its diversified, uncooperative bureaus, the Civil Aeronautics Act of 1938 appeared. It removed all of the air safety regulatory functions from the Department of Commerce and placed them in the hands of a new commission, the independent Civil Aeronautics Authority (CAA). The regulatory functions of the Interstate Commerce Commission were also given to the new authority, as were the responsibilities of national airways management. Later, President Franklin D. Roosevelt, under the Reorganization Act of 1939, placed all air regulatory functions back in the Department of Commerce as the Civil Aeronautics Administration. In 1940, the CAA retained the functions of administration and safe operation of the nation's airways and a separate Civil Aeronautics Board (CAB) took over policy making and rate setting. This remained the situation until the Federal Aviation Agency came about in 1958.

See also Aeronautics; Black-McKellar Act; Federal Aviation Act; McNary-Watres Air Mail Act.

References Bilstein, Roger E., *Flight in America* (1994); Corbett, David, *Politics and the Airlines* (1965); Komons, Nick, *Bonfires to Beacons* (1978); Whitnah, Donald R., *Safer Skyways* (1966).

Clay, Henry (1777–1852)

Henry Clay was born in Hanover County, Virginia, on 12 April 1777 and died in Washington, D.C., on 29 June 1852. He studied law in Richmond and practiced his profession at Lexington, Kentucky, where he became a member of the state legislature. Elected to the U.S. House of Representatives (1811–1821, 1823–1825), Clay was a noted nationalist and a "War Hawk," pushing for the war of 1812 against Great Britain and for his American System of managed economic growth. As U.S. senator (1806–1807, 1809–1810, 1831–1842, and 1849–1852), he was noted for his sponsorship of the Missouri Compromise (1820), the Compromise Tariff of 1833, and the Compromise of 1850, all of which delayed the rupture between the North and South until 1860 and earned him the title of "the Great Pacificator." Clay was a clever diplomat (Treaty of Ghent, 1814) and secretary of state during the John Quincy Adams administration (1825–1829), noted for his support of Latin American revolutions for independence from Spain and pan-American cooperation. He was also an unsuccessful aspirant to the presidency (1824, 1832, 1844) under the banner of the National Republican and Whig parties.

Outwardly, "Harry of the West" was born to please. He was tall, lanky, towheaded, with gray-blue eyes and a mouth so wide that he complained that he could never learn to spit properly. At times high tempered and meddlesome, he got through life relying on his indolent charm, although he was not above engaging in an occasional duel. He was a superb conversationalist and could talk for hours on nearly any topic, sitting comfortably with snuffbox in hand. A gambler and alleged ladies man, Clay would stay up until all hours of the night, engaging in both pursuits. He did everything with captivating vitality, which endeared him to friend and foe alike. His political philosophy was expressed in his American System. His greatest fault, according to Secretary of the Treasury Albert Gallatin (1801–1814), was that Clay was "devoured with ambition."

Clay's shenanigans in the 1824 presidential election, the so-called Corrupt Bargain, which assured John Quincy Adams' victory, merely proved Gallatin's point. In a four-way race, Clay had come in last to Andrew Jackson, John Quincy Adams, and William Crawford, in that order. Since there was no candidate holding a majority vote (even though Jackson was close), the election was thrown into the House of Representatives to determine which of the top two men had

won (Adams or Jackson). As Jackson was far and away the more popular of the two selections nationwide, most expected the House, led by its speaker, Clay, would elect Old Hickory.

But Clay, impelled by a similarity of political philosophy with Adams (the American System, the heart of which was transportation improvements), threw his supporters to Adams. Then President Adams nominated Clay for secretary of state in his new administration. The implication was, as the secretaries of state had traditionally been the next presidential candidate in early U.S. history, that Clay would eventually succeed Adams and cut out the popular Jackson altogether. This was too blatantly corrupt on its face for both the public and Jackson. Adams fell in four years later to a renewed Jackson campaign and Clay, a perennial presidential candidate in later years, could never shake the onus of cutting the Corrupt Bargain, and he would never attain the highest office to which he aspired. The taint of corruption did much to delay public acceptance of federal assistance to transportation until the Civil War.

See also American System; Maysville Road Veto; Van Buren, Martin.

References Carroll, E. Malcolm, *Origins of the Whig Party* (1925); Dangerfield, George, *The Era of Good Feelings* (1952); Eaton, Clement, *Henry Clay and the Art of American Politics* (1957); Poage, George Rawlings, *Henry Clay and the Whig Party* (1936); Van Deusen, Glyndon, *The Life of Henry Clay* (1937).

Clayton Act (1914)

Along with the Federal Trade Commission Act, the Clayton Act tightened the strictures of the 1890 Sherman Antitrust Act by prohibiting corporations engaged in interstate commerce from acquiring stock, or under-the-table deals, that excluded the products of competitors or any other company in interstate commerce *if* competition would be diminished thereby (an important concession obtained by conservatives upon President Woodrow Wilson's tactical error in abandoning the Clayton Bill in mid-passage for the Federal Trade Commission Act). The act became the controlling law in railroad antitrust cases. It also exempted labor and agricultural organizations from antitrust laws, by which the federal courts had been limiting their effect, causing the measure to be called "labor's Magna Carta." But this praise was a bit premature, and the labor question would not be settled until the New Deal. In 1920, testifying before a Congress about to consider the Transportation Act of 1920, the railroads asked to be set free from Clayton Act restrictions so that they might voluntarily consolidate. Congress agreed without repealing the Clayton Act, creating a dichotomy—the Clayton Act discouraged forming conglomerates, while the 1920 Act encouraged them. The result was an increase in cases before the Interstate Commerce Commission involving alleged Clayton violations, the opposite of what the 1920 Act intended.

See also Mann-Elkins Act; Railroads from Appomattox to Deregulation; *Ripley Report*; **Transportation Acts.**

References Blaisdell, Thomas C., Jr., *The Federal Trade Commission* (1932); Blum, John Morton, *Woodrow Wilson and the Politics of Morality* (1956); Leonard, William Norris, *Railroad Consolidation under the Transportation Act of 1920* (1946); Link, Arthur S., *Woodrow Wilson and the Progressive Era* (1954); Martin, David Dale, *Mergers and the Clayton Act* (1959); Saunders, Richard, *The Railroad Mergers and the Coming of Conrail* (1978); Swindler, William F., *Court and Constitution in the 20th Century* (1969).

Clayton-Bulwer Treaty (1850)

During the James K. Polk administration (1845–1849), the United States was suspicious of British interest in constructing a Central American canal. The fear stemmed from Britain's establishment of a protectorate along the Mosquito Coast, which became British Honduras (today's nation of Belize). Polk's envoy to Nicaragua concluded an unauthorized agreement that permitted the United States right-of-way across the isthmus in return for protecting Nicaraguan sovereignty from British encroachments, an understanding affirmed by the Zachary Taylor administration in late 1849. Great Britain, in turn, seized Tiger Island, which was in the U.S. sphere of interest in the Bay of Fonseca.

Seeking to avoid a clash of arms, Secretary of State John Clayton turned to the British minister to the United States, Sir Henry Lytton Bulwer, and the two men hammered out the Clayton-Bulwer Treaty. Both nations agreed never to obtain nor exercise exclusive control over an isthmian canal, never to fortify such a canal, to keep any canal neutral and secure from the domination of others, to keep the canal open to themselves equally, and not to colonize any part of Central America. This treaty remained in effect until superseded by the Hay-Pauncefote Treaty in 1901.

See also Hay-Pauncefote Treaty; Panama Canal.

Clinton, De Witt (1769–1828)

A powerful, sagacious New York State politician, De Witt Clinton was born in New Britain, New York, in 1769. He attended Columbia University and graduated with honors in 1786. He was admitted to the state bar in 1788 and became secretary to his

As governor of New York from 1817 to 1823, De Witt Clinton was instrumental in building the Erie Canal.

uncle, George Clinton, a seven-term governor of New York, and two-term vice-president of the United States under Presidents Thomas Jefferson and James Madison.

The Clinton family members were Republicans—not in the modern sense, the party of Abraham Lincoln—in the classical sense, opponents to the Constitution of 1787 and Anti-Federalists in favor of strong states' rights government thereafter. De Witt Clinton was briefly a U.S. senator (1801–1803), but resigned his seat to become mayor of New York City. His administration (1803–1815 with two breaks, 1807–1808 and 1810–1811) was noted for the introduction of free public schools. He ran for president unsuccessfully against James Madison in 1812 with Federalist support, a move that alienated stringent Republicans like Martin Van Buren, who instituted the Albany Regency political machine to counter Clinton's hold on the state. But Clinton's strength was not to be broken until the mid-1820s.

Clinton continued his state service in the assembly, where he stood for the abolition of slavery, relief of those in debtor's prisons, and the advancement of steam navigation. He also introduced the "spoils system" into American politics, which rewarded loyal followers with state jobs so long as they performed responsibly—a proviso his successors soon forgot. He served as commissioner to examine and survey the route of the Erie Canal, and as governor (1817–1823) was instrumental in its construction. When the Regency removed him as governor and canal commissioner in 1823, in a quarrel over his seeming embrace of nationalist political philosophy (common among older Republicans like Clinton nationwide) and control of state patronage, public reaction was so much in Clinton's favor that it led to his reelection as governor in 1824. He was noted for honest, efficient administration and his economic farsightedness. Clinton's Erie Canal became the basis of New York's pre–Civil War prosperity, which helped to center U.S. commercial and financial interests in New York City.

See also Erie Canal; Van Buren, Martin.

References Bobbé, Dorothie, *De Witt Clinton* (1933); McBain, Howard L., *De Witt Clinton and the Origin of the Spoils System in New York* (1906); Ostrogorski, M., *Democracy and the Organization of Political Parties* (1902); Remini, Robert V., *Martin Van Buren and the Making of the Democratic Party* (1951).

Clipper Ships

Just as steam conquered the inland rivers, the clipper ship mastered the open seas until conquered by steam in the nineteenth century. But there was a little irony in the fact that its sails did not fold gracefully. The nineteenth century marked some of the finest triumphs of the old sailing ships, and Americans led the way with a new style of ship, the clipper.

The clipper ship was the outgrowth of the trans-Atlantic packet competition, an informal contest of who could transfer goods and passengers by ship the fastest, but she rarely engaged in that trade. Long in length and narrow abeam, the clipper has been described as "a knife with sails." And what sails! Yards and yards of canvas on three tall masts that stretched nearly 200 feet toward the heavens. They appeared like great white birds, one sea captain said, sails so massive that they could catch every zephyr that passed. Especially dashing was the smaller two-masted variation known as the Baltimore Clipper, with masts raked back at a foppish angle (two or three inches per foot of mast) toward the stern. Baltimore Clippers were the very picture of speed, and they never failed to deliver. Some of the early Baltimore types existed before the Revolution. They specialized in smuggling, slave trading, and any activity that called for outrunning the law or the competition. Few clippers ever carried a gun. There was not a pirate ship or customs cutter that could touch them once at sea. Captains spared no canvas regardless of the weather, causing many a clipper to reach her destination missing part of a mast. The crews were a motley lot, slow to obey at first—until they realized that if they did not follow orders with alacrity, all of them might drown.

The shipbuilders were legends in their own times. There was Donald McKay of Boston, who built the *Flying Cloud* for Enoch Train. But agents of Grinnell, Minturn & Company liked what they saw and offered Train $90,000 for her before she left the builder's stocks. After seeing her at sea, Train later opined as how it was the worst deal he had ever made. But New York had its own master shipbuilders. One was William Webb, who laid down the *Challenge*, a massive 2,006-ton speedster for N. L. & G. Griswold. Neither owner could wait to race the other to California. The two ships did not sail together; rather each captain set sail at different times and followed his favorite course. The *Flying Cloud* won by 18 days—the *Challenge* had hit a storm blowing the wrong way in the Straits of Magellan rounding the Horn. But when she came into San Francisco, not a single sail had been lost, despite the weather. The *Flying Cloud* was sold to an English concern in 1862 and burned to the waterline in 1874. The *Challenge* outlasted her two years, being wrecked off the French coast.

The clipper did not have much room for cargo. The hold was too narrow for that. But what she offered was unbelievable speed. She could round the Horn and sail to China and back before most vessels were fairly under way. Clipper captains specialized in hauling tea and opium from China to England. It did not take too many such lucrative cargoes to pay off the creditors, either. The first clipper hit the waves in 1845. In a matter of years the California gold trade offered another market where a smart ship and a reliable captain could get rich quick. And the argonauts paid dearly to make the trip from Boston or New York City to the Golden Gate in record times. Gold waited for no one.

A clipper trip of less than 90 days (16,000 miles) around the Horn was not unusual—the *Flying Cloud* did it regularly. One craft, the *James Baines*, sailed around the world in 132 days, taking in Australia on the way.

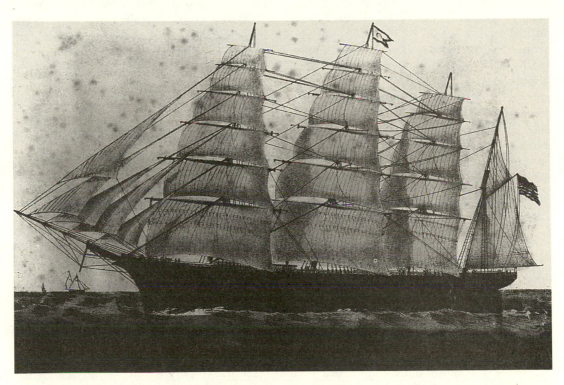

Clipper ships, such as the Great Republic, *pictured here, were more than twice as fast as any other vessel in the mid-nineteenth century.*

The *Baines* set a speed record of 21 nautical miles per hour. Another vessel, the *Lightning*, aptly named, sailed 436 miles in 24 hours. But already she was beaten by the *Marco Polo* and the *Champion of the Seas*, the latter of which lived up to her name by doing 465 miles in the same time span. These records held for a generation. The *David Crockett*, built in 1853 at a cost of $93,000, was a 1,619-ton marvel that sailed without a problem for 37 years. Converted to a coal tender in 1890, the proud ship foundered and sank in 1905 on Romer Shoals, New York. She had earned her builders over a half million dollars in profit before her demotion to fuel tender—all of it in competition with steam-powered craft.

In 1851, American speed sailors received an up-to-date chart that accurately recorded winds, currents, and weather conditions on preferred sea lanes around the world. And the clippers went even faster, aided by Matthew Fountaine Maury's years of research. Maury learned that a straight line was not the shortest distance at sea—rather an arc was. In this he presaged the Great Circle routes used by airliners flying, for example, from San Francisco to Tokyo. One did not go to Midway Island in the Pacific. The short route was through Fairbanks far to the north. By 1853, over 270 clippers had been built. By 1860, steam finally began to catch up in the speed category, and with bigger holds, too. The day of the clipper was over by the time of the Civil War. They filled a void between sail and steam, a truly American answer to the problem of speed on the high seas.

See also Early Steamboats; Merchant Marine; Ocean Liners; Steamboats.

References Chapelle, Howard Irving, *History of American Sailing Ships* (1935); Chapelle, Howard Irving, *The Baltimore Clipper* (1965); Chatterton, E. Kenle, *Sailing Ships and Their Story* (1935); Clark, Arthur H., *The Clipper Ship Era* (1910); Cutler, Carl C., *Greyhounds of the Sea* (1930); Firestone, Harvey S., Jr., *Man on the Move* (1967); Fletcher, R. A., *In the Days of the Tall Ships* (1928); Howe, Octavius A., and Frederick C. Matthews, *American Clipper Ships* (1926–1927); Jennings, John, *Clipper Ship Days* (1952); Rydell, Raymond A., "The California Clippers," *Pacific Historical Review* (1949) 18: 70–83.

Coffin, Lorenzo S. (1823–1915)

An Iowa farm boy, Lorenzo Coffin was a farmer, a railroad real estate agent, a Baptist preacher, a Civil War chaplain, and a member of the board of Iowa Railroad Commissioners. In 1874, he witnessed a railroad brakeman loose the two remaining fingers of his right hand while trying to couple some cars with the link and pin method. Coffin was especially moved to find out that the man he had witnessed had lost his other two fingers the year previously. The brakeman had to stand between the cars and guide the link into the receiver by hand to engage the pin. The slightest miscalculation would result in the loss of a finger or two, if he were lucky. Others lost a hand, and more were killed in the crush of the cars. Coffin also learned that many breakmen fell from the cars during bad weather when they ran along the roofs to tighten the brakes by hand. This incident made Coffin a lifelong reformer of workers' conditions on the rails. He lobbied Congress for years and finally got it to pass the Safety Appliance Act of 1893. It required that all railroads use Westinghouse air brakes, handrails, and the Janney knuckle coupler in their operations. It not only provided a safety margin for the crews but also standardized all cars so that they could be run on any line. When he signed the act, President Benjamin Harrison said it was one of the highlights of his political career.

See also Janney, Eli Hamilton; Safety Appliance Act; Westinghouse, George.

References Hubbard, Freeman, *Encyclopedia of North American Railroading* (1981); Natte, Roger B., "Lorenzo S. Coffin," in Robert L. Frey (ed.), *EABHB: Railroads in the Nineteenth Century* (1988), 53–57.

Commercial Motor Vehicle Safety Act of 1986

Effective in 1992, the Commercial Motor Vehicle Safety Act ensures national standards for the commercial driver's license (CDL). No person can operate legally unless they have passed written and driving tests, shown expertise in air-brake procedure and preinspection skills, and taken a physical examination. As the states still administer the CDL, there is wide leeway as to what constitutes a passing score. Several states really test very little at all. Sometimes examiners have been accused of being open to bribes.

See also Trucking.

Reference Agar, Michael H., *Independents Declared* (1986).

Commuter Trains

Commuter trains had their American beginnings in 1840 when a predecessor to the Boston & Maine Railroad was asked to stop at numerous local stops to discharge local passengers who wanted to use the trains to ride to work. Rather than clog up the running of intercity passenger trains, the railroad experimented with a single locomotive and one coach. Tickets could be bought that were good for a number of rides or a specific short period. The sales rose each year, causing the railroad to increase the number of trains and cut the price of tickets in half.

Prior to automobiles, trains provided a convenient manner for city dwellers to get to work. Commuter trains are rarely cost effective and often tie up more crews and equipment than any other service, and their use is conditioned by rush-hour traffic. Moreover, commuters are chronic grumblers and often quite fickle in their loyalty. But as the suburbs grew after World War II and the highways became clogged with single-driver vehicles, commuter trains have gained new supporters. Although intercity passenger service was assumed by Amtrak in 1971, commuter services were unaffected. Several railroads still operate commuter traffic (Amtrak, CSX Corporation, Canadian National, CP Rail, Chicago & North Western, Long Island Rail Road, Norfolk Southern, Southern Pacific) and several jurisdictions have their own separate commuter trains (Metro in Chicago, CalTrains in Los Angeles, BART in San Francisco, MBTA in Boston, MUCTC in Montréal, NJ Transit between Trenton and New York City, and PATrain in Pittsburgh are examples).

See also Amtrak; Buses; Greyhound Corporation; Trains in Cities.

References Brandes, Ely M., and Alan E. Lazar, *Rail Passenger Traffic in the West* (1966); Grow, Lawrence, *On the 8:02* (1979); Hilton, George W., and John F. Due, *The Electric Interurban Railways in America* (1960); Holle, Gena, "The Coaster Comes to California," *Passenger Train Journal* (October 1994) 25: 32–33; Hubbard, Freeman, *Encyclopedia of North American Railroading* (1981); Sebree, Mac, "BART's Billion Dollar Expansion Program," *Passenger Train Journal* (October 1994) 25: 20–23; Sebree, Mac, "DART and RDC's: Texas-Style Commuter Rail," *Passenger Train Journal* (October 1994) 25: 34–35; Van Wilkins, "Commuter Rail Is Booming in Maryland," *Passenger Train Journal* (October 1994) 25: 24–31.

Conrail

Shortly after Penn Central Transportation Company went bankrupt in 1970, Congress passed the Regional Rail Reorganization Act of 1973 (amended by the Railroad Revitalization and Regulatory Reform Act of 1976), which created the United States Railway Association (USRA) to plan a reorganization of the Penn Central and act as its receiver. One of the major reasons that the government went from indirect control of the railroads (regulation) to actual interference in every aspect of their lives (just short of outright nationalization) was the demand of some congressmen, representing 16 of some of the most populous states in the Union, that their rail service be saved. The result was the 1976 start-up of the Consolidated Rail Corporation, or Conrail, which combined railroads once serving 100 million people and 55 percent of all American manufacturing plants. The new corporation was made up of Penn Central (which included the old Pennsylvania Railroad, the New York Central System, and the New York, New Haven & Hartford) and the so-called anthracite coal roads (Central of New Jersey, Lehigh Valley, Erie Lackawanna, Lehigh & Hudson River, and the Delaware, Lackawanna & Western). The only anthracite road to steer clear of the merger was the Delaware & Hudson. It was also the only one that was not broke at the time.

Conrail began with $2.1 billion in federal funds invested in Conrail stock. Right away the new line sold much of the Northeast Corridor (Boston to Washington) trackage to Amtrak. Then it abandoned many unprofitable track sections, operating some, like the old Ann Arbor Railroad, with state subsidies. Finally, it got rid of commuter lines everywhere in the system. It then rebuilt or purchased new roadbed, rails, and equipment. The key to the whole program was congressional funding (supposedly loans) expected to total about $6.8 billion over a ten-year period. Conrail was managed by a board of directors, with 13 drawn from the private sector, 6 from USRA appointees, and 5 chosen by the bankrupt railroads. There was also a chairman, chief executive officer, and a chief operations officer. Eighty-five percent of the initial stock was bought by the federal government, with the rest falling in private hands. Conrail was permitted to use a different system of accounting than other railroads. Called "depreciating accounting," it allowed capital to be depreciated over its useful life. The normal "betterment accounting" system common to the other railways produces an initial heavy depreciation followed by lesser amounts that skews the corporate financial reports, particularly early on.

As it was, Conrail's labor-intensive terminals and switching operations caused it to expend over 63 cents of every dollar in an area where other lines were expending 53 cents. The whole physical plant, especially the tracks and roadbed, was a mess. Conrail's failure to perform well (a $295 million loss was posted in the first nine months) caused many critics to accuse the government of creating another post office. To alleviate the labor difficulties, Conrail managed to consolidate its 285 labor contracts into 34 single agreements. The result was a reduction in the number of crew members required on all trains, mainline or switching. There was much doubt if Conrail, so dependent on federal subsidy, could survive the budget cuts of the 1980s, but its predicted demise had been exaggerated.

Hiring L. Stanley Crane from Southern Railway (he had had a mandatory age retirement there), Conrail began to enter the new age of modern railroading. Crane increased the marketing of the line, a forgotten aspect of the earlier days of successful rail companies. He brought in new, articulated container platforms to cut costs, purchased state-of-the-art locomotives with computerized controls, added to automatic track control systems, and put more trains over the existing track. Although it came a year later than projected, held up by excessively bad winters, Conrail showed a profit in 1981 of $39 million. This quadrupled the following year. Employee production was up 38 percent and the number of employees decreased by two-thirds, helped by the switching of all passenger and commuter service to Amtrak. The quasi-nationalized Conrail was a success. It even managed to hold it own against the trucking industry, always a big competitor in the upper Midwest and Northeast. Up until 1994, Conrail actually surpassed trucks in service in its running area. All this happened in an era of rising fuel costs, industrial depression, strong foreign competition, and unusually bad weather. The key was the Staggers Rail Act that partially deregulated the trains in 1980.

President Ronald Reagan's administration was pleased with the progress of Conrail but most uncomfortable with its political philosophy. Led by conservatives, Congress passed the Northeast Rail Services Act in 1981 that called for the sale of Conrail to the private sector. The law said that when the U.S. Railway Association certified to the Department of Transportation that certain profitability tests had been passed, Conrail was to be sold as a single entity. The sale was to be made to the bidder that would protect Conrail's success. Chief among the potential buyers was Norfolk Southern, whom many members of Congress opposed, preferring Conrail's independence or continuance as a quasi-governmental corporation. A stock sale in 1987 returned Conrail as an independent railroading company to the private sector, one of the largest in the nation. It has continued its aggressive marketing, especially in piggyback and container freight, and still turns a tidy profit today, with United Parcel Service, American President Lines, and the U.S. Postal Service providing one-third of its intermodal freight.

See also Anthracite and Bridge Line Railroads; New York Central System; Penn Central Transportation Company; Pennsylvania Railroad; Regional Rail Reorganization Act of 1973; United States Railway Association.

References Drury, George H., *The Historical Guide to North American Railroads* (1985); Drury, George H., *The Train-Watcher's Guide* (1990); Grow, Lawrence, *On the 8:02* (1979); Hilton, George W., *The Northeast Railroad Problem* (1975); Hubbard, Freeman, *Encyclopedia of North American Railroading* (1981); Musolf, Lloyd, *Uncle Sam's Private, Profitseeking Corporations* (1983); Nock, O. S., *Railways of the USA* (1979); Orenstein, Jeffrey, *United States Railroad Policy* (1990); Saunders, Richard, *The Railroad Mergers and the Coming of Conrail* (1978); Saunders, Richard, "Conrail," in Keith L. Bryant, Jr. (ed.), *EABHB: Railroads in the Age of Regulation* (1988), 92–94; Sobel, Robert, *The Fallen Colossus* (1977); Stephens, Bill, "Conrail Caters to Customers," *Trains* (August 1994) 54: 62–69.

Containers

One of the more dramatic changes in the transportation of freight on land or sea in the twentieth century has been the development of the container industry. Containers are big steel boxes that measure 8 feet tall (although taller sizes are available) and 8 feet wide and come in lengths of 20, 40, 45, 48, and 53 feet. There are also some domestic sizes of 28-foot lengths, but the international trade still relies on the Forty Foot Equivalent (which includes the 20-foot shorty). The modern concept of container cargo began in 1929 when Seatrain began to ship full boxcars between the United States and Cuba. During World War II, the vast amounts of cargo threatened to overwhelm the dock facilities and employees. To try and speed up the process, the shippers filled their ships with crates of the same size. After the war no one seemed willing to go on with the concept until the late 1950s, when the Sea-Land, Grace, and Matson companies in the Pacific and Moore-McCormick in the Atlantic offered room on the top of vessels

and then launched specially built ships to carry container cargoes. The change in a ship's time in port dropped from one-half of the trip time to one-fifth. Labor costs also dropped dramatically, assisted by the Mechanization and Modernization Agreement negotiated with the unions.

At first, the container ship had to provide its own shipboard cranes to load and unload, but new facilities soon sprung up to augment this service and provide storage. This meant that ships now were nothing more than floating boxes that transported all-weather containerized cargoes that were stored outside in huge marshaling lots. The containers also provided a defense against theft and assisted yardmasters in keeping track of small cargoes. The container could be packed at the plant, sent to the sea by truck or rail, shipped overseas, and taken to its destination by truck or rail. It never had to be handled until its arrival at its final destination, when it was unpacked for local distribution. In 1971, Seatrain developed the concept of the "landbridge" that allowed cargoes to be shipped across the ocean to a U.S. port, placed on special flatcars on a freight train and sent to the opposite coast, and then reloaded for more sea travel. The landbridge saved ten days over the trip from New York City to Tokyo via the Panama Canal. In 1984, American President Lines introduced a new wrinkle by outfitting trains with special double-stack container cars that could haul twice as much on the same run. Others have followed suit, and container trains make up the bulk of transcontinental railroading and have become so efficient with the computerization of ordering and shipping that companies can operate on a "just in time" inventory process, manufacturing products from parts that arrive only when needed.

See also Bridges, Harry; Intermodal Freight; Intermodal Surface Transportation Efficiency Act of 1991; Merchant Marine.

References DeBoer, David J., *Piggyback and Containers* (1992); Pedraja, René de la, *The Rise and Decline of U.S. Merchant Shipping in the Twentieth Century* (1992); Transportation Research Board, *Intermodal Marine Container Transportation* (1992).

Continental Airlines

Beginning as the Southwest Division of Varney Speed Lines in 1934, Continental Airlines made the airmail jaunt between Denver and El Paso with four Lockheed Vega aircraft. In 1936, Robert Six purchased the company and ran it for the next 44 years. He changed the name of the company to Continental in 1937, and used the slogan "Fly the Old Santa Fe Trail." His logos were successively the head of a Spanish Conquistador, the head of a Pueblo Indian, and a thunderbird before the adoption of the impressionistic sun emblem. Six put his headquarters in Denver and began to expand over the western plains. He went public with the stock in 1938 to finance the move. By World War II, his airline flew into Kansas, New Mexico, Texas (El Paso), Colorado, and Oklahoma (Tulsa). During the war, Six repaired and modified U. S. Army Air Force bombers.

At the end of the war, he was among the first to purchase DC-3 surplus aircraft to modernize his fleet. By 1950, he had graduated to Convair 240s and "coach fare" with the slogan "Fly the Blue Skyway." He obtained landing rights in Houston, but expanded most of his service through pairing with other bigger airlines like American, Frontier, and United. This brought him into the West Coast market for the first time. By the mid-fifties, he served all of Texas and a new route between Chicago and southern California. During the next decades he would acquire an exclusive route between Texas and California, with stops in New Mexico and Arizona, and extend his flights into the Pacific to Micronesia.

With the advent of deregulation, Continental was in the hole $13 million and Robert Six had retired. The airline was ripe for the plucking, and Frank Lorenzo saw the opportunity first. He purchased a controlling interest over the attempts of employees to block him with their own offer. The result was a bitter fight with unions that saw the airline debt mount, as Lorenzo cut routes and restructured management to his liking. Finally, Lorenzo declared bankruptcy to foil continued employee resistance. He then laid off large numbers of workers. In 1987, Lorenzo had worked out of the bankruptcy court and purchased Peoples Express and New York Air, which he added to Continental. Lorenzo has since sold his interest in the airline, which still flies today.

See also Aeronautics; Lorenzo, Frank.

References Cornett, Lloyd H., Jr., "Continental Airlines," in William M. Leary (ed.), *Encyclopedia of American Business History and Biography* (1992), 119–122; Davies, R. E. G., *Continental Airlines* (1986); Murphy, Michael, *The Airline That Pride Almost Bought* (1986); Serling, Robert J., *Maverick* (1974).

Corduroyed Roads

Corduroying is a process of providing a solid road surface by cutting unpeeled logs and laying them crosswise across a roadbed to provide solid traction for wagon traffic. It was commonly used by both armies in the American Civil War to move supply wagons and artillery across wet and swampy land.

See also Plank Roads.

CP Rail

CP Rail is the modern name (1968) for the old Canadian Pacific Railway, Canada's privately owned transcontinental line. Its logo is a modern rendition of the old beaver within a circular shield. Now the stately animal has been abstracted into a black triangle covering 90 degrees on the edge of a white circle, each side of which is a radius of the circle. The company is well diversified, owning ships, hotels, and an airline.

See also Canadian Pacific Railway.

Crandall, Robert L. (b. 1935)

Born in Westerly, Rhode Island, Robert L. Crandall had a very mobile childhood, attending 12 schools in 14 years before graduating high school, where he was voted the most ambitious and most affectionate member of his senior class. He married his high school sweetheart the same year he graduated from the University of Rhode Island (1957). Crandall served in the U.S. Army and returned to attend the Wharton Business School of the University of Pennsylvania for his MBA. He was a financial officer in several firms before coming to the airline industry, initially with TWA, then transferring to American Airlines (AA). His business colleagues failed to see the affectionate side of Crandall that his high school buddies praised. He became known as an intensely focused, straight-arrow sort, who drove himself and others very hard. He is an extraordinarily quick study, which has allowed him to change fields within a company and bypass others less adept. He also understands computers and has a hands-on experience with them, a quality lacking in most executives in the 1970s.

Crandall took over American in 1980. For a man opposed to deregulation, he has become the master of its economic realities. Crandall says that he has new respect for the free market that he lacked earlier. But he also has benefited from one of the best computer reservation systems in the industry, SABRE (Semi-Automated Business Research Environment) from IBM. Originally developed for C. R. Smith, American's first CEO, in the 1950s, this program allowed American to get an edge on its competition that has lasted for decades. Installed in over a third of all travel agents' offices, it has permitted Crandall to develop SuperSaver fares and the first frequent-flyer program, and to fill jets in a practice known as "yield management," a mix of fares and passenger types that produces a maximum return per seat per plane. These practices allow AA to achieve a return average of 12 cents per seat-mile as opposed to the no-frills airlines' 8 cents.

Crandall has moved on other fronts to make American the United States' supreme airline in passenger use. He cut an aging air fleet of dated Boeing 747s and smaller jets. By coincidence, Douglas Aircraft had developed a new twin jet, the Super 80, that was sitting unsought in a dwindling cash economy. Crandall arranged to rent the planes for AA with the option to turn them back in anytime with 30 days' notice. The savings allowed him to purchase Boeing 757s for longer flights. He sold off all peripheral businesses like hotels and moved the airline's headquarters to the new Dallas–Fort Worth airport. In the process, Crandall instituted the hub-and-spoke system that funneled all travelers to D-FW and connected them to other American flights for the completion of their trips. He developed another hub at Chicago, with minihubs at Nashville, Raleigh-Durham, Miami, San Jose, California, and San Juan, Puerto Rico. Although some of the hubs have not lived up to expectations, most have served AA well.

Crandall also infused the American Eagle System of commuter flights into these hubs to enhance AA's passenger draw even more. His creative approach to the problem of employee wages and benefits was different than Frank Borman's at Eastern (to give in) or Frank Lorenzo's at Continental (to declare bankruptcy and hire a new crew). By a narrow union vote, Crandall instituted a double-tier system of wages and benefits. The older employees stayed on at their current rate, while new employees came in on a newer cheaper scale. He granted profit sharing to all, and lifetime employment. This has resulted in a one-third reduction of fixed costs in wages. At the same time, he promised expansion that would allow all employees to advance within the company ranks more quickly. Part of this was in domestic service, but most was international in scope. Buying into TWA's European and Eastern's Latin American routes, Crandall found that the right to fly did not bring with it the right to land at the same old places. So he instituted a system of taking off and landing in interior cities not used by most airlines. This allowed AA to utilize major airports in say, Chicago and Manchester, where traffic was not so congested, and to fly smaller planes (fully loaded) more often. He staked his draw on the fact that AA provided service that other carriers, especially European ones, did not.

Critics point out that Crandall has merely delayed facing up to the inevitable crunch. The two-tier employee system has its detractors, the price of oil is dependent upon the soundness of a Middle East known for its instability, he lacks the wide-bodied planes for developing the international routes, some of his hubs have not paid off, and he has had to resist an attempted take-over by New York City real estate financier Donald Trump. But as the mid-1990s approach, American Airlines is still the airline to beat in the American market, leaving one with the feeling that Crandall must be doing a lot more things right than he is wrong. His well-known flexibility, the ability to change tack on a dime, bodes well for his and AA's future.

See also Aeronautics; American Airlines.

References Cornett, Lloyd H., Jr., "Robert L. Crandall," in William M. Leary (ed.), *Encyclopedia of American Business History and Biography* (1992), 126–129; Davis, L. J., "And Now, Can Bob Crandall Have It All?" *New York Times Magazine* (21 September 1990): 25, 42, 44, 46.

Crédit Mobilier of America

After the passage of the Pacific Railroad Act in 1862 and its amendment in 1864, railroad investment became increasingly attractive to various entrepreneurs in the United States. It was slowly becoming obvious that the Civil War would soon end and with it would go the lucrative government contracts for war matériel. A new field for moneymaking was needed and railroad first-mortgage bonds now looked to fill that need. As lucrative as the rails might be, the construction and management of the trans-continental railroad offered more to those wise in the ways of maximizing profit at public expense. Their efforts went into establishing a construction company to build the railroad across the Plains and mountains. That company was called the Crédit Mobilier of America—to differentiate it from the corrupt French company involved in the construction of the Suez Canal—and which should have been an omen of things to come.

To this day no one knows the names of all of those involved in the American version of the Crédit Mobilier. Suffice it to say the estimated six dozen did not lose face in financial wizardry. They came from Boston, Chicago, Philadelphia, and New York City. They included William B. Ogden, John Murray Forbes, Charles Butler, Thomas A. Scott, John Edgar Thomson, Erastus Corning, John V. L. Pruyn, John I. Blair, Russell Sage, August Belmont, J. F. D. Lanier, and Samuel J. Tilden. They all stood forth when the Union Pacific Railroad was a patriotic project to propel the power of the nation westward. But they all disappeared from sight when the Crédit Mobilier came into existence, so their involvement is a matter of debate, not certainty.

The Crédit Mobilier was set up in Pennsylvania under charter from the state legislature at the behest of Thomas Durant, a manipulator of stocks in what later became the Rock Island Lines. He was also interested in the Union Pacific (UP) Railroad, and he looked around for a company whose charter was a little vague and lax in the things that mattered, like strict accountability. He found one in Pennsylvania: the Pennsylvania Fiscal Agency. Durant purchased it in his role as vice-president of the UP, and renamed it the Crédit Mobilier of America. The Crédit Mobilier was a construction company, so far as the public knew, with which the UP contracted to build the rail line to the west. What the public did not know was that essentially the Crédit Mobilier was run by the same men who directed the railroad. They bought items cheap and sold them back to themselves dear, charging the federal government the higher price and pocketing the difference. If the profits were not in cash, they came in the form of securities that allowed the men to control the railroad and its attendant land grants, particularly the timber and mineral rights that came with them.

It was nothing new—business was done that way then, quite openly actually, by today's standards. At first the Crédit Mobilier contracted to lay the rails onto the Plains for the first 200 miles at a profit to themselves of just over $5 million. That was a poor showing. The Boston investors complained, so congressman (House Committee on Pacific Railroads) and shovel-maker Oakes Ames was put in charge. He laid the next 600 miles of track and overcharged the government and first-mortgage common stockholders (the manipulators never used their own money) almost $30 million. The system was beginning to hum. But the problem was the five directors appointed by the federal government. What if one of them blew the whistle? What if the rumors of profit caused some crusading congressman to investigate? Ames had the solution. He went around among the directors and his political peers and distributed shares in the Crédit Mobilier "where it would do the most good," he said sagely later—free to some or at a small cost to others. This also was not unusual during that era, later remembered by Mark Twain as the "Gilded Age." Among those blessed with Crédit Mobilier shares were the vice-president of the United States, the speaker of the house, future President James A. Garfield, and perennial presidential hopeful James G. Blaine. Everyone was in on the take.

Almost everyone. The problem lay in the fact that some of those paid off believed that they had been cheated out of their fair share of the greed. One of them took Oakes Ames to court. Now, this was not a smart tactic to take. Trials had a way of engaging the public's usually diverted attention. Then in 1871, well after the transcontinental railroad had been finished and nearly everyone paid off, a combination of directors elected Thomas A. Scott as president of the UP. Scott was big in the Pennsylvania Railroad, and his election looked like a power grab to many. The "Pennsy" would control the whole east-west transportation system of the United States. These critics also backed the litigation against Ames. So others on the board banded together and threw Scott out of his presidency. The Scott group then leaked old letters in which Ames stupidly named those whom he had bribed. The muckraking New York Sun got hold of the letters and the story went public with a bang—right in the middle of the election of 1872. President Ulysses S. Grant, all of Congress, and one-third of the Senate were up for reelection. And although the president was clean, the rest of his administration was not.

There was no way around it. Congress would have to investigate. Of course everyone professed wide-eyed innocence. But the facts were out and the government had to take the Crédit Mobilier to court. Naturally, the suit was civil not criminal (one does not send such upstanding citizens to jail) and eventually the Supreme Court ruled that the government could not collect, even on the fraud, until 1895, 30 years after the first bonds went out as stipulated in the federal charter. The only one who really suffered was Oakes Ames. He lost his congressional seat—but he kept his cash. (Grant won a second term, running against reformer Horace Greeley, who died before the electoral count could be made.) The stock of the UP fell 25 points in the wake of the scandal, and the financial jackals Russell Sage and Jay Gould moved in to strip its carcass. But before they could act, the great banking house of Jay Cooke & Company had to default on a new Northern Pacific Railroad bond it was floating. The public had tired of railroad mania at last, and the Panic of 1873 put an end to future moves for some years to come. Only Sage survived in any shape to move up, and to him went what was left of the Union Pacific.

See also Forbes, John Murray; Gould, Jay; Huntington, Collis Potter; Pacific Railroad Act of 1862; Sage, Russell; Vanderbilt, William H.

References Fogel, Robert W., *The Union Pacific* (1960); Galloway, John, *The Transcontinental Railroad* (1950); Griswold, Wesley S., *A Work of Giants* (1962); Hipp, James W., "Oakes and Oliver Ames," in Robert L. Frey (ed.), *EABHB: Railroads in the Nineteenth Century* (1988), 12–14; Howard, Robert W., *The Great Iron Trail* (1962); Lyon, Peter, *To Hell in a Day Coach* (1968); Summers, Mark W., *Railroads, Reconstruction, and the Gospel of Prosperity* (1984).

Crocker, Charles (1822–1888)

Born in Troy, New York, and the son of a failed businessman, Charles Crocker went into debt at age 12 to buy a newspaper agency and help support his parents. In 1836, he cleared land and worked a farm in Indiana where he met and married Mary Donnelly. Vain, stubborn, and at times stupid, Crocker was a big man who seldom weighed less than 250 pounds. He later moved to Maryland and operated an iron mill and smithy. In 1850, he went to California to join a brother who had made a small fortune in the general store business. They expanded their operations, and Charles was elected to the city council of Sacramento, where he met Mark Hopkins, Leland Stanford, and Collis P. Huntington. By 1862, Crocker and Company had contracted to build the first 18 miles of the Central Pacific Railroad, with Huntington and Hopkins as silent backers.

Although Crocker had no railroad experience, he learned quickly and lived in an old coach that he had shunted up and down the line. Crocker hired J. H. Strobridge as his track foreman, and the latter drove the crews mercilessly. After much complaining, Crocker brought in Chinese laborers and the work proceeded smoothly. He made $275,000 cash and $150,000 in Central Pacific bonds for this first section of tracks. Crocker rode up and down the construction sites on an old mare. He was resoundingly hated, but twice each month he insisted on paying the crews in cash and in person. In 1871, after the sudden death of his brother, by then a judge, Crocker retired from the railroad, selling out to his partners. He lived comfortably at Monterey until his death.

See also Hopkins, Mark; Huntington, Collis Potter; Judah, Theodore D.; Railroads from Appomattox to Deregulation; Stanford, Leland.

References Hubbard, Freeman, *Encyclopedia of North American Railroading* (1981); Lewis, Oscar, *The Big Four* (1938); Meyers, Gustavus, *History of the Great American Fortunes* (1910).

CSX Corporation

The CSX Corporation is the acronym for Chessie and Seaboard, the two rail giants that make up this conglomerate of 17 railroads with track in 22 states, and various nationwide holdings in nonrail industries like newspapers, coal and forestlands, aircraft management, oil and gas exploration, hotel management, and real estate development. This merger took place in 1980 with the approval of the Interstate Commerce Commission. At the time, it was America's

largest rail network, but now it has been surpassed by Burlington Northern. Each of the 17 railroads still operates as a separate entity, but is coordinated with the whole for improved service and operational savings. It has links from the Great Lakes to the Gulf of Mexico and from the Atlantic to the Mississippi. One of the road's biggest businesses is coal hauling, which the combined railroads can do more cheaply than the truckers, who had decimated their business before the joining of the increased capacity and cheaper carriage ability of CSX.

See also Chessie System; Family Lines System.

References Drury, George H., *The Historical Guide to North American Railroads* (1985); Drury, George H., *The Train-Watcher's Guide* (1990); Hubbard, Freeman, *Encyclopedia of North American Railroading* (1981).

Cullom Law (1887)

See Interstate Commerce Act.

Cumberland Road

The Cumberland Road was the first long, planned road in American history, and it was the first good, well-built road to cross the Appalachian Mountains. But it took until well after the War of 1812 for it to replace the traffic that went west on Daniel Boone's Wilderness Road in Kentucky, and even longer to intercept the trade from the U.S. Middle West that flowed down the Mississippi and its tributaries to New Orleans. The Cumberland Road had one great advantage over all other roads and canals during the early national period of American history; however, it went west directly out of the national capital, Washington, D.C., and it had the implicit sanction of saintly George Washington himself, following as it did the pathways of his early wanderings and military campaigns.

Originally, what would become the Cumberland Road was a trail that had been blazed in 1751 by a friendly Delaware Indian and named for him as Nemacolin's Trail. It was no more than 2 feet wide, an Indian trail in all but the blaze marks on the trees it passed. George Washington went out in 1754 to demand that the French withdraw from Ohio lands claimed by Virginia and the British Crown. In the process, he widened the trail with about 60 axemen, a task so arduous that Washington pretty much gave up the idea of wagons going west. British Colonel Edward Braddock determined to widen and improve Washington's Road to accept the guns and wagons of his army. Braddock employed over 600 men with axes, ten times Washington's effort. The resulting road was 12 feet wide, a virtual swath through the forest, now named Braddock's Road.

The improved section of Braddock's Road, about 100 miles, left a lot to be desired. The whole road needed to be modernized and made to withstand the ravages of weather. But the advent of the American Revolution delayed work. After the war, the federal government and the states were too much in debt to act. At that time, states financed road projects, but few of them could afford to do so. Private companies were reluctant to act in so massive a project. As the Constitution made no direct provision for building roads, there were constitutional and political objections to the appropriation of federal moneys.

Washington understood the need for a road to connect east and west. The farmers now settling in the Middle West had no way to get their produce to market. They had to ship it down the Mississippi and its tributaries to New Orleans. There it was at the whim of Spanish colonial officials who closed the port on a regular and unannounced basis. Then the American cargoes were seized or bribes were accepted. It was all very chancy. The whole problem was driven home in 1794 during the Whiskey Rebellion. Western farmers had been converting their grains into hard liquor, which they packed in barrels and either rolled or shipped them to market. The profits were immense ($36 for a wagon of grain versus $220 per wagon of booze). When Congress taxed the profits, the farmers revolted. They ran the collectors out and defied the federal government to enforce the hated law. Washington sent out the federalized militia (the army was

pretty small then), 15,000 strong, under his secretary of the treasury, Alexander Hamilton (once a staff officer under Washington during the Revolution). The farmers surrendered, not expecting such a powerful response, and Hamilton hauled them into Philadelphia in chains. Washington admonished them and let them go—disappointing Hamilton, who wanted them hanged for treason. Much of the activity took place overland on Braddock's old road, now called the Cumberland Road, as it headed for Cumberland, Maryland.

As the Whiskey Rebellion waged (1794), a storekeeper at Wheeling, Ebenezer Zane, believed that a great rush of people would head west as soon as the Old Northwest Indians could be defeated. Before, during, and after the Whiskey Boys gave up, the army had turned to the task of subduing protesting Native Americans in what became Ohio State. In the process, the military forces of the United States suffered two of the greatest defeats it would ever know: Josiah Harmar's defeat occurred in 1790, when a coalition of tribes routed an expeditionary force near present-day Fort Wayne; Arthur St. Clair's defeat happened a year later when the entire regular army (some 600 strong) and a large militia force were literally cut to ribbons in an ambush on the upper Wabash, with losses exceeding 40 percent. Finally in 1794, General "Mad Anthony" Wayne marched a new force, well trained and disciplined, to near today's Toledo, Ohio, and scattered the Native Americans at the Battle of Fallen Timbers. Under the ensuing Treaty of Greenville, the tribal leaders gave up claim to most of Ohio, and Zane's prophecy came to pass.

Zane did more than just think about emigration; he actively assisted it to march past his store by building Zane's Trace from Wheeling to the valley of the Scioto River near Chillicothe. He surveyed a direct route from Wheeling to the west, and petitioned Congress for money to build it. Wise in the ways of government, Zane did not wait on Congress to act before he went in with gangs of slaves and free laborers and began to build his road. Meanwhile, Congress granted him three tracts of land to defray road-building expenses. Zane would be able to sell the land after he surveyed it at his own expense. On one of his land grants he founded a city, which he immodestly named after himself. Zane's Trace became the route of early settlers into Ohio and a part of the Cumberland Road system by 1802, with Ohio's admission to statehood.

Once again Ohioans turned to the federal government for aid to improve and extend the roads running west from Washington and Baltimore that joined at Frederick, Maryland, and headed through Cumberland to Wheeling and beyond. Although there were constitutional objections to federal aid, especially among President Thomas Jefferson's own Democratic Republican party, Jefferson knew that better communications between east and west could prevent another Whiskey Rebellion and numerous attempts to erect a new nation in a seceded West, one of which was soon to be led by his own vice-president, Aaron Burr. He turned to his secretary of the treasury, a man from the western Pennsylvania area that produced the Whiskey Rebellion, for help. And the secretary, Albert Gallatin, fashioned a program that met constitutional objections and led to an act to build an improved Cumberland Pike, to be called the National Road.

See also National Road; Roads and Highways, Colonial Times to World War I.

References Bruce, Robert, *The National Road* (1916); Durrenberger, Joseph Austin, *Turnpikes* (1931); Hart, Val, *The Story of American Roads* (1950); Hulbert, Archer Butler, *Historical Highways of America* (1902–1906); Ierley, Merritt, *Traveling the National Road* (1990); Jordan, Philip D., *The National Road* (1948); Lacock, John Kennedy, "The Braddock Road," *Pennsylvania Magazine of History and Biography* (1914) 38: 1–38.

Cummins, Clessie L. (1888–1968)

C. L. Cummins' claim to fame was the adaptation of the heavy marine diesel engine to motor truck use in the 1920s. He first powered a Packard automobile in 1930, driving it from Indianapolis to New York City. He then put the engine on a truck

chassis and drove the rig from New York City to Los Angeles the following year. He entered several races for publicity. World War II made his reputation as he powered numerous heavy vehicles for armed forces use. Although Cummins retired in 1956 and died 12 years later, his engines have made his name live on. The quality of the Cummins Diesel was such that he could keep up with larger manufacturers like Ford and General Motors—they even powered their vehicles with his motors. Indeed, by 1986 every truck manufacturer offered models powered by Cummins engines. One of the more popular trucks among farmers and ranchers in the 1990s is the Dodge Ram pickup, with Cummins power.

See also Buses; Trucking.

References May, George S., "Cummins Engine Company," in George S. May, (ed.), *EABHB: The Automobile Industry* (1989), 90–91; Motor Vehicle Manufacturers Association of the United States, *Automobiles of America* (1974); Wren, James A., and Genevieve J. Wren, *Motor Trucks of America* (1979).

Curtiss, Glenn Hammond (1878–1930)

Born at Hammondsport, New York, Glen Curtiss' father was a harnessmaker who died when the boy was but six years old. He attended public schools, became a messenger, developed an interest in bicycles and motorcycles, and set up to manufacture them. He was an avid racer and won many contests. Curtiss became connected with Thomas S. Baldwin, a balloonist, and together they motorized balloons and went into construction of dirigibles. In 1907, Curtiss met Alexander Graham Bell, who turned his attention to airplanes. Curtiss built his first aircraft soon after. In 1910, he dropped oranges from a plane to demonstrate the possibilities of aerial bombing. By 1911, he was teaching military cadets how to fly, and had developed a seaplane, which he sold to the United States Navy as well as to the military services of England, Germany, Italy, France, and Czarist Russia. Curtiss invented the moveable aileron on the wing tip, but the Wright brothers maintained that it infringed upon their patent for warping the wings. Although Curtiss eventually received the patent, it cost him a lengthy court battle and a damage claim to the Wrights.

During World War I, Curtiss introduced mass production into his Curtiss Aeroplane and Motor Company, the makers of the famous JN series of trainers better known as "Jennies." Located at Garden City, Long Island, it was the largest manufacturer of aircraft in the country. But the end of the war and the government's sale of all surplus aircraft cut the bottom out of the manufacturing of planes for years. Curtiss continued to experiment with aerodynamic forms and won many world's records for speed, climb, and altitude with his *Wasp*. He also developed Florida real estate, especially Hialeah Country Club Estates. In 1929, Curtiss and Wright merged their companies into Curtiss-Wright, which he directed until his death a year later.

See also Boeing, William Edward; Douglas, Donald W.; Martin, Glenn Luther.

References Biddle, Wayne, *Barons of the Sky* (1991); Ingham, John H. (ed.), *Biographical Dictionary of American Business Leaders* (1983), 80–81; Roseberry, Cecil, *Glenn Curtiss (1972)*.

Dartmouth College v. Woodward 4 Wheaton 518 (1819)

Dartmouth is the U.S. Supreme Court decision in which Chief Justice John Marshall wrote the decision for the majority, which stated the sanctity of contracts in terms so broad as to give contracts implied powers of absoluteness, placing legislature-granted charters of private corporations outside the control of the states that had granted them. The state of New Hampshire had a change in government between political parties in 1816, and the new group wished to "democratize" all state institutions by issuing new charters. One institution affected was Dartmouth College, which was chartered originally under British colonial rule in 1769. The old board of trustees sued the new board, claiming that its old colonial charter was still in effect and sacrosanct. Marshall ruled that the old charter was for all practical purposes a contract and protected under the contracts clause of the U.S. Constitution of 1789. The result led to many corporate economic abuses that tended to grant exclusive rights that stifled new inventions, products, and corporate development, which had to be modified by later federal court decisions.

See also *Charles River Bridge Company v. Warren Bridge Company*; *Gibbons v. Ogden*.

References Kelly, Alfred H., and Winfred A. Harbison, *The American Constitution: Its Origins and Development* (1948); Swisher, Carl B., *The Taney Period* (1974); Warren, Charles, *The Supreme Court* (1922); White, G. Edward, and Gerald Gunther, *The Marshall Court, 1815–1825* (1988).

Death Valley Scotty (n.d.)

Walter Scott was a gold miner who struck it rich, real rich, in the Death Valley region. On 1 July 1905, he came into the Santa Fe station at Los Angeles and rented a train (baggage car, diner, sleeper) and set out for Chicago to beat the speed record, then at 46.5 hours. Scott paid the Santa Fe agent $5,500 and the train, named the Death Valley Coyote, set out on the legendary journey. Using a combination of ten wheelers (4-6-0), Prairies (2-6-2), and Atlantics (4-4-2), Scott caught the imagination of the nation as he and his wife sped eastward. Normal traffic was sidelined. Crews refused to slow down for the tightest curves, commonly ran at 90 miles per hour on the plains, and reached 106 mph on straightaways across the Illinois prairies. To keep the train safe, switchmen spiked their turnouts open to let Scotty pass. En route, he sent a telegram to President Theodore Roosevelt: "An American cowboy is coming east in a special train faster than any cowpuncher ever rode before." He made the run of 2,265 miles in 44 hours and 54 minutes, in the process becoming a national hero and setting records for crossing mountains, deserts, prairies, and plains that remained unbroken for decades. When asked why he did it, he said it was a sort of bender, a celebration of his happiness at striking it rich.

See also Henry, John; Jones, John Luther "Casey"; Locomotives, Steam Locomotives.

References Hubbard, Freeman, *Encyclopedia of North American Railroading* (1981); Johnson, Hank, *Death Valley Scotty* (1974); Marshall, James, *Santa Fe* (1945).

Debs, Eugene Victor (1855–1926)

A native of Terre Haute, Indiana, Eugene V. Debs went to work as a paint scraper on the Vidalia Railroad at 50 cents a day in 1870. He then fired switching engines at $1 a night before graduating to fireman on road engines. In 1873, he became secretary to the newly formed Brotherhood of Locomotive Firemen and edited its union magazine. By 1880, he was editor-in-chief and also an elected member of the Terre Haute City Council. Debs believed that all members of the working classes needed to cooperate to gain concessions from management. He began to expand his union's membership to include brakemen, switchmen, telegraphers, shopworkers, and laborers. In 1893, he resigned his Brotherhood of Locomotive Firemen positions to devote himself full time to this concept of one union for all trainmen, the American Railway Union.

In 1894, the new union took on James J. Hill's Great Northern Railroad, which had just reduced laborers' salaries in response to growing economic depression. Carefully letting only the mail trains through, Debs brought Hill to his knees and gained a return to former salaries for the laborers. His success buoyed all trainmen and when George Pullman pulled the same stunt against his shopworkers as Hill, the union voted overwhelmingly to take on Pullman as well. Debs was not sure that the relatively new union had such power, but he agreed to lead the strike in view of the members' vote. Over a quarter of a million men walked out on 20 railroads in sympathy with the Pullman strikers. This made the Pullman strike more national than the Great Northern walkout, and the federal government stepped in with court injunctions and troops, even though the governor of Illinois, John Peter Altgeld, begged them to stay out. Debs and others were soon in jail, and the government refused his request for a jury trial on real charges beyond contempt of court and the right to testify and call upon witnesses. Instead, the railroads, with the exception of the Rock Island, blacklisted union supporters.

Debs' quarrel with management and government led him into the ranks of the Socialist Party. He was an avid public speaker, organized party and union groups, edited several magazines, and wrote extensively. He served as chancellor of the People's College at Fort Scott, Kansas, an institution that worked with working people who desired to advance their education through correspondence courses and regular attendance. He ran for president on the Socialist ticket in 1900, 1904, 1908, 1912, and 1920, the last time from a jail cell to which he had been sentenced for antiwar activities in violation of the Espionage Act of 1917. He was pardoned by President Warren G. Harding in 1921 and died five years later.

See also Pullman, George Mortimer; Railroad Unions.

References Ginger, Ray, *The Bending Cross* (1949); Hubbard, Freeman, *Encyclopedia of North American Railroading* (1981); Karsner, David, *Debs* (1919); Lindsay, Almont, *The Pullman Strike* (1942); Lyon, Peter, *To Hell in a Day Coach* (1968); Shannon, David A., "Eugene V. Debs: Conserva-

American Railway Union founder Eugene Victor Debs

tive Labor Leader," *Indiana Magazine of History* (1951) 47: 357–364; Tussey, Jean Y. (ed.), *Eugene V. Debs Speaks* (1970); White, W. Thomas, "Eugene Victor Debs," in Robert L. Frey (ed.), *EABHB: Railroads in the Nineteenth Century* (1988), 79–83.

Defense Highway Act (1941)

Because of the strong possibility of American entry into World War II, funds already appropriated under the Federal Highway Act of 1940 could be used to plan a strategic road network for national defense without states providing matching funds. By 1941, the Bureau of Public Roads, the Department of the Army, and the Department of the Navy had declared about 78,000 miles of roads as a part of this network. The Defense Highway Act of 1941 appropriated funds to construct this network, with the states not to pay over 25 percent. It also provided $10 million for postwar highway planning. Because of shortages of materials, equipment, and labor caused by the war, normal road building came to a virtual halt. Materials were diverted to the military road network. Substitutes were to be used in all other projects, with an emphasis on maintenance over new construction. This was the philosophy of road building adhered to throughout the war.

See also Roads and Highways since World War I.

Reference U.S. Department of Transportation, Federal Highway Administration, *America's Highways* (1976).

Delta Airlines

Delta began with the Huff-Daland crop-dusting effort out of Talullah, Louisiana, in the early 1920s. Bought by a consortium of Monroe planters and businessmen, Delta received its name and the mail route from Monroe to Dallas, after first losing out to the 1930 contract frauds. Its first passenger-and-mail-carrying planes were Stinson Tri-motors, which differed from the Ford and Fokker models in that they had low wings with shrouded engines. By 1936, Delta had advanced to Lockheed L-10B Electras and began an aggressive advertising campaign under the slogan, "Southern Gentlemen and Southern Belles Fly Delta." It also moved its home base to Atlanta as it enlarged its sphere of operations. The stock went public in 1941 as the airline acquired its first DC-3s.

During World War II, most of Delta's aircraft and crews flew for the United States Army Air Force. With its contribution to the victory over the Axis powers, Delta won routes to Miami and Chicago. It bought DC-4s to fly the new runs. This put it in direct competition with Eastern Airlines, a process that would last until Eastern's demise. Delta also made a wise labor choice. With the inception of the new "third man in the cockpit" rules, Delta made the flight engineer's position that of a third pilot. This allowed it to avoid the mid-fifties strikes that hurt Eastern so much. But in general, as a southern-operated business, Delta used nonunion labor in most areas of its operations. Delta continued to make wise choices in its day-to-day operations. In 1959, it held off from buying Boeing's 707 jets and opted for Douglas DC-8s instead. The DC-8 flew longer with less maintenance, and with minor alterations, lasted for years past the 707's demise. Continued mergers with smaller airlines allowed Delta to reach the West Coast

and enter the New England market. Delta also refused to enter the "sporty games" of buying various wide-bodies and jumbo jets, sticking with the more conservative Lockheed L-1011. It also instituted the "hub-and-spoke" system with all flights going through Atlanta, where one could connect with other Delta flights rather than a competitor. This led to some raised eyebrows from those who had to fly from St. Louis to Baton Rouge via Atlanta, but presaged the trend that would predominate after deregulation by some years. According to the old Dixie saw, "To get to Heaven or Hell one has to change planes in Atlanta."

The result was that by the time of deregulation, Delta was in great shape. It already had cheaper nonunion labor; economical aircraft like Boeing 737s (short hauls), 767s (medium range), and 757s (long runs); the hub-and-spoke system; and a record as the least-complained-about airline by its customers in the business. Its coffers were full and growing as Delta moved into European travel. Although Delta had previously opposed deregulation (it did not consider it necessary), it became its foremost advocate later as its competitors went broke one after the other and Delta picked up the pieces. The only mar on its service record were a pair of fatal crashes in the mid-1980s. Today, it shares half of the U.S. market with American and United, but some airline analysts believe that Delta is due for a long-term financial problem, one that might lead to a foreign merger with, possibly, Japan Air Lines, after the model of what has happened to Northwest and KLM or USAir and British Airways. Meanwhile, Delta has come out clean in a lawsuit filed by Pan American Airways claiming that Delta had reneged in an earlier financial deal that would have saved Pan Am from bankruptcy.

See also Aeronautics.

References Davies, R. E. G., *Delta* (1990); Davis, Sidney F., *Delta Air Lines* (1988); Lewis, W. D., and W. P. Newton, *Delta* (1979); Lewis, W. D., and W. P. Newton, "Delta Air Lines," in William H. Leary (ed.), *Encyclopedia of American Business History and Biography* (1992), 145–150; Newhouse, John, "The Battle of the Bailout," *New Yorker* (18 January 1993) 68: 42–51.

Denver & Rio Grande Western Railroad (D&RGW)

A Civil War veteran cavalryman despite his Quaker upbringing, William J. Palmer had dreamed for years of taking a railroad down Colorado's Front Range, the foothills of the Rocky Mountains. He got his wish in 1871, after gaining much valuable experience on the Pennsylvania, Kansas Pacific, and Union Pacific Railroads. Palmer began what was at first a narrow-gauge line down toward modern-day Colorado Springs, a town he would help found. He was headed for El Paso. By 1871, his Denver & Rio Grande Railroad had nearly reached New Mexico when it ran head-on into Santa Fe Railroad building crews coming in from the plains. But the route to Santa Fe would have to wait. There was bigger game in the Colorado mountains to the west—silver was discovered at Leadville.

In the 1870s Leadville was the highest city in North America at 10,000 feet. It was also a booming mining town, producing so much silver the wagons could not haul it away fast enough. The key to Leadville was the canyon of the Arkansas River. Whoever held the canyon would supply rail service to the mines at great profit to himself and his company. Palmer knew that he would have to act quickly. The Santa Fe was an aggressive road, and their armed gunmen had recently driven out D&RG's preliminary survey crews working at Ratón Pass and taken the route for themselves. (It would take the Rio Grande until 1895 to reach Santa Fe by another route out of Alamosa, nicknamed the "Chili" Line.) Not to be outdone in the Grand Canyon of the Arkansas, Palmer sent an armed train into the contested area at night. But W. R. Morley, a Santa Fe construction engineer, heard of the move and rode his horse through the canyon to beat the train. He made it, but killed the horse in the effort. The next morning he managed to scrape together a half dozen of his crewmen, armed them with rifles, and stood to receive Palmer's train.

"We got here first," he boomed out at the D&RG men. "Anyone interfering will stop a bullet between the eyes." Old railroaders played for keeps in those days. Palmer took one look at Morley and decided that the Quaker ways of his ancestors had much merit. The courts, he reckoned, would be a wiser battlefield. He was wrong. Santa Fe had an option on the old Cañon City & San Juan Railroad, a clear title. The Denver & Rio Grande seemed doomed to eventual bankruptcy. But the Santa Fe was not exactly flush with money either, and did nothing to put its rails through. Both sides kept the usual armed men staring at each other and a stalemate ensued. By 1879, Palmer had new capital and a new judge. The ruling was for the Colorado-born D&RG over "foreign" companies like the Santa Fe. Immediately, Palmer sent 50 men and a copy of the judge's orders to the canyon and ordered the Santa Fe loyalists out, "by the authority of the [Colorado] Supreme Court and the 50 rifles you see here."

The court opinion might have more influence in the long run, but the 50 rifles carried the day. Palmer's men dragged Santa Fe crews from their cabs and tents and returned them to Pueblo, Santa Fe's last bastion, held by none other than notorious gunman and onetime Dodge City marshal (the two images were often synonymous) Bat Masterson and a posse. And Masterson had a trump card—a small canon forcibly borrowed from a state militia arsenal. He finally agreed to withdraw in the face of the state militia, and the D&RG "deputies" shot it out with the remaining Santa Fe managers, killing two and wounding two more.

But the victory was fleeting. The U.S. Court of Appeals now ruled on behalf of Santa Fe. Palmer's operations had to go into receivership. But still, Santa Fe could not deliver on the rail service to the mountain mining communities. Rather than fight it out, Santa Fe offered the Rio Grande a deal. Santa Fe would take Ratón Pass and the route into New Mexico and give D&RG title to the canyon line if Palmer's company would pay for the improvements (track and the fabulous Royal Gorge Bridge) made to the roadbed. Each was to keep out of the other's zone, and the route to Denver would be shared, with the Santa Fe renting the right-of-way. Palmer raised enough cash to close the deal ($1.8 million). The Palmer road would go through three more receiverships before becoming solvent again. The board of directors now forced Palmer out of the Front Range operations, but he was not through. He turned to the mountains and built a railroad through them to Salt Lake City. By 1900, he sold this to the old Denver & Rio Grande, which now added the name "Western" to its title. He doled out the $1 million profit to his entire staff, with the laborers alone getting $5,000 each.

The Rio Grande tapped much of the Colorado mountains, serving the various silver towns until federal monetary policy demonetized silver in the late 1890s. Then it began to concentrate on the vast coalfields in western Colorado and eastern Utah. The railroad also capitalized on its scenic route through the Rockies and ran some of the best passenger trains in the nation like the *California Zephyr*, calling itself "the Scenic Line of the World." When Amtrak decided to drop the Colorado Rockies from its schedules, the Rio Grande continued to run its own passenger operations until 1983, well past the decline of such service on other private roads. It is now an Amtrak passenger road. Two of the old Rio Grande narrow-gauge lines in southern Colorado are still in operation as day scenic routes: the Durango & Silverton, run by the Rio Grande itself, and the Cumbres & Toltec, run by a private company out of Chama, New Mexico. Recently (1988), the Rio Grande and the Southern Pacific have merged operations, seeking to become more competitive in the changing world of American railroading.

See also Mears, Otto; Santa Fe Railway; Southern Pacific Lines; Western Pacific Railroad.

References Athearn, Robert C., *Rebel of the Rockies* (1962); Drury, George H., *The Historical Guide to North American Railroads* (1985); Drury, George H., *The Train-Watcher's Guide* (1990); Fisher, John S., *A Builder of the West* (1939); Hauck, Cornelius W., and Robert W. Richardson, *Steam in the Rockies* (1963); Hofsommer, Don L., "Denver & Rio Grande Western Railroad," in Keith L. Bryant, Jr. (ed.), *EABHB: Railroads in the Age of Regulation* (1988), 114–115; Hubbard, Freeman, *Encyclopedia of North American Railroading* (1981); McCoy, Dell,

and Russ Colman, *The Rio Grande Pictorial* (1971); MacGregor, Bruce A., and Ted Benson, *Portrait of a Silver Lady* (1977); Nock, O. S., *Railways of the USA* (1979); Schmidt, William C., "Rail Buffs Bid Adieu to Rio Grande Zephyr," *New York Times* (24 April 1983): 36; Thode, Jackson C., "Denver & Rio Grande," in Robert L. Frey (ed.), *EABHB: Railroads in the Nineteenth Century* (1988), 87–90; Wilson, O. Meredith, *The Denver & Rio Grande Project* (1982).

Department of Transportation (DOT)

Originally organized as an engineering advisory committee in the "good roads" era of the 1890s, the Bureau of Public Roads (BPR) had grown into a highly diverse and complex federal regulatory agency by the 1960s. Specialist employees included economists, historians, planners, behavioral scientists, real estate appraisers, landscape architects, contract experts, safety experts, and civil rights advocates. By the end of 1966, the bureau employed 4,839 persons, including temporary staff and 157 overseas employees. On 16 October 1966, Congress sought to make some sense of the complex organization by reorganizing over 30 transportation agencies or functions into one massive department with cabinet status, the Department of Transportation. Its divisions were the Federal Aviation Administration (FAA), Federal Railroad Administration (FRA), U.S. Coast Guard, the St. Lawrence Seaway Development Corporation, the Urban Mass Transit Administration, and the Federal Highway Administration (FHWA), consisting of the Bureau of Public Roads, Motor Carrier Safety Bureau, and the National Highway Safety Bureau.

The new entity had 900,000 employees and a budget of $6 million, two-thirds of which involved highway programs. Almost immediately the bureau was reshuffled again. The National Highway Traffic Safety Administration, formerly part of the FHWA, became a separate seventh administration. The remaining FHWA sections were broken into their component parts: Planning, Research, and Development; Right-of-Way and Environment; Engineering and Traffic Operations; Motor

Carrier and Highway Safety; and Administration. The old Bureau of Public Roads no longer existed. Although the new DOT was a bureaucrat's dream, at least on paper, the new organization actually weakened the connection between the federal government and the states as far as highways were concerned, as the BPR employees were scattered to the winds. This temporarily wrecked decades-long cooperation that had been taken for granted. A whole new system of personal networking had to be rebuilt and personality clashes became common as new authorities were staked out, and it took some years before the smooth workings of prior decades could be restored. The transition was hampered by the federal practice of hiring inexperienced engineers, usually college graduates, and placing them in charge of the experienced state highway engineers who actually build the projects.

See also Roads and Highways since World War I.
References Seely, Bruce E., *Building the American Highway System* (1987); U.S. Department of Transportation, Federal Highway Administration, *America's Highways* (1976).

Dismal Swamp Canal

Running between Portsmouth, Virginia, and Albemarle Sound in North Carolina, the Dismal Swamp Canal was built to haul lumber and pitch. The Dismal Swamp Company was created in 1787, but the canal was not completed until 1828. It was eventually replaced by the Intracoastal Waterway.

See also Canals; Intracoastal Waterway.

Dixie Highway

One of the "named highways" popular in the teens and twenties of the twentieth century, the Dixie Highway was used by local chambers of commerce and tourism and the American Automobile Association to stimulate travel on the "good roads" and increase income in the towns and states through which they passed. The 1915 Dixie Highway was named after its goal, the Deep South, particularly Florida's Gold Coast. There were two highways that claimed the

name Dixie. One began in Detroit and went south through Cincinnati and crossed the Appalachian Mountains at the Cumberland Gap, utilizing the old Wilderness Road, and joining the Atlantic Highway at Augusta, Georgia. The other began in Sault Ste. Marie, Michigan, and ran down the west side of the state's "thumb" to South Bend, Indiana, then straight south through Indianapolis, where it met a branch starting in Chicago, passing through Danville and coming into Indianapolis from the west. The Dixie then went on to Louisville and Bowling Green, Kentucky, thence to Nashville and Chattanooga, Tennessee, and down through Atlanta, to Macon, where it split, the eastern branch going to Jacksonville, Florida, while the western branch went via Thomasville to Tallahassee and then south through central Florida to Gainesville, Orlando, and Marco before coming into Miami from the west. The route roughly parallels today's U.S. Highway 31 to Nashville (U.S. Highways 45, 150, and 136 out of Chicago), U.S. Highway 41 to Macon, and U.S. Highway 23 to Jacksonville. The branch to Tallahassee parallels U.S. Highways 41 and 319, and then U.S. Highway 27 to Orlando and U.S. Highways 17 and 41 to Miami. Parts of Interstates 94, 196, and 96 in Michigan, 57 and 74 in Illinois and Indiana, 65 in Indiana to Tennessee, 24 to Chattanooga, and 75 southward very roughly parallel this old route.

See also Roads and Highways, Colonial Times to World War I; Roads and Highways since World War I.

Reference Hart, Val, *The Story of American Roads* (1950).

Dodge, Grenville Mellen (1831–1916)

A Danvers, Massachusetts, native, Grenville Dodge was educated as a civil engineer at Norwich University in Vermont. His interest in railroads began at an early age when he helped build a short line to an icehouse. In 1851, he went to Illinois and helped survey the Illinois Central roadbed. Later, he moved to Iowa and worked for the Rock Island in its race with the Chicago & North

Western and the Illinois Central to be the first at Council Bluffs, Iowa. In 1859, Dodge spoke to Abraham Lincoln, then visiting Council Bluffs while looking ahead to the 1860 presidential contest. He asked Dodge where the beginning of the transcontinental railroad ought to be. Dodge told him Council Bluffs was the ideal choice because of its access to the Central Overland Route and the number of railroads already building between it and Chicago.

In Iowa, Dodge had been involved in the state militia, and when the Civil War began, he became colonel for the Fourth Iowa Volunteer Infantry. He was wounded at Pea Ridge and more severely shot up at Atlanta. His command abilities were recognized in his promotions to brigadier and major general. He resigned his commission in 1866 and was made chief engineer of the Union Pacific (UP) Railroad, organized during the war in the Pacific Railroad Act of 1862. Remembering his conversation with Dodge, Lincoln strove successfully to have it begun across the Missouri River from Council Bluffs at a new town named Omaha. Union Pacific promoters undoubtedly hoped that Dodge's influence with Generals W. T. Sherman and U. S. Grant (president in 1868) would help the railroad with sticky political issues.

But Dodge's main job was to lay out the route to the West. Most of the survey followed the old Central Overland Route, but Dodge made several changes to assist the locomotives across the mountains. At the Laramie range, he found Frazer Pass after an Indian ambush forced his party to seek shelter there. His skillful engineering kept the grades to less than 2 percent, important in those days when engines were relatively weak in horsepower. A 700-foot bridge across Dale Creek and blasting through solid rock onto the Wyoming plains were a few of his many feats. The Union Pacific received its materials from the Chicago & North Western, beginning a partnership that would extend well into the twentieth century, especially in joint passenger operations from the Windy City to the Pacific Coast. The main material shortage was in crossties, some of which had to be transported across the treeless plains so far as to cost $6 apiece. In winter, the crews had to burn the precious ties just to survive the cold. The main construction problem was crossing the Wasatch Mountains, which added $10 million to the red side of the ledgers.

The tracklaying became a race across the Great Basin between the UP and its western rival, the Central Pacific (CP). The railroads received their federal subsidies based on the number of miles of track put down. It was not uncommon for crews to lay as much as five miles a day. For awhile, tracklaying crews laid track side by side, leaving it to the politicians and managers to sort out who owned what. This they did before the Golden Spike was driven at Promontory Summit in 1869. Two years later, Dodge was elected to the UP board of directors. But the offer of Pennsylvania Railroad's Thomas Scott to build another line, the Texas & Pacific (T&P), drew Dodge out on the Plains once again.

The T&P was to extend from Marshall, Texas, to San Diego and be as long as the UP and CP combined. Unlike the northern plains, Dodge had to contend with yellow fever quarantines that held up much-needed supplies. Then the Panic of 1873 hit, ruining Tom Scott and Jay Cooke, who had financed the new line. Jay Gould and Russell Sage took over the T&P and Dodge extended the line to Fort Worth. He also built several subsidiary railroads at the same time, eventually building a line from Laredo to Mexico City. He was prevented from working on the trans-Siberian Railway only because of a cholera epidemic. After the Spanish-American War, Dodge went to Cuba to build another rail line there. Dodge spent his later days writing his personal recollections of the Atlanta Campaign, the construction of the UP, and his memories of Lincoln and Grant.

See also Central Overland Route; Crédit Mobilier; Railroads from Appomattox to Deregulation; Union Pacific Railroad of America.

References Boatner, Mark M., III, *The Civil War Dictionary* (1959); Due, John F., "Grenville M. Dodge," in Robert L. Frey (ed.), *EABHB: Railroads*

Dodge, John F., and H. Elgin

in the Nineteenth Century (1988), 94–98; Griswold, Wesley S., *A Work of Giants* (1962); Hubbard, Freeman, *Encyclopedia of North American Railroading* (1981); Perkins, J. R., *Trails, Rails, and War* (1929); Riegel, Robert E., *The Story of the Western Railroads* (1944); Sabin, Edwin L., *Building the Pacific Railway* (1919); Trottman, Nelson, *History of the Union Pacific* (1973).

Dodge, John F. (1864–1920), and H. Elgin (1868–1920)

The Dodges were machinists who became interested in bicycles and ball bearings. Bought out by a Canadian firm, the Dodges went to Detroit and opened a machine shop. Soon they were making transmissions for Oldsmobile. In 1903, Henry Ford offered each brother 50 shares of Ford stock if they would manufacture engines for him. The result was that they owned one-tenth of Ford. Ford made vast profits, which he plowed right back into the company, despising banks and stockholders. In 1917 the Dodges sued for their stock dividends. The court ordered Ford to pay $19 million to all stockholders including the Dodges and himself ($11 million). In 1919, Ford bought them out for $25 million on the original investment of $20,000.

With this kind of capital the Dodges had the money and the know-how (John being the businessman and Elgin the technocrat) to enter the manufacturing process and compete directly with their former employer. Their first four-cylinder model (1915) had the first all-steel body in the industry. When they announced that they would produce such a vehicle, they were swamped with 22,000 applications for dealerships. Literally overnight, the Dodges were number three in motor production and sales. They developed great rapport with their employees, offering free beer and sandwiches at 9 a.m. and 3 p.m., visiting the floor, and providing a "playpen" for retirees to tinker in. Caught in the overexpansion of the auto industry that followed World War I, the Dodges put the plant up for sale, and Walter P. Chrysler took it over to give him the production and distribution facilities necessary to expand his new company.

See also Automobiles from Domestics to Imports; Automobiles in American Society.

References Halberstam, David, *The Reckoning* (1986); Latham, Caroline, and David Agreda, *Dodge Dynasty* (1985); May, George S., "John F. and Horace Elgin Dodge," in George S. May (ed.), *Encyclopedia of American Business History and Biography: The Automobile Industry* (1990), 125–137; Motor Vehicle Manufacturers Association of the United States, *Automobiles of America* (1974); Pitrone, Jean Maddern, *Tangled Web* (1989); Pitrone, Jean Maddern, and Joan Potter Elward, *The Dodges* (1981); Shook, Robert L., *Turnaround* (1990); Thomas, Robert Paul, *An Analysis of the Pattern of Growth of the Automobile Industry* (1977).

Dodge, Martin (1851–1915)

An avid proponent of good roads in the 1890s, Martin Dodge served on the Ohio State Roads Commission, where he helped build the first brick-surfaced rural road in the United States. The road ran just outside Cleveland for four miles at a cost of $16,000 a mile. Built in 1893, the project boosted Dodge's image as a great publicist for the Good Roads Movement. In 1898, he was appointed interim director of the Office of Road Inquiry, to fill in for General Roy Stone who had gone off to fight in the Spanish War. When Stone went over to the private sector upon his return, the directorship went to Dodge permanently.

Dodge worked hard to make information available to state authorities and recommended a national postgraduate school of road engineering, based on a French model, which came to fruition in 1905. He also fought with Congress over the organization and financing of the road office, desiring to make it a permanent part of the government with adequate long-term financing. Congress belatedly heard his plea and joined the division of materials testing with the road office and called it the Office of Public Road Inquiry. Congress also saw to it that the head of the department had to have a "scientific" education, which forced Dodge's retirement in 1905—a sort of Pyrrhic victory.

See also Roads and Highways, Colonial Times to World War I.

Reference U.S. Department of Transportation, Federal Highway Administration, *America's Highways* (1976).

Dodge Line

U.S. Banker Joseph Dodge created the modern Japanese industrial recovery with a nine-point program called the Dodge Line. It included items like cutting the national budget, improving tax collections, cutting back on government waste, cutting government aid to laggard industries, and stabilizing the currency at 360 yen to the dollar to gain a favorable trade balance. The result was the agonizing decade of the 1950s, involving much belt-tightening and increased unemployment. The Dodge Line also led to labor unrest and left-wing popularity in politics opposing its policies. But by mid-decade, the toughness had paid off, and exports, employment, and savings increased, allowing a Japanese economic miracle that surpassed Europe's without the aid of a Marshall Plan. This prosperity has continued into the present with only minor setbacks until the major recession of the 1990s. It also has allowed the retention of the *zaibatsu* system, allegedly destroyed by the post–World War II occupation forces, whereby businesses are run by certain traditionally powerful families on an intimate relationship with the government bureaucracy, one of the chief beneficiaries of which has been the Japanese auto industry.

See also Automobiles from Domestics to Imports; Automobiles in American Society.

References Halberstam, David, *Reckoning* (1986); Sobel, Robert, *Car Wars* (1984).

Douglas, Donald W. (1892–1981)

A Brooklyn native, Donald Douglas was educated at Trinity Chapel School and appointed to the U.S. Naval Academy. He was there but a year before he became interested in aviation and resigned to enter the Massachusetts Institute of Technology. He was MIT's first graduate in aeronautical engineering. After staying on to teach for a year, he joined the Connecticut Aircraft Company to build dirigibles for the navy. Within a couple of years he had traveled to Los Angeles where he was hired as the chief engineer of the Glenn Martin Company. He also worked for the U.S. Army Signal Corps, helped Martin build the first American bomber during World War I, tried to start his own company but failed, built some of the navy's first torpedo planes, and restarted his own firm, which became Douglas Aircraft Company by 1928.

Although he continued to make military planes, Douglas was more interested in the new passenger aspects of air transport. In 1931, he began the development of the Douglas Commercial (DC) line with the DC-1. In 1933, TWA bought 40 of his DC-2 models. But these were quickly eclipsed by the revolutionary DC-3, affectionately called the "Gooney Bird" for its graceful lines in flight. American Airlines ordered 448 of them, and the larger four-engine DC-4 became the first presidential aircraft after Franklin D. Roosevelt employed one for his personal transportation. After World War II, President Harry Truman would use the better DC-6. During the war, Douglas made numerous types of military aircraft, both combat and transport. He had factories in Santa Monica, El Segundo, and Long Beach, California, and Tulsa, Oklahoma. He employed 29,000 people in southern California alone. He had also won the Collier Air Medal and the Guggenheim Gold Medal for his inventiveness in aircraft development. He brought his son, Donald, Jr., into the firm before the war and turned all operations over to him in 1957.

See also Boeing, William Edward; Curtiss, Glenn Hammond; Martin, Glenn Luther.

References Biddle, Wayne, *Barons of the Sky* (1991); Francillon, René J., *McDonnell Douglas Aircraft since 1920* (1987); Ingham, John H. (ed.), *Biographical Dictionary of American Business Leaders* (1983), 80–81.

Drew, Daniel (1797–1879)

Once described as a "gaunt, wily, and pious" outwardly appearing man who really was "a shambling, mealy-mouthed coward, saved from mediocrity by the almost insane cunning of his weasel mind," Daniel Drew was born on a farm near Carmel, New York. At 15 he began driving livestock into New York City. He liked to buy the herds cheaply in the countryside and sell them

Daniel Drew

torious money-grubbers, but Drew decided instead to take Vanderbilt in league with the others. Then Gould and Fisk played with the stock once again without letting Drew in on it, destroying his financial empire's ability to survive the Panic of 1873. He never regained his wealth and died a financial derelict. Before he lost his fortune, he built and supported various churches—Drew Theological Seminary in New Jersey and Drew Seminary for Young Ladies in his hometown of Carmel—and had educated Vanderbilt's son, Billy, in his devious ways.

See also Fisk, James, Jr.; Gould, Jay; Vanderbilt, Cornelius.

References Ginger, Ray, *Age of Success* (1965); Hubbard, Freeman, *Encyclopedia of North American Railroading* (1981); Josephson, Matthew, *The Robber Barons* (1934); Lyon, Peter, *To Hell in a Day Coach* (1968); Meyers, Gustavus, *History of the Great American Fortunes* (1910); Weinstock, Charles B., "Daniel Drew," in Robert L. Frey (ed.), *EABHB: Railroads in the Nineteenth Century* (1988), 106–111; White, Bouck, *Book of Daniel Drew* (1910).

dearly in the city. One day he dumped salt in the pen where the cattle were stored and shortly before the buyer arrived (a brother of fur magnate John Jacob Astor), he turned them loose to water. When his mark arrived, the cattle looked fat and weighed in the same. When the news of this deal got out, Wall Streeters chuckled and coined a new term, "watered stock." It was a term Drew would make famous again and again.

Drew was not exceptional in his ethics, or lack of them. His attitude was standard in the nineteenth century—Drew was just better at it than most. He challenged Commodore Cornelius Vanderbilt for the Hudson River trade, opened a prosperous brokerage house on Wall Street, and turned his eye toward railroads. By 1855, he had loaned the Erie Railroad $2 million and called it in. The directors were caught short and had to surrender the control of the line to Drew. When Vanderbilt bought a controlling share, he mistakenly kept Drew on board as one of the directors. Vanderbilt had hoped that Drew would watch Jay Gould and Jim Fisk, the other two directors, who were no-

DT&I Conditions 275 ICC 45 (1950)

As railroads sought to merge, customers and passengers were often left out in the cold as service was cut indiscriminately to meet bottom-line cost realities. Stemming from Pennsylvania Railroad's desire to control the Detroit, Toledo & Ironton Railroad, the DT&I Conditions stated that merging railroads must maintain all routes and channels of trade through existing junctions and gateways (key cities) and all previous traffic relationships. But the railroads noted that no enforcement procedures accompanied the decision. In an effort seeming to follow the DT&I regulation, the bigger railroads merely changed their schedules at will in an attempt to force less economically viable companies out of business or into a hostile merger by fouling up the critical interchange of shipments and potential merger savings in a cutthroat effort to kill the lesser lines off. The ICC gave in and recognized the loophole in the Transportation Act of 1958, which not only permitted the railroads to ignore DT&I conditions legally but overruled concurrent state regulations that disallowed any cut in service, opening the way to increased cuts and renewed mergers.

See also Reed-Bullwinkle Act of 1948; Staggers Rail Act of 1980; Transportation Acts.

Reference Saunders, Richard, *The Railroad Mergers and the Coming of Conrail* (1978).

Dudley, Plimmon Henry (1843–1924)

Born on an Ohio farm, P. H. Dudley studied engineering and metallurgy and went to work for a local railroad. Here he built the first of his inventions, the "dynamometer car." This device told rail officials exactly what results they would get from the expenditure of steam power. By 1880, he was employed by the New York Central System. He improved the technology and design of steel rails and reduced the incidence of accidents from faulty or broken rails 24-fold. He also invented the track indicator, a device that measured the track gauge and its relation to the roadbed centerline. If a track was more than an inch off, a small dab of green paint was shot onto the rails for the track crew's later repair. A third device, the "stemmatographer," was placed under the rail to record the stresses of each wheel that passed over it. The New York Central placed all three devices in a single car costing $150,000. The car also had living quarters for Dudley and his wife, so they could travel throughout the system testing trains and rails. Dudley's inventions, plus his new stronger, lighter rail, permitted the higher speeds and greater weight that made American twentieth-century railroading possible.

See also New York Central System; Railroads from Appomattox to Deregulation.

Reference Hubbard, Freeman, *Encyclopedia of North American Railroading* (1981).

Durant, William C. (1860–1947)

Formerly a two-wheeled cart manufacturer, in the early twentieth century William C. Durant bought up Buick and made it into one the biggest competitors in the mid-price range in four short years. But along with the head of Maxwell-Briscoe Company, Benjamin Briscoe, Durant believed that the day of a single car line was limited. He and Briscoe deemed it much better to have several models in several price ranges to absorb the shock and fickleness of the buyers and the general economic fluctuations that regularly occurred and drove so many others (about 20 percent of early entrepreneurs each year) from the industry. He believed that about four different models would assure the continued success of each other—hopefully no more than one would "go bad" at any given time. In addition, he believed that bigness had a production advantage. All of the divisions could share plant space and marketing. Finally, this approach would create a near-monopoly situation, which, as any businessman knows, is safer and more profitable to the participants.

Durant and Briscoe tried first to unify Buick, Maxwell, Reo, and Ford. They hoped to buy the others by issuing stock in the new firm in lieu of cash. Such a combination would gain about half of the existing auto market. Durant especially was interested in bringing in others. Henry Ford was willing to sell, but only for cold cash. Reo also agreed, but wanted cash that Durant and Briscoe were unable to raise. Then Briscoe himself, on the advice of banker J. P. Morgan, withdrew Maxwell from the stock merger and said he wanted cash. The result was that Briscoe and Durant parted company. Durant went on alone. He chartered General Motors (GM) Company in New Jersey in 1908. Within two years he put together Buick, Oldsmobile, Cadillac, and Oakland (later the name was changed to Pontiac). He also bought parts and engine companies and many lesser auto production firms. Most historians credit Durant with defensive motives—merely trying to save Buick. But it appears that he was on the offensive—attempting to gain a monopoly position within the industry. That he failed to do so was probably because of the strength of his competitors rather than from a lack of trying.

Durant's GM was an instant success. The conglomerate made $10 million profit in its first year. But much of it had to be plowed back into the weak units of the company. The result was a lot of debt. Durant toured the nation looking for a savior. Finally a group of investors agreed to finance the debt if Durant would step down as active manager and be part of the board of directors. Durant hated to comply, but financial success demanded it. He may have taken some smug satisfaction later in the fact that the position of GM actually worsened in the industry after he left its active control. It was his old Buick and Cadillac divisions that kept GM alive until the 1920s.

Durant meanwhile went over to the Chevrolet division. He had backed the experiments of racing car driver Louis Chevrolet (1878–1941), who had designed and built five cars. One soon made it into the medium-price range market. Durant worked to get another entry in the lower price range. Within six years, Durant was back as big as before, having built Chevrolet into a company with three car lines and with its own parts sections and retail branches across the United States. His new concept

was to decentralize the fabrication of the autos to district plants that fed units into the whole system. But he still charged dealers for transportation from Detroit and the difference allowed him to compete with Ford. By 1915, Chevrolet was fifth in the industry. After World War I, Durant put Chevrolet in direct competition with Ford. Although the Chevy was more expensive, it had all sorts of nice options included as standard (like an electric starter and demountable rims). To get these items on a Ford, one had to pay extra. After all that was done, the prices were less than $100 apart.

By 1921, Durant's success had placed him back in the driver's seat at GM. He was known in the industry as "Fabulous Billy"— but no one dared say it to his face. Wise men called him "Mr. Durant." He purchased Fisher Body Works, but the postwar recession hit him hard and he had to step down in favor of Pierre DuPont, who came in under the condition that Durant get out of GM entirely. But DuPont had to rely on Durant's subaltern, Alfred P. Sloan, Jr., so

William Durant, known in the automobile industry as "Fabulous Billy," talks with his wife, Catherine, in this 1928 photograph.

Durant's influence would nonetheless be with GM forever. It was the epitome of the American auto idea: lots of models at varied prices, lots of options and gadgets, and an annual design change that put the notion of planned obsolescence into the whole formula. Durant went into other auto firms and Mason trucks, but was wiped out for the final time in the Great Depression. He died in obscurity.

See also Automobiles from Domestics to Imports; Automobiles in American Society; Briscoe, Benjamin; Sloan, Alfred P., Jr.

References Gustin, L. R., *Billy Durant* (1973); Motor Vehicle Manufacturers Association of the United States, *Automobiles of America* (1974); Rae, John B., "The Fabulous Billy Durant," *Business History Review* (1958) 25: 255–271; Rothschild, Emma, *Paradise Lost* (1973); Scharchburg, Richard P., *W. C. Durant* (1973); Shook, Robert L., *Turnaround* (1990); Sobel, Robert, *Car Wars* (1984); Thomas, Robert Paul, *An Analysis of the Pattern of Growth of the Automobile Industry* (1977); Weisberger, Bernard, *The Dream Maker* (1979); Weisberger, Bernard A., "William Crapo Durant," in George S. May (ed.), *Encyclopedia of American Business History and Biography: The Automobile Industry* (1990), 151–164.

Eads, James B. (1820–1887)

Born in Indiana, James Eads began his adult life as a dry-goods clerk in St. Louis at age 13. Six years later he went to work on a steamboat and became a skilled boatbuilder and salvager of river wrecks. He advised the Abraham Lincoln administration in 1861 on river defense, and received a contract to build eight river ironclads in 100 days. He also built other river war-craft, including a series of mortar boats. After the war, Eads constructed an arched bridge across the Mississippi at St. Louis and cleared out the South Pass at the river's mouth. He also developed plans for deepening the Mississippi as far as the mouth of the Ohio by means of jetties and for a railroad to haul ships across the isthmus of Tehuántepec, but they never came to fruition. He was the first American to receive the Albert Medal of the Society of the Arts in 1884, and died at Nassau, the British Bahamas, three years later.

See also Bridges; Steamboats at War.

Earhart, Amelia (1898–1937?)

Born in Atchison, Kansas, Amelia Earhart graduated from Chicago's Hyde Park School and attended the Ogontz School for Girls in Rydal, Pennsylvania. In 1918, after a mere ten hours' instruction, she soloed in an airplane at Los Angeles. She attended Columbus University and a summer session at Harvard, and did social service work at the Denison House at Boston. She was invited by Wilbur Stutz and Louis Gordon to be copilot on their flight across the Atlantic in the late 1920s. The successful completion of the trip, from Newfoundland to Wales, made her the first woman to fly the Atlantic in 1928, a feat she duplicated in 1932, setting a new speed record of 13.5 hours, this time flying alone from Newfoundland to Ireland. For this feat, she was made a Chevalier of the Legion of Honor of France and received the U.S. Distinguished Flying Cross (the first woman to do so) and the Gold Medal of the National Geographic Society. She married George P. Putnam, a noted publisher (who helped publicize her flights) in 1931. Additionally, she served as aviation editor of *Cosmopolitan*, was vice-president of a pair of smaller airlines, and wrote three books about her flying episodes. She also endorsed commercial products like cigarettes (she did not smoke) that simply horrified the common people of the day and led to much unwarranted criticism of her really conservative lifestyle (beyond flying airplanes, that is), much to her own chagrin.

Subsequent to several other record-setting feats, Earhart decided to attempt to circle the globe, accompanied by Fred Noonan as navigator. After a false start, she took off from Miami, Florida, flying east. All went relatively well until she took off from New Guinea for Howland Island in the Pacific. It was believed at the time that her radio setting was inexplicably different from that of the Coast Guard ship *Itasca*, leading to her missing the island and being lost at sea. Recent research by Fred Goerner posits the thesis that she and Noonan were actually scouting Japanese bases in the mandated islands of the South Pacific, a feat that had cost the lives of numerous agents already. Desperate to get a look at these areas, the story goes, the navy sent her across them, figuring that her fame and public knowledge of her around-the-world trip would protect her. It was a miscalculation. According to Goerner, Noonan was executed early on and Earhart later in World War II as Americans approached Saipan. He also claims that witnesses saw her Lockheed Electra plane taken by American authorities later, never to be seen again. Others, however, claim to have found parts of her plane and the sole of her shoe on an island near Howland.

Whatever Earhart's real fate, she was and continues to be an inspiration to women fliers the world over. Although she was not the first American woman to fly—an honor reserved for Harriet Quimby, who flew the English channel in 1912 only to crash and die at a Boston air show soon after—Earhart publicized the ability of women to compete in a field then seen as only for the most rugged and daring of men. She broke the barriers of condescension during the 1930s, along with Phoebe Fairgrave, Neta Snook, Ruth Nichols, Bobbi Trout, the equally legendary Florence "Pancho" Barnes, and Janet

Amelia Earhart at the 1933 National Air Races in Los Angeles

H. W. Bragg, America's first black woman to make a name in flying at the famed Tuskeegee Flying School.

Earhart's real contribution came with the organization of the Ninety-Nines, a women's flying group named after the number of its charter members at the 1929 National Air Races, and in her inspiration in the organization of the Women's Air Force Service Pilots (WASPs), the Women's Flying Training Detachment (WFTD), the Women's Auxiliary Ferry Squadron (WAFS) in World War II, and the Civil Air Patrol (CAP). These women took the place of men sent into the air war in Europe and the Pacific and trained pilots, patrolled American coastlines, and took aircraft of every imaginable size and style to bases overseas. Women organized as civilian adjuncts to the armed services, assisted by the example of the British Air Transport Auxiliary (ATA), following the advocacy stance of the New Deal and especially the outspoken role assumed by First Lady Eleanor Roosevelt. Led by Nancy L. Harness and Jacqueline Cochran, the women got the ear and tacit support of Army Air Force Generals Robert Olds and Henry "Hap" Arnold, who were short of male flyers anyhow. Although many women wanted to actually enter combat (of World War II participants, only the Russians permitted this), they were limited to behind-the-lines activity.

But in 1944, an anonymous male wrote a confidential report that doomed these women's service organizations' continued contribution to the war effort. Asserting that women lacked mechanical ability and the capacity to perform many tasks at one time—so necessary to flying (the reporter obviously forgot much about his mother's child-rearing efforts)—were sloppy and devoid of military discipline, and not worth the money invested in their training, falsely accusing them of larceny and disobedience, the report recommended that the program be terminated. Although hidden deep in one paragraph, it seems the real reason behind the report was the fear that women would compete with men after the war for anticipated plush civilian flying jobs with the airlines. Or, in other words, they were getting to be too good as pilots. As one WASP pointed out, the only difference between their training and a combat pilot's was the emphasis on aerobatics the men received. Yet when a group of male pilots refused to fly the Martin B-26 bomber, known as a "widow maker" because of its idiosyncrasies, an enraged General Arnold pointed out that the women could do it, and threatened to send every slacker to the infantry. The revolt against women pilots thus ended, and Amelia Earhart would have been proud.

It was not until 1976, as the Air Force announced its "first" program to train women pilots, that the WASPs and the others finally received recognition long overdue. After a bitter fight, President Jimmy Carter signed the "WASP bill" that recognized the women's contribution to World War II. But it took until 1984 before the women flyers received their World War II Victory Medals and the American Theater Medals. Today, women fly civilian airliners and combat and support planes for the armed services, engage in various air sports (air racing, parachuting, wing walking, ballooning, and soaring), own their own aviation businesses, and participate in the federal aeronautical agencies like the Civil Air Patrol, the Federal Aviation Administration, the National Transportation Safety Board, and Air Traffic Control (civilian and military). The aviation world is still a tough place to survive for women, but pioneers like Amelia Earhart and those who preceded and followed her helped make today's diverse roles for women in aviation possible.

See also Aeronautics.

References Bilstein, Roger E., *Flight in America* (1994); Douglas, Deborah, *United States Women in Aviation* (1991); Earhart, Amelia, *The Fun of It* (1932); Goerner, Fred, *The Search for Amelia Earhart* (1966); Holden, Henry M., and Lori Griffin, *Ladybirds I* (1991); Holden, Henry M., and Lori Griffin, *Ladybirds II* (1993); Lovell, Mary S., *The Life of Amelia Earhart* (1989); MacDonald, Anne, *Feminine Ingenuity* (1992); Planck, Charles E., *Women with Wings* (1942); Roseberry, C. R., *The Challenging Skies* (1966); Verges, Marianne, *On Silver Wings* (1991).

Early River Travel

From time immemorial, rivers were the transportation arteries of human endeavor. America was no exception. The Native Americans used them as prebuilt roads. The trails these peoples frequented very often connected one navigable river to another. The whites changed this use of portages with the technology of canals, which as often as not connected unnavigable parts of rivers with each other. As important as canal and road building was to early commerce, rivers always claimed an important chunk of trade; they still do.

The heyday of river transportation came prior to the Civil War, before the steel rails dominated the American landscape. No wonder—the Mississippi River system opened the trans-Appalachian West to white settlement, and the canals and roads all headed for one of its numerous branches, mostly the Three Rivers area where the Ohio was formed by the junction of the Allegheny and the Monongahela. It was no accident that the French and Indian War began here or that Pontiac's Rebellion occurred nearby, that primitive Fort Duquesne would become bustling Pittsburgh, or that Daniel French and Henry Shreve would start the building of river boats here just after the War of 1812—boats that could go with or against the current as one chose, powered by steam.

But that would have to wait. Initial journeys in the West were made as the locals did, by canoes, some made of birch bark, others hollowed out of logs by chopping or fire, known as "dugouts" in the North and "pirogues" in the bayou country. Farther west where there were few trees, bullboats made of hides stretched across a stick frame were common. The French *coureurs de bois*, the "runners of the woods" (early trappers), went by water. French (later Dutch and British) trade with the native peoples became so extensive as to eat into the very fabric of their ancient civilizations, making them more and more dependent on manufactured goods and causing them to war with each other for trade routes. To accommodate the demand, the traders used larger

Emigrants travel along the Tennessee River in a flatboat.

canoes. When white settlers established themselves at outposts like Natchez, Pittsburgh, Cincinnati, Vincennes, St. Louis, Cahokia, Kaskaskia, Fort Madison, and Galena, the demand for finished goods grew in size and so did the river craft.

The problem was that most trade had to go downstream to New Orleans. Because of the currents of the western rivers, upstream travel was difficult and restricted to the shallows. The freight canoes soon gave way to the keelboat, a narrow craft with a single-story superstructure for cargo and living quarters in inclement weather (any self-respecting keelboatman slept ashore when weather and rain permitted). The keelboat could be polled upstream by men who would find bottom and walk the deck to the rear, shoulders pushing against saplings braced in the water. Then they would step to the inside and carry the pole back to the bow and repeat the process. When topography allowed, the men would go ashore and pull the boat in a rope harness called a "cordelle." Lucky was the boat that had animal power for this latter job. Sometimes a stout tree was available for a block-and-tackle winching job known as "warping." The manpower version was used by Meriwether Lewis and William Clark in their expedition to explore the Louisiana Purchase up the Missouri River. Lewis and Clark also utilized another twist in the keelboat trade; they hoisted a sail whenever the wind blew upstream. A light canon or two was normally mounted for defense.

Downstream travel was more informal. One could simply lash a lot of logs together and float a cargo to any destination lower down. Often wigwams were erected on board for shelter, and fires built in dirt-filled boxes. A more complicated craft, and safer as it was better controlled, was the flatboat. These vessels could be rather sophisticated and have a structure to protect goods and crew, often built so sturdily that bullets and arrows could not penetrate it. The flatboats usually had large sweeps for steering, at least one on each side. On their long, spindly handles, the paddles stuck over the side gave the flatboats the nickname "broadhorns."

When loaded, they drew a deep draft, which restricted their use to mid-channel or spring-flooded waterways.

Once the flatboatmen and rafters reached New Orleans, they would sell the craft for lumber, sell their cargo, and walk home. At Natchez, they often branched away from the Mississippi and took a short-cut to Nashville and on to the headwaters of the Ohio, the so-called Natchez Trace. Still a modern highway, the trace wound through deep forest and swamp and was the headquarters of all sorts of riffraff like the John Murrell gang, mostly white. Erosion put the trail in a sunken pathway, sometimes three or four feet deep. The disappearance of a money-laden boatman was not uncommon, and bodies often were never found. The playground for river men was Natchez-Under-the-Hill, a two-mile-long strip of gambling, prostitution, and drinking parlors of varying rip-roaring character. Above, on the bluffs, stood the antebellum town of Natchez—charming, clean, and law abiding, the center of the cotton culture. The contrast was stultifying, to say the least. Similar districts existed at New Orleans and Memphis, and on a lesser scale everywhere the boats docked. But after Henry M. Shreve drove his flat-bottomed side-wheel steamer, *Washington*, upstream in 1817, a new era was on. The boatmen could ride home the same way they came, and everyone else could, too.

See also Early Steamboats; French, Daniel; Natchez Trace; Shreve, Henry Miller; Steamboats.

References Baldwin, Leland D., *The Keelboat Age* (1941); Donovan, Frank, *River Boats of America* (1966); Flexner, James Thomas, *Steamboats Come True* (1944).

Early Steamboats

Although Robert Fulton is given popular adulation for the invention of the steamboat, he did not deserve it. Many had preceded him by as much as 20 years, particularly Americans John Fitch, James Ramsey, and Oliver Evans and Englishman William Symington. But even these obvious candidates were preceded by earlier inventors and tinkerers. In 1618, David Ramsey of England applied for a patent for a boat driven by some sort of steam engine. He claimed that the engine could also pump water out of "lowe pitts." But nothing came of it. An American gunsmith, William Henry, built a steam-powered boat that sank on its maiden voyage in Pennsylvania's Conestoga River in 1763, although some dispute this. A half dozen men in France were experimenting with steam-powered vessels at the time of the American Revolution, only to be defeated by the lack of sufficient power. Indeed, it is probable that as many as 48 candidates existed before Fulton's effort. No wonder he was mired in legal problems with his claim to exclusivity, and he and his partner, Robert Livingston, ultimately failed to gain a monopoly on riverboat travel for their company, either on the Hudson or the Mississippi.

Why did Fulton get the credit? Probably because his vessel was practicable and made money. It also came about at the right time and place. Moreover, he had a reputation as a gentleman and a scholar and the backing of the powerful Livingston family, which gave him connections to publicity and respectability. And although the first successful trip up the Hudson River was made by a Fulton boat popularly called the *Clermont*, that, too, is a misconception. Its actual name was *The North River Steamboat*. Later, an eminently wise Fulton changed the name to *The North River Steamboat of Clermont*, Clermont being the name of Livingston's Hudson River estate. In 1817, Cadwallader Colden, the first biographer of Fulton, called it simply the *Clermont*, the name by which it is generally known today.

Out in Pittsburgh, a keelboatman named Henry M. Shreve, tired of polling upriver, bought the first Fulton boat he saw, the *Enterprise*, and set out for the Gulf. In 1814, he ascended the Mississippi and Ohio Rivers in the *Enterprise*, the first time this had been done. But the trip was possible only because of the spring flood tide. In 1816 he built the flat-bottomed shallow-draft stern-wheeler *Washington*, which rode on the water rather than in it. Although she ran aground and suffered a boiler explosion and two dozen casualties horribly scalded by escaping steam (another river "first" of doubtful honor), the *Washington* was repaired and continued on its trip to New Orleans. Then Shreve turned around and made the upstream trip in just over three weeks, a feat that took a keelboat four to six months to accomplish. Soon Shreve rebuilt the *Washington* into a side-wheeler, with each wheel operated by a separate engine. His design became a riverboat standard for power and control.

Over on the Missouri, Secretary of War John C. Calhoun decided to build a government-sponsored steamboat to challenge the British, operating out of Canada, for the upper Missouri River trade. In 1819, the *Western Engineer*, painted up like a fire-breathing dragon to impress Native Americans, negotiated the tricky Missouri up to Council Bluffs, where it conked out. Primitive engine technology was not yet up to conquering the shallow Missouri as it had the deeper Mississippi and Ohio. Spurred on by the development of the Santa Fe Trail and other emigrant roads out of Independence, Missouri, and the burgeoning upriver fur trade, John Jacob Astor's American Fur Company took notice of the newer, improved Mississippi boats by 1830. Under the impetus of Pierre Chouteau, Jr., Astor's St. Louis representative, the company built the *Yellowstone* (one of four craft to hold that name in the nineteenth century) and sent it up the Missouri to the mouth of the Yellowstone River, where the company's main depot, Fort Union, lay. At last, the Missouri had been proved navigable, and it joined the Mississippi and Ohio as an important inland waterway.

See also Early River Travel; Evans, Oliver; Fitch, John; Fulton, Robert; Rumsey, James; Shreve, Henry Miller; Steamboats; Symington, William.

References Chittenden, Hiram M., *History of Early Steamboat Navigation on the Missouri River* (1903); Donovan, Frank, *River Boats of America* (1966); Flexner, James Thomas, *Steamboats Come True* (1944); Foreman, Grant, "River Navigation in the Early Southwest," *Mississippi Valley Historical Review* (1928) 15: 34–55; Hunter, Louis C., "The Invention of the Western Steamboat," *Journal of*

Economic History (1943) 3: 202–220; Petersen, William J., "Steamboating on the Missouri River," *Iowa Journal of History* (1955) 53: 97–120.

Eastern Air Lines (EAL)

Once the most profitable carrier in the country, Eastern Air Lines is now defunct, a victim of poor management decisions, unreal employee demands, deregulation, and smugness. The company had its beginnings in the late 1920s when it obtained the airmail route from New York City to Atlanta, with stops in Philadelphia, Baltimore, Washington, and several smaller cities in Virginia and the Carolinas. Later the route was extended southward to include Miami. The original founders went in with Curtiss-Wright in 1930 and took on the title of Eastern Air Transport (EAT). One of the real benefactors of the airmail reshuffle of 1930, EAT's opponents and competitors challenged the selection methods, leading to congressional hearings and a new airmail law in 1934. It had little effect on EAT's business, which by now monopolized all air traffic along the American Atlantic Coast. But to keep the tarnish of the airmail scandals off its corporate image, EAT changed its name to the more familiar Eastern Air Lines.

At the same time as the name changed, EAL brought in a new manager, former World War I air ace Eddie Rickenbacker. The new manager completely reorganized the carrier, bringing in new aircraft like Lockheed Electras and Douglas DC-2s. He also extended its reach into the West through New Orleans to the Texas Gulf Coast, and into Chicago and St. Louis. Then Rickenbacker brought in the DC-3, in gleaming silver aluminum, promoted his airline as the Great Silver Fleet, and turned a cool $1.5 million profit by 1940. During World War II, Rickenbacker's airplanes flew for the United States Army Air Force. It would be the apex of the carrier's business cycle. After the war, the long downward slide began—some of it because of bad luck, the rest from unfortunate management decisions.

The first assault came from the federal government, the new Harry Truman administration, which began to break up the accepted prewar monopoly runs. EAL now had to compete along the East Coast with hungry companies like National and Delta. Whenever Eastern or other prewar giants competed for new routes, the government tended to award them to the newer upstarts. Hence the transcontinental routes went to Delta and National instead of EAL. Worse yet, when the government required a third man on the flight deck as flight engineer, Eastern put flight engineers there. This meant that it suffered much in the mid-1950s when the Air Line Pilots Association struck to make this person a pilot-in-training. Thus competitors (Delta had chosen to make the third man a pilot from the beginning) flew all traffic when EAL's planes were grounded by labor troubles. This made Eastern look unreliable to customers, and EAL's service became such a farce that dissatisfied passengers organized a national "We Hate Eastern Air Lines" group called WHEAL that publicized every gaffe. Malicious reports placed the stewardesses in the cockpit serving the flight crew instead of the customers.

Eastern also held off from the new jet planes, preferring to go to the intermediate step of the turboprop. This hurt its image and speed on long hauls, but it did give them an advantage on the New York City–Washington shuttle run, its one bright spot. But when Rickenbacker retired, his successor, Floyd Hall, began "Operation Bootstrap," designed to change past performance and public image. On-time flights were emphasized, company morale raised, in-flight amenities went back to the paying customer, new jets were bought, and EAL became Walt Disney World's official airline at Orlando. But Hall's well-intended program fell to many forces, some of which EAL could not predict. It suffered a disproportionate number of air-piracy attempts as it flew into the Caribbean, strikes plagued its operations at home, the Hall and old Rickenbacker factions quarreled, the new jets put the company into much debt, and one of its Lockheed L-1011 jets crashed into the

Florida Everglades, generating much adverse publicity.

Hall knew that he had to move on, and he chose EAL vice-president Frank Borman as his replacement. Borman had not been in favor of many of Hall's decisions, but he had worked loyally within the company to effect change. Now Hall believed the ex-astronaut might straighten out Eastern as only a military man could. Borman imposed strict discipline upon operations, renegotiated labor contracts and substituted profit sharing for wage hikes, got rid of the ponderous executive departments, bought more efficient and modern planes, and began an aggressive advertising campaign. At first, Borman's system boomed. EAL turned a profit for the next four years (1976–1979). But EAL had gone beyond the ability of any one person's skill to save it. Deregulation changed the whole picture. Suddenly, with one act the government had upset Borman's whole rescue mission by changing its economic realities, dominated by fixed costs like labor and debt. EAL was forced to cut fares to keep up with the new, cheaper competitors that deregulation spawned and who took the cream off the top of the better routes that Eastern had held more or less inviolate under regulation.

Borman's lack of business experience may have hurt him in this fight. He feared that EAL could not survive a strike, so he talked a tough line but yielded to labor's demands. The unions accused Borman of duplicity and trying to cheat workers out of their fair share of profits. In reality, Borman understood better the adverse results on wages and benefits that deregulation would have for organized labor in all transport companies. But he could not convince his employees. Reluctantly, he turned EAL over to Frank Lorenzo in a buyout and retired. Lorenzo took on the unions frontally. When they refused to meet his demands he declared a Chapter 11 bankruptcy and began to sell off Eastern's assets to cover its debt. The unions split between trades, each scrambling for survival. But Lorenzo literally sold off everything before a federal bankruptcy judge called a halt to further

proceedings and forced Lorenzo to step down. The fuel price increase during the Gulf Oil Crisis in 1990 was the last straw for Eastern's weak finances. EAL went out of business in January 1991, a victim of the demise of federal regulations that once made it America's most profitable airline.

See also Aeronautics; Borman, Frank Frederick, II; Lorenzo, Frank.

References Bernstein, Aaron, *Grounded* (1990); Lewis, W. David, "Eastern Air Lines," in William M. Leary (ed.), *Encyclopedia of American Business History and Biography* (1992), 160–168; Mailhout, Ernie, et al., *The Eastern Airlines Strike* (1991); Rickenbacker, Edward V., *Rickenbacker* (1969); Serling, Robert J., *From the Captain to the Colonel* (1980).

Eastman, Joseph B. (1882–1944)

Joseph Bartlett Eastman was born in Katinah, New York, in 1882. His father was a Presbyterian minister, and Eastman grew up in the Puritan heritage of New England. He moved with his family to a Pennsylvania coal town as a teenager, and attended college at Amherst in Massachusetts. He was an above-average but not outstanding student. He stood five feet, nine inches tall, forsook formal religion, and never married.

Eastman had no formal plans after school. He took up a fellowship at South End House, a settlement house in Boston. It was here that his social conscience was awakened for the first time. He became a protégé of Louis D. Brandeis (later an associate justice on the U.S. Supreme Court) and worked with him in many of his cases to defend the common peoples' rights against the privileged. He did not like the use of inflated yellow journalism in support of his positions—Eastman preferred to debate issues cordially and rely on the copious use of fact. This attitude gained him an appointment to the Massachusetts Public Service Commission in 1916. Originally a regulator of railroads, the commission had withered during the decades into a rubber stamp for the railroad barons. Eastman was, for all practical purposes, a socialist, and he favored government ownership not only of utilities but of all forms of the means of production. He came to represent the government regulation of private capital, but was always open to the exchange of ideas that differed with his.

With his open attitude, Eastman impressed many in government. In 1919 President Woodrow Wilson appointed him to the Interstate Commerce Commission (ICC). He was to serve for 25 years there and in other federal regulatory positions until his death. He worked long days and complained that he had too little time to mull over properly many of the difficult issues presented to the commission. As always, Eastman believed in extensive research and investigation in all cases. His general philosophical position became that he believed the theory of private enterprise did not work, and that governmental regulation was essentially a wasteful duplication of managerial functions. But he was impressed with the success of the American Railroad Administration in untangling U.S. transportation during the Great War. He wanted to combine all types of transportation under several strong business firms, but realized that the nation would not allow such monopolies. So he settled for government regulation of all transportation in a unified plan as an alternative. This was the man appointed federal coordinator of transportation under the Federal Emergency Railroad Transportation Act of 1933.

Eastman's role as coordinator was to organize the railroads into an efficient system, investigate competitive forms of transport (like trucks), and design a comprehensive program of regulation. Unlike World War I, however, the charge failed to be met. The only success that Eastman could point to was the Motor Carrier Act of 1935, which placed the truckers under the ICC for the first time. The main reason for his success here, limited though it was (he wanted all forms of transport regulated heavily), was because the truckers wanted to be regulated to bring a stability to their business that it lacked previously—or, to be blunt, to force out the dynamic forces that kept shipping costs low.

The ICC put Eastman in charge of the new motor truck division after the act's passage. It soon became apparent that the regulators were overworked. Eastman was often outvoted by his free-enterprise colleagues on the semijudicial investigative boards. He kept all proceedings public and continued to work in a pragmatic fashion, emphasizing what could be done rather than the ideal. By the beginning of World War II, Eastman and the truckers had stabilized the industry with a strong federal role through ICC regulation. He died in 1944 as the director of wartime transportation before he could complete his tasks (as he saw them) defined in the Federal Emergency Railroad Transportation Act of 1933—the coordination of all transportation into one system working to benefit the nation at large.

See also Federal-Aid Highway Acts, Federal-Aid Highway Act and Highway Revenue Act of 1956; Federal-Aid Highway Act of 1976; Federal-Aid Highway Amendments of 1975; Motor Carrier Acts, Motor Carrier Act of 1935; NRA Trucking Codes; Surface Transportation Assistance Acts, Surface Transportation Assistance Act of 1982; Transportation Acts, Transportation Act of 1920, Transportation Act of 1940; Trucking.

References Childs, William R., *Trucking and the Public Interest* (1985); Fuess, Claude Moore, *Joseph B. Eastman* (1964); Latham, Earl, *The Politics of Railroad Coordination* (1959).

Elkins Act (1903)

As the first major revision of the Interstate Commerce Act of 1887, the Elkins Anti-Rebate Law stated punishments for discriminatory pricing and fixed criminal penalties for railroad owners who deviated from ICC-agreed-upon rates. The statute was more important in the signal that it sent (enlarging the powers of the ICC) than for its actual content. But it relieved the railroads from having to respond to rebate demands by large shippers, promoting a more open competition. A corporate lawyer from the Pennsylvania Railroad allegedly drew up the first draft.

See also Hepburn Act; *Northern Securities Company v. U.S.*; Sherman Antitrust Act.

References Keeler, Theodore E., *Railroads, Freight and Public Policy* (1983); Kolko, Gabriel, *Railroads and Regulation* (1965); Lyon, Peter, *To Hell in a Day Coach* (1968); Martin, Albro, *Enterprise Denied* (1971); Mowry, George E., *The Era of Theodore Roosevelt* (1958); Swindler, William F., *Court and Constitution in the 20th Century* (1969).

Emergency Railroad Transportation Act (1933)

Based upon a plan suggested by Boston banker Frederick H. Prince, one-time president of the soon-to-be-defunct Pere Marquette Railroad, the Emergency Railroad Transportation Act called for the radical consolidation of American railroads with an eye to preserving competition and service by putting maximum traffic on minimum trackage. Because of the Great Depression and the falling of commodity prices, the railroads had to restructure rates and work on a principle of economy lest the commodity traffic be eliminated altogether. The entire nation would be divided into seven major systems, which would rent the railroads as needed from their owners. All labor would be protected by receiving their guaranteed jobs at half to three-fourths of their current salaries.

Intrigued by anything different, President Franklin D. Roosevelt's administration sent the Emergency Transportation Act through Congress in 1933. It created a federal coordinator of transportation to encourage all carriers to reduce duplication and reorganize their finances. Consolidation was one way this could be done, but not the only way. This measure amended the Transportation Act of 1920 in that it no longer tied railroad rates to a fair return on a fair value of their properties, a provision that led to increasing rates in a constricting economy. Now, the effect of rates on the movement of traffic and the public need for cheaper transportation were more important. It also abandoned the "recapture clause" and ordered the funds returned to the railroads that had deposited them. The Interstate Commerce Commission's (ICC) authority was extended to noncarrier companies with railroad interests. In return, the act placed a great emphasis on consolidation as a means of reducing costs by preventing wasteful duplication . Finally, it provided for labor representation on the administrative regional committees and declared that none of the cost-saving measures could be directed to shrinking the labor force, which pretty well ended a lot of potential savings.

Any employee transferred to another location was to have the transfer paid for by the company.

Joseph Eastman was appointed federal coordinator of transportation, but he lacked any coercive powers and the Association of American Railroads, a management organization designed to work with him, opposed any of his suggestions, rendering any reform moot. The law was very vague in its goals, but it stimulated the railroads to set up their own lobbying institution, the Association of American Railroads, to keep regulation in check in the future. As a business cartel, it fully cooperated with the Blue Eagle program of the National Recovery Administration. The measure was temporary and expired without renewal in 1936.

See also Eastman, Joseph B.; National Industrial Recovery Act of 1933; Railroad Labor Act of 1926; Railroad Retirement Act of 1934; Railroad Unification Act of 1931.

References Latham, Earl, *The Politics of Railroad Coordination* (1959); Leonard, William Norris, *Railroad Consolidation under the Transportation Act of 1920* (1946).

Emergency Relief and Construction Act (1932)

As part of the response of the Herbert Hoover administration to the onset of the Great Depression, the Emergency Relief and Construction Act was a $120 million advance to the states to allow them to continue to match federal funds for highway construction and repair. It was repayable in ten years. The idea was to guarantee jobs in this area of the economy, as the states were vastly overextended on bond payments contracted for during the boom years of the 1920s, the combined payments on which were $90 million and climbing. Opponents had warned that bond issues were deceptive—merely delaying payments until a future date, which now saw the states literally broke—but legislatures had followed the lead of Illinois in 1919 and bonds became one of the more popular ways to finance highways. The new federal law required that current wage standards be upheld to defeat the deflationary pressures inherent in the national economy then, and did much to push the later ideas of a minimum wage and the Davis-Bacon Act, which guaranteed that federal project wages reflect the highest prevalent wages of any similar civilian project.

See also Roads and Highways since World War I.

Reference U.S. Department of Transportation, Federal Highway Administration, *America's Highways* (1976).

Emergency Relief Appropriation Act (1935)

A continuation of the policies set forth in the National Industrial Recovery Act, the Emergency Relief Appropriation Act set aside $200 million for highway construction and $200 million for the elimination of hazards at railroad grade crossings. The money was in the form of unmatched funds.

See also Hayden-Cartwright Act; National Industrial Recovery Act of 1933; Roads and Highways since World War I.

Reference U.S. Department of Transportation, Federal Highway Administration, *America's Highways* (1976).

Erie Canal

The old American folk song "The Erie Canal" is reputed to have over 100 verses, many as ribald and rowdy as they are deadly serious, lending much credence to the definitive statement on the canal's place in history as propounded by its foremost advocate De Witt Clinton: "Conceived in sin, fed by ignorance and brought forth in iniquity, it disappointed no observing man."

The New York legislature had expressed an interest in western canals as early as 1784. The Erie Canal concept grew from earlier experiences, especially that of the Western Inland Lock Navigation Company. This firm, backed by George Clinton, Philip Schuyler, and Elkanah Watson, tried to develop the Mohawk Valley by building canals around the various falls and open a reliable water route to Oswego. Then another canal was to be built around Niagara Falls to connect to Lake Erie. Later, in 1807–1808, Jesse Hawley, a New York City merchant confined as a debtor at Canandaigua for 20 months, wrote 14 essays from jail proposing

a so-called Genesee Canal across the whole state. He claimed to be the Erie Canal's originator, but his claim was ignored to his death in 1841.

At the same time as Hawley's essays, Secretary of the Treasury Albert Gallatin proposed a route along the Mohawk with a canal to Oswego and another bypassing Niagara Falls to Buffalo, all to be sponsored by the federal government. Washington refused to come through before the War of 1812, and the project reverted to the state. Previously, the canal commission was essentially Federalist in politics, but De Witt Clinton's entry on the scene in 1810 brought the Republicans into the picture. He and Governor Morris wrote a positive presurvey report in 1811, and Clinton wrote a popularly received memorial in 1815.

Like the rest of the nation, New York turned enthusiastically nationalistic in 1815, which peaked interest in transportation projects. The state legislature set up a seven-man canal board composed of Federalists like Morris and Stephen van Rensselaer, and Republicans like Peter B. Porter, Governor Daniel B. Tompkins (both of whom hated Clinton), and Clinton. Constant infighting among the board members was overcome by the nationalism of the Era of Good Feelings, the demise of the Federalist Party, and the unification of all political parties under the Republican label. But the canal was delayed by further surveys and the ultimate failure of federal aid. There were other problems as well, including a scarcity of civil engineers, then an unknown profession in the New World; a lack of excavating machinery, which the canal builders would wind up inventing; a lack of building contractors able to undertake the project; an unknown route through forests and marshes; ardent opposition by those bypassed by the surveyed route west; and the need of the highway system to collect goods at key spots along the canal route, which absorbed most state capital until 1810.

The canal's attachment to Clinton's popular gubernatorial campaign in 1816 led to its passage by the state legislature as a state-funded internal improvement in 1817, with the route to be overland all the way to Buffalo, not by way of Oswego and Lake Ontario. Construction began on 4 July 1817 at Rome, going both east and west simultaneously, amid the usual hoopla. It was to be built concurrently in three sections: Rome to the Hudson, Rome to the Seneca River, and Buffalo to the Seneca.

The New York canal board wanted William Weston to be chief engineer. Weston was known for building the Schuylkill River Bridge in Philadelphia and the New York City water system, made by damming the Bronx River. But he hemmed and hawed and the offer was withdrawn in 1812. The men in charge were Benjamin Wright and James Geddes, who had surveyed the whole inland route in 1808, and offered to engineer the route on the condition that they would have full support of the board. Their calm, self-assured attitude convinced the board and they were hired, regardless of their lack of previous experience. In reality, they were attorneys who merely knew how to survey land titles, which made up the bulk of their previous business.

Wright and Geddes had to learn on the job. Indeed, former American canal builders proved more of a hindrance than a help; less than 30 theoretical tracts were available for instruction. Geddes got his experience by building the Hudson and Lake Champlain Canal by 1820. When Benjamin Wright surveyed the central section around Rome, he discovered Canvass White as one of his surveyors. At Clinton's suggestion, Wright sent the sharp young White to England to examine British canals, reputedly the best in the western world. White's biggest find was the construction methods of the locks. The main problem was the type of cement (hydraulic cement) to be used for the rock work that lined the banks and locks. It had to be waterproof. Quite by accident, White found at Chittenango in Madison County a local man who made a cement that proved superior even to European grades.

By 1819, Wright and Geddes had a large staff of engineers, aged 27 to 47, many of whom went on to build other canals and later even railroads. They solved the prob-lem of the canal's water level by keeping the summit level lower than that of Lake Erie. Nathan Roberts designed the locks and Wright built the 800-foot aqueduct across the Genesee at Rochester (one of 18 such structures that gave the canal its distinctive look), drained the Montezuma Marshes near Syracuse, and put up the one-mile-long embankment at Irondequoit across the creek, which ran under the canal through a culvert. Every day mechanics suggested innovative and altered equipment in plows, dredges, and tree-felling and uprooting devices. Stephen Van Rensselaer's development of the Technical College that bears his name came partly from his experience as a canal commissioner.

After eight years of construction, the 363-mile Erie Canal opened on 26 October 1825. The canal is pictured here in Syracuse, New York, in 1900.

The myth that Irish immigrants built the Erie is not entirely true. Most of the labor was homegrown until 1821, when immigrants from Wales and Ireland appeared in greater numbers than before. Oftentimes, work on the canal was the only source for jobs along its route. The route was essentially wilderness, full of forests and swamps. Disease was rampant among the laborers and managers alike. Working conditions were damp and malarial. Nonetheless, the canal was completed in eight years and opened on 26 October 1825. The finished canal was 363 miles long, 40 feet wide at the surface and 28 feet at the bottom, and 4 feet deep (the common depth in canal building then). The locks were 90 feet long and 15 feet wide. They were closed by iron-bound rock-slab gates, equipped with ingenious sluices and wickets that raised and lowered water levels inside the closed gates, and so well balanced that they could be opened by one man using a long wooden pivot arm. It was not uncommon to see 60 to 70 boats waiting their turns at the locks.

The Erie Canal ran from Buffalo through Lake Oneida to Rome and parallel to the Mohawk River, entering the Hudson just north of Troy. There were 84 locks that raised the water level 689 feet between Troy and Buffalo. Both banks were towpaths just wide enough for two draft animals to operate, pulling the barges through a singletree arrangement. Toll rates started at $18 per ton-mile in 1826 and eventually dropped decade by decade until they were less than $1 per ton-mile by 1850. The average speed of freight was 55 miles in 24 hours; passenger packets—speedy vessels, 75 feet long and 11 feet wide with dining rooms and sleeping areas—frequently made 100 miles in 24 hours. It took four minutes per boat to pass through a single lock. At Lockport, a ladder of five locks raised or lowered boats, comprising the largest single rise (or drop) on the whole canal.

"Clinton's Big Ditch" cost $7,143,790 to build. Tolls and tonnage on the Erie-Champlain system were so great by 1819 that the opening of the finished parts helped finance the unfinished sections. Total maintenance expenses to 1882, when tolls were abolished, were $78,862,154 and total income during the same period of time was $121,461,871. In the 1840s, the canal provided work for over 25,000 persons, attracting both immigrants and the native-born from several surrounding states. It was unrivaled as the main commercial and public transport system west until the 1850s, when railroads began to compete, but its greatest tonnage year was in 1880.

The success of the Erie Canal set off a nationwide craze for canal building east of the Mississippi. New York fell to the fever by building extensions on the Erie Canal. Some proved to be valuable, as were the branches to Oswego and the Black Water branch out of Rome, but others heading southward were not. As early as 1835, the system was so overworked that the state ordered an enlargement, increasing the width at the surface to 70 feet and the depth to 7 feet, which took until 1862 to complete. Reconstruction occurred again in 1915–1918 when the Erie Canal became part of the New York Barge Canal System with 34 modern locks and a 10-foot depth.

See also American System; Canals; Gallatin Report; Geddes, James; Van Buren, Martin; White, Canvass; Wright, Benjamin.

References Andrist, Ralph K., *The Erie Canal* (1964); Bourne, Russell, *Floating West* (1992); Johnson, Emory R., *Elements of Transportation* (1914); Krout, John A., "New York's Early Engineers," *New York History* (1945) 24: 269–277; MacGill, Caroline E., et al., *History of Transportation in the United States before 1860* (1917); O'Donnell, Thomas C., *Snubbing Posts* (1949); Shaw, Ronald E., *Erie Water West: A History of the Erie Canal, 1792–1854* (1966); Taylor, George Rogers, *The Transportation Revolution, 1815–1860* (1951); Whitford, Nobel E., *History of the Canal System of the State of New York* (1906).

Erie Lackawanna Railroad (EL)

From its seedy past strewn with stock manipulations and fraud, the Erie Railroad became known as the "Scarlet Woman of Wall Street." But by the twentieth century it had managed to become a prime carrier of perishable and finished goods and a passenger route of some note. It experimented with the gigantic triplex, the Matt Shay, in its day the largest of American steam locomotives with three banks of steam cylinders and drivers in a 2-6-6-0 pattern. But the trials failed. No matter. The Erie had another reputation that was even more critical to its future than the financial shenanigans of its past: It was a trunk railroad that went from New York to Chicago and missed every major city in between. This meant that even a well-run Erie, and that was its reputation since the 1880s, went nowhere.

Or, as the cynics on Wall Street put it, when Erie common stock paid a dividend, Hell would freeze over.

Like Erie, the Lackawanna Railroad also had a past difficult to live up to. But in Lackawanna's case it was a past that regularly paid 20 percent dividends on its stock. In 1909, the Lackawanna was doing so well that it paid its dividends plus a Christmas bonus—a total that reached an incredible 50 percent. Beginning in the Pennsylvania coalfields, its mainline paralleled the Erie's for some distance between Binghamton and Elmira, New York, before Lackawanna turned north to Buffalo and Erie headed west to Chicago. The Great Depression, however, gave Lackawanna more similarity to Erie than a parallel route. Both nearly went broke. Then came World War II, and both came back into the black. So in 1945, Erie and Lackawanna began anew from roughly the same point on the ledger sheet.

But the profitability of the postwar era began to end with a freak of nature. In 1955, Hurricane Diane wiped out about 75 miles of mainline. Next came a long, bitter steel strike, then a cement strike, followed by a longshoreman's strike. And in 1958, the severest of the postwar recessions put the final nail in the coffins of Erie and Lackawanna. The two railroads had much in common, especially in the location of their physical plant in the East. Their terminals were nearly adjacent from Hoboken to Elmira. Coordination along the common stretches of mainline had been going on for years. Why not formally merge and cut out the duplications? It seemed so logical that no one in the two corporations opposed it. Yet, in the end, it would become the prime example of why mergers were no panacea to railroad problems.

Since 1956, Erie and Lackawanna had been talking merger. Also involved was the Delaware & Hudson (D&H), another coal hauler. But unlike the other two, D&H was still profitable, a fact that led its board to reject the merger and leave Erie and Lackawanna to go it alone. It was believed by people at the time that the merger could not fail because it was based on the first exten-

sive computer study of the time. But it also revealed the truism of the information age: "garbage in, garbage out." It turned out that the estimates in savings were based on 1956, the last profitable year on the two lines. This skewed all the figures to the optimistic side. It also did not give much background into how many of the cost estimates were arrived at. It was a good example of how figures could be twisted to get whatever conclusion the report writers wanted.

The result was that, for all the talk, there was little actual savings to be realized in the merger. The report called for the Lackawanna mainline to be abandoned; yet it was one of the best in the nation. But Erie served the most businesses, and business was a key protester against the merger before the Interstate Commerce Commission. So "give a little, and (hopefully) gain a lot" became the byword. Labor was especially angry because more than half of the new corporation's savings was to come out of their jobs, and the cities bypassed or suffering job cuts saw the merger as an attack on their very existences. Other railroads wanted interchanges guaranteed, especially the competing anthracite-hauling lines and the so-called bridge lines that took Lackawanna freight westward. They wanted to be sure that Erie would not undercut them to Chicago. The only competitor that did not complain was the Pennsylvania Railroad (PRR), probably because it saw the merger as a failure in the long run that would help the "Pennsy" gain a better position overall. But no one else seemed to anticipate this.

The merger went through, and PRR sat back and watched. It did not have to wait long. Right away there were problems. The alleged savings did not materialize. The recession deepened and EL went into the red. Premerger planning was nonexistent. The two railroads were one company but labor and accounting were kept separately. Abandoning Lackawanna facilities in New York State was a mistake. The Erie mainline trains could not use the Lackawanna yards, kept because of their capacity and modernity. Old shippers on the bridge lines (Wabash and Nickel Plate) refused to ship via EL beyond Buffalo, supposedly one of the great advantages of merger. The old routes stayed the same, except now the Erie main to Chicago was actually used less. Pennsylvania moved in to grab the Erie's old Chicago trade. EL tried to stave off the inevitable by sprucing up its passenger service and getting rid of its commuter lines. Then the bridge lines all merged with Norfolk & Western (N&W), leaving EL more isolated than ever.

It seemed that Pennsy knew what it was doing. A true merger would have put together Erie Lackawanna, Lehigh Valley, Nickel Plate, and Wabash. But PRR and N&W would have had none of that, and the necessary capital in that age of recession was unavailable. Besides, that particular merger would have had clout. It would have worked. PRR was fortunate that the investors saw only the short-term profit, a problem that has haunted most of American industry in the late twentieth century. But there was some irony in it after all. Not only did EL take the dive, but the Pennsylvania Railroad was not as well-off as it had hoped. Soon it would try to stave off economic defeat by its own merger with the rival New York Central System. That failure would put Pennsy into the federal concoction called Conrail—along with a half dozen anthracite railroads like Lehigh Valley and the operation they had tried to checkmate all along, Erie Lackawanna.

See also Anthracite and Bridge Line Railroads; Conrail; Drew, Daniel; Fisk, James, Jr.; Gould, Jay; Locomotives, Steam Locomotives; Penn Central Transportation Company; Vanderbilt, Cornelius.

References Adams, Charles F., and Henry Adams, *Chapters of Erie* (1956); Casey, Robert J., and W. A. S. Douglass, *The Lackawanna Story* (1951); Drury, George H., *The Historical Guide to North American Railroads* (1985); Drury, George H., *The Train-Watcher's Guide* (1990); Grow, Lawrence, *On the 8:02* (1979); Hubbard, Freeman, *Encyclopedia of North American Railroading* (1981); Hungerford, Edward, *Men of Erie* (1946); Larkin, Daniel F., "Erie Railroad," in Robert L. Frey (ed.), *EABHB: Railroads in the Nineteenth Century* (1988), 115–117; Lyon, Peter, *To Hell in a Day Coach* (1968); Mott, Edward H., *Between the Ocean and the Lakes* (1899); Saunders, Richard, *The Railroad Mergers and the Coming of Conrail* (1978); Saunders, Richard, "Erie Railroad," in Keith L. Bryant, Jr. (ed.),

EABHB: Railroads in the Age of Regulation (1988), 136–138; Wresting, Frederick, *Erie Power* (1970).

Evans, Oliver (1755–1819)

An American inventor born in Newport, Delaware, Oliver Evans had a practical turn of mind from an early age. He went into the milling business with his brothers and soon invented the elevator, the conveyor, the drill, the hopper boy, and the descender, all powered by water, and which revolutionized the milling industry for all time. He tried without success to invent a steam carriage, an amphibious craft that came up the Schuylkill River and lumbered around Philadelphia's Independence Square, belching smoke and hissing, which also gave him claim to the invention of the first steamboat. His engines differed in principle from most in use at the time, relying on high-pressure steam, and he discovered that they could be applied to his earlier milling inventions to produce more reliable and flexible power. Later English applications came from Evans's sending the plans to correspondents there who capitalized on them. Evans's high-pressure steam engine became the basis for the Mississippi River flat-bottomed riverboats, as adapted by Daniel French and improved by Henry Shreve. Evans moved to New York in his later years, where he died shortly after developing a steam-powered dredging barge.

See also Early Steamboats; Fitch, John; Fulton, Robert; Rumsey, James; Shreve, Henry Miller; Steamboats; Stevens, John, Jr.

References Donovan, Frank, *River Boats of America* (1966); Flexner, James Thomas, *Steamboats Come True* (1944).

Express Cases 117 US (1886)

A major Wells Fargo Express Company suit against the Northern Pacific Railroad, which had its own exclusive express company, was known as the *Express Cases*. The U.S. Supreme Court ruled that a monopolistic position of an express company on any railroad was actually a public service that prevented confusion and duplication of services, and competition need not be allowed.

This cost Wells Fargo its attempt to break into the Northern Pacific service area as a second company beside the railroad's own express company.

See also Wells Fargo & Company.
Reference Warren, Charles, *The Supreme Court* (1922).

Family Lines System

The Family Lines was an eight-year economic endeavor that united a dozen and a half southern railroads controlled by the Louisville & Nashville Railroad and the Seaboard Coast Line Industries, itself a combination of the Seaboard Air Line Railroad and the Atlantic Coast Line Railroad. It was hoped that together they could compete better with the Southern Railway. But by 1980, the Family Lines proved unequal to the task and merged with the Chessie System to form CSX Corporation, a move countered by the merger of Southern with Norfolk & Western as Norfolk Southern Railroad.

See also CSX Corporation; Louisville & Nashville Railroad; Norfolk Southern Corporation; Seaboard Coast Line Railroad.

References Drury, George H., *The Historical Guide to North American Railroads* (1985); Drury, George H., *The Train-Watcher's Guide* (1990); Saunders, Richard, *The Railroad Mergers and the Coming of Conrail* (1978).

Fargo, William G. (1818–1881)

William G. Fargo was born in Pompey, New York, in 1818. He worked as a store clerk, tried to open his own business but failed, and instead became an agent for the new Auburn and Syracuse Railroad (later part of the New York Central System). In 1842, he became a messenger for Pomeroy and Company Express, and there met one of Pomeroy's partners, Henry Wells. Like Wells, Fargo believed that the future for the express business lay to the west. Intrigued by his enthusiasm, Wells helped Fargo organize Western Express. Wells soon sold his interest to William A. Livingston, and the firm became Livingston, Fargo & Company. The company didn't have much business at first, but made a big step forward by transferring bank notes back and forth between exchange houses. By 1850, business between Buffalo and the West was booming, and when the eastern companies coming into Buffalo organized American Express Company, they invited Livingston and Fargo to be their western connection as full partners.

With the discovery of gold in California, American Express organized a subsidiary company to exploit the gold trade and compete with Adams Express, which had a three-year head start. The result was Wells Fargo & Company, initially capitalized at $600,000. American and Wells Fargo divided the nation between them at the Mississippi and Missouri Rivers. After surviving the depression of the mid-1850s, Wells Fargo had the whole West Coast to itself. It also expanded out onto the Great Plains by acquiring the Holladay Stage Lines. This last transaction nearly proved to be too much for the company. Wells and Fargo had been very contemptuous of the transcontinental railroad and had failed to gain a foothold on it. By 1869, the old way of doing business had come to an end. But Wells Fargo had no rail connections. Wells resigned and Fargo took over, doing his best to save the company. He sold much of the unprofitable stage line and bought out the Central Pacific's express contract, giving up one-third of the company's stock to achieve it. By 1872, the company

William G. Fargo profited as a partner in Wells Fargo & Company during the mid-nineteenth century.

had come under the dominance of the Central Pacific (later Southern Pacific) crowd.

A Democrat in a business that was dominated by Republicans, Fargo was a bit of an oddity. He saw to it that all of his employees who enlisted in the Civil War received their normal salaries in addition to the meager army pay. Like all other expressmen, Fargo had packages to and from soldiers sent at half price during the war. Fargo, North Dakota, on the Northern Pacific Railroad (once a Fargo carrier), was named after him. He gradually retired from the business and died in Buffalo in 1881.

See also Wells, Henry; Wells Fargo & Company.

Reference Harlow, Alvin F., *Old Waybills* (1934).

Federal-Aid Highway Acts

The Federal-Aid Highway Acts are a series of congressional measures designed to assist the states through matching funds in building the national highway network. By putting federal money in the mix, Washington could set minimal standards and assure overlying symmetry to the plan. Some of the more important examples follow.

FEDERAL-AID HIGHWAY ACT OF 1934

This measure, for the first time, allowed the states to spend up to 1.5 percent of their federal matching funds on surveys, plans, and engineering investigations for future road projects. The bill intentionally avoided the use of the word "planning" as it had fallen into disrepute among many. Although some states tried to apply such moneys to actual construction, public roads chief Thomas M. MacDonald refused to allow anything but planning efforts in the expenditure of such funds. The 1934 act had another provision that required that one-fourth of highway matching funds be applied to secondary and feeder roads. This was the first time that road classification was made a part of the federal funding system. Before this, states could spend the money on any roads they pleased. Now the 25 percent set aside guaranteed that all roads would receive some attention.

FEDERAL-AID HIGHWAY ACT OF 1938

Because of the continued interest in beautifying American roadsides, Congress passed the act of 1938, which provided for landscaping and roadside development, particularly in sanitary facilities. This marked the first time that the federal matching funds could be used in the finishing touches to a highway that made for such items as roadside rest and picnic areas. It also marked the joining of the parkway concept, where roadside beauty and convenience had been extensively practiced, to the common highway, where this type of finishing touch had been largely ignored. The measure was permissive only, which meant that many states chose to ignore it. It was not until 1965 that such roadside amenities received separate funding under the Highway Beautification Act.

FEDERAL-AID HIGHWAY ACT OF 1940

In anticipation of American entry into World War II, this act of 1940 provided that the secretaries of the army and navy, or any other cabinet-level agency, could ask the federal works administrator to expend federal highway-aid matching funds on projects necessary for the national defense. The funds did not require the states to match them and could be used to survey such projects and pay for supervision of their construction. Although it was not realized at the time, it was the last federal-aid act to be passed until the end of the war—all those during the war were seen as outright defense measures.

FEDERAL-AID HIGHWAY ACT OF 1944

With the Allied victory in World War II merely a matter of time, Congress passed the 1944 highway act with the postwar world in mind. It authorized the expenditure of $500 million a year for three years plus $25 million for Forest Service roads; $225 million was to be spent on the federal highways, $125 million on urban extensions, and $150 million on secondary and feeder roads, as selected by the states. Up to one-third of federal matching funds could be used to purchase rights-of-way (including those strictly for beautification). The construction of the 40,000-mile interstate, limited-access, divided highway system was authorized, but no money was appropriated for it. The interstate routes would be chosen by the states through which they ran, but with the concurrence of adjoining states and the federal government. The act preserved the essential federal-state relationship but liberalized the amount of federal assistance. It marked a defeat for those who desired a federally owned trunk highway system, or toll road. But the interstate highway system was put off for some time in the future, allowing much debate as to its final form. Another clause required the states to uniformly sign all roads with the approval of the Bureau of Public Roads, and a final paragraph authorized the expenditure of 1.5 percent of matching funds for highway "research." By 1962, the research funds would be required to be spent as such, and not revert to the ordinary building fund at the discretion of the states. It is generally seen as a far-reaching measure that paved the way for future legislation.

FEDERAL-AID HIGHWAY ACT OF 1948

This measure ordered a study of the interstate and primary federal highways, over- and underpasses, and bridges, with an eye toward future defense needs and to increased truck traffic and weights. It generated the congressional report, *Highway Needs of the National Defense*, the basic thesis of which was that the highway was an integral part of the defense assembly line, allowing a decentralization of defense plants throughout the nation.

FEDERAL-AID HIGHWAY ACT OF 1950

This act allowed the states to borrow funds in the bond market against future federal-aid highway appropriations. As it did not make any new money available or do anything for the states' bond ratings, nor guarantee that future federal funds would be forthcoming, few states availed themselves of its authorization. Other clauses called for

public hearings to discuss the bypassing of any city by the interstate system, the appropriation of $3.5 million for two years for Forest Service roads, and the authorization of other moneys (some of which were never appropriated) for the Pan American Highway.

FEDERAL-AID HIGHWAY ACT OF 1952

Increasing the aid package to $550 million for the next two fiscal years, this measure also authorized spending $25 million on the interstate highways at the same time. State matching funds for the interstate were at the ratio of 50–50.

FEDERAL-AID HIGHWAY ACT OF 1954

This congressional legislation increased the aid package to $875 million a year and the interstate aid to $175 million. The federal-state ratio was 60–40. It also allowed the states to use federal money for their secondary roads virtually without federal supervision. It finally called for an extensive investigation of the needs of the interstate highway system and of the use of toll roads and their relation to the new system. The result was the report *Progress and Feasibility of Tolls Roads and Their Relationship to the Federal-Aid Program*. It confirmed that toll roads were not the way that the federal aid should be spent (a principle first set forth in 1916), but permitted them to be included in the interstate system if they were up to its standards and could be bypassed by other highways.

FEDERAL-AID HIGHWAY ACT AND HIGHWAY REVENUE ACT OF 1956

Among the most important highway legislative measures of all time, the acts of 1956 set up the interstate highway system with funding for completion. The Federal-Aid Highway Act (or Title I) contained the program features. The name of the new road network was to be the National System of Interstate and Defense Highways. It was set up for 41,000 miles (later increased in 1968 to 42,500 miles). It created standards of construction to accommodate the traffic predicted for 1975, nearly 20 years hence. Ramps and interchanges were to be limited to the original plan to keep access truly controlled, although some changes could be made with the approval of the secretary of commerce.

The system established by Title I was to have funding at $27 billion, and the federal-state ratio was 90–10. Increased gasoline taxes made up the public's direct contribution. It was to be paid for on the pay-as-you-go principle. The first appropriations for the first three years were to be on the traditional federal-state formula (half according to population, half according to the 1916 law), but thereafter the funding was to be on the basis of need to finish the whole system, regardless of the local governing entity. Needs were to be based on the cost estimates to finish the entire project. Salaries of labor were to be paid out on the Davis-Bacon principle—at the highest going rate for the area in which the project was built. As this measure had only been used in federal projects before, and the interstate was essentially a state project with 90 percent federal funding, this was a new approach. The interstate was to be treated as one whole project, much like a flood control scheme or the building of the transcontinental railroad. This meant that it was not considered finished until all of the component parts were in place.

In addition, the 1956 act said that no service facilities were to be on the interstate right-of-way (unlike the Florida Turnpike, for example, where such facilities are franchised for such locations). Existing highways were to be utilized as much as possible to determine the route of the interstates. Public hearings had to be held whenever a town was to be bypassed, but this was not a democratic process. Final decisions were made by state and federal highway officials. Seven toll roads were to be incorporated into the system, on condition that they be toll-free as soon as their original debt was retired. These (some 2,300 miles) included the Indiana Toll Road, the Northern Illinois Toll Highway, the Kentucky Turnpike (the first to go free in 1975), the Maine

Turnpike, the New York State Thruway, the Ohio Turnpike, and the Richmond-Petersburg Turnpike. This effectively ended toll roads as an effective alternate to federal funding. The Highway Revenue Act established the Highway Trust Fund under Title II, which absorbed all highway user taxes and fees for highway construction for the first time. This required a major overhaul of the internal revenue code. The fund received all of the tax income and dispensed all of the payment vouchers to the states.

Finally, under the Federal-Aid Highway Act of 1956, all vehicle weights and measurements were to be federally determined. Early highway truck size and weight limits had been applied in a haphazard fashion. States began to regulate the limits before World War I, but the wartime emergency caused these limits to be largely ignored, to the detriment of American roadways. After the war, the states once again adopted size and weight limits, and by 1933 almost all states had them. The usual regulations relied heavily on a Pennsylvania law of 1913, and provided for a maximum axle weight of 18,000 pounds. But the variation among jurisdictions ranged from 16,000 pounds per axle in Alabama (the amount originally recommended by the American Association of State Highway Officials [AASHO]) to 24,640 pounds per axle in the District of Columbia. Of course, unless truckers wanted to risk being caught, a vehicle had to be loaded for the state with the lightest weight and shortest length criteria through which they passed. Otherwise lots of unloading and reloading entered the picture, along with inflated costs. World War II led to a general lifting of weight and size limits once again. After the war, AASHO recommended that they be increased to Pennsylvania's 18,000 pounds per axle.

With the advent of the federal interstate limited access, divided highway program, the Federal-Aid Highway Act of 1956 provided that 18,000 pounds per axle be made the national standard. Tandem axles were limited to 32,000 pounds and gross vehicle weight to 73,280 pounds. This legislation allowed operation at higher weights that were legal in some states under a "grandfather clause." It also called upon AASHO to conduct tests to find the optimum weight for interstate operations.

FEDERAL-AID HIGHWAY ACT OF 1958

By 1858, the United States was in an economic recession and the government decided to spend its way out of the slump. The result was an increase of interstate appropriations from $2 billion annually to $2.2 billion for 1959 and $2.5 billion for 1960 and 1961 (fiscal years). This was in part a recognition that annual costs were increasing. Further, the 1958 act permitted the pay-as-you-go provision be set aside for two years. This allowed expenditures to exceed the amounts taken in by the Highway Trust Fund. Changes in the highway taxes and user fees followed in 1959 (which floated upward to cover the balance).

FEDERAL-AID HIGHWAY ACT OF 1961

After the change of administration from President Dwight D. Eisenhower to John F. Kennedy (Republican to Democrat), the new administration decided to return to the pay-as-you-go principle. Accordingly, the Highway Trust Fund was bolstered by another increase in taxes and user fees. Also, a 10 percent excise tax on trucks, buses, and trailers was devoted solely to the fund. This amounted to a new authorization to fund and finish the interstate program.

FEDERAL-AID HIGHWAY ACT OF 1962

This piece of legislation introduced the continuing reevaluation of the existing interstate program through a process called 3-C, which stood for "continuing, comprehensive, cooperative planning." It required states and localities with more than 50,000 in population to develop future programs that took into account other forms of transportation and to act in accordance with the input of appropriate federal agencies. In practice this meant lots of planning but little cooperation. In addition, the states had to prove that they were giving those persons

and businesses displaced by new rights-of-way advisory assistance and access to the limited federal funds set aside for moving them. Again, the states removed the people but provided little monetary assistance. Finally, the act called for a survey of the road situation in Alaska (recently made a state) and a report to Congress. This report led to the Federal-Aid Highway Act of 1966, in which $14 million annually for five years went to improve Alaskan roads and highways.

FEDERAL-AID HIGHWAY ACT OF 1968

Besides designating an additional 1,500 miles of interstate, this measure created the program known as TOPICS—Traffic Operations Program to Increase Capacity and Safety—for improving highway traffic operations in urban areas, and authorized additional funds for primary and secondary roads. It also created a program to create parking facilities next to interstate rights-of-way, a program that became permanent in 1970. Moreover, the act established a revolving fund to purchase rights-of-way for future construction, a provision restricted the following year by the National Environmental Policy Act that required environmental impact statements be made ahead of any purchase. Finally, the payment of relocation costs became mandatory and could actually be higher than the lost property's assessed value to cover actual replacement cost. Another alternative was to move a house and its occupants to a new site at the government's expense.

FEDERAL-AID HIGHWAY ACT OF 1970

This congressional mandate required that the states give on-the-job training to further the goals of the Equal Employment Opportunity Commission and the civil rights of minorities. All hiring on the federally aided highway projects was not to discriminate on the basis of race, color, or national origin. The federal government created the National Highway Institute to develop these training programs with the states. All public hearings on interstate location had to look at the economic, social, and environmental impact of the new road. New housing as a replacement for those displaced by highway construction was made available. Noise abatement standards were to be created to further reduce the impact of interstates on established residential areas. An inspection of all bridges was to be made and inadequate structures brought up to standard. Finally, Forest Service programs were placed under the Highway Trust Fund.

FEDERAL-AID HIGHWAY ACT OF 1973
This measure restated the 1916 federal-state relationship, pledging that no project would be undertaken in any state without its explicit permission. It also allowed Highway Trust Fund money to be used for urban feeder routes to the interstate of not more than 10 miles in length, urban mass transit (including purchase of buses and rail facilities), bike-ways, pedestrian walkways, and the entire cost of motor vehicle safety programs. A series of amendments creating a program for constructing, reconstructing, and improving roads not currently in the federal system was appended. Finally, money was provided for constructing noise abatement walls and other devices prescribed under the study launched three years earlier.

FEDERAL-AID HIGHWAY ACT OF 1976
This act completely reconstituted the financial process in the federal-aid highway program, creating more flexibility in the expenditure of funds, consolidating the numerous accounts, and permitting the allocation of funds for any single year to be available for up to three years if not used immediately.

As can be readily surmised from these acts, the federal role in highway construction and maintenance serves as an entrée into the lives of the states and their people for more than mere road building. It encompasses all federal programs including highway finance, employment practices, highway standards, research and development of new procedures and materials, environmental regulations, mass-transit man-

dates, securing of rights-of-way, and relocation of businesses and existing residents. Federal transportation's growth from an office of "inquiry" into a large federal department employing nearly 1 million persons is a statement on the impact of the federal government of American everyday life in the twentieth century. It is truly something that the Founding Fathers, with the exception of men like Alexander Hamilton, never contemplated as possible or desirable 200 years ago. It shows not only the flexibility of the Constitution, but questions its very meaning as a continuing document of intent.

See also Eastman, Joseph B.; Federal-Aid Highway Amendments of 1975; Motor Carrier Acts, Motor Carrier Act of 1935; NRA Trucking Codes; Roads and Highways, Colonial Times to World War I; Roads and Highways since World War I; Surface Transportation Assistance Acts, Surface Transportation Assistance Act of 1982; Transportation Acts, Transportation Act of 1920, Transportation Act of 1940; Trucking.

References Burnam, John Chenowyth, "The Gasoline Tax and the Automobile Revolution," *Mississippi Valley Historical Review* (1961–1962) 48: 435–455; Transportation Research Council, *Twin Trailer Trucks* (1986); Transportation Research Council, *Truck Weight Limits* (1990); U.S. Department of Transportation, Federal Highway Administration, *America's Highways* (1976).

Federal-Aid Highway Amendments of 1975

Under tests conducted by the American Association of State Highway Officials (AASHO) since 1956, AASHO recommended in 1964 that truck sizes and weights be increased to 20,000 pounds per axle (tandems to 34,000 pounds), and gross vehicle weight be determined by a formula designed to protect bridges, but generally standing in at 80,000 pounds. Vehicles that spread their weight over more axles and length were allowed to carry more tonnage than short-coupled rigs. This same legislation reduced interstate highway speeds to 55 mph in response to the Arab oil embargo. A grandfather clause allowed trucks exempted from federal weight standards in 1956 to continue that exemption, regardless of the bridge formula, the idea being that more weight per trip saved on fuel consumption.

See also Eastman, Joseph B.; Federal-Aid High-way Acts, Federal-Aid Highway Act and Highway Revenue Act of 1956, Federal-Aid Highway Act of 1976; Motor Carrier Acts, Motor Carrier Act of 1935; NRA Trucking Codes; Surface Transportation Assistance Acts, Surface Transportation Assistance Act of 1982; Transportation Acts, Transportation Act of 1920, Transportation Act of 1940; Trucking.

References Transportation Research Council, *Twin Trailer Trucks* (1986); Transportation Research Council, *Truck Weight Limits* (1990).

Federal-Aid Road Act (1916)

Prompted by the rapid increase in motor vehicle registrations, the potential of trucking, and the disconnected efforts of the states to build their own highways, Congress passed the first comprehensive measure designed to bring some order to the process, the Federal-Aid Road Act of 1916. Many of its principles are still valid today. Congress reserved to the states the rights to participate in the program, initiate projects, let contracts on them, or do the work themselves. But to qualify for federal assistance, the states had to satisfy the administrative requirements of organizing state highway departments and creating financing arrangements. Completed projects were to be inspected by the federal government and those approved were to receive federal matching funds on a 50–50 basis, not to exceed $10,000 per mile. The highways were to be tax-supported and free from all tolls. The funds had to be spent on a select portion of the states' roads designated as part of the federal highway system (actually, the government simply refused to match funds used elsewhere). Maintenance was a local responsibility. Finally, funds were appropriated for a five-year period (later extended for two more years) according to a formula based in equal parts upon area, population, and post-road mileage. The available funds were $5 million in 1917, increasing by $5 million a year until the sum of $25 million was reached in 1921. An additional $10 million was appropriated for roads in national parks and forests.

See also Roads and Highways, Colonial Times to World War I.

Reference U.S. Department of Transportation, Federal Highway Administration, *America's Highways* (1976).

Federal Airport Act (1950)

After World War II and the subsequent increase in domestic and international air travel, the Civil Aeronautics Authority (CAA) continued to promote air traffic, particularly airport construction and expansion assisted by government grants and loans. The Federal Airport Act of 1950 actualized this interest in air travel, airports being seen as essential national security. This act, along with the Interstate Highway Act in 1956, sealed the fate of the nation's railroads, now cut off from governmental subsidy for the sake of newer modes of transportation.

See also Aeronautics; Federal-Aid Highway Acts, Federal-Aid Highway Act and Highway Revenue Act of 1956.

Reference Bilstein, Roger E., *Flight in America* (1994).

Federal Aviation Act (1958)

As more commercial airliners filled the skies after World War II, control became a critical problem. Elementary traffic control had begun at Chicago, Cleveland, and New York City in 1936. By the outbreak of World War II, 11 more cities had entered the system and the first six-instrument landing systems allowed all-weather landings and takeoffs at some airports. By 1950, vertical omnirange (VOR) radio-controlled airways were the standard, replacing the old prewar single-beam radio-direction system. More sophisticated ground-controlled systems were available and used by military airports, but the commercial pilots balked at losing more selective pilot control to non-flyers. The increased pace of airline flights caused several near disasters. In 1954, nasty weather over New York City kept 300 airliners stacked up for hours. A similar incident occurred in 1956, when New York–bound airliners could not land for half a day.

Reservations were canceled throughout the nation and planes landed at every available airport. It took Eastern Airlines three days to find all of its diverted planes. The fear of a midair collision came true that summer. A United Airlines DC-7 and a Trans World Airlines Constellation collided in the air over the Grand Canyon, killing 128 and demonstrating how inadequate air traffic control was. Other less spectacular crashes followed and called the whole CAA operation into question.

Congress responded with the Federal Aviation Act of 1958, which completely reordered the control of commercial airways. The measure created the Federal Aviation Agency (FAA) as an independent entity from the Department of Commerce, essentially combining the old CAA and the Civil Aeronautics Board (CAB), and gaining the sole responsibility for American domestic airspace. In 1967, the name of the FAA was changed to the Federal Aviation Administration and transferred into the new Department of Transportation (DOT). The secretary now held the functions of the old FAA, minus the safety responsibilities. The old CAB's policy functions went to the National Transportation Safety Board (NTSB). The DOT/FAA/CAB/NTSB system remains in effect today, and has recently begun pushing for federal safety regulation of operators flying tourists over national parks like Arizona's Grand Canyon and Hawaii's Mauna Loa and Kilauea volcanoes.

See also Aeronautics; Civil Aeronautics Act of 1938; National Transportation Safety Board.

References Bilstein, Roger E., *Flight in America* (1994); Rochester, Stuart, *Take-off at Mid-Century* (1977); Whitnah, Donald R., *Safer Skyways* (1966).

Federal Control Act of 1918

After President Woodrow Wilson appointed William G. McAdoo to head the United States Railroad Administration, in December 1917 Congress needed to give its sanction to government regulation of the trains. This it did in March 1918 in the Federal Control Act. The measure outlined compensation to the railroad owners, determination of rates, appropriations to cover federal expenses, and ordered the courts to delay any final execution of pending or future antitrust cases.

See also McAdoo, William G.; Railroad War Board; United States Railroad Administration.

References Kerr, K. Austin, *American Railroad Politics* (1968); Leonard, William Norris, *Railroad Consolidation under the Transportation Act of 1920* (1946).

Federal Highway Act (1921)

Because the Federal-Aid Road Act expired in 1921, Congress was compelled to create a new roads measure in 1921, the Federal Highway Act. The federal aid to the states as the main road builders was reconfirmed, and the assistance confined to federal highways chosen by the states and not to be more than 7 percent of the total roads in each state. Not more than 60 percent of federal matching funds could be used on a state's primary roads; the rest was reserved for lesser roads. This ended the debate between advocates of local and long-distance roads by giving something to each side. Design standards had to emphasize materials durability; thus, the act of 1921 became the first legislation to support sustained road building and materials research. It also confirmed the U.S. government's bias against toll roads, and required that each state's highway department be a functioning entity capable of administering the federal matching funds, not a mere paper agency. The aid was limited to $20,000 per mile, twice that of 1916. Any state that did not properly maintain selected federal highways could be billed for work done through the Bureau of Public Roads to bring the roads in question up to par. Congress appropriated $75 million in federal matching funds for this one year, but appropriations for two or three multiple years began in 1923. Forest and Park Service roads increased and the bureau created a western regional office in San Francisco to expedite matters in the West. Western states with large amounts of public land could receive funds based on a sliding scale that took the amount of nonstate lands into consideration. Along with the act of 1916, which it modified, the act of 1921 completed the basic philosophy of federal aid to states for highways that still holds true today.

See also Roads and Highways since World War I.

Reference U.S. Department of Transportation, Federal Highway Administration, *America's Highways* (1976).

Federal Highway Administration (FHWA)

Organized as a part of the Department of Transportation in 1868 to replace the functions formerly carried out by the Bureau of Public Roads (dispensing federal assistance to the states and auditing the same monetarily and physically, and planning, education, and research, particularly as regards the interstate highway system), the Federal Highway Administration originally included three bureaus: Public Roads, Motor Carrier Safety, and the National Highway Safety Bureau. It had at that time just over 5,000 employees, including temporary staff and 140 hirees in foreign countries. In 1970, the FHWA was again reorganized. The National Highway Safety Bureau became an administrative branch of the Department of Transportation, and the Bureau of Public Roads and Motor Carrier Safety were abolished. In the latter's place, new component branches were instituted: Planning, Research, and Development; Right-of-Way and Environment; Engineering and Traffic Operations; Motor Carrier and Highway Safety; and General Administration. Nowadays, however, many agencies besides FHWA are involved in the highway aid picture. These include the Environmental Protection Agency; the Departments of the Interior, Commerce, Labor, Housing and Urban Development, and Justice; the Occupational Safety and Health Administration; the Office of Economic Opportunity; the Urban Mass Transportation Administration; the National Highway Traffic Safety Administration; the Corps of Engineers; and numerous boards, councils, and commissions.

See also Roads and Highways since World War I.

Reference U.S. Department of Transportation, Federal Highway Administration, *America's Highways* (1976).

Fess-Parker Bill

Under the Transportation Act of 1920, the Interstate Commerce Commission (ICC) was to look into and recommend a compulsory consolidation plan for American railroads based on the unified operations that were instituted under the United States Railroad Administration during World War I. Several such plans were proposed, the most important by William Z. Ripley in 1921, but none came to fruition, mainly because the railroads did not wish to cooperate with their competitors or the government. In 1926, with the defeat of Senator Alfred Cummins of Iowa for reelection, the rail executives drafted a measure that was introduced by Representative James S. Parker of New York and Senator Simeon D. Fess of Ohio. This measure freed the ICC of any obligation to write up a consolidation measure, allowed a majority of stockholders to condemn the securities of any minority that might frustrate majority will (common in any voluntary merger), and placed a seven-year limit on the ICC's consolidation effort, after which it was to submit a full report to the Congress on its activities.

The Fess-Parker Bill failed to come to the floor for debate for two consecutive congressional sessions and eventually melted away in the impending Great Depression. The main reason it failed was due to the suspicious nature of its motives. There was a fear that if voluntary consolidation was not adequately monitored, certain larger railroads would reap excessive profits at the cost to the public of service and rates. This was especially evident when committee recommendations that profits from mergers be limited were opposed by the same railroads that had backed the original measure. Finally, the interest of short lines in the measure waned as they grew stronger in the late 1920s, oblivious to the economic disaster that loomed on the horizon in 1929.

See also Railroad Unification Act; *Ripley Report*; **Transportation Acts.**

Reference Leonard, William Norris, *Railroad Consolidation under the Transportation Act of 1920* (1946).

Financing Highways

Five ways of financing highways have been used in the United States: bonds, federal aid, state aid, taxes, and tolls. Bonds are interest-bearing certificates issued by a public or private entity, payable over a period of time, usually in multiples of five or ten years. In the early twentieth century, many states tried without success to float bonds for road construction. In 1918, however, Illinois managed to get the populace to approve, with a large voter majority, $60 million in bonds to pay for the construction of a carefully selected trunk highway system. In the 1920s, road expansion was often financed by state bonds that adversely affected the states' ability to put money into the economy during the Great Depression, which led to measures like the Hayden-Cartwright Act of 1934 to relieve their indebtedness. Most city streets were financed through this method, as were big single items like bridges and state toll roads like New Jersey's Garden State Parkway and the Pennsylvania Turnpike. These projects were usually managed by "authorities"—public corporations set up specifically for this purpose, usually based on the example of the Port Authority of New York harbor.

Beginning in 1916, federal aid has tended to replace most other forms of financing. Much of the old National Road was financed by allowing the states to sell federal lands within their boundaries granted to them for highway purposes. Other roads in the advancing western frontier were built by the army. More recently, there has been a ratio between federal aid and state responsibility. Originally 2–1 in favor of the states in the early part of the twentieth century, this ratio has shifted to 9–1 in favor of the U.S. government under the building of the interstate highway system. Paralleling this shift has been the increase of federal controls that inevitably follows monetary grants, even if they are matching funds. Nowadays, the feds determine environmental, civil rights, beautification, and roadway standards to a degree never before dreamed possible. Naturally, managing and auditing of the federal moneys is a part of the picture, too.

A third method of financing roads is through state aid. Originally, roads were the responsibility of local governmental entities like counties or even road districts. As the dawn of the age of the automobile occurred, local government found it did not have enough resources to finance adequate roads. Beginning with Mecklenburg County, North Carolina, in the 1880s, local authorities have sought to broaden the financial bases for road building. By the 1890s, it had become evident that the states had to assume the responsibility for an extended road network. Iowa, then Massachusetts, New Jersey, and New York developed highway departments to coordinate state road expenditures. At first, these state coordinating agencies were under departments of agriculture (as were the early federal agencies) because road building was seen as a rural problem. But gradually by the turn of the century, they became independent departments in their own right. Although state aid is still important and federal highway programs are conditional upon state highway department management under federal guidelines, the amount of state aid has declined in relation to the cross-country and interstate highways. But it is still a critical factor in secondary farm-to-market roads.

Sooner or later, no matter which governmental entity is responsible for highway building and maintenance, it all boils down to taxes. These taxes come in many forms: use taxes on larger vehicles like trucks and buses based on size and weight (wear and tear on the roadway); licensing fees of drivers and vehicles; sales taxes on the purchase of vehicles, gasoline, tires, and lubricating oils; and even property taxes all figure in the tax picture. In some states one not only buys the state license plate but also an add-on tag or sticker from the county and/or city. On the federal level, these various excises disappeared into the general fund, out of which came highway aid expenditures as well as hundreds of other items, until 1956 when, under pressure from states, truckers, and auto associations, Congress established the Highway Trust Fund to receive all road-related moneys and dispense them to the localities.

Finally, there have been toll roads from the beginning of American history. Tolls are popular because the fees are directly paid by those who use the facility. They also offer a way to pay for single large projects. The first highways were usually toll roads built by a joint-stock company, the tolls building and maintaining the road and the profits going to the investors. Few of these made any money until the Lancaster Pike, running west out of Philadelphia in the late 1790s. Most were too expensive to maintain to justify the toll. Tolls also played havoc with the American notion that roads were public conveniences that benefited all. Attempts to place tolls on the first federal project of note, the National Road, failed. Besides, in a country as vast and with as fluctuating a population as the United States, there was always another way to travel and avoid the hated tolls. But the automobile changed all that. The hard surface was necessary to the free movement of the automobile—definitely not a cross-country vehicle in its early days especially. There were two toll road eras in the twentieth century, the first coming between the wars, the culmination of which was the Pennsylvania Turnpike, and the second after World War II before the introduction of the freeway. The concept of the freeway, especially its Los Angeles application, killed the chance that toll roads would survive. Those toll roads that eventually became a part of the interstate system did so on the condition that the tolls would cease as soon as the original debt of construction was retired.

Regardless of the manner in which the costs of road making are met, the whole process is not without criticism. Many critics point out that the highway system created more problems than it solved. Highway financing is a giant Molloch that consumes resources better used elsewhere. This money-grubbing monster is endorsed by a vast lobby that consists of state highway officials, contractors, auto and truck manufacturers, engineers, congressional representatives (405 of 435 districts have part of the interstate system passing through), state legislators, newspaper publishers, and road user groups, all of whom know better. So much of America's resources have been sunk into the interstates and supporting roads that little is left over for other forms of travel, except airlines for long distances where time is important. City dwellers and homeowners in the path of the juggernaut are displaced to somewhere else. Businesses that relied on the old federal highway system have been bypassed. It is one thing to put in a superhighway between cities; it is quite another to put it through established city neighborhoods. This is all done in the name of progress.

But is it truly progressive? Boston put freeways into the city during the 1960s and lost 9 percent of its retail sales. San Francisco halted its freeway construction in the late 1960s, opting instead for mass transit (BART trains), and saw its retail sales go up 16 percent. Highway planners call for more cement and more ramps. Yet the problems persist. Pollution increases as more motor vehicles stall in the congested highway system. Neighborhoods are torn apart as the freeways pass through. Worse yet, there seems no end to the construction. New branches are added, old ones are repaired and widened. It is as if a perpetual-motion machine has gone into action, never to stop.

One Washington "think tank" has proposed that roads be financed in a new manner based on congestion and wear and tear. The first important change would be to charge vehicles an extra fee for the use of a highway at peak hours, with no exceptions. The result would be to encourage carpooling and different delivery times. The second key element would be to revise vehicle weight charges from gross vehicle weight to axle weight, which really determines wear on a roadway, and include all governmental vehicles that are normally exempt. Such a change would actually lower the costs that an over-the-road 18-wheeler would pay and increase the amounts that a small van with a heavier axle load would owe. The collection of such fees would depend on the development of new electronic technology and use stickers, much of which is already available experimentally. The proponents of such changes think that revision would eventually replace the current system of licenses and use taxes and produce more income by charging those who use the highways in the most devastating form and at the worst times.

See also Federal-Aid Highway Acts; Federal-Aid Road Act; Federal Highway Act; Hayden-Cartwright Act; Highway Trust Fund; Roads and Highways, Colonial Times to World War I; Roads and Highways since World War I; Statute Labor.

References Brodsly, David, *L.A. Freeway* (1981); Burnham, John Chenowyth, "The Gasoline Tax and the Automotive Revolution," *Mississippi Valley Historical Review* (1961) 48: 435–459; Leavitt, Helen, *Super Highway—Super Hoax* (1970); Owen, Wilfred, et al., *Financing Highways* (1957); Robinson, John, *Highways and Our Environment* (1971); Small, Kenneth, et al., *Road Work: A New Highway Pricing and Investment Policy* (1989); U.S. Department of Transportation, Federal Highway Administration, *America's Highways* (1976).

Fisher, Carl G. (1873–1939)

By 1912, few people had considered driving a car across the United States. Not many people had even traveled more than ten miles from home. If they did, they went by rail. Usually that meant fighting in a foreign war. But now something new had occurred that would change American society forever. The family auto brought mobility and change. If one so desired, one could pack up the car and take off on vacation, or even move across the state or across the nation. And these new personal travel devices were getting cheaper and more reliable all the time. They were no longer just playthings of the rich.

One man saw what the auto revolution meant for Americans of the twentieth century. This was Carl G. Fisher. He was in a place to know—he was the founder of the Prest-O-Lite Company, makers of carbide auto headlights before cars had the fancy electrical systems that adorn them presently. Fisher was known for more as well. He had built up the Indianapolis Motor Speedway and paved it with bricks—it is still known as "the Brickyard" by racing aficionados today. He also loved yachting and ballooning. He once floated a car over Indi-

anapolis by balloon as a stunt. He had built bicycles (which almost all who made it big at that time seemed to do—the Wright brothers for instance) and raced cars against the first man to go a mile a minute, the famous Barney Oldfield ("Who do you think you are," Americans in those days would ask anyone going too fast, regardless of conveyance, "Barney Oldfield?"). Born in Greensberg, Indiana, in 1873, and possessing only a common school education, Fisher first made it big developing Lake Michigan beach resorts. He would go out as he came in, making a mint in Miami Beach real estate. But in the interim he looked at cross-country travel and deemed it necessary for the average American.

In the fall of 1912, he came up with one of the most fantastic ideas of his age: Americans should build a transcontinental highway, and not just a dirt road either. This was to be one of pavement and well-marked junctions, equipped with motorist services, that even Barney Oldfield would find pleasure in driving. He called it the Coast-to-Coast Rock Highway at first. Fisher was a promoter first and foremost, and the name soon became one that would sell any red-blooded American patriot—it would be the Lincoln Highway. He figured that $10 million would do the job. He and his Lincoln Highway Association would buy only materials. Localities would provide the labor and machinery. He hoped to finish the job in two short years, so that 25,000 auto-borne Americans could attend the San Francisco's Panama-Pacific Exposition a continent away. That would be one terminus for the highway, and the other of course would be America's biggest city, New York. He really had no preference for the cities between; any would do.

To fund the project, Fisher took donations from the auto industry. He thought that 1 percent of each year's gross would be sufficient. But anyone could join his association as an individual for $5. He had $300,000 in hand 30 minutes after he proposed the idea, from the Goodyear Tire and Rubber Company. Chairman Charles A. Sieberling made the donation without even consulting the board of directors. Fisher was not the first to propose a transcontinental highway—the American Automobile Association did it in 1902. But he had financing and a vision. He published the *Ocean-to-Ocean Bulletin* announcing contributors, goals, and news. But his big obstacle was Henry Ford. The auto magnate refused to contribute, although members of his family did and his son Edsel served on the association board. Henry B. Joy of the Packard Motor Company put up $150,000 and kept the idea going. By now it was obvious to everyone that two years was not enough time to act. It was he who proposed the notion of the highway as a tribute to Abraham Lincoln, an idea Fisher quickly took up as his own, even as he resented Joy's influence in the association.

The next problem was the route. Many of the donations came with a condition—the highway must pass through their towns or their states. And once again, Joy made his choice over all objections, favoring a road that roughly paralleled the old Central Overland Route of the previous century. Kansas and Colorado were furious, but the decision stuck. Then Fisher decided to use what money they had for education through the construction of "seedling miles," short sections of concrete demonstrating to the public what their donations might do. That year, 1914, was the first time more automobiles sold than wagons. By 1915, Carl Fisher had removed to Florida. His interest in the highway waned as his investments in Florida real estate boomed. To bring the buyers down, Fisher created another road club, the Dixie Highway Association. It had multiple routes through almost every southern and midwestern state. Joy and the Lincoln Highway Association thought Fisher had gone mad—and maybe he had, just a little. But his legacy lived on. Highway associations became part of the new American way of doing things. By 1925, they numbered over 100, and their roads and schemes covered the country.

Fisher, meanwhile, was going broke making Miami Beach more than a home for alligators. Just when he was about to go

under, a miracle happened. People began to come to Florida on the Dixie Highway, as he had hoped so many years before. By 1925, he was worth millions. Will Rogers maintained that Fisher *was* Florida, and that "he rehearsed the mosquitoes till they wouldn't bite you until after you bought." He died in wealth and happiness at his magnificent creation, the island across Biscayne Bay from Miami, thinking about expanding his highway operations onto a new set of islands already developed by rail magnate Henry Flagler: the Florida Keys.

See also Lincoln Highway; Roads and Highways, Colonial Times to World War I; Roads and Highways since World War I.

Reference Hokanson, Drake, *The Lincoln Highway* (1988).

Fisk, James, Jr. (1835–1872)

A Vermonter who made money as a peddler, filling supply contracts for the Union army, and buying and selling cotton during the Civil War, Jim Fisk became an agent for the noted stock manipulator Daniel Drew in 1866. With Drew's help, Fisk, who had a

Cartoonist Thomas Nast's caricature of James Fisk, Jr., in 1866

modicum of formal education but a lot of what is now called "street smarts," opened his own brokerage house and made a small fortune. In 1868, Drew got Commodore Cornelius Vanderbilt to put Fisk on as a fourth on the Erie Railroad's board of directors, which then included Vanderbilt, Drew, and Jay Gould. There Fisk came into his own as he joined Drew and Gould to swindle Vanderbilt out of his control, and then assisted Gould to do the same to Drew. Most of the transactions resulted from watered stock (i.e., stock with no real value), and a cartoon of the time pictures the malefactors hard at work printing, with Fisk saying, "If this printing press don't break down, I'll be damned if we don't give the old hog [Vanderbilt] all he wants of Erie." It was typically Fisk: brash, boisterous, and a bit crude. He was a high liver, and he did it all in the public eye, by choice.

Vanderbilt swore out a complaint and the trio of Fisk, Gould, and Drew fled to New Jersey, tipped off by informants. The outraged Vanderbilt pursued them with the police to the dock on lower Manhattan, each man gripping a suitcase and carpetbag full of money and stocks. On the Jersey shore, Fisk garbed himself in a naval uniform and labeled himself "the Admiral," with obvious implications that he outranked the old Commodore. "The Commodore owns New York, the stock exchange, the streets, the railroads, and most of the steamship lines," Fisk told an inquisitive newspaper reporter. "As ambitious young men," he continued with a twinkle in his eye, "we saw there was no chance for us there to expand, and so we came over here. Yes," he concluded with a flourish, "tell Mr. [Horace] Greeley [famous editor of the *New York Tribune*] from us that we're sorry now that we didn't take his advice sooner—about going West."

Things stood at a stalemate until Fisk and the others cut a deal whereby they legalized the stock and bought it back, and Vanderbilt dropped all charges. Returning to New York, Fisk stayed with Gould at Erie throughout the rest of the 1860s, both to his gain and loss. He backed up Gould's ploy to ship cattle over Vanderbilt's railroads after a price war with Erie had driven the price down from $125 a carload to $1. Fisk also was involved in fleecing his old mentor, Drew, with fraudulent stock issuances. But he stayed with Gould one trick too many and took a dive himself when the pair tried to corner the gold market and brought on Black Friday, a crash in gold prices that caused not a few suicides in the New York City financial district. Gould pulled out early and saved his ill-gotten gains because of a tip-off that the government was about to step in to stabilize the price. Fisk was not told and took the loss. But he and Gould merely saw it as a part of the game.

Later, Fisk set himself up at New York's Grand Opera House, where he kept an office connected to the stage by a semisecret passageway. Here he wined and dined numerous ladies fascinated by this handsome rake from the financial district (he wasn't known as "Jubilee Jim, the Prince of Erie" for nothing). But Fisk's attentions to Josephine Mansfield threatened to blow up all of Erie's private business. She and her boyfriend Ned Stokes had been blackmailing Fisk over something. But Fisk had cut off the payments, and now Josephine was bringing him to court over a minor matter in retaliation. Probably as many people wanted to see Fisk asked questions under oath as did not. But neither side got its chance. Stokes shot Fisk dead after a compromising liaison with Josephine at a local hotel. His body lay in state at the opera house before burial back home in Bennington, Vermont. The famous cartoonist Thomas Nast (who invented the ass for the Democrats and the elephant for the Republicans) drew a cartoon of the funeral, showing Gould and New York Democrat and political boss William M. Tweed of Tammany Hall standing over Fisk's grave, looking much relieved. The caption: "Dead Men Tell No Tales."

See also Drew, Daniel; Gould, Jay; United States Express Company; Vanderbilt, Cornelius.

References Fuller, Robert H., *Jubilee Jim* (1928); Ginger, Ray, *Age of Success* (1965); Hubbard, Freeman, *Encyclopedia of North American Railroading* (1981); Hungerford, Edward, *Men of Erie* (1946);

Josephson, Matthew, *The Robber Barons* (1934); Swanberg, William A., *Jim Fisk* (1959); Weinstock, Charles B., "James Fisk, Jr.," in Robert L. Frey (ed.), *EABHB: Railroads in the Nineteenth Century* (1988), 12–27.

Fitch, John (1743–1798)

Born on an East Windsor, Connecticut, farm (work he hated for the rest of his life), John Fitch grew up in an unhappy home from which he fled, first to school and then to the sea at age 17. He returned, got married, fathered a son, deserted his wife and child, and wandered for the rest of his life. Fitch served with the Continental army as a gunsmith during the Revolutionary War. He was also a passable silversmith. He toured the West after the war and was captured by Native Americans but escaped. At Warminster, Pennsylvania, inspired by laborious boating experiences on the Ohio River, he made a model of a steamboat with a wheel on each side, which he later replaced with a bank of mechanical oars. Within two years (1787), he had a full-sized prototype, which made a trial run on the Delaware River at Philadelphia. Later improvements led to larger vessels and a passenger service that ran from Philadelphia to Wilmington, Delaware, during the summer months. His ship logged 2,000 or 3,000 miles in the process and ran half again faster than Fulton's later *Clermont*.

During this period, Fitch learned for the first time that others were interested in steam navigation. He met and talked with William Henry, and through a conversation with George Washington, learned of James Rumsey. Washington, however, refused to divulge any of Rumsey's methods, except to say that the two inventors were not in conflict. Fitch failed to gain further backing from conservative Philadelphians, probably because he was a rude, often drunken man, and his competitor Rumsey was not. The result was that Rumsey took the field. Under the influence of St. John de Crevecour, one of the few who saw more merit in Fitch's approach than in Rumsey's, Fitch went to France to continue his efforts.

At the time, France was the center of a vigorous look into the possibilities of steamboating, but Fitch was compromised by the 1787 Revolution. According to the tale, he deposited his steamboat plans with the American consul at L'Orient, who, after Fitch's departure for the New World, turned them over to Robert Fulton. In any case, the New York legislature ruled that Fulton's patents as presented to them in 1817 by Robert Livingston were an outright copy of Fitch's earlier designs. John Fitch, however, "inventor of steamboats" (in his own words), never lived to see the expropriation of his idea nor its vindication. Arriving back in the United States penniless, he worked his way to Bardstown, Kentucky, where he committed suicide in 1798, overdosing on opium pills and whiskey, leading to the nickname that has followed him since: "Poor John Fitch."

See also Early Steamboats; Fulton, Robert; Rumsey, James; Shreve, Henry Miller; Steamboats; Stevens, John, Jr.

References Boyd, Thomas, *Poor John Fitch* (1937); Donovan, Frank, *River Boats of America* (1966); Flexner, James Thomas, *Steamboats Come True* (1944).

Florida East Coast Railway (FEC)

Henry M. Flagler was a partner of John D. Rockefeller's who, in 1883, wanted to develop southeastern Florida into a national playground. He bought out several small rail lines and created the Florida East Coast Railway. The FEC was designed to bring people to Flagler's hotels and beaches. He also bought steamship lines and dredged Miami harbor to make it more useful. But the FEC did not extend much beyond Daytona, so Flagler started to build southward. He passed through Palm Beach and wound up in Miami, a small trading post for the benefit of the Seminoles. Ten years later he reached Homestead and began to extend the line out along the Florida Keys. He finally arrived at Key West, where his steamships would transfer people to Havana, Cuba, thus making all of southern Florida and Havana an extension of New York City.

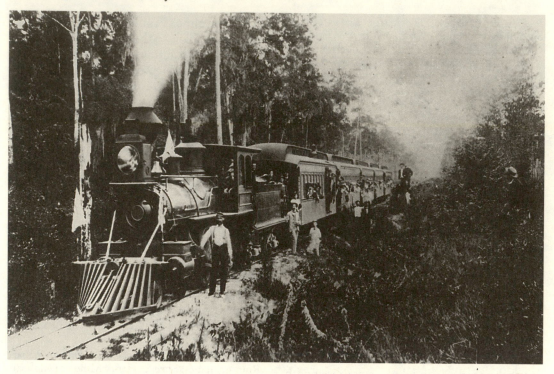

At the time this 1880s photograph was taken, the Florida East Coast Railway was used to attract tourists to Florida. The Florida East Coast Railway is credited with surviving a series of storms and hurricanes, as well as one of the longest railroad strikes in history.

The line across the Keys had to bridge 37 miles of water. Flagler brought in tons of rock and fill, structural steel, and concrete to establish a roadbed upon which to lay his rails. He planned to construct 17 miles of bridges and lay the rest over viaducts and the islands themselves. Although the construction had to be repeated because of several hurricanes, the giant storm of 1896 caught the crews unprepared. Almost 100 men disappeared in the inundation, and much of the previous work had to be repeated. In 1909, another big storm came in but the crews had some warning and managed to save much of the work and themselves. By 1913, Key West had been reached and the railroad, an amazing engineering feat for its day, was opened. The route was marked by 6 steel bridges, 4 drawbridges, and 29 viaducts built in water ranging in depth from 3 to 38 feet. Knight's Key Bridge was 7 miles long, and Long Key viaduct ran 3 miles with 180 concrete arches

over a 50-foot span. It was the first large concrete bridge built anywhere. All of the tracks were 30 feet above high tide.

In 1935, another hurricane swept in from the Gulf of Mexico and caught a full train on the passageway. Rails were washed out and the train overturned with large loss of life. With that disaster, the "railroad that died at sea," as the FEC became known, retreated to Homestead and turned the remnants over to the Florida state highway department, which built the current road to Key West. By the time of the Great Depression, the FEC was in bankruptcy. It remained so for 30 years until Edward Ball took it over. Ball attempted to restructure the line, laying off employees and cutting recent pay raises negotiated nationally among all railroads and their unions. The result was a vicious strike. Ball retaliated by firing the strikers and rehiring nonunion personnel, including college students. The railroad now ran trains from Jacksonville to Miami with two-man crews, a trip that formerly took three five-man union crews, each paid a full eight-hour day for going 200 miles (usually in half that time), according to collective bargaining.

After 14 years of violence and sabotage, with crews shot at from ambush, switches tampered with, bridges destroyed, and trains wrecked and derailed, the FEC won the right to keep its restructuring in federal court. It did this without any support from the federal government, which sided with the strikers. The strike formally ended in 1976, with the FEC able to claim a number of unique achievements throughout its controversial history: It had built the longest across-water route and survived one of the longest rail strikes; its labor costs were among the lowest in the nation (30 cents on the dollar, when the national average was 53 cents and bankrupt Conrail was at 60); it ran its line faster than the national freight average of 59 miles per hour; and it plowed an unusual amount (29 cents on the income dollar versus a national average of 17 cents) back into the operation, making it one of the better-maintained roads in the country, truly amazing for an independent, unabsorbed line.

See also New Orleans Conditions; Railroad Unions; Seaboard Coast Line Railroad.

References Bramson, Seth H., *Speedway to Sunshine* (1984); Bramson, Seth H., "Henry M. Flagler," and "Florida East Coast Railway," in Keith L. Bryant, Jr. (ed.), *EABHB: Railroads in the Age of Regulation* (1988), 159–161, 162–163; Drury, George H., *The Historical Guide to North American Railroads* (1985); Drury, George H., *The Train-Watcher's Guide* (1990); Hubbard, Freeman, *Encyclopedia of North American Railroading* (1981); Parks, Pat, *The Railroad That Died at Sea* (1968).

Forbes, John Murray (1813–1898)

Unlike so many of the business magnates of his time, John M. Forbes was a man of some culture. Born in Bordeaux, France, where his parents had moved to educate their children, Forbes finished his education in Boston and went to work for his uncles who were in the China trade. At age 17, he was their representative in Canton. Home after a seven-year stint, Forbes had a small fortune, which he invested in railroads. Even-

tually, he put together the lines that made up the Chicago, Burlington & Quincy (CB&Q) Railroad.

Forbes actually believed that the rails operated for the public's good. He eschewed construction companies like the Crédit Mobilier (and his participation in it is arguable) and paid full dividends to stockholders. He built his rails soundly and proceeded slowly to build his rails westward. He was a part of the Iowa Pool, an organization of the CB&Q, the Chicago & North Western, and the Rock Island set up to divide the trade with the Union Pacific at Omaha and Chicago. The Iowa Pool was unusual—it worked and continued to do so for decades, because Forbes kept it honest. Unlike other pools, the parties of the Iowa Pool did not begin to covet the trade of other members, a rare quality in business deals of that age. Forbes believed that the railroads were products that ought to deliver a fair deal—pay their investors, carry their passengers and freight at reasonable prices, and serve to better the nation at large. He was not so much a robber baron as he was what historian Burton W. Folsom calls a market entrepreneur, that is, one who innovated, cut costs, and competed in an open market to bring services, jobs, and an improved lifestyle to the American people through up-to-date transportation.

See also Gould, Jay; Huntington, Collis Potter; Pacific Railroad Act of 1862; Sage, Russell; Scott, Thomas A.; Vanderbilt, William H.

References Folsom, Burton W., Jr., *The Myth of the Robber Barons* (1991); Grodinsky, Julius, *The Iowa Pool* (1950); Hughes, Sarah Forbes (ed.), *Letters and Recollections of John Murray Forbes* (1889); Larson, John Lauritz, "John Murray Forbes," in Robert L. Frey (ed.), *EABHB: Railroads in the Nineteenth Century* (1988), 128–132; Lyon, Peter, *To Hell in a Day Coach* (1968); Pearson, Henry G., *An American Railroad Builder* (1911).

Forbes' Road

When British General Edward Braddock landed in the New World to begin his campaign from Frederick, Maryland, to Fort Duquesne (now Pittsburgh, Pennsylvania), he urged upon the colonial governors that another shorter route out of the granary of the American colonies, the Pennsylvania Dutch country west of Philadelphia, be constructed. Pennsylvanians did head west to clear the roadway, but upon hearing of Braddock's massacre, they quickly returned to the safer pastures of home. The road had not passed beyond Bedford.

The route to Bedford was the Old Trading Path, known to local Native Americans from time immemorial. But Braddock's suggestion was not forgotten. In 1758, General John Forbes arrived in the colonies with a new army and began to construct a real road to Fort Duquesne. A former medical student, he had abandoned medicine for the army. He was a marked contrast to Braddock—much less pompous and more direct, an endearing quality in the colonies. Along with the usual militia, Forbes had the Royal American Regiment (a British regular unit recruited in the 13 colonies) and a contingent of Scots Highland Infantry. But this 6,000-man force had to get to Fort Duquesne first, and that called for a supply route into the wilderness.

Forbes first thought to use the old Braddock route out of Maryland. But he soon learned that the Pennsylvania route was shorter, closer to the Lancaster granary, and hence easier to extend and supply. In doing this he went against the advice of Virginians, led by George Washington. But Forbes undoubtedly remembered the problems that the colonial colonel and his British mentor had had earlier, and determined to avoid them. Forbes sent forward the Virginia and Pennsylvania militia and Royal Americans under Lieutenant Colonel Henri Bouquet, their Swiss-born commander serving the English king. As with Braddock's Road earlier, the colonial militia did most of the axe work. Also like the earlier campaign, the advance guard was ambushed and defeated. But Forbes refused to retreat. Unlike the 1755 campaign, that in 1758 also had a little luck. British victories at Fort Frontenac to the north had cut the French lines of supply and communication. By the time Forbes' full column had reached the junction of the Monongahela and Allegheny, the French had withdrawn voluntarily to contest for more important holdings in Canada. Forbes named the burned remnants of the place Pittsburgh, after the British prime minister, William Pitt. Shortly after, the general died, his body wracked with fever and pain that had dogged him since his arrival in America.

As he had advanced, Forbes fortified his road at Carlisle, Shippensburg, Chambersburg, Loudon, Littleton, Bedford, Ligonier, and finally Pittsburgh. This became the direct route to the west from Philadelphia. It had the advantage of being shorter than the Braddock route to the south and was closer to New York City. It was the supply path down which the frontier was maintained by Colonel Henri Bouquet during Pontiac's Rebellion (his Battle of Bushy Run was the first Anglo-American victory over the Indians on Pennsylvania's western border), and was also defended during the Revolution by General George Rogers Clark. Providing the northern route to Kentucky, it was a straight shot to Ohio. Using the Lancaster Pike, it ran from Carlisle to the port city of Philadelphia. It was known as Forbes' Road, the Old Glade Road, or the Pennsylvania Road.

Forbes' Road was still active after Braddock's Road had disappeared into the wilderness. It took the bulk of westward traffic into Ohio while the Cumberland Road and the later National Road were still being built. It nearly went under, faced with the competition from the Erie Canal and the Baltimore & Ohio Railroad. But its route returned to prominence when the mainline of the Pennsylvania Railroad opened. Its slogan, "Look at the Map," meant that the trip from the Atlantic to Pittsburgh was 84 miles shorter along the rails that followed the old Forbes' Road.

See also Braddock's Road; Lancaster Pike.

Reference Hulbert, Archer Butler, *Historic Highways of America* (1902–1906).

Ford, Edsel B. (1894–1943)

Never tough enough to suit his father Henry, his kindness being seen as a weakness, Edsel Ford never made a decision that the old man did not have to sanction. That kind of ill luck seemed to daunt him for most of his life. For one thing, Edsel Ford had massive stomach problems. But when he drank milk for a supposed ulcer, prescribed by his father from the family dairy farm, it proved to be tainted and he got undulant fever. His unsympathetic father said his stomach problems resulted from a poor lifestyle, but the malady turned out to be stomach cancer. Edsel Ford died in 1943 at age 49.

Often seen as the inferior member of the family, Edsel's accomplishments prove that criticism unfair. Edsel Ford was a decent man who had to work around a domineering, stubborn father. The miracle is not that he did so little, but that he accomplished what he did. To his credit he saw the threat of General Motors and wished to alter the Ford offerings to compete with it (his father disagreed), he designed the outward appearance of the Model A, and he was instrumental in setting up the Ford Foundation in 1936, which has done much to make up for Henry Ford's arrogance and opinionated ideas. It says much for Henry Ford's rough exterior that the tragic death of his only son shook the old man to his core.

See also Automobiles from Domestics to Imports; Automobiles in American Society; Ford, Henry.

References Collier, Peter, and David Horowitz, *The Fords* (1987); Halberstam, David, *The Reckoning* (1986); May, George S., "Edsel Bryant Ford," in George S. May (ed.), *Encyclopedia of American Business History and Biography: The Automobile Industry* (1989), 138–140; Shook, Robert L., *Turnaround* (1990).

Ford, Henry (1863–1947)

Born a farm boy on 30 June 1863 near Dearborn, Michigan, Henry Ford grew up with an interest in what made things work. As he said in his later years, "my toys were all tools—they still are." By age 12 he worked in a machine shop, and soon after he became a mechanic's apprentice and then a chief engineer for Edison Illuminating Company. During his spare time, he tinkered with internal-combustion engines. His made his first car in 1896, and fitted it with four bike wheels. Seven years later he founded Ford

Motor Company. He produced his cars and named them after the letters of the alphabet, hence the first Model A appeared in 1903. By 1906, his abrasive personality had caused some of his original investors to sell out, and Ford owned 58 percent of the company. He made 19 models of cars, some two-cylinder, most four-cylinder, and one six-cylinder, before settling on the Model T in 1908. He and his son Edsel created the second Model A just before the Great Depression, and Henry conceived of the V-8 engine in the early 1930s, perhaps one of his finest moments.

Ford revolutionized the auto industry. He used assembly-line production and interchangeable parts, paid a high minimum wage, offered low-priced cars, and emphasized one model with few yearly changes. This philosophy became known as "fordism" (indeed the first Japanese word for auto was "fordo"). The sale of 10,000 units in 1909–1910 caused him to buy 60 acres at Highland Park, Michigan, for the biggest factory the world had seen. This was the essence of Ford—he saw the expansion of capital plant as thrilling, while modern managers see it as a regrettable necessity. Ford's true love was technology. Unlike such men as William C. Durant and Alfred Sloan at General Motors, Ford's idea of an advertisement (if he had to have any at all) was a simple line drawing, short sentences, and colloquial language, emphasizing economy, safety, serviceability, and reliability. "We have remade this country with automobiles," he once bragged. Indeed, he envisioned most ideas of the modern production plant, even the use of robots, long before the Japanese used them in the 1970s.

Ford saw inspection as the keynote of production. His worst public relations problem was the harshness of regimented work, which was lambasted in Charlie Chaplin's movie *Modern Times*. Ford achieved the epitome of Frederick Taylor's concept of the elimination of wasted motion through his moving assembly line. He used unskilled workers to achieve rapid production through unbelievable coordination in an operation where thousands of bolts arrived when needed, wheel rims joined tires, and interiors were matched to exteriors. It was a tough system based on discipline and doing one's own job—no more and no less. This discipline, a trait ascribed by the English to the Germans and by others to the America of the 1930s or the Japan of the 1970s, was probably produced by rapidly expanding economies in every case. On top of it all, Ford introduced the eight-hour shift at $5 per day wages, which got his workers enough money to buy their own cars. Although he was considered a traitor by most industrialists of the day, Ford's good working conditions allowed him to select his workers carefully from the long lines who came to sign up.

With such success Henry Ford became one of America's early billionaires. In late 1915, he chartered the *Oscar II*, the so-called peace ship, and sailed off with a bunch of do-gooders to settle World War I. He al-ways considered war as an interference with good business and accused Jews and others of war conspiracy. He was an active anti-Semite all his life. But he was enough of a businessman to produce war materials for the U.S. government. In 1918, he ran for the U.S. Senate and lost. In 1919, he turned the management of the company over to his son, Edsel, but no one really doubted where the real authority lay—not even Edsel. At first, Henry blamed the Great Depression upon money-changers (code word for Jewish bankers). He further reduced the price of his cars and raised wages to $7 a day, but he miscalculated. When overall car sales dropped by 75 percent, he had to lay off staff and reduce wages to $4 day. He unwisely accepted a civilian award from Hitler and stood with Charles Lindbergh as opposed to the U.S. entry into World War II, but did support the war effort after Pearl Harbor.

Always controversial, Ford could fly off

Henry Ford stands beside his Racer 999 in this undated photograph. Ford was to become one of America's first billionaires.

the handle at a moment's notice. He engaged in many lawsuits; two of the most noteworthy were his action against the Association of Licensed Automobile Manufacturers, which freed up the patents of the four-stroke engine, and his defense in the suit, initiated by John and Elgin Dodge to force him to pay dividends to stockholders. When the court ruled, Ford had to pay off $19 million (including $11 million to himself), and he began a process of buying up all of the company stock for himself (or in the names of family members). It cost him $105 million, but he thought it was worth it. This made Ford Motor Company a unique, completely family-owned business. Not even business genius John D. Rockefeller had controlled more than 27 percent of Standard Oil in his heyday. Ford held out against unionism longer than any other manufacturer, partly through high salaries, partly through intimidation of organizers and employees. When his people went out on strike in 1941, only the intervention of his wife, Clara, on labor's behalf prevented a long, drawn-out, potentially bloody confrontation.

Ford suffered a mild stroke in 1938 and a worse one in 1941. Devastated by Edsel's tragic death in 1943, he took over the firm again. But the U.S. government worried about a major defense contract being supervised by what detractors thought was a senile old man. Aware of the criticism, Ford asked for and got his grandson Henry released from the U. S. Navy to help him out. But he would not let him run the operation without interference until Edsel's widow threatened to sell her stock to outsiders if the old man did not step aside. Henry Ford died in 1947, receiving eulogies from men with as varied political philosophies as President Harry S Truman, former Prime Minister of Great Britain Winston S. Churchill, and Soviet Premier Joseph Stalin.

See also Automobiles from Domestics to Imports; Automobiles in American Society; Ford, Edsel B.; Ford, Henry, II.

References Arnold, Horace Lucien, and Fay Leone Faurote, *Ford Methods and the Ford Shops* (1915); Burlingame, Roger, *Henry Ford* (1954); Collier, Peter, and David Horowitz, *The Fords* (1987); Folsom, Richard B., "Henry Ford," in George S. May (ed.), *Encyclopedia of American Business History and Biography: The Automobile Industry* (1990), 192–222; Ford, Henry, *My Life and Work* (1922); Halberstam, David, *The Reckoning* (1986); Jardim, Anne, *The First Henry Ford: A Study in Personality and Business Leadership* (1970); Lacey, Robert, *Ford* (1986); Leonard, Jonathan Norton, *The Tragedy of Henry Ford* (1932); Motor Vehicle Manufacturers Association of the United States, *Automobiles of America* (1974); Nevins, Allan, and Frank Ernest Hill, *Ford* (3 vols., 1954–1963); Nye, David E., *Henry Ford* (1979); Rothschild, Emma, *Paradise Lost* (1973); Shook, Robert L., *Turnaround* (1990); Sobel, Robert, *Car Wars* (1984); Sward, Keith, *The Legend of Henry Ford* (1948).

Ford, Henry, II (1917–1987)

Also referred to as Hank the Deuce, Henry Ford II had gone to Yale and unwittingly handed in his crib notes with an exam, which got him suspended without a degree in 1938. Some years later as he gave a speech to the campus, he waved his notes saying, "And I didn't write this one either." A navy officer in World War II, the Deuce really preferred to stay in the war when he was ordered to go back to manage Ford at the behest of his grandfather. But the company was too big a defense contractor to let his grandfather run it. Henry just observed the plant at work at first. But he was feared by many as an interloper. Henry Ford had to be forced to hand over reins to the Deuce under the threat that the rest of the family would sell their stock to outsiders.

The first thing the Deuce did was clean out the old man's loyalists, who had tried to keep the grandson out. Then he brought in Ernest R. Breech of Bendix and Charles "Tex" Thornton's "whiz kids" to run the place. This was quite innovative at the time—using men who had not grown up talking and thinking about cars. Rather, these men were financial wizards. Thornton brought with him ten army air force buddies who had all decided to offer their military skills (they had been procurement officers, seeing to it that the service got the right items in the right quantity at the right time in the right place with the right quality) as a group after World War II.

Henry Ford II saw these ex-military men

as just the answer to his grandfather's lackadaisical management policies. They were young men (between 26 and 34 years old), and two of them, Arjay Miller and Robert McNamara (later secretary of defense during the Vietnam years), rose to the presidency of Ford Motor Company under the Deuce's tutelage. But at first the younger Ford looked to have made a mistake. The newcomers knew absolutely nothing about producing motor vehicles. They roamed the plant floor asking questions, earning them the derisive nickname "the quiz kids" after a popular radio show of the time featuring preteen geniuses showing off their knowledge. But as Henry Ford II had hoped, after a brief hiatus, the new management team began to pay off in good decisions that led to efficient operations. Then Thornton's men received the more congratulatory moniker, "the whiz kids."

Henry II was smart enough to know he could not do it alone. Under his leadership, the "whiz kids" ran the company's first real audit and found that vast sums of money had been wasted by his grandfather's sloppy procedures. The Deuce and his men cut out the dead wood, introduced the postwar cars of 1948, and watched profits go wild. Unlike his grandfather, Henry was a good friend to Jews and an important supporter of the State of Israel, for which the company received a private 20-year Arab boycott until 1976. He also supported the civil rights aspirations of African Americans, made the first public stock offering in 1956 (since the original one that Henry Ford had bought back), and introduced the Edsel, Mustang, and Thunderbird. Henry had a fiery temper just like Henry I. He fired Lee Iacocca as too big a competitor for the top job. He was also a true internationalist and interested in European ventures, and approved of the program that has brought Ford back to the top of American auto production without receiving government bailouts. After a prolonged fight with marital problems and heart trouble, he died of pneumonia at age 70.

See also Automobiles from Domestics to Imports; Automobiles in American Society; Ford, Henry.

References Collier, Peter, and David Horowitz, *The Fords* (1987); Halberstam, David, *The Reckoning* (1986); Lasky, Victor, *Never Complain, Never Explain* (1981); May, George S., "Henry Ford II," in George S. May (ed.), *Encyclopedia of American Business History and Biography: The Automobile Industry* (1989), 145–158; Rothschild, Emma, *Paradise Lost* (1973); Sobel, Robert, *Car Wars* (1984); Shook, Robert L., *Turnaround* (1990); Wik, R. M., *Henry Ford and Grass-Roots America* (1972).

Forty-Niners

The "forty-niners" is the nickname given to the gold rushers who went to exploit the mineral bonanza in California in the mid-nineteenth century. Since the first ones traveled in the year of 1849, they received the forty-niner appellation.

See also California Trail.

Freighting and Teamsters

Vehicles of any kind were scarce in colonial America. This was especially true of commercial conveyances. It was not until the middle of the eighteenth century that stagecoaches began to roll on the miserable roads that ran inland and paralleled the East Coast. The venerable Conestoga wagon was not invented until approximately the same time. Most traffic went by canals or by sea and river. But when pioneers reached the Mississippi River and crossed into the vast hinterland, there were no deep rivers reliable enough for transportation. Even the venerable Missouri could be considered treacherous at best. This meant that roads (and later railroads) would be essential to the expansion of the Unites States to the Pacific.

The standard commercial vehicle of early America was a homegrown product first produced by German immigrants in Lancaster County, Pennsylvania. As the product came from near the Conestoga River, the vehicle was called a "Conestoga wagon." This vehicle was a conversion of the usual two-wheeled cart that had dominated trade up to then. It was set on four wheels that had a peculiar bend in the spokes that put the wheel rim out from the axle hub, like a dish. This configuration made for flexibility and a heavy load-carrying capacity. It also forced the wheel's pressures inward on the axle and strengthened the frame. The tires were made of iron, heated by a blacksmith and shrink-cooled to fit the rim. Generally the wheels were six feet in diameter and two to four inches in width. Actually, the wider tire was an aid to movement as it required less than half the power to move as a narrow one. But it was correspondingly harder to heat and shrink-fit properly.

The body of the wagon bowed down in the center from front to back, giving it a distinct boatlike shape that prompted its nickname, "Prairie Schooner." Indeed, the wagon passing through the tall grass of the plains with its white canvass top did look much like a ship plowing through the sea. There were two reasons for the bowed shape of the cargo base. First, it allowed cargo to hang over the front and back, keeping the wheelbase short for easy turns. It also kept the cargo in the box, sliding to the center. The top was a canvas cover stretched over a frame that leaned outward on each end, giving all-weather protection to its cargo. The entire frame was mortised to hold it in place.

The Conestoga first made its national

A column of cavalry, artillery, and wagons, commanded by General George Custer, crosses the Dakoka Territory in this 1874 photograph.

debut during the Braddock Campaign in 1755. Pulled by six massive draft horses (or sometimes with an odd number of horses known as a "spike"), it became a standard on the turnpikes of the East. Teamsters usually rode the near-side wheel horse, reserving the whole bed for cargo. As the teamsters became more competitive, they painted their wagons distinctive colors and put a tuned set of bells on the hames (sides of the horses' collars). Sometimes each team in a six-horse hitch had a different ring, and a loaded wagon and its hitch could make a powerful racket coming down a hard-surfaced pike. It was this type of wagon that supplied the Continental army and ran up and down the interior roads outside British reach. To accommodate these six-bell-team Conestogas, Congress, state legislatures, and private companies lobbied to build America's early roads.

At first, trans-Mississippi transportation was by pack train. The army soon set the standards. An average army pack train contained 50 mules, 14 riding animals, and a bell horse. Led by a packmaster, the crew consisted of his assistant, ten packers, a cook, and a farrier. Each mule carried a pack saddle that was preceded by a *corona*, or sheepskin blanket, and a saddle blanket. Before the old sawbuck pack saddle, packers used a leather coverall called an *aparejo* with a crupper attached. In any saddle used on a mule, both a breast strap and breaching were necessary as the animal has such narrow shoulders and hips that the saddle slides up and back too easily. Over the aparejo came the *sobre jalma*, or as Americans called it, the hammer cloth, which kept the load off the mule's back and on the saddle.

Packers were crusty individuals who could throw a rope hitch around a mule in mere minutes that would keep the cargo in place all day. Various pack saddles came into vogue, ranging from the old wooden crossed sawbucks to the more complicated Decker, with its iron rings and hoops. Small items were loaded into boxes known as *paniers* (French for "basket," often misspelled as "pannier"), usually pronounced "panniard" in the trade. Larger items could be piled up

between the paniers and the sawbucks and secured by single- or double-diamond hitches. These ropes were tied in an intricate pattern that actually worked like a spring, flexing with the movement of the load, automatically tightening as the packer tied it on. Usually it helped for the packer to tie one back leg off the ground to keep impatient animals in line while loading, keeping kicking under control. Bad cases could get a blindfold and the "scotch hobble," as the leg tying was called.

Generally, one man could manage five mules (the army standard) on the trail, but longer strings per man were not uncommon. The mules usually were "tailed," with the lead rope of one tied to the tail or pack saddle of the animal preceding it. Smart packers used a thin line to make the final hookup—just in case there was a "wreck." If someone got stubborn and pulled up suddenly the line could part and leave the others unmolested. Others preferred to snub up the lead rope around the animal's neck and let it walk free. Such strings were always led by a gray mare with a tinkling bell. The fascination of a mule for the gray mare still is not fully understood, but it is a combination that is pretty near infallible. At night, the only animal that needed to be tied or hobbled was the mare. The mules stayed close by listening for the jingle of her neck bell, sleeping or munching the grass.

But mule trains could only carry a limited amount of weight. Soon the tons of goods needed by towns, mines, forts, and various other enterprises in the West had to be carried by large wagons. But the Conestoga was too heavy for the long haul over the Plains. And their six-horse hitches could not handle the heavy pull upgrade from the Missouri to the Rockies on the sparse feed available on the Plains. It was a peculiar feature of the western wagon trade that the loads generally went one direction—either away from the Missouri River or the Pacific coast. This made the river towns important shipping points. By the end of the Civil War, Atchison, Kansas, was the farthest west one could send goods by boat or rail. Some 54 million pounds of goods passed through Atchison in 1865. Some 5,600 men, 4,500 wagons, 30,000 oxen, and 7,300 mules worked the levees and the trails out of town. It was a lucrative business. Local farmers often filled in for extra cash.

In New Mexico and on the Red River of the North, two-wheeled carts still moved the majority of the trade. The *carretas* or Chihuahua carts had long been a familiar sight in the Southwest since Spanish colonial times. They were pulled by a team of animals, often burros or mules, but mostly by oxen. Large loads were double- or triple-teamed. The wheels were the carreta's most spectacular feature. Some were solid, but generally they were made in three parts—two semicircular rim pieces fitted to a rectangular center that also served as part of the rim. The whole thing was pinned together by large dowels. The carreta ranged in size from small carts to the large freight vehicles 7 feet long, 1.5 feet wide, and 5 feet high.

By the middle of the nineteenth century, a similar vehicle, made of updated materials, came into prominence along the border with Canada west of the Great Lakes. These vehicles generally hauled hides and furs in exchange for finished goods. As the main center of this trade was Pembina south of the border on the Red River of the North, the vehicles came to be called Pembina Carts. Each two-wheeled cart was pulled by one draft animal and could haul a half ton about 20 miles a day. The wheels were set with an extreme dish, which gave them the look of being about to collapse. They were never greased, so the rubbing of the hub against the axle made a hideous screech that could be heard for miles. A whole train of such howling vehicles was downright nerve-wracking. At the peak of their use, some 5,000 to 8,000 such carts engaged in the trade until the arrival of the rails put them out of business in the 1870s. The Pembina Cart was rugged and cheap, two requisites for the frontier. The axle on this and most two-wheel carts was offset to the rear to give the tongue weight and prevent the vehicle from dumping its load off the rear.

If the Conestoga wagons were not commonly used west of the Mississippi, the tradesmen had their pick of several famous wagon brands, most of them based on a modified Conestoga design. One of the most popular, especially in the Santa Fe trade, was the vehicle produced by Joseph Murphy of St. Louis. Murphy's wagon was much larger and lighter than the Conestoga, but it was renowned for its quality. Murphy hired German craftsmen to build his wagons. Only selected hardwoods were put into the boxlike body, and the wheels were constructed of white oak and hickory. The holes in the wood pieces were not drilled but bored with a hot iron, which kept them from splitting. In fact, the hallmark of Murphy's wagon was the toughness of the running gear, an essential quality when working the western trails. There was no set form to Murphy's wagons—he made them to order. But all proudly carried the name J. Murphy on the builder's plate.

Most freighters liked wagons of single-ton capacity for speed. But those interested in hauling more tonnage went for the 4-to-6-ton capacity Murphy. This wagon was 15 to 20 feet long and 4 feet wide, with varying box heights. All wagons were covered by a tarp to protect the load in transit. Most wagons carried dedicated equipment: a spare axle, maybe a spare wheel, axe, shovels, side barrels and boxes for water, small items, and food for man and beast.

Another company that competed with Murphy was Studebaker Brothers of South Bend, Indiana. Known for using woods that had been air dried and aged three to five years, Studebaker became synonymous with quality. The black hickory axles were boiled in oils for toughness. Their spokes sloped outward as on the earlier Conestogas. Unlike Murphy, Studebaker offered standard designs of many weights and capacities, all listed in the company's voluminous catalogue.

As usual the army had a standard wagon that it preferred. The Civil War made these vehicles plentiful, and later many were transferred to civilian service through surplus auctions. The standard wagon was hauled by six mules, with the driver mounted on the near-wheel mule. It had straight sides and a slight upsweep in the floor, with boxes in front and back that could be detached and used for feed troughs. It was these same wagon boxes that ambushed soldiers used as an improvised fort on the Bozeman Trail in 1866 to hold off a Sioux war party in the so-called Wagon Box Fight. As the years passed and Congress got stingier with the national defense dollar, the number of mules was reduced to four and the wagon redesigned to accept a spring seat for the driver. These vehicles continued in use until the end of World War I.

But there were massive Carson Wagons, too. Used mostly in ore processing in the Great Basin mining zones (hence named for Carson City, Nevada, the center of the mines), these massive, tall-sided wagons could take up to 10 tons. These wagons were often run in tandem, like a modern semitrailer rig. In the Death Valley region of California, two massive Carson Wagons and a water tanker (after all, the lack of that commodity gave the place its ominous name) were pulled by 20-mule teams. These hitches were so long that the teams in the middle of the hitch (called swing teams) were trained to jump the drag line and pull at right angles to turns. This kept the chain curved around sharp bends. As the teams progressed through a turn, they would jump back across the chain and pull ahead normally, reversing the process. Such hitches were guided by a single "jerk line" to the near lead animal. A jerking motion turned him right, a steady pull, left. The off lead animal had his bit connected to the breast collar of his mate, and the turning motion was transferred across the pair. The others followed the leaders. The driver rode the near-wheel animal, sometimes a heavy draft horse instead of a mule. A swamper rode on the second tall wagon and worked the brakes for it and the water tanker.

Wagons often traveled in trains for protection and assistance in emergencies. On the Plains they usually traveled four abreast. At night the whole train forted up by pulling the wagons into a box or circle, with wagon tongues to the inside. The encircled wagons then became a corral for the animals and shelter against attack. But when no danger was apparent, the teamsters let the animals graze nearby under the watchful gaze of a nighthawk. Some wagon trains, especially those going to Santa Fe, hauled a cannon or two to overawe marauding Indians. Each wagon was hauled by a half dozen yoked oxen, horses, or mules. It never hurt to have a skittish mule for the lead rider. Many a train was saved by an alarm-sounding animal catching the whiff of unseen danger ahead. Whenever a wagon train approached a grade or a river ford, it was common practice to stop and use double or triple hitches to move the wagons up the grade. Braking was applied by blocks rubbing against the wheels. They could be applied by the driver pulling on a rope attached to the brake lever or by a swamper riding at the lever for that purpose. A runaway wagon was nothing short of disaster for men, animals, and vehicle alike.

The men in the train had a definite social hierarchy that was rigidly observed. At the top was the wagon master, who had near dictatorial powers. Next came the drivers, the mule skinners, and the bullwhackers. At the bottom echelon were the swampers and greasers—the young, often Hispanic, men who maintained the wagons, and from which work the derogatory slur "greaser" was derived. As driving men went, the bullwhackers and mule skinners took a back seat to riverboatmen, who considered themselves superior to royalty, and stagecoach "jehus," the "Dukes of the Road." All of them looked about the same—dirty, dust covered, wearing tall boots with tucked-in pants legs, checkered shirts, and broad-brimmed hats. They quarreled and fought and drank heavily, but rarely had a fatal set-to. And they were basically honest. It was not unusual to ride into a freighting town like Dodge City and pass dozens of wagons loaded down with the tools of the trade, unlocked and lying about on seats, and nothing ever being disturbed except by its rightful owner.

Teamsters had a lot of ideas when it came to draft animals. Oxen were inexpensive, readily available, hard to steal, tractable, and not easily stampeded. They could haul a heavy load at a steady pace all day. They ate what grew beside the road, had few gastric problems, and could be eaten with gusto if the situation called for it. They generally worked in a yoke, a wooden collar that held the team together. American yokes worked off the animals' shoulders; those in Mexico worked off the horns to which they were tied. The men who drove them, called "bullwhackers," walked alongside and controlled them with a long whip (experts allegedly could snap a fly off the lead steer) and yells of "gee" (right), "haw" (left), "ya" (get going), and the universal "whoa." One had not truly lived until he experienced an ox stampede, wagon and all, to a watering site after a long, hot, dry stretch of trail.

Mules also had their advocates. They moved faster than oxen and were stronger and more sure-footed than horses, as well as less disease prone, with a stronger gastric system. But they needed supplementary feed carried along, although they could be kept at one-third the cost of a horse. They could go across deserts with less water than horses or oxen. But if they broke down, no respectable white man would eat the meat. It was considered too tough and common. Many Native Americans were rumored to like mule meat, however. Maybe that is why mules made excellent "watchdogs" on the trail and in camp. Mules had the ability to endure harsh treatment and the worst language, a real merit considering the quality of many a mule skinner. For some reason, Mexican mules had a better reputation for docility when compared to their Missouri and Tennessee cousins.

An old mule story, probably apocryphal (but if it isn't true, it ought to be), has a mule skinner getting religion at one stop and taking the pledge not to swear. The next day when he hitched up his teams, he mounted the near-wheel mule and asked the hitch to step out. Not one animal moved. The reformed mule skinner repeated the effort with the same result. Then he lost his temper and newfound religion simultaneously, letting out a string of cuss words that colored the air blue for a week. Dutifully, the mules leaned into their harnesses, satisfied that their real driver was there, not some effete impostor. (The Apaches did not call the white men "goddamies" for nothing.) In the end, the real problem with mules was that they were smarter than their masters.

While some preferred oxen or mules, everyone in the West liked horses. But they were expensive and not as hardy in the harness as their four-legged counterparts. But they could be eaten with a modicum of respectability if they broke down, and they rode better. Their main problem was that Native Americans admired good horseflesh, too. For a wagon train to use horses, the wagonmaster had to be interested in a lighter cargo and speed. He also needed to watch for Indian horse thieves. Many a young warrior increased his *remuda* (herd) by cutting out horses from inside wagon train corrals at night, considered a deed of bravery and guile in the Plains societies, not stealing. But it was dangerous, as whites shot first and asked few questions later.

The wagonmen carried a chip sack on each vehicle. On the treeless Plains, everyone was expected to pick up buffalo chips for cooking fires. Organized trains, like those of the first-class plains freighters, Russell, Majors & Waddell, divided their crews into messes of five men each, one of whom was designated "cook." Fare tended to be simple: crackers, beans, bacon, and coffee so thick one could float iron in it. Sweetening was provided by molasses. Each man carried his eating utensils as a part of his kit. No buffalo chips meant that everyone ate cold. It also meant that the food lacked the "character" that burning chips imparted to what they cooked. A clean plate was one that had the prior meal rubbed out with a little dirt and the swipe of a greasy palm. For a whiskey substitute, wagoneers drank a brew called "tangle leg," descriptive of how one walked after swilling it. The contents were alcohol, nitric acid, pepper, and tobacco juice. Legend has it that a dude would go weak-kneed when he approached within 400 yards of the stuff. No wonder the drivers could swear so profoundly.

Until the arrival of the motorized truck,

the freight haulers were teamsters, as their modern union's name still implies. They hauled the cargo wherever the railroads and the steamboats could not or would not go. As such, they did much to chart, create, and utilize the road system that took the pioneers, miners, and soldiers west. Without their form of transportation the West could not have been won.

See also Camels in the West; Russell, Majors & Waddell Company.

References Briggs, Harold E., "Early Freight and Stage Lines in Dakota," *North Dakota Historical Quarterly* (1929) 3: 229–261; Back, Joe, *Horses, Hitches and Rocky Trails* (1959); Dunlop, Richard, *Wheels West* (1977); Eggenhofer, Nick, *Wagons, Mules, and Men* (1961); Elser, Smoke, and Bill Brown, *Packin' in on Mules and Horses* (1980); Gregg, Josiah, *Commerce of the Prairies* (1884); Harsha, Max, *Mule Skinner's Bible* (1987); Hooker, William F., *Prairie Schooner* (1918); Hooker, William F., "The Frontier Freight Train Wagon Boss of the 1870s," *Union Pacific Magazine* (1925) 4: 9–10; Hough, Emerson, "A Study in Transportation: The Settlement of the West," *Century Magazine* (1902) 41: 212; Jackson, W. Turrentine, *Wagon Roads West* (1952); Majors, Alexander, *Seventy Years on the Frontier* (1893); Paden, Irene, *Wake of the Prairie Schooner* (1943); Settle, Raymond W., and Mary Lund Settle, *Empire on Wheels* (1949); Settle, Raymond W., and Mary Lund Settle, *War Drums and Wagon Wheels* (1966); Walker, Henry Pickering, *The Wagonmasters* (1966); Winther, Oscar Osburn, *The Old Oregon Country* (1950); Winther, Oscar Osburn, *The Story of the Conestoga* (1954); Wyman, Walker D., "Freighting: A Big Business on the Santa Fe Trail," *Kansas Historical Quarterly* (1931) 1: 17–27; Wyman, Walker D., "Bull-Whacking: A Prosaic Profession Peculiar to the Great Plains," *New Mexico Historical Review* (1932) 7: 297–310; Wyman, Walker D., "The Military Phase of Santa Fe Freighting, 1846–1865," *Kansas Historical Quarterly* (1932) 2: 415–428.

French, Daniel (n.d.)

Located at Pittsburgh, Daniel French built the first non-Fulton-designed and licensed steamboats in the West. The *Comet* appeared in 1813, followed a year later by the *Enterprise*, a deep-draft stern-wheeler 80 feet in length, that utilized Oliver Evan's discovery of high-pressure steam for increased torque, rather than Fulton's low-pressure engine. The ship was taken south to New Orleans by Henry M. Shreve, got caught up in the preparations for the battle against the British, and was conscripted by General Andrew Jackson to run supplies to the American army south of the city. After the battle, in the spring of 1815, the *Enterprise* became the first steamboat to go upriver all the way to the falls at Louisville, demonstrating that French's high-pressure engine was the key to upriver travel. But French gained little credit from the expedition, as Shreve feared that the trip was made possible only by the spring flood. French refused to change his concept, which led Shreve to design his own shallow-draft boat, the *Washington*, that became the standard for western waters thereafter.

See also Evans, Oliver; Shreve, Henry Miller; Steamboats.

Frost et al. v. Railroad Commission of the State of California 271 US 583 (1926)

In 1926, the U.S. Supreme Court decided the Frost case. The circumstances were that the state had passed a law requiring truckers to obtain certificates of convenience and necessity to use the highways. Since the California edict did not specifically refer to the state's use of police powers, the Court majority ruled in favor of the law based on the precedent set in *Michigan Public Utilities Commission et al. v. Duke Cartage Company.* The Court found that California's licensing purpose was to control competitive conditions within the state to the benefit of all. The implication was that states could control trucking so long as it had to do with guaranteeing the conditions of competition. The Court was concerned only with the surface appearances of the regulation, not its results. The dissenting opinion held out for the state's absolute right to regulate an industry that used its highways.

Five years later, in *Smith v. Cahoon* 283 US 533, the Court expanded the *Frost* decision. It required the states to define contract (owner-operated) and common (public) carriers and regulate them separately. Private carriers (those who hauled their own company's goods) were still exempt. The former could be regulated by the state with impunity to protect the latter and be required to obtain permits from the state to operate. Contract carriers were also refused the right to undercut the rate schedules of the common carriers. The notion that the common carrier could be regulated through the state's police powers in the public interest and the contract carrier merely by the necessity to control competitive conditions within an industry was retained.

See also Michigan Public Utilities Commission et al. v. Duke Cartage Company; *Sproles et al. v. Binford*.

Reference Childs, William R., *Trucking and the Public Interest* (1985).

Fulton, Robert (1765–1815)

Born in Lancaster County, Pennsylvania, at Little Britain (now named Fulton) into an immigrant Irish family, Robert Fulton had a mechanical turn of mind from his youth. He experimented with paddle wheels on fishing boats before he turned to art. He was a painter of miniatures, and produced mechanical and landscape drawings. He lived in Philadelphia and was a friend of Benjamin Franklin. At age 20, Fulton traveled to London where he lived and studied with Benjamin West. Later, he practiced his art for rich patrons at various country estates, including that of the Duke of Bridgewater, a canal builder, and the Earl of Stanhope, an inventor of a printing process.

Fulton's mechanical mind was encouraged by his mentors, and he turned to invention, developing a double-inclined plane designed to assist canal boats from one level to another. He patented a marble saw, a machine to spin flax, and a cast-iron aqueduct of the style used across the River Dee and other locations. Fulton then turned his talent to canal boats, developing designs for both light and heavy cargo haulers. He wrote extensively on canal building in the London *Morning Star*, and these works were collected in a treatise, *The Improvement of Canal Navigation*. In 1794, he moved to Paris where he lived with the family of Joel Barlow, an expatriate author. Here he painted the first panorama seen in France and experimented with submarines in the Seine River, but failed to convince the revolutionary government of their efficacy.

Robert Fulton introduced the steamboat in 1807.

The more sea-oriented British, however, were not interested in seeing a genius like Fulton's go unappreciated into French employ. Stanhope got Fulton to return to England and continue his submarine experiments there. Interested especially in his torpedo concepts, the British navy employed them against the French at Boulogne, but the design proved faulty. Later, in 1805, his improved torpedo sank a target ship in an experiment in England. In 1806, Fulton returned to America. The U.S. government spent $5,000 in further experiments with submarines and torpedoes and, although the navy department was unimpressed, Fulton took out patents on several torpedo designs.

In addition to undersea warfare, Fulton had experimented with steam engines and paddle wheels since 1793. His first ship sank in the Seine in 1803, and a rebuilt effort could not get up enough power to be practicable. He continued the trials in New York, ordering a new, more sophisticated steam engine from Watt and Boulton in 1807. Constructing a ship named the *North River of Clermont*, basically a deep-draft vessel that looked like a sailing ship with side paddle wheels, Fulton made the first successful trip up the Hudson against the current to Albany that same year, capitalizing on a power concept first tried by John Fitch of Connecticut in 1787. Fulton's triumph led to counterclaims and court suits by a host of others, the defense against which threatened his livelihood. Nonetheless, he patented his work in a preliminary stage in 1809 and in a more improved form two years later. These patents and the Fulton system led to a boom in steamboat building by a multitude of companies besides his own, because as long as others did not duplicate his mechanical parts, Fulton's patents were not interfered with. Fulton tried but could not patent the paddle wheel, it being held a common property from antiquity. Fulton also invented a steam ram (a steam-powered ramming vessel) and an armed steam-powered warship designed to protect harbors. He turned to submarines again in the midst of the War of 1812, but he died in 1815 with only the keel of his *Nautilus* laid.

See also Early Steamboats; Evans, Oliver; Fitch, John; Rumsey, James; Shreve, Henry Miller; Steamboats; Symington, William.

References Flexner, James Thomas, *Steamboats Come True* (1944); Sutcliffe, Alice, *Robert Fulton and the "Clermont"* (1909).

Gallatin, Albert (1761–1849)

Born in Switzerland, Albert Gallatin came to the New World in 1780 after he graduated from Geneva Academy, eventually settling in the Pennsylvania backcountry. An ardent Jeffersonian Republican, Gallatin was denied a seat in the first U.S. Senate on the grounds he had not lived ten years in the country. He took a moderate stand during the Whiskey Rebellion, which helped avert much bloodshed, and was reelected to the Congress in 1795. He served until 1801, when his able grasp of the difficult subject of finance, a topic previously dominated by the Federalist Alexander Hamilton, led to his appointment as Thomas Jefferson's secretary of the treasury, a post he also held under James Madison until 1814. He was a member of the treaty commission at Ghent (1814), minister to France (1816–1823) and England (1826–1827), and president of the Bank of New York City (1831–1839). He is also remembered as the "father of American ethnology," having founded the American Ethnological Society, and wrote a well-received synopsis of American Indians. Meriwether Lewis and William Clark named one of the tributaries of the Missouri River after him during their exploration of the West. As revealed in his *Report* of 1808, he became a supporter of federal aid to internal improvements, which cost him political position later under the Jacksonians. He died in Astoria, New York, in 1849.

See also Gallatin Report.

Reference Adams, Henry, *The Life of Albert Gallatin* (1879).

Gallatin Report (1808)

Interest in internal improvements had grown to such an extent that in 1807 Congress authorized Secretary of the Treasury Albert Gallatin to investigate and report on the problem and its possibilities. Gallatin's report represented the first real concern by the federal government in transportation and marked the beginning of a constitutional debate that ranged up to and even beyond the Civil War. Gallatin proposed a nationally planned and financed program of transportation projects. He grouped them into four packages: (1) coastal canals across the four great necks of land behind Cape Cod; the New Jersey, Delaware, and the Virginia–North Carolina Capes, a visionary concept later enlarged in the twentieth century to become the Intracoastal Waterway; (2) interior canals from the coasts up the Santee, Potomac, Susquehanna, Roanoke, and James River systems, and a canal from Muscle Shoals to the Tombigbee, opening the interior to Mobile; (3) canals opening up the Great Lakes along the Mohawk Valley and around Niagara Falls, and up the Hudson to Lake Champlain, which later would be built by the state of New York; and (4) a system of interior canals and roads to fill in the gaps between the other proposals, typified by the National Road.

Gallatin saw all of this as being financed by the federal government because the end result would benefit the whole country. The Jeffersonian Republicans, however, had great constitutional reservations about federal financing and much preferred to eradicate the national debt, already inflated by funding, assumption, and the purchase of Louisiana (another constitutionally dubious project), rather than add to it. But Gallatin had a way around the objections of the "old" Republicans (men who opposed anything not exactly specified in the Constitution) to satisfy the "new" Republicans (men who wanted a less literal interpretation of the document). The secretary of the treasury proposed that the National Road (the first project of his plan placed into action) be built by a road-construction fund financed by 5 percent of the receipts of the sale of public lands in the states and territories through which it passed. This fund, later reduced to 2 percent, was the basis for the only road project fully financed by the federal government in American history, and effectively built the National Road from Cumberland, Maryland, to Vandalia, Illinois.

See also Canals; Erie Canal; Gallatin, Albert;

National Road; Roads and Highways, Colonial Times to World War I; Two Percent Fund.

Reference Gallatin, Albert, *Report of the Secretary of the Treasury on the Subject of Public Roads and Canals* (1808).

Geddes, James (1763–1838)

Born of Scots ancestry near Carlisle, Pennsylvania, James Geddes moved to New York State and engaged in the salt industry. He then went on to study law and was admitted to the bar in 1799. He was appointed justice of the peace and later judge of the county court and court of common pleas. He was also elected to the state assembly (1804 and 1822), and the U.S. Congress (1813). In Albany, he was approached about the possibility of digging a canal to Buffalo. Since he was from the area to be traversed, he undertook a study of the terrain for the most favorable route, and although he lacked technical training he made the first survey himself. His route was reported to the assembly and essentially became that of the Erie Canal. He also suggested the various side canals that became so critical to gaining statewide support for the project. When construction began after the War of 1812, Geddes was one of the principal engineers. He was later asked for help by other governmental entities in Ohio, Pennsylvania, Maine, and Washington, D.C.

See also Erie Canal; White, Canvass; Wright, Benjamin.

References Baker, Ray Palmer, "James Geddes," in Allen Johnson, et al. (eds.), *Dictionary of American Biography*, vol. 4, 204–205; Krout, John A., "New York's Early Engineers," *New York History* (1945) 24: 269–277; MacGill, Caroline E., et al., *History of Transportation in the United States before 1860* (1917); Whitford, Nobel E., *History of the Canal System of the State of New York* (1906).

Gibbons v. Ogden 9 Wheaton 1 (1824)

Gibbons is a landmark U.S. Supreme Court decision, written by famed Chief Justice John Marshall, in which the Court ruled that state governments could not interfere with the movement of interstate commerce or any goods that might potentially be in interstate commerce through legislation or licensing. The Robert Livingston and Robert Fulton heirs who held a monopoly on steam river trade on the Hudson and other rivers farmed out franchises to others, one of whom was Aaron Ogden, through licensing arrangements. Thomas Gibbons, a former partner of Ogden who broke with him over kowtowing to the Fulton interests, tried to run his own operation between New York and New Jersey without a North River Company (Livingston-Fulton) license. Ogden sued and the case wound up in the U.S. Supreme Court. Chief Justice Marshall ruled that the commerce clause in the constitution gave Congress broad powers of legislation in the field and construed interstate commerce to be anything that moved even inside the state boundaries, as it was potentially liable to cross them. The result was to free transportation from restrictive licensing agreements and state restraint. In the West, these licensing arrangements had been ignored all along, especially in the field of steamboat development, with popular support.

See also Charles River Bridge Company v. Warren Bridge Company; Shreve, Henry Miller.

References Kelly, Alfred H., and Winfred A. Harbison, *The American Constitution: Its Origins and Development* (1948); Swisher, Carl B., *The Taney Period* (1974); Warren, Charles, *The Supreme Court* (1922); White, G. Edward, and Gerald Gunther, *The Marshall Court, 1815–1825* (1988).

Gila Trail

There were three natural routes west of the Mississippi that led travelers to the Pacific. All of them were pioneered by Native Americans; although it is doubtful if any of them went coast to coast or even river to coast, they did go long distances utilizing these natural routes. The natural paths emphasized rivers and streams. Not only did these waterways provide ease of movement by canoe or bullboats, they were essential to horse travel and teemed with game needed for food.

Two of the natural trails west followed the Missouri River up from St. Louis. One went up to the headwaters of the Missouri, crossed the Continental Divide, and followed the Columbia River to the ocean. The other branched off from the first near Omaha, followed the Platte and Sweetwater Rivers west to the Continental Divide, crossed South Pass and hit the headwaters of the Green and Bear Rivers, and then followed the Snake River to the Columbia River and the ocean. The third trail west branched off at Independence, went out along the Kansas River and dropped down to the Great Bend of the Arkansas, followed the Arkansas to near Pueblo, Colorado, and went south on the Rio Grande to near Socorro, New Mexico, where the traveler turned west and followed the Gila River to old Fort Yuma. Here, one had to head out across the desert to Warner Springs and come into San Diego from the north, through the area where the wild animal park is today. This last route and its various branches made up the Gila Trail, the southern route to the Pacific before the Civil War.

The first Europeans who discovered the Gila route came out of Old Mexico. These were the priests and soldiers of Spain, the *conquistadores*. According to legend, when the Moors had taken the great city of Mérida, Spain, seven Catholic bishops had fled capture to a foreign land called Cíbola, where they had built seven cities of gold. Most educated persons doubted the legend, but the masses believed it, and after the subjugation of the wealthy Aztec and Inca empires, even the scoffers wondered if it might not be true.

In any case, the mythical seven cities of Cíbola drove men like Fray Marcos de Niza, Melchoir Díaz, and Francisco Vásquez de Coronado on long journeys north from modern Mexico, especially after Cabeza de Vaca and his companions reported rumors of great cities inland during their wanderings along the Gulf Coast. Led by a slave, Esteban, who had accompanied Cabeza de Vaca, Marcos de Niza advanced down the San Pedro to the Gila, which he followed upstream to the San Francisco River. Here he learned that Esteban, whom de Niza had sent on ahead, had overreached himself among the Native Americans and

had been killed by members of the Zuñi pueblo. De Niza returned to Mexico with tales of a great city of gold—which he had never seen. Justifiably suspicious of de Niza's veracity, the viceroy dispatched a new expedition under Díaz to check the tale out. Díaz went in secret to keep the possible gold discovery from others until the viceroy could ensure his primary share. He became the first white man to mark and explore the Gila Trail westward from the San Pedro to the Colorado, returning to near where de Niza had stopped. There he camped for the winter.

But de Niza's rumors of a city or cities of gold swept the New World. Refusing to wait on others, Coronado organized an expedition in 1540. Coronado explored all the way up into present New Mexico and out onto the Kansas plains, but found no gold. His trips around the Rio Grande opened up more of the Gila Trail, but killed off the desire of all but missionaries to go there. The most important of the churchmen was Eusebio Kino, who established numerous missions in present-day Sonora, Mexico, and Arizona, an area known to the Spanish as Pimería Alta (the Upper Pima Land), in the last quarter of the seventeenth century. Kino's death marked the high point of Spanish influence for three-quarters of a century. Then in 1774, Juan Bautista de Anza, commandant of Tubac (in today's Arizona), received orders to open a land route to the missions recently established in California. De Anza's journey established the route of the Gila Trail from the Colorado River to Los Angeles across the Imperial Desert. Father Tomás Garces set up mission stations on the Arizona side to keep the trail open, but his murder by the Yuma Indians, who were disgusted with the dishonest activities of nonmission personnel, caused the abandonment of the Gila Trail until the arrival of the American fur trappers in the 1820s.

The first Americans to explore the Gila Trail were part of the James Ohio Pattie expedition in 1824. They proceeded south on the road down the Rio Grande to near Socorro and turned west to the copper mines at Santa Rita (near Silver City, New Mexico). The party then proceeded down the Gila to the San Pedro, where they trapped beaver. After Apaches rustled their horses and confiscated their fur, Pattie and the survivors returned to New Mexico on foot. Later, an Apache leader, Mangas Coloradas (Red Sleeves), came into the settlements decked out in fur and what Pattie recognized as his red flannel underwear. Pattie believed that the chief got his moniker from the underwear, but Apache legend attributes it to a fight in which the man emerged with his arms covered by an opponent's blood.

After Pattie, Ewing Young took a party down the Gila to its junction with the Salt, and trapped the Salt and Verde Rivers northward to near present-day Flagstaff, Arizona. He then turned westward to California, blazing a path that later became the famed Route 66. His youngest adherent was named Kit Carson. Carson remained in the mountains trapping for years, and by the time of the Mexican War, he knew more of the Southwest than any other American. He guided John Charles Frémont on two expeditions, one along the Central Overland Route to California and another along the Oregon Trail. The latter journey turned into a lengthy trip into California, where Frémont and Carson joined the Bear Flag Rebellion. Frémont then sent Carson east to report his great deeds to Washington. The redoubtable Carson went by the Gila Trail. Near Socorro, he met the invading American army, under Stephen Watts Kearny, which had just captured Santa Fe.

Kearny took Carson's dispatches, read that Frémont was governor of California, a post reserved for Kearny, and resolved to get there as quickly as possible and secure his privilege. Carson led him and his mounted dragoons on a trip that became famous for its sufferings in the canyons of the Gila and the deserts of California. Meanwhile, Lieutenant Philip St. George Cooke led a battalion of Mormon infantry by an easier route to the south of the Gila River through Las Cruces and Tucson and up the Santa Cruz River to the Gila Trail, where he followed Kearny's route to California. With some modifications, Cooke's better route became the main Gila Trail from there on out, and after the discovery of gold in California, a popular southern route to the placer sites. It had the advantage of being able to support wagon traffic because the Mormon Battalion had built a road as they traveled.

The gold rushers used two Gila Trail routes, one running from El Paso through Janos in Mexico, up to Tubac and Tucson. The other went north out of El Paso to Las Cruces and westward directly to Tucson. This latter trail, pioneered by Texas Ranger Captain Jack Hays, was the last modification in the Gila Trail. It had the advantage after the Gadsden Purchase in 1854 of being completely within the boundaries of the United States, unlike part of the Cooke Wagon Road. Caught up in the slavery fight in Congress, two routes, the Central Overland and the Gila Trail, were improved for fast travel to the goldfields. Speed and all-weather access being essential, Southerners wanted the Pacific mail contract let out on the Gila Trail; Northerners of course preferred the Central Route.

After Texas had been secured by the Mexican War, numerous expeditions sought to explore the area west of San Antonio, known only as Comanche and Apache country. Three major routes were established by the time of the Civil War: one running from San Antonio south to San Patricio and then to Ringgold Barracks on the Rio Grande, and the two others running from San Antonio to El Paso del Norte at the U.S.–Mexican border. The first of these ran north from San Antonio to Fort Mason, where it was joined by the road west from Austin. Then the road swung in a semicircle to the old Comanche ford at Horsehead Crossing on the Pecos and followed the river north to the Guadalupe Mountains, approaching El Paso from the northeast. This later was the route of the Texas and Pacific Railroad. Another road came out of San Antonio west to Fort Inge and looped northward to Camp Hudson on the Devil's River and Fort Lancaster on the Pecos. The road continued westward to Forts Stockton and Davis and then looped west and north to run up the Rio Grande to enter El Paso from the southeast. This eventually became the route of the Southern Pacific Railroad and much of the interstate highway. Before the Civil War, travelers on both roads risked attack from either Comanches or Lipan and Mescalero Apaches. But otherwise they were usable 12 months a year. All joined the Gila Trail at El Paso.

Led by Senator Thomas J. Rusk of Texas, who was supported by Secretary of the Interior Jacob Thompson and Secretary of War Jefferson Davis, both of Mississippi, southern route advocates had great political clout. Unfortunately, the man chosen to improve the road was James B. Leach. He proved less than competent, so much so that he ultimately faced a federal indictment for misuse of funds. The original promoters had wanted to take the mail out of St. Louis to Independence, down the Santa Fe Trail, and follow the Hays Cutoff across southern New Mexico and Arizona to California. But a condition of the contract was that the route had to leave Memphis (hometown of the postmaster general), meet the St. Louis run at Fort Smith, and pass through Arkansas and Texas to the Hays Cutoff. There it would follow the recommended route of the railroad survey, through Railroad Pass in Arizona and up the San Pedro to the Gila. But the actual route went south of this, for reasons of water supply, through Apache Pass, and west to the Santa Cruz at Tucson. It became known as the "Ox Bow Route" of the Gila Trail.

But the Civil War and a decade-long Apache war soon put an end to John Butterfield's stage route in 1861, three years after its birth. After the Civil War, the Gila Trail would be reopened to freighting and followed successfully by the Southern Pacific Railroad, U.S. Highway 90, and Interstate 10, eventually running all the way from Jacksonville, Florida, to San Diego.

See also Camino Real (California); Camino Real (Texas); Central Overland Route; Lewis and Clark Trail; Central Overland Trail; Roads and Highways, Colonial Times to World War I.

References Bieber, Ralph P., "The Southwestern Trails to California in 1849," *Mississippi Valley Historical Review* (1925) 12: 342–375; Dumke, Glenn S., "Across Mexico in '49," *Pacific Historical Review* (1949) 18: 33–44; Dunlop, Richard, *Great Trails of the West* (1971); Egan, Ferol, *The El Dorado Trail* (1970); Faulk, Odie B., *Destiny Road* (1973); Hague, Harlan, *The Road to California* (1878); Harris, Benjamin, *Gila Trail* (1960); Jackson, W. Turrentine, *Wagon Roads West* (1952); Martin, Mabelle E., "California Emigrant Roads through Texas," *Southwestern Historical Quarterly* (1924–1925) 18: 287–301; Moody, Ralph, *Old Trails West* (1963).

Goethals, George Washington (1858–1928)

Born in Brooklyn, New York, on 29 June 1858, George W. Goethals attended the City College of New York (1873–1876) before graduating from the U.S. Military Academy at West Point in 1880. His commission was as an army engineer. He received regular promotions and during the Spanish-American War served as chief engineer of the volunteer force and brevet lieutenant colonel. Returning to the regular army as a major, Goethals attended the Army War College in 1905. In 1915 he

George Washington Goethals

attained the rank of major general and retired in 1916.

Goethals served on numerous engineering projects during his career, including the Muscle Shoals Canal, and was a member of the committee on harbor and coastal fortification. But his greatest work was as chief engineer of the Panama Canal (1907–1914). Goethals received this post because President Theodore Roosevelt was tired of having civilian engineers resign from their canal jobs as soon as they learned the ropes, the worst instance being that of Chief Engineer John F. Stevens. Roosevelt reasoned that a military man could be kept at his assignment by the rigors of army discipline. Goethals did not disappoint, and when the canal opened in 1914, President Woodrow Wilson made him the first civil governor of the Canal Zone. Goethals brought to the job military discipline and organization, the ability to command men, and an excellent engineering background. He was an able delegator of power, and expected his subordinates to take full responsibility for their work. Under his rigorous administration, work went so smoothly that it finished a year ahead of schedule. After his retirement, Goethals continued to assist the army as a civilian employee in the logistics department during World War I. He also took on several state government engineering positions in New York and New Jersey, and died at New York City in 1928 after a ten-year stint as head of his own engineering consulting firm.

See also Panama Canal.

Good Roads Movement

During the last two decades of the nineteenth century, Americans began to move out of their cities and farms. The city dwellers did so for recreation, their method of travel being the new, more rideable bicycles that became the national craze. Farmers were interested in selling their surplus crops. Both found that the nation's roads were in worse shape than they had been in 100 years. Even proud old byways like the National Road had disintegrated into a sea-

sonable morass. Since the Civil War, America had been on a railroad binge to the exclusion of every other form of travel. Something had to be done to improve the roads—not just for cyclists but for the economic well-being of the country. The result was a public crusade called the Good Roads Movement.

The first inklings that something was to be done came from Mecklenburg County, North Carolina. The county decided to tax all property holders for road maintenance in 1879. The idea did not come easily—the following year the county commissioners repealed the tax. But they got back their nerve and reinstalled it in 1881. By the end of the decade Mecklenburg County had the best roads in the state—indeed, perhaps in the nation. It had higher tax rates, but the farmers and merchants noticed that business, hence prosperity for everyone including the city residents of Charlotte, was up. Wagons could haul cotton to town and the railroads in a matter of hours. Traditionally, it had taken days or weeks to dispose of the yearly crop. Mules and horses did not break down as often. Each wagon could haul more load with less horsepower and were safer than before.

Other states took notice of their deplorable roads. In 1883 Iowa held the first state road convention. It was said that one could find more negotiable roads in mountainous Switzerland than in the rolling hills that made up the heart of the Corn Kingdom. The convention recommended payment of specially dedicated road taxes, the end of statute labor in lieu of cash tax payments, consolidation of road districts by county, and the use of responsible road contractors—an indication that things have not changed much in certain areas of the construction trades. The state legislature saw the merit in these suggestions and adopted them outright. But political realities being what they were, the law was passed as a county option, not a mandate.

Other states did what North Carolina and Iowa had done. But the real impetus to the Good Roads Movement came from the weekend bicycle riders. New designs made bikes safer (one was not as likely to be propelled over the handlebars as the size of the front wheel was reduced) and pneumatic tires made them more practical to ride without losing one's teeth as they rattled over what passed for roads. "Wheel clubs" came into being all over the country. Planned excursions to spots in the country became common, roads were mapped out with something akin to precision, and propaganda as to the health benefits of cycling inundated the nation. The wheelmen, as bike riders were nicknamed, organized nationally as the League of American Wheelmen. The pressure for good roads now became a club imperative, and some of the Wheelmen knew the right people, like President Benjamin Harrison, for example. They also put out a national publication, *Good Roads*. Published by I. B. Potter, its main goal was to prepare the public to accept the taxes and standards of better travel. Potter praised those areas with good roads. He wrote of the advances made in Europe and of how the United States lagged behind. He published articles on how to build good roads.

Potter's magazine was an instant success. State after state formed good-roads associations. In 1894, a national road conference met and passed resolutions asking state legislatures to get behind the program. Led by New Jersey, where the Wheelmen were especially strong, states began to pass laws granting statewide aid for road building. New Jersey had its board of agriculture administer the first year's grant of $75,000. A couple of years later, New Jersey, following the lead of Massachusetts, established a public roads commission. Massachusetts already had an annual highway budget of $300,000. By 1900, there were over 100 local good-roads associations and six national bodies.

The most aggressive of the national groups was the National Good Roads Association (NGRA). It had no permanent membership list and depended on donations to operate. Led by Colonel William Moore of St. Louis, the NGRA tapped not only the public for operating revenue, but auto manufacturers, various civic groups,

makers of road machinery, materials distributors, and even railroads. Moore's biggest brainstorm was the National Good Roads Train. The railroads (each one tried to outdo its competitors in this greatest of the day's public relations stunts) responded with an 11-car special, the federal government supplied national specialists, and through able advance propaganda, Moore made wide swaths of the country knowledgeable about the needs for improving America's highways.

But it was not all roses. There was some tension between city motorists and cyclists and the farmers with their heavy wagons, plodding along down the highways behind horses and mules. But the farmers soon got motorized, too, and everyone was headed for the open road. The problem then became one of long-distance highways versus local farm-to-market roads. Despite arguments, the Good Roads Movement swept the country and resulted in a series of federal agencies (beginning with the Office of Road Inquiry in 1893) that led to the Bureau of Public Roads and the passage of the Federal-Aid Road Act of 1916. Gradually, the need for a separate public service association dedicated to good roads died out, and by the 1930s good roads had become a national imperative managed by state and federal employees.

See also League of American Wheelmen; Roads and Highways, Colonial Times to World War I.

Reference U.S. Department of Transportation, Federal Highway Administration, *America's Highways* (1976).

Gorgas, William Crawford (1854–1920)

Born in Mobile, Alabama, in 1854, William C. Gorgas was educated at the University of the South and Bellevue Hospital Medical College. He received a military appointment as a surgeon (doctors were private contractors then with the automatic rank of captain) and as chief sanitary officer in the Cuban Campaign of the Spanish-American War (1898–1902). His claim to fame was his conquest of tropical diseases like yellow fever, malaria, and typhoid fever, in which, by expanding on the work of Cuban researchers, he recognized the active role of insects, particularly mosquitoes, in their transmission. A chief reason for French failure in building their own Panama Canal arose from an inability to prevent pestilence, so Gorgas was a natural choice as chief sanitary officer of the American effort in 1904. He set to work draining swamps, spraying oils on ponds, and generally cleaning up the work areas. He also instituted a regular quinine ration for all men. As much of the work crew consisted of Caribbean blacks, and following the standard racial practices of the time, Gorgas divided the rationing process into Gold Employees and Silver Employees. The colors referred to the common cups that dispensed the liquid quinine—gold for white supervisors and mechanics and silver for the black laborers.

William Crawford Gorgas

By 1913, he had pretty much eradicated tropical disease as a major problem on the isthmus. He also served on the canal commission, was head of the American Medical Association, and the recipient of honorary degrees for his work. In 1914, he became surgeon general of the United States. Gorgas died while on a trip to London, England, in 1920.

See also Panama Canal.

Gould, George Jay (1864–1923)

Son of railroad mogul Jay Gould, George Gould hoped to succeed where the old man had failed—by building a rail empire that stretched from the Atlantic to the Pacific. George Jay received 6,000 miles of track from his father's will in 1892. He parlayed his father's empire into one that included the Denver & Rio Grande Western, Missouri Pacific, Texas & Pacific, St. Louis & Southwestern, and the International & Great Northern in the West and the Wabash, Western Maryland, West Virginia Central, and the Wheeling & Lake Erie in the East. There was one minor problem—the whole system had a gap at Pittsburgh.

An industrial giant with more freight traffic than any other three cities in the United States, Pittsburgh was the keystone to the fortunes of the Pennsylvania Railroad. And the "Pennsy" was not about to let Gould into its bailiwick. But Gould was adamant. He got Congress to pass a bill allowing a streetcar company (really a Gould front) to build a new bridge into Pittsburgh. The Pennsy sued in court but lost the case. Meanwhile, the American economy was booming and the Pennsylvania Railroad could not haul all of the goods that had to pass through Pittsburgh. So Gould stepped in with large sums of money and greased the wheels of local government. He also had the backing of John D. Rockefeller, Andrew Carnegie, and New York rail magnate Russell Sage, all of whom wished to break Pennsy's hold on Pittsburgh.

It took Gould four years to build his Wheeling & Lake Erie line into Pittsburg, then America's steel capital. The route was torturous. He had to build 60 bridges and 20 tunnels (the Pennsylvania Railroad and other early comers already had the good routes). Finally, at a cost of somewhere around $40 million, Gould reached his dream. But he had spent so much reaching Pittsburgh that he could not build the facilities necessary to move the freight. Gould also ran afoul of E. H. Harriman. Then came the Panic of 1907. The overextended Gould empire collapsed overnight. Gould had to sell everything but the Rio Grande, most of it going to Harriman. He died some years later after a visit to the tomb of the ancient Egyptian boy-pharaoh, Tutankhamen, allegedly a victim of the burial site's curse.

See also Gould, Jay; Harriman, Edward Henry.

References Ginger, Ray, *Age of Success* (1965); Holbrook, Stewart H., *The Age of the Moguls* (1953); Hubbard, Freeman, *Encyclopedia of North American Railroading* (1981); Josephson, Matthew, *The Robber Barons* (1934); Klein, Maury, "George J. Gould," in Keith L. Bryant, Jr. (ed.), *EABHB: Railroads in the Age of Regulation* (1988), 167–171; Lyon, Peter, *To Hell in a Day Coach* (1968); Meyers, Gustavus, *History of the Great American Fortunes* (1910); Moody, John, *The Masters of Capital* (1919).

Gould, Jay (1836–1892)

Once described by a historian as a small, quiet, private, outwardly respectable sort with a "reptilian" looking face, Jay Gould was one of the princes of those nineteenth-century malefactors of great wealth known collectively as the "robber barons." Born on an upstate New York farm, Gould worked in a rural store, became a surveyor, invented a mousetrap (there is something very appropriate in this, given his later life), and even wrote a history of Delaware County, New York. He built a tannery at what is now Gouldsboro, Pennsylvania (named after him), stole money from his partner, and invested in a bank. He cheated his banking partner, too, and the man killed himself in despair.

By age 24, Gould was in New York City looking for bigger and better things. He married Ellen Miller, whose father owned a railroad in upstate New York and Vermont. Gould borrowed cash from his father-in-

law and took over the line himself. He improved the railroad and sold it at a profit to what became the Delaware & Hudson. For the rest of his life Gould would see a profit in manipulating railroad stock. And he was good at it. His general pattern was to buy a poor railroad with a strategic location, raise the paper value of the stock, and sell out at a profit. Unlike his father-in-law's railroad, Gould never bothered to improve what he bought in actuality. Gould became an expert in forcing stocks down, buying, forcing the price up, and selling. He also learned the fine art of bribing politicians and never let a friendship stand in the way of profit. He ruined several men on his way up in life, but once he started he never looked back.

Gould's career became synonymous with the New York, Lake Erie & Western Railroad, commonly called the Erie. It ran from New York City to Buffalo by way of Binghamton and Elmira, in direct competition with Cornelius Vanderbilt's New York Central, which followed the old Erie Canal route. To counter Vanderbilt's great influence, Gould ingratiated himself with Daniel Drew, the "Great Bear of Wall Street." Drew had loaned the Erie some $2 million and called in the loan. The directors could not pay and Drew and his erstwhile compatriot, Gould, now had their own rail line. But Vanderbilt did not want competition in the trade to and from Buffalo. So he started buying Erie stock. When Vanderbilt controlled enough stock, he took over, keeping Drew and Gould on the board and adding James Fisk (another financial evildoer) as the final member. Vanderbilt then continued to buy up Erie stock on the sly, intending to dump the others at the appropriate time. The result was the "Erie War."

Eventually Gould, Fisk, and Drew, known as the "Unholy Three" on Wall Street, found out what was happening. If Vanderbilt wanted to buy stock, they decided to accommodate him. They printed all of the watered stock that the Commodore would buy. When Vanderbilt found out he had been bilked, he swore out a complaint against his partners (he practically owned the law enforcement personnel anyway). The Unholy Three, forewarned by a leak in the court system (there was always extra money to be made by the more enterprising informants), fled in a taxi ahead of Vanderbilt's coach, carrying their money in carpetbags to the waterfront. Grabbing a waiting boat, they wound up safe and rich in a New Jersey hotel. Laughing at their close call, Fisk mimicked the unfortunate Commodore by declaring himself "the Admiral" and walking about in a ridiculous uniform and sword.

The furious Vanderbilt hired a gang of thugs to kidnap the trio back into New York jurisdiction. The Unholy Three hired their own force to protect them, with three cannon mounted at the waterfront. They also incorporated their Erie system in New Jersey, where Vanderbilt had no influence. Meanwhile, realizing that they could never get back to New York City (where the real action was) without being arrested, Gould slipped off to Albany with $500,000 of ill-gotten gains to "cultivate" the state legislature. The job was well done, and all of the watered stock was declared legal, leaving Vanderbilt holding the bag. Then Gould and his men bought back Vanderbilt's share. By then Drew had had enough, and he withdrew with Vanderbilt, leaving Gould and Fisk in sole control of the Erie.

Still Vanderbilt sought revenge. He started a rate war against the Erie. Cattle went from Buffalo to New York City at $125 a carload. The Commodore cut the rate to $100. Erie responded with $75; Vanderbilt dropped it to $50; Erie went to $25; Vanderbilt mercilessly cut it to $1. But he reckoned without Gould, who had been buying up all the cattle around Buffalo he could get his hands on. Bumping Erie's rate back up to $125 a carload, to ensure no one would ship cattle on it, Gould and everyone else sent their steers over the New York Central. Gould and Fisk made a fortune while the price held. Once again Vanderbilt was the laughingstock of America's financial community. But Gould and Fisk spent so much time messing with Vanderbilt's fortune that they had let the railroad fall to ruin. Crews slept at their posts, equipment

was falling apart, and wrecks were common. Newspapers dubbed it the "Erie Massacre."

But Gould was still busy. In league with Fisk, he began to buy gold to force up its price. The plan was to buy and buy until the market became overheated and then suddenly sell, leaving the speculators with the crash when reality struck. The whole plan depended on the U.S. government keeping its supply of gold off the market. If the government stepped in, the price would crash prematurely, leaving Fisk and Gould in the lurch, too. The Erie magnates thought they had the cooperation of President Grant to hold the treasury in check, but Grant never understood what was going on and authorized the treasury to inject its gold into the market to stabilize it. Gould found out about the government move; Fisk did not. Gould saw no reason to tell his partner in crime as he shifted all of his options to sell. The next day, Fisk went under with the rest of the speculators and Gould alone made money. Fisk died a few years later, probably agreeing with Daniel Drew's comment on Gould: "His touch is death."

Fisk's stock went to an independent group of capitalists who quickly audited the Erie's books and found that Gould had misappropriated $12 million. They had Gould arrested. The Great Manipulator soon proved he had not lost his touch. He promised restitution. Erie stock prices soared. He reneged; Erie stock plummeted. He promised restitution again and the stock rose again. Gould made a fortune selling short on his own lousy reputation. When he paid the Erie back, he had lost only $200,000 instead of $12 million.

Knocked off the board of directors on the Erie, Gould lined up other financial men, like Russell Sage, and turned to the Union Pacific, suffering under the Crédit Mobilier scandal. Then he went to work on the Kansas Pacific, Missouri Pacific, Central Pacific, Texas & Pacific, and the Wabash. He wrapped up a stock package of these smaller roads and offered it to the Union Pacific (UP) at a one-to-one trade. UP refused until Gould threatened to wage a fares war. The UP had too much debt to survive, so

UP traded its stock worth $66 per share for the others worth $13, taking a managed loss to survive. Gould pocketed the difference, about $10 million. That he acted against a company on whose board he sat was immaterial to Gould. His wealth at the age of 45 amounted to some $100 million.

By now, Gould rode roughshod over American financial markets. He ignored unions, bought and sold telegraph companies, and cut employee wages at will. He owned the *New York World* (formerly owned by the Pennsylvania Railroad's Tom Scott), and dominated the editorial policy of the *New York Times* and, by virtue of shares owned in Western Union, he could influence the Associated Press. But the activity had taken a great toll on his own health. His enemies had been waiting for this moment. They took him to the tune of $20 million during the Panic of 1884, as the once brilliant Gould could no longer keep up. Gould retired to his home to regain his health, but it was too late. He died in less than a decade; the Great Manipulator had finally met his match in a force more potent than he.

See also Drew, Daniel; Fisk, James, Jr.; Forbes, John Murray; Gould, George Jay; Huntington, Collis Potter; Pacific Railroad Act of 1862; Sage, Russell; United States Express Company; Vanderbilt, Cornelius; Vanderbilt, William H.

References Adams, Charles F., and Henry Adams, *Chapters of Erie* (1956); Fuller, Robert H., *Jubilee Jim* (1928); Ginger, Ray, *Age of Success* (1965); Grodinsky, Julius, *Jay Gould* (1957); Hubbard, Freeman, *Encyclopedia of North American Railroading* (1981); Hungerford, Edward, *Men of Erie* (1946); Josephson, Matthew, *The Robber Barons* (1934); Klein, Maury, *The Life and Legend of Jay Gould* (1986); Klein, Maury, "Jay Gould," in Robert L. Frey (ed.), *EABHB: Railroads in the Nineteenth Century* (1988), 138–147; Lyon, Peter *To Hell in a Day Coach* (1968); Mott, Edward H., *Between the Ocean and the Lakes* (1899); White, Bouck, *Book of Daniel Drew* (1910).

Grand Trunk Railway

Incorporated in 1852, the Grand Trunk was envisioned by the Dominion Parliament as an operating and management entity for various sections of railroad either built or under construction throughout eastern Canada, with some interconnection with other lines in the United States. Thus it became North America's first international railroad by connecting Montréal with Portland, Maine, in 1853. The system spread throughout Ontario, connecting with Detroit by 1863 and extending to Chicago by 1880. From then until the turn of the century, the Grand Trunk increased its mileage by buying up smaller competing railroads in Michigan and Ontario. The Grand Trunk also bought out the Vermont Central, solidifying its position in northern New England. Steamships and a car ferry were added on the Great Lakes, especially in the area of Georgian Bay. As it increased its size, the Grand Trunk used its window on the Atlantic at Portland to increase its traffic, it being closer to Europe than Canadian ports.

The railroad had many engineering superstructures once considered among the biggest or most unique of their class, including the Victoria tubular (suspension) bridge, opened in 1860 and rebuilt as an arched structure with double track and roadways and foot paths in time for the Diamond Jubilee of Queen Victoria and renamed as such; a similar suspension bridge at Niagara Falls, also rebuilt as an arched structure; the mile-long bridge at Fort Erie; and the St. Clair Tunnel under the straits at Detroit. In 1920, the Grand Trunk joined the Canadian National Railways system and lost its name except in the United States, where it was known for many more years as the Grand Trunk Western. Further short line purchases have taken the line as far south as Cincinnati.

See also Canadian National Railways.

References Drury, George H., *The Historical Guide to North American Railroads* (1985); Drury, George H., *The Train-Watcher's Guide* (1990); Henwood, James N. J., "Grand Trunk Western Railroad," in Keith L. Bryant, Jr. (ed.), *EABHB: Railroads in the Age of Regulation* (1988), 172–173; Hubbard, Freeman, *Encyclopedia of North American Railroading* (1981); Stevens, George R., *History of the Canadian National Railways* (1973).

Granger Cases

Under the Constitution of 1789, Americans had an inherent conflict between the right of the federal government (the commerce clause, which regulates trade across state lines) or the states (police powers, which permit regulation of businesses for the local good) to regulate trade. The Supreme Court flip-flopped over who had the more important interest here, the earlier courts ruling for the federal government and later ones holding for the states. Because of the Civil War and the passage of the Fourteenth Amendment during Reconstruction, new cases arose probing where this right of regulation lay and what it was. These cases were collectively known as the Granger Cases.

This series of nineteenth-century Supreme Court cases involved laws that were enacted in midwestern states under the influence of a farmers' rights group formally called the Patrons of Husbandry, or colloquially, the Grange. Its members were thus Grangers. These cases included *Munn v. Illinois; Chicago, Burlington & Quincy Railroad v. Iowa; Peik v. Chicago & Northwestern Railroad Company; Chicago, Milwaukee & St. Paul Railroad Company v. Ackley; Winona & St. Paul Railroad Company v. Blake;* and *Stone v. Wisconsin.* In these cases the court posited that historically the police powers had been used in both the United States and England to supersede the rights of individuals or corporations when in the public interest. It ruled that when a private use was part of the public good, it changed its very nature to a controllable right. The complaint that state-sponsored Granger laws or regulations prevented business from earning a fair profit was one for legislatures or city governments to solve, not the courts.

Finally, the court held that when the federal government did not exercise a power granted it under any clause of the Constitution, the field was properly left open to the states and local governing entities under the Bill of Rights. It was the referral of prerogatives in this area to the state legislative branch that would lead directly to the Interstate Commerce Act ten years later, because the problems hoped to be solved were interstate in nature, and if profit were unduly limited by state and local police powers, it amounted to a constitutional violation under the Fourteenth Amendment.

See also Munn v. Illinois.

Great Lakes Freighters

Beginning with the Native Americans and their canoes, inhabitants of the Great Lakes have long used the huge waterway for travel and the movement of goods. The largest inland freshwater lake system in the world, the lakes can take one from the Atlantic to Minnesota and Alberta. There are only two points of constriction, or "portages" in the language of yesteryear: One lies at the falls on the Niagara between Lakes Ontario and Erie, and the other at the rapids of Sault Ste. Marie between Lake Superior and the Mackinac Straits to Lake Michigan, Lake Huron, and Georgian Bay. Both of these have been circumnavigated by canals since the mid-1850s.

The first European vessels on the lakes were Indian canoes employed by the fur traders and trappers in an age-old manner. But the demands of the lucrative fur trade soon called for bigger boats, and the French brought over shipwrights to build sailing ships in the late 1600s. Robert Cavalier, le Sieur de la Salle, launched the first four ships on the lower lakes in 1678, followed by the *Griffon* the next summer to explore and exploit the upper lakes. As La Salle departed for further explorations in the Mississippi Valley, the *Griffon* disappeared after departing Green Bay, taking a full cargo of furs to her watery grave, the first of over 10,000 ships to suffer a similar fate somewhere on the expanse of the Great Lakes. For the next century, both France and Britain sponsored the ships that coursed the lakes. The trade was so great that the ships available to the British after the American Revolution could only move half of it. It was not until after the Treaty of Greenville in 1796 that Americans were able to get to the Great Lakes, blocked by both the British occupation of American forts (in retaliation for the U.S. seizure of Tory properties) and the hostilities of local Native American warriors toward land-hungry American settlers. It took until the end of the War of 1812 and the demilitarization of the lakes in the Rush-Bagot Agreement of 1817 before Americans could fully exploit their access to the waterway.

With the neutrality of the Great Lakes a reality, both the United States and Canada began to exploit its waters freely. The trade generally went down the lakes and the St. Lawrence to Montréal and Québec until 1826, when the Erie Canal sucked most of it to New York City via Buffalo. Immediately, steamboats appeared on the waters, and the route between Buffalo and Detroit boomed as settlers went west and raw materials moved east. Early lake steamer design pointed to the lucrative "packet trade" by placing cabins on the main deck in preference to easy access to the cargo holds. The lake steamers soon had their engines placed in the stern and the pilothouse moved forward above the cabins. It was a design that was to endure and become more emphasized as the ships began to lengthen and emphasize cargo, as passenger service went to the railroads in the era preceding the American Civil War. The sleek, single-deck lake packet boats never assumed the towering cabin castles so common to the Mississippi steamboats. Instead, they ran more like an oceangoing operation as befitted the vast expanse of water that made up the Great Lakes.

The key to lake traffic became the rich pockets of iron ore first discovered in 1844 near Marquette on Michigan's Upper Peninsula. To fully exploit the ore beds, it became obvious that the primitive locks and canal at Sault St. Marie (the "Soo" to linguistically limited Americans) would have to be modernized. Finished in the mid-fifties, the new canal and locks transported massive amounts of ore each year, stimulated by the bloody fighting during the Civil War. Giant ore docks at Marquette permitted trains of ore to dump their cargoes into bunkers that loaded lake-going ships in a matter of hours. The war forced the development of the first mechanical unloading system to speed up the process at the other end. The system of hand-loaded tubs that were winched out of the ship holds to be carried off in wheelbarrows seems almost primitive today, but it cut unloading time in half. After the war, Bothwell and Ferris added steam power to the winches and cut the time in half again. Now it took only 12 hours to unload a cargo of up to 200 tons.

In 1869, Peck's Shipyard at Cleveland launched the *R. J. Hackett*, the first of the real lake ore haulers and the basis of design for all ships that followed down to the present. Long gone were the deck cabins, replaced by giant cargo hatches amidships. The engines were still in the stern, connected directly to the propellers. Above them was a small stack of cabins, mostly accommodations for the crew. The only other superstructure was a forward deck house where the captain and helmsman controlled the ship. Early models still had auxiliary masts and sails, but gradually these disappeared, too. Until the turn of the century, the ore ships were made of wood. Because of the properties of wood, lengths were limited to around 200 feet. Interior holds and outer skins had to be braced to prevent warping or "hogging."

As iron and then steel hulls appeared during the 1880s, they took on the same basic construction plan. Bracing still appeared throughout the holds that interfered with the ease of cargo unloading. But in 1904, the *Augustus B. Wolvin* appeared—the first lakes ship with no interior bracing. This left the entire hold open for cargo. The entire load was supported by steel frame members integral to the ship's outer skin. Ballast tanks sandwiched between the outer skin and the inner hold gave the ship weight to steady it without a full cargo. This allowed the recently invented Hulett crane, a special clamshell that had its operator riding just above the bucket for accurate operation, to empty the holds cleanly without worrying about damaging the interior braces. Each Hulett had its own storage bunkers that straddled several rail tracks and moved with the crane to make the unloading operation speedy and fully mechanical.

The big thing now became to make the longest, widest, and deepest ships possible, given the restrictions of construction technology, harbor facilities, and the Sault St. Marie locks. Each time the locks were altered to take four or more ships through at one time, some shipyard built a bigger vessel, only one or two of which could pass through at one time. Big ships meant more cargo, which meant more profit per trip. From the old 200-foot lengths of the post–Civil War era, lake ships reached 600 feet in length by the turn of the century. By the mid-twentieth century, the ore carriers were 1,000 feet long, in some cases. Older craft had their centers cut in half and new, longer sections spliced in to keep up with the tonnage wars. In 1925, the shipyard at Manitowoc, Wisconsin, built the *Charles C. West*. It had each hold slanted downward toward the center where a conveyor belt could unload the cargo at 1,800 tons an hour. Earlier self-unloaders had employed an internal bucket system, but did little over the speed of a Hulett dockside crane. The conveyor belt system became standard on all new ships, often replacing the aft crew quarters, which were moved to under the forward pilothouse.

The construction of the oceangoing Liberty and Victory ships during World War II gave the maritime industry a vast surplus of vessels after the conflict ended. Several of these ship types were cut in half and had long cargo sections inserted and their superstructures lowered to became lake freighters. Other post–World War II craft had streamlined superstructures and dimensions (730 feet long) that permitted the full use of the St. Lawrence Seaway after it opened in 1959. Cargo holds were redesigned to allow for more ballast to steady an empty ship on the lakes. The Great Lakes are so vast that they actually have storms that take on the attributes of ocean disturbances. Travel on the lakes had always been risky, and sudden storms have claimed many a ship and its crew. The older vessels carried two-sided, rigid life rafts that sported two air tanks for flotation. After spending a night in one of these revolving doors, lake crews came to prefer the more flexible oceangoing style of raft with a canopy for protection.

Even today, lake ships continue to alter their appearances. The *James R. Barker* is one of a fleet of 1,000-footers that has its unloading machinery, crew quarters, and pilothouse all located in the stern. Its holds have three unloading belts, instead of the usual single center conveyor. The "Queen of the Lakes," that is, the longest steamer afloat, is the 1,013-foot *Paul R. Tregurtha*, with all of its accommodations and controls located in the stern housing. Although the ships of the Great Lakes may be surpassed in size and efficiency by many oceangoing craft, as a whole, the Great Lakes fleets of the United States and Canada boast the highest operating efficiency of any fleet anywhere in the world.

See also Canals; St. Lawrence Seaway; Sault Ste. Marie Canal; Steamboats.

References Barry, James P., *Ships of the Great Lakes* (1973); Havighurst, Walter, *Long Ships Passing* (1942); Strang, Jacques Les, *Cargo Carriers of the Great Lakes* (1981); Thompson, Mark L., *Queen of the Lakes* (1994); Wilson, James A., "A Critical Look at our Marine Transportation," *Seaway Review* (September 1983): 11–13.

Great Northern Railroad

Built by the great railroad magnate James J. Hill, the Great Northern (GN) was the last transcontinental line to connect the Great Lakes with the Puget Sound area, not receiving its name until 1889. Hill was blind in one eye, the result of a childhood accident, which led those opposed to his policies to call him "that one-eyed sonofabitch." The Panic of 1873 was the entrée that Hill used to begin his rail empire, buying up the bankrupt St. Paul & Pacific Railroad. Hill's policy was to run his trains through country that had potential settlement value. Then Hill's agents went to Europe with propaganda to attract immigrant settlers, promising a veritable heaven on earth.

Since the rival Northern Pacific had picked many of the best routes earlier, the government refused to give him the land grants that had financed the Union Pacific, Northern Pacific, and the other great railroads. So Hill used the proceeds of his immigrant program to continue the track laying and, in 1890, he reached Puget Sound, crossing the Rockies in places surveyed by Lieutenant John Mullan for his Mullan Road years before. The chief engineer for the crossing there and the eight-mile Cascade Tunnel later was John F. Stevens, who also worked on the Panama Canal in the meantime. Hill added many short branches to tap the agricultural areas of the Great Plains, and signed a cozy deal with the Chicago, Burlington & Quincy (CB&Q) to reach Chicago over its tracks. There he set up the Northwest Steamship Company that monopolized traffic on the Great Lakes. Other Hill steamships handled trade with the Orient, especially lucrative in cotton shipped out of the South on the Illinois Central and to Japan via Hill's rail and steam lines.

Hill and the rival Northern Pacific bought up the CB&Q for its Chicago access, and set up the Spokane, Portland & Seattle to tap jointly the whole Puget Sound and Pacific Coast area. By now, Hill had a large share of the Northern Pacific, but E. H. Harriman began an insidious attempt to buy a controlling share. Hill soon realized what was happening, and with the backing of J. P. Morgan, attempted to halt Harriman's purchases. Northern Pacific stock rose to $1,000 a share—it had been worth a mere $58 originally. Then Hill realized that Harriman's majority lay in preferred stock that could be retired at will. Hill offered a compromise in the form of a holding corporation, the Northern Securities Company, that would control the Great Northern, the Northern Pacific, and the CB&Q. The Supreme Court later declared the corporation an unconstitutional violation of the Sherman Antitrust Act. The dissolving of Northern Securities cost Hill and his side $40 million.

The Great Northern has the distinction of being the only railroad to cross a national park (Glacier), and Hill's use of the Rocky Mountain goat as his symbol was not accidental. The line crosses some of the more rugged terrain in the West. The many long tunnels led the GN to electrify its mountain routes, using big, box-cab electric motors to power the trains. The GN's main passenger train, the *Empire Builder*, an orange and green streamliner, was named after Hill, replacing the older *Oriental Limited* in 1932.

After World War II, the *Empire Builder* kept to a 45-hour schedule, cutting a half a day from its previous time. It still runs today under the same name on Amtrak.

See also Burlington Northern Incorporated; Hill, James Jerome; Mullan Road.

References Drury, George H., *The Historical Guide to North American Railroads* (1985); Drury, George H., *The Train-Watcher's Guide* (1990); Folsom, Burton W., Jr., *The Myth of the Robber Barons* (1991); Ginger, Ray, *Age of Success* (1965); Hediger, Jim, "Great Domes of the Empire Builder," *Model Railroader* (June 1984) 51: 73–76; Hidy, Ralph W., et al., *The Great Northern Railroad* (1986); Hill, James J., *Highways of Progress* (1910); Hofsommer, Don L., "Great Northern Railroad," in Robert L. Frey (ed.), *EABHB: Railroads in the Nineteenth Century* (1988), 152–153; Hofsommer, Don L., "Great Northern Railway," in Keith L. Bryant, Jr. (ed.), *EABHB: Railroads in the Age of Regulation* (1988), 178–179; Hubbard, Freeman, *Encyclopedia of North American Railroading* (1981); Josephson, Matthew, *The Robber Barons* (1934); Lyon, Peter, *To Hell in a Day Coach* (1968); Martin, Albro, *James J. Hill* (1976); Mercer, Lloyd J., *Railroads and Land Grant Policy* (1982); Meyers, Gustavus, *History of the Great American Fortunes* (1910); Nock, O. S., *Railways of the USA* (1979); Pyle, Joseph Gilpin, *The Life of James J. Hill* (1926); Renute, Alfred, *Trains of Discovery: Western Railroads and the National Parks* (1990); Sperandeo, Andy, "The 1947 Empire Builder," *Model Railroader* (December 1991) 58: 108–123.

Great Wagon Road

Much like their Spanish and French counterparts, the English came to the New World searching for gold, God, glory, and the all-water route to China—the Northwest Passage (so named because it supposedly would be northwest of the continental land mass). Under these forces, Englishmen moved westward, reaching the Shenandoah and Cumberland Valleys by the mid-1600s. There they found an established Native American trail system, called the Warriors' Path, that stretched from northern Georgia across the Appalachians to New York and beyond. By the early 1700s, Virginia's royal governor, Colonel Alexander Spotswood, believed that England had found El Dorado—it was not a base metal, however, it was land. The surveying and sale of western land became the basis for many an early American fortune. In the bombastic style of the times, he dubbed his explorers the "Knights of the Golden Horseshoe," and gave each a medal. Its inscription read, *Sic Juvat Transcendere Montes* ("Thus We Cross the Mountains").

Treaties with the Iroquois Nation's six tribes gave Virginians the right to use the Warriors' Path, and gradually they did so. They were joined by Palatine Germans (Pennsylvania Dutch) and French Huguenots, who had penetrated the low mountains that marked the eastern edge of the Great Valley (the Shenandoah-Cumberland) in Pennsylvania. Preceded by the Scots-Irish (Scots Protestants settled in Ulster to pacify the Catholic Celts, a policy that troubles Britain to this day), who were the cutting edge of the English westward drive, these settlers and the Virginians moved into the Shenandoah and Cumberland valleys and then turned south, looking for an easy way around the mountain massif of the Appalachians. Again they used the Warriors' Path, which, by this time, was more of an unimproved road. With them, the Germans brought their industrial skills: wagon building, gunsmithing, cabinet making, tanning, and modern agriculture.

The Society of Friends (Quakers), which had first settled Pennsylvania as a religious haven, disliked the earthy German, French, and Scots-Irish, who were hard drinkers and fighters, but the newcomers served a purpose. The more of them who settled the West, the more protected those in the East were from Indian incursions. The other side of the coin was that the western settlers were more willing to war against the Native Americans, something that the Quakers abhorred. Thus began a political split that would plague Pennsylvania for a century. But the Friends were good businessmen, too, and the new western settlements meant prosperity, trade, and profit. By 1744, under pressure from the colonial French and English wars, treaties with the Iroquois Confederation had secured the exclusive use of the Warriors' Path for the whites. The woodland trail was more and more becoming a major wagon road.

Those whites who used it were becoming different, too. They were moving west in increasing numbers to avoid English rule, exploiting the land, losing some of their ethnicity, and becoming Americans. And the road accelerated the process, compounded by the English victory of 1763 in the French and Indian War, which secured the whole known West for them alone. It had been one of the dirtiest, bloodiest wars Americans had ever fought. Atrocities were commonplace. It cost the English treasury a fortune, and in 1763, King George III decreed that everything west of the Appalachians was Indian Country and off-limits to white settlers. The American subjects of the king wondered what they had fought and suffered for if it were not access to western lands.

The Proclamation of 1763 caused many settlers to move south, looking for a route across the mountains that the king's men did not control. As they moved they extended the Great Wagon Road. By 1765, a system of county responsibility had grown up. Each county was accountable for clearing the roadway and repairing it. Road work became a good way for the farmers to get a little off-season spending money. The Pennsylvania Dutch had developed the Conestoga covered wagons—huge vehicles for their day, drawn by magnificent six-horse teams. In addition, road traffic included pack trains, livestock drovers, and the new settlers. Traffic was so great that ferries sprang up, complimented by taverns, warehouses, and dozens of towns—all to service the road and its users. By the time of the Revolution, regular stage and wagon schedules had appeared.

In 1768, British Indian agents managed to negotiate a new treaty that opened the western sections of Kentucky and Tennessee. The whites were already there anyway—those who thought that proclamation lines and treaties could limit western settlement were a bit naive. These documents never really caught up with men like Daniel Boone, who was deep into Kentucky, exploring lands that companies had begun to mark for sale. Although he did not discover it, Boone was utilizing what would become the greatest early route west, the Cumberland Gap, in his ventures. His route would become the Wilderness Road, an adjunct to the Great Wagon Road that would cause the Great Valley route to hum well into the next century. And as settlers moved into Kentucky and Tennessee, the Great Wagon Road took a turn southeast at Big Lick, Virginia, and moved across the Carolinas to Augusta, Georgia. Up and down the road came names that, like Boone's, would have great impact in later years: Henry Clay, Andrew Jackson, John Sevier, Sam Houston, and William Blount.

Interest in the Great Wagon Road was not limited to businessmen. It also was the route of the Great Awakening, the religious revival that swept the American colonies after 1740. The revival was a reaction to the staid, Puritan religious practices of the established denominations that began in Massachusetts with Jonathan Edwards. It came south with George Whitefield, and found its greatest expression in the activities of a young English immigrant, Francis Asbury. The epitome of the circuit rider—a man of no denomination who represented all denominations—Asbury was technically a Methodist, sent by John Wesley to bring religious reform to the colonies. He stayed on during the Revolution, and when the American church broke from its English counterpart, he became its first bishop. And he made his reputation preaching up and down the Great Wagon Road and its branches into the West. In four months he logged over 2,500 miles in the service of God, and a 5,000-mile year was common. Most of it was made possible by the valley road.

During the American Revolution, the Great Wagon Road offered Americans a route sheltered from British influence, based on sea power, to move men and supplies safely between the Continental armies. It was the Great Wagon Road that brought in the frontiersmen who won a decisive battle at King's Mountain. It was also down the road that the Americans transported Quakers and other pacifists who refused to fight or swear allegiance to the new government

to safe spots removed from the war theaters. And it was up the Great Wagon Road that the war in the South was fought by Lord Cornwallis and Banastre Tarleton against Nathaniel Green, Horatio Gates, and Daniel Morgan.

After the war, the Great Wagon Road saw traffic increase. Not only did the freighters and pioneers pass daily, but new stagecoach routes carrying the mails appeared. It soon became obvious that an improved dirt surface could not manage the traffic's needs. After the example of the Lancaster Pike in Pennsylvania, the new macadam surface of graduated sizes of gravels appeared and the road surface was widened and stabilized. Virginia spent much money improving the section through the Shenandoah Valley, which became a toll road in parts to maintain its quality. Under common law, farmers going to and from market could travel free, and many travelers tried to pass without charge, disguised with a small load of grain. To pull the wagons and carry the people, horse breeding became of great interest. Draft animals bred for strength but a bit lighter for speed, called Conestogas, were preferred. Virginia, Kentucky, and Tennessee bred fine riding animals, finally producing the Tennessee Walker, a horse that could pace along the roads and trails with an easy gait that meant speed and comfort, especially in the Old South.

The coming of the railroads began to eat into road profits by the time of the Civil War. But the war itself saw numerous campaigns fought along the Valley Turnpike, part of the Great Wagon Road. Because of the northeast–southwest tilt of the Shenandoah, the valley was a natural invasion route into Pennsylvania or Washington, D.C., covered by the Blue Ridge and South Mountains. At the same time, although the Union forces had to occupy the valley to deny its use to the Confederacy, it led away from Richmond and other areas of importance to Union victory. The result was a series of Southern victories that made the reputation of generals like Stonewall Jackson and Jubal Early, until late in 1864, when the Yankees under Phil Sheridan finally ravaged the upper valley to deny its use to the South, both as an invasion route and as the breadbasket of Robert E. Lee's Army of Northern Virginia.

After the war, the rise of the railroads caused the old road to be split up into its component parts within each state. Much of the roadbed went to seed. But the Good Roads Movement and the advent of automobile and truck traffic has restored the Great Wagon Road to its preeminence. First called U.S. Highways 11 and 25, now Interstates 77 and 81, and paralleled by the Blue Ridge Parkway in Virginia, the Great Wagon Road stills moves masses of Americans and their goods up and down the Appalachian foothills as in days of yore.

See also Roads and Highways, Colonial Times to World War I; Roads and Highways since World War I; Wilderness Road.

References Durrenberger, Joseph A., *Turnpikes* (1931); Rouse, Parke, Jr., *The Great Wagon Road* (1973).

Greyhound Corporation

"Go Greyhound—and leave the driving to us" has been one of the best-known advertising slogans for over 30 years. The flashy buses with their stylized logo of a racing hound in full stride have been an important part of Americana and the transportation scene since the company's founding at Hibbing, Minnesota, in 1914 (although the actual name was a creation of the 1930s). Today, the company that began with Carl E. Wickman driving a seven-passenger Hupmobile from his failed auto dealership to nearby towns, hauling miners to work and play, owns over 3,500 buses that can haul seven times what Wickman could for a grand total of 45 million people and 300 million miles annually. Greyhound has its own manufacturing and maintenance facilities and not only runs buses, but has interests in temporary service help agencies, convention and exhibitors' services, vehicle rentals, package express, and airplane ground services. Or at least it did. By 1994, Greyhound finally hit the wall of deregulation competition and faced a $98 million

debt that bondholders have promised to wipe out for 55 percent of the company (Greyhound's counteroffer is 32 percent).

It is a sad end for a company that got its name from an off-duty operator who pointed out a Fageol bus speeding by the cafe in which he was eating and proudly asserted it was as "fast as a greyhound!" Wickman and his partners did not own all of the bus lines that carried the canine name. They provided coordinating services and schedules, trained and uniformed drivers, and handled advertising, unity, and image. But Greyhound was more cohesive than its major competition, Continental Trailways, which was made up of independent companies in partnership with each other. Railroads bought up much of Greyhound's early stock offerings, seeing the buses as an extension of their service, not as competition. The Great Depression nearly did Greyhound in. It was saved when General Motors invested heavily, giving the bus line a new infusion of needed cash. Historians credit the company's true success to a providential accident—Claudette Colbert and Clark Gable had some of their romantic Hollywood *tête-à-têtes* occur on a Greyhound bus. By the mid-thirties, Greyhound owned 3 bus lines outright and had 11 affiliates that covered the United States. It would soon reduce these to seven divisions for purposes of management and labor control.

Like the trucking industry, interstate buses had to accommodate federal regulation for the first time through the Motor Carrier Act of 1935. This was both good and bad. The federal measure called for strict passenger safety standards and adequate service. It restricted new entrants into the field, and also restricted mergers and affiliations, the method by which Greyhound had grown. Hereafter, the Interstate Commerce Commission would have to concur in all major business decisions. Greyhound faced up to its new responsibilities by hiring a safety expert, setting strict guidelines for drivers, and then hiring unmarked motorcycle riders to check up on the buses during their trips. The buses themselves were new sleek aluminum vehicles, Supercoaches, devised by Raymond Loewy of railroad design fame in 1935, marking the first time that a bus company had standardized its vehicles into one style. They would dominate the market until the 1950s brought new, bigger buses into vogue.

World War II brought Greyhound into an era of prosperity, as the company transported troops of all branches of the service. It also marked the use of women drivers to make up for the shortage of men gone to the military services. The postwar years were marked by much expansion of terminals and maintenance facilities. Greyhound also produced its own bus, the double-decker Scenicruiser model still familiar to bus riders today. Greyhound was proud of its "firsts" in the bus industry: diesel engines, engines in the rear, air suspension for comfort of ride, central heating and air-conditioning, power steering, on-board lavatories, automatic transmissions, and turbocharged engines. It also introduced massive psychological, mental, and physical testing of all personnel. The testing revealed just how much the company had changed and demonstrated that the second generation of management was going to run things a mite differently. Rapid expansion put inexperienced people in the field to confront the customer. Labor unrest stymied operations more. Diversification spread limited monetary and personnel resources too thin. The company went into meat production (Armour Company) and its own computer services. By 1982, nearly three-fourths of the company's revenue came from nontransportation sources.

Under the impetus of the deregulation of transportation and the economic recession of the time, Greyhound found itself in much the same position as the major airlines. It had grown too fat under government supervision. Now independent companies could enter the bus business and pick off the best routes. They had nonunion drivers, fewer fixed costs, and cheaper tickets. Deregulated airlines could offer comparable rates to distant places. The high cost of meat caused the public to patronize the company's biggest subsidiary less. All of this was com-

pounded by a massive strike in 1983. The company had been trying for years to get all of its bus employees into one union to simplify wage-benefits negotiations. It had succeeded, and now the union walked off the job. Greyhound had to cut its fixed costs in wages and benefits because they were 50 percent higher than its rivals. Cognizant of similar problems in the airline industry and the numbers of jobs lost to those workers who failed to cooperate, and threatened with massive layoffs and the hiring of nonunion personnel, the Amalgamated Transit Union finally gave in and accepted a much-reduced contract. But the uncertainty of fuel costs and the sell-off of affiliated businesses for cash-flow purposes has put Greyhound into a bind that still threatens to crush the company.

See also Automobiles from Domestics to Imports; Automobiles in American Society; Stagecoaches and Other Horse-Drawn Conveyances; Trucking.

References Jackson, Carlton, *Hounds of the Road* (1984); Schisgall, Oscar, *The Greyhound Story* (1985).

Guggenheim Fund for the Promotion of Aeronautics

More important in late 1920s than federal airmail subsidies to the emerging commercial airline system was the interest of the Guggenheim family in the new mode of transportation. Philanthropists Daniel and Harry Guggenheim created the Guggenheim Fund for the Promotion of Aeronautics in 1926. Lasting until 1930, this fund (especially when combined with the awe-inspiring trans-Atlantic flight of Charles Lindbergh, which demonstrated how far air travel had come and its potential) allowed American aviation to catch up with European efforts and finally to surpass them. It laid the foundation for aeronautical education, conducted basic research on principles of flight, navigation, and "blind" flying (creating the artificial horizon, gyrocompass, and altimeter), marked towns to differentiate locations, put on demonstrations to interest the public in air travel, and even set up a model airline along the Pacific coast using the Fokker trimotor, the standard passenger liner of its day. The benefits of the fund have continued to the present through the Guggenheim Aeronautical Laboratory at the California Institute of Technology—famous for its 1930s work on jet-assisted take-off (JATO) and filleted wing farings that made the single wing strong and streamlined in its attachment to the fuselage—which conducts ongoing research in aerospace problems. The Guggenheims have also funded the Air Law Institute at Northwestern University (Illinois) and its journal, *Air Law Review*.

See also Aeronautics.

References Bilstein, Roger E., *Flight in America* (1994); Lomask, Milton, *Seed Money* (1964).

Gulf, Mobile & Ohio Railroad (GM&O)

The Gulf, Mobile & Ohio was the brainchild of Isaac B. "Ike" Tigrett. Ike Tigrett was the son of a Baptist preacher-farmer who parlayed an $800 inheritance into a banking fortune in Jackson, Tennessee. Through banking he became interested in railroading because he needed someone reliable to supervise the payment of his notes. He took on the job himself. He liked to travel the trains, talking with employees and learning the way things were in the eyes of the men who did the actual work. As he traveled, he surveyed small railroads that might extend his burgeoning rail empire. He developed port facilities at New Orleans and Mobile and emphasized Central American fruit and South American coffee and beef. He absorbed some of Jim Hill's activities with the Great Northern and improved farming methods along his lines to increase their use and curry a favorable public image.

In 1940, Tigrett combined all of his rail segments into one empire that he named after its largest components, the Gulf, Mobile & Ohio. Some had histories extending back into the 1840s, and the Mobile & Ohio had received a land grant in a rider to the Illinois Central bill in 1850. The old Mobile & Ohio had been home road to the legendary Casey Jones. But Tigrett wished to

push his empire out of the South beyond Cairo, Illinois, to Chicago. So he bought the old Chicago & Alton line. Realizing that there was still much suspicion toward the South and Southerners, Tigrett sought to allay fears by emphasizing the Northern aspects of the merger. He had been running a railroad called the "Rebel Route" and his named passenger train was *The Rebel*, the South's first streamliner—complete with trained hostesses, women of vivacious beauty who topped the much-vaunted Harvey Girls of the Santa Fe Railway.

Tigrett, in a brilliant public relations move, now called his rail empire the "Alton Route" and added the named passenger trains *Abraham Lincoln* and *Ann Rutledge*. To keep the runs long and efficient, he used company buses to take passengers from the larger stops back to the smaller stations the trains normally bypassed. He even put his own privately run post office cars in the consists, and called the whole operation "Gulf Transport" service. After Tigrett's death in 1954, the reality of rail consolidation caught up with the GM&O. As one of the more successful medium-sized railroads in the country, it was an attractive merger target. Even though it ran through country characterized as so barren "even a rabbit would have to pack a lunch," it regularly had earned 10 percent a year, especially during the Tigrett administration. In 1972, it became a part of its major competitor, the Illinois Central, in a railroad called the Illinois Central Gulf.

See also Illinois Central Gulf Railway; Illinois Central Railroad.

References Drury, George H., *The Historical Guide to North American Railroads* (1985); Drury, George H., *The Train-Watcher's Guide* (1990); Hubbard, Freeman, *Encyclopedia of North American Railroading* (1981); Kennan, George, *The Chicago & Alton Case* (1916); Lemy, James H., *The Gulf, Mobile & Ohio* (1953); Lemy, James H., "Gulf Mobile & Ohio Railroad," and "Isaac B. Tigrett," in Keith L. Bryant, Jr. (ed.), *EABHB: Railroads in the Age of Regulation* (1988), 181–182, 432–436; Lemy, James H., "Mobile and Ohio Railroad," in Robert L. Frey (ed.), *EABHB: Railroads in the Nineteenth Century* (1988), 262–264; Nock, O. S., *Railways of the USA* (1979).

Hamilton, Alexander (1755–1804)

Born out of wedlock to a Scottish father and West Indian mother (which opponents never let him forget) on the island of Nevis in the British West Indies, Alexander Hamilton began work at the age of 12 as a clerk on St. Croix. He showed an immediate skill with numbers and company politics. He came to New York City in 1773 and entered King's College (Columbia), where he wrote pamphlets for the colonial cause. He organized an artillery battery and fought with General George Washington in the battles around New York City in 1776 and the retreat across New Jersey. Washington soon noted Hamilton's skill with headquarters intrigue and courage in military matters and made him aide de camp with the rank of lieutenant colonel. At his own request, Hamilton received a troop command at Yorktown and led an assault on the last British lines.

Hamilton met the daughter of New York governor Philip Schuyler and married her in 1780. Shortly after the Yorktown battle, he resigned from Washington's staff after the general reprimanded him for a delay in a trifling matter. He stood for and was elected to Congress (1782–1783). After a single term, Hamilton went into a law practice in New York City, and dabbled in politics on the side. As a delegate to the Annapolis Convention (1786) he drafted a report critical of the Articles of Confederation that helped lead to the Constitutional Convention in 1787, where he served as one of New York's representatives. At the convention, Hamilton became one of the outspoken delegates for a strong central government and even the restoration of a domestic monarchy. He wrote some of the Federalist Papers and worked wholeheartedly to get the Constitution ratified by the various states, especially New York, which had much opposition to a new government.

After the ratification of the Constitution and election of the new federal government, President Washington appointed Hamilton as the first secretary of the treasury (in effect, as aide de camp again). Hamilton quickly became the most important member of the cabinet, and controversial to boot. He issued a *Report on Manufactures* in 1791 that relied strongly on the notion that the new government had many "implied powers" not specifically stated in the constitutional document. This interpretation, usually referred to as "loose construction" of the Constitution, became one of the pivotal political philosophies in American history. Relying on such phrases as "general welfare," Hamilton asserted that the government had wide-ranging authority to effect the future goals of the nation. Hamilton called for high protective tariffs to nurture American industry and bounties to assist the farmers, and hoped much of the moneys raised could be used for massive internal improvements to join the domestic market and production together in a vast economic cornucopia.

He was opposed in his efforts by James Madison and Thomas Jefferson, Washington's secretary of state, who felt obliged to resign after the president sided with Hamilton. These Virginians maintained that unless the Constitution were read literally, the restraints on the intrusive megalith of central government against the states and people would be useless. The Bill of Rights was placed against the federal government as a further safeguard against a Hamiltonian philosophy, but through an expansive reading of the later Fourteenth Amendment, these rights set up to protect the states have been turned against them by the modern Supreme Court. Hamilton and his believers foresaw a bustling, urban, industrial America that needed unity and big government to succeed. Madison and Jefferson fought for a simpler agrarian life. Theirs was to be a losing battle.

At the end of Washington's second term, Hamilton resigned, pushed out by allegations that he had paid blackmail to his mistress' husband from federal funds (which was never proven). He declined an offer of the chief justiceship of the U.S. Supreme Court and returned to local politics and his law practice. He resumed government service during the Quasi-War with France (1798) as second in command of the army. He became irritated with John Adams' policies, which he blamed for the loss of New York to the Jeffersonians in 1798. He worked against Adams, and as a result, Jefferson won the presidential election of 1800. Through a quirk in the Constitution, later cleared up by the Twelfth Amendment, Jefferson and his ally Aaron Burr wound up with the same number of electoral votes. The Founding Fathers had not reasoned that there would be permanent political parties under professional politicians, just temporary coalitions of interests among wise men. Hamilton's allies thought it would be funny if Jefferson would loose out to Burr in the House of Representatives, but Hamilton threw his influence behind the hated Jefferson to make him president. As Hamilton's opponent in New York State, Burr was widely known as a rascal—at least Jefferson was honest in his convictions.

The fight between Hamilton and Burr increased during the ensuing years, with Hamilton working behind the scenes to defeat Burr for governor in 1804. Burr challenged Hamilton to a duel on the basis of a trumped-up insult. Hamilton believed that his political influence would be seriously hampered if he backed down. The two met at Weehawken Heights, New Jersey (dueling being illegal in New York), on 11 July 1804. Hamilton's shot went astray in the treetops, but Burr shot true and mortally wounded his opponent. Hamilton died the next day, and Burr's reputation followed him into the grave. Nearly a century and a half later, museum gunsmiths tore apart and rebuilt Hamilton's dueling pistols, the ones used by both men that fateful day at Weehawken. They found to their surprise that each had a secret hair trigger, engaged by pushing the firing trigger forward before squeezing it back for the actual shot. It seems now that Hamilton may have fumbled nervously while engaging the hair trigger and it cost him his shot into the trees. The fact that Burr shot so precisely with the ordinary heavy trigger pull seems to indicate he was a fabulous shot—or possibly he found the

hair trigger just in time to use it to increase his accuracy.

Much of American political history can be read in light of Hamilton's idea of "implied powers" of the federal government through a loose reading of the Constitution—with the Jeffersonians winning the fight until the Civil War, then the Hamiltonian view slowly being instituted, until by the time of the New Deal it became the dominant one. Hamilton's philosophy also became a key to federal aid for transportation projects. The Jeffersonians decided to take a practical tack (the greatest short-term advantage of American politics and at the same time possibly its greatest long-term weakness) and through the efforts of Albert Gallatin found a way around the constitutional proscriptions against government funding. After all, internal improvement projects were politically popular.

But Madison and James Monroe were uncertain about whether Jefferson and Gallatin were correct. The Jacksonians reinstituted the strict constructionist view completely, restricting internal improvements to the states. The Republicans then won the Civil War and used their victory to help build the railroads. The return of the Progressive Democrats under Woodrow Wilson led to all highways being declared to be Post Roads and thus able to receive massive government aid. Federal aid and the intrusive management of local and state matters from Washington so feared by Madison in the 1790s has only increased since. Thus the chronicle of transportation in America becomes little more than the constitutional history of the nation in microcosm. The irony of it all is that Hamilton secretly admitted in a 1799 letter to Jonathan Dayton, speaker of the House of Representatives, that particularly where internal improvements were concerned, Jefferson was probably right that a constitutional amendment was necessary. But custom and expediency beat out law and Constitution, a tribute to American practicality, if not perspicacity.

See also Gallatin, Albert; Maysville Road Veto; Post Office Appropriations Acts.

References Bowers, Claude G., *Jefferson and*

Hamilton (1925); Bradford, M. E., *Original Intentions* (1993); Brant, Irving, *James Madison* (1941–1961); Charles, Joseph, *The Origins of the American Party System* (1956); Cooke, Jacob Ernest, *Alexander Hamilton* (1982); Cunningham, Nobel E., Jr., *The Jeffersonian Republicans* (1957); Dauer, Manning J., *The Adams Federalists* (1953); Frisch, Morton J., *Alexander Hamilton and the Political Order* (1991); Hammond, Bray, *Banks and Politics in America* (1957); Ketcham, Ralph, *James Madison* (1971); McDonald, Forrest, *Alexander Hamilton* (1979); Malone, Dumas, *Jefferson and His Time* (1948–1981); Miller, John, *Alexander Hamilton and the Growth of the New Nation* (1959); Mitchell, Broadus, *Alexander Hamilton* (1957–1962); Peterson, Merrill D., *Thomas Jefferson and the New Nation* (1970); White, Leonard D., *The Federalists* (1948).

Harnden & Company Express

Beating out Alvin Adams by one year, William F. Harnden invented the idea of an express company to haul packages, mail, and valuables over scheduled long distances (others had done it earlier over short distances) in 1839. He consulted with boat companies, stage lines, and even railroads to get special rates for his service, and passed the savings on to his customers. He was the first to use the name "Express" to describe his service, took full liability for the goods in transit, and extensively manipulated the local newspapers for free advertising, hauling news items from surrounding areas free in exchange for the mention of his company. Another idea of his was to use "crates," moveable boxes of freight that could be hauled by various conveyances and transferred quickly at will, a small-scale forerunner of today's containerized operations.

Harnden extended his operations from Boston to New York, relying extensively on coastal steamers for speed. Later he added other cities like Philadelphia, utilizing the new railroads for carriage. He also specialized in sending items to Europe and Latin America. A sickly man since his youth, Harnden had tuberculosis, a malady from which he died prematurely at age 33 in 1845. His partners continued the business a few years, then sold out to Adams Express. Others tried to use the Harnden name over the years, but none lasted long. His name

was synonymous with safety, speed, and quality service.

See also Adams Express Company; American Express Company; American Railway Express Company; Central Overland California & Pike's Peak Express Company; Leavenworth & Pike's Peak Express Company; Pacific Union Express Company; Russell, Majors & Waddell Company; United States Express Company; Wells Fargo & Company.

Reference Harlow, Alvin F., *Old Waybills* (1934).

Harriman, Edward Henry (1848–1909)

A small man with a walrus mustache and thick eyeglasses, E. H. Harriman was born the son of an Episcopal rector and educated at Trinity School in New York City. At age 15 he went to work as an office boy for a brokerage house and by age 23 had bought his own seat on the exchange and opened his own financial firm, E. H. Harriman & Company. He learned his trade competing against the likes of Daniel Drew, Jay Gould, Jim Fisk, and Cornelius Vanderbilt. As Harriman watched the malefactors of great wealth milk various railroads dry for their personal gain, he found the process distasteful—he had no qualms about making money, but he came to see that a good businessman could take one or a series of railroads and manage them well for his own and the public good.

Harriman really did not enter the world of railroad finance until he married Mary Averell, whose father owned the Ogdensburg and Lake Champlain route in upstate New York. Her dowry became the nucleus to the Harriman fortune. Part of it included directorships for Harriman and his friend Stuyvesant Fish. Harriman bought another line and improved it before offering it up for sale. It was bought by the Pennsylvania Railroad, with the New York Central running up the price in a vain effort to capture Harriman's route for itself. Harriman soon turned his eyes westward to the Illinois Central Railroad. It was located in a growing area and had little competition or debt. He bought a large number of shares and ensconced himself on the board of directors. Friend Fish went along, too. The whole operation had the covert backing of the August Belmont organization, who gave Harriman a blank check to draw on for $1 million at any time, no questions asked.

Harriman liked to buy railroads in the same way he bought stocks and securities. He looked for weak entities that had the potential for growth and pounced on them. He only built one railroad in his own life, a short line that became part of the Illinois Central (IC). By 1885, he had placed his friend Fish as president of the IC, himself as vice-president, and launched a program to extend the route over 1,000 miles. His reputation as a businessman was so good that he could borrow money at 4 percent—half of the going rate to other rail magnates. In the process, he ran afoul of J. P. Morgan and made a powerful enemy when he forced Morgan to sell stock in a Harriman short line at below par. But the health of the financial world troubled Harriman. A sixth sense told him that a crash was coming, so he persuaded the Illinois Central board to retrench in the midst of prosperity—no mean feat. In 1893, Harriman's feelings were sustained when the United States fell into a great depression. Dozens of overextended rail lines fell into bankruptcy, but the Illinois Central weathered the storm.

The depression found Jay Gould in trouble with the Union Pacific (UP), which had to go into receivership. Harriman had long coveted the western line and used the Panic of 1893 to achieve his goal. He and a consortium paid out $85 million for the prize. They had earned it all back within three years under Harriman's guiding hand. He cut freight rates by 15 percent and doubled business in the process. He supported Theodore Roosevelt until he considered "TR" to be a troublemaker for business. After he withheld money from Roosevelt's successful presidential campaign, the president sicked the Interstate Commerce Commission on Harriman. An investigation of one of his rail deals showed that he had watered the stock from $30 million to $94 million. But Harriman kept his composure and managed to avoid any recriminations beyond bad publicity.

E. H. Harriman

After the death of his enemy, Collis P. Huntington, Harriman bought the Southern Pacific (SP) and Central Pacific (CP). He handled them as he had the UP and rerouted the rails to shorten miles traveled. His prime improvement was the Lucin Cutoff across the Great Salt Lake that knocked 44 miles off the CP's main line. It was the farthest cutoff of a railroad from a shoreline constructed up to that time. It also led to the eventual abandonment of the 1869 Golden Spike site at Promontory Summit. Harriman believed that idle men and idle capital were the bane of good business. He got himself a seat on the Santa Fe Railway's board of directors by beating them to filing claims at a land office by 20 minutes after a tip-off from an informant. He bought the Erie Railroad out from under his old foe Morgan, helping to lessen the effect of the Panic of 1907. Finally, he even dumped his old buddy, Stuyvesant Fish, from the Illinois Central after a quarrel.

Had Harriman lived longer he probably would have secured controlling interests in the Santa Fe, the Penn Central, and the Baltimore & Ohio. He controlled a huge trust company, America's largest bank, and had a piece of many other corporations. Even after his compromise with J. P. Morgan and Jim Hill over control of the Great Northern–Chicago, Burlington & Quincy had soured when the Supreme Court declared their jointly run Northern Securities Corporation to be an illegal trust, Harriman managed to clear $40 million. His last foray was into Mexico where he built a rail line for President Porfirio Díaz. Harriman died in 1909, just after he finished a magnificent mansion in New York's Ramapo Mountains near Arden. His fortune, bequeathed to his wife, was estimated to be as high as $600 million.

See also Hill, James Jerome; Illinois Central Railroad; *Northern Securities Company v. U.S.*; Southern Pacific Railroad; Union Pacific Railroad.

References Eckenrode, H. J., and P. W. Wright, *E. H. Harriman* (1933); Ginger, Ray, *Age of Success* (1965); Hubbard, Freeman, *Encyclopedia of North American Railroading* (1981); Josephson, Matthew, *The Robber Barons* (1934); Kahn, Otto H., *Edward Henry Harriman* (1911); Kennan, George, *E. H. Harriman* (1922); Lyon, Peter, *To Hell in a Day Coach* (1968); Mercer, Lloyd J., "Edward Henry Harriman," in Robert L. Frey (ed.), *EABHB: Railroads in the Nineteenth Century* (1988), 155–164; Meyers, Gustavus, *History of the Great American Fortunes* (1910); Moody, John, *Masters of Capital* (1919).

Harvey, Frederick Henry (1835–1901)

Born in England, Fred Harvey emigrated to the United States at age 15 and got a job as a busboy in a New York City cafe at $2 a week. He graduated to a packet boat, then took a job as a mail sorter on the Hannibal & St. Joseph Line, the first railroad to have mail cars. Eventually, he became a general freight agent for the Chicago, Burlington & Quincy (CB&Q). Harvey took many business trips associated with his jobs and hated the lousy food served to travelers. Service was so poor that eaters often were not served until the train was about to leave. There were no dining cars then, so everyone had to detrain and go to a local lunchroom to eat. Harvey thought about the problem, then proposed a radical change to his bosses at the CB&Q. They refused to consider it. So Harvey went over to the rival Santa Fe line.

On the new railroad, Harvey was given a lunch counter to run as an experiment. His success was so phenomenal that he received the Santa Fe's main hotel and restaurant to run. Harvey brought in a chef from Chicago's famed Palmer House to manage the operation. Harvey then began to set up a series of roadhouses along the Santa Fe mainline. He was a stickler for correctness. He inspected his restaurants with white gloves, looking for dust. Improperly set tables were overturned, chipped crockery was smashed to the floor. He brought in alkali-free water in tank cars and imported fresh vegetables from Mexico—nothing came from cans.

Harvey's places generally stood by or adjoined the railroad station. En route, conductors would ask passengers on the trains if they preferred to eat at the counter or in the dining room. The information was telegraphed ahead and the food made ready. When the train stopped, the passengers were met by the Harvey Girls, neatly attired in black and white. Harvey's main principles were that no customer should have to eat rushed and that no train departed leaving anyone behind still waiting for his food. The Harvey Girls were his secret. They were single, pretty, between 18 and 30 years old, efficient (one served 16 full meals in 25 minutes), and set a high moral tone on and off the job. When they signed on it was much like going off to the army. They took lengthy training classes, lived in dormitories, and had their hours regulated by the company. The girls signed a promise not to get married, but quite a few broke it— Harvey Girls were considered quite a catch among the young bachelors of the West. Harvey Girls not only served meals to passengers but to the crews as well, and working for the Santa Fe was considered a good deal by professional railroad men. "Meals by Fred Harvey" became synonymous with quality.

In 1893, Harvey took over the Santa Fe's dining cars. As dining cars always lost money, the railroad reimbursed Harvey for the difference. The news that Fred Harvey would run the Santa Fe's diners brought in so many customers that the railroad never felt the loss. When Harvey died he had 15 hotels (including one with 270 rooms), 47 restaurants, 30 dining cars, and food services on San Francisco car ferries and at St. Louis's Union Station, not even on the Santa Fe line. Working for Harvey wasn't like it was portrayed in the MGM movie, but it had character.

See also Santa Fe Railway.

References Bryant, Keith L., Jr., *History of the Atchison, Topeka and Santa Fe Railway* (1974); Holbrook, Stewart, *The Story of American Railroads* (1947); Hubbard, Freeman, *Encyclopedia of North American Railroading* (1981).

Hastings Cutoff

Hastings Cutoff was a section of the California Trail, the existence of which was put forth by Lansford Hastings, a publicist for the settlement of California before the 1849 gold rush. Concerned that Americans were overlooking a great opportunity to seize California from Mexico, much as Oregon had been secured for the Union by out-settling the British there, Hastings published his *Emigrant's Guide to Oregon and California* in 1845. In it, he postulated that the California Trail running out of Fort Hall could be shortened greatly by turning instead at Fort Bridger and, circling south of the Great Salt Lake, heading straight west to the Humboldt River. He had never seen this route, and its description of it was quite vague. He traveled eastward along his route in 1847 and found it to contain a desert much more vast than he expected. Nonetheless, Hastings still encouraged settlers to use it over the proven route, leading to a near-disaster for the Harlan-Young group and the tragedy of the Donner party in the High Sierras. The Mormons, however, successfully managed to use part of the cutoff to reach their Promised Land and establish the Mormon Trail.

See also California Trail; Mormon Trail; Oregon Trail.

Reference Moody, Ralph, *Old Trails West* (1963).

Hay–Bunau-Varilla Treaty (1904)

This document, negotiated between U.S. Secretary of State John Hay and the new Republic of Panamá's minister to the United States, Phillipe Bunau-Varilla, in 1903, granted the United States in perpetuity the control and use of a "canal zone" ten miles wide across the isthmus at the Chagres River, the right to fortify the zone, and the ownership of the Panama Railway and the New Panama Canal Company (in which Bunau-Varilla had an interest), so long as the zone remained neutral within the terms of the Hay-Pauncefote Treaty. The United States guaranteed the independence of the Republic of Panamá and agreed to pay $10 million and an annual fee of $250,000 beginning nine years after ratification (February 1904), in effect after the United States constructed the canal.

See also Hay-Herrán Convention; Panama Canal.

Hay-Herrán Convention (1903)

After the ratification of the Hay-Pauncefote Treaty and the passage of the Spooner Act, the United States had to get Colombia to agree to allow the construction of a canal across the isthmus in its northern province of Panamá. Colombian politics were extremely tenuous at the time. The nation had just concluded an expensive (in terms of blood and cash) civil war. Both sides jockeyed for position. It was obvious that the executive had to present any U.S. demands as an ultimatum, merely to prevent his expulsion from power. Opponents wanted to use any agreement as an excuse to eject the ruling party from power. These problems were also evident in Washington, where negotiations went through three Colombian representatives before Dr. Tomás Herrán took over.

Herrán moved very carefully with the seeming approval of his government to reach an agreement with U.S. Secretary of State John Hay. The convention provided that in exchange for an outright payment of $10 million, and an annual rent of $250,000, Columbia would allow the United States a

99-year lease with option for renewal over a six-mile-wide strip of land centered on the Chagres River. None of the money ($40 million) paid earlier to the Panama Canal Company would go to Colombia. The Colombian Congress demanded that the nation receive at least $25 million outright, and deferred action until after the expiration of the Panama Company's charter, hoping to snare the whole $40 million, which it desperately needed to help retire the gigantic $800 million national debt. Not only did this embarrass the current Colombian administration, which had indicated that Herrán's terms were acceptable (at least he thought they had, and so informed the Americans), it outraged President Theodore Roosevelt, who also thought he had a done deal. The result was that Roosevelt moved to overthrow the Colombian presence in Panamá by supporting local revolutionaries and secessionists, with whom the United States could negotiate with confidence.

See also Hay–Banau-Varilla Treaty; Panama Canal.

Hay-Pauncefote Treaty (1902)

Determined to build a canal across Panamá, the Theodore Roosevelt administration sought to abrogate the Clayton-Bulwer Treaty of 1850, which guaranteed British approval of and participation in American plans. Fortunately for the United States, Britain was in trouble with the world community for its heavy-handed prosecution of the Boer War and needed friends wherever it could find them. In 1900, the first Hay-Pauncefote Treaty was signed. In it, Great Britain agreed to renounce its joint rights to an isthmian canal, permitting the United States to build, control, and maintain it. America promised to maintain the canal's neutrality and not to fortify it. President Theodore Roosevelt especially was incensed because the treaty would allow any nation's warships through anytime, and invited world participation in the canal's security, a breech of the Monroe Doctrine. The

Senate ratified the agreement after adding provisos that allowed U.S. fortifications and kept the rest of the world out of the process. The British found all this unacceptable, but finally proposed a renegotiation, fearing its total international isolation. Roosevelt accepted, as he wished to bring the two nations closer together, having the inflated feeling about Anglo-Saxon unity, that was fashionable among the East Coast college-educated of his day.

The result was the second Hay-Pauncefote Treaty. It openly abrogated the Clayton-Bulwer Treaty and permitted the United States to construct an isthmian canal, to control it, and to fortify it; the canal was to be open to all nations on an equal footing; and neutrality would be maintained under U.S. auspices only. The new treaty was ratified on 16 December 1902, clearing the way for America to build the canal alone.

See also Clayton-Bulwer Treaty; Panama Canal.

Hayden-Cartwright Act (1934)

During the Great Depression in 1932, Congress passed the Emergency Relief and Construction Act, which appropriated $120 million for advances to the states to help them match federal highway funds. The sums were to be repaid over a ten-year period. This was necessary because the states had issued many highway bonds during the prosperous 1920s and now had to curtail highway programs to pay them off. With the insertion of federal money, the states could continue to build roads and provide jobs, cutting the rampant unemployment that marked the depression. The act also set up a standard of minimum wages, the first in American history.

The following year saw a change in presidential administrations and economic policies. Franklin D. Roosevelt's New Deal had "pump priming" as part of its domestic economic policy, designed to inject large amounts of federal money (usually borrowed from future generations' tax payments) into the domestic economy to provide jobs. One of the important pieces of legislation was the National Industrial Recovery Act. It gave $400 million in road-building moneys to the states without the necessity of matching funds. For the first time, the money could be spent inside cities and on secondary roads not a part of the declared federal highway system. Hours of employment were limited to a 30-hour week, to force the hiring of additional workers. Convict labor was prevented from being used on these federal projects.

But the biggest boost in highway building came through the Hayden-Cartwright Act of 1934. This measure canceled the need of the states to pay back the funds given to them under the 1932 Emergency Relief and Construction Act. Hayden-Cartwright appropriated $200 million as a federal donation to the states in highway construction in 1934, an additional $200 million for 1935, and $200 million more for improving railroad grade crossings. The measure also provided a return to the principle of matching funds (with states having large amounts of federal lands getting proportionately more money) for the years 1936 and 1937. One percent of the money had to be used to improve roadsides by ditching, drainage, wider shoulders, and increasing the standard right-of-way from 60 to 100 feet. Some of the money also went into development of divided parkways and roads in Forest and Park Service areas.

President Roosevelt protested this measure as tying the hands of the executive budget director in handling the depression with flexibility. Senator Carl Hayden of Arizona said that was exactly the purpose of the measure sponsored by him and Representative Wilburn Cartwright of Oklahoma—to guarantee highway funds with considerable lead time to allow proper research, planning, and increased road safety measures, without diversion of the funds to any other project. As such, Hayden-Cartwright returned America to the matching-funds principle after injecting a large amount of "free" money into the states. It kept the principles of minimum wage and aid to city and secondary roads (25 percent of the total), but added the ideas of safety, investigation, and planning to federal funding proposals. It literally built the highways that took American into World War II and into the development of the interstate highway system two decades later.

See also Roads and Highways since World War I.
Reference U.S. Department of Transportation, Federal Highway Administration, *America's Highways* (1976).

Helicopters

From the fourth century B.C.E., when the Chinese developed a top with upward-angled feathers that would fly in a hovering manner, to the twentieth century, when powered, vertical flight became a reality, humans have been fascinated not only by flight, but by the ability to hover in flight. Leonardo da Vinci even drew a proposed full-scale helicopter and the Russian Mikhail Lomonosov actually built a similar object that rose into the air powered by a screw device. But Lomonosov's was only a small model. Actually the real problem was not to get into the air but to stay there. Propulsion seemed to be a perpetual enigma that stumped British, French, and Italian tinkers—and even the genius of the American, Thomas A. Edison.

But in the twentieth century, two French inventors, Louis Breguet and Paul Cornu, managed to get contraptions to hover from a few seconds to a couple of minutes. Breguet had his held steady by four assistants to keep a sudden gust of wind from dumping the whole project. Cornu was more daring and achieved the first free helicopter flight of five feet off the ground. Austrian military experiments attempted to replace the vulnerable aerial observation balloon with a gasoline-powered helicopter, but it crashed (fortunately it was unmanned at the time) before anything positive was achieved. Similar experiments continued after World War I, encouraged by the Spanish Marquis Pateras Pescara's invention of "autogyroing," a process that allowed the rotors to continue to turn in the event of a power failure, allowing the craft to descend softly (sort of) to Earth. But all efforts to get a practical helicopter to fly under rotor power failed, be they Belgian, Italian, British, Hungarian, Dutch, or American. Only the Frenchman Etienne Oehmichen got his machine to fly a one-kilometer closed course. Others, like the Spaniard Juan de la Cierva, managed to get lift from a rotor attached to what amounted to an airplane. These contraptions were called "autogyros."

But in the late 1930s Louis Breguet returned to helicopter design and flew a machine without wings that had two flexible rotors (a new concept), one on each side of the cabin, that rotated in opposite directions. More ominous for its military potential was the invention of the German Heinrich Focke. Claiming all sorts of altitude and speed records, Focke faced the skepticism of the world. So Adolph Hitler's favorite personal aviatrix, Hanna Reitsch, flew one of Focke's machines in a Berlin sports arena

and amazed onlookers as she rose vertically and maneuvered at will. But Focke's invention still was a cross between an airplane and a true helicopter, with dual rotors at the tip of each wing skeleton.

Meanwhile, with the outbreak of World War II, Igor Sikorsky was using the funds appropriated by Congress in 1938 to build an experimental helicopter. He decided to stray from the plans submitted to the army and reduce the various rotors to two, one spinning horizontally overhead with cyclic pitch and another mounted vertically on the tail as a stabilizer. All appearances of an airplane's wings disappeared from the craft's smooth fuselage. By 1942, Sikorsky could fly to several thousand feet in altitude, hover, and fly cross-country like an airplane, all with rotor action alone. The true helicopter was born. The armed forces ordered

An aerial ambulance arrives at a mobile army surgical unit tent in 1951.

two dozen or so immediately. By the end of the war, Sikorsky had delivered 100 choppers of various size to the military services, the last ones equipped with hoists to lift cargo. Bodies were reconfigured to include streamlined Plexiglas noses, sleek underpinnings, and an enclosed tail housing. The new machine was proving to be very adaptable to all sorts of situations. One had already ferried medicines to a disabled ship at sea and another had probed the new volcano that had suddenly appeared in a farm field in Mexico.

Although the end of the war killed many of the governmental programs, numerous small companies like Bell, Piasecki, Hiller, Kaman, and Hughes were formed to exploit the civilian aspects of helicopter development and use along with the veteran Sikorsky. Charter and scheduled airline operations, crop-dusting, forest fire fighting, power line surveying, rescue operations, medical evacuation, law enforcement, and business applications for the helicopter came into being. But still most important were the military uses. The navy found out that a hovering helicopter made for safer landings and takeoffs from its carriers at sea. During the Korean conflict, the army found out that air evacuation of wounded soldiers from frontline combat areas to mobile hospital complexes in the rear areas saved lives formerly lost (and gave birth to a book, movie, and television series, *M*A*S*H*). Payloads increased and grew more varied. Turbojet propulsion was added for more power and speed, and in the late 1950s the UH-1 Huey, the machine that was adapted for every task asked of it in the Vietnam War, was born. It was so adaptable to the fighting role that Bell made a special fighting machine, the AH-1 Cobra. Sikorsky contributed the single-rotor giant CH-54 Flying Crane that could lift giant loads into combat or a civilian construction site. The Piasecki tandem rotor system was sold as the best way to get more load-carrying capacity without an expensive investment in new engines and power trains, and allowed the dropping of the tail rotor. The result was the CH-47 Chinook, the cargo workhorse of Vietnam.

The Gulf War of 1991 showed just how far military helicopter design had come. New tank-killing choppers like the Hughes AH-64 Apache, the Bell AH-63 Super Cobra, and Sikorsky's S-61 Blackhawk (the first helicopter that could do loops, "split Ss," and rolls) hid behind landforms and vegetation only to spring up and eliminate enemy tanks with "smart" weapons that rarely missed their target. Indeed, the main problem seemed to be target acquisition, particularly the identification and separation of friend from foe. One slip-up in turning on the proper electronic identification signal could result in a tragic "friendly fire" incident in which the ever-accurate attack helicopters hit their own forces with deadly precision. Nearly one in four American casualties in the Gulf War came from such "friendly fire" incidents, an all-time high for a military expedition.

For the future, the direction of helicopter development only seems to be going up. Problems to be solved include noise abatement, vibration reduction (many a Vietnam infantryman swore the Chinooks he rode would disintegrate before his destination was reached), increased all-weather capabilities, more fuel efficiency, improved safety and rideability, and less frequent maintenance. New rotor configurations, power systems, and payload packages will likely put the helicopter into common usage as passenger and cargo carriers.

See also Aeronautics.

References Boyne, Walter J., and Donald S. López (eds.), *Vertical Flight* (1984); Carey, Keith, *The Helicopter* (1986); Fay, John, *The Helicopter* (1987); Gablehouse, Charles, *Helicopters and Autogiros* (1967); Young, Warren R., *The Helicopters* (1982).

Hennepin Canal
Between Rock Island on the Mississippi inland to the Illinois River at Great Bend, the Hennepin Canal was built very late in the canal era (1892–1907) and soon fell to rail competition and was relegated to a drainage canal for floodwaters.

See Canals.

Henry, John (?–1888?)

No written documents provide conclusive evidence of the singular Mississippi ex-slave John Henry, well known to several regions (especially Kentucky and West Virginia) for his prowess and vigor with a single-jack (one-man), nine-pound driving hammer. Many interviewed in the post–Civil War era claimed not only to remember him, but also the essential details of the contest that made him and his name a legend for all time. John Henry was a "steel driver"—a tunnel builder who struck his hammer against a steel drilling rod clenched between the hands of a fellow worker, who twisted the drill slightly every stroke to aid in the penetration of rock. When the hole reached sufficient depth, a charge of black powder was inserted and a fulminate of mercury primer was used to induce an explosion, lengthening the tunnel.

According to material researched during the 1930s on a grant from the Works Progress Administration, the John Henry legend arose from an 1870s competition held at the Big Bend Tunnel on the Chesapeake & Ohio Railroad in West Virginia, where the raw-boned, powerful African American was pitted against a newfangled steam drill, and bored two standard seven-foot blasting holes to the steam drill's one-and-a-third holes in 35 minutes. Others claim the feat took place in 1888 at Alabama's Oak Mountain Tunnel, where a monument stands today. Wherever rail links spread, the story was repeated and often embellished. The famous ballad of his feat eventually reached 14 stanzas in number, 10 of which were once published by the University of North Carolina Press. In 1939, African-American singer Paul Robeson starred in the title role of a Broadway stage adaptation of the tale.

All versions of the story of John Henry, whether in the form of play, song, or prose, have been adapted to other geographical regions and conditions, such as the operation of a cotton-rolling steam winch. Several playwrights and authors of prominence have chosen to refer to the mythical John Henry as the "black Paul Bunyan of the workingman," the most popular railroad man next to Casey Jones—maybe even ahead of him nowadays, song-wise. But the greatest tribute of all may have been the Chesapeake & Ohio Railroad's naming its last, largest, and most powerful, modern steam locomotive the *Jawn Henry* in the 1950s.

See also Death Valley Scotty; Jones, John Luther "Casey."

References Botkin, Benjamin A., and Alvin F. Harlow, *A Treasury of Railroad Folklore* (1953); Hubbard, Freeman, *The Train That Never Came Back* (1952); Hubbard, Freeman, *Encyclopedia of North American Railroading* (1981); Lomax, Alan, *Folk Songs of North America* (1960); Sandburg, Carl, *The American Songbag* (1927); Smith, Ronald D., and William L. Richter, *Fascinating People and Strange Events from American History* (1993).

Hepburn Act (1906)

As the second major overhauling of the 1887 Interstate Commerce Act, the Hepburn Act broadened the law to apply to pipelines and other forms of transportation beyond railroads. The rulings of the Interstate Commerce Commission (ICC), set up by the 1887 act, were binding unless changed by the courts, which placed the burden of proof upon the carriers. It also had a commodities clause, stating that no railroad could own a producing property like a mine that had a product shipped in interstate commerce. It gave the ICC the right to set maximum railroad rates and created a uniform system of accounting. It was an attempt to subordinate the capitalistic system to the government and the people, which had failed most of the time so far. In the notion that the ICC could establish principles of auditing and bookkeeping and set rates without reference to a court, the Hepburn Act was revolutionary. But the railroads got the right to appeal any ICC decision to the very friendly federal courts. President Theodore Roosevelt was criticized by many as too anxious to compromise, yet his advocates praise his political ability and willingness to trade tariff support for the regulation of railroads. In response to his often very vocal and vicious critics, Roosevelt dismissed them as "muckrakers" (a label in which his opponents actually gloried).

See also Elkins Act; Man-Elkins Act.

References Hoogenboom, Ari, "Hepburn Act," in Keith L. Bryant, Jr. (ed.), *EABHB: Railroads in the*

Age of Regulation (1988), 198; Keeler, Theodore E., *Railroads, Freight and Public Policy* (1983); Kolko, Gabriel, *Railroads and Regulation* (1965); Martin, Albro, *Enterprise Denied* (1971); Mowry, George E., *The Era of Theodore Roosevelt* (1958); Swindler, William F., *Court and Constitution in the 20th Century* (1969).

Highway Research Board (HRB)

Established in 1920 as the National Advisory Board on Highway Research, its name was changed to the Highway Research Board in 1925 and to the Transportation Research Board in 1974 to conform to the regulations of the relatively new Department of Transportation. Its purpose was to coordinate a program of highway research and dispense the information to interested persons and societies, and collect results from these persons and entities and coordinate them. The board had members from the Bureau of Public Roads, the National Research Council Division of Engineering, and the American Association of Highway Officials. Investigative committees are organized and terminated according to needs. Outside specialists from research organizations and colleges and universities are often put on committees. Typical topics of concern include the economic theory of highway improvement, structural design of roads, character and use of road materials, highway traffic analyses, highway finance, and highway maintenance. Technical papers are published annually in its *HRB Proceedings*. Other publications are *HRB Bibliography*, *Highway Research Abstracts*, and HRB's *Annual Report*. A highway information library was set up in 1946, and more recently a computerized data base, Highway Research Information Service (HRIS), emphasizing research in progress and abstracts of results, is in operation.

See also Roads and Highways since World War I.

Reference U.S. Department of Transportation, Federal Highway Administration, *America's Highways* (1976).

Highway Revenue Act (1956)

Also known as Title II of the Federal-Aid Highway Act of 1956, the Highway Revenue Act provides the funding mechanism of the interstate highway system through the creation of the Highway Trust Fund.

See also Federal-Aid Highway Acts, Federal-Aid Highway Act of 1956; Highway Trust Fund; Roads and Highways since World War I.

Reference U.S. Department of Transportation, Federal Highway Administration, *America's Highways* (1976).

Highway Trust Fund

Prior to the enactment of the 1956 Federal-Aid Highway Act, all federal road funds came from the general fund of the U.S. Treasury. Although the feds collected many fees and taxes from motor uses of highways and related items like gasoline, oils, tires, and parts, none of this went automatically to construction and maintenance of the federal highway network. Title II of the 1956 act, the Highway Revenue Act, changed all of this. It increased existing fees and taxes and instituted many new ones to fund completion of the new interstate system. But all items collected in relation to road use were now to go into the Highway Trust Fund, a receptor of income, which then would dispense the federal matching highway moneys to the states.

For years, states had complained that user fees and taxes were being lost inside the general fund, going to other projects. State representatives maintained that this represented a shortfall of money that should be applied to the purpose for which it was ostensibly collected—federal roads. The effect was that Congress increased user fees and taxes dramatically but softened the $25 million price tag on completing the interstate system by putting it on a pay-as-you-go basis through the money in the Highway Trust Fund. If the planned road building in any one year was to drain the Highway Trust Fund beyond its income, the secretary of the treasury could advance money from the general fund to make up the difference. But if the same occurred in the following year, the secretary had to reduce the projects to a manageable size until income filled up the trust fund again. Money not used one year could be carried over to the next.

The mini-depression of 1958 caused Congress to suspend the work of the Highway Trust Fund and permit deficit spending to relieve the deflationary influence of the economic recession. But the normal pay-as-you-go features were restored in 1961 after the effects of the recession had been overcome. In reality, recession or not, the Highway Trust Fund is merely an accounting convenience that uses paper transfers. It has no money physically on deposit. And Congress has to release the accrued sums each year through its ordinary annual appropriation process. The interstate system is a matching-funds project at a federal-state ratio of 90–10. Normal federal highway projects were funded at a 50–50 ratio until 1973, when Congress changed this to a 70–30 basis. Currently the whole process is audited by the executive branch's Office of Management and Budget, which keeps track of the income and outflow of money into the trust fund and makes adjustments to keep the balance in the black. This is not seen as an impoundment of funds (a total halt of spending regardless of prior appropriation) but a regulation on how fast appropriations are spent, keeping fluctuations in the fund predictable.

See also Federal-Aid Highway Acts, Federal-Aid Highway Act of 1956; Roads and Highways since World War I.

References Owen, Wilfred, et al., *Financing Highways* (1957); Rose, Mark H., *Interstate: Express Highway Politics, 1841–1956* (1978); U.S. Department of Transportation, Federal Highway Administration, *America's Highways* (1976).

Hill, James Jerome (1838–1916)

Canadian-born (Rockwood, Ontario) James J. Hill was blind in one eye, the result of a childhood accident. His father died when Hill was 15, thrusting him rather suddenly into the business world. He wandered from job to job for a number of years, finally settling in St. Paul, Minnesota. There he became a riverboat shipping clerk, bought up several plots of land, and married. At night he studied geography, geology, and economics. Several of his shipping contracts were with local railroads, mostly nascent short lines that would later be in Hill's rail

empire. He began that empire by knitting together stage, river, and rail carriers into the Red River Transportation Line that ran from St. Paul to Winnipeg.

The Panic of 1873 was the entrée that Hill used to begin his rail empire. Together with George Stephen (financial wizard), Donald Alexander Smith (political pull), and Norman W. Kittson (engineering and politics), Hill conceived a scheme that allowed them to buy up the bankrupt St. Paul & Pacific Railroad. Both rails and farmers had been hurt not only by the economic depression but by a horde of locusts that had plagued the Old Northwest for five years. Hill knew that the locusts would not last forever, but Dutch investors were anxious to unload, and the innocent-looking Hill seemed a perfect sucker. He took them for 25 cents on the dollar.

Soon the Red River Valley of the North began to prosper with wheat, and Hill and his associates had to build westward or lose potential federal land grants. As they built, they sold the land to finance the track laying. At the same time, Hill and company began to move the Canadian Pacific Railroad westward in Canada. There was much criticism in both countries about this, and Hill responded by becoming an American citizen in 1880. His partners decided to go with the Canadian operation, which left Hill the sole owner of the future Great Northern Railroad. Hill's policy was to run his trains through country that had potential settlement value. "Land without people is a wilderness; people without land is a mob," he once said. Western railroads had to cross many barren areas that cost them freight-hauling opportunities. Hill went to Europe and developed an organized immigration plan to fill up the Plains with farmers. Agents flooded Europe with propaganda, promising a veritable heaven on earth.

Since the rival Northern Pacific had picked many of the best routes earlier, Hill had to cross a lot of Indian and military land, which necessitated congressional approval. Jay Gould (of the rival Union Pacific) paid many influential people to block Hill and other potential rail magnates. When public demand proved too much, the government allowed Hill access to federal areas, but refused to give him the land grants that had financed the Union Pacific, Northern Pacific, and the other great railroads. So Hill used the proceeds of his immigrant program to continue the track laying and, in 1890, he reached Puget Sound, crossing the Rockies in places surveyed by Lieutenant John Mullan for his Mullan Road years before.

Hill added many short branches to tap the agricultural areas of the Great Plains, and signed a cozy deal with the Chicago, Burlington & Quincy (CB&Q) to reach Chicago over its tracks There he set up the Northwest Steamship Company that monopolized traffic on the Great Lakes. Other steamships handled trade with the Orient, especially lucrative in cotton shipped out of the South on the Illinois Central and to Japan via Hill's rail and steam lines. His old land purchases happened to have large deposits of iron ore, which now paid off big. For the first time in 1888, he called his railroad, the only western road to the Pacific built without normal government land grant aid, the Great Northern. He constantly plowed profits back into the system. On the rails he emphasized low grades, big motive power, longer trains, larger-capacity cars, and fewer empties. Hill let no detail escape his grasp. He was a hard man to work for (he never forgot a slight or a foul-up) and even harder to get an advantageous freight rate out of. Hill's monopolistic domination of traffic across the Plains led farmers to coin a phrase: "After the grasshoppers, we had Jim Hill." His personal fortune of $400 million competed with those of Cornelius Vanderbilt, Jay Gould, and E. H. Harriman.

In the 1890s, things began to change in the West. Hill and the rival Northern Pacific bought up the CB&Q for its Chicago access, and set up the Spokane, Portland & Seattle to tap jointly the whole Puget Sound and Pacific Coast area, which stopped E. H. Harriman's efforts to do the same thing. Harriman had taken over the Union Pacific upon Gould's death and was now interested in the western railways in a big way. By now, Hill had a large share of the Northern Pa-

cific, but Harriman began an insidious attempt to buy a controlling share. Hill soon realized what was happening, and with the backing of J. P. Morgan, attempted to halt Harriman's purchases. Northern Pacific stock rose to $1,000 a share—it had been worth a mere $58 originally. Then Hill realized that Harriman's majority lay in preferred stock that could be retired at will. Hill offered a compromise in the form of a holding corporation, the Northern Securities Corporation, that would control the Great Northern, the Northern Pacific, and the CB&Q. The Supreme Court later declared the corporation an unconstitutional violation of the Sherman Antitrust Act.

The dissolving of Northern Securities cost Hill and his side $40 million. He managed to keep his rail lines, but he emerged from the contest a much-embittered man. He resented what he saw as Harriman's playing with stocks for personal gain, while he relished his own title, "The Empire Builder." Hill saw himself as a positive force developing the industrial and agricultural prospects of the Pacific Northwest for the benefit of the nation, not just himself. He brought in agricultural ideas from Europe, publicized fertilizers, and increased farm outputs many times over. Of course he made money hauling the bounty over his rails at the same time. When property he bought turned out to hold the Messabi Iron Range, Hill sold it to shareholders in the Great Northern at the price he paid for it years before. This puts him in a league of industrialists that go beyond the vulgar term "robber barons." Hill belongs to that class of men who built the country and made it strong, as opposed to normal interpretation of the robber barons as crass manipulators of everyone else's wealth.

See also Chicago, Burlington & Quincy Railroad; Great Northern Railroad; Harriman, Edward Henry; Mullan Road; Northern Pacific Railway; *Northern Securities Company v. U.S.;* Villard, Henry.

References Folsom, Burton W., Jr., *The Myth of the Robber Barons* (1991); Ginger, Ray, *Age of Success* (1965); Hill, James J., *Highways of Progress* (1910); Hubbard, Freeman, *Encyclopedia of North American Railroading* (1981); Josephson, Matthew, *The Robber Barons* (1934); Martin, Albro, *James J. Hill* (1976);

Martin, Albro "James J. Hill," in Robert L. Frey (ed.), *EABHB: Railroads in the Nineteenth Century* (1988), 169–178; Meyers, Gustavus, *History of the Great American Fortunes* (1910); Pyle, Joseph Gilpin, *The Life of James J. Hill* (1926).

Holladay, Benjamin (1819–1887)

Kentucky born, Ben Holladay went to Missouri with his parents as a boy. By age 20 he was operating a store and saloon at Weston. He next moved into trading with Plains Indians and also bought a hotel at Weston. During the war with Mexico, he freighted supplies to the army, operating down the Santa Fe Trail. He purchased surplus oxen and wagons from the army at the war's end and, in partnership with Theodore F. Warner, took 50 wagonloads of supplies to Salt Lake City at some profit. In 1850, he drove a herd of oxen to California, and made a big profit. During the 1850s he bought livestock for the big freighting firm, Russell, Majors & Waddell. He also joined William H. Russell in a contract to deliver flour to the army in Utah. In 1860, he advanced money to begin the operation of the Pony Express, which gave him a mortgage on the whole company that he cashed in two years later, buying what remained of the then-bankrupt operation and reorganizing it as the Overland Mail and Stage. He also dabbled in steamship service to California. As befitted a man of his wealth, he kept ostentatious homes in Washington, D.C., and White Plains, New York. By 1866, seeing the end of the profitability of horse-drawn overland transportation in the face of the transcontinental railroad, he sold his operations to Wells Fargo. He soon sold his steamship company and invested in Oregon railroads. In 1876, he lost control of the railroad company and retired from business. He died in Portland in 1887.

See also Russell, Majors & Waddell Company; Stagecoaches and Other Horse-Drawn Conveyances.

References Schwantes, Carlos A., "Benjamin Holladay," in Robert L. Frey (ed.), *EABHB: Railroads in the Nineteenth Century* (1988), 179–181; Settle, Raymond W., and Mary L. Settle, *War Drums and Wagon Wheels* (1966).

Hopkins, Mark (1813–1878)

Less is known about Mark Hopkins than about any other of the men associated with the Central Pacific Railroad, the transcontinental railroad branch built out of California in the 1860s to link up with the Union Pacific in Utah. Described as tall, thin, cautious, and stubborn, he was essentially a clerk. He reached the goldfields in 1849 and went into business with Collis P. Huntington in a general store at Sacramento. In 1861 he was at a meeting with Theodore D. Judah, Huntington, Charles Crocker, Leland Stanford, and four others that led to the organization of the Central Pacific.

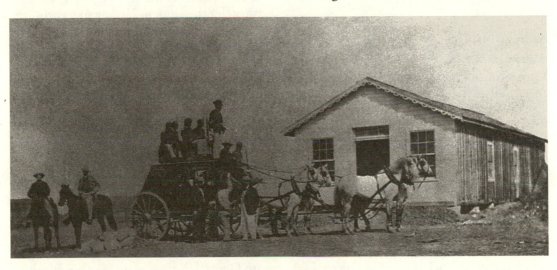

In 1860, Ben Hollady provided the capital to begin the Pony Express.

Construction began two years later, and in 1869, the transcontinental route was finished. But the four major financial backers of the route—Hopkins, Crocker, Huntington, and Stanford—merely had their appetites whetted for wealth and power. They went on to take over other railroads, steamship lines, docks, cable cars, and interurban transit lines. When Hopkins died, many biographical documents relating to him disappeared. The whole Central Pacific was under investigation for monopolistic practices by Congress at the time, and no one wanted the items to reach probate. Instead of his estate going his heirs, it was pumped back into the railroad to bolster its sagging fortunes. Worse yet, the papers of his three partners mention little about Hopkins except that he was treasurer of the system and a member of the board of directors. It all leaves one with the uneasy feeling that there is more to the Mark Hopkins story than meets the eye.

See also Crocker, Charles; Huntington, Collis Potter; Judah, Theodore D.; Southern Pacific Lines; Stanford, Leland.

References Butler, Dan, "Mark Hopkins," in Robert L. Frey (ed.), *EABHB: Railroads in the Nineteenth Century* (1988), 184–186; Dagget, Stuart, *Chapters on the History of the Southern Pacific* (1922); Hubbard, Freeman, *Encyclopedia of North American Railroading* (1981); Latta, Estelle, and M. L. Allison, *Controversial Mark Hopkins* (1953); Lewis, Oscar, *The Big Four* (1938).

Hughes, Howard Robard, Jr. (1905–1976)

A pilot, motion picture producer and studio owner, aircraft designer and manufacturer, airline owner and operator, hotel and casino owner, entrepreneur, and playboy, Howard Hughes was Charles Lindbergh, Donald Douglas, and Juan Trippe all rolled into one. Born in Houston, Hughes was the only child of a tool and die maker and his wife. His father struck it rich early in the Texas oil boom when he accidentally bumped into a man in a Shreveport bar who sold him the idea for a drilling bit that would break through any bedrock to the black gold. For $150 the elder Hughes went on to become

a billionaire at a time when $1 million was big money. The Hughes Rotary Drill Bit would finance his son's various careers and whims, making him a free man to do anything he wanted when he wanted. It was an ideal sought after by many but reached by very few.

The younger Hughes soon had a bench at his father's company where he tinkered and motorized his bicycle, built a radio transmitter, and generally exercised his inquisitive mind. A loner from the start, Howard Hughes, Jr., liked to ride horseback in the Los Angeles hills behind the private school he attended. He also played the saxophone and took up golf. The early death of his parents had caused him to be raised by his aunt and uncle, who was a screenwriter in a Hollywood that was just beginning to take off. Hughes had inherited most of his father's business—a Texas judge with whom the 19-year-old played golf made a favorable ruling that declared him an adult and allowed Hughes to buy the rest of the Hughes Tool Company. Hughes put the business in charge of Noah Dietrich, a trusted friend, and went off to seek the world.

Hughes' first stop was Hollywood. His uncle had introduced him to this fascinating world, which became even more fun after he ditched his Texas socialite wife—or did she get rid of him? It was hard to say as neither saw each other much. He began to produce pictures of his own. Later he would own RKO Radio. He bought and sailed his own yacht. He also took up and advanced his flying skills. He particularly like fast flying and entered many air races and set several transcontinental records. He would fly around the world in 1938, a trip that led him into the business of aviation both as an owner of Trans World Airlines (TWA, called Trans West in those days) and an aviation inventor. Both the famous *Constellation* (or "Connie"), designed and built in league with Lockheed, and the giant six-engine flying boat known as the *Spruce Goose* from its glued wooden construction, built with Henry J. Kaiser, were Hughes-inspired designs.

The Connie was a big four-engine, streamlined aircraft with a pressurized cabin, distinct triple tail fins, 60 seats, and a 3,500-mile range that made it better than anything that flew. It was Hughes' way of teaching other airlines and plane builders not to sell TWA short as they had in the past. In 1941, the Connie was ten years ahead of anything the competition had. Typically, Hughes took the whole Civil Aeronautics Board up and cut two of the engines to prove its safety performance. He built the Constellation series at the Hughes Tool Works at a cut rate exclusively for TWA. The *Spruce Goose* was a huge military transport, the largest until the C-5 in the 1970s. But the armed forces could not envision any need for it after winning World War II, and it sat abandoned by the government for which it was built, much of it having been financed by the inventor's own money. It is now on display at Long Beach, California.

After World War II, during which Hughes turned the *Constellation* over to the United States Armed Forces for the war effort, he worked on a new plane, a high-altitude photo reconnaissance craft, the XF-11. As usual, Hughes took it up on its first flight. All went well until the landing, when one propeller went into reverse pitch unexpectedly. The resulting crash nearly killed Hughes. But he walked out of the hospital five weeks later to the amazement of on-lookers. Many of his ideas would be used later in Lockheed's successful U-2 spy plane.

In the mid-fifties Hughes' world began to slowly unravel. He had turned TWA into one of the finest airlines in the country. But his director of operations, Ralph Damon, died in 1956, and Hughes seemed rudderless without him. When airlines began to convert to jets, Hughes was cash-short for the first time in his life. He managed to work with Lockheed to update and lengthen the *Constellation* (the L-1649A) so that he could fly nonstop from New York City to Frankfurt. But the money he borrowed to keep his empire afloat was called in by the Equitable Corporation. Hughes sold his empire in 1968 to pay his legal and financial debts. The shares went in 20 minutes and brought him $566 million. With the leftover money, Hughes reentered the airline industry, purchasing Air West, a small airline made up of a merger of West Coast, Pacific, and Bonanza Airlines. Hughes refurbished the carrier with bright yellow jets, "Flying Bananas" to friend and foe alike. He lived more and more as a recluse in his various hotels, and was labeled as an eccentric by the media, unfairly rumored to have been roped in by the Church of Latter-Day Saints (Hollywood turned this into the slick flick entitled *Melvin and Howard*). Hughes died aboard his private jet in the air above Mexico in 1976. He was a legend to the very end.

See also Aeronautics; Trans World Airlines.

References Barton, Charles, *Howard Hughes and His Flying Boat* (1982); Davies, R. E. G., *Rebels and Reformers of the Airways* (1987); Dietrich, Noah, and Bob Thomas, *Howard* (1972); Keats, John, *Howard Hughes* (1966); Murphy, Charles J. V., and Thomas A. Wise, "The Problem of Howard Hughes," *Fortune* (January 1959) 59: 79–82; Phelan, James, *Howard Hughes* (1976); Rummel, Robert W., *Howard Hughes and TWA* (1991); Serling, Robert J., *Howard Hughes' Airline* (1983); Tinnin, David B., *Just About Everybody vs. Howard Hughes* (1973).

Pilot and movie producer Howard Hughes poses in front of his new Boeing pursuit plane in the 1940s.

Hull-Alfaro Treaty (1936)

With the accession to power of the Franklin D. Roosevelt administration, a new Good Neighbor policy was undertaken toward Latin America, which emphasized negotiations rather than military intimidation. Roosevelt held a conference with Panamanian President Harmodio Arías in 1933 that issued a declaration that Panamá would be permitted the commercial rights of a sovereign state in the Canal Zone. Roosevelt also promised to negotiate changes in the Hay–Bunau-Varilla Treaty (1904) under which the canal was built and administered.

The Hull-Alfaro Treaty increased annual rent payments from $250,000 to $450,000, incorporated joint action of both nations in defense of the installation, and allowed the United States to expand its facilities or begin new construction. The treaty was not ratified by the U.S. Senate until 1939 because of the objections of army and navy authorities and key senators who feared that the inclusion of Panamá in defense procedures would compromise American administration of the canal.

See also Panama Canal.

Huntington, Collis Potter (1821–1900)

Born in Harwinto, Connecticut, Collis P. Huntington's first job was hawking watches and clocks on the street at age 14. He then opened a store at Oneonta, New York, with his brother and shipped goods to the California goldfields. In 1850, he followed one of his shipments to Sacramento and opened a store with Mark Hopkins, specializing in picks, shovels, axes, nails, and gold pans. He was approached by Theodore D. Judah to help finance the Central Pacific Railroad, from which he made a fortune. As an adult, Huntington was a big man, ruthless, grim, cold, and crafty, or as one unknown but acute observer once opined, "scrupulously dishonest."

Huntington and the others had what the eastern railroad men could only dream of—a monopoly. And Huntington was not going to let anyone else tread on his turf.

Despite the millions he had taken from the federal government, the state of California, and the people of the United States, Huntington never changed his frugal lifestyle one iota. Frugality, tenacity, and industry were his bywords; he cared little for the finer things in life—but his wife made up for all that. Like her husband, she brooked no defeat. She just enjoyed the fruits of their labors more. Huntington lavished no excess on himself. His office was a small, dreary, seventh-floor room in New York City with no carpet nor curtains on the window, just a table topped with a felt cover, a few high-backed chairs, and papers strewn everywhere. The only picture on the wall was of the shipyards at Newport News, Virginia, which he owned. He spent two days a week in New York City, one in Boston, and four in Washington, lobbying for his interests (i.e., buying congressmen and senators).

To ensure his control of California railroading, Huntington proposed to block the two open southern routes into the state, the one at Fort Yuma and the other at the Needles up the Colorado River, by getting there first. When Thomas A. Scott got congressional permission to build the Texas & Pacific into San Diego from El Paso, Huntington saw to it that there was an additional paragraph authorizing the Southern Pacific to build south and west from Los Angeles to meet it "at or near" Fort Yuma. To Huntington this meant he had to build eastward, and fast, to as far as he could. He reached El Paso far ahead of anyone else. But he would lose the Needles route to the Atlantic & Pacific (later the Santa Fe). He was well hated in California by everyone except those who had invested in Southern Pacific stock—and as a matter of fact they did not like him much either. They hated his lack of dividend payments, as he plowed it all back into the system.

Huntington died in Raquette Lake, New York, in 1900. He left a large collection of paintings to the Metropolitan Museum of Art in New York City and endowed two black colleges, Hampton Institute in Virginia and Tuskegee Institute in Alabama. His widow Arabella, she of palatial houses, fancy art collections, and a feisty mind in her own right, later married one of Huntington's nephews, also an heir to the fortune. As one might say, two fortunes are better than one.

See also Crocker, Charles; Forbes, John Murray; Gould, Jay; Hopkins, Mark; Judah, Theodore D.; Sage, Russell; Scott, Thomas A.; Southern Pacific Lines; Stanford, Leland; Vanderbilt, William H.

References Evans, Corinda W., *Collis Potter Huntington* (1954); Hubbard, Freeman, *Encyclopedia of North American Railroading* (1981); Lavender, David, *The Great Persuader* [Collis P. Huntington] (1970); Lewis, Oscar, *The Big Four* (1938); Lyon, Peter, *To Hell in a Day Coach* (1968); McCague, James, *Moguls and Iron Men* (1964); Redinger, Matthew A., "Collis P. Huntington," in Robert L. Frey (ed.), *EABHB: Railroads in the Nineteenth Century* (1988), 188–193.

Iacocca, Lee A. (b. 1924)

Born Lido Anthony to Italian immigrant parents, Lee Iacocca graduated in engineering from Lehigh University and Princeton College. He wanted to be a Ford employee. The company recruited college graduates and gave them extensive in-house training. In 1945, the hiring limit was 50, but Iacocca sold himself so well that he became the exceptional fifty-first. These men had to compete with the so-called whiz kids, two of whom made it to the presidency of Ford—Robert McNamara and Arjay Miller. Although Henry Ford I saw the expansion of capital plant as thrilling, these modern managers saw it as a regrettable necessity brought on by model changes. Iacocca believes to this day that this is the main difference between American and Japanese approaches to business.

At Ford, Iacocca often played on corporate fears (as he did in saving Chrysler from the Japanese). He took credit for the success of the Mustang model, to the exclusion of others, and was also the "father" of the Pinto and Mustang II. He believes that American auto workers are pretty well off, but not in utopia by any means. He and Henry Ford II did not get along. It was a classic conflict of egos; Henry ruled like his grandfather with an I-decide-everything approach, but Iacocca saw the "I" as the initial of his last name. As a result, Iacocca got fired. But the crude manner in which the firing was done gained him much public sympathy. Iacocca went to Chrysler in 1978, as did some other Ford executives. There Iacocca pulled off the deal of the century by swinging a $1.3 billion government loan. He paid it back early, saving the taxpayers millions in interest, by making his own pseudo-patriotic commercials. He became a hero again and his books were number-one best-sellers, especially his autobiography (or "AUTObiography," as one reviewer put it). He increased his patriotic credentials by assuming charge of the Statue of Liberty restoration and appealing successfully for public donations. Iacocca was reputedly interested in doing with Chrysler what

Durant and Briscoe had done before World War I in establishing General Motors and United States Motors, but this time creating a sort of Global Motors. He never achieved his goal before his recent retirement.

See also Automobiles from Domestics to Imports; Automobiles in American Society; Ford, Henry, II.

References Abodaher, David, *Iacocca* (1982); Flink, James J., "Lido Anthony Iacocca," in George S. May (ed.), *EABHB: The Automobile Industry* (1989), 197–217; Gordon, Maynard M., *The Iacocca Management Technique* (1985); Halberstam, David, *The Reckoning* (1986); Iacocca, Lee, and William Novak, *Iacocca* (1984); Rothschild, Emma, *Paradise Lost* (1973); Shook, Robert L., *Turnaround* (1990); Sobel, Robert, *Car Wars* (1984); Stuart, Reginald, *Bailout* (1980); Wyden, Peter, *The Unknown Iacocca* (1987).

Illinois and Michigan Canal

The first canal constructed in the state, the Illinois and Michigan Canal ran along the old portage route between the Chicago and Des Plaines Rivers and connected the Mississippi system with the Great Lakes. The result was a business boom in the 1830s and 1840s for Chicago, which transshipped goods from the interior to the Erie Canal via the lake route.

See also Canals.

Illinois Central Gulf Railway (ICG)

Formed in 1972 by the combination of the Illinois Central and the Gulf, Mobile & Ohio systems, the Illinois Central Gulf is a 13-state company that bridges the country between the Great Lakes and the Gulf of Mexico. The company also has bus and truck interests, extensive coal reserves, and connections throughout one of America's highly industrialized regions. It has emphasized computer control of freight, keeping empty cars to a minimum, tracking loaded cars, and coordinating use of cars from other carriers. It has also experimented with a special intermodal concept called "Slingshot," developed by a joint labor-management team. Slingshot allowed short piggyback trains between Chicago and St. Louis to be operated with two-man crews, a concept that has since become universal on most railroads, eliminating the caboose in favor of a computerized monitoring box attached to the rear coupler and signal lines of the last car. This system reduces the five-man standard freight crew to the engineer and conductor, both riding in the engine cab. As with most mergers, the promise of the new company of better service has yet to be seen over the whole operation. Some individual customers sometimes suffered. Crown-Zellerbach at Bogalusa, Louisiana, found its rail service cut in half from two to one train a day. The merger was opposed by both the federal government and the state of Mississippi, but the new company's willingness to take on several faltering smaller lines won the day. More recently, however, ICG has led the way in downsizing its rail operations, spinning off unwanted portions of its empire into independent short lines and reducing its mainline from over 9,000 miles to under 3,000.

See also Gulf, Mobile & Ohio Railroad; Illinois Central Railroad.

References Drury, George H., *The Historical Guide to North American Railroads* (1985); Drury, George H., *The Train-Watcher's Guide* (1990); Hubbard, Freeman, *Encyclopedia of North American Railroading* (1981); Nock, O. S., *Railways of the USA* (1979); Saunders, Richard, *The Railroad Mergers and the Coming of Conrail* (1978).

Illinois Central Railroad (IC)

Authorized in the first railroad land grant in American history in 1850, the Illinois Central received 3.6 million acres of federal land in alternate sections only in the state of Illinois in what proved to be a forerunner of federal policy within ten years under the administration of President Abraham Lincoln, once one of IC's attorneys. The railroad was not allowed to sell any of its land until the federal lands next to the grant had been occupied, a process that took a mere two years. But during this time the railroad company was essentially without money. The original charter allowed the railroad to construct its line from the southern terminus of the Illinois and Michigan Canal to the junction of the Ohio and Mississippi

Rivers at Cairo, with branches to Chicago and Dubuque, Iowa. It would take until 1869 to bridge the Mississippi on the latter leg.

Using former Erie Canal engineers and later, Civil War heroes like George B. McClellan and Grenville M. Dodge, the IC pushed forward to complete its mainline by 1856. Otherwise it would lose all of its land grants. Using every expedient including rails laid so fast and haphazardly that train crews expressed great reservations about using them, the job was done. The IC did not miss a lick with the general public. Parties were thrown as the railhead passed through small towns, and agricultural information, advice, educational grants and schools, and even blooded livestock were handed out at every turn. In Chicago the IC built a four-and-a-half-mile breakwater to keep Lake Michigan out of the city during storms. The IC also helped develop southern Illinois coalfields, which provided much of its freight over the years.

Meanwhile, the IC took its rail cargoes south from Cairo in its own fleet of steamboats. It was two IC-owned steamboats, the *Natchez* and the *Robert E. Lee*, that engaged in one of the most famous races in American history in 1870. Learning that the Mississippi Central Railroad was in financial trouble after the Civil War, the IC moved quickly to secure this line and move to complete it for direct access to New Orleans. More than 100 smaller lines eventually went into the makeup of the IC rail empire. It set an all-time one-day record for passengers carried by a railroad during the 1893 Columbian Exposition at Chicago when the IC brought 263,282 in specials and 241,832 in regularly scheduled trains. Among its engineers on this day was the legendary Casey Jones. To increase the ease of commuter traffic into Chicago, the IC pioneered so-called double-enders, engines that ran as easily backward as forward. Other IC firsts were interlocking switches that threw a series of turnouts at one time, guaranteeing safety, refrigerator cars to haul fresh fruit, and labor-management teams that jointly sought better ways to gain more business.

Illinois Central passenger trains were famous for quality. Its emblem was the green diamond (many coal roads like the IC used the diamond, including the Reading, Lehigh Valley, and Erie, coal being "black diamonds" in rail slang). The Diamond Special, the Day Light Special, the Panama Limited, the Green Diamond (a unique one-unit, articulated streamliner, where the cars shared the trucks of those that preceded and followed them), and the famous City of New Orleans cut the running time between Chicago and New Orleans to under 16 hours. But the automobile made heavy inroads on passenger use, and the once-proud trains began to fade from use, now only celebrated in song and fable. In 1971 IC joined with competitor Gulf, Mobile & Ohio to form the Illinois Central Gulf Railroad. It was the first merger or reorganization from adverse economic pressures in IC's history.

See also Gulf, Mobile & Ohio Railroad; Illinois Central Gulf Railway.

References Drury, George H., *The Historical Guide to North American Railroads* (1985); Drury, George H., *The Train-Watcher's Guide* (1990); Grow, Lawrence, *On the 8:02* (1979); Hubbard, Freeman, *Encyclopedia of North American Railroading* (1981); Lyon, Peter, *To Hell in a Day Coach* (1968); Nock, O. S., *Railways of the USA* (1979); Somers, Paul M., "Illinois Central *Green Diamond*," *Model Railroader* (May 1990) 57: 84–89; Stover, John F., *History of the Illinois Central Railroad* (1975); Stover, John F., "The Illinois Central Railroad," in Keith L. Bryant, Jr. (ed.), *EABHB: Railroads in the Age of Regulation* (1988), 222–224, and in Robert L. Frey (ed.), *EABHB: Railroads in the Nineteenth Century* (1988), 193–195.

Illinois Waterway

Utilizing the various indigenous river systems, old transportation canals, and the Chicago sanitary canals, Illinois completed the Illinois Waterway, a modern shipping channel that is 327 miles long and a direct route between Chicago and the Deep South in the twentieth century.

See also Canals.

Inland Waterways

Inland waterways are composed of navigable rivers, canals, and tidal estuaries and bayous behind coastal islands, as opposed to the oceans or high seas.

See also Canals; Intracoastal Waterway.

Inter-American Highway

That part of the Pan American highway extending south from Laredo, Texas, to Panama City is called the Inter-American Highway and was the first foreign-aid sponsored highway in American history.

See also Pan American Highway; Roads and Highways since World War I.

Reference U.S. Department of Transportation, Federal Highway Administration, *America's Highways* (1976).

Intermodal Freight

Intermodal is one of those new words that does not appear in many dictionaries or encyclopedias. It essentially means moving an item in one receptacle by more than one carrier during a single journey. It is related to two other concepts: "piggyback," where the receptacle is a truck semitrailer with wheels and "container," where the receptacle is a trailerlike box without wheels. Technically, a packed barrel is a form of intermodal freight, so although the word is new, the concept is not. Intermodal is merely the most recent solution to an age-old problem—how to handle less-than-carload (LCL) freight efficiently and profitably.

One of railroading's biggest problems historically has been that much of the freight was not in boxcar-sized loads, no matter the size of the car. This meant that the cargo had to be man-handled on board at the beginning rail terminal and removed the same way at each interchange or transfer point and at the end of the trip. The result was a lot of jobs, but a real logjam in the flow of traffic, as the cargo had to be split up into its component parts at each step of the journey. In the nineteenth century, the first real practitioners of modern intermodal freight loading were circuses. The circus train is little more than a preview of the modern container-on-flatcar (COFC) or trailer-on-flatcar (TOFC or piggyback) concepts. The same thing was done in various geographic areas (New York, for example) when railroads would load up farmers, their horses, and produce-filled wagons on trains and carry them to market and back. The loading of the animal cages and wagons over the end sills of the freight cars by a ramp is still called "circus loading."

In the twentieth century, the concept of "land bridge" has come into vogue. This is the notion that cargoes coming in from the Pacific Rim countries can cross North America faster by the sea-land (hence the name of a modern container shipper, Sea-Land) connection than by using the Panama Canal. This is true, but only if the cargoes are loaded into boxes at the beginning of the journey, transferred from conveyance to conveyance, and never have to be unloaded until the end. Hence intermodal freight got its biggest boost from international trade, a phenomenon of the post–World War II era. But its beginnings were solely domestic, stemming from the nineteenth-century circus approach to handling LCL cargoes by rail car.

The more a cargo is handled the less profit a carrier makes hauling it. This is the basic problem of LCL freight. A whole train of LCL boxcars can mean very little profit per ton-mile traveled, and a lot of freight is LCL. The result was the entrance of trucking into the freight market early in the modern era. Trucks could carry the LCL freight with less handling. But soon the trucks became more than an extension of railroad freight carriage. They became active competitors. Among the first rail carriers to approach a solution to this dilemma were the New York Central Lines and the Pennsylvania Railroad. They invented small (6 x 9 x 7.5 feet) steel containers that could haul 6,000 pounds of cargo. But the weight tradeoff was high as the empty containers weighed 2,800 pounds apiece. The New York Central put these containers on gondolas in a dozen pairs (on a subline called LCL Company), the Pennsy on flatcars in a configuration of six laid end-to-end (known as Keystone Container Car Company). But the concept was the same—an efficient handling of LCL freight.

Like the two railroads, Acme Fast Freight Line, a private hauling company, created small containers that they placed on their own private flatcars in eight pairs. The containers were constructed of plywood with steel reinforcing on the end joints and doors, and rode on spring-cushioned floors that sprung up to hold the cargo snug and safe. To make the haul attractive the railroads priced the goods by the mile regardless of what was carried or who originated the haul. But the Interstate Commerce Commission (ICC), acting on a trucker's complaint, forced the costs to be figured by class of cargo, a restriction that plagued containerized freight until its deregulation by the 1980 Staggers Rail Act. Meanwhile, in Chicago, the North Shore commuter line instituted a policy of hauling two trailers per flatcar to expedite the movement of goods through the city and its environs. This was the first commercialized use of piggyback (TOFC) operations. But it was limited in its approach in that the trailers had to be specially made to conform to special clearances imposed by the trackage of its elevated inner-city section.

The coming of the Great Depression put the railroads in a real bind. The whole economy fell off rapidly, which resulted in a decrease of rail traffic (as much as 50 percent in some cases) but a rise in costs. The Chicago Great Western (CGW) Railroad, a Granger line characterized as a mountain railroad in a prairie serving a traffic vacuum, was about to go under. Such pressure brought about innovation, and it came from the railroad's transportation of the circus throughout the Midwest. In 1935, the CGW began moving trailers lashed to common flatcars from Chicago to Dubuque. The CGW was joined in its efforts by the eastern-based New Haven in 1937, which carried trailers from New York to Boston. All that was needed in either case was a trailer modified by the addition of lashing rings to its four corners to secure the cargo. The New Haven also added a new twist— for each loaded trailer carried, a shipper could send or return an empty. Soon the Chicago, Burlington & Quincy and the

Chicago & Eastern Illinois added similar service to their offerings. The modern intermodal era had truly begun.

The success of the 1930s was delayed by the advent of World War II. The railroads were now hauling massive bulk cargoes for the war effort, and the LCL freight nearly disappeared. After the war, intermodal was slow to recover until an ex-trucker with an interest in railroading, Gene Ryan, came along. In 1952, Ryan organized a private piggyback company called Rail-Trailer that was to specialize in the creation and carrying of TOFC cargoes. In cooperation with General Motors (GM), he solved two problems—he designed a special car that would carry two 35-foot (the highway length limit then) semitrailers and he developed a forklift device that would load and unload trailers, obviating the need for the presence of a tractor and a skilled driver who could back up several hundred feet without a mishap. The only problem was that a specialized trailer terminal had to be built to utilize the system, with the tracks sunk into the ground.

But Ryan had gotten the ball rolling. Shortly thereafter, rail giant Southern Pacific (SP) entered the intermodal world. It decided to try out the Ryan system with a few new twists. SP would use the TOFC service solely within the state of California to bypass the ICC rate rulings, and it would develop its own truck line, Pacific Motor Transport, to handle the ground travel away from and to the train. The entrance of SP into the TOFC market forced other railroads to compete. The New Haven decided to file 20 questions (later reduced to 12) with the ICC to change the rate structure of TOFC. The result was a ruling that allowed several variations in TOFC: a system where the whole operation could be owned by the railroad, where it could be split between the railroad company and the shipper, or where the railroad could haul private trailers on private cars, all owned by different companies. Now piggyback services had spread from the East to the Midwest and jumped to the Pacific Coast. The Illinois Central took the concept south, although this area would

always trail the other regions in its adoption of TOFC. The only section not yet in the TOFC picture were the transcontinental western lines.

The slow adoption of TOFC was the direct result of its experimental nature and complexity. It took up to 40 pieces of tie-down equipment per car (the invention of the moveable, collapsible fifth wheel hitch, conceived on the back of a lunch napkin, solved this). There was a labor argument as to which labor group would represent the workers, the Teamsters or traditional rail unions (a deal cut with Jimmy Hoffa to protect truck jobs cleared this up). Finally, the technology of car building had to be advanced further. Ryan's GM flatcar had not panned out. Trailers were still carried on common flats. Several car builders came up with ideas on how to haul trailers and tie them down. Trailers themselves had to be strengthened to stand up under the stresses of rail traffic, something that Fruehauf quickly did. One plan even called for trailers to be built with highway and rail wheels that could eliminate the need for special rail cars all together, but the system proved unstable. Finally, an old idea, the container, had spread to international shippers. Several steamship lines, especially in the Pacific, were utilizing containers in 20- and 40-foot lengths (later extended to 48 and 53 feet as state and federal highway regulations were modified). The trailer was about to be joined by wheeless boxes that had to be accommodated on new or existing rail cars.

The most successful device to come out of this "first generation" of intermodal equipment was a Fruehauf-developed system known as Flexi-Van. This consisted of a specially built flatcar that had a swiveled platform at each end. The truck would back up perpendicular to the car and engage its trailer on a pair of guide rails on the swivel platform. Then the trailer wheels would be disconnected and braked, and the trailer (now a container) would be backed on to the platform, which was swiveled 90 degrees and locked in place. Unloading was the exact reverse process. The New York Central mainly used the Flexi-Van system, although it also made an appearance on the Milwaukee Road, the Seaboard Airline, and the Illinois Central.

The success of Flexi-Van led to a pooling of all intermodal interests into a new entity named Trailer Train (TTX). The second generation of intermodal had begun. Trailer Train began to develop new flats designed to haul two trailers of the longest lengths legally allowed on America's highways. The resulting cars went from 75 to 85 feet in length and created real worries among railroaders that they were too long to be horizontally stable. To meet that concern, TTX developed a "safe" 50-footer. But the tradeoff in weight and maintenance of the shorter equipment was not as cost effective. Meanwhile the new company began to sign up rail lines as participants. For the first time, the transcontinentals joined. Large trailer-leasing agencies like Gene Ryan's Van Pool, XTRA (which introduced the idea of intermediate "rest stops" where the lease could be put on hold a few days until a new cargo developed), and Realco (a creation of the nearly defunct Railway Express Agency) sprang up anew, eventually to absorb Van Pool, which ultimately was sold to Transamerica. All were established to fulfill the traffic requirements of TOFC's expansion.

One of the biggest private users of TOFC was United Parcel Service (UPS). Originally a delivery service for downtown stores to their suburban customers, UPS was nearly put out of business by the shopping center and the automobile. Shifting to parcel service in competition with the U. S. Post Office, UPS started with shipments between San Diego and Los Angeles. They then expanded into the Great Lakes region and the Florida peninsula. It was the Florida expansion that caused UPS to turn to TOFC—the incoming to outgoing ratio was 15 to 1, much too lopsided to make Florida profitable any other way. The railroads began to use UPS's TOFC to replace their failing passenger services. UPS did much to bring the TOFC concept to the transcontinentals as it bridged the whole nation in the 1970s. Terminals were modernized with forklift devices called Piggypackers that could unload cars from the side without any special ramps or sunken tracks. Other terminals used new self-propelled Drott cranes (originally used in the lumber industry) that straddled the tracks and could position trailers and containers on or off the cars with precision from the top—especially important for containers.

On the rails, more experiments marked the second generation of intermodal. The Santa Fe became interested in the land bridge concept and suggested that it and New York Central develop a joint program of hauling freight between Los Angeles and New York City by way of Chicago. The system, called Super C, would use multiple passenger-geared diesels (for speed). After speed-testing on Santa Fe's Illinois Division (using an engine-to-weight ratio of 7.8 horsepower per ton), the pilot run made the trip from New York to Los Angeles in just over 51 hours, 8 hours faster than hoped for. Speeds ranged up to 90 miles per hour. But Southern Pacific (SP) had a prior agreement to ship perishables to New York City from California, and threatened to pull this profitable trade if the Santa Fe deal went through. The financially strapped New York Central needed the SP "car count" and pulled out of the pending TOFC deal. Santa Fe went on alone, but without its eastern partner the program failed. But it did reveal the fact that handling heavier intermodal loads at high speeds called for redesigned cars with a lower center of gravity, better braking, elimination of slack, and smooth power evenly distributed throughout the consist, provided by streamlined motive units like the ones that once pulled the passenger trains.

As Santa Fe struggled with its Super C program, other railroads advanced intermodal. The Illinois Central (IC) managed to negotiate the reduction of its crew on intermodal between Chicago and St. Louis to two men in the locomotive cab. These speedy runs, known as Slingshot, had capitalized on the potential loss of jobs. IC guaranteed jobs if they could provide a profitable, cost-effective service. Inspired by the

IC's success and bolstered by a federal government loan, the failing Milwaukee Road inaugurated a similar program, which it nicknamed Sprint. Burlington Northern, Norfolk Southern, Santa Fe, and Southern Pacific soon followed, initiating their own speedy intermodal programs and reduced crews. Norfolk Southern's program relied on the rebirth of the trailer with road and rail wheels idea, dubbed the Mark IV Road-Railer, in a program called Triple Crown Services. But the high initial costs of equipping the trailers spelled doom for the carless rail trailers. A similar program on the Illinois Central failed when the unions refused to permit the trains to run without traditional caboose crews, despite the success of the earlier Slingshot trains.

But the 1970s gave way to a new decade that began with the deregulation of the railroads through the Staggers Rail Act of 1980. It was critical to the expansion of intermodal traffic because it eliminated restrictions on price and service charges and allowed railroads to combine their intermodal services with company-owned truck firms without fear of antitrust violations. The result was an unprecedented growth spurt, assisted by the arrival of important third-generation rail car technology that affected both TOFC and COFC carrying methods. The first development was the "spine car," in which all of the car's superstructure was cut away except for a foothold for the trailer wheels. In addition, the cars were joined or articulated in groups of six or ten, each carrying one trailer, with the intermediate cars sharing a pair or "truck" of rail wheels. Only the end cars had the normal automatic coupler; the rest were permanently joined with an inflexible pin that acted as a bolster. Commonly called six-packs or ten-packs, Santa Fe, which developed the concept, labeled them "fuel foilers" because that is what they did—saved fuel. A similar concept was the Front Runner, a spine car with European-style fixed wheels—a pair on a single axle at each end. At first the Front Runner had bad stability problems, but TTX refitted the cars at some expense, convinced of their efficacy.

After the spine cars came the depressed-well container car. Built by Budd Company, a former specialist in passenger cars that had seen its business decline precipitously, the well cars could carry two 40-foot containers stacked on top of each other. The result was a very low center of gravity and a car and load that would clear most current track obstructions. It too was run in articulated fashion, usually five to a unit. The BUDX 2000 well car is known as a Thrall Car after its ultimate marketing contractor. A similar unit, also run as an articulated five-car combination, was the ACF double-stack. Developed by American Car Foundry (ACF) and Southern Pacific for SP's customer Sea-Land, the ACF double-stack held its containers in place and took their weight on its sides, eliminating the need for a center sill. It is commonly referred to as a Gunderson car after the name of its final contractor. More unique was the Santa Fe experiment called the A-Stack. It was a spine car without platforms to receive trailer wheels. Instead it had a special fiberglass container that looked like a squashed "A" and rode over the spine. These could be double-stacked since their roofs fit into their bases. Santa Fe made only one set of these—the fiberglass containers carried so much product that they violated over-the-road truck weights, even for the interstates.

Two other new concepts that had their origins in the near past were the Pogie Bogie and the Iron Highway. The Pogie Bogie was a two-trucked platform that received the rear wheels of one trailer and the front wheels of another. It was not connected with a spine, but relied on the semitrailer for its center. Only an air/signal hose ran between the bogies. It was conceived for short hauls from rural terminals to an intermodal hub, but it has made its name in urban areas like New York City, where it is used to hook up trailers quickly to circumvent crowded city traffic by utilizing the Long Island Rail Road commuter line. The Iron Highway is a "high-productivity integral train" (H-PIT) that has a control cab at each end and 28-foot platforms (the size of a domestic container) that form a continuous, slack-free bed with power to multiple axles through an automatic-transmission–fluid torque converter—almost like front-wheel-drive automobiles. Each ramp can be lowered to the ground for loading or unloading, giving the unit maximum flexibility. It is still in the experimental stages.

The final newcomer is the so-called 125-ton Maxi-Stack car. Constructed by Thrall and Gunderson in three series, it is currently a five-car articulated unit that can accept 48-foot containers in the well, topped off by the even longer 53-foot containers. Because the domestic container market uses different length containers (28, 48, and 53 feet long) than the overseas shippers (20- and 40-footers), the loads of a pair of domestic containers mounted on an international one can exceed the 125-ton limit. Hence, manufacturers have created the Husky Stack, a stand-alone, depressed-well car that lacks an articulated end, both ends being supported by double-axle trucks with automatic couplers like a standard rail car. These units can carry a 48-foot well container topped off by two 28-footers. Because the 28-foot domestic containers are singly shorter but combined longer than any bottom container, a special rack known as an Ingrahm saddle fits over the lower container to provide a bed for the uppers. The efficacy of double-stack containers can be seen in the fact that they cost $100 less per container per 1,000 miles to haul than any other type of intermodal freight.

Intermodal has come a long way in its 60 years since the Chicago Great Western began its service between Chicago and Dubuque. Combined with deregulation, it has saved the American railroad. Although the TOFC market is still strong, 1992 saw COFC units exceed trailers for the first time. Given the increasingly international nature of trade and the preferred use of special container ships, there seems to be no end to its future as a mainstay of American and international transportation.

See also Containers; Intermodal Surface Transportation Efficiency Act of 1991; Merchant Marine; Railroads from Appomattox to Deregulation.

References Buford, Curtis D., *Trailer Train Company* (1982); DeBoer, David J., *Piggyback and Containers* (1992); Dozell, Gary W., "The Train They Call Sprint," *Trains* (April 1981) 41: 26–33; Frailey, Fred W., "Super C: Hottest of the Hotshots," *Trains* (May 1986) 46: 42–53; Frailey, Fred W., "Al Perlman Was Right," *Trains* (August 1994) 54: 70–71; Grant, H. Roger, "The Chicago Great Western Railroad: Piggyback Pioneer," *Trains* (January 1986) 46: 31–34; Grant, H. Roger, "Piggyback/Trailers-on-Flatcars," in Keith L. Bryant, Jr. (ed.), *EABHB: Railroads in the Age of Regulation* (1988), 348–349; Ingles, J. David, "Milwaukee Road—Still Sprinting Along," *Trains* (September 1983) 43: 17; Margetts, F. C., "The Marriage of Road and Rail: Trains for Tomorrow," *Trains* (April 1976) 36: 40–47; Morgan, David P. "Piggyback: The Most Realistic Approach," *Trains* (May 1955) 15: 7; Odegard, Gordon, "Santa Fe 10-Pack," *Model Railroader* (September 1982) 49: 58–61; Saunders, Richard, "Alfred E. Perlman," in Keith L. Bryant, Jr. (ed.), *EABHB: Railroads in the Age of Regulation* (1988), 341–348; Sperandeo, Andy, "Santa Fe Piggyback Conversions," *Model Railroader* (December 1984) 51: 104–109; Transportation Research Board, *Intermodal Marine Container Transportation* (1992); Treiman, Larry, "Containers Instead of a New [Panama] Canal: The Ultimate Land-Bridge," *Trains* (May 1975) 35: 36–39.

Intermodal Surface Transportation Efficiency Act of 1991 (ISTEA)

Sometimes referred to as the Motor Carrier Act of 1991, the Intermodal Surface Transportation Efficiency Act (ISTEA) established a new view of national transportation that was to be efficient, environmentally sound, capable of competing favorably with the world economy, and that would move people and goods in an energy-efficient manner. Modern theorists posit that the mode of transportation is relatively unimportant. What counts now is quality, cost, time, and safety. The old emphasis on a single mode is to be set aside; for the first time in history the impetus is toward an intermodal movement of goods and people in an integrated network called the National Transportation system (NTS). The NTS will focus on varied transportation of cargoes (sea, land, air) in a partnership of governmental and private entities. As of 1994 it was estimated that 37 percent of all freight is carried in an intermodal manner using containers.

The magnitude and importance of the problem can be seen in just one transportation mode of the city of Chicago where daily traffic includes 83 commuter trains, 4 Amtrak trains, and 60 to 100 freight trains with a 98 percent on-time factor. This excludes traffic on the Great Lakes, highways, and in the air that must also meld with the rail movement. A major problem in big cities has been the congested intercity areas and thoroughfares where businesses have located in the past. The first area to integrate all modes of transportation into one modern facility has been the Dallas-Fort Worth area, whose DFW International airport is now an intermodal hub for the whole region with container, auto, truck, train, and air freight at one easily accessible location. In 1994 the nation spent $226 billion on integrating its transportation with 33 percent of the money coming from federal funds, 17 percent from state authorities, and 50 percent from private sources. In conjunction with the national political inclination toward state and local management of national problems to meet unique local conditions, the ISTEA has emphasized working with Municipal Planning Organizations (MPOs) to achieve a locally responsive answer to national and even international transportation demands.

See also Containers; Intermodal Freight; Motor Carrier Acts.

Reference U.S. Department of Transportation, National Committee on Intermodal Transportation, *Toward a National Intermodal Transportation System* (1994).

Internal Improvements

A term commonly used prior to the American Civil War to describe transportation projects, especially roads and canals.

International Brotherhood of Teamsters (IBT)

The main changes affecting the character of the intercity trucking industry from 1940 to 1980 were the introduction of federal regulation through the Interstate Commerce Commission (ICC) and the rise of the International Brotherhood of Teamsters. By 1983, the IBT was the nation's largest union with 1.6 million members. It controlled not only truck drivers but workers in a host of related and unrelated industries. Its members were organized in 750 locals, 48 joint councils, and 5 area conferences. Ultimate authority rests with the general union conference, which meets every five years. Between conventions the authority rests with its elected officials: the general president, the general secretary, and the executive board. It is no secret that the IBT has been embroiled in what one historian called "far from exemplary" leadership and politics, which have led to an extended legal confrontation with the federal government.

The teamsters trace their heritage back to pre–Civil War days when eastern city draymen began to organize to gain safer, more reasonable working conditions. Gradually, the drivers came to be differentiated from small drayage operators and by 1899, the teamsters were part of the American Federation of Labor (AFL). Membership was limited to those who drove or operated businesses with six or fewer teams. As many of the drivers owned their teams, the first organization efforts produced increased freight rates as opposed to higher wages. In 1902, the drivers who did not own any teams organized separately as the Teamsters National Union. The AFL merged both groups in 1903 into the IBT, and added truck drivers to their number with a name change in 1910 that included warehousemen, chauffeurs, and helpers.

Several jurisdictions remained outside the national organization until the mid-1930s, principally in Chicago. But in its early days, teamsters and truckers tended to stay in a local jurisdiction, even with the beginnings of cross-country trucking in the 1920s. Cross-country drivers were considered the cream of the talent and were so highly paid that they needed no union assistance. But all that changed with the Great Depression. Then three men, Dave Beck of Seattle, Jimmy Hoffa of Detroit, and Farrell Dobbs of Minneapolis, began maneuvering to represent over-the-road drivers. They saw the road men as the key to the whole industry. But by 1940, none of these three had gone national.

The reason for the lag in a national organization was the autonomy and strength of the locals. The first national union head, Dan Tobin, realized this power of the locals and ran the union to permit such decentralization on a platform of honest but weak leadership. This allowed the locals to be as honest or corrupt as they desired. The powerful local leaders resented the notion advanced by Beck, Hoffa, and Dobbs for national leadership as it would compromise their positions. Meanwhile, the three potential national organizers used secondary boycotts and strikes in areas where they were strong to expand their control regionally as much as possible. They were assisted in this by the legislation of the New Deal and the use of thugs and intimidation when drivers failed to see where their future lay. The National Labor Relations Board chose to see such tactics as "inducement" rather than illegal coercion.

In 1952, Dave Beck achieved the union leadership and Hoffa became a vice-president who would step into the top position when Beck ran afoul of the campaign of John McClellan's Senate Rackets Committee and its vigorous counsel, Robert F. Kennedy. As Beck became enmeshed in his legal problems, which led the IBT to withdraw from the AFL in 1957, Hoffa advanced his notion of national control and the policy by which he hoped to achieve that—the National Master Freight Agreement (NMFA). Before 1953, the various labor contracts never were unified beyond the area command, and often even lower down than that. Hoffa first sought to equalize the rates of all drivers, a policy that was highly attractive to places with a low wage scale, such as the South. This also made them dependent on the national for their standard of living. It took him until 1961 to bring all of the locals under his control.

Within three years, Hoffa had negotiated the NMFA—one standard contract nationwide. It was a triumph of his organizational and negotiating genius. The truck owners liked it because it kept everything rolling with few disruptions—something that had plagued the industry from the start. Hoffa was assisted involuntarily by government policy under the Motor Carrier Act of 1935, which set high standards for new owners to come into the industry. By the 1960s, the number of owners had declined precipitously as mergers and attrition cut them back. But Hoffa still had to give the locals more leeway than he liked to gain their support for his administration. Such autonomy meant wildcat strikes, something the owners hated. Worse yet, Hoffa also followed Beck into the federal prison system in 1967, leaving a lesser breed of men to run things so laboriously built up over the years. None of them could approach the popularity of "Little Jimmy" among the drivers, something that may have contributed to his failed attempt to regain union leadership privileges after his pardon and his mysterious death.

Hoffa and his successors managed to negotiate six NMFAs between 1964 and 1980, when the industry was deregulated and the power of the union driver began to decline in favor of the nonunion independent, less-than-truckload cargoes, the small-business fleet owner, and the rebirth of rail competition for the more profitable long hauls in the form of trailer-on-flatcar (TOFC) cartage. The Great Shakeout, as it has been called, split the industry into a form that only old Dan Tobin might have recognized. The NMFAs negotiated in 1985 now had to be drawn up between union drivers and multiple new trucking industry representatives. New hires were to be paid a lower rate, and the haulers agreed not to attempt to de-unionize their operations. But deregulation operates in transportation industries like a snowball rolling down a hill—it has just grown bigger and faster and more destructive to the world that Dave Beck, Jimmy Hoffa, and Farrell Dobbs created years ago.

See also Motor Carrier Acts; Trucking.

References Garnel, Donald, *The Rise of Teamster Power in the West* (1972); James, Ralph C., and Estelle Dinnerstein James, *Hoffa and the Teamsters* (1965); Levinson, Harold M., "Collective Bargaining and Technological Change in the Trucking Industry," in Gerald G. Somers (ed.), *Collective Bargaining* (1980), 4–84; Levinson, Harold M.,

"Trucking," in Gerald G. Somers (ed.), *Collective Bargaining* (1980), 99–149; Perry, Charles R., et al., *Deregulation and the Decline of the Unionized Trucking Industry* (1986).

Interstate Commerce Act (1887)

Also known as the Cullom Law, the Interstate Commerce Act was designed to achieve consistent enforcement of certain principles embedded in common law. It called for just and reasonable rates, prohibited discrimination between shippers or persons, prohibited undue preferences among geographical areas, and forbade charging more for a short haul than a long haul. Most important, it created the Interstate Commerce Commission (ICC) to regulate the act. The act was designed to stop railroad pooling, drawbacks, and rebates (collusions to control the amount of service provided beyond agreed-upon levels), forcing rail magnates to resort to other methods like traffic agreements and consolidations. The act's tenets were later modified by the Transportation Act of 1920 to permit more centralized control through voluntary consolidation over governmentally enforced competition. Its advantage to the railroads was that it established rates high enough to guarantee better profits than had pooling (which had actually lowered rates overall), something the public seemed not to be aware of, and maybe the real reason Congress voted it in. It was pretty well gutted when the U.S. Supreme Court ruled in *Counselman v. Hitchcock* 142 US 547 (1892) that witnesses before the ICC did not have to testify unless given total immunity to all related prosecution.

See also Interstate Commerce Commission; Sherman Antitrust Act.

References Counselman v. Hitchcock, 142 US 547 (1892); Faulkner, Harold U., *Politics, Reform, and Expansion* (1959); Garraty, John A., *The New Commonwealth* (1968); Haney, Lewis Henry, *A Congressional History of the Railways in the United States* (1910); Hoogenboom, Ari, "Interstate Commerce Act," in Keith L. Bryant, Jr. (ed.), *EABHB: Railroads in the Age of Regulation* (1988), 230–232; Hoogenboom, Ari, and Olive Hoogenboom, *A History of the Interstate Commerce Commission* (1976); Keeler, Theodore E., *Railroads, Freight and Public Policy* (1983); Leonard, William Norris, *Railroad Consoli-*

dation under the Transportation Act of 1920 (1946); MacAvoy, Paul W., *The Economic Effects of Regulation* (1965); Purcell, Edward A., "Ideas and Interests: Businessmen and the Interstate Commerce Act," *Journal of American History* (1967) 54: 561–578; Saunders, Richard, *The Railroad Mergers and the Coming of Conrail* (1978); Swindler, William F., *Court and Constitution in the 20th Century* (1969).

Interstate Commerce Commission (ICC)

Created by the Interstate Commerce Act, the Interstate Commerce Commission has been dismissed by historians of all viewpoints as a failure. But the historians do not agree on why. Some fault a proper balance between the interests of transportation businesses and the public, represented by government, in guaranteeing fair profits and adequate service at a reasonable cost. Others find that the ICC was taken over by the very businesses it was set up to regulate. This second group finds that the railroads and others wanted the ICC to regulate commerce to take the heat off from critics and reduce the ill-effects of cutthroat competition. A third view is that the ICC overdid its mandate and regulated the railroads so well that it in effect killed them off by driving investors to other, more profitable enterprises. Still others claim that any government administrative agency has a life cycle that includes hopeful birth, vigorous youth, devitalized maturity, and doting old age. The ICC is no exception. A final contention is that the ICC chose to fail. This hypothesis holds that through unimaginative administrators and an entrenched bureaucracy anxious to preserve the status quo, the personnel of the ICC chose not to challenge the forces ranged against them but to accommodate and record violations of its mandate. It got into a rut early on and never chose to get out of it.

The ICC came in the wake of agrarian and labor protest of the late nineteenth century that proved that the states did not have the clout necessary to fully regulate interstate commerce. Under the Constitution this is a federal function, but such grants of power go by default to the next lower level of government when not exercised. Not until 1887 did the national government assert its power in the regulatory functions of commerce through the Interstate Commerce Act. The process got off to a good start as the first administrators moved to curtail railroad combinations deemed in restraint of trade, as the Sherman Antitrust Act of 1890 put it. But throughout the 1890s, the ICC faced a hostile federal court system that undercut its mandate by granting witnesses the right to refuse to testify without immunity grants, and applied the idea of restraint of trade against labor rather than management. Moreover, Congress added safety supervision to the ICC's list of responsibilities (railroads were horrifically bad environments in which to work or travel then) without a necessary increase in personnel or appropriations.

Ignored by the railroads and angered by the court decisions—which probably revealed the complexity of the problem and Congress' sloppy lawmaking as much as an outright conspiracy to negate the process—Congress passed a series of measures during the Theodore Roosevelt, William H. Taft, and Woodrow Wilson administrations to tighten the process up. The Elkins Anti-Rebating law in 1903, the Hepburn Act in 1906 (which defined the intent to regulate fully and spelled out the penalties for disobedience for the first time in no uncertain terms), the Mann-Elkins Act of 1910 (which put the burden of proof on the accused business violators), and the Clayton Act of 1914 (the high point of government legislation during this so-called Progressive Era, which detailed what an illegal business combination was) all gave the ICC a wide variety of weapons with which to attack the allegedly unresponsive business leadership in its creation of pools, trusts, and holding companies. The ICC had a powerful ability to negate business decisions, but it did little constructively at this time. Indeed, its refusal to permit railroads to increase rates, so as to improve the poorly constructed nineteenth-century roadbeds so they would accommodate the increased and heavier traffic requirements of the twentieth century, may have been instrumental in their collapse in the advent of World War I.

By December 1917, it was obvious that the railroads could not meet the necessities of wartime traffic. The Wilson administration put the consolidation of the lines and their efficient management under the control of the United States Railroad Administration, separate from the ICC. This experiment allowed the railroads to violate the various anticonsolidation requirements of the previous congressional legislation, to raise rates, and to combine in a more efficient manner—everything that the rail managers had claimed that they needed to do since the passage of the Interstate Commerce Act in 1887. But when the government hinted that it might continue its operation of the rails after the war, the rail executives demurred and Congress agreed.

The return of the railroads to civilian control and ICC regulation once again under the Transportation Act of 1920 merely led to more confusion of the nature that had preceded the war. The few vigorous administrators were stymied by their compatriots on the board, unimaginative bureaucratic underlings, and the foot-dragging railroads. The result was that the Great Depression threw the railroads into a crisis that looked unsolvable. If they could not reduce their indebtedness and consolidate during a time of relative wealth like the 1920s, how could they survive the depression-ridden 1930s? With large fixed operating expenses, the railroads were in deep trouble as the Great Depression plunged the economy into a tightening-demand situation. Income fell rapidly. Government-underwritten loans and exemptions from antitrust legislation under government supervision failed to solve the rail problem. Of course the railroads acted as if they did not wish it solved. They organized the Association of American Railroads to keep the government at bay, and managed to get trucking and waterborne transport placed under laws similar to those that proscribed rail operations.

New laws like the Motor Carrier Act of 1935 and the Transportation Act of 1940 merely gave the ICC new duties to perform, but Congress did not insist that the ICC actually accomplish something. So the bureaucratic recording of conditions and the generation of statistics and reports continued with the reorganization of the ICC's departments and the addition of more minor bureaucrats. The efforts of imaginative men like transportation coordinator Joseph Eastman disappeared under the stultifying voting majorities of the board and the career bureaucrats. But the salvation of the railroads, as with so much of American industry and agriculture, came not so much from the effects of the ICC's administration of the New Deal as from the expansion of demand called forth by World War II. Franklin Roosevelt did not place the railroads under federal control as had Wilson. He placed Ralph Budd, a railroad man, in a position under Eastman to suggest what federal policy might be if federal control existed. The railroads, anxious to keep the government out of their business as much as possible, took the hints and the rails functioned magnificently throughout the war period, and profits soared.

But the victory ended all that. After the war, the railroads received an exemption to the antitrust laws in the form of the Reed-Bullwinkle Act, but the supervision of the ICC continued. The ICC process for everything by now had become a ponderous thing. Regulated businesses had to wait so long for ICC decisions that the reasons for them actually disappeared by the time permission was secured. Established procedure was the watchword of the day. Red tape and bureaucracy were the norm. By the middle of the 1950s, people began to suggest that the problem with transportation, particularly railroads, was too much regulation, not too little. The Transportation Act of 1958 began to codify this view by permitting changing rates and discontinuation of passenger service with less government interference. But the entrenched habits of the ICC continued with the best of intentions.

President John F. Kennedy added his voice to the critics of American transportation policy, calling for more open competition and less government regulation, but he had other, more-pressing problems to consider during his short term. The ICC failed to come to grips with the notion of intermodal transport (trailers and containers moved by ship, rail, barge, and truck combinations). When the Southern Railroad came up with an innovative, giant aluminum covered hopper car called the Big John, the ICC refused to allow the railroad to cut prices as it might adversely affect other modes of transportation. Of course such a decision undercut the desire to spend any more money in research and development of such cost-saving procedures thereafter—and adversely affected the railroads. The ICC also worked its influence to prevent all forms of transport to keep up with inflation. Reacting to public criticism, the ICC overcompensated and began to permit rail mergers right and left. Many were necessary, but the stench from the failed Penn Central merger hung heavy over the ICC's failure to check out the facts independently. When the ICC did check things out more fully, as in Judge Nathan Klintenic's suggested merger of all western railroads into four strong systems, it placed unrealistic conditions on the railroads. It vacillated back and forth so much in the case of the Rock Island Line, where it seemed best to let the slowly sinking railroad be merged with the Union Pacific (UP), that the ICC alienated the UP and caused the Rock Island to fall precipitously into bankruptcy.

The ICC did much better in the case of the Trunk Line crisis. Trunk lines were the several railroads that hauled goods between Chicago and St. Louis and the East Coast. They hauled about half of the rail traffic in the United States for over half of the population. Nonetheless, several lines sunk into serious financial difficulties in the 1970s, and the ICC worked with Congress to help create the Consolidated Rail Corporation (Conrail) to clear the problem up and eventually chart the course that took the combined trunk lines back into profitable operation. It also allowed the creation of Burlington Northern in the West, a combination of the Chicago, Burlington & Quincy, the Great Northern, and the

Northern Pacific. The ICC decision to combine these three lines into one giant rail operation reversed the U.S. Supreme Court's decision in the 1905 Northern Securities case, the hallmark of Theodore Roosevelt's trust-busting reputation. The ICC also showed great imagination in permitting the Chicago & North Western Railway (C&NW) to be reorganized as an employee-owned corporation.

The Conrail, Burlington Northern, and C&NW cases were the wave of the future. But this future, one of deregulation of transportation industries, has actually placed the ICC at jeopardy—a sort of suicide, as it were. As the Airline Deregulation Act of 1978, the Motor Carrier Act of 1980, and the Staggers Rail Act of the same year demonstrated, the role of the ICC began to diminish proporionately as the need for regulation declined. Entrance restrictions into transportation fields, the centerpiece of the New Deal, have fallen away. Combinations of railroads, the opposition to which was the reason for setting up the ICC in the first place, are now commonplace.

The deregulation drive has done something that the ICC regulators never seemed able to grasp before. It has made many big companies more viable by their consolidation and dropping of unprofitable services in favor of the money-earners of the current age, intermodal traffic. At the same time it has opened up the way for the creation of a multitude of smaller companies to assume the once unprofitable branch lines that the regulated industry had to operate as a condition of business. These smaller firms can operate the short lines to the consumer's advantage. The key is in flexible rates set without the interference of the federal government. The main loser in this process has been unionized labor. The numerous smaller firms operate on a close profit margin that precludes the higher wages that were once a standard of big industry. And downsizing means lower wages, fewer jobs, and more independent contractors competing for business—conditions not amenable so far to traditional labor organization.

Deregulation is still partial; the ICC does have a supervisory role, be it much reduced. How far deregulation may go is problematic, but the House of Representatives voted in 1994 to abolish the ICC because of its reduced functions under deregulation policies, and because it now costs $47 million a year to keep up at a time when the competition for dollars by government programs has tightened up. Whether the Senate and the executive branch will ever concur remains a matter of conjecture. But much of the paperwork that unregulated industries like trucking were required to submit to the ICC was canceled in August 1994, leading one to think that more deregulation is on the way. And one of the casualties of governmental reform in the Republican congressional landslide of November 1994 is rumored to be the ICC.

See also Interstate Commerce Act; Safety Appliance Act; Sherman Antitrust Act.

References Aitchison, Clyde B., "The Evolution of the Interstate Commerce Act: 1887–1937," *George Washington University Law Review* (March 1937) 5: 289–403; Carson, Robert B., *Main Line to Oblivion* (1971); Fellmeth, Robert C., *The Interstate Commerce Omission* (1970); Friedlaender, Ann F., *Dilemma of Freight Transport Regulation* (1969); Hilton, George W., "The Consistency of the Interstate Commerce Act," *Journal of Law and Economics* (1966) 9: 87–113; Hoogenboom, Ari, and Olive Hoogenboom, *A History of the ICC* (1976); Kolko, Gabriel, *Railroads and Regulation* (1965); MacAvoy, Paul W., *The Crisis of the Regulatory Commissions* (1970); McCraw, Thomas K., "Regulation in America: A Review Article," *Business History Review* (1975) 49: 159–183; Marshall, Jonathan, "Cheap Truckin'," *National Review* (7 November 1994) 46: 54–56; Martin, Albro, *Enterprise Denied* (1971); Martin, Albro, "The Troubled Subject of Railroad Regulation in the Gilded Age—a Reappraisal," *Journal of American History* (1974) 61: 339–371; Martin, Albro, *Railroads Triumphant* (1992); Moore, Thomas Gale, "Rail and Trucking Deregulation," in Leonard Weiss and Michael W. Klass (eds.), *Regulatory Reform* (1986), 14–39; Porter, Glenn, *The Rise of Big Business* (1973); Sharfman, Isaiah Leo, *The Interstate Commerce Commission* (1937); Shenefield, John H., and Irwin M. Stelzer, *The Antitrust Laws: A Primer* (1993); Wilner, Frank N., "Interstate Commerce Commission," in Robert L. Frey (ed.), *EABHB: Railroads in the Nineteenth Century* (1988), 200–201.

Intracoastal Waterway

Although originally given to the inland waterway stretching along the Atlantic coast from New York City to Miami, Florida, the name Intracoastal Waterway has been extended informally to include the Gulf inland waterway running from Brownsville, Texas, to Appalachicola, Florida, which is also a part of the Mississippi River system and more accurately called the Intracoastal Canal. Secretary of the Treasury Albert Gallatin first considered the idea of an inland waterway paralleling the Atlantic coast in his *Report* of 1808. As various tidewater canals were constructed in the Middle Atlantic states during the nineteenth century, the Intracoastal was put into operation in many separate projects that were combined and regularized in the 1930s into one system for protected shipping. The canalized portions of the Intracoastal measure at least 12 feet in depth and about 90 feet across the bottom of the channel. Whenever possible the route follows coastal sounds behind sea islands, reefs, and shoals. At one time, plans were had for the development of a cross-Florida canal and the modernization of the old Delaware and Raritan Canal to cut across the neck of New Jersey, but World War II intervened and they were never completed. Nowadays, modern environmental concerns would make such projects doubtful, to say the least.

Augmenting the Intracoastal Waterway are the inland rivers, important in moving cargoes from the earliest times. Initially, the direction was only downstream, by rafts, canoes, flatboats, and keelboats that were usually broken up and sold for their lumber once their destination, usually New Orleans, was reached. Canoes could make the return upstream by staying out of the current in the shallows. Keelboats could travel upriver, but then only by superhuman (or animal) effort through polling, tow ropes and, if the wind were good and true, by sail. A keelboat, for example, took Meriwether Lewis and William Clark up the Missouri on their famous exploration of the Louisiana Purchase. But generally the current of the mighty Mississippi was too much, until

the advent of the steamboat and Captain Henry Shreve's modifications made them the queens of the inland rivers. Most boatmen, too poor to afford a steamboat ride, walked home to find a new cargo, much as future President Abraham Lincoln did in the 1820s.

To be of use, an inland river must be commercially navigable, that is, not too shallow, not too swift, and improved enough to take shallow-draft cargo vessels without danger of waterfalls, driftwood, or floating stumps (known as "sawyers"). Most such waters are tributaries of the Mississippi. The largest nonnavigable river in the lower 48 states is the Colorado. In the United States, however, 19 of its largest cities are located on ocean or inland waterways or both; the same can be said of its 26 largest states and of 90 percent of its population.

Important navigable river systems in the East include the Atlantic Intracoastal Waterway, which progresses from Long Island Sound and the lower tributaries of the Susquehanna, the Delaware, the Potomac, the Rappahannock, and the James, to the rivers entering the North Carolina Sounds—the Cape Fear, the Santee, the Savannah, and the St. Johns. Also important is the New York Barge Canal, which is comprised of the old Erie Canal, the Lake Champlain Canal, and the Hudson River, all connected to the Atlantic Intracoastal via the St. Lawrence Seaway. In the Far West, California has the Sacramento and San Joaquin Rivers as far as Stockton, and Oregon and Washington possess the Columbia-Snake basin and Puget Sound. Alaskan rivers are often the only routes to the interior, the most important system being the Yukon River and its branches.

But the East and the West are outshone by the Mississippi River and its tributaries. Including the Missouri River, the Mississippi system is one of the longest in the world at 4,000 miles. The actual source of the Mississippi is the Missouri, one of its three big branches—the others being the Ohio and the Upper Mississippi (not its true geographic source despite its name). The Mississippi system drains about 40 percent of the entire nation, and one can travel from western New York to Montana on its waters. It possesses half of the navigable waters in the United States, and carries half of the ton-miles of freight moved inland. It is the Mississippi that has the largest "tows" (a tug and its barges) and moves some of the largest bulk cargoes like coal and grain.

Of the Mississippi's branches, the Missouri is one of the longest open rivers (without dams and locks below Yankton, South Dakota), and thus one of the most difficult to navigate, as there are few pools of slack water and its upper sections go shallow to dry in summer. The Upper Mississippi above St. Louis is hampered by ice in the winter, but handles large amounts of cargo through a system of locks. In effect, it is a large canal. The Ohio River is the busiest in the country. Running from Pittsburgh to Cairo, Illinois, it has important tributaries like the Tennessee, the Cumberland, the Kannawha, the Allegheny, and the Monongahela Rivers. Like the Upper Mississippi, the Ohio is more of a canal, with dams and locks to assist navigation. Before modernization, which lengthened the locks to 1,200 feet, the tows used to "double-lock," that is to say, they would be broken into sections to fit the locks. Also important to the Mississippi is the Illinois River system that begins just north of St. Louis and is canalized to Chicago, where it funnels the Mississippi system into the St. Lawrence Seaway and eventually the New York Barge Canal. The Illinois waterway suffers from the canal section at Chicago, which is narrow, crossed by low bridges, and has small locks.

All of these branches flow into the Lower Mississippi (below Cairo), an open river, the great depth and width of which lend itself to the largest tows. The banks are packed with industry, especially petrochemicals in Louisiana. And at its mouth is New Orleans, with access to the sea and the Intracoastal Canal, actually part of the Mississippi River system. The Intracoastal can move cargoes south to Brownsville and east to Florida with connections to the Mobile River and, via the Tombigbee, to the Tennessee via the Tenn-Tom Canal, and up the Chattahoochee along the Georgia–Alabama border.

The principal means of locomotion on the inland rivers, especially the Mississippi system, is the barge towboat. Although cargoes are often towed behind the boat on the East and West Coasts, on the inland rivers the barges are pushed ahead of the propelling craft. Pushing is more effective than pulling. It also gives the captain more control of the "tow" (the assembly of barges). As tows can have 40 barges or more connected together in parallel rows that stretch for a quarter mile, the pilothouse is often 40 feet in the air for visibility. The towboats are big and powerful and house a crew of a dozen or more. Radar and modern communications permit all-weather operation. But the biggest limitation on water traffic is the inflexibility of river routes relative to highway and railroad systems.

The barges are merely floating steel boxes that carry cargo, or the payload, as they say in the trade. Barges are carefully designed to save fuel and engine effort. They come in three types: those raked (turned up) at the bow and stern, those raked at one end only, and those with no rake at all, having square ends. Each has a specific purpose. Those pushed one at a time are raked on both ends, allowing the barge to rise up over the water rather than dig into it. But if double-raked barges are placed in a long tow (an "unintegrated" tow), turbulence develops between facing rakes that means more power for certain speeds must be used. More power means more fuel expense. Most tows, then, are combinations of single-raked barges at the front and back of the tow with square-ended barges in the center positions (an "integrated" tow). This allows the tow to act as a long ship for purposes of movement and takes much less fuel to propel it to its destination. A mixture of raked and square barges at random is called a "semi-integrated" tow. Like rail flatcars, barges are either open topped, covered on top, or simple decks with cargo lashed to them.

To provide the most flexible transportation with the fewest transfers of cargo, as with railroads moving trailers and containers piggyback, barges move other means of transportation "fishyback." Many barges have rail on them to accept rail cars or roadways to accept semitrailers or containers. Others have tanks to accept liquids or gasses. Some barges carry liquid sulfur in thermos-bottle-like tanks, designed to keep it hot and liquid rather than allowing it to cool and solidify. As in the last century, inland water transport remains a key component of American industry and the overall standard of living.

See also Canals; Steamboats.

References Brady, Edward M., *Tugs, Towboats and Towing* (1967); Stewart, William H., Jr., *The Tennessee-Tombigbee Waterway* (1971); Wattenburg, Ben, *Busy Waterways* (1964).

James River & Kanawha Canal

Began at the urging of George Washington and Edmund Randolph, among others, the James River Company was formed to exploit the 33-mile gap between the James and branches of the Great Kanawha River, which flowed into the Ohio River at Point Pleasant, Virginia (West Virginia today). Unlike most early ventures, the James River stock was subscribed to in large amounts, generating much capital for its initial effort: a series of short canals around the falls at Richmond and other obstructions upriver. By 1805, the venture was showing a profit, and in 1808, Albert Gallatin favorably mentioned it as one of the key routes to tap the western Virginia coalfields and other traffic on the Ohio. But the company's inability to raise the capital necessary to continue across the Appalachians led the state of Virginia to purchase it at the time of the War of 1812 and contract the work out to the company.

Failure of the company to satisfy the state's construction requirements led to a reorganization in 1823. Benjamin Wright came in from New York's Erie Canal project and Claudius Crozet from South Carolina's Santee Canal to make many of the surveys. The construction soon became mired in sectional jealousies between the Tidewater and Mountain areas of Virginia that ultimately would contribute to the creation of West Virginia years later. The legislature was dominated by Tidewater interests and tended to be tight-fisted with spending on internal improvements. At the same time, the railroads were siphoning off interest in any canal project, nationwide.

Led by U.S. Chief Justice John Marshall and Joseph C. Cabell, canal supporters managed to get the state to charter a new company, now labeled the James River & Kanawha Canal. By 1840, this enterprise completed the so-called First Division, a

The James River and Kanawha Canal served as a central passageway for transporting Confederate military supplies during the Civil War.

canal all the way to Lynchburg. Much of the work was done by slave labor. The Second Division over the mountains proved a harder task. Finally, the canal was completed as far as Buchanan at a total cost of slightly over $8 million for all the construction from Richmond, about the same as the Erie Canal's total cost. The final stretch had 38 locks. Contracts for the Third Division were let during the 1850s but little construction took place. Instead, a great ship lock at Richmond opened the port to ocean-going vessels. Nonetheless, traffic was impressive, and the canal was a major artery for Confederate military supplies during the Civil War. But rail competition prevented the canal from reaching its full potential, and it was finally sold to a subsidiary of the Chesapeake & Ohio Railroad in the 1880s.

See also Canals.

Reference Dunaway, Wayland Fuller, *History of the James River and Kanawha Company* (1922).

James River Company

See Canals; James River & Kanawha Canal.

Janney, Eli Hamilton (1831–1912)

A Virginia farm boy, Eli Janney served on General Robert E. Lee's staff as a quartermaster for the Army of Northern Virginia. After the war, Janney clerked in a grocery store. During a lull one day, he hit upon the idea for a different style railroad coupler by joining his hands vertically with his knuckles bent. By flexing his fingers he could hold or release his hands. He soon made a working model on the principle of a vertical plane with a few moving parts. The knuckle automatically closed itself as the cars were shunted together. The greatest value was the knuckle's ability to be released by a bar that ran the width of the car. This allowed the brakeman to release the cars without going between them, as was necessary with the link-and-pin system then in use. Many a trainman died or was crippled guiding a pin into the link; Janney's coupler stopped most of that. They were also stronger overall. He sold the patent to McConway & Torley

Corporation and retired to a farm where he lived and worked until his death.

In 1877, McConway & Torley put Janney's system on passenger cars on a branch of the Pennsylvania Railroad. It proved an instant success. The Pennsylvania Railroad made them standard on all cars, freight or passenger. Up to then, various railroads had tried out 39 varieties of automatic couplers on 80,510 cars. None of these types could couple with another brand. In 1887, the Master Car Builders Association decided to test 42 styles, automatic and otherwise, in an attempt to find the best and hopefully standardize couplers throughout the nation. Twelve of the varieties were selected for further testing, and the following year the Janney knuckle coupler defeated all comers as the best available. It was made standard on all new cars, but many railroads refused to go along with the expensive retrofitting. But in 1893, Congress passed the Safety Appliance Law, which made it the standard of the industry by fiat. The coupler has been modified over the years and is now bigger and stronger, but it is essentially the same one that Janney introduced 120 years ago.

See also Coffin, Lorenzo S.; Safety Appliance Act; Westinghouse, George.

References Carter, Charles F., *When Railroads Were New* (1926); Frey, Robert L., "Couplers," in Robert L. Frey (ed.), *EABHB: Railroads in the Nineteenth Century* (1988), 76–78; Hubbard, Freeman, *Encyclopedia of North American Railroading* (1981).

Jones, John Luther "Casey" (1864–1900)

Unlike John Henry, there is no doubt that a specific Casey Jones existed. Born in Kentucky or Missouri during the Civil War, Jones worked as a brakeman on the Mobile & Ohio and fireman on the Illinois Central, becoming an engineer on the latter road in 1890. One of his first jobs—odd because he is identified with the Deep South—was taking passengers into Chicago from Champaign for the Columbian Exposition in 1893. He adopted his nickname from Cayce, Kentucky, where he had once lived. Jones was known as a different sort of guy—he had his own whistle built and installed on the engine he ran. It truly wailed and was well known up and down the tracks where he worked. He also was not above stretching the rules to suit himself—he had been called on the carpet several times for infractions that included things like not closing a switch, negligence in train orders, and running signals. But he never had a serious accident or lost a life except his own. He was fearless and a teetotaler—a rarity in those days of hard-drinking trainmen.

In 1900 Jones received the best position available. He ran the first leg out of Memphis to Canton, Mississippi, on the Central's crack freight No. 1, the *Cannonball.* Jones ran his engine by "feel." He could literally feel how the steamer was running by its touch and sound. He had a knack of being able to coax the last mile out of a locomotive, and he never came up short before the water tower, a common fault among enginemen then. The *Cannonball* deserved the best driver around, and Casey Jones was he. On 29 April, Jones took the *Cannonball* out of Memphis. He was 95 minutes late through no fault of his own. It was rainy and foggy, the clouds were dark and low, as they can be only in a Mississippi springtime. His fireman was Slim Webb, a black man, a common practice on engine crews in the South. Jones opined that he could make up the 95 minutes at a mile every 50 seconds. Webb was a good stoker—he kept the fire hot and the steam up. Suddenly, as they rounded the curve at Vaughn, six miles from his destination, Webb, who had the best view on the curve, which bent toward his side of the cab, saw red lights on the track ahead. Webb screamed a warning and Jones ordered him to jump.

When Webb awoke 30 minutes later, he found out that a local freight had left three cars on the main track. Jones was dead inside the *Cannonball,* an iron bolt through his neck, covered with seed corn and hay from the boxcars he hit. No one else had been injured. For some years the site was marked by cornstalks growing wild, remnants of the seed corn strewn across the track during the wreck. Jones' death was remembered in a song written by a black roundhouse hostler, Wallace Saunders ("Come all you rounders, I want you to hear/The story of a brave engineer"). Later, T. Lawrence Siebert put it into formal music and it became a popular turn-of-the-century hit. Eventually the U.S. government would issue a postage stamp honoring the dead engineer, Casey Jones.

See also Death Valley Scotty; Henry, John.

References Hubbard, Freeman, *Railroad Avenue* (1945); Hubbard, Freeman, *Encyclopedia of North American Railroading* (1981); Lee, Fred J., *Casey Jones* (1939); Lomax, Alan, *Folk Songs of North America* (1960).

Jones Act

See Merchant Marine Acts, Merchant Marine Act of 1920.

Judah, Theodore D. (1820–1863)

A construction engineer who designed and built bridges, canals, and the Niagara Gorge Railroad, Theodore D. Judah came west in the 1850s and built California's first railway, between Sacramento and Folsom. Some of the roadbed turned up pieces of gold, and Judah had a ring made with the inscription, "First gold ever taken from earth used in making a railroad bank." He played a major role in organizing the financing for the Central Pacific (later the Southern Pacific lines) by getting Leland Stanford, Collis P. Huntington, and others interested in the project. At first, the investors could not comprehend the vast scope of the project Judah had in mind. But when he went to Washington and lobbied the Pacific Railroad Act through Congress, they began to catch on. They at least understood that the rails would go through the Washoe, the silver mines of Nevada, and that they would have the only direct access to thousands of miners who needed finished goods stocked at their San Francisco stores.

The actual roadbed was begun in 1863. Within three months the investors had managed to get more than $3 million from local people, the state, and some counties. After all, this was a public project, wasn't it?

Stanford, as governor, got the state to pay the interest on the company's 7 percent bonds. But there was trouble in store. Judah wanted to build a railroad, a lasting monument that would have value for the next century. The Big Four—Stanford, Hopkins, Huntington, and Crocker—wanted a quick return on their investment. The split came when the beginning of the High Sierras had to be marked. Judah actually wanted to mark them accurately! That was the end of that naiveté. The others forced him out of the company, and the Big Barbecue was on. There is no record of how much it cost to get rid of Judah. Evidence points to at least $90,000 in stock and $10,000 in gold. Soon he was on his way east again, probably plotting to oust his old partners. But he contracted yellow fever on the Panama crossing and died a week after his arrival in New York City. His ouster and early death has largely caused him to be forgotten as the man who dreamed the impossible dream and made it begin to happen. He is remembered today only by a granite monument at the old Southern Pacific station at Sacramento.

See also Crocker, Charles; Hopkins, Mark; Huntington, Collis Potter; Stanford, Leland.

References Beebe, Lucius, *The Central Pacific and Southern Pacific Railroads* (1963); Butler, Dan, "Theodore Judah," in Robert L. Frey (ed.), *EABHB: Railroads in the Nineteenth Century* (1988), 213–215; Hubbard, Freeman, *Encyclopedia of North American Railroading* (1981); Jones, Helen H., *Rails from the West* (1969); Lewis, Oscar, *The Big Four* (1938); Lyon, Peter, *To Hell in a Day Coach* (1968); Sabin, Edwin J., *Building the Pacific Railway* (1919).

Kelly Air Mail Act (1925)

In 1925, federal officials returned all mail service, managed by the Post Office since World War I, to private carriers. Congress accordingly passed the Kelly Air Mail Act, which granted a subsidy to fly airmail. Many of these contractors also carried passengers, and American commercial aviation received its first governmental financial boost.

See also Aeronautics; McNary-Watres Air Mail Act.

References Bilstein, Roger E., *Flight in America* (1994); Whitnah, Donald R., *Safer Skyways* (1966).

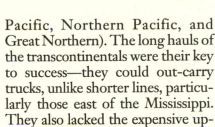

Klitenic Plan

Nathan Klitenic was a federal administrative law judge who wound up in charge of the dissolution of the Chicago, Rock Island & Pacific Railroad in the 1970s. He propounded the then-novel theory that the existence of the midwestern Granger railroads was obsolete and the cause of railroad bankruptcies in the region. He believed that it was wrong to expect that a few western transcontinental lines would feed freight into a half dozen Granger roads, who in turn would feed the traffic into the East and South. He rejected combining the Grangers (in this case, the Rock Island and the Chicago & North Western) and proposed instead a wide-ranging plan to completely restructure all railroads west of Chicago.

Judge Klitenic's plan had its birth in the declining economic position of American railroads in the late 1960s and the manner in which the lines proposed to deal with it. At the core of the whole problem was the seasonal nature of the Granger railroads' business. Grain hauling was available only part of the year. What made the Granger lines (the Rock Island; Chicago & North Western; Milwaukee Road, even though it had a Pacific branch; Chicago, Burlington & Quincy; and other numerous smaller lines) survive was the funneling of freight into them from the transcontinentals (Southern Pacific, Santa Fe, Denver & Rio Grande Western/Western Pacific, Union Pacific, Northern Pacific, and Great Northern). The long hauls of the transcontinentals were their key to success—they could out-carry trucks, unlike shorter lines, particularly those east of the Mississippi.

They also lacked the expensive upkeep of commuter lines (only the Southern Pacific had a small one at San Francisco), multiple-tracked mainlines, and resort-bound passengers (with the exceptions of the Great Northern, with Glacier National Park on its main, and the Santa Fe, with its Grand Canyon National Park branch).

Western rail consolidation had begun in the 1920s with the provisions of the Transportation Act of 1920. The first to make a move had been Southern Pacific (SP), which absorbed outright the old, separately managed Central Pacific in Nevada and Utah, the mineral-rich and scenic El Paso and Southwestern in Arizona and New Mexico, and, in the biggest coup of all, the St. Louis-Southwestern or Cotton Belt. A poverty-stricken, Texas-based road, the Cotton Belt gave SP entrée into St. Louis, access which had been provided by the Rock Island from El Paso under a freight rental agreement. Without the SP money, the Rock Island was a dead duck.

Further SP moves were made against the Western Pacific (WP). The WP ran a tighter ship than most and had access over the Sierra Nevada through a pass much lower than its competitors'. It turned its freight over to the Rio Grande (D&RGW) at Salt Lake City, and the D&RGW gave it to the Grangers at Denver. It ran the *California Zephyr*, one of the best passenger runs in the nation. Control of the WP would also threaten traffic agreements between the WP and the Great Northern into Oregon, and the Santa Fe into the Bay Area. Now SP would be able to dictate entrance terms to all. Already the SP and WP shared their tracks across Nevada, using them as a double-tracked main. The Department of Justice blocked the SP move, refused to accept a counterproposal by the Santa Fe, and eventually, after the WP went broke in the 1970s, dealt it to the Union Pacific.

But the core of western mergers involved the "Northerns"—the Great Northern and the Northern Pacific, both of whom divided control of the Chicago, Burlington & Quincy between them for access to Chicago, and the Spokane, Portland & Seattle for access into the West Coast. Their main competition was the Milwaukee Road's new Pacific branch, electrified and maintained to a fault. To keep the Milwaukee Road from outdoing them, the Northerns prevented any freight from coming into their West Coast yards, unless it had been hauled by the Northerns from the Twin Cities. There had been several attempts to merge the Northerns, the most celebrated being the Northern Securities Case before the Interstate Commerce Commission (ICC) in the early 1900s. Another attempt in the 1920s was dropped when the condition of merger was the divesting of the Northerns of the Burlington.

In 1961, however, the Northerns were back with a new proposal. Their claim that they could provide better service through more efficient use of parts of both of their transcontinental lines was false. The two had been forced to compete with the Milwaukee Road and had improved their service each time they had to. As the historian of rail mergers put it, paraphrasing an economist of the day, for the Northerns asking to merge to compete with the Milwaukee Road would be like Ford and General Motors asking to merge to compete with Packard. The real reason for the merger was to compete with trucking. The trucks were cutting into the traffic, and united they could undercut them easier. Also, the Milwaukee Road had a better piggyback service that they had. Once again the Northerns were put off, complaints coming not only from the Milwaukee Road, but also from every state through which the Northerns ran, plus labor, plus every trackside business involved.

Which brings us back to Judge Klitenic and the Rock Island. The problem with the Rock Island line was that it went nowhere that someone else could not get to faster and straighter. It had always been a hard-luck railroad. Shipments by the "Rock" took a day longer than any other line. Now that was all about to end, and Union Pacific was to be the new owner. That was, until the Chicago & North Western's (C&NW) Ben Heineman made a proposal directly to the stockholders, over the heads of UP and Rock Island's management. The attractive offer was a mixture of C&NW stock, bonds, and cash. Had not the C&NW failed to register its prospectus with the Securities and Exchange Commission, it would have gone through. But the legal gaffe killed the chances of a C&NW takeover. It would all go to UP, if Judge Klitenic agreed. The Rock was attractive because it had fewer Granger side lines and much mainline that would complement UP's and get it into Chicago without C&NW or Milwaukee Road traffic agreements.

Rejected in its attempt to block UP, C&NW had to settle for the rival Chicago & Great Western, a Granger line that made a habit of pulling extra-long trains so it had to offer only once-a-day service. The farmers and manufacturers hated this arrangement, and welcomed C&NW's better schedules and management in 1968. At the same time, C&NW bought the Minneapolis & St. Louis, another small Granger railroad, and diversified its holdings into clothing, shoes, steel, coal, and chemicals. Prompted by a proposal by the Northerns that they would not block a C&NW merger with Milwaukee Road if the two Grangers would not block the Northerns' merger, the smaller line took the bait. The C&NW offered itself, lock, stock, and barrel, to the Milwaukee Road. But the latter could not come up with the capital. Meanwhile, the Northerns gave in to the conditions of labor and customers and, using the appointment of new commissioners, approached the ICC with their plan. It won approval, appeals, and a subsequent ruling by the U.S. Supreme Court. Burlington Northern (BN) was a reality by 1970.

Realizing that it had been taken by the Northerns, C&NW moved to bloc UP's takeover of Rock Island. All sorts of computerized diagrams accompanied the briefs of both proponents and opponents of the merger. Judge Klitenic issued three rulings in the Rock Island case. First, he analyzed the railroads and their traffic patterns. Second, he discussed the demands of all and the effect of the demands on others. Finally, he issued the Klitenic Plan, outlining the destruction and division of the Rock Island and every other railroad for or against the UP takeover. Essentially, he created four massive, highly competitive railroads west of the Mississippi River: Burlington Northern, Union Pacific, Santa Fe, and Southern Pacific. Each would serve two of the four midwestern gateway cities of St. Louis, Chicago, Memphis, or New Orleans. All would reach the Pacific coast. Each line was strong in certain areas of the West, balanced by its weaknesses in other parts (for example, Santa Fe was weak around Chicago but strong in California, and UP was strong in the central corridor but weak in California). The division of the Rock Island, and the compulsory absorption of the other Granger roads, was the price of competition.

Often one can gauge the effectiveness of a proposal by its opponents. Every railroad in the West screamed at Judge Klitenic's plan. Not one of them actually wanted what he granted—fair competition. Each wanted some corporate economic advantage over all the others. The ICC lacked the courage and political independence to stick by the judge. It dropped the Klitenic Plan immediately, and divided up the Rock among the vultures, but kept all of the other Granger roads, each protected by a traffic guarantee from the transcontinentals. The only line to get the shaft was the Milwaukee Road. Left hanging in the wind, it seemed but a matter of time before Burlington Northern and the interstate highway system took it down. But BN refused to merge as promised to the ICC. Instead, the federal government wound up subsidizing the Milwaukee Road by a stock buyout, leaving her in existence as another weak sister in the discordant family that Judge Klitenic had sought to harmonize on an equal basis.

See also Burlington Northern Incorporated; Chicago & North Western Railroad; Milwaukee Road; Regional Rail Reorganization Act of 1973; Rock Island Lines; Santa Fe Railway; Southern Pacific Lines; Union Pacific Railroad.

Reference Saunders, Richard, *The Railroad Mergers and the Coming of Conrail* (1978).

Knudsen, William S. (1879–1948)

A driving force behind Henry Ford's assembly lines, William Knudsen was a bicycle maker and automobile axle machinist who had set up 14 plants for Ford in less than two years. Known as "Big Bill," Knudsen stood in at 6 feet and 230 pounds. A Dane, he claimed that he could yell, "Hurry up!" in 15 languages. He smoke, drank, and swore, but he was a hard worker, which saved him from the Puritan Henry until the 1920s. An advocate of change in the industry, Knudsen wanted to modify and improve the Model T. Big Bill and Ford disagreed on the idea of two or four doors for the revised Model T. Henry Ford came to regard him as disloyal, even though his son, Edsel, agreed with Knudsen. It was the last straw. Knudsen walked out on a $50,000-a-year job, to be replaced by Charles "Cast Iron" Sorenson, who was smart enough never to argue with Henry over his darling car.

Knudsen then went to General Motors (GM), where he performed well, making their production as good as Ford's. Added to Alfred P. Sloan's marketing philosophy, Knudsen's production revisions helped make GM number one by 1928, especially with the six-cylinder Chevrolet, his pet idea, brought over from his arguments with Ford. Knudsen's success with Chevy forced Ford to drop the outdated Tin Lizzie and introduce the Model A. Knudsen became president of GM in 1937 and joined the war effort as a troubleshooter, ultimately being awarded a general's rank and the Distinguished Service Medal. He was ever a decent man (cynics would label him a "soft touch") who, in the midst of the "sit down" strike at GM in the late thirties, asked a friend to get milk for the strikers' children and paid for it out of his own pocket.

See also Automobiles from Domestics to Imports; Automobiles in American Society.

References Beasley, Norman, *Knudsen* (1947);

Bryan, Ford R., *Henry's Lieutenants* (1993); Flink, James J., "William S. Knudsen," in George S. May (ed.), *EABHB: The Automobile Industry* (1989), 265–283; Halberstam, David, *The Reckoning* (1986); Motor Vehicle Manufacturers Association of the United States, *Automobiles of America* (1974); Shook, Robert L., *Turnaround* (1990).

Kuhler, Otto (1894–1977)

One of the three most influential industrial designers in the early twentieth-century American railroad scene, Otto Kuhler was employed by the American Locomotive Company as an engine streamliner, and by several railroads to redesign passenger equipment. His most noted engine job was the shrouding of the Milwaukee Road's Hiawatha, an Atlantic-type (4-4-2) passenger engine (a *shroud* is a steel, streamlined cover over the boiler of a steam engine). Kuhler altered the cab so that the engineer could see down the tracks farther and clearer. He needed to. When finished, these small engines could make two miles a minute pulling a full train. Kuhler, unlike many other designers of his day, liked the side-rod action and left the main drivers clear of the shroud for maximum view and ease of maintenance. He also introduced the then-new and experimental fluorescent bulbs in the Lehigh Valley's John Wilkes passenger cars. He streamlined cars for the New York subway system and designed trolley cars, station interiors, passenger cars, and a bus for the Baltimore & Ohio. He became an avid etcher and painter in later life, employing both oils and watercolors, emphasizing steam power in southwestern scenes.

See also Loewy, Raymond; Pennsylvania Railroad; Railroads before and during the Civil War; Railroads from Appomattox to Deregulation.

References Hubbard, Freeman, *Encyclopedia of North American Railroading* (1981); Kuhler, Otto, *My Iron Journey* (1967).

La Follette Seamen's Act (1916)

Although neither Republican Senators Knute Nelson of Minnesota nor Robert La Follette of Wisconsin had many constituents concerned with the sea, both men were old-time Progressives who believed in identifying wrongs and curing them through legislation. Such was the case with the lack of constitutional rights available to American seamen (and American Indians, coincidentally) as confirmed by the U.S. Supreme Court in *Robertson v. Baldwin*, also known as the the Arago case. Nelson had drafted a measure designed to alleviate the situation, providing sailors normal constitutional guarantees available to all American citizens, better living conditions aboard ship, fair wages, and the ability to achieve classification as able-bodied seamen, but he could not sell it to Congress, which at the time was influenced by vigilant ship owners. La Follette ("Battlin' Bob" was his moniker), however, was a personal friend of Andrew Furuseth, the seamen's advocate in Washington, D.C. He took Nelson's bill and added several items that would strike Congress favorably in the wake of the recent *Titanic* disaster, such as requirements for life rafts, lifeboats, life preservers, drills, and other safety accouterment. Then he waited until the end of the March 1916 session of Congress and introduced the measure quietly, obtaining passage that had so far proved illusive. The measure reached President Woodrow Wilson's desk, where Secretary of State William Jennings Bryan pointed out that the United States had several international agreements contrary to the proposed law. He advised a quiet pocket veto after Congress adjourned. Wilson mulled the decision over for days. La Follette came in with Furuseth to plead their cause, Furuseth reputedly throwing himself on his knees in supplication. Wilson signed the measure into law one hour before Congress went out of session. But during the interwar period nearly every court ruling went against the measure and it became a dead letter except for the safety requirements that substituted for America's refusal to ratify international safety acts after the sinking of the *Titanic*.

See also *Robertson v. Baldwin*; Shipping Acts.

References Pedraja, René de la, *A Historical Dictionary of the U.S. Merchant Marine and Shipping Industry* (1994); Standard, William L., *Merchant Seamen* (1947); Weintraub, Hyman, *Andrew Furuseth* (1959).

Lancaster Pike

By the end of the 1750s, trade in the original 13 colonies was beginning to boom. But now it turned from the traditional north–south routes and began to flow from east to west, as settlers moved onto the Great Valley beyond the first mountains. By 1792, this trade with the new West was critical, and the Commonwealth of Pennsylvania decided to tap the rich agricultural region around Lancaster with a road. As Lancaster (pronounced "Lank'ster" by those in the know) was the largest inland town in the United States not situated on a waterway but rather at the meeting place of the roads that stretched down the Cumberland and Shenandoah Valleys, and since its farms were the breadbasket of Philadelphia, this new road would not be just any highway—it was to be the first truly planned and well-built road in American history. The surface for the whole 62 miles was macadamized (i.e., covered with crushed stone of various sizes, with the larger rocks on the bottom and finer gravel on the top). There would be no ruts in this road, regardless of the weather. The more traffic the better, as each passing vehicle packed the surface harder. It was 24 feet wide, with a berm of 15 feet on each side, and grades limited to a then-moderate 4 percent so that traffic could pass in both directions with ease. Bridges crossed all creeks and rivers. The Lancaster Pike took ten years and $465,000 to construct.

The vast sum needed to build the Lancaster Pike was obtained by selling stock in the road company at $300 a share. In turn, the company was allowed to charge tolls to make up its investment and pay for repairs.

There were nine toll booths spaced roughly seven miles apart, and the fees ranged from a penny to 13 cents a mile, depending on the number of wheels and horses used on the early wagon traffic. Unlike many other such endeavors, the Lancaster Pike made money. Freight houses and taverns sprang up along the route. Big Conestoga wagons pulled by six horses were commonplace, and the teamsters considered themselves a fraternity apart from the coaches and common travelers. The road was considered so efficient and well maintained that when New York State decided to build the Erie Canal, cost and profit projections (the Lancaster Pike returned up to a whopping 15 percent) were based on direct comparison with the fees charged on the Lancaster Pike, America's first real highway.

See also Great Wagon Road; Macadamized Roads and Other Surfaces; Roads and Highways, Colonial Times to World War I.

References Durrenberger, Joseph A., *Turnpikes* (1931); Hart, Val, *The Story of American Roads* (1950); MacGill, Caroline, et al., *History of Transportation in the United States* (1917); U.S. Department of Transportation, Federal Highway Administration, *America's Highways* (1976).

Samuel Langley

Langley, Samuel Pierpont (1834–1906)

Massachusetts-born Samuel Langley was a physicist and astronomer. Educated as an architect and civil engineer, Langley traveled in Europe before becoming an assistant at the Harvard Observatory. He became a professor of mathematics at the Naval Academy at Annapolis, and director of the Allegheny Observatory by 1867. He organized an expedition to Mount Whitney, California, where he redeveloped the color constant and expanded the invisible light spectrum. By 1887, he was secretary to the Smithsonian Institution and an organizer of the National Zoological Park and the Astrophysical Observatory. He was also president of the American Association for the Advancement of Science.

But Langley's greatest renown came from his experiments with motorized flight. In 1896, the Smithsonian Institution credited him and his machine with the first successful flight, a claim challenged by the Wright brothers, who saw Langley's quarter-size craft as unworthy of the title of first practicable aircraft. At the time of the Spanish-American War, Assistant Secretary of the Navy Theodore Roosevelt got him a congressional grant of $5,000 to continue his investigations. Unfortunately his full-sized experiments, refined and flown by Charles Manly, proved unsuccessful and Langley's failures, highly publicized, led to much skepticism as to the feasibility of sustained human flight. A decade later, however, after Langley's death, Glenn Curtiss would repower Langley's plane and prove his principles valid. Many governmental research facilities, including an airfield, and a Virginia town are named after Langley.

See also Aeronautics; Wright, Orville and Wilbur.

References Bilstein, Roger E., *Flight in America* (1994); Crouch, Tom D., *A Dream of Wings* (1981).

League of American Wheelmen

In 1880 at Newport, Rhode Island, the League of American Wheelmen came into being in response to the latest American transportation craze—the bicycle. The bike had been around for over 100 years, and by now it had been improved into something to behold. It had style and grace in lines, new pneumatic tires, and a chain drive. Eventually it even got brakes with handgrips that applied pressure on one or both tires, and finally the Bendix coaster brake, applied by reversing the path of the pedals. By 1900, over 300 companies made bikes, producing over 1 million units, in an industry capitalized at $30 million. Bicycles were not just for the sporty rich. They even spread to the trans-Mississippi West. It was an economical touring device that many used to go to work on. It allowed one to explore one's surroundings freely, and it was easier to care for than a horse.

The Wheelmen were not the only cycle organization, merely the biggest. They made much of the health aspects of cycling—getting the blood churning, purging the body of poisons, and so forth. The bike was a mental purgative, too. It drove the pressures of modern life from the mind. Besides, bicycle clubs allowed one to have a social life among those who felt the same way. Full-fledged bike tours, picnics, and other activities became common. A national journal, *The Wheelman*, gave hints as to bike use and care. Special departments in national magazines contributed their share, and the association's *The Road and Handbook* contained a new twist: national and regional road maps. Now people could know ahead of time where they were going—and even find their ways back.

As cyclists roamed into the hinterlands, one salient fact came to them: American roads were seriously in disrepair. Ever since before the Civil War, roads had been allowed to disintegrate as public concern turned to the railroads. Besides, few people had wheeled vehicles that they took into the country anyhow. But things were changing.

The first national meet of the League of American Wheelmen took place in Newport, Rhode Island, in 1880.

Cyclists started to campaign nationally and locally for more and better roads—marked roads that went somewhere. No one caught the long-distance bike fever more than Thomas Stevens, who logged 3,700 miles in a cross-country bike tour in 1884. He wore out several changes of clothes, but the little machine he rode withstood all the unimproved roads that rural America could throw at it and more. He forded streams, rode in the rain, and saw a part of the West that few had experienced since the days of the pioneers. It took him 12 weeks to make the trip from San Francisco to Chicago. And now the need for macadamized roads was obvious to all devoted wheelmen everywhere.

One of the wheelmen's greater banes was the poor old horse. Serving mankind since the beginnings of time, the wheelmen now condemned Old Dobbin as a polluter, dangerous, and a perennial road hog. Their owners were reviled as even worse. The wheelmen failed to remove the horse from American life—it would take the automobile to do that—but the cyclists did do much to raise awareness about good roads. The associations had "good roads days," where they set up information booths loaded with propaganda and some real information on how to go about getting local government to finance and build better highways. Farm journals backed up their crusade, one that farmers, despite their reliance on the much-maligned horse, could sympathize with. Good roads meant more goods taken to town for sale and brought home from the store to improve rural life. In 1892, Wheelmen chairman Charles L. Burdet finally got to someone who counted in American life, President Benjamin Harrison. Burdet presented good highways as a potential boon to their biggest enemy, the railroads. With good highways, he argued, rail business would expand as they moved the goods sold or bought by local road users. (No one had heard of or even dreamed of the independent trucker yet.) Harrison agreed and began the debate to deal with improving American roads.

The League of American Wheelmen did much to popularize the idea of good roads as an economic benefit to the nation at large. So persuasive were their arguments, and so interested were the new motorists and their horseless carriages, that there emerged groups like the National League for Good Roads and the National Good Roads League to capitalize on their erstwhile efforts. As Americans looked into the twentieth century, the movement for decent national highways was blooming—all because a group of devoted bicyclists wanted to travel more widely. The automobile had yet to make its impact on the American psyche, and if the wheelmen thought the horse and buggy were nuisances, they hadn't seen anything yet.

See also Good Roads Movement.

References U.S. Department of Transportation, Federal Highway Administration, *America's Highways* (1976); Winther, Oscar O., *The Transportation Frontier* (1964).

Leavenworth & Pike's Peak Express Company

A subsidiary of the freighting firm of Russell, Majors & Waddell, the Leavenworth & Pike's Peak Express Company was established by William H. Russell and John S. Jones in 1859 to take advantage of the traffic going to the new Colorado goldfields near Denver. Set up over the protests of Alexander Majors and William B. Waddell, both of whom found themselves committed without their permissions, the express utilized the Smoky Hill route straight west across Kansas, although the stage run is believed to have traced its own route parallel to and slightly north of the older trail. The service made Denver the key city in Colorado, but started its parent company on the road to doom, the original investment never being made good. As soon as Russell and Jones took over the Central Overland Route, the separate Smoky Hill route was eliminated in favor of combined operations over the Oregon Trail, and the Leavenworth & Pike's Peak line was discontinued as a separate entity.

See also Adams Express Company; American Express Company; American Railway Express Company; Central Overland California & Pike's Peak Express Company; Harnden & Company Express; Pacific Union Express Company; Russell, Majors & Waddell Company; United States Express Company; Wells Fargo & Company.

Reference Harlow, Alvin F., *Old Waybills* (1934).

Lee Highway

One of the "named highways" popular in the teens and twenties of the twentieth century, the Lee Highway was used by local chambers of commerce and tourism and the American Automobile Association to stimulate travel on the "good roads" and increase income in the towns and states through which they passed. Named after the Civil War's premier Confederate general, the Lee Highway began in New York and came south to Washington on what would become U.S. Highway 1. There it swung west to New Market, Virginia, and headed southward through the Shenandoah Valley, following the route of current U.S. Highway 11 and Interstate Highway 81 to Chattanooga. Turning west, it passed through Huntsville and Corinth and on to Memphis, on a route now numbered U.S. Highway 72. Following current U.S. Highway 70 out of Memphis, the Lee Highway crossed Arkansas by way of Little Rock, Hot Springs, and De Queen, and Oklahoma through Durant, Ardmore, and Frederick. It dropped south to Vernon, Texas, and crossed the high plains through Plainview on future U.S. Highway 70. It followed the same route through New Mexico, passing by way of Roswell, Alamogordo, Las Cruces, Deming, and Lordsburg. It turned north at the latter spot and headed into the Arizona mountains, still following the route that would become U.S. Highway 70 into Globe and Phoenix. There it followed the Gila River to Yuma and cut across the Imperial Desert to San Diego on what is now Interstate 8. In California, the Lee Highway wended its way north to San Francisco on the Pacific Highway, the old Camino Real, the route along the coastal range's Spanish missions.

See also Camino Real (California); Roads and Highways since World War I; Valley Turnpike.

Reference Hart, Val, *The Story of American Roads* (1950).

Leiper, Thomas (1745–1825)

A Philadelphia tobacco exporter, Thomas Leiper was born in Scotland before migrating to the New World at age 18 and serving as a cavalryman for the American cause during the Revolution. After the war, Leiper became a rich man; he not only handled tobacco but also dabbled in mills and quarries. In 1806 or 1809 (depending on whose account is followed), Leiper built a 180-foot experimental track of wood rails near Bull's Head Tavern. It worked so well that he transferred the operation to one of his quarries and used the rails to transport rock to the nearby river. Although only three-fourths of a mile long, the horse-drawn cars operated until 1828, three years after his death. If the date 1809 is accepted for Leiper's railway, the honor of the first wooden railway goes to Silas Whitney who put tracks on Beacon Hill in 1808. Several other quarries and mines in Massachusetts and Pennsylvania operated animal-drawn "trains" as a part of their industrial operations in the early 1800s before the Baltimore & Ohio Railroad was set up in the 1830s.

See also Railroads before and during the Civil War.

Reference Hubbard, Freeman, *Encyclopedia of North American Railroading* (1981).

Lewis and Clark Trail

When the United States learned of the availability of the Louisiana Purchase, President Thomas Jefferson was so enthused that he abandoned his constitutional scruples and nearly broke up his political party to buy it. Democratic-Republican Jefferson had made his reputation opposing Federalist Alexander Hamilton's loose constructionist interpretation of the written Constitution of 1787, maintaining along with his fellow Virginian, James Madison, that strict construction, meaning a literal reading of the words, would preserve essential American liberties. As there was no actual provision in the document for land purchases, which purists believed necessitated an amendment before buying Louisiana, Jefferson by rights ought to have sought one. But that was a too-lengthy process for such a once-in-a-lifetime bargain. Jefferson needed to move at once, and he did. He thus created not only the great American West, but the beginnings of an intraparty quarrel.

Part of Jefferson's interest in Louisiana was his fear that Napoleon I would compromise American interests in the New World, particularly by closing New Orleans permanently to the American West as the Spanish had done off and on for years. Then there was the potential of an untapped continent and its possible access to China and the Pacific. The problem was that no one—not Jefferson who bought it, not the French who sold it, nor the British who opposed its purchase—knew where Louisiana began and ended. It would take the Adams-Onís Treaty with Spain to define its southern boundary, and the Rush-Bagot, Webster-Ashburton, and Oregon Treaties with Great Britain to extend its northern boundary to the Pacific; but in 1803, it was all up for grabs. The United States asserted its claims through a series of explorations, the most notable of which was the Lewis and Clark expedition of 1804–1805.

Jefferson knew from an American sailor, John Ledyard (who had accompanied England's Captain James Cook on a search for the Northwest Passage—the fabled water route around North America), that the Pacific Northwest teemed with furs. Especially valuable were sea otter pelts, which could be sold in China for a fortune. Ledyard told Jefferson that he could cross Russia, find Vancouver Island (where he had been), and backtrack from there across North America. He would open the Northwest Passage that had intrigued Europeans and Americans for centuries. It would be the all-water route to China sought by Christopher Columbus. This was in the 1780s, and Jefferson, as American minister to France, agreed to the fantastic scheme. But the Russians arrested Ledyard in Siberia (unbelievably, he had crossed in midwinter) and deported him westward, ending the search. Ledyard died shortly thereafter—heartbroken and a lot worse for the wear.

But Jefferson never forgot Ledyard's dream, especially after American Captain John Gray sailed up the coast and found the Columbia River, establishing an American claim to the area. In 1790, Great Britain and Spain agreed to allow the English to settle and exploit any territory above San Francisco in the Nootka Sound Convention. Later, the British also got the Russians to agree to the line 54° 40' as the southern boundary to their Alaskan claim in the Anglo-Russian Treaty of 1825, following a similar treaty signed between the United States and Russia the year before. But in 1803, there was the possibility that the United States might be shut off from the Pacific forever by a then unsympathetic Britain. A land expedition based on Ledyard's hopes, this time crossing the North American continent, would do to reassert U.S. claims and find out what Jefferson had purchased. It would also contest with the British Hudson's Bay Company for the inland fur trade, now that a decade of greed had destroyed the great sea otter herds.

Jefferson chose his personal secretary, Meriwether Lewis, to lead the expedition. His second in command would be Lieutenant William Clark, whose brother George Rogers Clark had done much to secure the Old Northwest for America during the Revolution. Assembling at St. Louis, the Corps of Discovery, as it was called officially, set off up the Missouri River in May 1804 in a keelboat with a company of about 50 men. Little was known of what lay ahead except what French fur trappers could relate. But their knowledge did not cover the headwaters of the river or the Continental Divide. The party spent their first winter at the Mandan Indian villages near present-day Bismarck. There, they were augmented by two, a mixed-race Frenchman named Charbonneau and his bought teenage wife Sacagawea, who had been stolen from her native Shoshone people some years before. As no one in the party had any language skills, Sacagawea's ability to speak several tongues and make universal sign language proved important. The problem was that she spoke little English and would have to converse with Charbonneau in French.

Then he would try and tell Lewis and Clark what was said in his broken English. It was a poor solution, but it generally worked.

In the spring of 1805, Lewis sent everyone back but 26. The advance party included Lewis and Clark; a French-Canadian guide, George Droulliard; Clark's black slave, York; Charbonneau; and Sacagawea with her baby carried on a back cradle. They traveled by canoe to Great Falls, where they cached all but essentials and continued on foot. It took two months to ascend the Continental Divide. The party was soon in great trouble, having seen no Native Americans to trade and exchange information with. Finally they contacted a band of Shoshone, who turned out to be Sacagawea's people, a great stroke of luck. Trading for horses and information, the company rode on. Sacagawea insisted on coming along, too. By now she had a crush on Clark, which pleased the red-headed American, but angered Charbonneau, who came along to protect his "investment." The expedition ran out of food and had to eat the horses, but it reached the Clearwater River and made contact with the Nez Percés. Building dugout canoes, Lewis and Clark continued down the Clearwater to the Columbia and to the ocean. Raising a fort, which they named Clatsop, they spent a cold, uneventful winter there.

Lewis and Clark returned by the same route. After crossing the Continental Divide, however, the party split into three groups. Lewis went northward to check out the drainages into Canada. There he had a fight with the Blackfeet, which caused them to hate Americans ever after, egged on by the Hudson's Bay men, who wished to limit the American's northward advance. Clark crossed over to the Yellowstone River and followed it to its junction with the Missouri. The third group, under Sergeant Nathaniel Pryor, went to Great Falls and picked up the canoes and cached supplies. All joined together at the mouth of the Yellowstone and proceeded to St. Louis, ending the journey. When Jefferson's representatives had bought Louisiana, the French foreign minister, Charles Maurice de Talleyrand-

Périgord, in referring to the vagaries of its boundaries, had cautioned the Americans, "make the most of it." By sending Lewis and Clark out to the Pacific, Jefferson did just that.

See also Central Overland Route; Mullan Road; Oregon Trail.

References Bakeless, John, *Lewis and Clark* (1947); Dillon, Richard, *Meriwether Lewis* (1965); Moody, Ralph, *The Old Trails West* (1963); Satterfield, Archie, *The Lewis and Clark Trail* (1978).

Lincoln Highway

One of the "named highways" popular in the teens and twenties of the twentieth century, the Lincoln Highway was used by local chambers of commerce and tourism and the American Automobile Association to stimulate travel on the "good roads" and increase income in the towns and states through which they passed. The Lincoln Highway passed from New York City to Philadelphia where it followed a route that is now U.S. Highway 30 and Interstate 80 to Salt Lake City, Utah. There it went southwest roughly across what are now U.S. Highways 93 and 93A (the actual route was across the modern prohibited-access Wendover-Dugway-Deseret Proving Grounds) to Ely, Nevada. Turning west, the road passed over to Reno on what became U.S. Highway 50. Taking the Truckee Summit route, it crossed the Sierras into California where it wound up at Sacramento by a route approximating current Interstate 80.

The Lincoln Highway Association was the first of the named-highway associations, designed to promote the use of the automobile and its related products and services in a safe manner. At the time, it was pretty near impossible for a traveler to cross the continent without a guide. None of the existing roadways were marked, and few were paved. Few people knew where roads passing their farms and houses went beyond, say, the nearest town. Organized in 1912 by Carl Fisher, a promoter of the Indianapolis Speedway, the Lincoln Highway Association made a program of mapping these roads (eventually 3,150 miles of them), setting up standards, and creating the first transcontinental highway. The association collected millions of dollars in public subscriptions from states, interested organizations and businesses, and even pennies from schoolchildren to finance their road and its improvements. Local auto clubs handled the sections of the highway in their locales, and the American Automobile Association helped through the publication of their "Blue Book" that marked accommodations along the way. In 1915, Lewis Stubbs of St. Joseph, Missouri, suggested marking telephone poles with a series of stripes to indicate proper route. The auto club of his home town did just that on the Pike's Peak Ocean-to-Ocean Highway.

Fisher's idea caught on in a big way, and by the 1920s associations popped up all over the United States plugging their local highway for speed, safety, tourism, and scenic qualities. By mid-decade, there were over 100 associations, each issuing information, booklets, and travel hints. Some were valid projects; others existed merely to provide salaries for their organizers. Each trail overlapped its competitors', and one piece of highway carried 11 association markers. The National Highways Association (1914) published a map that recommended 50,000 miles of roads that it asserted should be built, improved, and maintained by the federal government. But it would take World War II and the example of the German *autobahn* before such a sweeping use of federal money would be endorsed.

State highway planners went crazy trying to keep up with the associations and their constant new standards of road building and repair. In 1922 the Lincoln Highway Association assembled its own board of highway engineers and put forth the "ideal" American road. It was to be four lanes wide, two for each direction, each lane to be 10 feet wide of concrete construction, with a total right-of-way of 100 feet. Traffic to be carried past a given point in a 24-hour period was projected to be 15,000 autos and 5,000 trucks. The association constructed segments of this type of road and some on a smaller scale as instructional and educational demonstrations throughout the course of the Lincoln Highway's pathway. Public response was good.

Another publicity stunt that had much value from the viewpoint of national defense was the army's First Transcontinental Motor Convoy of 1919. Two motor companies and support units comprised of 79 vehicles and nearly 300 officers and men (one of whom was a Major Dwight D. Eisenhower, who never forgot the experience) made the two-month trip from Washington to San Francisco. Average speed was 18 miles per hour. Bridges had to be reinforced throughout the trip, and the trucks, which averaged 8 tons in weight, literally tore up light roads in the West. All of it proved that highways left much to be desired in the United States.

Finally, federal and state engineers met and tried to formulate a national system of road markers. Six regional meetings helped get input from local regions, but the board explicitly kept association members from propagandizing them for their own trails. The board eventually got up a list of over 80,000 miles of roads of interstate importance and, in consultation with the various states, pared this down to 50,000 miles. But localities about to be left out of the system lobbied Washington hard and another list came out with over 75,000 miles of roads on it. No one wanted to be bypassed, just as in the railroad era. By 1926, the final list had 96,626 miles on it, all to be designated U.S. Highways and marked with the familiar black-and-white shield. The day of the highway associations were numbered after this, although many did not go out of existence for some years.

See also Fisher, Carl G.; Roads and Highways, Colonial Times to World War I; Roads and Highways since World War I.

References Hart, Val, *The Story of American Roads* (1950); Hokanson, Drake, *The Lincoln Highway* (1988); Lincoln Highway Association, *The Lincoln Highway* (1835); U.S. Department of Transportation, Federal Highway Administration, *America's Highways* (1976).

Lindbergh, Charles A. (1902–1974)

A Detriot, Michigan, native, Charles A. Lindbergh grew up in Little Falls, Minnesota. He entered the state university as a student in mechanical engineering but dropped out to go to a Lincoln, Nebraska, flying school in 1922. Working as a para-chute jumper and wing-walker, he purchased a plane in 1923 and began flying solo. He slept in a hammock slung between his Curtiss JN-4 Jenny's wings. The following year, he entered the army reserve as a flying cadet at Brooks Field, San Antonio, eventually attaining the rank of colonel in

Charles Lindbergh made the first nonstop flight from New York to Paris in 1927.

the Missouri National Guard. He flew airmail from Chicago to St. Louis until the allure of Raymond B. Orteig's $25,000 prize for the first nonstop flight from New York to Paris inspired him to make an attempt. He obtained local financing in St. Louis and had a special Ryan monoplane with a new Wright J-5 radial engine built for the trip, which he christened *The Spirit of St. Louis*. He flew the aircraft from San Diego to New York City, stopping in St. Louis to bid his friends farewell, in a quick flying time of 21 hours and 20 minutes.

On 29 May 1927 Lindbergh took off from Long Island and headed for France. He landed at Le Bourget Air Field 33 hours and 33 minutes later, a hero to all the world. He was accorded a ticker-tape parade in New York City and made an 82-city tour of all 48 states. Later, he flew on a goodwill tour of Latin America and the Caribbean and wrote on aviation. He also penned a modestly short autobiographical account, *We*. He later commented on the paradoxes of solo flying: "I may be flying a complicated airplane, rushing through space, but this cabin is surrounded by a simplicity and thoughts set free of time." Lindbergh marveled at "this air, stirring around me. That air, rushing by with the speed of a tornado, an inch beyond. These minute details in my cockpit. The grandeur of the world beyond. The nearness of death. The longness of life."

Lindbergh soon married Anne Morrow and together they made an air trip to China, which she wrote about, and a 30,000-mile trip up and down both sides of the Atlantic, looking for future air routes. In 1932, their son, Charles A., Jr., was kidnapped and killed. After an agonizing trial, a German immigrant, Bruno Hauptmann, was convicted of the child's death and, although there remains some doubt as to whether he did the deed, did it alone or in league with others, or merely knew who did it, Hauptmann was later executed. Shunning publicity, always just a shy midwesterner who never drank a drop (unlike most who flew then), Lindbergh and his wife went into self-imposed exile in Europe until 1939. He became impressed with the new Luftwaffe, and spoke out in favor of isolationism on the eve of World War II. But ever a patriot in spite of vicious rumors to the contrary, Lindbergh made a survey of American air needs and served in the South Pacific during the war. He later wrote anew of his life in the 1953 volume, *The Spirit of St. Louis*.

Lindbergh's initial trans-Atlantic flight was one of the most moving moments of the twentieth century. It focused the eyes of the common people and their business and political leaders on the potential of air transportation. Airline stocks and mergers increased markedly as the new industry moved to cash in on the "Lindbergh boom." Military men, like General Billy Mitchell, talked about future wars being won in the air. As the growing airlines were to demonstrate, the distances that had historically protected nations from each other were now mere fiction. It was a haunting, complex revision of the world. Although most Americans did not realize it, isolationism was a thing of the past. In the twentieth century, every nation was to be affected by the problems and conflicts of others.

Even Lindbergh himself had trouble coming to grips with this revolutionary new concept. It had taken Ferdinand Magellan's ship 1,090 days to circumnavigate the globe in 1521. The *Graf Zeppelin* did it in 20 days in 1929, and Wiley Post did it in under 9 days by plane in 1931. But the Lindbergh saga also reveals another dilemma of the information age. His life shows the difficulty of carrying on a normal life after one becomes a public property, and how a decent person can be destroyed by the well-intended (or not) dreams of others. And the dream that Lindbergh brought true was a reaffirmation that one person—daring, shy, unassuming, the son every mother always wanted—could make a difference in a positive way. After the carnage of World War I, it was indeed exhilarating.

See also Aeronautics; Pan American Airways.

References Bilstein, Roger E., *Flight Patterns* (1983); Davis, Kenneth S., *The Hero* (1959); Ward, John William, "The Meaning of Lindbergh's Flight," *American Quarterly* (1958) 10: 3–16.

Locomotives

One of the most important inventions of the modern era has been the railroad locomotive, of which there are three basic types in the United States. The following sections cover each of these in detail.

DIESEL ELECTRIC LOCOMOTIVES

By the end of the nineteenth century, the time had come to rethink the means of propelling trains. Steam engines had the advantages of powerful energy, familiarity, and flexibility, but they were expensive to maintain. They were especially hard on the tracks, as each thrust of the drive wheels tended to wear and bend the rails. The new craze was electricity, but while it was relative easy to maintain it had the disadvantages of high initial investment and inflexibility—an electric engine could not run on any track like a steamer. There had to be a power wire overhead or alongside. Then in 1905, W. R. McKeen of the Union Pacific's department of motive power designed a new rail vehicle. He used a 100-horsepower gasoline engine to power an ordinary passenger car with the engineer and the motor taking up the baggage compartment. His innovation offered great advantage to the small passenger service lines that had been wasting a steam locomotive to pull a couple of cars, but it could not pull "drag" freights, common to the twentieth century: those massive, more than a mile-long consists of heavy tonnages, headed by powerful double-engine Mallets and "articulateds." Something else would have to be invented to displace steam.

There was such an invention in Europe. Dr. Rudolph Diesel had been experimenting with his new internal combustion engine. But Diesel had disappeared on a cross-channel trip to England. Presumably he fell overboard and drowned, but cynics claimed that his willingness to consult with the British government had caused German military agents to assist in his descent into the sea. His early demise probably set the technology back considerably. Others, however, went forward in his stead. In 1913 General Electric (GE), inspired by the McKeen cars, created a gasoline-powered railcar that used the gasoline engine's torque to power a generator that ran a pair of traction motors that turned the wheels. The ugly boxlike engine, No. 100, was such a success that the McKeen principle of the gas-mechanical car was replaced by the gas-electric. An attempt to build several V-8 diesel-powered electrics for the army in World War I failed because of mechanical difficulties, probably in part because of the extra weight of the heavily armored cab.

Further efforts from GE in the decade after the war did better. GE combined its efforts with Ingersoll-Rand and the American Locomotive Company (Alco) to produce the first successful diesel-electric freight locomotive in 1922. Baldwin Locomotive works produced a couple of models independently, but they proved too fragile for hard rail use. Baldwin withdrew from the competition until the late 1930s. During this same period GE, Ingersoll-Rand, and Alco split into two companies, GE and Alco. In 1928, Alco produced a box-cab electric, the 1500, that was so capable that it worked right through World War II before being scrapped. This and other models allowed the New York Central to clean up the smoke pollution that had covered Manhattan Island for decades.

As Alco progressed, so did others. Buying up the Electro-Motive Corporation (EMC) in 1930, General Motors (GM) entered the diesel race. In 1934, EMC put out a diesel in a railcar; Edward G. Budd (a company specializing in all types of custom-built railcars, passenger cars, and now specialized freight equipment) streamlined its exterior and created the *Pioneer Zephyr* for the Chicago, Burlington & Quincy. The *Pioneer Zephyr*, a three-car articulated train (the inner car rode on the trucks of the outer cars), weighed as much as one normal passenger car of its day. It was an instant success, even starring in a Hollywood movie. Other rail lines ordered similar trains, the Illinois Central's *Green Diamond* and the Union Pacific's *M-10000* being the best-known examples. The Baltimore & Ohio and the

Santa Fe bought larger styled box-cabs for their "name trains." These units often ran in pairs, back-to-back, and the modern diesel "lash-up" was born. The diesel spread into the switcher realm, and almost every engine maker in the country (Cummins, Ingersoll-Rand, Baldwin, Alco, EMC, and GE) was putting out motors for rail locomotives.

In 1938, Electro-Motive put out the 567-cubic-inch diesel in an effort to challenge steam in freight power. But the engine made its name in streamlined passenger locomotives called the "E" series. Sporting sleek, raked-back cowls and fancy paint jobs that were continued on the cars that followed, the Es were giant locomotives with 12-cylinder, 2,000-horsepower motors driving two six-axle trucks. The E was powered on only the end axles of each truck, or "A-1-A" in rail parlance (all axles powered would be called "C-C"). They would continue through nine model changes and pull every important passenger train ever fielded by American railroads right down to Amtrak in the 1970s.

Hard on the heels of the E units came the "FT." Designed by EMC with a V-16 diesel developing 1,350 horsepower (later increased in succeeding models), the FT rode on two-axle trucks in a power pattern called "B-B." The Santa Fe (SF) Railway was the first buyer, ditching its steam fleet as quickly as it could. The FT offered SF a great advantage. Trains could be powered more exactly by multiple lash-ups that did not waste as much power as the steamers. Santa Fe steam engines were oil burners anyway, as it crossed that coal-barren West. The change made sense, and the FT powered SF freights during World War II, never failing. The FT was so successful that GM reorganized the Electro-Motive Corporation by adding the Winton Motor Company and called the result the Electo-Motive Division (EMD). EMD would produce an entire F series (F-3, F-7, F-9) and power freights on nearly every American railroad. The Fs would later be replaced by the "GPs" (B-B power) and SDs (C-C power) beginning in the 1960s. EMD's success prompted Baldwin, Alco, and Fairbanks-Morse to enter the freight market, too, but wartime restrictions limited EMD to road engines and the others to switchers.

After World War II, the horsepower race began. Steam was dead, although it was a lingering death on some roads. The first volley in the horsepower race came from Fairbanks-Morse, which produced the aptly named Trainmaster in 1953. It was a versatile engine designed to switch or haul on the main line. These road switchers would come to dominate American locomotive design up to the present time. The first models came with a long hood cab and a short hood configuration, all with the same roof height. Western roads tended to run the short hood forward for better visibility; eastern roads tended to run the long hoods forward. Then, in the 1960s, someone at EMD cut the short hood and installed a full windshield for better visibility for the crew. The "snoot" became a standard version for all makers thereafter.

Attrition among the producers has reduced the field to EMD and GE. Alco had crankshaft problems, Fairbanks-Morse was undercapitalized, and Baldwin could not keep up and turned to heavy machinery. Although EMD had a head start, GE has managed to close the gap. Today both companies produce computer-regulated engines that give the crew more control; wide, so-called comfort cabs; and enough horsepower in each unit to out-pull a half dozen FTs. Diesel took on and replaced steam because it is more efficient. It requires less maintenance and chews up the track less because its power is smoother, being delivered through geared power wheels spread throughout its length, rather than heavy drivers linked by side rods. It is still resented by rail aficionados as an ugly intrusion over the magnificence of American steam locomotives, but it is here to stay—until nuclear-powered engines come along, if ever.

ELECTRIC LOCOMOTIVES
Electrification of train engines began with toy trains as early as 1835, and graduated to the powering of a full-sized locomotive with

batteries in 1857. Thomas A. Edison's claim to have invented the electric locomotive was challenged by German investor Wilhelm Siemans, who invented it the year before. By 1895, General Electric's No. 1 engine pulled a complete steam train (engine and all) through the 7,300-foot-long Howard Street Tunnel in Baltimore. Electricity was clean and made for use in the big cities of America. Manhattan Island, for example, prohibited the use of steam after 1908. It was also ideal for use in long tunnel situations that had forced the Southern Pacific railroad to create the cab-forward steam locomotive to keep the engine crew from being asphyxiated by its own exhaust in the tunnels of the Sierra Nevada.

Because of its terminal in New York City, the New York Central (NYC) was among the first to use outside third-rail direct-current electric locomotives. It built two powerhouses that could charge the whole line to White Plains, where the motive power was changed to steam. Other lines, notably the New Haven, followed the NYC's example, electrifying the road out to Stamford, Connecticut. Eventually, the New Haven electrified the whole route between New York City and New Haven. Most of the later electric locomotives ran off an overhead catenary line that ran on alternating current because it has better transmission qualities over distance. The power was picked up by extending a pantograph up from the engine roof. The outside third rail, on the other hand, was picked up by a "shoe" that could be retraced and folded alongside the engine. Motormen could switch between the two forms of power by flipping a simple lever inside the cab.

Following the success of New Haven with electric power, the Pennsylvania Railroad (PRR) took a look at it. Electrification made possible the tunneling under the harbor into Manhattan Island's Penn Station. But the Pennsy, as it was affectionately called, wanted more. It had been experimenting with a powerful passenger and freight hauler run by electricity. During the Great Depression (which gives one an appreciation as to the financial soundness of the PRR in those days), the Pennsylvania Railroad electrified much of its route between New York City and Philadelphia. By 1940, the PRR had electrified 2,667 miles of track, 40 percent of the nation's electrified rails. It had the engine to use it, too. This was the powerful, streamlined GG-1, geared for 90-mile-per-hour operation. At first an passenger locomotive, later GG-1s were geared for freight hauling. They cut nearly an hour off the trip between New York City and Washington, D.C.

Out West, the Great Northern (GN) and the Milwaukee Road used electric power to run through their tunnels under the Rocky Mountains. The GN's Cascade bore was two and a half miles long, the longest tunnel in North America. The tremendous box-cab electrics in the West were two engines semipermanently coupled back-to-back, and had a wheel combination of 2-B+B and B+B-2. They were over 112 feet long. During World War II the Milwaukee Road bought a group of electric locomotives designed for the Soviet Union through the lend-lease program, but never delivered. The units, nicknamed "Little Joes" after the Soviet leader Joseph Stalin, were almost 90 feet long and powered in a 2-D-D-2 arrangement. Later, the Milwaukee's staff developed a remote control that allowed its engineers to run diesels on the same train, an unusual combination of different power types. A later electric used "regenerative traction," a method whereby the motor becomes its own generator, using the motor to assist braking and actually returning power to the overhead wires. A similar technique called "dynamic braking" is used on modern diesels.

Electric power has several advantages besides its cleanliness. It develops higher torque on a grade, there is less maintenance than a diesel or steamer, and the fuel costs less after the initial heavy capital investment in the overhead lines or third rail. It even works better in cold weather, a distinct plus in the Rockies and other mountain ranges. But the initial capital outlay essentially doomed electricity as well as steam to the powerful, more flexible diesel.

STEAM LOCOMOTIVES

The first American locomotive was built by John Stevens in 1825—a four-wheeled flat-car with an upright boiler. He ran it around a small circle of track on his Hoboken, New Jersey, estate. Four years later the Delaware and Hudson (D&H) Canal (forerunner of the D&H Railroad) imported from England a locomotive named the *Stourbridge Lion*. Developed by Robert Stephenson & Company, one of the first builders of practical locomotives in the world, the *Lion* proved to be too heavy for the D&H's bridges and was dismantled. But the *Lion* was the first locomotive to pull cars in America. In 1830, Peter Cooper, a Baltimore merchant and philanthropist, designed and supervised the building of the first practical locomotive made in the United States, the *Tom Thumb*. The first rail line to use steam from the start was the South Carolina Canal and Railroad Company. Its locomotive was the *Best Friend of Charleston*, a small four-wheeler that blew up when its fireman lashed down the safety valve. He had grown tired of its noise.

As the demand for locomotives grew, the American engine-building industry expanded to met the need. The first major producer of railroad steam engines was Paterson, New Jersey. Led by men like Thomas Rogers, William Swinburne, John Cooke, and Charles Danforth, the town, located on the falls of the Passaic River, had to construct its own railroad to reach the nearest mainline to deliver its products. Various companies in the town produced the old diamond-stacked locomotives made famous to modern Americans in Hollywood movies and amusement parks.

A steam locomotive is essentially a boiler turned on its side. Fired from the rear of the tube by wood, oil, or coal, hot gases are carried into the tube, which has been partly filled with water in pipes, heating it until steam is formed. After the beginning of the nineteenth century the steam was reheated a second time to create superheated steam, a more efficient propellant at higher pressures. This steam was then forced into the cylinders at the front of the engine and fed against the pistons alternately from the front and back of the cylinder to cause a back-and-forth motion that was imparted to the driving wheels by a pair of drive rods. All of the drivers were counterweighted, quartered (so each side would be powered as the other recovered), and linked together with side rods to work in cooperation with each other. The only thing that changed over the years was the design of the locomotives (bigger pistons and improved valve gear) and the pressures of the steam (beginning with 100 pounds per square inch in early nineteenth-century models, doubling by the end of the century, and then as high as needed as boiler technology advanced). The basic principles remained the same.

The engineer and fireman worked the whole mechanism from inside the cab, a standard box at the back of the boiler by the 1850s. Early cabs were quite luxurious, made of fine, polished woods, and even having interior and exterior decorations. Inside, the fireman fed the fire by hand, until the advent of the automatic stoker, and watched the fire and pressure gauges. The engineer worked the "Johnson lever" that imparted forward or rearward power to the cylinders. To put the Johnson bar in neutral would cause the engine to stand still. The throttle went to the steam dome and regulated how fast the engine ran. To go too quickly or slow too fast could separate the train. The drawbar pressure had to be maintained by a constant shifting of throttle and brakes, a fine art when the train weighs several hundred tons and is running up and down slight grades at 50 or more miles an hour. Engineers developed a real attitude about the skills of their job and were just as cocky as any stagecoach driver of earlier times. The conductor might be in charge of the train, but nobody moved unless the engineer pulled the right levers.

Steam locomotives are differentiated by the combinations and numbers of wheels or axles under it. There are various systems, but the most common is the Whyte classification system (who Whyte was has been lost in history). This system is based on counting up the paired wheel types from the front

A front view of streamlined diesel and steam trains. Efficient diesel-powered locomotives derailed steam trains in the early twentieth century.

(cowcatcher or pilot) to the rear and placing them in a formula. Each locomotive is listed by the number of small pilot wheels at the front, followed by the number of drivers, then the number of trailing wheels under the firebox. If any one component is missing it is given the value of zero. For example, an engine with a pair of leading pilot wheels on one axle, six drivers on the middle three axles, and a pair of trailing wheels on a rear axle is a 2-6-2, or in railroad slang, a Prairie. The more wheels in a truck preceding the drivers, the smoother and easier a loco comes into a switch or a curve. Hence, most passenger engines have four of them. The more wheels under the firebox, the bigger it can be. Thus the larger engines have more of them. A 4-8-4 (Northern) is a speedy, high-powered engine that can be used in passenger or freight work. A 2-6-0 (Mogul) is a small freight hauler. A 4-6-0 (Ten-wheeler) or 4-4-2 (Atlantic) is a small passenger engine.

Mallet (double sets of drivers) steam engines, named after the Swiss inventor Anatole Mallet, came into use in the United States at the beginning of the twentieth century. A true Mallet uses the steam twice—once in the rear driver high-pressure cylinders and a second time on the front driver low-pressure cylinders. An "articulated" engine is of the same outward appearance except it has high-pressure steam chests on the front and back drivers and its frame is hinged in the middle to take curves. On a sharp curve, in some models that had the boiler connected only to the last half of the frame, the front of the engine tube would swing wide to the side. An example of such an engine would be a 2-8-8-2, a common freight engine, or a 4-6-6-4, a Union Pacific (UP) combination freight/passenger engine known as a Challenger, one of the best all-around locomotives ever produced.

The biggest practical articulated engine was the UP's Big Boy, a 4-8-8-4, whose small drivers made it a freight hauler par excellence. The Santa Fe tried a 2-10-10-2 combination but it proved impractical. So the Santa Fe broke them in half and rebuilt them as 2-10-2s. But the Virginian Railway had better designed 2-10-10-2s that functioned quite all right. The Erie used a Triplex (three sets of drivers and steam chests) for nine years until 1925 that had a 2-8-8-8-2 combination. High-pressure steam drove the middle set of drivers; low-pressure steam powered the fore and aft set. It had greater tractive effort than the later Big Boy, but unlike the Union Pacific engine, it proved to be too complicated to be of value. Since switchers have to negotiate lots of sharp corners, they usually lack the leading and trailing trucks. A small switcher might be a 0-4-0, indicating it was resting on four drivers on two axles; a big switcher would be a 0-10-0. A switcher without a tender that carried its own water and coal in an onboard bunker would have a "T" added after the wheel combination. They were often called tank locomotives. Early commuter trains were pulled by a variety of larger tank locos that had normal passenger wheel arrangements.

Until the advent of new power sources at the beginning of the twentieth century, steam was king. But the addition of electric and diesel power changed all of that. By the end of World War II, diesel was cheaper to operate than coal. It required less servicing over distance, affected the track less, and was cleaner to operate, not requiring the elimination of ashes nor the use of water chock full of boiler tube-clogging minerals. In 1945, coal cost around $4 a ton, and diesel was 7 cents a gallon. The combination of several low-power units allowed the railroad to select pulling power more closely related to the load hauled. Economy and flexibility demanded shifting the power source. The process was accelerated by the fact that many steam engines ran on low-grade oil and the government encouraged the use of petroleum products, which seemed plentiful at the time. Sadly, most steam engines were turned into junk, except for a few relics kept behind for rail fans and publicity uses.

After the energy crises of the 1970s threw the future of oil in doubt, the American Coal Enterprises produced a modern, redesigned steam engine to utilize America's plentiful supply of that fossil fuel. With coal running at $15 a ton as opposed to fuel oils at over $1 a gallon, the price differential so important in ending steam engines a half century ago had ended. Now the steam engine can operate at $1.60 per million BTUs versus the diesel's $6 per million BTUs. This meant that by 1980 the switch back to coal looked better on the accounting books than did the original dumping of steam propulsion in the 1950s.

The ACE 3000 looked more like a passenger diesel on the outside, but it was all brute, coal-fired steam power on closer examination. The leading power unit produced 4,000 horsepower with diesel-equivalent tractive force, 80-mile-an-hour speed, a 500-mile range on its coal load, and 1,000 miles on its on-board water. The tender, called a "support unit" in today's government-speak jargon, had a complex system of condensation fans that recondensed water from the steam to be used over and over, making it highly efficient. It could work hand in hand with other coal units or with diesels, if the ACE 3000 led the lash-up. The coal was burned well within Environmental Protection Agency guidelines, and all coal and burned ash were added or removed in modular containers designed not to break the streamlined skin of the locomotive and to enhance speed and cleanliness. Servicing of water (called "condensate") and sand were performed at ground level. Although the proposal looked good, in the poignant words of one author, "neither General Motors nor General Electric have sold their diesel locomotive divisions." Changing oil prices and improved diesels have kept the reintroduction of coal-fired locomotives a dream at best.

See also Blomberg, Martin; Kuhler, Otto; Loewy, Raymond; McCoy, Elijah; McKeen, William Riley, Jr.; Neuhart, David E.

References Alexander, Edwin P., *Iron Horse* (1941); Barnard, Charles F., "Santa Fe's 3000 Class Mallets," *Model Railroader* (May 1989) 56: 85–91; Bezilla, Michael, "Electrification," in Keith L. Bryant, Jr. (ed.), *EABHB: Railroads in the Age of Regulation* (1988), 130–131; Comstock, Henry B., *The Iron Horse* (1993); Cook, Richard J., *Super Power Steam Locomotives* (1966); Drury, George H., "Dieselization," in Keith L. Bryant, Jr. (ed.), *EABHB: Railroads in the Age of Regulation* (1988), 119–121; Drury, George H., *Guide to North American Steam Locomotives* (1993); Duke, Donald, and Edmund Keilty, *RDC* (1990); Flower, George L. (ed.), *Locomotive Dictionary* (1972); Frey, Robert L., "Locomotives," in Robert L. Frey (ed.), *EABHB: Railroads in the Nineteenth Century* (1988), 228–239; Grant, H. Roger, "Electric Traction," in Keith L. Bryant, Jr. (ed.), *EABHB: Railroads in the Age of Regulation* (1988), 129–130; Hollingsworth, Brian, *Illustrated Encyclopedia of North American Locomotives* (1984); Hubbard, Freeman, *Encyclopedia of North American Railroading* (1981); Keefe, Kevin P., "Landmark Locomotive: Union Pacific's Challenger," *Trains* (January 1995) 55: 54–62; McGowan, George F., *Diesel Electric Locomotive Handbook* (1951); Marre, Louis A., and Jerry A. Pinkepank, *The Contemporary Diesel Spotter's Guide* (1979); Middleton, William D., *When the Steam Roads Electrified* (1951); Olmstead, Robert P., *The Diesel Years* (1975); Pinkepank, Jerry A., *The Second Diesel Spotter's Guide* (1977); Richards, Gilbert F., *Budd on the Move* (1975); Sinclair, Angus, *Development of the Locomotive Engine* (1970); Sperandeo, Andy, "Presenting the ACE 3000: A Steam Locomotive for Today's Railroads," *Model Railroader* (June 1982) 49: 77–79; Tuplin, William A., *The Steam Locomotive* (1975); White, John H., Jr., *American Locomotives* (1968); White, Roy V. (ed.), *The Locomotive Cyclopedia of American Practice* (1941); Zimmermann, Karl R., *The Milwaukee Road under Wire* (1973).

Loewy, Raymond (1893–1987)

French-born and raised, Raymond Loewy became a U.S. citizen in 1938. He wanted to streamline Pennsylvania Railroad (PRR or "Pennsy") locomotives, but the company put him to work designing station trash-can shrouds instead. Loewy went ahead and submitted a design for his first locomotive anyhow. The proposal became the origin of the GG-1, one of the most important electric engines in the history of American railroading. Loewy's design called for one all-welded, sleek, unbroken shell with no rivets or joints showing. The lack of broken lines made for easier maintenance and even cut construction costs. He had the engine painted in the traditional Brunswick green or Tuscan red, offset by five thin gold stripes running the length of the body and curving to a pointed V at the front and back pilots (both ends were duplicate cabs, allowing the engine to run in either direction without being turned). The stripes were adorned with the name of the road, "Pennsylvania," stretched out the full length of the sides. Power was from an overhead electric catenary system, imparted to the engine through one (the rearward, usually) of a pair of pantographs on top of the hood. The railroad bought 130 of them for its eastern corridor travel; they lasted into the modern era, the 40 survivors being taken over by Amtrak until a change in railroad overhead electricity from 25 to 60 Hz put them out of work in the mid-1970s.

Loewy then went on to streamline the steam fleet used for passenger service. He made over 100 wind-tunnel tests so that his shrouds not only looked good but were functional as well. In the 1940s he completely redesigned the Pennsy's *Broad Way Limited* into a lightweight streamliner. He did freelance jobs for the Fairbanks-Morse Locomotive Company's new diesels, and passenger cars for the Delaware & Hudson, Missouri Pacific, Boston & Maine, Northern Pacific, and Monon. He also redesigned the Norfolk & Western's Roanoke station. Loewy was one of three premier designers of American Railroad equipment during the golden age of passenger service, the other two being Otto Kuhler and Henry Dreyfuss. He did much to make American passenger trains among the most attractive and stylish in the world.

See also Kuhler, Otto; Locomotives; Pennsylvania Railroad.

References Hubbard, Freeman, *Encyclopedia of North American Railroading* (1981); Loewy, Raymond, *Never Let Well Enough Alone* (1951); Loewy, Raymond, *Designs of Raymond Loewy* (1975); Zimmerman, Karl R., *The Remarkable GG-1* (1977).

Long Island Rail Road (LIRR)

Originally, the Long Island Rail Road was chartered in 1834 to be built from New York to Boston. As the Connecticut shore was thought impracticable for railroads because of its numerous rivers and coves, the LIRR would run from Brooklyn to Greenport on Long Island, where passengers would detrain and board ships to cross the sound and reboard Boston-bound trains at Stonington, Connecticut. The line flourished for about five years when the predecessors to the New Haven Railroad proved the shorter onshore route was able to be built. By 1850, the LIRR was in receivership. The new managers then set another goal: carrying passengers to communities on Long Island and connecting to Manhattan-bound ferries. By 1895 it reached Montauk, just in time to carry soldiers to and from the military camp there for the Spanish-American War.

By buying out competing lines, the LIRR soon had a monopoly on all rail traffic to Long Island. It was the first railway to use electric trains, the first to use all-steel cars, and the first to abandon its wooden equipment completely. It was controlled by an automatic speed controller that allowed only one train at a time in a specific block of track to prevent head-on and tailend wrecks, common before its introduction. It reached an agreement with the Pennsylvania Railroad (Pennsy) to tunnel under New York Harbor. The LIRR had the permits but no money to build; the Pennsy had plenty of cash but no permits. The Pennsylvania Railroad built a tunnel for each road and the terminal at Penn Station. LIRR became a Pennsylvania subsidiary in exchange. By the 1950s, however, the LIRR had lost 80 percent of its business to the automobile. Pennsylvania sold the bankrupt railway to the New York Transportation Authority for $465 million.

The new owners began to upgrade equipment and operate on a full schedule, retaining the LIRR name. Electricity was extended out to Huntington, grade crossings were eliminated by fly-overs, and welded rail was installed to smooth the ride. Pushed on by the Arab Oil Embargo of the 1970s, ridership rose to nearly 73 million.

The Long Island Rail Road was the first railway to replace wooden equipment with all-steel cars. Today, the Long Island Rail Road is the busiest commuter train in the United States.

Today, it runs special racetrack, fishing, and parlor car excursions. It is the second oldest railroad to operate under its original name (Georgia Railroad being the oldest), and the only one in the nation to make more money off of passenger service than freight. It is the busiest commuter train in America, still operating out of Penn Station, where it rents space from Amtrak.

See also Commuter Trains; Pennsylvania Railroad; Trains in Cities.

References Condit, Carl W., *The Port of New York* (2 vols., 1980–1981); Drury, George H., *The Historical Guide to North American Railroads* (1985); Drury, George H., *The Train-Watcher's Guide* (1990); Grow, Lawrence, *On the 8:02* (1979); Henwood, James N. J., "Long Island Rail Road," in Keith L. Bryant, Jr. (ed.), *EABHB: Railroads in the Age of Regulation* (1988), 258–259; Hubbard, Freeman, *Encyclopedia of North American Railroading* (1981); Kramer, Frederick A., and John Krause, *Long Island Rail Road* (1978); Seyfried, Vincent F., *The Long Island Rail Road* (1961–1972); Zeil, Ron, and George W. Foster, *Steel Rails to the Sunrise* (1965).

Lorenzo, Frank (b. 1940)

Born Francisco Anthony Lorenzo in New York City of Spanish immigrant parents, Frank Lorenzo is a modern Horatio Alger to admirers and an uncaring egotist to his detractors. Either way, he remains one of the movers who realized the effects of deregulation on modern airline development of the 1980s. Lorenzo was educated in New York City schools, including a college degree at Columbia. He graduated from Harvard Business School with an MBA and joined Trans World Airlines (TWA) as a financial analyst. He soon moved over to rival Eastern Airlines in the same capacity. But Lorenzo was not one who likes to work for others—he was and is his own man. It did not take long before he opened his own entrepreneurial business with a college classmate, Robert J. Carney.

After some minor deals, Chase Manhattan Bank asked Lorenzo and Carney to assist a faltering airline client, Texas International. Lorenzo insisted that he become the head of the carrier and Chase Manhattan agreed. Once in power, Lorenzo cut unprofitable routes, trimmed the number of employees, weathered an employees' strike with a victorious antilabor stance, established new routes and so-called peanut fares, and brought the debt-plagued airline into the black in short order. It was a pattern that he would remain faithful to throughout his airline career. He used Texas International as the basis for his holding company, Texas Air Corporation, for his future ventures.

With the coming of deregulation in 1978, Lorenzo moved to expand his holdings before someone did the same to him. He was one of the first to truly understand the implications of the decline in government regulations that had protected unprofitable routes for decades. His first foray into airline expansion was to attempt to buy National Airlines, but he lost out to TWA because he was loaded down with debt from earlier business moves. In the process he earned the title "Lorenzo the Presumptuous" when he dismissed doubts of his financial stability with a haughty claim that he could always raise the necessary cash as in the past. True to his word, Lorenzo then bought out New York Air, with its nonunion employees and cheap fares, and moved into the prosperous Atlantic Coast market in competition with Eastern Airlines. One of his associates, Donald C. Bun, left to form People's Express, using Lorenzo's success formula. Lorenzo would later merge with People's and bring it back into his own stable.

By 1980, Lorenzo was ready for the move that would bring him fame and infamy. He took over struggling Continental Airlines. The company was loaded with debt and high union-scale wages, but Lorenzo wanted its fleet of wide-body DC-10 jets. Learning of his move, employees tried to raise the capital to stop him but failed. When the federal government refused to see Lorenzo's takeover as a possible antitrust violation, the deal was done. Lorenzo immediately merged everything he owned into Continental and proceeded with his tried-and-true formula. He laid off 15 percent of the old Continental staff outright. The rest went on strike to stop him. Using new federal bankruptcy laws that allowed filing without actually being broke, Lorenzo filed Chapter 11. He then said Continental was to become a discount airline and dropped three-fourths of its routes and two-thirds of the employees. Those who remained had their wages and benefits slashed. Then he cut his own salary—a clever move more than a real deed as he had more than enough income from other sources. Pilots and flight attendants walked off their jobs, asserting that the airline was unsafe. Lorenzo went on with nonstrikers and new employees and rebuilt Continental to 10,000 workers and 70 routes, including some he had dropped earlier. At this time, he managed to absorb the smaller People's Express and Denver-based Frontier.

By now Lorenzo was so controversial that he was blocked in his efforts to merge with other major airlines. No one wanted to take the risk of the prolonged fight he seemed to bring with him everywhere he went. But there was one carrier that had problems as big as Continental's. That was Eastern. The employees there saw Frank Borman as a double-dealing, untrustworthy executive and welcomed Lorenzo as a breath of fresh air. It was to be a major error on their part. Borman was actually much more sensitive to his employees than the unions, blinded by their own antimanagement propaganda, realized. Lorenzo quickly dispelled any lingering doubts and instituted the usual formula: lower wages and benefits, cheap fares, cutbacks in staff and unprofitable routes. The militant Mechanics Union led the employees in a massive strike. Lorenzo retorted by selling Eastern's routes and other assets to meet his debts. Pilots and flight attendants went back to work trying to save their jobs at any cost. The federal government refused to interfere and in the end, Lorenzo literally sold Eastern out from under the still-striking machinists and ground crews. Lorenzo then got rid of his interests in the remaining shell of Eastern and the rest of his empire and retired from the airline business a wealthy man.

Lorenzo remains a controversial figure in American transportation history to this day. Opponents see him as a sort of ogre who made money at the expense of the working people under him. He defends himself with a simple statement, "We are not union busters. We are airline builders." Like all true believers, Lorenzo saw the future clearly and did what he thought had to be done under the environment in which he functioned. And like those who know where they are going, he often was tactless with those who marched to a different drummer. But he got where he was going—the others, sadly, did not.

See also Aeronautics; Continental Airlines; Eastern Air Lines.

References Bernstein, Aaron, *Grounded* (1990); Mailhout, Ernie, et al., *The Eastern Airlines Strike* (1991); Murphy, Charles E., *The Airline That Pride Almost Bought* (1986); Preston, Edmund, "Frank Lorenzo," in William M. Leary (ed.), *Encyclopedia of American Business History and Biography* (1992), 275–282.

Louisville & Nashville Railroad (L&N)

Chartered in Kentucky in 1850, the Louisville & Nashville ran between its namesakes before the American Civil War, a ten-hour trip in those days. At one time, its iron bridge over Kentucky's Green River was the longest in the country. Although the track was laid on a six-foot gauge, it was changed to five feet before the first train ran in 1859. It changed once again in the 1880s to the new standardized four feet, eight and a half inches. Its critical location from the Ohio River into Tennessee made it fair game for both Northern and Southern forces during the Civil War. Each side moved troops and supplies on it and destroyed the sections controlled by the enemy. During the Reconstruction that followed the war, the L&N expanded rapidly southward, reaching Memphis in 1871 and Birmingham, Alabama, in 1872. The latter place was barely a small town when the first trains came in, but the L&N's extensions into the coal-rich Appalachians and to St. Louis, Pensacola, Mobile, and New Orleans made Birmingham's steel plants boom. By 1881, the line had crossed the Ohio into Cincinnati.

Because of the iron ore in northern Alabama, the L&N became a prime coal hauler throughout the Middle South. It gave attractive rates for coal and iron, and had some of the better track locations in the area, making for slighter grades in roadbed and higher tonnage and higher speeds per train. In 1925, L&N leased the Clinchfield Railroad, an Appalachian coal route, splitting the lease with the Atlantic Coast Line. As the L&N was a major coal carrier, it changed to diesels rather reluctantly in 1957.

The freight-hauling L&N did not neglect its passenger service. It ran the crack *Panama Limited* between Cincinnati and New Orleans. The *South Wind* went from Chicago to Miami via the L&N and other roads. The latter was unusual because it hauled special tenders for its steam engines, carrying 27.5 tons of coal and 20,000 gallons of water. This eliminated the numerous water stops and made it the longest-running, nonstop, regularly scheduled, steam-powered passenger train in the nation, running 205 miles between Nashville and Birmingham. In 1950 the L&N carried 2.6 million passengers. By the time it turned passenger service over to Amtrak, it had dropped 74 passenger trains and 34 mixed passenger-express trains from its schedule—a poignant reminder of what the automobile meant to all railroads in the 1950s and 1960s. It expanded its operations northward in 1971 by absorbing the Monon Route, an X-shaped Indiana railroad that ran from Chicago to Indianapolis and Michigan City to Louisville. A year later, increased financial problems endemic to all American railroads forced the L&N to become a part of the Family Lines System.

See also Family Lines System.

References Herr, Kincaid A., *The Louisville & Nashville Railroad* (1964); Hubbard, Freeman, *Encyclopedia of North American Railroading* (1981); Klein, Maury, *History of the Louisville & Nashville Railroad* (1972); Klein, Maury, "The Louisville & Nashville Railroad," in Keith L. Bryant, Jr. (ed.), *EABHB: Railroads in the Age of Regulation* (1988), 268–269; Nock, O. S., *Railways of the USA* (1979); Stover, John F., *Railroads of the South* (1955); Stover, John F., "The Louisville & Nashville Railroad," in Robert L. Frey (ed.), *EABHB: Railroads in the Nineteenth Century* (1988), 236–241; Tilford, John E., *L&N: Its First 100 Years* (1951).

Lowe, Thaddeus S. C. (1832–1913)

An inventor and scientist, Thaddeus Lowe was born in Jefferson, New Hampshire. He was interested in mechanics and chemistry at an early age and often dreamed of human flight. He constructed many balloons to study atmospherics, created a process to make artificial ice, invented oil and gas stoves, a water-gas apparatus, and the Lowe coke oven and founded Lowe Observatory in California. In 1858 he built the largest balloon of his day, christened the *New York*, in which he hoped to cross the Atlantic Ocean. A lack of hydrogen gas prevented its takeoff from New York City, and when he moved his operations to Philadelphia, an accidental piercing of the gasbag caused the project to be postponed indefinitely. The outbreak of the Civil War led to its permanent cancellation. During the war, Lowe was instrumental in using observation balloons to reconnoiter Confederate positions, especially during the Peninsular Campaign in 1862. Although his balloons were credited for several Union victories, they never caught on with the army and Lowe went back to his civilian pursuits.

See also Aerostatics.

References Haydon, Frederick S., *Aeronautics in the Union and Confederate Armies* (1941); Millbank, Jeremiah, Jr., *The First Century of Flight in America* (1943); Pineau, Roger, "Ballooning in the United States from Straw to Propane," in Eugene M. Emme (ed.), *Two Hundred Years of Flight in America* (1977), 41–67.

McAdam, John L. (1756–1836)

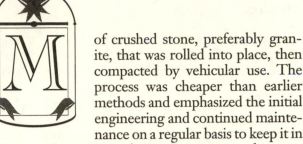

A Scotsman, John L. McAdam (also spelled Macadam) was sent to New York City where he spent the American Revolution selling prizes captured on the high seas by the British navy. He returned to Great Britain after the war and was involved in naval supplies and commissary work. In 1815, he was appointed surveyor general at Bristol and became interested in the process of road building. He had thought on the matter for some time previous, and spent his own money in experimenting with a process now called "macadamizing." Later, Parliament reimbursed him for his costs, considering his work a national treasure. His process was to grade the roadbed into the native soil and to stabilize it by covering it with a 6- to 12-inch bed of granite stone of varying sizes, not to exceed 2.5 inches. The surface was rolled by the passage of traffic and could be replaced as it wore by like material. It differed from the French process of J. P. M. Trésaguet in its lack of heavy underlying stone, which made it cheaper and easier to install and maintain. If it had a drawback, it was that if the underlying soil became wet through a lack of maintenance the whole pavement could shift. Hence, maintenance was the key principle of his road style (the system of reduced stones had been known for centuries) and his actual historical contribution, along with improved engineering of the initial layout. Both methods were used in the United States, but McAdam's came to be preferred because of its simplicity and cost.

See also Roads and Highways, Colonial Times to World War I; Trésaguet, Jean Pierre Marie.

Reference U.S. Department of Transportation, Federal Highway Administration, *America's Highways* (1976).

Macadamized Roads and Other Surfaces

A process of road building invented by the Scotsman, John L. McAdam, whereby the native soils were graded to accept a roadbed of crushed stone, preferably granite, that was rolled into place, then compacted by vehicular use. The process was cheaper than earlier methods and emphasized the initial engineering and continued maintenance on a regular basis to keep it in shape. Macadamization was used extensively in the early nineteenth century on American roads. Their deterioration during the neglectful last half of the century merely illustrated McAdam's wisdom in emphasizing the key role that continued repair meant to roads that endured constant heavy use.

As the interest in good roads picked up in the late nineteenth century, so did the use of different construction materials. Macadamized roads alone soon broke down under increasing motor vehicle traffic. Bituminous (oil-added) composites like asphalt had their beginnings in eastern cities, like New York and Washington, by the 1870s. Asphalt became popular because of its smoothness, silence, lack of dust, and ease of cleaning. It is also fairly easy to maintain, requiring tar sealing of cracks and a "seal coat" of road oil and gravel on a regular basis. It can also be "half-soled" in spots where the wear gets away from the normal upkeep. Its pliability often leads to its use as a patch in roads originally built with other materials.

Brick roads began in Cleveland, Ohio, in 1893. Concrete was first laid at Bellefontain, Ohio, in 1905, although federal records now give the honor to Wayne County, Michigan, in 1909. The first concrete road was two lanes, each 9 feet wide, laid in two "pours" (the first was 4 inches of cement, sand, and limestone mixed in a ratio of 1-2.5-5, and the second was 2.5 inches of cement, sand, and crushed cobblestones mixed 1-2-3); both were laid in 25-foot lengths separated by expansion felt. Current roads have surfaces, some reinforced by steel bars, that are 10 inches deep over a prepared roadbed of 4 to 20 inches of granular material before the natural soil is reached.

See also McAdam, John L.

McAdoo, William G. (1863–1941)

A Georgian, William G. McAdoo was educated at the University of Tennessee and admitted to the bar in 1885, even though he never finished college because of financial difficulty. McAdoo married Sarah Fleming in 1885. He practiced law in Chattanooga until 1893, when he moved to New York City. McAdoo had a lifelong interest in railroads, beginning with a street railway in Knoxville that soon went broke. In Manhattan, he conceived of the idea of tunneling under the Hudson River and in 1902 completed his scheme. He became vice-chairman of the Democratic National Committee in 1912, and President-elect Woodrow Wilson asked him to be secretary of the treasury the following year. McAdoo severed his rail connections and devoted himself to the creation of the Federal Reserve System. He later raised the money needed to fight World War I. At the end of 1917, the American transportation system had collapsed under the assaults of a full harvest, labor unrest, war production needs, and the harshest winter in decades. Wilson appointed McAdoo to run the United States Railroad Administration as director of railroads, a job he held until 1919, even after resigning the treasury post. In 1920 and 1924, he was an unsuccessful candidate for the presidency on the Democratic ticket and served as U.S. senator from California (1933–1938). As his first wife had died in 1912, McAdoo courted and married Eleanor Wilson, the president's daughter, in 1914. He later divorced her in 1935 and remarried a third time. He died in 1941 in Washington, D.C.

See also Railroads from Appomattox to Deregulation; United States Railroad Administration.

References Broesamle, John J., *William Gibbs McAdoo* (1973); Broesamle, John J., "William Gibbs McAdoo," in Keith L. Bryant, Jr. (ed.), *EABHB: Railroads in the Age of Regulation* (1988), 283–285; Cunningham, William J., *American Railroads* (1922); Godfrey, Aaron Austin, *Government Operation of the Railroads* (1974); Hines, Walker D., *War History of American Railroads* (1928); Kerr, K. Austin, *American Railroad Politics* (1968); Leonard, William Norris, *Railroad Consolidation under the Transportation Act of 1920* (1946); Lyon, Peter, *To Hell in a Day Coach* (1968); McAdoo, William G., *Crowded Years* (1931); Saunders, Richard, *The Railroad Mergers and the Coming of Conrail* (1978).

William Gibbs McAdoo

McCallum, Daniel Craig (1815–1878)

Scottish-born, Daniel McCallum came to New York with his parents and studied architecture. He patented his own arched-truss bridge and ran the McCallum Bridge Company. He was noted for the spindly look of his bridges, but they never collapsed. During the Civil War, and after the passage of the Military Railroad Act (1862), McCallum was made head of Union military railroads. With his headquarters in Washington, he operated 2,105 miles of track, and built or rebuilt 641 miles of track and 26 miles of bridges, much of the fieldwork being accomplished by his subordinate, Herman Haupt. In the Atlanta campaign, McCallum moved supplies for 100,000 men and 60,000 horses and mules over a 60-mile stretch of single-track railroad under the constant threat of attack. His major principle was to unload all cars upon reaching their destinations, never using them for storage. This maxim was ignored in World War I, leading to the near-collapse of the American rail system from a lack of rolling stock and the substitution of over-the-road trucks; but in World War II, McCallum's principle was followed to the army's advantage. McCallum received the rank of colonel and aide de camp, and was brevetted brigadier general (1864) and major general (1866) for war service.

See also Railroads before and during the Civil War; United States Railroad Administration.

References Boatner, Mark M., III, *Civil War Dictionary* (1959); Hubbard, Freeman, *Encyclopedia of North American Railroading* (1981); Ward, James A., "David Craig McCallum," in Robert L. Frey (ed.), *EABHB: Railroads in the Nineteenth Century* (1988), 246–248.

McCoy, Elijah (1844–1929)

A Canadian-born black whose parents had fled slavery in Kentucky, Elijah McCoy was a well-educated man with a degree from Edinburgh University in engineering. He applied for work on the Michigan Central (a part of the New York Central system that also crossed Ontario Province), but was forced to work as a fireman because of racial discrimination against black civil engineers. As he fired the locomotives, McCoy noticed that a lot of wasted time went into lubrication stops. After two years of experimentation, he invented an automatic oil cup that did the job while the train was running (1872). White railroad crews dismissed the idea as "the nigger oil cup," but his bosses reacted differently. They bought the cup for all of their engines, rewarded McCoy, and had him instruct the engine drivers in its use. He tinkered with other railway problems over the years and eventually had 50 patents.

In 1915, new superheated locomotives overpowered the old oil cup's ability to lubricate. So at age 70, McCoy invented a new graphite lubricator, generally considered his best invention. It proved to be efficient, saving lubricants, time, and wear and tear on the engines. Soon railroads retrofitted the graphite lubricator on all locomotives. His invention was considered one of the key ingredients in keeping rail movements going during the increased demands of World War I. Like many inventors, McCoy died in poverty. Years later, the state of Michigan affixed a plaque to his old Detroit home, making it a historic site.

See also Locomotives, Steam Locomotives.
Reference Hubbard, Freeman, *Encyclopedia of North American Railroading* (1981).

MacDonald, Thomas H. (1881–1957)

Born at Leadville, Colorado, Thomas Harris MacDonald was raised in Iowa, where he attended Iowa State College and received a degree in engineering. His thesis was on the tractive effort necessary for a horse to draw a wagon over different kinds of roads. He worked for the state as a highway engineer and during his tenure helped Iowa become one of the first states to develop a statewide highway plan. As the soils were very difficult to stabilize, his success in hard-surfacing much of the system was noted nationwide. In 1919 he took over as chief of the Bureau of Public Roads—an office he held through seven presidential administrations. He retired in 1951 but stayed on as interim head until 1953.

A partial list of his achievements include creating the forerunner of the Highway Research Board, being the prime mover behind the Federal Highway Act of 1921 (and its idea of federal assistance administered by the states, which is still standard), sponsoring the Pan American Congress and its highway, setting up the first highway safety conference, being commissioner and builder of the Alaska Highway, and acting as liaison between the federal government and the American Association of Highway Officials.

MacDonald was among the first to see highways in a broader picture than mere convenience—he thought that roads were an integral part of the whole American economy, which affected the movement of goods and services and the growth of cities and states, and determined patterns of settlement. He believed in cooperation between the different levels of government and ran his bureau in the same manner. He liked to delegate authority and give it free rein amid certain standards of excellence. He was a talker among men, one who liked to air all views and involve as many in decision making as possible. He believed in inclusion rather than exclusion in his management. These attitudes made him adept at gaining the cooperation of the states, who were jealous of losing power to the federal government. Though in the end they lost most of that power, MacDonald got them to like it and work for it. His 49 years in government at state and federal levels made him one of the major movers in the American highway system.

See also Roads and Highways since World War I.

Reference U.S. Department of Transportation, Federal Highway Administration, *America's Highways* (1976).

McKeen, William Riley, Jr. (1869–1926)

An enterprising inventor (he held over 2,000 railroad patents) who produced an air-conditioning system for passenger cars, William McKeen was best known for his building of a unique rail self-contained motor car, which he produced at his McKeen Motor Car Company beginning in 1908. He produced about 157 such cars, run by 100-horsepower marine gasoline engines. His cars had a pointed prow and rounded stern to lessen air resistance, the depressed center doors now so familiar on commuter lines, and circular windows like portholes. McKeen's cars could make up to 75 miles an hour, but ran best at 50 mph. A string of seven of his cars sent out to the Southern Pacific is reputedly the first all-steel train run west of the Mississippi. They were used to fill in for short passenger hauls where a regular train would have been run at a loss. McKeen's principle of Rail Diesel Cars (RDCs) was taken over and expanded by the Budd Corporation, which still produces railroad equipment today.

See also Locomotives; Trains in Cities.

References Duke, Donald, and Edmund Keilty, *RDC* (1990); Hubbard, Freeman, *Encyclopedia of North American Railroading* (1981).

McLean Trucking Co. v. U.S. 321 US 67 (1944)

McLean involved a 1944 U.S. Supreme Court decision that treated the dichotomy between the stated desire to merge common carriers for more efficiency and better service and the 1914 Clayton Act, which spoke against mergers. The court ruled that the merger was valid if the advantages of consolidation outweighed the disadvantages of reduced competition. It would decide similar mergers on a case-by-case basis, with no hard and fast rules. This decision, in effect, set aside the more stringent provisions of previous antitrust laws.

See also Reed-Bullwinkle Act of 1948; *Rochester Telephone Corporation v. U.S.*; Transportation Acts.

Reference Saunders, Richard, *The Railroad Mergers and the Coming of Conrail* (1978).

McNary-Watres Air Mail Act (1930)

As the types of civilian aircraft improved and the aviation business became more complex, more federal legislation appeared. In 1930 Congress enacted the McNary-Watres Air Mail Act. This measure was an attempt by Postmaster General Walter Brown to organize the airline industry into three large companies that might provide better passenger and mail service (the mail contracts gave bonuses to companies that also provided passenger service). It was hoped that the larger companies might survive more financially secure and obviate the need for future subsidies altogether. But in 1933, a major scandal in awarding the contracts turned up, with payoffs from airline operators to the government being alleged. To clean up the mess, the government turned the airmail contracts over to the army. But military aviation was not up to the task, and a dozen airmen quickly lost their lives. This caused Congress to take another look at the airline industry during the New Deal under the Black-McKellar Act.

See also Aeronautics; Black-McKellar Act; Kelly Air Mail Act.

References Bilstein, Roger E., *Flight in America* (1994); Komons, Nick, *Bonfires to Beacons* (1978); Whitnah, Donald R., *Safer Skyways* (1966).

Maine Central Railroad (MEC)

With one of its antecedents chartered in 1832, the Maine Central is the product of nearly 150 years of mergers and sell-offs that has produced a rarity in modern American railroading in New En-gland—a profitable line. In 1933, the MEC entered into an agreement with the Boston & Maine (B&M) Railroad that provided for joint management. MEC was basically a tourist's railroad, taking people to resorts and operating coastal steamers and bus lines. It also ran an airline with Amelia Earhart as a vice-president. Freight generally involved supplies and finished products for the local paper mills. By 1952, however, the MEC had begun to leave the B&M, a process completed in 1955, when it started to paint its locomotives pine-needle green instead of maroon. During the bicentennial in 1976, MEC named several of its diesels after American Revolutionary War heroes, but the procedure has not become general. In 1980, U.S. Filter took over the MEC, but the parent company's sale to Ashland Oil led to the railroad being sold to the Guilford Transportation Industries, managers also of the B&M and the Delaware & Hudson.

See also Anthracite and Bridge Line Railroads; Boston & Maine Railroad; Vermont Railway.

References Baker, George P., *The Formation of the New England Railroad Systems* (1937); Drury, George H., *The Historical Guide to North American Railroads* (1985); Drury, George H., *The Train-Watcher's Guide* (1990); Harlow, Alvin F., *Steelways of New England* (1946); Hickcox, David H., "Maine Central Railroad," in Keith L. Bryant, Jr. (ed.), *EABHB: Railroads in the Age of Regulation* (1988), 274–275; Hubbard, Freeman, *Encyclopedia of North American Railroading* (1981); Johnson, Ron, *The Best of Maine Railroads* (1985); Lindahl, Martin L., *The New England Railroads* (1965); Peters, Bradley, *Maine Central Railroad Company* (1976).

Majors, Alexander (1814–1900)

From Franklin County, Kentucky, Alexander Majors moved with his family to Missouri as a small boy. He married and became a farmer. He was successful, but his children were all girls, which led him to believe that he needed a different career since farming depended so much on large families of boys for labor. In 1846, he began trading with reservation Indians over the line in what would become Kansas. He got his first contract in the Santa Fe wagon trade in 1848, making the round-trip in 92 days, the fastest on record. Although he was doing well on his own, he joined with William H. Russell and William B. Waddell in 1855 as Russell and Majors, and later as Russell, Majors & Waddell.

Majors was the fieldman for his partners. He knew men and animals and how to get the most out of each. He hired and fired, loaded wagons, and saw to it they got on the road. He was famous for the pledge that all his employees had to agree to: no profanity, no drunkenness, no gambling, no cruel treatment of animals, and to conduct oneself as a gentleman or be discharged. He recommended Bible reading for all, and expected the company to be run on its principles from top to bottom and back up again. In many ways, it was his supervision that kept the company functioning in the field, day after day, year after year. And the tough men of the frontier seemed to like him.

When the firm failed in 1861, Majors never again went into government-backed freighting, staging, or financing. So far as can be determined, he left his partners and never saw them again. He was only 46, but had a difficult time starting over. He did some private freighting and eventually moved to Salt Lake City, where he became a personal friend of Brigham Young. He attended the Golden Spike ceremony of the joining of the transcontinental railroad. Then he went into silver mining, at which he never prospered. After roaming around a bit, Majors settled in Denver. There a former employee, William F. Cody, already famous as "Buffalo Bill," found him living in poverty, the floor of his shack covered with pages from a manuscript of his life as a freighter. Cody got Majors to finish the work and had it published for him (*Seventy Years on the Frontier*). It is a priceless piece of memorabilia, as noteworthy for what it leaves out or skips over as for what it says. He lived at Cody's Nebraska ranch briefly, and was a featured guest at several western business conventions. In 1900, he went to Chicago on a business trip where he contracted pneumonia and died.

Major's life spanned much of the nineteenth century. He saw many advances, some of which he made possible through his use of transportation and freighting. He crossed the Plains countless times and lived to see them transformed from the Great American Desert into the breadbasket of the world. When he was born, the War of 1812 was about to end. Transportation relied on the horse. When he died, the Wright brothers were tinkering with flight. It was a big change, and he witnessed it all.

See also Russell, Majors & Waddell Company.

Manifest Destiny

One of the driving forces in the building of the American nation, necessitating the technological advances in transportation to keep such a large land mass intact, was the ideology of Manifest Destiny. Although Henry Eddy, editor of the *Illinois Gazette*, asserted that the Unites States was "manifestly called to a destiny" in 1824, the actual term was coined by John L. O'Sullivan, a New York newspaperman, during the 1840s. It was a period of American interest in Texas, New Mexico (Santa Fe in particular), California, and Oregon. It was also the time of James K. Polk's political campaign calling for "54–40′ or fight," the "reannexation of Texas," and "the reannexation of Oregon," implying that somehow the United States had been robbed of its natural and legal rights to these areas and was going to get them all back.

The United States is not unique in its devotion to such a thought scheme. In fact, most nations throughout the world believe in their uniqueness over others. Some, however, lack the muscle to carry it out—others, like the United States, glory in the opposite, assisted by technological advances in transportation (wagons and stagecoaches, railroads and steamships) that carry the ideology forward. Manifest Destiny was, and is, the notion that the United States has a preeminent social worth and a unique right in its application of moral principles—the American mission to the world. Religious in its justifiability, although God's grace is not the sole determining factor in its makeup, there is also a natural right or secular quality to its composition—a right of self-determination and geographic predestination that supersedes all others' claims to language superiority, institutional superiority, or boundaries. It was the notion that the United States has a right to expand to the natural boundaries of the oceans that surround it, until stopped by nature itself. It involved America's superior use of the soil in an intensive agriculture that pushed the more nomadic Native Americans aside with scarcely a backward glance. It represents the northern European culture and American language that supplanted the Hispanic control of the great Southwest and drove Americans into Oregon and California, looking for the natural western boundary of the Pacific Ocean. Justified as an effortless growth, the filling of a void, manifest destiny encompassed the belief that no one was there unless white Americans were.

Manifest Destiny is also a special dispensation: the belief that America must extend the blessings of liberty, democracy, and constitutional government to those less fortunate (i.e., anyone in the way at the moment). It is a dispensation that cannot be denied, even by Americans. Whenever the American right to a piece of land or its policies are challenged by another nation or people with a seemingly equal or better claim under positive law, an appeal to the highest law of all, natural law (secular) or God's law (religious), suffices to assert special, final, superior U.S. claim. It is nationalism writ large. It also involves the extension of the old Puritan concept of a City on a Hill, now best seen as a form of isolationism. The United States no longer is to be an example to the world under Manifest Destiny—America will become the world, the world will become America, and modern technology like planes, ships, and vehicles in the form of rapid-moving armed forces will make it all possible.

Manifest Destiny is quite arrogant in its assumptions. It asserts that others will find themselves drawn to American ideals and control merely because the United States represents national goodness and purity more than any other country. This gave Americans a missionary zeal to extend this wonderful blessing even to those too "ignorant" to accept it outright. Moreover, the United States could not stop this process. The nation had to advance because it was a natural thing, willed by the powers that made the universe. Americans could not resist it any more than those who were conquered by it. It involved more than inevitable destiny. It was also called the White Man's Burden—to do what is right for our "little brown brothers" overseas; if necessary, to "civilize them with a Krag" (an infantry rifle of the 1890s). It involved a paramount interest, as in the American building and ruling of the Panama Canal, and Panamá itself. It gave the United States an exaggerated idea of self-defense, including the right to intervene in Latin American countries, or anywhere in the world, for that matter. It was the international police power, be it disguised by the League of Nations, the United Nations, the North Atlantic Treaty Organization, or any other international organization. And it represented a presumed political affinity, such as why America has a special interest in Canada—a condescending quality that still galls Canadians to the bone, to the wonderment of their neighbors to the south.

Manifest Destiny, then, has had many forms. During the American Revolution and the War of 1812, it was the drive to save Canada from British rule. During the nineteenth century it was the expansion to the Pacific and the desire to take all of Mexico in 1848, the latter blunted only by the slavery conflict at home. It was the secession of the South in 1860–1861, and the defense of the Union and Reconstruction that followed. It was the rise of the jingoistic imperialism of the 1890s, with the United States conquering the Spanish "oppressors" in the Caribbean and the Philippines, only to set up its own "better" empire. It was Woodrow Wilson's need to "make the world safe for democracy" and set up the League of Nations. All of this was made possible by extending American power overseas.

With the rise of air transportation to buttress the ship-borne extension of American influence, Manifest Destiny took on a truly worldwide aspect. It was Franklin D. Roosevelt maneuvering the United States into World War II against the non–Anglo-Saxon ideal of Germany and Japan, and helping to create and preserve Israel for the victims of that war. It was the Cold War, stopping the erosion of freedom everywhere. It was the Gulf War, saving America's alleged paramount interest in an area preeminent for oil—the key to modern transportation and industry; and as rocketry becomes more sophisticated, it extends into the reaches of space itself. It is the opposite of nonintervention, a continual theme and debate in American political life from its beginnings to the present.

See also Lewis and Clark Trail.

References Graebner, Norman A., *Empire on the Pacific* (1955); Graebner, Norman A., *Manifest Destiny* (1968); Merk, Frederick, *Manifest Destiny* (1963); Perkins, Dexter, *The Monroe Doctrine* (1933); Pratt, J. W., *Expansionists of 1898* (1936); Steel, Ronald, *Pax Americana* (1967); Weinberg, Albert K., *Manifest Destiny* (1935).

Mann-Elkins Act (1910)

Written by Senators Stephen B. Elkins of West Virginia (author of the earlier Elkins Act) and James R. Mann of Illinois, the Mann-Elkins Act prohibited higher rates for short hauls over long hauls without prior Interstate Commerce Commission approval, and gave the Interstate Commerce Commission (ICC) the right to suspend proposed rate changes without having to await a shipper's complaint. The burden of proof in all disputes rested with the carrier. Its jurisdiction was extended to communications as well as all transportation industries. The law established a commerce court to administer ICC decisions, but the court appointees proved so probusiness that Congress disbanded it in 1913 (a creature of President William H. Taft, the commerce court had been created only by a tie vote in the Senate as it was). Other proposals establishing a net worth of railroads and regulation of railroad securities were dropped. Further weakening of the bill was prevented, however, when Republican Progressives threatened to delay adjournment and force Congress to meet through the hot, humid Washington summer. By then, the ICC had all the power that the 1887 act had intended, but the courts and railroads had managed to find loopholes to avoid.

See also Clayton Act; Hepburn Act.

References Hays, Samuel, *The Response to Industrialism* (1957); Hoogenboom, Ari, "Mann-Elkins Act," in Keith L. Bryant, Jr. (ed.), *EABHB: Railroads in the Age of Regulation* (1988), 276; Keeler, Theodore E., *Railroads, Freight and Public Policy*(1983); Kolko, Gabriel, *Railroads and Regulation* (1965); Martin, Albro, *Enterprise Denied* (1971); Mowry, George E., *The Era of Theodore Roosevelt* (1958); Swindler, William F., *Court and Constitution in the 20th Century* (1969).

Martin, Glenn Luther (1886–1955)

Born in Macksburg, Iowa, Glenn Martin grew up in Liberal and Salina, Kansas, where his father ran hardware stores. As a young man he was interested in kites, many of which he designed, built, and sold to others. His mother encouraged his mechanical abilities, but his father was more skeptical. Martin attended Kansas Wesleyan University, but soon quit to become an auto mechanic. The family then moved to Santa Ana, California, where Martin opened his own garage. He became interested in flying and built his own plane in which he became the third man in the nation to fly in a self-made ship. He soon opened a factory and employed three assistants to build more aircraft. In these planes, Martin became nationally renowned as a stunt flyer—a birdman or barnstormer, as they were called then. He pioneered an airmail flight in California and was one of the first to fly over the ocean to Catalina Island. He advocated military uses of reconnaissance aircraft and bombers, the possibilities of which he demonstrated by dropping bags of flour on a designated target area.

Evidently the army was interested and ordered Martin's TT model training plane.

He also sold machines to the Dutch. During World War I, he cooperated with the Wright brothers but withdrew from their association at war's end. In 1918 he organized the Glenn Martin Company at Cleveland, Ohio, and built the first American bomber, which he managed to sell to the army even though the war was over. It was the prototype of all biplane bombers that followed. It was this plane that General Billy Mitchell used to sink the German battleship *Ostfriesland* off the Virginia Capes in 1921. During this period, Martin constructed many American "firsts," including the first plane for airmail service, the first bomber with an alloy-steel fuselage, and the first all-metal monoplane. Martin rarely shared information with anyone, and was known as a lone wolf. Recent biographers claim that he lived a homosexual "lifestyle" although no specific evidence can be pointed to.

Martin gradually turned from design to the administration of his business complex, and turned his attention to seaplanes, which he built on the Chesapeake Bay near Baltimore. From this factory came a series of flying boats and bombers that the Allies widely employed during World War II. One of the more significant models was the B-10 bomber that dominated the army air corps before the advent of the Boeing B-17. By 1941, Martin was the largest manufacturer of aircraft in the United States and expanding, as he constructed a new plant at Omaha, Nebraska. But the war that made him rich on the surface actually did him in. Martin was not a good practitioner of the government red-tape procurement process, a procedure in which other companies excelled. This allowed the competition to catch up with and outsell him, perhaps by as much as fourfold in machines produced. It was a continual problem that would ultimately force Martin's merger with Marietta in the 1960s into a corporation that in the 1990s carried out another union this time with competitor Lockheed into the corporate giant which would be, in the words of one analyst, "a one-of-a-kind company" that the "government won't let anything happen to …." But by this time, Glenn Martin had

Glenn Martin designed the first American bomber in 1918—it was to become a prototype for all biplane bombers.

long since retired (1952) and died (1955).

See also Boeing, William Edward; Curtiss, Glenn Hammond; Douglas, Donald W.

References Biddle, Wayne, *Barons of the Sky* (1991); Ingham, John H. (ed.), *Biographical Dictionary of American Business Leaders* (1983), 80–81; Rae, John B., *Climb to Greatness* (1968).

Mason, George W. (1891–1954)

Known among auto manufacturers as a genius, Mason's reputation was not a public commodity. He was employed at Charles Nash's plant at Kenosha, Wisconsin, where he transformed this moribund company into a real competitor with a new kind of car—the compact. Many others have received credit for Mason's pioneering work. He had been a small-engine salesman for his father, graduated from the University of Michigan in engineering, and had worked here and there in the auto industry and as an ordnance officer in World War I, finally winding up at Chrysler, where he looked like management material. But instead he went over to Kelvinator Refrigerator, which he saved from bankruptcy. This brought him other offers, one of which was from Charles Nash, whose auto firm had just barely survived the depression. Mason agreed to Nash's offer only if Kelvinator was a part of the deal. Thus was born Nash-Kelvinator in 1937.

In the end, the refrigerators saved the autos. Nash was hurt by its size, not its product. The company just lacked the scale necessary to compete with the likes of Ford and General Motors (GM). This meant higher costs of production for units that had to sell at the leaders' prices, for less profit per unit produced. It was a problem that plagued all smaller auto manufacturers. They tended to offer neat little gadgets and rely on former customers for their sales. It could not last. Mason went to work developing a uni-body—a welded frame and chassis instead of a bolted one. This innovation reduced rattles, made for production shortcuts, increased efficiency, and saved costs.

Interrupted by World War II, Mason thought over the auto situation as he produced aircraft engines. He came to the conclusion that the independents had to unite

in a miniature GM of their own, each independent being a new division of the firm and concentrating on one model and price level. Studebaker refused, but the plan went ahead with Packard (at the expensive end) and Hudson (in the middle price range). Mason reserved the low-end price for Nash. In the end, only Hudson would come in to American Motors, as the new firm would be called, and events caused the Nash to be dropped from production. Mason proceeded to make a smaller uni-body car of great economy at a time when everyone else was upgrading. He would call it the Rambler, using a respected name from the Nash 1930s line, and a "compact" to avoid American distaste for the word "small." The man who would sell this notion to the buying public was George Romney, a public relations man and company lobbyist.

The new Rambler was 20 inches shorter than the Ford or Chevrolet, got 20 percent better gas mileage, but was priced almost as much as the competition. But Rambler included a standard option package that cost other companies' buyers an extra $150, so Rambler's end price looked better. A little station wagon followed, as did a really small version of the sedan called the Metropolitan. But in the 1950s United States, size was status, and the buyer of a Rambler was unwittingly admitting to the world that he lacked status. The Metropolitan could not even shake the hold Volkswagen had on economy-minded Americans. The whole thing was beyond the power of one man, especially working with an independent, to change. The fifties was a time of glitz, size, and chrome. On 3 October 1954, America's farsighted car guru, George Mason, died of a heart attack, a prophet without a product—a man who had seen the 1990s 40 years too soon.

See also Automobiles from Domestics to Imports; Automobiles in American Society; Romney, George W.

References Langworth, Richard M., *Hudson* (1977); May, George S., "George W. Mason," in George S. May (ed.), *EABHB: The Automobile Industry* (1989), 316–320; Motor Vehicle Manufacturers Association of the United States, *Automobiles of America* (1974); Sobel, Robert, *Car Wars* (1984).

Maysville Road Veto

Ostensibly intended as a branch of the National Road to open the Bluegrass region to further economic exploitation, the Maysville Road extended from Maysville, just across the Ohio River from Cincinnati, to Lexington, Kentucky. Most conveniently, the road ran right past the plantation home of Kentucky political power Henry Clay, and would have as a by-product his ease of contact with Washington, D.C. The proposal for the road was put forth by Clay during President Andrew Jackson's first term and was designed to expose Jackson's state's rights position against internal improvements. Clay and the National Republicans hoped that the voters in the upcoming 1832 election would be offended by Jackson's expected veto. Jackson reserved for Clay's measure a special privilege in American history—the first use of a presidential "pocket veto." Since the bill was passed just as Congress went out of session, Jackson just let it sit on his desk (or in his "pocket," in popular parlance) for 14 days and the Maysville Road Bill automatically expired under a never-before-utilized section of the Constitution.

Clay denounced Jackson's action as dictatorial and against the interests of the American people's need for better transportation routes. Jackson, who under the Constitution did not need to give his reasons for a pocket veto, did so anyway. In the "Maysville Road Veto Message," the president said that he had no objections to internal improvements so long as they were truly national in scope and purpose. Internal improvements that did not meet that test were better left to the states and local entities to fund. Jackson deemed Clay's short addition to the National Road to be contrary to that philosophy because it benefited only one state, and hence was potentially an unnecessary abuse of federal power. The result was that such internal improvements as the Maysville Road became prerogatives of the states, which effectively stifled federal expenditures and helped keep the U.S. government in the black for most of the post–Civil War period. Operating under such a theory, Jackson became the first president to completely retire the national debt.

Jackson and his successors, however, did not cut road building entirely. The national government made a continuing contribution in road exploring, surveying, building, maintenance, and planning, up until the railroads became the prime movers of American goods after the Civil War. In addition, the civilian contracts let for supplying the army in the West, and mail and telegraph subsidies, contributed to road extensions onto the Plains and into the mountains. Jackson himself spent more money on roadwork than did his predecessor, whom Jackson criticized as a spendthrift. There was a lot of politics and public impression involved in the Maysville Road Veto, not the least of which was a chance for Jackson to embarrass his perennial political opponent, Henry Clay.

See also American System; Clay, Henry; Erie Canal; Van Buren, Martin.

References Jackson, W. Turrentine, *Wagon Roads West* (1952); Remini, Robert V., *Andrew Jackson and the Course of American Freedom, 1822–1832* (1981); Van Deusen, Glyndon, *The Jacksonian Era, 1828–1848* (1959).

Mears, Otto (1841–1926)

Originally the operator of a toll road and freight wagon service, Otto Mears created a one-state rail empire composed of three lines that connected the mineral-rich central Rockies with the Denver & Rio Grande at Silverton, Colorado. The first of Mears' railroads was the Silverton Railroad to Albany, following the twisting gorge of Mineral Creek. The roadbed was noted for its hairpin curves and switchbacks and its unique roofed turntable. The second line was the Silverton, Gladstone, and Northerly. It came down from Gladstone, following Cement Creek. The third of Mears' railways was the Silverton Northern, which followed the Animas River from its headwaters to Silverton. These roads hauled some passengers and freight, but they made their money off of the silver ore they brought down to the smelter at Silverton. All three ran at elevations ranging from 9,300 to 10,600 feet. The Mears lines issued passes painted on white buckskin and filigreed in gold and silver. The railroads fell into disuse as the mines played out and federal monetary policy changed in the early twentieth century. The last line, the Silverton Northern, closed during a miners' strike in 1941. Later it became a part of the Denver & Rio Grande system.

See also Denver & Rio Grande Western Railroad.

References Beebe, Lucius, and Charles Clegg, *Narrow Gauge in the Rockies* (1958); Crum, Josie, *Three Little Lines* (1900); Hubbard, Freeman, *Encyclopedia of North American Railroading* (1981); Kaplan, Michael, *Otto Mears* (1982); Schneide, James G., "Otto Mears," in Robert L. Frey (ed.), *EABHB: Railroads in the Nineteenth Century* (1988), 248–255; Sloan, Robert E., and Carl A. Skowronski, *The Rainbow Route* (1975).

Merchant Marine

Technically, a nation's merchant marine comprises all civilian vessels and personnel engaged in waterborne commerce, but generally it is restricted to oceangoing trade, excluding intracoastal and inland waterways. During a time of war, the merchant marine becomes an adjunct of the U.S. Navy, but its essential purpose is to transport goods and passengers across the high seas. The first whites came to North America by ship, and for several centuries thereafter sea and river travel were the prime means of travel and transport in the New World. The sea also provided much of the sustenance for early settlers, and fishermen were among the first to go to sea in the American colonies, utilizing grants provided by the king to set up permanent settlements to cure fish here for shipment to the Old World. One of the first domestic industries in the future United States was shipbuilding in the mouth of Massachusetts' Mystic River. This industry became crucial to America's survival in war and for the development of that unique nineteenth-century form of American ship, the "clipper."

By the middle of the nineteenth century, England had repealed her Navigation Acts, opening her shores to unrestricted shipping regardless of national flag. The Americans were the first to jump in and garner the profits. It was a wonderful relationship. England recognized implicitly the American principle of freedom of the high seas and the Yankee sailors profited from the Royal Navy's control of them without having to support their own armed fleet through high taxes. Perfect examples were the enforcement of the Monroe Doctrine and American entry into the Orient, all permitted by the Royal Navy's tacit cooperation and protection. This symbiotic relationship was made more formal in the 1850 Clayton-Bulwer Treaty that guaranteed the future cooperation of the English-speaking nations in the building of a canal across the Central American Isthmus of Panamá.

But this cooperative relationship did not last long. Except for a brief period between 1845 and 1858, Americans lacked a national subsidy that European nations traditionally provided for their ships of trade. This meant that other nations capitalized on the introduction of steam while American ships still plied the seas under sail. The clipper ships could outrun the steamers, but the speedy Americans could not haul enough cargo, limited by their ships' sharp beams. In addition, the excess shipping released by the Crimean War, the collapse of the California gold boom, the restrictions of the Civil War, and the new boom in inland railroads nearly did in the American merchant marine, placing it at one of its low points. Between 1858 and 1866, the amount of U.S. trade carried in American bottoms (cargo vessels) dropped from 73 to 25 percent. One-third of American registries went over to other flags during the war.

After the Union victory, other factors came into play to prevent the American merchant marine from expanding sufficiently to make up for the wartime decline. Americans failed to take up the construction of iron ships, preferring to stick with outdated wooden hulls. Even though an American, John Ericsson, invented the screw propeller, American steamers still employed the side paddle wheel extensively on its few steamers. As the American West expanded in the last half of the century, most of the nation's energy went into the westward movement. This expansion of population brought new landlocked states into the Union that voted against any national subsidy of ships, and for aid to railroads. Finally, American waterborne shipping concentrated on the intracoastal and inland water trade. Oceangoing transport decreased from 1.5 million tons in 1870 to 800,000 tons in 1910, while coastal and inland trade went up dramatically, increasing two-and-a-half times on the Great Lakes alone. American overseas trade was carried by ships belonging to other nations. The Supreme Court seemed to endorse that practice when it ruled in *Robertson v. Baldwin* (1896) that American sailors lacked the basic civil rights guaranteed all citizens under the Constitution after they signed on to a ship's service.

By the turn of the century, a new force swept the ruling circles of American government that boded better times for overseas shipping. This force was the renewed imperialism that emanated from the Spanish-American War, the building of the Great White Fleet (as the navy's new battleships were called), and the interventionism in foreign lands that marked Theodore Roosevelt's administration and American policy in general throughout the twentieth century. A small federal mail subsidy was the stumbling beginning in 1891, so meager that of 53 lines available only 8 were bid on. But things began to move as Congress forced American military supplies to be hauled in American-registered ships in 1904, and the Panama Canal opened in 1914. Finally, the reports came in from maritime investigatory commissions inaugurated during the Roosevelt and William H. Taft years.

The result was two congressional measures passed during the first Woodrow Wilson administration, the La Follette Seaman's Act and the Shipping Act of 1916. For the first time, American seamen were given constitutional guarantees of their civil rights, better food, and testing as to their abilities, and American-registered ships were restricted to having crew members of whom 75 percent spoke English. With the outbreak of the Great War in Europe, the neutral U.S. flag became an asset, and by 1916, many ships had changed over to American registry. To cope with this fact, Congress passed the Shipping Act of 1916, which established the U.S. Shipping Board, a government regulatory agency resembling an Interstate Commerce Commission of the high seas that controlled rate practices, which before had been unregulated.

But American entry into the war on the side of the western Allies caused the Shipping Board to be used in a wholly different manner than the law desired. It was assigned the task of building a "bridge to France"— the construction of hundreds of cargo ships to save the Allied war effort from German defeat in France. Nearly $3 billion was earmarked for this Emergency Fleet Corporation by the end of the war to be used for shipyard construction and shipbuilding alone. Although the total number of ships needed to take American troops and supplies to France were never built, the government impressed existing American-registered shipping and borrowed more from England to get the job done. But by the time of the Treaty of Versailles, American shipbuilding had surpassed that of Great Britain; 2,300 new ships were constructed, one-third of which were actually built after the armistice. Most of the wartime ships were of doubtful value, but the Hog Island freighters were considered to be of excellent quality and became an American standard for the interwar period. The government-owned ships were required to be sold to private concerns by law, and the Merchant Marine Act of 1920 provided for that sale and credit terms of purchase. It also gave a monopoly in trade between American ports to U.S.-registered vessels.

By the end of the 1920s, the World War I ship sale was complete and Congress passed a new Merchant Marine Act designed to place American vessels into competition with those of other nations on the high seas. The method was a subsidy to carry the mails through new ships built in U.S. shipyards. But American ships still operated at a disadvantage to those of other nations. U.S. vessels had higher costs of operation brought on by the lack of subsidies in construction and operation, the 1928 Act notwithstanding. Most of them still used coal; the American use of new maritime diesel engines was years behind the vessels of other nations. American ships also had a higher required standard of living for sailors mandated by law. Finally, wages on U.S.-registered vessels were higher than those of other nations. American vessels faced even more problems when the New Deal passed several safety measures that provided for licensed seamen, including provisions that three-quarters of the crew be American citizens, that a three-watch system and the eight-hour day be observed, that strict inspection of seamen's shipboard quarters be carried out, and that rigid control of flammable cargoes and installation of sprinkler systems for fire control be implemented. All of these measures were good for the sailors but cost the operators more overhead that was then passed on to the customer, who usually engaged a ship of another registry to save money.

The Franklin D. Roosevelt administration sought to regularize all measures related to ocean shipping in the Merchant Marine Act of 1936. It abolished all previous governmental boards, corporations, and subsidies and replaced them with the U.S. Maritime Commission. The commission was authorized to grant subsidies for operation and construction amounting to the difference between American and other nations' costs, a jobs program to combat the Great Depression that took a turn for the worse at about that time. It would also administer the seamen's qualifying tests, set wages and conditions, and create essential trade routes. After a survey of the merchant marine fleet, only two vessels of which had been constructed after the end of World War I, the commission determined that most of it would be obsolete by 1942. Seventy-three freighters and the liner *America*, all built to commission standards, were built and put into service by 1940. But their scope of service was initially narrowed when the Neutrality Act closed most European ports

to American ships in 1939 after the beginning of World War II.

As the war swept over Europe, it became evident that the British would be hardpressed to fight the Germans without help from their English-speaking relatives across the Atlantic. At least that was how President Roosevelt and British Prime Minister Winston Churchill viewed it. But Congress was not as enthusiastic, an accurate reflection of the American people at the time, and opted for neutrality. In January 1941, Roosevelt announced an Emergency Program of shipbuilding for American "defensive" use of 260 vessels of a standardized plan, called Liberty Ships. Coincidentally, the plans corresponded to a design that the British wanted built for their own use, but such oddities were best left unexplored. Most of the building was consigned to established shipyards, but notable among the newcomers was Henry J. Kaiser on the West Coast. By war's end, Kaiser would be responsible for 27 percent of all the Liberty Ships built, and his management techniques became widely copied elsewhere.

Spurred on by the damaging German submarine campaign in the Atlantic, the numbers of vessels to be built increased, often on a monthly basis. By November 1943, 1.5 million Americans worked at these shipyards, producing more ships than anyone could have imagined in 1939. By utilizing prefabricated assemblies, relatively unskilled laborers (many of them women with no prior job experience outside the home) could put together a whole vessel in a matter of hours (Kaiser was launching a new ship every day) that had taken skilled workers months to assemble piecemeal before the war.

To prevent any labor problems, worker strikes and management lockouts were prohibited. Shipyards were not allowed to outbid each other for labor. The country was divided into zones of production, run under close government supervision. Builders received bonuses for every day less than the 150-day limit a ship took to be built. Late production quotas were penalized also. The production quotas were met with such alacrity that the United States not only fought a two-front war, but also supplied Allied forces in both oceans at the same time. It could be argued that the logistical effort was the least hailed but the most important contribution America made to the defeat of the Axis powers. Thanks to its own production and the efficiency of the *U-booten* of the German Kriegsmarine, the United States emerged from the war as the supreme maritime power in both military and merchant marine vessels.

The end of World War II left large parts of Europe and Asia devastated. It also left two superpowers with differing economic, social, and political systems—the United States and the Soviet Union. Lest the weakened nations fall prey to the other side's aggression, the United States sought to restore much of the economic balance that had existed before the war. The instruments to achieve this were the Marshall Plan's economic aid and the Merchant Ship Sales Act of 1946, which put the vast World War II supply fleet up for sale at bargain prices. Almost immediately, many American-owned ships changed their registry to that of other nations, particularly Panamá, Liberia, and Honduras. In the case of Liberia, the registry was custom-built by American shipowners to get around U.S. regulators. The reasons were simple: lower operating and acquisition costs, greater operating flexibility, and lower taxes. Nonetheless, by 1954 the U.S. merchant fleet still stood second to none. American-flagged ships carried 27 percent of the nation's seaborne freight by tonnage and 40 percent of all cargoes available. After the passage of the Cargo Preference Act, guaranteeing that half of all military supplies would move in U.S.-owned ships, the change of registry was not perceived as a major political issue.

But in 20 years the whole picture had changed. The American merchant marine now moved less than 4 percent of the nation's foreign trade by weight, or 28 percent of cargoes available. The country had slipped from first to eleventh in numbers of ships in overseas trade. In absolute numbers, American ships had declined to 500, less

than half of the 1954 number. Clearly something had happened that had not been foreseen. The American merchant marine had slipped back into the doldrums of pre–World War II lethargy. Its massive foreign trade deficit was being hauled to its shores in foreign bottoms, a fact blamed on rigid government regulation (subsidy, cargo preference, and cabotage) and high operational costs. Japan, Norway, and Greece have advanced into the forefront of modern shipbuilding and merchant marine fleets by emphasizing modernity, size, speed, new demand (containers), automation, and computer technology. The United States has rested on its World War II laurels, often while providing the very technology that others use against it. The fact that its military forces now rely on airborne lift capability made possible by massive flying transports probably has not helped.

One analyst, historian René de la Pedraja, blames the decline of the American merchant marine on a series of trends. The U.S. government has steadfastly refused to recognize the value of foreign-flag operations. Since the Civil War, the flag of choice had been Great Britain. But World War I and the breakup of the British Empire caused shippers who wished to operate in a businesslike manner without government subsidies and controls to register their vessels under "flags of convenience" like those of Panamá and Liberia, among others. Another problem is the American reluctance to sanction large monopoly-like companies. This same trend was evident in railroading, with the same result: the collapse of an industry rather than its salvation. This highlights a third problem—America's blind faith in competition by a multitude of small companies that were too insignificant to survive a world shipping challenge backed by other governments without mergers.

Advanced technology has proven to be a demigod that has not helped the American merchant marine much either. The world is too technologically keen to allow any one nation to invent a process that others cannot copy overnight. Often the leader in technology makes costly mistakes and solves problems, which in turn allows the slower nations and companies to jump forward more cheaply—a sort of civilian version of the Dreadnought Decision of the British navy that allowed Imperial Germany to catch up in capital ships by omitting the in-between classes that had kept England supreme for a century. The United States, in pioneering containers and computers, cleared the way for others to do the same more cheaply after all the initial problems were solved. The fact that American companies received no governmental help on a large scale, like European and Asian governments did, means that the U.S. subsidies program has served only to prevent the weak from immediate failure in preference for a slow and agonizing death. And as they die, these companies blackmail the government for more and more assistance.

The American government has attempted to limit the regulations that its merchant marine operates under by passing the Shipping Act of 1984, which was roundly praised by a review committee in 1992; but critics claim that has not been enough. Many blame America's free-trade policies and call for a return to high-tariff, semimercantile policies of the past that made the country rich before World War II. They point out that Great Britain opted for free trade in the mid-nineteenth century and the United States filled that void, much as Japan fills the need for U.S. consumers today. But how a decline in foreign trade could help the declining American merchant marine, especially in light of the General Agreement on Tariffs and Trade (GATT), is a concept that seems to contradict the world trend toward less regulation and more reliance on free-market forces. The real security may rather be in large, diversified corporations active in many fields of economic endeavor, thus providing a strong financial background to absorb technological advance. It may be that the federal government will have to take an even bigger role in planning and bankrolling oceanic transportation in the future because of its ultimate strategic value in the defense of the nation, but the motion by victorious Republican conservatives in 1994 to abolish the House Committee on Merchant Marine and Fisheries leads one to suspect otherwise.

See also Bridges, Harry; Cargo Preference Act of 1954; Containers; Intermodal Freight; La Follette Seamen's Act; Merchant Marine Acts; Military Transportation Act of 1904; Oil Pollution Act of 1990; Panama Canal Act of 1912; Port and Tanker Safety Act of 1978; *Robertson v. Baldwin*; Shipping Acts.

References Buchanan, Pat, "Free Trade and the Rise in Poverty," *Washington Times* (National Weekly Edition), October 24–30 (1994): 34; Carlisle, Rodney, *Sovereignty for Sale* (1981); Frankel, Ernst G., *Regulations and Policies of the American Shipping Business* (1982); Hutchins, John G. B., *The American Maritime Industries and Public Policy* (1941); Jantscher, Gerald R., *Bread upon the Waters* (1975); Kilgour, John G., *The U.S. Merchant Marine* 1975); Kilmark, Robert A. (ed.), *America's Maritime Legacy* (1979); Lane, Frederic C., *Ships for Victory* (1951); Morison, Samuel Eliot, *The Maritime History of Massachusetts* (1921); Pedraja, René de la, *The Rise and Decline of U.S. Merchant Shipping in the Twentieth Century* (1992); Pedraja, René de la, *A Historical Dictionary of the Merchant Marine and Shipping Industry* (1994); Sawyer, L. A., and W. H. Mitchell, *The Liberty Ships* (1985); Schoenknecht, Rolf, et al., *Ships and Shipping of Tomorrow* (1983); Taylor, George Rogers, *The Transportation Revolution* (1951); Whitehurst, Clinton H., Jr., *The U.S. Merchant Marine* (1983); Whitehurst, Clinton H., Jr., *The U.S. Shipbuilding Industry* (1986).

Merchant Marine Acts

In a usually vain attempt to aid the development of the civilian sea service, Congress legislated certain subsidizing and regulating measures called Merchant Marine Acts. As with many such complicated economic measures, the acts often prolonged rather than alleviated the problems of the Merchant Marines. The various measures follow.

MERCHANT MARINE ACT OF 1891
Sometimes called the Ocean Mail Act, the act of 1891 was the first general subsidy bill that Congress had passed for maritime industries since before the Civil War. Individual companies had received some congressional largess since the fratricidal war, but this measure permitted the Post Office Department to grant five- or ten-year mail contracts to any American-owned company sailing American-built ships on

the high seas. Although it did not reverse the decline of the American merchant marine, it did halt the many transfers of American registry to foreign flags and save a skeleton fleet of oceangoing ships to be available with the coastal vessels for the world war to come.

MERCHANT MARINE ACT OF 1920

Also known as the Jones Act, the act of 1920 was rammed through Congress by Senator Wesley Jones. It reserved all coastwise and intracoastal shipping trade to vessels with American flag registry, a practice called "cabotage," and extended it to American territories with the exception of the Philippine Islands. The measure allowed for the lifting of cabotage restrictions during times of national emergency (as it was in World War I). The Jones Act also created the American Bureau of Shipping to determine the seaworthiness of registered vessels, reaffirm the principles set forth in the Shipping Act of 1916, and dispose of excess ships built as a result of the Great War. It tried in effect to return the American merchant marine to the protectionist principles of the earlier seventeenth-century mercantile era, but failed as it had no punitive provisions of enforcement.

MERCHANT MARINE ACT OF 1928

Since the Shipping Act of 1916 and the Jones Act of 1920 had failed to curb the steady decline of the American merchant marine, Congress decided to act once again, especially since the British Cunard Line had recently placed ships in the lucrative Miami–Havana trade that Americans had traditionally thought of as their exclusive domain. Mail contracts were to be awarded at a higher rate for faster and newer ships. This, along with a shipbuilding loan, was hoped sufficient to change the aging American merchant fleet over to newer, more modern vessels. Instead, the quickly drawn-up measure led to a bidding war for mail contracts among those companies determined to continue business as usual, which caused much corruption until the Hugo

Black Committee exposed these flagrant abuses along with the concurrent airmail scandals. Those companies on the brink of business failure were pushed over the edge; thus the measure actually had the exact reverse effect of its design—it shrunk the dwindling American merchant marine even further.

MERCHANT MARINE ACT OF 1936

Prompted by the disaster of the 1928 measure, Congress now approached the merchant marine problem under the auspices of the New Deal. The act of 1936 would be the operational measure for the merchant marine for the next 50 years. The legislation centralized all governmental supervision of the industry in the new U.S. Maritime Commission, an independent board of five members serving staggered six-year terms. It canceled all previous mail contracts and introduced the notion of parity. This was a government subsidy paid to American flag carriers to equalize their competition with foreign vessels in the international market. The parity extended to shipbuilders and ship owners alike. The act was really a confused compromise, little understood by the representatives who, overwhelmed in the press of other New Deal measures, voted it in and really satisfied no one. What it did was prolong what might have been the quick collapse of the American maritime industry by substituting a slow death. It did virtually nothing to help the industry get into competitive shape for the future.

MERCHANT MARINE ACT OF 1970

The first significant change to the act of 1936, the Merchant Marine Act of 1970 came about when a foreign-flagged ship refused to transport matériel to the Vietnam war zone. The act of 1970 extended subsidies, as outlined in the 1936 act, to bulk carriers exempt from its benefits heretofore. It produced few results, as most bulk carriers saw little reason to transfer from flags of convenience to American registry. Shortfalls in recent national budgets have made it difficult for the dozen carriers that did transfer to American registry to collect the full payments mandated under the law for their doing so.

See also Merchant Marine; Shipping Acts.

References Frankel, Ernst G., *Regulations and Policies of the American Shipping Business* (1982); Hutchins, John G. B., *The American Maritime Industries and Public Policy* (1941); Jantscher, Gerald R., *Bread upon the Waters* (1975); Pedraja, René de la, *The Rise and Decline of U.S. Merchant Shipping in the Twentieth Century* (1992); Pedraja, René de la, *A Historical Dictionary of the Merchant Marine and Shipping Industry* (1994).

Meridian Highway

One of the "named highways" popular in the teens and twenties of the twentieth century, the Meridian Highway was used by local chambers of commerce and tourism and the American Automobile Association to stimulate travel on the "good roads" and increase income in the towns and states through which they passed. Roughly following the ninety-eighth meridian, the highway began in Winnipeg, Manitoba, and came south through Grand Forks, Fargo, and Yankton in the Dakotas; then to Norfolk and Columbus, Nebraska; Salina and Wichita, Kansas; Enid, Chickasha, and Duncan, Oklahoma; and down to Fort Worth, Texas. The route paralleled today's U.S. Highway 81. From Fort Worth, the Meridian Highway headed south to Waco, Austin, San Antonio, and Laredo, on what are currently Interstates 35 and 35 West. The route allegedly continued through Old Mexico by way of Monterrey to Mexico City. Another route branched off at Waco and continued southeastward to Houston, the present route of Texas State Road 6.

See also Roads and Highways, Colonial Times to World War I; Roads and Highways since World War I.

Reference Hart, Val, *The Story of American Roads* (1950).

Miami and Erie Canal

The Miami and Erie Canal ran from Cincinnati to Toledo and was completed by 1845. It was part of a vast network of Ohio state canals that connected the Ohio River with Lake Erie and utilized the Erie Canal through New York State to the sea.

See also Canals.

Michigan Public Utilities Commission et al. v. Duke Cartage Company 266 US 570 (1925)

The first case before the Supreme Court to treat specifically the legal problems related to trucking, *Michigan v. Duke* concerned a Michigan statute that required both intra- and interstate truckers to get a state permit before they could haul goods in the state. To receive a permit the operator was to prove that his service met the test of public service and necessity. It was a vague phrase. Duke Cartage hauled between Detroit and Toledo, Ohio. The company asserted that in was engaged in interstate commerce and hence liable to federal regulation (of which, conveniently, there was none at the time) but not the state's. The Supreme Court met Duke's objections and declared that the Michigan law had no valid relation to public safety or order and that the law interfered with interstate commerce, a federal function. The court also maintained that Duke was a private carrier, not a common public carrier, because it hauled specific items for a specific business under contract, a limited function. All the state could do was collect reasonable license fees to compensate for use of the highways.

In a related Washington State case, *Buck v. Kuykendall* 267 US 307 (1925), a permit to operate a bus was denied to Buck because the state held that four bus lines already provided enough public service. The court ruled in Buck's behalf, holding that Washington's action had blatantly interfered with the movement of interstate commerce. But the court declined to rule whether the state could have limited Buck's right to enter business had he been in operation solely within Washington minus the Oregon permit he already had. These decisions corresponded to more general business regulation cases decided at the same time. The major dissenter in these cases was Justice James C. McReynolds, who thought that the motor industry was so new that the various states might best approach the problem and work out many of its difficulties on their own. He thought that the Court or Congress would be mistaken to thrust the industry into any straitjacket by decision or law prematurely.

See also Bush, *George W. and Sons v. Maloy*; *Tyson and Brothers–United Theater Ticket Offices, Inc. v. Blanton.*

Reference Childs, William R., *Trucking and the Public Interest* (1985).

Middlesex Canal

This 27-mile man-made waterway joined the Boston Harbor at Charlestown with the Merrimac River. It was incorporated in 1789, begun in 1790, and opened in 1804. It cost a half million dollars to build and maintain until 1815. It was a mere 3 feet deep, 30 feet wide at the top, and 27 feet wide at its base. It had 20 locks and a rise of 104 feet, each measuring 70 feet long and 11 feet wide. Its income was $245,000 annually by 1815, and the land values along its banks increased by a third. Its success had much to do with other canal projects of the era, especially the Erie Canal.

See also Canals.

Military Air Transport Service (MATS)

During the cold war, the United States, as the preeminent Western superpower, had occasion to move troops and supplies to far reaches of the globe at a moment's notice. As seaborne movements took too long, airlift capabilities became of prime importance. The result was the concentration of all army and navy (and later, air force) air transports into the Military Air Transport Service in 1948.

MATS was called upon almost immediately to show its capabilities when the Soviets shut off Allied access to Berlin. In postwar divided Germany, Berlin was 100 miles behind the Iron Curtain but occupied by France, Britain, the United States, and the Soviet Union. Seeking to drive out Allied influence, Soviet troops closed all land and river routes in June 1948. The city had a month's provisions. Rather than risk war, the Harry Truman administration decided to fly in all the goods the city needed to survive. At first beginning with the old DC-3s, called C-47s in military lingo, the airlift began. Russian fighters buzzed the route but did not commence hostilities. Given the failure of the Luftwaffe to supply German troops cornered in Stalingrad in 1942, they could not believe the West would be any more successful with a larger civilian population. Within weeks the bigger four-engine Douglas C-54 Skymasters began to haul ten-ton loads on a regular around-the-clock schedule, made possible by new advances in ground control and lengthened runways. A plane arrived every three minutes and unloaded in half an hour, supplying Berlin with 80 percent of its food and coal throughout the winter. The blockade was lifted in the spring of 1949, ending the first display in how organized air supply could work wonders.

But the C-47 and C-54 were military conversions of civilian-designed airliners and not up to what MATS hoped to be able to achieve in the long run. MATS called for specially designed planes to increase its capability. The aircraft industry responded with the twin-boomed Fairchild C-82 Flying Boxcar and Fairchild C-119 Packet. With the tail structures extending back from the wing-mounted engine nacelles (or housings), these transports had no encumbrances at the fuselage rear and could be loaded and unloaded with speed. Impressed, MATS pushed for larger planes with intercontinental capabilities. The result was the Douglas C-124 Globemaster. With twin clamshell front doors, the Globemaster had a more conventional shape, but it was the last piston-engine transport developed. The future belonged to turboprops and jets. The first turboprop was the Douglas C-133 Cargomaster. With a range of 4,400 miles, it could haul items as large as intercontinental ballistic missiles. Lockheed responded with the C-130 Hercules, a medium-range transport with a high tail under which were the load doors. As it could land on an inordinately short runway, it became the "brush fire" conflict master of the world.

But the turboprops soon gave way to jet-powered transports of unbelievable size. The Lockheed C-141 Starlifter entered service in the 1960s and could carry 154 troops for 6,000 miles. But nothing matched the Massive Lockheed C-5 Galaxy series. With an 8,000-mile range, the C-5 could carry 345 soldiers or two M-60 battle tanks or 125,000 tons of cargo. A controversial plane of innumerable cost overruns that also suffered the embarrassment of losing a wheel on its first public demonstration landing, the C-5 gave the United States a true global presence in a matter of hours. The versatility of these transports was aptly demonstrated in the Vietnam conflict, during which MATS had its name changed to Military Airlift Command (MAC) in 1966. The more recent Desert Storm campaign in the Persian Gulf region graphically demonstrated the airlift capacity of MAC to its fullest.

See also Aeronautics.

References Bilstein, Roger E., *Flight in America* (1994); Bowie, Beverly M., "MATS: America's Long Arm of the Air," *National Geographic* (March 1957) 111: 283–317; Davidson, Walter P., *The Berlin Blockade* (1958); Gething, Michael J., *Air Power 2000* (1992).

Military Transportation Act of 1904

Because the Spanish-American War had caught the United States with inadequate shipping to meet military requirements for the invasion of Spanish colonies, the War Department had to buy and charter foreign-flagged vessels. Embarrassment was avoided only because the war was mercifully short. In an effort to enlarge the American merchant marine, Congress required that all military supplies be carried in the future aboard American-flagged ships. There were exceptions allowed during national emergencies—and the world tour of the Great White Fleet was one of these—but the act did work to cause the navy to build up its own transport fleet. But the real shortage was among privately owned vessels, and to close this gap, Congress would pass the Cargo Preference Act in 1954, putting military supplies on these ships, too.

See also Cargo Preference Act of 1954; Merchant Marine Acts; Shipping Acts.

References Frankel, Ernst G., *Regulations and Policies of the American Shipping Business* (1982); Hutchins, John G. B., *The American Maritime Industries and Public Policy*; Jantscher, Gerald R., *Bread upon the Waters* (1975); Pedraja, René de la, *The Rise and Decline of U.S. Merchant Shipping in the Twentieth Century* (1992); Pedraja, René de la, *A Historical Dictionary of the Merchant Marine and Shipping Industry* (1994).

Milwaukee Road

Actually named the Chicago, Milwaukee, St. Paul & Pacific Railroad, the Milwaukee Road began operations in 1850 from Milwaukee to Wauwatosa, Wisconsin. By 1857, the line had been extended to the Mississippi River at Prairie du Chien. After the Civil War, the original railroad was joined to another line running from La Crosse to Milwaukee. Further mergers and construction took the railway out to Fargo, Omaha, and Kansas City. The road received its full modern name by 1880.

Another of the so-called Granger lines, the Milwaukee Road served farmers on the Plains. Its interchanges controlled by E. H. Harriman and James J. Hill, at the turn of the century the Milwaukee Road decided to strike out for the Pacific on its own. At first the board of directors chose Eureka, California, but then shifted their gaze to Seattle instead. It took nearly a decade to reach the Puget Sound area, and much of the mainline was within sight of the Northern Pacific. The cost of construction overran the estimates by four times, not helped any by the decision to electrify the 650-mile section through the Rockies. The purchase of two small short lines in Indiana and Illinois, plus the cost of construction, put the Milwaukee Road into receivership by 1921. By the beginning of the Great Depression the Milwaukee Road came out of receivership only to go back into reorganization in 1936, 1945, and 1977.

The indebtedness produced much resourcefulness in the shops, if not in the offices. Much of its streamlined passenger equipment, for such trains as the *Olympian* and the *Columbian*, was homemade. The Milwaukee Road had been the first railroad to use electric lights in its passenger equipment in the 1880s. Innovations in design followed with the shrouded steamers that pulled the "name train," the *Hiawatha*, between Chicago and St. Paul at an average speed of 63 miles per hour. It also managed to share trackage with the Union Pacific's passenger trains, giving the Omaha-based line a route into Chicago for its city-named trains after 1955. Dropping all passenger service in favor of Amtrak came too late to save the Milwaukee Road. It completely reorganized itself in 1977, cutting all of the rails west of Miles City, Montana, and gaining $40 million from Burlington Northern (BN) for the sale. Later, Union Pacific bought $23 million in trackage in Washington State. An exclusive piggyback express between Chicago and the Twin Cities called the Sprint did something to revive the Milwaukee Road's once proud image as a carrier of coal and agricultural and forest products. But the route was something of an orphan, too. Denied participation in BN, the Milwaukee Road eventually tried to become a part of the Canadian National's Grand Trunk Western subsidiary in the 1980s. The Interstate Commerce Commission demurred on this and the Soo Line came in and bought much of the Milwaukee Road (1986), spinning the rest off to several other nearby railroads.

See also Klitenic Plan; Soo Line.

References Clark, Milton R., "Chicago, Milwaukee & St. Paul Railway," in Robert L. Frey (ed.), *EABHB: Railroads in the Nineteenth Century* (1988), 49–50; Derleth, August W., *The Milwaukee Road* (1948); Drury, George H., *The Historical Guide to North American Railroads* (1985); Drury, George H., *The Train-Watcher's Guide* (1990); Field, H. H., *History of the Milwaukee Road* (1941); Grow, Lawrence, *On the 8:02* (1979); Hubbard, Freeman, *Encyclopedia of North American Railroading* (1981); Lyon, Peter, *To Hell in a Day Coach* (1968); Martin, Charles F., *Milwaukee Road Locomotives* (1972); Nock, O. S., *Railways of the USA* (1979); Odegard, Gordon, "Milwaukee Road Hiawatha," *Model Railroader* (January 1984) 51: 112–123; Olmstead, Robert P., *Milwaukee Rails* (1980); Schwantes, Carlos A., "The Milwaukee Road's Pacific Expansion," *Pacific Northwest Quarterly* (1981) 72: 30–40; Schwantes, Carlos A., "Chicago, Milwaukee, St. Paul & Pacific Railroad," in Keith L. Bryant, Jr. (ed.), *EABHB: Railroads in the Age of Regulation* (1988), 76–78; Scribbins, Jim, *The Hiawatha Story* (1970); Wood, Charles R., and Dorothy M. Wood, *Milwaukee Road—West* (1972).

Missouri-Kansas-Texas Railroad (MKT)

Known popularly as the Katy, the Missouri-Kansas-Texas was the first railroad to enter Texas from the north. The MKT had begun the race for the Indian Nations (present-day Oklahoma) in 1870 as the southern branch of the Union Pacific out of Junction, Kansas. The name change came a year later. The Katy was in a hurry to build because the federal government had limited the land set aside to the first line to come into the Neosho Valley. The Native Americans had to agree first, and did so reluctantly. The Katy celebrated this victory in the palm leaves on its original emblem. The investors in the Katy included the usual bigwigs: August Belmont, J. P. Morgan, Levi P. Morton (investment banker and ultimately vice-president of the United States), John D. Rockefeller, Levi Parsons, and George Denison. The latter two, as president and vice-president respectively of the MKT, had towns along the line named for them, one in Kansas, the other in Texas.

Running through the Indian Nations had its drawbacks. The Katy was the only line for decades, a nice monopoly, but it was also the only target for banditry. The last robbery of an MKT train took place in 1923 near Okesa, Oklahoma. The first probably was the purchase of the line by Jay Gould as the keystone to his southwestern empire in the 1880s. By the end of the decade, however, Gould was gone and the Katy returned to independent ownership. Narrowly surviving the Panic of 1893, the MKT extended itself to the Gulf Coast at Galveston and into Shreveport, St. Louis, Tulsa, and Oklahoma City. The oil boom made the MKT a rich railroad during the twentieth century. But the traffic ruined the rails and equipment, and little was plowed back into capital investment. The result was that the Katy nearly went under in the late 1950s. Only cutting all passenger traffic, downsizing the personnel pool, and rebuilding the engines and roadbed saved the MKT for further profit in the 1970s. The main carriage now is in grain and coal. The MKT has looked upon the numerous mergers of other midwestern lines with much trepidation, but has managed to do quite well. In the 1990s, however, the Burlington Northern, Santa Fe, and others have begun to make overtures of merger, leaving the future of the Katy as an independent in doubt.

See also Chicago & North Western Railroad; Chicago, Burlington & Quincy Railroad; Milwaukee Road; Missouri Pacific Railroad; Stillwell, Arthur Edward.

References Drury, George H., *The Historical Guide to North American Railroads* (1985); Drury, George H., *The Train-Watcher's Guide* (1990); Hofsommer, Don L., *Katy Northwest* (1976); Hofsommer, Don L., "Missouri-Kansas-Texas Railroad," in Keith L. Bryant, Jr. (ed.), *EABHB: Railroads in the Age of Regulation* (1988), 302–303; Hubbard, Freeman, *Encyclopedia of North American Railroading* (1981); Masterson, Vincent V., *The Katy Railroad and the Last Frontier* (1952).

Missouri Pacific Railroad (MoPac)

Known locally as the "MoPac" or the "Route of the Eagles," the Missouri Pacific was begun on the nation's seventy-fifth birthday in 1851. Its original goal was to build west out of St. Louis to Jefferson City and then on to the Pacific. Like so many railroads, the MoPac never saw the California surf, partly because Congress never gave it land grant assistance, and partly because the roadbed was ripped up by the Civil War, which in Missouri was a particularly vicious and destructive fight. It took until 1865 to reach Kansas City. In 1874, the MoPac's original two lines were consolidated and two years later the name Missouri Pacific was formally given to the whole system.

The history of the Missouri Pacific is bound up with the history of its Lone Star State subsidiary, the Texas and Pacific (T&P). Began in 1871, the T&P became a key participant in the Compromise of 1877, the end of the Civil War and Reconstruction, marked by the withdrawal of federal troops from the South. Part of this deal allegedly involved federal monetary assistance to this Southern effort to cross the vast southern high plains to California. Never mind that the assistance never came through. It was an effort by Southern conservatives to get in on the Great Barbecue known in Mark Twain's unforgettable term, the "Gilded Age." But the nation was tired of railroad greed at the public's expense, and the T&P, hence the MoPac, was stymied again. Jay Gould stepped into the picture and bought up the MoPac, the T&P, and numerous shorter lines to create his expansive Southwest System. Gould immediately began to extend the lines westward into New Mexico and Colorado. But as with all things Gould touched, the spurt was temporary. By the early 1880s, he was selling his empire to finance other plans.

The MoPac got along better without Gould. It moved into Louisiana and bought several Texas short lines that gave it access to Brownsville and another coastal line to New Orleans. In the twentieth century, MoPac became among the first to organize its own trucking company and the "piggyback" concept that came with it. It also dieselized early and by 1940 was running its all-streamliner, blue-and-gray Missouri Pacific *Eagle* (from which came one of its pseudonyms, "Route of the Eagles") with the new motive power. The *Colorado Eagle* and the *Sunshine Special* followed. More recently, the MoPac has acquired the Chicago & Eastern Illinois and its access to the center of all American railroads, the Windy City. It also formally merged the T&P into its organization, dropping the Texas line's name. In the 1980s the MoPac became a subsidiary of the Union Pacific, a process that has continued to advance with the old Eagle colors being dropped to incorporate Union Pacific's yellow-and-gray paint scheme, although the engines still carry the Missouri Pacific name on their sides in red.

See also Union Pacific Railroad.

References Collins, Joe G., *MoPac Power* (1980);

Collins, Joe G., *The Missouri Pacific Lines in Color* (1993); Drury, George H., *The Historical Guide to North American Railroads* (1985); Drury, George H., *The Train-Watcher's Guide* (1990); Hubbard, Freeman, *Encyclopedia of North American Railroading* (1981); Jenks, Downing B., *The Missouri Pacific Story* (1977); Kerr, John Leeds, *The Story of a Western Pioneer* (1928); Mercer, Lloyd J., *Railorads and Land Grant Policy* (1982); Miner, H. Craig, *The Rebirth of the Missouri Pacific* (1983); Miner, H. Craig, "Missouri Pacific Railroad," in Keith L. Bryant, Jr. (ed.), *EABHB: Railroads in the Age of Regulation* (1988), 303–305.

Mitchell, William "Billy" (1879–1936)

Born of American parents temporarily living in Nice, France, William Mitchell attended George Washington University and graduated in 1899. He enlisted in the army as a private to fight in the Spanish-American War, received a commission, attended the Army Staff College in 1909, and eventually attained the rank of brigadier general. Mitchell was chief of American military aviation in France in World War I and responsible for the Allied air cover and strategic bombing associated with the St. Mihiel–Meuse–Argonne offensives. After the war he was promoted to chief of army aviation. His career was considered brilliant and his future solid.

But Mitchell ran into bureaucratic problems after the war. He was enthused over the possibilities of military aviation and uncompromising in his critique of the stodgy thinking of those above him, civilian and military, who did not understand the air service and cut its potential through inadequate funding. He sunk the captured German warship *Ostfriesland* using army bombers, an exercise that disturbed (rather than enlightened) the military brass who had denied its possibility. Mitchell was outspoken in his positions, often getting into the press releases of his day, both accidentally and by his own design. Among other things, he predicted that planes would travel over 250 miles per hour and eventually cross the Pacific on regular service to China and the Orient. Not one to mince words, Mitchell publicly accused his overlords of

Brigadier General William Mitchell poses beside a pursuit plane, one of the fastest military planes in 1930.

"incompetency, criminal negligence, and almost treasonable administration of national defense."

This outburst led to his court martial and suspension from the service for five years without pay or allowances. President Calvin Coolidge reduced the sentence to suspension, full allowances, and half pay. Mitchell resigned his commission and retired to a Virginia farm and raised livestock. The winner of numerous medals from all of the Allied nations during the world war, Mitchell also authored three books on air power and numerous articles in magazines and pamphlets. He died at New York City in 1936.

See also Aeronautics.

References Bilstein, Roger E., *Flight in America* (1994); Davis, Burke, *The Billy Mitchell Affair* (1967); Hurley, Alfred E., *Billy Mitchell* (1964); Levine, Isaac Don, *Mitchell* (1972).

Montana Trail

Running from Great Salt Lake City to Fort Benton on the Missouri River, with branches to Deer Lodge and Virginia City, the Montana Trail was a north–south version of the Central Overland Route and branched off from it. Its purpose was to service Mormon settlements in Idaho (Utah was originally set up as the Latter-Day Saints' nation of Deseret, which ran from San Diego to Idaho's Salmon River) and the Gentile goldfields in Montana. As such, it competed with the Missouri River steamboat trade from St. Louis and with the Bozeman Trail out of Fort Laramie. But it had an advantage over its rivals: reliability. Except for a brief period during the Civil War when the Shoshone warred against travelers, soon put down by Union troops from California under General Patrick E. Connor, the trail contested only the elements—formidable enough, but conquerable. The Missouri River froze in winter and went shallow in summer and fall, not allowing steamboat use except during high water. And the Bozeman Trail crossed the land of the Lakota (Sioux), never a healthy prospect. The razing of the Bozeman's forts and withdrawal of its protective garrisons threw

trade back to the one sure route to Montana out of Utah.

The area of the Montana Trail had been used by various Native American tribes, primarily the Shoshone, for eons before fur trappers discovered its benefits in the early nineteenth century. They were led by Hudson's Bay Company (HBC) men like Peter Skene Ogden, who hoped to trap out the area as a part of his establishing a "fur desert" to keep opposing Americans out of the Oregon Territory. But Ogden had not moved fast enough. Free trappers dealing through the Ashley and Rocky Mountain fur companies, men like Etienne Provost, Jedediah Smith, and Jim Bridger, to name but a few, flooded the area of their own free will, beating the organized HBC effort with grasping free enterprise. It was the Americans who ultimately denuded the Rockies of their beaver and held an annual rendezvous in the contested area. The creation of Fort Hall on the upper Snake River assured American domination by the 1840s. The stationing of the Regiment of Mounted Riflemen (later the Third Cavalry) in the area gave protection and created a need for wagon traffic to the fort itself.

With the arrival of the Mormons to the Great Basin in the late 1840s, followed by the discovery of gold in California, the interest in the Continental Divide north of Fort Hall grew in many circles. Mormon frontiersmen advanced north, establishing Fort Lemhi and outlying trading posts to trade and proselytize among the Native inhabitants. And as the geography of California's goldfields was studied, these modern argonauts decided that similar foothills settings might prove rich, too. The result was rushes to the Fraser River in British Columbia, the Cherry Creek at Denver, the Washoe at Carson City, and the Montana diggings around Virginia City at the time of the Civil War. Supplies for the settlers and gold seekers needed to come overland or around Cape Horn. As the latter route was already well developed to California, it was natural for suppliers to utilize the Old Spanish Trail to Salt Lake City (open all year) and the California Trail (open only in summer) out of San Francisco as the Mormons and the soldiers at Camp Floyd did, and transship to the Montana gold strike over Monida Pass at the Continental Divide. Some early efforts were made to supply Montana over the Mullan Road, but Washington Territory lacked the port facilities of California, the less-harsh winters, and the intermediate customers and profits that dotted the Utah routes. The arrival of the railroad after the war only increased the convenience of the Montana Trail.

It was the shipping of mail and passengers along the Montana Trail that led to the Great Portneuf Canyon Stage Robbery in 1865. Thieves fired 75 charges of buckshot into the coach body, killing seven passengers. Failing to finish off one survivor, who pleaded he was dying anyway, proved to be the outlaws' undoing. The witness survived, as did the coach driver, which struck local authorities as odd. After the driver returned to Salt Lake City and began to spend lots of money, he was trailed to Denver and confronted. He confessed his part as the inside man in the holdup and fingered the rest of the gang. Eventually all were caught and hanged. An even worse threat was the Henry Plummer gang, operated by Sheriff Plummer in the goldfields. As in California earlier, the corruption of elected officials was met with vigilantism. Plummer unwisely had a list of gang members on his person when hauled in by the kangaroo court, which made the lynchers' task much easier. Wells Fargo & Company stationed guards in Portneuf Canyon and sent two shotgun messengers on many runs to stop the plague of robberies.

The freight and passengers flowed north for eight months of the year, until snows closed Monida Pass. Needless to say, the lack of homegrown produce in the goldfields placed a premium on things like flour in the spring. Mormon crop surpluses were in great demand. Many churchmen supplemented their farming by operating wagon companies and ferries along the route. Mormon and Gentile alike roped off sections of the trail and charged tolls to pass. Often, they built competing facilities and towns.

Stage service came in the form of Jack Oliver's Bannack Express, later taken over by Ben Holladay, the "Stagecoach King," who sold out to Wells Fargo & Company to avoid the inevitable loss of trade to the railroads. Gilmer & Salisbury bought out the Wells Fargo concession and continued until the Utah Northern Railroad, a narrow-gauge subsidiary of the Union Pacific, covered the route in the early 1880s. The Missouri River trade had lost out in the same way to the Northern Pacific coming across the northern Plains. With the arrival of the railroads, the "jehus," as the stage drivers were called, had to seek greener pastures elsewhere. The railroads provided fast, capacious, and safe haulage to Montana and made the trail superfluous. By 1885, travel had petered out to a few hardy souls and little else as the Montana Trail became history, like the Oregon, Mormon, and California Trails before it; today, U.S. Highway 91 and Interstate 15 approximate the route of the old road through Monida Pass.

See also Bozeman Trail; Mullan Road.

References Athearn, Robert G., "Utah and Northern Railroad," *Montana Western History* (1968) 23: 2–23; Madsen, Betty M., and Brigham D. Madsen, *North to Montana* (1980).

Morey, Samuel (1762–1843)

A Vermonter who showed an early talent for mechanical things, Samuel Morey was interested in canals, log chutes, and steam power. He built an early steamboat in 1793 that ran up the Hudson, and interested Robert Livingston. Offered $7,000 for the invention, Morey refused to sell. He did experiment with an improved version, hoping to win the $100,000 said to have been offered by Livingston for an "eight-hour" steamer. In 1797, he displayed the new craft at Philadelphia and became the rage of the Middle Atlantic Coast. He attracted a large number of investors, but the company failed to operate. Morey is one of numerous claimants for inventing the steamboat, and Robert Fulton had seen his plans before beginning his own work in New York. Morey also patented several other inventions, and is given credit for the type of paddle wheels used on Mississippi steamboats and others, although the principle was one known from the time of the Egyptians.

See also Steamboats.

Morgan, John Pierpont (1837–1913)

Born in Hartford, Connecticut, educated in Boston and at the University of Göttingen in Germany, J. Pierpont Morgan began his career in New York City as the representative of various banking firms engaged in gold and foreign-exchange speculations. By the end of the Civil War, he was in control of several banking businesses, one of which he inherited from his father. Morgan became interested in railroads and began to acquire control of line after line, beginning with the Erie, which he took from Jim Fisk and Jay Gould. His later acquisitions included the New York Central (NYC) System, the New Haven, the Reading, the Lehigh Valley, the Southern, the Chesapeake & Ohio, and the Northern Pacific. In 1893, the Grover Cleveland administration called upon him to relieve the depression by lending the government gold. Shortly afterward, he organized the United States Steel Corporation. He tried to organize a shipping trust to control trade on the high seas between the United States and Great Britain, but failed. He did control the soft- and hard-coal trusts. He was the best-known American financier in Europe and floated a large subscription for the national defense of England. He was investigated by Congress many times for his consolidation activities, and was both lauded and vilified for his great wealth.

As a railroad tycoon, Morgan began his spectacular rise to power when he edged the Vanderbilts out of the New York Central System in 1879. Morgan believed that the main problem with U.S. railroads was that the promoters had overbuilt the lines. They had twice the track they could utilize and had issued four times the number of securities they could pay interest on. Everyone seemed bent on building a new railroad to undercut someone else. Only in California, where Collis P. Huntington kept all inter-

lopers out, was this not so. There were six lines contending for the traffic between New York City and Chicago, with a seventh under construction. Passengers traveled the whole route for a dollar, and grain went at half the cost it took to ship it. As Morgan's banking empire had large sums out to the two prime culprits, the Pennsylvania Railroad and the New York Central, he called a meeting on his yacht to stop the nonsense. No one got off until the rate war ceased. He did the same thing with the so-called anthracite roads later.

Railroad tycoon J. P. Morgan

Then Morgan proceeded to reorganize everything—a particular talent of his. It was called "re-Morganization," and involved the paying off of the floating stocks, refinancing of the bond load, and an immediate assessment on all stockholders, who, if they did not pay up, were purged from the ownership roles with their stocks reverting to the company. Of course Morgan wound up with the majority of the stock in the end. Then Morgan saw to it that the railroads obeyed a sort of community interest—the rail community's interest, that is. There were to be no rate wars. Rather, the lines entered into large pools that controlled competition and rates. This kept everything artificially high and guaranteed profit. And it led directly to the Interstate Commerce Act and the creation of the Interstate Commerce Commission (ICC).

But the new government commission had little power. It could not fix rates, enforce its own decisions, or stop under-the-counter rebates. As for the competition that the ICC endorsed, that would eventually ruin the railroad companies. So Morgan stepped in and rescued the country from itself, as it were. He financed railroads going broke in the new rate wars brought on by the Interstate Commerce Act. Then he tried to bring order out of the whole mess. For three years he worked at it, but he could not get an agreement among the rail magnates, each of whom distrusted the others. But Morgan knew that rate cutting and expansion would bring the malefactors to his house soon, hats in hand. They were running out of money—Morgan was not.

The crisis that brought everyone to Morgan's point of view was the Panic of 1893. The overstretched rail barons folded by the hundreds. Morgan set about letting the unneeded lines collapse and picking up the strategically located ones. His prize was the creation of the Southern Railway System, a re-Morganized collection of numerous loans, with restructured debt and restructured mainlines and feeders. Another prize was the Northern Pacific (NP). Its promoters had looted the public lands but failed to manage a rail line. He wanted to combine the Great Northern (GN) and the Northern Pacific under James J. Hill, but that merger was deemed illegal. According to the antitrust laws, no railroad could own another. But the same individuals could own many railways. So Morgan bought up the Northern Pacific and sold most of the stock to Hill. It was the beginning of the consolidation that would lead to a war with

E. H. Harriman of the Union Pacific (UP), the Panic of 1903, and the Northern Securities case as the two sides sought to divide up the Chicago, Burlington & Quincy (CB&Q) between them.

Until the Northern Securities incident, the government mattered little. Morgan did not obey government, anyway; he bought it. Besides, the Supreme Court had practically whittled the ICC away to nothing. Many of the judges and more of the government (Republican or Democrat, it did not matter) were railroad lawyers. Strikes were enjoined and strikers driven away by police or the army when necessary. By 1900, railroads in the United States were divided into six major cartels: the Vanderbilt group (the New York Central [NYC], Lackawanna, and the Chicago & North Western[C&NW]); the Morgan group (the Southern, Atlantic Coastline [ACL], the Erie, and the Anthracite roads); the Harriman group (Illinois Central [IC], Union Pacific [UP], and Southern Pacific [SP]); the Pennsylvania group (the Pennsylvania Railroad [PRR], the Chesapeake & Ohio [C&O], the Baltimore & Ohio [B&O], the Norfolk & Western [N&W], and the Long Island Rail Road [LIRR]); the Gould group (Wabash, Missouri Pacific [MoPac], Texas & Pacific [T&P], Denver & Rio Grande Western [D&RGW], and Missouri-Kansas-Texas Railroad [MKT]); and the Hill group (Great Northern [GN] and Northern Pacific [NP]). There were many independents (Chicago, Burlington & Quincy [CB&Q], Atchison, Topeka, & Santa Fe [AT&SF]), and a so-called Belmont group based on the Louisville & Nashville [L&N]), but they were pretty much small fry in a big pond. And even the big boys were not as strong financially as they would have liked, which made many of them dependent on the good graces of the House of Morgan.

The real quarrel was between Harriman and Morgan over the inclusion of the CB&Q in Hill's empire in 1901. The Q had something lacked by most transcontinentals—a link to Chicago. Harriman's newly reorganized Union Pacific needed the same. But Hill refused to share. So Harriman began to buy the NP right out from under Hill to get even. Only Harriman's timidity in the face of his backers, who advised caution, kept him from getting the last 30,000 shares he needed to gain control. Into the breach stepped Morgan. He bid the price up until many who had promised to sell to Harriman reneged and went over to Morgan. Speculators did the rest. NP went from $110 a share to $1,000. Shares were sold that did not exist. Every other rail stock fell precipitously. The Panic of 1903 was the result.

Morgan, meanwhile, caring nothing that thousands of small investors had been ruined, began to form the Northern Securities Company. It would hold all the GN and NP stock—an entity so big that no one could buy it. That was the last bit of arrogance that President Theodore Roosevelt, a bit arrogant himself, would allow. Calling for a "square deal," he had the justice department bring suit against Morgan's holding company, forcing it to release the stock to its owners. The Elkins Act, restricting rebates, and the Hepburn Act, allowing the Interstate Commerce Commission to set maximum rates, soon followed. Temporarily foiled, Morgan turned to other fertile fields, organizing the railroads of New England through the manipulation of the New York, New Haven & Hartford. Morgan's attempt to organize all transportation in New England was so heavy-handed that the effects of his looting stayed with the New Haven until it became a part of Conrail in 1970. But that did not affect Morgan. He died peacefully in his bed on a European vacation in 1913.

See also Forbes, John Murray; Gould, Jay; Harriman, Edward Henry; Huntington, Collis Potter; *Northern Securities Company v. U.S.*; Railroads from Appomattox to Deregulation; Sage, Russell; Scott, Thomas A.; Southern Railway System; Vanderbilt, William H.

References Allen, Frederick Lewis, *The Great Pierpont Morgan* (1949); Corey, Lewis, *The House of Morgan* (1930); Frey, Robert L., "J. Pierpont Morgan," in Robert L. Frey (ed.), *EABHB: Railroads in the Nineteenth Century* (1988), 272–279; Hovey, Carl, *Life Story of J. Pierpont Morgan* (1912); Lyon, Peter, *To Hell in a Day Coach* (1968); Satterlee, Herbert L., *J. Pierpont Morgan* (1939); Winkler, John K., *Morgan the Magnificent* (1930).

Mormon Trail

The victories in the diplomatic struggle with England over Oregon and the war with Mexico in 1848 opened the whole Pacific Coast and all that lay between Texas and the Missouri River to American settlement. But strangely, the first settlers did not seek the best lands, but the worst. These were members of the Church of Jesus Christ of Latter-Day Saints, better known as Mormons. Persecuted all across the United States, the Mormons were looking for a place where no one else would bother them again. At Palmyra, New York, Prophet and First Seer Joseph Smith had translated and transcribed the Book of Mormon from pre-Columbian golden records that told of a lost tribe of Israel and its sojourn to America, Christ's ministry in the New World among them, the resultant internal quarreling, division, and the final war (the evil victors of which had their skins darkened to survive as the Native Americans). Hated by the local populace for their numbers, cohesiveness, and exclusivity, the church members moved to Kirtland, Ohio, where their communal religious and economic practices were challenged and "Mormon" was translated into "MORe MONey" by unsympathetic neighbors. Departing for Far West (now Independence), Missouri, where the Mormons believed was located the true biblical Garden of Eden hidden since a cataclysmic tilting of the earth's axis, the faithful were once again driven out by jealous local militia. They retreated back to Nauvoo, Illinois, where an angry posse arrested Smith and his brother on trumped-up charges and murdered them.

After the execution of Joseph and Hyrum Smith at the sheriff's office in Carthage, Illinois, the president of the Council of the Twelve Apostles, Brigham Young, decided that the Saints (as they styled themselves) ought to find a haven in the West. Thus began a migration of thousands that was of unprecedented scope and organization in the annals of western Americana. For Brigham Young did not merely think in the terms of the Saints at Nauvoo. He thought more in terms of the "Gathering," bringing all of God's children, including converts from all over the world, into one community of Zion located, in the words of Isaiah (51:3), in a "wilderness like Eden," where the elect could make the "desert like the garden of the Lord." It was the American Dream improved with scripture and endowed with sacred legend, a sort of religious Manifest Destiny. Not until 1891 did the church concede that Zion could be anywhere the pure in heart dwelled, and not necessarily in the sacred valleys of Utah.

The Mormons brought other important concepts into the West. One of these was community planning. Mormon towns did not just grow. They were set up at the outset as economically viable entities, with wide streets that adapted well to modern traffic demands without alteration. Lots were organized so that houses did not face each other for privacy, yet were close enough to offer mutual protection. They were large enough to allow truck farming, but major crops were grown in communal lands outside of town. Another idea was stewardship. The Mormons believed that one held land for the church as the Lord's earthly representative. All were to share equally in land, water (the Mormons produced one of the finest irrigation systems in the modern world, much copied all over the Southwest), public works, and merchandise. One was expected to use this grant wisely or have it rescinded. They also maintained that it was their purpose to rejuvenate the earth and reestablish a new Garden of Eden. This would produce economic independence, frugality, unity, and cooperation. All of this, heightened by previous persecutions and a strong, centralized church government, resulted in a close-knit, well-managed, cooperative, and prosperous society that drew jealous, violent criticism from their Gentile neighbors wherever they went.

Young was well aware of John Charles Frémont's journals and the many emigrant's guides of the day. He and the Council of Twelve knew where the Saints were going before they started. The trip was planned well, the one thing that differentiated Mormons from most western travelers.

In midwinter of 1846, advance parties crossed the Mississippi River on the ice and headed through southern Iowa. As they traveled, families would be left behind at crucial points to build "hay stations"—supply depots that grew crops and made goods to assist those who followed. This was a key factor in the success of the Mormon Trail. At Council Bluffs, Young constructed "Winter Quarters," a camp and temporary church headquarters until the main body could move on in 1847.

While the Saints were camped at Winter Quarters, news arrived of the Mexican War. Army recruiters needed infantry support for all of the cavalry they had raised in Missouri. Young saw an opportunity to send part of the congregation to the Great Basin at government expense and the Mormon Battalion was born—500 foot soldiers for the Santa Fe expedition. The only problem was that the Missourians were the same people who had driven the Mormons out of the Independence area years before. But General Stephen Watts Kearny kept the Mormons several days behind the Gentiles on the trail and no clashes occurred. As some of the Saints wondered why they should aid a government that failed to protect them, Young found it provident to "call" the "volunteers" to the colors as a part of their religious duty.

In 1847 Young sent advance parties west. As the Mormons came onto the Platte River from the north, and Gentiles bound for Oregon and California came up from the south, they marched on opposite sides of the river. The Mormons used the same system that got them across Iowa. The advance parties set up supply depots and ferry crossings and built a road for those who followed. The Mormon Trail stayed on the north side of the Platte all the way to Fort Laramie, where it joined the Oregon Trail to Fort Bridger. Jim Bridger warned Young that no one could live in the Great Basin, and offered to pay $1,000 for the first bushel of corn grown there. The Saints pushed on, following the same route as the ill-fated Donner party of the previous year. When the Mormons reached the canyons leading to Great Salt Lake, they stopped and scouted a better way. By midsummer, the advance party was already growing new crops when Young and the first settlers arrived.

Another distinction of Mormon settlement was that they settled the whole Great Basin all at one time. In a matter of years, they had settled the whole route of the Old Spanish Trail from Salt Lake City to San Diego, California, their seaport on the Pacific. Oddly, it was the saintly Mormons who first set up shop at Las Vegas. The southern clime was very popular with settlers, and often one crop or industry was emphasized, like cotton, leading southern Utah to be called "Dixie" to this day. The church organized entire towns and sent them off to preselected spots to dwell. Young also saw to it that they wrote their own honest guidebook of the trail west, authored by William Clayton.

On a trip to Utah, officers were appointed for each group of 100, 50, and 10. Each 10 had fording ropes, each 50 had a blacksmith and a wagon maker. Loads were inspected for weight and necessity. People walked to keep their livestock fresh. The day started at five in the morning and they traveled until dusk. All were asleep by nine. Half of Saturday and all of Sunday were days of rest, religion, and vehicle repair. Straggling was forbidden. In this manner, the Mormons could take twice as many in each wagon train as Gentiles. They also cut wagons in half and pulled them by hand, creating the famous "handcarts." These conveyances actually worked, despite the fate of one late party that got caught in the snow and had to be rescued by an expedition from Utah. But the rescue went well, as one would expect from Mormon efficiency. The Saints never tired of learning from their mistakes, and generally only made them once.

As many Mormons were poor, especially the recent immigrants from the European missions, the church set up a Perpetual Emigration Fund. All or part of one's trip could be paid by the church. The condition was that one traveled under church orders.

The immigrants were organized at their port of departure much like the overland wagon trains. Only essentials were allowed, and because of church discipline, Mormon travelers usually got along well with ship and train crews. No matter how they traveled, Mormon settlers traveled better-fed, cleaner, and healthier, with church and school in progress the whole way. Over 4,000 Saints made the transcontinental trek over the Mormon Trail in 1855 alone.

But Mormons had not counted on the effects of Manifest Destiny of the greater United States. No sooner had they settled in the Great Basin, Mexican Territory when they got there, than the new Eden became part of the United States again under the Treaty of Guadalupe Hidalgo (1848). Worse yet, gold in California meant that the argonauts traveled the shortest route by way of the Mormon Trail and the Hasting's Cutoff to El Dorado, the fabled city of gold. They complained mightily about Mormon control of roads, supplies, and ferries, and about their smugness. Although it took some years because of the issue of slavery in the territories, the Compromise of 1850 provided for the organization of the Territory of Utah (including today's Nevada and some of Colorado and Wyoming). But the Saints did not have the leisure of the Congress. They created their own theocracy, the State of Deseret, composed of the territory north of the Gila River, south of the Salmon River, the whole Great Basin between the Continental Divide and the Sierras, with an outlet to the Pacific at San Diego.

The rules for Deseret were those of the Council of Fifty, the political organization of the elect, not the United States. As the church held the land in trust from God, U.S. land laws were quickly suspended. Unable to do much else, President Millard Fillmore merely endorsed men of the council, recommended by Young, as the territorial government. His wisdom was endorsed forever when the Mormons named Millard County, with its seat of government at Fillmore. Unfortunately President Franklin Pierce had bigger patronage problems. When the territorial government (Gentiles from the East) arrived, they soon found that U.S. courts, laws, and officials had no influence. Not that the Mormons were not law abiding; quite the reverse—but they obeyed the laws revealed by God to church and civil leaders of the State of Deseret, and none other. Protests by the federal appointees, hack politicians all, caused Young to send them packing.

As the Republican Party platform of 1856 censured the twin evils of polygamy and slavery extension, President James Buchanan, a Democrat, felt obliged to do something about the "rebellion" in Utah. His will was fortified after Paiute Indians and Mormon leaders at Cedar City foolishly ambushed a Gentile emigrant wagon train (from Missouri and Arkansas, where the Saints had had prior troubles) headed for California on the Old Spanish Trail, now called the Mormon Corridor. Never mind that these self-styled "wildcats" acted abominably toward Mormon settlements as they passed, or that the Saints were in a period of religious revival that made them suspicious of all outsiders. The result was the Utah War in 1857 and the sending of a large portion of the U.S. Army to install a new territorial government by force. The Mormons proved excellent practitioners of guerrilla warfare. Realizing from their annual expeditions over the Mormon Trail how important supply was, their militia, the Sons of Dan or the Danites, ran Jim Bridger out of his fort (the nearest supply base) and burned it to the ground; besides, Bridger was considered a Gentile spy and critic. Raids against supply columns left the U.S. Army isolated in the Wyoming snow at the burned-out fort. The war had caused Bridger to lose more than that $1,000 he had offered for the first bushel of Utah corn.

Meanwhile, Thomas Leiper Kane, a Pennsylvania politician and Gentile friend to the Mormons, came around the Horn to California, up the Old Spanish Trail to Salt Lake City, and worked out a compromise. Utah was occupied, but the troops were stationed far from Mormon towns, and the church agreed to accept a new territorial government. But the Council of Fifty acted

as a "ghost government" until statehood, repassing all laws favorably considered by the territorial government. Military occupation continued during the Civil War, with volunteer soldiers from California providing the garrison. Little more happened except a Shoshone war along the Montana Trail after gold was discovered up north. After the war, the Mormon Trail, like all of the Central Overland Route, became superfluous with the arrival of the Union Pacific Railroad.

As an exclusivist, communal society run on a different basis than most of America, believing in Christianity with an uniquely American twist, practicing polygamy until it became a social burden that threatened statehood, and disciplined by a well-organized, principled, rigorous church hierarchy in a world where the secular has come to dominate the rest of society, the Latter-Day Saints have intrigued many, then and now. Arthur Conan Doyle made them and their alleged theocratic excesses the centerpiece of, *A Study in Scarlet*, featuring the famous consulting detective, Sherlock Holmes. Zane Grey made the church elders and their Danite militia the evil protagonists in his *Riders of the Purple Sage*. Charles Bronson faced the same antagonists in a bloody, popular 1988 movie, *Messenger of Death*, based on Rex Burns's book, *Avenging Angels*.

Mark Twain, fleeing Civil War service to be with his brother, secretary to the territorial government in Nevada, subjected the Saints to his irreverent, scathing pen in his memoirs of his overland stage trip in *Roughing It*—his basic thesis: The Mormons are a curious people, "their religion is singular but their wives are plural." Yet the fact remains that much of the criticism arose from their success in creating their Zion in the Great Basin, the State of Deseret, the seed of modern Utah. And they, more than any other emigrant group, wrote a big page in transportation history through their organized travel on the Mormon Trail, a "how to do it" masterpiece in America's move west.

See also California Trail; Central Overland Route; Manifest Destiny; Montana Trail; Old Spanish Trail; Oregon Trail.

References Anderson, Nels, *Desert Saints: The Mormon Frontier in Utah* (1942); Arrington, Leonard J., *Great Basin Kingdom: An Economic History of the Latter-Day Saints* (1958); Billington, Ray Allen, *The Far Western Frontier* (1956); Brooks, Juanita, *The Mountain Meadows Massacre* (1950); Clark, James R., "The Kingdom of God, the Council of Fifty, and the State of Deseret," *Utah Historical Quarterly* (1958) 26: 131–148; Cooley, Everett L., "Carpetbag Rule: Territorial Government in Early Utah," *Utah Historical Quarterly* (1958) 26: 107–129; Creer, Leland H., "Lansford W. Hastings and the Discovery of the Old Mormon Trail," *Western Humanities Review* (1949) 3: 175–186; Drago, Harry S., *Roads to Empire* (1968); Dumke, Glenn S., "Mission Station to Mining Town: Early Las Vegas," *Pacific Historical Review* (1939) 8: 257–270; Dunlop, Richard, *Great Trails of the West* (1971); Fielding, R. Kent, "The Mormon Economy in Kirtland, Ohio," *Utah Historical Quarterly* (1959) 27: 331–356; Furniss, Norman, *The Mormon Conflict, 1850–1858* (1960); Ganoe, John T., "The Beginnings of Irrigation in the United States," *Mississippi Valley Historical Review* (1938–1939) 25: 59–72; Hafen, LeRoy R., "Handcarts to Utah, 1856–1860," *Utah Historical Quarterly* (1956) 24: 309–317; Hart, Val, *The Story of American Roads* (1950); Hunter, Milton R., "The Mormon Corridor," *Pacific Historical Review* (1939) 8: 179–200; Larsen, Gustive O., "The Perpetual Emigration Fund," *Mississippi Valley Historical Review* (1931–1932) 18: 184–194; Moody, Ralph, *Old Trails West* (1963); Mulder, William, "Mormonism's Gathering: An American Doctrine with a Difference," *Church History* (1954) 23: 248–264; Olsen, John Alden, "Proselytism, Immigration and Settlement of Foreign Converts to the Mormon Culture in Zion," *Journal of the West* (1967) 6: 189–204; Poll, Richard D., "The Political Reconstruction of Utah Territory, 1866–1880," *Pacific Historical Review* (1958) 27: 111–126; Sperry, Sidney B., *The Book of Mormon Testifies* (1952); Stegner, Wallace, *The Gathering of Zion* (1964); Van Der Zee, Jacob, "The Mormon Trails in Iowa," *Iowa Journal of History and Politics* (1914) 12: 3–16.

Motor Carrier Acts

As the twentieth century progressed it became evident that much transportation involved newer technologies based on the gasoline and diesel engines. To place these modes of transportation under the regular auspices of the Interstate Commerce Commission (ICC) as earlier acts had done with railroads was the purpose of the Motor Carrier Acts.

MOTOR CARRIER ACT OF 1935

Prompted by Joseph B. Eastman, the federal coordinator of transportation, Congress undertook to pass a measure that would regulate land, water, and air carriers. But under pressure from the American Trucking Associations (ATA), Eastman's concept of comprehensive regulation of all public carriers was reduced to an act that handled trucking alone. This was accomplished by imposing the old National Recovery Administration's (NRA) truck code of 1934 through the extension of regulatory control of the ICC over the trucking industry for the first time.

Essentially, the truck owners had convinced Congress that their interest was the public's. The ICC was to issue operating permits, set minimum rates, supervise mergers and consolidations, and establish hours of service and safety. Most of all, the ICC was to provide a mechanism of enforcement that the NRA codes had lacked. Included were the independent truckers (wildcatters) and all interstate operations that the states could not handle before. In cases involving the operating rights and complaints of a trucker not hauling in over three states, an official from each state involved would constitute a mandatory joint board to adjudicate them with the inherent powers of an ICC examiner. In cases involving more than three states, the ICC set up its own joint board.

But this act was noteworthy because it marked the first time that the federal government had transferred its powers to state officials. The main goal of the act was to stabilize the industry by creating a legal cartel that limited competition to the few so that they might prosper. Truck businesses in operation when the act was passed were "grandfathered" in automatically. But it severely limited the entry of new firms into the cartel through regulations that stifled all but the biggest who were able to compete "fairly" with those already in business. Fair competition was guaranteed by eliminating competition, in violation of pure capitalist theory. Not until the era of deregulation would these federal entry regulations be liberalized in the Motor Carrier Act of 1980. But the states could impose further regulations of their own, in any case.

MOTOR CARRIER ACT OF 1980

Once the trucking industry had been regulated by the Motor Carrier Act of 1935, neither the regulated nor the regulators were much inclined to change. For 45 years the same rules and regulations applied even though economists challenged their relevance to the modern world. But the skyrocketing prices of petroleum upset the norm enough to finally cause change. To ship economically one needed to be able to get around regulations that were initially set up to encourage full employment, mandated circuitous routing, and validated cartel rate making. And with the rail and air industries burgeoning, mergers abounded as the 1970s fuel crisis deepened. The initial changes came from the regulators in the 1970s whose efforts at change were enshrined into law in 1980. The result was the Motor Carrier Act of that year. It was not as comprehensive a deregulation as was occurring in other transportation industries, principally because there was more fear that to deregulate trucking completely might upset the whole economy.

The act eased the criteria for common-carrier certification; curtailed the right of existing carriers to protest new entries; liberalized the rules on commodities to be carried, points served, or routes traversed; extended the old agricultural exemptions; permitted a motor carrier to operate both as a common and contract carrier; established a "zone of reasonableness" in which rates could be adjusted without interference from the Interstate Commerce Commission; called for simplified procedures; permitted hauling of regulated and exempt commodities concurrently; and narrowed the exemptions from antitrust laws. Basically, the emphasis was changed from an industry controlled by business cartels and unionized drivers to one that encouraged the independent owner-operator. But the Motor Carrier Act of 1980 did not go as far as the Airline Deregulation Act of 1978 or the Staggers Rail Act of 1980. An applicant still had to show public benefit from entry into the field; the ICC could still rule on case-by-case applications rather than on general findings and make a mandatory filing of tariffs and rates, which could still be investigated by the ICC, and there were still restrictions involving places and routes.

MOTOR CARRIER ACT OF 1991

Better known as the Intermodal Surface Transportation Efficiency Act (ISTEA), the Motor Carrier Act of 1991 further deregulated the trucking industry by coping with the increased use of containers, especially the new 28-foot domestic varieties. In a combination of federal, state, and local government activities and financing (nearly 50 percent of which were actually private endeavors), the 1991 measure sought to increase the modernization of container terminals and relieve inner-city congestion so common in old downtown terminal areas. The dropping of more restrictive ICC regulations and agreements between railroads, truckers, and the International Brotherhood of Teamsters growing out of this act have permitted the loading of 28-foot containers or semitrailers on flatcars as less-than-carload freight, just like international 20-foot equivalent loads.

In 1994 Congress struck at trucking regulations again, obliquely through the Federal Air Port Act. A rider to the act took away the right of the 41 states that still regulated truckers operating under their jurisdictions, providing that the trucking firm in question made over 15,000 transactions a day. Led by a successful Federal Express suit in the western states, United Parcel Service (UPS) got Kentucky (home of UPS's largest distribution facility) Senator Wendell Ford to introduce the measure in Congress. Assisted by Kansas (Yellow Freight) Senator Robert Dole and North Carolina (Carolina Freight Corporation) Senator Jesse Helms, Ford tacked the measure on a very popular airport funding measure to assure its passage. Before its passage, it was cheaper to ship from San Francisco to Reno (200 miles, unregulated) than from San Francisco to Oakland (15 miles, regulated), or to ship packages within Indiana boundaries by sending them out of state and back again to get the 1980 Motor Carrier Act benefits. Advocates expect the new law to save truckers and their customers $7 billion a year in addition to the $15 billion saved annually under the 1980 Motor Carrier Act. The current trend is to modify laws enough to permit shippers to maximize their benefits under the "just-in-time" inventory methods made possible by the computer revolution, reducing warehouse costs.

See also Airline Deregulation Act of 1978; Eastman, Joseph B.; Federal-Aid Highway Acts, Federal-Aid Highway Act of 1956, Federal-Aid Highway Act of 1976; Federal-Aid Highway Amendments of 1975; NRA Trucking Codes; Shipping Acts; Staggers Rail Act of 1980; Surface Transportation Assistance Acts; Transportation Acts; Trucking.

References Cheng, Philip C., *Accounting and Financing for Motor Carriers* (1984); Childs, William R., *Trucking and the Public Interest* (1985); Felton, John Richard, and Dale G. Anderson (eds.), *Regulation and Deregulation of the Motor Carrier Industry* (1989); Fishbein, Meyer D., "The Trucking Industry and the National Recovery Administration," *Social Forces* (1955–1956) 34: 171–179; Keeler, Theodore E., *Railroads, Freight and Public Policy* (1983); MacAvoy, Paul W., and John W. Snow (eds.), *Regulation of Entry and Pricing in Truck Transportation* (1977); Marshall, Jonathan, "Cheap Truckin'," *National Review* (7 November 1994) 46: 54–56; Nelson, James C., "The Motor Carrier Act of 1935," *Journal of Political Economy* (1936) 44: 464–504; Perry, Charles R., et al., *Deregulation and the Decline of the Unionized Trucking Industry* (1986); Robyn, Dorothy, *Braking the Special Interests* (1987); Wagner, Warren H., *A Legislative History of the Motor Carrier Act of 1935* (1935); Winston, Clifford, et al., *The Economic Effects of Surface Freight Regulation* (1990).

Mullan Road

As late as the 1850s, the only road into the Pacific Northwest was the Oregon Trail. People to the north of the Columbia River, still part of Oregon Territory, organized the Cowlitz Convention and petitioned Congress for a separate territorial government. Agreeing to such action, Oregon's delegate to Congress, Joseph Lane, suggested that

Washington, D.C., pay more attention to the road needs of the upper part of the Pacific Northwest, and set up a new territory to supervise this concern. In 1853, President Franklin Pierce sent Major Isaac I. Stevens to be the new governor of Washington Territory.

A former military man recently gone into politics, Stevens was interested not only in roads but railroad routes into the Puget Sound area. His major problems were how to cross the Cascade Range and the Continental Divide. Stevens began his survey from two points. In Washington Territory, Captain George B. McClellan was to start from Puget Sound proper. Stevens would come across the Plains from Minnesota. They planned to meet at Fort Walla Walla. McClellan was to build a road as he went, connecting Puget Sound with the fort near the Columbia River. McClellan established his base near present-day Ellensburg, convinced that the best path across the Cascades emanated from there. But McClellan never surveyed a route. He also refused to build the road, leaving that to a civilian contractor appointed by Stevens, Abiel W. Tinkam. He chose Naches Pass, but movement of the center of population up Puget Sound to Seattle caused pioneers to mark their own route through Snoqualmie Pass. Both routes began at Walla Walla.

Similar problems haunted the building of a road from Old Fort Vancouver to Puget Sound. Stevens cleverly suggested to the federal authorities that such a route was of prime military importance and merely needed completion, not construction from scratch, as was the case. But Congress, for as yet still unexplained reasons, refused to consider the proposal. The result was that the road north from the Columbia had to be built by civilian donations and territorial appropriations. By 1860, it was completed, but it was only wide enough and smooth enough to accept mule packtrains.

Meanwhile, another more massive road project was under way in eastern Washington. In the early 1850s, Asa Whitney, a New Yorker interested in the China trade, had proposed that Congress finance a northern route from the Great Lakes to Puget Sound, but he was dismissed as a dreamer. Even when it came to the Pacific railroad surveys, Congress had overlooked the possibilities of the forty-seventh parallel as a potential route, even though it would be followed in part by the Milwaukee Road and the Northern Pacific and Great Northern Railroads in the twentieth century. With the problems of the Yakima War in the 1850s, the army was interested in more roads in what is now Washington State, and eventually located one from Puget Sound to Fort Walla Walla. There, branches connected to the emigrant trails farther south.

It was obvious that a northern route would have to cross some of the highest passes and most rugged terrain of the whole Continental Divide. It was this job that was entrusted to Lieutenant John Mullan. Coming to Washington with the surveying party of Captain Isaac Stevens, an army officer soon to become territorial governor, Mullan had been assigned to find a route across the Bitterroot Mountains out of Fort Benton on the eastern slope. The result was his discovery of Mullan Pass, still a major crossing. He continued his explorations and crossed the Continental Divide six times in 1854, surveying all major routes available from the headwaters of the Missouri River. Then he selected the route through the Coeur d'Alene Mountains into Walla Walla.

Like all survey parties, Stevens knew that he was to select both road and rail possibilities, and in 1855 he was elected territorial delegate to Congress, where he lobbied for a northern route and recommended Mullan as its engineer. The government responded with an appropriation, because the impending Mormon War had fired up all sorts of interest in alternate routes through the mountains. In 1858, Mullan received authorization to construct a road west across the Rockies from the head of navigation on the Missouri at Fort Benton to Fort Walla Walla. The project was delayed for a year when local Native Americans, irked by the activity of miners along the proposed route, went to war and defeated the army

detachment sent to suppress them. Mullan joined a new successful punitive expedition and used the campaign to familiarize himself with more of the terrain. In 1859, Mullan took a party of 250 into the mountains to build the road. The party was fairly large—there was much work and fear that the Blackfeet, always distrustful of Americans, would attack.

Mullan followed his old route east out of Walla Walla, building his road and marking the path with posts containing the letters M.R. (Military Road) plus the mileage from the beginning. The route went north to near today's Spokane, where it turned east. Most of the terrain was level and well drained, so Mullan just had to set up his markers and move on. Wet spots were corduroyed and fords marked, but no bridges were constructed. Then he advanced up into Sohon Pass (named for his Indian guide). This work was more demanding, and some bridging was required. Worse, there were 100 miles of forest to the St. Regis Borgia River, and the undergrowth was so tangled it became a major project just to clear it. The delays were long and winter caught the party in the St. Regis Borgia Valley. Travel back to Washington Territory revealed that the Native Americans had used a route farther north, and the following spring the road was moved over to Clark's Fork. Scurvy and freezing were common problems throughout the operation.

In 1860, Mullan traded with friendly Flatheads (Salish) for horses and continued his work. It took six weeks to grade the approaches to Big Mountain and follow the Bitterroot River to Mullan Pass. The party crossed the divide and reached Fort Benton by midsummer. Mullan picked up a detachment of recruits and returned to Walla Walla, improving the route as he traveled. There he proposed that another road be extended from the one he had just built to connect the Fort Benton area to the Overland Trail, presaging the creation of the Bozeman Trail. In May of 1861, he started a new party forward to Montana by the Mullan Road, making repairs and changes in the route when necessary. Winter caught them in the Bitterroot Valley. This winter of 1861–1862 was even worse on his crew than the previous year's. But by spring, except for the construction of one bridge, which he let out to a civilian contractor, the road was finished.

Although the Mullan Road was ostensibly built as a military road, the discovery of gold in the foothills of the Montana Rockies brought much civilian use. In 1865, Mullan published all of his observations and notes as an emigrant's guide. But few wagons actually used the Mullan Road. It remained too rough. Even large mule trains reported that the way presented numerous difficulties. Fallen timber and destroyed bridges caused the Washington territorial legislature to beg federal assistance to reopen the northern route into Montana, but it would never be a serious rival to the Central Overland Route with its Bozeman and Montana Trails. Additional routes from Lewiston, Idaho, through the Lolo Pass on the west and across the northern Plains from Minnesota to the east also failed to materialize, even after initial surveys. The most common reason given for failure to finance such projects was the winter snow, which made them impassable at least four months of the year. As for the Plains routes, they would entail altering federal Indian policy, which was in enough of a mess already. It remained for the railroads to open the Mullan Road to full public use on their all-weather tracks of steel at the end of the nineteenth century, after the Indian reservations and the people on them had been reduced to a "manageable" size.

See also Bozeman Trail; Montana Trail.

References Addison, Howard, "Captain John Mullan," *Washington Historical Quarterly* (1934) 25: 185–202; Bemis, Samuel Flagg, "Captain John Mullan and the Engineer's Frontier," *Washington Historical Quarterly* (1923) 14: 201–205; Dunlop, Richard, *Great Trails of the West* (1971); Elliott, T. C., "The Mullan Road: Its Local History and Significance," *Washington Historical Quarterly* (1923) 14: 206–209; Jackson, W. Turrentine, *Wagon Roads West* (1952); Talkington, Henry L., "Mullan Road," *Washington Historical Quarterly* (1916) 7: 301–306; Winther, Oscar O., "Early Commercial Importance of the Mullan Road," *Oregon Historical Quarterly* (1945) 46: 22–35.

Munn v. Illinois 94 US 113 (1877)

The idea of governmental control of transportation has a long Anglo-American legal history. By 1518, the idea of a public service had been differentiated from private ones. The concept of public duty also assumed the notion that the carrier was responsible for the safe delivery of a cargo without spoilage or damage through neglect on the part of the carrier. Later American custom held that a shipper must charge equal rates to all who shipped similar goods over similar routes.

Under the Constitution of 1789, Americans had an inherent conflict between the right of the federal government (the commerce clause, which regulates trade across state lines) and that of the states (police powers, which permit regulation of businesses for the public good) to regulate trade. The Supreme Court flip-flopped over who had the more important interest here, the early Courts ruling for the federal government and later ones holding for the states. Because of the Civil War and the passage of the Fourteenth Amendment during Reconstruction, new cases arose probing where this right of regulation lay and what it was. These cases were collectively known as the Granger Cases.

The most important Granger case regarding regulation was *Munn v. Illinois*. In it, warehousemen in Chicago complained that local regulations of prices were unconstitutional under the Fourteenth Amendment's concept of due process. They further held that any regulatory right was federal because of the commerce clause. The Court, in a decision written by Chief Justice Morrison R. Waite, ruled that historically the police powers had been used in both the United States and England to supersede the property rights of individuals or corporations when in the public interest. The Court found that the maximum price controls in Chicago followed that pattern. It ruled that when a private use was part of the public good, it changed its very nature to a controllable right. The complaint that such laws or regulations prevented the warehousemen from earning a fair profit was one for the legislature or city council, not the courts.

Finally, the Court ruled that when the federal government did not exercise a power granted it under any clause of the Constitution, the field was properly left open to the states and local governing entities. It was the referral of prerogatives in this area to the state legislative branches that would lead directly to the Interstate Commerce Act ten years later, because the problems to be solved were interstate in nature, particularly when the dissenters in the case, led by Justice Stephen J. Field, said that the majority had been neglectful of the rights of private property. And the Court would tend toward the dissenting view in later cases, maintaining that the states' police power was not absolute. If profit were unduly limited by police powers, it amounted to a constitutional violation. In the end, the Court held in the 1890s that this balance was so fragile that each regulatory action would have to be ruled on by the courts piecemeal (*Smyth v. Ames* 169 US 466 [1898]). The Court also

divorced production from the public interest wholly (*U.S. v. E. C. Knight Co.* 156 US 1 [1895]). The legislatures could still regulate and appoint commissions to administer the regulations, but the courts would have the final say if the regulated protested, which they usually did. The result was the formation of the Interstate Commerce Commission in 1887, an attempt to put federal teeth in transportation regulation, which itself would go through the same emasculating process until the New Deal.

See also Interstate Commerce Commission; *Tyson and Brothers–United Theater Ticket Offices, Inc. v. Blanton*.

References Buck, Solon J., *The Granger Movement* (1913); Childs, William R., *Trucking and the Public Interest* (1985); Kelly, Alfred H., and Winfred A. Harbison, *The American Constitution* (1948); Miller, George H., *Railroads and the Granger Laws* (1971); Scheiber, Harry N., "The Road to Munn: Eminent Domain and the Concept of Public Purpose in the State Courts," *Perspectives in American History* (1971) 5: 327–402; Swindler, William F., *Court and Constitution in the 20th Century* (1969–1974).

Nader, Ralph (b. 1934)

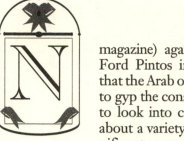

Born of Lebanese immigrant parents and a graduate of Harvard Law School, Ralph Nader gives the public impression of an austere, humorless, unrelenting individual, undoubtedly honest, but one who is seen by opponents as self-righteous, socialistically inclined, surprisingly ill-informed, with pronounced vigilante leanings. In his groundbreaking fight against General Motors (GM), however, he came off as St. George slaying the dragon, particularly when he testified before Senator Abraham Ribbicoff of Connecticut, encouraged by Senator Robert F. Kennedy. Nader raved against the alleged instability of GM's popular Corvair model, which was once *Motor Trend* magazine's car of the year. His noted 1965 book, *Unsafe at Any Speed*, has a provocative opening sentence: "For over a century the automobile has brought death, injury, and the most inestimable sorrow and deprivation to millions of people." His general theme was that auto manufacturers brought out cars by cutting costs and ignoring safety. Surely, his opponents and even some friends argue, the auto has done more than merely maim Americans.

But Nader's charges provoked lots of lawsuits and public feeling against the automakers, especially GM. The company responded stupidly, putting detectives on Nader's trail. The snoops got caught, and GM had to apologize and pay an out-of-court settlement of $425,000. The foul-up made Nader a national hero. That crusader Nader could kill an American car model, made by GM no less, showed to what depths the U.S. auto industry had fallen. Nader's subsequent attacks have influenced several government regulatory agencies, and can been seen as the American consumer movement's greatest success story. His concern has brought about the whole concept of product recalls. Nader has been aided in his quest by dissident company dealers. The Center for Auto Safety owes its influence to Nader. He has also criticized recreational vehicles as unsafe (especially in their suspensions), launched the attack (with *Mother Jones* magazine) against the "exploding" Ford Pintos in 1970, and argued that the Arab oil crisis was contrived to gyp the consumer. He continues to look into consumer complaints about a variety of products, a magnificent curmudgeon to the end. As one former employee said, the pleasure of eating a hot dog means nothing to Nader— "he tastes only the nitrates."

See also Automobiles from Domestics to Imports; Automobiles in American Society.

References Dowie, Mark, "Pinto Madness," *Mother Jones* (1977) 2: 18–32; Halberstam, David, *The Reckoning* (1986); Holsworth, Robert D., *Public Interest Liberalism and the Crisis of Affluence* (1981); McCary, Charles, *Citizen Nader* (1972); May, George S., "Ralph Nader," in George S. May (ed.), *EABHB: The Automobile Industry* (1989), 338–341; Nader, Ralph, *Unsafe at Any Speed* (1965); Rothschild, Emma, *Paradise Lost* (1973); Shook, Robert L., *Turnaround* (1990); Sobel, Robert, *Car Wars* (1984); Whiteside, Thomas, *The Investigation of Ralph Nader* (1972).

Natchez Trace

Running from the bluffs overlooking the Mississippi River at the town that gives it its name, the Natchez Trace winds northward away from the Father of Waters toward Nashville, Tennessee, home of some of the best hunting grounds in pre-Columbian America. Originally a game trail enlarged and used by Native Americans, the trace became a route followed by white men returning from New Orleans after they had sold their cargoes and flatboats, now made useless by the mighty river's current for the trip north. It was first crossed by the Spaniards under Hernando de Soto in the 1540s, and his brutalities seemed to mark the trace forever. It was not for nothing that it became a robber's trail—the returning farmers, trappers, and rivermen often carried fat purses of gold. It was also the road on which President Thomas Jefferson's one-time clerk and western pathfinder, Meriwether Lewis, on returning to answer charges against his territorial administration in Louisiana, was murdered—or did he, a moody man whose stint as territorial governor was under investigation for monetary irregularities, commit suicide? On the Natchez Trace, nobody really cared. It also took General Andrew Jackson and the riflemen of Kentucky and Tennessee to their great battle with destiny below New Orleans, victory in which made him the seventh president of the United States.

The Natchez Trace had numerous names attached to it during its long history. It was the Road to the Choctaws, the Chickasaw Trace (both being tribal residents along its route), and once Congress set up a mail run on it and labeled it the Columbian Highway. Most called it the Natchez Road or the Nashville Road, depending on where they were headed. Some idealist in a weak-minded moment even named it the Path of Peace—it was more correctly described by its ancient moniker, the Devil's Backbone. Abe Lincoln passed by in the 1820s returning from New Orleans, gaining a hatred for African slavery that never left him. One of the greatest duels in American history, the Sand Bar Fight, was fought nearby on an island in the river—known for the Bowie fighting knife that made a participant famous for carving his opponent apart in one vicious thrust, and preserved him for a different fate at the Alamo. As the returning whites moved north, they passed slave coffles headed south to open up some of the finest cotton land the world would ever see, and produce one of the richest societies on the American frontier. This heritage is still honored in the fine plantation homes now opened up for inspection by gawkers and dreamers each spring.

The white man's permanent interest in Natchez came with the French. In 1716, Jean Baptiste Le Moyne, Sieur de Bienville, built a fort on the bluffs, which he named Fort Rosalie. It was at Natchez that John Law hatched his famous scheme to recoup the fortunes of the king of France by selling stock in lands along the Mississippi. He marketed the lands, using sales techniques that would make a Madison Avenue advertiser's mouth water. He slipped out of Paris as the bubble burst, the first in a long line of slick promoters of American lands to run

away with the profits. Meanwhile, settlers infected the local Indians with smallpox, bought scalps, and sold whiskey, all much to the detriment of the original inhabitants. This policy resulted in a 1729 uprising by the tribe for which the modern city is named that practically cleaned out the white settlement at Fort Rosalie. The French wiped out the Natchez in turn, using their own Native American allies, the Choctaw, for the dirty work. The French also tried to destroy the pro-British Chickasaw at the same time, but they proved too tough.

The French and Indian War transferred the Natchez Trace area from the French to the British, with New Orleans and all land east of the Mississippi being given to the Spanish. The American Revolution replaced the British but left the Spanish at the Crescent City. At the same time, James Robertson, the Father of Tennessee to some, established the settlement that would become Nashville at the northern end of the trace. Now there were settlements of Americans at both ends of the trace, and Robertson moved to improve the road for travel. With the prospects of improved transportation, people were ripe for another land fraud, as "Mississippi Fever" swept the new American nation's eastern shores. Under the American scheme of things, the Natchez Trace area was then part of the state of Georgia, which sold over 35 million acres of Mississippi land to four companies. Crying foul, as many of the legislators had been bribed by the land companies, a new "honest" legislature rescinded the sale the following year. Shortly thereafter, Georgia ceded her claim to any western lands to the United States and, to settle outstanding issues, President Jefferson awarded 5 million acres to the holders of the original grant.

But Jefferson had reckoned without gaining support of his most ideological supporters in Congress. Angry with the president's abandonment of a strict reading of the Constitution in purchasing Louisiana from the French (who had secretly obtained it from the Spanish), these Democratic Republicans blocked the necessary congressional appropriation. After all, the Constitution never said anything about compounding a fraud by the remotest stretch of the imagination, ran their argument. Eventually, the claimants would get $4.52 million in 1814, but now the territory through which the Natchez Trace ran faced lengthy court cases over the validity of the Yazoo Frauds, as they were popularly billed. The U.S. Supreme Court settled the whole thing on behalf of the land companies, Chief Justice John Marshall maintaining that it was not for the Court to inquire as to how the lands were sold, but to honor the sanctity of the contract under the Constitution.

The settlement of the Yazoo Frauds was important, but the key issue was American access to the port at New Orleans. Farmers in the West could not afford the costs of transporting their surplus products across the miserable roads to the East Coast. It was easier and cheaper to send them to New Orleans on the Mississippi and its tributaries, and then transship them from there to New York City or Philadelphia. At that time in U.S. history, westerners strongly believed that the new national government cared little for their problems. When they liquefied their corn harvests to ship them easier, the government passed a whiskey tax that drained up profits. When the farmers protested in time-honored American fashion, in what was called the Whiskey Rebellion, by riding tax collectors out of the territory on rails as they had done to the British in 1776, the federal government sent in the army to subdue them and collect the tax. Many thought of seceding from the Union, and under Aaron Burr (who hated Jefferson for blocking his shady ascent to the presidency) and General James Wilkinson (who received a pension from the Spanish) they found men who could lead them.

Tired of these rumblings from the West, and elected with western support, Thomas Jefferson decided to ask Napoleon I to sell New Orleans (the transfer of Louisiana from Spain to France was supposed to be a secret, but Americans were adept spies in those days). The emperor surprised the American negotiators by offering a final arrangement for all of Louisiana at a price too good to pass up. The deal was done and the Mississippi opened up to American river trade from all the Old Northwest and Southwest. This meant that the boatmen would be returning north up the only good road available, the Natchez Trace. To make the place irresistible, businessmen (gamblers, grifters, whiskey peddlers, and the like) constructed Natchez-Under-The-Hill, a mile-long den of iniquity, no holds barred. No boatman worth his salt could refuse a stop at Natchez before proceeding up the trace. Many lost so much money at Natchez that they were hardly worth stopping to rob further up the trail. But they were stopped anyway—the Natchez Trace had a reputation to uphold. Gangs like Joseph Hare's, Wiley Harpe's (he and his brother had terrorized Kentucky's Wilderness Road for years before moving to this greener pasture, as it were), and John Murrell's robbed, murdered, ran stolen slaves, and dealt in pilfered goods until authorities scattered, hanged, or whipped them into submission.

Because of the increased traffic on the Natchez Trace, the army came in after 1800 and widened and improved the roadbed and set up more ferries at river crossings. In 1811, however, the beginning of the end was in sight. It was a strange year: There was a close passage of a comet; the New Madrid earthquake, probably the most violent in American history, changed the course of the Mississippi, causing it to flow backward for a time; Tecumseh established his great eastern Indian alliance, from which Natchez was saved from the fate of massacre, unlike neighboring Alabamians at Fort Mims, by the refusal of Chief Pushmataha to permit his Choctaw to join; and the first steamboat came downriver, a Robert Fulton boat of deep draft that could ply the river between New Orleans and Natchez. The War of 1812 merely delayed the inevitable—the new flat-bottomed steamers of Henry Shreve would doom the trail to near extinction. Who would suffer the trials and tribulations of dangerous overland travel when the steamboat was so cheap, classy, and fast?

So the Natchez Trace fell into disuse. It

had not been too good a road from the beginning. The government spent a little over $20,000 on it during the same time that almost $2 million was spent on the National Road. But then the trace did not have the same amount of traffic either. In the early twentieth century, the Daughters of the American Revolution and the Daughters of the War of 1812 began to mark the old route with boulders. In some places, no one really knew where it had run. Then in the 1930s, Congress passed a law creating a new roadway, the Natchez Trace Parkway. President Franklin D. Roosevelt needed spending measures to get a bill out of congressional committee, and the committee was controlled by a Mississippian. Eventually, the federal government threw in $15 million, a considerable sum in 1935. Construction began soon thereafter, and the Natchez Trace sprang back into existence, where it remains today.

See also Steamboats.

References Daniels, Jonathan, *The Devil's Backbone* (1962); Davis, William C., *A Way through the Wilderness* (1995); Harrison, C. William, *Outlaw of the Natchez Trace* (1960); Hart, Val, *The Story of American Roads* (1950); Kane, Harnett T., *Natchez on the Mississippi* (1947); Keating, Bern, "Today along the Natchez Trace," *National Geographic* (November 1968) 134: 641–667; Magrath, C. Peter, *Yazoo* (1966).

National Advisory Committee for Aeronautics (NACA)

American airplane engines were much less advanced than those of European countries fighting the Great War, as was pointed out in the report of Dr. Albert F. Zahm, on contract to the Smithsonian. His report prompted President Woodrow Wilson to establish the National Advisory Committee for Aeronautics in 1915. Although it had no facilities until 1920, the NACA conducted scientific studies of the problems of flight, including aerodynamics, instruments, fabrics, and air-cooled, radial engines.

The increased importance of aircraft in both civilian and military capacities after the Great War led to the creation of an actual NACA research facility at Langley Field, Virginia, in 1920. NACA had one of the first wind tunnels for testing aerodynamics. The tunnel seemed a failure until the arrival of the German aeronautical theorist Ludwig Prandtl. He had the air in the tunnel compressed to 20 atmospheres and used exact models at one-twentieth of their actual size. In 1923, NACA received a congressional appropriation to build a variable pressure, full-size wind tunnel with a throat of 20 feet in diameter. This improvement helped sort out problems of wind drag on such items as fixed landing gear, and particularly engine cowls. Before these tests, exposed flat-faced radial engines had created up to one-third of the drag on an airframe. The wind tunnel also led to improved mono-wing design that replaced biplanes, with their external struts and wire bracing, with cantilevered internal braces. The NACA also led the field in stressed-skin, streamlined bodies that aided the cantilevered wings in distributing stresses equally throughout the aircraft.

NACA continued its 1930s successes with military research during World War II. It developed ice-prevention systems, but angered the top brass with its failure to keep up with foreign developments in jet engines. This led to a separate and independent research facility for the air force at Wright-Patterson Field at Dayton, Ohio. But NACA continued its work nonetheless. It cooperated with both military and industry representatives in the rocket-powered X-series of record-setting aircraft. It also developed the "pinched waist" concept that helped increase the speed of jet fighter aircraft by reducing transonic drag. But in the multitude of industry and military branch research facilities, it became but one voice in a large choir rather than the solo role it enjoyed during the first two decades of its existence and was absorbed by the National Aeronautics and Space Administration in 1958.

See also Aeronautics; National Aeronautics and Space Administration.

References Bilstein, Roger E., *Flight in America* (1994); Gray, George W., *Frontiers of Flight* (1948).

National Aeronautics and Space Administration (NASA)

After public consternation at the Soviet launching of *Sputnik* and the embarrassing sight of so many similar American attempts blowing up on the launch pad, Congress responded by reorganizing the U.S. space program under one massive coordinating agency in the National Aeronautics and Space Act of 1958. Named the National Aeronautics and Space Administration, the new organization had a strong civilian element so that it would not be limited to military exploitation of the heavens alone. Today NASA includes over a dozen different agencies: its Washington headquarters, the Ames Research Center, the Dryden Flight Research Facility, the Goddard Space Flight Center, the Jet Propulsion Laboratory, the Johnson Space Center (which in turn administers the White Sands Test Facility), Langley Research Center, Lewis Research Center, Marshall Space Flight Center (which directs the Michoud Assembly Facility and the Slidell Computer Complex), the National Advisory Committee for Aeronautics, the National Space Technology Laboratories, the Wallops Flight Facility, Vandenburg Space Transportation Systems, and the Plum Brook Station.

Although its budget fluctuates year by year as its political overseers revisualize its importance and critics decry its becoming another stale bureaucracy that has seemingly lost the leading-edge assertiveness of its early moon-race days, NASA has made many contributions to American society. Not only through manned space flight (the Mercury, Gemini, Apollo, and Space Shuttle programs), but also by way of the numerous unmanned probes of deep space, NASA projects have revealed much essential information about how the earth came about, and the relationships between the planets and the various solar systems of the Milky Way. Needless to say, any satellite that has peaceful applications can with very little alteration become a potent military weapon or intelligence-gathering apparatus. More important to the person on the street have been the various spin-off projects that util-ize space applications for the betterment of everyday life. A partial list includes the miniaturizing of countless items that in turn reduces cost and increases practicability; medical-systems reporting over long distances that can put a doctor in touch with an emergency medical team; advanced aircraft design and related products; reduction of drag in various land, sea, and air vehicles; solar power research; water filtration; speech aids; removal of interference in radio, television, and X-rays; and the development of "cool suits" to prevent heat exhaustion.

See also Astronautics; National Advisory Committee for Aeronautics.

References Bilstein, Roger E., *Flight in America* (1994); DeWard, E. John, and Nancy DeWard, *History of NASA* (1984); Hall, R. Cargill, "Instrumented Exploration and Utilization of Space: The American Experience," in Eugene M. Emme (ed.), *Two Hundred Years of Flight in America* (1977), 183–212; McCurdy, Howard, *Inside NASA* (1993).

National Industrial Recovery Act of 1933 (NIRA)

One of the cornerstones of Franklin D. Roosevelt's New Deal, the 1933 National Industrial Recovery Act was designed to revive industrial and business activity and reduce unemployment. It was based on the idea of industry self-regulation with government supervision operating through the National Recovery Administration (NRA), which enforced a series of fair competition codes, many of which had been in effect since World War I. If a group of businessmen refused to draw up such codes, the president through the NRA could impose them. All such codes were exempt from antitrust laws. Perhaps most important was Section 7(a), which permitted labor to organize and bargain collectively—the first time that labor unions had received federal endorsement. Initially successful, code violations and cutthroat competition soon became rampant despite the NIRA. The NIRA also set up the Public Works Administration (PWA) for the construction of roads, public buildings, and other projects. This whole process was called "pump priming," a process whereby the national treasury got business moving again so that unemployment would end. The PWA spent $4.25 billion in its efforts, but was ultimately declared unconstitutional in the Supreme Court case *Schechter Poultry Corp. v. U.S.*, the so-called sick chicken case in which the Court ruled that Congress had unconstitutionally delegated its powers to the president and interfered in businesses that were not interstate in nature.

See also Emergency Railroad Transportation Act; Hayden-Cartwright Act; Roads and Highways since World War I.

References Fishbein, Meyer H., "The Trucking Industry and the National Recovery Administration," *Social Forces* (1955–1956) 34: 171–179; Latham, Earl, *The Politics of Railroad Coordination* (1959); Leuchtenburg, William E., *Franklin D. Roosevelt and the New Deal* (1963); Perkins, Dexter, *The New Age of Franklin D. Roosevelt* (1957); U.S. Department of Transportation, Federal Highway Administration, *America's Highways* (1976).

National Old Trails Highway

One of the "named highways" popular in the teens and twenties of the twentieth century, the National Old Trails Highway was used by local chambers of commerce and tourism and the American Automobile Association to stimulate travel on the "good roads" and increase income in the towns and states through which they passed. Its association formed in 1913, the National Old Trails Highway followed several historic trails, the first of which was the National Road out of Baltimore to St. Louis (eventually U.S. Highway 40). It then continued out to Kansas City on what is roughly modern Interstate 70, and followed the old Mountain Division of the Santa Fe Trail out of Kansas City into New Mexico through Ratón Pass. At Santa Fe the road turned west across northern New Mexico and Arizona, alongside the tracks of the Atchison, Topeka, and Santa Fe Railroad, the old Thirty-fifth Parallel Way once explored by Captain Amiel Whipple and Edward Beale and what would later be labeled U.S. Highway 66 and Interstate 40, to Barstow, California. There it turned south to San Bernardino and Los Angeles on what is today Interstate 15.

See also Roads and Highways, Colonial Times to World War I; Roads and Highways since World War I.

Reference Hart, Val, *The Story of American Roads* (1950).

National Rail Passenger Act of 1971

The National Rail Passenger Act provided a government subsidy to run passenger service on U.S. railroads through a federal entity, Amtrak, which had its own equipment and rented use of the lines from the private freight roads.

See also Motor Carrier Acts; Railroad Revitalization and Regulatory Reform Act of 1976; Regional Rail Reorganization Act of 1973; Staggers Rail Act of 1980; Transportation Acts.

References Hilton, George W., *Amtrak* (1980); Keeler, Theodore E., *Railroads, Freight and Public Policy* (1983); Musolf, Lloyd, *Uncle Sam's Private, Profitseeking Corporations* (1983).

National Railroad Passenger Corporation

The National Railroad Passenger Corporation is the official name of the federal rail corporation better known as Amtrak, which was established in 1970 to run all U.S. passenger traffic except commuter trains. The corporation actually buys track space over which to run its passenger services from a dozen and a half private railroads all devoted to freight movement.

See also Amtrak.

National Road

When George Washington left office, the old Braddock Road was so rough that it actually improved when covered with snow and ice. The problem inherent in federal subsidization of highway building was how to justify financing the building of a national road to the west in a manner that would not compromise states' rights guaranteed in the Constitution. This dilemma means little to a modern American; the Constitution has been so stretched that it may be used to justify anything nowadays, and it is rarely read anymore. But to Americans in 1800, as Thomas Jefferson came to power under the guise of states' rights and a weak central government, it was a key issue. Secretary of the Treasury Albert Gallatin solved the problem to Jefferson's satisfaction. Gallatin urged that 2 percent of the income from the sale of public lands be held aside to build the National Road. Later the sum was raised to 5 percent (to keep the state from selling the lands for taxes), and ultimately $20 million was spent. In 1806, Congress passed an act authorizing the construction of a National Highway between Cumberland, Maryland, and Wheeling, Virginia (West Virginia not being a separate state until 1863). The clearing was to be 66 feet wide and ruling grades limited to 8.75 percent. Current interstate highway legislation allows up to a 7 percent grade, so the standards of the National Road were quite modern. Only one small, very rugged section of the National Road failed to meet the standard grade. As with more recent road projects, the route meant life or death for the towns included or bypassed by the highway. Pennsylvania withheld her approval until the survey was changed to include Uniontown and Washington (the process was for the federal government to get permission to build from the state and then advance the money needed against the future sales of land). It was decided that the capitals of the states and territories through which it passed would always be included (Columbus, Ohio; Indianapolis, Indiana; and Vandalia, Illinois). Because of political delays and the War of 1812, it took until 1818 to complete the section to Wheeling. The finished roadbed was 20 feet wide and made of graduated crushed stones and gravels compressed with a three-ton roller (a so-called macadamized roadbed). Bridges (some of which still stand) crossed waterways. The real problem came when it was discovered that Congress had even less constitutional authority to maintain the road than to build it. So the road stayed toll-free and poorly kept up.

Even though land sales rarely kept up with the financial demands of construction and repair, the government kept on building from Wheeling (1818), to Columbus (1833), and to Vandalia (1839). At least that

was what was planned—the actual road never quite got to Vandalia. Before construction, it took six to eight weeks for goods to travel from Baltimore to Pittsburgh; after the National Road came into use, the time was shortened to two weeks. Unlike most roads of its day, the National Road had drainage ditches on each side, giving it an all-weather look. Stagecoaches and three-teamed Conestoga wagons plied its surface daily, stopping at one of the numerous roadhouses for the night. The wagonmen were avid cigar smokers, by the way, and the peculiar long, cheap black tobacco came to be known as "Conestogas," a term eventually shortened to "stogie."

Hauling the federal mails led many coaches to carry as much as $50,000 a trip, and the result was a plague of robberies. But these highwaymen had a bit more class, as might be expected of men working the main government-funded road in America. Dr. John F. Braddee, for instance, had his medical offices overlooking the stage yard at Uniontown. He connived with stage employees to hand the mailbags through a hole in an adjoining fence, looted the bags, and returned them to speed on their way. He was caught by mail detectives and received a ten-year prison sentence. While incarcerated, he pricked his gums to fake a lung hemorrhage, probably to be sent to the hospital for a possible escape, and died of blood poisoning. The other noted thief of the National Road mails was a stagecoach company owner, "General" Otho Hinton, who worked out of Columbus. He took the mailbags out of coaches and looted them as the horses and coaches were changed. Suspicious of him after a prolonged investigation, the Post Office Department set him up with a lucrative mailbag and arrested him in the act. He jumped bond and fled to the West Coast, or maybe even Australia; rumors differed.

With the Maysville Road Veto in 1830, President Andrew Jackson began a project of divesting the road and turning it back to the states. Under no constitutional restraint, the states made their sections into toll roads. Construction had been handled by the

Army Corps of Engineers, and they went back to relocate some of the steeper and rougher older sections as they continued to build westward. But it took so long to build the National Road that it began to suffer from fierce competition, particularly from the Erie Canal and the later railroads. The highway's heyday was pretty much over by the 1840s.

An odd effect of the National Road was that civilization changed north and south of it, irrespective of state boundaries. North of the highway, Yankee mores ruled. South of the highway, society had a distinct southern feel, so much so that Illinois tried to institute slavery upon statehood in violation of the Northwest Ordinance of 1787, which prohibited it north of the Ohio River. During the Civil War, the southern parts of Ohio, Indiana, and Illinois were decidedly lukewarm to federal policies like the military draft and emancipation. Organizations, lumped together under the title of "copperheads," even planned active war opposition. One of their members took his trial by military tribunal to the U.S. Supreme Court and got it overruled.

Following the Civil War, the National Road, like most highways, began to suffer mightily after the railroads took over. The Baltimore & Ohio, for instance, was a direct competitor along the very same route. In 1893, the federal government set up an Office of Road Inquiry, prompted by bicyclists, farmers, and the rise of the automobile. It was fitting that the congressman most interested in "good roads" was from Detroit and a personal friend of Henry Ford. Later, Carl Fisher, also of Detroit, came up with the idea of a national coast-to-coast highway, financed by private contributions. The result was the Lincoln Highway to San Francisco. But other roads associations came to the fore, too, such as the Dixie Highway, the Atlantic-Pacific Highway, and the Old Spanish Trail. Highway One, the National Old Trails Route, included the National Road.

In 1912, the federal government openly gave aid to national post roads for the first time. After World War I, the Federal High-way Act of 1921 set up a program of federal aid to highways designed to connect all the states. Like everything federal, the highways were numbered and the National Road became U.S. Highway 40. In 1956, the Interstate Highway Act set up a new system of highways based on the German Autobahnen of World War II that had so impressed General (now President) Dwight Eisenhower as he led Allied forces to victory in Europe in 1945. The National Road changed to Interstate 70, often built so close to the original pathway that one cannot find the old roadbed anymore.

See also Cumberland Road; Gallatin, Albert; Roads and Highways, Colonial Times to World War I; Two Percent Fund.

References Bruce, Robert, *The National Road* (1916); Durrenberger, Joseph Austin, *Turnpikes* (1931); Hart, Val, *The Story of American Roads* (1950); Ierley, Merritt, *Traveling the National Road* (1990); Jordan, Philip D., *The National Road* (1948); Lacock, John Kennedy, "The Braddock Road," *Pennsylvania Magazine of History and Biography* (1914) 38: 1–38; U.S. Department of Transportation, Federal Highway Administration, *America's Highways* (1976).

National Transportation Safety Board (NTSB)

When Congress passed the act establishing the Department of Transportation in 1966, it combined many small and independent government regulatory bodies under the new cabinet-level agency. One of these was the Civil Aeronautics Administration and its safety commission, the Civil Aeronautics Board (CAB). The CAB became the National Transportation Safety Board, with all of its previous functions transferred intact. Right away the NTSB ran into trouble with its parent organization, the Federal Aviation Administration (FAA), on whose policies the NTSB blamed many air crashes of the 1960s. Naturally, the FAA was miffed and it found a ready ally in the functionaries of the Richard Nixon administration who accused the NTSB of not being a "team player."

In an effort to reposition the NTSB, the Nixon people recommended that the president appoint new board members who would be more "reliable." The Democratic

Congress, however, was not about to permit a Republican administration to change policies in entities of its own creation. In 1974, Congress passed a new measure, the National Safety Board Act, that guaranteed that the president could not appoint the head of the NTSB without Senate confirmation, a concurrence not needed before. Further, NTSB rulings against any Department of Transportation (DOT) agency now had to be answered formally within 90 days and no longer ignored. To prevent other executive punitive measures, Congress prohibited the Office of Management and Budget from cutting appropriations to the NTSB—a needed measure in view of the fact that the NTSB had ten times less money than other safety agencies while airline traffic was increasing markedly throughout the 1970s.

The problem with the NTSB has not been that it has failed to do its job. If anything, it is perhaps too diligent. This has created enemies among competing agencies, regulated businesses, and professional unions like the Airline Pilots Association and the Air Traffic Controllers Organization, which are routinely blamed for accidents (after all, they set the policies and manage and fly the planes). With the division between the political parties controlling the White House and the legislative branch, a reoccurring problem since 1968, interagency quarrels, no matter how pertinent or petty, become a political football. The NTSB is important enough to have clout in its decisions (even though its punitive rulings can be appealed to unsympathetic administrative court judges and overturned) but not visible enough to draw undue public attention when it is attacked by outside interests. Because it is often made up of persons who are technically proficient but not politically astute in announcing their decisions, the NTSB has made political gaffes in public statements that then become fodder for those more adept at controlling public opinion. With an increase in the safety jurisdiction of the NTSB, these problems are bound to increase rather than decline in the near future.

See also Department of Transportation; Federal Aviation Act.

Reference Burkhardt, Robert, "National Transportation Safety Board," in William M. Leary (ed.), *Encyclopedia of American Business History and Biography* (1992), 306–309.

Nebbia v. New York 291 US 502 (1934)

After the departure of Chief Justice William Howard Taft on 3 February 1930, the Supreme Court minority became assertive and began to undo his concept of what constituted a business operating in the public interest rather than privately. In 1934, under the influence of New Deal reforms, the Supreme Court decided that the old *Munn* decision was a better line of reasoning, and in *Nebbia v. New York* the Court returned to the Munn ideal, which held that all a state had to do was show that the business activity in question posed a danger to the public. Then the state could impose its own police power to regulate the businesses' activities. If the state merely passed a law, it showed it had followed the due process required in the federal Constitution. If there were a protest, the Court would not take the case if that one prerequisite was made. Protests were hereafter deemed to be political matters settled by the individual state legislatures.

See also Munn v. Illinois; Tyson and Brothers–United Theater Ticket Offices, Inc. v. Blanton.

References Childs, William R., *Trucking and the Public Interest* (1985); Swindler, William F., *Court and Constitution in the 20th Century* (1969–1974).

Neuhart, David E. (1901–1973)

Originally hired on as a car cleaner in 1818, David Neuhart transferred to the mechanical department in 1926, and by 1949 had become general superintendent of motive power for the Union Pacific Railroad. Neuhart's basic idea was to put on the rails engines that produced the most horsepower in the least number of multiple lash-ups. The result was the biggest freight haulers anywhere in the world, a quality that made Union Pacific renowned among railroad men. Neuhart and the Union Pacific made it a principle never to be locked in to any one locomotive producer. Under Neuhart, the Union Pacific had the world's largest switcher (Fairbanks-Morse's M-2-44), some of the first low-nosed, general-purpose GM diesels, and was the first and only to use General Electric's new massive gas turbine electric locomotives. The latter operated on the Union Pacific between 1958 and 1969, and were capable of pulling long freights both on the prairie and up and down mountain grades. The first were 4,500-horsepower units that did so well that the railroad ordered 8,500-per units soon after. These units ran only 12 miles per hour, but pulled 735 cars of a seven-mile-long train on a level track. They regularly hauled 5,000 tons on grades of 1.53 percent in Utah's Echo Canyon; the equivalent in motor trucks would be 170 rigs with trailers carrying 25 tons of cargo each. There was even a super turbine, 16 feet high, 179 feet long, with a top speed of 76 miles per hour, on four three-axle trucks. Unfortunately, these locos burned too much fuel (800 gallons an hour under full load) and had their efficiency affected by weather (they liked it cool) and altitude (the lower the better). The crowning glory to Neuhart's reign was Alco's DD-40X, a gigantic diesel that ran on all-powered eight-wheel trucks, that was produced in 1969 for the road's centennial. Neuhart left the company the following year under its mandatory retirement policy.

See also Locomotives; Union Pacific Railroad.

References Banks, William W., and Harold E. Banks, *Motive Power of the Union Pacific* (1958); Hubbard, Freeman, *Encyclopedia of North American Railroading* (1981); Keekley, Harold, *Big Blow* (1975); Keekley, Harold, *U 50s* (1978); Lee, Thomas R., *Turbines Westward* (1975).

New Orleans Conditions

Under the drive for railroad consolidation, labor was often left holding nothing. When management spoke of cutting costs and saving money, the first thing they meant was letting employees go. It was obvious that some sort of agreement had to be reached or no merger would go through without labor opposition before the Interstate Commerce Commission, in the federal courts, and in the field through strikes. When the Emergency Transportation Act of 1933 expired, labor made its move. The result was the Washington Agreement, an informal pact that whenever a merger forced an employee to take a lesser job, that worker would receive a monetary allowance to make up the difference in pay. If one were laid off under a merger, the employee could receive 60 percent of the previous salary. All benefits lasted for a period of five years, beginning when the person was affected, providing that that was three years after the merger. In lieu of these provisions, an employee could accept a lump sum settlement, freeing the employer and employee from future obligation.

The unions preferred that the Washington Agreement remained informal, subject to the pressures of collective bargaining. But in 1940 an attempt was made to outlaw any merger if it resulted in cut salaries or switched or lost jobs. This was eventually compromised by the Harrington Amendment, which allowed any worker four years of 100 percent protection from the day the merger took effect. On top of that, one could receive 60 percent from the day one's job was changed. During World War II (1944), the matter was changed again under the pressures of the drive for victory. Railroads were allowed to change anyone's job so long as that employee retained the former salary for four years. This amendment was called the Oklahoma Condition.

But in 1948, when the New Orleans railroads petitioned to build a new station, the construction took longer than the allotted four years, permitting massive layoffs. So the New Orleans Conditions were arrived at. The new plan was for the Oklahoma Condition to last for four years, as usual, whereupon the labor force would be protected by the Washington Agreement. These New Orleans Conditions became the basic protection for labor as the postwar mergers got under way, until the merger of the Southern Railroad with the Central of Georgia occurred in the mid-1960s. Because the New Orleans conditions did not mention fringe benefits normally included in salary negotiations, the New Orleans Conditions were administered differently by local brotherhoods, and recent federal court decisions had closed off most appeal routes; the unions asked that these anomalies be clarified.

The Interstate Commerce Commission (ICC) decided to simplify the whole prior history of the conditions and produce a definitive document. Unfortunately the process was a mite sloppy. The resulting Southern–Central Conditions left out much of the Washington Agreement as concerned advance notice of layoff, merging of seniority rosters, and lump sum payoffs. Southern Railroad decide that it would follow the letter of the law and dumped 1,500 Central of Georgia employees out of hand. The result was three years of litigation that wound up with the ICC angrily denouncing the Southern Railroad and restating the Southern-Central Conditions to include former precedents and forcing Southern to pay up under the New Orleans guidelines from the day of the merger. The railroad protested that it would cost $55 million and destroy them. The ICC refused to budge, returning everything to where it had been in 1948.

See also Florida East Coast Railway; Railroad Unions; Transportation Acts.

Reference Saunders, Richard, *The Railroad Mergers and the Coming of Conrail* (1978).

New York Barge Canal System

The barge canal system is a twentieth-century modernization of the old Erie Canal, which included widening and deepening the channel, resetting the locks, and acting as a part of the Great Lakes–St. Lawrence Seaway water routes.

See also Erie Canal.

Reference Vosburgh, Frederick G., "Drums to Dynamos on the Mohawk," *National Geographic* (July 1947) 92: 67–110.

New York Central Securities Co. v. U.S. 287 US 12 (1932)

New York Central Securities stated a simple test for public interest for railroad and other mergers. The Court stated that the merging carrier merely had to prove that its action had a direct relation to the adequacy of transportation and was thus essential to economy and efficiency in the public domain.

See also National Industrial Recovery Act of 1933; Transportation Acts.

Reference Saunders, Richard, *The Railroad Mergers and the Coming of Conrail* (1978).

New York Central System (NYC)

Using the old Erie Canal route, the New York Central System extended its rails north and west from New York City to Chicago and St. Louis with few steep grades, passes, or tunnels. Eventually, the Central would stretch its rails across 11 states and 2 Canadian provinces. Its oval-shaped emblem was a product of the 1904 St. Louis Louisiana Purchase Exposition. The line also coined the term "red cap" and equipped its porters with such uniforms after a black porter took to wearing a piece of red flannel on his hat to attract customers.

The New York Central began as the Mohawk & Hudson Railroad (M&H). Built by Stephen Van Rensselaer and George W. Featherstonehaugh in 1831, the M&H was the state's first railway. Its first locomotive was the *De Witt Clinton*, its first cars looked like Concord stagecoaches on railroad wheels, and the first scheduled run was from Albany to Schenectady. In 1853, Erastus Corning and John V. L. Pruyn merged the M&H with nearly a dozen short lines and created the New York Central Railroad from Albany to Buffalo. After the Civil War, Cornelius Vanderbilt joined his Hudson River Valley line to the Central and created the New York Central and Hudson River Railroad, with service from New York City to Buffalo, which was then extended further to Chicago with the purchase of the Lake Shore & Michigan Southern in 1915.

At the same time, the Central electrified its New York City operations and put the whole system underground, creating Grand Central Terminal, replacing the old Vanderbilt Grand Central Station on the same site. The main problem faced by the Central was getting more trains into the same land area. It took nearly a decade to put the trains underground and the streets and buildings over, but the job was done. It cost $65 million to complete the terminal, and trains hauled more than 400 carloads of rubble out each day of construction. When finished, Grand Central Terminal had two tiers of tracks, 66 on the upper level and 57 on the lower. Some of the tracks are loops, but most are stubs into which trains are backed up to the platforms. The yard and its approaches contain 34 miles of rail. In its heyday, up to 180 trains arrived or departed each day. An attempt to alter the structure led to its being placed on the National Register of Historic Places. Since Amtrak has pulled passenger service over to Penn Station, Grand Central has declined in modern railroad importance but still remains a formidable piece of transportation architecture and ingenuity.

The New York Central was famous for its passenger service. In competition with the Pennsylvania Railroad for the New York to Chicago business, the Central pioneered powerful express locomotives that could run along the water-level mainline at consistent speeds not possible on other more mountainous lines. The epitome of its 4-4-0 American-style steamers was No. 999, which possessed the land speed record of 112.5 miles per hour on the Batavia to Buffalo run in the 1890s. The engine pulled the *Empire State Express* to the Chicago Columbian Exposition in a bid to secure a lion's share of passenger traffic out of New York. Later, in the 1930s, the NYC developed the J-3 series Hudson-type locomotive, a 4-6-4 wheel arrangement, some of which were streamlined so beautifully that they are considered by many to be the most beautiful steamer of all time. To keep speed up, the Central would take on water by lowering a scoop from the tender bottom into a pan between the rails. Without slowing down, the tender would be filled in a quarter mile and the scoop raised.

The New York Central System was at the forefront of modern, innovative railroading in other aspects as well. The Central established the first railroad workers'

apprentice school at Elkhart, Indiana, in 1872. It also developed the first workable system of measuring the drawbar pull exerted by a train. It developed a new high-powered brake designed for the new heavier all-steel passenger cars in 1910, and followed with the first all-steel boxcar two years later. In 1925, it experimented with Automatic Train Control (ATC), an electronic system designed to tighten up schedules and run more trains more safely. By 1927, ATC had become a system standard. In 1928, the NYC was the first American railroad to run a diesel freight engine, a harbinger of the future when its light gray engines and their white "lightening" pinstripes would dominate freight and passenger service. Later, the Central developed an air-cushioned ride for freight to keep transit damage to a minimum. It also introduced jet-powered snowplows in the 1950s and in 1967 it formulated the world's first low-cost, specially formulated diesel fuel.

The most famous of the NYC streamliners was the *Twentieth Century Limited*, arguably the finest of its type. The *Limited* was so long that it had to be pulled in seven sections, each leaving the terminal on 30-minute intervals. The average speed was 70 miles per hour for the whole trip, including stops. The consist of 16 Pullman cars with engine and tender cost $1.4 million to build, and only pulled in $2.61 in revenue per mile (the Milwaukee Road's *Hiawathas* made $3.79 per mile). But the *Limited* was as much a prestige item as it was functional. Each section had two dining cars to serve the patrons, and the combined sections hauled as many as 1,000 people a trip. The whole consist, engine and tender included, was painted a sleek, two-tone gray with silver and blue accents, created by noted industrial designer Henry Dreyfuss.

The *Twentieth Century Limited* was the hallmark of luxury: A patron could visit a barber, dictate correspondence to a railroad-provided secretary, take a shower, dine in splendor, play bridge or some other card game, and retire to a private roomette with a bed and mattress 3 feet wide and 80 inches long. After World War II, the *Limited* was reintroduced with diesel power and lighter cars, but the effect was not the same. Already the railroad knew that the airlines would take away their intercity speed traffic and the automobiles the rest. But the *Twentieth Century* made the trip between New York and Chicago in 18 hours on average, meeting the competition of the Pennsylvania Railroad's *Broad Way Limited*, which had 60 fewer miles to travel.

In 1954, Robert E. Young took over the NYC and appointed Alfred E. Perlman to bring it out of the doldrums into which it had sunk, propelled by post–World War II highway and air competition. Perlman modernized the roadbed and equipment but failed to stem the tide of late-twentieth-century passenger preferences. But he was instrumental in introducing Flexi-Van, the first containerized freight system, in the late 1950s, one copied by others including the Milwaukee Road. In 1962, the Central and its longtime main competitor, the Pennsylvania Railroad, merged their operations into the Penn Central Transportation Corporation. Legal action managed to postpone the union until 1968, when the New York Central System disappeared from the annals of American railroading forever.

See also Conrail; Penn Central Transportation Company; Pennsylvania Railroad; Vanderbilt, Cornelius; Vanderbilt, William H.

References Beebe, Lucius, *20th Century* (1962); Condit, Carl W., *The Port of New York* (2 vols., 1980–1981); Drury, George H., *The Historical Guide to North American Railroads* (1985); Drury, George H., "New York Central System," in Keith L. Bryant, Jr. (ed.), *EABHB: Railroads in the Age of Regulation* (1988), 317–319; Drury, George H., *The Train-Watcher's Guide* (1990); Frailey, Fred W., "Al Perlman Was Right," *Trains* (1994) 54: 70–71; Grow, Lawrence, *On the 8:02* (1979); Harlow, Alvin F., *The Road of the Century* (1947); Hubbard, Freeman, *Railroad Avenue* (1945); Hubbard, Freeman, *Encyclopedia of North American Railroading* (1981); Hungerford, Edward, *Men and Iron* (1938); Larkin, F. David, "New York Central Railroad," in Robert L. Frey (ed.), *EABHB: Railroads in the Nineteenth Century* (1988), 282–285; Lyon, Peter, *To Hell in a Day Coach* (1968); Marshall, David, *Grand Central* (1946); Middleton, William D., *Grand Central* (1977); Miekle, Jeffrey L., *Twentieth Century Limited* (1979); Morgan, David P., "The Greatest Century of All," *Model Railroader* (April 1988) 55: 76–91; Nock, O. S., *Railways of the USA* (1979);

Sobel, Robert, *The Fallen Colossus* (1977); Staufer, Alvin F., *Steam Power of the New York Central System* (1961); Stevens, Frank W., *Beginnings of the New York Central Railroad* (1926); Wayner, Robert J., *New York Central Cars* (1972).

New York, Chicago & St. Louis Railroad
See Anthracite and Bridge Line Railroads.

Norfolk & Western Railway (N&W)
Begun as an eight-mile track between City Point and Petersburg, Virginia, in 1838, the Norfolk & Western ultimately ran through 16 states and 2 Canadian provinces. It is chiefly an east–west line running from the Atlantic coast westward as far as Omaha, Nebraska. The original line was acquired through a series of mergers that extended the railroad into the bituminous coal country in southwestern Virginia, eastern Tennessee, Kentucky, and West Virginia. After the usual bouts with receiverships in the depression-ridden late nineteenth century, it was reorganized under its twentieth-century name in 1896.

The various components of the modern N&W include the New York, Chicago & St. Louis (called the Nickel Plate because of its once high-priced stock), the Wabash, the Akron, Canton & Youngstown, the Pittsburgh & West Virginia, the Delaware & Hudson, the Virginian, and the Sandusky section of the Pennsylvania Railroad. The Erie Lackawanna was once dished out to the N&W by the Interstate Commerce Commission, but soon withdrew to join Conrail. The main cargo for the N&W was coal. The huge coal drags caused the N&W to develop giant Mallet–style steam engines like the A-1 (a 2-6-6-4), the Y3a, the Y4b (later bought by the Santa Fe Railway to be used as helper engines on the grades through Ratón Pass in New Mexico), the Y5, Y6b, and Z1b (all 2-8-8-2s). In 1954, the railroad also tried to develop a massive, coal-powered, streamlined, turbine electric engine, the Jawn Henry, in a vain effort to keep diesels from replacing the coal users.

But it proved too complicated and not cost effective, and N&W fell to the diesel on-slaught soon after.

N&W passenger trains were pulled by streamlined Js (4-8-4), painted in two-tone maroons and dark reds to match the passenger cars. N&W's named passenger trains included the *Cavalier*, the *Tennesseean*, the *Birmingham Special*, the *Powhatan Arrow*, and the *Pocohantas*. Ever-thirsty engines regularly hauled massive coal and water tenders (one style of which was lovingly called "Big Emma"), whose 18,000 to 22,000 gallons of water were supplemented by auxiliary tenders (A-tenders) holding 20,000 gallons more. This meant longer hauls with fewer stops. But the addition of the mid-western lines broadened its freight to include auto parts, finished autos, primary steel products, grain, furniture, chemicals, forest products, and stone quarry products. This wider scope of carriage has undoubtedly aided in the railroad's survival into the late twentieth century. In the 1980s, the N&W joined with the Southern Railway to create one of two major shippers in the South under the name Norfolk Southern Railroad System.

See also Locomotives, Steam Locomotives; Norfolk Southern Corporation; Southern Railway System.

References Drury, George H., *The Historical Guide to North American Railroads* (1985); Drury, George H., "Norfolk & Western Railroad," and "Virginian Railway," in Keith L. Bryant, Jr. (ed.), *EABHB: Railroads in the Age of Regulation* (1988), 324–325, 459–460; Drury, George H., *The Train-Watcher's Guide* (1990); French, Vern, *The Norfolk & Western Railway* (1992); Hubbard, Freeman, *Encyclopedia of North American Railroading* (1981); Lyon, Peter, *To Hell in a Day Coach* (1968); Nock, O. S., *Railways of the USA* (1979); Rehor, John A., *The Nickel Plate Story* (1965); Reid, H., *The Virginian Railway* (1983); Saunders, Richard, *The Railroad Mergers and the Coming of Conrail* (1978); Striplin, E. F. Pat, *The Norfolk & Western* (1981).

Norfolk Southern Corporation

The Norfolk Southern Corporation is a combination of the Southern Railway System and the Norfolk & Western Railroad that was capitalized in the early 1980s at $5.7 billion, with earnings projected at $100 million annually. The new logo is a forward-leaning white "NS" preceded by four stripes and complemented by the figure of a rearing thoroughbred stallion, depicting its southern heritage and it speedy image of efficiency. Some idea of its solvency can be gleaned from the fact that it offered to buy Conrail from the federal government but was turned down by the House of Representatives for fear of its economic impact against other competing lines.

See also Norfolk & Western Railway; Southern Railway System.

Northeast Rail Services Act of 1981

A congressional measure that called for the eventual return of Conrail to the private sector when it met certain profit conditions, the Northeast Rail Services Act of 1981 was an initiative of the Ronald Reagan administration to deregulate and privatize former governmental efforts at intervention in the national economy.

See also Railroad Revitalization and Regulatory Reform Act of 1976; Staggers Rail Act of 1980.

References Keeler, Theodore E., *Railroads, Freight and Public Policy* (1983); Orenstein, Jeffrey, *United States Railroad Policy* (1990).

Northern Pacific Railway (NP)

The Northern Pacific received a federal charter in 1864, the purpose being to link the Great Lakes with Puget Sound. It would take 20 years for this goal to be met. The first rails were laid at Carlton, Minnesota, in 1870. Shortly thereafter, a second track crew began work in Washington Territory and headed east. Much of the material and equipment, including its first steam engine, had to be carried around Cape Horn by sea. By 1873, the line had been completed in Washington and the Plains had been breached as far as Bismarck, so named to attract German settlers and investment in the new railroad. But the financial panic of that year, compounded by the Sioux Wars and the need to bridge the Missouri River at Bismarck, delayed construction until 1879. By 1883, the golden spike ceremony was ready at Gold Creek, Montana, with former President U. S. Grant doing the honors.

Much of the NP mainline followed the old exploration route of Meriwether Lewis and William Clark. Only a short section in Washington remained to be completed, which was done the following year. But the Columbia River was not bridged until 1918, the trains having to be ferried across before then. Branches connected the NP with the many farmers it served in the northern Plains and one also ran to the boundary of Yellowstone National Park. An imaginative advertisement of the time had Alice in Wonderland describing her enchanted journey along the NP. The railroad also saw to it that the delegates choosing the capital of Dakota Territory (North and South combined) were wined and dined until they picked Bismarck over Yankton. In conjunction with the Great Northern, the NP controlled the Spokane, Portland & Seattle Railroad that connected those cities with their mainlines. Eventually the NP and the Great Northern Railroads fell under the control of James J. Hill, but formal unification was defeated by the U.S. Supreme Court in the Northern Securities case (1905), and again by the Interstate Commerce Commission in the 1920s, despite the necessity of such a combination to take on the rival powerhouse, the Union Pacific. In 1970, this fact was acknowledged when the Burlington Northern Corporation was formed with these lines and the Chicago, Burlington & Quincy as its main components.

See also Burlington Northern Incorporated; Hill, James Jerome; Villard, Henry.

References Butler, Dan, "Spokane, Portland & Seattle Railway," in Keith L. Bryant, Jr. (ed.), *EABHB: Railroads in the Age of Regulation* (1988), 412–413; Drury, George H., *The Historical Guide to North American Railroads* (1985); Drury, George H., *The Train-Watcher's Guide* (1990); Frey, Robert L., and Lorenz P. Schrenk, *Northern Pacific Supersteam Era* (1985); Frey, Robert L., "Northern Pacific Railway," in Keith L. Bryant, Jr. (ed.), *EABHB: Railroads in the Age of Regulation* (1988), 331–333; Hubbard, Freeman, *Encyclopedia of North American Railroading* (1981); Lyon, Peter, *To Hell in a Day Coach* (1968); Mercer, Lloyd J., *Railroads and Land Grant Policy* (1982); Meyers, Rex C., "Northern Pacific Railroad," in Robert L. Frey (ed.), *EABHB: Railroads in the Nineteenth Century* (1988), 287–289; Nock, O. S., *Railways of the USA* (1979); Wood, C. R., *The Northern Pacific* (1968).

Northern Securities Company v. U.S. 193 US 197 (1904)

Decided 14 March 1904, the Northern Securities case was deemed so important that many feared it might set off a panic on Wall Street. The issue was simple. James J. Hill (backed by banker J. P. Morgan) and his Northern Securities railroad holding company were accused of being in violation of the 1890 Sherman Antitrust Act. The act had been fairly well destroyed by adverse court decisions over the years, but this was a new Court and a new case. The Theodore Roosevelt administration was out to make an example of Jim Hill, accusing him of acting in restraint of trade by limiting railroad competition. He owned the Great Northern and the Northern Pacific Railroads and a good portion of the Chicago, Burlington & Quincy (CB&Q) Railroad. Now Uncle Sam (or was it Uncle Teddy?) was going to break up his empire legally. And the Court did just that, and there was no panic (the market actually improved); the trusts were on the run. The Big Stick had carried the day.

The railroads (and all big business) had mixed feelings about what happened to Hill. By and large, most saw it as useful in drawing the heat away from all the rest of them. Sure, Hill went down in smoke, but the public's attention was short, and Roosevelt would find other villains to campaign against. Northern Securities was a cheap way to get off the hook. The public at the time had a weird love-hate relationship with the railroads. They loved the conveniences and high standard of living that the railroads made possible. A big wheat harvest was no good to the solitary Kansas farmer, but it was essential to the big-city baker, and the railroads got the two together. But they hated the monetary and political costs that that standard of living entailed.

Originally, the railroads had been pioneers under single management. After the Civil War, competition grew and rivals raced each other to absorb feeder lines. This lasted until the Panic of 1893 weeded out the overextended. The survivors wound up with the big empires, many of which lasted until the collapse of railroading in the 1960s under the highway and airline assault. Now the railroaders wanted to control the destructive competition between themselves. But open trusts like Northern Security made easy targets for public wrath and political reformers eager for votes. The result was the Hepburn Act in 1906, which plugged the loopholes in the old Sherman Act. Then in 1910, the Mann-Elkins Act was drawn up to plug the holes in the Hepburn measure, followed by the Clayton Act to wind it all up in one nice package.

But the farsighted saw that the regulations would not last. Economic reality dictated a different solution. As one banker said after the Northern Securities decision: "That which will be incredible to men fifty years from now is that [Jim Hill] should have been assailed as a wrong doer." The creation of the Burlington Northern system which, in the 1960s, proved that Hill had been a prophet before his time. The Northern Securities decision went for naught.

See also Elkins Act; Harriman, Edward Henry; Hill, James Jerome; Interstate Commerce Commission; Morgan, John Pierpont; Railroads before and during the Civil War; Railroads from Appomattox to Deregulation.

References Leonard, William Norris, *Railroad Consolidation under the Transportation Act of 1920* (1946); Saunders, Richard, *The Railroad Mergers and the Coming of Conrail* (1978).

Northwest Airlines

Today, half of the American air traffic market is controlled by American, United, and Delta, and the other half is divided between the rest of the carriers, with Continental and Minneapolis-based Northwest Airlines splitting half of that. This makes Northwest one of the major medium-sized airlines in the country. Formed in 1927 to fly the airmail route between Chicago and the Twin Cities, Northwest took on passengers and expanded its routes slowly across the northern Plains and Rockies to Seattle during the 1930s. It originally flew Lockheed L-10 Electras, but by 1939 had added modern DC-3s to its plane inventory. During

World War II, it flew cargo and passengers for the armed forces and managed to add a New York City route to its civilian arm. This made it the fourth-ranked transcontinental carrier along with giants like American, United, and TWA. After the war, Northwest used its wartime experience to obtain the great circle route to the Pacific, flying by way of Alaska to China and the Philippines. It became Northwest Orient for a number of years, and as such was a critical component to the Korean War effort, flying Boeing 377 Stratocruisers and DC-4s. Unfortunately, a series of domestic accidents left the carrier reeling by 1954.

At this moment Donald W. Nyrop entered the scene and saved Northwest from collapse. He got rid of the older planes and reduced costs wherever possible. In 1960 he shifted the air fleet to jets like the DC-8 domestically and later the Boeing 747 internationally. By 1978 and deregulation, Northwest had had an annual profit of 7.8 percent each year for ten years, making it the most profitable airline in the business. This meant that it could fly with its planes less full than other airlines, which allowed it to approach deregulation and its problems slowly. It eventually took over Republic Airlines, but then became a target for takeover itself. To forestall this possibility, Northwest worked out a deal with KLM, the Royal Dutch Airlines. Although Northwest received collapsing Eastern's gates at Washington National Airport, it has taken on much debt of late and enters the 1990s stable but needing to cautiously advance with an eye to profit lest the debt assume a more commanding influence over its balance sheets.

See also Aeronautics.

Reference Leary, William M., "Northwest Airlines," in William M. Leary (ed.), *Encyclopedia of American Business History and Biography* (1992), 319–321.

NRA Trucking Codes

During the Great Depression, one American industry seemed exempt to all economic law and theory that was wreaking havoc throughout the nation—the truckers. Everything else was constricted drastically, causing massive unemployment. But the trucking industry actually expanded and hired on more drivers. New firms joined established companies. True, the competition was rough, both economically and physically; management and union quarrels were downright vicious, but by and large the truckers did pretty well. The trucks operated at lower costs than other forms of transportation and they were very flexible in their response to shippers' needs.

But politicians led by Franklin D. Roosevelt's New Deal administration sought to intervene in the economic problems under the theory that government had a duty to guide the economy for the betterment of all. Besides, the voters demanded something, anything, to get some improvement in the employment arena and to boost production. The result was the National Industrial Recovery Act that established the National Recovery Administration (NRA), the first federal agency to concern itself with regulating trucking, and the Federal Emergency Railroad Transportation Act, which established the position of Federal Coordinator of Transportation, an office held by Joseph B. Eastman. But Roosevelt's habit of serving all political needs regardless of conflict led to a mess of confusing, often contradictory regulations that tried to satisfy all interests. This unfortunate result was especially present in the NRA.

The NRA was a product of a perceived need in 1933 to reform business and save capitalism and through it, the economy. The notion was to set up codes of fair competition, something that was a holdover from the creation of the Federal Trade Commission in 1914, but had never come to fruition. These codes were designed to promote cooperation, eliminate unfair trade practices, increase purchasing power, reduce unemployment, and conserve the nation's resources. It was a tall order that soon collapsed. But the NRA did stabilize automobile manufacturing and gave labor a voice in politics heretofore denied. More importantly, it benefited trucking more

than most industries, because trucking had the most to gain.

Before the NRA, truckers had no national association. The NRA trucking code established one. But there were two major groups within the trucking industry, and each saw the code through a different light. The first group wanted to eliminate wildcat truckers, set rates, and stabilize the highly competitive business. These men feared federal regulation would raise rates and eliminate the natural advantages truckers had enjoyed so far. The second group wanted federal regulation to eliminate the conflicting state rules and bring uniformity within the industry. They feared that self-regulation would fail and that the Interstate Commerce Commission would be a fairer monitor.

Both groups were in violation of the spirit of the NRA code, which was to establish the joint interests of management, labor, and shippers. The conflict threatened to ruin the whole program until Ted V. Rogers, a truck manager from Pennsylvania, forged all parties into a single committee. As the elected president of the newly formed American Trucking Associations, Incorporated (ATA), he worked with the government regulators of the NRA to produce a uniform code. After much bickering among the factions, the code created the trucking business as a cartel that operated over the public highways. Moving companies, farmers, and farm cooperatives were declared exempt. Hours and wages were set for drivers and clerical personnel, and overtime was computed on the basis of "time and one-third" over 54 hours per week, not to exceed 12 hours in any two-week period.

The code was considered to be a very liberal one, especially as regards labor. But the real problem was putting it into effect. There was a national code office in Washington and a subordinate office in each of the states plus Washington, D.C. and New York City. Rogers was elected president of the national office. Each state office was to have a board of competing truck interests, plus a neutral member, to represent everyone in the business. In California alone this meant 25 members. They could agree on little. Other states presented similar problems. The interstate nature of much of the business undermined jurisdictions. Drivers refused to pay the $3 registration fee. Others merely rented vehicles and avoided the code altogether, by which they could also avoid the whole federal process and engage in cutthroat competition. Before a trucker could display the blue eagle of compliance, he had to file a schedule of rates. Registration, compliance, and enforcement were the bases of the whole system. Even if registration and compliance came automatically (which they did not), enforcement was haphazard to say the least. Offenders simply ignored any adverse decision rendered against them. The U.S. Supreme Court decisions that declared various codes unconstitutional simply supported recognition that they did not work among the truckers.

But there was some maturity that came as a result of the code episodes. The ATA held its national convention in Chicago in 1935 and acted more harmoniously. By now it was obvious that truckers by themselves could not regulate their industry. They also did not wish to put up with a mass of differing regulations from the individual states. This left the federal government and its traditional transportation organ from the 1880s, the Interstate Commerce Commission, to do the job. All it would take was a federal law to put the truckers under its wing, which came later that year in the Motor Carrier Act of 1935, and the ATA would see that it reflected industry interests.

See also Eastman, Joseph B.; Federal-Aid Highway Acts, Federal-Aid Highway Act of 1956, Federal-Aid Highway Act of 1976; Federal-Aid Highway Amendments of 1975; Motor Carrier Acts, Motor Carrier Act of 1935; Surface Transportation Assistance Acts, Surface Transportation Assistance Act of 1982; Transportation Acts, Transportation Act of 1920, Transportation Act of 1940; Trucking.

References Bellush, Bernard, *The Failures of the NRA* (1975); Childs, William R., *Trucking and the Public Interest* (1985); Fishbein, Meyer H., "The Trucking Industry and the National Recovery Administration," *Social Forces* (1955–1956) 34: 171–179; Himmelberg, Robert F., *Origins of the National Recovery Administration (1976).*

Object Lesson Roads

Developed by General Roy Stone, head of the federal Office of Road Inquiry, object lesson roads were short (a mile or so) highways built to the best standards of the time in different sections of the United States at the beginning of the twentieth century to popularize the notion of good, all-weather roads and what they could mean for the local community. The roads were financed by the federal government or by interested private or public parties as a form of public education to expand interest and expertise in road building using many products, including clay, gravels, concrete, and asphalt. Although discontinued by the time of World War I, the notion was revived in 1969 in the Demonstration Projects Program, which did the same with new products like prestressed and reinforced concrete, and new concepts like controlling the erosion of shoulders, better bridge decks, modern safety measures, noise abatement projects, recycled materials use, and translating technical jargon into plain English to gain public support for these items.

See also Roads and Highways, Colonial Times to World War I.

Reference U.S. Department of Transportation, Federal Highway Administration, *America's Highways* (1976).

Ocean Liners

In early January 1818, the first passenger ship, or "sailing packet" as it was called then, left New York for England on a scheduled run. The unusual thing was that it sailed regardless of cargo or passengers booked. Until then, ships had waited until their holds were filled before departure—no matter how long it took. Neither were the old sailing ships made for passenger comfort. It was not unusual for ships that had been used in the slave trade to be pressed into service in the North Atlantic hauling immigrants to the New World. They were not called "coffin brigs" for nothing.

But the *James Monroe* was different. It was built with two passenger decks, and the upper had small staterooms or "sleeping closets" seven feet square, with marble entrances and satinwood interiors. There was even a dining room or saloon with fresh bread baked daily and unspoiled meat. Although the packets were designed to haul only first-class passengers, they did so only on the "downhill" (eastward, with the wind) leg of the trip. Soon it proved profitable to allow steerage passengers on the "uphill" leg, the unwashed proletariat or "white cargo" from the rural and urban poverty centers of Europe. These were people who paid £5 each (judging from the fact that they had to bring all their own provisions, it was nearly pure profit) to travel to the "land of milk and honey," where gold supposedly rolled down the streets itching for someone to pick it up.

Steerage was usually filled with an unbelievable stench of excrement and overcrowded bodies in close, fetid quarters. There were congressional laws granting each adult 14 clear feet of deck space, but they were honored more in the breech than in compliance. "Ship fever" spread like wildfire below decks—so did rape, as no separation by sex was provided for. But there was 1 public toilet per 100—the emphasis being on "public." The United States solved the problem by charging captains twice the immigrant's cost of passage for each dead body hauled into port. Of course, captains usually threw all unwanted things overboard before docking.

Actually, the crews were treated worse than the immigrants. They were beaten at the slightest offense, or the appearance of one. The captain was akin to God Almighty at sea. He was truly a law unto himself, no questions asked. The crew all lived up forward in the forecastle, where sea spray came in through poorly chinked planks, light was dim, and tobacco smoke filled the air. They lived off of boiled beef, salt pork, boiled rice, and hardtack—usually moldy or infested with crawling mites of protein. Sailors ate out of a common pot, cutting their meat off the joint with a dirty clasp knife. They shared their hammocks with the aggressive rats that the ships abounded with. The crews were driven like slaves to set transoceanic speed records: the faster the ship, the more the profit. Overloaded and piling on all the sail that could be carried, one in six of such ships sailing the Atlantic were soon wrecked, at a rate of around 90 a year. But the passenger packets had the best safety records of all ships at sea.

This was an era when Americans dominated the waves with their speedy clipper ships. They also experimented with the first steamship to cross the Atlantic, the *Savannah*. Of course, any smart investor saw to it that a steamship had sails, too, in case the engines failed. Early steamers had the habit of running out of coal. They had side paddle wheels, and it took a sharp hand at the rudder to keep the ship on course as the ship yawed and alternately dipped one wheel in the water while the other spun freely. But the *Savannah* set the style for what was to follow as the companies of every nation afloat began to follow her example. It was not until the Canadian ship *Royal William* crossed all the way under steam alone that it was proved that a steamer did not need a coal mine to power its engines or an iron mine to make its machinery, as many old salts proclaimed.

But trans-Atlantic steamer service was a dream until the 1840s. It took an American transplanted to England, Junius Smith, to get the ball rolling. He believed that four steamers would be able to do the job of the 12 sailing packets now plying the waters between Britain and the United States: two American-built, two English-built, just to keep things even. He could obtain money in England, and the result was that Americans would be forever engaged in a race of catchup with the British, if they even ran at all. With the newly built steamers *Great Western* and the *Royal Victoria Smith* beginning to make sailing history, Smith was soon overtaken by another company headed by Samuel Cunard and his family. Cunard, a transplanted Nova Scotian, bid on and took the royal mail contract to the Americas, and in 1841 his ship *Canada* beat the renowned clipper *Sovereign of the Seas* by two days on

the downhill leg from the New World to Britain. In 1840, Cunard opened up a scheduled service between Liverpool and Boston that would last the next 125 years. Soon his four steamers (same formula as Smith) were taking 20 percent of all cargoes. The rest went to the 150 competing sailing vessels.

As Smith and Cunard fought for the British side of the oceanic trade, Americans began to feel a bit embarrassed that they were not able to beat their cousins across the sea. The result was the *Washington*, a ship that introduced the concept of respectable second-class passenger accommodations as a slot between the cabin and steerage. But although built to be fast, the *Washington* was a real tortoise at sea and soon failed. But it stimulated the rise of Edward K. Collins, who brought the United States as close to glory in the Atlantic crossing as one man could. Collins first introduced a new ocean ship design, one with a flat bottom, all named for popular actors of the day, the lone dissenter being the *Roscius*, named after a Roman thespian. His ships were large, airy, and comfortable. Learning from a friend in the Post Office Department that Congress was interested in letting a U.S. mail contract, Collins secured it by appealing to national pride and pointing out his prior success. As a part of the contract he would build five steamers. The designs of these ships followed his earlier bathtub look, rode high out of the water and spray, had steam heat, individual bathrooms, and a barber shop, and were heavily carpeted with plush furniture and loaded with wall mirrors and windows.

Although Collins' first ship was badly damaged in an ice field (captains tended to run through ice and fog at full speed to make the inconvenience disappear quickly), the return trip after repairs set a new Atlantic record of just under 11 days. As his ships steamed into the record books, so did the amount of red ink on his account books. It was costing him $17,000 a trip (beyond subsidy and income) to provide his by now well-known luxuries. He managed to get Congress to double his subsidy and, at the same time, exempt him from building his fifth ship. After a series of accidents at sea, Collins's star began to wane. Congressmen from western and southern states began to question so big a subsidy to one business in New York City. The result was a cutting back of the subsidy to its original level, and Collins soon went broke.

Collins had another competitor besides the British. This was Cornelius Vanderbilt, better known by his moniker, "Commodore." Vanderbilt operated by the same strict accounting principles as Cunard—he was cheap but cost effective. Vanderbilt had been providing transportation across New York Harbor and through Long Island since the War of 1812. He had also ferried gold seekers to the isthmus of Central America. His annual income was at least $3 million—at age 59 he could pretty much do whatever or buy whomever he wanted. Now, the Commodore wanted a trans-Atlantic steamship empire. Before he went under, Collins had wind of Vanderbilt's ambition and tried to cut a deal where the Commodore would ask for as much government subsidy as Collins needed. No deal, smiled Vanderbilt, it was every man for himself. But Vandy did not relish a fight with Cunard after the latter returned to the Atlantic following the Crimean War. Vanderbilt satisfied himself with a New York–Le Havre connection and took off on a pleasure cruise of Europe in his own yacht, the *North Star*. Further desires in the world of oceanic business fell before the onslaught of the American Civil War and the Commodore's newest interest—railroads.

After the Civil War, the ocean trade seesawed between a series of newcomers, each of whom built new vessels with more speed and fancier appointments. Each new company killed off its predecessors with one exception: The old Cunard Line steamed on, unspectacular, slow but sure, but always in the black. Americans did poorly in large part because they were still wedded to the wooden hull and sail, falling farther behind in the race for passengers and steam-driven speed. Their clippers only hauled small, precious cargoes on routes the trans-Atlantic

companies rarely bothered with. The greatest inventions of the mid-nineteenth century were the screw propeller and the steam turbine. Not only did they provide ships with great speed, but they also changed an age-old tradition, the notion that royalty and other important personages ought to ride aft over the deck. Because the new propeller was a noisy device, the plushest quarters now moved amidships and forward, and the builders began to stack the cabins above each other much like the river steamers had done for over a half century. The epitome of this new style was the British White Star Line's steamer *Oceanic*.

As the race for plushness and speed went mostly to the White Star Line (as did the worst disaster of the century, the grounding of the *Atlantic* off Nova Scotia with the loss of 700 passengers and crew), Cunard decided to change its stale image and go for the glory. Old Samuel Cunard had died and with him went the conservative bookkeeping. The result was the *Servia*, fast and plush, the kind of ship, according to one chronicler, that used up the energies of all competitors and kept them busy trying to beat it, but killing each other off instead. Cunard introduced electric lighting, refrigerators, hot-water heaters, twin and triple screws, and life jackets. The height of Cunard's change in image came with the *Campania* and the *Lucania*. Between them they had enough speed to exchange the coveted Blue Riband, a massive pennant 20 feet wide and 40 feet long, flown at the foremast by the Atlantic crossing's current record holder at will.

Finally, late in the century the Americans made a move to recapture the Atlantic trade by allowing the bankrupt British Inman Company to come under U.S. registry, provided it build two ships in American shipyards under the supervision of the U.S. Navy. The result was the American Line, with four ships, two old ones and the new navy-approved *St. Louis* and *St. Paul*. These two new ships were really on the ugly side, as Atlantic steamers went. Big and bulky, their interiors were sparsely decorated (perhaps too paramilitary in design), but they were fast. American honor was restored until the Spanish-American War and the arrival of Imperial Germany put an end to it until 1952.

At the turn of the century, Kaiser Wilhelm II's Germany entered the world stage, rich, brash, and brusque. If England (he liked to compare his growing empire with the biggest and best) had ocean liners, then Germany had to have them, too, only bigger, faster, and better. This was done in typical German fashion, with everything planned, organized, and executed with military precision by Germany's two steamship carriers, the Hamburg-Amerika and the Bremen-based Norddeutscher Lloyd. With the *Kaiser Wilhelm der Große*, Germany seized the Blue Riband and moved into first place. Nicknamed "the Rolling Billy" because of its propensity to yaw, the *Kaiser Wilhelm* and other imperial ships dominated the seas until World War I. After the war, those that had not been destroyed were dealt to the Allies as a part of war reparations. Renamed, they joined other fleets in the twenties.

As the Germans moved out to claim the Atlantic they were joined by an American, J. Pierpont Morgan. The financier of America's railroads, and the American and British governments when necessary, Morgan reasoned that if the United States could not build and man the winning ships of the Atlantic crossing, they (or more specifically, he) could monopolize their ownership. He began to buy up lesser companies in the United States and Britain. Then he got control of the White Star Line. The British considered his plot a near act of war. Worse yet, Morgan was eliciting a favorable response from the Germans, whom he invited to enlist in his financial scheme. Cunard went to Parliament and laid out the facts. Either the government bailed it out or Morgan would take it over, too.

The British were not about to let the Germans replace them on the high seas. Parliament responded with a £2.6 million loan at 2.75 percent and an annual subsidy of £150,000. Cunard was determined to reclaim the Blue Riband with new designs, the *Lusitania* and the *Mauritania*. Although the world remembers the former's sinking by a German submarine as the reason for America's entry into World War I, the latter became the ship of the day and won the trans-Atlantic speed record on her in 1907. The *Mauritania* kept the Blue Riband for 22 years, all the while gaining the reputation as the most consistent ship ever made. The vessel never varied in her cross-Atlantic times more than ten minutes each time. It took 22 trains hauling 300 tons of coal each to fuel these ships' bunkers. They burned 1,000 tons a day at sea, and had a "black gang" of 324 firemen and trimmers per ship to keep them going. Morgan surprisingly wound up in trouble at home when the New York Stock Exchange refused to list his combine on the big board as the stock was feared excessively watered. The result was that the combination fell apart almost as fast as it had begun, although Morgan held on to White Star for two decades before returning it to British hands.

Although owned by Morgan, the White Star Line was run by British interests whose managers had decided by 1910 to build the three biggest, fastest, and finest-appointed ocean liners in the world: the *Olympic*, *Titanic*, and the *Britannic*. The *Olympic* lived a long and fruitful career. But the *Titanic* was doomed to strike an iceberg on her maiden voyage and sank losing 1,500 of the 2,200 aboard, still the worst maritime disaster in history. The oddest thing about the disaster was that seaman and novelist Morgan Robertson had written a story about a ship named the *Titan* that had suffered exactly the same fate as the White Star liner—but he wrote it ten years before the actual incident. Fully as ill-fated as her sister ship, the *Britannic* was converted to a hospital ship in World War I and sank after hitting a mine in the Aegean Sea. Fortunately, it was empty of wounded at the time.

Even though fattened by German prizes after the war, the Atlantic liners went into a period of decline. The United States closed it doors to immigrants through quota laws, leaving a big gap in the passenger lists. The steamship lines began to tout third class as a fine place to travel to and from Europe for young people as tourists. Smaller lines went into the business of tour cruises that took the wealthy around the Mediterranean or the Caribbean with lavish entertainment and food spreads that were the envy of gourmands everywhere.

The biggest cruise aficionados were Americans, well-heeled rubes, really, who seemed to fall for the glitzy advertising. Actually, the first such American trip had been a well-documented jaunt to the Holy Land organized by the Reverend Henry Ward Beecher after the Civil War. The commentator was a dry wit named Mark Twain. The book was called *Innocents Abroad*, an apt description that still held. Companies tried for the Blue Riband with much intensity, and even the Germans reemerged with new candidates. The Norddeutscher Lloyd ship *Bremen* made the trip in 4 days, 17 hours,

and 42 minutes, a record that held until broken by the American liner *United States* in 1952. But overhead flew Charles Lindbergh and the German airships *Graff Zeppelin* and *Hindenburg*. The age of sea travel had already been eclipsed. The airships could make the trip in less than two and a half days.

Great ships were still being built. The British combined the Cunard and North Star Lines into one company, which launched the *Queen Mary* and the *Queen Elizabeth*, ships so speedy that they sailed the U-boat–infested Atlantic without escorts during World War II. Eventually the *Queen Mary* would retire to a Long Beach pier, near another relic from the past, Howard Hughes' multiengine, wooden sea plane that flew only once, the *Spruce Goose*. The French had the *Normandie*, which was sabotaged in its New York berth in 1942 during

In 1910 White Star introduced three luxury ocean liners, the Olympic, Britannic, *and* Titanic. *Of the three, the* Olympic, *pictured here in 1911, is the only one that did not sink.*

its conversion into a troop ship to be named the USS *Lafayette*. The basic difference between the Anglo and Gallic designs, said one observer, was that the British built a beautiful ship and put a hotel in it, while the French built a beautiful hotel and put a ship around it.

After the war, the Italians came forward with their masterpieces *Andrea Doria*, tragically sunk off the American coast in a collision in 1965, and *Michelangelo*, almost destroyed in 1966 by a freak wave in a manner reminiscent of the novel *The Poseidon Adventure*. But regardless of the luck, the Italians had the most beautiful ships, inside and out, of the postwar era. France and Britain still competed with the stately *Ile de France* and the computerized *Queen Elizabeth 2*. One of the last great ships afloat, the *QE 2* was recently remodeled extensively to take advantage of the cruise trade only to be embarrassed by making its initial voyage with a half-finished interior. The *America* and the *United States* (the quintessential record-setting ship of the 1950s) marked a resurgent U.S. interest in trans-Atlantic travel. The latter was made under naval supervision and set a record on her maiden voyage of 801 miles in one day, which still holds. Indeed, the *United States* was faster than a lot of navy destroyers and could make up to 48 land miles an hour wide open. It was the last ship to claim the Blue Riband, never to relinquish it. The ocean liner as a concept had come back to its land of origin only to be surpassed by air travel in 1955 and totally ruined by the jet airliner in 1960. The great age of oceanic sea travel was over, replaced by the cruise trade so romantically portrayed on the popular television series *The Love Boat*.

See also Clipper Ships; Merchant Marine; Morgan, John Pierpont; Vanderbilt, Cornelius.

References Albion, Robert G., *Square-Riggers on Schedule* (1938); Bonsor, N. R. P., *North Atlantic Seaway* (1975); Brinnin, John Malcolm, *The Sway of the Grand Saloon* (1971); Cutler, Carl C., *Queens of the Western Ocean* (1961); Hanson, Marcus Lee, *The Atlantic Migration* (1940); Jackson, C. G., *The Story of the Liner* (1931); Jones, Maldwyn Allen, *American Immigration* (1960); Newell, Gordon, *Ocean Liners of the 20th Century* (1963); Spratt, H. P., *Outline History of Transatlantic Paddle Steamers* (1951).

Office of Public Road Inquiry (OPRI)

Created in 1899 and lasting to 1905 as a section of the Department of Agriculture, the Office of Public Road Inquiry was the successor to the Office of Road Inquiry founded in 1893. Headed by Martin Dodge of Cleveland, Ohio, a local politician with good knowledge of how the American political process works, the OPRI continued its educational effort, albeit with inadequate funding. Dodge made it one of his prime duties to get the office set up on a permanent basis with adequate funding. He hounded Congress at every opportunity. He divided the nation into four geographical areas with an assistant in charge of each. But all were part-time employees. Dodge and his assistant traveled around the country publicizing good roads, often at their own expense. They continued to construct "object lesson" roads and worked with the Good Roads Movement and their traveling train of exhibits. Dodge also made the first national road inventory, not only listing all roads but investigating public funding sources, road laws, and total expenditures state by state. In 1905, Dodge finally got Congress to bow to his wishes and create a permanent road office with increased funding. But as revenge for all of the years that he had begged for money, Congress made the chief's position that of a road professional. As Dodge lacked these qualities, he had to resign and return to local politics as his office went out of business.

See also Dodge, Martin; Roads and Highways, Colonial Times to World War I.

Reference U.S. Department of Transportation, Federal Highway Administration, *America's Highways* (1976).

Office of Public Roads (OPR)

Successor to the Office of Public Road Inquiry (OPRI) in 1905, the Office of Public Roads was a branch of the Department of Agriculture until 1915. As the end product of the merging of the OPRI and the Division of Tests of the Bureau of Chemistry, Congress required its new head be a professional civil engineer. Logan Waller Page took over from lawyer Martin Dodge immediately. He was given increased funding, a staff of six clerks, a chief of records, and an instrument maker.

Although there was undoubtedly some animosity between Dodge and Congress, it was true that road projects had come a long way from the old macadamized roads of the past, and more technical expertise was needed at the helm. Page had studied road building in France, where some of the world's best existed, and had experimented and tested road materials for years. He expanded the "object lesson" road project, using new techniques and materials to see how they stood up to modern motor traffic. He was especially interested in oil-based products like asphalt mixtures. As a proponent of the French system, Page emphasized continual maintenance as the critical factor in good roads. He publicized dragging dirt roads on a regular basis to allow good drainage and smooth surfaces. He called the massive effort of road construction, funding, and maintenance the "model systems" approach. To facilitate federal road management he updated the national road inventory begun in 1904.

Page continued to publicize new methods in newspapers and magazines devoted to informing the average citizen. He was also responsible for supporting the Good Roads Movement and the American Road congresses, a series of meetings of interested professionals and citizens. This led to the formation of the American Association of State Highway Officials in 1914. When the federal aid program was initially set up as an improvement of the post roads, the project wound up at the Office of Public Roads. In the Federal-Aid Road Act of 1916, Congress expanded the functions of the OPR and changed its name to the Office of Public Roads and Rural Engineering.

See also Dodge, Martin; Page, Logan Waller; Roads and Highways, Colonial Times to World War I.

Reference U.S. Department of Transportation, Federal Highway Administration, *America's Highways* (1976).

Office of Public Roads and Rural Engineering (OPRRE)

Established by the Federal-Aid Road Act of 1916 as a part of the Department of Agriculture, the Office of Public Roads and Rural Engineering existed until the end of World War I in 1918. Still under the leadership of Logan Waller Page, the OPRRE now had to manage the dispersal of federal-assistance highway funds to the states. With the onset of the war, however, the office soon became involved in traffic management as large convoys of trucks and matériel moved to the East Coast to be shipped to France. Page acted to coordinate the federal highway selection in the states and tried to get these roads to connect at state borders. His death in 1918 of a massive heart attack, however, left a void in the federal program. Delayed by the incapacitation of President Woodrow Wilson and an extensive debate in Congress over the future of the federal aid program, Page was not replaced for seven months. Finally, Congress passed a new post roads law that declared every road in the nation as a postal delivery system. When Thomas H. MacDonald received the appointment in July 1919, the office's name had been changed by the same law to that of the Bureau of Public Roads.

See also Bureau of Public Roads; Page, Logan Waller; Roads and Highways, Colonial Times to World War I.

Reference U.S. Department of Transportation, Federal Highway Administration, *America's Highways* (1976).

Office of Road Inquiry (ORI)

In existence from 1893 to 1899 as a part of the Department of Agriculture, the Office of Road Inquiry was created by Secretary of Agriculture J. Sterling Morton under the Agriculture Appropriations Act of 1893 to investigate and disseminate information on modern road-building techniques. The first head of the office was General Roy Stone, who published numerous bulletins, many of which were so popular they went through several printings. Stone also created the "good roads" map, a visual representation of all gravel and macadamized roads in the United States county by county. One of the office's best projects was the development of the "object roads" program, where the office would advise a locality on how to build a modern stretch of road to illustrate its advantages to local inhabitants. Both Stone and his assistant were indefatigable speakers and writers, doing much to educate the public on the need for improving America's roads. Stone's bureau was superseded by the Office of Public Road Inquiry in 1899.

See also Roads and Highways, Colonial Times to World War I; Stone, Roy.

Reference U.S. Department of Transportation, Federal Highway Administration, *America's Highways* (1976).

Ohio and Erie Canal

Built during the great canal boom of the 1820s and 1830s, the Ohio and Erie Canal connected the Great Lakes with the Ohio River between Cleveland on Lake Erie and Portsmouth on the Ohio, utilizing the Scioto River Valley. It tapped this region's production and linked it to New York City through the Erie Canal–Hudson River route.

See also Canals.

Oil Industry

Petroleum is organic matter that has been compressed under millions of tons of rock and through eons of history into pools of liquid hydrogen and carbon matter, tainted (at least as far as refiners are concerned) with elements of oxygen, nitrogen, and sulfur. It comes from the ground as the only known liquid mineral, known as "crude oil." It is cracked and refined into gasoline, kerosene, diesel, fuel oils, and various lubricants, and is the basis of numerous "ersatz" products like synthetic rubbers and plastics. The prosperity of the twentieth century, the Oil Century, has its basis in transportation largely fueled by petroleum.

But oil is not new. Humans have used it since 4000 B.C.E. (at least in the form of asphalt); Egyptian mummification has its basis in oil derivatives, and there are many biblical references to it. Hand-dug wells produced petroleum products in Asia at least 3,000 years ago, and early European references to its use as a medicine, lubricant, and source of illumination are common. Native Americans employed it for similar reasons and used it as a base for paints. Tar pits and "bituminous springs" were employed as a source for the product in its natural state. As Europeans moved inland from the Atlantic coast they began to drill artesian wells for salt brine. Many of these wells in western Pennsylvania and other Appalachian areas were contaminated with crude oil. Most of it was used as "rock oil" in medical applications, particularly to clear the bowels, or distilled as "coal oil," a somewhat odoriferous source of illumination.

As petroleum was distilled and experimented with, numerous products emerged, making the skimming of crude from salt wells a very inadequate source. Since many of the salt mines had been drilled into the ground, about the time of the American Civil War a group of investors decided to drill for oil alone in western Pennsylvania. The result was "Colonel" Edwin L. Drake's Titusville discovery, which proved that vast pools of oil lay beneath the earth's surface, awaiting exploitation. Out of this realization came the field of geology concerned with finding, not so much oil itself, but rock formations that might yield oil. Quickly, steam was applied to the concept of bringing oil to the surface, and the walking beam or cricket pump, so familiar to oil production, was introduced in its primitive forms. The drill hole was cased in wrought-iron pipe to channel the flow of oil and gas and keep the petroleum from being contaminated with underground water.

Legally, the well owner's rights were an application of the old English right of percolating waters. This held that a driller was entitled to the fruits of all that lay beneath the ground he owned. Unlike riparian (surface) water rights, the user was not responsible to keep the waters flowing along to his neighbor. This was so because no one knew what lay deep in the ground. So technically, an oilman could drain the same underground pool as his neighbor, even if it denied him later or concurrent exploitation. This was known as the "rule of capture."

The practice has led to numerous wells being sunk into one underground pool, thereby wasting pumping capacity and drilling costs, and causing higher consumer prices, rapid exhaustion of the reservoir's energy to assist pumping, and lower recovery rates from any one pool.

As most wells were operated under lease, there was a theoretical difference in the method of exploitation between lessee and owner. The actual landowner would want to obtain the full amount of oil in the least amount of time to maximize profits. But the driller often wanted the exploitation of a reserve to take a number of years, as the lessee operated with a limited amount of employees and equipment. Courts ultimately gave the lessee the right to delay exploitation for whatever reason, but the actual owner had the right to collect rent or foreclose on the lease anytime before drilling commenced. These were "correlative rights."

Legalities aside, one of the biggest problems for the early oil tycoons was how to transport the oil to refining and storage facilities, and the finished product from there to the user. It soon became obvious that teamsters hauling barrels in wagons could not gather the oil as efficiently as pipelines. Already in use in larger cities for water supplies, the introduction of oil pipelines allowed the individual wells to be located almost anywhere. Most of the early ones were gravity-fed, but the introduction of pumps allowed them to traverse any type of terrain. The oil then came down to a loading port with storage tanks for delivery to the next stage of its movement to market. As the pumps and materials for the pipes improved, these collection systems became larger and larger until they replaced flatboats and rail cars for the trip to the refinery. Originally, the crude oil was put in barrels and floated down the Allegheny River in flatboats to Pittsburgh for transfer to the railroads. It did not take long before various branches and short lines probed into the oil country, aiming to cut out the rivermen. This initially gave the Erie Railroad an advantage as the most direct line between the oil country and New York City. Soon the mighty Pennsylvania Railroad moved in to secure these small lines and divert the oil back to Pittsburgh. The railroads undercut each other, gave rebates and drawbacks, drew up traffic agreements and broke them, and generally mucked up the transportation scene until Standard Oil cornered oil production and John D. Rockefeller brought them to heel with a dictated traffic agreement that he could enforce by denying oil to any railroad that failed to cooperate.

Regardless of the rail line used, the packing of oil into barrels (often poorly made as the demand was so high) and loading them on flats and gondolas for transport was too costly. At the end of the Civil War, Amos Densmore developed the first railroad tank car, a flatcar with two gigantic, allegedly leak-proof vertical tanks set over its trucks. As the railroads moved to create vast tank fleets, it was discovered that Densmore's wooden tanks were top heavy, sloshed oil around too much, and began to develop leaks over time, regardless of care in construction. In response, iron tanks positioned in a horizontal fashion close to the track for a low center of gravity were created, with a top dome to allow for expansion, the first of which were built by J. F. Keeler. The modern tank car was born, although nowadays cars 100 feet in length can haul closer to 100,000 gallons and dwarf Keeler's diminutive 80-gallon 25-footers. But the elimination of individual barrels and loss of product due to leaks significantly reduced the cost of shipping. As with most merchant marine-based industries, however, the United States failed to keep up with the Europeans, particularly the Russians, in the export trade. The Russians dominated the export trade by developing oceangoing tankers under sail and steam in the late 1880s.

The early petroleum product of choice was kerosene (60 million barrels were produced annually by the turn of the century), and often refiners destroyed all other by-products lighter or heavier than it. Gradually, more sophisticated refining methods came to the fore and the lighter fractions of oil (those with a lower boiling rate for distillation) were made into naphtha, gasoline, naphtha gas, and liquefied petroleum gases like rhigolene and cymogene. The heavier fractions that had a higher boiling rate than kerosene produced fuel oils, light and heavy lubricants, deodorized or natural oils, mineral oils, paraffin, and petroleum jelly. By 1900 over 200 petroleum byproducts were available. Of course different products, many of which were unknown to the early refiners, now dominate the refinery scene. Early refineries were concentrated in Pittsburgh and Cleveland, rail hubs south and north of the production fields.

As the nineteenth century came to a close, oil production began to spread into Ohio and Indiana. These oils were high in sulfur content, but a method for precipitating and removing it eliminated that problem. There was a particular American habit associated with most oil production that continued to be evident as new discoveries abounded. This was wastage of product above and below ground, typified by the burning off of natural-gas pockets in oil fields. Sloppy refining procedures were evident as illumination oils often blew up in the public realm because of excessive amounts of volatile naphtha. But as new uses came into vogue for naphtha, more care was exercised to eliminate this problem. In general, prices for all products (but dominated by kerosene) dropped precipitously in the 40 years from the Civil War to the Spanish-American War, from 45 cents a gallon to 6 cents retail. Although Standard Oil controlled much of the industry, it did so through transportation monopolies as much as production methods. The discovery of new fields in Illinois, Texas, Kansas, Oklahoma, Wyoming, and California would open up competition once again (with new companies like Gulf, Union, Sunoco, and Texaco), and shift much of crude-oil transportation to a system of continental pipelines. The increased use of tankers accompanied the drilling in California and the completion of the Panama Canal. More recent efforts have been concentrated in the California and Texas–Louisiana offshore regions and the North Slope of Alaska.

Concomitant with the new twentieth-century discoveries of oil came a new use for petroleum as the dominant means of transport propulsion for the entire century. At the same time, the increased demand from the public opened up another field of petroleum use, that within the industry to power the continuous refining processes that changed and improved as new products were developed in the petrochemical industry. But nothing beat out the use of petroleum in powering automobiles, airplanes, and rockets, land and marine diesel engines, and even oil-burning steam locomotives, which topped the market by the time of the Great Depression. Oil (as asphalt) even paved the roads that made the tremendous fuel consumption necessary. The company-leased gas station became a new building at the center of Americana. Tetraethyl lead was added to gasoline to prevent knocking. Thermal cracking allowed refiners to break up the petro-hydrocarbons into smaller ones, which increased the supply of refinable gasoline in a given amount of crude. Catalytic cracking further improved the amounts and quality of gasoline, especially in high-octane aviation gas for the Allied war effort in World War II.

Domestically, one of the big questions between the world wars was the conservation of oil for national emergencies. There was some doubt as to whether the government could interfere on the state or national level to regulate the amount of production and corruption in the storage process leading to scandals like Teapot Dome. The Great Depression and the increased regulation of all industries to stimulate price control and employment hit the oil industry with the Market Demand Act of 1932, the National Industrial Recovery Act of 1933, and the Connelly Hot Oil Act of 1935. These measures confirmed the federal government's right, and in its absence the state's, to regulate the production of oil on a monthly basis based on the prediction of national needs as determined by the Interstate Oil Compact Commission and the Bureau of Mines.

As the domestic demand for petroleum

products increased in the United States, foreign sources of production began to grow. In Europe, the Soviet Union became the largest producer, followed by Romania. In Asia, Burma and the Dutch East Indies (currently Indonesia) were the big leaders in the Far East as Persian Gulf nations began to expand their oil fields. In the Western Hemisphere, Venezuela increased its production as Mexico's fell. But the United States still exported 30 percent of its own production overseas, a level that remained fairly constant until the beginning of World War II. Numerous measures were undertaken to increase the flow of domestic oil such as water injection, a procedure by which water was injected into the bottom of an oil pool as gas was forced into the top, causing more of a given pool to be recovered for refining.

The thirties also saw oil production attacked by the government from another aspect. The "Mother Hubbard" suit charged over 20 companies with fixing prices and restricting competition, a process made easier for them by the extensive use of pipelines for the transportation of crude and refined products. Another companion suit accused various pipeline companies of giving oil producers transportation rebates in violation of long-standing antitrust laws. Because of the onslaught of World War II and the emergency needs for oil, the government settled these suits gently by limiting any rebates to 7 percent of the product shipped. Most companies signed this agreement to avoid further prosecution. The settlement also avoided the complete divorce of production from shipping, a consideration enforced against railroads for years and long desired by oil industry critics.

By the end of World War II, the U.S. domestic demand for petroleum products was staggering, of which the raging demand for gasoline was just a superficial part. Asphalt, one of the more mundane derivatives, was used for road oils, paving (imagine the amounts needed for the Interstate Highway System alone), paper saturants, fuel briquetting, shingles, roofing papers, roof coatings, insulating compounds, rust preventatives, and paint additives. Petrochemical raw materials made up a list that would run on for a page, and is still increasing daily. Oil was and is the basis of hundreds of products, many of which never occur to the average person as being oil derivatives, like synthetic fabrics and plastics.

In the 1950s the United States was king of world oil. Texas alone produced twice the oil of the Soviet Union and more than the whole Middle East combined. Today, the balance is changing constantly. Imports in crude oil from overseas have risen from 5 percent in 1946 to over 50 percent today. America is reliant on foreign imports of oil and possesses only about 5 percent of the world's remaining proven reserves of crude. Cheap foreign producers have made the exploitation of remaining U.S. reserves uneconomical. Texas has in effect gone broke, and the rest of the nation is following rapidly, the pathway being greased by foreign oil. The dependency of the United States on oil imports has been highlighted by the effects, real or imagined, of the Arab oil embargoes of the 1970s, and of supertankers, oil spills, and the Gulf War of the 1990s.

The various "oil crises" of the 1970s have led to a reexamination of fuel uses and a rethinking of transportation alternatives. Transportation accounts for about 25 percent of America's total energy consumption, but oil comprises 90 percent of transportation's energy sources. Several methods have been employed to counter this dependence on natural resources that are increasingly becoming non-American in origin. Better mileage in automobiles is very important because over half of any family's energy costs go into powering its motor vehicles. The same applies to the trucking industry, only more so. Various methods have been used, such as lower-weight vehicles, computerized fuel delivery to the engine, streamlined exteriors, and conversion to diesel (which gets a fourth more mileage per gallon). But the latter creates more problems of its own in the form of more pollution, which generally has restricted its use to heavy trucks and buses. Natural gas and liquid propane are transportation energy alternatives that avoid polluting side effects, and are becoming increasingly popular with smaller vehicles, especially company and governmental fleets operated inside cities. Improved maintenance and the increased use of commuter trains, buses, bicycles, mopeds, car pools, and van pools are other common methods of reducing daily petroleum use.

But conservation merely circumvents the problem; it does not hit it head-on. Critics of America's oil policies cannot come to an agreement as to what course to pursue. On the one hand, many are suspicious of the oil industry and its motives. These critics offer a litany of scandals and shady dealings, with the government and the consumer backing their point of view, best summed up in the words of New Deal guru Harold Ickes: "An honest and scrupulous man in the oil business is so rare as to rank as a museum piece." On the other side are those who feel that government regulations, not the industry or a shortage of oil, are the problem. If the government would simply free an energetic energy industry from unnecessary, burdensome, and foolish restraints, energy sources would once again be abundantly available. Their viewpoint in a nutshell might be seen in the plaintive pronouncement of Standard Oil of Indiana's John E. Swearengin: "It is automatically assumed that we are liars and connivers instead of trying to be decent citizens like newspaper people and senators are." The truth lies somewhere in between the extremes, and the real crux of the issue remains the nation's inability to say intelligently, without being blinded by the usual demagoguery, where.

See also Organization of Petroleum Exporting Countries; Pipelines; Rockefeller, John D.

References Clark, J. Stanlet, *The Oil Century* (1958); Hodel, Donald Paul, and Robert Dietz, *Crisis in the Oil Patch* (1994); Rose, Harvey, and Amy Pinkerton, *The Energy Crisis, Conservation and Solar* (1981); Schurr, Sam H., et al., *Energy in the American Economy* (1960); Sherill, Robert, *The Oil Follies* (1983); Williamson, Harold F., and Arnold R. Daum, *The American Petroleum Industry* (1959).

Oil Pollution Act of 1990

In reaction to the tragic oil spill from the Exxon *Valdez* into Prince William Sound, Congress passed one of the strictest antipollution measures it has ever considered. Hearings had been under way for some time prior to the spill about changes in the Port and Tanker Safety Act of 1978, but the *Valdez* mishap caused a transportation measure to become an environmental protection one. It was particularly embarrassing because the accident involved an American-owned and manned ship. The 1990 law worked in two areas. First, it strengthened the ability of the U.S. Coast Guard to examine qualifications of personnel serving aboard tankers, going into their lives ashore previously considered off-limits because of privacy legislation. Even driver's license offenses were considered relevant. Second, Congress imposed the double-hull requirement on all tankers entering U.S. waters, and a detailed time chart as to how fast the conversions must take place. On their part, the oil companies have resorted to expensive tugboat escorts out of Prince William Sound, and the first company to convert totally to double-hulled vessels, Conoco, has made it a part of their domestic advertising.

See also Merchant Marine; Pipelines.

References Easton, Robert, *Black Tide* (1972); Lord, Nancy, *Darkened Waters* (1992); Pedraja, René de la, *A Historical Dictionary of the Merchant Marine and Shipping Industry* (1994).

Old Spanish Trail

In 1598, Juan de Oñate founded San Gabriel 30 miles north of Santa Fe in today's New Mexico, to connect up with the trade the Ute Indians made with Taos, some 40 miles up the Rio Grande. The settlement eventually failed, replaced by Santa Fe to the south, but the first step had been taken to advance Spanish rule up what became the Old Spanish Trail. At the time, New Spain was managed by the *encomienda*, a system of labor that granted the *encomendero* (holder of a land grant) the right to exploit native peoples, providing they were civilized and Christianized in the process.

As adult Native Americans refused conversion and made inefficient and rebellious slaves, the demand shifted to children who could be raised "properly" from the beginning. Driven by the slave trade in young Native Americans, especially girls, the Pueblo villages revolted against Spanish rule in the Uprising of 1680. For a decade, the Pueblos lived without European presence, one of the only true Native American victories in hundreds of years of warfare with the whites in North America. But by the turn of the century, the Spanish were back in force to stay, and the slave trade in Indian children began anew, this time thriving on captives brought down from the north by the powerful Utes, conveniently allowing the Spanish to keep their hands and consciences fairly clean in the transaction and allowing the Pueblos to live in some peace. Although the church managed to reconvert local Pueblo villages in time, the Comanche, Navajos, and Hopis all remained hostile. The Apaches of course had never been friendly with anyone. It was the route the Utes took from the interior of what is now modern Nevada and Utah that became the Old Spanish Trail or the Great Slave Trail.

In the mid-eighteenth century, the chore of supplying Spanish missions in California by sea had become nearly impossible. Juan Bautista de Anza's route through Sonora and Arizona involved too much hard desert travel. Both methods were too costly in terms of men and animals. At Zuñi Pueblo in New Mexico, Father Silvestre de Escalante thought he had a solution—one that would help bring increased prosperity to the region. He proposed that the old Ute trading route be utilized. True, it was long and indirect, but it was negotiable and could connect to the trade route up the Rio Grande from El Paso and Chihuahua. He offered to go along to keep the faith and a written record. In 1776, as the American Revolution raged miles to the east, Escalante set out from Abiquíu, the northernmost post in New Mexico.

Led by Ute guides, Escalante traveled far north to escape the canyon country of the Four Corners area. Then he crossed west to Utah Lake. He turned south, hoping to reach the latitude of Monterey, California. In the process he saw the Sevier River, an inland stream with no outlet to the sea, and Sevier Lake, the river's destination. By now, Escalante calculated he should turn west, but he had run out of supplies, and California was hundreds of miles west across the desert. The party turned to go back to Santa Fe, moving more or less southeast. He discovered the headwaters of the Virgin River and forded the Colorado at the Crossing of the Fathers, a spot since covered by the waters of Lake Powell behind the Glen Canyon Dam. He returned through the Hopi villages and the western New Mexico pueblos to Santa Fe.

Soon thereafter, the California missions reported themselves to be pretty much self-sufficient, so interest in the route to the Pacific diminished. But the eastern leg of the trail to Utah Lake was used by men who traded with the Utes. About that time, the American mountain men arrived and established their winter quarters at Taos. Among the Americans was an unusual trapper, Jedediah Smith, unusual because he could read and did so voraciously. In one of the atlases Smith read, an author had speculated that the area south of the Great Salt Lake had to drain into the Pacific somewhere. So he had invented a river, the Buenaventura, to accomplish the job. As co-owner of the American Fur Company, facing the hostilities of the Blackfeet and the competition of the British Hudson's Bay Company to the north, Smith decided to find this southern route to California. He hoped that the Buenaventura and its branches teemed with beaver like all Rocky Mountain streams.

In 1826, Smith set out from the rendezvous areas (mountain meadows where trappers came in and sold their furs each year) and went south past Great Salt Lake. His journey would establish the western half of the Old Spanish Trail. Following roughly the same route as Escalante, Smith kept going down the Virgin instead of turning east. He eventually reached the Colorado and followed it down to about where Needles, California, is today. Then he headed west across the Mojave Desert, becoming the first white man to cross it, and wound up at San Gabriel near Los Angeles. He would make a second trip a year later after a roundabout return to the Great Salt Lake directly across Nevada from Lake Tahoe.

After Smith's journeys, the Old Spanish Trail came into more general use. William Wolfskill and George Yount led the first expedition to traverse the whole trail from beginning at Santa Fe to end at Los Angeles. Reaching the Sevier Lake region in the winter snows, which obliterated landmarks, they became lost and struck out across the country and shortened one of the roughest sections of the route. Later Antonio Armijo, in 1829–1830, followed Escalante's return route to southern Utah and established the final leg of the journey through present-day Las Vegas, avoiding the Mojave villages at the Needles, which had grown hostile to white travelers. The whole trail now was complete, a vast circular route that avoided Apache, Navajo, and Mojave hostiles and took the shortest way across the desert to California. The caravans carried finished goods from the United States and Mexico to California and returned with horses and mules and goods from the China trade over the Pacific.

To regulate the trade, caravans were supposed to get operating licenses at both ends of the journey. Americans generally ignored these edicts. The result was that many of them received rough handling on the part of Mexican officials. The mountain men were a rather independent lot, not prone to allow any treatment they thought was unfair, legalities be damned, so they retaliated. The result was an illicit trade in stolen California horses and mules that made the Old Spanish Trail infamous. The slave trade continued, with the market in New Mexico vigorous to the end. After the Mexican War, the Territory of Utah passed a law against the traffic in humans, but had little power to enforce it. A U.S. duty on goods that moved across the trail from New Mexico, enacted by the

military government of California, put an end to all transactions in 1848. Combined with the gold rush and the emphasis on the more direct Gila Trail, the Old Spanish Trail gradually petered out. Some of it is used today to get into the Canyonlands National Park area. The section from California to Salt Lake City was kept active by the Mormons as an outlet to the ocean, but the section to Santa Fe disappeared. The western branch became the roadbed for the Union Pacific Railroad, then U.S. Highway 91, and finally Interstate 15, and is still important today.

See also Gila Trail; Roads and Highways, Colonial Times to World War I; Roads and Highways since World War I; Santa Fe Trail.

References Hafen, LeRoy, and Ann Hafen, *Old Spanish Trail* (1955); Moody, Ralph, *The Old Trails West* (1963); Morgan, Dale L., *Jedediah Smith and the Opening of the West* (1953); Weber, David J., *The Spanish Frontier in North America* (1992).

Old Spanish Trail Highway

One of the "named highways" popular in the teens and twenties of the twentieth century, the Old Spanish Trail Highway was used by local chambers of commerce and tourism and the American Automobile Association to stimulate travel on the "good roads" and increase income in the towns and states through which they passed. Coming out of Jacksonville, Florida, this route is almost exactly what is known today as Interstates 8 and 10 or old U.S. Highway 90, including the branch to Del Río and Van Horn out of San Antonio, while the main road went west through Kerrville, Junction, Sonora, Fort Stockton, and Van Horn. The major cities on the route included Jacksonville, Tallahassee, Pensacola, Mobile, Pascagoula, New Orleans, Beaumont, Houston, San Antonio, El Paso, Deming, and Lordsburg in New Mexico, and Tucson, Phoenix, and Yuma in Arizona. The road followed the same route as the Lee Highway to San Diego. It is still one of the most traveled routes across the United States.

See also Roads and Highways, Colonial Times to World War I.

References Hart, Val, *The Story of American Roads* (1950); U.S. Department of Transportation, Federal Highway Administration, *America's Highways* (1976).

Olds, Ransom E. (1864–1950)

By the early 1900s, it had become evident that there was much demand for an auto that cost less than $1,000. The demand actually had been discovered quite accidentally ten years earlier by Ransom E. Olds, a pioneer auto tinkerer. Olds produced the first horseless carriage that sold. His curved-dash runabout was nothing more than a buggy with a reliable one-cylinder engine; it weighed 500 pounds and cost $650. It was called the Oldsmobile (as in the refrain from the old song, "Come away with me Lucille/in my merry Oldsmobile"). The little car was so popular that it captured nearly a quarter of the whole auto market and one-half of the under-$1,000 market.

Olds' success was due partly to manufacturing and partly to distribution. His car was mechanically well designed and used existing technology available from the bicycle industry. This meant that Olds had a supply of already-trained workers. The Olds used wire spoke wheels, a chain drive, and a tubular steel frame, and subcontracted all parts to existing companies. He built his own engine on a crude assembly line, a harbinger of things to come. He also pioneered routing materials to the assembly area to keep the assembly line fully employed. He got 30 to 90 days credit from his suppliers and forced dealers to pay cash upon delivery. This was a necessity brought about when fire destroyed his first plant and he had to rebuild at considerable debt. But the market was so hot that Olds got away with it.

On the distribution side, Olds had retail outlets in Boston, New York City, Philadelphia, Chicago, Omaha, Minneapolis, and Los Angeles. Olds engaged in all sorts of state fairs and primitive auto shows. He even had a professional driver motor between Detroit and New York in a previously unheard-of seven days. He gave away the distribution rights to area dealers, who in turn hired local showroom representatives.

These arrangements allowed Olds to concentrate on Detroit manufacturing, and his company made it "Motor City" until a fire caused him to move his operation to Lansing. Before the introduction of the French design, a whole new car without the carriage façade, Ransom E. Olds and the Oldsmobile made the horseless carriage an American institution. Others would have an easier time because of his pioneering effort. After he was bought out by General Motors, Olds started Reo Car Company and continued to experiment with the internal combustion engine. He also invented the first power lawn mower.

The success of Ransom Olds' Oldsmobile took the automobile industry by surprise.

See also Automobiles from Domestics to Imports; Automobiles in American Society.

References Motor Vehicle Manufacturers Association of the United States, *Automobiles of America* (1974); Niemeyer, Glenn A., *The Automotive Career of Ransom E. Olds* (1965); Thomas, Robert Paul, *An Analysis of the Pattern of Growth of the Automobile Industry* (1977).

Omnibus Reconciliation Act of 1981

This congressional measure eliminated the quasi-private status of Amtrak by issuing preferred stock to the secretary of transportation and eliminating the private railway company representatives from the board of directors. In effect, Amtrak has gone the opposite route of Conrail. At the same time, however, the government has refused to state that Amtrak is a nationalized rail organization—a part of the political history of a nation that has blanched at the idea of calling socialism by its real name even when it is obviously present.

See also Amtrak Improvement Act of 1978; Conrail.

References Hilton, George W., *Amtrak* (1980); Musolf, Lloyd, *Uncle Sam's Private, Profitseeking Corporations* (1983); Orenstein, Jeffrey, *United States Railroad Policy* (1990).

Oregon Trail

In 1827, a New England schoolmaster and an avowed Anglophobe, Hall J. Kelley, wrote a pamphlet urging Americans to travel to Oregon, then under joint occupation with the British, and by force of numbers make the place American. He knew of Robert Stuart's report and William Ashley's use of wagons hauling goods east and west across the plains in the fur trade, and had read Lewis and Clark's journals. He took the most glowing of these, filled in the gaps with his own fertile imagination, and painted a picture of an easy highway leading to a promised land. The only one to be inspired was a fellow Bostonian, Nathaniel Wyeth. A successful young businessman, Wyeth decided to research the trip to Oregon on his own. He found that there was no highway, but, still convinced that Oregon was a Garden of Eden on the Pacific, contacted Kelley. It was then that Wyeth realized that Kelley was a mere publicist. If Oregon were to be settled by Americans, Wyeth would have to do it himself. So he did in 1832.

Wyeth advertised for 50 single young men who would brave the wilderness. He proposed to train them in a sort of frontiersmen's boot camp and send them overland to Oregon, where they would meet a supply ship sent around Cape Horn. Each man would sign a contract to repay his personal costs of the expedition. Travel was to be by a special keelboat, one equipped with wheels in case the rivers ran shallow. Two dozen signed up. When the expedition reached St. Louis with three wagon boats, Wyeth met Milton Sublette and convinced him to guide them west. Sublette agreed, providing the keelboats on wheels were dispensed with. Wyeth consented reluctantly (they were, after all, magnificent craft) and the party set off.

Leaving Independence, Missouri, on horseback, the troop turned north on the Little Blue River and cut across to the Platte. Following the Platte west, the party jogged around the confluence of the South Platte and met the North Platte at Courthouse Rock, a major landmark. Then they followed the North Platte to the Sweetwater River and crossed the Continental Divide at South Pass. Sublette then asked the remaining members of the party if they wished to go south to Bridger's Fort and then north to the Snake River, or follow the rendezvous caravan they had been traveling with to Pierre's Hole. The lure of the rendezvous was too much to refuse. Wyeth turned north, although the Oregon Trail would take the other route, as a matter of course. This northern branch would be known ever after as the Sublette Cutoff. Wyeth and his proper Yankees were astounded and shocked by the excesses of the rendezvous, but they survived the experience, little worse for the wear. Just west of the Twin Falls, Sublette left the group to attend to business of his own and told Wyeth to follow the river to the coast.

Either Sublette did not make it clear, or did not know the route well, because Wyeth should have crossed to the northern bank. He did not and got lost briefly, but managed to follow Indian trails to Walla Walla, home of a Hudson's Bay trading post. Resupplied, with the horses exchanged for a river barge, they floated down to Fort Vancouver, opposite the Willamette. Here they found out that their supply ship had been lost at sea and no supplies awaited them. Wyeth did not despair. He decided to return to Boston and do the whole thing all over again. He hoped to finance the trip by trading the Native Americans a shipload of trinkets for salmon, which would sell at 10 cents a pound in Boston. He accidentally met Sublette on the Green River, and the latter agreed to buy a wagon train of goods if Wyeth returned in time for the next rendezvous.

Refinanced, Wyeth left Boston in 1834 for another go. His party was bigger this time and included Methodist missionaries intent on converting Native Americans. But the weather on the Plains did not cooperate; it was very wet that year, and he reached the mountains after the rendezvous had disbanded. At Fort Bridger, Sublette refused to buy his goods. Undaunted, Wyeth proceeded north to the Snake and built his own fort to house the goods until next year's rendezvous. He would now be first at the meet and gain the best furs. He called his place Fort Hall, after one of his Boston backers. He then went down the north bank of the Snake River to the Columbia, crossed to the south side, and tried to build a wagon trail around the Dalles Rapids and Mount Hood that entered the Willamette Valley opposite Fort Vancouver. But the forest defeated him and for years after settlers were compelled to float through the Dalles in a dangerous rafting operation until the Barlow Road skirted the area. His ship failed to arrive until after the salmon run, but his colony prospered, and he became the first to open the Oregon country.

Spurred on by the fact that Methodists were already on the scene, thanks to Wyeth's second expedition, the American Board for Foreign Missions (Presbyterians and Congregationalists) organized their own effort in 1836. They selected Marcus and Narcissa (she married him so he would qualify) Whitman, and Henry and Eliza Spaulding, a farmer and a mechanic, to go to Oregon and spearhead the work. They accompanied the rendezvous caravan

"Oregon Fever" swept the nation in the mid-nineteenth century. Americans traveled the Oregon Trail mainly by foot—enduring exposure, snakebite, and disease.

westward, as Wyeth had earlier. Like all emigrants, the party carried too much gear and wound up jettisoning a lot of it. Their scout, veteran mountain man Thomas Fitzpatrick, transferred his items to pack animals at Fort Laramie. Whitman refused, determined to take a wagon on through to the Columbia for the first time. At the rendezvous, the white women created quite a stir. The trappers had not seen one in years, and the local Native Americans never had. The draft horses gave out, and Whitman built himself a cart on two wheels. His items had already been put on horseback, but Whitman declined to abandon the wagon's remnants, even if empty.

Having met Wyeth at the rendezvous (he had sold Fort Hall and its contents and made his stake up at last), Whitman received a letter of introduction that got him in a party returning from the Oregon settlements. Finally, at the mouth of the Boise River the cart gave out, but Whitman had gotten farther on wheels than anyone else to date. Arriving at Fort Walla Walla, they sent messages downriver to oceangoing ships, extolling the beauties of Oregon and the ease of travel—a slight exaggeration. But the travelers came on anyway, and by 1839 the trail was passable to wagons all the way to Portland.

In 1840, the Catholic church sent a Jesuit priest, Father Pierre Jean de Smet, a Belgian by birth, to compete in the missionary "wars." He liked to travel alone, and like the priests in northern Mexico, he was successful at it. In 1841, Fitzpatrick took de Smet on a route that cut the Sublette Cutoff in half, crossing an almost desertlike region between various headwaters of the Green River straight into Fort Hall. That same year, U.S. Senator Thomas Hart Benton concocted a scheme to convince more settlers to go to Oregon—through his hometown of St. Louis, of course. He had his new son-in-law, army Lieutenant John Charles Frémont, appointed to map the Oregon Trail, taking Benton's 12-year-old son with him to prove the trail's safety. As guides, Frémont hired Kit Carson and Lucien Maxwell. All sorts of scientific instruments

and a German topographer completed the expedition.

Now anyone short of blind could follow the ruts of those who passed before, but Benton knew that while Frémont might not be shucks as a soldier, he could write tremendous prose. His story of the uneventful journey was a masterpiece, printed up at government expense, and went through the East like wildfire. In 1843, the rush to Oregon was on with hundreds of caravans going each year. "Oregon Fever" had hit the nation hard at last, just as Hall J. Kelley had hoped a decade and a half earlier. In 1845, 3,000 Americans made the trip. Total U.S. residents outnumbered the 700 British subjects (mostly trappers) by seven to one. In 1846, Samuel Barlow finally managed to find a route around the Dalles and built a toll road behind Mount Hood that entered the Willamette Valley from the east, relieving the long lines waiting to negotiate the treacherous Columbia River gorge. The land route to Oregon was fully opened at last.

It was an expensive trip. It has been estimated that one traveler died for every 80 yards of road, a total of 30,000 for the whole migration. Most of the deaths were due to exposure, snakebite, and disease. Probably less than 100 ever had a hostile run-in with Native Americans. They let the trains pass along the "Great Medicine Trail," thinking the whites to be a little batty, often negotiating right of passage for trade goods and even offering food to the trekkers, who soon tired of beans, bacon, and coffee.

It was also an arduous trip. Everyone but the very old, the very young, or the infirm walked. The wagons only offered a space 4 feet wide and around 10 feet long for provisions, clothing, and any "treasure" the family might want to take along. Usually the prized bedstead, grandmother's piano, or whatever, was discarded by the time it reached South Pass, as the animals began to tucker out. The nicer persons left notes on their discards offering them to anyone who followed. The more crass destroyed their discards to keep them selfishly for themselves, if only in memory. The trail was marked by the skeletons of dead animals, the graves of dead people, and the litter of overloaded wagons. A lot of dreams died, too, left unmarked along the way.

Many travelers "saw the elephant," that is, experienced some level of tragedy on the trip. It could be almost anything from death to accident, or from loss of animals to destruction of the wagon going down a steep hill. The worst trail danger was negotiating the Snake River near Boise at Three Island Crossing, the islands breaking up the torrential current—a little. The most gratifying section was probably Farewell Bend and McFarland Pass, where the travelers left the Snake gorge and saw trees (the real primeval forest—not scrub—of the Blue Mountains) for the first time since Missouri. The quiet matting of the noise of the wheels as they rolled through the pine duff was at first disquieting, then pleasing, to an ear accustomed to the thumping jolts of the plains and mountains.

Family emigration by wagon over the Oregon did what the diplomats had failed to do—it presented the British with a fait accompli. Oregon Territory (present-day Oregon, Washington, and British Columbia) was divided at the forty-ninth parallel the next year, with the rich Columbia River basin being in the American part. It was a transportation victory that spread the American nation to the Pacific coast, with nary a shot being fired. One hundred and fifty years later, it is still possible to see the ruts of the emigrants in places, but major parts of the Oregon Trail have disappeared forever in the sands of passing time.

See also Barlow Road; California Trail; Central Overland Route; Manifest Destiny; Mormon Trail; Roads and Highways, Colonial Times to World War I; Roads and Highways since World War I.

References Bell, James C., *Opening a Highway to the Pacific* (1921); Brown, Jennie B., *Fort Hall on the Oregon Trail* (1932); Drago, Harry S., *Roads to Empire* (1968); Drake, Harrison C., "The Organization of the Oregon Emigrating Companies," *Oregon Historical Quarterly* (1915) 16: 205–227; Dunlop, Richard, *Great Trails of the West* (1971); Dunlop, Richard, *Wheels West* (1977); Eggenhoffer, Nick, *Wagons, Mules, and Men* (1961); Gibbons, Boyd, "The Itch To Move West: Life and Death on the Oregon Trail," *National Geographic* (August 1986)

174: 147–177; Hafen, LeRoy, and Francis M. Young, *Fort Laramie and the Pageant of the West* (1938); Hart, Val, *The Story of American Roads* (1950); Hartman, Amos W., "The California and Oregon Trail, 1849–1860," *Oregon Historical Quarterly* (1924) 25: 1–35; Kroll, Helen B., "Books That Enlightened the Emigrants," *Oregon Historical Quarterly* (1944) 45: 103–120; Monaghan, Jay, *The Overland Trail* (1947); Moody, Ralph, *The Old Trails West* (1963).

Organization of Petroleum Exporting Countries (OPEC)

Perhaps nothing has so adversely affected transportation costs in the last 20 years as the rising price of fuel. It has put a premium on efficiency in management, labor, and equipment to prevent ruin. At the forefront of the rise in fossil fuel costs have been the policies of the combined oil producing countries through their cartel, the Organization of Petroleum Exporting Countries. Formed in 1960 in response to the manipulation of oil prices by western oil managers, the various nations met at Baghdad to form OPEC to maintain a higher, more stable price. The organization included the Arabian Gulf nations, many of them just becoming free of western imperial rule and resenting the continuation of this by the oil companies' policies; Libya and Nigeria in Africa; and Venezuela in Latin America. As the grip of imperialism slipped throughout the 1960s, more small Gulf emirates joined. The association placed its headquarters at Vienna, but really did little during the decade.

The do-nothing attitude of OPEC changed in the 1970s. Several forces combined to produce a more active cartel. One was nationalism and the entrance of various governments into the oil-pricing arena. The other was the Yom Kippur War in 1973, which galvanized the various Muslim countries to punish the West for its crucial military and economic support of Israel. In any case, beginning with the Tripoli Agreement and extended by the Tehran Agreement some months later, the OPEC countries began to cooperate to raise selling prices and limit production to make the higher prices stick. This produced the first oil shock, which saw prices of crude rise from 35 cents to $3, then $5, and finally to a peak of $17 a barrel. Finally, the crude oil price stabilized at $11.65 a barrel. The OPEC policies quickly revealed that it had found the Achilles' heel of western economic strength as gas lines and shortages spread throughout Europe and North America.

The price remained stable until 1979 when the Islamic Revolution hit Iran, one of the major producer states. Disrupted by the Iranian political turmoil, a vast section of the supply market was cut out overnight. Other oil-rich states could not make up the difference and the price for crude shot up to $34 a barrel. This time OPEC realized fully that its economic power could be translated into political punch, and the cartel moved to limit production to keep the price artificially high. The process, however, was not without its own weaknesses. The war between Iran and Iraq both interrupted oil production and made it imperative for national survival. Other states resented the leadership of Saudi Arabia in setting production quotas and prices. There were 40 percent more oil tankers than product to move. Energy alternatives like the new seaborne transportation of liquid natural gas (rather than burning it off at the wellhead) altered the traditional dependency on oil.

Many oil-producing states began to violate the quota, eschewing long-range profit and power for short-range economic gains. In 1985, both Saudi Arabia and Kuwait recognized that OPEC was crumbling and recognized free-market forces in the setting of oil prices. The price dropped below $20 and American fields were no longer able to produce petroleum and maintain a profit. The result was a prolonged depression, especially felt in the older fields in Texas. Saudi Arabia decided to overproduce enough to keep the price at $18 a barrel—high enough for a good profit at the wellhead in the Gulf, but low enough to take American production out of the picture.

With the two-decade price fluctuation driving western economies crazy and the crumbling Soviet empire fearing its own Muslim revolts, it was little wonder that the West, with tacit Russian approval, moved through the auspices of the United Nations to destroy Iraq's invasion of the largest Gulf producer, Kuwait, in the Gulf War of the early 1990s. There was simply too much at stake to allow the domination of the oil market by any one man, especially one so untrustworthy and unreliable as Saddam Hussein. For his part, as Desert Storm rolled over the Iraqi armed forces, Hussein wreaked revenge by attempting to destroy the Kuwaiti oil fields. The plan looked successful until western technology proved up to the task of extinguishing the fires in months rather than the expected years. Western victory, led by the United States, has led to the cheapest fossil energy in years—a process that America has sought to guarantee by moving against the latest threat by Iraq in 1994 with great swiftness.

See also Aeronautics; Automobiles from Domestics to Imports; Automobiles in American Society; Oil Industry; Rockefeller, John D.; Trucking.

References Chester, Edward W., *United States Oil Policy and Diplomacy* (1983); Fanning, Leonard M., *Foreign Oil and the Free World* (1954); Ffooks, Roger, *Natural Gas by Sea* (1979); Ghosh, Arabinda, *OPEC, the Petroleum Industry, and United States Energy Policy* (1983); Ratcliffe, Mike, *Liquid Gold Ships* (1985); Stover, Paul (ed.), *Oil and Gas Dictionary* (1988).

Pacific Highway

One of the "named highways" popular in the teens and twenties of the twentieth century, the Pacific Highway was used by local chambers of commerce and tourism and the American Automobile Association to stimulate travel on the "good roads" and increase income in the towns and states through which they passed. The Pacific Highway is the old route through the Siskiyous Mountains behind the Coast Range. It began in Vancouver, British Columbia, and came south through Seattle, Tacoma, Olympia, and Vancouver, Washington, to Portland, Oregon. There it wound up at the Willamette River, crossed the mountains, and came down the Sacramento River to Oakland, roughly following modern Interstate 5. The Pacific Highway then followed the old Spanish mission route through San Jose (a branch went up to San Francisco), Paso Robles, San Luis Obispo, and Santa Barbara to Los Angeles and San Diego, a route that is U.S. Highway 101 today.

See also Roads and Highways, Colonial Times to World War I; Roads and Highways since World War I; Siskiyou Trail.

Reference Hart, Val, *The Story of American Roads* (1950).

Pacific Mail Steamship Company

In 1847, after the United States had taken most of northern Mexico in the Mexican-American War, Congress authorized a mail contract from New York to San Francisco by way of the Isthmus of Panamá. William Aspinwall secured the contract and established the Pacific Mail Steamship Company to carry it out. Providentially located to take advantage of the rush of the argonauts in 1849, Aspinwall began with $.5 million in 1848, which he parlayed into $20 million by the end of the Civil War. Among other assets was his part ownership in the Panama Railroad. Disliked by Californians and other westerners for glorying in his monopoly, poor service, and high prices, Aspinwall inspired them to seek new mail routes. Challenged by the overland transportation

of the mails in the late 1850s, particularly by the speed and reliability of the Pony Express, the company lost most of its remaining mail and express business when the transcontinental railroad was finished in 1868, but continued operations until 1925, when the Panama Canal made it superfluous.

See also Central Overland Route; Merchant Marine; Panama Canal.

Reference Harlow, Alvin F., *Old Waybills* (1934).

Pacific Railroad Act of 1862

A key piece of Republican legislation that had it roots deep in American history in such items as Alexander Hamilton's Economic Program, Albert Gallatin's proposals on public roads, John C. Calhoun's idea of the Bonus Bill, and Henry Clay's American System (President Abraham Lincoln was a great admirer of Clay), the Pacific Railroad Act authorized two companies to build and operate a transcontinental railroad between Sacramento, California, and the Missouri River (from what became Omaha, Nebraska). To assist the companies in their initial capitalization, Congress gave them a strip of land 200 feet wide for their right-of-way and ten alternate sections of public land per mile on each side of the roadbed. This grant was similar to the Illinois Central grant in 1850 in that the land went to the railroad proper. It differed from the others that had gone before 1850, where the grants had gone to the states through which the utility would pass. In addition, each company was to be paid from $16,000 a mile on the flats to $48,000 a mile in the mountains. All of these subsidies were to be repaid and were secured by 30-year bonds at 6 percent, giving the federal government a first mortgage on the project. The railroad was to serve the public interest and be available to the government for purposes of national defense. To keep any one group of greedy entrepreneurs from getting rich on this deal, each individual investor was limited to 200 shares of the companies involved.

The lobbyist for this legislation was

Theodore D. Judah, "Crazy Judah" to acquaintances in his adopted home state of California, an engineer who believed that the railroad could be built across the High Sierras if the money was right. But it could be even better. Collis P. Huntington of the Central Pacific, a hardware store owner who had fleeced miners for years and one of the men Judah had interested in the transcontinental railroad, knew how to grease the wheels of government. He went to Washington and got together with his counterparts in the Union Pacific to change the Pacific Railroad Act—to make it even more lucrative. It took $436,000 worth of bribes, entertainment, and such to get an 1864 amendment to the original act that doubled the land grants along the right-of-way, canceled the limit on individual stock ownership, and allowed the companies to issue first-mortgage bonds of their own, relegating the government's bonds to a second mortgage.

One congressman, evidently not in on the take or not receiving enough, called the new act "the most monstrous and flagrant attempt to overreach the Government and the people that can be found in all the legislative annals of the country!" The others pocketed their share and voted for the changes, which President Lincoln, old "Honest Abe" himself, signed without a whimper. Huntington called the measure "an extraordinarily generous act," and began diverting all the materials he could from the war effort to California and the railroad project. The Central Pacific was supposedly limited to the California–Nevada border, but that would not stop its backers from rushing out into the Great Basin and grabbing all they could before the Union Pacific could get there from the Great Plains. There was a lot of money—real and potential—to be made, and these men would not be found wanting.

The transcontinental railroad race was on, even though 70 percent of the grants went to the Union Pacific, the Southern Pacific, the Northern Pacific, and the Santa Fe. And regardless of the shenanigans with the peoples' money, history has borne out the necessity of the land grants to spur railroad development in order to "build ahead of demand." In the case of the seven transcontinental railroads (Central Pacific, Union Pacific, Texas & Pacific, Santa Fe, the Great Northern, the Northern Pacific, and the Canadian Pacific north of the border) that were built with land grants, five of them made a positive contribution to the settlement and industrialization of North America, and a sixth (the Great Northern) made a qualified contribution, its construction coming late in the nineteenth century. In the case of the Texas & Pacific, the cancellation of its grants through congressional and federal executive action cut much of its impact.

See also Crédit Mobilier of America; Dodge, Grenville Mellen; Railroads before and during the Civil War; Raidroads from Appomattox to Deregulation; Union Pacific Railroad.

References Carstenson, Vernon (ed.), *The Public Lands* (1962), 121–180; Haney, Lewis Henry, *A Congressional History of the Railways in the United States* (1910); Lyon, Peter, *To Hell in a Day Coach* (1968); Mercer, Lloyd J., *Railroads and Land Grant Policy* (1982); Mercer, Lloyd J., "Railroad Land Grants," in Keith L. Bryant, Jr. (ed.), *EABHB: Railroads in the Age of Regulation* (1988), 353; Russell, Robert R., *Improvement of Communication with the Pacific Coast as an Issue in American Politics* (1948); Summers, Mark W., *Railroads, Reconstruction, and the Gospel of Prosperity* (1984).

Pacific Railroad Survey (1853–1855)

Although many explorations of the West had taken place since Meriwether Lewis and William Clark first crossed the Great Divide to the Pacific and opened up the Louisiana Purchase, not until after the Mexican Cession did the first real systematic official explorations occur. Their purpose was the same as those that preceded them—to find a practicable commercial route to the western ocean. It was little more than the same quest that drove Christopher Columbus and others since (i.e., to find the short route to Asia). In British colonial terms, it was the continuing search for the Northwest Passage, this time by land across the Great Plains, that vast treeless void people of the time called the Great American Desert, despite the fact that many Native American tribes had made this country their home for centuries.

The search for a quick route to the Pacific coast was made imperative by two factors. First, there was the Oregon Fever of the 1840s that culminated in American conquest of the New Northwest, and the Gold Fever that led to the fantastic burgeoning of settlement in California. Second, there was the haunting American past revealed in the machinations of Aaron Burr and General James Wilkinson; history showed that western territories not readily provided with transportation facilities and defense installations led to economic loss, political dissatisfaction, and possible secession, with the West falling victim to the grandiose dreams of would-be emperors.

Until the American victory in the war with Mexico, railroads were not technically capable of answering national transportation needs over the vast distances that were the trans-Mississippi West. But led by the propagandist Asa Whitney, who at his own expense clamored for rail expansion westward from Lake Michigan to Oregon, the project approached feasibility. Whitney asked for a strip of land 60 miles wide along his proposed route. He would pay for the allotment at 10 cents per acre. Whitney would build ten miles of track. If his work were acceptable, the government would reimburse him with half of the land for that strip, which he could sell for cash, encouraging settlement of the rail zone by future customers. The process would continue to Oregon, ten miles at a time. When he reached the Great American Desert, considered unsuitable for settlement, the government would sell its half of the tracts and apply the money to Whitney's construction, enabling the project to continue. He estimated the total cost to be $68.4 million.

Rail advocates like Whitney came to dominate the American political scene by 1850. Even John C. Calhoun, opponent of so much the government proposed to do, favored rails west—from South Carolina. He did much to push rail expansion in the South to put it in a favorable position as the eastern terminus of the Pacific route. *De Bow's Commercial Review*, a New Orleans publication of influence, estimated that a rail line west to California from Louisiana would comprise 1,491 miles at a cost of $22 million. Note how much cheaper than Whitney's route this estimate was. And therein lay the crux of the issue. No matter where the rails began, the country at that moment could afford only one concentrated, massive effort. In the America of 1850, this meant that the issue would become part of the North–South debate. Nothing could be more pernicious than that.

The first shot in the debate came from an important voice, Senator Thomas Hart Benton of Missouri. Naturally, Benton saw both the far north plans of Whitney and the far south proposal of Calhoun and De Bow as too extreme. He favored a route through the center of the nation out of St. Louis or Independence—anywhere in Missouri. He called it, in that wonderful self-promoting manner incumbent to all powerful politicians, the National Central Highway. The route he favored ran out from Independence along the Kansas River to the headwaters of the Rio Grande, across Utah Pass to the Great Basin and the Sierra Nevada, coming out at San Francisco. Naturally, Benton knew of this route based on the explorations of his bombastic son-in-law, John Charles Frémont. It would be financed by the sale of public lands, or by loans in anticipation of those sales.

But the survey was not to be a scientific endeavor devoid of politics. Immediately, various communities held commercial conventions, trying to stack the deck ahead of time. St. Louis endorsed Benton's basic idea of the National Central Highway, but suggested that the route follow the California Trail through South Pass. Benton presided, but could not sway the delegates' common-sense route selection with the exploits of Frémont in the Rockies. Memphis decried the idea of not using the natural advantages of the all-weather route along what would become the Butterfield Route out of Memphis through Arkansas and Texas in a wide loop to El Paso, and then west along the Gila Trail to southern California and up the great inland valley to San Francisco. Much of this route had already been surveyed by W. H. Slidell and Captain Randolph B. Marcy. The boundary commission that drew the international line with Mexico also noted the feasibility of this route. Possible starting points included Memphis, Vicksburg, and St. Louis.

Unfortunately for the cause of the central route, Benton had just retired from the Senate. This left leadership of the railroad debate in the hands of Senators William M. Gwinn of California (an open advocate of the South), Thomas J. Rusk of Texas, Solon Borland of Arkansas, and John Bell of Tennessee. That deck of cards was getting restacked again, Southern style. Benton's concern for a central route was taken up by Senator Stephen A. Douglas of Illinois. But as a Democrat and future presidential contender, Douglas knew that he had to appease the South to win, be it railroad route or higher office. The presidential election of 1848 demonstrated that Southerners would not stand by the Democrats for the mere sake of party. There were also principles and deep sectional interests involved.

Maybe Douglas feared what the surveys would find—a clear all-weather route from the South as the best route west. In any case, he had to overcome Southern advantages in geography with ones of westward movement. History had shown that Northerners moved west more rapidly and in denser population than Southerners. Why not create territorial governments to lure people west. There was a geographical advantage to the area west of Missouri—it was good farmland. The arid Mexican Cession would not be settled for decades, but people were already in Kansas. So Douglas introduced the Kansas-Nebraska Bill. The implication from the two territories was that Southerners would get Kansas and Northerners would settle in Nebraska. But there was more. Both territories lay above the southern border of Missouri. That 36° 30′ line had been the centerpiece of the 1820 Missouri Compromise—no slavery in the territories above it was countenanced. Slavery had to go west south of the line, into what is

today New Mexico and Arizona. But this was not plantation country. Kansas was, or at least that was what people thought.

So Douglas, in the name of American expansion and to populate the central route, thus making it more feasible for the new rail transportation revolution, developed a scheme to get around the Missouri Compromise without actually giving Southerners anything but constitutional theory. Douglas knew that Northern men would rush to Kansas. Given the natural flow of things, there was a good chance that Kansas would never be pro-slave or when the time came even elect senators and congressmen as pro-Southern as Gwinn in California. It would become a Free-Soil territory by the consequences of history—free farmers historically moved west faster than slaveholders.

His idea was to repeal the Missouri Compromise and replace it with a notion called Popular Sovereignty. Now, something similar had been tried before in 1848. Named Squatter Sovereignty, it had been the central idea of the defeated Democrat presidential candidate, Lewis Cass. Cass reasoned much the same as Douglas. The government would form a territory and let the people living there decide the issue of slavery. What could be more fair? What could be more democratic? The territorial legislature would take a simple vote and the question would be decided. It would end the divisive debate in Congress and allow it to get along with more important issues—like railroad subsidies. But Cass lost the election. He had based his plan on what Southerners saw as faulty constitutional reasoning. Douglas sought to reason more correctly.

Southerners maintained that an issue like slavery could not be decided except by the people acting in a sovereign capacity. A territorial legislature was the creation of Congress, and hence not sovereign. Much better, they reasoned, to have the vote taken during the final stage of territorial development as defined in the Land Ordinance of 1786—when the people gathered as a sovereign body in a constitutional convention draw up a proposed organic law as the territory seeks statehood. Besides this would al-

low Southerners to catch up with their settlement and have a fairer shot at introducing
a pro-slave constitution. They would have
gotten away with it in Illinois in 1818, had
not the Northwest Ordinance reserved the
area as Free Soil in 1787. Douglas gave the
South its constitutional victory, believing
that free institutions would win the move
west. But he did not tell the South about his
ace-in-the-hole.

Northern antislavery forces, however,
understood the loophole Douglas had
placed in the law. They flooded Kansas with
Free-Soil settlers. Southerners cried foul.
This was not the usual pattern of settlement.
Missouri residents, slaveholders by sympathy, crossed the border to drive the Free-
Soilers out. They had to. Douglas was right.
The North would win the race for Kansas.
The result was a miniature pre–Civil War
with atrocities on both sides that had to be
put down by the army. In the end, Kansas
would be a free state in 1861 after the South
left the Union, but it did little for Douglas'
political ambitions (another Illinoisan,
Abraham Lincoln, would gain the 1860
prize by forcing Douglas to admit the duplicity of his scheme in the Lincoln-
Douglas Debates of 1858) and it sure distracted the nation from building railroads
for a while.

Meanwhile, before the politicians and
their supporters went nuts over territorial
government and such, Congress put off any
decision on the rails west. It decided it did
not have enough information to make a wise
decision (that is, votes were lacking on all
choices). So it temporized and ordered a
study. Under orders from the president, the
War Department was to make four surveys
of probable railroad routes to the Pacific:
along the rough lines of the thirty-second
parallel (later roughly the Southern Pacific–
Texas Pacific lines), the thirty-fifth (the
Atchison, Topeka, and Santa Fe lines), the
thirty-eighth (the Rio Grande route), and
the forty-seventh parallels (the Northern
Pacific–Great Northern routes). This actually left out the well-used Central Overland
Trail to California and Oregon, but private
enterprise and common usage would outdo

government surveys in the end, leading to
its selection for the Union Pacific–Central
Pacific line.

The southern thirty-second parallel
route was surveyed in several sections. The
War Department deemed that an earlier
exploration by Lieutenant Colonel William
H. Emory from the Colorado River to San
Diego would suffice for that part of the job.
Lieutenant John G. Parke would handle the
section from the Colorado at Fort Yuma to
the Rio Grande near present-day Las Cruces by way of the Gila River, the Pima
Villages, and Tucson in Arizona. He would
duplicate some of the work of the earlier
boundary commission. Parke found the terrain would be easily traversed by a railroad
but was short of water. Upon reaching Fort
Fillmore on the Rio Grande, Parke found
that Lieutenant John Pope had taken up the
trek to the east across the *Llamo Estacado*, or
"Staked Plains"(the high plains of Texas
that today is the area around Amarillo, Lub-
bock, and the Panhandle) and Texas. So
Parke retraced his steps the following year,
exploring several alternative routes, particularly up the San Pedro River rather than the
Santa Cruz.

Pope meanwhile explored west Texas
carefully. He had several visits from Lipan
Apaches, Comanches, and Kiowas, but all
turned out friendly. Pope sent off several
smaller parties from the main group and
paid special attention to the feasibility of
boring artesian wells for a water supply. He
continued across northern Texas to the Red
River, where he stopped at a place northeast
of Gainesville. Like Parke, he found the
whole route easily adapted to railroad construction. As Douglas and other promoters
of different routes had feared, the Southern
run looked very good—too good.

At the same time Parke and Pope explored the southern route, Lieutenant
Amiel Whipple received the assignment to
inspect the possibilities from Fort Smith,
Arkansas, to Los Angeles by way of Albuquerque along the thirty-fifth parallel. Whipple's party went out the Canadian River,
crossed the upper Pecos, and arrived in Albuquerque after initial delays in securing his

surveying equipment. He, too, sent out smaller parties to check out various side routes. He found the Indians, especially in New Mexico, to be friendly and interested in selling food to the whites. Crossing northern Arizona, Whipple determined that the rails should stay south of the San Francisco Peaks, a recommendation followed decades later when the rails were laid. Part of this route had been looked at by a party under Captain Lorenzo Sitgreaves two years earlier.

Travel was rough, and Whipple eventually had to abandon all of his wagons. He reached the Colorado at the mouth of the Bill Williams River and explored the various side canyons, looking for a better route. He crossed the river near modern Needles, California, and headed northwest to the Mormon Road (the Old Spanish Trail). He ascended Cajón Pass and passed through the Mormon settlements near San Bernardino, arriving in Los Angeles. His trip between the Rio Grande and the Colorado opened up much new territory and the whole route was practicable for railroading, the only real problem being the mountains in Arizona, all of which had negotiable passes.

Like Whipple's route, the exploration along the thirty-eighth parallel, Benton's suggested National Central Highway, would cover much new ground. Its survey was led by Captain John W. Gunnison, considered somewhat of a Gentile expert on Mormon settlement in Utah, about which he had written based on previous service there. Gunnison's party went west from Fort Leavenworth, down the Santa Fe Trail to the Kansas River, west to the Smoky Hill and dropping south from it to the Great Bend of the Arkansas, which he followed past Bent's New Fort to the Rockies. Crossing the headwaters of the Rio Grande, he traversed through central Colorado by way of the river valley and later town site now named for him, across the Grand and the Green Rivers, and on through the mountains by the Old Spanish Trail to Fillmore, Utah.

As with the other parties, Gunnison sent out many smaller groups on ancillary explorations parallel to his route. Exploring around Sevier Lake, Paiutes attacked Gunnison's party, killing the captain. The men claimed that the Mormons had instigated the assault, but Lieutenant Edward G. Beckwith, now in command, did not. He worked with Brigham Young to obtain the return of the surveying instruments lost in the fight and continued north. The party wintered near Salt Lake City and examined various canyons into the Fort Bridger area for rail possibilities. The following year, Beckwith led them out across the Great Basin, eventually intersecting the Hastings Cutoff of the California Trail, crossed the Sierra Nevada and wound up near modern Redding, California, in the Sacramento Valley. Beckwith found the Great Basin easy to negotiate for a railroad, the only obstacles being the snow in the mountains and the grades through the passes.

The final exploration came under the command of the recently appointed governor of Washington Territory, Isaac I. Stevens, along the forty-seventh parallel. This route approximated that publicized by Asa Whitney a decade before. Stevens started from Fort Snelling, near St. Paul, Minnesota, taking an almost direct tack across the Red River of the North to Fort Union at the point where the Yellowstone flows into the Missouri. Subordinates took numerous side trips to expand the scope of the survey. He then traveled to Fort Benton on the upper Missouri, using the Milk River route through modern Havre, Montana.

At Fort Benton Stevens treated with the Blackfeet and sent out numerous side parties to explore the surrounding passes. He also met the party coming eastward from Fort Walla Walla under Lieutenant Rufus Saxton. Stevens continued his trip the following year, meeting another party that had been examining the passes in the Cascades under Captain George B. McClellen, and circling south by way of Walla Walla and the Columbia River gorge, arriving at Olympia on Puget Sound. He was among the more active in his dispatch of side scouts who thoroughly explored the gaps in the northern Rockies. Stevens was responsible for the construction of the Mullan Road to Montana, and became an active advocate of a Pacific railroad until his death as a Union general at the Battle of Chantilly, Virginia, in 1862.

The reports of the explorers went to the secretary of war, Jefferson Davis of Mississippi. Davis perused them and recommended the southern route as the shortest and least expensive path by which to build a railroad to California. He did try to give all routes a fair hearing, spending twice as much time on the northernmost as the southern ones, but the partisanship of the times overwhelmed reason. There was little chance that the rails would go west until the sectional discord had been solved. But that did not prevent men from trying to prove their choice was the better. The Butterfield Overland Stage mail contract was devised to show that the Gila River Trail was a safe, all-weather route; the Pony Express did the same for the Central Overland Route. But with the secession of the South in 1860–1861, the whole question became moot. The transcontinental railroad would be built by the victorious Union and the Republican Party, and they took the southernmost of the routes that all knew so well—the Central Overland became the Union Pacific, with a charter granted in 1862, in the midst of the greatest war Americans ever fought.

See also Butterfield Trail; Central Overland Route; Mullan Road; Pony Express.

References Albright, George L., *Official Explorations* (1921); Haney, Lewis Henry, *A Congressional History of the Railways in the United States* (1910); Russell, Robert R., *Improvement of Communication with the Pacific Coast as an Issue in American Politics* (1948).

Pacific Union Express Company
Organized by stockholders of the Central Pacific Railroad when Wells Fargo stupidly refused to bid for rail express service between Sacramento and Salt Lake City, the Pacific Union Express Company challenged its competitor at every point along the Central Overland Route, especially in the Nevada silver fields. Since the railroad had a ten-year contract with Pacific Union, Wells Fargo was literally cut off from transcontinental rail sources for trade. Wells Fargo had assumed that their Overland Stage Company could compete for service. They nearly went broke in the process. With the situation deteriorating rapidly, Wells Fargo had to buy out Pacific Union. Although Wells Fargo sought unsuccessfully to hide the embarrassing facts from the public, it cost the company nearly a third of its stock to do the job in 1868. The whole fiasco demonstrated that the express companies could ignore the new rail transportation technology only at their own peril.

See also Adams Express Company; American Express Company; American Railway Express Company; Central Overland California & Pike's Peak Express Company; Harnden & Company Express; Leavenworth & Pike's Peak Express Company; Russell, Majors & Waddell Company; United States Express Company; Wells Fargo & Company.

Reference Harlow, Alvin F., *Old Waybills* (1934).

Pacific Wagon Road Office
In 1857, Secretary of the Interior Jacob Thompson created the Pacific Wagon Road Office to coordinate all reports, surveys, and road building in the West. Politically, it marked the rise of Southerners (Thompson was a Mississippian, John Floyd at the War Department was a Virginian, and Howell Cobb at the Treasury was a Georgian) to the controlling positions on the several road projects and most of the patronage appointments elsewhere, just one of the myriad small but important details of government the election of Abraham Lincoln threatened to change in 1860. An argument could be made that many moderate Southerners opposed Lincoln's rise to the presidency because it challenged not only their influence in one office but in the entire executive department. They feared they would be cut out entirely from day-to-day governmental operations. Hence, secession was the belated recognition of an already established fact.

The problem of the federal financing of road projects had a long history under the

Constitution of 1789. Alexander Hamilton suggested it as an important economic activity as a part of his Report on Finances. Thomas Jefferson and James Madison argued that such projects were outside the scope of federal power as envisioned by the Founding Fathers. Nowhere in the Constitution did it specifically state that such things could be within the purvey of a central government. But after the Whiskey Rebellion in the early 1790s and various other western secession schemes not fully understood even today, reality demanded that something be done to join the West more firmly to the East.

The man who developed the constitutional rationale to accomplish this was Jefferson's secretary of the treasury, Albert Gallatin. He suggested that a percentage of the receipts from the sale of public lands within the states involved be diverted to building a National Road. Later, John C. Calhoun proposed that the "bonus" paid by the chartering of the Second U.S. Bank go to road building. But this concept received a presidential veto, both James Madison and James Monroe having doubts as to the government's role under the Constitution as written. With no amendment forthcoming, the problem continued. Although John Quincy Adams was more amenable to federal projects, Andrew Jackson issued the Maysville Road Veto, which reserved federal action only for projects of truly national scope and benefit.

But Jackson's stand was more show than substance. Even after the Maysville Road Veto, Jackson, and all of the succeeding presidents down to the Civil War, continued to spend money on roads in the West. Die-hard state's righters were given the nearly completed National Road as a sop to their point of view, but were ignored when they protested federally financed road building in the western territories. A workable majority of congressmen, north and south, accepted the notion that such projects were constitutional under the clause providing for military and post roads. And no western politician worth his salt refused to ask for such aid.

In reality there was only one technically qualified group of men in America who could carry out such projects, the Army Corps of Engineers. Founded in 1802, the corps was joined by another army department, the Topographical Engineers, in 1813. Their duties were conflicting until Secretary of War Joel Poinsett restricted the Corps of Engineers to military fortifications and the Topographical Engineers to civil works—roads, harbors, and rivers. Hence, the only road that the Corps of Engineers worked upon was the western end of the National Road, the eastern or Cumberland Road section being handled exclusively by civilian contractors. But the only place to find adequate capital to finance any such project was in the Congress.

Admittedly, there were some mighty doubtful military roads built under the constitutional sanctions available, but Congress made the most of them. By the time of the Mexican War, military roads had been constructed west of the Mississippi, most notable being the one from Fort Towson in the Indian Territories to Fort Laramie on the Great Plains. Congress winked openly to the fact that the real users of military roads were civilians interested in settling in the areas through which the pathways passed. As in the twentieth century, Congress appropriated the funds and made the president and his executive cabinet members responsible for their proper use. This gave great patronage to department heads in this era of the "spoils system." Political loyalty was often more important than engineering capability, although most surveys were militarily supervised. This was especially true after the absorption of Texas, Oregon, and the Mexican Cession into the Union in 1848.

The admission of California to statehood in 1850 put immediate pressure on the various presidential administrations to connect the far-flung western empire to the rest of the nation through roads, then telegraphs and railroads. Californians suggested that the Central Overland Route be used, a proposal that Northerners cheered. But the Southern-dominated Democratic administrations of Franklin Pierce and James Buchanan favored the use of the old Gila Trail. Politically wise Californians said they really would like three routes, the two mentioned above (from St. Louis and New Orleans, respectively) and a third from Minnesota to South Pass. To make the patronage system function at its political best, the whole project was transferred from the stuffy old soldiers of the War Department to the results-oriented political appointees (one senator called them "practical men") of the new Interior Department. Numerous regional commercial conventions and lesser gatherings each petitioned Congress on behalf of their favored route. Many passed the hat to get the ball rolling in their behalf.

Congressmen and delegates did their best to carry out these mandates. But the North–South quarrel stalled everything. Finally, compromise was achieved by approving every route conceivable and calling upon the Topographical Engineers to survey them. Even then, improvements were to be restricted to only those sections of roadway that needed them most. To facilitate the work, Secretary Thompson set up a subordinate entity, the Pacific Roads Office, to supervise the work. The problem was that the real administrative experience lay with the Topographical Engineers, and the political hacks who oversaw the various road projects could not account properly for the moneys spent and tended to be jealous of the more knowledgeable engineers under them. They also underestimated the immense logistical problems of working on the Great Plains, the Great Basin, the Rocky Mountains, and the Sonoran Desert.

The result was that much of the work had to be delegated or assumed by the army to get it done. The Pacific Roads Office, then, was a stopgap measure designed to placate westerners and Mississippi Valley residents, who wanted action on roads, by skirting the slavery issue and delegating all power to the Department of the Interior. It asserted the continuing desire of Congress to finance roads in the West by shifting the responsibility from military to civilian control. But Congress failed to consider whether the ci-

vilian arm had the necessary experience to supervise such a program outside political influence, as had the army. The Civil War put an end to the problem. From there on out, federal aid was to be an important platform of Republican politicians, but emphasis shifted from road building to the new technology of railroads at the expense of everything else.

See also Butterfield Trail; Central Overland Route; Pacific Railroad Survey.

Reference Jackson, W. Turrentine, *Wagon Roads West* (1952).

Page, Logan Waller (1870–1918)

The first professional road engineer to hold the positions of the head of the Office of Public Roads and the later Office of Public Roads and Rural Engineering, Logan Waller Page was instrumental in getting the first federal highway aid package through Congress and managing the roads to enhance the American war effort in the Great War.

See also Office of Public Roads; Office of Public Roads and Rural Engineering; Roads and Highways, Colonial Times to World War I.

Reference U.S. Department of Transportation, Federal Highway Administration, *America's Highways* (1976).

Pan American Airways (PAA)

As the U.S. government began to let airmail contracts in the mid-1920s, three companies vied for the route from Miami to Havana, Cuba. Government administrators feared that the American companies would in effect kill each other off, leaving the field open for single national companies from Germany and France that might threaten the Panama Canal. So the government forced the American entities to merge as one and Juan Trippe, who already held the exclusive Cuban landing rights by prior negotiation, became the president of the new Pan American Airways. Trippe was an excellent lobbyist both at home and abroad. Under his tutelage PAA spread its tentacles throughout the Caribbean islands, Mexico, and Central America. Although he spoke no Spanish (despite the sound of his name) and disliked most Latin Americans, Trippe knew when to keep his mouth shut and when to speak. His excellent diplomacy opened up new markets in South America at a time when "Yanqui" imperialism was especially hated, and stymied German and French interests. He also managed to stop his only American competition, the New York, Rio, Buenos Aires line (NYRB). Because of his congressional contacts, Trippe managed to hold up his rival's government subsidy until the NYRB collapsed and PAA could take over. Throughout this period until the end of World War II, Trippe financed PAA through his own contacts and personal friends.

Originally, Trippe flew Fokker trimotors over his empire, but they were underpowered and needed loading facilities that many Latin American countries lacked and could ill-afford to build. So Trippe shifted PAA's interest over to flying boats that could land in existing harbors and use steamship services. He was not loyal to any one maker. He dropped Sikorsky's S-42, which had produced his Caribbean flying boats, for Glenn Martin, whose M-130 was dubbed the *China Clipper*, and flew new routes across the Pacific via Hawaii, Midway, and Wake Island to the Chinese mainland. When Trippe expanded his routes across the Atlantic, using a route through the Azores recommended by Charles Lindbergh, he dropped Martin for Boeing's new 314 flying boat, which Trippe nicknamed the *Yankee Clipper*. It boasted service that would rival any first-class ocean liner or German Zeppelin airship. Many of Trippe's routes received secret support from the American armed forces to counter Japanese moves in the Pacific and Nazi influences in Latin America. In the latter instance, Trippe's diplomacy in achieving flying rights paved the way for World War II cooperation.

The end of World War II brought new challenges to PAA. No longer did the U.S. government support a single overseas airline. Many of PAA's routes received competitors. Trippe tried to get domestic rights in exchange, but failed as the Harry Truman administration sought to strengthen smaller carriers. The 1950s saw Trippe working with Douglas and Boeing to produce the first jet airliners. The company also diversified and went into defense contracts in missile tracking, nuclear testing in Nevada, and investing in French jet manufacture and the largest hotel chain in the world, all run through the largest office building in New York City. As the 1970s approached, Pan Am led the way in the wide-body and jumbo-jet wars, converting to the DC-10 and Boeing 747.

But the Arab oil embargo caught PAA heavily in debt with a management team (since Trippe had retired in 1968) that could not agree on how to solve problems. With deregulation, PAA merged with National Airlines to get the domestic base it had always wanted. Unfortunately the merger cost more than it was worth. National had extensive Lockheed equipment that was not compatible with PAA's Boeing fleet, and the large debt forced Pan Am, in a self-destructing process, to sell off many of its oldest and most profitable overseas routes for ready cash. The airline was also held negligent in the 1988 terrorist bombing of its Flight 103 over Lockerbie, Scotland, another drain on its cash flow. With the addition of its already high fixed-labor and equipment costs, it was not hard for the Persian Gulf War and the fuel crisis it brought on to destroy PAA in 1991. The collapse lingered on in the courts, with Pan Am losing a case in December 1994 in which the beleaguered company blamed its fall on the refusal of competing Delta Airlines to come through on a planned financial bailout.

See also Aeronautics; Lindbergh, Charles A.; Trippe, Juan Terry.

References Davies, R. E. G., *Pan Am* (1987); Newton, Wesley P., "Pan American Airways," in William M. Leary (ed.), *Encyclopedia of American Business History and Biography* (1992), 343–349; O'Neill, Ralph A., *A Dream of Eagles* (1973).

Pan American Highway

Since the days when John Quincy Adams was president, Latin American nations and the United States and Canada have had so-

Construction of the international Pan American Highway began during World War II. Today, the highway connects South and Central American cities with U.S. and Canadian highways.

called Pan American congresses. At Rio de Janeiro in 1929, after several earlier meetings in previous years, the various nations worked out an international road plan that would connect them all together, north to south, and named the project the Pan American Highway, once the dream of sixteenth-century Spanish King Charles V. Each nation was to build its own road and by agreement they were to meet their neighbors' roads at a prearranged border point. It was not a new concept. At the height of railroad fever in the United States during the 1880s, some had suggested a Pan American Railroad. But the time was not right. Nor was it especially right in the early twentieth century. The Pan American Highway started slowly. By the time of World War II, about 1,000 miles of paved road and 600 miles of all-weather road existed from Laredo, Texas, to Panama City, but not all of it was continuous. The Japanese attack on Pearl Harbor changed all

that. The Panama Canal assumed a vital importance in the United States' war plans, and the need for a road across Central America and Mexico received new interest.

With the exception of Mexico ("poor Mexico: so far from God, so close to the United States," goes the old saw), the Central American nations accepted American appropriations (on a two-to-one basis with the United States paying the larger share) and technical assistance and began building the Pan Am Highway in earnest. Mexico did all the work within its boundaries on its own. Panamá paid the difference necessary to make its section concrete. U.S. engineers faced many of the same problems that existed in building the Alaska Highway at the same time—most of them related to weather, equipment maintenance, and the health of the crews. The jungle threw some massive problems in the road builders' way: massive trees that, as a rule, had to have their stumps blown out by as many pounds of dynamite as they were tall; wild animals that most men have never dreamed of threatened the unwary, like packs of wild boars that actually attacked and devoured their victims, clothes and all; swamps full of tropical dangers, especially malaria, yellow fever, and poisonous snakes; men and domestic animals driven insane by droves of insects; rain that fell ten months of the year; and Costa Rican mountain passes that climbed 11,000 feet in a matter of miles to cross the Continental Divide. Given all these obstacles, paving of the Central American section was completed only in 1973.

Nonetheless, by the 1990s the Pan Am has been finished from Fairbanks, Alaska, in the north, through Edmonton, Alberta, and Denver, Colorado, to Laredo, Texas, and south through every capital in every nation through which it passes—Mexico City, Guatemala City, San Salvador, San José, Panama City, Bogotá (with a branch coming in from Caracas), Quito, Lima (with a branch going south to Santiago de Chile), La Paz, and Buenos Aires (other branches go to Asunción, Montevideo, and Rio de Janeiro). All that remains to be built of its 30,000 miles is a treacherous piece of jungle between Panama City and Colombia, the Darien Gap. Whether it will ever be built is a debatable question. Already the route has been moved from the Pacific coastal mountains to the junglelike Caribbean side of the isthmus. Not only do the governments concerned have many more important domestic issues to face, but environmental and social concerns that previous generations never thought of are coming to the fore. These include the diminishing of the rain forests, the actual decline in rainfall, the extinction of flora and fauna, drug trafficking, and Indian civil and property rights. In 1994, Colombia had begun an environmental impact statement for the Interamerican Development Bank, but the actual date of any construction remains problematic.

Although the Darien Gap still looms wide, others have seen the Pan American Highway and the Alaska Highway as roads of great potential. Since the signing of the North American Free Trade Agreement, and the desire of many South American and Central American nations to climb on board, and the successful opening of the British-French "Chunnel" under the English Channel, American engineers have even toyed with the idea of linking Asia and North America by road via a tunnel under the Bering Strait. One wonders if the adverse winters of Siberia and Alaska might not dictate its success or failure, but the building of such a route is definitely within the engineering technology of today, as is the completion of the Darien Gap.

See also Alaska Highway; Roads and Highways since World War I.

References Hart, Val, *The Story of American Roads* (1950); Hindley, Geoffrey, *A History of Roads* (1971); U.S. Department of Transportation, Federal Highway Administration, *America's Highways* (1976).

Panama Canal

The string of events that led to the construction of the Panama Canal had its origins not only in the American imperialistic movement of the late nineteenth century, but also in the history of Panamá itself. Panamá had long been tied to the nation of Colombia. In 1518, King Charles V of Spain gave primary administration of the isthmus to the viceroyalty of New Granada at Bogotá. The province declared its independence from Spain in 1821 and joined Simón Bolívar's Gran Colombia (including present-day Equador, Colombia, and Venezuela). But the dissolution of Bolívar's dream for a United States of South America led Panamanians to consider secession from the newly formed state of New Granada (present-day Colombia and Panamá). They acted on these notions in 1830, 1831, 1845, 1895, and 1898, but failed to achieve separation. By the end of the century, New Granada had been further centralized and strengthened as the Republic of Colombia, and was determined to reassert vigorously its claim to the isthmus.

Meanwhile, the United States has had its own interest in the isthmus, much of it originally stimulated by the need of a route to the California goldfields. The forty-niners knew that the fastest path to West Coast riches lay by utilizing the sea. But the 8,000-mile trip around Cape Horn was fraught with delays and danger. If one cut across the isthmus at Panamá, much time could be saved. But the terrors of tropical disease and banditry loomed large. In an attempt to lessen these dangers, the United States made a treaty with New Granada granting American travelers access to the shortcut and guaranteeing Colombian sovereignty. Under this agreement, an American company constructed the Panama Railroad to ease passage (1850–1855) and built the terminal of Colón on the Atlantic side.

By the end of the Spanish-American War in 1899, it was obvious to Americans that if they wished to have the defensive capability of a two-ocean navy (and they did), it would be necessary to transfer ships from coast to coast with much greater speed than that displayed by the battleship USS *Oregon*. Straining to join the Atlantic fleet from Puget Sound in time to assist in the Cuban Campaign, the *Oregon* had spent 68 days at sea rounding Cape Horn. One of those who noticed was a former assistant secretary of the navy, Rough Rider, and vice-president of the United States, Theodore Roosevelt.

Assuming the presidency upon William McKinley's assassination, Roosevelt moved to assure his dream of an isthmian canal. It was not an idea unique to Roosevelt and his henchmen. A canal had first been proposed in 1534 by Alvaro de Saavedra, a follower of Hernan Cortés, conqueror of Mexico. The Spanish considered four routes, and they remained the favored ones to the end: Darien, Nicaragua, Tehuántepec, and Panamá. These routes and five others were discussed by the famous German explorer Alexander von Humboldt at the end of the eighteenth century. At the Pan American Conference in 1825, Henry Clay wowed the audience with his vision of a canal, and a year later, Aaron H. Palmer of New York actually contracted with the Central American Republic to construct one. But technology was not yet sophisticated enough to handle the job, and Congress refused President John Adams' entreaties to act.

In 1850, Great Britain and the United States signed the Clayton-Bulwer Treaty in which both sides agreed not to proceed on a canal project without the approval and participation of the other. Unofficial American freebooters, known as *filibusteros*, made numerous attempts to seize parts of Central America for fame and profit in the 1850s, but all came to naught. Further U.S. concern with Panamá was delayed by the festering slavery issue and Civil War (during which President Abraham Lincoln considered settling freed slaves there to guarantee future U.S. interests); the initiative passed to the preeminent canal diggers of their day, the French.

In 1879, Count Ferdinand de Lesseps, builder of the Suez Canal, purchased all outstanding concessions and organized the Compagnie Universel du Canal Interoceanique de Panamá. He proposed to build a sea level canal 30 feet deep, 72 feet wide at the bottom, and about 48 miles long, using his Egyptian experience. The whole world endorsed the project, and all expected that the great de Lesseps would succeed. But Panamá was not the Egyptian desert. It was a jungle with an eight-month rainy season that rendered it swampy and overrun with insects, poisonous snakes, and tropical diseases. Moreover, the earth was highly unstable and prone to landslides when ditched. For nine years de Lesseps and the French tried to conquer the isthmus in vain. Ignoring the latest scientific medical knowledge, the French operated on the outdated notion that tropical maladies were a product of swamp gasses, ignoring the mosquitoes that carried the sicknesses. It cost the French company $266 million, thousands of lives (75 percent of those who entered hospitals died), and a scandal in stock purchases that nearly destroyed the French government. De Lesseps was a great promoter, but not much of an engineer. He went home in disgrace.

By now, the Americans were interested in assuming the canal project. Many preferred the competing Nicaraguan route, but after an acrimonious debate, Congress passed the Spooner Act (1902), authorizing the purchase of the French effort for $40 million, provided that the Panama Railroad was included and Colombia signed a satisfactory treaty. Already, Secretary of State John Hay had negotiated with Britain the Second Hay-Pauncefote Treaty (the first was rejected as too pro-British in not allowing the United States to defend the ditch adequately), which gave America the right to go on alone, provided the United States guaranteed the canal's international access. Hay then negotiated an agreement with Colombia, the Hay-Herrán Convention, granting the United States sole ownership and management of the canal; rights to the Panama Railroad; and the right to construct the canal, harbors, and two free ports, to maintain hospitals and sanitation facilities, and to install a waterworks and sewerage plant in Panama City and Colón. In exchange, the United States agreed to the canal's neutrality (but received the right to defend the canal and station troops there), did not abrogate Colombia's sovereignty in the Canal Zone, and assumed a 100-year lease with annual payments on a strip 10 kilometers wide across the isthmus.

The Hay-Herrán Convention was immediately ratified by the U.S. Congress. But to everyone's surprise (at least in the United States), it was rejected by the Colombian Congress. Having just emerged from a costly civil war and anxious to embarrass the nation's current president, it did not take kindly to the ease with which his emissary, Tomás Herrán (the third of Colombian negotiators), gave away Colombian territory without securing any of the $40 million slush fund paid to the defunct French company. But that did not stop the United States. Acutely aware that the people in the Province of Panamá were incensed at Colombian rejection of their economic future and desirous of ridding themselves of the warring factions in Bogotá, Roosevelt backed another isthmian revolt against Colombian "tyranny," dismissing the Colombian government as "inefficient bandits" and "homicidal corruptionists." Operating in this state of mind, Roosevelt sent the USS *Nashville* and a few support ships to intercept the Colombian army's counterinsur-

gency effort. In a matter of days, Philippe Bunau-Varilla, formerly of de Lessep's old canal company and a friend of powerful Ohio Republican politician Mark Hanna, had communicated with the rebels, drawn up a constitution, designed a national flag, and become the new Republic of Panamá's representative in Washington. He then signed the Hay–Bunau-Varilla Treaty (1904), almost a duplicate of the Hay-Herrán Convention, except that Panamá was now the other party and the United States got more rights to interfere domestically in the new republic. And of course Bunau-Varilla, who resigned his diplomatic post after concluding the pact, and his American and Panamanian friends wound up with a large portion of the $40 million.

The United States took control of the Canal Zone on 4 May 1904, and construction began. The chief engineer was John F. Stevens, builder of the Great Northern Railroad over the Rocky Mountains. In league with Dr. William C. Gorgas, his first step in construction was to control the insect population and eradicate most of the diseases plaguing the zone. Gorgas attacked the problem by draining the swamps and putting oil over the insect breeding places. He also cleaned up the physical plant and provided fresh, clean water and sewerage systems. The result was 12,000 fewer sick per day than the French sustained, most of whom recovered to work again. The total human loss on the U.S. project over ten years was 6,630 men, and the canal was completed ahead of schedule. Gorgas estimated that vigorous sanitation measures had saved over 70, 000 lives. But each mosquito killed probably cost $10.

The most difficulty came from the digging of the Culebra Cut across the Continental Divide. The ditch was 8 miles long, 50 feet deep, and 300 feet wide. The men and the steam shovels loaded 200 trains a day. There were 50 to 60 steam shovels going at one time. The locomotives moved at an exact pace so that each time a shovel scraped up a load and spun around, there was an empty car to dump the dirt into. The dirt (three and a half times that taken from the Suez Canal) was removed to the site of the dam, and each train was unloaded by a special sweep all at one time. Sixty million pounds of dynamite assisted the earth moving. As temperatures commonly reached 120 degrees, the TNT became very unstable and often blew up prematurely. This caused fires that had to be put out by the Panama Fire Department. Others were deafened by the noise of the work; so much so, that some wandered into the paths of trains and were crushed. A monument stands in the middle of the Culebra Cut (the Spanish word means "snake," an ominous reminder of what the canal workers went through, now more pleasantly renamed the Gaillard Cut, after Lieutenant Colonel D. D. Gaillard, an early Panama Canal engineer and administrator of note) to commemorate those who lost their lives building the canal.

The canal's locks were constructed in pairs so that traffic could move both ways through them. There were three pairs of locks that lifted and lowered boats 85 feet to clear the mountain section. They were 1,000 feet long and 110 feet wide. They had massive gates that weighed 700 tons each, but were so finely balanced that a 40-horsepower electric motor could close them. Electricity for all the gates and the little engines that pulled the ships through the locks (called "mules") was generated at the Gatun Dam. Water for the locks, equal in amount to that flowing over two Niagara Falls a day, came through tunnels big enough for a train. The locks and tunnels were the largest concrete project of their time, and it is common for shipyards worldwide to build their vessels to clear the canal lock dimensions.

President Roosevelt visited the canal in 1906, the first time a sitting president had left the country. He came in November, the worst part of the rainy season, and was so impressed with the work that he decided to have the Philadelphia Mint strike off a medal for everyone who worked at least two years on the project. The medal had a profile of Roosevelt on its front. It was fabricated from melted-down junk left over from the French effort in the 1880s. A short time later Chief Engineer Stevens resigned. He was fed up with political interference and had signed on for two years merely to start the project anyway.

But President Roosevelt ignored his earlier promise to Stevens and unfairly interpreted the resignation as an act akin to treason. He appointed a regular army engineer, George Washington Goethals, in his place. Goethals made the whole operation function with military precision. On 20 May 1913, the mountain cuts were finished, and four weeks later a final charge of dynamite freed the Chagres River to fill the lake and cuts. The first vessel to negotiate the canal was a local crane boat, *Alex La Valley*, on 7 January 1914. On 3 August 1914, the first oceangoing ship, the *Cristóbal*, sailed through the canal—an eight-hour trip. It takes a crew of 8,000 to operate and maintain the canal, much of the work being done by hand as in 1914. Because of continued landslides in the Gaillard Cut, one of which closed the canal for seven months shortly after its opening, the canal cut was widened to 500 feet by the 1960s, a project that removed more dirt than the original dig. Constant dredging keeps the ever-filling channel free of sludge.

The United States threw a gigantic exposition at San Francisco to celebrate America's entry on the world stage as a power to be reckoned with. But the world was busy elsewhere, as the Great War had just begun in Europe. Colombia recognized the inevitable and accepted Panamanian independence in 1914 along with a $25 million indemnity from the United States, reestablished diplomatic relations with Panamá in 1924, and established a border between the two nations in 1925. Since then, in response to periodic riots, the United States has revised the treaty governing the Canal Zone, bringing the Hay–Bunau-Varilla Treaty more into line with the original Hay-Herrán Convention. The Hull-Alfaro Treaty (1936), for example, renounced the American right to interfere in Panamá's domestic politics, raised the rents, brought local laborers' salaries more into line with the Americans', and provided for the lease of certain military bases.

But there were other Panamanian demands left unsatisfied. Part of the problem was national pride and dignity, a national inferiority complex created by Panamá's subordinate position under the treaties. The rest was economic. Panamá understood that its geographic position in the world is one that creates wealth—a richness compromised by American domination. Panamanians wanted more of the income generated by the canal and open access to supervisory and administrative positions. After riots in Panama City in the mid-1960s, President Lyndon Johnson agreed to talks designed to settle these problems. He also set up an Interoceanic Canal Commission to survey possible alternate routes for a larger sea level canal. The commission seemed to favor a Nicaraguan route and the use of nuclear explosives to open up the ditch and cut costs, but Central American political instability, U.S. cold war policies, and environmental worries have delayed any real action.

By the agreement of 1979, President Jimmy Carter agreed to most of Panama's demands and the United States promised to surrender all control of the canal to Panamanian sovereignty on the last day of 1999. Although there was much anti-American activity until this treaty was signed, today many on both sides wonder if the U.S. military presence should be completely withdrawn, as it means $300 million annually to the Panamanian economy. But neither side has yet proposed a change, and the sea-land route across the United States by railroad and containerized freight threatens to make the canal obsolete in the next century.

See also Canals; Goethals, George Washington; Gorgas, William Crawford; Stevens, John F.

References Beale, Howard K., *Theodore Roosevelt and the Rise of America to World Power* (1956); Bunau-Varilla, Philippe, *Creation, Destruction, and Resurrection* (1914); DuVal, Miles P., Jr., *And the Mountains Will Move* (1947); DuVal, Miles P., Jr., *Cadiz to Cathay* (1947); Goethals, George W., *The Panama Canal* (1916); Gorgas, Marie D., and Burton J. Hendrick, *William Crawford Gorgas: His Life and Work* (1924); Gorgas, William C., *Sanitation in Panama* (1914); Hays, Samuel P., *The Response to Industrialism* (1957); Kemble, John H., *The Panama Route* (1943); Klette, Immanuel J., *From Atlantic to Pacific* (1967); McCain, W. D., *The United States and the Republic of Panama* (1937); McCollough, David, *The Path between the Seas* (1977); Miner, Dwight C., *The Fight for the Panama Route* (1940); Mowry, George E., *The Era of Theodore Roosevelt and the Birth of Modern America* (1958); Padelford, Norman J., *The Panama Canal in Peace and War* (1942); Rydell, Raymond A., *Cape Horn to the Pacific* (1952); Stevens, John, *An Engineer's Recollections* (1936).

Panama Canal Act of 1912

Designed to set up rules for the opening, maintenance, operation, protection, governing, and sanitation of the Panama Canal, this measure guaranteed the availability of the canal to the nations of the world without discrimination during a time of peace as already recognized by international treaty. It also set up rules that affect the American merchant marine and business worlds. No ship that passed through was to be owned by any U.S. railroad. Hereafter, any other ships owned by American railroads had to receive special dispensation from the Interstate Commerce Commission (ICC). The railroads retaliated with stepped-up schedules and reduced rates that practically made coastal shipping via the canal prohibitive. The deregulation of the 1980s removed the restrictive ownership clauses and CSX Corporation has acquired Sea-Land with the approval of the ICC, but Sea-Land had no intention of using the canal because the continental land bridge is faster and cheaper. But critics point out that the Panama Canal Act remains an anachronism that ought to be repealed to aid American merchant marine interests. Such a change may be forced by the return of the canal to Panamanian control by the end of the twentieth century.

See also Merchant Marine; Panama Canal.

Reference Pedraja, René de la, *A Historical Dictionary of the Merchant Marine and Shipping Industry* (1994).

Pell Plan

First advocated in 1962 by the senator from Rhode Island, Claiborne Pell, this proposal created the Northeast Corridor or Megalopolis Project, an eight-state authority for high-speed rail passenger service between Boston and Washington, D.C. It was not uncommon then for Canadian National Railroad's *Rapido* trains to make the distance between Toronto and Montreal one hour faster and at 50 percent less ticket cost than the similar distance between New York and Chicago over the old New York Central System. Pell was at first dismissed as a nice crank; the airlines, highway builders, and truckers talked his plan down in Congress, but the senator hit a soft spot in the collective heart of the American people. Besides, he was quietly persistent, had tons of facts supporting his position, and pestered the White House continually.

The Boston-Washington line was (and still is) one of the most traveled routes in the country, and Pell finally managed to interest President Lyndon Johnson's administration in high-speed rail; after all, everyone else—at least the French and Japanese—were working on it, and Johnson did not like to be caught short on any new idea for his Great Society. The result was a $90 million appropriation from Congress and backing from public interest groups, the steel industry, the rail unions, and even the railroads themselves. The goal was a four-hour transit between Boston and Washington, with speeds in excess of 100 miles per hour—not really a problem as the Chicago North Western's *400* had done that in the 1930s between Chicago and the Twin Cities. So had its competition, the Milwaukee Road's *Hiawatha* and the Burlington's *Twin Cities Zephyr*. It took many years of track upgrading and new equipment and management, but with the transfer of the corridor's passenger service to the control of Amtrak and the infusion of millions of federal dollars, the Northeast Corridor is now up to standard for high-speed travel by Amtrak's *Metroliners*.

See also Amtrak; Transportation Acts.

References Lyon, Peter, *To Hell in a Day Coach* (1968); Orenstein, Jeffrey, *United States Railroad Policy* (1990); Pell, Claiborne, "Our Run-Down Railroads," *The New Republic* (2 May 1964) 150: 11–14.

Penn Central Transportation Company (PC)

Formed in 1968 by the Pennsylvania Railroad (PRR) and the New York Central (NYC) System, the Penn Central Transportation Company was an answer to the competition of airlines and interstate highways to what had been one of the most lucrative rail routes in the nation, the New York City–Chicago run. The NYC and the PRR had run neck and neck in dominating the corridor until the Great Depression had permitted the tighter-run Pennsy to forge ahead. Both lines had foreseen the competition of other forms of transportation and had de-emphasized passenger travel in favor of freight operations. By the time of the recession of 1958, adverse national economic conditions made the merger an imperative. Neither firm liked the other. Despite the obvious economic advantage, there was pure hatred among managers and the rank and file, nurtured by decades of competition. The wonder was that they could talk to each other at all, much less join ranks. The force of inevitability pushed the PRR and NYC into bed with each other. Labor disliked the plan and opposed it because ending the duplication of facilities meant the loss of thousands of jobs. But the U.S. Supreme Court approved of the merger and in February 1968 the Penn Central came into being, the largest rail merger up to that time.

The Penn Central's poor economic position turned worse when the Interstate Commerce Commission made it absorb the bankrupt New York & New Haven Railroad. The extra $22 million in New Haven debt was too much. Combined with a depression in the steel and automobile industries, other factors moved the Pennsy closer and closer to bankruptcy. A lack of cooperation from connecting railroads, which delivered cars to whatever yard they felt like, closed or not, and then complained about PC's unreliability in setting out or picking up interchanges; a corresponding loss of carload after carload of goods that could not be traced, which angered shippers, who had to shut down from lack of inventory; different labor contracts that caused old NYC engine crews not to operate Pennsy trains and vice versa, which was compounded as equipment got mixed up with joint use; stupid decisions, money wasted in flashy corporate suites, vicious corporate intrigue, disappearing slush funds—all of which was wrapped up in the term "executive jet"; and a devastating hurricane, which wrecked much of the rails, roadbed, and bridging finally caused the Penn Central to declare bankruptcy in the middle of 1970, shocking the American industrial world.

The fact that many large stockholders sold out just before the crash lent a taint of corruption to the process. This was compounded by the fact that Penn Central had been represented by President Richard Nixon's old law firm, many of whom now held key cabinet positions. The proper House of Representatives committee had as its chair the last of the business-bashing demagogues of Populism, Wright Pattman of Texas, who leaked a lot of embarrassing material to Jack Anderson, a muckraking journalist of national audience. Soon the country was up in arms over the whole thing, classed as the most miserable fiasco in American business. Four million dollars disappeared into a Liechtenstein bank, annual losses of $100 million, 352 boxcars stolen from PC by a neighboring short line, then repainted and rented back to PC—the litany went on and on. After six years the Penn Central was released from receivership, but it never entered railroads again. It now emphasized amusement parks, real estate, hotels, and a pipeline. The rail interests had been taken over by Consolidated Rail Corporation (Conrail) in 1976.

See also Conrail; New York Central System; Pennsylvania Railroad.

References Carson, Robert B., *Main Line to Oblivion* (1971); Daughen, Joseph R., and Peter Binzen, *The Wreck of the Penn Central* (1973); Drury, George H., *The Historical Guide to North American Railroads* (1985); Drury, George H., *The Train-Watcher's Guide* (1990); Hubbard, Freeman, *Encyclopedia of North American Railroading* (1981); Keisling, Phil, "The Great Train Robbery: How to Make a Billion from a Bankrupt Railroad," *Washington Monthly* (July–August 1982) 14: 24–29, 32–35; Salsbury, Stephen, *No Way To Run a Railroad* (1982); Saunders, Richard, *The Railroad Mergers and the Coming of Conrail* (1978); Saunders, Richard, "Penn Central," in Keith L. Bryant, Jr. (ed.), *EABHB: Railroads in the Age of Regulation* (1988), 334–336; Sobel, Robert, *Fallen Colossus* (1977); Stover, John F., *The Life and Decline of the American Railroad* (1970).

Pennsylvania Main Line Canal

The greatest rival for New York's preeminent spot in the canal wars was Pennsylvania. It was obvious with the success of the Erie Canal and the destruction of the Second Bank of the United States headquartered at Philadelphia that the state had to move decisively to compete on a more equal basis for western trade. The result was a combination of canals and railroads that became known as the Pennsylvania Main Line. It turned out to be an expensive boondoggle that doomed the state to a second-class position in canals, but prepared it for the new railroad boom. But in many respects, the state never again caught up to where it had been in earlier times before canals changed the face of the American economy.

Pennsylvanians had begun their initial forays into the canal wars by connecting the Delaware, Susquehanna, and Schuylkill Valleys. Efforts lagged until Canvass White came in off the Erie Canal with several of his assistants. He found an easier route for the Union Canal but the company's preference for smaller, cheaper locks fatally doomed it to obsolescence from the start. New routes of the Main Line would have to bypass and duplicate the earlier projects. The goal of the new Main Line was to cross the Appalachian Mountains through the Juniata Valley and reach Pittsburgh on the Ohio River, and intercept trade now going to the Erie Canal. Branches would bring Pennsylvania anthracite coal into the eastern seaboard cities. It was an ambitious project that turned out to be a disaster.

The Main Line was publicized by Matthew Carey's Pennsylvania Society for the Promotion of Internal Improvements. Their goal was not to lose out to New York City or Baltimore in the drive for the west.

The society also acted as a lobbying force in the state legislature and attempted to blunt opposition within the state from those who felt canals would ignore their needs by being routed elsewhere. Carey wrote, debated, and orated extensively on the benefits of internal improvements, a topic dear to his heart, as his naming his son Henry Clay Carey, after the Kentucky politician who popularized government-sponsored transportation projects, demonstrated. He was assisted in his goals by William Lehman, described by one historian as the De Witt Clinton of Pennsylvania, who got the state legislature behind the Main Line.

The problem in Pennsylvania was that the canal started on the two extremities, not in the middle as had been done in New York. Yet the center was the critical bottleneck that had to be surmounted first to generate any traffic at all. The dimensions of the canal were the same as those of the Erie Canal, probably because many of its engineers (Canvass White, James Geddes, Nathan S. Roberts) had gained their experience on that effort. The other problem was that to get the legislature's continual backing, the laws provided for the construction of the feeder lines concurrently and often in preference to the Main Line. The result was stagnation that affected expected revenues adversely. Finally, the crests of several mountains were traversed by rail at a time when locomotives were underpowered for such a task. The result was an extensive use of inclined planes to hoist cars at a cost in time and money. The Erie Canal was faster and cheaper, from start to finish.

The construction was magnificent, as with most nineteenth-century improvement projects. A 1,140-foot aqueduct brought the canal across the Allegheny into Pittsburgh. Although impressive, worries about its possible collapse led John Roebling to build an even more stunning suspension bridge with the canal on it as a replacement. A massive tunnel took the canal over to the Monongahela to connect with the expected terminus of the Chesa-peake & Ohio Canal. Other tunnels, as long as 1,000 feet each, carried the Main Line through parts of the Alleghenies. A dam on the Connemaugh at Johnstown on the western slope provided water for that section. It would collapse decades later as a part of the famous Johnstown flood. Engineer Moncure Robinson designed the Portage Railroad to connect east and west at the apex of the mountains. It was a double-tracked inclined plane, built to exacting standards, often literally hung from the cliffs, and one of the engineering marvels of the century. The railroad tunnel at Johnstown was the first one in the nation.

The Main Line was completed in 1835, nine years after it started. It stretched 395 miles, had 174 locks, 49 aqueducts, and 3 tunnels, and cost just over $12 million. But also to be built were 435 miles of branch lines, which proved too much for the state's coffers and ran up an imposing state debt. The final bill by 1860 was an impressive $100 million, more than any other state spent on internal improvements during the antebellum years. The whole works was sold for debt just before the Civil War. It was inevitable. The English investors who held two-thirds of the stock were angry, and the newer railroads were garnering all the competition. The Erie Canal had beat it to the west, and the financial drain of the canal projects had allowed the Baltimore & Ohio Railroad to beat Philadelphia to Pittsburgh. Even Boston was linked to Albany before the Pennsylvania Railroad got to the Ohio River on a competitive basis. Pennsylvania had had the canal-building fever in a big way, and Philadelphia's once preeminent economic position in the nation was never the same afterward.

See also Canals.

References Baer, Christopher T., *Canals and Railroads of the Mid-Atlantic States, 1800–1860* (1981); Bishop, Avard Longley, "Corrupt Practices Connected with the Building and Operation of the State Works of Pennsylvania," *Yale Review* (1907) 15: 391–411; Hartz, Louis, *Economic Policy and Democratic Thought: Pennsylvania, 1776–1860* (1948); McCullough, Robert, *The Pennsylvania Main Line Canal* (1962); Shaw, Ronald E., *Canals for a Nation: The Canal Era in the United States, 1790– 1860* (1990).

Pennsylvania Railroad (PRR)

Chartered in 1946 by a group of Philadelphians, the Pennsylvania Railroad (PRR, or Pennsy) replaced one of the most ambitious rail-canal projects in American history, the Pennsylvania Main Line. The PRR owed much of its early success to its chief engineer, John E. Thomson, once described as "one of the greatest all-round railroad men America has ever known." He gradually extended the Pennsy to Harrisburg, then across the mountains via the spectacular Horseshoe Curve (eventually having a four-track mainline) to Pittsburgh by 1848. Reaching the Middle West, the PRR began an aggressive policy of buying out and renting small, local lines, and headed eventually to Chicago. In the East, the PRR moved into New Jersey opposite New York City and southward to the nation's capital. When completed, the Pennsy had bought up 600 corporations, a railroad record.

The Pennsylvania Railroad has always had a great pride in its rail business, calling itself "the Standard Railroad of the World." It was not all bravado, either. It rapidly changed from wood to coal, the state being one of the great coal producers in the East. It had the first cowcatcher ("pilot" to railroad buffs), the first use of modern T-shaped rails, the first uniformed conductors, and some of the finest varnish (passenger equipment) and steam locomotives ever built. It was among the first to adopt Westinghouse air brakes and the Janney knuckle coupler. It was the first to standardize its motive power and rolling stock, both passenger and freight.

The Pennsylvania Railroad experimented with hard and soft coal and developed a fondness for the Belpaire firebox, giving its locomotives a distinctive square top look aft. The PRR developed a stem injector to spray feed water into the boiler, making the achievement of higher temperatures and greater pressures possible. It built one-third of its steam locos in its own shops, of which Altoona was the most famous. The Pennsy used cast-iron centers and wrought-iron treads on its tires during the Civil War, considered an advance over previous cast

wheels. In 1904, the PRR set up a locomotive testing laboratory as a part of the St. Louis Louisiana Purchase Exposition. By that time, Pennsy steam was a standard for the business. The tractive force of various PRR steam engines rose 53 percent during the twentieth century. Passenger engines like the K-4 Pacific type (4-6-2) were the best in the world. Heavy steam for freight consists used eight- and ten-wheeled driver combinations, some in Mallet double engines. The Pennsy also developed a steam turbine engine (6-8-6) that emitted a distinct "whoosh" as it passed, but proved impracticable in the long run.

For most of the nineteenth century, the PRR was limited in its competition for the New York market by being unable to enter the city directly. Passengers and freight had to be off-loaded on the Jersey side and taken over by boat. But through its subsidiary, the Long Island Rail Road, recently purchased for just that reason, the necessary permits were obtained. Tunneling began immediately, supervised by William G. McAdoo, later head of the U.S. Railway Administration. Giant boring machines cut a half dozen tunnels under New York Harbor, and electrified engines brought the trains over to a new 57-track yard at Penn Station. Although since razed and replaced by a newer station now used by Amtrak, the original Penn Station was a magnificent structure built of pink granite. Station clocks measured 7 feet in diameter. Italian marble graced the interior, and public services were many, including chartering deep-sea fishing boats. At one time, the Pennsy, the Long Island Rail Road, the Lehigh Valley, and the New Haven all ran trains into Penn Station on leasing and traffic agreements.

Because of its interest in the Atlantic Corridor from New York to Washington, and the need to go into New York pollution-free, the Pennsylvania had a great interest in electric locomotives. It designed one type, the DD-1, specifically to haul trains in and out of the tunnels at New York City. The mainline southward was often four to six tracks wide and electrified the whole way. At first a charged outside third rail was used, but this soon gave way to catenary lines overhead. The famous GG-1 streamlined electric engine made this run famous, an engine so well designed that it survived the Amtrak takeover of all passenger service in the early 1970s. The existence of so much coal caused the PRR to shift to diesel power reluctantly. But as early as 1929, the Pennsy used diesel switchers of its own design in the New York area.

After World War II, the Pennsylvania moved gradually into diesel, and by 1954, the whole line except for the Atlantic corridor ran on the new motive power. The engines were painted the standard Tuscan red or Brunswick green with five gold stripes running the length of the body, topped off with the word "Pennsylvania" in gold letters. Passenger equipment followed the same pattern. The PRR's name train was the all-Pullman, all-bedroom *Broad Way Limited*; though not as fancy as the New York Central's *Twentieth Century Limited*, the more practical Pennsy never missed a dividend payment during the Great Depression as did the Central and so many others. Incidentally, the *Broad Way* (original spelling) was not the New York street but a reference to the four- and six-track PRR main line. Pennsy was among the first railroads to radio-equip its engines, observation cars, and cabooses. It also offered New York City to Los Angeles service with a side trip to the Grand Canyon in no-changes-necessary sleepers hauled in cooperation with the Santa Fe out of Chicago.

The *Pennsylvania Limited* and the *Broad Way Limited* made due with standard steam equipment (especially at night when no one was the wiser) over shrouded locomotives, older dining cars, and standard head-end (baggage, express, and mail) cars where people did not ride, anyway. But it easily matched the Century's time since it had 60 fewer miles to Chicago from New York City. One trip was made in 15.5 hours, a record that still holds. Normal time for both the PRR and the NYC was 18 hours—about 60 miles an hour on the Pennsy route until the run

was dieselized and cars modernized in 1949 and the time cut to 16 hours. Moreover, the PRR had been the first to fully electrify its passenger equipment (everything east of Harrisburg, Pennsylvania), and everything was air-conditioned, giving it the largest fleet of cooled passenger cars in the world. The Pennsy was proud of its organization, efficiency, and volume of traffic—the largest in the United States. It traversed 13 states and the District of Columbia. Unlike the western railroads, the Pennsy's network was compact and ran between the largest population centers in the country. But it lost out to the same forces that did in all railroads—federally financed airlines and highways. Its proud use of the Keystone State emblem on the front of all locomotive fronts came to an end in 1968 when it merged with the lesser New York Central to form the Penn Central Transportation Company. It was the end of an era when the name and policies of the Pennsylvania Railroad were standards for well-run business the world over.

See also Conrail; Locomotives, Steam Locomotives; Long Island Rail Road; New York Central System; Penn Central Transportation Company; Scott, Thomas A.

References Alexander, Edwin P., *The Pennsylvania Railroad* (1947); Alexander, Edwin P., *On the Main Line* (1971); Botkin, Benjamin A., and Alan F. Harlow, *A Treasury of Railroad Folklore* (1953); Burgess, George H., and Miles C. Kennedy, *Centennial History of the Pennsylvania Railroad* (1949); Condit, Carl W., *The Port of New York*, 2 vols. (1980–1981); Drury, George H., *The Historical Guide to North American Railroads* (1985); Drury, George H., *The Train-Watcher's Guide* (1990); Grow, Lawrence, *On the 8:02* (1979); Holbrook, Stewart H., *The Story of American Railroads* (1947); Hubbard, Freeman, *Encyclopedia of North American Railroading* (1981); Lyon, Peter, *To Hell in a Day Coach* (1968); McGonigal, Robert S., "The 1949 Broad Way Limited: The Flagship Streamliner of the Pennsylvania RR's Blue Ribbon Fleet," *Model Railroader* (October 1994) 61: 84–99; Nock, O. S., *Railways of the USA* (1979); Schotter, H. W., *Growth and Development of the Pennsylvania Railroad Company* (1928); Sinclair, Angus, *Development of the Locomotive Engine* (1970); Ward, James A., "Pennsylvania Railroad," in Keith L. Bryant, Jr. (ed.), *EABHB: Railroads in the Age of Regulation* (1988), 313–315; Wilson, W. B., *History of the Pennsylvania Railroad Company* (1895).

Philadelphia Wagon Road

The road running west from Philadelphia and southward through the great inland valleys of the Cumberland and the Shenandoah to Augusta, Georgia, is sometimes called the Philadelphia Wagon Road, but was better known as the Great Wagon Road. It provided an inland route paralleling the coast, but was so far inland that it could not be intersected militarily by the British during the American Revolution. It later incorporated the Lancaster Pike and the Valley Turnpike as a part of its length.

See also Great Wagon Road; Lancaster Pike; Valley Turnpike.

Pike's Peak Ocean-to-Ocean Highway

One of the "named highways" popular in the teens and twenties of the twentieth century, the Pike's Peak Ocean-to-Ocean Highway was used by local chambers of commerce and tourism and the American Automobile Association to stimulate travel on the "good roads" and increase income in the towns and states through which they passed. Often called "the Appian Way of America," this 1916 road passed from New York City south to Philadelphia, where it turned west to Harrisburg. From the Pennsylvania capital the route wound through the Appalachians, following the course of today's U.S. Highway 22 through Lewistown south of Altoona to Pittsburgh. It crossed the Ohio River at Weirton, West Virginia, and continued west by way of Steubenville to Coshcoton and Bellefontaine, following what would become U.S. Highway 36. The road then passed into Indiana at Anderson and proceeded westward to Danville, Illinois. Heading through Decatur and Springfield (modern Interstate 72), the route crossed the Mississippi at Hannibal, Missouri. Still on what would be U.S. Highway 36, it crossed Missouri to St. Joseph and continued through Kansas to Norton, where the Oceanto-Ocean Highway dropped down to Colby, now part of modern Interstate 70. At Limon the route turned to Colorado Springs and wound its way past Pike's Peak and on through the Rockies by way of Gunnison to Grand Junction. Following what would become U.S. Highway 6, the Ocean-to-Ocean Highway passed through Utah's coal country at Price, following the Old Spanish Trail down to Los Angeles via Las Vegas, the route of present-day Interstate 15.

See also Roads and Highways, Colonial Times to World War I; Roads and Highways since World War I.

Reference Hart, Val, *The Story of American Roads* (1950).

Pipelines

Pipelines are used to transport bulk products cheaply in a gaseous, liquid, or semi-liquid form. In the United States such products include petroleum, gasoline, natural gas, and various forms of slurry—a mixture of water and coal, for instance. A pipeline is much like a railroad in its layout, with a trunk line and many feeder lines. At suitable intervals there are pump houses that push the product through the line under pressure, and valves and control devices that increase or limit the flow. It is standard practice to bury pipelines, except sections of the Alaska pipeline that were built on the surface to monitor the joints and preserve the permafrost because of the special weather conditions there. The whole construction process, once a lengthy one filled with much hand labor, is now fully mechanized. Pipe was once joined by bell and spigot, screw, and packed sleeves. Now it is welded and inspected by electronic bugs that float through the lines on a regular basis.

The idea of petroleum pipelines in the United States was first broached in the 1860s in Pennsylvania. The first successful pipeline was constructed after the Civil War and transported the oil from the wellhead to a local refinery. In 1878, a pipeline was laid from the Pennsylvania fields to the Atlantic coast. Pipelines expanded as the exploration for gas and oil did, into Indiana and Illinois in the 1890s; Kansas, Oklahoma, and Texas in the early 1900s; and into California and then Wyoming later in the century.

Natural gas lines have kept pace with the petroleum lines. The Chinese first transported natural gas through bamboo pipes a thousand years ago. The first American gas pipeline was in Fredonia, New York, in 1825. By 1870, a 12-inch wooden pipeline with 4-inch walls handled natural gas under pressure at Rochester, New York. Shortly afterward, the first iron pipeline to transport natural gas was laid at Titusville, Pennsylvania. The use of natural gas spread throughout the East in the 1890s. The first high-pressure natural gas line carried fuel from northern Indiana to Chicago in 1891. It was an 8-inch line that operated under 525 pounds of pressure and moved the gas over 120 miles. The use of natural gas lines followed the expansion of the petroleum explorations, where it was an important by-product of the drilling process.

Pipelines were a highly controversial means of transportation initially. Originally, they were seen as a method for collecting products for transshipment to barge, ship, and rail lines. But as the need to move liquids and gasses increased, the other carriers began to lobby to include the pipelines under the same federal controls they had to operate under. The Hepburn Act of 1906 placed pipelines under the jurisdiction of the Interstate Commerce Commission (ICC) as a common carrier. Another federal law allowed the pipelines to cross sections of Oklahoma owned by Native Americans in 1909. The Mann-Elkins Act of 1910 increased the ICC's control over pipeline operations, and the U. S. Supreme Court upheld the federal supervision of the pipeline companies in the Pipe Line Cases in 1913.

Later, the National Labor Relations Act outlawed the company unions that had been used to stifle labor influence among employees prior to the days of the New Deal. The Natural Gas Policy Act of 1978 proved the political volatility of gas lines when it set up three classifications of gas, some to be deregulated immediately, some to be deregulated by 1985, and a third to continue to be regulated. Wellhead prices were deregulated in 1989. The Federal Energy Regulatory Commission continues to monitor the flow of pipeline products that are "unbundled" and given different rates depending on the service provided (transportation, storage, marketing, or purchasing). Because of their energy relationship, pipelines are among the most regulated of transportation services in modern America.

The use of pipelines received a real boost with the advent of World War II. German submarines interrupted the tanker traffic that kept the United States supplied. The amount of petroleum available on the East Coast fell from 1.5 million barrels a day in 1941 to 77,000 by 1943. The War Productions Board developed a completely new system of moving oil and natural gas relying on pipelines and railroads, reasoning that land movement was impervious to enemy interdiction. Key to the plan was a 24-inch pipeline from Longview, Texas, to Norris City, Illinois (and later, to Phoenixville, Pennsylvania), known in industry parlance as the "Big Inch." In Illinois the petroleum was shipped by ordinary pipelines to eastern refineries. Later in the war, a new line 20 inches in diameter was laid to take heating oil directly to the big eastern cities from the Gulf Coast. This "Little Big Inch" line went into operation in 1944, at a time when heating oil had been reduced to a mere three days' supply. War Emergency Pipelines, Incorporated, a civilian company controlled by the federal government, built both of these lines under wartime authority, the necessary materials normally being restricted for the war effort overseas.

The government projects were soon joined by private efforts. Tennessee Gas built a 24-inch natural gas line from the Southwest to the East Coast. Texas Eastern bought out the government lines in 1947 and modernized them. At the same time, a consortium built a line from Texas to the West Coast. As more pipelines were built until they now crisscross every state, the larger diameters from 32 to 40 inches proved more efficient and came to be emphasized. Two such lines ran from the Southwest to Illinois and to the East Coast, built in response to striking maritime unions.

But these efforts paled in comparison to

the construction of the Alaska Pipeline, a 48-inch monster stretching from Valdez on Prince William Sound to the North Slope. The existence of oil in Alaska had been known from the earliest times—in places it actually rises to the surface naturally. Areas along Cooke Inlet have been exploited since the days of the Klondike gold rush. In the 1920s, President Warren G. Harding set aside 25 million acres in the Arctic for future oil exploration. Meanwhile, discoveries along the Kenai Peninsula fueled the growth of Anchorage. When Alaska became a state in 1959, it received (as do all territories that assume statehood) a large grant of federal lands to promote its economic growth. Among these land grants were certain areas along the North Slope that fairly oozed oil.

Many of the state's North Slope lands were near already explored petroleum reserves set aside by President Harding. In 1968, the Atlantic Richfield Company (ARCO) made a major oil discovery at Prudhoe Bay. In league with Humble Ohio and British Petroleum, Exxon formed the Trans Alaska Pipeline System (TAPS). The membership of TAPS changed over the years with the addition and subtraction of several other companies until the original three and Standard Oil of Ohio formed 90 percent of a new entity, the Alyeska Pipeline Service Company, which designed, built, and operated the whole project. The state immediately began to sell the rights to exploit the area and the oil rush was on. But Prudhoe Bay was 800 miles from the Gulf of Alaska and tanker transportation to the Lower Forty-Eight and the world. Although the process of meeting federal guidelines concerning Native American claims, the environment, earthquake security, and the cold was lengthy, oil began to flow south in 1977. Today 85 percent of the state's revenues come from oil taxes and royalties.

Although the recent oil spill from the bunkers of the Exxon *Valdez* are legend, the pipelines not only in Alaska but elsewhere have had a relatively safe history. Of 45 spills recorded by the Smithsonian Institution to 1971, for example, pipelines were involved in less than a handful. Two of these came from ships dragging anchor that ripped up a line laid at the bottom of a bay, one from a line ruptured in a storm in the Arabian Gulf, and the fourth from an actual leak in a pipeline on the U.S. Gulf Coast. Although pipelines are not totally secure from environmental accident, it would appear that the worst disasters come from the blowing of a well as happened at Santa Barbara in 1969, from loading poorly maintained ships like the tanker *Sansinena* incident at Long Beach in 1978, or from tanker mishaps such as occurred at Nantucket in 1978 or in Prince William Sound in 1989—all of which happen at least once a year on average worldwide. Pipelines have some advantage in that a spill is more manageable from various control devices and valves located along the line. They also handle less than 25 percent of all oil delivered annually to the United States (along with barges and rail cars), the rest being supplied by tankers.

See also Intracoastal Waterway; Port and Tanker Safety Act of 1978; Railroads from Appomattox to Degregulation; Trucking.

References Beard, William, *Regulation of Pipe Lines as Common Carriers* (1941); Easton, Robert, *Black Tide* (1972); Kennedy, John L., *Oil and Gas Pipeline Fundamentals* (1993); Loos, John L., *Oil on Stream!* (1959); Lord, Nancy, *Darkened Waters* (1992); *The Pipe Line Cases*, 234 US 548 (1913); Rister, Carl Coke, *Oil!* (1949); Roscow, James P., *800 Miles to Valdez* (1977); Williamson, Harold F., and Arnold R. Daum, *The American Petroleum Industry* (1959); Wolbert, George S., Jr., *American Pipe Lines* (1952); Wolbert, George S., Jr., *U.S. Oil Pipe Lines* (1979).

Plank Roads

As railroads and canals could not go to every part of the country, farmers needed a different approach to all-weather transportation of their goods to market. The answer, of course, lay in a modification of the dirt roads, one that would render them serviceable even after heavy rain or snow had drenched them. The result was the corduroying of dirt roads or, better yet, actual plank roads. Corduroying was a Russian concept, brought to the United States through Canada, of laying rough logs across a muddy road, making the surface hard once again. It had the advantage of speed and simplicity of construction, but was extremely rough on the vehicles and travelers as the log bumps were built into the roadbed. Corduroyed roads were used extensively in the American Civil War to speed the movements of troops, artillery, and supply wagons across swampy terrain of the kind that was prevalent in many parts of the South.

Plank roads were an extension of the corduroy principle and involved laying 3-inch planks across stringers, which, in turn, were laid parallel to the direction of travel. The planks were smoother than mere logs and took a heavy load over the wettest terrain. Some of the earliest turnpikes in the United States were plank roads. Usually, the plank road ran next to its dirt cousin, and the rule was that loaded vehicles had the right-of-way over those running empty, which had to pull off the planks onto the dirt. Needless to say, two loaded wagons meeting in a wet spot could lead to a fistfight to decide which teamster would yield.

George Geddes first brought plank roads into New York State from Canada in 1845. The cost of construction was around $1,500 per mile. The labor ratio of horses pulling a load was enough for one commentator to state that it "seemed more of a frolick than labour." Plank roads swept the United States until the Panic of 1857 caused the road companies to fail by the hundreds. The intervention of the Civil War, the competition of the railroads, and the expense of maintenance, which was more than regular roads that also could not meet upkeep expenses, forced entrepreneurs to direct their money elsewhere, and the common roads movement more or less died out until the advent of the motor car and truck transport around World War I.

See also Roads and Highways, Colonial Times to World War I.

References Kingsford, William, *History, Structure, and Statistics of Plank Roads* (1851); MacGill, Caroline, et al., *History of Transportation in the United States before 1860* (1917); Taylor, George Rogers, *The Transportation Revolution* (1951).

Platt, Thomas C. (1833–1910)

Of all the express company owners, Thomas C. Platt of United States Express was the most politically high-placed. Born at Oswego, New York, in 1833, Platt went to Yale but had to drop the program due to ill health. He returned home to enter business as a merchant. As with most successful businessmen of his day, he avoided Civil War service, but his poor health was undoubtedly a contributing factor. In 1865 he became president of a local bank. During the war, he first ran for office as county clerk and became attracted to the support of Roscoe Conkling. Later, Platt was chairman of the local Republican Party and elected to Congress in 1872 and 1874. By January 1881, his political fortunes had advanced to where the state legislature elected him to the United States Senate, there being no popular election of senators until 1913. At the same time, Platt became first manager and then president of U.S. Express, where he showed great ability in obfuscating the competition to his own profit.

Because President James Garfield routinely ignored senatorial courtesy by consulting senators on the appointment of local officials if the Senate had to approve of them, Platt followed the lead of Senator Conkling and both men resigned in disgust. Conkling was reelected but Platt chose to withdraw and work with the New York City Quarantine Commission. In 1884, Platt attended the Republican National Convention and thereafter, Platt rose in Republican circles in New York until he controlled the whole state party. He was known as the "easy boss" because he controlled for the love of power rather than money or personal advancement. He made instant judgments on men's abilities and was usually correct. He also remembered small details and knew how to use political rules to his advantage. He generally displayed a great deal of common sense; however, he opposed the popular reform elements of the party and was an avowed "gold bug," in favor of the gold standard over silver monetary inflation.

Platt later served two terms in the Senate

(1896–1910) and was instrumental in getting Theodore Roosevelt made vice-president to get him and his reformers out of New York politics. Needless to say, the assassination of William McKinley in 1900 at Buffalo put Teddy in exactly the right place to do the most damage—a fact that turned other conservatives' anger at Platt. As senator, Platt opposed the idea of parcel post legislation that would put the government in competition with the private companies. The legislation passed shortly after his death in 1910, a monument to his years of service that he could have well done without.

See also United States Express Company.
Reference Harlow, Alvin F., *Old Waybills* (1934).

Pony Express

Created by William H. Russell of the freighting firm Russell, Majors & Waddell, the Pony Express was established in 1860 to prove that the Central Overland Route could be traveled reliably all year-round. That would open up all sorts of investment possibilities, not the least of which was a transcontinental railroad through the mid-northern states. It was originally nothing but a big public relations stunt with wider implications. Russell chartered the whole operation as the Central Overland California & Pike's Peak Express Company. Although the scheme was a resounding success with the public and eventually led to a transcontinental railroad on the central route, it marked the final chapter in the saga of Russell, Majors & Waddell. The costs to income ratio could not meet their debt payments. By 31 December 1861, the firm of Russell, Majors and Waddell was bankrupt and the telegraph had ended the pony experiment.

See also Central Overland Route; Russell, Majors & Waddell Company.
References Bradley, Glenn D., *The Story of the Pony Express* (1960); Settle, Raymond W., and Mary Lund Settle, *Saddles and Spurs* (1955); Settle, Raymond W., and Mary Lund Settle, *War Drums and Wagon Wheels* (1966).

The Coming and Going of the Pony Express, *painted by Frederic Remington, portrays the excitement in running mail across the Central Overland Route. The operation only lasted a year and was replaced by the transcontinental telegraph in 1861.*

Port and Tanker Safety Act of 1978

In response to recent oil spills in American territorial waters at Nantucket Island by the grounded *Argo Merchant* and an explosion of the tanker *Sansinena* in port at San Pedro, California, Congress acted to strengthen the existing Tank Vessel Act of 1936 and Ports and Waterways Safety Act of 1972. These earlier measures had established national standards but lacked positive enforcement mechanisms. The 1978 act increased the authority of the U.S. Coast Guard to make inspections and deny entry into U.S. waters of suspect vessels. The measure imposed both civil and criminal penalties for violation and also held the ship's owner liable for any damages caused, for which the ship could be seized to guarantee payment. It also created strict standards of knowledge for ship operators and crew members that if not met would allow the Coast Guard to deny entry to ships of any nation into American waters.

See also Merchant Marine; Oil Pollution Act of 1990.

References Frankel, Ernst G., *Regulation and Policies of American Shipping* (1978); Pedraja, René de la, *A Historical Dictionary of the Merchant Marine and Shipping Industry* (1994).

Post Office Appropriation Acts

Many of the initial federal appropriations for assistance to early twentieth-century highways were lodged within post office appropriation acts, because the constitutional mandate for such federal action was clearer as concerned military and post roads than anywhere else. All of the more important measures follow.

POST OFFICE APPROPRIATION ACT OF 1912

After defeating 60 suggestions for federal involvement in improving post roads for free rural mail delivery, Congress passed a measure to look into the feasibility of providing federal aid to improve post roads and decide whether such improvements increased the efficiency of rural letter carriers, permitted an increase in their territory of delivery and the number of days they could deliver, and how much federal money in excess of normal state and local expenditures was required to make the program worthwhile. The act also provided $500,000 to be matched by the state on a two-to-one basis and specified that the moneys be apportioned per mile as to road surface (dirt, gravel, or macadam). The states soon raised $1.3 million, but the measure failed miserably. Many states refused to cooperate, others could not because of state constitutional objections, and most merely ignored the offer, federal money not being the panacea then that it is today.

POST OFFICE APPROPRIATION ACT OF 1919

This legislation declared rural post roads to be any road used, once used, or that could be used in the future to transport the mails and any connecting link not to exceed ten miles in length between such roads. As opponents pointed out, this measure declared every road in the United States to be a post road. This ended any argument as to the constitutional authority granted Congress to finance road building that had wracked the nation for over 100 years. It also added another $50 million to the assistance available to the states under the Federal-Aid Road Act of 1916.

POST OFFICE APPROPRIATION ACT OF 1922

This measure expanded the federal aid granted states for roads in the Federal Highway Act of 1921, which was limited to two years. It sweetened the pot for the years 1923, 1924, and 1925 by authorizing the future appropriation of $190 million. But the actual appropriation had to be reapproved each year. This became the standard federal procedure until 1956—authorizing (proposing) appropriations for several years in advance, then appropriating the authorizations (actually putting up the cash) each year they came due.

See also Roads and Highways since World War I.

Reference U.S. Department of Transportation, Federal Highway Administration, *America's Highways* (1976).

Potomac River Company

Organized in the 1780s, the Potomac River Company (George Washington was one of its original investors) became the nucleus of the Chesapeake & Ohio Canal.

See Canals; Chesapeake & Ohio Canal.

Presidential Trains

Beginning in 1858, when an incumbent U.S. senator from Illinois, Stephen A. Douglas, and his opponent, Abraham Lincoln, rode the same train around the state to engage in debate over the issues of the day, politics and railroads would be connected for a century. Douglas was a past master at the technique; he would come into town on his specially chartered campaign train and fire a cannon from a flatcar to announce his arrival. Although Lincoln lost the fight for the 1858 Senate seat, he won the Republican Party nomination two years later. He also won the 1860 election, traveling around to see local politicians to drum up support, using a specially converted coach in which he slept in his clothes on a mattress without sheets. He rode to his Washington inaugural on the train, taking a circuitous route through every northern state between Springfield, Illinois, and Washington, D.C. He had to change trains in Baltimore, a secessionist stronghold, and his security advisor, one E. J. Allen, advised that he do so in disguise at night. Lincoln knew Allen from his days when the rail-splitter was a corporate attorney for the Illinois Central Railroad, and Allen was the railroad detective Allen Pinkerton. The safe but surreptitious way in which he entered Washington ("cowardly," his critics maintained) caused him much political embarrassment early in his administration.

Lincoln's successor, Andrew Johnson, made a so-called Swing around the Circle, roughly the same trip as Lincoln with a few additions to fight congressional plans to reconstruct the South. The tour went for naught and Johnson lost his fight and the ensuing presidential election, not even receiving his party's nomination against U. S. Grant. President Rutherford B. Hayes and his opponent lined up support by train, as did Grover Cleveland and Benjamin Harrison. Although popular tradition had presidential candidates stay at home and let cronies campaign for them, improved transportation caused local bigwigs to desire the real thing. And as the twentieth century approached, William McKinley was one of the last to enjoy the luxury of a "front porch" campaign.

McKinley's opponent William Jennings Bryan hit the rails, riding coaches, sleepers, and cabooses, even taking buggy trips to isolated places. Bryan made 569 speeches, 24 of them in one 24-hour period. He lost anyway, but Bryan set the example for the coming century. Theodore Roosevelt and the perennial socialist candidate, Eugene V. Debs, joined Bryan riding the tail end of rail cars. William Howard Taft made a lot of railroad-catered campaign speeches, too, but a more reasonable 418 when compared to Teddy's 673, probably an all-time record. But TR had a penchant for talk that few could match, much less surpass. However, Taft did set another record (besides his weight, well over 300 pounds); he traveled 114,500 miles while serving as president. No one broke that total until Franklin D. Roosevelt, who traveled 375,847 miles as president in 390 separate Pullman cars. Woodrow Wilson was making a train campaign on behalf of the Treaty of Versailles and the League of Nations, vociferously opposed in the U.S. Senate, when he suffered his stroke in 1920.

As Wilson and the others could attest, speaking from the back of a train could be quite rough on one's voice after awhile, something Warren G. Harding solved by using the first public address system. Calvin Coolidge rode only one special train during his presidency, the one that took him to Washington to replace Harding, recently dead. Coolidge thought specials way too expensive. He was the only one who did, though. In 1928, the race was on again, with Al Smith riding the rails in an 11-car train complete with shower and barber shop. He had style but lost to Herbert Hoover in spite (or was it because) of it. Franklin D.

Roosevelt issued standing orders that the train was to pull out as soon as he finished his speech to avoid anticlimax. Often he wound up leaving distracted crew members behind or giving slow-moving local pols a free ride. His opponent in 1940, Wendell Willkie, could not match FDR's punctuality—he liked to drone on and fouled up many a schedule. Finally, the engineer was told to blow the whistle two minutes ahead of the time to leave, and Willkie would try to finish promptly.

The king of modern whistle-stoppers had to be Harry Truman in 1948. He covered 21,000 miles in 17 days to defeat Republican nominee Thomas Dewey and dissident Democrats Henry Wallace and J. Strom Thurman. By the time Truman rode the rails, the White House had a special presidential car, the *Air Force One* of its day. It was an armor-plated Pullman that had the ability to survive even if it sunk in water. When presidents traveled, switches would be preset and locked and then spiked into place. A pilot train ran ahead to scout the tracks. No one could follow closer than 15 minutes behind. The presidential car was the *Ferdinand Magellan*, converted and donated to the White House by the American Association of Railroads. It currently is preserved on the Gold Coast Railroad, a Hollywood, Florida, tourist line.

In addition to the special presidential trains for politicking, there were seven presidential funeral trains over the years. The first and most famous carried Abraham Lincoln back to Springfield from Washington over the same route he had followed to the presidency four years before. It had seven cars, all painted black and draped in black crepe. Bonfires lighted the way and thousands stood by in silent tribute to the man who had saved the Union. Ex-President James Buchanan came down at Lancaster, Pennsylvania, as did an honor guard at West Point. George Pullman had his new sleeping car, *Pioneer*, switched onto the train for the comfort of the president's family in Illinois. After being mortally wounded, President James Garfield was taken to the New Jersey coast in hopes that the breezes would assist in his recovery. Another train took him to Washington after he died and on to his farm in Cuyahoga County, Ohio. Their appearance was much the same as Lincoln's earlier. U. S. Grant was accorded the usual presidential honors when he died from cancer in 1885, almost ten years after leaving the White House and just two days after finishing his *Personal Memoirs*. He was carried past West Point to New York City where he was interred.

Far to the south in 1889, Grant and Lincoln's wartime opponent, Jefferson Davis, president of the Confederate States of America, received full tribute from admirers and the usual rail treatment in 1893 as his body was moved to Richmond. His body traveled in a glassed-in maroon observation car draped in black crepe, part of a special nine-car train sent by the various southern railroads that had kept the Confederacy alive during its short existence. In 1901, President William McKinley was shot at Buffalo, New York, at the Pan American Exposition. A special Lackawanna train, complete with medical personnel, was organized to speed the lingering president to New York. The trip received an unconditional green light and the engineer made 395 miles in 405 minutes, but the president could not be saved and died a week later. The Pennsylvania Railroad reserved two trains for McKinley, one to take him to Washington, the other to carry him home to Ohio. Every railroad in the nation stopped its operations for five minutes at the beginning of the funeral service in Canton.

The next president to be carried home was Warren G. Harding in 1923. He died in San Francisco of a stroke after a trip to Alaska to drive the golden spike on the Alaska Railroad. His special 11-car train draped in black was shipped over the Southern Pacific, the Union Pacific, the Chicago & North Western, and the Baltimore & Ohio mainlines to lie in state at the Capitol. Later, his body was carried to his home in Marion, Ohio. The various railroads had set record times in transporting the body to the capital. Harding's train was the last black-draped funeral train. When Franklin D.

Roosevelt died at Warm Springs, Georgia, a double-headed, 12-car undecorated Southern Railway train took him back to Washington, his body traveling in the *Ferdinand Magellan*. After lying in state at the Capitol, FDR's body was shipped to his Hudson River estate in the Pullman car *Conneaut*. His was the last funeral train got up for an American president. The bodies of John F. Kennedy, Lyndon B. Johnson, and Richard M. Nixon went by airplane.

See also American Freedom Train.

References Henry, Robert S., *This Fascinating Railroad Business* (1946); Hubbard, Freeman, *Great Trains of All Time* (1962); Hubbard, Freeman, *Encyclopedia of North American Railroading* (1981); Starr, John W., *Lincoln and the Railroads* (1927); Wesolowski, Wayne, "Abraham Lincoln's Funeral Train," *Model Railroader* (February 1995) 62: 92–97.

Professional Air Traffic Controllers Organization (PATCO)

Organized in 1968 by a half dozen New York–based air traffic controllers as a professional society and not as a union, the Professional Air Traffic Controllers Organization's purpose was to present their complaints of increasingly long hours and poor working conditions. The organization caught on immediately. In six months it had 5,000 adherents. At its peak in 1981, it had 15,000 members. PATCO was a professional organization because of President John F. Kennedy's executive order in 1962, which allowed government workers to join nonunion groups to affect limited collective bargaining without striking, an illegal act. PATCO's increasing membership was guaranteed by President Lyndon B. Johnson's expenditures on the shooting war in Southeast Asia and the so-called war on poverty at home. There was a lot of government money being spent, but air traffic control was not one of the favored programs.

The first administrator of PATCO was Michael J. Rock, assisted by high-profile lawyer F. Lee Bailey. Rock and Bailey wrote the book on job slowdown as a bargaining tactic. It was unspectacular but hit the airlines where it hurt—in the fuel bill ledger. Planes often stacked up around major air-

ports for three hours at a time. Because their stand was viewed by the citizenry as a principled one involving public safety, they had much passenger support. But in 1968, Rock and Bailey instituted the practice of taking union dues out of paychecks with members' permissions. This caused the government to question whether it was a union or a professional organization. When PATCO devised a bunch of "sick-outs" in 1969 and 1970, the government acted against it for calling illegal strikes. The unsympathetic Federal Aviation Administration (FAA) suspended 1,000 "sick" members and fired 52 outright (although 42 were later rehired). This action ended the Rock-Bailey administration of PATCO.

The new head of PATCO was Robert Leyden. He learned his lesson and went back to the slowdown route. The Richard Nixon administration responded to the lesser threat and Congress enacted several measures to improve working conditions. These included the Airport and Airway Development and Revenue Act (1970) and the Air Traffic Controllers' Career Program Act (1972). Radars and runways were improved and retirement was made easier to achieve, plus retirees received training for new jobs if they desired. At the same time, however, the government formally certified PATCO as a union. Leyden's favorite tactic was to call the slowdown during big holidays like Thanksgiving or Christmas. One in 1976 gained everyone an increase in pay and salary level. But another in 1978 found the nation increasingly weary and not inclined to humor the controllers. PATCO received a $100,000 fine and a warning that future slowdowns would lead to criminal prosecution. Leyden stepped down because of impaired health.

Robert Poli followed Leyden as president of PATCO. Poli represented the militant side of controller feelings. He instituted a strike fund and called for increased salaries that, in some cases, would pay a senior controller more than members of the cabinet of the president of the United States. After a long bargaining session, Poli signed a compromise pact with government negotiators.

Then he turned around and voted with his own union to reject it. Union members voted 13,495 to 616 for giving the government a strike ultimatum. Receiving no answer, PATCO struck on 3 August 1981. President Ronald Reagan ordered them back to work within 48 hours. PATCO refused. Reagan fired all but 4,199 who returned to their positions. He then ordered FAA administrators to pick up the slack and instituted the Flow Control 50 program—a safety cutback by airlines of 50 percent of their peak-hour flights. When the Reagan administration got through with PATCO it owed over $40 million in fines and had only $5 million in assets. PATCO had ceased to exist.

What the 1981 PATCO strike really underlined was the difficulties facing the control of aircraft in America's skies and the change in the unions' power position brought about by deregulation of the airline industry. The radar system used to mark flights within a tower's jurisdiction was an older and cumbersome system that relied on the controller to highlight each blip with a plastic marker known as a "shrimp boat." The marker had on it an identification code and abbreviated flight data. A nearby board had more detailed information available. Anytime an on-screen aircraft requested and received new flight data it had to be manually changed on the shrimp boat and the master board. Controllers were also responsible for monitoring incoming traffic not yet on the radar screen by telephone or teletype. It was a system that could drive one to distraction on a calm day, much less a hectic one.

The FAA sought to simplify the system through the use of a computer program, IBM's En Route Stage A. The new radar screen was computer controlled and displayed real-time information directly on the screen. No longer did the blips have to be hand coded. They came up on the screen with the codes already in place. It simplified the job of controllers and automatically handed each plane over to the next tower's radar system, each tower controlling about 600 square miles of airspace. As for union power, the decline marked by President Reagan's wrecking of PATCO would be repeated in other industries until unions learned that to save some jobs they would have to give up many of the gains they had fought so long and hard for during the previous 50 years. It was a new era in economics marked by job insecurity, lower salaries, and an emphasis on productivity. Like many of the companies that failed to adapt to the new order of things, America's organized working people paid a dear price for the new deregulation.

See also Aeronautics; Airline Deregulation Act of 1978; International Brotherhood of Teamsters.

References Kaplan, Daniel P., "The Changing Airline Industry," in Leonard W. Weiss and Michael W. Klass (eds.), *Regulatory Reform* (1986), 40–77; Komons, Nick A., "Professional Air Traffic Controllers Organization," in William M. Leary (ed.), *Encyclopedia of American Business History and Biography* (1992), 382–385; Pickerell, Donald, "The Regulation and Deregulation of U.S. Airlines," in Kenneth Button (ed.), *Airline Deregulation* (1991), 5–47; Williams, George, *The Airline Industry and the Impact of Deregulation* (1993).

Public Roads Administration (PRA)

In 1939 the Bureau of Public Roads (BPR) was renamed the Public Roads Administration and placed under the Federal Works Agency to harmonize it with the rest of the New Deal programs. This organization carried the federal highway programs through World War II until 1949, when the Bureau of Public Roads title was again used and the agency placed under the Department of Commerce. The latter organization held until the Department of Transportation was set up in the 1960s and the Federal Highway Administration was established in 1967, with the BPR being broken up into its component parts. Regardless of name, there was little change in its basic functions of administering highway construction, maintenance, and road safety.

See also Department of Transportation; Federal Highway Administration; Roads and Highways since World War I.

Reference U.S. Department of Transportation, Federal Highway Administration, *America's Highways* (1976).

Pullman, George Mortimer (1831–1897)

Born in upstate New York, George Pullman worked as a store clerk and in his brother's cabinet-making shop until he obtained enough knowledge to go out on his own. He first worked as a building mover. His first jobs involved setting back the buildings on a section of the Erie Canal so it could be widened. Impressed with his work, a Chicago businessman invited Pullman to come out and raise a whole city block. Pullman did it and enabled all of the merchants to continue in business as the job progressed. His fame spread accordingly.

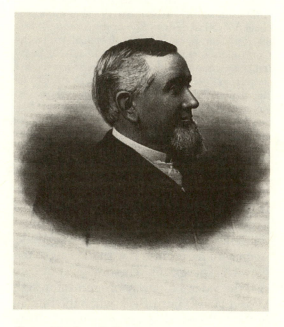

George Mortimer Pullman

But Pullman had other goals in mind. He spent a sleepless night on a three-tiered sleeper on a trip back to New York, and decided that he could build a better rail car. He hired Leonard G. Seibert, a master woodworker, and obtained a couple of coaches from the Chicago and Alton to experiment with. He and Seibert took a 14-foot-long car and put in ten berths, a linen closet, and two tiny washrooms. Each was finished in plush and heated by small box stoves. They rode on standard four-wheeled

trucks. The first run saw only four seats sold at 50 cents apiece, one of which was bought by Pullman himself. But he continued his car building for the Galena Railroad and later the Baltimore & Ohio. All of his cars were commandeered by the Union army during the Civil War.

During the war, Pullman continued to rethink the idea of a sleeper. In 1864, he had a master car builder build a car of Pullman's own design. It cost $20,000 and was named the *Pioneer*. And a pioneer it was. There was not a car as luxurious on any road in the country. But the new car was a foot wider and two and a half feet higher than any passenger car in existence. In fact, it could not fit by any passenger platform or through any bridge in rail service at that time. When people criticized Pullman for his alleged stupidity, he replied, "Change the platforms and the bridges." And that is exactly what happened. Upon the death of President Abraham Lincoln, his body was taken back to Illinois by train. Of course no car was better than Pullman's *Pioneer* for the now-sainted president, and Pullman offered it for free. Not wishing to appear less than respectful to the family of the assassinated Union leader, the Chicago and Alton widened the bridges and narrowed the platforms for the trip. A few months later General U. S. Grant returned to Galena on the same car. Again, the railroads changed the bridges and platforms. Pullman got plenty of free publicity in both cases.

As a matter of fact, the railroads took a new look at Pullman's car and decided that all new rail equipment would be built to its measurements. The Pullman car specifications remained in force until the advent of streamliners, the only changes being in the length of the cars. Meanwhile Pullman and Ben Field jointly patented a folding upper berth, and a year later they invented a lower that was convertible from the day seats. The new car was an instant success. Pullman and Field organized the Pullman Car Company with Robert Todd Lincoln (the dead president's son) as legal advisor. Later, Lincoln would succeed Pullman as president of the organization. Improvement followed improvement. Pullman junked the standard passenger trucks and designed his own with more springs and rubber reinforcement. He adopted the Miller Platform, the best designed underbody of its time. But most of all he made the interiors elegant. His cars soon spread to all parts of the world.

Pullman branched out into other cars, too. He built a combined restaurant-sleeper in 1867 and a dining car in 1868. With the completion of the transcontinental railroad, Pullman's designs were regarded as essential for long trips. He soon introduced a chair car with folding seat backs for cheaper fares. In his English cars, he installed the first electric lighting—in the United States he used Pintsch gas lighting in place of smelly oil lamps. As Pullman grew he absorbed his competition. He took over the Union Car Company by the end of the century, leaving the Monarch Sleeping Car Company, which served only one road in Ohio, and the Wagner Drawing Room Car Company, which had a monopoly on Harriman-owned lines. Wagner was a powerful competitor; he was backed by Cornelius Vanderbilt. So Pullman made a deal with Vanderbilt's enemy, Jay Gould, and equipped the Erie Railroad from New York to Chicago with Pullman Palace Cars. He installed the first vestibule cars on this run in 1887. Pullman also instituted a lengthy legal battle, which he won, bankrupting Wagner in the process. Both Wagner and Monarch fell to Pullman takeovers after George Pullman's death.

Pullman's record was forever marred by his niggardly treatment of his employees. He built a model city that sported a fabulous community center that was reserved for the use of company big shots, while his company housing lacked running water and indoor toilets. When the Panic of 1893 hit, Pullman laid off 4,000 workers and cut the pay of the rest by anywhere from a fourth to a third. But he refused to lower his rents, which ate up most of the employees' pay-checks. Pullman had bragged about the glories of his model community, but the employees were not impressed. They went on strike, led by Eugene V. Debs and the American Railway Union.

The resulting bloody confrontation spread from Pullman's plant to the hauling railroads before it was put down by federal soldiers and the strikers blacklisted. When a striker sued to obtain a letter of recommendation and won, Pullman and the General Managers Association issued letters on paper made by the Crane Brothers Paper Company. But Crane provided Pullman and the railroads with two watermarks, one with an erect crane and the other with a feeding crane. The latter was handed out to strikers so that future employers could identify them by holding the sheet up to the light. Among workers this became known as the "crane with a broken neck" and meant sure unemployment. Only the Chicago, Rock Island & Pacific resisted this solution and hired most of its former workers back.

Pullman died shortly after the strike was crushed, but his company continued to prosper and create newer and better passenger cars. First came all-steel cars, then roomettes, spring mattresses, all-aluminum cars, and double-decker cars. Pullman has altered its production with the decline of passenger service and gone into freight cars to keep up with the changes in modern railroading.

See also Coffin, Lorenzo S.; Janney, Eli Hamilton; Railroad Unions; Safety Appliance Act.

References Beebe, Lucius, *Mansions on Rails* (1959); Beebe, Lucius, *Mr. Pullman's Elegant Palace Car* (1961); Harding, Carroll R., *George M. Pullman* (1951); Hubbard, Freeman, *Railroad Avenue* (1945); Hubbard, Freeman, *Encyclopedia of North American Railroading* (1981); Husband, Joseph, *The Story of the Pullman Car* (1917); Lindsay, Almont, *The Pullman Strike* (1942); White, John A., "George Mortimer Pullman," in Keith L. Bryant, Jr. (ed.), *EABHB: Railroads in the Age of Regulation* (1988), 335–339; White, John H., Jr., *The American Railroad Passenger Car* (1978).

Rail Passenger Service Act of 1970

This congressional measure created the quasi-nationalized rail passenger entity, National Railroad Passenger Corporation (NRPC), known popularly as Amtrak. Made up of eight federally appointed directors and a chief executive, the NRPC established the process by which Amtrak became the only rail passenger carrier of the nation. The 1970 act was renewed in 1973, 1974, 1975, 1976, and 1978, the latter making it a more or less permanent institution.

See also Amtrak; Pell Plan; Transportation Acts.

Railroad Labor Act of 1926

Railroads and unions had been engaged in a vicious argument since the Panic of 1893, involving a workable system of labor contract negotiations. The result was the congressional act of 1926, a historic measure that provided for union recognition, collective bargaining, settlement of grievances, and the arbitration of disputes. At the time, the statute was considered a milestone in good labor-management relations, particularly by U.S. Supreme Court justice Felix Frankfurter, who praised its worker-management creation. But there was a flaw in the act: It provided for closed-shop conditions (compulsory union membership). There were two reasons for this condition. First, the unions believed that all who benefited in negotiations should have to support the costs of seeking better conditions, and second, management wanted all negotiations to be binding on every employee. This provision of the act was challenged successfully in *Texas & New Orleans Railway v. Brotherhood of Railway and Steamship Clerks* (1930), when the U.S. Supreme Court ruled that any employee had the right to choose whomever one desired for labor representation in collective bargaining. This court attitude would endure until challenged by the New Deal legislators and administrators by the Wagner-Connery Act (1935) that created the National Labor Relations Board (NLRB) to recognize, certify,

and deal with union representatives in all industries. The 1935 act was upheld in the U.S. Supreme Court case *NLRB v. Jones and Laughlin Steel Corporation* (1937).

See also Emergency Railroad Transportation Act; Transportation Acts.

References Latham, Earl, *The Politics of Railroad Coordination* (1959); *NLRB v. Jones and Laughlin Steel Corporation*, 301 US 1 (1937); Swindler, William F., *Court and Constitution in the 20th Century* (1969); *Texas & New Orleans Railroad v. Brotherhood of Railway and Steamship Clerks*, 281 US 548 (1930).

Railroad Retirement Act of 1934

Before the creation of the nationwide system of Social Security, Congress sought to create a retirement system within one industry on which to base its later program. The railroad workers were chosen because they represented the most organized group of industrial workers at that time. All railroads in interstate commerce (which, broadly defined, could include just about everyone) had to participate in providing a retirement and workers' compensation fund through worker and company contributions. Within a year the measure was overturned by the U.S. Supreme Court in the case *Railroad Retirement Board v. Alton Railroad Company*. The Court ruled that this was an obvious overextension of the commerce clause to matters that had no application to interstate commerce and violated the due process clause of the Fifth Amendment. After Congress passed the Social Security Law it rewrote the railroad retirement law as the Wagner-Crosser Act (1935), which set up a three-member board to administer the rail workers' retirement pension fund. With the upholding of the Social Security Act, the Wagner-Crosser Act was rewritten once again to conform totally to the former measure in 1937 as the Railroad Retirement Act.

See also Emergency Railroad Transportation Act; Transportation Acts.

References *Helvering v. Davis*, 301 US 619 (1937); *Railroad Retirement Board v. Alton Railroad Company*, 295 US 330; *Stewart Machine Company v. Davis*, 301 US 548 (1937); Swindler, William F., *Court and Constitution in the 20th Century* (1970).

Railroad Revitalization and Regulatory Reform (4-R) Act of 1976

With the disappointing merger of the Erie and Lackawanna Railroads, the even more spectacular collapse of the Penn Central, the federal government's demand that Illinois Central Gulf fix its roadbed so Amtrak could run on it safely (there were over 200 slowdown orders on the line between Chicago and New Orleans), and the Securities and Exchange Commission threatening to sue Burlington Northern to find out how much its equity had declined because of the general deterioration of its equipment and roadbed, the American railroads were in dire straits by the 1970s. The result was the Railroad Revitalization and Regulatory Reform Act of 1976.

Known as the 4-R Act, this congressional measure was to address the problems of mergers and the chopping off of unprofitable branch lines, so graphically illustrated by the ten-year end of the Rock Island. If there was to be increased merger demand, such shortcomings had to be rectified. According to this measure, the proceedings surrounding a merger had to be completed within 24 months. The Interstate Commerce Commission (ICC) was to reach its decision within 180 days following the investigation. Samplings of traffic diversion would have to follow strict guidelines to prevent exaggeration and misrepresentation. The Rail Services Planning Office of the ICC would represent public interest, and the Office of Public Counsel of the ICC would speak for small business and those who could not afford to engage in the expensive regulatory process. Finally, Congress provided massive federal subsidies to money-losing branch lines ($500 million), for the rehabilitation of mainlines ($1.6 billion), to upgrade the Amtrak Boston-Washington line ($1.75 billion), and for Conrail ($2.1 billion).

The Department of Transportation undertook a study of all rail lines to determine which were the most critical, in case the government had to bail out the entire industry should it go bankrupt like the Penn Central. When this report appeared in 1977, many wondered if the government was trying to save American railroading or kill it off, as it gutted the heart of the feeder lines to concentrate on the transcontinental mainlines and thus reduced rail traffic by 20 million gross tons a year. Yet none of this recognized the real problem—that Congress had created the rail mess by subsidizing airline and truck transport, which made the rail mergers of doubtful value and left the merger laws vague and outdated, still responding to conditions from 1920 and 1940. This left the merger process up to the rail management, which had gotten itself into the disaster in the first place, and the investors who refused to put their money in an industry that looked bad, making it worse. Labor of course saw no reason to cooperate with mergers that did nothing to stabilize jobs, but threatened instead to wipe out all of them. Indeed, the diffusion of blame meant that no one had to take responsibility for any of it, and no one did. This lack of goodwill, commitment, and leadership was the challenge that Congress would have to solve. It took the Staggers Rail Act of 1980 to provide the impetus for this reform.

See also Motor Carrier Acts; National Rail Passenger Act of 1971; Regional Rail Reorganization Act of 1973; Staggers Rail Act of 1980; Transportation Acts.

References Keeler, Theodore E., *Railroads, Freight and Public Policy* (1983); Saunders, Richard, *The Railroad Mergers and the Coming of Conrail* (1978).

Railroad Unification Act 1931

The Railroad Unification Act of 1931 was the Herbert Hoover administration's plan to revitalize the transportation industry in the face of the Great Depression, which called for more consolidation of railroads to provide adequate service, a more simplified rate structure, and lower operating costs. Hoover claimed that these were the goals of the Transportation Act of 1920, an overly optimistic viewpoint, as that act had done a lot of things but none involved the goals of the 1931 measure. The new act went a long way to vindicate the scientific management solutions put forth by the United States

Railroad Administration during World War I and which were junked by Congress in 1920. The measure came so late in Hoover's term that it had little effect, but it was built on by Franklin D. Roosevelt's New Deal and the idea of industry codes and consolidation to stimulate investment and increase job security and production.

See also Emergency Railroad Transportation Act; Fess-Parker Bill.

Reference Saunders, Richard, *The Railroad Mergers and the Coming of Conrail* (1978).

Railroad Unions

In the union-busting, blacklisting, economic fluctuations that followed the American Civil War, nearly one million rail workers roamed the countryside looking for work. Because of their transient nature they were known as "boomers." Using fake names to escape blacklists, police, or former wives, these men moved from job to job. The railroads hired them because of the seasonal nature of railroad work, especially at harvest time. But the regular rail workers were not transients, even though they were often treated as such. Working hours were irregular, and competition between rail lines on the lucrative Chicago–New York run was so intense that railroads began to lay off workers and double the size of their trains to make up the losses.

The result of these practices and the generally risky working conditions associated with rail work led to the first major rail strike in American history in 1877. The strike was supposed to begin in Indiana on a Pennsylvania Railroad subsidiary, but they balked and Baltimore & Ohio employees at Baltimore and Martinsburg, West Virginia, took the lead. Trains stopped between the Atlantic and the Mississippi and from Canada to Virginia. With the trains tied up completely and the local militia on the workers' side, President Rutherford B. Hayes sent in federal troops to open up the rails. Workers assaulted the armory at Baltimore but received a bloody repulse. More strikers controlled Pittsburgh and closed down the Pennsy main line.

As the Pennsylvania militia was unreli-able, the New York militia was sent in to quell the strike, with federal support. The troops had to fight their way down the rails, closed by wrecked engines and rolling stock. In Pittsburgh, rioters seized a gun works and used the arms to force the soldiers to take refuge in a Pennsylvania Railroad roundhouse. The strikers sent a flaming oil train in to smoke them out. The soldiers came out shooting, killing and being killed. They finally managed to escape. President Hayes ordered the regular army to quell the strike, which had by now spread to the coal mines. Beginning in Chicago and methodically working eastward, the soldiers reduced the strike. Most labor men had no desire to fight the army and its cannon and Gatling guns, and the violence petered out. Although labor never restored its lost wages, William H. Vanderbilt of the New York Central chose to believe that only a few of his employees were involved and distributed $200,000 among his loyal operators. But labor had shown that it had greater power and public sympathy than had been previously thought.

As the strike of 1877 demonstrated, many early attempts to organize American trainmen into comprehensive union organizations across all trades did not meet with success. Unlike other workers of the late nineteenth and early twentieth centuries, railroad men had their own craft unions, which, by and large, eschewed violence. But there were train employees in the Knights of Labor, an early attempt to organize American labor, regardless of craft, by industry, established by Clarence V. Powderly. The Knights called for the eight-hour day, arbitration between labor and management, a graduated income tax, and consumers' and producers' cooperatives.

Unfortunately for their continued well-being, the Knights' failure in several strikes (especially against the Texas & Pacific Railroad and against the national packinghouse industries), the interest in craft unions and the rising American Federation of Labor (which was a national organization of craft unions by Samuel Gompers), and economic depression led to the Knights' downfall in the 1880s. Instrumental in their demise was the Haymarket Square Incident in which the Knights, on strike for an eight-hour day in Chicago industries, were given the reputation of being uncompromising anarchists after an unknown person threw a bomb into the police deployed against them. Four strikers were executed and many others jailed. Two successive Illinois governors, Richard Oglesby and John Peter Altgeld, pardoned several of the jailed men, but the damage to the union had been fatal.

Eugene V. Debs attempted to salvage something from the affair by organizing all railroad employees in the American Railway Union (ARU) in 1893. After a strike against the Great Northern tied up the trains for nearly a week, the ARU won its demands. But when the union took on the Pullman plant in Chicago, it went down to defeat against the combined armed and legal forces of business and the federal government. Debs and others went to jail. The Industrial Workers of the World (IWW), known as the "Wobblies" and organized to hasten the fall of capitalism in the early twentieth century, had little impact on railroad labor relations. Some trainmen might give IWW men a ride, free lodging, or a meal as brother laborers, but little else came of it.

The main reason that the American labor movement had little impact on railroad workers was that they organized among themselves on the basis of craft before the industrial unions came into being. Railroaders engaged in what might have been the first real labor strike in America when, in 1855, the employees of the Boston and Thompson Railroad hooked up all 13 coaches of the line and rode into Boston to demand six months of back pay owed them. They sat there for three weeks, making occasional acts of sabotage against the rails until the company treasury went dry from lack of mill hauling and public sympathy waned. The 1,200 workers then scattered to the winds, never gaining their money. It took six months to hire new employees and repair the damage.

During the Civil War, the first railroad craft union organized in Marshall, Michi-gan, in protest to the Michigan Central's policy of cutting salaries and firing men who protested existing working conditions. Thirteen engineers formed a protective organization. If any were fired all would quit, paralyzing the railroad. They also demanded that their firemen be retained under the same threat. Successful with the Michigan Central, it dawned on the men that if all engineers stuck together on all roads they would have more clout. Representatives from a half dozen railroads met in Detroit and launched the Brotherhood of Locomotive Engineers (BLE). In 1867, they began to publish their own magazine, now called the *Locomotive Engineer*. In 1887 they formed a women's auxiliary for their wives. The BLE was involved with the violent strikes in 1877 and 1888, but not the Pullman Strike of 1894. In 1915, along with other labor unions, the BLE spearheaded the drive for the eight-hour day, which became a national standard in Congress' Adamson Act of 1916. After World War II, the BLE and other unions struck the railroads for better working conditions. President Harry S Truman threatened to draft the strikers into federal service to end the impasse. The BLE returned to work with an 18.5-cents-an-hour raise.

Shortly after the Civil War, the railroad conductors followed the engineers and organized themselves into what, after several name changes, became the Order of Railway Conductors (ORC). This union was organized on the Illinois Central (IC) in 1868 with an initial program that called for members to make themselves more valuable workers entitled to improved pay, working conditions, and job security through education, sobriety, and safety. The union at first was present only on the IC, but word spread to the Chicago, Burlington & Quincy (CB&Q). Angry CB&Q managers demanded that conductors forswear membership or lose their jobs. The attack backfired and the conductors met at Columbus, Ohio, and organized nationwide, electing a fired CB&Q employee as their head. Soon there was a women's auxiliary (for wives) and an executive committee to negotiate with management. By the 1890s, the union had formed a strike committee. The more militant stance for wages, hours, and safety brought 90 percent of all rail conductors into the union by 1910. Like the BLE, the ORC was instrumental in obtaining federal laws like the Sixteen Hour Act (no one would work more than 16 hours in 24), which cut accidents drastically, the eight-hour day, and the usual benefits packages associated with modern unions. In the early 1950s, its name was changed to the Order of Railway Conductors and Brakemen.

As with the engine drivers and conductors, railroad firemen organized their own union in 1873 at Port Jervis, New York, the Brotherhood of Locomotive Firemen and Enginemen. Membership included firemen and hostlers, who manned the engines in the yards and repair facilities. Their program was much the same, but the union contributed one of the truly important labor organizers in the figure of Eugene V. Debs, an early officer and editor of its publication, the *Locomotive Firemen's Magazine*. The switchmen formed their group in 1877 at Chicago as the Switchmen's Union of North America. Their goals concerned hours, wages, and safety. It suffered two disastrous losses to management in strikes against the Chicago & North Western and the CB&Q, which caused its early demise in 1894. Three months later, however, the union organized again and affiliated with the American Federation of Labor, the only rail union that did until well into the twentieth century.

The brakemen organized their union in a caboose at the Delaware & Hudson yard in Oneonta, New York, in 1883. Only eight men attended the first meeting. Their concern was the usual—wages, hours, and safety. Union-kept records after the Civil War show that 70 percent of all railroad workers were killed on the job between 1866 and 1870. Needless to say, they could not get accident insurance. The running joke was the manager telling a job applicant that he had no openings at that time, but if he would come back in a week someone would be killed by then. Among the brakemen's early supporters was Eugene V. Debs, who supported the change in the Union's name from the Brotherhood of Railway Brakemen to the Brotherhood of Railroad Trainmen (BRT). After the end of the American Railway Union in the Pullman strike, the BRT took up the slack and expanded its muster rolls to include conductors, brakemen, yardmen, roadmen, baggagemen, and even bus drivers. It became one of the largest railroad unions and engaged in many strikes for its members, including the joint action with the BLE during the Truman years.

While white railroad workers were organizing themselves for better wages and working conditions, black employees had not been included, mirroring the segregated nature of American society as a whole. African Americans had contributed much to the construction of the nation's rail lines, especially in the South. With the end of the Civil War, blacks found themselves no longer in bondage, but not really free either. In place of chattel slavery came a form of peonage and wage slavery. The mores of American white society restricted the freed people to the most menial of tasks at the lowest wages. In 1867, with the founding of the Pullman Palace Car Company, a new field opened in which to exploit black labor. As porters, they had a guaranteed job not in competition with whites. But as Pullman employees, they suffered as did their white counterparts from Pullman's low wages, long hours (on call for a 24-hour day), and little provision for food or comfort. If a Pullman car broke down, its porter had to stay with it even though a car on a siding had no heat, light, or food. Although black porters and maids did not join in the 1894 Pullman strike, they were not pleased with their working conditions.

The deprivation of jobs extended into the yard and engine crews. Few railroad companies hired blacks in any number unless they were needed to break a strike by white employees. The African Americans were so desperate for work that they felt compelled to take such offers. The striking union men, all white, merely had their racial stereotypes against blacks reinforced. Labor contracts regularly called for limiting employment of African-Americans. Those blacks who had jobs could not be promoted because contracts permitted union men alone in the higher positions. Racial strife was especially hard in the competition between black and white firemen in the Deep South. This forced blacks to rely on themselves to improve their own working conditions. The Association of Colored Railway Trainmen and Locomotive Firemen was established in 1913, but excluded from the American labor movement until the Congress of Industrial Organizations (CIO) accepted them in 1933. The Chicago (independent) Red Caps Union dropped its American Federation of Labor (AFL) affiliation when the parent organization threatened to combine them with a white affiliate, and remained unattached for five years before joining the CIO, a less discriminatory body, in 1942.

Although two black unions had sprung up during World War I in response to the War Labor Board's rulings (the Brotherhood of Sleeping Car Porters Protective Union [BSCP] and the Railway Men's Association [RMA]), neither was recognized by the United States Railroad Administration. While the RMA was the most independent of the Pullman Company, the car maker managed to replace both by 1920 with the Pullman Porters Benefit Association, a company union. By far the most influential African-American labor advocate was the Brotherhood of Sleeping Car Porters, formed in Harlem in 1925. Led by A. Philip Randolph, the BSCP had great difficulty getting the U.S. government to recognize its existence. When it struck Pullman in 1928, the Interstate Commerce Commission voted four to three to decline jurisdiction. The major force behind the union was Randolph, who survived company pressures against him because he was not a Pullman employee but a self-employed editor, writer, speaker, and labor organizer. Even many blacks asserted that Randolph was too radical, but he did manage to keep the union a unique African-American spokesman in labor relations.

In 1936, Randolph and the BSCP took in another predominantly black working force, the redcaps. Originally named in the 1890s for the piece of red flannel that decorated their caps at Grand Central Station to differentiate them from customers, the redcaps had received formal uniforms and red caps soon thereafter. They generally worked for tips and occasionally, depending upon the station, a nominal wage. But an enterprising redcap could make a good living. Randolph and the union got the redcaps bargaining rights and a minimum wage under the Railway Labor Act of the New Deal. The railroads began to charge for each piece of luggage carried on to make up the costs of this agreement. Randolph also obtained the exclusive right to represent all Pullman porters in a vote under the Wagner Act, displacing the company's union. A couple of years later, all maids and other sleeping-car employees were organized in a ladies auxiliary (representing real workers, not wives, in this case).

Since 1929, these standard rail unions have had the Railway Labor Executives Association (RLEA), an overall unit designed to handle all labor-management negotiations. In the 1930s, as its first big order of business the RLEA negotiated with the Association of American Railroads to create the federal legislation that set up the still-used retirement system. Meanwhile, the Brotherhood of Railroad Trainmen, the Order of Railway Conductors and Brakemen, the Brotherhood of Locomotive Firemen and Enginemen, and the Switchmen's Union of North America merged to form one massive union in 1969 called the United Transportation Union. Only the BLE decided to remain independent—engineers are sort of a breed apart anyway. Formal labor bargaining is currently handled by the Railway Labor Conference (RLC) and its National Carriers Conference Committee. The latter is comprised of representatives of ten major railroads and the chairman of the RLC. The Brotherhood of Sleeping Car Porters and Red Caps (the name was changed in 1936) has gradually disappeared as passenger service has declined. In 1978, it joined the racially integrated Railway and Airline Clerks as an autonomous member.

One of the more noted issues of the post–World War II period, particularly between railroad labor and management, has been the notion of "featherbedding." This make-work concept had been recognized in labor contracts forcing railways to hire more workers than needed. Part of the problem came from technological advances that allowed companies to drop employees for machines. A typical example is the supplanting of the end of the caboose and its two-man crew at the rear of the train by a little black box with some computer chips and a flashing red light. Hooked into the signal circuits of the train, the box can tell if the whole train is hooked up and running properly and notify the engine crew if not. Called a "FRED" in rail parlance, it stands for "Flashing Rear End Device." Another featherbedding argument concerns the number of train crew. Once as many as a half dozen men rode the train fore and aft; now the number is generally reduced to the engineer and conductor in the cab. The fireman, switchmen, and front and rear brakemen are gone except for local way freights that switch local industries and need a "go-fer" or two to throw the track turnouts. Featherbedding, a hot issue in the 1960s, has become a relatively minor problem in the 1990s.

See also Florida East Coast Railway; New Orleans Conditions; Pullman, George Mortimer; Railroads before and during the Civil War; Railroads from Appomattox to Deregulation; Randolph, Asa Philip; Safety Appliance Act.

References Anderson, Jervis, and Peter Stone, *A. Philip Randolph* (1973); Botkin, Benjamin A., and Alvin F. Harlow, *A Treasury of Railroad Folklore* (1953); Boyle, Ohio D., *History of Railroad Strikes* (1935); Brazeal, Brailsford R., *The Brotherhood of Sleeping Car Porters* (1946); Bruce, Robert V., *1877: Year of Violence* (1959); Burbank, David T., *Reign of the Rabble* (1966); Burgess, George H., and Miles C. Kennedy, *Centennial History of the Pennsylvania Railroad Company* (1949); Caleb, Walter F., *Brotherhood of Railroad Trainmen* (1937); Cooke, Richard J. (ed.), *A Brief History of the Brotherhood of Locomotive Engineers* (1977); Dougherty, Carroll R., *Labor Problems in American Industry* (1933); Drake, St. Clair, and Horace R. Clayton, *Black Metropolis* (1945); Eggert, Gerald G., *Railroad Labor Disputes* (1967); Foner, Philip S., *The Great Labor Uprising of 1877* (1978); Harris, Herbert, *American Labor* (1939); Hill, Herbert, *Black Labor and the American Legal System* (1977); Holbrook, Stewart H., *The Story of American Railroads* (1947); Hubbard, Freeman, et al., *Pennsylvania Songs and Legends* (1949); Hubbard, Freeman, *Encyclopedia of North American Railroading* (1981); Kaufman, Jacob J., *Collective Bargaining in the Railroad Industry* (1954); Knapke, William F., and Freeman Hubbard, *The Railroad Caboose* (1968); Leiter, Robert D., *Featherbedding and Job Security* (1964); Licht, Walter, "Railroad Unions and Brotherhoods," in Keith L. Bryant, Jr. (ed.), *EABHB: Railroads in the Age of Regulation* (1988), 354–357; Northrup, Herbert R., *Organized Labor and the Negro* (1944); Robbins, Edwin C., *Railway Conductors* (1970); Weinstein, Paul (ed.), *Featherbedding and Technological Change* (1965).

Railroad War Board

The Railroad War Board was a private attempt by railroad managers to produce the traffic needed to move war goods to the eastern ports for shipment to the Western Front in France during World War I. At least four attempts had already failed, but the vicious winter of 1917 had caused total collapse of the transportation facilities in the United States critical to the war effort. The board ordered equipment and rolling stock to be redistributed to the railroads with the goods to be moved, regardless of actual ownership. For example, Lackawanna was told to move 1,100 hopper cars to interchange points for use by other swamped lines without their own cars. The board's efforts failed to solve the problem, a fact many blamed on the Interstate Commerce Commission's failure to allow railroad consolidation prior to the war, egged on by politicians looking for popular votes. As with all voluntary efforts, it was hard to break former prejudices, or as one board member from the New York Central put it, "I've always wanted to issue orders to the Pennsylvania Railroad, and now I've got my chance." The idea collapsed as no rail executive in good faith would send his freight by another road. The results were cross shipments (Kentucky coal going east and Pennsylvania coal going west) and crowded eastern ports, while Gulf ports were underutilized. The failure of the

Railroad War Board led to the government takeover of the rails under the Army Appropriation Act of 1916 and the creation of the United States Railroad Administration.

See also Federal Control Act of 1918; McAdoo, William G.; United States Railroad Administration.

References Godfrey, Aaron Austin, *Government Operation of the Railroads* (1974); Kerr, K. Austin, *American Railroad Politics* (1968); Lyon, Peter, *To Hell in a Day Coach* (1968); Saunders, Richard, *The Railroad Mergers and the Coming of Conrail* (1978).

Railroads before and during the Civil War

If any one factor made the United States unique from the start it was its vast distances. The nation was truly continental in scope, stretching between the Atlantic and the Pacific, and from the Gulf to the Great Lakes. Canals could provide transportation in many areas in the East, but the arid west needed other means of transportation. Roads might help, but the distances were so great even east of the Mississippi that some mechanical means of propulsion seemed to be called for. The steamboat solved a lot of problems, but rivers did not always go where people did, and not all waterways were navigable. The real answer loomed on the horizon as early as the beginning of the nineteenth century—railroads, the first really big businesses of the American Industrial Revolution.

The railroad had proved its mettle by 1830 in England. It could go where canals and steamboats could not, and it could haul great loads at speed, something that humans and animals could not do. But although the railroad was developed and proven as a commercial venture in Europe, it was in the great expanses of the United States that it found it first real home. By 1840, before railroad building had even begun to burgeon, there were three times the miles of tracks in America as in all of Europe. The first railroads in the United States were mining company lines, generally less than one or two miles long, and often running as inclined planes and using horses and mules to power the little trains.

The state of New Jersey issued the first actual charter for a railroad to John Stevens in 1815, but it was never built. Nonetheless, Stevens went on to build the first operating steam locomotive, which he ran on a bit of circular track on his Hoboken estate. Others eventually expanded upon his original charter and had an actual railroad operating by 1839. The first operating railroad was the Granite Railway Company that ran from a quarry near Quincy to the Boston area in Massachusetts.

Railroads were initially viewed as some sort of demonic contrivance, designed to lead the gullible down the path to hell and in violation of existing scientific laws and plain common sense. After all, everyone knew it was dangerous to travel faster than a horse could gallop. The first person to envision the polluting effects of locomotive exhaust on the environment was Henry David Thoreau. Wily politicians, like Martin Van Buren of New York, spread these rumors in a vain effort to protect projects like the Erie Canal from future obsolescence. So did freighters, wagon builders, stage lines, and steamboat interests. But all of them were more than happy to assist in their own demise by hauling goods and supplies to the railroaders as they extended their twin lines of iron into uncharted territory.

The first railroad chartered as a common carrier (that is, it pledged to refuse service to no one, charge a reasonable price for services rendered, serve all equally, and take responsibility that passengers and cargoes would arrive safely) was the Baltimore & Ohio (B&O) in 1827. Construction began the following year. The B&O used standard passenger equipment of the day—a sort of stagecoach mounted on railroad wheels and freight cars that looked like wagons. But the first railroad to haul passengers was the Delaware & Hudson Canal Company, using the *Stourbridge Lion*, an imported locomotive from England. Its later import, the *John Bull*, was the first locomotive to have a pilot or cowcatcher mounted on its front beam.

The first American-made engine to pull cars was the *Best Friend of Charleston*, which eventually ran between that city and Hamburg (across from Augusta, Georgia) beginning in 1830, in an effort to intersect upstate trade that normally followed the river to Savannah. The Charleston & Hamburg Railroad was also the first railroad to commit itself completely to steam power. It was a daring idea; most early steam locomotives were not yet able to outpull a good team of horses. The following year, the *De Witt Clinton* engine pulled a train in the Mohawk Valley on what wound up as a part of the New York Central System. Many of these first locomotives had their steam cylinders mounted high over the rear wheels to which they were connected by drive rods, which made them look like insects from a distance, hence their name, "grasshoppers."

The early cars were not any more sophisticated than the engines that pulled them. They usually had four fixed wheels, which limited their size to whatever would negotiate the sharpest curve. It was not unheard-of for the train to flip over in a curve because of the rigid wheelbase of engine and cars. In the 1830s, a Delaware & Hudson engineer, John B. Jervis, developed the railroad truck, a two-axle, four-wheel device in a rigid frame that swiveled from its center and was attached by a kingpin to a crossbeam on the car above, known as a bolster. Still, the wheels seemed to derail upon occasion when the track was unevenly laid until Joseph Harrison of Philadelphia developed the equalizing beam, which put pressure on each wheel allowing them to float with the ups and downs in the track.

Like the cars and engines, early roadbeds were a haphazard thing; often the tracks were laid on the ground with a minimum of grading. Early rail was wood with strap iron laid on top. The metal often curled up at its joints when it became worn, leading to some nasty accidents until the idea of the all-iron (later steel) T rail came into being, an idea suggested by Robert L. Stevens in New Jersey. Wooden crossties came into vogue at the same time, another Stevens contribution, found out by accident when a load of rock piers failed to arrive to rest the rails on. The expedience of wooden crossties was so successful that it became the norm. They were imbedded in gravel for drainage and protection from frost heaves.

As the 1840s passed, the idea of a rail network came into being, although it was greatly hampered by the lack of a standard gauge (the distance between rails). The British had adopted the 4-foot 8.5-inch distance early on, and it spread to New England, which tended to import English equipment. But in the American South 5 feet was considered normal. Thus it was necessary to change trains several times whenever a long trip was taken. Pennsylvania and Ohio led the war of the gauges, with each having seven different track widths within their boundaries. The Erie Railroad decided to use 6 feet as its norm—the problem was that other lines in New York State used the British width, so Erie cut itself out of a lot of trade until it changed its whole system in one mighty effort. After the Civil War demonstrated the need for quick interchanges of passengers and freight, the whole nation did the same as the Erie, converting to the British standard in the 1880s.

By the time of the Civil War, there was still no single rail line that ran from New York to Chicago, or anywhere else, for that matter. One made such a trip by buying tickets on several railroads and changing trains when necessary. But at least the lines existed in the area north of the Ohio River. South of Kentucky, one could travel from east to west on only one line through eastern Tennessee. The three states with the most track were New York, Pennsylvania, and Ohio. Following close behind were Massachusetts, Indiana, Illinois, the Carolinas, Tennessee, and Georgia. As a matter of fact, the Southeast had more rails laid than it is generally given credit for, and they would become critical to the life of the Confederacy and its armies.

But generally the nation lacked the private capital to build railroads. This led to the notion of government subsidy, which got tangled up in the tariff and slavery debates because it affected what could be done under a Constitution that was vague about the financial responsibilities of such activity.

The states' rights South especially feared granting undefined powers to the central government and, led by the Jacksonian Democrats, a strong notion of states' rights blocked federal action for most of the prewar period. A few exceptions were government surveys of the routes of the B&O and the Charleston & Hamburg, and the land grant given to the Illinois Central Railroad in Illinois, Mississippi, and Alabama to connect North and South along a line from Chicago to Mobile.

By the time of the Civil War, railroad fever had produced congressional grants of lands in ten states totaling 18 million acres and benefiting 45 railroads, despite the sectional controversy. It was far from enough, causing railroad advocates to turn to the states. The problem with the states was that canal construction had already used up the public largesse, resulting in many states having constitutional prohibitions against internal improvements of any kind. In these cases, local and city governments stepped into the breech. By the Civil War the states alone had gone into debt $90 million on various rail projects. Private capital in the form of stocks and bonds also came to the fore, and with it came the first inklings of what would happen after the Civil War and during the remainder of the nineteenth century: massive public fraud and government manipulation. By granting free passes, buying out the newspapers, advertisements, and outright bribes, Robert F. Stockton made New Jersey the "Camden & Amboy State" after the name of his railroad. In neighboring New York, men like Daniel Drew, Cornelius Vanderbilt, Jim Fisk, Jay Gould, and others took note.

By 1860, the railroad had become the dominant transportation form in the United States. It offered simple, reliable, flexible, all-weather transportation that outshown its competition. When it came to dense traffic and great distances, railroads could move goods faster, in greater quantity, and cheaper than any other form of transport. And when well managed, they provided a good return on investment, jobs, and the incentive for increased agricultural

and industrial production. By the Civil War, it was becoming obvious that Chicago would be the center for this new means of transportation, the hub for the rails from the East, South, and West, with a connection to the Great Lakes trade besides.

Nothing illustrated the effect that the railroads had on the Civil War more than the famous Andrews' Raid, an undercover operation by a determined band of Northern soldiers dressed as civilians, who hoped to ride almost to Atlanta, steal a train, and flee back to Union lines, wrecking and burning the Confederate railroad that supplied its army in Tennessee. The whole episode was enshrined in the Walt Disney movie, *The Great Locomotive Chase*. Of course, the plan went awry, but the exploits of James Andrews and his 21 men as they tried to improvise in an attempt to carry out their mission was high adventure, as was the dogged pursuit of the raiders by the conductor, William A. Fuller, whose train they stole. On foot, by handcar, and with three locomotives, Fuller maneuvered around several oncoming trains and ambushes set by the raiders, allowing them no time to burn a single bridge. Finally arrested by Confederate cavalry, their train out of wood and water, Andrews and his men were convicted as spies and sentenced to be hanged. They staged a daring prison break but most were recaptured and Andrews and seven men hanged. The others were eventually exchanged, and the survivors received the first congressional Medals of Honor from the hand of President Abraham Lincoln himself.

As the Andrews raiders showed, the Civil War was one that revolved around railroads. But that was really nothing new. As early as 1838, General Edmund P. Gaines suggested that the United States consider railroads as a part of the nation's strategic defense. He proposed that a series of lines be built out of the center of the country (then Kentucky) so that troops could be shifted to defend the borders by rapid movement. His ideas were too revolutionary for that time and probably suggested the wrong approach. But within ten years, American troops from Pennsylvania made at least part

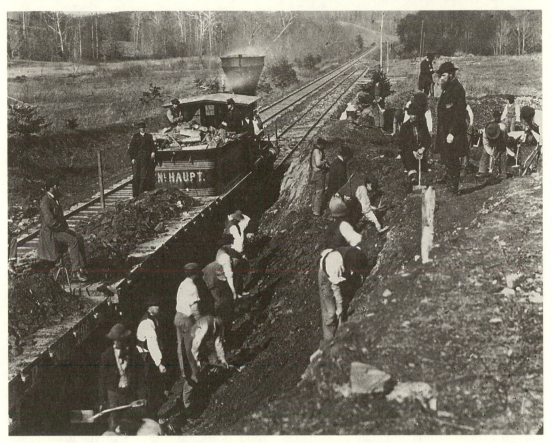

General Haupt (standing, right) oversees the U.S. Military Railroad Construction Corps' repair of the Orange &
Alexandria Railroad in 1863.

of their trip to Mexico by rail, the first such move in American military history. The rail movement was such a small part of the strategic advance on Mexico City that it went unnoticed, but the approaching Civil War would change all of that. It would be the world's first railroad war, and its innovations would be studied throughout the world, especially in the German states, where they would form the basis of a vast national mobilization embodied in the World War I Schlieffen Plan.

Numerous soldiers and regiments went to war North and South by rail from the first day of the Civil War. It simply was the easiest way to deploy men to Washington or Richmond (or anyplace else) if the rails were nearby. The North found out right away that the shifting of troops between trains could be hazardous as the pro-secession ri-

oters in Baltimore demonstrated. Even President Abraham Lincoln had to sneak through Baltimore at night in disguise to his inaugural in 1861. The Baltimore & Ohio Railroad had the advantage of being the most direct route between the national capital and the Old Northwest, but it ran through Virginia and Maryland.

Fortunately, in both cases, the rails went through pro-Union areas in both states, but that did not prevent Confederate cavalry raiders from wrecking the tracks on a regular basis throughout the war. The situation was so bad that the Federals raised the Sixth West Virginia (the state was formed from a rump government representing loyal Virginia in 1863) Railroad Infantry. This volunteer regiment was unique in that its sole purpose was to garrison strategic rail centers and bridge abutments and protect the cars and structures from Confederate attack. The soldiers never had to leave home as they were mustered in to guard, in effect, their own environs. That helped keep the trains rolling for most of the war.

But the battle of First Manassas demonstrated that the North had seriously misjudged the effect of railroads in modern warfare. Confederate armies used the Manassas Gap Railroad to shift troops in from the Shenandoah, where they disembarked just behind the field of conflict to give the rebels the first major victory of the war. A year later, the Confederates moved an entire army from one theater of war (Mississippi) to another (eastern Tennessee) by rail in a wide sweep through southern Alabama. The direct route had been interdicted by Yankee soldiers, but the rails allowed a long trip to be made in a matter of days, about the same time as a direct march. In 1863, after his retreat from the battle of Gettysburg, General Robert E. Lee shipped two of his divisions (about 18,000 men) and their supporting artillery from Virginia to northern Georgia, where they helped the Confederate army there win its only major victory of the war.

The rebels also tore up small irrelevant branch lines and extended their existing railroads through strategic areas in Alabama and Mississippi that had not received tracks before the war. In this manner they replaced what east–west rail connections they lost in the Union invasion of central and western Tennessee. They held onto eastern Tennessee as long as they could (which, like all strategic Southern rail areas, was pro-Union), as its rails provided the most direct route between Virginia and the Old Southwest. The rebels then saw to it that the rails that advanced southward in Virginia and Tennessee did not materially aid Yankee movements, making numerous strategic cavalry raids led by Generals J. E. B. Stuart, Nathan Bedford Forrest, Earl Van Dorn, and John Hunt Morgan.

At first, the Union forces seemed unable to effect a rational rail policy. The Confederates had done much more with considerably less infrastructure. The War Department determined that the problem needed the expertise of a real railroad man. Prompted by congressional passage of the Military Railroad Act of 1862, it called in a man who was building a railroad through the Berkshire Mountains in Massachusetts, Herman Haupt. Eventually given the rank of brigadier general, Haupt was to get the Union armies in Virginia back into supply. A graduate engineer from the Military Academy at West Point, Haupt had resigned his commission to work on railroads. His specialty was bridge building, although he would later be remembered for financing and boring the famous Hoosac Tunnel through the Berkshires (still used today).

Operating under the overall command of General David C. McCallum, Haupt took several companies of volunteers and turned them into a railroad-building machine. He rebuilt the Fredericksburg & Aquia Creek Railroad in a matter of days. He reconstructed the Orange & Alexandria further inland. He built long bridges with spindly trestle bents using green labor, sometimes in matter of hours. Of course Confederate raiders merely burned them down again. After the rebel interdiction of the Orange & Alexandria Railroad in August, a disaster that led to the Union debacle at Second Manassas, Haupt came up with a brilliant idea. He could prefabricate trestle bents ahead of time in Washington and other places. Each bent was standardized and catalogued. Thereafter, whenever the Rebs wrecked a bridge, Haupt and his boys could rebuild it as fast as it burned. Some bridges were wrecked and rebuilt six or seven times during the war. Using such a system late in the war, Haupt's aide, Colonel E. C. Smeed, built a bridge across the Chattahoochee River 780 feet long and 90 feet wide in a little over four days to help General William T. Sherman take Atlanta.

If Haupt could keep the trains moving, the Yankees were determined to show the Rebs how an industrialized nation could fight. When Lee slipped his men to northern Georgia, the Federals assigned railroad General D. C. McCallum to ship two corps of infantry to counter the move. Twenty-three thousand men and their artillery and wagons traveled 1,200 miles in just under eight days from Virginia to Chattanooga, Tennessee, to save the city from a Confederate siege. Like Haupt, McCallum had only one condition to the successful carrying out of his mission: complete control with no interference from the army chain of command. And McCallum had to cross his 23,000 men over the Ohio River twice, once on a pontoon bridge and another time on a ferry.

In addition to troop trains, the Civil War saw the first use of armored trains, railroad mounted artillery, and the evacuation of wounded from the battlefield to rear-area hospitals. Needless to say, tons of supplies were hauled to the fronts by both sides, although the transportation of animals, packed in close without water or feed particularly early in the war, left a lot to be desired. By 1865, however, Union railroad operations had emulated a fine-tuned machine.

Under McCallum's leadership, the government-run Military Railroad ran every soldier, animal, and bit of supplies needed for the final siege of Petersburg-Richmond from the James River to behind the trenches. But the siege was victorious only when General U. S. Grant managed to break through the half dozen railroads that kept his opponent, Lee, supplied in like manner. In the end, the poor state of the Confederacy's railroads, which had done so much initially in assisting the new nation in its fight for independence, helped cost it the war.

See also Canals; Dodge, Grenville Mellen; Drew, Daniel; Freighting and Teamsters; Leiper, Thomas; McCallum, David Craig; Pacific Railroad Act of 1862; Rails and Crossties; Stagecoaches and Other Horse-Drawn Conveyances; Steamboats; Steamboats at War.

References Black, Robert C., *Railroads of the Confederacy* (1952); Cleveland, Frederick A., and Fred Wilbur Powell, *Railroad Promotion and Capitalization in the United States* (1909); Cotterill, Robert S., "Southern Railroads and Western Trade, 1840–1850," *Mississippi Valley Historical Review* (1916–1917) III: 427–441; Cotterill, Robert S., "The Beginnings of Railroads in the Southwest," *Mississippi Valley Historical Review* (1921–1922) VIII: 318–326; Cotterill, Robert S., "Southern Railroads, 1850–1860," *Mississippi Valley Historical Review* (1923–1924) X: 396–405; Feuerlicht, Roberta S., *The Andrews' Raiders* (1967); Fish, Carl Russell, "The Northern Railroads, April 1861," *American Historical Review* (1916–1917) 22: 778–793; Goodrich, Carter, "The Revulsion against Internal Improvements," *Journal of Economic History* (1950–1951) 10: 145–169; Haney, Lewis Henry, *A Congressional History of the Railways in the United States* (1910); Hubbard, Freeman, *Encyclopedia of North American Railroading* (1981); Jensen, Oliver, *The American Heritage History of Railroads in America* (1975); MacGill, Caroline E., et al., *History of Transportation in the United States before 1860* (1917); Meredith, Roy, and Arthur Meredith, *Mr. Lincoln's Military Railroads* (1979); Phillips, U. B., *A History of Transportation in the Eastern Cotton Belt* (1908); Riegel, Robert E., "Trans-Mississippi Railroads during the Fifties," *Mississippi Valley Historical Review* (1923–1924) X: 153–172; Roberts, MacLennan, *The Great Locomotive Chase* (1956); Taylor, George Rogers, *The Transportation Revolution* (1951); Turner, George E., *Victory Rode the Rails* (1953); Van Fleet, James A., *Rail Transport and the Winning of Wars* (1956); Ward, James A., *That Man Haupt!* (1973); Ward, James A., "Herman Haupt," in Robert L. Frey (ed.), *EABHB: Railroads in the Nineteenth Century* (1988), 165–168; Weber, Thomas, *The Northern Railroads in the Civil War* (1952).

Railroads from Appomattox to Deregulation

All along, the big problem in railroad expansion westward had been that the expense was so great that only one transcontinental railroad project could be built. With the secession of the Confederacy, the United States Congress lost a big block of Democratic members who either were against government-sponsored internal improvements or ably jockeyed to have them oriented to the South. Now the Republican majority in Congress could act. In 1862, the Abraham Lincoln administration sponsored the Pacific Railroad Act, proposing a transcontinental railroad that loosely followed the Central Overland Route. Lobbied through by Theodore D. Judah, the measure called for two railroads to build simultaneously from Sacramento and Omaha and to meet somewhere in between.

The actual charter for the California-sponsored Central Pacific (CP) implied that it would only reach the California–Nevada border, but its management team of Leland Stanford, Mark Hopkins, Collis P. Huntington, and Charles Crocker kept right on and reached near Ogden, Utah, before the Union Pacific (UP) coming out of Omaha could do anything about it. The advance of the Central Pacific was fairly marvelous, considering the problems they faced in securing reliable labor and conquering the Sierra Nevada. Only half of the signed-up workers appeared when the line began its trek east. The rest deserted to the American River goldfields. Those who stayed only did so until they approached the Washoe silver strike. Stanford asked for Confederate prisoners of war and Union guards, but nothing came of it.

Then Stanford got a brilliant idea. What about Chinese laborers? Most of his labor bosses were vehemently against it. They considered the Chinese to be lazy. But Charles Crocker's brother was head of the CP legal department. Why not use the Chinese? he opined; after all, who had built the Great Wall of China? The line bosses agreed to give it a shot, convinced that the experiment would fail. But to their amazement, they were converted to the Chinese labor cause in one shift. The Orientals worked harder with fewer complaints than their white counterparts. Whites got the cushy supervisory and easy labor jobs, which allayed their initial hostility. Soon thousands of Chinese were working. "Crocker's pets," said some derisively; "the Asiatic contingent of the Grand Army of Civilization," retorted Crocker. Often working at only 8 inches a day, the Chinese laborers bored and hacked their way through the mountains, never faltering. They drilled and blasted in baskets hung from the sides of cliffs. Workers pulled the powder men up on winches after they lit the fuses, but sometimes the charges blew before everyone cleared the work area. Hundreds died (giving rise to the old American phrase of hopelessness, "a Chinaman's chance"), but many more retired relatively rich. Indeed, when the Northern Pacific faced the same obstacles 15 years later, Henry Villard, remembering the travails of the Central Pacific, hired 15,000 Chinese to build his transcontinental railroad.

The Central Overland line was completed in 1869 with the driving of the golden spike at Promontory Summit (not Promontory Point as some aver, which is on the Southern Pacific's Lucin Cutoff on the Great Salt Lake). The rail executives were to drive the golden spike. There were also several silver spikes, one each from the state of Nevada and the territories of Montana and Idaho, and a mixed alloy spike of gold, silver, and iron from Arizona Territory. A telegraph line had been rigged to make contact when the hammer hit the golden spike, but Leland Stanford missed his first attempt. The telegrapher was imaginative enough to hit the key anyway (the executives were better at stock manipulations than hammers and the telegrapher was not about to wait all day) and tap out the word "done." The nation went wild. The actual laurel tie and the precious metal spikes were removed and kept in museums. The golden spike is still at Stanford University, but the others have disappeared. The tie was destroyed in the San Francisco earthquake of 1906.

Despite the legend of the railroads, building transcontinental lines was not a lucrative business. It would take until the 1880s before a second line was established, and by the end of the century for a half dozen to be built. The process was marked by corruption and miscalculation. Typical in this manner was the Crédit Mobilier scandal of the early 1870s that revealed that Union Pacific contractors had been giving congressmen kickbacks to permit overcharging of the government for construction fees. Nonetheless, millions of acres of public lands were donated to the building efforts, and the railroads spent much time in luring settlers to come and make the Plains (the Great American Desert, as the area was known then) bloom. The money given to the railroad men was supposed to be a loan, but it was never really paid back. Instead, they spent their profits trying to manipulate their stock and merge with other lines to form massive rail empires.

Thousands of Chinese laborers were hired to work on the Central Pacific Railroad, pictured here in Sierra, Nevada, in 1877.

By World War I, there were several types of railroads spanning the continent. The West was covered by the transcontinentals, long haul lines like the Southern Pacific, Santa Fe, Union Pacific, Northern Pacific, and Great Northern. Soon they would be joined by the Chicago, Burlington & Quincy (CB&Q)/Denver & Rio Grande Western/Western Pacific combination and the Milwaukee Road. In the Midwest were the Granger railroads, those that supplied the nation's farmers. The Milwaukee Road and the CB&Q were a part of these as were the Chicago & North Western, the Frisco, the Rock Island, the Texas & Pacific/Missouri Pacific combination, and a half dozen others. The New England railroads were in a class by themselves, isolated from the rest of the country, with lines like the Boston & Maine and the New York, New Haven, and Hartford. Then there were the trunk lines, those that bridged between New York City and Chicago like the Erie, the New York Central, the Chesapeake & Ohio, the Baltimore & Ohio, and the Pennsylvania Railroad. Along the eastern coast and Piedmont lay the coal railroads, like the Lackawanna, the Delaware & Hudson, the Lehigh Valley, the Norfolk & Western, the Virginian, the Reading, and the Central of New Jersey. These coal lines were connected to Chicago by roads called bridge lines. Two important ones of these were the Nickel Plate and the Wabash. The South had its own giants like the Illinois Central, the Gulf & Ohio, the Southern, the Atlantic Coast Line, the Louisville & Nashville, and the Seaboard Air Line.

It would seem that everything looked good by 1914, and on the surface it did. In the 1880s, the various lines had facilitated interchange by adopting the 4-foot 8.5-inch gauge (distance between tracks) and Standard Time zones. In both cases, there were numerous deviations across the nation, many of which made little sense. In the realm of time, the railroads divided the North American continent into five zones (the one not familiar to Americans today is in eastern Canada). These changes became the norm in every community and were fully recognized by federal law in 1918, when Congress established the first daylight savings time. But underneath it all there was trouble. The railroads were not making money. The solution to this had been the establishment of great rail empires run by William Vanderbilt, George Jay Gould, E. H. Harriman, J. Pierpont Morgan, John Forbes, James J. Hill, and Cyrus Holliday. They had spent much time outfoxing themselves and the public to gain their domains, and it had cost everyone a fortune to do it. The Erie Railroad had been so ravaged by the railroad wars that it would never really recover well into the twentieth century. Others were better off, but only somewhat.

The result was higher fees and lower wages that led to agrarian unrest (most Americans were still on the farm) and labor strikes. These in turn led to government intervention. The government's role in the railroads was marked by rate and antitrust legislation and workers' safety and compensation laws. The first of these measures created the Interstate Commerce Commission (ICC) and prevented pools (private rate- and traffic-sharing agreements) and rebates at the expense of smaller customers. The Interstate Commerce Act was followed by the Sherman Antitrust Act, which outlawed conspiracies in restraint of trade. But the courts soon eviscerated both measures, as the rail barons fought to control their competition by mergers. Congress responded with a series of measures (the Elkins Act, Hepburn Act, and Mann-Elkins Act) designed to plug the legal loopholes of the earlier legislation. The crowning piece of legislation was the Clayton Act of 1914, which modified all that came before and tied it all up in one neat, little package. The Clayton Act forbade trusts and holding companies and the purchase of stock that would lessen competition, and made the

corporate directors personally responsible. Although court cases lessened the measure's effect, especially as regarded labor, it provided the rules for railroad consolidation measures until deregulation.

The Congress also moved to outlaw practices that affected labor. Railroading was a very dangerous job and thousands were killed or maimed each year doing their jobs. Violent strikes had plagued the industry as officials manipulated wages and working conditions just as malevolently as they did stock shares. Led by Levi Coffin, Congress passed the Safety Appliance Act in 1893. This measure called for air brakes, automatic knuckle couplers, and safety handholds on all cars. Later legislation and Interstate Commerce Commission directives limited hours of work, called for electric headlights and automatic warning bells, forced boiler inspections, and improved the stoking of engines. The Clayton Act also put labor organizations outside the antitrust definition, but labor would have to await the Wagner Act during the New Deal to get real legal protection. Nonetheless, railroad workers had strong unions early in labor's organizing history to combat dangerous working conditions.

By the time of American entry into World War I, the railroads were an integral part of the national transportation system. But the war caused the surface veneer to crack badly, revealing all of its inherent organizational and management defects. The goods for the soldiers piled up at warehouses, lacking rail cars to ship them in. Managers seemed more interested in cornering the market than providing service. Voluntary organization of railroad managers into the Railroad War Board failed several times. The executives were not good historians, failing to look back at the Civil War to see what had made rails function so well then. The key was to unload all cargoes upon delivery and not to have the rail cars act as storage houses.

Finally, faced with the total collapse of rail commerce intensified by the hard winter of 1917, Congress passed the Federal Control Act and put the railroads under government supervision. The head of the United States Railroad Administration (USRA) was William G. McAdoo. He standardized engines and rail cars, established uniform rates, and set schedules and coordinated trains, utilizing lines that had been cut out of the process by competition. The result was that the railroads were merged into one entity for the first time in their history. It was not that the rail barons objected to the forced consolidation—it was that they wished to do it themselves and reap the profits. As the war ended, they fought to regain civilian control of the unification process, confident that the postwar era would bring new profits and mergers they could live with.

At the end of World War I, the railroads were still under government control through the United States Railroad Administration. Even though the USRA was no longer headed by William G. McAdoo but by Walker D. Hines of the Santa Fe Railway, no railroader wanted it to continue. The government was making things just too cozy for the weak lines and not cozy enough for the big boys. The railroads wanted to end Clayton Act restrictions, terminate the USRA, and resume the railroad wars, whereby the strong could absorb the weak at their own volition.

Labor advanced the notion that the railroads ought to be controlled by a mixture of management, workers, and government, much as in Europe. But the railroad barons had the ear of Congress and the result was the Transportation Act of 1920. It put the rails back on a private footing supervised by the Interstate Commerce Commission, and encouraged mergers in the interest of better service to the public within the scope of the Clayton Act. Profitable railroads that earned over a certain percent on their investment had to pay the excess into a recapture fund that the government parceled out to the struggling lines. The railroads could get bigger—but not too big. The act also established a mandate for the ICC to draw up a plan to achieve this better rail network. The basis of the plan would be the *Ripley Report*, a 200-page document by a Harvard University professor that divided the country into six basic groups by geographic region. The railroads were not about to allow this—it was too level of a playing field. They countered with the Fess-Parker Bill that would put a time limit on government unification proposals. The result was that the twenties frittered away in endless debate and no action.

The Great Depression jolted the Roaring Twenties to a sudden stop. President Herbert Hoover sponsored the 1931 Railroad Unification Act, which called for more rail consolidation and a simplified rate structure, but his administration ended before the act had any effect. Hoover's measure was replaced by the Emergency Railroad Transportation Act of 1933. This legislation created the Federal Coordinator of Transportation and restructured the rates away from rail property value to traffic movement. The 1920 recapture clause, which mandated that the strong railroads pay the losses of the weak, ended.

The railroads countered with the Association of American Railroads, an organization designed to work with the coordinator, in theory. But in fact it put a check on any proposal that affected the status quo. But the roads supported the National Recovery Administration that set up industry cartels to set rates, something the rail managers had wanted for years but the Clayton Act had prevented. Finally, the government and the railroads rewrote the Transportation Act of 1920 as the Transportation Act of 1940, which provided that railroads could merge if it was consistent with the public interest. The earlier measure said merger had to promote the public interest. The difference was important, and by the end of World War II, the railroads were in as good a shape as they had been since the Civil War.

The railroads did well during World War II. They not only moved war goods and increased passenger service with troops and civilians restricted by curbs on highway travel, but they trained a series of U.S. Army Railroad Battalions. These special troops were headquarters personnel who could step in and take over rails captured in military offensives and get them into operation to support Allied offensives. The various soldiers could handle track and equipment maintenance, train operation, bridge building, telegraphing and communications, and schedule planning. The whole operation was run by General Carl R. Gray, a civilian railroader called up for that specific reason. The whole U.S. Military Railroad Service was actually one big rail line in its organization.

After the war, rail consolidation was pursued anew. The railroaders subscribed to the New Orleans Conditions that gave organized labor a stake in mergers. The rules provided that workers could be shifted from job to job to encourage a merger, provided they kept their former salaries. Those laid off would receive a percentage of their former pay for five years. Later, the Southern Railroad would try to circumvent this agreement, leading to a prolonged fight that the unions eventually won. On another front, railroad managers got Congress to pass the Reed-Bullwinkle Act that sanctioned the industry's establishment of its own price cartels, much like the outmoded NRA codes. It was another step away from the protections of the Clayton Act. Meanwhile the U.S. Supreme Court helped out in the *Schwabacher* case when it ruled that state laws against mergers could not prevent federal law for mergers from taking prior effect.

When the ICC ruled that railroad mergers had to take into account all local channels of trade and maintain interconnections, the so-called DT&I Conditions, the railroads noted that no enforcement procedure accompanied the decision, and they changed their schedules at will in an attempt to force competing lines out of business or into a merger. The Transportation Act of 1958 permitted the railroads to ignore DT&I Conditions legally and gave responsibility for passenger transportation solely to the federal government, cutting out state rules that disallowed any cut in service. Now railroads could drop their passenger services and they did so in droves. The decline in passenger service and the poor quality of that which remained drew the particular

attention of congressmen and senators from the eastern Atlantic states. Led by Claiborne Pell of Rhode Island, they backed the creation of a Northeast Corridor agency that would supervise rail traffic between Boston and Washington, D.C. Ninety million dollars was set aside to improve track and keep this busiest of all passenger routes open.

It was but a short step from the Pell Plan to a government passenger service plan for the whole country. In 1970 the Rail Passenger Act established the National Rail Passenger Corporation, a quasi-governmental agency that was to reestablish quality passenger service everywhere. Known by the acronym Amtrak, the agency took over all of the existing passenger equipment and began to set up schedules over the tracks of the private railroads, from which it rented access. It was a halting effort at first; the measure had to be renewed year by year to 1978, but by that time Amtrak had replaced all of its aging cars and engines with modern equipment, much of it designed especially for the corporation. By 1981, Congress recognized that passenger service would never exist as a private concern again. The national legislature passed a new set of laws that made the company fully federal in ownership and continued governmental subsidies unto the present.

The freight railroads, all private companies, went a different route than passenger service. Instead of more government supervision, they moved briefly into the government realm and then out of it into privatization and deregulation. By 1970, it was becoming clear that no railroad was ready to work in unison with any other to save the rail network as a whole. This had been demonstrated by their refusal to accept the plan drawn up by Judge Nathan Klitenic that would have divided up the Granger railroads of the Midwest among the transcontinentals so that each of four highly competitive systems resulted: the Santa Fe, Southern Pacific, Union Pacific, and Burlington Northern. Instead, each line wanted to see its competitors have to fight to stay alive. In the East, the mergers of the Pennsylvania Railroad and the New York Central into Penn Central, and of the Erie and Lackawanna, both failed, throwing rail transport from Illinois to Maine into limbo. This was exactly what the rejection of Klitenic's plan would lead to nationwide— an open war among railroads that only the very strongest would survive.

The failure of railroading in the nation's heartland, with the bankruptcy of Penn Central and Erie-Lackawanna, isolated New England from the rest of the country. This meant that rail service was out of commission for a majority of American industry and almost half of its population. Congress had to act. It passed the Regional Rail Reorganization Act in 1973 that set up a quasi-governmental corporation that became known as Conrail. In Conrail were the Penn Central, New Haven, and all of the so-called anthracite roads. The other coal roads in the Middle South and the rest of New England either joined the Chessie System (a combination of the Baltimore & Ohio and the Chesapeake & Ohio) or remained separate and private. Funded by federal money, Conrail was the freight equivalent of Amtrak. To keep the rest of the private rail companies from going into government receivership, another measure, the Railroad Revitalization and Regulatory Reform Act of 1976, was passed, allowing railroads to propose a merger and have it ruled on by the ICC within two years. A separate action by the Department of Transportation permitted railroads to abandon most feeder lines and reduce rail traffic by 20 million tons a year. Yet all of this was criticized as letting the people who caused the problem sort it out.

The whole question of rail viability was solved in 1980 with the Staggers Rail Act. Holding that free-market forces could solve the problem, the Staggers Act in effect deregulated the railroads, the very position that they had wanted since the passage of the Sherman Act in 1890. Mergers would receive federal approval or denial in less than nine months. The audit figures upon which abandonment and merger were based were changed from assessed value of property to also include traffic flow. No cartels like under the Reed-Bullwinkle Act were allowed. Each participant in a traffic route could set its own rates. To bring Conrail into the deregulated system, the Northeast Rail Services Act of 1981 provided for its sale when certain profit conditions were met. This occurred late in the 1980s, making Conrail one of the few successful government programs of economic intervention in American history. Today there remain numerous independents (the Soo Line is the biggest in revenues), short lines (they are growing without federal regulation to interfere with market forces), Amtrak, and seven major freight railroads: CSX, Norfolk Southern, Conrail, Union Pacific, Burlington Northern, Santa Fe, and Southern Pacific. The key to their profits has been dropping the cabooses for end-of-train devices (little black boxes hung on the trailing coupler that flash a red light and monitor brake and signal lines electronically) and an emphasis on intermodal freight like containers and trailers.

See also American Freedom Train; Amtrak; Association of American Railroads; Automobiles from Domestics to Imports; Automobiles in American Society; Conrail; Harriman, Edward Henry; Interstate Commerce Commission; Interstate Highway Act; Judah, Theodore D.; Klitenic Plan; Morgan, John Pierpont; New Orleans Conditions; Pacific Railroad Act of 1862; Pell Plan; Presidential Trains; Railroad Unions; Railroad War Board; Safety Appliance Act; Staggers Rail Act of 1980; Stillwell, Arthur Edward; Transportation Acts; Trucking; United States Railroad Administration; Vanderbilt, William H.

References Allen, John S., *Standard Time in America* (1951); Best, Gerald M., *Iron Horses to Promontory* (1969); Carper, Robert S., *The Railroad in Transition* (1968); DeBoer, David J., *Piggyback and Containers* (1993); Drury, George H., *The Historical Guide to North American Railroads* (1985); Drury, George H., *The Train-Watcher's Guide* (1990); Farrington, S. Kip, *Railroads at War* (1946); Godfrey, Aaron Austin, *Government Operation of the Railroads* (1974); Grodinsky, Julius, *Transcontinental Railroad Strategy* (1962); Hage, David, "On the Right Track: America's Railroads Are Chugging Their Way Back to Prosperity," *U.S. News & World Report* (21 March 1994) 116: 46–53; Haney, Lewis Henry, *A Congressional History of the Railways in the United States* (1910); Hines, Walker D., *War History of American Railroads* (1928); Horne, George R., "That Promontory Myth," *Trains* (May 1994) 54: 40–43; Hubbard, Freeman, *Encyclopedia of North*

American Railroading (1981); Itzkoff, Donald M., *Off the Track* (1985); Jensen, Oliver, *The American Heritage History of Railroads in America* (1975); Johnson, Emory R., *Elements of Transportation* (1914); Keeler, Theodore E., *Railroads, Freight, and Public Policy* (1983); Kerr, K. Austin, *American Railroad Politics* (1968); Latham, Earl, *The Politics of Railroad Coordination* (1959); Leonard, William Norris, *Railroad Consolidation under the Transportation Act of 1920* (1968); Lyon, Peter, *To Hell in a Day Coach* (1968); MacAvoy, Paul W., and John W. Snow (eds.), *Railroad Revitalization and Regulatory Reform* (1977); McCague, James, *Moguls and Iron Men* (1964); Nock, O. S., *Railways of the USA* (1979); Orenstein, Jeffrey, *United States Railroad Policy* (1990); Quiett, Glenn C., *They Built the West* (1934); Sabin, Edwin L., *Building the Pacific Railway* (1919); Saunders, Richard, *The Railroad Mergers and the Coming of Conrail* (1978); Sharfman, I. Leo, *The American Railroad Problem* (1921); Stilgoe, John R., *Metropolitan Corridors* (1983); Stover, John F., *The Life and Decline of the American Railroad* (1970); Wheeler, Keith, *The Railroaders* (1973); Ziel, Ron, *Steel Rails to Victory* (1970).

Rails and Crossties

The rails upon which trains roll have evolved over many years into the shape they have today. Originally, rails were wood stringers covered with an iron strap. The iron had a tendency to work loose on the ends after awhile and then to curl up and catch in the wheels of an oncoming train causing great damage and derailment. In 1830, Robert L Stevens, chief civil engineer of the Camden and Amboy Railroad in New Jersey, mulled the problem over and whittled a piece of wood into a T-shape. He took the model over to England where he was going to buy an engine for his tracks. Showing the carved wood piece to a relative in the foundry business, Stevens convinced him to roll out rails in that pattern for his train. Thus rails took a broad-based high T form that became standard with minor modification over the years. The wide portion of the T is the base, the smaller blocklike piece at the top is the head, and the steel between them is called the web. Each of their measurements differs depending on the use of the rail.

Stevens' T rail impressed a lot of American railroad men. Several all-iron rails had been used concurrently over the years, the most common being the inverted U rail, called an Evans rail. Stevens redesigned his product in 1845, reducing the height of the T into a more pear-shaped product. But the Pennsylvania Railroad adopted Stevens' original design in 1845, plus his rail spike and rail joiners. Mount Savage Rolling Mills in Maryland began to turn out American-made iron T rail for the first time, and they used the Pennsylvania standard T rail. The Bessemer process of steel making arrived at the American rolling mills by the end of the Civil War, the first steel T rails being produced in Chicago. The Bessemer process continued to produce rail until the early twentieth century, when the open-hearth process replaced it.

Rails ordinarily came in short pieces around 39 feet long that were bolted together, the joints causing the distinctive "clickety-clack" as the trains sped across them. Because of the shrinkage and expansion of the steel, the joints are never butted close together; they are gapped slightly, lest the rails buckle in hot weather. As rails shrink in cold weather the track joint opens slightly, increasing the clickety-clack of the rolling trains. In spite of the effort to take expansion and contraction into consideration, the rail lines warp in warm weather, especially the father south ones goes. Railroads used to employ gangs of men called "gandy dancers" to straighten out the snakelike waves in the track work by applying a pry bar to the offending sections and pulling them back in place.

With the advent of modern, heavy, high-speed railroading, the pounding that rail joints took became a prime factor in cost of maintenance. To alleviate this and make the track unit stronger as a whole, railroads now use welded rail. This eliminates the clickety-clack sound and produces a smoother ride. The rails are prewelded into quarter-mile sections at a central location and then hauled to the work site in specially designed flatcars, 33 to the quarter-mile section of track. Each set of flats carries about 54 lengths of prewelded track to the job site, enough to lay almost 7 miles of completed rail. Then the new rail is laid by a special car that pushes each rail out in a line next to that being replaced. As the rail weighs over 100 pounds per yard on mainline tracks (there are around 75 types of T rail by weight and use, like those for mainline, sidings, switch points, guard rails, etc.), a welded ribbon can be quite heavy to manipulate. The work is all done by machine, eliminating the need for large crews of gandy dancers to assist in the work.

Rails are held in place by the crossties, the wooden sleepers that hold the tracks apart at the correct distance, which is called the gauge. The proper gauge in the United States and Canada is 4 feet 8.5 inches, agreed upon in the 1880s when all tracks of different gauge were moved in one day. This standard was adopted from the British who got it from the Romans who used it as the distance between cartwheels. There are other gauges common to mountainous areas or industrial operations that differ, 3 and 2 feet being the most common in North America (called "narrow gauge"). The rails are held to the ties and kept in gauge by the tie plates. The tie plate keeps the rail from eating through the wooden tie that supports it. Each plate has four holes in it, a pair to a side, and a depression in the center to accept the rail base. Tie plates and rails are tacked down by spiking two of the holes in a plate. As ties outlive rails by three to one, this allows any new rail to be spiked down using the empty holes and fresh wood. This way each time rail is laid the spikes have "bite" in the tie.

Ties are made of pressure-treated wood. In the nineteenth century, when a rock shipment was delayed, Robert L. Stevens substituted wood laid crosswise to the rails as a temporary expedient. He discovered that wood had better shock-absorbing qualities and was more flexible than the stone piers he had laid his original rails on. So Stevens pulled all of the stone piers and replaced them with the wooden crosstie. The speed by which they could be laid made rail building much easier. Generally, the crosstie is 8 to 9 feet long, made from oak, pine, fir, beech, maple, or any of about 30 different kinds of wood. Often a tie can last

30 years with proper preservation. Pressure preservatives were first used on the Louisville & Nashville line at Pascagoula, Mississippi, in 1875.

It generally takes a green tie 18 months to dry enough to be pressure-treated. Formerly, railroads used a creosote or zinc chloride mixture, but with the outlawing of creosote for environmental reasons, other chemicals are being experimented with. Modern ties are often made of reinforced concrete, metals, and plastics, but nothing has yet replaced wood for its low cost, light weight, strength, and long life, if properly preserved. And a machine can move along the rails and replace ties without disturbing the rail above it. The rails and ties are set in a roadbed that is graded to keep ups and downs to a minimum and covered with varying sizes of rock and cinders called ballast. The ballast is hauled to the job site by special gondolas and hopper cars that allow it to be dropped right over existing rails. The ballast is kept in place by machines that pound it down on a regular basis. Its primary purposes are to cushion the ties and provide proper drainage to keep the roadbed smooth and intact.

See also Railroads before and during the Civil War.

References Frey, Robert L., "Rails, Roadbed, and Track Gauges," in Keith L. Bryant, Jr. (ed.), *EABHB: Railroads in the Age of Regulation* (1988), 340–344; Hubbard, Freeman, *Encyclopedia of North American Railroading* (1981); Palmer, William J., Lorenzo M. Johnson, and John J. Lipsey, *The War of the Gauges* (1961).

Randolph, Asa Philip (1889–1979)

From Crescent City, Florida, A. Philip Randolph grew up in the atmosphere of the African Methodist Episcopal Church, in which his father was a minister. The family ran a small tailor shop during the week, and the young Philip sold newspapers. He managed to gain a high school education, worked on a railroad track gang, and eventually went north to attend college. But Randolph soon found out that it made no difference where a black lived, North or South, or how much education he had, because only the most onerous drudgery awaited him in the workplace. Thus began his lifelong interest in improving the laboring conditions faced by blacks nationwide. Fired from a waiter's job for organizing labor protest, Randolph became a waiter at the rail terminal at Jersey City, New Jersey. He rejected both extremes of black nationalism and automatic obeisance to the white ruling structure. He believed that no race was better than another—he strove to keep contact between the races daily and constant.

Married in 1915, Randolph turned to socialism and journalism to support his family. He organized the New York City newspaper with Chandler Owen, the *Messenger*, and by 1917, 25 percent of the black voters in New York City supported the socialist ticket, which Randolph took as an indication of his influence. He actively organized black workers throughout the New York–New Jersey waterfront, and ran unsuccessfully as a socialist candidate for New York state assembly, secretary of state, and Congress. In 1925, Randolph organized the Brotherhood of Sleeping Car Porters (BSCP) in Harlem. He made the *Messenger* the union's official voice, and continued to work for the union as organizer and president even when funds were unavailable to pay him. The Pullman Company refused to recognize the union and fired 500 employees over the years for union activities. But the company could not touch Randolph as he never worked for them. Randolph's constant striving finally paid off when the Pullman Company agreed to allow organization of its employees and the American Federation of Labor admitted the BSCP to its ranks—the first charter granted to an all-black union in its history.

Randolph's work was recognized by two presidents—by Franklin D. Roosevelt in 1944 with a Worker's Defense League Medal and by Lyndon B. Johnson in 1964 with the Medal of Freedom, the highest award that can be given an American civilian. In 1978, the BSCP joined with the Railway and Airlines Clerks. A year later, Randolph died at age 90. In a eulogy, President Jimmy Cater described Randolph as a man of integrity and dignity. At death his estate was worth less than $500, but his honor was priceless.

See also Railroad Unions.

References Brazeal, Brailsford R., *The Brotherhood of Sleeping Car Porters* (1946); Hubbard, Freeman, *Encyclopedia of North American Railroading* (1981); Minton Bruce, and John Stuart, *Men Who Led Labor* (1937).

Reed-Bullwinkle Act of 1948

This piece of congressional legislation sanctioned the organization of rate-setting industry cartels, groups previously used by the railroads but declared in violation of the antitrust laws. This set up a structure that was exempt from antitrust laws and could protect the carriers from rate wars, assuring guaranteed prices and profits. It also protected weak companies from cutthroat competition from the stronger ones.

See also Clayton Act; *McLean Trucking Company v. U.S.*; National Industrial Recovery Act of 1933; Staggers Rail Act of 1980; Transportation Acts.

Reference Saunders, Richard, *The Railroad Mergers and the Coming of Conrail* (1978).

Regional Rail Reorganization (3-R) Act of 1973

The idea of Union Pacific management, which did not wish to loose the 25 percent of its traffic that was generated from or sent to the Northeast, First National City Bank, which was stuck with $120 million in defunct Penn Central securities, and the United Transportation Union, which stood to loose many jobs, the Regional Rail Reorganization Act of 1973 established the United States Railway Association (USRA). The act created a board of directors that included the federal secretaries of transportation and treasury, the chairman of the Interstate Commerce Commission, representatives of solvent railroads, representatives of the creditors of bankrupt railroads, shippers, labor, and state and local governmental agencies. It was to save railroading in the northeastern United States by planning and financing an entity that came to be called the Consolidated Rail

Corporation or Conrail, the directors of which the USRA would choose. It could also authorize loans off-budget, unlimited by the ceiling on the national debt or the constraints of the Office of Management and Budget. Up to $1.5 billion in loan guarantees went to Conrail, and other amounts went to state and local communities that wanted to buy and keep operating routes about to be abandoned, to Amtrak, and to railroads about to go under. Labor was appeased with a contribution of up to $250 million to their retirement board, but the number of employees who would lose jobs was staggering. Because so much of the background work was done by private sources, there was little committee work or debate on the floor of Congress. President Richard Nixon feared that it would cost the American taxpayer, but since the financing came mostly from banks, he finally signed the bill at the end of 1973, and Conrail was on its way to becoming one of the few successful federally subsidized businesses in history.

See also Conrail; Motor Carrier Acts; National Rail Passenger Act of 1971; Railroad Revitalization and Regulatory Reform Act of 1976; Staggers Rail Act of 1980; Transportation Acts.

References Keeler, Theodore E., *Railroads, Freight and Public Policy* (1983); Musolf, Lloyd, *Uncle Sam's Private, Profitseeking Corporations* (1983); Saunders, Richard, *The Railroad Mergers and the Coming of Conrail* (1978).

Reuther, Walter Philip (1907–1970)

The son of German immigrants, Walter Reuther was born in Wheeling, West Virginia. Educated in public schools, but greatly influenced by his union-supporting, socialist father to read widely at home, Reuther worked as a tool and die maker. He decided to go to Detroit to work for the high-paying Ford Motor Company. There he finished high school and attended what is today Wayne State University. He became a Socialist Party member and traveled to Europe, including a stint in the Soviet Union, where he worked at the Gorki tractor complex. He returned to the United States by way of the Trans-Siberia Railroad, China, and Japan.

In 1935, when Reuther returned home, it was the height of the Great Depression and automobile workers were ripe for union organization. The new federal Wagner Act gave them the right, but the auto company owners responded with a blacklist of agitators that soon included Reuther himself. As he could gain no work in the plants, Reuther went to work for the unions, at first for no pay. He soon advanced to more lucrative organizer positions and finally was elected president of the United Auto Workers' (UAW) Local 174. Meanwhile, he married Mary Wolfe, a schoolteacher and union supporter, who became as knowledgeable as he in union matters and his personal assistant and secretary. Reuther was involved in several strikes including the 1936 General Motors (GM) sit-down strike (where the workers sat at their machines to keep from being replaced by strike-breakers) and the bloody encounters at Ford (where private security police attacked picketers blocking company gates). He also worked to heal internal divisions between socialist and communist union members. Although not a Communist Party member, Reuther sought to compromise all difficulties in a "Popular Front" style of organization that was a favorite tactic of the day. World War II stopped all labor action beyond organization, but by 1945 the United Auto Workers had a membership list of 1.2 million, including 350,000 women.

As soon as the war was over, the UAW walked out at GM. The lone holdout for the union's insistence on higher wages and benefits and guaranteed jobs, the success of the strike propelled Reuther into the union presidency, a position he held until his death in 1970. He was liked as a moderate, anticommunist who got results. Indeed his opponents in the union liked to refer to him as "the Bosses' Boy." Reuther was assisted by the fact that the auto industry was among the most profitable in postwar America. Management could afford to meet union demands, and Reuther was not above promoting himself as the alleged genius behind this prosperity. An advocate of the unification of the American Federation of Labor

(AFL), which organized laborers by craft, and the Congress of Industrial Organizations (CIO), which organized laborers by industry, regardless of craft, as with the UAW, Reuther took second place to the AFL's George Meany in 1955. It was not a happy relationship. Reuther was not a man who normally settled for number two, and he disliked Meany's extravagant lifestyle at the expense of members' dues and his support of the Vietnam War. This disagreement led Reuther to withdraw the UAW from labor's organized front in 1965.

Walter Reuther's leadership of the United Auto Workers in its successful strike against General Motors landed Reuther a job as union president.

Reuther had a lot to do in the independent UAW. He urged the automakers to take notice of the increasing popularity of smaller foreign cars, and brought in black auto workers, often to the protests of the entrenched white leadership. "There are no white answers" to the problems facing the union, Reuther maintained. "There are no black answers. There are only common answers that we must plan together in the solidarity of humanity." It was in the pursuit of such answers that Reuther was killed in the crash of his private business plane in 1970.

See also Automobiles from Domestics to Imports; Automobiles in American Society.

References Bernard, John, *Walter Reuther* (1983); Bernard, John, "Walter Philip Reuther," in George S. May, (ed.), *EABHB: The Automobile Industry* (1989), 357–373; Gould, Jean, and Lorena Hickok, *Walter Reuther* (1972).

Ride, Sally Kristen (b. 1951)

A NASA mission specialist, Sally Ride was born and raised in the Greater Los Angeles area. Somewhat of a tomboy, her mother successfully tried to interest her in tennis to keep her away from football and baseball. She became so proficient that she earned a sports scholarship to prep school. She went to Swarthmore to study physics but dropped out to pursue a career in tennis. Despite encouragement from Billie Jean King to continue her sports career, Ride returned to school, this time at Stanford University. She earned two bachelor's degrees (in physics and English literature) and went on to study first English literature then astrophysics and received her master's degree in the latter subject. She received her Ph.D. in physics in 1978 and entered the astronaut training program at the same time. Ride learned to fly jets and trained on the space shuttle's robot arm, a device on which she became an expert operator. Because of her talent, she became the first American woman in space when she went up in the shuttle on 18 June 1983 in *Challenger*'s second flight to launch satellites out of the payload bay with the remote arm. She later flew a second shuttle mission with Kathryn Sullivan (the first woman to walk in space), and served at President Ronald Reagan's request on a panel that inquired into the explosion of the shuttle *Challenger*. Ride then did a stint at NASA headquarters. She resigned from government service in 1987 and entered private business to became a fellow at Stanford University. She has written of her space experiences in a book designed for preteens.

See also Astronautics.

References Cassutt, Michael, *Who's Who in Space* (1987); Hawthorne, Douglas B., *Men and Women of Space* (1992); Shepard, Alan B., and Donald K. Slayton, *Moon Shot* (1994).

Rio Grande Railroad

See Denver & Rio Grande Western Railroad.

Ripley Report (1921)

W. Z. Ripley was a Harvard University professor who specialized in problems relating to rail transportation and who recommended a plan of railroad consolidation to the Interstate Commerce Commission (ICC) at the commission's request under the provisions of the Transportation Act of 1920. Much of his plan was made a part of the final ICC report on consolidation issued in 1929. Insofar as the ICC plan differed with his original suggestions (mostly in his recommendations of which eastern railroad lines ought to be merged), Professor Ripley would criticize it as unsound.

In his 196-page presentation Ripley envisioned an American rail system that divided the country into six territorial regions: (1) five eastern trunk lines and one leftover regional (Pennsylvania Railroad, New York Central System, a new Baltimore & Ohio-Reading–Central of New Jersey–Monon, a proposed Erie–Wabash–Lehigh Valley–Delaware & Hudson–Bessemer & Lake Erie system, a revitalized Nickel Plate–Lackawanna–Western Maryland, and an isolated Pere Marquette Railroad in Michigan); (2) one New England line (all railroads united into one, based on the Boston & Maine and the New York, New Haven & Hartford); (3) two Chesapeake Bay railroads (consisting of the Chesapeake & Ohio–Virginian Railway and the competing Norfolk & Western, all coal haulers); (4) four Southeast roads (Southern Railroad, Louisville & Nashville–Atlantic Coast Line System, Seaboard Air Line–Illinois Central Railroad, and the isolated Florida East Coast Railroad; (5) six western transcontinentals (Union Pacific–Chicago & North Western System, Northern Pacific–Chicago, Burlington & Quincy System, Milwaukee Road–Great Northern Railway, Southern Pacific–Rock Island Lines, and the Santa Fe–Denver & Rio Grande Western–Western Pacific System); (6) and two Gulf-Southwest regional railroads (Frisco–Katy–Cotton Belt Line, and the Missouri Pacific–Texas & Pacific–Chicago & Eastern Illinois–Kansas, Oklahoma & Gulf Railroad).

Ripley claimed that to further consolidate would reduce competition, which he guaranteed by putting at least two different rail lines in each major city (except the Michigan and Florida peninsulas). He thought the weakest systems existed in the Gulf-Southwest region. He believed that his plan would institute the best of the United States Railroad Administration's control of railroads: long hauls, elimination of duplicate lines and equipment, and the establishment of uniform standards of operation and rolling stock. Naturally, no one could guarantee that any plan would be perfect—the ICC put out at least two modifications of Ripley's document, and Professor W. M. W. Splawn advanced a plan supported by Texas interests that would reorganize the West in a more north–south orientation to enhance that state's geographical position. But none of these ideas would have the force of compulsion behind them in the form of an act of Congress, and all were lost in the economic myopia that preceded the disaster of the Great Depression.

See also Fess-Parker Bill; Transportation Acts.

References Leonard, William Norris, *Railroad Consolidation under the Transportation Act of 1920* (1946); Lyon, Peter, *To Hell in a Day Coach* (1968).

River Travel

See Early River Travel.

Roads and Highways, Colonial Times to World War I

Early roads built in America before the Revolution were generally pack trails, unless they were located near a coastal city whereupon they became wide enough for wagons and carriages, and hard surfaced enough to withstand most inclement weather. The best roads were the stage routes in New England. Even Braddock's Road out of Maryland to Pittsburgh, chopped through the underbrush at a 12-foot width, soon reverted to forest. By 1758, two years after it was built, Braddock's Road was again nothing but a trace through the wilderness. Forbes' Road, out of eastern Pennsylvania to Pittsburgh, faired better and could pass wagons westward, but it too was little more than track through the eternal forest.

Part of the problem with roads was inadequate funding. Another was too little labor. Both resulted from the practice of leaving road building and maintenance to the town (New England) or county (elsewhere) authorities. Local people usually did not go anywhere and roads seemed superfluous. The economy until well after the Revolution was essentially one of subsistence and not able to generate raw materials or use many finished goods. Usually the roads and ferries were built by public-spirited citizens who were allowed to charge small fees for upkeep. Profit was nil.

After the Revolution, the American economy began to pick up and the need for roads became more acute. The first turnpike, named after the device that blocked entry until users paid a fee and the gate or pike was turned, was built in Virginia in 1785 from Alexandria to Berryville at one of the gaps in the Blue Ridge Mountains. But the first road to turn a profit was the Lancaster Pike out of Philadelphia to the west into the German country. Indeed, Pennsylvania was the first state to consider a comprehensive transportation plan in 1791. Its main feature was a guarantee that the road builder would have exclusive right to be free from competition for a set number of years so as to gain a return on the initial investment. The policy extended not only to roads but canal companies as well. By 1800, all states had some form of the Pennsylvania plan. Connecticut had 50 such companies alone with 770 miles of roads, New York had 67 with over 3,000 miles, and Pennsyl-

vania had a similar amount as the Empire State. Standards differed widely, as demonstrated by costs, which ran from $550 to $1,400 per mile.

Early roads had standards based on the French engineer, J. P. M. Trésaguet, whose work was well known to educated Americans like Benjamin Franklin. As France's director general of highways, Trésaguet believed on adequate right-of-way, lots of ditching to drain water, and the use of heavy foundation stones topped off by layers of gradually smaller rock, all packed into place. His roads were about 18 feet wide and 10 inches thick. But his most important contribution to the idea of highway building was well-organized and constant maintenance by trained and adequately paid workers.

About 1820, Trésaguet's system began to be replaced in America by a new one developed in England by John McAdam. He did not favor the use of large foundation stones. McAdam held that the native soil had to support all that went above it, so the stone layers were sufficient if they were consistently less than 2 inches in diameter and broken into angular pieces to be packed by the traffic using the road. Like the Frenchman, McAdam insisted that regular maintenance was the critical factor. His principles were first incorporated in the National Road from Boonesboro to Hagerstown, Maryland. But in either case, road building depended much on the skill and integrity of the contractors and the money available for the initial construction. That meant that a lot of variation could be had on the same road system.

As Americans moved west, it became obvious that the new territories needed transportation systems but lacked the monetary basis for instituting them. Without these systems, the West would not expand and be able to absorb the new immigrants coming from Europe. Nor would those in the East be able to sell the products of a burgeoning Industrial Revolution to farmers, who in turn could not sell their surpluses for finished goods. But the need for government-financed transport collided with the Constitution, which did not explicitly endorse such projects unless they were for postal or national defense needs. The architect of westward expansion, President Thomas Jefferson, already faced growing opposition within his own party over their literal reading of the Constitution that protected the individual and state rights guaranteed by it.

Jefferson turned to one of the more brilliant members of his cabinet, Secretary of the Treasury Albert Gallatin, to find a way around this problem. Gallatin had to act in a manner that would not endorse the Federalist notion developed by one of his predecessors, Alexander Hamilton, that gave a blank check to the development of federal powers through the "necessary and proper" and "general welfare" clauses of the Constitution that threatened to upset the original concept of a decentralized government. Of course that view has long since been destroyed by the results of the Civil War and the twentieth-century quasi-socialism of the Square Deal, Fair Deal, New Deal, and the Great Society, but in Jefferson's time these were unheard-of notions.

Luckily for road building, Gallatin was up to the task. He proposed that a percentage of the sales of public lands within any state be donated to the building of roads if that state agreed. The Ohio Enabling Act of 1803 incorporated the proposal, which became known as the Two Percent Fund. This idea was adopted by all of the states in the Old Southwest and Old Northwest, and even applied by some to railroad and school construction later on. By 1910, all new states beyond the original 13, except West Virginia and Texas, which through peculiar circumstances unique to each had no public lands, received like sums for internal improvements.

But Gallatin went further. He also submitted a report that suggested a sweeping nationwide plan for various kinds of internal improvements (roads, bridges, canals, river dredging), costing about $20 million. Opposition to the National Road, just a small part of the entire plan, and the intervention of the War of 1812 shelved the debate for the moment. But after the war the new nationalists of Jefferson's Democratic-Republican party, led by men like Henry Clay and John C. Calhoun, revived Gallatin's concept. In 1816 Calhoun introduced the Bonus Bill in Congress. It provided that the $1.5 million bonus paid by the directors of the recently chartered Second Bank of the United States should be given out to the states for internal improvements on the basis of their representation in the lower house of Congress. Using interest rates current at the time, Calhoun figured that the total moneys available would be $13 million over 20 years. Strict constructionists, those who did not see such a measure endorsed specifically in the Constitution, and those who wished such moneys applied to tax relief and ending the national debt, opposed the Bonus Bill. Although the measure passed Congress by a narrow margin, President James Madison, the original strict constructionist when a congressman in 1790, vetoed it. Congress failed to override the president's action.

But the National Road (or Cumberland Road, from its original starting point at the head of navigation of the Potomac River) was built through Gallatin's earlier funding and a separate congressional act passed in 1806. Although many easterners and the usual strict constructionists opposed the measure, the need to tie East and West together, as demonstrated by several attempts to have the West secede from the Union like the recent Aaron Burr conspiracy, carried the day for the transportation advocates. The resulting road was 30 feet wide with the central 20 feet built on Trésaguet's model. Ditches, drains, and bridges made it a first-class improvement. Cost was $14,000 a mile from Cumberland, Maryland, to Wheeling, Virginia, the head of navigation on the Ohio River when at ebb stage.

Traffic was so heavy and vandalism so prevalent that the road wore away almost as fast as it was built and repaired. Congress' attempt to collect tolls for maintenance received a veto from President James Monroe on strict constructionist grounds. He saw the collection of tolls as a sovereign power still vested in the people and the states.

Measures to fund it continued but by closer margins each time. Monroe's objections came more and more into vogue as time passed, and by 1835, the National Road reverted to state control for maintenance over its whole length. The construction methods had declined the farther west the process went, with the amount of stone for the graded roadbed declining in availability. There was also a growing feeling that roads and canals were things of the past and that the new railroads were more deserving of national support and investment. By the mid-1850s the roadway had been totally surrendered to the states through which it passed.

But the real death knell came in the Maysville Road Veto President Andrew Jackson issued in 1830. This and the already close votes in Congress on road building ended any hope for extending the program to local levels. Jackson also ended the obtaining of lands for roads through Indian treaties, a ploy to bypass the usual constitutional objections to congressional action. The army, however, continued to build many roads in the territories under the explicit grant in the Constitution for military roads. Some of these included the Natchez Trace, the Jackson Road from Nashville to New Orleans (soon abandoned and overgrown with forest), the Santa Fe Trail, Cooke's Wagon Road in southern New Mexico and Arizona, the Old Spanish Trail from St. Augustine to Pensacola, the Mullan Road in Washington Territory, and the 512-mile-long wagon road that came south out of Fort Snelling, Minnesota, to Fort Leavenworth, Kansas. Detroit benefited most from the military road policy—such highways radiated from it like spokes on a wheel.

The reliance on steam, be it on land or water, led to the gradual disintegration of the old road network. By the time of the Civil War, the railroads were supreme, a dominance in land transpiration that only increased after the war as the steel ribbons moved westward. Although 1.5 million miles of farm-to-market roads were constructed from 1850 to 1900, the period was

still known as the "dark age of the rural road." Especially in the West, with congressional approval in 1866, state legislatures tended to mark off one chain (66 feet) for public access split along section lines, giving the Plains their characteristic checkerboard look that remains today. In the East, property owners often donated rights-of-way as a public-spirited action (or, more selfishly, as an easier method to get to town). The main methods of finance remained local also. They were mostly built with property and poll taxes (worth $53.8 million in 1904 alone) and statute labor (work in lieu of taxes). The latter was rather inefficient, but in 1904 statute labor contributed work worth an estimated $19.8 million. But the large investment was spread pretty thinly and remained almost unnoticeable in a country as vast as the rural United States. High prices and low availability of finished goods and farm products reflected the lack of roads.

In the cities, heavy wagons required roads made up of granite or brick paving blocks. The conveyances all used iron tires and pulverized any other material to bits. In 1871, New York City and Philadelphia began to surface these old block roads with asphalt. This cut noise dramatically and made cleaning easier (horses have a tendency to be eclectic in their concept of bathrooms). Although traffic was heavy because of the concentration of industry, cities generally had fairly good transportation networks within their governmental limits. They also had a broader tax base to finance roads. Cities eliminated statute labor and relied on a professional workforce to build and maintain their roads. The population at large moved by public transit, which included horse-drawn trolleys and steam-powered trains. By the turn of the century, both kinds of power were gradually replaced by electricity to stem ever-increasing urban pollution.

The difference between urban and rural transportation was obvious to anyone who cared to take a look. And by the 1880s, more and more were observing. Part of the surmise came from the evolution of travel into

the countryside made possible by the bicycle. A horse was too expensive a luxury to keep in the crowded city. By the end of the 19th century, however, the bicycle had evolved into a form of conveyance that the common citizen could enjoy. It made possible trips into the surrounding rural areas on weekends and extended vacations to attractive spots nearby. The riders quickly noted the deterioration of roads as they left the city. Forming bicycle clubs such as the League of American Wheelmen, the cyclists began lobbying for improved roads. Various states also got into the act. Many legislators realized that poor roads hurt the economy. In North Carolina the legislature passed the Mecklenburg Law in 1885. This allowed Mecklenburg County to enjoy the highest taxes in the state—and the best roads. But the improved rural roads meant that by 1900 loads six times bigger could be hauled by the same team, a big savings in time and money and an expansion of service businesses to serve the road users. A similar program in Iowa allowed counties throughout the state the increased tax option to improve its roads. It was needed. In the 1880s Iowa actually had steeper grades on its rural roads than did most of Switzerland.

The movement for "good roads" continued. Led on by the Wheelmen and various good road automobile leagues, legislatures began to understand that much of the travel on county roads was between counties and hence statewide in nature. New Jersey began statewide road financing in 1891. Massachusetts went a step further and created the first highway department in 1892. It was charged with building an interconnected system of roads and emphasized the network rather than all roads, thus concentrating the financial effort where it would do the most good. By 1917, almost all states had a state highway commission operating on the Massachusetts principle.

As the states realized that the economics of good roads benefited everyone, so did the federal government. In 1892, the U.S. Senate tried to get the government to sponsor a display of new road-building techniques and equipment at the Columbian Exposi-

tion at Chicago. The effort failed, but the following year Congress established the Office of Road Inquiry to examine new road-building methods and disseminate this information through the nation's land-grant agricultural and mechanical colleges. General Roy Stone, a prominent New York civil engineer and good-roads man, became the head of the office. Stone issued numerous bulletins on the various road topics and soon found that he could not supply them fast enough to meet demand. Stone and his subordinates spoke at good-roads conventions and in 1894 began a national good-roads map, showing all macadamized and gravel roads in each county of the country. He compiled the information from maps sent in by county clerks or surveyors. The first complete maps included Pennsylvania, Indiana, and New Jersey. Stone also compiled figures that proved that the actual cost to send goods across America's roads in 1895 was 25 cents per ton-mile. Although the railroads could do the same for a half cent, the implication was that good roads were a national economic necessity.

To further disseminate information, Stone borrowed an idea from Massachusetts. There the state road commission had fastened on the plan of building 1-mile-long demonstration strips of properly built roads in each county, called "object lesson" roads. In this way the local population could examine and try out the strips and hopefully be converted to the concept of good roads and the expenses that went with them. Stone wanted the Office of Road Inquiry to do this on a national scale, but was limited by the usual lack of funds. So Stone got the states and localities to put up the money, equipment manufacturers to donate machines, and took it all on the road, so to speak. Soon he was deluged with requests to send his staff out to build demonstration sections in many areas. Stone also advised states legislatures on what to include in good-road laws. By this time, however, the Spanish-American War took Stone out of the country for military service. He would return after the Cuban Campaign, but not to the Office of Road Inquiry. He instead joined the National League for Good Roads as its president, where he suggested that three national demonstration highways be built, one up the Atlantic and Pacific coasts and another connecting them across the country between Washington, D.C., and San Francisco.

With Stone on military duty, the federal government pulled one of its usual bureaucratic stunts and renamed the Office of Road Inquiry. The new entity was the Office of Public Road Inquiry, now headed by Martin Dodge, former head of the Ohio state road commission. Like Stone before him, Dodge begged Congress to increase the office's $10,000-per-year budget. Finally in 1903, Congress tripled the annual sum. Meanwhile, Dodge divided the nation into four administrative areas, with a special agent in charge of each. The agents were part-time employees, but their rigorous schedule of trips to local conventions and research and writing of reports and bulletins belie this designation. The object lesson team was still shipped by rail to eight or nine places a year to build the 1-mile demonstration roads. Lectures by E. G. Harrison, the team leader, were published in local newspapers and widely read. After 1903, with the new increased budget, Dodge was able to field four such teams.

As Dodge struggled to propagandize the good-roads concept, he was aided by many private associations. In 1893 only one national association and three local ones existed. Ten years later there were over 100 such groups. The most important was the National Good Roads Association, founded at the Chicago Good Roads Convention in 1900. Like all associations, the National Good Roads Association had no real membership list. Rather it depended upon private donations and the aid from businesses involved in road-building equipment, materials suppliers, and even railroads. Under the leadership of William Moore of St. Louis, the association came up with the idea of a Good Roads Train that would travel the nation and educate the public. It worked much like a circus train, except the railroads contributed the cars and schedule time (well

hated by the antimonopolistic public, the railroads saw this as a good public relations ploy and a way to increase profits by hauling the business engendered by road traffic). Machinery companies picked up the tab, and the Office of Public Road Inquiry contributed the services of Special Agent Charles T. Harrison after the association offered to pay his salary and expenses. The trains were a rip-roaring success everywhere they went, especially in the South and West.

As the Good Roads Trains covered the country, Director Dodge continued his efforts in Washington. He compiled an inventory of all roads in the United States outside of cities (there were 2,151,570 miles of them and only 153,622 had any pavement). Dodge also went to Congress and asked that his office be made permanent and independent of the Department of Agriculture. In 1905, Congress complied and merged the Division of Tests of the Bureau of Chemistry with the Office of Public Road Inquiry and called it all the Office of Public Roads. But it required that the personnel be scientists by training, which cut Dodge, a lawyer, out. He was replaced by Logan Waller Page.

Page brought a new outlook to the federal road effort, that of the scientifically trained civil servant. In 1893, at the ripe old age of 23, he became director of the road materials laboratory at Harvard University. Later, he was a geologist and testing engineer for the Massachusetts state highway commission. He took what today would be seen as postgraduate training in France. Then he took his methods to Washington to the chemical laboratory that tested road materials for the Office of Public Road Inquiry, where his methods created a worldwide reputation. From there the step to director of the Office of Public Roads was a natural step.

Page had an advantage over his predecessors—a $50,000 budget. He also began to look into new materials like sand, clay, and common earth as opposed to the rocks and gravels of earlier processes. He believed that any local governing structure could afford to improve its roads using these easily available materials. Then it could use such roads as an infrastructure upon which to lay hard surfaces later. Page was aided greatly in his emphasis of native materials when D. Ward King of Maitland, Missouri, developed a simple log drag that could plane the surface of dirt roads so that they shed water more easily. Page also practiced burning the sticky clay until it lost its tacky qualities and made a usable surface material. He used the old demonstration mile to illustrate his methods for local civil engineers and the public.

Among the materials that Page looked into was blast furnace slag, which certain sections of the steel-producing regions had in abundance. He mixed this with limestone and road oil, the latter being a product developed in the Los Angeles basin to keep dust down. Page also cooperated with Jackson, Tennessee, in conducting extensive experiments on various residue oils left over from the normal refining process. As the number of automobiles increased (from 8,000 in 1900 to 468,500 in 1910), so-called bituminous materials (oils and tars) increased and asphalt mixes became more popular for the same reasons as they had been used in cities for decades.

But Page wished to try out the French maintenance system in the United States. Experience had shown that constant maintenance made for the best roads, and France had the best roads on Earth before World War I. He used Alexandria County, Virginia, to conduct his experiments. Each road was divided into short strips of a couple of miles and maintained by a paid patrolman who lived nearby. Page knew that the roads in Virginia south of the nation's capital were the heaviest traveled of their day. Yet he discovered that for the modest price of about $100 per mile per year the highways could easily keep up with traffic use. Most patrolmen were local farmers who had a team and a King drag.

By 1914, with such information in his files, Page next set up the longest demonstration highway ever used until then, combining roads passing through 49 counties in Virginia, the Carolinas, and Georgia from

Washington to Atlanta. Supervised by the federal agents, local maintenance men kept the highway open for the next three years, regardless of season or weather. Page curtailed the demonstration teams and sent them off as advisors who would look deeply into an area's road system and establish a building maintenance program. He called this the "model systems" program. In the process he discovered that the whole nation had one problem in common—not enough highway engineers. Even before Page, Dodge had recommended a national school for road engineers, but nothing had been done. Now Page developed an apprenticeship program whereby young engineering graduates could come to work for his office and be trained in the field. Much of their work was done in the national forests and national parks. He also advised state colleges on what to include in their own road engineering courses.

In 1908, Page sent a comprehensive exhibit on "road improvement" to the Alaska-Yukon-Pacific Exposition at Seattle. The effort was so successful that Page got the Smithsonian to lend him some model makers to do up a really big display that was loaned, complete with slide show and government staff lecturer, to state fairs. The Pennsylvania Railroad offered to carry such a show by rail and the Road Improvement Train, with full-sized construction equipment, toured the Pennsy line. Not to be outdone, a half dozen other railroads followed suit. Finally, Page organized the American Association for Highway Improvement (later the American Highway Association) in 1911. Its program included federal aid to highway construction (with the stipulation that no aid be forthcoming unless maintenance was provided for after construction), the creation of a highway department in every state, the employment of educated highway engineers, the use of prison labor as road gangs, the requirement that a white headlight and a red taillight be installed on all motor vehicles, prohibitions against horn-honking and muffler cutouts in urban areas, and the provisions that slow vehicles travel to the right of the roadway, that roads be marked in a uniform manner, and that speed regulations be posted and enforced.

It was inevitable that a lobbying group of professional highway officials be formed, and Page had a hand in that, too. In 1914, the American Association of State Highway Officials came together and made its first order of business the writing of a proposed bill for federal aid to highways for congressional consideration.

Federal highway aid had its roots in the creation of rural free mail delivery (RFD). Farmers in the late nineteenth and early twentieth centuries were very isolated. There were few modern amenities now taken for granted: no electricity, no phone, no mail. To get any of these things, even a newspaper, the farmer had to go into town. And abominable roads made such a trip a real adventure. The Patrons of Husbandry, an agricultural organization better known as the Grange, had as one of its goals the free delivery of rural mail. It had been a common practice in Europe for decades. In 1893, after much hemming and hawing at the Post Office Department, Congress set up a route in West Virginia. It was an instant success. Ten years later there were 8,600 carriers taking the mail to 5 million persons. But there was a catch—no rural delivery was forthcoming unless the roads were up to par, and the post office sent out inspectors to be sure there were no cheaters. Everyone wanted mail delivery, so now the clamor for post roads was added to that of the good-roads lobby.

In 1903, Congressman Walter Brownlow of Tennessee had introduced a bill asking for $20 million annually in federal aid to the states to create post roads. The measure failed but the drive was on. In 1912, after several other measures had failed to pass, Congressman Dorsey W. Shackleford of Missouri introduced a proposal that would authorize $25 million per year for rural free delivery. The money would be apportioned among counties on the basis of $15 per mile of graded earth roads, $20 for gravel roads, and $25 for macadamized roads—providing that the counties spent a like amount on these roads the preceding year. Shackleford called this an economy measure as RFD was losing $28 million a year, much of which could be made up in more efficient use of carriers over better roads. Shackleford's bill failed, but Congress did pass the Post Office Appropriation Act of 1913 to improve post roads if the territory of an individual carrier could be increased, and ordered the Post Office and Agriculture Departments to set up a board to examine the problem. Congress also set up committees to look into the matter of federal aid to highways.

When the states (which had to put up $2 to each federal dollar and could not use convict labor to build or maintain the roads) refused to participate, the two departments used the tried-and-true concept of setting up demonstration routes. The job was dropped in the lap of the Office of Public Roads, in addition to its other tasks, with no concomitant increase in funding or personnel. The major lesson learned was that federal aid of any kind ought to be dispensed through the 48 states and not the multitude of county governments. Meanwhile, various highway associations cropped up, each adopting a road to some faraway place of importance. The Lincoln Highway Association proposed to fund and construct a highway across the nation between New York City and San Francisco, the Dixie Highway Association opened up the Florida East Coast to northern tourists, the Pacific Highway Association opened up the West Coast from north to south, the Ozark Trails Association did the same in its area of concern, and so on.

By 1916, several measures proposing federal aid to highways awaited congressional action. They ranged from a proposal by Senator Hoke Smith of Georgia that would revamp the earlier Shackleford formula but dispense the money through the states, to one by Senator John H. Bankhead (the father of sardonic actress Tallulah) of Alabama that suggested forming a national bureau of highways to dispense at least $25 million annually on road building and maintenance. Most agreed that the states receiving federal money ought to be required to match it dollar for dollar. Shackleford introduced Smith's version of his earlier bill, a measure that would have the federal government "rent" roads annually dependent on their surface classifications. But city interests and the American Automobile Association worked successfully to defeat it as too rural in nature. One of the concepts that Shackleford introduced at this time was the notion that there were two basic types of highways—touring (rural, cross-country) and business (urban, city or local)—and that they were somehow incompatible. Others put it differently. They warned that the road program must not become scattered in its effect by becoming nothing but local pork barrel legislation, but concentrated to have the effect of bettering certain central routes.

In 1916, Shackleford introduced the first successful federal highway aid measure, the Federal-Aid Road Act. It appropriated up to $25 million annually for the next five years, of which each state was guaranteed $65,000. The rest was apportioned one-half on the basis of population and the other half on the mileage of certified RFD routes in the state (this overcame the opposition of states with large cities that had defeated earlier measures). The federal money had to be matched at least on a one-to-one basis by the states, but at no more than a two-to-one ratio. To receive aid after 1920, the state in question would have to have created a state highway department to supervise use of the funds. The states had to prepare the plans, apply to the federal government for approval, do the work under existing state laws (meaning less convict labor), permit federal inspection of the work, and send the proper ratio of bills to the federal government for payment.

There was much debate, but the bill's reliance on the Constitution's post roads formula and its resting the ultimate ownership of the roads in the states and localities overcame any constitutional doubts. The bill passed the lower house with a healthy margin and, through the able leadership of Senator Bankhead, a lifelong supporter of better roads, received unanimous approval in the Senate. The final measure included provisions for roads and trails in the national parks and forests. It also merged agricultural drainage, irrigation, and farm architecture into Walter Page's office, the new organization being labeled the Office of Public Roads and Rural Engineering.

See also American Automobile Association; Bonus Bill; Braddock's Road; Bridges; Calhoun, John Caldwell; Clay, Henry; Federal-Aid Road Act; Forbes' Road; Gallatin, Albert; Good Roads Movement; Hamilton, Alexander; League of American Wheelmen; Lincoln Highway; McAdam, John L.; Maysville Road Veto; Mullan Road; National Road; Office of Road Inquiry; Pacific Wagon Road Office; Page, Logan Waller; Post Office Appropriation Acts; Trésaguet, Jean Pierre Marie; Two Percent Fund.

References Billington, Ray Allen, *The Far Western Frontier* (1956); Hart, Val, *The Story of American Roads* (1950); Moody, Ralph, *The Old Trails West* (1963); Paxson, Frederick L., "The Highway Movement, 1916–1935," *American Historical Review* (1945–1946) 51: 236–253; Rose, Mark H., *Interstate* (1979); Tindall, George B., *The Emergence of the New South* (1967); U.S. Department of Transportation, Federal Highway Administration, *America's Highways* (1976); Winther, Oscar Osburn, *The Transportation Frontier* (1964).

Roads and Highways since World War I

The Good Roads Movement received a real boost almost immediately from the declaration of war against Germany. The war overtaxed the rail system in a matter of weeks. Goods piled up on loading docks and millions of men had to be moved to army camps, trained, and sent to Europe, and all of this effort had to be supplied—a major logistics problem. Because of the crowding of terminals and the lack of rail cars, the infant motorized trucking industry expanded enormously. The radius of delivery increased until trucks began hauling what the railroad traffic managers called "less than carload" freight (amounts that did not fill up a standard 40-foot boxcar) between cities. The result was that the American highway system began to crumble from excessive use. The inability of railroads to haul all of the war goods meant that there was little space for road materials. Established contractors emphasized wartime demands, leaving highway construction to the inexperienced and the crooked. Owners of the railroads unfairly held certain rail cars back for emergency use, whether such a demand existed or not. Coal shortages threatened with winter approaching.

The result was the creation of the Military Truck Route, by which motor vehicles designed for army use would be driven from their inland assembly plants to the East Coast ports under their own power in massive convoys to save rail space, each loaded with three tons of spare parts and munitions. The basic path was from Toledo to Akron, Pittsburgh, Harrisburg, Lancaster, and Philadelphia. Other military roads came later. The trip across the Alleghenies had never been done in winter before on a regular basis, but the trucks had to be delivered. As fate would have it, the winter of 1917–1918 was one of the stormiest in memory. The Pennsylvania Highway Department threw 200 men and every motorized machine and horse-drawn vehicle they had into the task of keeping the highway open. They succeeded even though drifts ran up to 6 feet in spots. During the gaps in the military convoys, civilian trucks and cars used the roads all winter for the first time in history. All of this demonstrated that roads could be kept open in any weather, if necessary, but it cost a lot per ton-mile to move such goods.

But everyone knew that the winter freeze was all that allowed this traffic to keep moving. In spring, the roads would break up under such wear. Army trucks were loaded with no consideration as to their effect on the roadway. That spring, one military truck with an 11-ton load broke up a whole Delaware highway it crossed in one trip. In New York, a highway that had been in service without a hitch for nearly ten years broke up after 30 military trucks crossed it in one day. Only Wayne County, Michigan, where the road surfaces had been built to twice the normal 5 inches in depth, survived the heavy truck use. And the factories turned out 19,000 new trucks a month during the war. The truckers could haul small shipments at intermediate distances more efficiently than railroads. They made up the initial higher cost by requiring less packing and delivering door-to-door. Paperwork was also reduced. The railroads had found a vigorous new competitor, and the highways of the nation were not merely overused, but in the long run, assisted by their increased importance. It was clearly time to create a national system of through roads, financed by increased federal appropriation.

The Federal-Aid Highways Act of 1916 had been predicated on the idea of getting the farmer out of the mud. No real national highway system had been envisioned. Most of the movement in this direction had come from private associations that pushed long-distance roads for specific goals like improved motoring to use more auto parts and related products, tourism, or simple motoring pleasure. But the destruction of the state highways by wartime traffic had changed the scope of American interest. Almost any road bill got immediate state support. Money and tax rates jealously guarded by state legislatures were no longer a problem. Everyone wanted improved roads and more of them, quickly, the cost be hanged. But the federal picture was complicated by the death of Walter Page, and a break between the advocates of farm-to-market roads as in the past and the cross-country highway advocates. The latter, led by E. J. Mehren of the *Engineering News-Record*, called for a federal system of highways of five east–west routes and ten north–south routes, composed of about 2 percent of existing state roads to be built, maintained, and administered by a federal highway commission

The Post Office Appropriation Bill of 1919 ended the last stand of those who insisted that highway money have some relation to the constitutional requirement that it be spent on postal or militarily related projects. By broadly defining a post road so as to include almost any road that could potentially carry the mails, the constitutional condition meant nothing. But there were more problems. There were so many independent state projects that construction firms could not keep up with the demand, even though hundreds of new road-building companies sprang up, partly aided by the auctioning off of World War I military road machines. Costs rose with the demand. By the end of the construction season in 1920, less than 20 percent of the desired work had been accomplished. The whole road program needed coordination. States were building great roads, when they could, that did little but end at their borders. Neighboring states did not coordinate their projects; the "good roads" literally went nowhere.

Under these conditions, Thomas H. MacDonald became the head of the Bureau of Public Roads, as the federal office was now called. He was to rule the agency for the next 34 years, and the modern system of American highways owes much to his positive influence. He knew that the federal government had to coordinate the use of money within the states, but that a program mandated solely by his office would draw opposition from the states as it would absorb all federal funding. He believed that the solution was to strengthen the state highway departments and let them spend the money as they chose, restricting a small proportion of them for an interstate system. He enrolled the help of state road engineers all over the country and the army and marked out a system of militarily important highways across the country, state by state. Then he classified all roads by national, state, or local importance.

Next MacDonald turned to Congress. All federal aid would terminate at the end of the 1921 fiscal year. A new congressional act was imperative. MacDonald worked with the legislative branch to create a measure that would correct the perceived ills of the 1916 law. The result was the Phipps-Dowell-Townsend Bill, which became the Federal Highway Act of 1921. The measure originated with Congressman Cassius Dowell of Iowa. He proposed (in league with MacDonald and others) that each state, in order to qualify for federal highway funds, had to designate not more than 7 percent of its roads as a state highway system, of which 43 percent were to be designated as federal interstate highways (meaning roads between the states, not to be confused with the present-day divided highway usage of the term). Sixty percent of all federal road money given to the state had to be spent on the interstate roads. The rest could be spent on any of the designated state highways.

Dowell went on to say that the states should match federal funds dollar for dollar (except in the West where so much of the land was federal and could be deducted from the ratio), and all money spent in construction and maintenance had to go through a state highway department. Failure to maintain the roads on which federal money was spent, upon investigation by the U.S. secretary of agriculture, would allow the federal government to repair such roads and bill the state, and to withhold all federal funds until the bill was paid. Senator Lawrence C. Phipps of Colorado amended the measure to allow states that had not spent all of their money under the old 1916 act to retain it under the present measure. And Senator Charles E. Townsend of Michigan changed his earlier bill that provided for federal ownership of the interstate roadways to provide for state ownership and maintenance under federally set standards. These included a paved roadway 18 feet in width. The whole measure had a $75 million price tag.

Just as important was the Post Office Appropriation Act of 1922. This measure established the principle of "contract authority." This meant that whenever the proper federal official (usually the secretary of agriculture then, and the secretary of the treasury now) approved of a state road plan, the federal government was obligated to fund the project even before Congress appropriated any actual money for it. This allowed the states to plan ahead, confident that Washington would back them up once the initial approval was obtained. It established a new continuity to the highway programs and made them more rational in nature and nationwide in scope.

The Federal Highway Act of 1921 had two immediate results. First, it marked the beginning of the end for the trails associations that had funded interstate roads through public contributions. No one could match the federal government when it came to money. They would continue on for many years as popularizers of certain routes, but dwindle to nothing by the Great Depression. The other effect was the numbering of the federally sponsored highway system in a uniform manner throughout the nation. Through a number of regional meetings and cooperation between state and federal highway officials, just under 100,000 miles of federal highways were designated and marked with the familiar black-and-white shield.

Originally, on east–west roads the numbers on the bottom two- thirds of the shield were even, with the lowest numbers being northernmost. Major routes were multiples of 10 up to 90. The odd-numbered routes ran north and south, with the lower numbers on the east side of the nation. The important north–south highways had two-digit numbers ending in 1 or 5, with the major exception of U.S. Highway 101, which ran the length of the U.S. Pacific coast. It was not unusual for numbered routes to have alternate courses. In these cases, the normal highway designator ended in an A, for "alternate" or, on north–south roads, an E for "east" or W for "west." The same was true with east–west routes, which had alternate routes marked with the usual route number followed by an N for "north" or S for "south." The top section of the shield was often marked with the name of the state through which the federal road passed. Three-digit numbers (except U.S. 101 again) originally meant that the road was a feeder for the highway depicted by the last two figures. The first cipher was the feeder number. State highways, also a part of the system, were marked with different emblems, quite commonly a depiction of the state's map outline. But some states used other symbols—Utah, for example, still uses the symbol for the old Mormon Territory of Deseret, a beehive.

Besides the numbering of the highways, MacDonald got Congress to fund programs for several years in a row, important because the state legislatures often met every other year. He endorsed the concept of building the highways by stages, the "wait and see" approach, especially in the West and South where travel was lighter. A state could lay out a dirt road, then cover it with gravel, and finally pave it, all in successive years. The result was massive numbers of miles laid during the early 1920s. MacDonald continued to experiment with road materials and construction and maintenance methods. There were two exceptions to this, however: Illinois had its own experimental highway, the Bates Road, and California had a test track built by Columbia Steel Company. The results of these tests showed that increasing the road width to 20 feet put less wear and tear on the edges and shoulders. In addition, soils were classified into eight basic standards, which aided planners in deciding how much to spend and what kinds of materials to use at what depth ahead of building. Most states participated in these Bureau of Public Roads tests at one time or another.

The highway construction boom of the 1920s was followed by another forced program of public works after the onset of the Great Depression. The 1930 Emergency Construction Act and the 1932 Emergency Relief and Construction Act advanced money to the states as loans to promote employment; the 1934 Hayden-Cartwright Act converted these loans to outright grants. The National Industrial Recovery Act of 1933 allowed highway money to be spent within the limits of cities for the first time. Again, it was seen as a form of "pump priming," so essential to the New Deal's attack on the Depression. Meanwhile, much of the money was spent in improving highway safety by straightening out the roadbeds. The result was thousands of miles of completely straight roads that unwittingly would introduce a sort of mesmerizing driver fatigue as the speed of motor vehicles and the length of trips increased.

Meanwhile, the military advantages of a reliable nationwide road network were not lost on planners. In 1921, Bureau Chief MacDonald had asked the army to indicate its requirements for national defense. The result was the Pershing Map, signed by

General John J. Pershing as chief of staff in 1922, marking out three classes of roads of military importance: primary, secondary, and tertiary. Pershing emphasized that the nation did not need wide transcontinental highways so much as it needed a full network that blanketed the country. His roads differed from the already-selected national highway for federal aid, and all those not already so chosen were added to the original list. Fifteen years later, the War Department restudied the national defense road network and passed its conclusions on to the Bureau of Public Roads. The result was the adoption of 26,700 miles of key roads to be a part of an interregional highways plan. This proposal was put out as the 1939 report, *Toll Roads and Free Roads*. It envisioned the system of restricted-access highways to be built in the future.

The real problem with securing governmental backing for a massive highway program involved the depression. Although road building created jobs and benefited the nation in the long run, highway jobs were limited, much of the work being done by machines. President Franklin D. Roosevelt did an inventive balancing act, juggling jobs and highway construction, keeping the highway expenses at a minimum until the approach of World War II changed his perspective. Then in the Federal Highway Act of 1940, Congress restricted most highway materials to use on the federal defense roads and military reservations, a restriction that continued until the defeat of Japan in 1945. This meant that most roads in the country had little or no maintenance during the war.

But the traffic requirements for war were many times those of World War I, and the result was much the same—the highways were pounded to death by military traffic. Congress gave the Interstate Commerce Commission the right to set weight limits, standardizing these for the first time and allowing easier passage of trucks between states. The states, led by Colorado, challenged the federal government's standards, especially since the truckers were allowed to exceed limits as a matter of course to further the war effort. States feared that the excessive weights would tear up their highways and create a new plateau of weight that after the war would entail their rebuilding any highway to the new limits. But the federal government insisted and suspended the limits, making the highways expendable for the final victory. Contractors asked to be released from state highway work that they might bid on the more lucrative federal jobs. Citizens parked their cars as the rationing of gasoline and other auto products went under the ration system. Revenues to the states declined accordingly.

Despite the decline of revenues, states still conducted highway planning, as did the federal government. Most of this was based on the Pennsylvania Turnpike, a controlled-access superhighway that duplicated German designs of their Autobahns. Opened in late 1940, the turnpike grossed $2.6 million in its first year of operation. New York, Maryland, Illinois, Maine, and Florida passed similar proposals in their states. Toll highways lost narrowly in the legislatures of Missouri, New Jersey, Oklahoma, and Wisconsin. California was looking into an urban freeway, the Bayshore, for San Francisco. Roosevelt did not like the restrictive idea of toll roads, nor the lack of federal participation in them, and suggested instead that the nation build its own limited-access highways after the war, when manpower and industrial capacity would be available in excess. Roosevelt wanted the federal government to condemn the land necessary for such a highway system and to sell it back to the states and public after the value went up from the road improvements put on it. The profit would finance the new highways.

But Congress declined to change the federal-state relationship so radically. In 1944, acting on a federal study that showed that most of the traffic on any highway would be generated within a 35-mile radius of any city as opposed to long-distance traffic, Congress passed the Federal-Aid Highway Act of 1944. It appropriated $500 million for the first three postwar years to be divided up between the declared federal highway system (45 percent), urban extension roads (25 percent), and principal secondary

After World War II, highways not only connected city to city but city to suburb.

roads (30 percent) selected by the states with the approval of the federal government. The federal government could help states obtain rights-of-way by contributing up to one-third of the money needed, but no change in ownership to Washington was to be had. The act also authorized 40,000 miles of "interstate" controlled-access highways, but no money was set aside for construction. The proposed system of "freeways" effectively set back the burgeoning toll road movement, but it was all potentially possible, depending on future appropriation.

At the end of World War II, all controls

on highway use were lifted. Automobile production rose from 69,500 in 1945 to 3.9 million in 1948. Truck registration jumped 34 percent in the same time. Highway usage went up 6 percent every year, a phenomenon that was to last for decades. But the highways were in the same condition as before the war—functionally obsolete, narrow, and lacking capacity and a rational network. The problem was compounded by the movement of people out of the cities to the suburbs, made more possible by entire suburban developments of reasonably priced housing like Long Island's Levittown. The result was increasing congestion. There were a few large-sized parkways, like the Arroyo Seco between Los Angeles and Pasadena, and the Westchester County and Long Island in New York State. But the throughways merely exacerbated urban sprawl. In its early days, federal highway aid had emphasized rural roads. No longer. Now the aid poured into urban access roads, as emphasized in the Federal-Aid Highway Act of 1944. To better understand this new suburban traffic problem, states and the federal government took "origin-and-destination" surveys. They literally stopped the commuters and found out how they drove in 30 large metropolitan areas and 135 smaller cities.

The states also updated their secondary routes under the 1944 act. The mileage of these select roads more than doubled in the decade following the war. But the newest concept was the 40,000 miles of proposed interstate highways. When the Public Roads Administration (PRA) asked each state to designate such roads, more than the quota were selected. As many of the extra miles involved city loops and access, the federal government decided to ignore these for awhile and concentrate on city-to-city connections. After reexamining the states' proposed routes, the PRA whittled the list down to about 38,000 miles and asked the states to approve of the choices made. By June 1947, all of the states and the federal agencies were in agreement as to selected miles for the new highway system.

But the standards of construction were something else. The original federal standards did not come up to those used for years on such gems as the Pennsylvania Turnpike. Current government regulations permitted railroad grade crossings and the intersection with other interstate roads, much like the outdated Airline Highway from New Orleans to Opelousas, Louisiana. States could build to 60- or 70-mile-per-hour standards, as they pleased. Rights-of-way could vary between 150 and 250 feet. Given these poor standards, and particularly the fact that roadside business access was not regulated, it appeared that the new superhighways would soon be clogged with converging traffic like the outdated roads they were to replace. Few states had laws of eminent domain to permit securing highways from businesses and residences through the controlled-access parkway principle. Added to the strained demand on federal resources for the cold war's Marshall Plan of extensive foreign aid, the United Nations' police action in Korea, and domestic housing, the shortage of road materials and a lack of trained highway engineers got the interstate system off to a slow start.

The states were as short of resources as the federal government. Attempts to transfer the responsibility for roads to Washington only resulted in a meager concession in 1950—the feds would help with up to 50 percent of right-of-way acquisition, but little else was forthcoming. This stagnation led to a renewed interest in toll roads, built and maintained by the states without Washington's participation. The inspiration for this trend was again the Pennsylvania Turnpike. Finished just before World War II, the turnpike at first seemed a bad deal. It lost money during the war. But when wartime controls on travel were lifted, the project boomed. It did so well that the turnpike was lengthened into Philadelphia to the east and to the Ohio state line to the west. A similar experience occurred in Maine, which built a 47-mile turnpike parallel to U.S. Highway 1 in 1946 and 1947. Charging a 1.5-cents-a-mile toll, the road operated comfortably in the black from the start. Massachusetts put in a free expressway to the New Hampshire

443

line. The short New Hampshire section between the two throughways was so congested that the Granite State finally put in a toll road of its own. It ran in the black so well that the state decided to build two more toll roads elsewhere.

But New Jersey was the state that hit the real jackpot. It sold its own bonds, avoiding the New York commission houses. At least 15 other states went into the turnpike business. Following a method used by the Port Authority of New York, the turnpikes were often overfinanced in tolls collection and the extra money was used to bolster weaker sections of the project or to fund other related projects. New Jersey prevented truck traffic from using its turnpike at first, relying solely on automobile usage for its income. The federal government refused to help finance these turnpikes, but later incorporated them into the interstate system so as to coordinate the movement of traffic across the nation. PRA chief MacDonald retired at this juncture, and Francis V. DuPont took over. Under his leadership, the Federal Highway Act of 1954 boosted the aid to the states by 50 percent to a new high of $875 million. DuPont hoped to deflate some criticism from the states that their citizens had paid more into the treasury in gasoline and other highway use taxes than they had received back. The 1954 act also set aside $175 million of the total amount for the interstate highways and loosened many of the controls on which roads were liable to receive the aid.

As the Federal Highway Act of 1954 demonstrated, the Dwight D. Eisenhower administration was acutely interested in updating the nation's road system. As head of the Allied effort in the European theater in World War II, Eisenhower had firsthand experience with the Germans' Autobahn—a sort of blueprint of what the United States' new highway program would build. The president pledged to the nation's governors that he would approve of spending up to $5 billion a year for ten years to bring American highways up to what he believed the nation needed. He also placed General Lucius D. Clay, with whom he had worked in

the occupation of Germany, in charge of a study group to recommend a measure for congressional consideration. Clay proposed that the highways be financed outside the usual budget constraints at $31 billion, using 32-year bonds, of which the states ought to contribute 5 percent.

But the Clay report, called *A 10-Year National Highway Program*, ran into a buzz saw in Congress. It was quickly shelved and more conservative pay-as-you-go proposals considered. No single measure could get the requisite votes in either house. Popular sentiment, however, backed Eisenhower, so the highway proposals came up for consideration again in 1956. The result was the Federal-Aid Highway Act or the Interstate and Defense Highway Act of 1956. The act went on the old pay-as-you-go principle. But the rest was a radical departure from the past. For the first time, all highway user taxes (gasoline, lubricants, rubber, etc.) were reserved for highway projects. Excise taxes on truck and bus use likewise went into highway construction. Next, the Davis-Bacon Act of 1935, which guaranteed that wages on jobs bid out by the federal government were not lower than the prevailing wage of the area in question, was to apply to all highway construction. Before this, wages could be bid in on federal highway jobs at a lower rural rate. Now more expensive union contracts in the nearby big cities became the minimum on all highway projects, necessitating a 15 to 40 percent rise in overall costs.

Finally, the Interstate Highway project was not to be as open-ended as prior road bills, but was to be built in a specific amount of time (16 years, later extended) under one authorization, much like the railroads of the century before—and this was a project of much the same scale for its day. Appropriations were not to be made on the basis of population, but on the nature of the work needing to be done in any one area to finish the job on time, and appropriations were to be administered by the Highway Trust Fund. The total appropriation was to be $25 million through 1969, with 90 percent of the money to be federal. Standards on weights and vehicle size and provisions to relocate utilities and salvage archeological finds completed the measure.

The interstate highways were indicated with a red, white, and blue shield, the services in white on blue signage, and information in white on green rectangular signs. They were numbered exactly opposite to the old federal system of 1921. North–south highways had odd numbers and began with the low numbers in the west. The east–west routes had even numbers and began with low numbers at the south. Loop roads around or through cities received three-digit multiples of the main route, beginning with an even-numbered digit. Such a road with an odd-numbered digit is a spur route. For example, Interstate 10 goes through Houston; its loop feeder is numbered Interstate 610. The spur north from Interstate 10 in Baton Rouge is Interstate 110. The longer transcontinental routes have one- or two-digit numerals ending in 5 or 0. On Interstate 10, shorter parallel routes are numbered I-12 in Louisiana and I-8 in Arizona and California. Interstate 5 runs along the whole Pacific coast, but Interstate 19 merely connects Tucson and Nogales in Arizona. The latter road is signed in metric—part of the nascent bureaucratic drive to force that "modern" system upon a population still enamored with the old English system.

The road-building explosion stimulated by the 1956 act forced the Bureau of Public Roads to decentralize its operations and move into the field to properly supervise the many individual projects. New congressional measures increased the amount of federal supervision required. In 1962, states had to institute long-range continuing, comprehensive, and cooperating planning processes (known as "3-C") on roads in urban areas of over 300,000 population. Further, all families displaced by the highway construction had to be advised of their options and of the availability of federal aid for their moving. In 1970, such aid was made automatic and broadened to include all federal programs under the Assistance Act of 1970.

The assistance given to those displaced by the new interstate system illustrated the increased emphasis on the social goals of the highway program. Consideration had to be taken of such things as increased safety, beautification, noise and other sorts of environmental pollution, soil erosion, racial and sexual discrimination, and the effect of the highways on wildlife, recreation, and historic sites. Under such guises, Congress acted again in 1965 to further modify the 1956 highway program. States had to show that they enforced federally prescribed measures to slow the rate of traffic accidents. This program was further expanded in the Highway Safety Act of 1966 and the introduction of the Traffic Operations Program to Increase Capacity and Safety (TOPICS). The same year saw the passage of the Highway Beautification Act, which regulated junkyards and sign advertising along the interstates and called for roadside landscaping or "scenic enhancement," as the bureaucrats like to call that sort of thing. Two years later, Equal Employment Opportunity regulations had to be made a part of all bids and labor contracts. In 1969 an environmental impact study and statement had to be done for each new road location.

By 1970, Congress called for economic growth centers to revitalize local areas bypassed by the new system, a new urban highway system, improved bridge standards, and a noise abatement program. Training programs for new workers added to the equal employment program's impact. In 1973, new programs for safer roads emphasized better highway markings, better primary routes through cities, and the use of carpooling and mass transit lanes. For the first time, gender discrimination in hiring was forbidden and minority companies were given preference in certain contracts. The following year, Congress enacted laws providing for handicapped and elderly access and higher limitations on vehicle weights and sizes. The speed limit was dropped to 55 mph as a part of the response to the Arab oil embargo (later rescinded outside major urban areas).

Advances in construction and maintenance have kept pace with modern developments. It became possible to pour a drier form of concrete that holds its form in a matter of minutes, obviating the need for the extensive building and tearing up of forms. The only form needed slides right along with the cement layer. Almost everything is done by heavy machinery, starting with the self-powered grader from the 1920s. Huge trucks and earthmovers can scrape the roadbed in hours, whereas it once required teams of mules and dozens of men as late as World War II. Chemical additives strengthen concrete and asphalt and make their application more varied and easy. Massive steel girders and prestressed concrete beams take bridges over the highways or highways over obstacles to limit the grade of the highway. Although the interstate highway system comprises less than 2 percent of the national road network (about 43,000 miles) and was not declared fully complete until 1990 (with a price tag of $275 billion), it carries about one-fourth of all motor vehicle traffic in the United States.

See also Automobiles from Domestics to Imports; Automobiles in American Society; Bridges; Emergency Relief and Construction Act; Federal-Aid Highway Acts; Federal Highway Act; Good Roads Movement; Hayden-Cartwright Act; Mac-Donald, Thomas H.; Post Office Appropriation Acts; Trucking.

References Batchelder, A. G., "The Immediate Necessity of Military Highways," *National Geographic* (November–December 1917) 32: 477–499; Belasco, Warren James, *Americans on the Road* (1979); Borth, Christy, *Mankind on the Move* (1969); Cron, F. W., "Highway Design for Motor Vehicles—A Historic Review," *Public Roads* (1975) 38: 163–174, *Public Roads* (1975) 39: 68–79, 96–108, 163–171, and *Public Roads* (1976) 40: 78–86, 93–100; Davis, Richard O., *The Age of Asphalt* (1975); Hindley, Geoffrey, *A History of Roads* (1971); Jordan, Robert Paul, "Our Growing Interstate System," *National Geographic* (February 1968) 133: 195–219; Lillard, Richard, *Eden in Jeopardy* (1966); McDade, Matt C., "New York State's New Main Street," *National Geographic* (November 1956) 110: 567–618; Moses, Robert, "The New Super-Highways: Blessing or Blight?" *Harper's* (December 1956) 213: 27–31; Partridge, Bellamy, *Fill 'er Up!* (1952); Paxson, Frederick L., "The Highway Movement, 1916–1935," *American Historical Review* (1945–1946) 51: 236–253; Robinson, John, *Highways and Our Environment* (1971); Rose, Mark H., *Interstate* (1979); Schmitt, Peter J., *Back to Nature* (1969); Seely, Bruce E., *Building the American Highway System* (1987); Simplich, Frederick, "U.S.

Roads in War and Peace," *National Geographic* (December 1941) 80: 687–716; U.S. Department of Transportation, Federal Highway Administration, *America's Highways* (1976).

Roberts, Nathan S. (1776–1852)

Born in Pine Grove, New Jersey, Nathan Roberts helped superintend the construction of the locks on the Erie Canal. He also acted as consulting engineer and member of the board of directors on the Chesapeake & Ohio Canal, was engineer of the western division of the Pennsylvania Main Line Canal, and served as an estimator and consultant for Democratic administrations of the federal government.

See Chesapeake & Ohio Canal; Erie Canal.

Robertson v. Baldwin 165 US 275 (1896)

In the 1890s, American seamen who deserted had no rights under the Constitution. The International Seamen's Union, led by Andrew Furuseth, managed to get Congress to pass the Maguire Act that forbade the imprisonment without trial of U.S. seamen who deserted while engaged in the coastal trade between American ports. The union then sought to extend rights to American seamen engaged in interoceanic trade, but failed. When four seamen deserted the ship *Arago* in Portland, engaged in trade between Chile and San Francisco via Oregon, the union brought suit hoping to get the courts to act where Congress had not, claiming that the seamen were held in violation of the Thirteenth Amendment, which forbade slavery and involuntary servitude. The result, however, was not what the seamen's representatives had wanted. In *Robertson v. Baldwin* the U.S. Supreme Court ruled that not only did the seamen in question not have any constitutional civil rights during their voyage while under shipping articles, but that the Maguire Act was also unconstitutional. The Court held that seamen were actually like minors or wards and subject to different concepts of contract than the ordinary citizen because of the transient nature of their occupation. Furuseth and his supporters labeled the Court's action a "Second Dred Scott Decision." In reality, however, there were so many seamen begging for work in ports that the right of arrest was rarely utilized. But the seamen disliked the notion of the law and Furuseth began a 20-year fight to end the Court's ruling that resulted in the La Follette Seamen's Act of 1915.

See also La Follette Seaman's Act; Merchant Marine.

References Pedraja, René de la, *A Historical Dictionary of the U.S. Merchant Marine and Shipping Industry* (1994); Schwartz, Stephen, *Brotherhood of the Sea* (1986); Standard, William L., *Merchant Seamen* (1947); Weintraub, Hyman, *Andrew Furuseth* (1959).

Rochester Telephone Corporation v. U.S. 307 US 125 (1939)

Rochester Telephone was a Supreme Court decision in which the Court ruled that the extent of control of public utilities and common carriers be set not by fixed, artificial standards, but by the special circumstances of each case. It was an important step in limiting control of the railroads by major holding groups or in allowing such control in light of public interest—also a substantive concept according to the Court.

See also Clayton Act; *McLean Trucking Company v. U.S.*; Transportation Acts.

Reference Saunders, Richard, *The Railroad Mergers and the Coming of Conrail* (1978).

Rock Island Lines

Conceived by a group of local businessmen in 1845, the Chicago, Rock Island & Pacific (CRI&P) began laying track out of Chicago for its namesake, the small town on the Mississippi River. Led by Henry Farnum, the track crews put down the 180 miles of rail necessary to reach Rock Island by 1853. The CRI&P then put the first bridge across the Father of Waters, a drawbridge that crossed to Davenport, Iowa. In the Hawkeye State, Grenville M. Dodge assisted the road in moving across the rolling plains to

Rock Island's 1900 advertisement claimed to have the "fastest passenger engines in the world."

Council Bluffs. After the Civil War, the Rock Island was reorganized several times, bought several minor routes, and came into its modern form as a Granger railroad (i.e., one that served the farmers on the Plains by bringing in supplies and manufactured goods and taking out their crops). The CRI&P also beat out the Chicago North Western for the U. S. mail contract, which made it attractive enough for Jesse James and his gang to rob the line twice. After that, the Rock Island was probably more than happy to transport the dead Jesse's body and family home for burial, free of charge.

The Rock Island expanded south and west into Kansas, Oklahoma, and New Mexico. But at the turn of the century the line suffered from a buyout and a $20 million stock manipulation that put it into receivership for decades. It also had a terrible wreck between two of its passenger trains, killing 52 and injuring three score others. This 1910 Green Mountain, Iowa, crash was instrumental in the changeover from wooden to steel cars. Nonetheless, passenger service on the CRI&P was considered good, its first-class trains being the several *Rockets* (the *Des Moines Rocket, Peoria Rocket, Kansas City Rocket, Texas Rocket,* and the *Denver Rocket*), white, red, and maroon partly articulated streamliners (where the cars shared the trucks of those that preceded and followed them); the *Rockets* were based on the Burlington's *Pioneer Zephyr*, but were pulled by normal diesels. But the Rock was one of numerous middle-sized railroads that suffered greatly from competition in the twentieth century. By the mid-1970s, it was bankrupt and eventually passed over to the Union Pacific system after selling its El Paso run to the Southern Pacific and much of its Kansas-Oklahoma-Texas lines to the Santa Fe Railway and the Missouri-Kansas-Texas (Katy) Railroad.

See also Klitenic Plan; Missouri-Kansas-Texas Railroad; Santa Fe Railway; Southern Pacific Lines; Union Pacific Railroad.

References Drury, George H., *The Historical Guide to North American Railroads* (1985); Drury, George H., *The Train-Watcher's Guide* (1990); Gardner, Ed, *Rock Island Lines* (1978); Grant, H. Roger, "Chicago, Rock Island & Pacific Railroad," in Keith L. Bryant, Jr. (ed.), *EABHB: Railroads in the Age of Regulation* (1988), 79–80; Grow, Lawrence, *On the 8:02* (1979); Hayes, William E., *Iron Road to Empire* (1953); Hubbard, Freeman, *Encyclopedia of North American Railroading* (1981); Larkin, F. David, "Chicago, Rock Island Railroad," in Robert L. Frey (ed.), *EABHB: Railroads in the Nineteenth Century* (1988), 45–46; Lyon, Peter, *To Hell in a Day Coach* (1968); Nevins, Frank J., *Seventy Years of Service* (1922); Schafer, Mike, and Harold Russell, "Rock Island's Rocket Streamliners," *Model Railroader* (May 1980) 47: 52–61.

Rockefeller, John D. (1839–1937)

Born in New York State and raised in Cleveland, Ohio, John D. Rockefeller became a dry-goods clerk, cashier, and bookkeeper. By the time of the Civil War, he had entered the burgeoning oil business as partners with his younger brother William and Henry Flagler of later Florida real estate and railroad fame. By the end of the war, the Rockefellers had built the beginnings of the Standard Oil Company with its first refinery located in Cleveland. In 1867, the brothers joined all of the various parts of their companies (New York, New Jersey, and Ohio) as one, incorporated in 1870 with a $1 million capitalization that increased to $3.5 million by 1874. After that date the true worth of Standard Oil cannot be accurately figured. Rockefeller brought economy and efficiency to a field in which most before him had gone broke. His prices were so cheap that kerosene beat out whale oil, coal oil, and electricity (for a while) as the prime product for power in the American home.

Using tactics that can best be called ruthless (but then, his opposition was not made up of Sunday school teachers), he drove competitors to join him or go broke. Those who resisted saw Standard cut its prices until opponents went broke. Rockefeller's empire covered so many states that he would make up his temporary losses in one area elsewhere. As soon as Standard controlled the desired competition, Rockefeller raised prices again. Users had little they could do but go along—if they wanted to use petroleum. In 1881 Standard became part of a large trust run by Rockefeller with the aid of shrewd legal and financial advisors. The oil trust was so successful that it was widely copied by other industries (steel, sugar, tobacco, and various railroad pools). In an era of dishonest business manipulators, however, Standard Oil always gave full value and eschewed any watering of stock. Unlike others of his era, Rockefeller alone managed his whole empire while owning a minority portion of stock. Even though the oil trust was broken up by the courts in the 1890s, by the turn of the century, John D. Rockefeller was acknowledged as the world's first (and at that time only) billionaire. And all this from kerosene; the automobile and petrochemical industries with their use of multiple petroleum products had not yet begun to boom.

Rockefeller never doubted that what he did was for the good of the oil industry and, in the end, of the consuming public. He destroyed the chaos present in any developing industry, established well-managed production of a needed product, and made it available in a reliable manner at a fair price. At the same time, he created jobs and a good standard of living for his employees. That he made a fortune doing it was merely a tribute to his fine management skills. His influence in American transportation came from his ability to make or break railroads that shipped his product. All of the trunk lines—Erie, New York Central, Pennsylvania, and the Baltimore & Ohio—wanted to become the exclusive shipper of Rockefeller oil. But the Pennsylvania had a subsidiary company that handled its oil shipments, the Empire Transportation Company, whose directors tried to break into the refining business and threatened Standard Oil's monopoly position.

When the going got sticky, Rockefeller merely cut off the Pennsylvania as his main transport consignee and shifted his product to competing lines. The Pennsylvania Railroad then became a party to destroying its own subsidiary, bought up by Rockefeller after he promised to return the railroad to its former status as chief shipper. Then Rockefeller made a broad agreement among the eastern railroads, assigning his product among them: 47 percent to the Pennsylvania, 21 percent each to the Erie and New York Central, and 11 percent to the Baltimore & Ohio. It was one example of how the shipper could manipulate the transporter, a rare thing in those days of manipulative railroad rates, and the railroads had to take it or go under.

In 1900, Rockefeller began to leave the day-to-day management of the business to his partners and advisors, but he still retained title of president. His business associates insisted that he keep it so that in case any of the court proceedings against the company resulted in jail sentences, Rockefeller would have to serve time, too. Rockefeller laughed, noting that any judge that ruled against Standard Oil would be dead a long time before his decrees would take effect—if they ever did (it took 20 years just to enforce the initial breakup of Standard Oil into its modern components). Rockefeller was right, of course. He now turned his attention to philanthropy. He gave $23 million to the University of Chicago, $50 million to the General Education Board, $100 million to the Rockefeller Foundation, $4 million to the Rockefeller Institution for Medical Research, presented over $.5 million in real estate to the city of Cleveland, contributed buildings and a Greek literature library to Vassar College, $1.3 million to Barnard College, almost $.5 million to the Baptist Missionary Union (Rockefeller was a practicing Christian all his life), a water tower to Tarrytown, New York, and some $500 million to other educational institutions. He died in Florida nearly 100 years after his birth, still unaffected by the adverse court decrees so feared by his cronies.

See also Oil Industry; Organization of Petroleum Exporting Countries; Pipelines.

References Folsom, Burton W., Jr., *The Myth of the Robber Barons* (1991); Josephson, Matthew, *The Robber Barons* (1934); Nevins, Allan, *Study in Power: John D. Rockefeller, Industrialist and Philanthropist* (1953); Tarbell, Ida M., *History of the Standard Oil Company* (1904); Williamson, Harold F., and Arnold R. Daum, *The American Petroleum Industry* (1959).

Romney, George W. (b. 1907)

A public relations man and lobbyist for American Motors in the 1950s and an effective and highly popular Michigan governor, George W. Romney was also a one-time U.S. presidential candidate in 1968, losing the Republican nomination to Richard Nixon when the former's intellectual and political abilities were questioned after he claimed he had been brainwashed about the Vietnam War. After Nixon's triumph, Romney served as the Department of Housing and Urban Development secretary from 1969 to 1972, and retired into obscurity. Seen often as an energetic lightweight, Romney's disarming quality served him well as he led American Motors after George Mason's heart attack. Romney was the giant-killer of the 1950s auto industry who defeated Volkswagen and threatened to turn the Big Three into the Big Four. Not until the emergence of Lee Iacocca in the late 1970s was there such a folk hero among the auto manufacturers.

A member of the Church of Jesus Christ of Latter-Day Saints, George W. Romney was born in Mexico where his family had gone in search of economic opportunity and religious freedom. The 1910 revolution put an end to such hopes, and his family returned to the United States. Young George grew up in Salt Lake City, worked at day labor, and became a devout church member. After the expected year-long missionary experience (he went to Great Britain), Romney became a political assistant to Senator Davis Walsh, a Massachusetts Democrat. Romney was a strikingly good-looking man; he had a distinguished look, the kind that can be a hit in various advertising media as a model. He was also a likable man—gregarious, polite, and sincere. He went from senatorial assistant to lobbyist for the aluminum industry and did a fantastic job. He switched fields in 1939, but his role was the same as director of the American Automobile Association. He represented them with the government during World War II, served on numerous boards, learned how the industry worked, and received several offers from different auto companies to join their public relations staffs. He refused all of them. In 1948, he almost accepted a vice-presidency from Packard, but turned it down for a role under George Mason at Nash-Kelvinator, which soon merged with Hudson to become American Motors.

At Nash, Romney spent several years wandering the plant and getting acquainted with the day-to-day operations. Although some have erroneously given him credit for the compact car idea (it was George Mason's, put into reality by Meade Moor), it was publicized by Romney. When Mason died and Romney took over, American Motors was in big trouble—it sold even less than Studebaker-Packard. Romney flirted with the idea of dropping the Rambler/Metropolitan side of the line and going with the upscale cars of Nash/Hudson. He even worked on a V-8 engine. But in the end he stuck to Mason's vision of the smaller cars. Romney then downsized both plant and labor force, dismantling the Nash/Hudson part of the company. Hudson had saved the company, but only through its dissolution. He worked hard improving the image of Rambler/Metropolitan with the buying public. Then a little luck entered the picture in the form of the worst recession since World War II, in 1958. Romney had guessed right—he had the small, cheaper cars that would enable Americans to survive tough times. American Motors' sales rose dramatically while those of the Big Three plummeted. The result was broad imitation throughout the industry—General Motors' Corvair, Ford's Falcon, Chrysler's Valiant, Studebaker's Lark, and the beginning of the size of car that is standard today.

See also Automobiles from Domestic to Imports; Automobiles in American Society; Mason, George W.

References Halberstam, David, *The Reckoning* (1986); Lazare, Michael, "George Wilcken Romney," in George S. May (ed.), *EABHB: The Automobile Industry* (1989), 387–393; Mahoney, Tom, *The Story of George Romney* (1960); Sobel, Robert, *Car Wars* (1984).

Roosevelt, Nicholas J. (1767–1854)

Nicholas Roosevelt established America's first engine-building plant at Belleville,

New Jersey, in 1794. Robert Livingston tried to get Roosevelt to finance his building of a steamboat in the late 1790s. After much negotiation, Roosevelt (a poor man then) could not refuse to buy into the steamboat scheme at a 12 percent share. But he lived to regret it, as Livingston interfered with the engineering provided by Roosevelt and John Stevens (Livingston's son-in-law) at every turn and used the cheapest materials available, hampering much of the effort's success. The final boat had a paddle wheel too heavy for the engine to turn, and the experiment failed.

After the invention of Fulton's steamboat, he and Roosevelt's old partner, Robert Livingston, set about to gain a monopoly on the Mississippi River, recognizing its possibilities as a steamboat route. They failed to achieve more than a monopoly at the mouth of the river in and around New Orleans. But the partners sent Roosevelt as their representative to survey the whole river system from Pittsburgh to the Gulf in 1809. Recently married, Roosevelt took his new wife and made a honeymoon trip of it. He built a special flatboat complete with bedroom, kitchen, sitting room, and a porch out back with an awning for nicer days. They floated through a wilderness full of pirates, snags, and numerous other perils, but they made the journey without incident.

Impressed with Roosevelt's report of trading potential, the Fulton concern ordered up the first Mississippi steamboat. The *New Orleans* was built at Pittsburgh and the redoubtable Mr. Roosevelt with his wife, Newfoundland dog, and a captain and crew of six, plus a cook, steward, and two maids (no one else would book passage) were off. Local women thought Roosevelt rather irresponsible in taking his wife, who by now was pregnant. A hardy woman, she gave birth as they passed through the rapids at Louisville, but that was the least of their problems. It was the year (1811) of the famous New Madrid earthquake, one of the most violent in American recorded history, and the river shook from Louisville southward. One night they moored to an island that disappeared by dawn. They pulled into the Mississippi, refusing to rescue the frightened multitudes in destroyed towns that begged rescue, for fear that the mob would literally swamp the boat. Outrunning the quakes, they put in at Natchez, where the captain married one of the maids before they continued on to New Orleans, completing the first downstream steamboat trip on the Mississippi.

But there was a great defect in the *New Orleans'* design—she was a deep-draft boat like the *North River of Clermont*, and so were her two sisters built at New Orleans. Hence, they never could go above Natchez, which left a lot of river to be covered by new men like Henry M. Shreve.

See also Fulton, Robert; Shreve, Henry Miller; Steamboats.

Route 66

Route 66 was the legendary number of the federal highway that ran from Chicago to Los Angeles through St. Louis and Springfield, Missouri; Tulsa and Oklahoma City, Oklahoma; Albuquerque, New Mexico; Flagstaff and Kingman, Arizona; and Needles and Barstow, California.

See also Will Rogers Highway.

Rumsey, James (1743–1792)

A Marylander, James Rumsey was educated as a blacksmith, learned mechanical engineering on his own, and worked as a miller. With pretensions at being a southern gentleman, he was too dreamy to be a good businessman, but it was a quality that made him a good inventor and solicitor of funds. But his affect was tempered by his seeming to be a con man. His first model was of two boats that had a pair of poles on their gunwales accentuated by a wheel and powered by water flow that "walked" the vessel upstream. He had a passion for secrecy and a disarming way of disguising his inventions in print. One of his earliest backers was George Washington. Virginia and Maryland gave him a ten-year monopoly on upstream water travel on the Potomac. He was the first engineer of the Potomac Company, which caused him to leave the actual boatbuilding to a brother-in-law, Joseph Barnes.

Later, Rumsey conceived the idea of a steam-propelled boat. The craft was moved by means of a steam pump, which forced a jet of water out the stern. Because the weight of a steam engine at the time was great and the plant bulky, he modified it to take a pipework that caused the load to lessen and the efficiency to increase. The innovation later became known as a tubular boiler. His initial run was in 1786 on the Potomac River. Soon thereafter, he submitted a letter of resignation in a quarrel with his assistant in the canal company, and to his shock, the board of directors accepted.

Rumsey now devoted full time to his boats. He confused the issue by shifting his attention between his pole boat, now mounted on one hull and steam powered, and the jet boat. He managed to get the pole boat to move several tons of cargo and spectators up the Potomac in 1786. In summer of the following year, he got the jet boat to move upstream past Shepardstown, to the amazement of local citizens. His steam engine in the jet boat, however, was not very sophisticated and cost him much power.

After his initial successes, Rumsey turned to confront John Fitch who was attempting to obtain support in Virginia and Maryland, territory Rumsey considered his own. Rumsey turned to print and sought to annihilate Fitch's competition. Then he moved his own operations to Philadelphia, the heart of Fitch's support. His suave, mannerly, compromising approach stood him well with the influential residents of the City of Brotherly Love, and his jet propulsion idea especially appealed to the elderly scientific genius of the century, Benjamin Franklin. The result was the Rumsean Society, formed at Philadelphia in 1788 and the rout of the heretofore more successful John Fitch. The argument as to who was the original mind and who was the usurper continues to the present day in a sort of North versus South format that does justice to the contribution of neither man.

Cognizant that an unchallenged Fitch would make a splash in Europe, the Rumsean Society loaded its man of the hour with money and letters of introduction from Franklin and sent Rumsey off to England. There he met with the Boulton and Watt Company, which offered him the rights to market their engine in the United States. This would have secured Rumsey's place in science and history permanently. But the American's irritating dickering for advantage alienated the British, and they terminated the arrangement before it got off the ground. The English steam men knew something that neither Rumsey nor Fitch realized—that the steamboat had to be precisely built and each part coordinated with the other to function properly. It was a gap represented by the head start that England had achieved in the Industrial Revolution. The English were sophisticated and scientific, while the Americans were still basically medieval craftsmen. But Rumsey did manage a British patent for his pole boat, his jet boat, and his pipe boiler.

With this, Rumsey set off to France to head off Fitch there, only to find that the French patents had been granted to their own citizens. But assured by the American diplomat, Thomas Jefferson, that this was merely a minor inconvenience, Rumsey returned to England, leaving his French future in Jefferson's hands. In England, Rumsey, who was broke, reluctantly entered into a partnership with Daniel Parker and Samuel Rogers. Unfortunately they were less solvent than he and were soon bankrupt. Rumsey hired out as a canal expert, calling on his Potomac Company experience, and invented a new milling process, which straightened out his finances. Within a year, his partners had also recovered financially and Rumsey was back at work on his jet boat. While at a meeting of the Society of Arts on hydrostatics, Rumsey suffered a fatal stroke. His partners were never to improve on the jet principle and the project fell victim to Fitch's better design as interpreted by Fulton a decade later.

See also Early Steamboats; Evans, Oliver; Fitch, John; Fulton, Robert; Shreve, Henry Miller; Steamboats; Symington, William.

References Flexner, James Thomas, *Steamboats Come True* (1944); Turner, Maria, *James Rumsey, Pioneer in Steam Navigation* (1930).

Russell, Majors & Waddell Company

If any one company typified pre–Civil War freighting on the Great Plains, it was Russell, Majors & Waddell. Organized by William H. Russell, Alexander Majors, and William B. Waddell in 1855, this company represented a monopoly on all freighting on the western frontier, mostly thriving on military supply contracts. The firm had its origin in the company begun by Russell and others to deliver supplies to the army as it advanced down the trail to Santa Fe in 1846. Five years later, Russell's expanding interests merged with Waddell. Both men were dry-goods clerks who had tired of working for others, but they were very much unlike each other otherwise. Russell was adventuresome, willing to try anything new to advance the business. Waddell was very deliberate and even sullen. Although the two men argued regularly, they had a sincere friendship and trusted each other. They made considerable money in 1853 freighting supplies to Fort Riley at $7 per 100 pounds and Fort Union at $16 per 100 pounds. They had to put only two or three trains on the road to do this.

But they lost the bid the following year, and sent a train to California to make up for it. In 1854, as the wagons rolled to California, the partners went to Westport and signed on Alexander Majors, a man who had competed with them in the military trade and had sent private goods to Santa Fe and various Indian reservations in Kansas and the Indian Nations (today's Oklahoma). A new accounting system was instituted whereby the company would charge a fixed sum per 100 miles per 100 pounds. Any goods sent after May of a given year cost more depending on how late they were contracted for service. The firm employed 1,700 men in various trades, both among the 300 to 350 wagons and the numerous way stations necessary to maintain their service on the Plains. Among them was 16-year-old William F. Cody, the later "Buffalo Bill," who hired on as a messenger. The firm cleared $150,000 in their first year of operations (1855), a feat repeated the following season.

In 1857, the army approached the firm and ordered 3 million pounds of supplies for the Utah expedition, a campaign against the Mormons. But the approach was made in mid-June, and the company's wagons were already on the road elsewhere. The army was quite insistent, however, and Russell, the company's business representative, agreed to haul the freight at $20 per hundredweight. In reality, the army eventually paid just over $14 per 100, a loss that Congress refused to take up (unfairly dismissing the company's expenses as near-fraudulent), in spite of the army's promise to pay in full. It was the first in a string of business decisions that eventually would bankrupt Russell, Majors & Waddell.

When the many wagons reached the proximity of Utah, Mormon militia captured several of the trains, allowing the teamsters to escape only with their personal belongings. Other wagon trains got caught in the winter storms, destroying goods and more ox teams. Estimated losses were $500,000. Worse yet, the 1858 contracts, separate from the Utah expedition, required more wagons and teams than ever before, requiring a heavy debt to purchase. And the ever-expanding Russell organized a subsidiary company that Russell, Majors & Waddell outfitted and that defaulted on its debt. Russell tried to resign from the army supply contract if the government would buy them out at a fair price set by a board of appraisers. Unfortunately, the government refused to buy them out or let the contract lapse.

The discovery of gold on Cherry Creek and the subsequent expansion of the rush and settlement of nearby Denver looked like real opportunity to Russell, worried as he and his partners were over their heads in debt. Merchandising and transportation of people and goods, not the shinny metal, were the issues for Russell, Majors & Waddell. Many gold seekers called on the firm for advice in traveling the Plains safely. To men who were accustomed to distances to Salt Lake City and Santa Fe, the trip to Denver looked pretty appealing. So Russell opined that many travelers might appreciate an organized conveyance for the journey.

The result was the Leavenworth & Pike's Peak Express Company, a stage line organized in 1859 by Russell and an independent group of investors led by John S. Jones. Evidently Russell had not consulted with Majors or Waddell, assuming that they would go along with his decision. Waddell was furious at the sideshow and refused to take part. Majors joined him. It made little difference, because the decision had already affected all three of the original partners. Many public persons of importance, bankers and investors, saw the venture as risky, to say the least. This further harmed the position of Russell, Majors & Waddell with the public.

To minimize future competition, the Pike's Peak company set out to find the shortest route to Denver. They went straight across the Plains past Fort Riley. Then they built a series of relay stations 25 miles apart to support the venture. Six men manned each station, providing changes of drivers and teams and food for the passengers. Drivers and crew contracted for 12 months. Half of their pay was withheld until the end of the contract, to be forfeit if they did not complete the term or behaved in a dishonorable manner. Total employees numbered 175, with salaries per month at $14,400. When other expenses were totaled, the venture cost $1,000 a day to run. One thousand mules and 50 new Concord stages completed the operating capital. All freight would be supplied by Russell, Majors & Waddell, year-round. Ominously, all of it was paid for on credit. The trip was a seat-numbing 20 days, day and night, with passengers sleeping on the coach, if they could sleep at all.

But Russell did not stop there. He and Jones immediately bought out another company and its contract to deliver U.S. mails from the Missouri River to Salt Lake City. This was another $144,000 expense (for wagons, coaches, stations, and animals), and the government had just reduced the carrying fee from $190,000 to $132,000 per year. To consolidate the Pike's Peak operations with the mail run and hopefully save on operating expenses, the stage route to Denver was shifted northward to the mail route along the Oregon Trail, with a branch going to Denver down Lodgepole Creek. Passengers paid $125 one-way, with meals costing extra. And the food was not that great either. It tended to go down in quality the farther west one traveled, although the 50 cents a meal at the start increased to a $1.50 further west. Mail was carried at 25 cents a letter. Small mail-order packages also made the trip and paid the company quite well until Russell interfered and put a 5 percent commission on them and increased general freight rates to 75 cents a pound. Although the company's prices were eminently fair, its monopolistic attitudes (pay up or be damned) were not popular.

Russell continued to try and recoup the fortunes of the parent company, Russell, Majors & Waddell. In 1859, the company negotiated a contract to supply flour to the army of occupation near Salt Lake City. Returning from Washington, Russell met an old friend in New York City, Ben Holladay. The army had not wanted to rely on the Mormons for provisions in their own military occupation, but Holladay believed that the Saints would be forthcoming at a price below that in St. Louis. The army agreed that Russell, Majors & Waddell could supply the flour from any source if the firm would guarantee delivery of the amount agreed to. In effect, by buying flour in Utah from Mormon suppliers at 7 cents a pound instead of in St. Louis at $22.50 (including freight charges), the company would make a bundle and save the wear and tear on wagons and animals crossing the Plains. The profit was about $170,000. All of this was all right until newspaper editor ("Go west, young man") Horace Greeley got hold of it. Angered that Brigham Young and the church had made a bundle building Camp Floyd barracks for the occupation, Greeley put the freighting firm in league with the Saints—all of whom were fleecing the taxpayer. The venture ultimately did Russell, Majors & Waddell little good in public relations.

Meanwhile, Majors and Waddell had changed their minds about the Colorado gold rush. Along with Russell, the three agreed to send Robert B. Bradford, a relative of Waddell's, to Denver to open a store. Bradford would get one-third of the profits, and all goods would be freighted by the company at 10 percent over cost. Bradford's reports from Denver were too rosy as far as the store was concerned. He did, however, believe that the stage company would go broke eventually. He also engaged in speculations of his own, which caused Russell and Waddell to charge him with neglect of the business. Bradford told his relative that if he did not like his operations in Denver to send someone else. The firm backed down. But by 1860, business conditions in the Rockies proved to have ebbed—the gold rush was over. Bradford sold out his interest in the store to Majors, acting on behalf of the company.

But Bradford proved to be correct in his estimate of the stage company. In fact it was in so much debt ($500,000) that Majors and Waddell feared that it might take the whole firm down with it. The company had lost the military freight contracts over the Oregon Trail and now merely had their Santa Fe forts. But there was another possibility. In 1856, Congress had authorized a transcontinental mail subsidy. Most agreed that, all things being equal, the shortest route, the Central Overland Route, was the best and shortest way to California. But they reckoned without Postmaster Aaron V. Brown. A Tennessean, Brown wanted this impetus for communication and the settlement that was bound to go with it to come through the South. So he had let the first contract to the Butterfield Overland Stage Company, which carried the mails from Memphis (Brown's hometown) and St. Louis to California by the southern trails, the so-called Ox Bow Route from the circle it made through America's heartland.

The main sticking point against the Central Route was winter weather. This the southern route lacked to a large degree, promising year-round travel and punctuality. The Mormons had set up their own private route for mail to the East, but gold demanded that the mail be delivered in a more determined manner designed to service all the public. Both Gentiles and Mormons bid on the mail service, and different companies handled it each year. The mail from Salt Lake City to Sacramento was handled by a company under George Chorpenning. Both ends of the route had Indian problems going into Salt Lake City. At this point, Russell stepped into the mail subsidy picture with something named the Pony Express. Whether the idea was original or Russell stole it has been a matter of debate ever since. The idea occurred to several people, some of them Russell, Majors & Waddell employees. It lay dormant in Russell's mind for about a year when suddenly he acted upon it.

But from the beginning, Russell knew that the idea was not going to make money—far from it. It would be a big expense. But there were bigger fish to fry. The real goal was to prove that the Central Overland Route could be traveled reliably all year-round. That would open up all sorts of investment possibilities, not the least of which was a transcontinental railroad. It was nothing but a big public relations stunt with broad implications. Russell chartered the whole operation as the Central Overland California & Pike's Peak Express Company. It was chartered to run stagecoaches on a weekly basis from St. Joseph, Missouri, to Sacramento, California, in return for a land grant at St. Joseph that was to be a rail terminal. Russell was thinking way far ahead of everyone else. He expected to run a mail and express service one day by rail to California. He had just bought its starting point. Again, the stations would have to be set up and equipped. Employees had to be hired and stages and animals bought. There were "home" stations, where crews and teams were changed, and "swing" stations, where just the teams were changed.

The Pony Express was merely the flashy part of the experiment of the transcontinental mails. Allegedly, Russell, Majors & Waddell spent $75,000 to equip it alone. They bought 400 to 500 fast horses, *mochilas* (a cover of saddlebags with four locked pockets in each corner) for the mail, and contracted with riders unafraid to travel alone. All of the equipment for the horses was specially designed. The whole rig weighed 13 pounds without mail. All that was necessary at each horse change was for the rider to grab the *mochila* and mount the awaiting horse. Speed was of the essence. It was a fast relay race against the clock and the *mochila* was the baton passed along the line. The first run took an hour under ten days. George Chorpenning saw the future and sold out the Central Overland California & Pike's Peak Express within days. The nation, used to the mail taking weeks, even months, to get to the West Coast, was ecstatic. The 75 to 80 pony riders became legends in their own time: Bill Cody, Pony Bob Haslam, and Boston Kelly were just some of the gutsy, lightweight, adventuresome, and well-paid ($100 a month and "found" [i.e., fed]) pony expressmen. But the Central Overland marked the final chapter in the saga of Russell, Majors & Waddell.

Part of the problem lay between Russell and the man selected to manage the Pony Express, Benjamin Franklin Ficklin. The latter considered the original "pony" idea to be his, grabbed without credit by Russell. Ficklin also wanted to increase service to twice a week. Russell knew the company could not afford it. Each considered the other to be an ignorant meddler. In the end, Ficklin had to go. And after refusing Ficklin's twice-a-week service idea, Russell had the nerve to propose a three-times-a-week mail contract with the government for $900,000 a year. The Post Office ignored it and gave the coach contract from the Missouri River to Denver to a rival line. Competition had entered the scene at last. Russell and the board of directors dropped their rates one-fourth and doubled their speed. The public loved it. But the costs-to-income ratio could not meet their debt payments, and the emphasis on the Central Overland had caused the company to fail to meet the demands of the army's New Mexico freighting contract. By 31 December 1861, the firm of Russell, Majors & Waddell was bankrupt. The holder of the assets was Ben Holladay, who would go on to be the Stagecoach King of the West, using the discontinued Butterfield equipment and contracts as his starting point. But he utilized the Central Overland Route that Russell, Majors & Waddell had proved to be viable after Texas secessionists cut off the Ox Bow Route from service. The completion of the transcontinental telegraph caused the Pony Express to end in October 1861, relieving Holladay of a great burden.

Then it was discovered that the government bonds that secured the private investors' moneys had been stolen by an Interior Department employee. Russell, Secretary of War John B. Floyd, and the thief were indicted on charges of defrauding the government. Eventually, Russell and Floyd were dropped from the indictment after Russell paid off the government for the bonds. The real thief was never prosecuted. But Russell, Majors & Waddell, with some help from Southern secessionists, proved the Central Overland Route, the most direct way to California from the center of the nation, to be a practicable, all-weather route, placing them in the forefront of cross-country American transportation history before the Civil War. By their efforts, the route was the one finally selected for the transcontinental railroad.

See also Central Overland California & Pike's Peak Express Company; Central Overland Route; Freighting and Teamsters; Leavenworth & Pike's Peak Express Company; Majors, Alexander; Pony Express; Russell, William Hepburn; Waddell, William Bradford.

References Drago, Harry S., *Roads to Empire* (1968); Dunlop, Richard, *Wheels West* (1977); Eggenhoffer, Nick, *Wagons, Mules and Men* (1961); Root, George A., and Russell K. Hickman, "Pike's Peak Express Companies," *Kansas Historical Quarterly* (1944) 13: 163–195, 211–242, 485–526, and *Kansas Historical Quarterly* (1945) 14: 36–92; Settle, Raymond W., and Mary L. Settle, *Empire on Wheels* (1949); Settle, Raymond W., and Mary L. Settle, *Saddles and Spurs* (1955); Settle, Raymond W., and Mary L. Settle, *War Drums and Wagon Wheels* (1966); Walker, Henry Pickering, *The Wagonmasters* (1966).

Russell, William Hepburn (1812–1872)

Born in Vermont, W. H. Russell moved to Liberty, Missouri, with his mother and stepfather, where he went to work as a store clerk at age 16. Aristocratic by nature, he made his whole life's work off the Great Plains—an environment that he visited but once late in his life. He never worked with his hands, abhorred hunting and fishing, and never cursed (his wife, Harriet, was a strict Baptist). He served as county treasurer for one term and spent the rest of his life in retailing. He entered the Santa Fe trade in the late 1840s and moved into freighting military supplies to the numerous forts set up after the American victory in the Mexican War. He also organized an insurance company and helped sponsor Lexington Baptist Female College. In 1855, he and William B. Waddell formed a freighting partnership that in 1858 became Russell, Majors & Waddell, the most famous pre–Civil War freight outfit on the Great Plains.

Russell was a vivacious, daring businessman and gave the company its daring from the start. He was full of nervous energy. He often acted in schemes on behalf of his partners without informing them of their implications, or merely giving a bare outline of the facts. As such, he was often at odds with his partners, whom he often brought into deals kicking and screaming. This unfortunate risk taking produced some of the most spectacular business opportunities and failures of their day. Upon an appeal to his patriotism, Russell pledged the company to the military campaign against the Mormons in Utah, which nearly broke them after the army failed to keep its promises of monetary support for all costs. From freighting, Russell took the firm into stagecoaching and mail subsidies, mercantile investments in Denver, transcontinental stagecoaching, and the famed Pony Express, by which he hoped to prove the viability of the Central Overland Route as an all-weather passage west. All of these ventures drained assets from the parent company. By the time of the Civil War, investors had called in their notes, and Russell was under indictment for receiving stolen government bonds, a charge later correctly dropped.

Russell never got out from under the pall cast by his later business deals. He sold his few assets to Ben Holladay, a friend who had invested heavily with him. Russell's debts ran into six figures, a fantastic sum for its day. Despite his monetary problems, Russell remains a motivating force and one of the first private businessmen who saw the potential that transportation across the Great Plains promised for the future of the United States. He had already invested in railroads before the Civil War and was a visionary who promoted travel and business through the use of the Central Overland Route, pioneering several shortcuts. In the end, he was reduced to selling patent medicine. He died at the home of his son in New York State in 1872, worn down by the adversity that haunted him from his old business failures.

See also Central Overland Route; Pony Express; Russell, Majors & Waddell Company.

References Settle, Raymond W., and Mary L. Settle, *Empire on Wheels* (1949); Settle, Raymond W., and Mary L. Settle, *War Drums and Wagon Wheels* (1966).

Safety Appliance Act (1893)

In the nineteenth century there were few industries more dangerous to work in than the railroads. The movement of the cars and engines, the difficulty of braking each car from a wheel located on the roof, the lack of handholds, the skill it took to guide a link into its receiver and slip a pin in to couple-up (which left a lot of brakemen named "Fingers" or "Lefty"), and the chance that the most careful worker might be caught by an engine that suddenly jerked all contributed to the thousands of killings and maimings for which railroading was noted.

Led by the lobbying of unions (formed to promote safety) and Lorenzo Coffin, Congress passed the Safety Appliance Act in 1893. This measure required railroads that had not already done so to install the Westinghouse air brake on freight cars, to replace the link and pin coupler with the Janney automatic knuckle coupler, and to install riveted-on handholds on the cars for the brakemen to operate around them more safely. It took the railroads ten years to comply with the measure. They found in the end that it was too much of a problem to retrofit their wooden freight cars. It was cheaper to build new ones and junk the old models.

But the real push for reform came in the early twentieth century when employees obtained the right to sue their employers for workers' accidents caused by faulty equipment. Led by Governor Robert "Fightin' Bob" La Follette of Wisconsin, states began to write workers' compensation laws that assisted those hurt in accidents. These laws had to modify the common law concerning an employer's responsibility to provide a safe workplace and properly maintained machinery and equipment, to instruct employees on how to use these items correctly, and to establish and enforce rules of safe conduct. The employees, for their part, were expected to follow such rules lest the employer be allowed a defense as to liability from the employee's negligence, from another employee's negligence (the "fellow servant" rule), or from normal risks inherent to the job. As early as 1855, Georgia had passed a law to make employers liable for on-the-job injuries. It was followed by Iowa, Kansas, Wisconsin, and Wyoming by 1880.

By 1910, almost every state had some form of employer's liability law, mostly but not exclusively directed against railroads or mines. The first federal law was passed in 1906, but only affected federal possessions and territories like Washington, D.C. But each law required the employee or his estate to sue to collect. The real benefit to workers came with the notion of workers' compensation laws, beginning in New York in 1910. Within ten years, all but eight states had such a law. The last state to pass such a law was Mississippi in 1949, making their effect nationwide. These laws applied to almost every working group except domestic and agricultural workers.

At the same time that employees were winning the right to sue and to compensation from a state-organized fund, the safety process was augmented by law. In March 1907 railroad workers were limited to 16-hour shifts. Two years later, ashpan boys were prohibited from going under the firebox to empty out the pans, a process that often resulted in serious burns. By 1910, railroads were required to use electric headlights. In addition, all accidents above a certain sum had to be reported to the federal government. A year later, compulsory boiler inspections and standards retired hundreds of substandard engines to the junk heap. That same year saw the requirement of automatic fire doors for all engines to keep the engine crew from getting blistered or burned by flashbacks and the heat of the open firebox.

There was a hiatus until the Great Depression, when more safety laws appeared. The Cab Curtain Act required that a curtain be placed at the rear of the cab to protect the crew from cold or inclement weather. This was deemed so necessary that the crews had been installing these for years out of their own pocket money. In 1938, the Interstate Commerce Commission took the lead from

Congress and mandated the use of mechanical stokers and automatic, mechanical bell ringers. Both issues revolved around the liability of the company for accidents if either of these devices were missing from a locomotive. Although steam locomotives were relatively noisy, the new diesels were not. Thus the practice since the advent of diesels has been to install an extra headlight, called a Mars light, that is always on and throws light ahead of the engine in an oscillating, figure-eight pattern to call attention to the approach of a train.

See also Coffin, Lorenzo S.; Janney, Eli Hamilton; Railroads from Appomattox to Deregulation; Train Control; Westinghouse, George.

References Armstrong, John H., *The Railroad—What It Is, What It Does* (1978); Auerbach, Carl A., et al., *The Legal Process* (1961); Hubbard, Freeman, *Encyclopedia of North American Railroading* (1981); Shaw, Robert B., *A History of Railroad Accidents, Safety Precautions, and Operating Practices* (1978).

Sage, Russell (1816–1906)

Born in a year that never saw summer—local chroniclers called it "Eighteen Hundred and Starve to Death"—Russell Sage never seemed to thaw out. He was chilly, a habitual liar, a perjurer, and a betrayer of associates. He was a convicted usurer who was spared a jail term only because his lawyer, Samuel J. Tilden, found a crooked judge to buy. Indeed, historian Peter Lyon finds it noteworthy that the area of Sage's birth in upstate New York and the decade preceding and following its date produced a large number of so-called Robber Barons—men who had a penchant for looting the public and the nation. These include Philip Armour, Marshall and Cyrus Field, Charles Crocker, Collis P. Huntington, Sidney Dillon, Jay Gould, George Pullman, Leland Stanford, and William C. Whitney. John D. Rockefeller and Mark Hopkins were born just north of this spot, Isaac Singer too soon, and George Westinghouse a little too late. Tongue-in-cheek, Lyon postulates it might be soil, climate, or a general lapse in moral training that produced these men, all of a time and place that emerges notorious in the annals of American transportation.

But Sage need take a back seat to none. He fattened off the misfortune of others. He corrupted at least two state legislatures. He was miserly, devious, and cheated on his second wife, the daughter of a man he had defrauded—which may say a lot about her, too. Need one mention that he was also a congressman? In short, Sage was a great partner for Jay Gould. No one knows why they worked together, Sage in the background, Gould in the public eye. Sage's biographer posits that he held notes signed by Gould that made him a safe bet. Peter Lyon figures that Sage had 20 years more experience in "chicane," and began to use Gould as he looted one railroad after another. Gould of course got the blame, then and now—not that he was an angel himself. Sage loved to buy up small feeder railroads and then sell them to the larger mainline in which he had an interest, looting the stockholders along the way, while he ran with the real cash. He probably had some interest in the famed Crédit Mobilier scandal, but kept his mouth shut, something he had a talent for.

When Sage had begun his career as a clerk in his brother's grocery, he met and married Margaret Slocum, a local schoolteacher. She took an active interest in his business affairs and ran the whole operation in the last five years of his life, making several astute business deals that must have thrilled her husband. After Sage's death, Margaret became a philanthropist and returned nearly half of the Sage $70 million fortune to public charities before her own death in 1918.

See also Forbes, John Murray; Gould, Jay; Huntington, Collis Potter.; Pacific Railroad of 1862; Scott, Thomas A.; Vanderbilt, William H.

References Lyon, Peter, *To Hell in a Day Coach* (1968); Sarnoff, Paul, *Russell Sage* (1965).

St. Lawrence Seaway

The St. Lawrence River, which runs from the easternmost Great Lake, Ontario, to the sea, has been an important waterway since the beginning of history. Used by Native

Americans and explored by early French seamen looking for the fabled Northwest Passage, the river opened up central Canada, the Great Lakes, and the midwestern United States mainly through the fur traders and their massive cargo canoes. The canoes were lightweight enough to be muscled around the land bridges between rapids and falls, known as "portages," that connect the five Great Lakes, but that very act limited the amounts of goods that could be transported. A product of the ice ages, the whole system includes not only the lakes and the St. Lawrence, but also the St. Mary's River between Lakes Superior and Huron, the Detroit River between Lakes Huron and Erie, and the Niagara River and its famous falls between Lakes Erie and Ontario. The whole waterway is about 2,000 miles long. The main problem is that the level of Lake Superior is 600 feet above that of the Atlantic. Combined with cliffs that constantly narrow the river courses, the result is the appearance of rapids along the way at strategic spots.

The St. Lawrence waterway had long been fought over. Algonquin and Iroquois Indians battled for key positions to control its trade. Later the Dutch, British, and French launched lengthy and repeated campaigns through its valleys as Europe struggled for colonial power. With the freedom of the United States from Britain, and the last of the Anglo-American armed conflicts in 1814, the parts of the lakes and rivers that marked the international border were declared henceforth neutral and unfortified in the Rush-Bagot Treaty of 1819. This demilitarization of the waterway permitted visionary men to contemplate the dream of centuries—the movement of oceangoing ships from the mouth of the St. Lawrence to the western tip of Lake Superior at Duluth.

The first to think of canalling the rough stretches of the St. Lawrence was Jacques Cartier in 1536. But his was an expedition of exploration. Permanent French settlement revived the notion in the mind of the priest Dollier de Casson in the late 1600s. But technology and friendly relations with the Native Americans were lacking, and by the time of his death in 1701 little had been done at the cost of 20,000 livres. In 1779, during the heat of the American Revolution, Colonel Frederick Haldimand, British governor of Québec, constructed the first lock canal in North America at Coteau du Lac. Like their counterparts in New York, with the arrival of the steamboat businessmen along the St. Lawrence saw the lakes and rivers as potentially profitable paths for the riches of the untapped West.

Shortly after the Rush-Bagot agreement, W. Hamilton Merritt organized and built the Welland Canal on the Canadian side of Niagara Falls. Poorly built in haste, the Welland profited by the example of the Erie Canal, and in 1841, after a decade of falling trade at Montréal (it was all going to New York City at one-tenth the cost to anywhere else, and Canadian exports were duty free to boot) and growing division between Upper and Lower Canada, the British government assumed control of the Welland. By 1846, the government had rebuilt the Welland and three other works farther downstream on the St. Lawrence, and traffic could move to the sea by 1848. The whole thing cost around $15 million, pretty cheap for the time. It also did much economically to unite the two Canadas at a critical time in their history.

As in the United States, the Canadian canals suffered from rail competition, primarily the Grand Trunk Railroad from Chicago to Portland, Maine, through Toronto and Montréal, but the St. Lawrence waterway had one advantage over American canals and the railroads—it actually flowed to the sea. With some planning and modernization, the whole length of the river could be made to handle oceangoing traffic straight into the lakes without the costly and time-consuming necessity of unloading and transferring cargoes. With this in mind, Canada, following the American success with the Sault Ste. Marie Canal (which carried one-third of all U.S. tonnage shipped by water by 1900), improved her canals, especially the Welland, once again. By 1937, the way was open to rethink the whole waterway, this time internationally.

But World War II loomed on the horizon and things were delayed.

One might argue that the war actually helped the St. Lawrence Seaway in the long run. The conflict against the Axis powers led to much enforced cooperation by the Allies, and Canada and the United States learned to work together on very big projects as never before. And in some ways, the idea of the seaway was too big to contemplate adequately before the defeat of the Axis powers in 1945. The preliminaries of the seaway began as an agreement between the United States and Canada over the development of shared hydroelectric power facilities needed by New York State and Ontario Province. Acting on a joint Canadian-American report first done in the 1920s, both nations saw that if the hydroelectric dams were placed in such a fashion as to put man-made lakes over certain rapids, the whole project could pay for itself over time. In 1932, a Great Lakes Waterway Treaty had missed ratification by a mere six votes in a short-sighted U.S. Senate dominated by rail, Appalachian coal, New York Barge Canal, and East Coast shipping interests, and distracted by the Great Depression. A second attempt to pass the treaty in 1943 had the same result.

By 1950, New York and Ontario had agreed to build two dams near Cornwall, Ontario—the Long Sault and Iroquois— and share the white power generated. But a new factor entered the picture. Buoyed by the discovery of new mineral wealth in the territories, Canada had wealth never before available to complete the project without American assistance. After new talks proved unable to bypass continued opposition in the U.S. Congress, Canada made the historic decision to go it alone. This put a new look on American opposition—whether the Unites States could afford to be cut out of the picture of a done project. After all, Canada could always elect to go up the Ottawa River to Georgian Bay and cut out the Americans all together, as the old fur trappers had done.

The election of Dwight D. Eisenhower as president in 1952 ended U.S delays. As former Allied supreme commander in World War II, and a Republican, Eisenhower could undercut powerful men in his party who feared that the seaway would compromise American sovereignty, especially on Lake Michigan. After a last stand in the courts, American opponents crumbled and, with the passage of the Wiley-Dondero Act in 1954, the Americans jumped aboard the seaway project, much to the disappointment of some Canadians who resented the johnny-come-lately attitude of those south of the border.

The two nations organized the St. Lawrence Seaway Development Corporation and got to work that same year. Argument developed over the location of the seaway in international sections of the St. Lawrence on the Canadian or American side. Once, as a joke, President Eisenhower suggested that Canada consider becoming the next state (Hawaii and Alaska still being territories). Canadians retorted that the United States might make a better eleventh province. But quick action by Canada to begin work on its side of the border and American hesitation solved the problem in Canada's behalf. Engineering problems encountered in completing the project were massive. The Jacques Cartier bridge was literally jacked up in the air to clear ocean vessels more easily. Major traffic routes had bridges duplicated on both ends of the locks to allow uninterrupted traffic by land or sea at all times. Coffer dams diverted the river out of building areas. The famous Thousand Islands scenic area at the head of the river was dredged without affecting its traditional beauty. Other areas, especially rapids, wound up at the bottom of the new lakes created by dams. One hundred square miles of valuable farm land disappeared under the water, displacing about 10,000 people. Many homes were moved by gargantuan, sensitive machines that allowed dishes to remain in cupboards and furniture on the floor. Churches, cemeteries, roads, sewerage systems, schools, factories, farms, and businesses were placed anew. Exchange negotiations with the Iroquois Nation solved the problem of inundation of their Canadian lands guaranteed by treaty, and the courts took care of the rest.

Then the dams, power stations, locks, and canals were built. One section was built through solid Potsdam sandstone at a cost of $50 million for a single mile. Americans and Canadians built the joint Moses-Saunders power dam using different construction techniques, equipment, languages, and problem solving, but when the structure met in the center of the river, everything came together perfectly. The St. Lawrence Seaway was officially opened by President Eisenhower and Queen Elizabeth II on 16 June 1959. The project allowed 80 percent of existing oceangoing ships (27-foot draft or less) to negotiate the route to Duluth. Tolls from the ocean to the beginning of the Lake Ontario section are divided, with 71 percent going to Canada and the rest to the United States.

But major problems remained. Most of the lake ports had to be dredged to accept vessels of such deep draft, and today 50 ports in both countries use the system. Unforeseen invasions of sea life from the oceans have ravaged local species and clogged traditionally free-running sewage and drainage lines. And shipping has increased over the years, forcing more improvement in the 27-mile Welland Canal, the biggest bottleneck in the system, by 1974. In 1829 it had taken 40 locks to lift ships from Lake Ontario to Lake Erie. In 1873, these were reduced to 25, and in 1913 to the current 7 lift locks and 1 guard lock to maintain water level. Still, the U.S. Army Corps of Engineers has recommended that an entirely new canal augment the Welland, located on the American side. Others would prefer to increase the size of the present locks to equal those of the Sault Ste. Marie.

The seaway remains the most modern and recent of the great canal projects in the New World—important enough to have actually created a fourth coastline for the United States. Over 37 percent of the U.S. population and over 80 percent of Canada's live in the states surrounding the Great Lakes. Fuel rates, so important in the years after the Arab oil embargo, as determined

by the U.S. government studies in the mid-1970s were: airplanes, 37 ton-miles per gallon of fuel used; trucks, 38 ton-miles per gallon; railroads, 200 ton-miles per gallon; waterways, 250 ton-miles per gallon; and pipelines, 300 ton-miles per gallon, making the seaway highly competitive. As to its cost of construction of $650 million for the seaway and as much more again for the hydroelectric project (financed by the two national governments but to be paid back by tolls to the seaway management companies by the twenty-first century), few could argue with the comment of one early advocate: "To hell with economics; it's a magnificent conception, and it has got to be built!"

See also Canals; Great Lakes Freighters; Panama Canal.

References Brown, Andrew H., "New St. Lawrence Seaway Opens Great Lakes to the World," *National Geographic* (November 1959) 116: 299–339; Chevrier, Lionel, *The St. Lawrence Seaway* (1960); Hills, T. H., *The St. Lawrence Seaway* (1959); Jackson, John N., *Welland and the Welland Canal* (1975); Les Strang, Jacques, *Seaway* (1976); Macbee, Carleton, *The Seaway Story* (1961); Tallamy, B. D., and T. M. Sedwick, *The St. Lawrence Seaway Project* (1940); Willoughby, William R., *St. Lawrence Waterway* (1961).

St. Louis & Southwestern Railroad (SL&SW)

Known as the Cotton Belt, the St. Louis & Southwestern Railroad began in northeastern Texas in 1877, and through a series of mergers reached St. Louis, Dallas, and Memphis. The SL&SW also had a shared trackage arrangement into Chicago via the Chicago & Eastern Illinois, which led to its acquisition by the Southern Pacific Lines.

See also Southern Pacific Lines.

St. Louis–San Francisco Railway

Known as the "Frisco," the St. Louis–San Francisco Railroad was chartered by the Missouri legislature after the Mexican War. It began to lay rail in 1851, and headed for Springfield, Missouri, and the Pacific Ocean. It made it to Springfield in 1870, but the Pacific remained an elusive goal for the life of the line. At Springfield the Frisco merged with the Atlantic and Pacific, a road that had the rights to the thirty-fifth parallel route. Its western half would be bought by the Santa Fe Railway, and the eastern half would be the basis of the Frisco's midwestern empire. Eventually, the Frisco would be a gigantic X-shaped system, running from St. Louis to Fort Worth in the west and from Kansas City to Pensacola in the east. Like many railroads in that region, the Frisco can be considered a Granger railroad, one that supplied farmers with finished goods and supplies and in return shipped produce to market. The result was many short feeder routes that tapped the mainlines. In the twentieth century, George H. Nettleton bought the Frisco and hoped to make it the largest railroad in the nation. He not only laid more track and bought short lines, he made working agreements with all neighboring railways, especially the Chicago, Rock Island & Pacific, to allow it more flexibility in destinations. Unfortunately, this empire was overextended and disintegrated in receivership. It took until 1947 before the Frisco could regain its solvency. It then had three decades of profitable operations before the Burlington Northern system took it over in 1980.

See also Burlington Northern, Incorporated; Missouri-Kansas-Texas Railroad; Rock Island Lines; Stillwell, Arthur Edward.

References Bain, William E., *Frisco Folks* (1961); Drury, George H., *The Historical Guide to North American Railroads* (1985); Drury, George H., *The Train-Watcher's Guide* (1990); Hubbard, Freeman, *Encyclopedia of North American Railroading* (1981); Miner, H. Craig, *The St. Louis–San Francisco Continental Railroad* (1973); Pomphrey, Martin M., "St. Louis–San Francisco Railway Company," in Keith L. Bryant, Jr. (ed.), *EABHB: Railroads in the Age of Regulation* (1988), 381–384; Stragner, Lloyd, *Steam Locomotives of the Frisco Lines* (1976).

St. Mary's Falls Canal
See Canals.

Santa Fe Railway (AT&SF)
The Atchison, Topeka & Santa Fe Railway, conceived by Cyrus K. Holliday in the 1860s, more or less runs the route of the old Santa Fe Trail's mountain division west

through Kansas and Colorado to the Front Range of the Rocky Mountains, and south across Ratón Pass to Santa Fe. The line has been lengthened through purchase and rebuilding to cover the added distance between the original tracks and Chicago and Los Angeles. Additional lines take the Santa Fe up the California coast between San Diego and Oakland and provide a shortcut on the mainline that avoids the steep Ratón Pass area in southern Colorado.

The railroad's main inspiration, Holliday, was from Carbondale, Pennsylvania. He began working with rail builders in that state and soon traveled to Kansas Territory in the days of the middle 1850s when it was called "Bloody Kansas," involved as it was in a sort of North-South battle prelude to the coming Civil War. But Holliday was not interested in ideology; his was a desire to expand rail transportation over the Great Plains. Under the land-grant rail legislation of the Republican Party passed during the war, new lines westward could receive alternate sections of land along the right-of-way. Holliday became involved with the Atchison, Topeka & Santa Fe in 1863, and by 1868 the corporation had finally raised enough capital to begin building toward its New Mexico goal. The first project was a bridge across the Kansas River to connect the Santa Fe with the old Kansas Pacific, which was used to ferry supplies out along the Santa Fe's proposed right-of-way. But the capitalization was not enough for the job, and Boston financiers backing the road insisted that someone be hired who could properly supervise the construction to the Colorado–Kansas border. Unless the Santa Fe reached this intermediate stage by March 1873, its land grants were forfeit. The man who accomplished the job was Albert A. Robinson, a career civil engineer who built a world's record of 5,000 miles of track during his lifetime. Robinson was assisted in his task by the cattle drives coming up from Texas, which provided income for the fledgling line.

Like all Plains railroads, the Santa Fe's mainline was made of unballasted ties laid with lightweight rail. Initial cost was kept to a minimum as the company could just manage to pay the workers $2 a day, much less buy the necessary equipment. Occasional skirmishes with Indians and employee theft also caused problems. But Robinson managed to make 3 miles a day and the Colorado line was reached two months ahead of schedule. The Panic of 1873 put the company in the red again, however, and construction came to a standstill, except for a survey excursion to present-day Pueblo, Colorado. Still, the Santa Fe would endure as its southern position in the trek across Kansas had undercut its competition with the Texas trail herds. The mass killing of the southern Plains buffalo also provided a lucrative trade in hides and bone fertilizer. In 1878, Fred Harvey began to popularize Santa Fe passenger accommodations with his famous restaurant stops and pretty, efficient waitresses, known as Harvey Girls.

As the track laying began again, the Santa Fe came into conflict with the Denver & Rio Grande (D&RG), which was coming south along the Front Range toward Ratón Pass right where the Santa Fe hoped to cross into New Mexico. Armed clashes finally gave way to litigation, and the D&RG received the right to the Royal Gorge through the Rockies westward and the Santa Fe to the passage south. Each was to stay clear of the other's territory; both were to share rights to Denver, which nowadays means sharing track along the Front Range to keep costs down. As the Santa Fe moved up the pass, it financed its project by land sales back in Kansas, where the population tripled during the decade of the 1870s. The Santa Fe brought immigrants directly from Europe, assisted by advertising there and in the eastern U.S., and aided them in adapting to the idea of dry-farming, drought, and vicious hail storms. When nature proved too tough to master, the railroad formed relief societies to keep the farmers able to plant another year—and shipping and buying goods brought by rail.

Crossing Ratón Pass proved to be a real challenge for the Santa Fe. The railroad either had to delay all traffic until the tunnels brought the grades down to where the trains could negotiate them, or a temporary track had to be laid to continue freight and passengers into New Mexico, where track had already been laid on the flatlands. The Santa Fe chose to continue business over a temporary line. The problem was that to achieve grades that could be climbed, railroads usually employed various curves between canyon sides, gradually rising in height. But there was no room for curves in the narrow confines of Ratón Pass. So the Santa Fe used a set of switchbacks. The trains would go up to the end of the tracks on one side of the pass and throw a switch behind the train. This allowed the consist to back up the next set of rising tracks across the canyon to the other side, and so on all the way to the 2,000-foot summit. This Ratón Mountain Switchback barely allowed trains to go on to Santa Fe. Later, tunnels reduced the grade from 6 percent (rising 6 feet vertically for every 100 horizontal feet) to a more manageable 2 or 3 percent by 1879. The Santa Fe also employed helper engines to pull a consist up the hills and developed special heavy steam engines to make the effort easier.

The Santa Fe never really reached the city of its destination with its mainline. It had to build a special 18-mile branch to do it. The main remained below at Lamy, ready to continue on in short order to California. Another branch ran south along the Rio Grande River to hook up with the Southern Pacific at Deming, permitting the Santa Fe to run trains to California by 1881 with rented trackage rights. The Santa Fe also bought into Mexican railroads and offered service to Guaymas on the Gulf of California. Eventually this line was traded to the Southern Pacific for the Needles–Mojave Desert crossing. Meanwhile, the construction department was crossing the northern fringes of New Mexico high desert and Arizona pine forests. At Diablo (Devil) Canyon, Robinson and his men built a spindly bridge that ran track 250 feet above the creek, which became a noted landmark for train buffs in later years. Using favorable court orders, the Santa Fe reached San Bernardino by the 1880s. It then bought the nascent California Western to get trackage rights into Los Angeles and San Diego by 1887.

Having reached the West Coast on its own tracks at last, the Santa Fe turned to the central part of the country again. Branches took the road to the Gulf of Mexico through Oklahoma (then Indian Territory) and Texas. These allowed the railroad to bypass the Ratón Pass branch with a line across the high plains to Belen, just south of Albuquerque. The further purchase of small lines took the mainline east to the biggest prize of all, Chicago. Returning to the West Coast, the Santa Fe moved up the San Joaquin Valley to Oakland, sharing the famous Teháchapi Loop (where the mainline crosses over itself, making a spectacular vista of the trains passing over their own cabooses in rising to the crest of the pass). But the railroad was overextended and got caught in the Panic of 1893. Thrown into receivership, the company was reorganized under the same men but with a new name. Instead of "railroad," the new entity was the Atchison, Topeka & Santa Fe Railway. New branches in Arizona to Phoenix and the Grand Canyon brought in more revenue. The Grand Canyon side trip was made part of a coast-to-coast tour deal with the Pennsylvania Railroad that saw occasional cars from each on the other's consists, although most passengers changed at Chicago.

The Santa Fe faced the same problem of all southwestern railroads—a lack of nearby coal deposits. The Santa Fe solved it in the usual manner by bringing in oil burners and using its own tank cars to replenish engine stops. The line east of Kansas tended to use coal burners, as a supply was available there. In one of its experiments in steam power, the Santa Fe developed a massive 2-10-10-2 locomotive that proved so ponderous that company shops cut them up into 2-10-2 configurations, a workhorse on freight consists on the Santa Fe for years. This experiment ended the Santa Fe's interest in Mallet-style engines. Instead, it went for big single-coupled steam engines like 2-10-2s, 4-8-4s, and 2-10-4s.

As it was already using low-grade oil, it was a natural for the railroad to shift over to more economical diesels just before and during World War II. Santa Fe pioneered an idea that became common among diesels—painting them in different freight and passenger models. The freight engines used a blue body with gold, red, and black stripes that curved around the nose, called "cat's whiskers." Later, the gold became more prominent and covered the whole nose in what was called the "warbonnet" look after its mimicking of the passenger cabs. Variations of this paint job still adorn Santa Fe freight units. The passenger units were among the flashiest in all of American railroading. They had silver (or stainless steel) bodies and full red noses set off with black and gold stripes. They were, in the style of the Santa Fe, the original "warbonnets." Each engine had the profile of the Santa Fe Chief, the line's logo, until its passenger service went to Amtrak.

In the 1980s, the Santa Fe and its rival, Southern Pacific, tried to work out a merger. As a part of the deal, each line began to paint its road equipment in a joint paint scheme, tagged "Kodachrome" because of its brightness. The units were painted with a yellow warbonnet and the body was a bright scarlet topped off with a black roof. As the new entity was to be called the SP/SF Railway, each line put its own initials on the body side, leaving a space for the other's letters once the merger was completed. But the Interstate Commerce Commission saw this as a potentially monopolistic combination and vetoed the merger scheme, leading one punster to declare that SP/SF stood for "Shouldn't Paint So Fast." Today the Santa Fe has revived its silver and red warbonnet look for its crack container and trailer trains (the so-called Super Fleet), which make up much of its profitable freight business, typified by the recent piggyback agreement with J. B. Hunt Trucking, called Quantum Service. Regular freight units still use the traditional blue and yellow paint pattern.

Although it had to finally admit defeat, the Santa Fe was among the last American railroads to cut its own passenger service. After World War II, when the automobile drained passenger revenues all over the nation, Santa Fe introduced lightweight streamliners, vista dome cars, and double-decker chair cars. The names of its crack passenger trains are famous: the *Chief, California Chief, Super Chief, Grand Canyon, Valley Flyer, Scout, El Capitan,* and *San Diegan.* Santa Fe passenger equipment was so modern that much of it, especially the double-decker *El Capitan* cars, went to make up the core of the original Amtrak consists. Indeed, some revitalized *El Capitan* cars can be seen still in the 1990s. And although the Santa Fe mainline has now bypassed the Ratón Pass route on the Belén Cutoff in the interests of speed and efficiency, Amtrak still uses its scenic vistas as one of its major attractions. Amtrak's cross-country Chicago–Los Angeles train is named the *Super Chief,* a tribute to bygone days when Santa Fe meant the finest in passenger accommodations.

In the wake of the North American Free Trade Agreement (1994), Santa Fe and Burlington Northern (BN) have initiated merger talks. If approved by the Interstate Commerce Commission, the new line would be the largest in the nation. Santa Fe would get access to Canada through BN and BN would obtain access to Mexico through AT&SF. Each line would complement each other, forming one vast circle route between Chicago and Los Angeles, touching the borders of the new economic order of the twenty-first century. But the Union Pacific (UP) has instituted what is seen by observers as a more unfriendly merger offer to Santa Fe, because unlike BN, which is a commodity hauler (grain, coal, lumber), UP is an intermodal railroad as is Santa Fe. Although UP and Santa Fe parallel each other in Midwest markets, a merger would give UP a shorter route into Los Angeles.

See also Burlington Northern Incorporated; Denver & Rio Grande Western Railroad; Harvey, Frederick Henry; Klitenic Plan; Locomotives, Steam Locomotives; Railroads from Appomatox to Deregulation.

References Bryant, Keith L., Jr., *History of the Atchison, Topeka & Santa Fe Railway* (1974); Bryant, Keith L., Jr., "Atchison, Topeka & Santa Fe Railway," in Keith L. Bryant, Jr. (ed.), *EABHB: Rail-roads in the Age of Regulation* (1988), 10–13; Clark, Gary, "Santa Fe's Curtis Hill," *Pacific RAILNews* (November 1994) 372: 40–41; Dalmas, Herbert, "The Super Chief: Luxury on Rails," *Coronet* (May 1954) 36: 38–42; Drury, George H., *The Historical Guide to North American Railroads* (1985); Drury, George H., *The Train-Watcher's Guide* (1990); Duke, Donald, and Stance Kistler, *Santa Fe* (1963); Greever, William S., *Arid Domain* (1954); Greever, William S., "Atchison, Topeka & Santa Fe Railway" and "Cyrus K. Holiday," in Robert L. Frey (ed.), *EABHB: Railroads in the Nineteenth Century* (1988), 15–17, 182–184; Hubbard, Freeman, *Encyclopedia of North American Railroading* (1981); Kogan, Denis J., et al., *Santa Fe's Hi-Level Cars* (1975); Lyon, Peter, *To Hell in a Day Coach* (1968); McKinley, Joe, *Santa Fe 's Diesel Fleet* (1974); McKinley, Joe, *Route of the Warbonnets* (1977); Marshall, James, *Santa Fe* (1945); Mercer, Lloyd J., *Railroads and Land Grant Policy* (1982); Nock, O. S., *Railways of the USA* (1979); Pope, Dan, and Mark Lynn, *Warbonnets* (1994); Renute, Alfred, *Trains of Discovery: Western Railroads and the National Parks* (1990); Renute, Alfred, "Celebrating Rails and Parks," *Trains* (October 1994) 54: 32–33; Repp, Stan, *Super Chief* (1980); Richmond, Al, *The Story of the Grand Canyon Railway* (1985); Rush, Elson, "BNSF: Biggest Merger of All," *Pacific RAILNews* (September 1994) 370: 16–21; Sperandeo, Andy, "The Super Chief, 1951–1953," *Model Railroader* (August 1993) 60: 74–89; Stagner, Lloyd E., *Santa Fe, 1940–1971* (1992); Worley, E. Dale, *Iron Horses of the Santa Fe Trail* (1965); Zimmermann, Karl R., *Santa Fe Streamliners* (1987).

Santa Fe Trail

Famous as the first great American thoroughfare west of the Missouri River, the Santa Fe Trail ran from Independence, Missouri, to the capital of the Mexican province of New Mexico. Like all early roads, its path was a composite of many parallel trails. Trade with northern New Mexico predated the arrival of the Spanish. Plains Indian tribes came into the Taos Pueblo for centuries to exchange goods and captives. The Spanish basically increased the market and moved it to Santa Fe. In the process, the Spanish taxed everything that moved. Goods from the United States could enter Mexico only through the port of Veracruz, a long detour for Americans along the Mississippi River, and at great costs to the purchasers at Santa Fe. The market was there; all knew it, but few dared challenge Spanish authority.

A pair of pioneers and their four horses cross Apache territory on the Santa Fe Trail as they make their way to San Diego.

One who did make the challenge was Zebulon Pike, for whom the distinctive peak in southern Colorado is named. In 1806, Pike explored the southern boundaries of the Louisiana Purchase for the United States. The southern boundary of the Louisiana Purchase was to be the Arkansas River, and Pike went out along its length to see where it was. In the process, he crossed over to the headwaters of the Rio Grande, got caught by Spanish soldiers, was detained at Santa Fe, and transferred to Chihuahua City as a prisoner. Although he was treated well, similar experiences by commercial traders would entail confiscation of goods and complete bankruptcy, as well as jail, as was the case with the Robert McKnight party in 1812. The Spanish wanted no Americans in their borderlands.

In 1815, however, Joseph Philibert, Auguste Chouteau, and Jules de Mun thought that Spanish policy had changed. Sending de Mun to Santa Fe to explain their desire to trap beaver and trade with Spanish citizens, the governor at Santa Fe welcomed the Americans. The trappers spent a whole season obtaining pelts, and returned to find that a new man was governor. He promptly confiscated packs and traps and jailed the entire party as trespassers. After threatening to shoot the Americans as spies, they were sent packing for St. Louis, glad to be alive. In 1821, William Becknell of Franklin (near Independence), a farmer in debt to at least five creditors and but one jump ahead of the sheriff and debtors' prison, outfitted a pack train and went out with a few adherents to trade with the Plains tribes. He followed the Kansas River to the Smoky Hill, dropped down to the Great Bend of the Arkansas, and followed it west. It was too late in the season, and he did little business. Upon reaching the foothills of the Rockies, Becknell decided to take a chance on a rumor he had heard. Spain had been thrown out of Mexico and the New Mexicans were starved for manufactured goods. He turned south, traveling through Ratón Pass to Santa Fe. To his surprise, the rumor proved true, and the officials welcomed him with enthusiasm.

Becknell and his men made a fortune. The whole region was so far beyond the old

Spanish frontier and so starved for finished goods that it wanted all the Americans could bring. Markups were as much as 1,000 percent, and the payment was in silver. When he returned to Franklin, Becknell cut loose his packs in a dramatic gesture and let the silver roll into the street. His creditors scrambled for their shares. Becknell returned to New Mexico the following year. This time he instituted another first—he brought his goods down by wagon. Becknell followed the traditional route to about where Dodge City stands today. Knowing that his wagons could not cross Ratón Pass, he set a compass course to the southwest. At night he used the stars. Although men and animals were pushed almost to collapse, he found the Cimarron River. Replenishing his water, he moved on across more desert and hit the Canadian River. A short trip around the end of the Sangre de Cristo Mountains and he was in Santa Fe. The shortcut became known as the Cimarron Cutoff. It was fast but dangerous; water was scarce but available if one was lucky. Those who were not died of thirst or fell victim to marauding Comanches, as did famed mountain man Jedediah Smith ten years later. Those who succeeded made a fortune.

In 1825, the U.S. government sent a surveying party to mark the trail on the American side of the Arkansas. The trade became regularized. An expedition would set out in the spring, each wagon moving out of Independence to Council Grove in Kansas. There the wagons were organized into a unified train and moved off down the trail, traveling three or four abreast for speed and protection. Often a small cannon or two was carried to keep Native Americans at bay. The caravan was ordered with military precision and a captain, who possessed all authority, was elected. Four lieutenants, also elected, commanded each column. At night the caravan formed a square and all livestock was driven inside for protection. Maintenance was provided by Mexicans, who were called "greasers" for the main work they did—greasing wagon wheels. The Americans became "gringos" for their penchant of singing the song "Green Grow the Lilacs."

When Wagon Mound was reached, near Santa Fe but still far from Mexican official notice, the wagons were reloaded and their numbers cut in half to avoid paying the wagon tax, or bribe, as the Americans saw it (everything went into the Mexican governor's pocket anyhow). Later caravans specialized in especially large Murphy wagons pulled by oxen or mules. Once Santa Fe was reached, the traders split up, selling their wares in small shops or right out of their wagons and packs. Most traders took payment in horses and mules brought in from California and in high demand back in the States (and by watching Plains Indians). Since some made their haul faster than others, the train returned to Missouri in several divisions, picking up their extra vehicles stashed along the way.

In 1829, the U.S. government sent along a column of infantry under Major Bennet Riley to escort the wagons through hostile Indian territory until the train left American soil. The troops would await the returning traders there and escort them and their profits back. The trip proved that unmounted troops were no match for the various horse-mounted tribes of the Plains. The result was the organization of the First and Second Dragoon regiments, basically mounted infantrymen.

Meanwhile, Charles and William Bent formed a partnership with Ceran St. Vrain and decided to establish a safe post of refuge on the upper Arkansas. Completed in 1834, Bent's Fort was an imposing adobe structure that could outfit whole hunting and trapping parties, trade with the Native Americans, and buy furs—beaver and buffalo mostly—from the mountain men. The man who kept the fort supplied with meat was Kit Carson. Bent's Fort was soon the largest trading center west of St. Louis.

During the Mexican War, the Army of the West under Colonel Stephen Watts Kearny came down the Santa Fe Trail on a mission of conquest. With regular army dragoons, two regiments of Missouri volunteer cavalry, and the Mormon infantry battalion, he reached Bent's Fort. Kearny was worried that the Mexicans might put up a vigorous defense at Apache Canyon, just outside Santa Fe. Under the influence of the Bent brothers, a large sum of American money wound up in the proper hands. When Kearny reached Apache Canyon, the route was open to Santa Fe and the city fell without a shot being fired. But the volunteer troops' vicious behavior toward the locals led to a revolt by the inhabitants of the Taos Pueblo, which cost Charles Bent, the newly appointed American governor, his life. In 1849, his brother blew up the family bastion as the revolt spread into the Plains tribes before it was curtailed.

U.S. military occupation soon revealed that New Mexico roads were marginal. During the 1850s army engineers constructed a series of roads in the territory. Most were improvements over the old Mexican cart roads. From Santa Fe, roads emanated northward to Canada, where they split into the Old Spanish Trail through Abiquiu and another extension of the Santa Fe Trail through Taos and Ratón Pass. To the southeast, the Santa Fe Trail through Apache Pass was improved to take the heavy traffic of military supply trains all the way to Fort Union. A side trail cut through Cañon Blanco to Albuquerque. Directly south, the old Camino Real was redone to Las Cruces, where it joined the Gila Trail. A string of new forts and a military occupation that cost more than $40 million kept the roads open for the next 15 years. Monthly mail and passenger service followed the army onto the Plains. After the Civil War, the Kansas and Pacific Railroad and the Atchison, Topeka and Santa Fe Railway (AT&SF) pushed their way westward, and by 1872, the AT&SF had reached Dodge City. By 1880, the rails had reached Santa Fe and the era of the trails was over. The Santa Fe Trail had lasted the longest of the western routes and been one of the bloodiest.

See also Gila Trail; Old Spanish Trail; Roads and Highways, Colonial Times to World War I.

References Atherton, Lewis F., "Business Techniques in the Santa Fe Trade," *Missouri Historical Review* (1940) 34: 335–341; Cleland, Robert G., *This Reckless Breed of Men* (1950); Drago, Harry S., *Roads to Empire* (1968); Duffus, R. L., *Santa Fe Trail* (1930); Dunlop, Richard, *Great Trails of the West* (1971); Dunlop, Richard, *Wheels West* (1977); Eggenhoffer, Nick, *Wagons, Mules and Men* (1961); Findley, Rowe, "Along the Santa Fe Trail," *National Geographic* (March 1991) 179: 98–122; Hart, Val, *The Story of American Roads* (1950); Jackson, W. Turrentine, *Wagon Roads West* (1952); Lavender, David, *Bent's Fort* (1954); Moody, Ralph, *The Old Trails West* (1963); Stephens, F. F., "Missouri and the Santa Fe Trade," *Missouri Historical Review* (1916) 10: 223–262, and *Missouri Historical Review* (1917) 11: 289–312; Vestal, Stanley, *Old Santa Fe Trail* (1939); Walker, Henry Pickering, *The Wagonmasters* (1966); Weber, David J., *The Spanish Frontier in North America* (1992); Young, Otis E., *First Military Escort on the Santa Fe Trail* (1952).

Santee Canal

Using the west branch of the Cooper River (Biggin Swamp), the Santee Canal connected the seaport of Charleston to the Santee River valley in the 1790s. It was put out of business by the advance of the railroads, in which South Carolina was a pioneer.

See also Canals; Railroads before and during the Civil War.

Sault Ste. Marie Canal

Begun in 1853 and completed as the St. Mary's Falls Canal in 1855, the Sault Ste. Marie Canal would be rebuilt several times, eventually winding up with locks 1,200 feet long, 110 feet wide, and 32 feet deep. From the beginning, the "Soo," as it is called, carried more traffic than any other canal, even the fabled Erie, and remains one of the most used canals in the world.

See also Canals; Great Lakes Freighters; St. Lawrence Seaway.

Sawyers Wagon Road

An extension to the east of the Bozeman Trail to the mouth of the Niobrara River in Nebraska, and first surveyed by James Sawyers of Sioux City, Iowa, in 1865, the Sawyers Wagon Road took so long to build (mostly because of Lakota [Sioux] opposition) that the transcontinental railroad put it out of business almost as soon as it opened—at least that is what more-or-less official sources would have one believe. Many historians question whether any of the $50,000 appropriated for the road was ever spent in a proper manner or any work done at all.

See also Bozeman Trail.

References Drago, Harry S., *Roads to Empire* (1968); Jackson, W. Turrentine, *Wagon Roads West* (1952).

Schwabacher Cases

Both an Interstate Commerce Commission (ICC) case (*Schwabacher v. ICC* [1948]) and a U.S. Supreme Court decision (*Schwabacher v. U.S.* [1944]), the *Schwabacher* ruling held that state laws or corporate charters granted by the state concerning the manner of payment of preferred and common stockholders could not interfere with federal law permitting the consolidation of railroads. It essentially cleared the way for more and bigger mergers after World War II. In the actual case, the Chesapeake & Ohio Railroad (C&O) had taken over the Pere Marquette Railroad in Michigan only to be challenged by the preferred stockholders, who complained that they should not only receive the exchange in C&O stock given common stockholders in the Pere Marquette, but also a monetary bonus, as they were now reduced to holding merely common stock in the C&O. Under Michigan law, preferred stockholders had to be settled with before common stockholders received anything; under federal law this was not so. Originally, the ICC held for the Michigan law only to be overruled by the Supreme Court on appeal, with the case referred back to the regulatory body for reconsideration.

See also DT&I Conditions.

References Saunders, Richard, *The Railroad Mergers and the Coming of Conrail* (1978); *Schwabacher v. ICC*, 72 F. Supp. 560 (1948); *Schwabacher v. U.S.*, 334 US 182 (1944).

Scott, Thomas A. (1824–1881)

Orphaned at age 12, Thomas A. Scott worked his way up from the bottom. Errand boy, clerk, station agent, superintendent of the Pennsylvania Railroad's (PRR) western division, and vice-president of the road at age 37, Scott had a real talent for spotting weakness in others and using it to corrupt. He saw to it that Pittsburgh, which welcomed any railroad to its environs, could not have any rail service beyond the PRR. He knew the city council would not stand for this, but the state legislature would if plied with the proper favors. He got one bill protecting the Pennsy from outside competition through the legislature and signed by the governor in 34 minutes. His business and political acumen made the Pennsylvania the strongest corporation in the nation.

His railroads crisscrossed the best American industrial regions, but lacked a western outlet. Scott desperately wanted one, and decided that the last great land-grant railroad, the Texas & Pacific, should be his. But there was a problem here. The Texas & Pacific was a southern railroad, and Scott's business goals conflicted with the realities of radical Republican Reconstruction. Parts of the South were still occupied by federal soldiers, and the votes of several southern states were still in the Republican column. The reason was simple—the soldiers kept blacks in those states voting, and voting Republican, long after the rest of the South had been "redeemed," that is, taken over by conservative, white-dominated governments. So when Scott worked out a deal in the controversial election of 1876 to get a Republican administration nationally (picking Republican war hero and family man Rutherford B. Hayes over Democrat Samuel B. Tilden, a bachelor railroad lawyer implicated in the Crédit Mobilier, but now governor of New York and marketed as an honest man for president), the soldiers withdrew from the southern states (leaving the recently freed slaves back at the mercy of their old masters and the Ku Klux Klan), and Scott received a southern land-grant railroad.

Then Collis P. Huntington offered to build his Southern Pacific with private financing, an offer too good for Congress to pass up. Scott and Huntington managed to compromise their differences and work out a masterful joint-defrauding of the treasury of nearly $90 million; but it all blew up in the great strike of 1877, when they increased their hauling rates by 50 percent and cut employee salaries by 10 percent to raise the necessary operating funds to gather their western empire together. The machinations of the railroad men, especially the pusillanimity of their money-grubbing tactics, caused "their" president, Rutherford B. Hayes, to declare that the Texas & Pacific deal smacked of Crédit Mobilier tactics (reminiscent of an earlier scandal), and he nixed the whole thing. Someone, probably Scott, should have told Hayes that an honest politician was one who, when bought, stays bought. In the aftermath of his failed policy, Scott stepped down from the directorship of the Pennsy. He died a few years later at Darby, Pennsylvania.

See also Forbes, John Murray; Gould, Jay; Huntington, Collis Potter; Missouri Pacific Railroad; Pacific Railroad Act of 1862; Pennsylvania Railroad; Railroads from Appomattox to Deregulation; Sage, Russell; Vanderbilt, William H.

References Bruce, Robert V., *1877: Year of Violence* (1959); Lyon, Peter, *To Hell in a Day Coach* (1968); Ward, James A., "J. Edgar Thomson and Thomas A. Scott: A Symbiotic Partnership?" *Pennsylvania Magazine of History and Biography* (1976) 50: 37–65; Ward, James A., "Thomas A. Scott," in Robert L. Frey (ed.), *EABHB: Railroads in the Nineteenth Century* (1988), 358–362; Woodward, C. Vann, *Reunion and Reaction* (1951).

Seaboard Air Line Railroad (SAL)

Originally the Weldon Railroad, an 1836 line out of Petersburg, Virginia, to Weldon, North Carolina, that played a key role in supplying Robert E. Lee's Army of Northern Virginia during the Civil War, the Seaboard Air Line was incorporated in 1914 as a conglomerate of many small Florida, Alabama, Georgia, South Carolina, North Carolina, and Virginia lines. In 1840, its 141 miles of track was the longest railroad in the United States. The name denoted speed, there being no airplane services implied. It operated over 4,000 miles of track and also operated a fleet of Atlantic coastal steamers and the famed *Orange Blossom Special*. Under a series of receiverships, the SAL was united with the Atlantic Coast Line in 1957, forming the Seaboard Coast Line Railroad. As

both roads essentially served the same area, it was hoped that combining the railways would allow a corresponding reduction in costs by avoiding duplication of tracks and equipment.

See also Atlantic Coast Line; CSX Corporation; Family Lines System; Seaboard Coast Line Railroad.

References Drury, George H., *The Historical Guide to North American Railroads* (1985); Drury, George H., *The Train-Watcher's Guide* (1990); Hubbard, Freeman, *Encyclopedia of North American Railroading* (1981); Stover, John F., *Railroads of the South* (1955); Ward, James A., "Seaboard Air Line Railroad," in Keith L. Bryant, Jr. (ed.), *EABHB: Railroads in the Age of Regulation* (1988), 394–395.

Seaboard Coast Line Railroad

A 1957 union between the Seaboard Air Line Railroad and the Atlantic Coast Line Railroad, to which was added the Piedmont & Northern Railroad in 1967, the Seaboard Coast Line dominated rail shipping in the South Atlantic states during this era until it merged with the Louisville & Nashville Railroad as part of the Family Lines. It boasted the longest single stretch of perfectly straight track in the United States—78.8 miles between Hamlet and Wilmington in North Carolina.

See also Atlantic Coast Line; CSX Corporation; Family Lines System; Florida East Coast Railway; Louisville & Nashville Railroad.

References Drury, George H., *The Historical Guide to North American Railroads* (1985); Drury, George H., *The Train-Watcher's Guide* (1990); Hubbard, Freeman, *Encyclopedia of North American Railroading* (1981); Ward, James A., "Seaboard Coast Line Railroad," in Keith L. Bryant, Jr. (ed.), *EABHB: Railroads in the Age of Regulation* (1988), 398.

Sherman Antitrust Act (1890)

Although it bore the name of revered Senator John Sherman (brother of the famed Civil War general, William T. Sherman), the Sherman Antitrust Act was the work of Senators George F. Hoar of Massachusetts and George F. Edmonds of Vermont. The Sherman Act was based on the implicit belief that competition no longer functioned in the railroad industry as classical economists had theorized. The measure passed with the support of business-oriented congressmen who knew that the public criticism of railroads could no longer be stayed. Better a fairly conservative "reform," most figured, than to invite worse by refusing to budge.

The measure outlawed conspiracies in restraint of trade. It was so vague that it would soon fall victim to adverse Supreme Court decisions. The case of *U.S. v. E. C. Knight* (1895), for instance, restricted the act to transportation, not manufactured goods. The Court restricted the law again to a "rule of reason" in *U.S. v. Trans-Missouri Freight Association* (1897) and *Addyson Pipe and Steel Company v. U.S.* (1899), stating the principle that there were "good" and "bad" trusts. In the *Northern Securities Company v. U.S.* case (1905), the Court rehabilitated the law against a railroad holding company, and in *Swift and Company v. U.S.* (1905) against a meat producer, but once again stating that there were good and bad trusts—these being bad ones. Actually, the only restraint of trade during this era was found to be in the activity of striking labor unions, not business.

The "rule of reason" became a stated principle in the 1911 cases *Standard Oil Company v. U.S.* (disbanded by the ruling as a bad trust) and *U.S. v. American Tobacco Company* (merely reorganized by the court's order as a "so-so" trust), which marked the end of the "trust busting" that had defined the Theodore Roosevelt administration and culminated in the Clayton Act. But in spite of declarations that the act gave labor the right to organize, such unions were held in restraint of trade until the New Deal in the 1930s. From a purely cynical point of view, the Sherman Act could be seen as a business concession on its face that in fact nullified labor's attempt to organize, rather than a reform to promote competition in railroading once again.

See also Clayton Act; Interstate Commerce Act; Interstate Commerce Commission; Mann-Elkins Act.

References *Addyson Pipe and Steel Company v. U.S.*, 175 US 211 (1899); Block, Michael K., *The Sherman Act* (1981); Leonard, William Norris, *Railroad Consolidation under the Transportation Act of 1920* (1946); *Northern Securities Company v. U.S.*, 193 US 197 (1905); Saunders, Richard, *The Railroad*

Mergers and the Coming of Conrail (1978); *Standard Oil Company v. U.S.*, 221 US 1 (1911); *Swift and Company v. U.S.*, 196 US 375 (1905); Swindler, William F., *Court and Constitution in the 20th Century* (1969); *U.S. v. American Tobacco Company*, 221 US 106 (1911); *U.S. v. E. C. Knight*, 156 US 1 (1895); *U.S. v. Trans-Missouri Freight Association*, 166 US 290 (1897); Walker, Albert Henry, *History of the Sherman Law of the United States* (1910).

Shipping Acts

Periodically, Congress would legislate certain subsidizing and regulating measures called the Shipping Acts. As with many such complicated measures (like the complementary Merchant Marine Acts), the acts often prolonged the problems of the Merchant Marines rather than alleviating them. The various measures follow.

SHIPPING ACT OF 1916

This measure initiated government regulation of the maritime industry as a process to be supervised by the Shipping Board, five members charged with defending and promoting the merchant marine. It was hoped that a coordinated approach might counter alleged monopoly practices undertaken by foreign shippers and governments. It was also hoped that the board might encourage the building and registration of ships under the American flag. The measure disallowed the most common rate kickbacks and discriminations, much as the Clayton Act had done against railroads. All cartel rates had to be filed with the board to be determined as valid. No nation had ever tried to regulate these cartel agreements before and the American law suffered from being the first in its field, plagued as it was with vagaries and inherent contradictions. The interruption of World War I saw many of the purposes of the act postponed or defeated, causing Congress to try to rehabilitate the act with further merchant marine legislation after the war.

SHIPPING ACT OF 1984

This legislation was the first comprehensive bill in 68 years to attack the problems of the

American merchant marine. Federal court decisions, the passage of time, technological inventions, and economic conditions had changed so much as to necessitate a new law from the 1916 enactment. The new law allowed shippers to book passage of cargoes via several different modes of transportation through one source. This made the new intermodal traffic possible from producer to user, which when combined with computer innovations, allowed manufacturers to use "just in time" inventory methods—using parts as they arrived at the plant without any storage on the premises. In effect, the measure deregulated the shipping industry as Congress had done earlier with other modes of transportation.

See also Airline Deregulation Act of 1978; Merchant Marine; Merchant Marine Acts; Motor Carrier Acts; Staggers Rail Act of 1980.

References Pedraja, René de la, *A Historical Dictionary of the Merchant Marine and Shipping Industry* (1994); Stafford, Jeffrey J., *Wilsonian Maritime Diplomacy* (1978); Transportation Research Board, *Intermodal Marine Container Transportation* (1992).

Shreve, Henry Miller (1785–1854)

Born in New Jersey, Henry Shreve went west as a young man to engage in river navigation. In 1807 Shreve took up keelboating on the Mississippi and Ohio. Bored by the monotony of the trips between St. Louis and Pittsburgh, he continued upriver to the Galena lead mines, then dominated by the French-Canadians and their British governors. The actual mines were overseen by the Sac-Fox tribe of Native Americans, whom Shreve won over by displays of physical strength. He managed to trade for a cargo of lead, which he took to New Orleans and transshipped to Philadelphia by schooner. He made $11,000 on the venture, no small deal in those days.

As Shreve passed a stranded keelboat headed upstream, it dawned on him that steam might offer a solution to the difficult journey against the river's powerful current. He was aware of Fulton's success on the Hudson, but he knew that such a deep-draft boat would not make it up the shallower western rivers. Nonetheless, he bought the first Fulton boat he saw, the *Enterprise*, built by Daniel French near Pittsburgh, and loaded it with powder and shot and set out for the Gulf. Conscripted by General Andrew Jackson, his boat helped supply the American forces at the Battle of New Orleans (1814). In 1815, he ascended the Mississippi and Ohio Rivers in the *Enterprise*, marking the first time this was done. But the trip was possible only because of the spring floods.

In 1816 he built the flat-bottomed, shallow-draft stern-wheeler *Washington*, modeled after the keelboats he knew so well. It rode on the water rather than in it. Cargo and passenger space came in the multiple decks reaching into the sky. Power came from a rebuilt high-pressure steam engine designed by Daniel French, which Shreve installed horizontally to save space. Although she ran aground and suffered a boiler explosion and two dozen casualties horribly scalded by escaping steam (another river first of doubtful honor), the *Washington* was repaired and continued on its trip to New Orleans. Then Shreve turned around and made the upstream trip in just over three weeks, a feat that took a keelboat four to six months to accomplish. All of it was in violation of the Fulton Company's patents and monopolies. When the Livingstons, Fulton's in-laws, tried to have Shreve arrested, New Orleans went mob crazy. No one in the West cared about monopoly, least of all Captain Henry Miller Shreve. Sixty more boats were built by various concerns in the next two years. Soon Shreve rebuilt the *Washington* into a side-wheeler, with each wheel operated by a separate engine. His design became a riverboat standard for power and control.

Shreve also invented a boat to remove snags from rivers, and a steam-powered ramming vessel for harbor defense. In 1826 he was made superintendent of improvements on western rivers. He was best known for removing the Red River raft, a historic jam of floating timber so solid that one could ride a horse across parts of it, that had prevented navigation of the Red above Alexandria, Louisiana; this allowed the army to supply the Choctaw and Chickasaw reservations in the Indian Nations. As soon as he accomplished the task, the army fired him and the river jammed up again. He left something else at the head of the logjam—a camp that became the town named for him, Shreveport. He retired in 1841 and died at St. Louis some years later.

See also Fulton, Robert; *Gibbons v. Ogden*; Steamboats.

Reference Donovan, Frank, *River Boats of America* (1966).

Siskiyou Trail

The Siskiyou Trail ran out of Fort Vancouver across from the mouth of the Willamette on the Columbia River, and then south past Klamath Lake to California by way of Mount Shasta and the Sacramento Valley. It is today the route of the Southern Pacific Railroad and Interstate 5, the great highway up the interior valleys from Mexico to Canada. But in the nineteenth century it was the route of conquest, coming down from Canada into the Oregon country, present-day British Columbia, Washington State, and Oregon. The men who opened up the Northwest were British subjects, employees of the Hudson's Bay Company (HBC).

The Hudson's Bay Company was founded on the king of France's shortsighted refusal to back up French fur trappers on the St. Lawrence River in their contest with the Dutch in New Amsterdam (today's New York) and their Iroquois allies to dominate the fur trade of the New World. Ménard Chouart, better know as the Sieur des Groseillers, and his partner, Pierre Esprit Radisson, came up with a plan to bypass the Dutch and get to the rich West via Hudson's Bay. But the French government could not see wasting any money on what appeared to be a harebrained scheme. Miffed, Groseillers and Radisson went to another king who would be thrilled to invest in their idea, Charles II of England. Through the agent of Prince Rupert, the king's cousin, a stock investment called the Hudson's Bay Company was set up to ex-

ploit the furs of North America through the back door at Hudson's Bay. The company was to become so powerful that at one time it was the government of most of Canada outside the St. Lawrence River Valley.

The HBC men (Americans in the West said that the acronym meant "Here Before Christ," in reference to the company's constant preemptive exploration efforts) cut across the Plains and were the first whites to see the Rockies. But like their American brethren to the south, they had to compete with another firm, the Northwest Company, organized in 1784 to exploit the Pacific Northwest. Under Alexander Mackenzie, the Nor'westers, as they were called, were the first to reach the Pacific in 1804, the same year Meriwether Lewis and William Clark set out from St. Louis on a similar mission for President Thomas Jefferson. After a brief war between the two Canadian companies, they merged in the 1820s under the older Hudson's Bay name. They ran into the Americans along the Columbia, under the banner of John Jacob Astor's Pacific Fur Company. But the Americans decided to sell out with the approach of British naval forces during the War of 1812.

Fortunately for the United States, the war ended in a status quo antebellum—all claims before the war remained valid. But it would be awhile before the Americans could return, and the British began to exploit the beaver-rich streams of the Columbia River basin. After a brief war with the Calapooya Indians, British-sponsored expeditions moved up the Willamette, but how far is still debated by historians. They probably did not reach present-day California. They had bigger game in mind—the Snake River and its tributaries into the Rockies, full of the best beaver trapping man has ever known. In 1824, after the two British fur companies merged, Dr. John McLoughlin became the head of the trapping brigades stationed at Fort Vancouver. Six-feet-four-inches tall, he had started out as a surgeon only to change over to trapping, rising to the top of his trade. He was a good host to all who came to Fort Vancouver and a noted conversationalist with a keen mind. He was an able adversary to the Americans in the contest for Oregon for over 20 years.

McLoughlin's chief leader in the field was Peter Skene Ogden. Ogden and his superior knew that in the long run, especially after the opening of the Oregon Trail, they would lose out to the Americans in much of Oregon. The problem was how much and when. Meanwhile, they decided to trap the whole region out as quickly as possible, creating a "fur desert" that would hopefully keep American interests farther south. Born of Tory parents who had fled the results of the American Revolution, Ogden was reputed to be honest, humorous, a bit eccentric, and a terror to Native Americans, the knifing of one causing his self-imposed exile into the wilderness two steps ahead of an indictment for murder. Yet he was no Indian-hater; he later married a Nez Percé woman and generally judged the various tribes on their merits. He disliked the Blackfeet, Shoshone, Bannocks, Diggers, and Paiutes because he considered them treacherous for raiding his prized horse herd.

Like the Americans, Ogden had heard rumors of the legendary Buenaventura River that supposedly drained the Great Salt Lake into the Pacific, many thought at San Francisco Bay. In 1825 he set off up the Willamette to explore the area toward Lake Klamath. In the next two years, he managed to cover the ground along the modern California-Oregon border, but it was left for Jedediah Smith to cross the Siskiyou Mountains from the south in 1828, a trip that almost cost his life when most of his party was massacred by the Kelawatset Indians. The following year, Ogden duplicated Smith's feat, advancing south to the Gulf of California on the east side of the Sierra Nevada and returning by California's central valleys. The first journeys over much of what would become the Siskiyou Trail had been completed. It remained for others to exploit what Ogden and Smith had done. In 1830, after passing a near-disastrous winter in the Siskiyou Mountains, Alexander McLeod and Michel Laframboise led their trapping brigade into the upper Sacramento Valley. McLeod, discredited by earlier mistakes and physically ill, was soon replaced by John Work. He and Laframboise continued into northern California, Mexican country.

The Hudson's Bay men feared that the lax Mexican rule created a vacuum into which the Americans would pour, and they wanted to assert their authority as far south as possible. For the next several years, Work, Laframboise, and others worked the streams that fed the Sacramento, going as far south as the mouth of the San Joaquin. Reporting that the area had little beaver, John McLoughlin withdrew the brigades and sent them to richer areas in the Rockies to the east. Right behind the withdrawing Hudson's Bay trappers came the Americans. Ewing Young was the first American to actually travel up the Siskiyou Trail since Jed Smith. In his party was a teenaged Kit Carson, a runaway from an apprenticeship in Missouri, once a cook but now a full-fledged mountain man. When the Young party reached the upper Sacramento Valley, it found that a brigade under Ogden had already trapped out most of the beaver. Tarrying with Ogden a few days, the Americans returned to the Mexican settlements. At the other end of the Siskiyou Trail, another Yankee, Nathaniel Wyeth, was already bringing in settlers and, despite McLoughlin's discouragement, exploring the upper Willamette for future sites of settlement.

In 1834, Young was back, driving a herd of California horses (most of them stolen) all the way to the Columbia. This marked a new advance for the Siskiyou Trail, and it grew year by year in the traffic it carried. Young settled on the upper Willamette and built a sawmill. Soon thereafter, Young and a group of investors bought cattle in California and drove them directly up the Sacramento River, shortening the Siskiyou Trail into its final form. Young built up his ranch and sawmill, importing Hawaiians to cowboy the herds, and wound up a rich man. Meanwhile Lieutenant George Foster Emmons of the U.S. Navy led an expedition up the Willamette through the Siskiyou Mountains and down the Sacramento to San Francisco. He mapped the whole route for the first time. He also found that it was possible to negotiate it later in the fall and earlier in the spring than believed before.

By the early 1840s, disenchanted American settlers in Oregon were regularly moving their families south to California, and John Bidwell had brought the first American farmers overland. Oregon had been rendered to the United States in 1846, thanks to the settlers who plied the trail in both directions. Old Hudson's Bay magnet John McLoughlin, once the most powerful man in the area, retired to the Willamette Valley and died an angry, lonely death in a foreign land, the Americanization of which he had tried in vain to stop. Landsford Hastings traveled from Oregon to California in 1846 to test his Hasting's Cutoff on the California Trail later that summer. When the Mexicans ordered John Charles Frémont out of California as a suspected spy after his survey of the Oregon Trail, he wintered up the Siskiyou Trail and then headed south by the Deschutes River gorge, disproving the idea of the Buenaventura River from Great Salt Lake to the coast forever. Frémont returned to lead the 1846 Bear Flag Revolt. The joining of California to the United States and the craze of the 1849 gold rush ended whatever few restraints international boundaries had placed on the Siskiyou Trail. Assisted by army engineers and military appropriations, a road was extended up the Willamette Valley to Grant's Pass, with a branch at its northern end to Astoria on the coast. Although the road would not pass wagons its whole length until after the Civil War, it eventually became the major inland highway up the Pacific coast; and so it remains to this day.

See also California Trail; Oregon Trail; Pacific Highway; Roads and Highways, Colonial Times to World War I; Roads and Highways since World War I.

References Baker, Burt Brown, *The McLoughlin Empire and Its Rulers* (1959); Binns, Archie, *Peter Skene Ogden, Fur Trader* (1967); Cline, Gloria Griffen, *Peter Skene Ogden and the Hudson's Bay Company* (1974); Dillon, Richard, *Siskiyou Trail* (1975); Hill, Joseph J., "Ewing Young in the Fur Trade of the Far Southwest, 1822–1834," *Oregon Historical Quarterly* (1923) 24: 1–35; Jackson, W. Turrentine, *Wagon Roads West* (1952); LaLande, Jeff, *First over the Siskiyous* (1987); Morgan, Dale L., *Jedediah Smith* (1953).

Slayton, Donald K. (b. 1924)

Of Norwegian-American parentage, Donald K. "Deke" Slayton was born at Sparta, Wisconsin. He attended a local elementary and high school and in 1942, with World War II being waged, he became a United States Army Air Force cadet. Graduated as a bomber pilot, Slayton flew B-25 and A-20 medium bombers and was a flight instructor. In 1946 he left the service and entered the University of Minnesota. Majoring in aeronautical engineering, he crammed the four-year program into two years. He graduated and went to work for Boeing Aircraft at Seattle. Meanwhile he kept active in the Minnesota Air National Guard and was called up for the Korean War, serving as an administrative officer. He soon went into test flying and, having been judged to have the "right stuff," advanced into the astronaut program.

Slayton was expected to be the first American to go into orbital flight. But the

Donald K. Slayton

first two suborbital flights went so well that NASA advanced John Glenn from the final suborbital program into the first orbital flight. Then Slayton was bumped by Scott Carpenter when it was determined that he had a heart fibrillation. The condition was fairly common among those in the civilian world, but the NASA doctors did not like its implications for space travel. NASA put Slayton into an administrative post, coordinating the other astronauts.

Resigning his commission, he continued at NASA as a civilian employee, directing crew operations. Meanwhile he stopped drinking coffee and most alcohol, quit smoking, and primed himself with vitamins and a strong exercise program. During a 1970 physical his heart appeared normal. Slayton immediately demanded flight status and began a rigorous training program, including the learning of the Russian language as a part of the Apollo-Soyuz joint American-Soviet docking in space. He flew this mission in 1975, his only space mission. He continued as a part of the ground crew in the early space shuttle program. Slayton was responsible for the 747 shuttle ferrying system and the first four such flights. In 1982, he resigned from NASA and went into private aerospace business, eventually writing a book with fellow astronaut Alan Shepard (the first American in space) about the space program.

See also Astronautics.

References Cassutt, Michael, *Who's Who in Space* (1987); Hawthorne, Douglas B., *Men and Women of Space* (1992); Shepard, Alan B., and Donald K. Slayton, *Moon Shot* (1994).

Sloan, Alfred P., Jr. (1875–1966)

President of General Motors (GM) between the world wars, Alfred P. Sloan, Jr., had started out in the roller bearings industry. He believed in variety marketing, a concept that he abstracted from William C. Durant's opposition to Ford that involved elaborate, expensive selling, planned obsolescence, and the slogan "a car for every purpose, a car for every pocket." He wanted no duplication between divisions, a concept

that never really took hold completely. In the 1930s, Sloan and "Sloanism" made GM into a modern corporation. He decentralized management, established industry divisions (each with its own corporate leaders and structure), emphasized more than manufacturing (unlike Ford) such as finance, marketing, and long-range planning, and introduced the organizational pyramid with advancement to the top possible for all.

His ideas were successful because of changes in the auto market in the 1920s, which altered it from a market dominated by new car owners to one in which former buyers wished to move up in status or rebuy old reliable products. He was successful in taking on and surpassing Ford because he hired away Norvel A. Hawkins to set up a revitalized distribution network and William S. Knudsen to reorganize production at Chevrolet. As Chevy approached Ford in price, Sloan filled in the gap with Pontiac from the old Oakland division. By the end of the decade, Sloan had created the first full-line auto company and surpassed Ford in business. He never looked back. He gave GM its industrial leadership position that has only been challenged in recent decades. Also a philanthropist, Sloan set up the Sloan Foundation and the Sloan-Kettering Institute for Cancer Research.

See also Automobiles from Domestics to Imports; Automobiles in American Society; Durant, William C.

References Halberstam, David, *The Reckoning* (1986); Motor Vehicle Manufacturers Association of the United States, *Automobiles of America* (1974); Rae, John B., "Alfred Pritchard Sloan, Jr.," in George S. May (ed.), *EABHB: The Automobile Industry* (1989), 402–413; Rothschild, Emma, *Paradise Lost* (1973); Shook, Robert L., *Turnaround* (1990); Sloan, Alfred P., Jr., *My Years with General Motors* (1964); Sobel, Robert, *Car Wars* (1984); Thomas, Robert Paul, *An Analysis of the Pattern of Growth of the Automobile Industry* (1977).

Smoky Hill Trail

As the California goldfields fell into the hands of bigger companies, the single prospectors began to fan out through the West, looking for similar geologic features that might signal the discovery of a new El Dorado. The process was compounded by the Panic of 1857, which put thousands of men out of work and desperate to find a means of making a living. On Cherry Creek near Denver, Colorado, the wandering miners made their strike, and the Pike's Peak (it was the closest geographic spot of note) gold rush was on. The rushers came to the Cherry Creek area and its new, bustling town of Denver by three trails. One route was up the Oregon Trail to near Lodgepole Creek, where they turned south following the Front Range to the headwaters of the South Platte and the diggings. The others were up the Arkansas River from the Deep South, or from St. Louis out the Santa Fe Trail to the Arkansas River, west to the Front Range (of which Pike's Peak is a prominent part), and north to Denver. Both these routes had the advantages of water and fewer hostile Indians.

But there were always those who dared to brave any odds in favor of speed. These hardy souls decided to pioneer a trail straight west from Independence, Missouri, to Denver, using the shorter Smoky Hill River. This route had the habit of running dry, offering great expanses of sandy desert, and pricking the ire of the Southern Cheyenne Indians. Shorter but deadlier, the Smoky Hill Trail also was utilized by Russell, Majors & Waddell's Leavenworth & Pike's Peak Express Company, although the stage is believed to have traced its own route parallel to and slightly north of the older trail. The Smoky Hill Trail helped make Denver the key city in Colorado, but monetary, safety, and water demands caused the stage line to eliminate the separate Smoky Hill route in favor of the Oregon Trail. The coming of the Civil War put a premium on all travel and the route stagnated until revived by the railroads after the conflict.

See also Leavenworth & Pike's Peak Express Company.

References Billington, Ray Allen, *The Far Western Frontier* (1956); Harlow, Alvin F., *Old Waybills* (1934).

Soo Line

The Soo Line is the result of a merger of the Canadian Pacific Railway's U.S. subsidiaries—the Wisconsin Central, the Duluth, the South Shore & Atlantic, and the Minneapolis, St. Paul & Sault Ste. Marie. The "Soo" name is the English-pronounced equivalent to the French "Sault." Its component parts can trace a history back to the Iron Mountain Railroad built in 1855. Originally a grain hauler, the Soo runs through seven of the United States along the Canadian border west into the Dakotas. It has the reputation of being an economical operation, running 65 percent more freight per gallon of fuel oil than the industry average. This is accomplished by maximizing the tonnage hauled per power unit used, installing fuel economy devices on engines, careful handling of fuel to avoid spills, coordination between crew assignments and locomotive availability, and shutting down any engine when it is not needed.

See also Canadian Pacific Railway; Milwaukee Road.

References Abbey, Wallace W., "Soo Line Railroad Company," in Keith L. Bryant, Jr. (ed.), *EABHB: Railroads in the Age of Regulation* (1988), 406–407; Dorin, Patrick, *The Soo Line* (1979); Drury, George H., *The Historical Guide to North American Railroads* (1985); Drury, George H., *The Train-Watcher's Guide* (1990); Gjevre, John A., *A Saga of the Soo* (1973); Hubbard, Freeman, *Encyclopedia of North American Railroading* (1981); Suprey, Leslie V., *Steam Trains of the Soo* (1962).

South Pass

The low area on the Continental Divide between the headwaters of the Sweetwater and Green Rivers that was a natural and relatively snow-free route over the Rocky Mountains in Wyoming was called South Pass. It received its name because it was south of the Lewis and Clark Trail, which was closed to American travel after Meriwether Lewis's disastrous 1806 encounter with the Blackfeet Indians alienated them against the advancing Americans for most of the pre–Civil War era. The first American to travel it was Robert Stuart in 1812, who traveled east by land from the Columbia

River in the employ of John Jacob Astor's Pacific Fur Company to report the sinking of the company's trade ship *Tonquin*.

See also Central Overland Route.

Southern Pacific Lines (SP)

The Southern Pacific railroad had to consolidate two ends of its empire to achieve railroad success. The Texas-Louisiana part was the oldest, beginning with the creation of the Buffalo Bayou, Brazos & Colorado, a line out of Houston to the west, in 1851. The following year the New Orleans, Opelousas & Great Western headed west toward Morgan City, Louisiana. After the Civil War, this road became the Texas & Louisiana and eventually all were absorbed into the Texas & New Orleans, a Southern Pacific subsidiary until 1961 when it lost its independence and name. The final leg of the eastern empire of the SP was the 1932 takeover of the St. Louis & Southwestern (SL&SW, also known as the Cotton Belt). This road had begun in northeastern Texas in 1877 and, through a series of mergers, had reached St. Louis. What interested the SP in it was the fact that the SL&SW had a direct connection into St. Louis and a shared-trackage arrangement into Chicago via the Chicago & Eastern Illinois. The drive for Chicago by a practicable route has been a recurring theme with SP management in the twentieth century. Needless to say, a lot of other lines have tried to keep the SP out and corner the market they established during the last century.

On the West Coast, the SP has its origins in the old Central Pacific, one of the elements of the first transcontinental route. Theodore D. Judah laid its first rails in 1855, and he later searched for and found the way across the Sierra Nevada, although others built the line. The SP did its best to secure an exclusive hold on the Golden State, aided by the machinations of the Big Four: Leland Stanford, who kept the politicos friendly; Charles Crocker, the ever-able engineer of roadbeds; Mark Hopkins, the financier extraordinaire; and Collis P. Huntington, the cutthroat business man-

ager. The result was that the SP pushed south toward Los Angeles and west across the Colorado into Arizona and New Mexico, reaching El Paso by the late 1880s.

As with most railroads that crossed the vast West, the SP needed to settle people along its right-of-way to create business. The Big Four had no intention of driving the SP to ruin and stripping it of all profits. They wanted a vast empire that stretched from Oregon to Chicago in a great arc that kind of paralleled the old Butterfield Stagecoach route. They sold their land grants at $1 to $10 an acre, and offered special immigrant rates to those who would come. In direct competition with the Santa Fe to the north, the line engaged in immigrant rate wars that saw the price of a ticket drop to $1 for awhile. As many of the areas were especially arid, the SP offered expert horticultural advice on how to grow crops and survive. The SP also pioneered ice cars to take the California produce to the East where it commanded high prices during the winter season.

By the mid-twentieth century, the Southern Pacific Transportation Company was a holding company with vast interests in all sorts of businesses, like oceangoing steamers, pipelines, and coal slurry lines. As coal was bulky to carry and the railroad had none it owned itself, the SP joined the Santa Fe in using fuel oil in its steam locomotives. Vast fleets of oil cars made the journey from the Texas fields, many owned by SP's Cotton Belt subsidiary, to provision the thirsty steamers. In 1901, E. H. Harriman bought the SP and modernized many of the old Central Pacific routes still in use; particularly, he built the Lucin Cutoff across the Great Salt Lake. The result was the abandoning of the old Promontory Summit site where the golden spike had been driven. Disastrous floods in California's interior valley cost the SP much produce business in 1905, and the following year the San Francisco earthquake destroyed the railroad's headquarters and yards. Nonetheless, the SP was the main artery for relief supplies. But by 1915, the damage was a thing of the past as the SP hauled 65 percent more passengers to San Francisco than ever before for the Panama-Pacific Exposition. Harriman worked out a shared refrigerator car program with his Union Pacific, and Pacific Fruit Express was born. Less perishable freight went by the Blue Streak Merchandise, a crack freight train that did almost anything to break speed records and undercut competition.

The SP has been a great user and innovator of distinctive motive power. One of the early railroads to use Mallet locomotives (two engines in one), the SP found that long tunnels in the Sierra Nevada caused the engine crew to nearly suffocate. So the SP shops turned the giant engines around and piped oil all the way from the tenders to the forward smoke box, now the cab. It was one of the truly great innovations in steam power, permitting the crew to enter the tunnel ahead of the smokestack. The cabs became more modernized and presaged the notion of streamlining that became common in later diesels. SP was one of the first lines to use radio communications between caboose, engine, and dispatcher in 1939. It started piggyback service (hauling trailers on flatcars) in 1951, and used all-steel welded rail for a smoother ride. The SP also was a developer of Hydra Cushion, a system of springing the coupler drawbars to protect freight from damage. And it had the first tri-level cars to haul automobiles; at first open, these cars are now totally enclosed to prevent damage from the elements or vandalism. SP also built the largest cutoff in recent years when in 1967 it bypassed New Orleans' congestion with 78 miles of new track. As with so much in the modern world, the SP is now computerized, allowing freight to be traced rapidly and accurately.

The SP has used as its logo the setting sun with the words Southern Pacific Lines written around and through it. Its crack, "named" passenger train was the *Sunset Limited*, which Amtrak still uses for its southernmost transcontinental run. Because much of the line across the desert between Tucson and El Paso is relatively boring and crowded with freight trains, SP used to send the passengers over their El Paso & Southwestern subsidiary. When Pancho Villa and his men attacked Columbus, New Mexico, in 1916, one of their goals was to stop the *Limited*, but somehow they got the wrong schedule and missed their train. Also important were the *Golden State Limited*, the *Argonaut*, the *Imperial*, and the *Daylight*. The latter, with its bright orange, scarlet, and black cars with silver lettering, gave its name to the flashiest of passenger colors on the best passenger trains, as opposed to the two-tone gray of most other rail coaches.

In the 1980s the SP tried to improve its financial picture in a more competitive world by merging with its arch-rival Santa Fe. The plans seemed to be well advanced. New paint jobs appeared on both companies' locomotives, a flashy yellow warbonnet on the hood followed by SP scarlet for the body. The SP/SF transportation company initials appeared on the red panels, each road using only its initials until final federal approval was obtained. But the Interstate Commerce Commission finally overruled the merger, causing the railroads to run these "Kodachrome" paint jobs for years before they disappeared. By the end of the decade, the SP managed its western merger, this time with the Denver & Rio Grande Western (D&RGW) in 1988. Their new paint jobs are the traditional lark gray and scarlet of the SP with new lettering in the racy "speedball" style of the D&RGW.

See also Crocker, Charles; Denver & Rio Grande Western Railroad; Harriman, Edward Henry; Hopkins, Mark; Huntington, Collis Potter; Klitenic Plan; Railroads from Appomattox to Deregulation; St. Louis & Southwestern Railroad; Santa Fe Railway; Stanford, Leland.

References Beebe, Lucius, *The Central Pacific and the Southern Pacific* (1963); Drury, George H., *The Historical Guide to North American Railroads* (1985); Drury, George H., *The Train-Watcher's Guide* (1990); Frailey, Fred W., *Southern Pacific's Blue Streak Merchandise* (1992); Hofsommer, Don L., *The Southern Pacific* (1986); Hofsommer, Don L., "St. Louis & Southwestern Railway," and "Southern Pacific Company," in Keith L. Bryant, Jr. (ed.), *EABHB: Railroads in the Age of Regulation* (1988), 383–384, 408–409; Hofsommer, Don L., "Southern Pacific Company," in Robert L. Frey (ed.), *EABHB: Railroads in the Nineteenth Century* (1988), 371–372; Hubbard, Freeman, *Great Trains of All*

Time (1962); Hubbard, Freeman, *Encyclopedia of North American Railroading* (1981); Lewis, Oscar, *The Big Four* (1938); Lyon, Peter, *To Hell in a Day Coach* (1968); Mercer, Lloyd J., *Railroads and Land Grant Policy* (1982); Nock, O. S., *Railways of the USA* (1979); Wilson, Neill C., and Frank J. Taylor, *Southern Pacific* (1952).

Southern Railway System

The Southern has it origins in the South Carolina Railroad, one of the first in the nation, designed to take away Savannah's trade advantages and help Charleston endure as a seaport, and the Richmond & Danville Railroad, one of General Robert E. Lee's lifelines during the 1864 Siege of Petersburg. It now comprises what were once 125 different railroads. The earliest had been wrecked during the Civil War; the later ones fell to the economic axe during the late-nineteenth-century depressions. Their names and initials lent themselves to not-so-praiseworthy monikers: the Georgia & Florida (G&F, God Forsaken), the New Orleans & Northeastern (NO&NE, No Omelets, No Eggs), the Georgia, Florida & Alabama (GF&A, Gophers, Frogs, and Alligators), Georgia Southern & Florida (GS&F, Go Slow and Flag), the East Tennessee, Virginia & Georgia (ETV&G, Eat Turnips, Vinegar, and Greens), and the Live Oak, Perry & Gulf (LOP&G, Lean Over, Push, and Grunt). In 1893, J. Pierpont Morgan created the Southern to exploit stock advantages he held in several small southern railroads. From there it expanded by absorbing its competition, becoming one of the major rail powers of the Atlantic and Deep South. Gone were the days of easy, southern-style management. This new railroad was to be lean and mean—totally "re-Morganized," as the saying went.

The first captain of the Southern was Samuel Spencer. Southern-born and raised, Spencer exploited the lumber, steel, coal, and textile industries that made the New South of the late nineteenth century famous. He was the sponsor of the Good Roads Movement and the Good Roads Train, seeing the highway as a railroad feeder and inadvertently sponsoring the very trend that would challenge railroad viability decades later. He doubled Southern's trackage and tripled its income. His successor, William Finley, built upon Spencer's success to ingratiate the railroads with the public and quell the distrust bred by the earlier Populist politicians. But his need to retrench during the days before World War I to keep the Southern from bankruptcy negated some of its effect. He did, however, standardize equipment, buy larger locomotives, and anticipate the increased traffic that the Panama Canal's opening brought south.

Finley was followed by Fairfax Harrison, who took the Southern through World War I and the Great Depression. He was president of the Railroad War Board, and under the United States Railroad Administration saw to it that the underused Southern port and rail facilities were made an integral part of the war effort. It was he who introduced the fabulous PS-4 Pacifics (4-6-2) painted in forest green and outlined in gold stripes for the *Crescent Limited* passenger train, whose matching cars made it one of America's classic trains of all time. He also developed the slogan, "The Southern Serves the South." But the Great Depression kept him from modernizing the company's capital holdings and introducing a modern management system.

After Harrison's departure, Ernest E. Norris came in to solve the problems left by the depression. The first Yankee to run the road, Norris moved to modernize the locomotive fleet, turning the Southern to diesels, and managed to raise the cash necessary to modernize the freight car fleet. By the time World War II came, Norris was ready to meet the challenge with a revitalized line. Many military training camps were in the South, and the Southern's increased passenger service reached most of them. He was the first to hire women to replace the men gone off to war. He replaced the old slogan with, "Look Ahead—Look South." After the war, Norris led the way into the electronic age with Centralized Traffic Control and a new signal system designed for more traffic, more speed, and more safety. His vision was shared by successors who took the Southern into the computer age and earned the railroad the image of one of the best-managed lines in the nation.

Throughout its history, the Southern Railroad earned the reputation as an innovator. In 1939, the Southern was the first railroad in the United States to use diesel electric locomotives (the original demonstrator FTs) to haul freight, a change symbolized in a 1953 ceremony that featured a replica of the Best Friend of Charleston, the last retiring steam engine 6330, and a modern diesel in clean white and green paint. It had already streamlined and dieselized its named passenger trains before World War II and invested in radio-controlled, computerized, and television-operated freight yards after the war. The change in motive power cost the railroad $120 million but expanded its engine fleet twofold and cut its costs of running it by half. The Southern led the postwar fight to remove firemen from the cab, holding that the job was now superfluous, and refusing to hire more until attrition did the trick 20 years later. But much of its good image was destroyed when it ignored the New Orleans Conditions and laid off Central of Georgia employees en masse, aided by a foul-up in the Interstate Commerce Commission in the early 1960s.

The Southern continued to lead the way in major rail innovations during the ensuing decades. It introduced the unit train—a train with all cars of the same type hauling the same load. It created the Autogard, all-door boxcar that hauled automobiles in an enclosed steel box, protecting them from vandalism, theft, and weather damage, yet unloading them with ease and speed. It developed a cushion-underframe tobacco boxcar, a massive monster 84 feet long and 11 feet high that could haul 98 hogsheads at a time. It led the way in tri-level auto haulers and experimented with container flats when they were still just an idea on other railroads. The Southern utilized forklifts to load lumber on specially built bulkhead flatcars to cut downtime. It created the *Big John* covered

hopper, an all-aluminum car that permitted bulk grain shipments at a decreased price— a practice once challenged by a less-than-brilliant Interstate Commerce Commission as unfair competition. In 1982, the Southern joined with the Norfolk & Western to create a rail empire that extends throughout the South.

See also Good Roads Movement; Morgan, John Pierpont; New Orleans Conditions; Norfolk & Western Railway; Norfolk Southern Corporation.

References Bryant, Keith L., Jr., "Southern Railway," in Keith L. Bryant, Jr. (ed.), *EABHB: Railroads in the Age of Regulation* (1988), 410–411; Davis, Burke, *The Southern Railway* (1985); Drury, George H., *The Historical Guide to North American Railroads* (1985); Drury, George H., *The Train-Watcher's Guide* (1990); Hubbard, Freeman, *Encyclopedia of North American Railroading* (1981); Lyon, Peter, *To Hell in a Day Coach* (1968); Nock, O. S., *Railways of the USA* (1979); Saunders, Richard, *The Railroad Mergers and the Coming of Conrail* (1978); Stover, John F., "Southern Railroad," in Robert L. Frey (ed.), *EABHB: Railroads in the Nineteenth Century* (1988), 372–374.

Spanish Trail

The Spanish Trail was the generic name given numerous old roads in the southeastern and southwestern United States where Spanish colonial administrations once ruled.

See also Old Spanish Trail; Old Spanish Trail Highway.

Spooner Act (1903)

With the ratification of the Hay-Pauncefote Treaty, the United States had to determine where to build a canal in Central America. It was by no means certain that Panamá would be chosen; indeed, most favored a Nicaraguan route, as the asking price for the purchase of the right-of-way from the New Panama Company was exorbitant. But then the price was reduced by two-thirds to $40 million under the influence of Philippe Bunau-Varilla. The result was the Spooner Act of 28 June 1902, which approved of the engineering recommendation that the Panamá route be used providing: (1) that the asking price for the New Panama Company stock not be over the $40 million that was appropriated, and (2) that Colombia grant a right-of-way over which the United States could have permanent control. If negotiations failed, the president was authorized to junk the Panamá route and go for the Nicaraguan one.

See also Hay-Herrán Convention; Panama Canal.

Sproles et al. v. Binford 286 US 374 (1932)

In 1931, Texas enacted laws designed to take advantage of the guidelines set down by the U.S. Supreme Court in *Frost et al. v. Railroad Commission of the State of California* and *Smith v. Cahoon*. Unregulated truckers, prompted by a rapid expansion of the state road system, had been hauling uncompressed cotton into the Galveston market from as far away as Oklahoma, undercutting the prices of the railroads and the interior cotton pressers. These interests prevailed upon the state legislature to regulate the truckers. The statute limited the trucks as to size and payload weight, and also size of individual cargo units. Of course, the only cargo units larger than legal size were uncompressed cotton bales. The law exempted contract truckers who hauled cargo from the producer to the nearest common carrier loading dock. This meant that one could haul almost anything to the nearest railroad but not all the way to Galveston (unless it was the nearest common carrier loading point).

In a unanimous opinion rendered in 1932, the U.S. Supreme Court upheld the Texas law. The court rejected evidence that the state roads could support the heavy uncompressed cotton bales if they were properly loaded. The Court maintained that constitutional principle did not rest with mere scientific advances but with the proper interpretation of the document itself. If the law was unreasonable, the truckers had to persuade the legislature, not the courts, to change it. The Court reasserted that states could act whenever the federal government left a field reserved to itself by the Constitution without law. The fact that truckers could get overload permits if they trans-

ferred cargo to the nearest loading point for common carriers left the flow of commerce essentially unrestrained. Further, the Court asserted that such law was a proper assertion of police power as it protected the use of and condition of the highways for the public good. In effect, the state could regulate trucking to protect the railroads, and the railroads represented the public interest. At least that seemed to be the underlying principle declared here. The future of trucking now rested on the agreement of a majority of a state legislature backed up by a majority of justices on the Supreme Court—not on technology, economics, or service.

See also *Frost et al. v. Railroad Commission of the State of California*; *Stephenson et al. v. Binford*.

Reference Childs, William R., *Trucking and the Public Interest* (1985).

Stagecoaches and Other Horse-Drawn Conveyances

Named from the fact that their trips went in stages from relief point to relief point, stagecoaches were the buses of the centuries preceding motorized transport. Stages were little more than coaches toughened up for daily use over poor or nonexistent roads. They were equipped with extra seats—usually three benches inside and often one or two roof benches in the older European versions that ran on American colonial roads.

Before the Revolutionary War, various companies ran passenger services between New York and Philadelphia, America's principal cities. But they were pretty minimal in service and comfort. Luggage was stored under the seats, and there was not a spring anywhere in the wagon, which led to a lot of jolts on even the best roads of the day. After the war, several companies experimented with leather springs running lengthwise under the passenger compartment. The bodies were generally egg-shaped, and the idea of the "boot," a compartment at the rear and another under the driver's seat for baggage, came along. But the roof was too curved to be of much use in carrying extra passengers or luggage.

If anyone can be credited with launching the stagecoach era in the United States it was Levi Pease of Connecticut. A blacksmith and teamster during the Revolutionary War, he saw the need for regular civil transportation after that conflict. With a friend, who had a little money, Pease launched a public conveyance between Boston and Hartford. He used wagons with bench seats in the bed for his first coach—there were no seat backs. Passengers had to crawl over each other to get in or out, but the idea caught on nonetheless. He received the first federal mail subsidy and set up taverns and added more wagons to meet the demand. Pease also created a new position, that of conductor. Before, the driver, called "captain" in seafaring style, was in charge of everything—horses, tickets, baggage, and so on. Now a second man rode next to him, and he was responsible for all passengers and baggage. He was also bonded and thus qualified to escort express packages, a new angle on the business. Pease also proposed that all stages in Boston have a central ticket office to complement each other's business. He developed the idea of the "Limited"— through-coaches with only four passengers. Every one of Pease's innovations was copied by the railroads later on. He also chartered a road-building project so his coaches could run faster, smoother, and cheaper.

But Pease was retired before two men came on the scene and removed American stagecoaches from the wagon-with-seats era. They were Lewis Downing and J. Stephen Abbot of Concord, New Hampshire. What the two did was revise the old English coach design and adapt it to American needs and conditions. They sold their first coach in 1825, the first of 3,000 made. It was called a Concord and was light, stoutly built, safe, and beautiful. Abbot and Downing brought John Burgum over from England—he specialized in making every coach an ornament of fine color and taste. The Concord was so well designed that two horses could pull it loaded on a macadamized road. (Since six horses were normal in the West, one can get some idea as to the quality of western highways.) And the lighter it got, the stronger they made it. Downing roamed the shop searching out inferior product. When he found a part not up to par, he smashed it with a hammer, ensuring irrevocable quality control.

The Abbot and Downing Concords went everywhere. They went around the Horn by ship to be used in the California goldfields. North, South, East, or West, the Concord was the standard public conveyance of the nineteenth century. It even served as a model for the first railway coaches pulled by the *De Witt Clinton* up the Hudson River Valley. On 15 April 1868, an entire trainload of stages went by rail from Concord to Omaha, consigned to Wells Fargo & Company. John Burgum took the photo of the train and painstakingly painted each coach the proper color. It was typical of Abbot and Downing—they made every coach by hand, no mass production here. It had taken one year just to produce that one trainload of coaches. The plant eventually covered six acres. Quality was the byword. As editor Horace Greeley wrote in his *New York Tribune*, the Concord coach emblazoned with the U.S. Mail insignia represented "Civilization, Intelligence, Government, [and] Protection" so much so that it somehow gave one the proof of the existence of "a terrestrial Providence."

The Concord coach traveled on heavy leather springs called "thorough braces." This allowed the coach to flex and roll over the rough roads, rather than bump. It also allowed the body to remain level regardless of the position of the wheels on the road. The seasoned wood—bass, elm, poplar, white ash, and white oak—was selected for its look as well as for strength. The seats and the two luggage boots in back and under the driver's seat were of the finest oxhide leather. All in all, 14 sides (a "side" was half a hide) of leather went into each coach. There were places inside for nine persons, using a jump seat. On top, next to and behind the driver, an exciting 8.5 feet above the ground, up to a dozen could be accommodated for short trips, weather permitting. The front wheels were 3 feet 10 inches in diameter, the rear ones 5 feet 1 inch. The iron tires were 3.5 to 4 inches wide and .75 inch thick. The whole coach weighed in empty at 2,500 pounds and was heavier than the eastern version, which had better roads to travel on. It cost 50 cents a pound to purchase.

No wonder that the stage driver, sometimes called a "jehu" or a "whip," was a cocky man. If steamboat captains were the kings of the river, the jehu was the Duke of the Road. As one declared to an unknowing customer: "Mister, when I drive this coach, I am the whole United States of America." If the president of the United States were on board, he would have to defer to the driver. He was God Almighty on wheels. He drove that way, too. No one in his right mind got in front of a stagecoach in motion, unless he wanted to get run down. Like all who drove animals in the West, the drivers were tobacco-chewing, hard-drinking experts in epithets. Swearing seemed to get the best out of driver and horse alike. Often they would treat a passenger with a trip up on the box and tell tall tales to pass the time. They were generally a gregarious bunch, more than happy to embellish a story for the incredulous greenhorn. On transcontinental trips on the Central Overland Route, a conductor rode along to attend to passenger needs, luggage, food, and rest stops. In the wilder areas, a shotgun messenger rode next to the driver. Oddly enough, no road agents robbed coaches east of the Mississippi. That was a truly western occupation.

The Concord was not the only public conveyance in the West, merely the best. John Butterfield used a Troy coach, a more boxlike stage made by Eaton, Gilbert and Company of Troy, New York. It also could seat passengers on top. Very popular for long hauls was the Celerity wagon. It was lighter than the Concord, with a rounded, leather-covered roof that permitted no passengers on top. But its seats could make up into beds, a distinct advantage to transcontinental travelers—providing the coach was not too crowded. Abbot and Downing made this coach, as well as the James Goold Company at Albany, New York. Another common coach was the "mud wagon." It was lighter than either the Concord or Celerity wagon and had a narrow tire that lent itself to speed, muddy roads (hence the name), and mountainous trails. All of these vehicles had thorough-brace construction. There was also a springless, broad-wheeled stage known as the Jerky. It was more like the eighteenth-century stage wagon used by Pease, which had been nicknamed a "Shake Guts" from the ride.

Private conveyances improved right along with the coaches and were often built by the same companies, with the exception of Studebaker Brothers of South Bend, Indiana, and James H. Birch of Burlington, New Jersey. As spring technology developed, steel springs took a lot of the jarring out of the ride. Most buggies had transverse springs at the axles, but Abbot and Downing made theirs with a thorough-brace pattern, fore and aft on each side. Commonly, farm wagons merely had the seats sprung, one of the favorites in the West being the multi-purpose buckboard.

Unlike the single horse or team that powered private conveyances, stages generally were pulled by four, six, (or in mud) eight horses. Many of them were wild mustangs, broken to drive. They lent speed and class to any operation. Their harnesses were light and quick to change. At the relay stations, the stock tender would leave the left tug loose until the driver had mounted the box, took the lines, and signaled he was ready. Then, with a snap of the chain, the whole rig was off. It generally took two miles at breakneck speed before the horses settled down and could be fully controlled. Six head required a steady hand and a lot of nerve to operate under the best circumstances, and driving eight was a veritable art.

Drivers knew that the slightest strange noise or change in the wind could cause the whole team to run away. It took a quick brake to stop them before the coach flipped. Often the brake was not enough, and some drivers would throw their right leg over the reins to exert extra pressure on the bits in emergencies. No wonder twentieth-century movie character actor Slim Pickens once said that learning to drive six-up was one of the highlights of his life. The coach routes had to have horse changes every 10 to 15 miles and crew changes less often, every 40 or 50 miles. The whole six-horse team could be let loose from the vehicle by pulling one pin, held in place by gravity. If the coach spilled over, it was hoped that the pin would drop out and free the team from the vehicle.

Home stations were usually the bigger ones and served meals (of a sort, and the fare got worse the farther west one went). Some passengers asserted that biscuits were hard enough to substitute for cannon shot. Most of the fare was greasy, fried, and eaten in a hurry. At one Central Overland stop a customer allegedly criticized the roast beef. "Help yourself to the mustard," was the indifferent reply. At home stations there were extra rooms for the crews to sleep in, but passengers went on with a new crew. Many became so tired that they approached insanity. At such times, the driver usually left them at a station to sleep a little before catching the next stage. The relay stations, by contrast, were generally one-room shacks or sod huts. Their main purpose was to tend the extra horses and change the teams quickly when a coach arrived. They had few amenities. In areas susceptible to Indian attack, they were miniature forts, with stock and stock tenders enclosed in loopholed rock walls. Often a backup dugout was available, stocked with food, water, guns, and ammunition, just in case the station was overrun in an attack.

Nothing beat a trip through the incessant rains of the Pacific Northwest or the winter snows of the Plains or the Rockies. Wheels were often placed on skids in the winter and tied together to prevent jackknifing. Drivers did their best to keep warm up on top, but frostbite and freezing were common. At times the cold hit a man so bad that amputation of a frozen extremity became necessary. Silken gloves protected a driver's hands and still allowed him to "feel" the lines and control the teams. When the blizzards rolled in from the northwest, there was nothing to do but fort up at a relay station until the storm blew over. It could be a long wait in very close quarters.

Stagecoaches thrived on carrying the mails. Although local mail contracts had been let to coaching companies, Congress in 1844 established the United States Postal Commission to make recommendations on improving the mail service. The commission recommended that mail rates be reduced to a nickel for all letters weighing less than one-half ounce and going less than 300 miles. All other letters cost a dime. In 1846, Congress enacted a law putting the commission's recommendations into effect. It also declared that the post office was a public institution that should be evaluated by its service rather than its income. The advent of the adhesive postage stamp permitted mail fees to be collected in advance rather than upon delivery. The result was the largest single annual increase in mail sent in U.S. history in 1848, and the need for more contract carriers to provide delivery. Congress further lowered the letter rates in 1851 to 3 cents for 3,000 miles and 6 cents for over that distance. Rates on all other packages and newspapers followed suit. The first western long-run mail contract went out in 1851 between the Missouri River and Salt Lake City. Another company had the route from Salt Lake City to Sacramento. A third outfit, Waldo, Hall and Company, took the mail down the Santa Fe Trail.

The contract to Santa Fe went to Dr. David Waldo, a longtime trail hand. He was to carry the mail in watertight coaches with elliptical springs and iron axles by way of the Cimarron Cutoff, the shortest route. Records are scarce, but it seems that the contract requirements of the vehicles used were liberally ignored. Most cargo was carried in small covered wagons, generally referred to as Dearborn or Jersey wagons, often used for conveying personal items for the crews of the larger Murphy wagons engaged in the Santa Fe trade. Army surplus ambulances probably hauled passengers separately. But no coaches appeared until after Waldo and his partners, Jacob Hall and William McCoy, also old-time Santa Fe hands, no longer bid the service. After 1861, when the mail route was switched to the more-populated mountain road of the Santa Fe

It was a bumpy ride during the stagecoach era. Even on the best of roads, passengers in the early nineteenth century felt every crevice (not to mention pothole) in these springless coaches.

Trail and Concord-type stages appeared, the coaches often used a "Mexican hitch," two wheel mules preceded by four mules abreast, rather than three teams in a column, or "American hitch."

Waldo and his partners also had a supply contract for the army in New Mexico, which might explain why they used traditional wagons rather than coaches after the first year. The eight-man crews carried Colt's revolvers and revolving rifles. Each man carried ten loaded cylinders in his pockets to exchange for empty ones, which meant that in a fire fight they could pour out 136 shots in quick succession, more than enough to hold off marauders. In 1854, Hall outbid his partners and gained the new contract without them. His new partner was William Hockaday, who later joined John Chorpenning in providing mail service from Salt Lake City to California on the Central Overland Route. In 1857, when the James Buchanan administration came into

office, there were over a dozen bidders for the Santa Fe run, but Hall still managed to win the contract in partnership with James Porter, who also had interests in the central route. Much of the business, however, was siphoned off by the Butterfield transcontinental line through El Paso to the south.

Increasing trouble from Comanche and Kiowa war parties, and the difficulty of co-ordinating runs with army escorts caused everyone to rethink the use of the Cimarron route. Besides, the army's power in the area lay on the mountain route, as did several small towns like Taos. In late 1860, tired of what they thought was unreasonable public criticism, Hall and Porter sold out to Preston Roberts, Jr., of the Missouri Stage Company. An experienced stage operator like his father before him, Roberts moved to expand service into southern Colorado to Cañon City and other mining towns. He had as his partners at various times W. G. Barkley and Samuel Slemmons.

With the Confederate campaign up the Rio Grande to Santa Fe, increased Indian difficulties, and Missouri rebel irregulars, the Civil War was a time of flux both in mail and passenger service and contractors. By the end of the war, the new Santa Fe Stage Company and its director, Jared P. Sanderson, had emerged as the holders of the Santa Fe contract. He claimed that his express rate was 25 cents less per pound than any other shipper. Bidding for the contract was fierce, and in 1866 Sanderson merged with Bradley Barlow, an unnoticed partner in some of the earlier Santa Fe mail companies, to make the run. They also obtained the contract to San Diego and used the old Butterfield route from the Rio Grande to the west. To keep up with the spirit of the increased service, they named their enterprise the Southern Overland Mail and Express Company. The 2,000-mile line stretched from Kansas City through Santa Fe to El Paso and from Mesilla (above El Paso) to San Diego. In 1869 alone they received $480,000 in mail subsidies, carried 3,000 pieces of mail each week, and served a territory of about 200,000 people.

Increased competition from stage lines coming out of Denver, domination of western coach travel by Wells Fargo & Company, and the westward movement of the railroads made exact scheduling, able drivers, fancy stages, fine horseflesh, and good service a key to survival for Barlow and Sanderson. But the use of stagecoach travel for both mails and passengers fell year by year as the Atchison, Topeka & Santa Fe Railroad moved west and south. In 1875, the railroad had reached the Animas River in southeastern Colorado. By 1880, as the Southern Pacific reached Tucson, Arizona, the Santa Fe entered the town for which it was named. The need for long-distance mail and passenger service by stagecoach on the Santa Fe Trail had come to an end.

In 1857, James E. Birch got the mail run from San Antonio to San Diego. He ran the route semimonthly and used mules to haul the coaches. A six-mule "mud wagon" made the first runs and a wrangler drove a *remuda* of 40 extra mules to spell the teams at regular intervals, as there were no relay stations. A group of armed guards kept curious Apaches at bay. It received the nickname "Jackass Mail," but it got the job done, slowly but surely.

Congress established the first truly transcontinental mail service by setting up the Ox Bow Route from St. Louis and Memphis to San Francisco by way of El Paso. This was the province of Butterfield Overland Mail. It was a political decision. California claimed the only mail and travel possible was through the Pacific Mail Steamship Company that used the isthmian route at Panamá. The steamship owners were portrayed as the most evil of monopolies. An alternate overland route promised relief. Since President James Buchanan owed much of his election to southern support, he appointed many southerners to his cabinet. One of them, Postmaster General Aaron V. Brown of Tennessee, wanted a southern transcontinental route used for the mail contract in 1857. John Butterfield, a personal friend of the president, reluctantly was willing to modify the route to include Memphis (Brown's hometown). So the contract was let.

The southern route was to begin at both St. Louis and Memphis, joining at Ft. Smith, Arkansas. Then it dropped southwest through Texas to El Paso and turned north to the Gila Trail. It crossed modern New Mexico and Arizona, turned up the Santa Cruz River to the Gila, and pushed on to Fort Yuma. Then it headed across the Imperial Desert to Los Angeles. From there, the run followed the San Joaquin Valley to San Francisco, crossing the mountains at Pacheco Pass. The trip was 2,795 miles long. It had to be done semiweekly and completed within 25 days. The 250 vehicles to be used (many of them Celerity wagons) were left up to Butterfield, but he had to use at least four horses or mules on each hitch by contract.

Laying out the route proved a prodigious task. Stations (141) had to built and staffed with men (800) and animals (1,000 horses and 500 mules). Most of the roads existed in one form or another, but Butterfield had to erect bridges and grade some of the roads. For the privilege of operating the route, Butterfield could charge 10 cents a letter and variable rates for express items. And despite criticism as to the southern route and bets that it could not succeed, the Butterfield Stage never missed its 25-day limit. Usually the run took only 21.5 days. It remained for the Civil War to close Butterfield's operations down. The whole operation, by order of Congress, was shifted to the preferred (in the North at least) Central Overland Route.

By now Butterfield had sold out to William B. Dinsmore, who sublet the eastern division of his contract to Russell, Majors & Waddell. William H. Russell had surreptitiously committed his partners to a stage route, the Central Overland California & Pike's Peak Express Company. The whole operation had been underfunded. On top of that, probably under political pressure from California, Russell had set up the Pony Express, another underfunded endeavor, to carry mail at $2 to $10 per ounce to California from the Missouri River in ten days. Both operations had to build the usual relay stations, hire labor, and purchase animals and coaches. By 1861, Russell, Majors & Waddell defaulted on a note held by Ben Holladay, another stagecoach entrepreneur. He changed the name to Overland Stage Company (1862), then to Holladay Overland Mail and Express Company (1866), and went to work expanding the territory covered by the firm.

Holladay soon spread his services into the vast western heartland. He had Russell, Majors & Waddell's mail contract on the Central Overland Route into the Great Basin. He gained new ones for lines out of Salt Lake City to the Montana goldfields, and up the Oregon Trail to the Dalles rapids. His stages served every major mineral strike and settlement except the Washoe and California. His only major competition was the smaller Butterfield Overland Dispatch (BOD), founded by D. A. Butterfield and running on the Smoky Hill route through central Kansas to Denver. But the smaller firm could not defeat Holladay. When

Cheyenne Indian attacks proved too costly to bear, Holladay made an offer and absorbed the BOD. Holladay was the new American "Stagecoach King," or as some opponents called him, the "Napoleon of the West." But he gloried in their derision and wore it as a badge of honor. The addition of the BOD to his empire gave him a total of 3,145 miles. His nine U.S. mail contracts netted him $1.9 million between 1862 and 1868. Other income records were destroyed in the San Francisco earthquake of 1906.

Beyond Salt Lake City to the west into Nevada and California, Wells Fargo & Company held sway. Incorporated in New York State in 1852, Wells Fargo was created to take advantage of the mail and express opportunities in California's goldfields. By 1855, it had outlasted its main competitor, Adams Express, and by 1860, the firm had 147 offices in the Golden State. Soon the company extended its services over the Sierras into Nevada. As William G. Fargo had been in with John Butterfield on the Southern Overland, they also took over the run from Sacramento to Salt Lake City—Russell, Majors & Waddell's old western division. It also had controlling interest in many "independent" lines throughout California. By 1866, a collision between Wells Fargo and Holladay was looming on the horizon. Wells Fargo had already tried to get hold of the BOD, but the merger failed to come to fruition. Holladay immediately stepped in and bought the BOD, saying of Wells Fargo, "let them be damned."

Suddenly the feisty Holladay sold his interests to those he had so recently condemned verbally to the netherworld. He had taken another look at the future, and it was not rosy. The Union Pacific Railroad was moving west, soon to join with the Central Pacific Railroad in Utah. His profitable mail contracts would undoubtedly be lost to the new transportation technology. He accepted $1.5 million in cash, $300,000 in Wells Fargo stock, and a directorship in the firm. Wells Fargo was now the conqueror of the "Napoleon of the West." Holladay thought he had bargained well; Wells Fargo saw the western stage and express monopoly as a springboard to negotiate better with the railroads.

But the arrival of the rails did not put an end to stage services in the West. The trains could not go everywhere. When the Black Hills gold strike was made, no railroad was within 200 miles of Deadwood Gulch. Two lines opened, one to the southern rail connection at Yankton, the other to the northern railhead at Bismarck. Another line connected the forts to the west until the Northern Pacific Railroad put it out of business in 1882. The rails put the long stage-express routes out of business by the 1880s, but there were always smaller lines that could serve areas where the rails could not (geographically) or would not (profitably) go. It was not until after the advent of autobus services in the 1920s that stagecoaching in the West came to an end. But the new technology could not kill them off totally. Every amusement park of any appreciable size runs a stagecoach ride, a throwback to the days when the stagecoach ruled the highways and byways of the Old West.

See also Buses; Butterfield Trail; Freighting and Teamsters; Greyhound Corporation; Russell, Majors & Waddell Company; Wells Fargo & Company.

References Banning, William, and George Hugh Banning, *Six Horses* (1930); Beebe, Lucius, and Charles Clegg, *U.S. West: The Saga of Wells Fargo* (1949); Conkling, Roscoe P., and Mary P. Conkling, *The Butterfield Overland Mail* (1926); Eggenhofer, Nick, *Wagons, Mules, and Men* (1961); Erskine, Albert Russel, *History of the Studebaker Corporation* (1924); Frederick, J. V., *Ben Holliday* (1940); Holbrook, Stewart H., *Old Boston Post Road* (1962); Hunt, Elmer Munson, "Abbott Downing and the Concord Coach," *Historical New Hampshire* (November 1945) 1: 1–22; Omwake, John, *The Conestoga Six-Horse Bell Teams of Eastern Pennsylvania* (1930); Root, Frank A., and William E. Connelly, *The Overland Stage to California* (1901); Root, George A., and Russell K. Hickman, "Pike's Peak Express Companies," *Kansas Historical Quarterly* (1944) 13: 163–195, 211–242, 485–526, and *Kansas Historical Quarterly* (1945) 14: 36–92; Sharp, Paul F., "Whoop-Up Trail: International Highway on the Great Plains," *Pacific Historical Review* (1952) 21: 129–144; Winther, Oscar Osburn, *Express and Stagecoach Days in Old California* (1936); Winther, Oscar Osburn, *Via Western Express and Stagecoach* (1945).

Staggers Rail Act of 1980

The most dramatic change in railroad law since the Interstate Commerce Act, the Staggers Rail Act completely reversed prior federal policies, some of which even predated 1887. It is based on the premise that the railroads no longer constitute a monopoly of American transportation as in the late nineteenth century. Transportation, through the addition of air, barge, and truck services, had become quite competitive. Rail transport was declining under the old-time regulatory burden. Hence federal regulation was reduced to a level necessary only to balance the various types of transportation and achieve a stable market under private carrier ownership. Much of this work had been started by the regulatory agencies during the Jimmy Carter presidency. The Staggers Rail Act incorporated these administrative decisions into statute law. To help achieve these goals, carriers were allowed to reduce services and/or raise prices to make such services profitable. Regulation was only to prevent cutthroat competition or monopoly conditions. The rate cartels allowed by the Reed-Bullwinkle Act of 1948 were eliminated. Rates now are set only by the participants competing in a particular trade, and rates deemed unfair can be appealed to the Interstate Commerce Commission (ICC). Many observers think that the Staggers Rail Act did much to allow the success of Conrail and the recovery of the other components of the American rail system.

The Staggers Act held that free-market forces will aid in more efficient rail systems, lower rates, and save energy and reduce inflation. To abet the process of consolidation and abandonment, the Staggers Act set a limit on the time for protests and evaluation, now 255 days, less than the earlier Railroad Revitalization and Regulatory Reform Act of 1976. The computation of figures to justify abandonment were also changed to include capital expenses as well as cash flow. Any subsidy to maintain a local unprofitable service for community good had to include a return on investment. The liberalization of government controls over the rail industry achieved in the Staggers

Act merely continued the trend evident since the Transportation Act of 1920. The ease by which unprofitable routes can be abandoned as interpreted by the ICC under the Staggers Act has amounted to nearly total deregulation of the rail industry. When combined with the Shipping Act of 1984, which allows U.S. steamship companies to book cargoes to their final inland destinations (as opposed to between port cities only, as before), the advantage of transporting imports via container freight and intermodal transfers has made for more profits than the rail lines have seen in 100 years.

See also Airline Deregulation Act of 1978; Motor Carrier Acts; National Rail Passenger Act of 1971; Railroad Revitalization and Regulatory Reform Act of 1976; Regional Rail Reorganization Act of 1973; Transportation Acts.

References Hilton, George W., "Staggers Rail Act of 1980," in Keith L. Bryant, Jr. (ed.), *EABHB: Railroads in the Age of Regulation* (1988), 417–418; Hubbard, Freeman, *Encyclopedia of North American Railroading* (1981); Keeler, Theodore E., *Railroads, Freight and Public Policy* (1983); Orenstein, Jeffrey, *United States Railroad Policy* (1990); Winston, Clifford, et al., *The Economic Effects of Surface Freight Deregulation* (1990).

Stanford, Leland (1824–1893)

Leland Stanford was born at Watervliet, New York. His father built roads and helped lay rail for part of the future New York Central. Educated as a lawyer (and the only one of his future California partnership who had much of a formal education), Stanford moved to Wisconsin in 1848 to practice his profession. There he married Jane Lathrop. Two years later his law office burned to the ground. Disgusted, Stanford decided to go to California and look for gold. He found much more. Stanford realized that the real money was in merchandising. He sold goods to the miners, first from San Francisco, then Sacramento. He met fellow businessmen Collis P. Huntington, Charles Crocker, and Mark Hopkins, and together they got interested in railroading after talking to construction engineer Theodore P. Judah.

The Big Four (less Judah) bankrolled the western end of the first transcontinental railroad. Stanford's roll was that of politician and lobbyist. He was big, stolid, ponderous, and vain. He was governor of California (1861–1863) and a U.S. senator (1885–1893), and influenced others to contribute much money and favorable grants to what was the Central Pacific and later became the Southern Pacific. In the style of the day, he overcharged the state and federal governments for his work. Company maps, for instance, showed several nonexistent mountain ranges across the right-of-way, permitting the inflation of construction costs and an $800,000 profit to the Big Four. Stanford's personal fortune was at least $50 million. Tragically, Stanford's only son died at age 15, and he and his wife, Jane, a sort of spittin' image of the elderly Queen Victoria, spent the rest of their lives donating money in the boy's name. The most important of these was the founding of Leland Stanford, Jr., University, set up at the family ranch at Palo Alto in 1891. The university received an initial grant of $20 million immediately and a further $18 million after Stanford's death.

See also Crocker, Charles; Hopkins, Mark; Huntington, Collis Potter; Judah, Theodore D.; Southern Pacific Lines.

References Bancroft, Hubert H., *History of the Life of Leland Stanford* (1952); Butler, Dan, "Leland Stanford," in Keith L. Bryant, Jr. (ed.), *EABHB: Railroads in the Age of Regulation* (1988), 376–379; Clark, George T., *Leland Stanford* (1931); Ginger, Ray, *Age of Success* (1965); Hubbard, Freeman, *Encyclopedia of North American Railroading* (1981); Josephson, Matthew, *The Robber Barons* (1934); Lyon, Peter, *To Hell in a Day Coach* (1968); Wilson, Neill C., and Frank J. Taylor, *Southern Pacific* (1952).

Statute Labor

Statute labor is the notion that local road assessments could be paid for through labor in lieu of cash, or that there was a pure labor assessment, regardless of taxation policies. Statute labor was common in the eighteenth and nineteenth centuries, but fell out of favor as road building and maintenance became professional activities requiring some technical expertise beyond that of the ordinary citizen.

See also Roads and Highways, Colonial Times to World War I.

Reference U.S. Department of Transportation, Federal Highway Administration, *America's Highways* (1976).

Steamboats

The nineteenth-century riverboats were of a varying genre. Each craft was a bit unique. There were two basic types, stern-wheelers and side-wheelers. The stern-wheelers came about initially to get around Robert Fulton's licensing requirements—his were side-wheelers. But the big stern paddle wheel weighed several tons and set up enormous stresses that side-wheelers avoided, even with two heavy wheels mounted amidships. Hence, most large boats in the 1830s were side-wheelers. In addition, a stern-wheeler had less maneuverability. Only one wheel meant that the pilot had to use the current to throw the boat's nose around objects the rudder could not avoid. The side-wheeler could back one engine and forward the other and turn "on a dime." But the stern-wheelers were protected against floating objects fouling the wheel by the superstructure and keel line (what little there was of it). With the stress problems largely solved by the 1840s, stern-wheelers competed with side-wheelers favorably thereafter, especially as they could run in shallower streams where they could raise and lower their wheels on a winch system to clear obstacles and shallows. Besides, they were cheaper to build and could use more of the available deck space for cargo. The little stern-wheelers dominated the trade on fickle western rivers like the Missouri, the Colorado, and those that drained into the Pacific Ocean.

Because the western rivers ran shallow especially in the late summer dry seasons, the steamboat drew very little draft; indeed, it was essentially flat bottomed. Hence any weight placed on the slab warped and rolled it, especially on the extremities fore and aft.

This warping was called "hogging." The designers kept the bottom flat by a series of braces and cables known as "hog chains." The bows and stern had a tendency to sink and the center to rise, hence "hogback," and by hooking a chain on or near the sinking areas and running the line over a stout wood spar brace set at the hump area, the deck slab could be straightened by pushing on the high spots and pulling the low ones. The tension could be adjusted through a series of turnbuckles on each line. The hogging took place laterally also, so that transverse cross-chains and braces were set up to counter this. Finally, any load on the deck, such as the superstructure above it, cargo, boilers, the paddle wheel(s), and engines, had their own stresses that in effect made the deck look like a piece of paper waving in a wind without the steadying of the hog chains and braces. If a boat went aground, the braces and chains could be readjusted to raise or hog (arch) the grounded area and the craft refloated and rehogged. It was a rather ingenious system.

Cargo was carried on the main deck, which was usually open with the machinery and boilers often showing or hidden in little houses of their own. This meant that if the boat ever went under water for any reason, a boiler explosion and scalding steam sprays would result. And as engine steam pressures increased over the years, such explosions became more spectacular and deadly. It was not uncommon to actually see the deck undulate an inch or so per engine stroke. If a part broke during operation the boat would "run through herself," scattering broken iron everywhere. Yet the engines were the strongest and most durable part of the ship. Old engines were taken from wrecked, sunken, or phased-out boats and put in newer craft, sometimes several times during their lives.

Samuel Morey, a Connecticut Yankee, invented the paddle wheel used on American rivers. Mounted on a heavy iron shaft, the arms were bolted to a shaft flange and flared like the spokes in a wagon wheel. The wheel was flanked on the outside rim by flat board paddles. Americans eschewed

European experiments like using buckets instead of paddles or feathering the paddle in a slight arc. "If it ain't broke, don't fix it," was a riverboat watchword.

Boilers were horizontally placed in a bank across the front of the main deck to counter the weight of the engine and paddle wheel, and could number as many as eight. They faced forward so that the motion of the boat increased the draft. The shifting of the deck caused gradual cracking of the original cast-iron boiler heads, and they sometimes blew off. The use of steel and more flexible mounting alleviated the problem. Although boilers had safety valves, engineers usually ignored gauges and valves (they were usually corroded and frozen or unreadable anyway) and went by the sound of the exhaust and the "feel" of the poppet valves, until the law required more accurate equipment monitoring in 1852. The quality of river water varied—clear upstream, dirty and muddy downstream—so the boilers had to be cleared of mud buildup on a regular basis.

The smoke stacks extended as much as 30 feet above the boilers, but they increased decade by decade until 90 feet became the norm by the 1850s. The increased height was believed to assist the "draw" of smoke and back pressure out of the boilers, but it was pretty cocky, too. The stacks were braced apart by fancy metal medallions and designed wrought iron that identified the ship or her owner. As bridging the rivers became more common, the stacks were hinged so they could be folded in half to clear any obstacle. Needless to say, pollution of the air and water with ash and trash were standard in those days before environmental concerns.

During cotton season, the bales were stacked on the main deck and extended up the sides of the boat nearly as high as the pilothouse. With such flammable cargoes commonplace, riverboat travel could be dangerous. In the pre–Civil War era, accidents generally fell into four categories: collision (no riverboat captain worth his mettle ever got out of the way of an inferior, especially a raftsman) accounted for 4.5 percent

of accidents; fire (it took just one spark from an open boiler into a load of cotton stacked to the pilothouse to finish a boat by destroying its control ropes, causing the introduction of chains in 1841), 17 percent; explosion (cast-iron boilers and machinery have a tendency to weaken and wear as they are heated and cooled incessantly), 21 percent; and snags and other obstructions (the channel changed each trip and at night the telltale white-water signs of underwater trouble were hard to see, putting a premium on a pilot who "knew" the river), 57.5 percent.

Unlike the mighty Mississippi and Ohio, the Missouri was a shallow, treacherous stream that brought out the best in a pilot. The channel changed each trip, sandbars abounded, and the river was full of floating obstacles—"freaks" or ice chunks in spring, and "sawyers" or bobbing, uprooted tree trunks that hovered just below the waterline the rest of the year. Here, stern-wheelers were a necessity. A side-wheeler would be ripped up in a minute by floating junk wood. Missouri riverboats were of such a shallow draft as to be said to "run on heavy dew" or the suds from a keg of beer. They had to be. It took seven years to learn enough of the river to open up the run from Fort Union to Fort Benton, the last post that could be reached by water. The traffic would not have made it at all were it not for the lure of Montana gold.

The most daring feat of a Missouri steamboat captain came during the 1876 Sioux War when Grant Marsh piloted the *Far West* up the Yellowstone and the Big Horn Rivers to the mouth of the Little Big Horn, freighting supplies for General George Armstrong Custer's Seventh Cavalry. The river's width was about the length of the craft, and it was impossible to turn around. Marsh's greatest contribution came when he took the casualties from the Custer fight back downriver to Fort Abraham Lincoln near Bismarck in five days. Not bad for nearly 1,000 miles of extremely dangerous river navigation, running day and night. He also brought the first news of the massacre, stories that kept the telegraph operator working at his key 22 hours straight. Like the Upper Mississippi, the Missouri could only rarely be negotiated in winter.

Regardless of the time of year, no one on any river ever turned back at the cry "man overboard." Besides, unless the victim dove for bottom immediately upon hitting the water, the paddle wheel chewed the unfortunate up. On the Missouri, anyone overboard probably stuck in the mud. Captains claimed that the Missouri River "never gave up its victims." The Ohio and Mississippi usually gave them up dead, but at least there was a bottom to dive to. One of the worst disasters in riverboat history came at a mooring dock. In St. Louis in 1849, an onshore fire hit the docks and cut loose the mooring ropes of several burning steamers, which were blown into others on down the line until 23 boats burned. But nothing beat the *Sultana* disaster. Returning 2,400 Union soldiers, many of whom were wounded or just released from prisoner-of-war camps, the *Sultana* blew her whole battery of boilers just above Memphis and sank. Because of wartime destruction of the levees, the river was so wide that rescue was impossible. Nearly 1,500 died, more than were lost in the *Titanic* disaster a half century later, their bodies caught up in trees and not discovered until the river dropped out of flood stage.

Needless to say, passenger travel on the low deck was dangerous, cheap, dirty, noisy, low class, and exposed to the weather. Real passenger accommodations were on the upper decks. The boiler deck had the cabins, generally set up for berthing two persons. The whole boiler deck was surrounded by a walkway known as the "guard," onto which transom windows and doors opened. Amidships of the cabin was the main saloon. Usually riverboats had just one deck with cabins, but it was possible to stack more cabin decks and create quite an imposing structure, and a saloon with passageways looking down on the main boiler deck floor. Every riverboat was known for the luxury of the decor of its saloon. Entertainment, dining, drinking, and gambling were mainstays of the saloon. Some vessels became "temperance" boats and preached reform, but most did not.

On top of the staterooms was the hurricane deck. The main superstructure poked through it amidships with transom skylights for the main saloon, topped by the skylight roof. On top of the skylight was a smaller set of staterooms for the crew, called the "texas." Atop the texas was the pilothouse, where the captain and the pilot supervised the ship's running. Communication between the pilothouse and the main deck mechanical area was through a set of bells and gongs. Rung in varying combinations, the captain could tell the engineer what speed and direction he wanted. And, as revealed in Mark Twain's famous novel, *The Adventures of Tom Sawyer*, all boys in every river town along the way knew these signals by heart as a matter of pride and dreamed of being riverboat pilots so they could actually ring them. The cry "steamboat's acomin'" made the day in many a small town in nineteenth-century middle America.

The riverboats ran on cordwood until the 1880s when coal came into use. A boat had to "wood up" twice a day, and the need caused the establishment of wood yards on the banks. Farmers often supplemented their incomes by leaving unmanned stacks of cordwood along the banks with a notice to leave payment. On an upstream haul, it was possible to pull a flatboat of wood alongside the riverboat and resupply on the move. Then the broadhorn was cut loose to drift back to the wood yard and load up again. This could not be done on downstream trips as the flatboat would be unable to move upriver. Care had to be taken to unload from the bow of the wood hauler, lest the weight of the cargo pull her head under and sink her.

Riverboats usually operated between two ports in a territory known as a "trade." They could be pretty exclusive about their trade, too. Unethical methods were common in luring passengers and cargo aboard before the competition got them. Touts, porters who grabbed luggage, exaggerated promises of safety (no boilers on this ship so we have no explosion risk), luxurious accommodations, placards, undercutting of prices, and any lie a sucker might accept were used to solicit customers. Downstream rates generally were about half of upstream prices. Carriage often added to the competition—one wished to travel with the least odoriferous cargo possible. To provide regular service and to stifle the competition, captains and owners formed pools and offered packet service. But mergers, liquidations, and breakups kept the public guessing. In their day, reliable packet lines were as well known as railroads and airlines later. The Cincinnati & Pittsburgh, the Eagle Line, the St. Louis & St. Joseph, the White Collar Line, the Five Day Line (the time between St. Louis and La Salle, Illinois), and the St. Louis & New Orleans were among some of the better thought of.

Not until after the Civil War did the riverboats reach their epitome in style. They truly became floating palaces—one even had a one-piece woven Belgian carpet for its saloon, which was the length of a football field. These pleasure boats cruised all of the major rivers, east or west. The *Mary Powell* was considered the supreme beauty in river vessels on the Hudson. It is said that cadets stood in formation at West Point in response to the *Mary Powell*'s bell—it was more accurate than Academy clocks. On the Mississippi, the *J. M. White* was just as grand. On her maiden voyage, the *White* broke all records from Pittsburgh to New Orleans, only to see them fall before the relentless surge of the *Natchez* in 1869, the same *Natchez* that was beaten by the *Robert E. Lee* the following year. The *White* had paneling and ceilings made of polished cherry wood, not the usual white and gold paint of other boats. Missouri boats usually were a little less gaudy, but their staterooms and dining halls were considered the last outposts of high-class civilization in the West.

These were the tourist places of the rich in their day, sort of floating Miami Beaches or Las Vegases, a mystique that modern Americans try to re-create in the gambling riverboats of today. To own a steamboat in the 1870s was the status symbol of the decade, and many rich "robber barons" did. Those who could not afford one would even print up catalogues with a make-believe boat on the cover in the firm's trade name

just to impress customers. The last great river event in the West was the New Orleans Cotton Exposition of 1884, when the levee was lined with boats as before the Civil War. The Hudson River excursion boats actually grew in size and magnificence until put out of existence by the new automobile turnpikes in the 1930s. Nowadays, there has been a revival of sorts in riverboats, many of them merely floating gambling dens. But the most noted example of a real steamboat is the *Delta Queen*, which, with her sisters, offers excursions of varying lengths for the traveler who wishes to step back 150 years to a time when every boat on the river was a queen held in awe by anyone who wished for the life of glamour the steamboat offered as she passed by.

See also Early Steamboats; Fulton, Robert; Great Lakes Freighters; Intracoastal Waterway; Shreve, Henry Miller; Steamboats at War.

References Bill, Fred A., "Early Steamboating on the Red River [of the North]," *North Dakota Historical Quarterly* (1942) 9: 69–85; Chittenden, Hiram M., *History of Early Steamboat Navigation on the Missouri River* (1903); Donovan, Frank, *River Boats of America* (1966); Havighurst, Walter, *Voices on the River* (1964); Hunter, Louis C., *Steamboats on the Western Rivers* (1949); Lane, Carl D., *American Paddle Steamboats* (1943); Leavitt, Francis H., "Steam Navigation on the Colorado River," *California Historical Society Quarterly* (1943) 23: 1–19, 151–174; MacMullen, Jerry, *Paddle-Wheel Days in California* (1944); Mills, Randall V., *Stern-Wheelers Up Columbia* (1947); Petersen, William J., *Steamboating on the Upper Mississippi* (1937); Petersen, William J., "Steamboating on the Missouri River," *Iowa Journal of History* (1955) 53: 97–120; Taylor, George Rogers, *The Transportation Revolution* (1951); Watson, Ken, *Paddle Steamers* (1985); Wright, Muriel H., "Early Navigation and Commerce along the Arkansas and Red Rivers in Oklahoma," *Chronicles of Oklahoma* (1930) 8: 65–88.

Steamboats at War (1861–1865)

Nothing stretched the development and use of riverboats more than the American Civil War. Confederate Secretary of the Navy Stephen Mallory seemed to have had little understanding of river fighting, and, as with the deep sea navy, the South was short of ships and matériel on the rivers. Most of the riverboats were Northern owned and built. But Mallory emphasized big, heavy, slow ironclads of the CSS *Virginia* class, which

A steamboat (center) delivers supplies on the James River in this undated photograph. Riverboats in the West gave the Union a considerable advantage over the Confederates during the Civil War.

were oceangoing vessels of a deep draft. In the West, most of these types were captured or destroyed before engaging the Yankees. The one exception was the CSS *Arkansas*, which wreaked havoc on the Mississippi before engine failure caused her destruction by her own crew at Baton Rouge.

It was in the West that riverboats gave the North its decisive momentum to win the war. The Northern river fleet was the invention of James B. Eads. He had tried to interest the Union government in a submarine, only to be turned down (which left the field to the Confederate CSS *Hunley* at Charleston). But he did gain a contract to build seven river ironclads. These were true riverboats—shallow in draft, armored at the front and opposite the engines, and armed with three heavy cannon pointed ahead (they were supposed to fight head-on) and six lighter guns at the sides and rear. Named

St. Louis, Carondelet, Cincinnati, Louisville, Mound City, Cairo, and *Pittsburgh,* they were called "pook turtles" because of the odd shape of their armored compartments. He also built two others of even greater size, the *Benton* and the *Essex*.

Meanwhile, Commodore John Rogers bought three old river steamers and stripped them to the decks. He rebuilt them with heavy oak timbers, 5 inches thick. Armed with an assortment of cannon, Rogers' boats, the *Lexington,* the *Tyler,* and the *Conestoga,* and the nine Eads boats became the Union river navy. Later they would be joined by a series of river rams, ships designed to smash in the sides of enemy vessels. Other than the navy crew that sailed them, all of these boats' guns were manned by infantry volunteers. They were also under army control until 1863.

River gunboats subdued Island No. 10

and defeated the Confederate river fleet at Memphis. Union General U. S. Grant took Forts Henry and Donelson by relying on armored riverboats. The ships alone, under Flag Officer Andrew Foote, caused Fort Henry to surrender. But Fort Donelson was on a bluff, and the plunging fire came in over the armor and cost Foote numerous casualties. Hereafter, the navy learned to avoid such forts unless active infantry cooperation was available. It was Foote's *Lexington* and *Tyler* that saved Grant's army from total defeat at Shiloh by taking the attacking Confederate line in the flank on the first day. Grant employed the same basic strategy in taking Vicksburg, as did his subordinates in capturing Fort Hindman on the Arkansas River. Without the riverboats to run by Vicksburg, Grant's army could never have crossed the Mississippi and taken the city from the rear.

Union supplies and troops, as well as the casualties of war, moved by river. The river gave the North an advantage over the much-heralded use of railroads. The latter were liable to interdiction and destruction by Confederate cavalry, while the rivers were not. The Union Red River Campaign relied on riverboat support, and the whole fleet came within a hair of being lost when the army was defeated at Mansfield and the Red River proved too shallow to let the fleet maneuver in retreat. Only by building a series of dams at Alexandria were the Federals able to raise the river enough to let the fleet pass. Although new ironclads were developed, Union river might relied mainly on plating existing riverboats and arming them with guns. These steamboats, called "thin-clads," were what gave the Federals their punch in the western theater, and the South was conquered by its rivers.

See also Eads, James B.; Steamboats.

References Gibbons, Tony, *Warships and Naval Battles of the U.S. Civil War* (1989); Milligan, John D., *Gunboats Down the Mississippi* (1965); Reed, Rowena, *Combined Operations in the Civil War* (1978).

Steamboats, Racing

One of the inevitable adjuncts of riverboat travel was steamboat racing. It did not take

much to get a couple of captains to contest for the next port or a certain landmark, cheered on by crew and passengers alike, bets being taken right and left. Besides, the first boat to the landing got the cream of passengers and carriage. The most famous race of all was between Captain J. W. Cannon of the *Robert E. Lee* and Captain T. P. Leathers of the *Natchez*. Although both denied they were racing, the word got out. They left the levee at New Orleans four minutes apart on 30 June 1870, and pounded north upriver for St. Louis. By the time they reached Memphis, the *Lee* was one hour ahead. Fog settled in at Cairo, slowing both ships. Most controversial, however, was the *Lee*'s interception of 100 tons of pine knots from a neighboring steamer for a midstream refueling. Worse, the *Natchez* had engine trouble and was laid up for several hours. The *Lee* pulled into St. Louis just before noon on 4 July, making the run in 3 days, 18 hours, and 30 minutes. When Leathers arrived 6 hours later, he figured that he actually beat the *Lee* by 12 minutes, measuring actual water time. Average speed was a sensational 15 miles per hour. The race created a stir internationally and drove the newspapers, and their reading public, wild. It has remained a popular historic event ever since.

See also Steamboats.

References Donovan, Frank, *River Boats of America* (1966); Watson, Ken, *Paddle Steamers* (1985).

Stephenson et al. v. Binford 287 US 251 (1932)

Such was the import of the *Frost et al. v. Railroad Commission of the State of California* (1926) and *Smith v. Cahoon* (1931) decisions of the U.S. Supreme Court, which permitted states to regulate common and contract carriers in the public interest, that in another statute the Texas legislature instructed its Railroad Commission (the common carrier regulating agency for trucks also) to establish rules and regulations not only for common carriers but for contract carriers, too. The state instructed that contract rates were not to be lower than those charged by common carriers by road or rail. The contract truckers sued, maintaining that the state had set up a legal fiction and regulated both forms of carriage similarly, not separately.

The Court, in *Stephenson et al. v. Binford*, endorsed the state's action and expanded the regulatory principle. The Court stated that Texas did have a traffic problem brought on by expanded highway building and its overutilization by heretofore unregulated contract truckers, which presented an unsafe condition for all motorists. If Texas wished to assure highway safety by regulating business through rate controls and protecting all common carriers, it was a proper application of state prerogatives. Again, the Court refused to look beyond the law and into its effect—protecting common carriers and their higher rates as a public interest, which contract truckers argued was unfair. In effect, the Court ruled that states could act in circumstances other than the public good to regulate a transportation or any other industry, even going so far as to create a public interest by legislative fiat in the absence of federal controls. This caused the truckers to push for a federal law that would have a unifying effect on the regulations affecting them, and resulted in the Motor Carrier Act of 1935.

See also Motor Carrier Acts, Motor Carrier Act of 1935; *Nebbia v. New York*; *Sproles et al. v. Binford*.

Reference Childs, William R., *Trucking and the Public Interest* (1985).

Stevens, John F. (1853–1943)

From West Gardiner, Maine, John F. Stevens won fame as the builder of railroads, especially the Great Northern route across the northern United States. In the late 1880s, Stevens explored the Rockies and the Cascades, looking for passes through which the rails might go. A big man who liked to smoke large cigars, Stevens was a blunt talker who liked to stomp mud on the carpets of big shots who irked him. His crossing the Rocky Mountains at Marias Pass and the Cascades at Stevens Pass by the Cascade Tunnel (later lengthened and electrified so that the engine crews would not suffocate from the smoke of steamers) for James Hill's

railroad led President Theodore Roosevelt to make him chief engineer of the Panama Canal in 1904. Much of the canal work was assisted by a massive railroad that hauled tons of earth out of the mountain cuts and redeposited it in an earthen dam 1.5 miles long and .5 miles wide at its base across the Chagres River. But Stevens found that the success of the canal's construction should be predicated on improved health conditions, and he set about, along with Dr. William C. Gorgas, to improve sanitary conditions on the isthmus.

Stevens helped develop the basic American approach to the canal, eschewing the French concept of a sea-level ditch in favor of one with two sets of massive locks and mountain cuts constantly filled by the dammed-up Chagres River. By 1907, Stevens had had his fill of canal politics and resigned his position, an act that enraged President Roosevelt, who thought it most unpatriotic. Stevens went back to railroads, and President Woodrow Wilson sent him and other American engineers to assist Alexander Kerensky's republican regime continue the Russian war effort after the fall of Czar Nicholas II. When the Bolsheviks toppled Kerensky, Stevens stayed on to keep the Trans-Siberian Railroad running, helping to evacuate the Czech Corps (40,000 prisoners of war once enlisted in the Czar's cause but now trapped behind the lines by the revolution) and to prevent Japanese takeover of the Chinese eastern branch of the rails. After his return to the United States in 1922, Stevens received many honors and awards, and wrote of his experiences. He died at his home in Southern Pines, North Carolina, in 1943. His age at his death (90 years) might say something wise about his not staying in the isthmus years earlier.

See also Great Northern Railroad; Panama Canal.

Reference Bachman, Ben, "Until the Thunder Dies," *Trains* (November 1994) 54: 48–55.

Stevens, John, Jr. (1749–1838)

A lawyer by education, John Stevens was born in New York City. He witnessed the imperfect steamboat built at Philadelphia by

John Fitch in 1787, and immediately turned to steam propulsion and experimented with it for the next 30 years. It was a difficult undertaking, especially as the patrician Stevens proved incapable in using his hands and tools. He planned a steamboat and petitioned New York State for exclusive rights to navigate the Hudson River, but his plan was deemed unworkable and the plea denied, especially in the light of Stevens' earlier support for John Fitch, who believed that all steamboats should have to pay him a fee as he was there first. Stevens next petitioned Congress in 1790 for protection of American inventors, which resulted in the patent system. In 1806, he built a screw propeller and ran a small open boat with it in combination with a steam engine. This success led to the full-sized *Phoenix*, which he perfected at his Hoboken estate a short time after Fulton's *Clermont*.

As Fulton and Stevens' brother-in-law, Robert Livingston, already had a monopoly on the Hudson, Stevens ran his vessels on the Delaware and the Connecticut Rivers. The trip there with the *Phoenix* marked the first ocean voyage powered by steam, a trip almost not completed because of intervening storms. Stevens later perfected a steam ferry that ran between Hoboken and New York City. Turning from steamboats to another topic in 1812, Stevens published a work that proposed government sponsorship of railroads. But it took until 1826 before he actually built such a locomotive himself, the first to run on a track in the United States.

See also Early Steamboats; Evans, Oliver; Fitch, John; Fulton, Robert; Shreve, Henry Miller; Steamboats; Symington, William.

References Donovan, Frank, *River Boats of America* (1966); Flexner, James Thomas, *Steamboats Come True* (1944).

Stillwell, Arthur Edward (1859–1928)

Born in Rochester, New York, Arthur E. Stillwell claimed to have built more miles of railroad than any other man. He first got his start by printing rail schedules, but soon moved to Kansas City, where he pledged to "save Midwestern farmers from unjust freight rates." He first got interested in belt switching (between the various railroads and the industries around town), and then began the construction of the Kansas City, Pittsburg (Kansas) & Gulf railway south into Oklahoma, Arkansas, Texas, and Louisiana. In 1895, Stillwell's outfit laid one-fourth of all rail put down in the United States that year. Although he had backing from George Pullman (of sleeping-car fame), Stillwell went bankrupt and had to sell out, his railroad changing its name to the Kansas City Southern. He is remembered for Port Arthur, Texas, which was named after him and whose oil boom came too late to save his finances.

But the financial setback only drove Stillwell on to new schemes. He planned and began to build the Kansas City, Mexico & Orient from its namesake to Topolobampo, Mexico, on the Gulf of California. Stillwell bragged that his new road would bring Kansas City 400 miles closer to the Pacific and 1,600 miles closer to Central America than San Francisco. But again he ran out of money and luck—Mexico had a revolution in 1910. In 1925, the Santa Fe bought out the 735 miles of track in the United States, and the Mexican government nationalized its 325 miles of rail after its purchase from the Santa Fe by a local *hacendado* (rancher). Stillwell died shortly afterward.

See also Missouri-Kansas-Texas Railroad; Railroads from Appomattox to Deregulation; Rock Island Lines; St. Louis–San Francisco Railway.

References Bryant, Keith L., Jr., *Arthur Edward Stillwell* (1971); Bryant, Keith L., Jr., "Arthur Edward Stillwell," in Keith L. Bryant, Jr. (ed.), *EABHB: Railroads in the Age of Regulation* (1988), 422–424; Hubbard, Freeman, *Encyclopedia of North American Railroading* (1981).

Stone, Roy (?–1901)

Brigadier General Roy Stone was the first federal road administrator as head of the Office of Road Inquiry (ORI) in the 1890s. Although from New York, he was a veteran of the crack Pennsylvania Reserves during the Civil War. Later a brigade commander, he was severely wounded on the first day of the Battle of Gettysburg. He innovated many of the ORI's earlier programs until he returned to military service for the Spanish-American War in 1898. After the war, he returned to civilian life as a member of New York's Good Roads Movement.

See also Office of Road Inquiry; Roads and Highways, Colonial Times to World War I.

Reference U.S. Department of Transportation, Federal Highway Administration, *America's Highways* (1976).

Studebaker

The family name of a lineage of blacksmiths and wagon builders who went into motor cars and trucks, the Studebakers came originally from Solingen, the German town noted for its cutlery. The family landed in Pennsylvania, and one of the boys moved from Gettysburg to Ashland County, Ohio. There he raised five sons, Henry (1826–1895), Clement (1831–1901), John Mohler (1833–1917), Peter E. (1836–1897), and Jacob F. (1844–1887). Henry and Clem soon grew up and left the family homestead for South Bend, Indiana, where they established a small blacksmith shop. Clem seems to have done most of the business, and Henry helped out and farmed. In 1852, they began building wagons. Henry and Clem were joined by the other brothers in their labor. John Mohler came, but decided to see the California goldfields. He traveled to Hangtown by wagon train, a five-month journey. There he wisely decided to take up the smithy trade, it being more certain to return a profit than gold. Years later, he would hire the man who employed him back in Indiana.

While John was in California, a fourth brother, Peter, came out to South Bend. There he drew up a contract to sell all the vehicles his brothers made. Peter moved to Missouri to be at the head of the many western trails. At first, the wagon shop turned out mostly wagon wheels, finely made, with an inward dish in the spokes that made it a difficult piece to build, but one that carried greater loads. The foundry profited greatly outfitting the Union army during the Civil War. In 1868 the firm was reorganized and Jacob was brought in as a roving sales representative. Now the whole family was in the business together. By 1874, sales were close to $1 million annually, and the Studebaker name was one renowned for its quality wagons and parts. Then a disastrous fire laid waste to the whole plant, but it was rebuilt bigger than before. But a new problem loomed—the new horseless carriage. At first, the conservative Studebakers scoffed at the new vehicle, but Clem, Jr., and Fred Fish, a son-in-law, became enthusiastic over the new invention. They brought the old wagon men into the twentieth century, horseless.

Many old Studebaker autos had quite a design flair, then attributed to French influence, and were among some of the first enclosed motorcars built in the United States. But their early trucks reflected their great wagon business—they were little but wagons with modifications and an engine. In 1910 Studebaker reaffirmed its commitment to the new automobile by acquiring the small-car builder, Everitt-Metzger-Flanders and, in 1911, changed the name of both companies to the Studebaker Corporation. All of the stock was family owned except for 10 percent in the possession of the House of Morgan. Studebaker did quite well to the Great Depression. It put out in-line four-, six-, and eight-cylinder models known for style, innovation, safety, and speed. In fact, it was one of only two American auto companies to improve sales during the post–World War I recession (the other being Ford). They flirted with electric autos and trucks, but soon turned their whole attention to gas-powered vehicles. In 1920, they phased out all of their horse-drawn lines.

In 1828 Studebaker took over the faltering Pierce-Arrow Company. When the Great Depression struck, Studebaker continued to pay stock dividends, even in the face of falling sales. Studebaker tried to absorb the White Truck Company, but failed when minority stockholders at White balked at the idea. The National Bank Moratorium of 1933 pushed the failing company into bankruptcy. There simply was no cash to borrow anywhere. It took Studebaker two years to raise the funds to buy the firm back. During World War II, Studebaker got back on its feet by producing trucks and airplane engines.

After the Allied victory, the company returned to domestic truck and car manufacture. It was among the first companies to get vehicles and customers together in the showroom, and became known for radical design. The first step was the "bullet nose" model that many compared to an airplane without a propeller—indeed, one enterprising purchaser added that item on his own! Studebaker also went into the futuristic Avanti design, an Italian-inspired sports model with the speed of a racer, and the Hawk—an American-designed vehicle with the Avanti engine. As the decade of the fifties moved along, however, Studebaker had the same problems as most independents—it was operated on too small a scale to survive, even with its massive truck line. This desperation forced the company to follow American Motors into the small-car field, the Studebaker contribution being the 1958 Lark. Like its independent competitor, Studebaker did well at first, pushed along by the 1958 recession. But even a merger with luxury-car maker Packard could not save the Studebaker line. In 1966, it closed its doors forever. Throughout 110 years, the Studebaker Company stayed true to their motto: Work hard, be honest, waste nothing, and "always give your customer more than you promise, but not too much or you will go broke." It is a credo that one might do well to remember today.

See also Automobiles from Domestics to Imports; Automobiles in American Society; Freighting and Teamsters; Stagecoaches and Other Horse-Drawn Conveyances.

References Cannon, William A., and Fred K. Fox, *Studebaker* (1981); Corle, Edwin, *John Studebaker, An American Dream* (1948); Critchlow, Donald T., "Studebaker Corporation," in George S. May (ed.), *EABHB: The Automobile Industry* (1989), 434–437; Erskine, Albert R., *History of the Studebaker Corporation* (1924); Hendry, Maurice D., "Studebaker: One Can Do a Lot of Remembering in South Bend," *Automobile Quarterly* (1972) 10: 228–257; Longstreet, Stephen A., *A Century on Wheels: The Story of Studebaker* (1952); Motor Vehicle Manufacturers Association of the United States, *Automobiles of America* (1974).

Surface Transportation Assistance Acts

As the United States freeway system neared completion and the size and speed of commercial vehicles increased, Congress moved to standardize the weights, widths, and lengths to override existing individual state highway laws to promote the interstate transfer of goods in the Surface Transportation Assistance Acts.

SURFACE TRANSPORTATION ASSISTANCE ACT OF 1978

Because of the increased weights allowed in the Federal-Aid Highway Amendments of 1975, some regulators and members of Congress became concerned with the increased wear and tear on the interstate highway system. Congress feared that some states were not fully enforcing the 1975 weight limits. The new measure in 1978 provided that the federal government withhold 10 percent of a state's portion of highway assistance funds should the state fail to comply with federal limits. Further, the act appropriated money for the purchase of highway scales to help the states comply with the mandate to check truck weights. The Federal Highway Administration reported that the penalty was way too low to be of much use against states that ignored federal guidelines. In response, the Congress ordered the Department of Transportation to investigate the issue of truck sizes and weights.

SURFACE TRANSPORTATION ASSISTANCE ACT OF 1982

Despite the new federal regulations, Montana and six Mississippi Valley states (Indiana, Illinois, Missouri, Arkansas, Tennessee, and Mississippi) retained lower limits. As the Mississippi Valley states were contiguous, they became known as the "barrier states" because a trucker had to limit his cross-country operations to their regulations or run illegally and hope not to be caught. Studies at the Department of Transportation revealed that the wear to highways would be more than offset by the increased revenues from expanded truck operations should the weights be raised uniformly throughout the nation.

In 1982, Congress required that all states come on line with the same federally mandated weight and size regulations. These included single-axle weights of 20,000 pounds, tandem-axle weights of 34,000 pounds, and gross vehicle weights of 80,000 pounds, as set forth in the Federal-Aid Highway Amendments of 1975. All states have regulations and procedures for exceeding these numbers, generally through obtaining a special permit. Vehicle width can be limited to 102 inches. Vehicle length can be limited to 48-foot single trailers and 28 feet for one trailer of a tandem rig, but overall length, including the tractor, cannot be limited. Truckers have also been using "longer combination vehicles" (LCVs) composed of two or three trailers that spread the load over more axles and allow more legal weight. Western states particularly have many kinds of LCVs that are prohibited in the heavier-trafficked East: Rocky Mountain Doubles consisting of a tractor and two trailers—one 45 to 48 feet in length, the other 27 to 28.5 feet in length—are permitted in 13 states; Turnpike Doubles consisting of a tractor and two trailers—each up to 48 feet long—are permitted in 9 states; and Triples consisting of a tractor and three 27 to 28.5 foot trailers are permitted in 10 states. And no matter what its local highway rules, each state must allow terminal access for trucks coming off the federal freeways.

See also Eastman, Joseph B.; Federal-Aid Highway Acts, Federal-Aid Highway Act of 1956, Federal-Aid Highway Act of 1976; Federal-Aid Highway Amendments of 1975; Motor Carrier Acts, Motor Carrier Act of 1935; NRA Trucking Codes; Transportation Acts, Transportation Act of 1920, Carrier Transportation Act of 1940; Trucking.

References Cheng, Philip C., *Accounting and Financing for Motor Carriers* (1984); Transportation Research Council, *Twin Trailer Trucks* (1986); Transportation Research Council, *Truck Weight Limits* (1990).

Symington, William (1763–1831)

Born in Leadhills, England, William Symington was educated at the Universities of Edinburgh and Glasgow for the ministry. He tired of that field and turned to civil engineering. He took out a patent for an improved steam engine in 1787 and used it to power a steam Brougham. Under the sponsorship of businessman Patrick Miller, Symington floated a steam skiff for Miller's private pond that outshone all efforts to date. But Miller quit him in disgust, probably operating under too high standards of success or dismissing the invention as a mere toy, and Symington did not seek other backers. In 1802, Lord Dundas, still intrigued by the earlier boat, financed Symington's new *Charlotte Dundas*, a sleek, full-sized vessel with an enclosed stern wheel that could pull a pair of barges, which British writers insist to this day was the completion of the invention of the steamboat, rather than American Robert Fulton's version. He gained the patronage of the Duke of Bridgewater, but the duke's death in 1803, and Dundas' fear that the boat would destroy river banks, left Symington broke and without sponsors. He wandered penniless, finally dying in abject poverty.

See also Early Steamboats; Evans, Oliver; Fitch, John; Fulton, Robert; Shreve, Henry Miller; Steamboats.

Reference Flexner, James T., *Steamboats Come True* (1944).

Telegraph

Having taken over the bankrupt Russell, Majors & Waddell Company, Ben Holladay and the Overland Mail were finding that the Pony Express was a drain on their firm's profits, just as it had been for their predecessor's. Under terms of their government contract, Overland Mail was compelled to reduce the charges on mail to $1 a half ounce. Holladay solved this drop in income by making Pony Express envelopes and stamps available at more places. The volume kept up the income—something that Russell, Majors & Waddell ought to have considered. But the final relief came from an entirely different source—the stringing of the transcontinental telegraph line.

Samuel F. B. Morse invented the practical wire telegraph in 1837. The concept was not new. Ancient civilizations, including Native Americans, had used telegraphic signals sent by mirrors or smoke. By 1800, Italian inventors had developed the battery, making available a reliable source of electricity for sending impulses over a pair of wires. By the 1830s, English inventors had developed the electromagnet, which Morse used to make the click by turning the current on and off in a rhythmic fashion called "dots and dashes." His Morse Code converted these into a readable signal that anyone conversant with the system could use. Soon the concept had spread throughout the eastern United States.

At first, the idea of the telegraph line to California was considered impractical. The potential contractors believed the Plains Indians would strip the wire down. Also, the lack of trees meant that poles had to be hauled out by wagon. But the impending Civil War pushed communication with the Pacific Coast to an emergency status. Edward Creighton, a telegraph contractor with construction experience in Maryland, Pennsylvania, and Ohio, decided to take the chance. He organized a company at his own expense (always a good way to impress the government) and inspected the route. He started at Omaha and headed straight west to the Central Overland Route. Then he followed the Pony Express route to Sacramento, the shortest of all of the several branches that made up the California Trail. Creighton made notes on all geographical

The Overland Pony Express rides by telegraph line construction in Salt Lake City, Utah. This wood engraving appeared in Harper's Weekly *2 November 1867.*

aspects of the run—including where wood might be found. He decided that 20 feet might be high enough for the wire and that cottonwoods might do for the poles in a pinch.

The Pony Express relay stations gave Creighton safe bases from which he could go out and make his inspections. This was especially valuable in Nevada, where the Paiutes were attacking small parties like his regularly. Creighton found that settlement was spreading rapidly onto the Great Plains, and the Mormons had moved all over the Great Basin. But for the military line between Fort Leavenworth and Fort Kearny, no rapid communication beyond the horse existed. Creighton then organized the Overland Telegraph Company in California and the Pacific Telegraph Company in Nebraska. He used equipment and manpower from the old Russell, Majors & Waddell firm, including Ben Ficklin, who had managed the Pony Express until he had a disagreement with William H. Russell.

The goal of the companies was to unite the Atlantic and Pacific Coasts by wire, winning a promised ten-year government subsidy at $40,000 a year. Creighton managed the construction from Omaha to Salt Lake City, and his partner James Gamble constructed the rest of the line from California east. Each divided their gangs in half and built from both ends of their divisions. Work began in July 1861 and was completed that October. Pony riders reported downed lines and thus aided in the construction and maintenance. Brigham Young sent the first message from Salt Lake City, and two days later the first message from California went through. The last Pony rider left with his mail on 26 October 1861, and no one noticed. The era of pre–Civil War transportation had come to an end. The telegraph was an essential prelude to new transportation technology—a single-track railroad that would bridge the country within the decade. It offered a safe method of train control as well as rapid miscellaneous communications of all kinds. Creighton's line would eventually become part of the Western Union Company.

See also Pony Express; Russell, Majors & Waddell Company.

References Drago, Harry S., *Roads to Empire* (1968); Du Boff, Richard B., "Business Demand and the Development of the Telegraph in the United States," *Business History Review* (1980) 59: 459–479; Harlow, Alvin F., *Old Wires and New Waves* (1936); Thompson, Robert Luthur, *Wiring a Continent* (1947).

Tire and Rubber Industry

The motor vehicle's dominance of twentieth-century transportation has its basis on wheels, or more specifically, the rubber tires that make up those wheels. The rubber industry is an important adjunct to the automobiles, trucks, and airliners that make up much of modern transportation. And just as motor vehicles and airplanes have changed and modernized, so have the tires that carry them. Rims have been curled to hold tires in place safely, yet allow them to be changed quickly. Black became the predominate color in about 1910 as carbon black was added as a rubber strengthener, although white sidewalls (the early ones were very wide add-ons held in place by the tire's pressure against the rim) remain popular, as does raised lettering. Low-pressure tires that cushioned the ride came forth in the 1920s; bias ply gave way to radial ply after World War II (less twisting of the belts in contact with the road meant lower operating temperatures and double the life of the tire); and puncture-proof outer belts were supplemented with steel and fiberglass inner belts that made for longer wear. The cross-profile of tires has become wider and flatter to carry bigger and heavier loads at greater speeds. Treads now shed water to cut hydroplaning on wet surfaces, studs make them grip in snow and ice, and lug treads negate the effects of mud.

At least 80 percent of all manufactured rubber goes into tires. This is a far cry from the rubber industry of the nineteenth century, where the greatest portion of its product went into boot and shoe soles, hoses, industrial belts, electric products, and various smaller items. Although the French knew how to break down natural rubber with turpentine in the 1700s and British inventor Charles Mackintosh had developed a method to waterproof cloth with a combination of coal tar and rubber in 1823, the big breakthrough occurred in 1839 when Charles Goodyear discovered the process of vulcanization, the heating together of raw rubber, sulfur, and white lead at 2,700°. This created a workable product that was impervious to water, heat, and cold. He patented the process in 1844, and until the patents expired in 1865 the rubber business was slow to expand. By 1892, Charles R. Flint combined several smaller firms into U.S. Rubber Company, much like Andrew Carnegie (steel), J. P. Morgan (railroads), and John D. Rockefeller (oil) did in their industries at the same time.

But beginning with the bicycling craze of the 1880s, tires became an industry that supported such names as U.S. Rubber, Goodyear, B. F. Goodrich (who started to make Akron, Ohio, the tire capital of the world), Dunlop, Armstrong, and Firestone. In various developments, not many of which began in America but all of which were capitalized here, the original solid-rubber bicycle tire became a changeable loop held onto a curved rim by a rubber bead, then became an inflatable hollow tube filled by a innertube filled with compressed air. But by the turn of the century the bicycle craze had begun to subside, leaving the Good Roads Movement—and the notion of the inflatable tire—as its enduring monuments.

The flagging tire industry was rescued by a new craze—one which still dominates the western world—the automobile. With the development of the family car and the increasing demand for motor vehicles by 1910, tire manufacture modernized to keep up with the new increased business, suffering several strikes in the process by displaced laborers. As the tire business became more reliant on mechanization and advanced chemistry, the smaller manufacturers began to fall away during the 1920s. Both Sears, Roebuck & Company (through Goodyear's production of Allstate Tires) and Montgomery Ward (whose contract was split between B. F. Goodrich and U.S.

Rubber) entered the mail-order tire market in a big way. It was no accident, by the way, that Henry Ford and Harvey Firestone vacationed together. Firestone provided tires for the Ford Motor Company.

The Great Depression caused the tire industry to fall with the rest of American business. There have historically been two basic tire markets: one for new original equipment, and the other for replacements for worn products. Each affected the supply and price of the other. Originally, the replacement tire field was well over two-thirds of the market. But as tire design and longevity has improved, it has dropped substantially. During the depression, the replacement tire market fell to nothing as money tightened, and the original equipment market declined as well with a failing auto industry. Tire makers tried to police their own industry prices and policies to no avail. They then turned to the government, and the National Recovery Administration established compulsory cartels, prices, and labor standards. By the time of the recovery of the late 1930s, five major producers dominated the field: Goodyear, Firestone, General Tire, Sieberling, and U.S. Rubber.

World War II was as much of a boon to the tire makers as it was to most of American industry. Recycling of old tires became a must to keep up with domestic and military demands. Retreads, which involved putting new tread on an old tire carcass, were popular. More important, however, was the government-led and -financed push for synthetic rubber as the Japanese overran Southeast Asia, a huge source of natural rubber. The original formula, called Buna-S from its use of copolymers of butadiene and styrene, had been developed during the 1930s by a consortium of the German firm I. G. Farben and Standard Oil of New Jersey using World War I research. Later, other forms came to the fore including Butyl (Standard Oil of New Jersey), Neoprene (Du Pont), Chemigum (Goodyear), and Koroseal (Goodrich). The government took all of these formulas and came up with GR-S (government rubber-styrene), and contracted with the various companies to produce it for military use. The government spent $673 million on synthetic rubbers developed during World War II. Natural and synthetic rubber were rationed and new natural sources cultivated. Eventually, the government plants were sold to the private companies that operated them, a process that was delayed by the Korean War until 1955.

Until about 1970, American tire producers pretty much had the domestic market to themselves. Then the Europeans and the Japanese began to crack the U.S. market, particularly with the introduction of radials. American makers countered with the belted tire, a bias ply with fiberglass and steel belts added for strength and longevity. Then congressional hearings revealed to the public that Firestone's "500" steel belt was liable to sudden blowouts. Firestone had countered such occurrences with a liberal replacement policy, but the manner in which the problem had been quietly handled looked bad and cost a lot of confidence in American makers. The result was the federal grading of tires and a new universal system of classification by 1980. With the Arab oil embargoes of the same period, fuel efficiency became more important, and the gas-saving radials took over the market. By 1990, only Goodyear remained as the major, solely American-owned tire company, with its major competitors being Michelin from France and Bridgestone from Japan.

See also Aeronautics; Automobiles from Domestics to Imports; Automobiles in American Society; Trucking.

References Babcock, Glenn D., *History of the United States Rubber Company* (1966); Burton, Walter E., *The Story of Tires Beads and Tires* (1954); French, Michael J., *The U.S. Tire Industry* (1990); Lief, Alfred, *The Firestone Story* (1951); Nelson, Daniel, *American Rubber Workers and Organized Labor* (1988); O'Reilly, Maurice, *The Goodyear Story* (1983); Tuttle, William M., Jr., "The Birth of an Industry: The Synthetic Rubber 'Mess' in World War II," *Technology and Culture* (1981) 22: 35–67; Walsh, James A., *The Armstrong Rubber Company* (1982).

Train Control

From the beginning, trains had to have some system of controls so that the usually single track could be utilized by more than one train at a time. Failure to implement such controls was often fatal, and railroad wrecks were common occurrences well into the twentieth century. Some of the first control "devices" were pretty simple and easily overcome by tragedy. The station agent would shinny up a pole and sit there until he spied a train coming, whereupon he would descend and ring a bell to announce its arrival. Posts were set up halfway between sidings (if there were any) and the first engineer to reach the post had the right-of-way—the other train had to back up until it could pull out of the way.

The most common form of control was for the engine crew to watch for smoke from an oncoming train and to pray that the approaching crew was doing the same. Often engineers were handed colored sticks that gave them the right-of-way to the next station. No train could move without the stick—a system also used by highway maintenance crews until the advent of hand-held two-way radios. Gradually, trains were expected to display lights on the front and rear, even if they were merely engines running without cars. Flags on the front often told if a train were being followed closely by another section (colors told how many sections) or whether it was clear behind it.

As railroading grew in complexity, the signals were displayed at the stations, which were connected together by telegraph by 1851. The information was displayed outside on a semaphore or ball that could be raised or lowered—giving derivation to the term "high ball" as a go-ahead or "fast run" signal. In reality, the reverse was true; a high ball or raised, horizontal semaphore blade meant "stop"—so much for convention. At the end of the nineteenth century, lights came into play. There were three original lights: red = stop, green = proceed with caution, and clear = go. But when the colored lens of a light was broken out on one signal, an engineer proceeded confidently through a closed switch and wrecked his train. So by 1914, amber came to mean "caution" and green to mean "go."

The usual manner of controlling traffic was to divide the tracks into sections called "blocks." Introduced in the United States from Great Britain in 1863, each block was allowed to have only one train in it on the mainline at one time; all others were to pull over for it. Any train that could not clear had to protect itself by setting up a flagman to wave down any approaching cars. Torpedoes and fusees—exploding and flared devices—helped to signal an oncoming engineer that all was not well ahead. Blocks were controlled by interlocking towers manned by switchmen who could throw signals and switches to expedite traffic flow. Turnouts were interlocked so that throwing one switch would mechanically change the signals and any other related switch to keep the system safe and whole. Modern electrical devices allow all of this to be done at one central location for a whole division (a series of blocks that generally can be traversed by a train on one work shift). Such an electrical system is called Centralized Traffic Control (CTC).

Because the colored-light signals along the track might fail or not be seen in bad weather, the Interstate Commerce Commission (ICC) forced certain larger railroads (95 of them) to install an Automatic Train Control (ATC) device on its road engines. The ICC-approved signal, an electrical impulse carried along the rails as are most track signals, would automatically release the air that kept the brakes open and stop the train. The Pennsylvania Railroad did not like the idea of taking the control of a train from the hands of its engineer, so it developed another device that displayed the trackside signal lights inside the cab on a miniature signal head. This allowed the train crew to stop at a more propitious spot than on a grade. The ICC, however, forced Pennsy to use a backup system that would engage the air brakes if the cab signal brought no response from the crew.

Signals are also transmitted by hand or by whistle or horn. Most people are familiar with the "long, long, short, long" of a highway crossing, but there are many more, including "approaching station" (one long), "call for signals" (four short), "back up" (three short), "read your signal" (two short),

and "look out" or "danger on the tracks" (a succession of shorts), just to name a few. Of the hand signals, the one for a hotbox (overheated journal that lubricates an axle) is most instructive—pinching the nose. It was often used by caboose crews as they passed and checked out each other's consists. Nowadays most of the caboose crew's role is handled by a small computer box called a FRED (Flashing Rear End Device). Placed on the coupler of the last car and hooked up to the air and signal lines, FRED also has a blinking red light to signal approaching engines of the end of the train.

The loads in the individual cars are tracked by computer to permit "just in time" delivery. That is, the producer/customer uses the materials right out of the boxcar in a matter of hours. If one car is delayed or lost, an entire assembly line can stall for lack of parts. Every shippable product is given a Standard Transportation Code (STC; there are more than 14,000 of them), and the STC must appear on the waybill. The numbers are standardized between carriers and the federal Department of Transportation. When combined with the Universal Machine Language Equipment Register (UMLER), which lists ownership, dimensions, capacity, weight, chief components, and hourly and mileage rates of use, a car can be assigned to a shipper and a carrier to keep materials flowing. All of the UMLER is kept in Washington at the headquarters of the Association of American Railroads. In addition, the railroads were among the first businesses to computerize. The original program they used was TeleRail Automated Information Network (TRAIN), which has since been upgraded several times over the years. The system could tell a railroader anything about a load on a Class I (the biggest and best) railroad, but when it rolled onto an independent line, it got "lost." This gap was filled by an additional program called Railroad Operations Modular Processing System (ROMPS) that monitors all other lines.

See also Railroads before and during the Civil War; Railroads from Appamattox to Deregulation; Safety Appliance Act.

Trains in Cities

References Armstrong, John H., *The Railroad—What It Is—What It Does* (1978); Hage, David, "On the Right Track: America's Railroads Are Chugging Their Way Back to Prosperity," *U.S. News & World Report* (21 March 1994) 116: 46–53; Hubbard, Freeman, *Encyclopedia of North American Railroading* (1981).

Trains in Cities

One of the many places that the train made initial headway, only to be challenged by the automobile until modern fuel shortages and traffic jams renewed interest in them, was in the American big city. These inner-city trains have taken many forms: trolley cars, subway and elevated lines, and commuter runs. One of the earliest applications of the idea of inner-city rail travel was in the form of the streetcar or trolley, the first of which was built in New York City in 1832. New Orleans soon followed suit, as did other towns of importance. Initial propulsion was by horses or mules, but by the end of the nineteenth century after experiments with various internal combustion engines, compressed air, and springs, electricity and cables had won out.

The cable car was a San Francisco devel-opment, brought about in the 1870s because many of the city's hills were so steep that draft animals could not take the workload. Andrew Halladie, a wire manufacturer, open the Clay Street Line in 1873. He had a steam-powered continuous cable laid in a trench slit below the pavement to which the cars could be attached by a gripping mechanism. Releasing the grip caused any one car to stop independent of the others. Although costly to install, the system was fairly easy to maintain when compared to the many horses necessary on a normal streetcar run (eight or ten per car per day on the flat streets). In the 1880s, many other cities installed cable car systems, including Seattle, Cincinnati, Philadelphia, Washington, New York, and Chicago (with one of the biggest).

But by the turn of the century, electric traction, or trolley, cars were replacing the cable cars, except in San Francisco's hills. The trolley went hand-in-hand with the development of mainline electric train engines. The first really successful system was the brainchild of Frank Sprague, the father of the American trolley (so named because

The first elevated railroad in New York City in 1868

510

the first models were pulled or trolled by the driver from a rope attached to an overhead wire). He developed the traction motor, an electric unit mounted to the trucks under the car and powering one of the two axles. Electricity was provided by an overhead catenary system. His first installation was in Richmond, Virginia, in 1888. Although there had been other electric trolleys in Montgomery, Alabama, and at Saratoga, New York, Sprague's system was more cost effective, dependable, and simple. An electric trolley could carry twice the weight a horse-powered unit could. As trolleys became more and more popular, the conductor often missed new arrivals and failed to collect the fare. The result was the restricted pay-as-you-enter (or leave) system run by the conductor at the front or rear door in 1905.

In 1916, Charles Birney built a light, enclosed, four-wheeled car that could be run by the driver alone. The doors were connected to the braking system, preventing anyone from entering or leaving while the car was in motion. But the year Birney invented his streetcar was the high-water mark of trolley ridership. From then on, trolley use declined under competition from the automobile and the gas-powered bus, a more flexible vehicle (no tracks or overhead wires needed). To meet this competition, the Electric Railway Presidents' Conference came up with a new unit—quiet, efficient, and comfortable—called the PCC. This kept streetcars operating until the 1960s. But within a decade, public awareness of air pollution, traffic jams, and rising fuel costs caused the reconsideration of the trolley's demise. The Department of Transportation sponsored a new trolley competition that has resulted in a modern PCC, an articulated two-unit car riding on three trucks. These or similar units have been placed in operation in San Diego, San Francisco, and Boston.

But the placing of vehicles on the ground has always meant slower travel for urban populations. Two other choices became available to avoid the ground congestion and leap into the realm of rapid transit. One was the elevated railroad, and the other was the subway. These systems were often combined with ground operations for a multiple approach to public transit. The first subway or underground train system was established in London, England, in 1863. It was an instant success, and the idea came to the United States in 1868, but as an elevated railroad in New York City. Set up by Charles T. Harvey, the "El" was at first pulled by a cable and sprocket combination, like a normal cable car. The system proved unsatisfactory and small steam engines were resorted to. Despite the pollution of smoke, sparks, and ashes, the public took to the El right off. The system spread to other boroughs around Manhattan, and by the turn of the century to Chicago, where the El created "the Loop" as it pulled through downtown in a circular path.

In the 1890s, Frank Sprague applied his electric traction motor to the elevated cars. The small steamers could not haul all of the cars needed to keep service up to the public's expectation. Sprague's electric motors were quiet and clean. Sprague fixed up a system of multiple unit controls that could be run from any one car. In this manner, one person could run a long train with each car providing its own power. The electricity was usually picked up by a "shoe" touching an outside third rail. Grades and tunnels were now no problem. Elevated lines still intrigue people today as a viable form of mass transit, although modern efforts are more often in the form of monorails.

Experimented with since the 1870s, monorails have received little attention in the United States beyond an early system, which had its steam engine accidentally blow up, and an effort in the California desert at Trona, designed to haul ores, which went bankrupt. Nowadays, more sophisticated monorails are present at several theme parks, and Seattle boasts a monorail connected to its 1962 World's Fair that actually functioned as a form of public transport afterward. Currently, the Germans are building a monorail called a Maglev (using "magnetic levitation") that boasts potential speeds of over 250 miles per hour. The train actually floats above the monorail and is propelled by opposed magnetic forces. Future plans call for trains of up to ten interconnected sections each carrying up to 90 passengers.

If tunnels could be built, the subway became a better place to conceal rapid transit. No longer would the ugly El towers be necessary. The noise would cease, too. There had been experiments in New York City with compressed air tubes that literally shot cars from one destination to another, but these were necessarily short distances of limited passenger-carrying capability. The city government refused to consider a subsidy. In 1897, the first United States subway line was constructed in Boston. The city found out that the speed was considerable because the stops were several blocks apart and there was no surface traffic to contend with. By adding Sprague's traction motors, the trains could be long and commodious. Subways spread rapidly, being constructed in Rochester, Philadelphia, Newark, and Cleveland. New York City organized the Interborough Rapid Transit Corporation (IRT) in 1900 to connect all of the boroughs by tunnels and to connect with existing El systems. It became the world's longest and most extensively used urban-suburban railroad. Subways have continued to spread. The Bay Area Rapid Transit (BART) and Washington's Metro are among the newer ones in the United States; Toronto, Montréal, and Edmonton have systems in Canada.

See also Commuter Trains; Locomotives, Electric Locomotives.

References Botzow, Hermann S. D., Jr., *Monorails* (1960); Harvey, Dereck G. T., *Monorails* (1965); Hilton, George W., *The Cable Car in America* (1971); Hubbard, Freeman, *Encyclopedia of North American Railroading* (1981); Miller, John A., *Fares Please!* (1960); Myers, William A., *Iron Men and Copper Wires* (1983); Rowsome, Frank, Jr., *Trolley Car Treasury* (1956); Walker, James B., *Fifty Years of Rapid Transit* (1918).

Trans World Airlines (TWA)

Formed in response to the Air Mail Act of 1930 to obtain the contract between New-

ark and Glendale, California, Transcontinental and Western Airlines (TWA; the official name was later changed) added passengers to its route in 1932. During the 1930s, it gained a reputation as the pilots' airline because it pioneered in numerous devices to improve flight safety like radio navigation and high-altitude flying, and in new aircraft like the DC-2 and the Boeing 307 Stratocruiser. It took money to finance this development, and TWA asked for financier and aircraft innovator Howard Hughes' help in 1938. Hughes was especially interested in new aircraft, and when Douglas and Boeing froze TWA out of its new planes, Hughes assumed ownership of TWA and turned to Lockheed to create the L-049 Constellation. It became a TWA standard, built at cost by Hughes' own tool company.

During World War II, TWA flew with the Military Air Transport Service and gained valuable experience for its pilots flying overseas routes. After the war, TWA got trans-Atlantic service routes at the expense of Pan Am. This led it to change its name to Trans World Airlines, still keeping the TWA acronym. It instituted west–east nonstop service between Los Angeles and New York City using the Constellation, and then established nonstop service between New York City and Rome and Los Angeles and Rome (using a polar circle route) with the more modern Lockheed L-1649A. It was one of the first to buy Boeing 707 jetliners for overseas flights. Because TWA had led the way in many innovative flight procedures, it wound up short of cash. Hughes had to borrow from bankers who put his stock in trust and then tried to force him out of TWA management. Hughes sued them in court and eventually won, but he sold his stock to pay his debts anyway. The new management diversified TWA by buying into hotels, a vending corporation, and a real estate company. But deregulation found it caught, like many older airlines, with many fixed costs in labor and maintenance. It was forced to sell many of its 747s to raise cash to meet its debts. In 1985, Carl Icahn took over the helm and has extensively restructured the management and labor contracts and added Ozark Airlines to substitute domestic routes for the Pacific runs abandoned earlier as unprofitable.

See also Aeronautics; Hughes, Howard Robard, Jr.

References Michaels, Patricia, "Trans World Airlines," in William M. Leary (ed.), *Encyclopedia of American Business History and Biography* (1992), 461–463; Rummel, Robert W., *Howard Hughes and TWA* (1991); Serling, Robert J., *Howard Hughes' Airline* (1983).

Transportation Acts

Throughout the twentieth century an argument raged as to what federal government regulations, if any, should be utilized to monitor private transportation companies. Initially, regulation was favored, but as the century progressed, less and less governmental supervision became the rule. Three of these measures were labled as Transportation Acts and operated through the Interstate Commerce Commission.

TRANSPORTATION ACT OF 1920

Prior to World War I, the Interstate Commerce Commission (ICC) had a narrowly construed concept of its job—it was there to protect the shipper. When railroads pointed out that they had to have increased freight charges to renew their capital investment in rails, cars, and locomotives, the ICC balked. The result was that when the Great War began, the railroads proved inadequate to ship the goods, opening the way for truckers. The federal government responded to the chaos by instituting the United States Railway Administration (USRA). Not only did this agency standardize the building of locomotives and railway cars, it also increased freight rates denied earlier by the ICC. The resulting efficiency and regulation proved to serve the railroads well, but traditional American fear and resentment of a powerful, central government won out and by 1920, the railroads returned to private hands completely, regulated once again by the ICC. The difference in 1920 was that the ICC's mandate was seen in a different light—that of regulating not to stymie railroad interests in favor of the shipper (or the public), but as an overall effort to guarantee a transportation network that functioned for the nation as a whole. In either case, the very existence of the ICC reflected the twentieth-century notion that men could use government benevolently to alter institutions to benefit the common good. The one-sided approach of the ICC before the war was not seen as an evil per se under this concept, but merely as misguided in its emphasis. The result was the Transportation Act of 1920, as Congress sought to promote the new concept of the ICC as the neutral guiding hand for transportation improvement and justice for all sides.

The Transportation Act of 1920 was also known as the Esch-Cummins Act after its two backers. U.S. Senator Albert Cummins, a three-term Republican governor of Iowa and an "archaic progressive," was the man who developed the notion that all railroads ought to be limited to a reasonable rate of return on their investments, say 6 percent, and the rest turned over to a special fund and "recaptured" to be parceled out to those lines that earned less. He was joined by John Esch, a Republican from Wisconsin and chairman of the House Committee on Interstate Commerce, who wished to return the railroads to private management after the World War I experience with the USRA.

Their principal rival was Glenn Plumb of the general counsel for the railway brotherhoods (unions), who put forth the idea that railroads ought to be owned and run by a mixed board of labor, public, and railway managers. After the explosive labor strikes and protests of 1919, the appearance of the International Workers of the World (Wobblies), and the Red Scare with its deportation of suspected "Bolsheviks," the Plumb Plan looked quite radical, although Plumb preferred to call himself a "pragmatist." Plumb felt vindicated when other western democracies in Europe did exactly what he proposed for the United States. But here, the result was the Transportation Act of 1920.

The 1920 act ordered the ICC to develop strategies to promote and enhance transportation nationwide. Not only would the public interest be protected through the regulation of shipping rates, the rates were to be set in such a manner as to safeguard the railroads in justified profits for reinvestment. The whole notion was to prevent a reoccurrence of the 1917 debacle. The ICC was to set minimum rates to head off any shipping wars. Fair return on company investment (eventually set at 5.75 percent) was guaranteed, but any excess was to be divided among the less fortunate rail companies. This was known as the "recapture provision." The ICC was also mandated to establish a rail consolidation plan that would rearrange railroads into several mutually capable competing groups that would promote movement of goods by rail and the sound financial condition of all lines. Rail lines could be ordered to pool equipment, share terminal facilities, and route shipments through the most efficient route, even if it crossed several lines. Thus the act sought to strengthen the railroads across the board and protect shippers alike.

Henceforth, the ICC was to monitor the rates structures to keep them fair and reasonable, its rulings were to have precedent over state charters previously issued, and consolidation of railroads was to be encouraged within the scope of the Clayton Act, but not made compulsory. The ICC would introduce merger suggestions in the public interest, the most important ones being the plan of William Z. Ripley in 1921 and another by the ICC (a rehashed Ripley plan) in 1929. But the railroads were free to reject them (which they did), preferring the right to attempt to monopolize any one market (to kill the goose that laid the golden egg, in effect). As far as the stronger railroads were concerned, the smaller ones could go down to bankruptcy, devil take the hindmost. To try to counter this feeling, the Transportation Act of 1920 also allowed the government to guarantee loans to smaller, less profitable rail lines—in contradiction to the overall merger trend.

Although Congress acted in what it perceived to be the public interest, the plan proved impossible to implement. The con-

cept of competition did not prove compatible with that of consolidation, and the railroads dragged their feet in cooperating with the government regulators—each hoping to gain as much and lose as little as possible within the limits of the law. On top of all that, Congress passed the Hoch-Smith Resolution in 1925 to have the ICC reexamine agricultural rates with an eye toward adjustment downward to assist ailing farmers. The ICC created a whole new division to handle this problem alone. But then came the Great Depression and the whole system was thrown into limbo. Meanwhile, the ICC was so busy with rail problems that it failed to regulate the new trucking industry at all. Trucks, the Panama Canal trade, pipelines, and even the nascent airlines all contributed to lower the tonnage moved by rail downward by nearly half, the worst loss being in less-than-carload (LCL) freight. Rail revenue followed suit.

TRANSPORTATION ACT OF 1940
As with much of the congressional legislation of the decade of the 1930s, this measure was the by-product of the depression and intense business competition. The act had two purposes: to restrain competition and to bolster the industries affected. But shippers and the general public were often opposed to this kind of mandate because it had the effect of raising users' costs. The arguments in favor of this act were common to others like it: The entrance into the industry for new firms needed to be restricted to those who could provide adequate service, coordination of industry could be provided by regulating capacity and rates, and all of this made the industry reliable and more efficient. But opponents charged that such enactments promoted bigger and more costly government, which in turn piled up more work on already extended government regulators and stifled competition and the efficiency it promoted in favor of a few large and established business firms. Ultimately the natural growth of the industry was managed artificially.

The act of 1940 initially limited itself to

the reorganization of the regulation of railroads, but it soon expanded into a comprehensive plan that affected all forms of transportation (including rail, trucks, inland waterways, and pipelines) except the airlines. The Transportation Act of 1920 had basically failed for three reasons: The strong railroads were against helping out the weak lines, the administrators appointed to the ICC were lukewarm in their enforcement of it, and the law was poorly written, being much too vague and lacking enforcement procedures. But the act of 1940 advanced the notion that maximum freedom from government controls to consolidate was consistent with the public interest, each case being judged on its own merits. In 1920 the restriction had been to consolidate in promotion of the public interest under direct government supervision and control.

The subtle shift was important. It meant that railroads now could evade the restrictions of the Clayton Act if they rationalized it with a bit of imagination that appealed to the public good, appeared to guarantee better service, and protected employees' jobs for a period later established as four years from the time of consolidation. A board of investigation and research was created to look into the economy and efficiency of the four modes of transportation, the extent that right-of-way or other special facilities had been provided by public funding, and the extent of taxes imposed on the carriers. The government was required to pay the going carriage rates without discount, and the Reconstruction Finance Corporation was authorized to make loans to troubled railroads to keep them out of receivership.

Although the rails received an expanded loan policy, critics charged that the act did not go far enough to protect them from economic realities and would lead to further foreclosures. In all industries, the investigating board received only the right to recommend the combination of weaker firms, but could not compel such. Moreover, consolidation seemed to contradict the provisions of the earlier Clayton Act. Nevertheless, the big rail mergers of the postwar era would be carried out under this 1940 measure.

In trucking, the investigation of complaints called for by the Motor Carrier Act of 1935 was considerably weakened. The full impact of the act was obscured by the advent of World War II and the emergency provisions to meet wartime needs. The act of 1940 modified the act of 1935 in that it limited the use of the joint boards to investigate complaints by and against truckers. Instead of boards that were convened in each case, usually at the trucker's convenience and often unattended by state authorities, the new law required that all truck contracts had to be made public. The idea was that publicity was a more potent weapon to curtail unfair trucking practices than government intervention that was haphazard at best. Then the market forces would put the offending trucker out of business or compel him to reform to compete.

TRANSPORTATION ACT OF 1958
Under the impetus of the 1958 recession, railroads lobbied for more flexibility to set rates. The federal act that followed permitted railroads to cut service without reference to other modes of transportation (truck, river, air) unless it adversely affected "the objectives of national transportation policy," or, stated another way, national defense. It also set up an improved credit plan for railroads, and the federal government assumed regulation of all passenger service (cutting out state and local authorities), permitting shutdown of those where public interest was not harmed and that constituted a drain on interstate commerce funding.

See also Amtrak; Clayton Act; Defense Highway Act; DT&I Conditions; Eastman, Joseph B.; Federal-Aid Highway Acts, Federal-Aid Highway Act of 1956, Federal-Aid Highway Act of 1976; Federal-Aid Highway Amendments of 1975; Motor Carrier Acts, Motor Carrier Act of 1935; New Orleans Conditions; NRA Trucking Codes; Reed-Bullwinkle Act of 1948; *Ripley Report*; Surface Transportation Assistance Acts; Trucking; United States Railroad Administration.

References Bingham, Truman C., "The Transportation Act of 1940," *Southern Economic Journal* (1941–1942) 8: 1–21; Childs, William R., *Trucking and the Public Interest* (1985); Cunningham, William J., *American Railroads* (1922); Hilton, George W., *The Transportation Act of 1958* (1969); Keeler,

Theodore E., *Railroads, Freight and Public Policy* (1983); Kerr, K. Austin, *American Railroad Politics* (1968); Leonard, William Norris, *Railroad Consolidation under the Transportation Act of 1920* (1946); Lyon, Peter, *To Hell in a Day Coach* (1968); Saunders, Richard, *The Railroad Mergers and the Coming of Conrail* (1978); U.S. Department of Transportation, Federal Highway Administration, *America's Highways* (1976).

Trésaguet, Jean Pierre Marie (n.d.)

Early American roads, like the eastern sections of the National Road, had standards based on the work of the French engineer Pierre Trésaguet, whose work was well known to educated Americans like Benjamin Franklin. As director general of highways, Trésaguet believed in adequate right-of-way, lots of ditching to drain water, and the use of heavy foundation stones topped off by layers of gradually smaller rock, all packed into place. His roads were about 18 feet wide and 10 inches thick. But his most important contribution to the idea of highway building was well-organized and constant maintenance by trained and adequately paid workers. About 1820, Trésaguet's system began to be replaced in America by a new, simpler, and cheaper one developed in England by John McAdam.

See also McAdam, John L.; Macadamized Roads and Other Surfaces; Roads and Highways, Colonial Times to World War I.

Reference U.S. Department of Transportation, Federal Highway Administration, *America's Highways* (1976).

Trippe, Juan Terry (1899–1981)

In spite of his first name, Juan T. Trippe was born to parents of northern European descent in Sea Bright, New Jersey. His father was a stockbroker and his mother independently wealthy from the results of a tragic railroad accident that took the life of her sister and the Trippes' eldest son. Afterward, the family doted upon Juan as the only surviving boy. Educated in private schools, Trippe was fascinated by the newfangled aeroplanes, as they were styled then. He went to Yale University's Sheffield Scientific School, where he was known more for his persistence and ability at debate than his academic prowess. It was said that Trippe had an unnerving way of smiling, captivating yet somehow menacing. A fairly good athlete despite his small size, Trippe enlisted in the U.S. Marine Corps for World War I. He wanted to fly, but marine aviation was not yet a fact, so he transferred to the navy courtesy of Assistant Secretary of the Navy Franklin D. Roosevelt. Trippe faked the eye test (he memorized the chart) and learned to fly. But the war was over before he could get into combat. Trippe returned to Yale, where he again excelled in nonacademic pursuits like the school newspaper, football, and flying. He graduated without honors and took over his father's seat on the stock exchange, the elder Trippe having recently died.

In 1923, Trippe finally entered aviation, the career that would dominate the rest of his life. With his engaging manner of conversation and Wall Street background, he was able to do it all on other people's money. Trippe's first venture was Long Island Airways (LIA). With the passage of the Kelly Air Mail Act, LIA bid for and won the contract for the New York City–Boston run. Here Trippe demonstrated the qualities that made him great—promoting self and company, lobbying Congress, and ingratiating himself with others of importance. The profit from the airmail route was immediate and Trippe looked overseas for more. Using the flight of Charles Lindbergh, Trippe began to lobby for international flight. He obtained the exclusive landing rights in Havana from the Cuban government and ultimately won the Miami to Havana airmail subsidy from Washington. His new airline, a combination of the three companies that had bid for the route, was named Pan American Airways (Pan Am).

Trippe thus began a long association with Latin America and the Caribbean. That he could win Hispanic confidence was a real credit to his persuasiveness, especially at a time when American interference through military occupation was widely hated. Ironically, Trippe did not particularly like Latin Americans. He especially disliked the Hispanic flavor of his first name, and preferred to be known as J. T. Trippe. It was his bilingual secretaries who used the "Juan" because they knew it predisposed their South American contacts to listen. And Trippe was astute enough never to let his likes and dislikes interfere with a good business deal. The result was that he alone of all *norteamericanos* was respected and listened to south of the border. He was respected at home, too. When a rival airline managed to win rights to fly the Atlantic coast in North and South America, Trippe went to his governmental contacts and got their mail route application held up for months, forcing the rival to sell out to Pan Am. A second attempt to enter "Trippe's World" had the same results in 1938. Trippe owed much to his old friend and navy mentor, now President of the United States Franklin D. Roosevelt.

Winning the diplomatic struggle was only part of Trippe's success. He also developed new technologies to assist in flying the Caribbean, like the loop antenna for direction finding. Realizing that Latin American nations were often short on capital for building airfields, he decided to use flying boats that could make use of existing harbor facilities. He worked with several airline manufacturers, dropping one for another at will, causing much dislike of him and his haughty business methods in the process. The first to build aircraft for Pan Am was Igor Sikorsky. Sikorsky developed several early flying boats on Trippe's promise to buy, among them the S-38, S-40, and the S-42. The latter became Trippe's carrier on the Caribbean routes. But when Trippe expanded his airways into the Pacific, he went over to Glenn Martin who built his M-130, leaving Sikorsky angrily holding the bag, as it were. Martin built a flashy flying boat that Trippe dubbed the *China Clipper*, envisioning the glory days when American clipper ships ruled the seas. When Trippe looked for new routes across the Atlantic (scouted by his friend Charles Lindbergh), however, he left Martin unceremoniously standing in the wings and went over to Boeing. Trippe

nicknamed the Seattle manufacturer's 314 the *Yankee Clipper*.

During World War II, Trippe's Latin American contacts proved vital to the war effort. In the early days, they provided information on clandestine Nazi activities and gave the United States a safe air route to North Africa and the Mediterranean. Later, they helped bring their countries into the Allied war effort, albeit as minor players. But Trippe himself foolishly refused to take over the Military Air Transport Service (MATS) upon the request of General "Hap" Arnold. This was a crucial mistake that would come back to haunt Pan Am after the war. Other airlines leapt at the chance to fly the MATS ships, and their companies would get an entree into the overseas trade because of it. Worse yet, as the others received portions of Trippe's old exclusive overseas network, Pan Am was denied compensating entry into the U.S. domestic market. There would be no single American flag fleet (all overseas flights combined under one government-backed management—under Trippe, of course) as Trippe proposed to checkmate his competitors either.

Nonetheless, Trippe continued to make it tough on his competition. He was among the leaders in developing the large jet aircraft (Pan Am was among the first airlines to go all-jet) as a way to beat the British Comets and other piston-driven American craft. This led to the so-called Sporty Games, in which American aircraft manufacturers bet their companies on the development of new planes. Trippe especially backed and used in large numbers the Boeing 747. Indeed, it was he who suggested the second-story lounge that made it unique. Trippe also diversified Pan Am into other nonairline- and airline-related ventures, all of which he supervised out of New York City's largest office complex, the Pan Am Building. He retired in 1968 and died of a cerebral hemorrhage in 1981, spared the humiliation of seeing his life's work go into ruin ten years later.

See also Aeronautics; Pan American Airways.
References Daley, Robert, *An America Saga*

(1980); Josephson, Matthew, *Empire of the Air* (1944); Newton, Wesley P., "Juan T. Trippe," in William M. Leary (ed.), *Encyclopedia of American Business History and Biography* (1992), 464–476.

Trucking

In 1898, Winton Motor Company of Cleveland built the first gasoline-powered delivery wagon in the United States. This was the beginning of what would become one of the biggest booms in motor vehicle production, especially if the popular pickup truck of the modern era is included. By 1905, there were already 1,400 trucks registered in the United States, a number that would grow to 2.5 million by 1925. The period before World War I saw trucks in their infancy. There were few standard vehicle types, but all had something in common—the driver sat on the right in an open cab that might have a partial roof over it and the cargo was fully covered, a holdover from old horse-drawn wagon days. Drivers were expendable, cargoes were not. Vehicles used either steam, electric, or gasoline engines. Final drive was through a series of chains and sprockets, a contribution from bicycles. The wheels were spoked and made of wood, and speeds were below 15 miles per hour. Carrying capacity ranged from .75 to 5 tons.

Although there were some companies that made short hauls before the American entry into World War I in 1917, the war can be seen as the birth of the over-the-road trucking industry. In that year there were 391,000 truck registrations in the whole nation. With the mobilization and the material needs of the armed forces, in-town terminals soon clogged up. To meet the needs of the war machine and civilians, truckers and railroads began to drop consignments off near the cities they were to serve. As the war lengthened, the radius of the drop-off points increased. It was but a short step to put the trucks on the road to fill the void left in the overutilization of the railroads by the government. One of the first runs was New York City to Boston. Then it was Akron, home of the rubber tire industry, to Detroit, home of auto and truck manufacturing.

This run was set up especially to test the roadability of pneumatic tires. As these first routes proved, it was often possible to avoid the transfer of goods between several railroads by using trucks instead.

The government itself gave trucking a big boost when it was decided that, rather than clogging up the overused rail lines with vehicle shipments, motor vehicles could be driven to eastern military embarkation centers under their own power. If they were going to make the trip anyway, why not haul a full load? By the winter of 1917, full convoys of trucks were headed east out of their midwestern factories. This effort was a disaster for American roads. The highways were built for light auto traffic, not 8- to 15-ton trucks with full, oftentimes overly full, loads. With the spring thaw came the destruction of the roadways as the asphalt and cement crumbled under the pounding of constant traffic. But these roads were declared National Military Truck Routes, and the war was still on. The War Production Board in Washington decided to classify trucks by weight to get a handle on the problem. To save the roads, military trucks were to be limited to 3-ton (class A) or 5-ton (class B) models.

The army's ordering of thousands of trucks changed the face of American transportation forever. In 1918, nearly 200,000 vehicles were built, almost doubling the number available the year before. The manufacturers numbered about 350, most of which are forgotten today. The Reo Speedwagon assured that gasoline would be the preferred means of propulsion, eliminating electric trucks from the competition. Along with White and Autocar, Reo dominated sales east of the Mississippi. Many of these outfits produced trucks and cars at first—but the trucks became so popular that their car lines were dropped. Out west a different kind of truck was needed. It had to be lightweight but be able to haul bigger payloads over longer distances. Kenworth (a combination of its owners names, H. W. Kent and E. K. Worthington, two maritime clerks who made good) of Seattle specialized in logging trucks at first, graduating to long-haul vehicles by the 1930s. To keep weight down and chassis strength up, aluminum bodies and axles (introduced by San Francisco's Fageol—modern Peterbilt—Company in the late 1920s) were emphasized.

Nothing, however, beat out Mack trucks in the old days. Jack Mack was a steam engineer who tinkered with trucks in his spare time. In 1905 he introduced two chain-drive trucks, the Mack Junior and the Mack Senior, differentiated by payload capacity. Mack himself retired from the company in 1912, but under E. R. Hewitt and Alfred Masery the truck building went on. They developed the Mack AB and the Mack AC, which became standards (4,100 produced) during World War I. An unnamed British Tommy was so impressed with the American prime mover that he dubbed it the "bulldog." The moniker stuck. With its peculiar cutoff nose and rear-mounted radiator, the Mack adopted the Bulldog name and affixed a model of the dog to its radiator cap (and its modern corporate headquarters). Mack kept the same design, including the chain drive that allowed for easy-change gear combinations to fit the job, until 1938. It was the construction vehicle of choice between the wars, working on skyscrapers and the Boulder Dam on the Colorado River. A specially developed Super Bulldog's reliability and big load capacity were credited with cutting construction time by several years on the latter project.

At the conclusion of World War I, army surplus gave the trucking industry a tremendous boost—and the leftovers included thousands of well-trained drivers, all of whom needed civilian jobs. By now Americans were aware that trucks gave transportation, especially locally, a great flexibility that the railroads had never met. Hauling what trainmen called LCL (less than carload) shipments, truckers could make a profit and avoid delays familiar to rail users. Besides, trucks could haul goods directly to the user, avoiding packing, transfer, and storage charges. The post office found that a motorized carrier could deliver a route twice as long as a horse-drawn carrier. After one year of having trucks haul its products,

Otis Elevator found that it had saved $100,000 in packing alone. Motor express became a booming industry. The next step was to run relief drivers who could spell each other and keep the vehicle moving 24 hours a day.

Trucks began to improve in their construction and payloads as they were increasingly used. Gasoline engines came to predominate the industry, generally of no more than 50 horsepower. Speeds still were relatively slow, but pneumatic tires allowed up to 35 mph on decent roadbeds. The driver was moved to the left side of the vehicle after 1915, in conformity to the same shift in automobiles. The cab was more enclosed but still lacked windshields. New transmissions of three and four speeds assisted the truck in moving heavier cargoes smoothly, as did the introduction of double-reduction rear axles, where the gears were reduced in the gearbox and again within the differential on the axle. At the same time, full and semitrailers were being introduced. Truck weights rose to 8 tons. Military purchases tended to standardize sizes and capabilities, but there was little federal control of trucking until the Great Depression.

It did not take trucking representatives long in joining the auto clubs in demanding well-built cross-country highways. They were both instrumental in backing the Federal Highway Act of 1921. But first the Bureau of Public Roads and the American Association of State Highway Officials had to create standards that would permit heavy trucks to use the roadways without tearing them up faster than they could be built and maintained. The key was recognized as a well-drained roadbed, reinforced by brick on concrete or reinforced concrete that was over 8 inches thick. Truckers asked for increased load limits to cut hauling costs. The difference in costs of the loads hauled by 3-ton and 5-ton trucks, for example, was 20 percent. The federal government agreed to a gross vehicle weight of 28,000 pounds on four wheels, but some states wisely built for more than this. Later research looked into driver behavior, speeds, curve radii, tire standards, origin and destination of cargoes, types of vehicles, and overall registration. Government authorities found that roads had to be built not for the posted speed, but for what drivers tended to drive, and that curves should be designed to allow that speed to be as constant as on straightaways.

By the postwar period, engines were almost universally moved to the front of the driver, who now sat behind a firewall rather than on top of the motor. Transmissions continued to become more sophisticated, now supplying up to seven speeds forward. Six-cylinder engines came into use and generated up to 100 horsepower. Tractors and semitrailers (first invented by wagon builder August Fruehauf in 1914 to be pulled by a converted Ford Model T chassis) increased in popularity as did multiple lash-ups of one or two full trailers and a semitrailer. Pneumatic tires became standard, and speeds and smoothness of ride improved vastly over solid steel or rubber tires. The cab became slowly enclosed and provided with a windshield and, in some instances, a sleeper arrangement behind the driver. Most importantly, brake systems improved to four-wheel types often using vacuum boosters to enhance their effect under loads. Trucks also became more specialized to the job—the best example was the building of cement mixers.

Although truck development was supposed to have stagnated during the Great Depression, the reverse was true. Small V-8 block gasoline engines and various styles of diesel engines came into use with the development of the Cummins diesel motor. C. L. Cummins' claim to fame was the adaptation of the heavy marine diesel engine to motor truck use in the 1920s. He first powered a Packard automobile in 1929, driving it from Indianapolis to New York City. He later put the engine on a truck chassis and drove that rig from New York City to Los Angeles in 1931. The result was power and economy to which was added a Rootes-blower supercharger, resulting in fuel cost reduction of up to 50 percent and higher horsepower and speeds.

As engines improved so did the truck's outer appearance and inner comfort. Cabs

became all-steel and more sleeper conversions were used on most over-the-road rigs. The "cab-over" tractor was reintroduced, with the capability of tilting it forward to service the engine, some of which were 12-cylinder "pancake" styles laid out flat under the cab. This allowed the cab to be relatively short in its wheelbase. Toward the end of the 1930s, producers began to take an interest in streamlining their rigs for style and reduction of wind friction. Steel disc wheels became standard as did pneumatic, low-pressure balloon tires. Trucks were now rated by gross vehicle weight (GVW) rather than payload ratings. The trend was toward three-axle trucks and cabs, with both rear axles being powered and sprung together. The New Deal's NRA Truck Codes, institutionalized under the Motor Carrier Act of 1935, placed some control over trucking, as did the Transportation Act of 1940. But by and large the industry was still under state-by-state authority for its operations.

The various changes had their downside, too. By World War II, the weight-width-length rules were a mess. Each state had its own rules. If one crossed several state lines, one could only haul the lightest state limit the whole trip without stopping to store the excess. Limits ranged from 7,000 to 36,000 pounds, too much of a variance to be conducive to ease of movement. As a war measure, Congress asked the Interstate Commerce Commission to set standard weight limits for the nation. The actual determination of limits fell to the Public Roads Administration, acting with the cooperation of the American Association of State Highway Officials. Lengths and heights of vehicles and the loads that could be hauled were limited to 18,000 pounds per axle. But when the states began to crack down on violators, truckers complained to the federal government that rigid enforcement was slowing their response to wartime necessities. Truck hauls were seen as a part of the war production line. Once again the roads became expendable for the war effort, and violations became commonplace.

During the war, truck production was once again stimulated and standardized by military demands. White, Autocar, and Diamond Reo specialized in half-tracks. Other companies made numerous trucks at varied GVWs for hauling light and heavy cargoes like troops, supplies, and tanks. Many military vehicles were all-wheel drive (4x4, 6x6) to traverse rough terrain devoid of roads. But none outshone the performance or flexibility of the Willys-Overland quarter-ton general purpose truck, the "jeep." The war stimulated many advances in trucking. Cab-over models became more popular as sleepers grew in use. The cabover feature allowed a roomy cab but remained within legal length limits. Diesel engines improved in performance, as did the arrival of power steering. Gasoline engines came out with higher horsepower capabilities per cubic inch of piston displacement. Stellite-faced valves and valve seat inserts, sodium-cooled valves, electrically hardened crankshafts, and hydraulic valve lifters made for longer engine life.

By the end of the war, the railroads began to realize that trucking was not merely an extension of their business as it been 20 years before. Now it was all-out competition. Soon the two industries began to attack each other by calling for increased taxes on each other's operations. Generally, the railroads lost out, as restrictive operating taxes levied on them (but not truckers) during World War II continued to be collected. But in one area, the railroads got a boost by carrying semitrailers on flatcars, known popularly as "piggyback" ("fishyback" if done on a river barge), or in railroad lingo as TOFC (trailer on flatcar). In 1954, the Interstate Commerce Commission ruled that railroads need not have a motor carrier certificate to haul TOFC. The result was the LCL cargoes could be hauled long distance and immediately picked up by a tractor cab without providing transfer or storage beyond a parking lot. The business was so big that special 89-foot flatcars and unloading machines that straddled the tracks were invented to speed up the operation.

The trend has continued into the present with container freight (COFC). But the volume, while profitable to railroads, never re-

ally interfered with the growing truck industry, especially the over-the-road independent drivers, the last of a self-employed breed. The result has been a progressive heightening of truck weights decade by decade. Truck ton-miles grew 89 percent between 1955 and 1971 alone. In the so-called Tri-State area of New York, New Jersey, and Connecticut, trucks hauled 75 percent of the tonnage and 97 percent of the value of all freight moved. The trucks, and even the airlines, had taken the cream of the freight transportation from the rails by 1975. New federal size and weight regulations in the Federal-Aid Highway Act of 1956, Federal-Aid Highway Amendments of 1975, Federal-Aid Highway Act of 1976, and Surface Transportation Assistance Act of 1983 all helped regularize and promote this service.

But there is another side to federal regulation. In 1988, the Federal Highway Administration instituted regulatory procedures for administering five drug tests: preemployment, postaccident, periodic, random sampling, and testing for due cause. Urine samples are taken at collection sites administered by a doctor, who interprets the results. Besides truckers, workers supervised by the Federal Aviation Administration, Coast Guard, Federal Railroad Administration, Research and Special Programs Administration, and Urban Mass Transit Administration have to submit to these or similar procedures.

Much of the growth in trucking was made possible by improved rigs. One of the chief developers of the modern truck was the Consolidated Freight Line (CFL). The brainchild of Leon James, CFL was the merger of many small companies and independent operators in the West into a topnotch association of drivers, who dressed in military-style caps and uniforms. To keep things as standardized and efficient as possible, James' mechanics developed their own prime mover by modifying existing truck tractors in their own shop. The result was the so-called Monkey (i.e., Montgomery) Ward Cab-Over, named for its mail-order appearance. The vehicle had a flat face with a distinctive bubble nose, and usually included a sleeper at the rear of the cab. The truck soon earned a reliable reputation and other firms started buying them. The manufacturing side became so profitable and CFL so big that the Interstate Commerce Commission forced the two functions to separate to prevent an antitrust judgment. The truck makers continued their side of the business as Freightliner.

Freightliner was not alone in its innovations. Fiberglass cabs have allowed weight reductions that were made up for in heavier payload weights. Improved gearing in the rear axles had made for lighter, more efficient, and flexible power trains. Double- and triple-trailer rigs became standard, except where prohibited by state law. Wide-based flotation tires allowed the use of single rather than double tires on each side of the rear axles (not widely accepted in the industry), and heavier front-end weights (widely accepted). Transmissions were improved, allowing for easier single-stick shifting, avoiding both the electrically assisted two-speed axle or the double-handed shifting (with the left arm slung through the steering wheel as the driver grabbed the second shifting stick) that the old Browning boxes necessitated. Half-cabs have become fairly common, especially with local, specialized working trucks, allowing more visibility.

Each pulling tractor has a fifth wheel, the receiver that locks the trailer to the power unit. Nowadays, these fifth wheels are moveable fore and aft so that truckers can adjust the axle weight at the scale, using the breaks and engine, in an effort to become legal. It is a matter of mixing good and bad. As the fifth wheel is jockeyed back and forth the quality of the ride in the cab can deteriorate, especially on a rough road. The same can be done with the trailer wheels. As the trailer wheels are moved back, the wheelbase is lengthened and turning ability reduced into a wider and wider radius.

There are dozens of kinds of trucks on the highway, classified by purpose (size and what they haul) and maker. Major truck manufacturers today include Peterbilt (considered the prince of luxury), Kenworth (one of the first with complete aerodynamic cabs), Freightliner (still a reliable, steady runner), Mack, Volvo/White/GMC, International, and Ford. But the most common model (90 percent of all trucks on the road) that comes to mind is the pickup, a half- or three-quarter-ton utility vehicle—the most popular of which have fully enclosed bodies with seats in the style of the old International Scout (Four-Runner, Explorer, Blazer, Pathfinder, and Cherokee, among others). There are also ten-wheelers, like dump trucks and flatbeds. These units mostly run "bobtail" (without a trailer), although combination rigs (with a trailer) are possible.

But when Americans say "truck" in the over-the-road sense, they are referring to the 18-wheelers of story and song. These are tractor-trailer units. The tractor is the power unit with a driver and sometimes an assistant inside. The trailer hauls the payload or cargo. It can be an open flatbed or enclosed (usually called a "box"). If perishables are hauled, the box can be heated or refrigerated (called a "reefer"—not in the modern marijuana sense, but the old railroad sense). All tractors have a steering axle attached to the front wheels and a drive axle or two. Double drive axles are called "tandems" or "twin screws" and allow the tractor to haul more weight. Some cabs are literally homes and have spaces in their rears called sleepers. This allows an assistant to rest or cuts the need for an expensive motel stay.

Truckers work for themselves as owner-operators or for a company. If a company delivers goods that it produces, it is a private carrier. If freight is hauled regardless of manufacture, the outfit is a public or for-hire carrier. If a trucker crosses a state line on the job, he or she comes under federal regulation by the Interstate Commerce Commission, regardless of the type of vehicle driven. By definition, almost all goods are interstate in nature. Some goods are exempt, usually those closest to nature in form. Everything else, especially anything worked by human hand, is regulated freight. To run a truck line before 1980, one had to

Defying the stereotype, a female trucker poses in her rig in 1978.

have operating authority under the Motor Carrier Act of 1935. This was extremely difficult to apply for as the intention of the act was to limit competition within the industry to make it strong. The result was that applicants were challenged by existing firms, lawyers were called in, and the permit denied. It was easier to buy a licensed carrier out than to be granted a new operating license. But under the deregulation intent of the act of 1980, the process has opened up.

If there is a real difference between company drivers and independents or owner-operators, it is that company employees generally are union members, do what they are told, and receive a regular paycheck and employee benefits. They see owner-operators as the bane of trucking—using drugs, chain-smoking, internalizing negative attitudes about employers, partying at truck stops, popping pills and booze, talking vulgarly over the CB radio, blasting their eardrums with loud music, always running late, or driving unsafely and illegally. Of course the owner-operators see the company drivers as the problem. They are commonly thought of as lackeys, rats, and squealers who lack the guts and integrity to go out on their own. But the self-employed have to pick up their own tab when it comes to truck payments, fuel, licenses, and insurance of all kinds for self and family as required by law. Often owner-operators, on the road the maximum ten hours per day allowed under the law, have to hire someone to unload their vehicles or do it themselves, free of charge. Company men, on the other hand, have unloaders, called "lumpers," available, or they can unload and receive $16 an hour for their trouble. Either way, one can be pretty tired at the end of the day. The Motor Carrier Act of 1980 asserts that a driver cannot be forced to hire a lumper, but the reality of getting rid of a cargo quickly mitigates much of the force of law ("if you don't like it, you can lump it," as the saying goes).

Freight comes in lots known as LTL or TL. Less-than-truckload freight (LTL) goes at a higher rate than TL—a full truckload of one item. But the problem is that each part of the LTL has to be delivered to a different place, which wastes time and money for the driver. Big companies like the TL business and leave much of the LTL for independents. Loads contain two types of cargo: industrial—like fuel, oil, pipe, and lumber—and commercial—like flour, coffee, vegetables, and such. The tradeoffs for commercial freight are safety on the road, travel restrictions on hazardous industrial goods on certain roads in populated areas, and delivery problems. The commercial freight is safer to haul but it usually has to be delivered to older parts of town with outdated streets and narrow loading docks. Quite often it is LTL, too.

Regardless of the type of cargo hauled, truck drivers behave as they do to gain autonomy over their work and freedom from the control of others. To gain sufficient income, truckers drive on the edge of safety and legality. They break laws, stretch safety regulations, and negotiate risky driving behavior—not as blatant radicals fighting the system, but as persons responding to fears that they might lose their livelihood in trucking. "We'll do anything to make a buck," one trucker told an interviewer. "If that means we have to screw the regs, so be it." Screwing the regulations can involve cutting corners in vehicle maintenance, disobeying traffic laws, skirting safe driving behaviors, and taking illicit drugs. Which is why dispatchers are sold on husband-wife teams. They tend to be safer, faster, cheaper, and more cooperative, and they cut down on prostitution at the truck stops. Their trucks also tend to stay cleaner, and they look after each other's welfare. They cut fewer corners and obey the law, and women drivers may lend a calmness and common-sense approach and awareness to the road.

Other behavior is a bit more rational. Many drive through the night to miss truck scales intentionally, particularly in the East. In the West, several states do not check weights and size of vehicles adequately. Inspectors just run identity cards through their recording machines. Most drivers try to look inconspicuous and not stand out whenever they come into contact with authorities. They see police citations as a conspiracy between the cops and the insurance business. The ticket is a one-shot cost, but their raised driving insurance rates go on for years. Their speed is a mental calculation, a matter of economics and judgment, not posted on a sign. In hundreds of thousands of miles a year, the difference between 65 and 75 mph is a lot of hours. Besides, rumor has it that police allow about 5 mph over on the radar gun before pulling a rig over.

The ultimate in safety concern by truck drivers concerns flicking lights to indicate when one vehicle has fully passed another and is able to safely pull back into the right lane. This is followed by the passer flicking his running and/or taillights to say, "Thank you." The citizen's band radio (CB) is a part of this safety concern and also a method by which truckers keep track of trouble on the road and elude crackdowns by authorities—generally referred to as "Smokies" or "Bears" (after the style of hat most highway patrols wear), "County Mounties" (the local sheriff's deputy), or "DOTs" (for the transportation department in which they work)—like speed traps or on-the-spot inspections. But the CB also does more. It allows the user to assume a whole anonymous identity as revealed in the "handles" (which range in aesthetics from Dusty Toad and Night Rider to Captain Marvel) employed in place of the allegedly required Federal Communications Commission registration letters and numbers.

The CB has other uses. Prostitutes have been known to pass a trucker in a recreational vehicle performing lewd and suggestive acts. If the driver responds to their conduct over standard channels (17 or 19), the prostitute might ask them to change to the channel made up of the last two numbers of their license plate to set up a tryst. No one not on the spot can really stop this kind of mobile sexual marketplace—except the trucker who refuses to be a part of it. Women known as "lot lizards" also entice drivers into a truck stop for paid romance, and tired gear-jammers have been bothered all night long at some stops by unwanted knocks at their doors as they try to sleep.

Truck stops often keep booths with phones so the drivers can call their dispatchers or families. These tables are reserved for truckers, and often drivers stop and call without making any purchase. But such activity is looked upon as a public service. Truckers generally stop to eat at places that have parking for big rigs available—though the quality of the food is secondary and sometimes suspect. Some drivers will not associate with anyone else, be they union men, independents, younger drivers, or older ones. They sit alone, eat quickly, use the phone, and leave. Quick service is appreciated as most have a long way to go. Others are quite gregarious, especially with old friends or someone driving the same direction, with introductions often established over the CB earlier. Convoys are not as popular in real life as they are in the movies, and occur pretty much accidentally because of road conditions. Two or three might hook up for a few hundred miles and "ratchet jaw" on the CB. Annoyed drivers within range might ask them to step up a few channels so 17 and 19 are left open for reports on police activity and road conditions.

Modern professional drivers are often compared to the cowboys of the Old West in their "go-to-hell" attitude of independence. Often a trucker will dress the role, complete with high-heeled boots and cowboy hat. Truckers often act like cowboys—looking with disdain on those four-wheelers who use the roads for pleasure rather than commercial reasons, much as the cowboy looked down on those who drove buggies or walked. But the independence of the owner-operator has its ups and downs. The more independent one tries to become, the more the system works to constrain that freedom. When an independent comes in, the dispatcher calculates the expenses and taxes for the trip. If the driver did not purchase enough fuel to cover the fuel tax, it is deducted from the payoff. If he buys too much fuel, he eats the excess. Other problems for independents are forced purchases of equipment (especially trailers), high interest on short-term loans or cash advances, delays and breakdowns with no assistance, cargo spoilage or breakage, insurance, routine maintenance, and delay of the final check. If one wishes merely to drive, he is better off working for a company rather than himself. Then if there is a problem, help is just a phone call away. About all deregulation has done is to make the independent haul for a lower rate with less protection from the ICC.

The relation between police and trucker is one of constant one-upsmanship and gaming theory. The Smokies cannot stop just any truck; they must have probable cause. But the probable cause can be pretty slim, such as an askew mud flap, an improperly displayed hazardous materials placard (a matter of inches from other names or load information), incorrectly colored lights, or any similarly minute traffic violation. States send out completely equipped vehicles that can test trucks on the spot for any safety violation. When a trucker has been stopped, the police are not looking for a single violation—in Arizona or California, for example, officers routinely try for a dozen or more. The authorities can write up a ticket, pull the vehicle off the road and refuse it permission to proceed, or allow the driver to move a set number of miles to get the illegality fixed. Police like to look for the very clean, very dirty, or a truck from a company with a poor reputation for legal running. Truckers warn each other about these spot checks, and the police counter with wolf-pack tactics that flood not only the main highway but possible pull-off routes with extra cops. Truckers usually get to know who is operating for the states, at what time, and their favorite methods in an effort to avoid them.

A safety stop starts with the pull-over, followed by (hopefully) a friendly greeting (smart truckers respond in kind), an inspection of legal forms (license, manifest, registration, insurance proof), and a visual inspection of the rig. Drivers concentrate on making their rigs look safe, hoping to keep the inspection cursory. When an officer begins to crawl under tractor and trailer, the driver knows it is going to be a long day.

Then the inspector takes a close look at the logbook. This is a ledger in which the driver lists all hours running, resting, and loading and unloading, in compliance with the Federal Motor Vehicle Safety Regulations. The only trouble with logs is that the definitions of "on-duty" and "off-duty" are not succinct, but more of a gray area open to interpretation. (One cynical driver told an interviewer that the whole industry was a vast gray area.) And naturally the driver sees one aspect of the rule, the dispatcher another, the questioning officer a third, and the ICC bureaucrat a fourth.

A sharp officer can compare hours driven with places of origin and determine if one could drive that far in the hours listed. Some will even drag out a road atlas for comparison. If something is out of order (or the trucker has been mouthy), the police might search the cab. To have drugs found there, or duplicate logs, can lead to real trouble. Truckers who want to avoid trouble generally use social skills to establish rapport, dress cleanly, and keep plenty of excuses handy ("I was too tired to fill out that log last night"). No matter how long the inspection, the clever trucker tries to manipulate the inspection subtly to his or her benefit. A warning ticket always beats the real thing or an actual arrest.

It is not unusual for professional drivers to see the interstates as their exclusive domain at the expense of others. The truckers are out there making a living; everyone else is merely "four-wheelin'." And four-wheelers do not have the responsibility for large pieces of equipment, thousands of dollars of cargo, constant schedules, and incompetent dispatchers—although many a harried vacationer might dispute that assessment. But many nontruckers drive dangerously around the big rigs and fail to understand that when one cuts directly in front of a semitrailer combination the safety cushion for stopping or evasive action is often eliminated. "Drafting" (tailgating so close as to be sucked along by the wind currents of the trailer) is another motorist tactic that runs chills up a trucker's back. Not only can they not see the four-wheeler, but if the big rig blows a tire or has to stop suddenly, the tailgater is dead. Unfortunately, the only tactic to stop four-wheelers from cutting in is for the trucker to tailgate and prevent it. To constantly drop back costs the big rigs too many revolutions per minute (rpms)—precious torque that takes miles to build up.

At the present time, diesel engines dominate the trucking business, and turbocharging is nearly standard. Aftercooling has helped reduce noise and emissions, but increasing federal interest in these matters may lead to great changes in the future. Interior cab noise is also subject to regulation. Antilock air brakes are required by federal law, and disc brakes are now available. Many manufacturers have entered the economy race and now offer truck packages that include fuel-efficient diesel engines, demand-actuated fans, radial tires, aerodynamic cab and trailer styling, axle ratios and engine speeds tailored for the 55 to 65 mph range, and transmission ratios that keep the engine turning over at its most effective speed range. The demands of federal and state law, plus the drive of an efficiency-oriented economy, are expected to increase these truck production factors in years to come. The lonely rounds of the driver and maybe an assistant of the single truck are a far cry from the days when the bullwhacker and ox-drawn wagon train dominated the carriage trade of the nation.

See also Buses; Cummins, Clessie L.; Federal-Aid Highway Acts; Federal-Aid Highway Amendments of 1975; Greyhound Corporation; Motor Carrier Acts, Motor Carrier Act of 1935; Organization of Petroleum Exporting Countries; Roads and Highways since World War I; Surface Transportation Assistance Acts; Tire and Rubber Industry.

References Agar, Michael H., *Independents Declared* (1986); Childs, William R., *Trucking and the Public Interest* (1985); Karolevitz, Robert F., *This Was Trucking* (1966); MacAvoy, Paul W., and John W. Snow (eds.), *Regulation of Entry and Pricing in Truck Transportation* (1977); Rothe, J. Peter, *The Trucker's World* (1991); Russell, P. J., *The Motor Wagons* (1971); Starr, Edward A., *From Trail Dust to Star Dust* 1945); Stern, Jane, *Trucker: A Portrait of the Last American Cowboy* (1975); Sternberg, Ernest R., *A History of Motor Truck Development* (1981); Sugar, James A., "Trucks Race the Clock from Coast to Coast," *National Geographic* (February 1974) 145: 226–243; Taff, Charles, *Commercial Motor Transportation* (1975); Thomas, James H., *Long Haul* (1979); Transportation Research Board, *Twin Trailer Trucks* (1986); Transportation Research Board, *Truck Weight Limits* (1990); U.S. Department of Transportation, Federal Highway Administration, *America's Highways* (1976).

Turnpike

Turnpikes are toll roads that usually had a gate at each end consisting of a bar or "pike" that blocked the road until it was swung up or aside. Hence to "turn the pike" was to allow access to the road, and the name "turnpike" or "pike" became synonymous with travel on the biggest and best roads, usually by paying a fee. The name has fallen into disuse with the demise of toll roads.

See also Roads and Highways, Colonial Times to World War I.

Two Percent Fund

The Two Percent Fund was a federally enacted method by which 2 percent of the proceeds of the sales of public lands in Ohio, Indiana, and Illinois would be applied to the construction of the National Road from Cumberland, Maryland, to Vandalia, Illinois. This legal fiction was created by Secretary of the Treasury Albert Gallatin to overcome constitutional objections to an actual congressional appropriation of building moneys by conservative members of his own Democratic-Republican Party in 1806. Congress appropriated moneys ahead of any actual receipts to begin the construction, a wise history lesson to those who think that legal and constitutional proscriptions can guarantee certain congressional action today.

See also Financing Highways; Gallatin, Albert; Gallatin Report; National Road; Roads and Highways, Colonial Times to World War I.

Tyson and Brothers–United Theater Ticket Offices, Inc. v. Blanton 273 US 418 (1927)

During the first part of the twentieth century, the Supreme Court wrestled with the concept of public regulation of transportation in light of the decision in *Munn v. Illinois* and the modifications that followed. Each case was decided in a piecemeal fashion, with the Court upholding some regulations and striking down others. Justice Oliver Wendell Holmes, Jr., tried to introduce a "stream of commerce" doctrine that would open up the business process to regulation much as *Munn* had done, but he was checked in this by the appointment of William Howard Taft as chief justice 1918. Taft got the Court to go along with the notion that states could not arbitrarily declare a business to be in the public interest and proceed to regulate it. There had to be a determination on a case-by-case consideration by the courts as to the validity of what constituted a public interest (*Wolff Packing*

Co. v. Court of Industrial Relations).

In 1927, in *Tyson and Brothers–United Theater Ticket Offices, Inc. v. Blanton*, Taft got the Court to spell out what was a public interest. A business was considered to be public if the state granted it a license, had traditionally and historically been treated as such, or if a business declared itself to be acting on the public's behalf by its own admission. But four of nine justices dissented to this prescription, leaving the field open to further modification in ensuing cases.

See also *Munn v. Illinois*; *Nebbia v. New York*.

References Childs, William R., *Trucking and the Public Interest* (1985); Swindler, William F., *Court and Constitution in the 20th Century* (1969–1974); *Wolff Packing Co. v. Court of Industrial Relations*, 26 US 522 (1923).

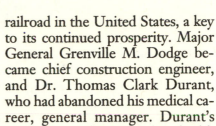

Uniform Relocation Assistance and Real Property Acquisitions Policy Act (1970)

As more and more people were dislocated by the acquisition of interstate highway rights-of-way, it became evident that fair market value was an inadequate sum to replace lost housing. There were often utility deposits, the disruption of moving, higher rents, and the pain of readjustment to be factored in. In 1962, Congress required that state highway departments advise those displaced of federal relocation advisory assistance, available to anyone displaced by any federal right-of-way acquisition. The Bureau of Public Roads could reimburse those displaced through the states. The advice was mandatory, but the payments were to be based on state law, and few states allowed them. So in 1968, Congress made the payments mandatory also. The full stress of the forced move had to be figured into the payments. But this still left a loophole where replacement housing was unavailable; Congress moved to solve this problem in the Uniform Relocation Assistance and Real Property Acquisitions Policy Act.

This 1970 legislation nullified earlier measures and provided federal last-resort housing whenever: (1) there was no other safe, sanitary, and decent housing from public agencies or private enterprise, (2) housing was unavailable for purchase at a cost of not over $15,000 more than the housing expropriated as highway right-of-way was valued at, or (3) such housing could not be rented for a period of four years at a price of $4,000 in addition to rent currently being paid before forced removal from the right-of-way.

See also Roads and Highways since World War I.

Reference U.S. Department of Transportation, Federal Highway Administration, *America's Highways* (1976).

Union Pacific Railroad (UP)

Chartered in the Pacific Railroad Act of 1862, the Union Pacific Railroad has the record for longest unbroken hauls of any railroad in the United States, a key to its continued prosperity. Major General Grenville M. Dodge became chief construction engineer, and Dr. Thomas Clark Durant, who had abandoned his medical career, general manager. Durant's first priority was to reach the hundredth meridian as quickly as possible. Only then would the federal grants come into effect to help finance the road, and the charter to operate be honored. All supplies had to be shipped to Omaha, the railroad's base on the western bank of the Missouri River. Outside of a few military posts up the Oregon Trail and several Indian reservations and encampments, the West was then virgin country. About 10,000 laborers, mostly Irish, later augmented by Civil War veterans, provided the labor force. Track was laid daily, and the amount put down tended to increase from a mile a day to five miles, depending on the terrain. Speed of track laying was important because each mile laid meant an additional $64,000 in federal bonds and 12,600 acres of federal lands to the company.

The railhead moved along with the men. It was not uncommon for the whole tent city to be packed up and moved to a new site in the matter of a day or two. Even the better buildings, those bars and houses of prostitution made of wood, were razed and rebuilt like magic. The towns that the railroad spawned (or expanded if they existed before) were infamously wicked places. One observer claimed that of 43 occupants of the local boot hill, only five died natural deaths. The railroads encouraged the gamblers and loose women—if a man blew his wages each payday, they reasoned, he would have to come back to work next Monday. Those with money tended to wander off. One of the spectacular incidents occurred at the end of the ordeal, when Charles Crocker of the Central Pacific bet Durant that his Chinese crew could put down 10 miles of track on one day. Durant put up $10,000, providing witnesses were present. The whole UP track crew took the day off and watched the spectacle. Crocker's men laid 10 miles and

1,800 feet in 11 hours, plus an hour off for lunch.

The funding of the UP was a critical problem; lack of capital had stopped many an early financier from building the railroad across so vast an unpopulated distance (that is, not populated with white customers— but then the railroad men ignored anyone or anything that got in their way). To build the UP, the corporation set up a construction company known as the Crédit Mobilier. Oakes and Oliver Ames (shovel makers whose excellent tools were considered legal tender by many on the frontier) and Durant contracted with the Crédit Mobilier to build the road. The idea was to overcharge the government and to kickback the profits. Oakes Ames soon ran Durant off, and to forestall a congressional investigation, bribed influential members of the august body, of which Ames himself was one.

But the newspapers got a hold of the details and it blew up in the midst of the 1872 national election. Ames was censured by the men he bribed (even though his tactics were standard for the era). President U. S. Grant, although not involved in the deal, was greatly embarrassed. But the general's popularity was so great as to surpass the damage and he won handily against Horace Greeley, the opposition candidate. Of course it did not hurt that Greeley had died during the campaign, being the only dead man to have received electoral votes in American history, a feat only matched by a lot of politically dead ducks.

For awhile the UP and its erstwhile partner in the transcontinental railroad scheme, the Central Pacific, built parallel tracks past each other until Promontory Summit was agreed upon as the dividing point for federal largess. The golden spike ceremony made the whole process formal in 1869. The UP had a difficult time during the rest of the nineteenth century. The line was extended to Portland, but mismanagement, overextension, and excessive debt took their toll. At the turn of the century, E. H. Harriman took control. He double-tracked the mainline, rebuilt a less steep line over Sherman Hill between Cheyenne and Laramie in Wyoming, and built another route from Salt Lake City to Los Angeles. By the teens, UP had to divest itself of its Southern Pacific (SP) holdings (another Harriman-controlled line), but SP had to solicit business to move eastward over the UP main.

As the prime transcontinental route since the beginning, the UP has been noted for its massive motive power. Its steam fleet began with the small Americans (4-4-0) and Moguls (2-6-0), but soon changed. The next engine class was the Consolidation (2-8-0), followed by the Mikato (2-8-2). In each case, more and more weight was placed over the drivers. The trailing trucks allowed a bigger firebox. Passenger trains graduated to the fast Atlantics (4-4-2) until the cars became steel; then Pacifics (4-6-2) came into use, but even they could not take Sherman Hill. This led to Mountain-type locomotives (4-8-2) for the passenger trains and Santa Fe engines (2-10-2) for the freights. As freights grew in length and weight, UP went into Mallet double engines like the 2-8-8-0.

But the early Mallets proved to be a bit unwieldy and the UP tried three-cylinder single engines (the third cylinder was hidden between the frame and wheels). The result was the 4-10-2 Overlands and the 4-12-2 Union Pacifics—powerful engines, but expensive to run. Passenger service graduated to the Northerns (4-8-4). The Northerns were cheap to run and could reach speeds of 100 miles per hour. To duplicate such economy and more speed in freight locomotives, the UP went back to the Mallets and produced the *Challenger* (4-6-6-4), so successful in "challenging" the grades between Ogden and Green River and so speedy that it could also pull passenger trains, and the lumbering *Big Boy* (4-8-8-4), the largest locomotive in the world. UP also experimented with various models of gas turbine engines, unique in American railroading.

By the era of the 1960s, UP went over to diesel exclusively. There, too, the UP ran diverse units built by nearly every company in North America. Besides being cheaper to operate, the diesels could be hooked up in consists of varying numbers as power demanded, making them more efficient than steam. UP passenger service was technically restricted to operate between Omaha and the Pacific Coast, like the *Overland Limited*. But it operated the City series of trains (*City of Los Angeles, City of San Francisco, City of Portland*) in cooperation with Chicago & North Western (to gain access to Chicago) and the Southern Pacific (to get into San Francisco). UP was among the first railroads to experiment with articulated streamliners in the 1930s (where the cars shared the trucks of those that preceded and followed them), producing the M-10,000 (*City of Salina*) and the M-10,001 (*City of Portland*) at the same time Burlington put out the *Pioneer Zephyr*. Later the takeover of Western Pacific would gain UP the San Francisco route in its own right, and the Missouri Pacific merger would extend its access to the Gulf of Mexico. Today, UP remains one of the most productive railroads in the United States, operating mostly containerized freight and piggyback services. In the 1990s, Union Pacific instituted what was seen by observers as an unfriendly merger offer to the Santa Fe Railway, a competing transcontinental intermodal railroad. Although UP and Santa Fe parallel each other in Midwest markets, the merger would have given UP a shorter route into Los Angeles on the Santa Fe mainline. It has since been outbid by Burlington Northern's 1995 merger offer with Santa Fe.

See also Chicago & North Western Railroad; Dodge, Grenville Mellen; Klitenic Plan; Locomotives, Steam Locomotives; Milwaukee Road; Missouri Pacific Railroad; Rock Island Lines; Western Pacific Railroad.

References Ames, Charles E., *Pioneering the Union Pacific* (1969); Athearn, Robert G., *Union Pacific Country* (1971); Banks, William W., and Harold E. Banks, *Motive Power of the Union Pacific* (1958); Beebe, Lucius, *The Overland Limited* (1963); Best, Gerald M., *Iron Horses to Promontory* (1969); Drury, George H., *The Historical Guide to North American Railroads* (1985); Drury, George H., *The Train-Watcher's Guide* (1990); Griswold, Wesley S., *A Work of Giants* (1962); Hubbard, Freeman, *U 50s* (1978); Hubbard, Freeman, *Encyclopedia of North American Railroading* (1981); Keekley, Harold, *Big Blow* (1975); Klein, Maury, "Union Pacific Railroad," in Keith L. Bryant, Jr. (ed.), *EABHB: Railroads in the Age of Regulation* (1988), 444–446; Klein, Maury, *Union Pacific* (1989); Kratville, William W., *Union Pacific Locomotives* (1967); Lee, Thomas R., *Turbines Westward* (1975); Lyon, Peter, *To Hell in a Day Coach* (1968); Mercer, Lloyd J., *Railroads and Land Grant Policy* (1982); Signor, John R., *Los Angeles and Salt Lake Railroad* (1988); Snoddy, Don, "Union Pacific Railroad," in Robert L. Frey (ed.), *EABHB: Railroads in the Nineteenth Century* (1988), 394–397; Sperandeo, Andy, "Challenger 3985 and Her Sisters," *Model Railroader* (January 1995) 62: 105–113; Wagner, F. Hol (ed.), *Union Pacific Motive Power Review* (1978).

United Airlines (UAL)

A union of four airlines in 1931, United Airlines flew early Boeing and Ford planes until 1933, when it provided the first test for the new Boeing 247. The new aircraft gave UAL a 50 percent speed advantage over its competition, which it increased with the creation of the first stewardesses for all flights. Its ties to Boeing backfired in the late 1930s when it saw its competition turn to the DC-2/3. But when United dropped its Boeing connection, as required by federal law, it, too, grabbed up the DC-3 to keep abreast of the times. United was in the forefront of aviation research in this decade, having its own laboratories. It helped develop static suppressers, terrain avoidance indicators, instrument landing systems, ground-to-air radios, and pressurized cabins.

After flying with the army air force in World War II, UAL decided that the best plan for the future was to back Juan Trippe's Pan Am as the international American air carrier and restrict itself and other airlines to domestic service. This plan failed when the Harry Truman administration opened all routes to more competition in response to increased air travel. Foiled in its attempt to contain costs, United kept at the forefront of aircraft development, buying DC-4s, DC-6s with pressurized cabins, Boeing 377 Stratocruisers, Convair 440s for short routes, and finally the first jets, eschewing the British Comet and Boeing 707 for the more modern Douglas DC-8. It was the first airline to convert completely to jetliners, a process that it had planned since 1946.

In 1961, it took over Capitol Airlines and advanced ahead of competitor American Airlines for the first time since 1934.

United went into the wide-body and jumbo-jet era with DC-10s and 747s. It anticipated deregulation better than most and, although it went into the red briefly, managed to renegotiate its labor contracts and lower other fixed costs to turn a profit again by 1982. It took over Hertz Rent-a-Car, moved into Dulles Field at Washington, D.C., and grabbed up Pan Am's Pacific routes in short order. An attempted buyout by its pilots, who disliked the diversification plan, led UAL to cut back its nonairline operations. By buying the new Boeing 757s and opening new European routes, UAL has managed to remain as one of three airlines (along with American and Delta) to currently share 50 percent of the U.S. airline market.

See also Aeronautics.

References Taylor, Frank J., *High Horizons* (1951); van der Linden, F. Robert, "United Airlines," in William M. Leary (ed.), *Encyclopedia of American Business History and Biography* (1992), 477–480.

United States Express Company

Organized by three prominent New York City businessmen, Charles Backus, Henry Dwight, and Hamilton Spencer, United States Express was capitalized at $500,000 in 1854. The company was to operate over the rails of the New York, Lake Erie, and Western, but the deal fell through—the details of which are still shady. American Express then appeared and took over the budding company at a bargain price. Most of its assets were confined to a large amount of custom-printed stationery.

Shortly thereafter, American Express wished to extend its operations along the Great Lakes, but found railroad proprietors reluctant to go along, as American used the competing lake boats extensively. Then American officials saw all of the old U.S. Express stationery on its shelves and conceived a clever notion—why not incorporate a second U.S. Express to go into Ohio

without revealing its connection with American? The scheme worked; the new company came out of Buffalo capitalized at $500,000, obtaining rail cooperation against American's use of the lake boats. The president of "States," as it was nicknamed, was D. B. Barney of New York City—also a large stockholder in American. Over the years, the board of directors of States decided to go into business for themselves. The States became a real master at utilizing federal contracts for profit. As each new board came in, States and American grew further and further apart. Eventually, they became full-fledged competitors and quite hostile.

This hostility played into the machinations of two stock manipulators, Jim Fisk and Jay Gould. Owners of the powerful Erie Railroad, Fisk and Gould notified States that their express contract for the next year across the Erie would cost the company $500,000 more. States refused to pay. Fisk and Gould then announced to the public that they would provide their own express services. They sent out representatives to do it. States stock fell from $60 per share to $16 overnight. Then Fisk and Gould saw a better opportunity. They bought up hundreds of shares of States' stock at the cheap price, scrubbed their notion of organizing their own express company, and instead awarded States the contract again with no new surcharge. States' stock rose above the old $60 figure, and Fisk and Gould sold their shares out at that price. The whole scheme netted them a cool $3 million.

But that was not all. Working hand-in-hand with States' new president, crafty New York politician Thomas C. Platt, Gould paid off States for its trouble by refusing to let his Rock Island and Pacific Railroad carry any express to be forwarded to points west of Omaha. Up to then, States had carried 40 percent of this business and American had had 60 percent by prior agreement. In effect, Gould cut American out of its share and gave it all to States because he owned the principal rails over which such shipments would have to travel. Through Platt, States said it was happy to hit on American because the latter had always put States into an inferior position. Just how much Fisk and Gould intended to do at the outset and how much came from sheer opportunism is unknown, but these ventures give some idea how all successful businesses operated during the Gilded Age. It should come as no surprise that the Erie Railroad cut States out again a couple of years later, organized its own express company for real, instituted a three-year rate war that involved all companies in the New York City–Chicago trade, and achieved nothing in the end but to restore rates and rail usage to a status quo ante. But then States was not wholly innocent. The company never had a stockholders' meeting from 1862 to its 1914 dissolution. Power and manipulation were goals in themselves. The important thing was the style in which such contests were carried off.

States fell to another rate war instituted in 1914, this time by the creation of the federal government's parcel post. Long opposed and blocked by New York's United States (it has a double meaning in his case) Senator Platt until his death in 1910, competition with the government with rates set by a hostile Interstate Commerce Commission cut $26 million from all express companies in the first year of operation (1913). States' balance sheet showed a net loss for the year of $109,000. Weakened by this and a corresponding drop of its stock that ended yearly dividends, States passed into liquidation "to prevent further losses by the stockholders." Its business was divided between American, Adams Express, and Wells Fargo. The survivors lasted only until the American entry into World War I, when federal reorganization of the express industry on a war footing changed the business forever.

See also Adams Express Company; American Express Company; American Railway Express Company; Central Overland California & Pike's Peak Express Company; Harnden & Company Express; Leavenworth & Pike's Peak Express Company; Pacific Union Express Company; Russell, Majors & Waddell Company; Wells Fargo & Company.

Reference Harlow, Alvin F., *Old Waybills* (1934).

United States Railroad Administration (USRA)

As the federal agency that took over the railroads on 29 December 1917, the United States Railroad Administration operated the railroads, but the ownership of the lines remained in private hands. Prompted by the collapse of rail service brought on by a harsh winter and the inability of the railway managers to voluntarily create a viable plan of cooperation in the war effort, President Woodrow Wilson appointed his son-in-law, William G. McAdoo, as administrator. Although accused of socialism, Wilson and McAdoo hardly relied on wide-eyed radicals to put the USRA into operation, as the board members were the heads of some of the bigger railroads in the nation. The rule was that traffic would be moved by an overall plan and that any route might be used or ignored depending upon the demands of the war effort. Competition, the bugaboo upon which the voluntary plans had wrecked, was out.

Among the many important deeds accomplished was the movement of 1.9 percent more ton-miles on 2.1 percent fewer trains, meaning that more trains were operating straight through to their destinations with less transfer or switching. Because of this straight-through operating concept, the USRA developed universal styles of locomotives and cars, all using standardized parts. The highly individualized rolling stock of prewar railroads could not wander far from their mainlines without special parts and individualized maintenance. The USRA-designed boxcar and Mikado light- and heavy-type locomotives (2-8-2) were among the finest and most popular designs of all time. Superfluous yards, warehouses, and terminals were eliminated. Maintenance was standardized. Common timetables were utilized. Everything worked so well under USRA that there was much public sympathy (orchestrated by McAdoo) for continuing this enforced consolidation of rail operations after the war, but Congress came up instead with the Transportation Act of 1920, which gutted the whole process (as the big railroads wanted) and returned railroad management to the dog-eat-dog existence of before the war. By the end of the 1950s, however, the railroads came to look upon the concept with more favor as they struggled with their very economic existence against trucks and airplanes. Today, Amtrak and Conrail are two examples of the precedents set by the USRA.

See also Amtrak; Federal Control Act of 1918; McAdoo, William G.; Railroads from Appomattox to Deregulation; Transportation Acts.

References Cunningham, William J., *American Railroads* (1922); Doezema, William R., "United States Railroad Administration," in Keith L. Bryant, Jr. (ed.), *EABHB: Railroads in the Age of Regulation* (1988), 447–448; Godfrey, Aaron Austin, *Government Operation of the Railroads* (1974); Hines, Walker D., *War History of the American Railroads* (1928); Kerr, K. Austin, *American Railroad Politics* (1968); Lyon, Peter, *To Hell in a Day Coach* (1968); McAdoo, William G., *Crowded Years* (1931); Saunders, Richard, *The Railroad Mergers and the Coming of Conrail* (1978).

United States Railway Association

A federal agency set up in the Regional Rail Reorganization Act of 1973 to plan a slimmed-down system of railroads in the northeastern area after the fall of Penn Central, the United States Railway Association created and financed Conrail.

See also Conrail; Railroads from Appomattox to Deregulation; Regional Rail Reorganization Act of 1973.

Reference Saunders, Richard, *The Railroad Mergers and the Coming of Conrail* (1978).

USAir

Originally formed as All American Air in the late 1930s, which changed its name to Allegheny Airlines in the 1950s, USAir was one of the initial cheap-fare airways (no reservations accepted), specializing in flight between Washington, D.C., Philadelphia, Pittsburgh, and Chicago. It flew turboprop planes that could get into smaller airports along the way. After merging with Lake Central and Mohawk Airlines, Allegheny had become a small trunk line when deregulation came on the scene. The 1978 deregulation was made for a small, booming company like Allegheny. It quickly added

on long-distance tourist and business routes to Florida, Arizona, and Texas and switched to Boeing 737 jetliners. In 1979, it changed its name to USAir to reflect this new concept. As always, its headquarters and central hub were in Pittsburgh.

When Frank Lorenzo expanded Texas International to include People's Express, Continental, and Eastern, USAir had to expand or be swallowed up. It bought rivals Pacific Southwest out of San Diego and Piedmont in the South. This, and fending off a hostile take-over from TWA, put USAir into the hole for the first time in a decade. With the carcasses of Eastern and Pan Am lying across its economic reputation, the George Bush administration hated to see another airline go under on its watch. As it was, Continental and TWA were in Chapter 11 bankruptcy, and Northwest was just steps behind. USAir looked shaky, and it flew through states where Bush hoped to pick up lots of votes in 1992. Airlines employ many people in towns in which they land. To let USAir go under would be political folly.

The pathway was opened when the Department of Transportation (DOT) permitted Northwest to unify operations with the Dutch line KLM, yet remain an independently operated domestic carrier. The infusion of foreign money put Northwest in the black again. The way was now open for a USAir deal. There was a buyer in line waiting for an opportunity to "crash" the U.S. domestic market with a merger. It was British Airways, which had exclusive landing rights at London's Heathrow Airport. But British Airways' proposed control of USAir and England's unwillingness to open the British market to all American aircraft led to a refusal of the deal in December 1993. Much of the DOT's decision was based upon protests by American, United, and Delta that another, closer U.S.-foreign merger would imperil their standing as leaders in the domestic market and invite other interlopers like Air Japan to buy out Delta, for instance. USAir was left hanging, its reputation for safety compromised by a series of unfortunate accidents over the last five years, until a new pact based on the Northwest-KLM deal unified it with British Airways at last.

See also Aeronautics.

References Bilstein, Roger E., *Flight in America* (1994); Lewis, W. David, and William F. Trimble, *The Airway to Everywhere* (1988); Newhouse, John, "The Battle of the Bailout," *New Yorker* (18 January 1993) 68: 42–51; Trimble, William F., *High Frontier* (1982); Trimble, William F., "Allegheny Airlines" and "USAir," in William M. Leary (ed.), *Encyclopedia of American Business History and Biography* (1992), 34–35, 483–484.

Valley Turnpike

The Valley Turnpike is the historical name of the road that follows the Shenandoah Valley throughout its length, and it achieved much fame as a route to the West, connecting to the Wilderness Road, and as the area of military fame for Confederate Generals Thomas J. "Stonewall" Jackson and Jubal Early and Union General Philip H. Sheridan.

See also Great Wagon Road; Lee Highway; Roads and Highways, Colonial Times to World War I; Wilderness Road.

References Ingalls, Fay, *The Valley Road* (1949); Weyland, John W., *The Valley Turnpike* (1967).

Van Buren, Martin (1782–1862)

Born in Kinderhook, New York, 5 December 1782, Martin Van Buren was the son of a tavern keeper. Listening to the patrons of his father's tavern taught him the art of politics. A lawyer, he served as surrogate of Columbia County (1808–1813), state senator (1812–1820), state attorney general (1815–1819), United States senator (1821–1828), governor of New York (1829), secretary of state (1829–1831), unconfirmed minister to Great Britain (1831), United States vice-president (1833–1837) under Andrew Jackson, and as president of the United States from 1837 to 1841. Described as short, stocky, and balding, the red-haired Van Buren was the quintessential, glad-handing politician. He was cheerful, tactful, suave, and a perfect gentleman. Even his most hated opponents admired his public persona. But his behind-the-scenes political maneuvering was something else. As one observer put it, Van Buren had a penchant of "rowing to his objective with muffled oars." He was so subtle and clever in his deals and plans that he earned deserved nicknames like "The Red Fox of Kinderhook" and "The Little Magician." An old story has the term "ok" being introduced into the English language from Van Buren's endearing moniker "Old Kinderhook." Others say it came from Andrew Jackson's misspelling of "all correct," a term he endorsed memos with. The barely literate Jackson spelled it "oll kworeckt," or "o.k." for short. But as Jackson allegedly maintained in his own defense, "It is a damned poor mind indeed that can't think of at least two ways of spelling any word."

Van Buren knew that it was important for New York politicians to force a "level" playing field in the area of internal improvements, especially after the failure of the state to obtain aid from the Monroe administration. Led by Governor Martin Van Buren, New Yorkers sought to prevent any other state from obtaining federal aid for their competing routes of roads and canals. After all, if New York had done it by itself, others could, too. In particular, Van Buren and his cronies wanted to prevent any more congressional assistance that might promote the business advantages of New York City's main competitors—Philadelphia, with its headquarters of the federally sponsored Second Bank of the United States, and Baltimore, beneficiary of the federally funded National Road project.

In reality, Van Buren preferred that the state build the canal as part of his Republican philosophy of government, which emphasized state primacy in government over the federal. But there was opposition to the canal inside the state, too. Peter B. Porter wanted the canal to exit at Oswego so that another canal would have to be built around Niagara Falls, through land he owned himself. Southern tier counties opposed the canal as a boon to the rest of the state but not themselves. This kind of opposition was somewhat mollified by the inclusion of state-funded turnpikes and branch canals to be built later. Worst of all, for Van Buren, the canal became attached to the political fortunes of De Witt Clinton, whom the Little Magician reviled as the main proponent of the "Monroe Heresy," that is, reading the federal Constitution loosely, like Alexander Hamilton did earlier. Van Buren saw in Clinton a Republican who really was a Federalist at heart, and he blamed President James Monroe's latent nationalism for giving such men patronage appointments over "real" party men like Van Buren and his cronies.

The problem was how to get rid of the constitutionally unsound Clinton without killing off the economic boon of the Erie Canal. Working with the Tammany Hall New York City Republicans, known as the Bucktails, Van Buren created a statewide political machine known as the Albany Regency. The Regency worked an ingenious plan whereby they could oppose Clinton politically and personally, but endorse the canal that promised so much economic prosperity to them and their constituents. Van Buren and his political allies managed to get a majority into the state legislature in 1822 and the governorship. Van Buren himself then went to Washington as U.S. senator. But without his tight hand, the Regency overstepped and fired Clinton from the canal commission. Instead of putting the final nail in Clinton's political coffin, this gaffe reinvigorated an already declining career. The population saw Clinton as a martyred hero who made the state prosperous through his scrupulously honest leadership in the canal building. They returned Clinton and his men to office in 1824, causing the Van Burenites to backtrack until the canal was finished and opened, and Clinton retired.

Working with certain southern politicians, and with the consent of ex-president Thomas Jefferson, Van Buren sought not only to throttle Clinton locally, but to keep the federal government out of the hands of pseudo-Federalists running for office under the Republican label. To achieve this, Van Buren backed William C. Crawford for president in 1824. But through complicated machinations in a four-man race that threw the election into the House of Representatives, John Quincy Adams, an ally of Henry Clay, the biggest federal spender of his day and a practitioner of the Monroe Heresy, was elected, with Clinton's proto-Federalist allies in Congress casting the decisive votes.

Andrew Jackson of Tennessee had received the most popular votes, however, and through the "corrupt bargain" between Adams, Clay, and the Republicans of Federalist antecedents, Van Buren now had his front man who could take the national executive by electoral storm in 1828 as the most popular states' rights advocate of the day. Doing this required an almost Byzantine flexibility on the issues confronting the nation—tariffs supported by New York and Pennsylvania, and the lack of federal regulation desired by the South and espoused by John C. Calhoun, with whom Van Buren sided on the denial of moneys to the states on internal improvements to keep the tariff as low as possible to protect nascent northern industry without hurting southern exports of staple crops (and safeguarding the Erie Canal from competition).

After electing Jackson and Calhoun in 1828, Van Buren moved to isolate Calhoun within the new administration and capture the vice-presidency during Jackson's second term. To do this, he got Jackson to give the Maysville Road Veto and destroy the Second U.S. Bank, headquartered in Philadelphia. This made New York's Wall Street able to surpass Philadelphia as a financial center, relying on the trade of the unchallenged Erie Canal to the west, an enviable position that New York City holds to this day. He also pointed out Calhoun's support of the nullifiers in his home state of South Carolina and other anti-Jackson stands, which drove the vice-president to resign to head off a violent confrontation with federal troops at Charleston and possible civil war. Then Van Buren had the New York congressional delegation help fashion the Compromise of 1833 to guarantee peace and the cotton export market. The sides drawn up in these conflicts led to the creation of the Jacksonian Democratic Party that dominated American politics until the Civil War.

By 1836, Van Buren was well placed to protect his home state's economic interests as president in his own right, elected as Jackson's heir apparent. As Van Buren's career demonstrates, the Erie Canal and the destruction of the Second Bank of the United States molded America's history more than the obvious population and economic growth that made the Empire State the road to the West. It also was the root cause of the development of the political party system that lasted until the American Civil War. Van Buren later sided with the antislavery wing of the Democrats in New York called the Barnburners, and returned to the regular party to oppose secession unsuccessfully in 1860. He died at Kinderhook on 24 July 1862.

See also Erie Canal; Maysville Road Veto.

References Cole, Donald B., *Martin Van Buren and the American Political System* (1984); Dangerfield, George, *The Era of Good Feelings* (1952); Niven, John, *Martin Van Buren: The Romantic Age of American Politics* (1983); Remini, Robert V., *Martin Van Buren and the Making of the Democratic Party* (1951); Remini, Robert V., *Andrew Jackson and the Course of American Freedom* (1981); Remini, Robert V., *Andrew Jackson and the Course of American Democracy* (1984); Risjord, Norman K., *The Old Republicans* (1965); Van Deusen, Glyndon, *The Jacksonian Era, 1828–1848* (1959).

Vanderbilt, Cornelius (1794–1877)

Born on Staten Island, Cornelius Vanderbilt (he signed it "Van Derbilt") was the son of a small farmer and grew up with little education. But his lack of formal education did not hold him back; with a loan from his mother of $100, he bought a small sailboat and operated a ferry between Manhattan and Staten Island. During the War of 1812, he ran supplies to American forts in the harbor. After the war he went to work for Thomas Gibbons at a pittance to learn about steam, which he saw as the future of shipping. He portrayed himself as the foe of monopoly, and devised numerous stratagems to avoid process servers as he ran passengers and cargo in violation of the Fulton Company's steam licenses. He became such a nuisance that Robert Livingston offered him a job at a 250 percent increase in salary. Vanderbilt refused, and came out on the winning side in a case that eventually went to the U.S. Supreme Court (*Gibbons v. Ogden*) and ended riverboat monopolies.

Vanderbilt bought out Gibbons and went to work. He would move into an area dominated by another company and cut rates until the opposition paid him to go elsewhere. This was considered standard practice at the time, was widely copied, and it made Vanderbilt a rich man. Unlike others who made a killing and retired, Vanderbilt kept working, developing steamboats of his own, and racing his competition up the Hudson in his sleek *Commodore Vanderbilt*, a title he himself had assumed to describe his vast shipping holdings. He now had vessels in transit on Long Island Sound, up the Hudson, and across to New Jersey and Staten Island.

After the discovery of gold in California, Vanderbilt realized another fortune of $10 million in a fast line to California, his passengers being transferred across the isthmus at Nicaragua's San Juan River. When a filibustering expedition led by William Walker threatened Vanderbilt's passage, he raised his own mercenary army and cooperated with Costa Rica in ejecting Walker from the area. Later Walker expeditions to Nicaragua were turned back by the U.S. Navy and the British Royal Navy, which turned Walker over to the Nicaraguan government. The "gray-eyed man of destiny," as Walker styled himself, was promptly executed as a nuisance.

By the time of the Civil War, Vanderbilt had garnered a fortune in various local and international shipping enterprises. He presented the steamer *Vanderbilt* to the Union navy and received a gold medal from a grateful Congress in return (it kept Congress from pursuing the fact he had also sold obsolete ships about to fall apart to the Union navy). But Vanderbilt had bigger game in mind as he turned his interest to railroading. This took quite a conversion, as he had been severely injured in 1836 in one of the first railroad wrecks in American history. When urged to invest in railroads shortly after, Vanderbilt snorted, "Nosiree. I'd be a damned fool to compete with steamboats." Now, 30 years later, he changed his mind, prompted by his son, William. Cornelius Vanderbilt sold his steamship interests and, in league with Daniel Drew, the noted stock manipulator, bought a small line that eventually became a part of the powerful New Haven empire.

Indeed, during his last ten years of life, beyond the ripe old age of 70, Vanderbilt increased his fortune tenfold. No mean task, considering the jackals he was running with.

Vanderbilt also bought up various Hudson Valley lines between New York City and Albany, consolidated them into the New York Central, and proceeded to extend his empire from Albany to Chicago. He cornered the stock in the line by wrecking numerous fortunes on Wall Street, so many that the Lincoln administration actually feared a possible depression brought on by Vanderbilt's actions in 1863. The worst loser was old Daniel Drew. After Vanderbilt blocked Jim Fisk and Jay Gould from the easy route to the West, forcing their competing Erie Railroad into the mountains, Drew talked him into buying the Erie. Then Gould issued false stock, conned Vanderbilt into buying it, and fled with Drew and Fisk to New Jersey with the profits, ahead of the law. According to the tale, Vanderbilt said that his dealings with Gould taught him a valuable lesson: "Never kick a skunk." (Another Vanderbilt maxim: "Never tell what you're goin' to do 'till you've done it.")

Unlike Fisk, Gould, and Drew, who were content to either gut their own companies or play the status quo, Vanderbilt proceeded to make the New York Central System into one of the showpieces of the age. The vastly improved line, extended into New York City as no other railroad had been allowed through his liberal bribing of the William M. "Boss" Tweed Ring, gave him a corner on freight and passenger service until the Pennsylvania Railroad managed to get rights to build Penn Station years later. Then Vanderbilt watered the stock, raising its paper value from $44 million to $85 million. As Charles Francis Adams once said, "Fifty thousand dollars of absolute water was poured every mile of track between New York and Buffalo." He became the wealthiest man in America and put the faith of the average citizen behind the railroads, but it cost them raised freight rates of the kind that would cause the Populist farmers' revolt by the 1890s.

Vanderbilt did not stop at Buffalo. He bought out several smaller lines, both in the United States and Canada, and entered Chicago in the early 1870s. He survived the Panic of 1873, and had the audacity to declare a dividend of $3 million in the midst of it. He then engaged in a disastrous rate war with the "Pennsy" (as the Pennslvania Railroad was nicknamed) and the Baltimore & Ohio Railroads that forced them to lower wages to recoup losses and precipitate the great strike of 1877, the first major labor walkout in American history. But Vanderbilt died before he had to witness the costs of his handiwork. Snow collapsed the roof of his Grand Central Station (predecessor to the current terminal) on the day he died. Although he would be considered a "robber baron" by many, Vanderbilt operated well within the ethics of the nineteenth-century American business community. His donation to a small southern college in Nashville began Vanderbilt University. This trust was kept up by his heirs with further contributions after Vanderbilt's death in early 1877. He left a fortune estimated at $100 million.

See also Drew, Daniel; Fisk, James, Jr.; Fulton, Robert; *Gibbons v. Ogden*; Gould, Jay; Ocean Liners; Steamboats.

References Croffut, William A., *The Story of the Vanderbilts and Their Fortune* (1886); Fitzmorris, C. C., Jr., *Commodore Vanderbilt and the Railroads* (1933); Hubbard, Freeman, *Encyclopedia of North American Railroading* (1981); Hungerford, Edward, *Men and Iron* (1958); Josephson, Matthew, *The Robber Barons* (1934); Lane, Wheaton J., *Commodore Vanderbilt* (1942); Larkin, F. David, "Cornelius Vanderbilt," in Robert L. Frey (ed.), *EABHB: Railroads in the Nineteenth Century* (1988), 398–408; Meyers, Gustavus, *History of the Great American Fortunes* (1910).

Vanderbilt, William H. (1821–1885)

Suffering from poor health all of his life, William H. Vanderbilt was the son of Cornelius Vanderbilt. Dismissed by his own father as somewhat of a dullard, Billy went to work as a clerk for Daniel Drew, one of the Commodore's competitors. The two were as thick as thieves, so to speak. Each worked to cheat the other and loved it. Alternately partners and rivals, the Commodore hoped that his son would learn a thing or two from Drew. He learned more than his father suspected and finally got the old man's attention by cheating him in a business deal. "There's something in the boy after all," the Commodore said admiringly. He put Billy in charge of a small Staten Island railway. Within two years, Billy made it run and the boy had become a man at age 42.

But no matter how much he learned at the shoulder of Daniel Drew or his father, the years of rejection had left their mark. William Vanderbilt was a much different man than his father. Unlike his brutal, autocratic, lustful, greedy, predatory father, William Vanderbilt was patient, cautious, and even stupid. He made a rebate deal with John D. Rockefeller for a pittance in Standard Oil stocks—the old man might have asked for half of the company. But he was not above getting together with his competition and raising rail rates to Chicago by 50 percent. Nor was he above cutting his employees' salaries by 10 percent, precipitating the rail strike of 1877, the first major labor disturbance in the country's history. Then he denied that his men were on strike at all. Called to testify before the New York legislature on excessive railroad rates, he professed ignorance of all aspects of his business. The legislature threatened to cancel the Consolidation Act of 1869 that had made his father's watered rail stock legal. Vanderbilt sold the whole thing to J. P. Morgan for $30 million. When his father had died in 1877, William inherited some $80 million and his annual income was $8 million.

He could have bought just about anything he wanted. He played around with the Union Pacific, toyed with the Rock Island, and even bought the Chicago & North Western, but whenever he was faced with a turf war against another rail mogul, William Vanderbilt withdrew and counted his money. When asked if he did not run his rail empire for the public, he responded with the classic, "the public be damned," often erroneously attributed to his gruffer father. It was a stupid thing to say to the press and came to typify the Robber Barons in the public and historical mind ever since. But on the other hand, he invested wisely and the family fortune grew. He gave much to various charities, almost as if to pay back the wrongs done by his father. In 1883, he turned his empire over to his sons and retired to his Staten Island estate where he died in 1885.

See also Forbes, John Murray; Gould, Jay; Huntington, Collis Potter; Pacific Railroad Act of 1862; Sage, Russell; Scott, Thomas A.; Vanderbilt, Cornelius.

References Andrews, Wayne, *The Vanderbilt Legend* (1941); Croffut, William A., *The Story of the Vanderbilts and Their Fortune* (1886); Fitzmorris, C. C., Jr., *Commodore Vanderbilt and the Railroads* (1933); Ginger, Ray, *Age of Success* (1965); Hoyt, Edwin P., *The Vanderbilts and Their Fortunes* (1962); Hungerford, Edward, *Men and Iron* (1958); Josephson, Matthew, *The Robber Barons* (1934); Larkin, F. David, "William H. Vanderbilt," in Robert L. Frey (ed.), *EABHB: Railroads in the Nineteenth Century* (1988), 410–415; Lyon, Peter, *To Hell in a Day Coach* (1968); Meyers, Gustavus, *History of the Great American Fortunes* (1910).

Vermont Railway (VTR)

Originally the Rutland Railroad with an 1843 charter, the predecessor to the Vermont Railway had a checkered history that included management by other railroads, floods, labor troubles, bankruptcy, and receivership. In 1961, the picturesque line was shut down by a lengthy labor walkout. The need for the trains was still there, but management and labor could not agree on terms. The state of Vermont bought out the remnants of the road and changed its name to the VTR, hiring Jay Wulfson to manage the line. Freed of labor problems and soon shucking its unprofitable Lake Champlain section, the VTR regained much of its lost business and obtained new business. It now had a large fleet of piggyback semitrailers and most of the Rutland's rolling stock. Success has led VTR to expand its services over many sections once abandoned as inoperable. It hauls granite, grain, petroleum products, and rock salt.

See also Bangor & Aroostook Railroad; Boston & Maine Railroad; Maine Central Railroad.

References Baker, George P., *The Formation of the New England Railroad Systems* (1937); Drury, George H., *The Historical Guide to North American Railroads* (1985); Drury, George H., *The Train-*

Watcher's Guide (1990); Lindahl, Martin L., *The New England Railroads* (1965).

VIA Rail Canada, Incorporated

VIA is the Canadian equivalent of Amtrak. It was established in 1978 as a Crown corporation independent of Canadian National Railways and Canadian Pacific Railway (CP Rail), with responsibility for all the Dominion's passenger system, less commuter lines. As in the United States, passenger traffic was going more and more to automobile and air traffic, leaving the railroads in a mess. Passenger service by rail is expensive, and with the decline in revenues, the cost overruns necessitated cuts in service and equipment maintenance. Parliament set up an independent passenger rail system to cut costs and be more responsive to customer demands. VIA brought on new "light, rapid, comfort" cars (LRCs) and upgraded the motive power. Although 4,000 employees from Canadian National and CP Rail signed on with VIA, they still remain paid by their parent companies. The VIA owns no track, merely cars and locomotives. Occasionally it operates in mixed consists, partly freight and partly passenger, especially in more remote areas where traffic is substantially less than necessary for full operations. The Dominion government pays a subsidy to each road over which VIA runs its trains. Like Amtrak, VIA has endured many cutbacks and modifications throughout its career.

See also Amtrak; Canadian National Railways; Canadian Pacific Railway.

References Drury, George H., *The Historical Guide to North American Railroads* (1985); Drury, George H., *The Train-Watcher's Guide* (1990); Gow, Harry, and C. Milliken, "VIA Faces New Cuts," *Passenger Train Journal* (June 1994) 25: 28–34; Gow, Harry, and C. Milliken, "VIA: Light Flickers at the End of the Tunnel," *Passenger Train Journal* (October 1994) 25: 18–19; Hubbard, Freeman, *Encyclopedia of North American Railroading* (1981); Nelligan, Tom, *VIA Rail Canada* (1982).

Villard, Henry (1835–1900)

Henry Villard was a penniless German immigrant when he arrived in New York City at age 18, on the run from his father who had threatened to put him in the Bavarian army. He was hampered by language difficulties, which he solved by going to work for German-language newspapers in the Middle West. He reported on the Lincoln-Douglas Debates, the Pike's Peak gold rush, and Abraham Lincoln's nomination and election as president in 1860. He was a friend of several Republican presidents and a lifelong party member, dedicated to equality under the law for all men. He later wrote eyewitness accounts of various Civil War campaigns for New York papers, the Associated Press, and his own news agency. He married the only daughter of abolitionist William Lloyd Garrison, and eventually bought the magazine, *The Nation*, which his son Oswald Garrison Villard (an original organizer of the National Association for the Advancement of Colored People) edited for years. Henry Villard returned to Germany because of ill health in the late 1860s, also reporting on the Austro-Prussian War for American newspapers. While there for medical treatment, he heard of the plight of Germans who had invested in mismanaged stock deals on railroads in the Pacific Northwest. Villard returned to the United States and traveled to Oregon to look into the complaints.

In Oregon, Villard became interested in railroading. He saw great potential in the Northwest and became president of several railroads and a receiver of the Kansas Pacific. But he could not compete with the advance of the Northern Pacific that was then crossing the Plains on the northern route. So Villard organized "Villard's Blind Pool," a stock company that soon gained majority interest in the Northern Pacific and elected Villard as president. He reorganized the construction crews, imported Chinese laborers, and built the line into the Puget Sound area. On 8 September 1883, he and ex-president U. S. Grant drove the final gold spike at Gold Creek, Montana. Villard then went to work bringing immigrants from northern Europe into the Plains and mountains. By the 1890s, the territories of Washington, Montana, and the Dakotas had enough population to become states.

But Villard had built too expansively. With over 500 miles of branch lines, the Northern Pacific was money-poor, and Villard was forced to resign as president. He managed to buy back into the railroad with German capital and become president again, only to see the line go into bankruptcy in the Panic of 1893, and then into the hands of J. P. Morgan and Jim Hill. But Villard himself remained an important force in finance and continued his influence with the Republican Party. He helped organize the Edison General Electric Company, took over Milwaukee's street railroad system, and bought the *New York Evening Post* before his death at Dobbs Ferry, New York, in 1900.

See also Hill, James Jerome; Morgan, John Pierpont; Northern Pacific Railway; Vanderbilt, William H.

References Due, John F., "Henry Villard," in Robert L. Frey (ed.), *EABHB: Railroads in the Nineteenth Century* (1988), 417–420; Hedges, James B., *Henry Villard and the Railways of the Northwest* (1930); Hubbard, Freeman, *Encyclopedia of North American Railroading* (1981); Macfarlane, Robert S., *Henry Villard and the Northern Pacific* (1954); Wood, Charles R., *The Northern Pacific* (1967).

Wabash and Erie Canal

In 1836, Indiana voted an extensive internal improvements program, the most important segment of which was the Wabash and Erie Canal, which was finally completed in 1853. At 450 miles, it was the longest canal in the nation in its day, but it had died from neglect and rail competition by 1872.

See also Canals.

Waddell, William Bradford (1807–1872)

Born in Fauquier County, Virginia, William B. Waddell grew up in Virginia and Kentucky. In 1824, he worked in the lead mines at Galena, Illinois. He grew weary of that and went to St. Louis, where he clerked in a store. He returned to his Kentucky home, married well, and inherited many slaves and much land. But he disliked farming and returned to store clerking. Drawn by tales of wealth in the West, he moved to Lexington, Missouri, where he set up a prosperous store and joined the local Baptist church. There he met William H. Russell. The two men went into several business opportunities together, and in 1851 became partners in Waddell & Russell.

Waddell was a quiet, cautious man, in direct contrast to his partner. The two men quarreled many times but always came together again. He joined Russell in some of the latter's business dealings, but criticized Russell's willingness to take chances. His ill-feelings were confirmed when the company of Russell, Majors & Waddell, organized to haul freight onto the Great Plains in the late 1850s, failed because of Russell's adventurousness. Seeing disaster coming, Waddell had wisely divested himself of much of his property in favor of his son. Hence he weathered the financial storm better than either of his two partners, Russell and Alexander Majors. He suffered much during the Civil War, being caught up in the Battle of Lexington in 1861 and being forced to sign the loyalty oath under the draconian measures that accompanied the vicious guerrilla war that ravaged Missouri. This and attempts to connect him to Russell's business misfortunes wasted much of his health away. He died in 1872, spending his last days as a banker and assisting in the rebuilding of the Lexington Female College, wrecked during the war. He would have been successful in small-town America that was the epitome of the mid-nineteenth-century United States, even had he not fallen under Russell's brilliant persuasiveness. He backed the wrong horse, but came out of it wealthier than either of his partners.

See also Russell, Majors & Waddell Company.

References Settle, Raymond W., and Mary L. Settle, *Empire on Wheels* (1949); Settle, Raymond W., and Mary L. Settle, *Saddles and Spurs* (1955); Settle, Raymond W., and Mary L. Settle, *War Drums and Wagon Wheels* (1966).

Wagner, Webster (1817–1882)

Born in Palatine Bridge, New York, Webster Wagner was apprenticed to his brother James, a wagon builder. He decided that railroading was the way of the future, and resigned his position to work as a station agent for nearly 20 years. As he watched the uncomfortable car passengers go through his station, Wagner began to think about improvements in passenger equipment. He got William H. Vanderbilt to let him reconstruct an old coach as a sleeping car. In 1868, Vanderbilt and his father, Cornelius the "Commodore," came down to see what Wagner had been doing all this time. Cornelius Vanderbilt was impressed. He asked Wagner how many of the cars he had. "Only one," came the answer. "Go ahead! Build more!" came back the order. Wagner went to his brother, and the two men opened up their own company. At first there was only a single tier of berths, but the Wagners soon decided that two, an upper and lower, would be better. To ventilate the uppers, they raised the center of the normally flat roof into an arch. It proved to be so successful that they installed it on their parlor cars, designed for day travel. Webster Wagner was killed while riding in one of his own parlor cars when it was involved in a train wreck just outside New York City in 1882. His company was absorbed into the competing Pullman Company after a long merger fight.

See also Pullman, George Mortimer; Woodruff, Theodore T.

References Hubbard, Freeman, *Encyclopedia of North American Railroading* (1981); Mencken, August, *The Railroad Passenger Car* (1957); White, John H., Jr., *The American Railroad Passenger Car* (1978); White, John H., Jr., "Webster Wagner," in Robert L. Frey (ed.), *EABHB: Railroads in the Nineteenth Century* (1988), 423–424.

Washington's Road

Part of the old Cumberland Road, Washington's Road was originally blazed in 1751 by a friendly Delaware Indian and named for him as "Nemacolin's Trail." It was no more than 2 feet wide, an Indian trail in all but the blaze marks on the trees it passed. In 1754, George Washington had gone out to demand that the French withdraw from Ohio lands claimed by Virginia and the British Crown. In the process, he widened the trail with about 60 axemen, a task so arduous that Washington pretty much gave up the idea of wagons going west. He also found out that he was not much of a military man, being caught at Great Meadows, where he had constructed the aptly named Fort Necessity, which he soon surrendered to the besieging French. An improved version of the pathway figured importantly in the French and Indian War as Braddock's Road.

See also Braddock's Road; Cumberland Road; National Road.

Reference Hulbert, Archer Butler, *Historic American Highways* (1902–1906).

Wells, Henry (1805–1878)

Originally a Harnden & Company Express agent at Albany, New York, Henry Wells was a transplanted Vermonter (born in Thetford) who saw a much bigger potential for express services than his employer. He begged William F. Harnden to expand his services westward. Harden refused, saying that there was no business out west as no one lived there. He told Wells that he could expand westward on money other than his.

Wells decided it was a fair challenge and met it head-on. He found George E. Pomeroy, a freight and passenger agent on the Erie Canal, and broached the idea of express services to the West. Pomeroy was open to the idea (he knew how many people were going west) and he had the money to act.

Employing his brother and Wells as messengers, Pomeroy soon began shipping large amounts of currency for banks. In those days, each bank issued its own currency that could be "cashed in" at various points for specie (coin of the realm). The banks in the West generally charged less than those in the East for this service, so Pomeroy levied a carrying charge just under the eastern rates to take the money out, obtain specie, and return it. The whole service operated without a loss and without a bond. The honesty of Pomeroy and his agents, like Wells, was impeccable. Letters and packages also made the trip, but most of the time the goods could be carried in a carpetbag. While in Buffalo, Wells hit on a new scheme to advance the company's business. Local restaurants wished to serve oysters on a regular basis. Wells agreed to bring them out. The idea made so much money that other spoilable goods like fish were soon added to the transportable list.

By now Wells and Crawford Livingston, another early messenger, were partners with Pomeroy. Postal service was so poor and expensive that many express companies, including Pomeroy, took letters as a part of their business. This angered the Washington bureaucrats, who never liked to be showed up by private initiative, and they decided to prosecute the express companies for violation of postal law. After all, the express companies charged so much less and their service was reliable! The postal authorities concluded there was something sinister in this. The result was the Postal War, in which investigators chased messengers, trying to catch them with the goods. Citizens often interfered with the chase, permitting the expressmen to escape, and Wells and Pomeroy were in the middle of it as the primary shippers to Buffalo.

Wells offered to take over the post office

services for the entire country. The post office pondered seizing the express companies, in effect nationalizing them. But it was too early in history for such a step to be taken (World War I would serve as the excuse for it) and the people backed Wells and the express companies. Besides, postmasters were local hack politicians, and for the government to lose such a lucrative part of the spoils system (political appointments for money and influence in the next elections) was at that time unthinkable. In 1845, the post office changed its concept of mail as an income producer, and decided to lower rates and subsidize mail delivery to make up the difference. About the same time, Pomeroy retired and sold his company to his partners. The result was called Livingston, Wells & Company.

Wells never gave up on continued western expansion of his service. As he moved into Ohio he met William G. Fargo, a former railroad ticket agent, whom he hired and placed at Buffalo. Fargo was in full sympathy with Wells' concept of expansion. Wells, Fargo, and another man organized the Western Express to ship west from Buffalo. As there were no rails in that part of the country, all shipment went by boat or stagecoach. Wells soon sold out his share and retired to New York City to devote full time to Livingston, Fargo & Company. Wells next turned to expansion across the Atlantic. His European service was a success, defeating all comers in service and low prices.

In 1847, Wells' partner, Livingston, died. The firm now became Wells and Company. At this same time, John Butterfield and a group of investors founded Butterfield, Wasson & Company to compete against Wells and Fargo to the west. The express business between the Hudson and Lake Erie had increased a hundredfold since Wells got started. Railroad car space sold at $100 a day to all companies. Wells saw the futility in this and suggested consolidation. The three firms became two (Wells and Butterfield joining together) and by another agreement, Fargo and eventually his brothers, James and Charles, were brought in and the new company entitled American Express.

With the discovery of gold in California, American Express organized a subsidiary company to exploit the gold trade and compete with Adams Express, which had a three-year head start. The result was Wells Fargo & Company, capitalized at $600,000. American and Wells Fargo divided the nation between them at the Mississippi and Missouri Rivers. Wells continued to lead the company to greater glory until he bought out Ben Holladay's transcontinental stage line on the Central Overland Route. Wells had not foreseen the rapid completion of the railroad, which by 1869 was putting all other forms of express out of business. Weary of the trade, Wells resigned his position in favor of Fargo and retired. He died ten years later.

See also Fargo, William G.; Wells Fargo & Company.

Reference Harlow, Alvin F., *Old Waybills* (1934).

Wells Fargo & Company

With the discovery of gold in California, the successful American Express Company organized a subsidiary company to exploit the gold trade and compete with Adams Express, which had a three-year head start. The result was Wells Fargo & Company, capitalized at $600,000. American and Wells Fargo divided the express business of the nation between them at the Mississippi and Missouri Rivers. Wells Fargo promptly put in an ocean service between New York City and San Francisco by way of the Isthmus of Panamá. They cut freight rates by one-third and spread throughout the goldfields. Within a year, they had service all the way north into the Willamette Valley of Oregon.

As there were many independents operating in the gold country, Wells Fargo (as did Adams) bought them out or drove them out by cutting prices. Each company met the mails at San Francisco and then raced their newspapers and letters to the hinterland, in a sort of preliminary Pony Express. They bragged extensively of their speed and prices, assisted by local newspaper editors who received their news by messengers. A conservatively run organization, Wells Fargo did not collapse in the gold panic of the mid-1850s, as did its major competitor, Adams Express Company. The collapse of Adams left Wells Fargo supreme in the West. By 1859, they controlled all shipments except for a few minor independent operations. Their famous detectives came into being to protect the gold shipments and trace those who stole them. Along with Adams, American, and National expresses, Wells Fargo joined the Butterfield Mail coalition to provide transcontinental overland mail on the southern route. The contract guaranteed the coalition $300,000 to make semimonthly service. But if the service ran weekly the amount would increase to $450,000, and if semiweekly, the payoff would be $600,000. Although Wells Fargo sent some shipments by stagecoach, most continued to travel by sea. There was more room in a ship than a stagecoach. But the impending split of the nation put an end to

the southern route, and the Butterfield line was shifted northward to the Central Overland Route under Ben Holladay. Wells Fargo assumed the mail service west of Salt Lake City and even continued their version of the Pony Express between Carson City and Sacramento.

In 1866 Wells Fargo bought the entire Holladay line and with it his mail contract. In effect, they now controlled all express west of the Missouri River. At this time, Wells Fargo made one of their major mistakes. Everyone knew that the Pacific Railroad was going to be built. Wells Fargo did its best to discourage the rails rather than abetting them or selling out as did Holladay. But Wells Fargo had bet that the rails would not be completed as soon as they were, within three years. Contemptuous of the Central Pacific Railroad, Wells Fargo forced the railroad barons to create their own express company, Pacific Express. Union Pacific Railroad already used another firm.

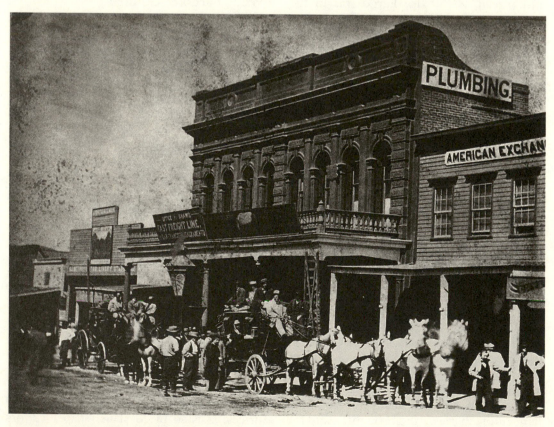

The Wells Fargo building in Virginia City in 1866

Thus, Wells Fargo had cut itself out of the express bonanza of the century. Also, the company had grown fat and complacent over the years, which affected adversely the speed and cost of its service, on which it had built its empire. Henry Wells resigned and retired from the business, leaving it in the hands of the Fargo brothers.

The Fargos did what had to be done. Their stage empire had been rendered useless by the transcontinental railroad. They sold off unprofitable parts of the stage line and gave one-third of their stock for the purchase of Pacific Express Company. They also did their best to conceal the terms of purchase from the public. Under leadership dominated by the defunct Pacific Express crowd, Lloyd Tevis became president of the firm and built it anew. Express contracts with the Southern Pacific and the Atchison, Topeka, & Santa Fe railroads gave Wells Fargo the transcontinental business between Chicago and California they needed. A new contract with the Erie Railroad gained Wells Fargo entry into the lucrative New York–Chicago markets. Their only real loss was a Supreme Court case against the Northern Pacific Railroad, known as the *Express Cases*, in which the Court ruled that competition among express companies on any single railroad need not be allowed. This cost Wells Fargo its attempt to break into the Northern Pacific as a second company in competition with the railroad's own express company.

Until 1913, when the U.S. Post Office created parcel post to help regulate fees through government competition, the only way to ship small packages and valuables was by express. Hence, Wells Fargo did its best to keep the federal government out of the express business through lobbying influential congressmen. By the turn of the century, Wells Fargo and other companies were listed among the smug malefactors of great wealth that stifled the free flow of goods through excessive charges. It also kept stockholders in the dark as to operations. With the advent of American entry into World War I, the government nationalized many transportation facilities, including the express companies. The major companies in operation then were Adams, Southern, American, and Wells Fargo. The government consolidated them under the name American Railway Express Company, with each firm subscribing to a portion of the stock. The government guaranteed them against loss, but they had to share profits, getting only 49.75 percent as their collective share. At the end of the war, none of the three companies desired to set up independently, so Railway Express continued in operation, this time as a private corporation. The glorious days of Wells Fargo had come to an end, although the company still exists and competes profitably in modern package express and bank security.

See also Adams Express Company; American Express Company; American Railway Express Company; Central Overland California & Pike's Peak Express Company; *Express Cases*; Harnden & Company Express; Leavenworth & Pike's Peak Express Company; Pacific Union Express Company; Russell, Majors & Waddell Company; United States Express Company.

References Beebe, Lucius, and Charles Clegg, *U.S. West: The Saga of Wells Fargo* (1949); Harlow, Alvin F., *Old Waybills* (1934); Hungerford, Edward, *Wells Fargo* (1949).

Western Pacific Railroad (WP)

The Feather River Canyon, named from the wild bird feathers that cover the water, is one of the truly wild gorges of America. In the days before the Civil War, a young Scottish engineer, Arthur W. Keddie, discovered that the twists and turns of the Feather River hid a route to Beckwourth Pass, a couple of thousand feet lower than Donner Pass, which the Central Pacific Railroad was in the process of negotiating. When Keddie informed Collis P. Huntington of the fact, Huntington ignored him—plans had already been made, and he was set in his ways. So the Feather River route, after a brief attempt by Keddie and Union General William S. Rosecrans to put a rail line in, went ignored for the rest of the century. But by the early twentieth century things had changed. E. H. Harriman had cornered the routes west run by the Union Pacific and Southern Pacific lines, cutting

George Jay Gould's Denver & Rio Grande Western off at Salt Lake City. But then someone remembered the Feather River Route. So in 1905, in an effort to bypass Harriman's monopoly on the passage to California, the Western Pacific Railroad began with the goal of reaching San Francisco from Salt Lake City a new way.

It was not easy. The Feather River Canyon wound up with 41 steel bridges and 44 tunnels, the track shifting from fork to fork and wall to wall in an effort to keep grades to 1 percent and curves as broad as possible. The Nevada high desert had to be crossed. Traffic agreements with the Santa Fe gave access to the entire southern California coast and the Orient. Gould gave up the line before it was finished, but a reorganization eventually put the Western Pacific under the control of Arthur Curtiss James, one of the last rail barons, who extended the line northward to meet the Northern Pacific (also run by James) at Bieber, California. It was said that 68-year-old Keddie, for whom a junction point on the new line was named, wept when his dream came true.

In 1910, freight and passenger traffic was instituted across one of the most scenic routes on the continent. Teaming up with the Chicago, Burlington & Quincy and the Rio Grande, the Western Pacific ran the flashy silver, domed streamliner (the first to carry them), the *California Zephyr*, rated consistently as one of the best passenger trains and most enjoyable trips in North American rail history. The schedule was made up so the beautiful Colorado and California canyons were crossed only during daylight hours, and the more boring plains and deserts at night. It was a slower trip than other transcontinental trains, but well worth the delay. Because of the Feather River Canyon, much of WP's motive power was copied from the Union Pacific, including use of massive 2-8-8-2s and 4-6-6-4s. Although Southern Pacific and Santa Fe wanted the Western Pacific when it reached bankruptcy in the 1970s, Union Pacific managed to get the Feather River line to complement its routes into Portland and Los Angeles in 1982. The Union Pacific

had reached San Francisco at last, 120 years after it started to do just that.

See also Chicago, Burlington & Quincy Railroad; Denver & Rio Grande Western Railroad; Klitenic Plan; Locomotives, Steam Locomotives; Union Pacific Railroad.

References Crump, Spencer, *Western Pacific* (1963); Drury, George H., *The Historical Guide to North American Railroads* (1985); Drury, George H., *The Train-Watcher's Guide* (1990); Dunscomb, Guy L., *Locomotives of the Western Pacific* (1963); Hubbard, Freeman, *Encyclopedia of North American Railroading* (1981); Kniess, Gilbert H., *Fifty Candles for the Western Pacific* (1953); Lloyd, Arthur C., "Western Pacific Railroad Company," in Keith L. Bryant, Jr. (ed.), *EABHB: Railroads in the Age of Regulation* (1988), 468–470; MacGregor Bruce A., and Ted Benson, *Portrait of a Silver Lady* (1977); Strapac, Joseph A., *Western Pacific's Diesel Years* (1980).

Westinghouse, George (1846–1941)

Inventor of the automatic air brake used by trains, streetcars, trucks, and buses, George Westinghouse was one of three brothers born at Central Bridge near Schenectady, New York. His farther was a mechanic who invented many items of his own, mainly associated with farm equipment. Returning from service in the Civil War, Westinghouse was intrigued by the slow, laborious manner in which trains were stopped—by brakemen who rushed from car to car to lock the brakes down by turning a wheel that was held in place by a wooden wedge bar, sort of like a pick handle. There was no such thing as an emergency stop, as he found out when he was delayed on a railroad trip by two freights that hit head-on. The engineers could not stop the moving trains, even though they had seen each other at some distance.

Westinghouse turned his mind to the invention of a brake system that could be operated from the engine cab. There had already been 305 patents for such a device in the United States and 650 in Great Britain, but none was satisfactory. Then he read a story of how Swiss tunnel engineers had powered their drilling machines by compressed air. In 1869, Westinghouse developed a straight air brake (the brake shut when air entered the lines to each brake cylinder). He offered it to several railroads, but they refused to take it. As Commodore Cornelius Vanderbilt was reputed to have said, "As I understand it, young man, you propose to stop trains with wind; I have no time to listen to such nonsense." He finally got a small railroad in Pennsylvania to try out his system on a train of four coaches. At Pittsburgh, as the train emerged from a tunnel at Grant's Hill, a team and a wagon had stalled crossing the tracks. The engineer threw Westinghouse's new air brakes, and to everyone's amazement, the train stopped with 10 feet to spare. It was the first emergency stop in rail history.

Westinghouse moved to capitalize on this event. He opened the Westinghouse Air Brake Company at Wilmerding, Pennsylvania, and by 1870, business was booming. The first railroad to install the brakes was the Michigan Central and the second the Chicago & North Western. In 1872, Westinghouse improved on his invention by putting the air lines under constant pressure, the reverse of the original system. This new twist allowed the train's brakes to set whenever air left the line. It meant that if a train parted, it automatically stopped, a great safety measure. Further refinements in 1877 resulted in a quicker application of brakes uniformly throughout the train and increased braking smoothness. In 1894, he made the brakes apply more gradually, eliminating the skidding common to cars when their wheels locked. Later, the types of air brakes available on trains differed from engine (6-ET, 8-ET) to freight (K, single cylinder A-B, double cylinder A-B) and passenger (UC, HSC) cars, depending on a unit's weight, speed, purpose, and load.

Westinghouse went on to take out 2,700 patents on various inventions. He was among the first to make alternating current feasible, as he demonstrated at the Columbian Exposition in Chicago in 1893, the beginnings of the modern electric industry. He invented numerous signaling devices for trains and a simple rerailer that allowed the engine to pull a derailed car back onto the track. He received several civilian medals in Europe, and became the president of 30 different companies. By the time of his death he had a personal fortune of some $50 million.

See also Coffin, Lorenzo S.; Janney, Eli Hamilton; Safety Appliance Act.

References Crane, Frank, *George Westinghouse* (1925); Frey, Robert L., "Brakes," in Robert L. Frey (ed.), *EABHB: Railroads in the Nineteenth Century* (1988), 27–32; Hubbard, Freeman, *Encyclopedia of North American Railroading* (1981); Prout, Henry G., *A Life of George Westinghouse* (1921); White, John H., Jr., "George Westinghouse," in Robert L. Frey (ed.), *EABHB: Railroads in the Nineteenth Century* (1988), 430–436.

White, Canvass (1790–1834)

A native of New York State, Canvass White struggled with ill health throughout his life. But his physical frailties were more than compensated for by the keenness of his mind, and by the time of his early death he was recognized as the chief civil engineer of his day. He worked as a storekeeper, and despite his health, shipped out as a merchant mariner and served in the War of 1812, where he was wounded at the capture of Fort Erie. He assisted Benjamin Wright in the early Erie Canal surveys and made an extended trip to Great Britain, home of the recognized canal builders of the western world, to examine their methods. In the process, he found that their waterproof cement could be reproduced from an American limestone found near the canal route in New York, a process he patented in 1820. He did much consulting work following his success on the Erie Canal, including the Union Canal and the Lehigh Canal in Pennsylvania, the waterworks at New York City, the Windsor Locks in Connecticut, and the Delaware and Raritan Canal in New Jersey. On the latter project, he collapsed and was advised to travel to a warmer clime for recovery. He went to St. Augustine, Florida, but died shortly after his arrival, leaving a wife and three children.

See also Erie Canal; Wright, Benjamin.

References Ford, James Kip, "Canvass White," in Allen Johnson, et al. (eds.), *Dictionary of American Biography*, X: 93; Krout, John A., "New York's Early Engineers," *New York History* (1945) 24: 269–277; MacGill, Caroline E., et al., *History of Transportation in the United States before 1860* (1917); Whitford, Nobel E., *History of the Canal System of the State of New York* (1906).

White Brothers Trucks

Windsor T. (1866–1958), Rollin H. (1872–1962), and Walter C. (1876–1929) White all began their careers working for their father's sewing machine company. Windsor and Rollin experimented with steam cars, producing a vehicle for sale in 1900. The following year Walter took the vehicle to London, England, for a demonstration, hoping to penetrate the export market. He returned in 1904 and continued to drive White vehicles in races and endurance runs. In 1906, the brothers organized the White Company with Windsor as president. The company shifted from steam to gasoline power and produced their first car in 1909 and their first truck in 1910. White dropped all auto manufacturing by 1918 to concentrate on trucks. In 1915, the brothers reorganized as the White Motor Company and Rollin left to form Cleveland Plow Company and concentrate on tractors. He later reentered the automobile business with the Rollin motor car, but quit production in 1925.

Along with companies like Reo, Diamond T, Autocar, Kelly-Springfield, Dodge, International Harvester, Studebaker, General Motors, and Ford, White became one of the premier truck and bus manufacturers in the United States. During World War II, it produced half-tracks, scout cars, and heavy tank transporters. During the 1950s it bought up most of its rivals, like Sterling, Reo, and Diamond T, and handled sales for Freightliner. It also tried to buy up Cummins Diesel, but the U.S. Department of Justice filed an antitrust suit to block the move. During the 1960s, under second-generation management, White made a tactical error and built their own diesel engine plant, which left them critically short of cash. Hit by increased fuel costs and tough foreign and domestic competition, White merged with Volvo and GMC in the 1980s to survive.

See also Buses; Trucking.

References Laux, James M., "White Motor Company," in George S. May (ed.), *EABHB: The Automobile Industry* (1989), 452–457; Motor Vehicle Manufacturers Association of the United States, *Automobiles of America* (1974); Sternberg, Ernest R., *A History of Motor Truck Development* (1981); Wagner, Richard, *Golden Wheels* (1975).

White Pass & Yukon Railroad

A product of the Klondike gold rush, the White Pass & Yukon follows one of the trails the *chechakos* or "novice miners" took to the interior goldfields from Skagway to White Horse, where the route meets the Alaska Highway. Originally, the goldfields were so remote across such rugged territory that attempts to supply the area by horse and wagon failed. It was obvious that rail would move more cargo faster and safer. Backed by British financiers and built by former Canadian Pacific Railway contractors, the White Pass & Yukon took over two years to construct. Finished by 1900, the builders had to partially drain a lake and literally hang the rails on the sides of nearly impassable coastal canyons to finish the job. Because of the terrain difficulties, the White Pass & Yukon is narrow gauge, unlike its Alaska Railroad neighbor to the north. The gold rush was over, however, and the traffic dwindled until trains ran but once a week. After World War II, mineral discoveries in Canada's northland have stimulated rail traffic once again. Tourism also provides enough income to run a regular passenger service, and flatcars are provided to haul cars and campers. A trip along the whole line takes about eight hours.

See also Alaska Highway; Alaska Railroad; Chilkoot Trail.

References Cohen, Stance, *The White Pass & Yukon Route* (1980); Drury, George H., *The Historical Guide to North American Railroads* (1985); Drury, George H., *The Train-Watcher's Guide* (1990); Hubbard, Freeman, *Encyclopedia of North American Railroading* (1981); Martin, Cy, *Gold Rush Narrow Gauge* (1974).

Wilderness Road

In 1671, a group of Virginians exploring the area around the Blue Ridge Mountains discovered the "Warriors Path," a trail that led north from the Tennessee lands of the Cherokee, over the Appalachian Mountains, and through the Shenandoah and

Cumberland Valleys to the Iroquois Nations in New York. Although they did not know it at the time, these white men had found the eastern terminus of what would one day become one of the first major routes of settlers into the new West, the Cumberland Gap. It would be the lifeline that opened the Old Northwest and Old Southwest to American occupation, producing the first new states admitted to the Union after the Revolution. It would also be part of the Valley Turnpike, which played a crucial role in the American Civil War, and would more recently be known as the Robert E. Lee Highway. The Wilderness Road was arguably the most important thoroughfare in America before the construction of the Erie Canal. It also produced an anomaly in American geography: Although the Cumberland Road did not cross the Cumberland Gap, the Wilderness Road did.

It was not its central location alone—one that tapped both North and South by way of the Great Valley—that made the Wilderness Road famous. It was also renowned for the man who built it, Daniel Boone, America's first real frontier hero. Although the 1673 discovery of the Cumberland Gap belongs to Gabriel Arthur, an unlettered indentured servant, it was Boone who made it famous by leading the first settlers to Kentucky over a road he built through the Cumberland Gap to the Kentucky River in 1775 for Richard Henderson's Transylvania Company, dealers in Kentucky lands. Henderson's company had bought the title to Kentucky from the Iroquois and the Cherokee—who probably had no right to sell it, at least the Shawnee never thought so, but if the whites were willing to pay for it, why not?

Faulty land titles notwithstanding, within 15 years 70,000 people had crossed the Cumberland Gap on the Wilderness Road, despite its reputation as "the worst on the continent." By then, Boone and many of the early settlers had been cheated out of their holdings, much as had been done to the Native Americans who had sold it to them. Boone went on to Missouri, seeking a new fortune. When Kentucky joined the Union as a state in the 1790s, the Wilderness Road was still the same stump-riddled pathway that Boone and his party had widened years before. Although new branches took the road into the Bluegrass State and beyond to the Ohio River, the Commonwealth of Virginia had not acted to carry out its Wilderness Road improvement bill of 1779.

Indeed, the Wilderness Road was so rough that the United States government had suspended mail service along its length, preferring to use the Ohio River route and the Potomac route, the old Braddock's Road. Something had to be done; during the 1790s, 150,000 more people would use the road to migrate into Kentucky. It was a procession that would cause historian Frederick Jackson Turner to theorize that one could see American civilization pass in successive waves, if one but stood patiently on the Wilderness Road at the Cumberland Gap: buffalo, Native American, hunter, fur trader, soldier, cattle raiser, miner, farmer, city dweller. Ever since, historians have to divide western history into "frontiers"—Indian frontier, military frontier, mining frontier, cattlemen's frontier, urban frontier, and so forth.

In 1796, the new Commonwealth of Kentucky, now separate from the restraints of Virginia to the east, took bids to redo the old road. James Knox and Joseph Crocket (both men were "colonels," a well-known Kentucky predilection) received the contract to refurbish the road. They went so far as to change the old route location, making all sorts of "modern" adjustments. The new route, which abandoned much of Boone's old trail, was for the first time officially called the Wilderness Road, although the name had been used informally for years. Banditry had sprung up in the form of the Harpe Gang, but the state quelled it by scattering the rogues and mounting the head of their leader on a nearby sapling for all to see and ponder.

The following year, Crocket received another contract to improve the roadbed. This time he was allowed to place a tollgate at the Cumberland Gap to obtain moneys to maintain the route. Crocket did so well that

Virginia followed suit and began to charge for their section of the Wilderness Road (although "their" section actually began in Tennessee). But traffic became so heavy that the tolls could not provide enough repairs. In 1835, in response to Andrew Jackson's Maysville Road Veto, Kentucky set up an internal improvements bureau to supervise road and river construction and maintenance. But the betterment of river navigation and building of ferries drained all the money. By 1840, the Wilderness Road seemed finished, replaced by the Ohio route to the north and north–south railroads that went directly to Tennessee from Virginia. Even the Civil War could not rejuvenate interest in the old road but briefly, and it disappeared once again from public view. After the war, coal, iron, and timber brought the Wilderness Road region back to economic prosperity. But the actual road still languished.

It was not until the beginning of the twentieth century that interest in rebuilding a modern road along the old route revived. Following the lead of the Lincoln Highway Association's enrolling subscribers to build a road from Detroit to California, businessmen in the Middle West and the South clamored for a modern route from Detroit to Miami. Joseph Bosworth, organizer of the Kentucky Good Roads Movement, saw to it that the Dixie Highway Association built its new thoroughfare from Detroit to Cincinnati, crossing the Ohio, and continuing down the old Wilderness Trail through the Appalachians at the Cumberland Gap, headed for Augusta and then Miami. The Federal Post Roads Act of 1916 gave it a number, U.S. Highway 25-E. Florida sunshine, improved automobiles, and new histories of Boone and the Wilderness Road attractive to the public brought people down the Warrior's Path once again. But in 1956, the Interstate Highway and Defense Act placed Interstate 75 to the west of the Cumberland Gap, and the Wilderness Road once more slipped into the byways of American transportation history.

See also Great Wagon Road; Lee Highway; Roads and Highways, Colonial Times to World War I; Roads and Highways since World War I.

References Addington, Bruce H., *Daniel Boone and the Wilderness Road* (1922); Bakeless, John, *Daniel Boone* (1939); Hulbert, Archer Butler, *Historic Highways of America* (1902–1906); Kincaid, Robert L., *The Wilderness Road* (1947); MacGill, Caroline E., et al., *History of Transportation in the United States* (1917); Rose, Mark H., *Interstate Express Highway Politics* (1979); Tindall, George B., *Emergence of the New South* (1967).

Will Rogers Highway

Perhaps no highway in the country is as well known as the Will Rogers Highway, old Route 66—but then few had a television program (*Route 66*) based on two young men and their adventures as they crossed the nation in a hot Chevy Corvette on what supporters touted as the "Main Street of America." Now the old road is about gone. In its place are the freeways—Interstate Highways 10, 15, 40, 44, and 55. One of the few pristine stretches of the old road, once bragged about as 2,200 miles of four-lane highway, is in northwestern Arizona, where the interstate cut miles off the loop to Peach Springs, Truxton, Valentine, and Hackberry (where, ironically, the first pavement of the future highway was laid in the state). Americans no longer hum Bobby Troup's jazz classic, "Get Your Kicks on Route 66." To coin a phrase, "You can get more on I-44," just doesn't hack it.

The Will Rogers Highway had its birth in the Good Roads Movement of the early twentieth century. Sure, the route had been explored before. The section across northern New Mexico and Arizona was the mainline of the Atlantic and Pacific, a subsidiary of the Santa Fe Railway. It had been explored by Lieutenant Amiel Whipple and Edward F. Beale. The latter had even used Arabian camels on his expedition. But the Will Rogers Highway was a little different than most "named" highways—it followed no real historical route. It was "the great diagonal" that cut across the nation from Chicago to Los Angeles. In the twentieth century, more than any of the others, it represented the American heritage of travel and the legacy of going west to better oneself. It was the route of the *Grapes of Wrath*, wherein the Okies and Arkies fled the Great Depression for the hoped-for riches of the inland valleys of California.

The biggest promoter of Route 66 was Cyrus C. Avery, real estate salesman, motel owner (in the days when they were called "tourist courts"), and small-time oilman. Born in Pennsylvania, the Avery family soon moved to Missouri. As a young man he farmed, taught school, and worked his way through college. He married and sold insurance in Oklahoma City. Then he joined Henry Sinclair and drilled for oil at Vinita. He finally wound up in Tulsa and speculated successfully in real estate. He quite naturally gravitated to the idea of good roads—real estate was not worth much out in the countryside without them.

Avery became a county commissioner and pioneered the use of D. Ward King's Missouri log drag, a way to grade roads with a team towing a simple set of logs hooked together in a rectangle. He was a member of the Tulsa Automobile Club, interested in the Ozark Trail (got those people closer to Tulsa, don'tcha know), and eventually became a member of the American Association of State Highway Officials. Then one day, Avery, Frank Sheets of Illinois, and B. H. Piepmeier of Missouri (all "good road" promoters and state highway officials) decided that they needed a modern highway that would bring people to their part of the country. It had to go somewhere—Los Angeles looked good—anywhere, said Avery, just so it went through Tulsa. The number 66 was available, but no one really knows why it was used. Avery was a born highwayman in the best sense of the word.

It took until 1940 to get the whole route paved. Most of it was concrete, 6 to 10 inches deep, with each lane 9 feet wide. Avery saw to it that the 66 Association pushed the project ahead. It was to be the best highway in America, and the Hayden-Cartwright (read Arizona-Oklahoma) Act of 1934 finally did the trick. Federal financing made Route 66 possible. But the same act emphasized long-range planning, and already the death knell for Route 66 and all highways like it was being sounded—the

studies spoke of divided highways and limited access and bypassing small towns that lived off the road trade, all harbingers of the interstate highway system.

One of the more successful businesses on 66 was Whiting Brothers Gas Stations. Begun in St. Johns, Arizona, in 1926, the white stations with their yellow and red signs ("It seemed like those colors would show up," one of four brothers said later) spread up and down the highway from California to Oklahoma. As a promotion, they handed out little white discount cards to travelers and regular customers alike that saved a penny a gallon. Gas was only 19 cents a gallon anyway. It worked like a charm—everyone wanted that penny discount card, and they all bought Whiting gasoline. Another outfit out of Oklahoma named Phillips Petroleum called their gasoline after the highway where it sold so well, Phillips 66. They offered ten free gallons with a fill-up. (No, the gasoline was not really named after the highway—its formula had a specific gravity of 66—but who cared? It sold like wildfire.)

The golden age of Route 66 came after World War II and before the completion of the interstate highways. More than 8 million Americans moved into the trans-Mississippi West, 3.5 million to California alone. They were returning GIs who had seen the sunshine and warmth of the Golden State and 100 places in between. One of the movers was Bobby Troup, going to Hollywood to be a songwriter. Along the way he and his wife wrote a classic. They really got their kicks on Route 66. But there was a lot of competition for the American motoring dollar. The old 66 Association sponsored a caravan to travel the Will Rogers Highway, as Route 66 was styled for the first time. All decked out like drugstore cowboys, it was one of the better publicity stunts of the era—almost as good as the sign at Holland Tunnel in New York City. "For Men/Winslow, Arizona," the westbound sign said, around the shadowed body of a young woman in hat, cowboy boots, short shorts, and a tight shirt opened at the neck. Yessir, that'll fetch 'em every time. Nowadays it's called sexism—then it was legitimate and effective advertising. Of course the sign failed to warn travelers to keep their eyes open. They just might miss Winslow at high speed.

But the 66 Association used more of a family appeal. They issued maps and brochures listing what the Will Rogers Highway—the Main Street of America, America's Most Improved Highway, with over 1,100 miles of new and rebuilt roadway—had to offer. The attractions included the Missouri Ozarks, the Will Rogers Memorial, Texas—Land of the Cowboy, the New Mexico Rockies, the Grand Canyon of Arizona, a side jaunt to Las Vegas (come to think of it, almost all of these were side trips), and Glamorous Hollywood. By 1985, the last piece of interstate was poured at Williams, Arizona, and the era of Route 66 had come to an end. All of the remaining Highway 66 shields were removed soon after.

"What they did," said one proponent of the old highway, "the interstate took all of us guys and ruined us. They could have named it Interstate 66. Now nobody knows what highway we're on, and before, everybody knew 66." Maybe the younger set doesn't know, but the older generations will never forget Route 66, the heartbeat of a nation on the move.

See also Roads and Highways since World War I; Route 66.

References Baylor, Roberts, J., "America on the Move," *National Geographic* (September 1946) 90: 357–378; Rittenhouse, Jack D., *A Guidebook to Highway 66* (1993); Scott, Quinta, and Susan Croce Kelly, *Route 66* (1988).

Willys, John North (1873–1933)

Best known for its World War II production of the army's general purpose 4x4 quarter-ton truck, popularly called the Jeep (for G.P. or "general purpose," its military designation), Willys-Overland was the creation of John N. Willys. In 1906, Willys had organized the American Motor Car Company to sell the output of the Overland Company. The panic of 1907 caused Overland to falter, and Willys bought the old Pope-Toledo plant and moved the whole

operation to Toledo in 1908. By 1915, he was second in car production only to Henry Ford. But the post–World War I recession caused Willys to put the company into bankruptcy. The banks asked Walter P. Chrysler to reorganize the firm. Willys meanwhile managed to raise enough money to buy the firm back and became prosperous by 1929, when he sold out for $21 million. But the stock market crash put the company into receivership again. Willys returned from retirement to save the firm but his death in 1933 stopped that. Joseph W. Fraser (1894–1973) managed to reorganize Willys-Overland and produced Delmar G. Roos' Jeep during World War II. After the war, Fraser went into business with Henry J. Kaiser and produced the Kaiser-Fraser automobile and in 1953 combined with Willys-Overland, but the company never proved viable and went broke in 1962.

See also Automobiles from Domestics to Imports; Automobiles in American Society.

References Baldwin, Nick, et al., *The World Guide to Automobile Manufacturers* (1983); May, George S., "John North Willys," in George S. May (ed.), *EABHB: The Automobile Industry* (1989), 462–466; Motor Vehicle Manufacturers Association of the United States, *Automobiles of America* (1974).

Woodruff, Theodore T. (1811–1892)

A Watertown, New York, native, Theodore Woodruff probably invented the first widely used passenger sleeping car for American railroads. A car builder for the Terre Haute & Alton, he patented his car on 2 December 1856, nearly three years before George Pullman. Manufactured in Springfield, Massachusetts, Woodruff's car had 12 sections, 6 on each side, double berths (upper and lower), with a center aisle. In 1872, Woodruff organized the Central Traction Company with $100,000 capital and began building in earnest. He put 20 cars on mostly midwestern railroads and was quite prosperous until a lawsuit brought against him by Pullman nearly broke him. He was accidentally killed by an express train at Gloucester, New Jersey, in 1892. His company continued for several years, merging with another firm to form the Union Palace Car Company. Eventually, however, this unit was absorbed by Pullman, which became the sole representative left in the field of sleeping-car builders.

See also Pullman, George Mortimer; Wagner, Webster.

References Beebe, Lucius, *Mansions on Rails* (1957); Hubbard, Freeman, *Encyclopedia of North American Railroading* (1981); Mencken, August, *The Railroad Passenger Car* (1957); White, John H., Jr., *The American Railroad Passenger Car* (1978); White, John H., Jr., "Theodore T. Woodruff," in Robert L. Frey (ed.), *EABHB: Railroads in the Nineteenth Century* (1988), 438–439.

Wright, Benjamin (1770–1842)

Usually recognized as the senior engineer on the Erie Canal project, Benjamin Wright was Connecticut born and educated. His family moved to the Mohawk Valley where he became a surveyor out of Fort Stanwix. As he surveyed the land, Wright became aware that there was little value beyond subsistence farming unless the farmers could get their produce to market. As the roads were abominable, he turned his study to canals. He particularly studied the Little Falls Canal on the Mohawk, built by the English engineer William Weston. Meanwhile, he was elected to the state legislature and appointed county judge. This gave him access to the state canal commission for which he began to make surveys that led to the Erie Canal. After the War of 1812, Wright was in charge of building the central section of the canal. He also went on to supervise the difficult eastern section after it lagged behind the others.

Wright was not only a self-taught engineer but an able executive. He gathered a brilliant crew of young men about him, including Canvass White, John B. Jervis, David Stanhope Bates, and Nathan S. Roberts, all of whom went on to sterling careers of their own. Wright's practical education of these young men on the Erie Canal project has led to his being called the "Father of American Civil Engineering." As with his students, Wright acted in a consultory manner on several other early canal projects in Connecticut, New Jersey, Pennsylvania, Maryland, and Canada. He also acted as consulting engineer for railroad projects in

Virginia, Illinois, New York, and Spanish Cuba. After a most productive life, he died in New York City at age 72.

See also Erie Canal; Roberts, Nathan S.; White, Canvass.

References Ford, James Kip, "Benjamin Wright," in Allen Johnson, et al. (eds.), *Dictionary of American Biography*, X: 543–544; Krout, John A., "New York's Early Engineers," *New York History* (1945) 24: 269–277; MacGill, Caroline E., et al., *History of Transportation in the United States before 1860* (1917); Whitford, Nobel E., *History of the Canal System of the State of New York* (1906).

Wright, Orville (1871–1948) and Wilbur (1867–1912)

Sons of a bishop of the United Brethren Church at Dayton, Ohio, the Wright brothers came from a family that not only encouraged scientific curiosity but opened up their kitchen to the boys' experiments. Neither boy had a formal education that extended beyond high school, but their mechanical bent continued as they entered the bicycle-racing business, published a weekly newspaper, and took on job printing. The Wrights became interested in the gliding experiments of the German pilot Otto Lilienthal, whose untimely death led them into studying problems of flight more formally. The Wrights read widely, including the works of L. P. Mouillard, Octave Chanute, and Samuel P. Langley. It is impossible to say who did what first, as the Wrights borrowed openly from others and were on the cutting edge of powered flight from the beginning. But encouraged by Chanute personally, they began to test various gliders at Kitty Hawk, North Carolina (a site suggested by the U.S. Weather Service after an inquiry), and in their own wind tunnel (a Wright brothers' first). It was Orville who discovered that varying the tips of a wing (they tried over 200 wing configurations) would allow an aviator to restore a machine's balance, which variable became the modern aileron and the basis of all of their patents.

After a few years of gliding, the Wrights applied a simple gasoline engine of their own design to their glider for power. They then connected the engine to propellers (used in ships at sea, the Wrights were among the first to test their application in air) with a bicycle chain. A flip of the coin in 1903 gave the first attempt to Wilbur, but the machine failed. Three days later, Orville got his chance and the device flew for 12 seconds and achieved an altitude of 120 feet. More attempts led to longer flights. Connecting the ailerons to the rudder's action helped to make controlled turns possible. They took out a patent the following year. Oddly, the secret of the Wrights' achievement was ignored for five years. Most people did not believe that powered flight was possible anyway, a fact bolstered by Langley's widely known failures. It was not until they negotiated a contract with the Department of War for a military scout plane that the public learned of the scope of the Wrights' achievement.

The Wrights publicized their aircraft by demonstrations in the United States and Europe. They were widely lauded in France, and their successes made for a profitable business venture as the American Wright Company. But the brothers never made as much money as they could have, lacking the necessary streak of avarice.

Orville tended to do the flying (nearly losing his life in one military test that killed his soldier passenger) while Wilbur was the businessman until his premature death from typhoid fever in 1912. The passing of his older brother shook up Orville badly, but he carried on to become a major in the Army Signal Corps flying service in World War I, and to develop the split wing flap that became the basis for the dive-bomber brake in World War II. Not until 1942 did the Smithsonian Institution change its award for the first practical flight from Langley to the Wrights. They were prodded by Orville for years, who finally sent their original plane for display and to prove his point. Orville died in 1948, a quiet Dayton, Ohio, man to the end.

See also Aeronautics; Curtiss, Glenn Hammond; Langley, Samuel Pierpont.

References Bilstein, Roger E., *Flight in America* (1994); Crouch, Tom, *A Dream of Wings* (1981); Freudenthal, Elsbeth E., *Flight into History* (1949); Hallion, Richard P. (ed.), *The Wright Brothers* (1978); Howard, Fred, *Wilbur and Orville* (1987); Kelly, Fred C., *The Wright Brothers* (1948); McFarland, Marvin W. (ed.), *The Papers of Wilbur and Orville Wright* (1953); Moolman, Valerie, *The Road to Kittyhawk* (1980).

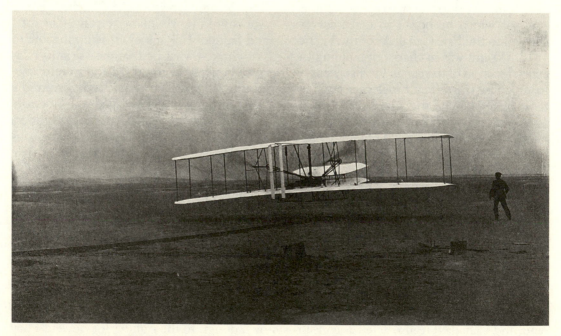

The Wright brothers made their first successful heavier-than-air flight on 17 December 1903.

X-Planes

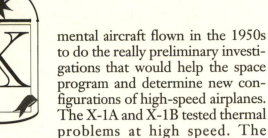

One of the more dramatic episodes of flight for the public was one of the more mundane from a technological point of view. This event was the breaking of the sound barrier, an event whose attendant "sonic boom" always turned heads to the sky. The air force managed this feat in 1947 above the Mojave Desert at Edwards Air Force Base Flight Test Center in California. The feat was made possible by the experimental (hence the prefix "X") rocket planes, the development of which began in the middle of World War II. The first successful type of these was the Bell X-1. Burning a mixture of alcohol, distilled water, and liquid oxygen, the engine could develop 1,500 pounds of thrust from each of its four thrust chambers. But it would exhaust its fuel supply in two and a half minutes. Hence, it would be launched from an airborne, modified B-29. The new craft was designed with the ballistics of a .50-caliber bullet, as little was known about which shape would do best. Dead-stick landings (without any engine power), release systems, and limited-speed powered flights took place in 1946. Then, flown by Captain Charles E. Yeager, the X-1 broke the sound barrier at 70,000 feet in 1947.

There was a succession of these experimental aircraft flown in the 1950s to do the really preliminary investigations that would help the space program and determine new configurations of high-speed airplanes. The X-1A and X-1B tested thermal problems at high speed. The Douglas D-558-I Skystreak brought forth information on air loads that could not be obtained from wind tunnels. The Douglas X-3 did not live up to its expected Mach 2 speed (twice the speed of sound), but solved inertial coupling problems that had rendered the North American F-100 Super Sabre dangerously uncontrollable, revealed the strengths and advantages of titanium construction, and solved the flight patterns necessary to produce the Lockheed F-104 Starfighter. Newer rocket planes like the Douglas D-558-II Skyrocket, the Convair XF-92A, the Northrop X-4, and the Bell X-5 reached new speeds and penetrated deeper space to test pilots' reactions to weightlessness, to develop flight suits that became the salvation of the first astronauts, and to probe the problems of variable swept wings and a myriad of other issues that led to the modern wider, longer, safer jetliners.

See also Astronautics.

References Bilstein, Roger E., *Flight in America* (1994); Hallion, Richard P., *Supersonic Flight* (1972); Hallion, Richard P., *Test Pilots* (1981); Yeager, Chuck, *Autobiography* (1985).

Yellowstone Trail Highway

One of the "named highways" popular in the teens and twenties of the twentieth century, the Yellowstone Trail Highway was used by local chambers of commerce and tourism and the American Automobile Association to stimulate travel on the "good roads" and increase income in the towns and states through which they passed. Coming out of Boston in 1914 with the slogan, "A good road from Plymouth to Puget Sound," the Yellowstone Trail went straight west on present-day U.S. Highway 20 through Albany to Buffalo, roughly paralleling the modern New York State Thruway and the old Erie Canal. At Buffalo, the Yellowstone Trail passed along the south shore of Lake Erie to Toledo, where it turned southwest to Fort Wayne, Indiana. From there it headed to Chicago, following what would become U.S. Highway 30 through Plymouth and Valparaiso. From Chicago the Yellowstone Trail went north to Milwaukee and westward through Oshkosh, Steven's Point, and Eau Claire to St. Paul, Minnesota. It crossed the Minnesota River at Ortonville and passed through South Dakota on what is now U.S. Highway 12 by way of Aberdeen, Mobridge, and Lemmon. Cutting across the extreme southwestern corner of North Dakota, the Yellowstone Trail passed through Miles City, Billings, and Livingston on what is modern Interstate 90. At Livingston, a branch of the Yellowstone Trail turned south to Yellowstone National Park, for which it was named. The main road continued westward to Butte, Missoula, and via Wallace and Coeur d'Alene, Idaho, to Spokane, Washington. It then dropped south to Walla Walla on what became U.S. Highways 195 and 12 and turned northwest through Ellensburg to Seattle via Snoqualmie Pass, the route of modern-day Interstates 82 and 90.

See also Mullan Road; Roads and Highways, Colonial Times to World War I; Roads and Highways since World War I.

Reference Hart, Val, *The Story of American Roads* (1950).

Zane's Trace

In the 1790s, an imaginative store-keeper and one of the founders of Wheeling, Virginia (now West Virginia), Ebenezer Zane, thought up a scheme to bring settlers into the Ohio country through Wheeling. He would petition Congress for aid and build a road from Wheeling to the fertile Scioto Valley at Chillicothe. Receiving three large land grants (one at each river, the Muskigum, Hockhocking, and Scioto, that his road crossed) to sell for expenses after he surveyed them at his own cost, Zane constructed a highway through his land grants to the west. Although as a veteran he was entitled to the land anyway, Zane got first pick ahead of the others, allowing him to choose the more advantageous locations for himself. In one of the grants, he laid out the town of Zanesville, Ohio, so that his name would be forever remembered by posterity. Zane's Trace was one of the prime routes into Ohio in the early 1800s, used by new settlers and flatboatmen returning from New Orleans. It was later absorbed by the National Road. Zane's Trace has the distinction of being the first federally funded road in American history.

See also Cumberland Road; National Road.

References Jordan, Philip D., *The National Road* (1948); U.S. Department of Transportation, Federal Highway Administration, *America's Highways* (1976).

Chronology

Prehistory
Various Native American trails, game trails, river routes.

1611 First "bridge" in America is a wharf at Jamestown.

1625 Paved (cobblestones) street in Pemaquid, Maine.

1630 Ferry opens between Boston and Charlestown.

1632 Virginia passes first road law making upkeep the responsibility of the counties.

1634 First real bridge built at Dorchester, Massachusetts.

1636 Early settlers learn of various Native American trails and began to name them and use them as roads.

1639 Beginnings of the Boston Post Road that eventually reached New York City.

1644 Shipbuilding begins in Massachusetts.

1654 First toll bridge at Rowley, Massachusetts.

1662 "Great Bridge" built over the Charles River at Cambridge, will last for 130 years until monopoly overruled in the Charles River Bridge case.

1673 Post route established between Boston and New York City.

1680 First ship built on Great Lakes by La Salle.

1698 First U.S. road map in *Tulley's Almanack* lists towns around Boston and their mileage from the bay.

1700 Whites began to use Mohawk Trail, later route of the Erie Canal and New York Central Railroad.

1713 First schooner built in Massachusetts.

1719 First fog-warning device, a cannon fired at measured intervals, at Boston.

1750 Connestoga wagons make appearance in Cumberland Valley.

Regular stage-wagons between Boston and New York City in service.

1751 A Delaware Indian, Nemacolin, blazes the trail to be known variously as Washington's Road, Braddock's Road, the Cumberland Road, the National Road, and also the route of the Baltimore & Ohio Railroad to the West.

Predecessor to the Lancaster Pike built in Pennsylvania on an old Native American route.

Chronology

1758 Forbes' Road crosses southern Pennsylvania directly to Pittsburgh.

1760 Tobacco-rolling roads in Virginia designed so that hogsheads of tobacco can be rolled to the river for shipment overseas.

1775 Daniel Boone builds the Wilderness Road through the Cumberland Gap.

1776 Father Escalante sets up the eastern half of the Old Spanish Trail.

1784 Thirteen-year-old Eli Warren takes the first balloon ride in North America.

1785 Little River Turnpike in Virginia is the first truly improved American road.

1786 Fitch steamboat built.

James Rumsey demonstrates his steamboat for George Washington.

1787 John Fitch runs his steamboat on the Delaware River at Philadelphia.

1789 First book of U.S. road maps is Christopher Colles' *Survey of the Roads of the United States of America*.

1790 Commercial canal at Richmond around the falls in the James River is first in America.

John Fitch inaugurates first steamboat service between Philadelphia and Trenton and goes broke in one summer.

1792 Pennsylvania puts in right-hand side of road rule on Lancaster Turnpike.

1793 First U.S. manned balloon flight.

Jean-Pierre Blanchard flies balloon from Philadelphia into New Jersey and is nearly killed by farmers who suspect he is some sort of witch.

1794 Whiskey Rebellion erupts, in part because of the lack of roads into the West.

1795 Little Falls Canal on the falls of the Mohawk River is the first in what will become the Erie Canal system.

Privately built Lancaster Turnpike becomes the best road in the nation.

1796 U.S. Congress approves of a post road between Wheeling and the Ohio River that will become a part of the National Road years later.

1800 Santee Canal built between the Santee River and Charleston, South Carolina, to divert upland produce to the port.

1802 James Rumsey builds the Potomac Canal around the falls north of today's District of Columbia at the behest of George Washington and others.

John Stevens builds the first propeller-driven steamboat. Stevens's boat navigates Hudson River.

1803 Natchez Trace is opened over the route of old Native American trail.

1804 Middlesex Canal in Massachusetts connects the Merrimack River to Boston Port.

New York becomes the first state to require right-hand travel on all roads in the state.

Oliver Evan's steam-powered amphibious vehicle goes through Philadelphia.

1806 Congress passes the Cumberland Road Act for the first part of the National Road.

First covered bridge in America.

Trenton Bridge over the Delaware River connects all states on the Atlantic coast in one system of roads.

1807 Beacon Hill (Boston) has a wooden-rail, horse-drawn transportation system.

Robert Fulton launches the first practical steamboat, the *North River of Clermont*.

1808 *Gallatin Report* proposes a unified national system of roads and canals.

1809 Canadian steamboat at Montréal on the St. Lawrence launched by beer magnate John Molson and others.

1811 Nicholas Roosevelt takes a Fulton boat down the Mississippi during the New Madrid earthquake and makes the first upstream voyage between New Orleans and Natchez.

1813 Lewis Downing opens coachworks at Concord, New Hampshire, and in partnership with J. Stephen Abbott will produce the stagecoach that tames the West.

1816 Captain Henry Shreve builds the first flat-bottomed, steam-operated riverboat.

John MacAdam publishes book on road-building methods.

1817 President James Madison vetoes Bonus Bill that granted money paid to incorporate the Second Bank of the United States to road building.

1818 Cumberland Road opened to traffic to Wheeling.

First tunnel in United States on Pennsylvania Mainline Canal.

1819 U.S. side-wheel steamship *Savannah* makes first trans-Atlantic Ocean voyage under steam.

1822 Santa Fe Trail opened to regular travel.

1824 *Gibbons v. Ogden* case breaks the Fulton monopoly on steamboats.

1825 Erie Canal opens that gives New York the East Coast lead in commerce never broken to this day.

John Stevens runs the first steam train on rails in North America.

1826 Jedediah Smith sets up the western half of the Old Spanish Trail.

Quarry railroad in Massachusetts is horse-drawn.

1827 Baltimore & Ohio Railroad becomes the first public rail carrier.

1828 Delaware and Hudson Canal opens, bringing Pennsylvania coal to New York City.

1829 Welland Canal opens allowing passage around Niagara Falls.

1830 Robert L. Stevens invents railroad spikes.

1831 Morris Canal opens in New Jersey bringing Pennsylvania coal into Newark.

1832 First New York City streetcars are horse-drawn and go to Harlem.

President Andrew Jackson vetoes the Maysville Road Bill and begins the restriction of federal aid to road building.

1833 First commercial Baltimore clipper ship built.

First fatal railroad accident in North America narrowly misses taking life of Cornelius Vanderbilt, later a rail magnate.

1834 First U.S. railroad tunnel at Staple Bend, Pennsylvania.

Pennsylvania Mainline Canal opens, a combination of canals and rails that is too expensive and slow to compete with the Erie Canal as Philadelphia businessmen had hoped.

1835 Richard Clayton makes balloon flight from Cincinnati to Monroe County, Virginia.

1836 Henry Campbell invents the "American" 4-4-0 locomotive, the standard nineteenth-century steam engine for U.S. passenger rails.

Illinois-Michigan Canal connects the Illinois-Mississippi River system to Lake Michigan at a little-known town called Chicago, which it will make the most important midwestern city, a matter compounded when railroads select the same hub.

1837 Adams Express organized.

Chief Justice Roger B. Taney issues opinion in the Charles River Bridge case that modifies the rule of contract if in the public interest.

First railroad sleeping car is a modified passenger coach on the Cumberland Valley Railroad, but no patent is issued.

1838 Congress declares all American railroads post routes.

1839 First iron bridge in United States.

William F. Harnden opens up the first successful express line.

1843 Oregon Trail opens up, which will carry enough settlers to the Pacific Northwest to make two-thirds of it American by 1845.

1844 Charles Goodyear perceives how to vulcanize rubber and make it stable and pliable under all conditions.

1845 Barlow Road marked to permit Oregon settlers to avoid the treacherous river route through the Dalles.

First iron railroad bridge in the United States.

The Miami-Erie Canal is finished, connecting the Ohio Valley to Lake Erie. It goes broke shortly from rail competition.

1846 Applegate Road gives a southern route into Oregon.

First plank road in the United States built at Syracuse, New York, using methods imported from Canada.

1847 The Mormon Trail parallels the Oregon Trail north of the Platte River until it turns into Deseret (Utah), the Latter-Day Saints' new home in the West.

1850 American Express organized.

Congress passes the first land grant for the Illinois Central Railroad—the land grant process will guarantee the building of so many other lines that it will do more to conquer the West and unify the nation economically, politically, and culturally than any other transportation subsidy.

Telegraph united with rail movements in New York State.

1851 The Hoosac Tunnel through the Berkshire Mountains begins, the longest tunnel in America until the Cascades are breached 24 years later.

1852 American Express organizes Wells Fargo in California and splits the country between them east and west at the Mississippi River.

1853 First all-rail line between New York City and Chicago, although trains had to be changed regularly.

1854 United States Express organized.

1855 First time word "caboose" used for the last car of a freight train.

Niagara River spanned by suspension bridge.

Panamá isthmus crossed by rail.

Russell, Majors & Waddell Company organized from several predecessor companies to carry freight on the Great Plains.

1856 Mormon handcart pioneers start for Utah.

Railroad built between Sacramento and Folsom is first on West Coast.

T. T. Woodruff obtains first sleeping-car patents.

1857 Beale's Wagon Road from Albuquerque to Los Angeles surveyed—later the route of the Santa Fe Railroad.

First refrigerated meat carried by train from Chicago.

U. S. Army experiments with camels as pack animals in the West.

1858 Butterfield "Ox Bow" route becomes the first transcontinental mail line.

1859 John LaMountain and John Wise fly a balloon from St. Louis to Henderson, New York, in 20 hours.

Oil discovered in Pennsylvania.

Pullman builds his first railroad sleeping cars.

1860 Pony Express demonstrates that mail and other items can be carried year-round on the Central Overland Route.

1861 Balloon Corps formed in Union's Army of the Potomac.

1862 Mullan Road in Washington Territory finished.

T. S. C. Lowe takes first aerial reconnaissance photographs of the Peninsula of Virginia and saves the Union army at Fair Oaks and Gaines Mill.

The Pacific Railroad Act establishes federal guidelines for public assistance to railroad construction, later to be extended and made even more generous.

1863 Steel rails first used on American railroads.

T. B. Watson, conductor, invents cupola for caboose to see train more clearly.

1864 Pullman builds his "Palace Cars."

1865 George Pullman offers his luxurious new car to the Abraham Lincoln family to carry the dead president home, forcing the railroads to widen their bridges and narrow their platforms overnight to let it pass.

1867 Elevated railroad built in New York City.

1868 Eli Janney builds first practical automatic coupler.

Fish market owner at Detroit, William Davis, receives a patent for a refrigerated freight car.

Fort Laramie Treaty ended the passage of travelers across Lakota land on the Bozeman Trail.

1869 George Westinghouse builds the air brake for railroad cars, which operates when the air line is filled from a reservoir.

Transcontinental railroad completed.

1870 Gustavus Franklin Swift perfects the rail refrigerator car by circulating the cold air over ice bunkers.

Pennsylvania Railroad develops the tender scoop that allows a train to pick up water from a tray between the tracks without stopping.

Vehicular tunnel built under the Chicago River.

1871 Chisolm Trail experiences its peak year with over a half million head of cattle driven to market.

Narrow gauge rails (any line less than 4 feet 8.5 inches in width) laid in Colorado mountains.

1872 Crédit Mobilier bribery of contractors and government officials involved with the transcontinental railroad revealed.

George Westinghouse receives patent for improved version of air brake, which operates when the air line is empty.

1873 Eli Janney receives patent for the "knuckle coupler."

Chronology

1874 Eads' iron bridge across the Mississippi River at St. Louis.

Engineers begin to drill tubes for rails under the Hudson River, a job that will take until the turn of the century to complete.

Stephen Field develops the outside third rail for electric locomotives.

1876 First vehicular (nonrailroad, noncanal) tunnel opens.

1877 First national strike by railroad workers.

Telephones become a part of rail traffic control.

The Granger Cases settled by the U.S. Supreme Court.

1879 George Selden obtains patents for his automobile engine that will cause other makers to pay him 1.25 percent royalty until Ford Motor Company finally breaks him in a court case 22 years later.

Street lights in Ohio.

1880 League of American Wheelmen organized to make roads better for bicyclists.

The first revolution in maritime technology as steel hulls begin to replace wood.

Thomas A. Edison experiments with electric railroad with no success.

1881 Steam heat becomes common to heat finer rail passenger cars.

1883 Brooklyn Bridge opens.

Standard time adopted throughout the United States in four time zones.

Transcontinental railroad between Great Lakes and Puget Sound completed.

1884 Lucius D. Copeland puts steam engine on a bicycle and invents the motorcycle.

1887 Interstate Commerce Act set up a government commission (ICC) to regulate railroad practices like pooling and rate discrimination.

Pennsylvania Railroad develops oil-burning locomotives.

Pennsylvania Railroad puts electric lights in passenger cars.

"Triple Valve" air brakes appear on the Chicago, Burlington & Quincy Railroad.

1888 Fred M. Kimball of Boston, Massachusetts, builds electric automobile.

1889 Octave Chanute begins to publish his theories of flight that influence the Wright brothers.

1890 Sherman Antitrust Act outlaws conspiracies in restraint of trade.

1891 Concrete highway built at Bellfountain, Ohio—220 feet long, 10 feet wide.

Jesse W. Reno invents the escalator.

Congress enacts the Ocean Mail Act.

1893 Agricultural Appropriation Act grants first federal monies for "good roads" since the days of President Andrew Jackson.

Duryea brothers' gas-powered auto is the first in the United States to be manufactured for the public.

First rural roads of brick constructed.

Henry Ford builds his first car.

New York Central Line's locomotive 999 exceeds 100 mph.

U.S. Office of Road Inquiry (predecessor to Department of Transportation) is established.

1894 Great Pullman strike led by Eugene V. Debs and the American Railroad Union.

1895 American Auto League become the first auto club in the States.

Boston has first U.S. subway line.

James Means begins to publish his up-to-date aeronautical information that assists men like the Wright brothers.

Railroads coming into Manhattan Island convert from steam to electricity just outside the city to stem pollution.

The Oldsmobile, which will be the first popular car, is constructed.

1896 First automatic transmission.

Rural free delivery (RFD) of mail begins.

Samuel P. Langley's steam-powered plane flies 3,300 feet and gives challenge to Wrights' claim to first powered flight for 30 years.

1897 U.S. Supreme Court announces that American seamen lack normal civil rights guaranteed under the Constitution in Arago case.

Frank J. Sprague invents multiple train controls that can operate rail cars from either end of the train, used in commuter service and subways even today.

Stanley Steamer becomes one of America's early popular autos.

1898 Chilkoot Trail takes more gold seekers into the Klondike than fought in the Spanish-American War of the same year.

First auto show in the United States at Boston.

John P. Holland invents the first true operational submarine.

1899 Chicago grants first auto license to a woman.

First auto fatality occurs when Henry H. Bliss is hit and killed as he descends from a streetcar into the path of an auto in downtown Manhattan.

First time an auto goes a mile a minute.

Percy Owen opens first auto showroom in New York City for Winton automobiles.

The Wright brothers fly their first biplane kite with wing warping controls that make it go where they want.

United States sets up Isthmian Canal Commission to investigate various routes across Central America to make communication and defense between the Atlantic and Pacific fleets faster, a need demonstrated in the Spanish-American War by the slow transfer of the battleship USS *Oregon* from the Pacific to the Cuban theater of war around the Horn.

1900 Auto manufacturers begin to use forward engine and steering wheel.

First U.S. auto show at Madison Square Garden.

Hendee Manufacturing begins manufacturing Indian Motorcycles at Springfield, Massachusetts.

National Good Roads Association organized from the Chicago Good Roads Association.

New York City installs first city buses.

1901 Automatic stokers appear on steam locomotives.

Curved-dash Oldsmobiles appear as the first mass-produced cars.

First long-distance auto race runs between New York City and Buffalo.

Gustave Whitehead of Bridgeport, Connecticut, claims to have made first controlled flight over one mile in length—no proof is offered.

New York and Connecticut begin to license autos and set up rules of the road.

New York City sets up first gas station.

Oil discovered at Beaumont, Texas.

1902 American Automobile Association (AAA) founded to unify all national car clubs.

David Buick opens up his motor car company in Detroit.

Wright brothers have controlled their gliders and now advance to engines.

1903 Elkins Act establishes penalties for discriminatory pricing on railroad services.

Ford Motor Company established.

Langley's plane, flown by Charles Manly, crashes into Potomac River.

William Harley and Arthur Davidson begin making motorcycles at Milwaukee.

Winton touring car make first coast-to-coast trip; spends one-third of time under repair.

Wright brothers make first sustained powered and controlled flight at Kitty Hawk, North Carolina.

1904 All-steel railroad passenger cars introduced.

Congress passes the Military Transportation Act, reserving military cargoes for American-registered ships.

First U.S.-made dirigible.

Sturdevant invents automatic transmission at Boston.

Wilbur Wright flies almost three miles in circles, making controlled turns.

1905 Agricultural Appropriations Act sets up Office of Public Road Inquiry.

American Motor Car Manufacturer's Association organized to fight Selden patent on auto engines.

Pennsylvania Railroad opens up 18-hour trips to Chicago out of New York City with *Broadway Limited*—New York Central follows suit with *Twentieth Century Limited* over track 60 miles longer.

Wright brothers introduce their *Flyer III*, the first practical airplane in history.

1906 Hepburn Act allowed the ICC to set up uniform railroad rates and accounting procedures.

Mack brothers (John, William, and Augustus) begin to make trucks in Allentown, Pennsylvania.

1907 Louis Breguet is the first person to fly off the ground in an early helicopter, hovering for about a minute 2 feet up.

New York motor taxis take the road, called "jitneys," a nickname for the nickel fare they charge.

Speed bumps installed at Glenco, Illinois, to slow fast cars.

U.S. Army establishes the Army Flying Corps, a branch of the Signal Corps.

1908 Delco develops the distributor cap and coil electrical system for autos.

First air fatality is Lieutenant Thomas E. Selfridge—Orville Wright severely injured in same crash and suffers from back pain for the rest of his life.

Fisher Coach Company begins to build one-piece enclosed auto bodies.

Ford produces Model T with left-side steering.

Glenn Curtiss flies the first plane of his design.

Kissimmee, Florida, issues the first aircraft regulations.

William C. Durant forms General Motors.

Wright brothers sell their airplane to U.S. Army.

1909 Autos begin to have workable fabric tops.

Edward Sperry produces first automatic pilot for aircraft.

Glenn L. Martin begins to make aircraft at Santa Ana, California.

Indianapolis Motor Speedway opens with brick track, hence the nickname "the Brickyard."

President William Howard Taft orders first car for the White House.

Wright brothers form a company to produce their airplane.

Wright brothers sue Glenn Curtiss for infringing upon their airplane patent.

1910 Auto headlights, horns, and brakes are made compulsory in some states; ignition timing linked to speed.

Blanche Scott is first female pilot to solo.

Glenn Curtiss makes first bomb run on a set of buoys in Lake Keuka, New York.

Curtiss takes off from platform on the cruiser USS *Birmingham*.

Glenn Curtiss builds his first flying boat.

Mann-Elkins Act granted ICC the right to suspend unfair railroad rates.

Penn Station opens in New York City.

1911 Cal P. Thomas flies coast to coast, crashing 19 times during the trip.

Glenn Curtiss lands an airplane on the modified battleship USS *Pennsylvania* near San Francisco and takes off again.

Electric starter introduced for autos, doing more to get women to drive than any other device as the physical work of cranking is eliminated.

First U.S. airmail contract let in New York State.

Harriet Quimby becomes first licensed female pilot.

Society of Automotive Engineers issues first handbook, standardizing parts.

Sperry invents electric gyroscope that always points north.

Wayne County, Michigan, paints first highway centerline.

1912 Auto windshield and electric lights become common.

Electric autos reach the peak of their popularity in America.

Salt Lake City installs electric stop lights.

1913 Ford builds first true assembly-line production plant.

Grand Central Station opens.

Gulf Oil gives away free road maps to promote driving.

Installment plan to sell cars introduced at San Francisco.

Milton J. Bryant uses skywriting to sell merchandise at Seattle.

1914 America's first commercial air flight.

Clayton Antitrust Act discourages formation of conglomerates that would diminish the flow of interstate commerce.

First Aero Squadron organized in the Army Signal Corps.

Opening of the Panama Canal.

1915 First all-steel auto body.

La Follette Seamen's Act reverses the 1897 Arago decision.

National Advisory Committee for Aeronautics established.

1916 Congress passes Federal Aid Road Act providing matching funds and standards for select roads.

Hand-driven windshield wipers appear on cars.

Hell Gate Bridge opened in New York City.

Congress enacts the Shipping Act, regulating oceangoing trade for the first time.

1917 Aircraft Manufacturers Association founded.

United States Railroad Administration organized to speed flow of war goods to port cities.

1918 August Fruehauf, a wagon builder, goes into making truck trailers.

Ethyl gasoline, a lead additive, introduced to delay air/fuel burn and retard engine "ping."

Express companies (Adams, Southern, Wells Fargo, American) unified by federal fiat as a war measure into American Railway Express.

Federal government orders all pilots to be licensed.

1919 First flight across the Atlantic by a U.S. Navy seaplane, made in stages.

First municipal airport created in Tucson, Arizona.

Glenn Curtiss invents the first mobile home trailer.

Robert Goddard publishes work on rocketry.

Post Office Appropriation Act declares almost any road in America to be a post road and thus able to receive federal aid for its improvement.

U.S. airmail routes set out.

1920 Donald Douglas leaves Curtiss to form his own aircraft company.

Holland Tunnel started from Jersey City to New York City—will take seven years to build.

Shock absorbers become common in autos to smooth the ride.

Diesel begins to replace coal on steamships in the second great technological transformation of maritime trade.

Jones Act reestablishes maritime cabotage privileges.

Transportation Act orders ICC to regulate transportation in such a way as to encourage its enhancement if within the public interest.

1921 Airmail goes coast to coast.

Congress enacts Federal Highway Act of 1921, continuing state matching-funds formula.

First crop-dusting from an airplane.

Frank and William Fageol built the Fageol Safety Coach, the first modern bus.

General William Mitchell sinks the ex-German battleship, *Ostfriesland*, off the coast of Virginia, confounding naval theorists.

Malcom Loughead (better known for his aircraft company, Lockheed) invents hydraulic auto brake.

Windshield wipers operated by engine vacuum introduced.

1922 Jimmy Doolittle flies coast to coast in one 24-hour period, from Pablo Beach, Florida, to San Diego.

Checker Cab founded.

Ford sells 1 million cars in one year.

Formation of the Lincoln Highway Association.

Harvey Firestone produces balloon tires, permitting a better ride and heavier loads.

U.S. Army uses helium in a dirigible.

Balloon tires for autos become common.

1923 American Locomotive Company builds the first practical diesel locomotive.

John Hertz founds the rent-a-car trade.

Moffat Railroad Tunnel begins in Colorado, making it the highest in elevation in the United States.

Pan American Highway proposed.

1924 "Duco" in use (cars painted different colors), ending Henry Ford's dictum "you can have any color you want as long as it's black."

First flight around the world by Douglas Aircraft.

Ford issues the cheapest Model T ever at $290 each, with no self-starter.

The oil filter appears on autos.

1925 American Association of State Highway Officials introduces uniform highway signs and numbering system.

Auto bumpers become standard.

Congress passes the Kelly Air Mail Act, turning the delivery over to private contractors.

General William Mitchell court-martialed for conduct unbecoming of an officer (i.e., disagreeing with his superiors' notions on the future of air warfare).

Robert Goddard fires a rocket that lifts its own weight.

The Cascade Tunnel, longest in the United States, is started—takes four years to build.

U.S. Navy airship *Shenandoah* destroyed in storm.

1926 Beginnings of U.S. Army Air Force as a separate unit.

Car heaters become common.

Congress enacts Air Commerce Act to regulate the skies.

Daniel Guggenheim Fund for the Promotion of Aeronautics created.

Greyhound Bus Line formed.

Safety glass that crumbles rather than shatters is put into auto windows.

Union Carbide introduces antifreeze.

1927 Centralized Track Control (CTC) installed on American railroads.

Charles A. Lindbergh flies the Atlantic Ocean, nonstop, alone.

National Advisory Committee for Aeronautics (NACA) builds first full-size wind tunnel.

Pan American Airways flies to Havana, Cuba, from Key West.

1928 AC Sparkplug Company invents the fuel pump, allowing the gas tank to be moved from the dangerous location under the hood to the safety of the trunk.

Aeronautics Branch of the Department of Commerce begins to investigate all air crashes.

Agricultural Appropriation Act permits federal government to build roads in national parks.

Amelia Earhart becomes the first woman to fly the Atlantic as a member of a crew of three.

C. S. Caldwell develops the variable-pitch propeller.

First syncromesh gearshift.

Merchant Marine Act establishes oceangoing mail subsidies.

The Seatrain *New Orleans* is the first "container" ship, carrying loaded railcars to Cuba.

1929 Air-conditioned Pullman cars developed.

Railway Express agency organized to replace the government-established American Railway Express Company.

1930 McNary-Watres Air Mail Act tries to reorganize mail delivery into three large conglomerates, which leads to corruption and collusion.

NACA recommends engines mounted in the wing, not above or below it, a standard procedure in multiengine aircraft thereafter.

Trans World Airlines becomes the first coast-to-coast airline flying between New York City and Los Angeles.

William Piper flies the prototype of the famous Piper Cub.

1931 Clessie L. Cummins produces the first truck diesel engine that revolutionizes the industry.

Congress passes the Railroad Unification Act calling for consolidation and simplified rates.

1932 Amelia Earhart is first woman to solo across the Atlantic—later that year she solos across the U.S. mainland.

Captain A. F. Hergenberger demonstrates blind flying (by instruments alone) at Dayton, Ohio.

Route 66 opens between Chicago and Los Angeles.

1933 Black Committee investigates awarding of mail contracts and finds corruption abounds.

Boeing introduces the first modern airliner, the 247.

Emergency Railroad Transportation Act creates a federal Coordinator of Transportation.

General Motors introduces knee-action front-end suspension for smoother ride and better control.

National Industrial Recovery Act creates industry cartels to set up competition codes.

U.S. Navy builds its first aircraft carrier (as opposed to converting an existing ship).

1934 Association of American Railroads organized to give a unified company view of rail problems.

Big Strike closes Port of San Francisco.

Black-McKellar Act excludes aircraft manufacturers from operating airlines.

First streamlined passenger train, the Chicago, Burlington & Quincy "Zephyr," is diesel powered.

Hayden-Cartwright Act has federal government assist states with plans, surveys, and engineering of public roads.

Hughes Aircraft Corporation established at Culver City, California.

1935 Boeing flies the predecessor to the four-engine B-17 bomber.

Congress passes the Motor Carrier Act to regulate trucking.

Douglas introduces the DC-3.

1936 Merchant Marine Act creates U.S. Maritime Commission to administer building and operating subsidies for American ship owners.

San Francisco-Oakland Bay Bridge opens.

1937 Amelia Earhart and Fred Noonan lost in Pacific.

Golden Gate Bridge opens.

Lockheed demonstrates the XC-35, the first pressurized cabin, which allows high-altitude flight.

Pan American Airways flies the Pacific to China.

1938 Boeing flies the 307 Stratoliner, a four-engine, pressurized-cabin airliner.

Congress passes the Civil Aeronautics Act to further control the skies.

Eddie Rickenbacker, World War I ace, takes over Eastern Airlines.

Washington, D.C., National Airport opens.

1939 Neutrality Act closes most European ports to American ships.

New York's La Guardia Field opens.

1940 First Los Angeles Freeway (Arroyo Chico) opens.

Pennsylvania Turnpike, America's first pay autobahn, opens from Carlisle to near Pittsburgh.

Igor Sikorsky flies first true helicopter.

Tacoma Narrows suspension bridge collapses.

Transportation Act allows ICC to exempt transportation from the restrictions of the Clayton Act if in the public interest.

1941 Defense Highway Act gives money to states without matching funds to construct highways for defense purposes.

Igor Sikorsky makes the first free flight in a modern helicopter with single overhead and tail rotors and variable pitch controls.

Santa Fe Railway puts the first FT diesels into operation hauling mainline freight.

Union Pacific Railroad puts the Big Boy, the largest steam locomotive in the world, into operation—the type will run until 1962.

1942 Alcan Highway begins at Dawson Creek, Yukon Territory, Canada, to reach Fairbanks, Alaska, USA.

DC-4 four-engine airliner built.

1944 Congress passes the Federal-Aid Highway Act that calls for interstate highways but appropriates no money.

First U.S. rocket plane, the MX-324.

First air-sea rescue by a helicopter.

U.S. Navy adopts container loading, a revolution in cargo handling rejected by civilian maritime personnel after the war.

1945 Chicago, Burlington & Quincy Railroad introduces the Vista Dome car.

Federal Communications Commission reserves select radio channels for railroads.

Federal government begins to finance the rocket program.

International Air Transport Association formed.

White Sands, New Mexico, Proving Ground opens.

1946 Bermuda Agreement opens up international airline rules.

First Great Circle flights from Hawaii to Egypt over the North Pole.

Kaiser-Fraser attempts to challenge the Big Three automakers (Ford, GM, Chrysler) and fails, the last time this is done domestically.

President Harry Truman signs the Federal Airport Act, providing $500 million in matching funds.

The Bell X-1 rocket plane flies for the first time.

The New York Yankees become the first sports team to fly to all of its away games.

U.S. Army launches a German V-2 rocket and a homegrown version, the WAC Corporal.

1947 Boeing B-47 becomes the first sweptwing, all-jet bomber in the new U.S. Air Force.

International Civil Aviation Organization founded.

Major Chuck Yeager breaks the sound barrier (670 mph) in the Bell X-1.

1948 B. F. Goodrich markets the first reliable tubeless tires.

Curtiss-Wright introduces the reversible-pitch propeller for shorter landings.

Idlewild (later JFK) Airport opens.

The Air Transport Command flies the Berlin Airlift.

U.S. Army launches a V-2 first-stage, WAC Corporal second-stage rocket.

1949 Air travel surpasses train travel for the first time in the United States.

American aircraft circles the earth without stopping because of air-to-air refueling.

Cape Canaveral established as the U.S. rocket test range.

Chrysler develops the first all-in-one key starter located in the steering column, replacing the on/off key and separate starter button in the dashboard.

Hiller model 12 helicopter flies across the United States commercially.

O'Hare airport begun at Chicago, completed in 1954.

U.S. Army establishes Redstone Arsenal at Huntsville, Alabama, as the center of its ballistic-missile program.

1950 First International Aeronautics Congress meets.

Hermes A-1 rocket replaces captured German V-2s in American programs.

Tinted glass and the McPherson strut suspension (shock absorber, coil spring, and wheel shaft all in one) introduced for automobiles.

1951 A monkey and 11 mice survive rocket trip into space.

Cape Canaveral missile range established.

Power steering put into automobiles.

U.S. Air Force begins to experiment with weightlessness.

1952 B-52 bomber put into operation.

More diesel than steam locomotives on American railroads.

1953 Corvette, America's only real sports car, hits the roads.

First American-made Redstone rocket launched.

John Hetrick invents first auto air-bag restraint.

1954 Cargo Preference Act reserves 50 percent of all military cargoes for civilian ships.

American Motors comes out of merger of Nash and Hudson.

President Dwight D. Eisenhower signs the St. Lawrence Seaway Act.

Walt Disney makes futuristic film *Man in Space*, which has much influence in the scientific community.

1955 Nuclear submarine *Nautilus* launched.

Remote control of railroad engines introduced, making longer consists possible.

1956 Douglas DC-7C is in service, able to cross Atlantic or Pacific nonstop.

Federal-Aid Highway Act passed, funding the interstate highway system.

First flight of Lockheed U-2 "spy plane."

Two airliners collide over the Grand Canyon.

U.S. Air Force project 7969 announced: to put a man in space at some future date.

1957 An intercontinental ballistic missile (ICBM) flies from Cape Canaveral, Florida.

First true "containerized" ship launched.

Julian Allen finds that blunt objects can dissipate heat better than bullet-shaped objects, especially if covered with ablative coatings; all American space vehicles will be shaped and coated this way until the space shuttle.

1958 After numerous failures, a Vanguard rocket puts up first American satellite.

Congress enacts the Federal Aviation Act reorganizing all air regulation into one superagency.

First time more passengers cross the Atlantic by air than by sea.

First U.S. Explorer satellites, followed by Pioneer and Vanguard satellites, are sent up to study radiation belts around Earth.

Ford introduces the Edsel, a grand failure.

Henry Bartrand invents the crash-sensitive air bag.

National Aeronautics and Space Administration (NASA) organized to concentrate and demilitarize space research and exploration.

National Airlines offers first U.S. jet passenger service.

Pan Am begins the first U.S. all-jet service over the Atlantic with Boeing 707s.

President Dwight D. Eisenhower broadcasts the first message from space at Christmas using Signal Communication by Orbiting Relay Equipment (SCORE).

Transportation Act permits railroads to cut passenger service.

TWA hires the first black stewardess.

Van Allen radiation belts discovered.

1959 Cape Canaveral builds launch sites for manned space program.

First telescopic "jetway" at San Francisco airport protects the passengers from the weather as they board planes.

St. Lawrence Seaway opens, making all Great Lakes cities Atlantic seaports.

The first seven U.S. astronauts selected.

United and Delta Airlines put the Douglas DC-8 jetliner in service.

The X-15 supersonic jet flies for the first time.

1960 "Echo" metallic balloons reflect terrestrial communications signals.

NASA creates global tracking-station network in treaties with host countries.

Nuclear submarine USS *Triton* duplicates Magellan's circumnavigation of the globe completely submerged.

Organization of Petroleum Exporting Countries (OPEC) formed.

The Apollo project for flight to the moon is envisioned.

Tiros satellites provide weather data with photographs from space.

1961 Alan Shepard is first U.S. man in space.

Dulles Airport at Washington, D.C., is the first designed for jet traffic, but because of its country location remains mostly unused until the 1980s.

Houston (later Johnson) Space Center becomes ground control for NASA.

President John F. Kennedy pledges an American man on the moon within a decade.

1962 First nuclear cargo ship launched.

John Glenn is first U.S. man to orbit Earth.

Mariner space probe flies by Venus.

Ranger satellites sent to the moon but fail in mission to crash-land until late in program (1965).

Relay military communications satellites launched.

Telestar is first privately funded satellite (AT&T) for telephone and television communications.

1963 Gates Learjet goes into operation.

1964 Capital Beltway opened in District of Columbia.

Chesapeake Bay Bridge/tunnel opens across the mouth of Chesapeake Bay.

First flight of the new reconnaissance plane, Lockheed's SR-71 *Blackbird*.

Ford introduces the Mustang, its most popular post–World War II model.

Fully automatic air-conditioning, "Climate Control," is introduced in Cadillac cars.

Mariner satellites begin to explore Mars with flybys and eventual orbiting.

U.S. Army Map Service finishes maps of the moon's known surfaces.

Verrazano Narrows Bridge opens.

1965 Bell AH-1 Cobra is first helicopter designed for military attack missions.

California creates the first compulsory auto emission tests.

First launch of the two-man *Gemini* spacecraft.

GEOS satellites study Earth from space orbits.

1966 Department of Transportation unifies all transportation agencies under its umbrella.

First docking in space between *Gemini 8* and a target vehicle.

Lunar Orbiter satellites confirm possible landing zones.

Ralph Nader publishes his *Unsafe at Any Speed* exposé of the Chevrolet Corvair, which helps lead to the National Traffic and Motor Vehicle Safety Law.

Surveyor satellites launch to soft-land on Moon and prepare the way for a manned landing.

The 251-passenger Douglas DC-8-61 is first "stretch" airliner.

1967 Robert H. Lawrence, the first black astronaut, dies in an air accident at Edwards Air Force Base.

Sikorsky S-61 is first helicopter to cross Atlantic nonstop.

Three U.S. astronauts die in ground test accident when spark ignites their pure-oxygen atmosphere.

Torrey Canyon involved in first major oil spill at sea in history.

TWA first airline to have all-jet fleet.

1968 *Apollo 8* circles the moon as astronauts read from the Bible on Christmas Day.

Lockheed C-5A Galaxy, largest cargo plane in the world, flies for first time.

1969 Boeing launches the 747 jumbo airliner.

First federal safety standards set for automobiles.

Man on the moon, *Apollo 11*.

Metroliner train runs between New York City and Washington, D.C., on regular schedule.

Worst year ever in American auto accidents, as 54,895 die; if projected to the year 2000, the annual number of casualties on America's roads would exceed the combined deaths of World Wars I and II.

1970 Clean Air Act sets national minimum auto emission standards.

DC-10 wide-body jet introduced (345 passengers) but has teething problems as baggage doors blow out and floors collapse on decompression, shearing control cables.

Federal-Aid Highway Act changes the standard 50-50 ratio between state and federal monies to 30 state–70 federal.

Lockheed L-1011 TriStar wide-body jet introduced.

Penn Central goes broke, shocking Congress and the American business community.

Rail Passenger Act creates National Rail Passenger Corporation or Amtrak.

Urban Mass Transportation Assistance Act puts federal money into public transit.

1971 D. B. Cooper commits the first airline highjacking, beginning an all-too-common crime.

Seatrain establishes the "landbridge" concept of cargo movement across the United States.

U.S. Senate rejects the American-built Supersonic Transport (SST) by one vote.

1972 European A-300B airbus enters market.

Last manned moon expedition.

Pioneer 10 heads to Jupiter and Saturn.

Space shuttle program is announced.

Washington, D.C., subway opens.

1973 Auto air bag offered as an option by General Motors; will take 20 years to become an industry standard.

Bay Area Rapid Transit (BART) opens up the longest underwater tunnel in America between San Francisco and Oakland, California.

Launching of *Skylab*.

McDonnell-Douglas DC-10-30CF wide-body has capability to convert between passenger and cargo (and vice versa) configurations overnight.

OPEC organizes the First Oil Shock by raising prices in response to the Yom Kippur War.

Regional Rail Corporation Act creates the Consolidated Rail Corporation, or Conrail, for the northeastern trunk lines.

1974 U.S. speed limit set at 55 mph in response to Arab oil embargo.

Westar satellites establish domestic communication network.

1975 Apollo-Soyuz Test Project (ASTP)—U.S. and Soviet spacecraft dock together in space.

French Concorde SST flies the Atlantic commercially as the United States declines to enter the competition.

Environmental Protection Act restricts the amounts of hydrocarbons, nitrogen oxide, and carbon dioxide emitted by industrial production and transportation.

Viking soft-lands on Mars.

1976 After receiving over 100,000 letters, President Gerald R. Ford names the first space shuttle the *Enterprise* after the spaceship on a popular television show, *Star Trek*, overruling NASA's choice, the *Constitution*.

Boeing 747-123 model is a special piggyback conversion that carries the space shuttle back and forth between its West Coast landing field and East Coast launch pad.

NASA pledges to put a woman into space.

Railroad Revitalization and Regulatory Reform Act eases railroad mergers.

1977 NASA receives 1,147 applicants for 30 space shuttle openings.

The Lockheed C141 Starlifter becomes one of America's two biggest transport planes.

1978 Airline Deregulation Act takes government control out of the first transportation segment.

America's first front-wheel-drive cars are the Dodge Omni and the Plymouth Horizon.

Amoco *Cadiz* oil spill.

First crossing of the Atlantic by a hot-air balloon.

NASA selects 35 astronauts for the space shuttle, six of whom are women, three black, and one a Japanese American.

1979 NASA names the four space shuttle craft *Columbia, Challenger, Discovery,* and *Atlantis* as the experimental *Enterprise* is retired to the Smithsonian.

OPEC raises oil prices in the Second Oil Shock, a response to the Iranian Islamic Revolution.

1980 Japan surpasses U.S. auto production.

Maglev train runs for the first time.

Motor Carrier Act deregulates trucking industry.

Space shuttle tiles that protect against reentry burnup are thicker and stickier.

Staggers Rail Act deregulates the railroads.

1981 Boeing 767 wide-body flies.

Columbia is the first space shuttle to go into orbit.

First crossing of the Pacific in a hot-air balloon.

Lockheed F117A stealth fighter is flown, will be kept secret for ten years.

Northeast Rail Services Act calls for the selling of Conrail to private investors.

Professional Air Traffic Controllers Organization strike is broken.

Boeing flies the 767 wide-body and the 757 regular-body, both being economical, fuel-saving planes.

1982 Helicopter (two-man crew) circumnavigates the earth.

Surface Transportation Act forces states to accept federally mandated truck weight and size limits larger than many states desire, a response to more expensive fuels.

1983 Guion S. Bluford becomes the first African American in space.

Sally K. Ride becomes first American woman in space.

President Ronald Reagan announces the Strategic Defense Initiative (SDI), also called Star Wars.

Dick Smith makes solo helicopter circumnavigation of the globe in a Bell JetRanger III.

1984 Astronauts Bruce McCandless and Robert L. Stewart become the first to make untethered space walks.

American President Lines introduces the idea of "Double Stack" container trains.

First seven-person space shuttle crew flies.

New York State is the first to require seat belts be worn by drivers, front-seat passengers, and all children under the age of ten.

Shipping Act deregulates the maritime industry.

1985 Ford Granada is the first American car with antilock breaks.

NASA looks for a teacher to fly on a shuttle mission—10,690 apply.

OPEC cartel no longer can keep its members in line on oil production quotas and Saudi Arabia abandons buttressing up prices.

Senator Jake Garn of Utah flies on a shuttle mission.

1986 *Challenger* explosion sets back U.S. space program one year.

Commercial Motor Vehicle Act requires national standards for drivers of any commercial vehicle carrying goods or passengers.

OPEC falls apart.

Voyager flies around the world on one tank of fuel.

1987 United States has double the railroad trackage of second-place Soviet Union, but hauls less freight and fewer passengers by train.

1988 Boeing 747-400 can carry up to 500 persons 8,000 miles—its sales (170) break all previous records.

Northrop B-2 Stealth Bomber revealed to the world.

1989 Exxon *Valdez* oil spill in Prince Edward Sound.

1990 Oil Pollution Act requires double hulls on all tankers using U.S. waters by 2015.

Space shuttle launches the Hubble Space Telescope into orbit.

1991 Federal Highway Administration estimates that half of America's highway bridges are inadequate and the general road infrastructure is failing.

Pam American, Eastern, and Midway Airlines all go broke.

1993 Space shuttle repairs the Hubble Space Telescope.

1994 Congress frees trucking industry from all state regulation.

Notes

For more on cars, see Motor Vehicle Manufacturers Association of the United States, *Automobiles of America:* "Milestones," "Pioneers," "Roll Call," "Highlights." Detroit: Wayne State University, 1974.

For maritime chronology, see René de la Pedraja, *A Historical Dictionary of the U.S. Merchant Marine and Shipping Industry.* Westport, CT: Greenwood Press, 1994.

For aerospace chronology, see Eugene M. Emme (ed.), *Two Hundred Years of Flight in America.* San Diego: Univelt, 1977.

In general, see Leonard C. Bruno, *On the Move: A Chronology of Transportation.* Detroit: Gale Research, 1993.

For Great Plains chronology, see Raymond W. Settle and Mary L. Settle, *War Drums and Wagon Wheels. Palo Alto, CA: Stanford University Press, 1949).*

Bibliography

Abbey, Wallace W. "Association of American Railroads." In Keith L. Bryant, Jr. (ed.), *EABHB: Railroads in the Age of Regulation.* New York: Facts on File, 1988, 9–10.

———. "Soo Line Railroad Company." In Keith L. Bryant, Jr. (ed.), *EABHB: Railroads in the Age of Regulation.* New York: Facts on File, 1988, 406–407.

Abbott, Carl. *The Metropolitan Frontier.* Tucson: University of Arizona Press, 1993.

Abernethy, Thomas P. *The Burr Conspiracy.* New York: Oxford University Press, 1954.

———. *The South in the New Nation, 1789–1819.* Baton Rouge: Louisiana State University Press, 1961.

Abodaher, David. *Iacocca.* New York: Macmillan, 1982.

Adams, Charles F., and Henry Adams. *Chapters of Erie.* Ithaca, NY: Cornell University Press, 1956.

Adams, Henry. *The Life of Albert Gallatin.* Philadelphia: J. B. Lippincott, 1879.

Addington, Bruce H. *Daniel Boone and the Wilderness Road.* New York: Macmillan, 1922.

Agar, Michael H. *Independents Declared: The Dilemmas of Independent Trucking.* Washington, DC: Smithsonian Institution Press, 1986.

Aitchison, Clyde B. "The Evolution of the Interstate Commerce Act: 1887–1937." *George Washington University Law Review* (1937) 5: 289–403.

Albion, Robert G. *Square-Riggers on Schedule.* New Brunswick, NJ: Princeton University Press, 1938.

Albright, George Leslie. *Official Explorations for Pacific Railroads, 1853–1855.* Berkeley: University of California Press, 1921.

Alexander, Edwin P. *Iron Horses: American Locomotives,1829–1900.* New York: W. W. Norton, 1941.

———. *On the Main Line: The Pennsylvania Railroad in the 19th Century.* New York: Crown, 1971.

———. *The Pennsylvania Railroad: A Pictorial History.* New York: W. W. Norton, 1947.

Allen, John Sinnickson. *Standard Time in America . . .* New York, 1951.

Allen, Lewis. *Only Yesterday: An Informal History of the 1920s.* New York: Harper and Brothers, 1931.

Allen, Oliver. *The Airline Builders.* Alexandria, VA: Time-Life Books, 1981.

Altrocchi, Julia. *The Old California Trail.* Caldwell, ID: Caxton Press, 1945.

Altschul, D. Robert. "Transportation in African Development." *Journal of Geography* (1980) 79: 44–56.

Ames, Charles E. *Pioneering the Union Pacific: A Reappraisal of the Builders of the Railroad.* New York: Appleton-Century-Crofts, 1969.

Anderson, Jervis, and Peter Stone. *A. Philip Randolph: A Biographical Portrait.* New York: Harcourt Brace Jovanovich, 1973.

Anderson, Nels. *Desert Saints: The Mormon Frontier in Utah.* Chicago: University of Chicago Press, 1942.

Anderson, Rudolph E. *The Story of the American Automobile.* Washington, DC: Public Affairs Press, 1950.

Anderson, Walter Truett. *Reality Isn't What It Used To Be.* New York: Harper and Row, 1990.

Andrews, Charles M. *The Colonial Period of American History.* 4 vols. New Haven, CT: Yale University Press, 1934–1938.

Andrews, Wayne. *The Vanderbilt Legend: The Story of the Vanderbilt Family.* New York: Harcourt, Brace and Company, 1941.

Andrist, Ralph K. *The Erie Canal.* New York: American Heritage, 1964.

Archer, Robert F. *A History of the Lehigh Valley Railroad.* Berkeley, CA: Howell North, 1977.

Armstrong, John H. *The Railroad—What It Is—What It Does.* New York: Simmons-Boardman, 1978.

Armstrong, Neil, et al. *First on the Moon: A Voyage with Neil Armstrong, Michael Collins, Edwin E. Aldrin, Jr.* Boston: Little, Brown and Company, 1970.

Arnold, Horace Lucien, and Fay Leone Faurote. *Ford Methods and the Ford Shops.* New York: Engineer Magazine Company, 1915.

Arrington, Leonard J. *Great Basin Kingdom: An Economic History of the Latter-Day Saints.* Cambridge: Harvard University Press, 1958.

Athearn, Robert C. *Rebel of the Rockies: A History of the Denver and Rio Grande Western Railroad.* New Haven, CT: Yale University Press, 1962.

———. "Utah and Northern Railroad." *Montana Western History* (1968) 23: 2–23.

Atherton, Lewis F. "Business Techniques in the Santa Fe Trade." *Missouri Historical Review* (1940) 34: 335–341.

———. *The Cattle Kings.* Bloomington: Indiana University Press, 1961.

Atkinson, Joseph D., Jay M. Shafritz, et al. *The Real Stuff: A History of NASA's Astronaut Recruitment Program.* New York: Praeger, 1985.

Auerbach, Carl A., et al. *The Legal Process: An Introduction to Decision-Making by Judicial, Legislative, Executive, and Administrative Agencies.* San Francisco: Chandler, 1961.

Babcock, Glenn D. *History of the United States Rubber Company: A Case Study in Corporate Management.* Bloomington: Indiana University Press, 1966.

Bachman, Ben. "Until the Thunder Dies." *Trains* (November 1994) 54: 48–55.

Back, Joe. *Horses, Hitches and Rocky Trails.* Chicago: Swallow Press, 1959.

Baer, Christopher T., et al. *Canals and Railroads of the Mid-Atlantic States, 1800–1860.* Wilmington, DE: Regional Economic History Research Center, 1981.

Bailyn, Bernard (ed.). *The Debate on the Constitution: Federalist and Antifederalist Speeches, Articles, and Letters during the Struggle over Ratification.* New York: Library of America, 1993.

Bain, William E. *Frisco Folks.* Denver: Sage Books, 1961.

Bakeless, John. *Daniel Boone.* New York: William Morrow, 1939.

———. *Lewis and Clark: Partners in Discovery.* New York: William Morrow, 1947.

Baker, Burt Brown. *The McLoughlin Empire and Its Rulers.* Glendale, CA: Arthur H. Clark Company, 1959.

Baker, George P. *The Formation of the New England Railroad Systems.* Cambridge: Harvard University Press, 1937.

Baker, Ray Palmer. "James Geddes." In *Dictionary of American Biography.* New York: Charles Scribner's Sons, 1964–1981, IV: 204–205.

Baldwin, Leland D. *The Keelboat Age on Western Waters.* Pittsburgh: University of Pittsburgh Press, 1941.

———. *Whiskey Rebels: The Story of a Frontier Uprising.* Pittsburgh: University of Pittsburgh Press, 1939.

Baldwin, Munson. *With Brass and Gas: An Illustrated and Embellished Chronicle of Ballooning in Mid-Nineteenth Century America.* Boston: Beacon, 1967.

Baldwin, Nick, et al. *The World Guide to Automobile Manufacturers.* New York: Facts on File, 1983.

Bancroft, Hubert H. *History of the Life of Leland Stanford.* Oakland, CA: Biobooks, 1952.

Banks, William W., and Harold E. Banks. *Motive Power of the Union Pacific.* Omaha: Barnhart, 1958.

Banning, William, and George Hugh Banning, *Six Horses.* New York, 1930.

Baranson, Jack. *The Japanese Challenge to U.S. Industry.* Lexington, MA: Lexington Books, 1981.

Barnard, Charles F. "Santa Fe's 3000 Class Mallets." *Model Railroader* (May 1989) 56: 85–91.

Barone, Michael. *Our Country: The Shaping of America from Roosevelt to Reagan.* New York: Free Press, 1990.

Barry, James P. *Ships of the Great Lakes.* Berkeley, CA: Howell-North, 1973.

Barton, Charles. *Howard Hughes and His Flying Boat.* Fallbrook, CA: Aero Publishers, 1982.

Batchelder, A. G. "The Immediate Necessity of Military Highways." *National Geographic* (November–December 1917) 32: 477–499.

Bateman, Carrol. *The Baltimore & OH: The Story of the Railroad That Grew Up with the United States.* Baltimore: Johns Hopkins University Press, 1951.

Baucom, Donald R. *The Origins of SDI, 1944–1983.* Lawrence: University Press of Kansas, 1993.

Bayley, Stephen. *Sex, Drink and Fast Cars: The Creation and Consumption of Images.* Boston: Faber and Faber, 1986.

Beale, Howard K. *Theodore Roosevelt and the Rise of America to World Power.* Baltimore: Johns Hopkins University Press, 1956.

Beard, William. *Regulation of Pipe Lines as Common Carriers.* New York: Columbia University Press, 1941.

Beasley, D. R. *The Suppression of the Automobile.* New York: Greenwood, 1988.

Beasley, Norman. *Knudsen.* New York: Whittlesey House, 1947.

Beaver, Roy C. *The Bessemer & Lake Erie Railroad, 1869–1969.* San Marino, CA: Golden West Books, 1969.

Beckett, Derrick. *Great Buildings of the World: Bridges.* London: Paul Hamlyn, 1969.

Bee, Roger, et al. *The Chicago Great Western in Minnesota.* Anoka, MN: Blue River Publications, 1984.

———. *The Central Pacific and Southern Pacific Railroads.* Berkeley, CA: Howell-North, 1963.

———. *Mansions on Rails.* Berkeley, CA: Howell-North, 1959.

———. *Mr. Pullman's Elegant Palace Car.* Garden City, NY: Doubleday, 1961.

———. *The Overland Limited.* Berkeley, CA: Howell-North, 1963.

Beebe, Lucius M. *20th Century: "The Greatest Train in the World."* Berkeley, CA: Howell-North, 1962.

———. *Narrow Gauge in the Rockies.* Berkeley, CA: Howell-North, 1958.

Beebe, Lucius M., and Charles Clegg. *U.S. West: The Saga of Wells Fargo.* New York: E. P. Dutton, 1949.

Belasco, Warren James. *Americans on the Road: From Autocamp to Motel, 1910–1945.* Cambridge: MIT Press, 1979.

Bell, James C. *Opening a Highway to the Pacific, 1838–1846.* New York: Columbia University Press, 1921.

Bellush, Bernard. *The Failures of the NRA.* New York: W. W. Norton, 1975.

Berger, John A. *The Franciscan Missions of California.* New York: G. P. Putnam's Sons, 1948.

Bernard, John. "Walter Philip Reuther." In George S. May, (ed.), *EABHB: The Automobile Industry*. New York: Facts on File, 1990, 357–373.

———. *Walter Reuther and the Rise of the Auto Workers*. Boston: Little, Brown and Company, 1983.

Bernstein, Aaron. *Grounded: Frank Lorenzo and the Destruction of Eastern Airlines*. New York: Simon and Schuster, 1990.

Berton, Pierre. *The Impossible Railway: The Building of the Canadian Pacific*. New York: Knopf, 1972.

———. *The Klondike Fever: The Life and Death of the Last Great Gold Rush*. New York: Knopf, 1958.

Best, Gerald M. *Iron Horses to Promontory*. San Marino, CA: Golden West Books, 1969.

Bestor, Arthur. "State Sovereignty and Slavery: A Reinterpretation of the Proslavery Constitutional Doctrine, 1846–1860." *Illinois State Historical Society Journal* (1960) 54: 117–180.

Bezilla, Michael. "Bessemer & Lake Erie Railroad." In Keith L. Bryant, Jr. (ed.), *EABHB: Railroads in the Age of Regulation*. New York: Facts on File, 1988, 31–32.

———. "Electrification." In Keith L. Bryant, Jr. (ed.), *EABHB: Railroads in the Age of Regulation*. New York: Facts on File, 1988, 130–131.

Biddle, Wayne. *Barons of the Sky*. New York: Simon and Schuster, 1991.

Bieber, Ralph P. "The Southwestern Trails to California in 1849." *Mississippi Valley Historical Review* (1925) 12: 342–375.

Bill, Fred A. "Early Steamboating on the Red River [of the North]." *North Dakota Historical Quarterly* (1942) 9: 69–85.

Billington, Ray Allen. *The Far Western Frontier, 1830–1860*. New York: Harper and Row, 1956.

Bilstein, Roger E. *Flight in America: From the Wrights to the Astronauts*. Baltimore: Johns Hopkins University Press, 1994.

———. *Flight Patterns: Trends of Aeronautical Development in the United States, 1918–1929*. Athens: University of Georgia Press, 1983.

Bingham, Truman C. "The Transportation Act of 1940." *Southern Economic Journal* (July 1941–1942) 8: 1–21.

Binns, Archie. *Peter Skene Ogden, Fur Trader*. Portland, OR: Binsford and Mort, 1967.

Bishop, Avard Longley. "Corrupt Practices Connected with the Building and Operation of the State Works of Pennsylvania." *Yale Review* (1907) 15: 391–411.

Black, Robert C. *Railroads of the Confederacy*. Chapel Hill: University of North Carolina Press, 1952.

Blaisdell, Thomas C., Jr. *The Federal Trade Commission: An Experiment in the Control of Business*. New York: Columbia University Press, 1932.

Block, Michael K. *Sherman Act Indictments, 1955–1980*. 2 vols. New York: Federal Legal Publications, 1981.

Blum, John Morton. *Woodrow Wilson and the Politics of Morality*. Boston: Little, Brown and Company, 1956.

Boatner, Mark M., III. *The Civil War Dictionary*. New York: David McKay Company, 1959.

Bobbé, Dorothie. *De Witt Clinton*. New York: Minton, Balch, 1933.

Bogen, Jules I. *The Anthracite Railroads: A Study in American Enterprise*. New York: Ronald Press Company, 1927.

Bolton, Herbert E. *Outpost of Empire: The Story of the Founding of San Francisco*. New York: Knopf, 1931.

———. *The Spanish Borderlands: A Chronicle of Old Florida and the Southwest*. New Haven, CT: Yale University Press, 1921.

Bonsor, N. R. P. *North Atlantic Seaway: An Illustrated History of Passenger Services Linking the Old World with the New in Four Volumes*. New York: Arena, 1975.

Borth, Christy. *Mankind on the Move: The Story of Highways*. Washington, DC: Automotive Safety Foundation, 1969.

Botkin, Benjamin A., and Alan F. Harlow. *A Treasury of Railroad Folklore*. New York: Crown, 1953.

Botting, Douglas. *The Giant Airships*. Alexandria, VA: Time-Life Books, 1980.

Botzow, Hermann S. D., Jr. *Monorails*. New York: Simmons-Boardman, 1960.

Bourne, Russell. *Floating West: The Erie and Other American Canals*. New York: W. W. Norton, 1992.

Bowers, Claude G. *Jefferson and Hamilton: The Struggle for Democracy in America*. Boston: Little, Brown and Company, 1925.

Bowie, Beverly M. "MATS: America's Long Arm of the Air." *National Geographic* (March 1957) 111: 283–317.

Boyd, Thomas. *Poor John Fitch*. New York: George Putnam's Sons, 1937.

Boyle, Ohio D. *History of Railroad Strikes*. Washington, DC: Brotherhood Publishing Company, 1935.

Boyne, Walter J., and Donald S. López (eds.). *Vertical Flight*. Washington, DC: Smithsonian Institution Press, 1984.

Bradford, M. E. *Original Intentions on the Making and Ratification of the United States Constitution*. Athens: University of Georgia Press, 1993.

Bradley, Glenn D. *The Story of the Pony Express*. San Francisco: Hesperian House, 1960.

Brady, Edward M. *Tugs, Towboats and Towing*. Cambridge, MD: Cornell Maritime Press, 1967.

Bramson, Seth H. "Florida East Coast Railway." In Keith L. Bryant, Jr. (ed.), *EABHB: Railroads in the Age of Regulation*. New York: Facts on File, 1988, 162–163.

———. "Henry M. Flagler." In Keith L. Bryant, Jr. (ed.), *EABHB: Railroads in the Age of Regulation*. New York: Facts on File, 1988, 159–161.

———. *Speedway to Sunshine: The Story of the Florida East Coast Railroad*. Erin, Ontario: Boston Mills Press, 1984.

Brandes, Ely M., and Alan E. Lazar. *Rail Passenger Traffic in the West*. Menlo Park, CA: Stanford Research Institute, 1966.

Brant, Irving. *James Madison*. 6 vols. Indianapolis: Bobbs-Merrill, 1941–1961.

Brazeal, Brailsford R. *The Brotherhood of Sleeping Car Porters*. New York: Harper and Row, 1946.

Briggs, Harold E. "Early Freight and Stage Lines in Dakota." *North Dakota Historical Quarterly* (1929) 3: 299–361.

Brinnin, John Malcolm. *The Sway of the Grand Saloon: A Social History of the North Atlantic*. New York: Delacorte, 1971.

Brinton, Crane. *The Anatomy of Revolution*. New York: Vintage Books, 1965.

Brodsly, David. *L.A. Freeway: An Appreciative Essay*. Berkeley: University of California Press, 1981.

Broesamle, John J. "William Gibbs McAdoo." In Keith L. Bryant, Jr. (ed.), *EABHB: Railroads in the Age of Regulation*. New York: Facts on File, 1988, 283–285.

———. *William Gibbs McAdoo: A Panic for Change, 1863–1917*. Port Washington, NY: Kennikat Press, 1973.

Brooks, Courtney, et al. *Chariots for Apollo: A History of Manned Lunar Spacecraft*. Washington, DC: Government Printing Office, 1979.

Brooks, Juanita. *The Mountain Meadows Massacre*. Palo Alto, CA: Stanford University Press, 1950.

Brooks, Peter W. *The Modern Airliner: Its Origins and Development*. London: Putnam, 1961.

Brown, Andrew H. "New St. Lawrence Seaway Opens Great Lakes to the World." *National Geographic* 116 (November 1959): 299–339.

Brown, Jennie B. *Fort Hall on the Oregon Trail: A Historical Study*. Caldwell, ID: Caxton Printers, 1932.

Bruce, Robert. *The National Road*. New York: National Highways Association, 1916.

Bruce, Robert V. *1877: Year of Violence*. Indianapolis: Bobbs-Merrill, 1959.

Bruchey, Stuart. *The Roots of American Economic Growth, 1607–1861*. New York: Harper and Row, 1965.

Brummett, John. *Highwire: From the Backroads to the Beltway: The Clinton Presidency*. New York: Hyperion, 1994.

Bibliography

Bryan, Ford R. *Henry's Lieutenants.* Detroit: Wayne State University, 1993.

Bryant, Keith L., Jr. "Arthur Edward Stillwell." In Keith L. Bryant, Jr. (ed.), *EABHB: Railroads in the Age of Regulation.* New York: Facts on File, 1988, 422–424.

———. *Arthur Edward Stillwell: Promoter with a Hunch.* Nashville, TN: Vanderbilt University Press, 1971.

———. "Atchison, Topeka & Santa Fe Railway." In Keith L. Bryant, Jr. (ed.), *EABHB: Railroads in the Age of Regulation.* New York: Facts on File, 1988, 10–13.

———. *History of the Atchison, Topeka & Santa Fe Railway.* New York: Macmillan, 1975.

———. "Southern Railway." In Keith L. Bryant, Jr. (ed.), *EABHB: Railroads in the Age of Regulation.* New York: Facts on File, 1988, 410–411.

Bryant, Keith L., Jr. (ed.). *Encyclopedia of American Business History and Biography: Railroads in the Age of Regulation, 1900–1980.* New York: Facts on File, 1988.

Buchanan, Pat. "Free Trade and the Rise in Poverty." *Washington Times National Weekly Edition* (24–30 October 1994): 34.

Buck, Solon J. *The Granger Movement: A Study of Agricultural Organization and Its Political, Economic, and Social Manifestations, 1870–1880.* Cambridge: Harvard University Press, 1913.

Buford, Curtis D. *Trailer Train Company, A Unique Force in the Railroad Industry.* New York: Newcomen Society in North America, 1982.

Buley, R. Carlyle. *The Old Northwest: Pioneer Period, 1815–1840.* 2 vols. Bloomington: Indiana University Press, 1950.

Bunau-Varilla, Phillippe. *Panama: Creation, Destruction, and Resurrection.* New York: McBride-Nast, 1914.

Burbank, David T. *Reign of the Rabble: The St. Louis General Strike of 1877.* New York: A. M. Kelley Publishers, 1966.

Burgess, George H., and Miles C. Kennedy. *Centennial History of the Pennsylvania Railroad Company, 1846–1946.* Philadelphia: Pennsylvania Railroad Company, 1949.

Burlingame, Merrill G. *John M. Bozeman, Montana Trail Maker.* Bozeman: Montana State University, 1983.

Burlingame, Roger. *Henry Ford.* New York: Knopf, 1954.

Burnham, John Chynoweth. "The Gasoline Tax and the Automotive Revolution." *Mississippi Valley Historical Review* (1961–1962) 48: 435–459.

Burton, Walter E. *The Story of Tire Beads and Tires.* New York: McGraw-Hill, 1954.

Butler, Dan. "Leland Stanford." In Keith L. Bryant, Jr. (ed.), *EABHB: Railroads in the Age of Regulation.* New York: Facts on File, 1988, 376–379.

———. "Mark Hopkins." In Robert L. Frey (ed.), *EABHB: Railroads in the Nineteenth Century.* New York: Facts on File, 1988, 184–186.

———. "Spokane, Portland & Seattle Railway." In Keith L. Bryant, Jr. (ed.), *EABHB: Railroads in the Age of Regulation.* New York: Facts on File, 1988, 412–413.

———. "Theodore Judah." In Robert L. Frey (ed.), *EABHB: Railroads in the Nineteenth Century.* New York: Facts on File, 1988, 213–215.

Caleb, Walter F. *Brotherhood of Railroad Trainmen.* New York: Albert and Charles Boni, 1937.

Callender, Guy S. "The Early Transportation and Banking Enterprises of the States in Relation to the Growth of Corporations." *Quarterly Journal of Economics* (1902–1903) 17: 111–162.

Campbell, E. G. *The Reorganization of the American Railroads, 1893–1900.* New York: Columbia University Press, 1938.

Cannon, William A., and Fred K. Fox. *Studebaker: The Complete Story.* Blue Ridge Summit, PA: Tab Books, 1981.

Capers, Gerald M. *John C. Calhoun—Opportunist: A Reappraisal.* Gainesville: University of Florida Press, 1960.

Carey, Keith. *The Helicopter: An Illustrated History.* Wellingborough, England: Patrick Stephens, 1986.

Carlisle, Rodney. *Sovereignty for Sale: The Origin and Evolution of the Panamanian and Liberian Flags of Convenience.* Annapolis, MD: Naval Institute Press, 1981.

Carper, Robert S. *Focus: The Railroad in Transition.* South Brunswick, NJ: A. S. Barnes, 1968.

Carroll, Charles C. *The Government's Importation of Camels.* Washington, DC: Government Printing Office, 1904.

Carroll, E. Malcolm. *Origins of the Whig Party.* Durham, NC: Duke University, 1925.

Carson, Robert B. *Main Line to Oblivion: The Disintegration of New York Railroads in the Twentieth Century.* Port Washington, NY: Kennikat, 1971.

Carstenson, Vernon (ed.). *The Public Lands: Studies in the History of the Public Domain.* Madison: University of Wisconsin Press, 1962.

Carter, Charles F. *When Railroads Were New.* New York: Simmons-Boardman, 1926.

Carter, Hodding, and Betty Carter. *Doomed Road of Empire: The Spanish Trail of Conquest.* New York: McGraw-Hill, 1963.

Caruso, John Anthony. *The Southern Frontier.* Indianapolis: Bobbs-Merrill, 1963.

Casey, Robert J., and W. A. S. Douglas. *Pioneer Railroad: The Story of the Chicago & North Western System.* New York: Whittlesey House, 1948.

———. *The Lackawanna Story.* New York: McGraw-Hill, 1951.

Cassutt, Michael. *Who's Who in Space: The First Twenty-Five Years.* Boston: G. K. Hall, 1987.

Chaisson, Eric J. *The Hubble Wars: Astrophysics Meets Astropolitics in the Two-Billion Dollar Struggle over the Hubble Space Telescope.* New York: HarperCollins, 1994.

Chambers, William Nisbet. *Political Parties in a New Nation: The American Experience, 1776–1809.* New York: Oxford University Press, 1963.

Chandler, Alfred D., Jr. "Anthracite Coal and the Beginnings of the Industrial Revolution." *Business History Review* (1980) 59: 459–479.

Chandler, Alfred D., Jr. (ed.). *Giant Enterprise: Ford, General Motors, and the American Automobile Industry.* New York: Harcourt, Brace and World, 1964.

Chapelle, Howard Irving. *The Baltimore Clipper: Its Origin and Development.* Hatboro, PA: Tradition Press, 1965.

———. *The History of American Sailing Ships.* New York: W. W. Norton, 1935.

Charles, Joseph. *The Origins of the American Party System.* Wiliamsburg, VA: William and Mary University Press, 1956.

Chatelain, Maurice. *Our Ancestors Came from Outer Space.* Translated by Oest Berlings. Garden City, NY: Doubleday, 1978.

Chatterton, E. Kenle. *Sailing Ships and Their Story.* Boston: Lauriat, 1935.

Cheng, Philip C. *Accounting and Financing for Motor Carriers.* Lexington, MA: Lexington Books, 1984.

Cherowyth, John. "The Gasoline Tax and the Automotive Revolution." *Mississippi Valley Historical Review* (1951) 48: 435–495.

Chester, Edward W. *United States Oil Policy and Diplomacy.* Westport, CT: Greenwood, 1983.

Chevrier, Lionel. *The St. Lawrence Seaway.* New York: St. Martin's, 1959.

Childs, William R. *Trucking and the Public Interest: The Emergence of Federal Regulation, 1914–1940.* Knoxville: University of Tennessee Press, 1985.

Chipman, Donald E. *Spanish Texas, 1519–1821.* Austin: University of Texas Press, 1992.

Chittenden, Hiram M. *The American Fur Trade of the Far West.* 3 vols. New York: Francis P. Harper, 1902.

———. *History of Early Steamboat Navigation on the Missouri River.* Minneapolis: Ross and Haines, 1903.

Christie, I. R. *Crisis of Empire: Great Britain and the American Colonies, 1754–1783.* New York: W. W. Norton, 1966.

Bibliography

Chrysler, Walter P. *Life of an American Workman.* New York: Dodd, Mead and Company, 1950.

Clark, Arthur H. *The Clipper Ship Era.* New York: G. P. Putnam's Sons, 1910.

Clark, Gary. "Santa Fe's Curtis Hill." *Pacific Rail News* (November 1994) 372: 40–41.

Clark, George T. *Leland Stanford.* Palo Alto, CA: Stanford University Press, 1931.

Clark, J. Stanley. *The Oil Century: From the Drake Well to the Conservation Era.* Norman: University of Oklahoma Press, 1958.

Clark, James R. "The Kingdom of God, the Council of Fifty, and the State of Deseret." *Utah Historical Quarterly* (1958) 26: 131–148.

Clark, John W. *The Grain Trade in the Old Northwest.* Urbana: University of Illinois Press, 1966.

Clark, Milton R. "Chicago, Milwaukee & St. Paul Railway." In Robert L. Frey (ed.), *EABHB: Railroads in the Nineteenth Century.* New York: Facts on File, 1988, 49–50.

Clarke, Mary Stetson. *The Old Middlesex Canal.* Easton, PA: Center for Canal History and Technology, 1974.

Cleland, Robert G. *From Wilderness to Empire.* New York: Knopf, 1959.

———. *Pathfinders.* Los Angeles: Powell Publishing Company, 1929.

———. *This Reckless Breed of Men: The Trappers and Fur Traders of the Southwest.* New York: Knopf, 1950.

Cleveland, Frederick A., and Fred Wilbur Powell. *Railroad Promotion and Capitalization in the United States.* New York: Longmans, Green and Company, 1909.

Cline, Gloria Griffen. *Peter Skene Ogden and the Hudson's Bay Company.* Norman: University of Oklahoma Press, 1974.

Clymer, Floyd. *A Treasury of Early American Automobiles, 1877–1925.* New York: Bonanza, 1950.

Coates, Kenneth (ed.). *The Alaska Highway: Papers of the 40th Anniversary Symposium.* Vancouver: University of British Columbia Press, 1985.

Cohen, Stan. *The White Pass & Yukon Route.* Missoula, MT: Pictorial Histories Puiblishing Company, 1980.

Coit, Margaret L. *John C. Calhoun: American Portrait.* Boston: Little, Brown and Company, 1950.

Cole, Donald B. *Martin Van Buren and the American Political System.* Princeton, NJ: Princeton University Press, 1984.

Coll, D. B., et al. *The Corps of Engineers: The Unites States Army in World War II.* Washington, DC: Government Printing Office, 1958.

Collias, Joe G. *The Missouri Pacific Lines in Color.* Crestwood, MO: M & M Books, 1993.

———. *MoPac Power.* La Jolla, CA: Howell-North, 1980.

Collier, Peter, and David Horowitz. *The Fords.* New York: Summit Books, 1987.

Collins, Michael. *Mission to Mars.* New York: Grove Weidenfeld, 1990.

Comstock, Henry B. *The Iron Horse: An Illustrated History of Steam Locomotives.* New York: Greenberg Publications, 1993.

Condit, Carl W. *The Port of New York: A History of the Rail and Terminal System from the Beginnings to Pennsylvania Station.* Chicago: University of Chicago Press, 1980.

———. *The Port of New York: A History of the Rail and Terminal System from the Grand Central Electrification to the Present.* Chicago: University of Chicago Press, 1981.

Conkling, Roscoe P., and Mary P. Conkling. *The Butterfield Overland Mail.* 3 vols. Glendale, CA: Arthur H. Clark Company, 1947.

Cook, Richard J. *The Beauty of Railroad Bridges in North America Then and Now.* San Marino, CA: Golden West Books, 1987.

———. *Super Power Steam Locomotives.* San Marino, CA: Golden West Books, 1966.

Cook, Richard J. (ed.). *A Brief History of the Brotherhood of Locomotive Engineers.* Cleveland: Brotherhood of Locomotive Engineers, 1977.

Cooke, Jacob Ernest. *Alexander Hamilton.* New York: Charles Scribner's Sons, 1982.

Cooley, Everett L. "Carpetbag Rule: Territorial Government in Early Utah." *Utah Historical Quarterly* (1958) 26: 107–129.

Corbett, David. *Politics and the Airlines.* Toronto: University of Toronto Press, 1965.

Corle, Edwin. *John Studebaker: An American Dream.* New York: E. P. Dutton, 1948.

———. *The Royal Highway.* Indianapolis: Bobbs-Merrill Company, 1915.

Cornett, Lloyd H., Jr. "American Airlines." In William M. Leary (ed.), *EABHB: The Airline Industry.* New York: Facts on File, 1992, 36–43.

———. "Continental Airlines." In William M. Leary (ed.), *EABHB: The Airline Industry.* New York: Facts On File, 1992, 119–122.

Cotterill, Robert S. "The Beginnings of Railroads in the Southwest." *Mississippi Valley Historical Review* (1921–1922) VIII: 318–326.

———. "Southern Railroads and Western Trade, 1840–1850." *Mississippi Valley Historical Review* (1916–1917) III: 427–441.

———. "Southern Railroads, 1850–1860." *Mississippi Valley Historical Review* (1923–1924) X, 396–405.

Coy, Owen C. *The Great Trek.* Los Angeles: Powell Publishing, 1931.

Crandall, Burton B. *The Growth of the Intercity Bus Industry.* Syracuse, NY: Syracuse University College of Business Administration, 1954.

Crane, Frank. *George Westinghouse: His Life and Achievements.* New York: Wise, 1925.

Cray, E. *Chrome Colossus: General Motors and Its Times.* New York: McGraw-Hill, 1980.

Creer, Leland H. "Lansford W. Hastings and the Discovery of the Old Mormon Trail." *Western Humanities Review* (1949) 3: 175–186.

Creighton, Donald. *The Forked Road: Canada, 1939–1957.* Toronto: University of Toronto Press, 1976.

Creighton, Roger L. *Urban Transportation Planning.* Urbana: University of Illinois Press, 1970.

Critchlow, Donald T. "Studebaker Corporation." In George S. May (ed.), *EABHB: The Automobile Industry.* New York: Facts on File, 1990, 434–437.

Croffut, William A. *The Story of the Vanderbilts and Their Fortune.* New York: Belford, Clarke and Company, 1886.

Cron, F. W. "Highway Design for Motor Vehicles—A Historic Review." *Public Roads* (1975) 38: 163–174; (1975) 39: 68–79, 96–108, 163–171; (1976) 40: 78–86, 93–100.

Crouch, Tom D. *A Dream of Wings: Americans and the Airplane, 1875–1905.* New York: W. W. Norton 1981.

———. "The Gasbag Era." *Aviation Quarterly* (1977) 3: 291–301.

———. "General Aviation, 1919–1976." In Eugene M. Emme (ed.), *Two Hundred Years of Flight in America.* San Diego: Univelt, 1977, 111–136.

Crum, Josie. *Three Little Lines: The Silverton Railroad, the Silverton, Gladstone & Northerly Railroad, and the Silverton Northern Railroad.* Durango, CO: Herald-News, 1900.

Crump, Spencer. *Western Pacific: The Railroad That Was Built Too Late.* Los Angeles: Trans-Anglo Books, 1963.

Cunningham, Nobel E., Jr. *The Jeffersonian Republicans: The Formation of a Party Organization, 1789–1801.* Chapel Hill: University of North Carolina Press, 1957.

Cunningham, William J. *American Railroads: American Government Control and Reconstruction Policies.* New York: A. W. Shaw, 1922.

Cusumano, Michael A. *The Japanese Automobile: Technology and Management at Nissan and Toyota.* Cambridge: Harvard University Press, 1985.

Bibliography

Cutler, Carl C. *Greyhounds of the Sea: The Story of the American Clipper Ship*. Annapolis, MD: United States Naval Institute, 1930.

———. *Queens of the Western Ocean*. Annapolis, MD: United States Naval Institute, 1961.

Dagget, Stuart. *Chapters on the History of the Southern Pacific*. New York: Ronald, 1922.

Dale, Edward Everette. *The Range Cattle Industry*. Norman: University of Oklahoma Press, 1930.

Dale, Harrison C. "The Organization of the Oregon Emigrating Companies." *Oregon Historical Quarterly* (1915) 16: 205–227.

Daley, Robert. *An America Saga: Juan Trippe and His Pan Am Empire*. New York: Random House, 1980.

Dalmas, Herbert. "The Super Chief: Luxury on Rails." *Coronet* (May 1954) 36: 38–42.

Dangerfield, George. *The Era of Good Feelings*. New York: Harcourt, Brace and World, 1952.

Daniels, Jonathan. *The Devil's Backbone: The Story of the Natchez Trace*. New York: McGraw-Hill, 1962.

Daniels, Winthrop M. *American Railroads: Four Phases of Their History*. Princeton, NJ: Princeton University Press, 1932.

Dauer, Manning J. *The Adams Federalists*. Baltimore: The Johns Hopkins University Press, 1953.

Daughen, Joseph R., and Peter Binzen. *The Wreck of the Penn Central*. New York: New American Library, 1973.

Davidson, Walter P. *The Berlin Blockade: A Study in Cold War Politics*. New Brunswick, NJ: Princeton University Press, 1958.

Davies, R. E. G. *Airlines of the United States since 1914*. Washington, DC: Smithsonian Institution, 1982.

———. *Continental Airlines: The First Fifty Years*. The Woodlands, TX: Pioneer Publications, 1986.

———. *Delta: An Airline and Its Aircraft*. Miami: Paladwr Press, 1990.

———. *A History of the World's Airlines*. New York: Oxford University Press, 1964.

———. *Pan Am: An Airline and Its Aircraft*. New York: Orion Books, 1987.

———. *Rebels and Reformers of the Airways*. Washington, DC: Smithsonian Institution, 1987.

Davis, Burke. *The Billy Mitchell Affair*. New York: Random House, 1967.

———. *The Southern Railway: Road of the Innovators*. Chapel Hill: University of North Carolina Press, 1985.

Davis, Kenneth S. *The Hero: Charles A. Lindbergh and the American Dream*. Garden City, NY: Doubleday, 1959.

Davis, L. J. "And Now, Can Bob Crandall Have It All?" *New York Times Magazine* (23 September 1990): 25, 42, 44, 46.

Davis, Richard O. *The Age of Asphalt: The Automobile, the Freeway, and the Condition of Metropolitan America*. Philadelphia: J. B. Lippincott, 1975.

Davis, William C. *A Way through the Wilderness: The Natches Trace and the Civilization of the Southern Frontier*. New York: HarperCollins, 1995.

DeBoer, David J. *Piggyback and Containers: A History of Rail Intermodal on America's Steel Highway*. San Marino, CA: Golden West Books, 1992.

Derleth, August W. *The Milwaukee Road*. New York: Creative Age, 1948.

Derr, Thomas S. *The Modern Steam Car*. Los Angeles: Clymer Publications, 1945.

Dethloff, Henry C. *Suddenly Tomorrow Came: A History of the Johnson Space Center*. Washington, DC: Government Printing Office, 1992.

DeWard, John, and Nancy DeWard. *History of NASA: America's Voyage to the Stars*. New York: Exeter Books, 1984.

Dickinson, John. *To Build a Canal: Sault Ste. Marie, 1853–1854 and After*. Columbus: Ohio State University Press, 1981.

Dietrich, Noah, and Bob Thomas. *Howard: The Amazing Mr. Hughes*. Greenwich, CT: Fawcett, 1972.

Dillon, Richard. *Meriwether Lewis: A Biography*. New York: Coward-McCann, 1965.

—. *Siskiyou Trail: The Hudson's Bay Route to California*. New York: McGraw-Hill, 1975.

Dobson, John M. *Politics in the Gilded Age: A New Perspective on Reform*. New York: Praeger, 1972.

Doezema, William R. "United States Railroad Administration." In Keith L. Bryant, Jr. (ed.), *EABHB: Railroads in the Age of Regulation*. New York: Facts on File, 1988, 447–448.

Donovan, Frank. *River Boats of America*. New York: Thomas Y. Crowell, 1966.

Dorin, Patrick C. *Amtrak Trains and Travel*. Seattle: Superior, 1979.

—. *The Canadian National Railways' Story*. Seattle: Superior, 1975.

—. *Chicago and North Western Power*. Burbank, CA: Superior, 1972.

—. *The Soo Line*. Seattle: Superior, 1979.

Dos Passos, John. *The Shackles of Power: Three Jeffersonian Decades*. Garden City, NY: Doubleday, 1966.

Dougherty, Caroll R. *Labor Problems in American Industry*. Boston: Houghton Mifflin, 1933.

Douglas, Deborah. *United States Women in Aviation, 1941–1985*. Washington, DC: Smithsonian Institution, 1991.

Dowd, Gregory Evans. *A Spirited Resistance: The North American Indian Struggle for Unity, 1745–1815*. Baltimore: Johns Hopkins University Press, 1992.

Dowie, Mark. "Pinto Madness." *Mother Jones* (1977) 2: 18–32.

Dozell, Gary W. "The Train They Call Sprint." *Trains* (April 1981) 41: 26–33.

Dozier, Howard A. *A History of the Atlantic Coast Line Railroad*. Boston: Houghton Mifflin, 1920.

Drago, Henry (Harry) Sinclair. *Canal Days in America*. New York: Clarkson-Potter, 1972.

—. *Great American Cattle Trails*. New York: Dodd, Mead and Company, 1965.

—. *Roads to Empire: The Dramatic Conquest of the American West*. New York: Dodd, Meade and Company, 1968.

Drake, Harrison C. "The Organization of the Oregon Emigrating Companies." *Oregon Historical Quarterly* (1915) 16: 205–227.

Drake, St. Clair, and Horace R. Clayton. *Black Metropolis*. New York: Harcourt, Brace and Company, 1945.

Drew, Elizabeth. *On the Edge: The Clinton Presidency*. New York: Simon and Schuster, 1994.

Drury, George H. "The Chicago, Burlington & Qunicy Railroad." In Keith L. Bryant, Jr. (ed.), *EABHB: Railroads in the Age of Regulation*. New York: Facts on File, 1988, 71–73.

—. "Dieselization." In Keith L. Bryant, Jr. (ed.), *EABHB: Railroads in the Age of Regulation*. New York: Facts on File, 1988, 119–121.

—. *Guide to North American Steam Locomotives*. Milwaukee: Kalmbach, 1993.

—. *The Historical Guide to North American Railroads*. Milwaukee: Kalmbach, 1985.

—. "New York Central System." In Keith L. Bryant, Jr. (ed.), *EABHB: Railroads in the Age of Regulation*. New York: Facts on File, 1988, 317–319.

—. "Norfolk & Western Railroad." In Keith L. Bryant, Jr. (ed.), *EABHB: Railroads in the Age of Regulation*. New York: Facts on File, 1988, 324–325.

—. *The Train Watcher's Guide to North American Railroads*. 4th ed. Waukesha, WI: Kalmbach, 1990.

—. "Virginian Railway." In Keith L. Bryant, Jr. (ed.), *EABHB: Railroads in the Age of Regulation*. New York: Facts on File, 1988, 459–460.

Du Boff, Richard B. "Business Demand and the Development of the Telegraph in the United States." *Business History Review* (1980) 59: 459–479.

DuBois, W. E. Burghardt. *Black Reconstruction in America: An Essay toward a History of the Part Which Black Folk Played in the Attempt To Reconstruct Democracy in America, 1860–1888*, New York: Russell and Russell, 1935.

Due, John F. "Grenvile M. Dodge." In Robert L. Frey (ed.), *EABHB: Railroads in the Nineteenth Century*. New York: Facts on File, 1988, 94–98.

———. "Henry Villard." In Robert L. Frey (ed.), *EABHB: Railroads in the Nineteenth Century*. New York: Facts on File, 1988, 417–420.

Duke, Donald, and Edmund Keilty. *RDC: The Budd Rail-Diesel Car*. San Marino, CA: Golden West Books, 1990.

Duke, Donald, and Stan Kistler. *Santa Fe: Steel Rails through California*. San Marino, CA: Golden West Books, 1963.

Dumke, Glenn S. "Across Mexico in '49." *Pacific Historical Review* (1949) 18: 33–44.

———. "Mission Station to Mining Town: Early Las Vegas." *Pacific Historical Review* (1939) 8: 257–270.

Dunaway, Wayland Fuller. *History of the James River and Kanawha Company*. New York: Columbia University Press, 1922.

Duncan, William. *U.S.-Japan Automobile Diplomacy: A Study in Economic Confrontation*. Cambridge, MA: Ballinger, 1973.

Dunlop, Richard. *Great Trails of the West*. Nashville, TN: Abington Press, 1971.

———. *Wheels West, 1590–1900*. Chicago: Rand McNally, 1977.

Dunscomb, Guy L. *A Century of Southern Pacific Steam Locomotives, 1862–1962*. Modesto, CA: Acme Printing, 1963.

———. *Locomotives of the Western Pacific*. Modesto, CA: Acme Printing, 1963.

Durrenberger, Joseph Austin. *Turnpikes: A Study of the Toll Road Movement in the Middle Atlantic States and Maryland*. Valdosta, GA: Southern Stationery and Printing Company, 1931.

DuVal, Miles P., Jr. *And the Mountains Will Move: The Story of the Building of the Panama Canal*. Palo Alto, CA: Stanford University Press, 1947.

———. *Cadiz to Cathay: The Story of the Long Diplomatic Struggle for the Panama Canal*. Palo Alto, CA: Stanford University Press, 1947.

Dwiggins, Don. *The Barnstormers: Flying Daredevils of the Roaring Twenties*. New York: Grosset and Dunlap, 1968.

Dykstra, Robert R. *The Cattle Towns*. New York: Knopf, 1968.

Dziuban, Stanley W. *Military Relations between the United States and Canada: The United States Army in World War II*. Washington, DC: Government Printing Office, 1959.

Earhart, Amelia. *The Fun of It: Random Records of My Own Flying and of Women in Aviation*. New York: Harcourt, 1932.

Earle, Alice Morse. *Stagecoach and Tavern Days*. New York: Macmillan, 1935.

Easterbrook, Gregg. "NASA's Space Station Zero." *Newsweek* (11 April 1994) 123: 30–33.

Easton, Robert. *Black Tide: The Santa Barbara Oil Spill and Its Consequences*. New York: Delacorte, 1972.

Eaton, Clement. *Henry Clay and the Art of American Politic*. Boston: Little, Brown and Company, 1957.

Eckenrode, H. J., and P. W. Wright. *E. H. Harriman: The Little Giant of Wall Street*. New York: Greenberg, 1933.

Edmondson, Harold A. *Journey to Amtrak*. Milwaukee: Kalmbach Publishing, 1972.

Egan, Ferol. *The El Dorado Trail: The Story of the Gold Rush Routes across Mexico*. New York: McGraw-Hill, 1970.

Eggenhofer, Nick. *Wagons, Mules, and Men: How the Frontier Moved West*. New York: Hastings, 1961.

Eggert, Gerald G. *Railroad Labor Disputes: The Beginnings of Federal Strike Policy*. Ann Arbor: University of Michigan Press, 1967.

Elser, Smoke, and Bill Brown. *Packin' in on Mules and Horses*. Missoula, MT: Mountain Press, 1980.

Emme, Eugene M. "Origins and Development of the Vanguard and Explorer Satellite Programs." *The Airpower Historian* (1964) 11 (no. 4): 101–112.

———. (ed.). *Two Hundred Years of Flight in America*. San Diego: Univelt, 1977.

Ephraim, Max, Jr. "Martin Blomberg, Designer Extraordinaire." *Trains* (October 1994) 54: 46–49.

Erskine, Albert Russel. *History of the Studebaker Corporation.* South Bend, IN: Studebaker Corporation, 1924.

Evans, Corinda W. *Collis Potter Huntington.* 2 vols. Newport News, VA: Mariners' Museum, 1954.

Ezell, Edward C. "The Heroic Era of Manned Space Flight." In Eugene M. Emme (ed.), *Two Hundred Years of Flight in America.* San Diego: Univelt, 1977, 231–253.

Fabre, Maurice. *A History of Land Transportation.* London: Leisure Arts, 1963.

Fanning, Leonard M. *Foreign Oil and the Free World.* New York: McGraw-Hill, 1954.

Farrington, S. Kip. *Railroads at War.* New York: Coward-McCann, 1946.

Faulk, Odie B. *Destiny Road: The Gila Trail and the Opening of the Southwest.* New York: Oxford University Press, 1973.

———. *The Last Years of Spanish Texas, 1778–1821.* The Hague, Netherlands: Mouton, 1964.

———. *The U.S. Camel Corps: An Army Experiment.* New York: Oxford University Press, 1976.

Faulkner, Harold U. *Politics, Reform, and Expansion, 1890–1900.* New York: Harper and Row, 1959.

Fay, John. *The Helicopter: History, Piloting, and How It Flies.* New York: Hippocrene, 1987.

Fellmeth, Robert C. *The Interstate Commerce Omission.* New York: Grossman, 1970.

Felton, John Richard, and Dale G. Anderson (eds.). *Regulation and Deregulation of the Motor Carrier Industry.* Ames: Iowa State University Press, 1989.

Feuerlicht, Roberta S. *The Andrews' Raiders.* New York: Crowell-Collier, 1967.

Ffooks, Roger. *Natural Gas by Sea: The Development of a New Technology.* London: Gentry Books, 1979.

Field, George, and Donald Goldsmith. *The Space Telescope.* Chicago: Contemporary Books, 1989.

Field, H. H. *History of the Milwaukee Railroad.* Chicago: CMSt.P & P Railroad, 1941.

Fielding, R. Kent. "The Mormon Economy in Kirtland, Ohio." *Utah Historical Quarterly* (1959) 27: 331–356.

Findley, Rowe. "Along the Santa Fe Trail." *National Geographic* (March 1991) 179: 98–122.

Firestone, Harvey S., Jr. *Man on the Move: The Story of Transportation.* New York: G. P. Putnam's Sons, 1967.

Fish, Carl Russell. "The Northern Railroads, April 1861." *American Historical Review* (1916–1917) 22: 778–793.

Fishbein, Meyer D. "The Trucking Industry and the National Recovery Administration." *Social Forces* (1955–1956) 34: 171–179.

Fisher, John S. *A Builder of the West: The Life of General William Jackson Palmer.* Caldwell, ID: Caxton Printing, 1939.

Fisher, Joseph A. *The Reading's Heritage, 1833–1958.* New York: Newcomen Society in North America, 1958.

Fitch, Edwin M. *The Alaska Railroad.* New York: Praeger, 1967.

Fitzmorris, C. C., Jr. *Commodore Vanderbilt and the Railroads.* Princeton, NJ: Princeton University Press, 1933.

Fletcher, R. A. *In the Days of the Tall Ships.* London: Bretano's, 1928.

Flexner, James Thomas. *Steamboats Come True: American Inventors in Action.* New York: Viking, 1944.

Flink, James J. *America Adopts the Automobile.* Cambridge: MIT Press, 1974.

———. *The Automobile Age.* Cambridge: MIT Press, 1974.

———. *The Car Culture.* Cambridge: MIT Press, 1974.

———. "Lido Anthony Iacocca." In George S. May (ed.), *EABHB: The Automobile Industry.* New York: Facts on File, 1990, 197–217.

————. "William S. Knudsen." In George S. May (ed.), *EABHB: The Automobile Industry*. New York: Facts on File, 1990, 265–283.

Flower, George L. (ed.). *Locomotive Dictionary*. Novato, CA: Newton K. Gregg, 1972.

Fogel, Robert W. *The Union Pacific Railroad: A Case Study in Premature Enterprise*. Baltimore: Johns Hopkins University Press, 1960.

Folsom, Burton W., Jr. *The Myth of the Robber Barons: A New Look at the Rise of Big Business in America*. Herndon, VA: Young America's Foundation, 1991.

Foner, Philip S. *The Great Labor Uprising of 1877*. New York: Pathfinder Press, 1978.

Ford, Henry. *My Life and Work*. Garden City, NY: Doubleday, Page and Company, 1922.

Ford, James Kip. "Benjamin Wright." In Allen Johnson, et al. (eds.), *Dictionary of American Biography*. New York: Charles Scribner's Sons, 1964–1981, X: 543–544.

————. "Canvass White." In Allen Johnson, et al. (eds.), *Dictionary of American Biography*. New York: Charles Scribner's Sons, 1964–1981, X: 93.

Foreman, Grant. "River Navigation in the Early Southwest." *Mississippi Valley Historical Review* (1928) 15: 34–55.

Frailey, Fred W. "Al Perlman Was Right." *Trains* (August 1994) 54: 70–71.

————. *Southern Pacific's Blue Streak Merchandise*. Milwaukee: Kalmbach, 1992.

————. "Super C: Hottest of the Hotshots." *Trains* (May 1986) 46: 42–53.

————. *Zephyrs, Chiefs & Other Orphans: The First Five Years of Amtrak*. Godfrey, IL: RPC Publications, 1977.

Francillon, René J. *McDonnell Douglas Aircraft Since 1920*. Annapolis, MD: Naval Institute Press, 1987.

Frankel, Ernst. *Regulation and Policies of American Shipping*. Boston: Auburn House, 1982.

Frantz, Joe B., and Julian E. Choate, Jr. *The American Cowboy*. Norman: University of Oklahoma Press, 1955.

Frederick, J. V. *Ben Holliday: The Stagecoach King*. Glendale, CA: Arthur H. Clark Company, 1940.

Freehling, William W. *Prelude to Civil War: The Nullification Controversy in South Carolina, 1816–1836*. New York: Harper and Row, 1968.

French, Michael. *The U.S. Tire Industry: A History*. Boston: Twayne, 1990.

French, Vern. *The Norfolk & Western Railway: Williamson Terminal—1953*. Denver: Rocky Mountain Publishing, 1992.

Freudenthal, Elsbeth E. *The Aviation Business: From Kitty Hawk to Wall Street*. New York: Vanguard, 1940.

————. *Flight into History [: the Wright Brothers]*. Norman: University of Oklahoma Press, 1949.

Frey, Robert L. "Brakes." In Robert L. Frey (ed.), *EABHB: Railroads in the Nineteenth Century*. New York: Facts on File, 1988, 27–32.

————. "Couplers." In Robert L. Frey (ed.), *EABHB: Railroads in the Nineteenth Century*. New York: Facts on File, 1988, 76–78.

————. "J. Pierpont Morgan." In Robert L. Frey (ed.), *EABHB: Railroads in the Nineteenth Century*. New York: Facts on File, 1988, 272–279.

————. "Locomotives." In Robert L. Frey (ed.), *EABHB: Railroads in the Nineteenth Century*. New York: Facts on File, 1988, 228–239.

————. "Northern Pacific Railway." In Keith L. Bryant Jr. (ed.), *EABHB: Railroads in the Age of Regulation*. New York: Facts on File, 1988, 331–333.

————. "Philadelphia & Reading Railroad." In Robert L. Frey (ed.), *EABHB: Railroads in the Nineteenth Century*. New York: Facts on File, 1988, 322–323.

————. "Rails, Roadbed, and Track Gauges." In Keith L. Bryant, Jr. (ed.), *EABHB: Railroads in the Age of Regulation*. New York: Facts on File, 1988, 340–344.

Frey, Robert L. (ed.). *Encyclopedia of American Business History and Biography: Railroads in the Nineteenth Century*. New York: Facts on File, 1988.

Frey, Robert L., and Lorenz P. Schrenk. *Northern Pacific Supersteam Era, 1925–1945*. San Marino, CA: Golden West Books, 1985.

Friedlaender, Ann F. *Dilemma of Freight Transport Regulation*. Washington, DC: Brookings Institution, 1969.

Friedman, George H. "Rail Travel: Using Trains for Business Travel." *Passenger Train Journal* (October 1994) 25: 36–41.

Friedman, Jon, and John Meehan. *House of Cards: Inside the Troubled Empire of American Express*. New York: G. P. Putnam's Sons, 1992.

Friedman, Milton, and Anna Jacobson Schwartz. *A Monetary History of the United States, 1867–1960*. New Brunswick, NJ: Princeton University Press, 1963.

Frisch, Morton J. *Alexander Hamilton and the Political Order*. New York: University Press of America, 1991.

Fuess, Claude Moore. *Joseph B. Eastman: Servant of the People*. New York: Columbia University Press, 1964.

Fuller, Robert H. *Jubilee Jim*. New York: Macmillan, 1928.

Furniss, Norman. *The Mormon Conflict, 1850–1858*. New Haven, CT: Yale University Press, 1960.

Gablehouse, Charles. *Helicopters and Autogiros: A Chronicle of Rotating-Wing Aircraft*. Philadelphia: Lippincott, 1967.

Gallatin, Albert. *Report of the Secretary of the Treasury on the Subject of Public Roads and Canals*. Washington, DC: R. C. Weightman, 1808.

Galloway, John Debo. *The First Transcontinental Railroad*. New York: Simmons Boardman, 1950.

Ganoe, John T. "The Beginings of Irrigation in the United States." *Mississippi Valley Historical Review* (1938–1939) 25: 59–72.

Gard, Wayne. *The Chisolm Trail*. Norman: University of Oklahoma Press, 1954.

Gardner, Ed. *Rock Island Lines: A Pictorial Review*. Mountain Top, PA: Ed Gardner, 1978.

Garnel, Donald. *The Rise of Teamster Power in the West*. Berkeley: University of California Press, 1972.

Garrard, Lewis. *Wah-to-Yah and the Taos Trail*. Norman: University of Oklahoma Press, 1955.

Garraty, John A. *The New Commonwealth, 1877–1890*. New York: Harper and Row, 1968.

Garreau, Joel. *Edge City: Life on the New Frontier*. Garden City, NY: Doubleday, 1991.

Gatland, Kenneth (ed.). *Space Technology: A Comprehensive History of Space Exploration*. New York: Harmony Books, 1981.

Gething, Michael J. *Air Power 2000*. London: Arms and Armour Press, 1992.

Ghosh, Arabinda. *OPEC, the Petroleum Industry, and United States Energy Policy*. Westport, CT: Quorum, 1983.

Gibbons, Boyd. "The Itch To Move West: Life and Death on the Oregon Trail." *National Geographic* (August 1986) 74: 147–177.

Gibbons, Tony. *Warships and Naval Battles of the U.S. Civil War*. Limpsfield, Surrey, England: Dragon's World, 1989.

Gies, Joseph. *Bridges and Men*. Garden City, NY: Doubleday, 1963.

Ginger, Ray. *The Age of Excess*. New York: Macmillan, 1965.

———. *The Bending Cross: A Biography of Eugene Victor Debs*. New Brunswick, NJ: Rutgers University Press, 1949.

Gipson, Lawrence Henry. *The British Empire before the American Revolution*. 12 vols. New York: Knopf, 1936–1965.

Gjevre, John A. *A Saga of the Soo*. La Crosse, WI: Milzahn Press, 1973.

Glad, Paul W. *The Trumpet Soundeth: William Jennings Bryan and His Democracy, 1896–1912*. Lincoln: University of Nebraska Press, 1960.

Glenn, Porter. *The Rise of Big Business, 1860–1910*. New York: Thomas Y. Crowell Company, 1973.

Godfrey, Aaron Austin. *Government Operation of the Railroads*. Austin, TX: Jenkins, 1974.

Goerner, Fred. *The Search for Amelia Earhart*. Garden City, NY: Doubleday, 1966.

Goethals, George W. *The Panamá Canal: An Engineering Treatise*. 2 vols. New York: McGraw-Hill, 1916.

Goetzman, William. *Army Exploration in the American West, 1803–1863*. New Haven, CT: Yale University Press, 1959.

Goldman, Eric. *Rendezvous with Destiny*. New York: Vintage, 1956.

Goodrich, Carter. *Government Promotion of American Canals and Railroads, 1800–1890*. New York: Columbia University Press, 1960.

———. "National Planning of Internal Improvements." *Political Science Quarterly* (1948) 63: 16–44.

———. "The Revulsion against Internal Improvements." *Journal of Economic History* (1950–1951) 10: 145–169.

———. "The Virginia System of Mixed Enterprise: A Study of State Planning of Internal Improvements." *Political Science Quarterly* (1949) 64: 35–87.

Goodrich, Carter, et al. *Canals and American Economic Development*. New York: Columbia University Press, 1961.

Gordon, Maynard M. *The Iacocca Management Technique*. New York: Dodd, Mead and Company, 1985.

Gorgas, Marie D., and Burtron J. Hendrick. *William Crawford Gorgas: His Life and Work*. Garden City, NY: Doubleday, Page and Company, 1924.

Gorgas, William C. *Sanitation in Panamá*. New York: Appleton and Company, 1914.

Gould, Jean, and Lorena Hickok. *Walter Reuther: Labor's Rugged Individualist*. New York: Dodd, Mead and Company, 1972.

Gow, Harry, and C. Milliken. "VIA Faces New Cuts." *Passenger Train Journal* (June 1994) 25: 28–34.

———. "VIA: Light Flickers at the End of the Tunnel." *Passenger Train Journal* (October 1994) 25: 18–19.

Graebner, Norman A. *Empire on the Pacific: A Study in American Continental Expansion*. New York: Ronald Press, 1955.

Graebner, Norman A. (ed.). *Manifest Destiny*. Indianapolis: Bobbs-Merrill, 1968.

Grant, H. Roger. "Chicago & North Western Railroad." In Keith L. Bryant, Jr. (ed.), *EABHB: Railroads in the Age of Regulation*. New York: Facts on File, 1988, 69–71.

———. "Chicago & North Western Railroad." In Robert L. Frey (ed.), *EABHB: Railroads in the Nineteenth Century*. New York: Facts on File, 1988, 43–44.

———. "The Chicago Great Western Railroad: Piggyback Pioneer." *Trains* (January 1986) 46: 31–34.

———. "Chicago, Rock Island & Pacific Railroad." In Keith L. Bryant, Jr. (ed.), *EABHB: Railroads in the Age of Regulation*. New York: Facts on File, 1988, 79–80.

———. *The Cornbelt Route: The History of the Chicago Great Western Railroad Company*. DeKalb: Northern Illinois University Press, 1984.

———. "Electric Traction." In Keith L. Bryant, Jr. (ed.), *EABHB: Railroads in the Age of Regulation*. New York: Facts on File, 1988, 129–130.

———. "Piggyback/Trailers-on-Flatcars." In Keith L. Bryant, Jr. (ed.), *EABHB: Railroads in the Age of Regulation*. New York: Facts on File, 1988, 348–349.

Gray, Colin S. "The Transition from Offense to Defense." *Washington Quarterly* (1986) 9 (no. 3): 59–72.

Gray, George S. *Frontiers of Flight: The Story of NACA Research*. New York: Alfred A. Knopf, 1948.

Gray, John S. "Blazing the Bridger and Bozeman Trails." *Annals of Wyoming* (1977) 49: 23–51.

———. *Custer's Last Campaign: Mitch Boyer and the Little Bighorn Reconstructed*. Lincoln: University of Nebraska Press, 1991.

Gray, Ralph D. *The National Waterway: A History of the Chesapeake and Delaware Canal, 1769–1965*. Urbana: University of Illinois Press, 1989.

Green, Constance M., and Milton Lomask. *Vanguard: A History*. Washington, DC: Smithsonian, 1971.

Greene, Bob. "Another Look at Highway Freedom." *Chicago Tribune*, reprinted in the *Tucson Citizen* (12 December 1994): 8A.

Greenly, Albert Harry. *Camels in America*. New York: Bibliographical Society of America, 1952.

Greever, William S. *Arid Domain: The Santa Fe Railroad and Its Western Land Grant*. Palo Alto, CA: Stanford University Press, 1954.

———. "Atchison, Topeka & Santa Fe Railway." In Robert L. Frey (ed.), *EABHB: Railroads in the Nineteenth Century*. New York: Facts on File, 1988, 15–17.

———. "Cyrus K. Holiday." In Robert L. Frey (ed.), *EABHB: Railroads in the Nineteenth Century*. New York: Facts on File, 1988, 182–184.

Gregg, Josiah. *Commerce of the Prairies*. Norman: University of Oklahoma Press, 1990.

Griswold, Wesley S. *A Work of Giants: Building the First Transcontinental Railroad*. New York: McGraw-Hill, 1962.

Grodinsky, Julius. *The Iowa Pool: A Study in Railroad Competition, 1870–1884*. Chicago: University of Chicago Press, 1950.

———. *Jay Gould: His Business Career*. Philadelphia: University of Pennsylvania Press, 1957.

———. *Railroad Consolidation, Its Economics and Controlling Principles*. New York: Appleton-Century, 1930.

———. *Transcontinental Railroad Strategy, 1869–1893*. Philadelphia: University of Pennsylvania Press, 1962.

Grossman, Peter Z. *American Express: The Unofficial History of the People Who Built the Great Financial Empire*. New York: Crown, 1987.

Grow, Lawrence. *On the 8:02: An Informal History of Commuting by Rail in America*. New York: Mayflower Books, 1979.

Gustin, L. R. *Billy Durant: Creator of General Motors*. Grand Rapids, MI: William B. Erdmanns, 1973.

Hacker, Barton C., and James M. Grimwood. *On the Shoulders of Titans: A History of Project Gemini*. Washington, DC: Government Printing Office, 1977.

Haethorne, Douglas B. *Men and Women of Space*. San Diego: Univelt, 1992.

Hafen, LeRoy R. "Handcarts to Utah, 1856–1860." *Utah Historical Quarterly* (1956) 24: 309–317.

———. *The Overland Mail, 1849–1869*. Cleveland: Arthur H. Clark Company, 1926.

Hafen, LeRoy R., and Ann Hafen. *The Old Spanish Trail*. Glendale, CA: Arthur H. Clark Company, 1955.

Hafen, LeRoy R., and Francis M. Young. *Fort Laramie and the Pageant of the West, 1834–1890*. Glendale, CA: Arthur H. Clark Company, 1938.

Hage, David. "On the Right Track: America's Railroads Are Chugging Their Way Back to Prosperity." *U.S. News & World Report* (21 March 1994) 116: 46–53.

Hague, Harlan. *The Road to California: The Search for a Southern Overland Route*. Glendale, CA: Arthur H. Clark Company, 1978.

Hahn, Thomas F. *Chesapeake and Ohio Canal Old Picture Album*. Shepherdstown, WV: American Transportation Center, 1976.

Halberstam, David. *The Reckoning*. New York: William Morris, 1986.

Hall, R. Cargill. "Instrumented Exploration and Utilization of Space: The American Experience." In Eugene M. Emme (ed.), *Two Hundred Years of Flight in America* San Diego: Univelt, 1977, 183–212.

———. *Lunar Impact: A History of Project Ranger*. Washington, DC: Government Printing Office, 1977.

———. "Origins and Development of the Vanguard and Explorer Satellite Programs." *The Airpower Historian* (1964) 11 (no. 4): 101–112.

Hallion, Richard P. "Commercial Aviation, 1919–1976." In Eugene M. Emme (ed.), *Two Hundred Years of Flight in America*. San Diego: Univelt, 1977, 155–180.

———. *Supersonic Flight: Breaking the Sound Barrier and Beyond.* New York: Macmillan, 1972.

———. *Test Pilots: The Frontiersmen of Flight.* Garden City, NY: Doubleday, 1981.

Hallion, Richard P. (ed.). *The Wright Brothers.* Washington, DC: Smithsonian, 1978.

Hammond, Bray. *Banks and Politics in America: From the Revolution to the Civil War.* New Brunswick, NJ: Princeton University Press, 1957.

Haney, Lewis Henry. *A Congressional History of Railways in the United States.* Madison: University of Wisconsin Press, 1910.

Hanson, Marcus Lee. *The Atlantic Migration, 1607–1860.* Cambridge: Harvard University Press, 1940.

Harding, Carroll R. *George M. Pullman, 1831–1897, and the Pullman Company.* New York: Newcomen Society in North America, 1951.

Harlow, Alvin F. *Old Towpaths: The Story of the American Canal Era.* New York: Appleton and Company, 1926.

———. *Old Waybills: The Romance of the Express Companies.* New York: Appleton-Century, 1934.

———. *Old Wires and New Waves: The History of the Telegraph, Telephone, and Wireless.* New York: Appleton-Century, 1936.

———. *The Road of the Century: The Story of the New York Central.* New York: Creative Age Press, 1947.

———. *Steelways of New England.* New York: Creative Age Press, 1946.

Harris, Benjamin. *Gila Trail.* Norman: University of Oklahoma Press, 1960.

Harris, Herbert. *American Labor.* New Haven, CT: Yale University Press, 1939.

Harrison, C. *William Outlaw of the Natchez Trace.* New York: Ballantine, 1960.

Harsha, Max. *Mule Skinner's Bible.* N.p.: Max Harsha, 1987.

Hart, Louis. *Economic Policy and Democratic Thought: Pennsylvania, 1776–1860.* Cambridge: Harvard University Press, 1948.

Hart, Val. *The Story of American Roads.* New York: William Sloane Associates, 1950.

Hartman, Amos W. "The California and Oregon Trail, 1849–1860." *Oregon Historical Quarterly* (1924) 25: 1–35.

Harvey, Dereck G. T. *Monorails.* New York: George Putnam's Sons, 1965.

Harwood, Herbert H., Jr. *Impossible Challenge: The Baltimore & Ohio Railroad in Maryland.* Baltimore: Bernard Roberts and Company, 1979.

———. "Oris Paxton Van Sweringen and Mantis James Van Sweringen." In Keith L. Bryant, Jr. (ed.), *EABHB: Railroads in the Age of Regulation.* New York: Facts on File, 1988, 450–458.

Hastings, Philip R. *Chicago Great Western Railway: Iowa in the Merger Decade.* Newton, NJ: Carsten Publications, 1981.

Hatcher, Harlan. *The Great Lakes.* New York: Oxford University Press, 1944.

Hauck, Cornelius W., and Robert W. Richardson. *Steam in the Rockies.* Golden, CO: Colorado Railroad Museum, 1963.

Havighurst, Walter. *Long Ships Passing.* New York: Macmillan, 1942.

———. *Voices on the River: The Story of the Mississippi Waterways.* New York: Macmillan, 1964.

Haydon, Frederick S. *Aeronautics in the Union and Confederate Armies with a Survey of Military Aeronautics Prior to 1861.* Baltimore: Johns Hopkins University Press, 1941.

Hayes, William E. *Iron Road to Empire: The History of 100 Years of Progress and Achievements of the Rock Island Lines.* New York: Simmons-Boardman, 1953.

Hays, Samuel P. *The Response to Industrialism, 1885–1914.* Chicago: University of Chicago Press, 1957.

Hebard, Grace R., and E. A. Brininstool. *The Bozeman Trail.* Cleveland: Arthur H. Clark Company, 1922.

Hedges, James B. *Henry Villard and the Railways of the Northwest.* New Haven, CT: Yale University Press, 1930.

Hediger, Jim. "Great Domes of the Empire Builder." *Model Railroader* (June 1984) 51: 73–76.

———. "This Highway Is Not on Your Oil Company Map." *Trains* (December 1974) 35: 22–32.

Hellman, Hal. *Transportation in the World of the Future.* New York: M. Evans and Company, 1974.

Hendry, Maurice D. "Studebaker: One Can Do a Lot of Remembering in South Bend." *Automobile Quarterly* (1972) 10: 228–257.

Henrich, Frederick K. "The Development of American Laissez Faire: A General View of the Age of Washington." *Journal of Economic History* (Supplement) (1943) 3: 51–54.

Henry, Robert S. *This Fascinating Railroad Business.* Indianapolis: Bobbs-Merrill, 1946.

Henwood, James N. J. "Central Railroad of New Jersey." In Keith L. Bryant, Jr. (ed.), *EABHB: Railroads in the Age of Regulation.* New York: Facts on File, 1988, 63–64.

———. "Grand Trunk Western Railroad." In Keith L. Bryant, Jr. (ed.), *EABHB: Railroads in the Age of Regulation.* New York: Facts on File, 1988, 172–173.

———. "Long Island Rail Road." In Keith L. Bryant, Jr. (ed.), *EABHB: Railroads in the Age of Regulation.* New York: Facts on File, 1988, 258–259.

———. "Reading Company." In Keith L. Bryant, Jr. (ed.), *EABHB: Railroads in the Age of Regulation.* New York: Facts on File, 1988, 364–365.

Herbert, Hill. *Black Labor and the American Legal System.* Washington, DC: Bureau of National Affairs, 1977.

Herr, Kincaid A. *The Louisville & Nashville Railroad.* Louisville, KY: Louisville & Nashville Railroad, 1964.

Hickcox, David H. "*Bangor & Arrostook Railroad.*" In Keith L. Bryant, Jr. (ed.), *EABHB: Railroads in the Age of Regulation.* New York: Facts on File, 1988, 25–26.

———. "Boston & Maine Railroad." In Keith L. Bryant, Jr. (ed.), *EABHB: Railroads in the Age of Regulation.* New York: Facts on File, 1988, 35–36.

———. "Maine Central Railroad." In Keith L. Bryant, Jr. (ed.), *EABHB: Railroads in the Age of Regulation.* New York: Facts on File, 1988, 274–275.

Hicks, John D. *The Populist Revolt: A History of the Farmers' Alliance and the People's Party.* Minneapolis: University of Minnesota Press, 1931.

Hidy, Ralph W., et al. *The Great Northern Railroad: A History.* Boston: Harvard Business School, 1986.

Higginbotham, Don. *The War of American Independence: Military Attitudes, Policies and Practice, 1963–1989.* New York: Macmillan, 1971.

Higgs, Robert. *Crisis and Leviathan: Critical Episodes in the Growth of American Government.* New York: Oxford University Press, 1987.

Higham, Robin. *Air Power: A Concise History.* New York: St. Martin's Press, 1972.

Hill, James J. *Highways of Progress.* New York: Page, 1910.

Hill, Joseph J. "Ewing Young in the Fur Trade of the Far Southwest, 1822–1834." *Oregon Historical Quarterly* (1923) 24: 1–35.

Hills, T. L. *The St. Lawrence Seaway.* New York: Praeger, 1959.

Hilton, George W. *The Cable Car in America.* Berkeley, CA: Howell-North, 1971.

———. "The Consistency of the Interstate Commerce Act." *Journal of Law and Economics* (1966) 9: 87–113.

———. *The Northeast Railroad Problem.* Washington, DC: American Enterprise Institute, 1975.

———. "Staggers Rail Act of 1980." In Keith L. Bryant, Jr. (ed.), *EABHB: Railroads in the Age of Regulation.* New York: Facts on File, 1988, 417–418.

———. *The Transportation Act of 1958: A Decade of Experience.* Bloomington: Indiana University Press, 1969.

Hilton, George W., and John F. Due. *The Electric Interurban Railways in America.* Palo Alto, CA: Stanford University Press, 1960.

Himmelberg, Robert F. *Origins of the National Recovery Administration: Business, Government, and the Trade Association Movement, 1921–1933.* New York: Fordham University Press, 1976.

Hindley, Geffrey. *A History of Roads.* London: Peter Davies, 1971.

Hines, Walker D. *War History of the American Railroads.* New Haven, CT: Yale University Press, 1928.

Hinshaw, Clifford Reginald. "North Carolina Canals before 1860." *North Carolina Historical Review* (1948) 25: 1–56.

Hipp, James W. "Delaware, Lackawanna & Western." In Robert L. Frey (ed.), *EABHB: Railroads in the Nineteenth Century.* New York: Facts on File, 1988, 85–86.

———. "Oakes and Oliver Ames." In Robert L. Frey (ed.), *EABHB: Railroads in the Nineteenth Century.* New York: Facts on File, 1988, 12–14.

Hodel, Donald Paul, and Robert Dietz. *Crisis in the Oil Patch: How America's Energy Industry Is Being Destroyed and What Must Be Done To Save It.* Washington, DC: Regnery Publishers, 1994.

Hodgsen, Bryan. "The Pipeline: Alaska's Troubled Collosus." *National Geographic* (November 1976) 150: 684–717.

Hofsommer, Don L. "Denver & Rio Grande Western Railroad." In Keith L. Bryant, Jr. (ed.), *EABHB: Railroads in the Age of Regulation.* New York: Facts on File, 1988, 114–115.

———. "Great Northern Railroad." In Robert L. Frey (ed.), *EABHB: Railroads in the Nineteenth Century.* New York: Facts on File, 1988, 152–153.

———. "Great Northern Railway." In Keith L. Bryant, Jr. (ed.), *EABHB: Railroads in the Age of Regulation.* New York: Facts on File, 1988, 178–179.

———. *Katy Northwest: The Story of a Branch Line Railroad.* Boulder, CO: Pruett, 1976.

———. "Missouri-Kansas-Texas Railroad." In Keith L. Bryant, Jr. (ed.), *EABHB: Railroads in the Age of Regulation.* New York: Facts on File, 1988, 302–303.

———. "St. Louis & Southwestern Railway." In Keith L. Bryant, Jr. (ed.), *EABHB: Railroads in the Age of Regulation.* New York: Facts on File, 1988, 383–384.

———. *The Southern Pacific, 1901–1985.* College Station: Texas A & M University Press, 1986.

———. "Southern Pacific Company." In Keith L. Bryant, Jr. (ed.), *EABHB: Railroads in the Age of Regulation.* New York: Facts on File, 1988, 408–409.

———. "Southern Pacific Company." In Robert L. Frey (ed.), *EABHB: Railroads in the Nineteenth Century.* New York: Facts on File, 1988, 371–372.

Hofstadter, Richard. *The Age of Reform: Bryan to F.D.R.* New York: Vintage, 1955.

Hokanson, Drake. *The Lincoln Highway: Main Street across America.* Iowa City: University of Iowa Press, 1988.

Holbrook, Stewart H. *The Age of the Moguls.* Garden City, NY: Doubleday, 1953.

———. *The Old Post Road.* New York: McGraw-Hill, 1962.

———. *The Story of American Railroads.* New York: Crown, 1947.

Holden, Henry M., and Lori Griffin. *Ladybirds: The Untold Story of Women Pilots in America.* Mt. Freedom, NJ: Black Hawk, 1991.

———. *Ladybirds II: The Continuing Story of American Women in Aviation.* Mt. Freedom, NJ: Black Hawk, 1993.

Holle, Gena. "The Coaster Comes to California." *Passenger Train Journal* (October 1994) 25: 32–33.

Hollingsworth, Brian. *Illustrated Encyclopedia of North American Locomotives.* New York: Crown, 1984.

Holsworth, Robert D. *Public Interest Liberalism and the Crisis of Affluence.* Rochester, VT: Schenkman, 1981.

Hoogenboom, Ari. "Hepburn Act." In Keith L. Bryant, Jr. (ed.), *EABHB: Railroads in the Age of Regulation.* New York: Facts on File, 1988, 198.

———. "Interstate Commerce Act." In Keith L. Bryant, Jr. (ed.), *EABHB: Railroads in the Age of Regulation*. New York: Facts on File, 1988, 230–232.

———. "Mann-Elkins Act." In Keith L. Bryant, Jr. (ed.), *EABHB: Railroads in the Age of Regulation*. New York: Facts on File, 1988, 276.

Hoogenboom, Ari, and Olive Hoogenboom. *A History of the ICC: From Panacea to Pallative*. New York: W. W. Norton, 1976.

Hooker, William F. *Prairie Schooner*. Chicago: Saul Brothers, 1918.

———. "The Frontier Freight Train Wagon Boss of the 1870s." *The Union Pacific Magazine* (1925) 4: 9–10.

Hopkins, George E. "Air Lines Pilots Association." In William M. Leary (ed.), *EABHB: The Airline Industry*. New York: Facts on File, 1992, 17–19.

———. *Flying the Line: The First Half Century of the Air Line Pilots Association*. Washington, DC: Airline Pilots Association, 1982.

Hopkins, Henry James. *A Span of Bridges*. New York: Praeger, 1970.

Hough, Emerson. "A Study in Transportation: The Settlement of the West." *Century Magazine* (1902) 41: 212.

Hough, Richard, and L. J. K. Streight. *A History of the World's Motorcycles*. London: George Allen and Unwin, 1973.

Howard, Fred. *Wilbur and Orville: A Biography of the Wright Brothers*. New York: Knopf, 1987.

Howe, Octavius A., and Frederick C. Matthews. *American Clipper Ships, 1833–1858*. 2 vols. Salem, MA: Marine Research Society, 1926–1927.

Hoyt, Edwin P. *The Vanderbilts and their Fortunes*. Garden City, NY: Doubleday, 1962.

Hubbard, Freeman. *Encyclopedia of North American Railroading*. New York: McGraw-Hill, 1981.

———. *Great Trains of All Time*. New York: Grosset and Dunlap, 1962.

———. *Railroad Avenue*. New York: McGraw-Hill, 1945.

———. *The Train That Never Came Back and Other Railroad Stories*. New York: McGraw-Hill, 1952.

Hubbard, Freeman, et al. *Pennsylvania Songs and Legends*. Philadelphia: University of Pennsylvania Press, 1949.

Hudson, Kenneth. *Air Travel: A Social History*. Totowa, NJ: Rowman and Littlefield, 1972.

Hudson, Kenneth, and Julian Pettifer. *Diamonds in the Sky: A Social History of Air Travel*. London: Bodley Head and the British Broadcasting Corporation, 1979.

Hughes, Sarah Forbes. *Letters and Recollections of John Murray Forbes*. Boston: Houghton Mifflin, 1899.

Hulbert, Archer Butler. *Historic Highways of America*. 16 vols. Cleveland: Arthur H. Clark Company, 1902–1906.

Hungerford, Edward. *Men and Iron: The History of the New York Central*. New York: Thomas Y. Crowell Company, 1938.

———. *Men of Erie*. New York: Random House, 1946.

———. *The Story of the Baltimore & Ohio Railroad*. New York: G. P. Putnam's Sons, 1928.

———. *Wells Fargo: Advancing the American Frontier*. New York: Random House, 1949.

Hunt, Elmer Munson. "Abbott-Downing and the Concord Coach." *Historical New Hampshire* (November 1945) 1: 1–22.

Hunt, George T. *The Wars of the Iroquois: A Study in Intertribal Trade Relations*. Madison: University of Wisconsin Press, 1967.

Hunter, Louis C. "The Invention of the Western Steamboat." *Journal of Economic History* (1943) 3: 202–220.

———. *Steamboats on the Western Rivers*. Cambridge: Harvard University Press, 1949.

Hunter, Milton R. "The Mormon Corridor." *Pacific Historical Review* (1939) 8: 179–200.

Huntley, Theodore A., and R. E. Royall. *Construction of the Alaska Highway.* Washington, DC: Government Printing Office, 1945.

Hurley, Alfred E. *Billy Mitchell: Crusader for Air Power.* New York: Franklin Watts, 1964.

Husband, Joseph. *The Story of the Pullman Car.* Chicago: A. C. McClurg and Company, 1917.

Hutchins, John G. B. *The American Maritime Industries and Public Policy, 1789–1914: An Economic History.* Cambridge: Harvard University Press, 1941.

Hyman, Harold M. *A More Perfect Union: The Impact of the Civil War and Reconstruction on the Constitution.* New York: Knopf, 1975.

Iacocca, Lee, and William Novak. *Iacocca: An Autobiography.* New York: Bantam, 1984.

Ierley, Merritt. *Traveling the National Road: Across the Centuries on America's First Highway.* Woodstock, NY: Overlook Press, 1990.

Ingalls, Fay. *The Valley Road.* Cleveland: World Publishing Company, 1949.

Ingells, Douglas J. *The Plane That Changed the World: A Biography of the DC-3.* Fallbrook, CA: Aero, 1966.

Ingham, John H. (ed.). *Biographical Dictionary of American Business Leaders.* 4 vols. Westport, CT: Greenwood, 1983.

Ingles, J. David. "Milwaukee Road—Still Sprinting Along." *Trains* (September 1983) 43: 17.

Itzkoff, Donald M. *Off the Track: The Decline of the Intercity Passenger Train in the United States.* Westport, CT: Greenwood, 1985.

Ivins, Molly. "Let's Get Busy on Roads and Dams, and Give Workers Jobs To Work On." *Fort Worth Star-Telegram,* reprinted in the *Arizona Daily Star* (7 February 1994): 12A.

Jackson, C. G. *The Story of the Liner.* London: Sheldon Press, 1931.

Jackson, Carlton. *Hounds of the Road: A History of the Greyhound Bus Company.* Bowling Green, OH: Bowling Green University Press, 1984.

Jackson, Donald D. *The Aeronauts.* Alexandria, VA: Time-Life Books, 1980.

Jackson, John N. *Welland and the Welland Canal: The Canal By-Pass Project.* Belleville, Ontario: Mika Publishing Company, 1975.

Jackson, W. Turrentine. *Wagon Roads West.* Berkeley: University of California Press, 1953.

James, Ralph C., and Estelle Dinnerstein James. *Hoffa and the Teamsters: A Study in Union Power.* Princeton, NJ: D. Van Nostrand and Company, 1965.

Jantscher, Gerald R. *Bread upon the Waters: Federal Aids to the Maritime Industries.* Washington, DC: Brookings Institution, 1975.

Jardim, Anne. *The First Henry Ford: A Study in Personality and Business Leadership.* Cambridge: MIT Press, 1970.

Jastrow, Robert. "Reagan vs. the Scientists: Why the President Is Right about Missile Defense." *Commentary* (January 1984) 77: 23–32.

Jenkins, Stephen. *The Old Boston Post Road.* New York: G. P. Putnam's Sons, 1913.

Jenks, Downing B. *The Missouri Pacific Story.* New York: The Newcomen Society in North America, 1977.

Jennings, John. *Clipper Ship Days: The Golden Age of American Sailing Ships.* New York: Random House, 1952.

Jensen, Merrill. *The New Nation: A History of the United States during the Confederation, 1781–1789.* New York: Knopf, 1950.

Jensen, Oliver. *The American Heritage History of Railroads in America.* New York: American Heritage, 1975.

Johannsen, Robert W. *Stephen A. Douglas.* New York: Oxford University Press, 1973.

Johnson, Allen, et al. (eds.). *Dictionary of American Biography.* 10 vols. and 9 supplements. New York: Charles Scribner's Sons, 1964–1981.

Johnson, Emory R. *Elements of Transportation.* New York: Appleton and Company, 1914.

Johnson, Hank. *Death Valley Scotty.* Corona del Mar, CA: Trans-Anglo Books, 1974.

Johnson, Ron. *The Best of Maine Railroads.* Portland, ME: Ron Johnson, 1985.

Johnston, Bob. "The Train They Call Number One." *Trains* (December 1994) 54: 82–90.

Johnston, Jay. "Waterway to Washington, The C&O Canal." *National Geographic* (March 1960) 117: 419–439.

Jones, Chester L. *The Economic History of the AnthraciteTidewater Canals.* Philadelphia: University of Pennsylvania Press, 1908.

Jones, Helen H. *Rails from the West: A Biography of Theodore D. Judah.* San Marino, CA: Golden West Books, 1969.

Jones, Maldwin Allen. *American Immigration.* Chicago: University of Chicago Press, 1960.

Jordan, Philip D. *The National Road.* Indianapolis: Bobbs-Merrill Company, 1948.

Jordan, Robert Paul. "Our Growing Interstate System." *National Geographic* (February 1968) 133: 195–219.

Jordan, Terry G. *Trails to Texas: Southern Roots of Western Cattle Ranching.* Lincoln: University of Nebraska Press, 1981.

Josephson, Matthew. *Empire of the Air: Juan Trippe and the Struggle for World Airways.* New York: Harcourt, Brace and Company, 1944.

———. *The Politicos, 1865–1896.* New York: Harcourt Brace and Company, 1938.

———. *The Robber Barons: The Great American Capitalists.* New York: Harcourt, Brace and Company, 1934.

Kahn, Otto H. *Edward Henry Harriman.* New York: C. G. Burgoyne, 1911.

Kalata, Barbara N. *A Hundred Years, A Hundred Miles: New Jersey's Morris Canal.* Morristown, NJ: Morris Canal Historical Society, 1983.

Kane, Harnett T. *Natchez on the Mississippi.* New York: William Morrow, 1947.

Kaplan, Daniel P. "The Changing Airline Industry." In Leonard W. Weiss and Michael W. Klass (eds.), *Regulatory Reform: What Actually Happened.* Boston: Little, Brown and Company, 1986, 40–77.

Kaplan, Michael. *Otto Mears: Paradoxical Pathfinder.* Silverton, CO: San Juan County, 1982.

Karaska Gerald J., and Judith B. Gertler (eds.). *Transportation, Technology, and Society: Future Options.* Worcester, MA: Clark University, 1978.

———. *This Was Pioneer Motoring: An Album of Nostalgic Automemorabilia.* Seattle: Superior Publishing, 1968.

Karolevitz, Robert F. *This Was Trucking: A Pictorial History of the First Quarter Century of Commercial Motor Vehicles.* Seattle: Superior Publishing, 1966.

Karsner, David. *Debs: His Authorized Life and Letters.* New York: Boni and Liveright, 1919.

Kaufman, Jacob J. *Collective Bargaining in the Railroad Industry.* New York: King's Crown, 1954.

Keating, Bern. "Today along the Natchez Trace." *National Geographic* (November 1968) 134: 641–667.

Keats, John. *Howard Hughes.* New York: Random House, 1966.

Keefe, Kevin P. "Landmark Locomotive: Union Pacific's Challenger." *Trains* (January 1995) 55: 54–62.

Keekley, Harold. *Big Blow: Union Pacific's Super Turbines.* Omaha, NE: George R. Cockle and Associates, 1975.

———. *U 50's: Union Pacific's Twin Diesels.* Omaha, NE: George R. Cockle and Associates, 1978.

Keeler, Theodore E. *Railroads, Freight and Public Policy.* Washington, DC: Brookings Institution, 1983.

Keisling, Phil. "The Great Train Robbery: How to Make a Billion from a Bankrupt Railroad." *Washington Monthly* (July–August 1982) 14: 24–29, 32–35.

Kelly, Alfred H., and Winfred A. Harbison. *The American Constitution: Its Origins and Development.* New York: W. W. Norton, 1948.

Kelly, Fred C. *The Wright Brothers.* New York: Harcourt, Brace, and Company, 1948.

Bibliography

Kemble, John H. *The Panama Route, 1848–1869*. Berkeley: University of California Press, 1943.

Kennan, George. *The Chicago & Alton Case*. New York: Country Life Press, 1916.

———. *E. H. Harriman: A Biography*. Boston: Houghton Mifflin, 1922.

Kennedy, Charles J. "Boston & Maine Railroad." In Robert L. Frey (ed.), *EABHB: Railroads in the Nineteenth Century*. New York: Facts on File, 1988, 25–26.

Kennedy, John L. *Oil and Gas Pipeline Fundamentals*. Tulsa, OK: PennWell Books, 1993.

Kerr, John Leeds. *The Story of a Western Pioneer, the Missouri Pacific: An Outline History*. New York: Railway Research Society, 1928.

Kerr, K. Austin. *American Railroad Politics, 1914–1920: Rates, Wages, and Efficiency*. Pittsburgh: University of Pittsburgh Press, 1968.

Ketcham, Ralph. *James Madison: A Biography*. New York: Macmillan, 1971.

Key, V. O., Jr. *Southern Politics in State and Nation*. New York: Knopf, 1949.

Kilgour, John G. *The U.S. Merchant Marine: National Maritime Policy and Industrial Relations*. New York: Praeger, 1975.

Kilmark, Robert A. (ed.). *America's Maritime Legacy: A History of the U.S. Merchant Marine and Shipping Industry since Colonial Times*. Boulder, CO: Westview, 1979.

Kincaid, Robert L. *The Wilderness Road*. Indianapolis: Bobbs-Merrill Company, 1947.

Kingsford, William. *History, Structure, and Statistics of Plank Roads, in the United States and Canada*. Philadelphia: A. Hart, 1851.

Kirk, Russell. *America's British Culture*. New Brunswick, NJ: Transaction Publishers, 1993.

———. *John Randolph of Roanoke: A Study in American Politics*. Indianapolis: Liberty Press, 1978.

Kirkland, Edward C. *Men, Cities, and Transportation: A Study in New England History, 1820–1900*. 2 vols. Cambridge: Harvard University Press, 1948.

Klein, Maury. "George J. Gould." In Keith L. Bryant, Jr. (ed.), *EABHB: Railroads in the Age of Regulation*. New York: Facts on File, 1988, 167–171.

———. *History of the Louisville & Nashville Railroad*. New York: Macmillan, 1972.

———. "Jay Gould." In Robert L. Frey (ed.), *EABHB: Railroads in the Nineteenth Century*. New York: Facts on File, 1988, 138–147.

———. *The Life and Legend of Jay Gould*. Baltimore: Johns Hopkins University Press, 1986.

———. "The Louisville & Nashville Railroad." In Keith L. Bryant, Jr. (ed.), *EABHB: Railroads in the Age of Regulation*. New York: Facts on File, 1988, 268–269.

———. "Union Pacific Railroad." In Keith L. Bryant, Jr. (ed.), *EABHB: Railroads in the Age of Regulation*. New York: Facts on File, 1988, 444–446.

———. *Union Pacific: The Rebirth, 1894–1969*. Garden City, NY: Doubleday, 1989.

Klette, Immanuel J. *From Atlantic to Pacific: A New Interocean Canal*. New York: Harper and Row, 1967.

Knapke, William F., and Freeman Hubbard. *The Railroad Caboose*. San Marino, CA: Golden West Books, 1968.

Kneiss, Gilbert H. *Fifty Candles for the Western Pacific*. San Francisco: Western Pacific Railroad, 1953.

Kogan, Dennis J., et al. *Santa Fe's Hi-Level Cars*. Danvers, MA: Prototype Modeler, 1975.

Kolb, Charles. *White House Daze: The Unmaking of Domestic Policy in the Bush Years*. New York: Free Press, 1994.

Kolko, Gabriel. *Railroads and Regulation, 1877–1916*. New Brunswick, NJ: Princeton University Press, 1965.

Komons, Nick. *Bonfires to Beacons: Federal Civil Aviation Policy under the Air Commerce Act, 1926–1938*. Washington, DC: Government Printing Office, 1978.

Kramer, Frederick A., and John Krause. *Long Island Railroad.* Newton, NJ: Carstens Publications, 1978.

Kratville, William W. *Union Pacific Locomotives.* Omaha, NE: Kratville Publications, 1967.

Kroll, Helen B. "Books That Enlightened the Emigrants." *Oregon Historical Quarterly* (1944) 45: 103–120.

Krout, John A. "New York's Early Engineers." *New York History* (1945) 24: 269–277.

Kuhler, Otto. *My Iron Journey: An Autobiography of a Life with Iron and Steel.* Denver: National Railway Historical Society, 1967.

Kuhn, Arthur J. *GM Passes Ford, 1918–1938: Designing the General Motors Performance-Control System.* University Park: Pennsylvania State University Press, 1986.

Labich, Kenneth. "How Airlines Will Look in the 1990s." *Fortune* (1 January 1990) 121: 50–51, 54–56.

Lacock, John Kennedy. " Braddock Road." *Pennsylvania Magazine of History and Biography* (1914) 38: 1–38.

Lacy, Robert. *Ford: The Men and the Machine.* Boston: Little, Brown and Company, 1986.

Lakoff, Sanford, and Herbert York. *A Shield in Space? Technology, Politics, and the Strategic Defense Initiative.* Berkeley: University of California Press, 1989.

LaLande, Jeff. *First over the Siskiyous: Peter Skene Ogden's 1826–1827 Journey through the Oregon-California Borderlands.* Portland: Oregon Historical Society Press, 1987.

Lamb, W. K. *The History of the Canadian Pacific Railway.* New York: Macmillan, 1977.

Lanati, Edward E. *A Brief Account of the Windsor Locks Canal.* Windsor Locks, CT: 1976.

Lane, Carl D. *American Paddle Steamboats.* New York: Coward-McCann, 1943.

Lane, Frederic C. *Ships for Victory: A History of Shipbuilding under the U.S. Maritime Commission in World War II.* Baltimore: Johns Hopkins University Press, 1951.

Lane, Wheaton J. *Commodore Vanderbilt: An Epic of the Steam Age.* New York: Knopf, 1942.

Langworth, Richard M. *Hudson: The Postwar Years.* Osceola, WI: Motorbooks International, 1977.

Langworth, Richard M., and Jan P. Norbye. *The Complete History of the Chrysler Corporation, 1924–1985.* New York: Beeckman House, 1985.

Larkin, F. David. "Chicago, Rock Island Railroad." In Robert L. Frey (ed.), *EABHB: Railroads in the Nineteenth Century.* New York: Facts on File, 1988, 45–46.

———. "Cornelius Vanderbilt." In Robert L. Frey (ed.), *EABHB: Railroads in the Nineteenth Century.* New York: Facts on File, 1988, 398–408.

———. "New York Central Railroad." In Robert L. Frey (ed.), *EABHB: Railroads in the Nineteenth Century.* New York: Facts on File, 1988, 282–285.

———. "William H. Vanderbilt." In Robert L. Frey (ed.), *EABHB: Railroads in the Nineteenth Century.* New York: Facts on File, 1988, 410–415.

Larkin, Katherine. "Delaware & Hudson Railroad." In Robert L. Frey (ed.), *EABHB: Railroads in the Nineteenth Century.* New York: Facts on File, 1988, 83–85.

Larrowe, Charles P. *Harry Bridges: The Rise and Fall of Radical Labor in the U.S.* New York: Lawrence Hill, 1972.

Larsen, Gustive O. "The Perpetual Emigration Fund." *Mississippi Valley Historical Review* (1931–1932) 18: 184–194.

Larson, John Lauritz. "Chicago, Burlington & Quincy Railroad." In Robert L. Frey (ed.), *EABHB: Railroads in the Nineteenth Century.* New York: Facts on File, 1988, 47–48.

———. "John Murray Forbes." In Robert L. Frey (ed.), *EABHB: Railroads in the Nineteenth Century.* New York: Facts on File, 1988, 128–132.

Lasky, Victor. *Never Complain, Never Explain: The Story of Henry Ford II.* New York: Richard Marek Publishers, 1981.

Bibliography

Latham, Caroline, and David Agreda. *Dodge Dynasty: The Grand Family That Rocked Detroit*. San Diego: Harcourt Brace Jovanovich, 1985.

Latham, Earl. *The Politics of Railroad Coordination, 1933–1936*. Cambridge: Harvard University Press, 1959.

Latta, Estelle, and M. L. Allison. *Controversial Mark Hopkins*. New York: Greenberg, 1953.

Laut, Agnes. *Overland Trail: The Epic Path of the Pioneers to Oregon*. New York: Frederick A. Stokes Company, 1929.

Laux, James M. "White Motor Company." In George S. May (ed.), *EABHB: The Automobile Industry*. New York: Facts on File, 1990, 452–457.

Laux, James M., et al. *The Automobile Revolution: The Impact of an Industry*. Chapel Hill: University of North Carolina Press, 1982.

LaValle, Omer. *Van Horne's Road*. Montréal: Railfare Enterprises, 1975.

Lavender, David. *Bent's Fort*. Garden City, NY: Doubleday, 1954.

———. *The Great Persuader [Collis P. Huntington]*. Garden City, NY: Doubleday, 1970.

Lay, M. G. *Ways of the World: A History of the World's Roads and the Vehicles That Used Them*. New Brunswick, NJ: Rutgers University Press, 1992.

Lazare, Michael. "George Wilcken Romney." In George S. May (ed.), *EABHB: The Automobile Industry*. New York: Facts on File, 1990, 387–393.

Leary, William M. "Northwest Airlines." In William M. Leary (ed.), *EABHB: The Airline Industry*. New York: Facts on File, 1992, 319–321.

Leary, William M. (ed.). *Encyclopedia of American Business History and Biography: The Airline Industry*. New York: Facts on File, 1992.

Leavitt, Francis H. "Steam Navigation on the Colorado River." *California Historical Society Quarterly* (1943) 23: 1–19, 151–174.

Leavitt, Helen. *Super Highway—Super Hoax*. Garden City, NY: Doubleday, 1970.

Lee, Fred J. *Casey Jones*. Kingsport, TN: Southern Publications, 1939.

Lee, Thomas R. *Turbines Westward*. Manhatten, KS: A. G. Press, 1975.

Lee, Ulysses. *The Employment of Negro Troops: The United States Army in World War II*. Washington, DC: Government Printing Office, 1966.

Leiter, Robert D. *Featherbedding and Job Security*. New York: Twayne, 1964.

Lemy, James H. *The Gulf, Mobile & Ohio: A Railroad That Had To Expand*. Homewood, IL: Irwin, 1953.

———. "Gulf, Mobile & Ohio Railroad." In Keith L. Bryant, Jr. (ed.), *EABHB: Railroads in the Age of Regulation*. New York: Facts on File, 1988, 181–182.

———. "Isaac B. Tigrett." In Keith L. Bryant, Jr. (ed.), *EABHB: Railroads in the Age of Regulation*. New York: Facts on File, 1988, 432–436.

———. "Mobile and Ohio Railroad." In Robert L. Frey (ed.), *EABHB: Railroads in the Nineteenth Century*. New York: Facts on File, 1988, 262–264.

Leonard, Jonathan Norton. *The Tragedy of Henry Ford*. New York: G. P. Putnam's Sons, 1932.

Leonard, William Norris. *Railroad Consolidation under the Transportation Act of 1920*. New York: AMS Press, 1968.

Les Strang, Jacques. *Cargo Carriers of the Great Lakes*. New York: American Legacy Press, 1981.

———. *Seaway: The Untold Story of North America's Fourth Seacoast*. Seattle: Salisbury Press, 1976.

Lesley, Lewis Burt (ed.). *The Purchase and Importation of Camels by the U.S. Government*. Austin: Texas State Historical Association, 1929.

Leuba, Walter. *The Pennsylvania Mainline Canal*. York, PA: American Canal and Transportation Center, 1981.

Leuchtenburg, William E. *Franklin D. Roosevelt and the New Deal, 1932–1940*. New York: Harper and Row, 1963.

———. *In the Shadow of FDR: From Truman to Ronald Reagan.* Ithaca, NY: Cornell University Press, 1983.

———. *The Perils of Prosperity, 1914–1932.* Chicago: University of Chicago Press, 1958.

Levine, Isaac Don. *Mitchell: Pioneer of Air Power.* New York: Arno Press, 1972.

Levinson, Harold M. "Collective Bargaining and Technological Change in the Trucking Industry." In Harold M. Levinson (ed.), *Collective Bargaining and Technological Change in American Transportation.* Evanston, IL: Transportation Center at Northwestern University, 1971, 4–84.

———. "Trucking." In Gerald G. Somers (ed.), *Collective Bargaining: Contemporary American Experience.* Madison, WI: Industrial Research Association, 1980, 99–149.

Lewis, David L., and Laurence Golstein (eds.). *The Automobile and American Culture.* Ann Arbor: University of Michigan Press, 1983.

Lewis, Oscar. *The Big Four.* New York: Knopf, 1938.

Lewis, Richard S. *The Voyages of Apollo: The Exploration of the Moon.* New York: Quadrangle, 1974.

Lewis, W. David. "Eastern Air Lines." In William M. Leary (ed.), *EABHB: The Airline Industry.* New York: Facts on File, 1992, 160–168.

———. "Frank Borman." In William M. Leary, (ed.), *EABHB: The Airline Industry.* New York: Facts on File, 1992, 62–73.

Lewis, W. David, and Wesley P. Newton. "Delta Air Lines." In William H. Leary (ed.), *EABHB: The Airline Industry.* New York: Facts on File, 1992, 145–150.

———. *Delta: The History of an Airline.* Athens: University of Georgia Press, 1979.

Lewis, W. David, and William F. Trimble. *The Airway to Everywhere: A History of All American Aviation, 1937–1953.* Pittsburgh: University of Pittsburgh Press, 1988.

Lewis, William S. "The Camel Pack Trains in the Mining Camps of the West." *Washington Historical Quarterly* (1928) 9: 271–284.

Licht, Walter. "Railroad Unions and Brotherhoods." In Keith L. Bryant, Jr. (ed.), *EABHB: Railroads in the Age of Regulation.* New York: Facts on File, 1988, 354–357.

Lief, Alfred. *The Firestone Story: A History of Firestone Tire and Rubber Company.* New York: Whittlesey House, 1951.

Lillard, Richard. *Eden in Jeopardy: The Southern California Experience.* New York: Knopf, 1966.

Lincoln Highway Association. *The Lincoln Highway: The Story of a Crusade That Made Transportation History.* New York: Dodd, Mead and Company, 1935.

Lindahl, Martin L. *The New England Railroads.* Boston: New England Economic Research Foundation, 1965.

Lindsay, Almont. *The Pullman Strike.* Chicago: University of Chicago Press, 1942.

Link, Arthur S. *Woodrow Wilson and the Progressive Era, 1910–1917.* New York: Harper and Row, 1954.

Lively, Robert A. "The American System: A Review Article." *Business History Review* (1955) 29: 81–96.

Lloyd, Arthur C. "Amtrak." In Keith L. Bryant, Jr. (ed.), *EABHB: Railroads in the Age of Regulation.* New York: Facts on File, 1988, 7–8.

———. "Western Pacific Railroad Company." In Keith L. Bryant, Jr. (ed.), *EABHB: Railroads in the Age of Regulation.* New York: Facts on File, 1988, 468–470.

Loewy, Raymond. *Designs of Raymond Loewy.* Washington, DC: Smithsonian Institution, 1975.

———. *Never Let Well Enough Alone.* New York: Simon and Schuster, 1951.

Logsdon, John M. *The Decision To Go to the Moon: Project Apollo and the National Interest.* Cambridge: MIT Press, 1970.

Lomask, Milton. *Seed Money: The Guggenheim Story.* New York: Farrar, Straus, 1964.

Lomax, Alan. *Folk Songs of North America in the English Language.* Garden City, NY: Doubleday, 1960.

Longman, Phillip. "The Great Train Robbery: How the Railroad Retirement System Swindles Taxpayers, Robs Young Workers, and Derails Amtrak." *Washington Monthly* (December 1987) 19: 12ff.

Longstreet, Stephen A. *A Century on Wheels: The Story of Studebaker*. New York: Henry Holt, 1952.

Loos, John L. *Oil on Stream! A History of the Interstate Oil Pipe Line Company, 1909–1959*. Baton Rouge: Louisiana State University Press, 1959.

Lord, Nancy. *Darkened Waters: A Review of the History, Science, and Technology Associated with the Exxon Valdez Oil Spill and Cleanup*. Stevens Point, WI: Worzalla Press, 1992.

Lovell, Mary S. *The Life of Amelia Earhart*. New York: St. Martin's Press, 1989.

Lyon, Peter. *To Hell in a Day Coach: An Exasperated Look at American Railroads*. Philadelphia: Lippincott, 1968.

McAdoo, William G. *The Crowded Years: The Reminiscences of William G. McAdoo*. Boston: Houghton Mifflin, 1931.

MacAvoy, Paul W. *The Crisis of the Regulatory Commissions: An Introduction to a Current Issue of Public Policy*. New York: W. W. Norton, 1970.

———. *The Economic Effects of Regulation: Trunkline Railroad Cartels and the Interstate Commerce Commission before 1900*. Cambridge: MIT Press, 1965.

MacAvoy, Paul W., and John W. Snow (eds.). *Regulation of Entry and Pricing in Truck Transportation*. Washington, DC: American Enterprise Institute, 1977.

McBain, Howard L. *De Witt Clinton and the Origin of the Spoils System in New York*. New York: AMS Press, 1906.

Macbee, Carleton. *The Seaway Story*. New York: Macmillan, 1961.

MacBeth, Roderick G. *The Romance of the Canadian Pacific Railway*. Toronto: Ryerson Press, 1934.

McCague, James. *Moguls and Iron Men*. New York: Harper and Row, 1964.

McCain, W. D. *The United States and the Republic of Panama*. Durham, NC: Duke University Press, 1937.

McCary, Charles. *Citizen Nader*. New York: Saturday Review Press, 1972.

McCullough, David. *The Path between the Seas: The Creation of the Panama Canal*. New York: Simon and Schuster, 1977.

———. *Truman*. New York: Simon and Schuster, 1992.

McCullough, Robert. *The Pennsylvania Main Line Canal*. Martinsburg, PA: Cove Herald, 1962.

McCormick, Richard P. *The Second American Party System: Party Formation in the Jacksonian Era*. Chapel Hill: University of North Carolina Press, 1966.

McCoy, Dell, and Russ Colman. *The Rio Grande Pictorial*. Denver: Sundance, 1971.

McCraw, Thomas K. "Regulation in America: A Review Article." *Business History Review* (1975) 49: 159–183.

McCurdy, Howard. *Inside NASA: High Technology and Organizational Change in the U.S. Space Program*. Baltimore: Johns Hopkins University Press, 1993.

McDade, Matt C. "New York State's New Main Street." *National Geographic* (November 1956) 110: 567–618.

MacDonald, Anne L. *Feminine Ingenuity: Women and Invention in America*. New York: Ballentine Books, 1992.

McDonald, Forrest. *Alexander Hamilton*. New York: W. W. Norton, 1979.

———. *E Pluribus Unum: The Formation of the American Republic, 1776–1790*. Boston: Houghton Mifflin, 1965.

———. *Novus Ordo Seclorum: The Intellectual Origins of the Constitution*. Lawrence: University of Kansas Press, 1985.

———. *We the People: The Economic Origins of the Constitution*. Chicago: University of Chicago Press, 1958.

McFarland, Marvin W. (ed.). *The Papers of Wilbur and Orville Wright*. 2 vols. New York: McGraw-Hill, 1953.

Macfarlane, Robert S. *Henry Villard and the Northern Pacific*. New York: Newcomen Society in North America, 1954.

MacGill, Caroline E., et al. *History of Transportation in the United States before 1860*. Washington, DC: Carnegie Institution of Washington, 1917.

McGonigal, Robert S. "The 1949 Broadway Limited: The Flagship Streamliner of the Pennsylvania RR's Blue Ribbon Fleet." *Model Railroader* (October 1994) 61: 84–99.

McGowan, George F. *Diesel Electric Locomotive Handbook*. New York: Simmons-Boardman, 1951.

MacGregor, Bruce A., and Ted Benson. *Portrait of a Silver Lady: The Train They Called the California Zephyr*. Boulder, CO: Pruett, 1977.

McLaughlin, Charles L. "The Stanley Steamer: A Study in Unsuccessful Innovation." *Explorations in Entrepreneurial History* (1954-1955) 7: 37–47.

McMillan, Joe. *Route of the Warbonnets*. Woodridge, IL: Joe McMillan, 1977.

———. *Santa Fe's Diesel Fleet*. Burlingame, CA: Chatham, 1974.

MacMullen, Jerry. *Paddle-Wheel Days in California*. Palo Alto, CA: Stanford University Press, 1944.

Madsen, Betty M., and Brigham D. Madsen. *North to Montana: Jehus, Bullwhackers, and Mule Skinners on the Montana Trail*. Salt Lake City: University of Utah Press, 1980.

Magill, Frank (ed.). *Magill's Survey of Science: Space Exploration Series*. 5 vols. Pasadena, CA: Salem Press, 1989.

Magrath, C. Peter. *Yazoo: Law and Politics in the New Republic: The Case of Fletcher v. Peck*. New York: W. W. Norton, 1966.

Mahoney, Tom. *The Story of George Romney: Builder, Salesman, Crusader*. New York: Harper, 1960.

Mailhout, Ernie, et al. *The Eastern Airlines Strike: Accomplishments of the Rank-and-File Machinists and the Gains for the Labor Movement*. New York: Pathfinder, 1991.

———. *The Anti-Federalists: Critics of the Constitution, 1781–1788*. Chapel Hill: University of North Carolina Press, 1961.

Main, Jackson Turner. *Political Parties before the Constitution*. Chapel Hill: University of North Carolina Press, 1973.

———. *The Sovereign States, 1775–1783*. New York: Franklin Watts, 1973.

Majors, Alexander. *Seventy Years on the Frontier*. Chicago: Rand McNally, 1893.

Malone, Dumas. *Jefferson and His Time*. 6 vols. Boston: Little, Brown and Company, 1948–1981.

Manchester, William. *The Glory and the Dream: A Narrative History of America, 1932–1972*. Boston: Little, Brown and Company, 1974.

Mandell, Susan Meikle, et al. *A Historical Survey of Transit Buses in the United States*. Warrendale, PA: Society of Automotive Engineers, 1990.

Mansfield, Henry C. *Vision: A Story the Sky*. New York: Duell, Sloan and Pierce, 1956.

Marcus, Robert D. *Grand Old Party: Political Structure in the Gilded Age, 1880–1896*. New York: Oxford University Press, 1971.

Margetts, F. C. "The Marriage of Road and Rail: Trains for Tomorrow." *Trains* (April 1976) 36: 40–47.

Marre, Louis A., and Jerry A. Pinkepank. *The Contemporary Diesel Spotter's Guide*. Milwaukee: Kalmbach Publications, 1979.

Marshall, David. *Grand Central*. New York: McGraw-Hill, 1946.

Marshall, James. *Santa Fe: The Railroad That Built an Empire*. New York: Random House, 1945.

Marshall, Jonathan. "Cheap Truckin'." *National Review* (7 November 1994) 46: 54–56.

Marshall, S. L. A. *Crimsoned Prairie: The Indian Wars on the Plains*. New York: Charles Scribner's Sons, 1972.

Martin, Albro. *Enterprise Denied: Origins of the Decline of American Railroads, 1897–1917*. New York: Columbia University Press, 1971.

———. "James J. Hill." In Robert L. Frey (ed.), *EABHB: Railroads in the Nineteenth Century*. New York: Facts on File, 1988, 169–178.

———. *James J. Hill and the Opening of the Northwest*. New York: Oxford University Press, 1976.

———. *Railroads Triumphant: The Growth, Rejection, and Rebirth of a Vital American Force*. New York: Oxford University Press, 1992.

———. "The Troubled Subject of Railroad Regulation in the Gilded Age—A Reappraisal." *Journal of American History* (1974) 61: 339–371.

Martin, Charles F. *Milwaukee Road Locomotives*. Chicago: Normandie House, 1972.

Martin, Cy. *Gold Rush Narrow Gauge*. Corona del Mar, CA: Trans-Anglo Books, 1974.

Martin, David Dale. *Mergers and the Clayton Act*. Berkeley: University of California Press, 1959.

Martin, Mabelle E. "California Emigrant Roads through Texas." *Southwestern Historical Quarterly* (1924-1925) 18: 287–301.

Masterson, Vincent V. *The Katy Railroad and the Last Frontier*. Norman: University of Oklahoma Press, 1952.

Matusow, Allen J. *The Unraveling of America: A History of Liberalism in the 1960s*. New York: Harper and Row, 1984.

Maxcy, George. *The Multinational Automobile Industry*. New York: St. Martin's Press, 1981.

May, George S. *A Most Unique Machine: The Michigan Origins of the Automobile Industry*. Grand Rapids, MI: Eerdmans, 1975.

———. "Benjamin Briscoe." In George S. May (ed.), *EABHB: The Automobile Industry*. New York: Facts on File, 1990, 48–53.

———. "Cummins Engine Company." In George S. May (ed.), *EABHB: The Automobile Industry*. New York: Facts on File, 1990, 90–91.

———. "Edsel Bryant Ford." In George S. May (ed.), *EABHB: The Automobile Industry*. New York: Facts on File, 1990, 138–140;

———. "George W. Mason." In George S. May (ed.), *EABHB: The Automobile Industry*. New York: Facts on File, 1990, 316–320.

———. "Henry Ford II." In George S. May (ed.), *EABHB: The Automobile Industry*. New York: Facts on File, 1990, 145–158.

———. "John F. and Horace Elgin Dodge." In George S. May (ed.), *EABHB: The Automobile Industry*. New York: Facts on File, 1990, 125–137.

———. "John North Willys." In George S. May (ed.), *EABHB: The Automobile Industry*. New York: Facts on File, 1990, 462–466.

———. "Ralph Nader." In George S. May (ed.), *EABHB: The Automobile Industry*. New York: Facts on File, 1990, 338–341.

———. *Encyclopedia of American Business History and Biography: The Automobile Industry, 1896–1920*. New York: Facts on File, 1990.

May, George S. (ed.). *Encyclopedia of American Business History and Biography: The Automobile Industry, 1920–1980*. New York: Facts on File, 1989.

Mayer, George H. *The Republican Party, 1854–1966*. New York: Oxford University Press, 1967.

Maynard, Theodore. *The Long Road of Father Serra*. New York: Appleton-Century-Crofts, 1954.

Mencken, August. *The Railroad Passenger Car: An Illustrated History of the First Hundred Years*. Baltimore: Johns Hopkins University Press, 1957.

Mercer, Lloyd J. "Edward Henry Harriman." In Robert L. Frey (ed.), *EABHB: Railroads in the Nineteenth Century*. New York: Facts on File, 1988, 155–164.

———. "Railroad Land Grants." In Keith L. Bryant, Jr. (ed.), *EABHB: Railroads in the Age of Regulation*. New York: Facts on File, 1988, 353.

———. *Railroads and Land Grant Policy: A Study in Government Intervention*. New York: Academic Press, 1982.

Meredith, Roy, and Arthur Meredith. *Mr. Lincoln's Military Railroads*. New York: W. W. Norton, 1979.

Merk, Frederick. *Manifest Destiny and Mission in American History*. New York: Knopf, 1963.

———. *The Monroe Doctrine and American Expansionism*. New York: Knopf, 1966.

Merrill, Horace Samuel. *Bourbon Leader: Grover Cleveland and the Democratic Party*. Boston: Little, Brown and Company, 1957.

Meyer, John R., and Clinton V. Oster, Jr. *Deregulation and the Future of Intercity Passenger Travel*. Cambridge: MIT Press, 1987.

Meyers, Gustavus. *History of the Great American Fortunes*. 3 vols. Chicago: Charles H. Kerr and Company, 1910.

Meyers, Rex C. "Northern Pacific Railroad." In Robert L. Frey (ed.), *EABHB: Railroads in the Nineteenth Century*. New York: Facts on File, 1988, 287–289.

Michaels, Patricia. "Trans World Airlines." In William M. Leary (ed.), *EABHB: The Airline Industry*. New York: Facts on File, 1992, 461–463.

Middleton, William D. *Grand Central: The World's Greatest Railway Terminal*. San Marino, CA: Golden West Books, 1977.

———. *When the Steam Roads Electrified*. Milwaukee: Kalmbach Publications, 1951.

Miekle, Jeffrey L. *Twentieth Century Limited: Industrial Design in America*. Philadelphia: Temple University Press, 1979.

Millbank, Jeremiah, Jr. *The First Century of Flight in America*. Princeton, NJ: Princeton University Press, 1943.

Miller, George H. *Railroads and the Granger Laws*. Madison: University of Wisconsin Press, 1971.

Miller, John A. *Fares Please!* New York: Dover, 1960.

Miller, John C. *Alexander Hamilton and the Growth of the New Nation*. New York: Harper, 1959.

Miller, Ronald, and David Sawers. *The Technological Development of Modern Aviation*. London: Praeger, 1970.

Milligan, John D. *Gunboats Down the Mississippi*. Annapolis, MD: Naval Institute Press, 1965.

Mills, Randall V. *Stern-Wheelers Up Columbia*. Palo Alto, CA: Stanford University Press, 1947.

Miner, Dwight C. *The Fight for the Panama Route: The Story of the Spooner Act and the Hay-Herran Treaty*. New York: Columbia University Press, 1940.

Miner, H. Craig. "Missouri Pacific Railroad." In Keith L. Bryant Jr. (ed.), *EABHB: Railroads in the Age of Regulation*. New York: Facts on File, 1988, 303–305.

———. *The Rebirth of the Missouri Pacific, 1956–1983*. College Station: Texas A&M Press, 1983.

———. *The St. Louis–San Francisco Continental Railroad*. Lawrence: University of Kansas Press, 1973.

Minton, Bruce, and John Stuart. *Men Who Led Labor*. New York: Modern Age, 1937.

Mitchel, Broadus. *Alexander Hamilton*. 2 vols. New York: Macmillan, 1957–1962.

Monaghan, Jay. *The Overland Trail*. Indianapolis: Bobbs-Merrill, 1947.

Moody, John. *The Masters of Capital*. New Haven, CT: Yale University Press, 1919.

Moody, Ralph. *The Old Trails West*. New York: Thomas Y. Crowell Company, 1963.

Moolman, Valerie. *The Road to Kittyhawk*. Alexandria, VA: Time-Life Books, 1980.

Moore, Thomas Gale. *Freight Transportation Regulation: Surface Freight and the ICC*. Washington, DC: American Enterprise Institute for Policy Research, 1972.

———. "Rail and Trucking Deregulation." In Leonard Weiss and Michael W. Klass (eds.), *Regulatory Reform: What Actually Happened*. Boston: Little, Brown and Company, 1986, 14–39.

Morgan, Dale L. *Jedediah Smith and the Opening of the West*. Indianapolis: Bobbs-Merrill, 1953.

Morgan, David P. "The Greatest Century of All." *Model Railroader* (April 1988) 55: 76–91.

Bibliography

————. "Piggyback: The Most Realistic Approach." *Trains* (May 1955) 15: 7.

Morgan, H. Wayne. *From Hayes to McKinley: National Party Politics, 1877–1896*. Syracuse, NY: Syracuse University Press, 1969.

Morison, Samuel Eliot. *The Maritime History of Massachusetts, 1783–1860*. Boston: Houghton Mifflin, 1921.

Moritz, Michael, and Barret Seaman. *Going For Broke: The Chrysler Story*. Garden City, NY: Doubleday, 1981.

Moses, Robert. "The New Super-Highways: Blessing or Blight?" *Harper's* (December 1956) 213: 27–31.

Motor Vehicle Manufacturers Association of the United States. *Automobiles of America: Milestones, Pioneers, Roll Call, Highlights*. Detroit: Wayne State University Press, 1974.

Mott, Edward H. *Between the Ocean and the Lakes: The Story of Erie*. New York: J. S. Collins, 1899.

Mowry, George E. *The Era of Theodore Roosevelt and the Birth of Modern America, 1900–1912*. New York: Harper and Row, 1958.

Mulder, William. "Mormonism's Gathering: An American Doctrine with a Difference." *Church History* (1954) 23: 248–264.

Murphy, Charles J. V., and Thomas A. Wise. "The Problem of Howard Hughes." *Fortune* (January 1959) 59: 79–82.

Murphy, Michael E. *The Airline That Pride Almost Bought: The Struggle To Take Over Continental Airlines*. New York: Franklin Watts, 1986.

Murray, Charles, and Catherine Bly Cox. *Apollo: The Race to the Moon*. New York: Simon and Schuster, 1989.

Murray, Edward P. *Camels to the Colorado*. Tucson, AZ: PIP Printing, 1980.

Musolf, Lloyd. *Uncle Sam's Private, Profitseeking Corporations*. Lexington, MA: D. C. Heath, 1983.

Myers, William A. *Iron Men and Copper Wires*. Glendale, CA: Trans-Anglo Books, 1983.

Nader, Ralph. *Unsafe at Any Speed*. New York: Grossman, 1965.

Nelligan, Tom. *VIA Rail Canada: The First Five Years*. Park Forest, IL: PTJ Publishing, 1982.

Nelligan, Tom, and Scott Hartley. *The Route of the Minuteman*. New York: Quadrant, 1980.

Nelson, Daniel. *American Rubber Workers and Organized Labor, 1900–1941*. Princeton, NJ: Princeton University Press, 1988.

Nelson, James C. "The Motor Carrier Act of 1935." *Journal of Political Economy* (1936) 44: 464–604.

Nevins, Allan. *The Emergence of Lincoln: Douglas, Buchanan and Party Chaos, 1857–1859*. New York: Charles Scribner's Sons, 1950.

————. *Study in Power: John D. Rockefeller, Industrialist and Philanthropist*. 2 vols. New York: Charles Scribner's Sons, 1953.

Nevins, Allan, and Frank Ernest Hill. *Ford*. 3 vols. New York: Charles Scribner's Sons, 1954–1963.

Nevins, Frank J. *Seventy Years of Service from Grant to Garman*. Chicago: Poole Brothers, 1922.

Newell, Gordon. *Ocean Liners of the 20th Century*. Seattle: Superior Publishing, 1963.

Newhouse, John. "The Battle of the Bailout." *New Yorker* (18 January 1993) 68: 42–51.

————. *The Sporty Game*. New York: Knopf, 1982.

Newton, Wesley P. "Juan T. Trippe." In William M. Leary (ed.), *EABHB: The Airline Industry*. New York: Facts on File, 1992, 464–476.

————. "Pan American Airways." In William M. Leary (ed.), *EABHB: The Airline Industry*. New York: Facts on File, 1992, 343–349.

Nicholi, A. "The Motorcycle Syndrome." *American Journal of Psychiatry* (1970) 126 (no. 11): 1588–1595.

Nichols, Roy. *The Disruption of American Democracy*. New York: Macmillan, 1948.

Niemeyer, Glenn A. *The Automotive Career of Ransom E. Olds*. East Lansing: Michigan State University Press, 1965.

Niven, John. *Martin Van Buren: The Romantic Age of American Politics*. New York: Oxford University Press, 1983.

Nock, O. S. *Railways of the USA*. New York: Hastings, 1979.

Northrup, Herbert R. *Organized Labor and the Negro*. New York: Harper and Row, 1944.

Nugent, Walter T. K. *The Money Question during Reconstruction*. New York: W. W. Norton, 1967.

Odegard, Gordon. "Milwaukee Road Hiawatha." *Model Railroader* (January 1984) 51: 112–123.

———. "Santa Fe 10-Pack." *Model Railroader* (September 1982) 49: 58–61.

O'Donnell, Thomas C. *Snubbing Posts: An Informal History of the Blackwater Canal*. Boobville, NY: Black River Books, 1949.

Olmstead, Robert P. *The Diesel Years*. San Marino, CA: Golden West Books, 1975.

———. *Milwaukee Rails*. Woodridge, IL: McMillan Publications, 1980.

———. *Prairie Rails*. Woodbridge, IL: McMillan Publications, 1979.

Olsen, John Alden. "Proselytism, Immigration and Settlement of Foreign Converts to the Mormon Culture in Zion." *Journal of the West* (1967) 6: 189–204.

Omwake, John. *The Conestoga Six-Horse Bell Teams of Eastern Pennsylvania*. Cincinnati: Ebbert & Richardson, 1930.

O'Neill, Ralph A. *A Dream of Eagles [The New York, Río, Buenos Aires Airline]*. Boston: Houghton Mifflin Company, 1973.

Ordway, Frederick I., and Mitchell R. Sharpe. *The Rocket Team*. New York: Thomas Y. Crowell, 1979.

O'Reilly, Maurice. *The Goodyear Story*. Elmsford, NY: Benjamin Company, 1983.

Orenstein, Jeffrey. *United States Railroad Policy: Uncle Sam at the Throttle*. Chicago: Nelson-Hall, 1990.

Ostrogorski, M. Moisei. *Democracy and the Organization of Political Parties*. New York: Macmillan, 1902.

Otto, Dixon P. *On Orbit: Bringing on the Space Shuttle*. Athens, OH: Main Stage, 1986.

Outland, Charles F. *Stagecoaching on el Camino Real: Los Angeles to San Francisco, 1861–1901*. Glendale, CA: Arthur H. Clark Company, 1973.

Overton, Richard C. *Burlington Route*. New York: Knopf, 1965.

Owen, Wilfred, et al. *Financing Highways*. Princeton, NJ: Tax Institute, 1957.

Padelford, Norman J. *The Panama Canal in Peace and War*. New York: Macmillan, 1942.

Paden, Irene. *Wake of the Prairie Schooner*. New York: Macmillan, 1943.

Palmer, R. R. *The Age of Democratic Revolution: A Political History of Europe and America, 1760–1800*. New Brunswick, NJ: Princeton University Press, 1959.

Palmer, William J., Lorenzo M. Johnson, and John J. Lipsey. *The War of the Gauges*. Colorado Springs, CO: Western Books, 1961.

Parkman, Francis. *France and England in North America*. 7 vols. in 2 vols. New York: Library of America, 1983.

Parks, Pat. *The Railroad That Died at Sea*. Brattleboro, VT: Greene Press, 1968.

Parmet, Herbert. *Eisenhower and the American Crusades*. New York: Macmillan, 1972.

Partridge, Bellamy. *Fill 'er Up!* New York: McGraw-Hill, 1952.

Paul, Günter. *The Satellite Spin-Off: The Achievements of Space Flight*. Translated by Alan and Barbara Lacy. Washington, DC: Robert B. Luce, 1975.

Paxson, Frederic L. "The Highway Movement, 1916–1935." *American Historical Review* (1945–1946) 51: 236–253.

———. *History of the American Frontier*. Boston: Houghton Mifflin, 1924.

Payne, Keith B. "The Soviet Union and Strategic Defense: The Failure and Future of Arms Control." *Orbis* (1986) 29: 673–689.

Pearson, Henry G. *An American Railroad Builder: John Murray Forbes*. Boston: Houghton Mifflin, 1911.

Pedraja, René de la. *A Historical Dictionary of the U.S. Merchant Marine and Shipping Industry*. Westport, CT: Greenwood, 1994.

Bibliography

———. *The Rise and Decline of U.S. Merchant Shipping in the Twentieth Century.* New York: Twayne, 1992.

Pell, Claiborne. "Our Run-Down Railroads." *The New Republic* (2 May 1964) 150: 11–14.

Perkins, Dexter. *The Monroe Doctrine, 1826–1867.* Baltimore: Johns Hopkins University Press, 1933.

———. *The New Age of Franklin D. Roosevelt, 1932–1945.* Chicago: University of Chicago Press, 1957.

Perkins, J. R. *Trails, Rails, and War.* Indianapolis: Bobbs-Merrill, 1929.

Perry Charles R., et al. *Deregulation and the Decline of the Unionized Trucking Industry.* Philadelphia: The Wharton School, University of Pennsylvania, 1986.

Perry, Robert E. "Military Aviation, 1908–1976." In Eugene M. Emme (ed.), *Two Hundred Years of Flight in America.* San Diego: Univelt, 1977, 137–154.

Peters, Bradley. *Maine Central Railroad Company.* .Portland, ME: MEC Railroad, 1976.

Petersen, William J. "Steamboating on the Missouri River." *Iowa Journal of History* (1955) 53: 97–120.

———. *Steamboating on the Upper Mississippi: The Water Way to Iowa.* Iowa City: University of Iowa Press, 1937.

Peterson, Merrill D. *Thomas Jefferson and the New Nation.* New York: Oxford University Press, 1970.

Phelan, James. *Howard Hughes: The Hidden Years.* New York: Random House, 1976.

Phelps, J. Alfred. *They Had a Dream: The Story of African-American Astronauts.* Novato, CA: Presidio, 1994.

Phillips, R. A. J. *Canada's Railways.* New York: McGraw-Hill, 1968.

Phillips, U. B. *A History of Transportation in the Eastern Cotton Belt to 1860.* New York: Columbia University Press, 1908.

Pickerell, Donald. "The Regulation and Deregulation of U.S. Airlines." In Kenneth Button (ed.), *Airline Deregulation: International Experiences.* London: David Fulton Publishers, 1991, 5–47.

Pineau, Roger. "Ballooning in the United States from Straw to Propane." In Eugene M. Emme (ed.), *Two Hundred Years of Flight in America.* San Diego: Univelt, 1977, 41–67.

Pinkepank, Jerry A. *The Second Diesel Spotter's Guide.* Milwaukee: Kalmbach Publications, 1977.

Pirsig, Robert M. *Zen and the Art of Motorcycle Maintenance.* Toronto: Bantam, 1975.

Pitrone, Jean Maddern. *Tangled Web: Legacy of Auto Pioneer John F. Dodge.* Hamtramck, MI: Avenue, 1989.

Pitrone, Jean Maddern, and Joan Potter Elward. *The Dodges: The Auto Family's Fortune and Misfortune.* South Bend, IN: Icarus, 1981.

Planck, Charles E. *Women with Wings.* New York: Harper Brothers, 1942.

Plowden, David. *Bridges: The Spans of North America.* New York: Viking Press, 1974.

Poage, George Rawlings. *Henry Clay and the Whig Party.* Chapel Hill: University of North Carolina Press, 1936.

Podhoretz, John. *Hell of a Ride: Backstage at the White House Follies, 1989–1993.* New York: Simon and Schuster, 1993.

Pole, J. R. *Foundations of American Independence, 1763–1815.* Indianapolis: Bobbs-Merrill, 1972.

Poll, Richard D. "The Political Reconstruction of Utah Territory, 1866–1880." *Pacific Historical Review* (1958) 27: 111–126.

Pollack, Norman (ed.). *The Populist Mind.* Indianapolis: Bobbs-Merrill, 1967.

Pomphrey, Martin M. "St. Louis-San Francisco Railway Company." In Keith L. Bryant, Jr. (ed.), *EABHB: Railroads in the Age of Regulation.* New York: Facts on File, 1988, 381–384.

Pope, Dan, and Mark Lynn. *Warbonnets: From Super Chief to Super Fleet.* Englewood, CO: Wiesner Publications, 1994.

Porter, Glenn. *The Rise of Big Business, 1860–1910.* New York: Thomas Y. Crowell Company, 1973.

Pratt, Fletcher. *Civil War on Western Waters.* New York: Henry Holt, 1956.

Pratt, Julius W. *Expansionists of 1898: The Acquisition of Hawaii and the Spanish Islands.* Baltimore: Johns Hopkins University Press, 1936.

Prince, Richard E. *Atlantic Coast Line Railroad.* Green River, WY: Richard Prince, 1966.

Prout, Henry G. *A Life of George Westinghouse.* New York: American Society of Mechanical Engineers, 1921.

Prucha, Francis Paul. *Broadax and Bayonet: The Role of the United States Army in the Development of the Northwest, 1815–1860.* Lincoln: University of Nebraska Press, 1967.

Purcell, Edward A. "Ideas and Interests: Businessmen and the Interstate Commerce Act." *Journal of American History* (1967) 54: 561–578.

Pyle, Joseph Gilpin. *The Life of James J. Hill.* New York: Doubleday, Page and Company, 1926.

Quiett, Glenn C. *They Built the West.* New York: Appleton-Century, 1934.

Rader, James. *Penetrating the U.S. Auto Market: German and Japanese Strategies.* Ann Arbor, MI: UMI Research, 1980.

Rae, John B. "Alfred Pritchard Sloan, Jr." In George S. May (ed.), *EABHB: The Automobile Industry.* New York: Facts on File, 1990, 402–413.

———. *American Automobile Manufacturers.* Philadelphia: Chilton, 1959.

———. *Climb to Greatness: The American Aircraft Industry, 1920–1960.* Cambridge: MIT Press, 1968.

———. "The Electric Vehicle Corporation: A Monopoly That Missed." *Business History Review* (1955) 22: 298–311.

———. "The Fabulous Billy Durant." *Business History Review* (1958) 25: 255–271.

Rainey, Froelich. "Alaska Highway: An Engineering Epic." *National Geographic* (February 1943) 83: 143–168.

Ramsay, Bruce. *PGE: Railway to the North.* Vancouver, BC: Mitchell Press, 1962.

Ratcliffe, Mike. *Liquid Gold Ships: A History of the Tanker.* London: Lloyd's of London Press, 1985.

Rawley, James A. *Race and Politics: "Bleeding" Kansas and the Coming of the Civil War.* Philadelphia: Lippincott, 1969.

Redinger, Matthew A. "Collis P. Huntington." In Robert L. Frey (ed.), *EABHB: Railroads in the Nineteenth Century.* New York: Facts on File, 1988, 188–193.

Rehor, John A. *The Nickel Plate Story.* Milwaukee: Kalmbach Publishing, 1994.

Reid, H. *The Virginian Railway.* Milwaukee: Kalmbach Publishing, 1983.

Remini, Robert V. *Andrew Jackson and the Course of American Democracy, 1833–1845.* New York: Harper and Row, 1984.

———. *Andrew Jackson and the Course of American Freedom, 1822–1832.* New York: Harper and Row, 1981.

———. *Martin Van Buren and the Making of the Democratic Party.* New York: W. W. Norton, 1970.

Remley, David. *Crooked Road: The Story of the Alaska Highway.* New York: McGraw-Hill, 1976.

Renute, Alfred. "Celebrating Rails and Parks." *Trains* (October 1994) 54: 32–33.

———. *Trains of Discovery: Western Railroads and the National Parks.* New York: Reinhart, 1990.

Repp, Stan. *Super Chief: Train of the Stars.* San Marino, CA: Golden West Books, 1980.

Riabchikov, Evgeny. *Russians in Space.* Edited by Nikolai P. Kamanin; translated by Guy Daniels. Garden City, NY: Doubleday, 1971.

Richards, Gilbert F. *Budd on the Move: Innovation for a Nation on Wheels.* New York: Necomen Society in North America, 1975.

Richmond, Al. *Cowboys, Miners, Presidents, and Kings: The Story of the Grand Canyon Railway.* Flagstaff, AZ: Grand Canyon Pioneers Society, 1985.

Rickenbacker, Edward V. *Rickenbacker: His Own Story.* New York: Fawcett, 1969.

Riegel, Robert E. *The Story of the Western Railroads*. Lincoln: University of Nebraska Press, 1944.

———. "Trans-Mississippi Railroads during the Fifties." *Mississippi Valley Historical Review* (1923–1924) X: 153–172.

Riesenberg, Felix , Jr. *The Golden Road*. New York: McGraw–Hill, 1962.

Risjord, Norman K. *The Old Republicans*. New York: Columbia University Press, 1965.

Rister, Carl Coke. *Oil! Titan of the Southwest*. Norman: University of Oklahoma Press, 1949.

Rittenhouse, Jack D. *A Guidebook to Highway 66*. Albuquerque: University of New Mexico Press, 1993.

Robbins, Edwin C. *Railway Conductors: A Study in Organized Labor*. New York: AMS Press, 1970.

Robert, C. Fellmeth. *The Interstate Commerce Omission: The Public Interest and the ICC*. New York: Grossman, 1970.

Roberts, Christopher. *The Middlesex Canal, 1793–1860*. Cambridge: Harvard University Press, 1938.

Roberts, J. Baylor. "America on the Move." *National Geographic* (September 1946) 90: 357–378.

Roberts, MacLennan. *The Great Locomotive Chase*. New York: Dell, 1956.

Roberts, Robert. "Amtrak Goal: Reduce Costs, Improve Service." *Modern Railways* (May 1983) 39: 30–37.

Robinson, David Z. *The Strategic Defense Initiative: Its Effects on the Economy and Arms Control*. New York: University Press, 1987.

Robinson, Douglas H. *Giants in the Sky*. London: Foulis, 1973.

Robinson, John. *Highways and Our Environment*. New York: McGraw-Hill, 1971.

Robyn, Dorothy. *Braking the Special Interests: Trucking Deregulation and the Politics of Policy Reform*. Chicago: University of Chicago Press, 1987.

Rochester, Stuart. *Take-Off at Mid-Century: Federal Civil Aviation Policy in the Eisenhower Years*. Washington, DC: Government Printing Office, 1977.

Root, Frank A., and William E. Connelly. *The Overland Stage to California*. Topeka, KS: Long's College Bookstore, 1901.

Root, George A., and Russell K. Hickman. "Pike's Peak Express Companies: The Platte Route." *Kansas Historical Quarterly* (1945) 14: 36–92.

———. "Pike's Peak Express Companies: The Solomon and Republican Routes." *Kansas Historical Quarterly* (1944) 13: 163–195, 211–242, 485–526.

Roscow, James P. *800 Miles to Valdez: The Building of the Alaska Pipeline*. Englewood Cliffs, NJ: Prentice-Hall, 1977.

Rose, Harvey, and Amy Pinkerton. *The Energy Crisis, Conservation and Solar*. Ann Arbor, MI: Ann Arbor Science Publishers, 1981.

Rose, Mark H. *Interstate Express Highway Politics, 1941–1956*. Lawrence: Regents Press of Kansas, 1979.

Roseberry, Cecil R. *The Challenging Skies: The Colorful Story of Aviation's Most Exciting Years, 1919–1939*. Garden City, NY: Doubleday, 1966.

———. *Glenn Curtiss: Pioneer of Flight*. Garden City, NY: Doubleday, 1972.

Rostow, Walt W. *The Stages of Economic Growth: A Non-Communist Manifesto*. 3rd ed. Cambridge: Cambridge University Press, 1990.

Rothe, J. Peter. *The Trucker's World: Risk, Safety, and Mobility*. New Brunswick, NJ: Transaction Publishers, 1991.

Rothe, J. Peter, and Peter J. Cooper (eds.). *Motorcyclists: Image and Reality*. Vancouver: Insurance Corporation of British Columbia, 1987.

Rothman, David J. *Politics and Power: The United States Senate, 1869–1901*. Cambridge: Harvard University Press, 1966.

Rothschild, Emma. *Paradise Lost: The Decline of the Auto-Industrial Age*. New York: Random House, 1973.

Rouse, Parke, Jr. *The Great Wagon Road from Philadelphia to the South*. New York: McGraw-Hill, 1973.

Rowsome, Frank, Jr. *Trolley Car Treasury*. New York: McGraw-Hill, 1956.

Rubin, Julius. *Canal or Railroad? Imitation and Response to the Erie Canal in Philadelphia, Baltimore and Boston*. Philadelphia: American Philosophical Association, 1961.

Rush, Elson. "BNSF: Biggest Merger of All." *Pacific RAILNews* (September 1994) 370: 16–21.

Russell, Carl P. "Wilderness Rendezvous Period of the American Fur Trade." *Oregon Historical Quarterly* (1941) 42: 1–47.

Russell, P. J. *The Motor Wagons: The Origin and History of Long-Distance Truck Transportation*. Akron, OH: Pioneer Motor Traffic Club of Akron, 1971.

Russell, Robert R. *Improvement of Communication with the Pacific Coast as an Issue in American Politics, 1783–1864*. Cedar Rapids, IA: Torch Press, 1948.

Rydell, Raymond A. "The California Clippers." *Pacific Historical Review* (1949) 18: 70–83.

———. *Cape Horn to the Pacific: The Rise and Decline of an Ocean Highway*. Berkeley: University of California Press, 1952.

Sabin, Edwin L. *Building the Pacific Railway*. Philadelphia: Lippincott, 1919.

Sagan, Carl. *Pale Blue Dot: A Vision of the Human Future in Space*. New York: Random House, 1994.

———. "Wanderers." *Parade* (18 September 1994): 14–17.

Salsbury, Stephen. *No Way To Run a Railroad: The Untold Story of the Penn Central Crisis*. New York: McGraw-Hill, 1982.

Sandburg, Carl. *The American Songbag*. New York: Harcourt, Brace, and Company, 1927.

Sanderlin, Walter S. *The Great National Project: A History of the Chesapeake and Ohio Canal*. Baltimore: Johns Hopkins University Press, 1946.

Sarnoff, Paul. *Russell Sage: The Money King*. New York: I. Oblensky, 1965.

Satterfield, Archie. *The Lewis and Clark Trail*. Harrisburg, PA: Stackpole Books, 1978.

Saunders, Richard. "Alfred E. Perlman." In Keith L. Bryant, Jr. (ed.), *EABHB: Railroads in the Age of Regulation*. New York: Facts on File, 1988, 341–348.

———. "Delaware & Hudson Railway." In Keith L. Bryant, Jr. (ed.), *EABHB: Railroads in the Age of Regulation*. New York: Facts on File, 1988, 110–111.

———. "Lehigh Valley Railroad." In Keith L. Bryant, Jr. (ed.), *EABHB: Railroads in the Age of Regulation*. New York: Facts on File, 1988, 256–258.

———. "New York, Chicago & St Louis Railroad." In Keith L. Bryant, Jr. (ed.), *EABHB: Railroads in the Age of Regulation*. New York: Facts on File, 1988, 320–321.

———. "Penn Central." In Keith L. Bryant, Jr. (ed.), *EABHB: Railroads in the Age of Regulation*. New York: Facts on File, 1988, 334–336.

———. *The Railroad Mergers and the Coming of Conrail*. Westport, CT: Greenwood, 1978.

Sawyer, L. A., and W. H. Mitchell. *The Liberty Ships: The History of the "Emergency" Type Cargo Ships Constructed in the United States during the Second World War*. London: Lloyd's of London Press, 1985.

Schafer, Mike, and Harold Russell. "Rock Island's Rocket Streamliners." *Model Railroader* (May 1980) 47: 52–61.

Schallenburger, Moses. *The Opening of the California Trail*. Berkeley: University of California Press, 1953.

Scharchburg, Richard P. *W. C. Durant: "The Boss."* Flint, MI: GMI Press, 1973.

———. "Walter P. Chrysler." In George S. May (ed.), *EABHB: The Automobile Industry*. New York: Facts on File, 1990, 52–64.

Scheiber, Harry N. *Ohio Canal Era: A Case Study of Government and the Economy, 1820–1861*. Athens: Ohio University Press, 1987.

———. "The Road to Munn: Eminent Domain and the Concept of Public Purpose in the State Courts." *Perspectives in American History* (1971) 5: 327–402.

Schisgall, Oscar. *The Greyhound Story: From Hibbing to Everywhere*. Chicago: J. G. Ferguson, 1985.

Schmitt, Peter J. *Back to Nature: The Arcadian Myth in Urban America*. New York: Oxford University Press, 1969.

Schneide, James G. "Otto Mears." In Robert L. Frey (ed.), *EABHB: Railroads in the Nineteenth Century*. New York: Facts on File, 1988, 248–255.

Schneider, Norris F. *The National Road: Main Street of America*. Columbus: Ohio Historical Society, 1975.

Schneider, Paul. *Burlington Northern Diesel Locomotives: Three Decades of BN Power*. Milwaukee: Kalmbach, 1993.

Schorr, Eugene. *The Politics of International Aviation*. New York: Macmillan, 1991.

Schotter, H. W. *The Growth and Development of the Pennsylvania Railroad Company 1846 to 1926 Inclusive*. Philadelphia: Allen, Lane and Scott, 1928.

Schurr, Sam H., et al. *Energy in the American Economy, 1850–1975: An Economic Study of Its History and Prospects*. Baltimore: Johns Hopkins University Press, 1960.

Schwantes, Carlos A. "Benjamin Holladay." In Robert L. Frey (ed.), *EABHB: Railroads in the Nineteenth Century*. New York: Facts on File, 1988, 179–181.

———. "Chicago, Milwaukee, St. Paul & Pacific Railroad." In Keith L. Bryant, Jr. (ed.), *EABHB: Railroads in the Age of Regulation*. New York: Facts on File, 1988, 76–78.

———. "The Milwaukee Road's Pacific Expansion." *Pacific Northwest Quarterly* (1981) 72: 30–40.

Schwartz, Stephen. *Brotherhood of the Sea: A History of the Sailors' Union of the Pacific, 1885–1985*. New Brunswick, NJ: Transaction Books, 1986.

Schwinn, Frank W. *Fifty Years of Schwinn-Built Bicycles*. Chicago: Arnold, Schwinn and Company, 1945.

Scott, Quinta, and Susan Croce Kelly. *Route 66: The Highway and Its People*. Norman: University of Oklahoma Press, 1988.

Scribbins, Jim. *The 400 Story*. Park Forrest, IL: PTJ Publishing, 1982.

———. *The Hiawatha Story*. Milwaukee: Kalmbach Publishing, 1970.

Sears, Stephen W. *The American Heritage History of the Automobile in America*. New York: American Heritage Press, 1977.

Sebree, Mac. "BART's Billion Dollar Expansion Program." *Passenger Train Journal* (October 1994) 25: 20–23.

———. "DART and RDC's: Texas-Style Commuter Rail." *Passenger Train Journal* (October 1994) 25: 34–35.

Seely, Bruce E. *Building the American Highway System: Engineers as Policy Makers*. Philadelphia: Temple University Press, 1987.

Seibel, Clifford W. *Helium: Child of the Sun*. Lawrence: University of Kansas Press, 1969.

Seip, Terry L. *The South Returns to Congress: Men, Economic Measures, and Intersectional Relationships*. Baton Rouge: Louisiana State University Press, 1983.

Serling, Robert J. *Eagle: The History of American Airlines*. New York: St. Martin's Press, 1985.

———. *From the Captain to the Colonel: An Informal History of Eastern Air Lines*. New York: Dial Press, 1980.

———. *Howard Hughes' Airline: An Informal History of TWA*. New York: St. Martin's/ Marek, 1983.

———. *The Jet Age*. Alexandria, VA: Time-Life Books, 1982.

———. *Maverick: The Story of Robert Six and Continental Airlines*. Garden City, NY: Doubleday, 1974.

Sessions, G. M. *Traffic Devices: Historical Aspects Thereof*. Washington, DC: Institute of Traffic Engineers, 1976.

Settle, Raymond W., and Mary Lund Settle. *Empire on Wheels*. Palo Alto, CA: Stanford University Press, 1949.

———. *Saddles and Spurs: The Pony Express Saga*. Harrisburg, PA: Stackpole, 1955.

———. *War Drums and Wagon Wheels: The Story of Russell, Majors, and Waddell.* Lincoln: University of Nebraska Press, 1966.

Seyfried, Vincent F. *The Long Island Railroad.* 5 vols. Garden City, NY: Felix F. Reifschneider, 1961–1972.

Shank, William H. *The Best from American Canals.* 4 vols. York, PA: American Canal and Transportation Center, 1972–1986.

Shannon, David A. "Eugene V. Debs: Conservative Labor Leader." *Indiana Magazine of History* (1951) 47: 357–364.

Sharfman, Isaiah Leo. *The American Railroad Problem.* New York: Century, 1921.

———. *The Interstate Commerce Commission: A Study in Administrative Law and Procedure.* 4 pts. New York: Commonwealth Fund, 1937.

Sharkey, Robert P. *Money, Class, and Party: An Economic Study of Civil War and Reconstruction.* Baltimore: Johns Hopkins University Press, 1959.

Sharp, Paul F. "Whoop-Up Trail: International Highway on the Great Plains." *Pacific Historical Review* (1952) 21: 129–144.

Shaughnessy, Jim. *Delaware & Hudson.* La Jolla, CA: Howell-North, 1967.

Shaw, Robert B. *A History of Railroad Accidents, Safety Precautions, and Operating Practices.* Potsdam, NY: Northern Press, 1978.

Shaw, Ronald E. *Canals for a Nation: The Canal Era in the United States, 1790–1860.* Lexington: University of Kentucky Press, 1990.

———. *Erie Water West: A History of the Erie Canal, 1792–1854.* Lexington: University of Kentucky Press, 1966.

Shayler, David. *Shuttle Challenger.* New York: Prentice-Hall, 1987.

Shenefield, John H., and Irwin M. Stelzer. *The Antitrust Laws: A Primer.* Washington, DC: AEI Press, 1993.

Shepard, Alan B., and Donald K. Slayton. *Moon Shot: The Inside Story of America's Race to the Moon.* Atlanta: Turner Publications, 1992.

Sherril, Robert. *The Oil Follies of 1970–1980: How the Petroleum Industry Stole the Show (and Much More Besides).* Garden City, NY: Doubleday, 1983.

Shook, Robert L. *Turnaround: The New Ford Motor Company.* New York: Prentice-Hall, 1990.

Signor, John R. *Los Angeles & Salt Lake Railroad: Union Pacific's Historic Salt Lake Route.* San Marino, CA: Golden West Books, 1988.

Simplich, Frederick. "U.S. Roads in War and Peace." *National Geographic* (December 1941) 80: 687–716.

Sinclair, Angus. *Development of the Locomotive Engine.* Edited by John H. Whire, Jr. Cambridge: MIT Press, 1970.

Skowronek, Stephen. *Building a New American State: The Expansion of National Administrative Capacities, 1877–1920.* Cambridge: Harvard University Press, 1982.

Sloan, Alfred P., Jr. *My Years with General Motors.* Garden City, NY: Doubleday, 1964.

Sloan, Robert E., and Carl A. Skowronski. *The Rainbow Route.* Silverton, CO: Sundance, 1975.

Small, Kenneth, Clifford Winston, and Carol A. Evans. *Road Work: A New Highway Pricing and Investment Policy.* Washington, DC: Brookings Institution, 1989.

Smelser, Marshall. *The Democratic Republic, 1801–1815.* New York: Harper and Row, 1968.

Smith, Henry Ladd. *Airways Abroad: The Story of American World Air Routes.* Madison: University of Wisconsin Press, 1950.

———. *Airways: The History of Commercial Aviation in the United States.* New York: Knopf, 1942.

Smith, Richard K. "The Airship in America, 1904–1976." In Eugene M. Emme (ed.), *Two Hundred Years of Flight in America.* San Diego: Univelt, 1977, 69–108.

Smith, Robert A. *A Social History of the Bicycle: Its Early Life and Times in America.* New York: American Heritage Press, 1972.

Smith, Robert W. *The Space Telescope. A Study of NASA, Science, Technology, and Politics.* New York: Cambridge University Press, 1989.

Smith, Ronald D., and William L. Richter. *Fascinating People and Strange Events from American History.* Santa Barbara, CA: ABC-CLIO, 1993.

Snoddy, Don. "Union Pacific Railroad." In Robert L. Frey (ed.), *EABHB: Railroads in the Nineteenth Century.* New York: Facts on File, 1988, 394–397.

Sobel, Robert. *Car Wars: The Untold Story.* New York: E. P. Dutton, 1984.

———. *The Fallen Colossus: The Great Crash of the Penn Central and the Crisis of the Corporate Giants.* New York: Weybright and Talley, 1977.

Somers, Paul M. "Illinois Central Green Diamond." *Model Railroader* (May 1990) 57: 84–89.

Sosin, Jack M. *The Revolutionary Frontier, 1763–1783.* New York: Holt, Reinhart, and Winston, 1967.

Speidel, William C. *Sons of the Profits; or, There's No Business Like Grow Business: The Seattle Story, 1851–1901.* Seattle: Nettle Creek Publishing Company, 1967.

Sperandeo, Andy. "Challenger 3985 and Her Sisters." *Model Railroader* (January 1995) 62: 105–113.

———. "The 1947 Empire Builder." *Model Railroader* (December 1991) 58: 108–123.

———. "Presenting the ACE 3000: A Steam Locomotive for Today's Railroads." *Model Railroader* (June 1982) 49: 77–79.

———. "Santa Fe Piggyback Conversions." *Model Railroader* (December 1984) 51: 104–109.

———. "The Super Chief, 1951–1953." *Model Railroader* (August 1993) 60: 74–89.

Sperry, Sidney B. *The Book of Mormon Testifies.* Salt Lake City, UT: Bookcraft, 1952.

Spratt, Hereward Philip. *Transatlantic Paddle Steamers.* Glasgow, Scotland: Brown, Son and Ferguson, 1951.

Stacey, May H. *Uncle Sam's Camels: The Journal of May H. Stacey, Supplemented by the Report of Edward Fitzgerald Beale.* Glorieta, NM: Rio Grande Press, 1970.

Stafford, Jeffrey J. *Wilsonian Maritime Diplomacy, 1913–1921.* New Brunswick, NJ: Rutgers University Press, 1978.

Stagner, Lloyd E. *Santa Fe, 1940–1971.* 4 vols. Edison, NJ: Morning Sun Books, 1992.

Standard, William L. *Merchant Seamen: A Short History of Their Struggles.* New York: International, 1947.

Stapleton, Darwin H. *The Transfer of Early Industrial Technologies to America.* Philadelphia: American Philosophical Society, 1987.

Starr, Edward A. *From Trail Dust to Star Dust.* Dallas: Transportation Press, 1945.

Starr, John W. *Lincoln and the Railroads.* New York: Dodd, Mead and Company, 1927.

Staufer, Alvin F. *Steam Power of the New York Central System.* Medina, OH: Alvin F. Staufer, 1961.

Steel, Ronald. *Pax Americana.* New York: Viking, 1967.

Stegner, Wallace. *The Gathering of Zion: The Story of the Mormon Trail.* New York: McGraw-Hill, 1964.

Steinman, David B., and Sara Ruth Watson. *Bridges and Their Builders.* New York: Putnam, 1941.

Stephens, Bill. "Conrail Caters to Customers." *Trains* (August 1994) 54: 62–69.

Stephens, F. F. "Missouri and the Santa Fe Trade." *Missouri Historical Review* (1916) 10: 223–262; and (1917) 11: 289–312.

Stern, Jane. *Trucker: A Portrait of the Last American Cowboy.* New York: McGraw-Hill, 1975.

Sternberg, Ernest R. *A History of Motor Truck Development.* Warrendale, PA: Society of Automotive Engineers, 1981.

Stevens, Frank W. *The Beginnings of the New York Central Railroad: A History.* New York: G. P. Putnam's Sons, 1926.

Stevens, G. R. *History of the Canadian National Railways*. New York: Macmillan, 1973.

Stevens, John F. *An Engineer's Reflections*. New York: McGraw-Hill, 1936.

Stewart, William H., Jr. *The Tennessee-Tombigbee Waterway: A Case Study in the Politics of Water Transportation*. Tuscaloosa: University of Alabama Press, 1971.

Stilgoe, John R. *Metropolitan Corridor: Railroads and the American Scene*. New Haven, CT: Yale University Press, 1983.

Stine, G. Harry. *The Third Industrial Revolution*. New York: G. P. Putnam's Sons, 1975.

Stover, John F. *American Railroads*. Chicago: University of Chicago Press, 1961.

———. "Baltimore and Ohio Railroad." In Keith L. Bryant, Jr. (ed.), *EABHB: Railroads in the Age of Regulation*. New York: Facts on File, 1988, 23–25.

———. "Baltimore and Ohio Railroad." In Robert L. Frey (ed.), *EABHB: Railroads in the Nineteenth Century*. New York: Facts on File, 1988, 20–22.

———. "Chesapeake & Ohio Railroad." In Keith L. Bryant, Jr. (ed.), *EABHB: Railroads in the Age of Regulation*. New York: Facts on File, 1988, 65–67.

———. "Chesapeake & Ohio Railroad." In Robert L. Frey (ed.), *EABHB: Railroads in the Nineteenth Century*. New York: Facts on File, 1988, 41–43.

———. *History of the Baltimore & Ohio Railroad*. West Lafayette, IN: Purdue University Press, 1987.

———. *History of the Illinois Central Railroad*. New York: Macmillan, 1975.

———. *Iron Road to the West: American Railroads of the 1850s*. New York: Columbia University Press, 1978.

———. *The Life and Decline of the American Railroad*. New York: Oxford University Press, 1970.

———. "The Louisville & Nashville Railroad." In Robert L. Frey (ed.), *EABHB: Railroads in the Nineteenth Century*. New York: Facts on File, 1988, 236–241.

———. *The Railroads of the South, 1865–1900: A Study in Finance and Control*. Chapel Hill: University of North Carolina Press, 1955.

———. "Southern Railroad." In Robert L. Frey (ed.), *EABHB: Railroads in the Nineteenth Century*. New York: Facts on File, 1988, 372–374.

Stover, Paul (ed.). *Oil and Gas Dictionary*. New York: Nichols Publishing, 1988.

Stragner, Lloyd. *Steam Locomotives of the Frisco Lines*. Boulder, CO: Pruett, 1976.

Strapac, Joseph A. *Western Pacific's Diesel Years*. Muncie, IN: Overland Models, 1980.

Striplin, E. F. Pat. *The Norfolk & Western: A History*. Roanoke, VA: Norfolk & Western Railroad, 1981.

Stuart, Reginald. *Bailout: The Story behind America's Billion Dollar Gamble on the "New" Chrysler Corporation*. South Bend, IN: And Books, 1980.

Sugar, James A. "Trucks Race the Clock from Coast to Coast." *National Geographic* (February 1974) 145: 226–243.

Summers, Mark W. *Railroads, Reconstruction, and the Gospel of Prosperity: Aid under the Radical Republicans*. Princeton, NJ: Princeton University Press, 1984.

Suprey, Leslie V. *Steam Trains of the Soo*. 2nd rev. ed. Mora, MN: B & W Printers and Publishers, 1962.

Sutcliffe, Alice. *Robert Fulton and the Clermont*. New York: Century Company, 1909.

Swanberg, William A. *Jim Fisk: The Career of an Improbable Rascal*. New York: Charles Scribner's Sons, 1959.

Sward, Keith. *The Legend of Henry Ford*. New York: Reinhart and Company, 1948.

Swenson, Lloyd S., et al. *This New Ocean: A History of Project Mercury*. Washington, DC: Government Printing Office, 1966.

Swindler, William F. *Court and Constitution in the 20th Century*. 3 vols. New York: Bobbs-Merrill, 1969.

Swisher, Carl B. *The Taney Period, 1835–1864*. New York: Macmillan, 1974.

Bibliography

Sydnor, Charles. *The Development of Southern Sectionalism, 1819–1848.* Baton Rouge: Louisiana State University Press, 1948.

Taaffe, Edward J., Richard Morill, and Peter R. Gould. "Transport Expansion in Underdeveloped Countries: A Comparative Analysis." *Geographical Review* (1963) 53: 503–529.

Taff, Charles. *Commercial Motor Transportation.* Cambridge, MD: Cornell Maritime Press, 1975.

Tallamy, B. D., and T. M. Sedwick. *The St. Lawrence Seaway Project.* Buffalo, NY: Niagara Frontier Planning Board, 1940.

Tarbell, Ida M. *History of the Standard Oil Company.* 2 vols. New York: McClure, Phillips and Company, 1904.

Taylor, Frank J. *High Horizons: Daredevil Flying Postmen to Modern Magic Carpet—The United Air Lines Story.* New York: McGraw-Hill, 1951.

Taylor, George, and Irene Neu. *The American Railroad Network, 1866–1890.* Cambridge: Harvard University Press, 1956.

Taylor, George Rogers. *The Transportation Revolution, 1815–1860.* New York: Rinehart and Company, 1951.

Taylor, J. W. R. *Combat Aircraft of the World from 1909 to the Present.* New York: G. P. Putnam's Sons, 1969.

Taylor, Morris F. *First Mail: Stagecoach Lines on the Santa Fe Trail.* Albuquerque: University of New Mexico Press, 1971.

Taylor, Stuart Ross. *Lunar Science: A Post Apollo View; Scientific Results and Insights from the Lunar Samples.* New York: Pergamon Press, 1975.

Thode, Jackson C. "Denver & Rio Grande." In Robert L. Frey (ed.), *EABHB: Railroads in the Nineteenth Century.* New York: Facts on File, 1988, 87–90.

Thomas, James H. *Long Haul: Truckers, Truck Stops, and Trucking.* Memphis, TN: Memphis State University Press, 1979.

Thomas, Robert Paul. *An Analysis of the Pattern of Growth of the Automobile Industry, 1895–1929.* New York: Arno Press, 1977.

Thompson, Gregory Lee. *The Passenger Train in the Motor Age: California's Rail and Bus Industries, 1910–1941.* Columbus: Ohio State University Press, 1993.

Thompson, Mark L. *Queen of the Lakes.* Detroit: Wayne State University Press, 1994.

Thompson, Robert Luthur. *Wiring a Continent: The History of the Telegraph Industry in the United States, 1832–1866.* New Bunswick, NJ: Princeton University Press, 1947.

Tilford, John E. *L & N: Its First 100 Years.* New York: Newcomen Society in North America, 1951.

Tindall, George B. *The Emergence of the New South, 1913–1945.* Baton Rouge: Louisiana State University Press, 1967.

Tinnin, David B. *Just About Everybody vs. Howard Hughes.* New York: Doubleday, 1973.

Torres, George. *Space Shuttle: A Quantum Leap.* Novato, CA: Presidio, 1986.

Tragatsch, Erwin (ed.). *The Illustrated History of Motorcycles.* London: Quarto Publishing, 1979.

Transportation Research Board. *Intermodal Marine Container Transportation: Impediments and Opportunities.* Washington, DC: National Research Council, 1992.

———. *Truck Weight Limits: Issues and Options.* Washington, DC: National Research Council, 1990.

———. *Twin Trailer Trucks: Effects on Highways and Highway Safety.* Washington, DC: National Research Council, 1986.

Treiman, Larry. "Containers Instead of a New [Panama] Canal: The Ultimate Land-Bridge." *Trains* (May 1975) 35: 36–39.

Trimble, William F. "Allegheny Airlines." In William M. Leary (ed.), *EABHB: The Airline Industry.* New York: Facts on File, 1992, 34–35.

———. *High Frontier: A History of Aeronautics in Pennsylvania.* Pittsburgh: University of Pittsburgh Press, 1982.

———. "USAir." In William M. Leary (ed.), *EABHB: The Airline Industry*. New York: Facts on File, 1992, 483–484.

Trottman, Nelson. *History of the Union Pacific*. New York: Ronald, 1973.

Tuplin, William A. *The Steam Locomotive*. New York: Charles Scribner's Sons, 1975.

Turnbull, Archibald, and Clifford L. Lord. *A History of United States Naval Aviation*. New Haven, CT: Yale University Press, 1949.

Turner, Frederick Jackson. "The Significance of the Frontier in American History." In his *The Frontier in American History*. New York: Henry Holt, 1920.

Turner, George E. *Victory Rode the Rails*. Indianapolis: Bobbs-Merrill, 1953.

Turner, Maria. *James Rumsey, Pioneer in Steam Navigation*. Scottsdale, PA: Mennonite Publishing House, 1930.

Tussey, Jean Y. (ed.). *Eugene V. Debs Speaks*. New York: Pathfinder Press, 1970.

Tuttle, William M., Jr. "The Birth of an Industry: The Synthetic Rubber 'Mess' in World War II." *Technology and Culture* (1981) 22: 35–67.

Unger, Urwin. *The Greenback Era: A Social and Political History of American Finance, 1865–1879*. Princeton, NJ: Princeton University Press, 1964.

U.S. Department of Transportation, Federal Highway Adminstration. *America's Highways*. Washington, DC: Government Printing Office, 1976.

Utley, Robert M. *Cavalier in Buckskin: George Armstrong Custer and the Western Military Frontier*. Norman: University of Oklahoma Press, 1988.

Van Der Zee, Jacob. "The Mormon Trails in Iowa." *Iowa Journal of History and Politics* (1914) 12: 3–16.

Van Deusen, Glyndon. *The Jacksonian Era, 1828–1848*. New York: Harper and Row, 1959.

———. *The Life of Henry Clay*. Boston: Little, Brown and Company, 1937.

Van Dyke, Vernon. *Pride and Power: The Rationale of the Space Program*. Urbana: University of Illinois Press, 1964.

Van Every, Dale. *Ark of Empire: The American Frontier, 1784–1803*. New York: William Morrow, 1963.

Van Fleet, James A. *Rail Transport and the Winning of Wars*. Washington, DC: Association of American Railroads, 1956.

Van Horne, George R. "That Promontory Myth." *Trains* (May 1994) 54: 40–43.

Vaughn, Walter. *The Life and Work of Sir William Van Horne*. New York: Century, 1920.

Verges, Marianne. *On Silver Wings*. New York: Ballantine, 1991.

Vestal, Stanley. *Old Santa Fe Trail*. New York: Houghton Mifflin, 1939.

Vigness, David M. *Spanish Texas, 1519–1810*. Boston: American Press, 1983.

Vladimirov, Leonid. *The Russian Space Bluff*. Translated by David Floyd. New York: Dial, 1973.

Voelker, Frederick E. "The Mountain Men and Their Part in the Opening of the West." *Missouri Historical Society Bulletin* (1947) 3: 151–162.

Vosburgh, Frederick G. "Drums to Dynamos on the Mohawk." *National Geographic* (July 1947) 92: 67–110.

Wagner, F. Hol (ed.). *Union Pacific Motive Power Review*. Denver: Motive Power Review, 1978.

Wagner, Richard. *Golden Wheels*. Cleveland: Western Reserve Historical Society, 1975.

Wagner, Warren H. *A Legislative History of the Motor Carrier Act of 1935*. Denton, MD: Rue, 1935.

Walker, Albert Henry. *History of the Sherman Law of the United States*. Westport, CT: Greenwood, 1910.

Walker, Henry Pickering. *The Wagonmasters: High Plains Freighting from the Earliest Days of the Santa Fe Trail to 1880*. Norman: University of Oklahoma Press, 1966.

Walker, James B. *Fifty Years of Rapid Transit*. New York: Law Printing Company, 1918.

Walsh, James A. *The Armstrong Rubber Company: Seventy Years of Progress in the Tire Industry*. New York: Newcomen Society in North America, 1982.

Ward, James A. "Atlantic Coast Line." In Keith L. Bryant, Jr. (ed.), *EABHB: Railroads in the Age of Regulation*. New York: Facts on File, 1988, 13–15.

———. "David Craig McCallum." In Robert L. Frey (ed.), *EABHB: Railroads in the Nineteenth Century*. New York: Facts on File, 1988, 246–248.

———. "Herman Haupt." In Robert L. Frey (ed.), *EABHB: Railroads in the Nineteenth Century*. New York: Facts on File, 1988, 165–168.

———. "J. Edgar Thomson and Thomas A. Scott: A Symbiotic Partnership?" *Pennsylvania Magazine of History and Biography* (1976) 50: 37–65.

———. *J. Edgar Thomson: Master of the Pennsylvania*. Westport, CT: Greenwood, 1980.

———. "Pennsylvania Railroad." In Keith L. Bryant, Jr. (ed.), *EABHB: Railroads in the Age of Regulation*. New York: Facts on File, 1988, 313–315.

———. *Railroads and the Character of America, 1829–1887*. Knoxville: University of Tennessee Press, 1986.

———. "Seaboard Air Line Railroad." In Keith L. Bryant, Jr. (ed.), *EABHB: Railroads in the Age of Regulation*. New York: Facts on File, 1988, 394–395.

———. "Seaboard Coast Line Railroad." In Keith L. Bryant Jr. (ed.), *EABHB: Railroads in the Age of Regulation*. New York: Facts on File, 1988, 398.

———. *That Man Haupt! A Biography of Herman Haupt*. Baton Rouge: Louisiana State University Press, 1973.

———. "Thomas A. Scott." In Robert L. Frey (ed.), *EABHB: Railroads in the Nineteenth Century*. New York: Facts on File, 1988, 358–362.

Ward, John William. "The Meaning of Lindbergh's Flight." *American Quarterly* (1958) 10: 3–16.

Warren, Charles. *The Supreme Court in United States History*. 2 vols. Boston: Little, Brown and Company, 1922.

Watson, Ken. *Paddle Steamers: An Illustrated History of Steamboats on the Mississippi and Its Tributaries*. New York: W. W. Norton, 1985.

Wattenburg, Ben. *Busy Waterways: The Story of America's Inland Water Transportation*. New York: John Day Company, 1964.

Wayner, Robert J. *New York Central Cars*. New York: Wayner Publications, 1972.

Weber, Art. "Transportation—Who Has a Right to What?" *Trains* (January (1994) 54: 80.

Weber, David J. *The Spanish Frontier in North America*. New Haven, CT: Yale University Press, 1992.

Weber, Thomas. *The Northern Railroads in the Civil War*. New York: King's Crown, 1952.

Weinberg, Albert K. *Manifest Destiny*. Baltimore: Johns Hopkins University Press, 1935.

Weinstein, Allen. *Prelude to Populism: Origins of the Silver Issue, 1867–1878*. New Haven, CT: Yale University Press, 1970.

Weinstein, Paul (ed.). *Featherbedding and Technological Change*. Boston: D. C. Heath, 1965.

Weinstock, Charles B. "Daniel Drew." In Robert L. Frey (ed.), *EABHB: Railroads in the Nineteenth Century*. New York: Facts on File, 1988, 106–111.

———. "James Fisk, Jr.." In Robert L. Frey (ed.), *EABHB: Railroads in the Nineteenth Century*. New York: Facts on File, 1988, 12–27.

Weintraub, Hyman. *Andrew Furuseth: Emancipator of the Seamen*. Berkeley: University of California Press, 1959.

Weisberger, Bernard. *The Dream Maker: William C. Durant, Founder of General Motors*. Boston: Little, Brown and Company, 1979.

Weiss, Leonard W., and Michael W. Klass. *Regulatory Reform: What Actually Happened*. Boston: Little, Brown and Company, 1986.

Wesolowski, Wayne. "Abraham Lincoln's Funeral Train." *Model Railroader* (February 1995) 62: 92–97.

Weyland, John W. *The Valley Turnpike: Winchester to Staunton.* Winchester, VA: Winchester-Frederick County Historical Society, 1967.

White, Bouck. *Book of Daniel Drew.* New York: Doubleday, Page, 1910.

White, G. Edward, and Gerald Gunther. *The Marshall Court, 1815–1825.* New York: Macmillan, 1988.

White, John H., Jr. *American Locomotives: An Engineering History, 1830–1880.* Baltimore: Johns Hopkins University Press, 1968.

———. *The American Railroad Passenger Car.* Baltimore: Johns Hopkins University Press, 1978.

———. "George Mortimer Pullman." In Keith L. Bryant, Jr. (ed.), *EABHB: Railroads in the Age of Regulation.* New York: Facts on File, 1988, 335–339.

———. "George Westinghouse." In Robert L. Frey (ed.), *EABHB: Railroads in the Nineteenth Century.* New York: Facts on File, 1988, 430–436.

———. "Theodore T. Woodruff." In Robert L. Frey (ed.), *EABHB: Railroads in the Nineteenth Century.* New York: Facts on File, 1988, 438–439.

———. "Webster Wagner." In Robert L. Frey (ed.), *EABHB: Railroads in the Nineteenth Century.* New York: Facts on File, 1988, 423–424.

White, Leonard D. *The Federalists: A Study in Administrative History, 1789–1801.* New York: Macmillan Company, 1948.

———. *The Jacksonians: A Study in Administrative History, 1829–1861.* New York: Macmillan Company, 1954.

———. *The Jeffersonians: A Study in Administrative History, 1801–1829.* New York: Macmillan Company, 1951.

———. *The Republican Era: A Study in Administrative History, 1869–1901.* New York: Macmillan Company, 1958.

White, Lonnie J. (ed.), "Hugh Kirkendall's Wagon Train on the Bozeman Trail, 1866: Letters of C. M. S. Miller." *Annals of Wyoming* (1975) 37: 45–58.

White, W. Thomas. "Eugene Victor Debs." In Robert L. Frey (ed.), *EABHB: Railroads in the Nineteenth Century.* New York: Facts on File, 1988, 79–83.

Whitehurst, Clinton H., Jr. *The U.S. Merchant Marine: In Search of an Enduring Maritime Policy.* Annapolis, MD: Naval Institute Press, 1983.

———. *The U.S. Shipbuilding Industry: Past, Present, and Future.* Annapolis, MD: Naval Institute Press, 1986.

Whiteside, Thomas. *The Investigation of Ralph Nader.* New York: William Morrow, 1972.

Whitford, Noble Earl. *History of the Canal System of the State of New York.* Albany, NY: J. B. Lyon, 1906.

Whitnah, Donald R. *Safer Skyways: Federal Control of Aviation, 1926–1966.* Ames: Iowa State University Press, 1966.

Wik, R. M. *Henry Ford and Grass-Roots America.* Ann Arbor: University of Michigan Press, 1972.

Wilkins, Van. "Commuter Rail Is Booming in Maryland." *Passenger Train Journal* (October 1994) 25: 24–31.

Will, George F. "Spending Restraints May Cripple Government." Reprinted in *The Arizona Daily Star* (10 February 1994): 15A.

Williams, George. *The Airline Industry and the Impact of Deregulation.* Brookfield, VT: Ashgate, 1993.

Williamson, Harold F., and Arnold R. Daum. *The American Petroleum Industry.* 2 vols. Evanston, IL: Northwestern University Press, 1959.

Willoughby, William R. *St. Lawrence Waterway: A Study in Politics and Diplomacy.* Madison: University of Wisconsin Press, 1961.

Wilner, Frank N. "Interstate Commerce Commission." In Robert L. Frey (ed.), *EABHB: Railroads in the Nineteenth Century.* New York: Facts on File, 1988, 200–201.

———. "Predecessors to the Association of American Railroads." In Robert L. Frey (ed.), *EABHB: Railroads in the Nineteenth Century*. New York: Facts on File, 1988, 333–334.

Wilson, James A. "A Critical Look at Our Marine Transportation." *Seaway Review* (September 1983) 14: 11–13.

Wilson, Neill C., and Frank J. Taylor. *Southern Pacific: The Roaring Story of a Fighting Railroad*. New York: McGraw-Hill, 1952.

Wilson, O. Meredith. *The Denver & Rio Grande Project, 1870–1901: The History of the First Thirty Years of the Denver & Rio Grande Railroad*. Salt Lake City, UT: House Brothers, 1982.

Wilson, W. B. *History of the Pennsylvania Railroad Company*. Philadelphia: H. T. Coates, 1896.

Wilson, William H. *Railroad in the Clouds: The Alaska Railroad in the Age of Steam, 1914–1945*. Boulder, CO: Pruett, 1977.

Wiltse, Charles M. *John C. Calhoun*. 3 vols. Indianapolis: Bobbs-Merrill, 1944–1951.

Wiltsee, Ernest A. *The Pioneer Miner and Pack Mule Business*. San Francisco: California Historical Society, 1931.

Winston, Clifford, et al. *The Economic Effects of Surface Freight Deregulation*. Washington, DC: Brookings Institution, 1990.

Winther, Oscar Osburn. *Express and Stagecoach Days in Old California*. Palo Alto, CA: Stanford University Press, 1936.

———. *The Old Oregon Country*. Palo Alto, CA: Stanford University Press, 1950.

———. *The Transportation Frontier: Trans-Mississippi West, 1865–1890*. New York: Holt, Reinhart and Winston, 1964.

———. *Via Western Express and Stagecoach*. Palo Alto, CA: Stanford University Press, 1945.

Wolbert, George S., Jr. *American Pipe Lines, Their Industrial Structure, Economic Status, and Legal Implications*. Norman: University of Oklahoma Press, 1952.

———. *U.S. Oil Pipe Lines*. Washington, DC: American Petroleum Institute, 1979.

Wolfe, Tom. *The Right Stuff*. New York: Farrar, Straus and Giroux, 1979.

Wood, Charles R. *The Northern Pacific: The Main Street of the Northwest*. Seattle: Superior Publishing Company, 1967.

Wood, Charles R. and Dorothy M. Wood. *Milwaukee Road—West*. Seattle: Superior Publishing, 1972.

Wood, Gordon S. *The Creation of the American Republic, 1776–1787*. Chapel Hill: University of North Carolina Press, 1969.

Woodbury, George. *The Story of a Stanley Steamer*. New York: W. W. Norton Company, 1950.

Woodward, Bob. *The Agenda: Inside the Clinton White House*. New York: Simon & Schuster, 1994.

Woodward, C. Vann. *Reunion and Reaction: The Compromise of 1877 and the End of Reconstruction*. New York: Doubleday, 1951.

———. *The Strange Career of Jim Crow*. New York: Oxford University Press, 1966.

Worley, E. Dale. *Iron Horses of the Santa Fe Trail*. Dallas: Southwest Railroad Historical Society, 1965.

Wren, James A., and Genevieve J. Wren. *Motor Trucks of America*. Ann Arbor: University of Michigan Press, 1979.

Wresting, Frederick. *Erie Power: Steam and Diesel Locomotives of the Erie Railroad from 1840 to 1970*. Medina, OH: Alvin F. Staufer, 1970.

Wright, Muriel H. "Early Navagation and Commerce along the Arkansas and Red Rivers in Oklahoma." *Chronicles of Oklahoma* (1930) 8: 65–88.

Wyden, Peter. *The Unknown Iacocca*. New York: William Morrow, 1987.

Wyman, Walker D. "Bull-Whacking: A Prosaic Profession Peculiar to the Great Plains." *New Mexico Historical Review* (1932) 7: 297–310.

———. "Freighting: A Big Business on the Santa Fe Trail." *Kansas Historical Quarterly* (1931) 1: 17–27.

———. "The Military Phase of Santa Fe Freighting, 1846–1865." *Kansas Historical Quarterly* (1932) 2: 415–428.

Yates, Brock. *The Decline and Fall of the American Automobile Industry*. New York: Empire Books, 1983.

Yeager, Chuck. *Yeager: An Autobiography*. New York: Bantam, 1985.

York, Herbert F. *Race to Oblivion*. New York: Simon and Schuster, 1970.

Young, Jeremiah S. *Political and Economic Study of the Cumberland Road*. Chicago: University of Chicago Press, 1932.

Young, Otis E. *First Military Escort on the Santa Fe Trail, 1829; from the Journal and Reports of Major Bennet Riley and Lieutenant Philip St. George Cooke*. Glendale, CA: Arthur H. Clark Company, 1952.

————. *The West of Philip St. George Cooke, 1809–1895*. Glendale, CA: Arthur H. Clark, 1955.

Young, Warren. *The Helicopters*. Alexandria, VA: Time-Life Books, 1982.

Ziel, Ron. *Steel Rails to Victory*. New York: Hawthorn, 1970.

Ziel, Ron, and George W. Foster. *Steel Rails to the Sunrise*. New York: Hawthorn, 1965.

Zimmermann, Karl R. *The Milwaukee Road under Wire*. New York: Quadrant Press, 1973.

————. *The Remarkable GG-1*. New York: Quadrant Press, 1977.

————. *Santa Fe Streamliners: The Chiefs and Their Tribesmen*. New York: Quadrant Press, 1987.

Index

Acme Fast Freight Line, 250
Adams, Alvin, 3, 37, 229
Adams, John Quincy, 40, 101, 119, 120, 130, 228, 378
Adams and Company of California, 3
Adams Express Company, 3–4, 37, 39, 177, 229
Adams-Onís Treaty, 278
Advanced Design Buses (ADB), 98
Adventure of Captain Bonneville, 102
Aerial photography, 10
Aeronautical Corporation of America, 11
Aeronautics, 4–21
Aeronautics Branch, Department of Commerce, 27, 80
Aerostatics, 21
Agricultural and Mechanical College, 27
Agricultural Appropriation Acts, 26–27
Air Commerce Act of 1926, 27
Air Force One, 17
Air Law Institute, Northwestern University, 226
Air Law Review, 226
Air Line Pilots Association (ALPA), 12, 27–28, 167
Air Mail Act of 1930, 512
Air Traffic Controllers' Career Program Act, 400
Air Traffic Controllers Organization, 341
Air West, 243
Airline deregulation, 19, 291
Airline Deregulation Act (ADA) of 1978, 28–30, 260
Airline Pilots Association, 341
Airmail, 12, 13, 80
Airport and Airway Development and Revenue Act, 400

Airships, 24–26
Alaska Central Railroad, 34
Alaska Highway (Alcan), 30–33, 297
Alaska Railroad (ARR), 33–34, 95
Alaska Steamship Company, 125
Aldrin, Edwin E. "Buzz," Jr., 54, 55, 56, 57
All American Air, 534
Allen, E. J., 398
Allen, James, 23
Alyeska Pipeline Service Company, 394
Amalgamated Transit Union, 225
American Airlines (AA), 4, 15, 34–36, 37, 139, 140
American Association of Railroads, 399
American Association of State Highway and Transportation Officials, 36
American Association of State Highway Officials (AASHO), 36–37, 180, 181, 182, 297, 357, 520
American Automobile Association (AAA), 36, 37, 280, 312, 338
American Bureau of Shipping, 311
American Car Foundry (ACF), 253
American Coal Enterprises, 288
American Eagle System, 36, 139
American Ethnological Society, 207
American Export Airlines, 35
American Express Company, 37–38, 39, 99, 177, 532
American Federation of Labor (AFL), 28, 255, 410, 427–428
American Freedom Train, 38
American Fur Company, 166, 363
American Locomotive Company (Alco), 128, 272, 283
American Motors Corporation, 63, 64, 65, 67, 304

American President Lines, 137
American Railway Association, 45
American Railway Express Company, 4, 38, 39
American Railway Union (ARU), 147, 403, 408
American Road congresses, 357
American System political philosophy, 39–40
American Telephone and Telegraph, 47–48
American Truckers Associations (ATA), 326, 349
Ames, Oakes, 141, 530
Amtrak, 40–41, 95, 135, 293, 387, 406
Amtrak Improvement Act of 1978, 41
Anders, William A., 55
Anglo-Russian, Treaty of 1825, 278
Annapolis Convention, 227
Anthracite and bridge line railroads, 41–43
Anza, Juan Bautista de, 106, 209
Apollo, 46, 55, 56, 83
Applegate, Jesse, 43–44
Applegate, Lindsay, 43–44
Applegate Road, 43–44
Armijo, Antonio, 364
Armour Company, 225
Armstrong, Neil A., 54, 56
Arnold, Henry "Hap," 163
Asbury, Francis, 223
Ashley, William, 117, 118
Asphalt roads, 295
Aspinwall, William, 371
Associated Press, 217
Association of American Railroads (AAR), 45, 170, 421
Association of Colored Railway Trainmen and Locomotive Firemen, 410
Association of Licensed Automobile Manufacturers, 62, 197
Association of Railway Executives, 45
Astor, John Jacob, 117, 166
Astronautics, 45–59
Atchison, Topeka & Santa Fe Railway (AT&SF), 60, 76, 95
Atlantic and Pacific Railroad, 75
Atlantic Coast Line Railroad (ACL), 60, 177
Atlantic Highway, 60
Atlantic Richfield Company (ARCO), 394
Augustus B. Wolvin, 219
Auto Train, 61
Automatic Train Control (ATC), 344, 509
Automobiles
   in American society, 68–72
   from domestics to imports, 61–68
Averell, Mary, 229
Aviation Corporation (AVCO), 34

Backus, Charles, 532
Bailey, F. Lee, 400
Baja California, 105
Baldwin, Thomas S., 144
Baldwin Locomotive, 283, 284
Ball, Edward, 192
Balloons, 21–24
Baltimore & Ohio Railroad (B&O), 3, 73–74, 92, 112, 120, 121, 277, 283, 340, 412, 415, 567
Baltimore Clippers, 132
Bangor & Aroostook Railroad (BAR), 74
Barlow, Samuel K., 74–75
Barlow Road, 74–75
Barnes, Florence "Pancho," 162
Barnum, P. T., 23
Bartleson, John, 102
Bay Area Rapid Transit (BART), 512
Beale, Edward F., 75, 105
Beale's Wagon Road, 75–76
Bean, Alan L., 56
Beck Dave, 255–256
Beechcraft Bonanza, 12
Behncke, David L., 27
Bell, John, 374
Bell Aircraft, 7, 50
Belmont, August, 230, 315
Ben Holladay's Overland Stage Company, 116
Benton, Thomas Hart, 368, 373, 374
Benz, Karl, 62
Bermuda Agreement of 1946, 76
Bessemer & Lake Erie Railroad (B&LE), 76
Bicycle clubs, 77, 274–276
Bicycle riders, 212–213
Bicycles, 77–80
Bidwell, John, 102
Big Medicine Trail, 80, 86, 118
Biplanes, 6, 302
Birney, Charles, 511
Black, Hugo, 311
Black-McKellar Act of 1934, 80–81, 298
Blaine, James G., 141
Blanchard, Jean-Pierre, 21, 22, 24, 566
Blanchard, W. L., 128
Blomberg, Martin, 81
Blue Riband, 356
Bluford, Guion S., Jr., 57
Boeing, William Edward, 81–82
Boeing Aircraft, 6, 7, 8, 14, 16, 18, 82, 531
Bollman, Wendel, 93
Bonneville, Benjamin L. E., 102
Bonus Bill, 82
Book of Directions, 12
Boone, Daniel, 222, 566

Borland, Solon, 374
Borman, Frank Frederick, II, 54, 55, 83–84, 139, 168, 292
Boston & Maine Railroad (B&M), 84–85, 299
Boston and Thompson Railroad, 408
Boston Metropolitan Transit Authority, 84
Boston Post Road, 85–86, 565
Bozeman, John M., 86
Bozeman Trail, 86–89, 318, 329
Braddee, John F., 339
Braddock, Edward, 89, 143, 193, 194
Braddock's Road, 89, 143, 430
Bragg, Janet H. W., 163
Brand, Vance D., 57
Brandeis, Louis D., 168
Braniff, 19, 29
Breakmen, 134
Breech, Ernest R., 197
Breguet, Louis, 234–235
Brick roads, 295
Bridge lines, 43
Bridger, Jim, 90, 101, 323, 325
Bridger Trail, 86, 87, 89–90
Bridges, Harry, 90
Bridges, 90–94, 565
Briscoe, Benjamin, 94–95, 157
Briscoe, Frank, 94
British Air Transport Auxiliary (ATA), 163
British Airways, 20
British Columbia Railway (BC Rail), 75, 95, 110
British Great Eastern Railroad, 95
British Petroleum, 394
Broad Gauge Company, 86, 87
Brooklyn Bridge, 69, 93
Brotherhood of Locomotive Engineers (BLE), 408
Brotherhood of Locomotive Firemen, 147
Brotherhood of Locomotive Firemen and Enginemen, 409
Brotherhood of Railroad Trainmen (BRT), 409
Brotherhood of Sleeping Car Porters, 410, 426
Brown, George, 73
Brown, Walter, 298
Bryan, Francis, 118
Bryan, John R., 23
Bryan, William Jennings, 273, 398
Bucareli, António María, 106
Buchanan, James, 325, 399
Buck v. Kuykendall, 312
Budd, Edward G., 283
Budd, Ralph, 259

Budd Corporation, 253, 298
Buick, 62, 63, 64, 94, 129, 157, 158
Bullwhackers, 203
Bulwer, Henry Lytton, 131
Bun, Donald C., 291
Bunau-Varilla, Phillipe, 232, 384
Buntline, Ned, 126
Burdet, Charles L., 276
Bureau of Air Commerce, 80
Bureau of Public Roads (BPR), 95, 148, 151, 152, 179, 184, 185, 213, 297
Bureau of Railway Economics, 45
Burlington Northern Incorporated (BN), 95–96, 122, 123, 142, 315, 347, 348
Burnett, Peter H., 44
Burns, Rex, 325
Burr, Aaron, 144, 228
Burr, Theodore, 91
Buses, 96–99
Bush, George W., and Sons v. Maloy, 99
Butler, Benjamin, 23
Butterfield, John, 99, 100, 107, 211
Butterfield Trail, 99–100
Butterfield, Wasson and Company, 37

C&O Canal, 113
Cabell, Joseph C., 265
Cabeza de Vaca, Alvar Nuñez, 107
Cable cars, 510
Cadillac, 62, 63, 64, 65, 66, 67, 94, 129, 158
Caldwell, John, 107
Calhoun, John Caldwell, 82, 101, 166, 373, 378, 538
California Highway Commission, 107
California Institute of Technology, 226
California Trail, 101–104, 117, 232
Camels in the west, 104–105
Camino Real (California), 105–107
Camino Real (Texas), 107–109
Campbell, Henry, 567
Canadian Broadcasting Corporation, 110
Canadian National Railroad (CN), 95, 110, 217, 315, 387, 542
Canadian Northern, 110
Canadian Pacific Railway (CP Rail), 110–111, 138, 542
Canal locks, 111
Canal zones, 232
Canals, 111–116
Cannonball, 267
Cañon City & San Juan Railroad, 150
Capper-Cramton Act (1930), 116
Carey, Matthew, 39, 388–389
Cargo Preference Act of 1954, 116, 309, 314
Carnegie, Andrew, 214

Carnes, Peter, 21
Carney, Robert J., 291
Carpenter, M. Scott, 53
Carrington, Henry B., 87
Carroll, Charles, 73
Carson, Kit, 102, 210, 368
Carson Wagons, 202
Carter, Jimmy, 19, 163, 386
Cartwright, Wilburn, 234
Cass, Lewis, 374
Cattle trails, 126, 127
Cavelier, René Robert, Sieur de la Salle, 108, 218
Cayley, George, 4
Center for Auto Safety, 333
Central Gulf Railroad, 249
Central of New Jersey (CNJ), 42
Central Overland California & Pike's Peak Express Company, 116–117, 396
Central Overland Route, 80, 103, 117–119, 153, 189, 318, 396
Central Pacific Railroad (CP), 142, 153, 177, 178, 216, 230, 241–242, 244, 267, 372, 417
Centralized Traffic Control (CTC), 509
Century Airline, 28
Century series, 9
Cernan, Eugene A., 54
Cessna airplanes, 11
Cevor, Charles, 23
Chaffee, Roger, 55
Chain Bridge, 92
Challenge, 133
Challenger, 49, 58
Champion, 63
Chanute, Octave, 4
Charles, Jacques Alexandre Caesar, 21
Charles River Bridge Company, 119, 565
Charles River Bridge Company v. Warren Bridge Company, 119
Chase Manhattan Bank, 38
Chatelain, Maurice, 56, 57
Chesapeake and Delaware Canal, 114
Chesapeake & Ohio Canal (C&O), 112, 119–120
Chesapeake & Ohio Railway (C&O), 113, 120–121, 266, 320
Chessie System, 121, 142, 177
Cheves, Langdon, 23
Chevette, 66
Chevrolet, Louis, 63, 158
Chevrolet, 64, 129, 158
Chicago & Alton line, 226
Chicago & Eastern Illinois, 251
Chicago & Great Western Railway, 122

Chicago & North Western Railway (C&NW), 121–123, 260, 270
Chicago, Burlington & Quincy Railroad (CB&Q), 37, 95, 123–124, 221, 240, 250, 283, 321, 408, 409
Chicago, Burlington & Quincy Railroad v. Iowa, 218
Chicago Great Western Railroad (CGW), 250
Chicago, Milwaukee & St. Paul Railroad Company v. Ackley, 218
Chicago Motor Bus Company, 96
Chicago, Rock Island & Pacific Railroad, 269, 403
Chilkoot Trail, 124–126
Chisholm, Jesse, 126
Chisholm Trail, 126–127
Chorpenning, George, 127–128
Chouteau, Pierre, Jr., 166
Chrysler, Walter P., 64, 128–129, 154
Chrysler Corporation, 63, 64, 65, 66, 67, 247
Chrysler-American Motors, 94
Churchill, Winston, 308
Cierva, Juan de la, 235
Citizen's band radio (CB), 525
Civil Aeronautics Act of 1938, 27, 28, 81, 129
Civil Aeronautics Authority (CAA), 129, 183, 184
Civil Aeronautics Board (CAB), 28, 29, 129, 184, 340
Civil Air Patrol (CAP), 11, 163
Civilian Conservation Corps (CCC), 32
Clark, William, 165, 278–279
Clay, Henry, 39, 129–130, 305, 383
Clayton, John, 131
Clayton, William, 324
Clayton Act of 1914, 130–131, 258, 298, 348, 420, 421
Clayton-Bulwer Treaty of 1850, 131, 233, 383
Clemens, Samuel. *See* Twain, Mark.
Clermont, 166, 191
Cleveland, Grover, 320, 398
Clinchfield Railroad, 293
Clinton, De Witt, 131–132, 171, 537–538
Clinton, George, 171
Clipper ships, 132–134
Cobb, Howell, 377
Coburn, Frank G., 34
Cochran, Jacqueline, 163
Cody, William F., 299
Coffin, Levi, 420
Coffin, Lorenzo S., 134
Colden, Cadwallader, 166
Colles, Christopher, 566

Collins, Edward K., 352–353
Collins, Michael, 54, 56
Colter, John, 117
Columbia, 58
Columbia Broadcasting Company, 74
Commercial aviation, 12–21
Commercial driver's license (CDL), 134
Commercial Motor Vehicle Safety Act of 1986, 134–135
Commercial Space Launch Act of 1985, 50
Communications Satellite Corporation (Comsat), 48
Commuter trains, 135
Compact cars, 64, 304
Compromise of 1850, 130, 324
Compromise Tariff, 130
Computer reservation systems, 139
Concrete roads, 295
Conestoga wagons, 198, 199, 200, 201, 222, 565
Congress of Industrial Organizations (CIO), 90, 410
Connecticut Aircraft Company, 155
Connelly Hot Oil Act of 1935, 360
Connor, Patrick E., 87, 318
Conrad, Charles "Pete," Jr., 54, 56
Conrail, 42, 43, 84, 135–137, 259, 388, 423, 427
Consolidated Freight Line (CFL), 521
Consolidated Rail Corporation. *See* Conrail
Consolidation Act of 1869, 541
Constellation, 242–243. *See also* Hughes, Howard Robard, Jr.
Constitutional Convention, 227
Container-on-flatcar (COFC), 249, 253, 521
Containers, 137, 249
Continental Airlines, 20, 29, 84, 138, 139, 291–292
Continental Trailways, 224
Cooke, Philip St. George, 210
Coolidge, Calvin, 318, 398
Cooper, L. Gordon, 53, 54, 57
Cooper, Peter, 73, 286
Cord, E. L., 28
Corduroyed roads, 138, 394–395
Corning, Erastus, 343
Cornu, Paul, 234
Coronado, Francisco Vásquez de, 209
Corporate automobile fuel efficiency (CAFE), 66
Corvair, 65, 333
Corvette, 64
COSTAR, 48
Counselman v. Hitchcock, 257
Covered bridges, 566

CP Air Lines, 111
Crandall, Robert L., 36, 138–140
Crane, L. Stanley, 136
Crane Brothers Paper Company, 403
Crates for moving freight, 229
Crawford, William C., 538
Crédit Mobilier of America, 140–141, 418, 530
Creighton, Edward, 505–506
Crevecour, St. John de, 191
Crocker, Charles, 141–142, 268, 418
Crop-dusting, 10
Crossman, George H., 104
Crossties, 424–425
Crozet, Claudius, 265
CSX Corporation, 61, 121, 142, 177
Cullom Law, 257
Cumberland Road, 142, 566, 567
Cumbres & Toltec, 151
Cummins, Albert, 513
Cummins, Clessie L., 144, 520
Cummins Diesel, 144
Cunard, Samuel, 352–353
Cunningham, R. Walter, 55
Curtiss, Glenn Hammond, 5, 144–145, 274
Curtiss Aeroplane and Motor Company, 10, 145
Curtiss-Wright Company, 6, 7, 34, 145, 167
Custer, George, 88

Daimler, Gottlieb, 62
Dartmouth College, 147
Dartmouth College v. Woodward, 119, 147
Daughters of the American Revolution, 336
Daughters of the War of 1812, 336
David Crockett, 134
Davis, Jefferson, 75, 104, 118, 211, 377, 399
Davis, Phineas, 73
Davis-Bacon Act, 171, 180
Dayton, Jonathan, 228
De Bow's Commercial Review, 373
De Smet, Pierre Jean, 368
de Soto, Hernando. *See* Hernando de Soto.
Death Valley Scotty, 147
Debs, Eugene Victor, 147–148, 398, 403, 408, 409
Defense Highway Act, 148–149
Delaware & Hudson (D&H) Canal Company, 42, 135, 174, 215, 286, 412, 567
Delaware and Raritan Canal, 114
Delaware, Lackawanna & Western, 42
Delta Airlines, 20, 149
Demonstration Projects Program, 351
Denison, George, 315

Densmore, Amos, 359
Denver & Rio Grande Western Railroad
    (D&RGW), 150–151, 214, 305–306
Depreciating accounting, 136
Detroit, Toledo & Ironton Railroad, 156
Dewey, Thomas, 399
Díaz, Melchoir, 209
Diesel, Rudolph, 283
Diesel electric locomotives, 283–284
Diesel engine, 81, 144
Dietrich, Noah, 242
Dinsmore, William B., 3
Dirigibles, 24–26
Discovery, 58
Dismal Swamp Canal, 112, 152
Dismal Swamp Company, 113
Dive bombers, 7
Dixie Highway, 152
Dixie Highway Association, 189
Dobbs, Farrell, 255–256
Dodge, Elgin, 197
Dodge, Grenville Mellen, 152–154, 529
Dodge, Horace, 64
Dodge, John F., 64, 154, 197
Dodge, Joseph, 155
Dodge, Martin, 27, 154, 356, 434
Dodge Line, 155
Dole, Robert, 327
Dominion Parliament, 217
Donaldson, Washington H., 23
Donner, George, 103
Donner, Jacob, 103
Douglas, Donald W., 155
Douglas, Stephen A., 374–375, 398
Douglas Aircraft, 8, 14, 16, 18, 34, 139, 149,
    155, 313
Doyle, Arthur Conan, 325
Draisine, 77
Drake, Edwin L., 358
Drew, Daniel, 155–156, 189, 190, 215, 216,
    539–540
Dreyfuss, Henry, 289, 344
Drive-in windows, 71
Drivers' licenses, 68
Driving on the right, 69
DT & I Conditions, 156–157, 422
Dudley, Plimmon Henry, 157
Dulle, John Foster, 17
Dunlop, John Boyd, 77
DuPont, Pierre, 63, 158
Durango & Silverton, 151
Durant, Charles F., 22
Durant, Thomas Clark, 140, 529–530
Durant, William C., 63, 94, 157–159
Duryea, Charles, 62

Duryea, Frank, 78
Dwight, Henry, 532
Dynamometer car, 157

E. H. Harriman & Company, 229
Eads, James B., 93, 161
Earhart, Amelia, 11, 161–163
Earl of Stanhope, 205
Early river travel, 164–165
Early steamboats, 165–167
Eastern Air Transport (EAT), 167
Eastern Airlines (EAL), 20, 83, 139, 149,
    167, 184
Eastman, Joseph B., 168, 170, 349
Eddy, Henry, 300
Edison General Electric Company, 543
Edison Illuminating Company, 195
Edsel, 65, 198
Eisele, Donn F., 55
Eisenhower, Dwight D., 17, 45, 49
Electric locomotives, 284–285
Electric Vehicle Corporation, 94
Electro-Motive Corporation (EMC), 283,
    284
Electro-Motive Division (EMD), 284
Electromotive Division of General Motors
    (GM), 81
Electronic Counter Measures (ECM), 9
Elgin, H., 154
Elkins, Stephen B., 301
Elkins Act, 169, 322
Elkins Anti-Rebating law, 258
Ellet, Charles, Jr., 93, 120
Emergency Fleet Corporation, 307
Emergency Railroad Transportation Act, 170
Emergency Relief and Construction Act,
    170–171, 234
Emergency Relief Appropriation Act, 171
Emergency Transportation Act of 1933, 45,
    342
Emigrant's Guide to Oregon and California,
    102, 232
Empire Builder, 221
Endeavor, 58
Energy Policy and Conservation Act, 66
Enoch Train, 133
Enterprise, 6, 58, 166, 204
Environmental Protection Act (1975), 66
Equal Employment Opportunity
    Commission, 181
Ericsson, John, 306
Erie and the Pennsylvania Main Line, 92
Erie Canal, 112, 113, 114, 115, 132,
    171–173, 208, 566, 567
Erie Lackawanna Railroad (EL), 173–175

Erie Railroad, 42, 92, 156, 190, 230, 288, 532

Escalante, Silvestre de, 363, 566

Esch, John, 513

Esch-Cummins Act, 513

Escort/Lynx, 66

Espionage Act of 1917, 148

Evans, Oliver, 62, 165, 175, 566

Explorer, 45, 47

Express Cases, 175–176

Express companies, 229

Exxon, 394

Fageol and White, 96

Fairbanks-Morse, 284

Fairchild Aerial Camera Corporation, 10

Fairchild Aircraft Corporation, 10, 34, 313

Fairgrave, Phoebe, 162

Family Lines System, 177, 293

Fargo, William G., 177–178

Farmers' Anti-Automobile Association, 68

Featherstonehaugh, George W., 343

Federal aid, 186, 228

Federal Air Port Act, 327

Federal Airport Act, 183

Federal Aviation Act of 1958, 183–184

Federal Aviation Administration (FAA), 9, 15, 151, 184, 340, 400, 401. *See also* Federal Aviation Agency (FAA).

Federal Aviation Agency (FAA), 129, 184

Federal Control Act of 1918, 184, 420

Federal Emergency Railroad Transportation Act of 1933, 169

Federal Energy Regulatory Commission, 393

Federal Highway Acts, 36, 148, 184–185, 340

Federal Highway Administration (FHWA), 151, 185, 401

Federal Motor Vehicle Safety Regulations, 526

Federal Railroad Administration (FRA), 151

Federal Reserve System, 296

Federal Trade Commission (FTC), 349

Federal Trade Commission Act, 130

Federal-Aid Highway Acts, 178–182, 238

Federal-Aid Road Act of 1916, 183, 184, 213, 397

Fess, Simeon D., 185

Fess-Parker Bill, 185

Fetterman, William J., 87

Ficklin, Ben, 506

Field, Ben, 402

Fighting Insects from Airplanes, 10

Fillmore, Millard, 324

Financing highways, 186–188

Findlay, Francois, 86

Finley, James, 92

Firestone, Harvey, 507, 508

First Aero Squadron, 5

First Transcontinental Motor Convoy of 1919, 280

Fish, Stuyvesant, 229, 230

Fisher, Carl G., 68, 188–189, 279, 340

Fisher Body Works, 158

Fisk, James, Jr., 156, 189–191, 215, 216, 320, 532, 540

Fitch, John, 165, 191, 206, 566

Fitzpatrick, Thomas, 102, 117, 118, 368

Flagler, Henry M., 191

Flashing Rear End Device (FRED), 509

Flexi-Van, 251–252, 345

Flint, Charles R., 507

Floatplanes, 6

Florida East Coast Railway (FEC), 191–193

Florida Turnpike, 180

Floyd, John, 377

Flxible, 97, 99

Flying boat, 16

Focke, Heinrich, 235

Fokker, Anthony, 13

Food service on trains, 230–232

Forbes, John Murray, 193, 194

Forbes' Road, 193–194, 430, 566

Ford, Edsel B., 194–195

Ford, Henry, 62, 65, 154, 157, 189, 195–197, 247

Ford, Henry, II, 197–198

Ford, Wendell, 327

Ford Foundation, 195

Ford Motor Company, 62, 63, 64, 66, 67, 94, 129, 157, 195, 247

Forrestal class carriers, 9

Fort C. F. Smith, 87

Fort Laramie Treaty, 89

Fort Necessity, 89

Fort Phil Kearny, 87, 88

Fort Reno, 87

Forty Foot Equivalent, 137

Forty-Niners, 198

Four-engine land plane, 16

Frankfurter, Felix, 405

Franklin, Benjamin, 21, 85

Freedom, 53, 58

Freeways, 70

Freight canoes, 165

Freight diesel, 81

Freighting and teamsters, 198–204

Frémont, John Charles, 44, 210, 323, 368, 373

French, Daniel, 175, 204

Frequent flyer program, 139

Friction brake, 77

Friendship 7, 53
Frontier Airlines, 20, 292
Frost et al. v. Railroad Commission of the State of California, 204–205
Fruehauf, 251
Fulton, Robert, 93, 113, 165, 166, 191, 205–206, 208, 319, 566
Funeral trains, 399
Furuseth, Andrew, 90, 273

Gagarin, Yuri, 53
Gaillard, D. D., 385
Gaines, Edmund P., 414
Galaxy, 48
Galileo, 48
Gallatin, Albert, 130, 144, 171, 207, 228, 261, 265, 339, 378, 431, 527
Gallatin Report, 207–208, 567
Gamble, James, 506
Garces, Tomás, 209
Garfield, James A., 141, 395, 399
Garn, Senator Jake, 58
Gasoline motors, 63
Geddes, George, 395
Geddes, James, 172, 208
Gemini, 46, 54, 57, 83
General Agreement on Tariffs and Trade (GATT), 310
General aviation, 9–12
General Dynamics F-111 fighter-bomber, 9
General Electric, 283, 285
General Motors Company (GM), 38, 62, 63, 65, 66, 67, 94, 97, 98, 99, 157, 158, 224, 251, 271, 283, 333, 365, 427
Genesee Canal, 171
Geos, 48
Gibbons, Thomas, 208, 539
Gibbons v. Ogden, 208, 539, 567
Gila Trail, 106, 208–211
Gillette, James N., 107
Glenn, John, 53
Glenn Martin Company, 155, 302
Gliders, 4
Global airways, 76
Global Positioning System satellite, 50
Goddard, Robert, 50
Goerner, Fred, 161
Goethals, George Washington, 211–212, 385
Gold rush, 86, 198
Goldin, Daniel S., 58
Gompers, Samuel, 407
Good Roads, 213
Good Roads Movement, 212–213, 357
Goodrich, B. F., 507

Goodyear, Charles, 507, 508
Goodyear Tire and Rubber Company, 25, 26, 96, 188
Gordon, Donald, 110
Gordon, Louis, 161
Gordon, Richard F., 54, 56
Gorgas, William Crawford, 213–214, 384
Gould, George Jay, 141, 153, 156, 190, 214–215, 215–217, 230, 239, 240, 315, 316, 403, 532, 540
Grand Central Terminal, 344
Grand Trunk Railway, 110, 217, 315
Granger cases, 217–218, 330
Granger railroads, 122, 269, 314, 419
Grant, Ulysses S., 399, 402, 530
Grapes of Wrath, 71
Gray, Carl R., 422
Gray, John, 278
Great Bridge across the Charles River, 91
Great Lakes freighters, 218–220
Great Northern Pacific & Burlington Lines, 124
Great Northern Railroad, 95, 123, 147, 220–221, 239–240, 270, 285, 322, 347
Great Slave Lake Railroad, 110
Great Stone Bridge, 92
Great Wagon Road, 221–224
Greek George, 105
Greeley, Horace, 530
Grey, Zane, 325
Greyhound Corporation, 224
Grinnell, Minturn & Company, 133
Grissom, Gus, 53, 54
Ground controllers, 19
Grumman Corporation, 98
Guggenheim Fund for the Promotion of Aeronautics, 225–226
Guilford Transportation Industries, 42, 84, 299
Gulf, Mobile & Ohio Railroad (GM&O), 226, 249
Gunnison, John W., 103, 376
Gustavson, Charlie, 79
Gwinn, William M., 374

Haise, Fred W., Jr., 56
Hall, Floyd, 167
Halladie, Andrew, 510
Hamilton, Alexander, 39, 119, 143, 227–229, 277, 378
Hamilton and Standard, 82
Harding, Warren G., 34, 394, 398, 399
Harlan-Young party, 103
Harley-Davidson, 80
Harmar, Josiah, 143

Harnden, William, 3
Harnden & Company Express, 229
Harness, Nancy L., 163
Harriman, Edward Henry, 73, 215, 221,
    229–231, 240, 314, 321, 530
Harrington Amendment, 342
Harris, Moses "Black," 43
Harrison, Benjamin, 134, 398
Harrison, Charles T., 434
Harvey, Charles T., 511
Harvey, Frederick Henry, 231–232
Haskell, D. H., 3
Hastings, Lansford, 102, 103
Hastings Cutoff, 103, 232
Haupt, Herman, 84, 93, 296, 416
Hawley, Jesse, 171
Hay, John, 232, 384
Hay-Bunau-Varilla Treaty, 232, 244, 384
Hayden, Carl, 234
Hayden-Cartwright Act (1934), 27, 186,
    233–234
Hayes, Rutherford B., 398, 407
Hay-Herrán Convention, 232–233, 384
Hay-Pauncefote Treaty, 131, 233
Hays, Jack, 210
Hays Cutoff, 211
Hedström, Oscar, 79
Heineman, Ben W., 122, 270
Helicopters, 234–236
Helium, 25
Helms, Jesse, 327
Hendee, George, 79
Henderson, Tom, 79
Henderson, William, 79
Hendrick v. Maryland, 99
Hennepin Canal, 115, 236
Henry, John, 237
Henry, William, 166
Hepburn Act, 237–238, 258, 322, 348, 393
Hernando de Soto, 64, 129, 333
Herrán, Tomás, 232–233, 384
Hewitt, E. R., 519
Hidalgo, Francisco, 108
Highway building, 233–234
Highway Needs of the National Defense, 179
Highway Research Board (HRB), 238, 297
Highway Revenue Act, 180, 238
Highway Trust Fund, 181, 182, 186,
    238–239
Hi-Jolly, 105
Hill, James Jerome, 110, 147, 148, 220, 221,
    239–241, 314, 321, 347, 348
Hindenburg, 24, 25
Hines, Walker D., 421
Hinton, Otho, 339

Hitler, Adolf, 65
Hoch-Smith Resolution, 514
Hoey, John, 3
Hoffa, Jimmy, 255–256
Hoge, William M., 32
Holladay, Benjamin, 241, 505
Holladay Stage Lines, 177
Honda, 66, 80
Hoover, Herbert, 170, 398
Hopkins, Mark, 142, 241–242, 244, 268
Horses, 203
Howe, Elias, 91
Hub-and-spoke system, 19, 139
Hubble, Edwin, 48
Hudson, 62, 63, 64, 304
Hudson's Bay Company (HBC), 318
Huey P. Long Bridge, 93
Huff-Daland Manufacturing, 10
Hughes, Howard Robard, Jr., 242–243, 512
Hughes Rotary Drill Bit, 242
Hughes Tool Works, 243
Hulett crane, 219
Hull-Alfaro Treaty, 244
Humble Ohio, 394
Hunt, Wilson, 117
Huntington, Collis Potter, 142, 230,
    244–245, 268, 320, 372

Iacocca, Lee A., 63, 66, 198, 247
Icahn, Carl, 512
Ickes, Harold, 362
Illinois and Michigan Canal, 114, 247
Illinois Central Gulf Railway (ICG), 226,
    247–248
Illinois Central Railroad (IC), 37, 115, 121,
    230, 248–249, 251, 252, 266, 283, 398,
    408
Illinois Waterway, 249
Imperial, 64, 129
Import quotas, 67
The Improvement of Canal Navigation, 205
Indiana Toll Road, 180
Indianapolis Motor Speedway, 68, 188
Industrial Workers of the World (IWW),
    408
Ingersoll-Rand, 283
Inland waterways, 249
Inman Company, 353
Intelligence applications for satellites, 47
Inter-American Highway, 249
Interborough Rapid Transit Corporation
    (IRT), 512
Intercoastal Waterway, 261–263
Intercolonial (Prince Edward Island), 110
Intermodal freight, 249–254

Intermodal Surface Transportation Efficiency Act of 1991 (ISTEA), 254–255, 327
internal combustion engine, 62
International Air Transport Association (IATA), 17, 76
International & Great Northern, 214
International Astronautical Federation, 50
International Brotherhood of Teamsters (IBT), 255–257
International Civil Aviation Organization, 76
International Convention on Civil Aviation, 76
International Geophysical Year, 45, 46, 50
International Longshoremen's Association, 90
International railroads, 217
Interoceanic Canal Commission, 386
Interstate 70, 340
Interstate Commerce Act of 1887, 169, 218, 257
Interstate Commerce Commission (ICC), 80, 96, 122, 123, 129, 131, 142, 156, 169, 170, 174, 185, 224, 230, 237, 250, 251, 255, 257–260, 270, 301, 307, 315, 321, 322, 326, 342, 343, 347, 349, 386, 393, 406, 410, 420, 429, 509, 513, 514, 522, 526
Interstate Highway Act of 1956, 183, 340
Intracoastal Waterway, 113
Iowa Pool, 193
Iranian crisis, 66
Iron bridge builders, 93
Iron Highway, 253
Irving, Washington, 102

Jackson, Andrew, 40, 101, 130, 305, 339, 378, 538
Jacobs, John M., 86
James River & Kanawha Canal, 112, 113, 120, 265–266
James River Company, 265
Janney, Eli Hamilton, 266
Jay Cooke & Company, 141
Jefferies, John, 21
Jefferson, Thomas, 144, 227, 228, 277, 334, 335, 378, 431
Jemison, Mae C., 57
Jersey Central, 73
Jervis, John B., 413
Jet propulsion, 18
Jet-assisted takeoff (JATO), 226
Johnson, Andrew, 398
Johnson, Clarence "Kelley," 7
Johnson, Hiram, 107

Johnson, Jack, 68
Johnson, Lyndon Baines, 386, 387, 400
Jones, John Luther "Casey," 266–267
Jones, John S., 116, 276
Jones, Wesley, 311
Jones Act, 311
Joy, Henry B., 189
Juchereau, Louis, de St. Denis, 108
Judah, Theodore D., 244, 267–268, 372, 417
Jupiter, 6

Kaiser, Henry J., 242
Kaiser-Frazer, 64
Kane, Thomas Leiper, 325
Kansas Pacific, 216
Kearny, Stephen Watts, 210, 323
Keelboat, 165
Keeler, J. F., 359
Kelley, Hall J., 366, 368
Kelly Air Mail Act, 27, 81, 269
Kelvinator Refrigerator, 304
Kennedy, John F., 46, 56, 259, 400
Kennedy, Robert F., 333
Kentucky Turnpike, 180
Khrushchev, Nikita, 55
King, Samuel A., 23
King, Stephen, 71
Kino, Eusebio, 209
Kipling, Rudyard, 62
Klitenic, Nathan, 259, 422
Klitenic Plan, 269–271
Klondike goldfields, 124
Knights of Labor, 407
Knuckle coupler, 266
Knudsen, William S., 63, 78, 271–272
Komarov, Vladimir, 55
Kraft Foods, 38
Kuhler, Otto, 73, 272, 289

La Follette, Robert, 273
La Follette Seamen's Act, 273, 307
La Pierre, Charles, 50
Labor leader, 90
Lackawanna Railroad, 43, 174
Lake ships, 220
Lakota, 86, 87, 88, 89
LaMountain, John, 23
Lancaster Pike, 273–274, 566
Land Ordinance of 1786, 374
Landbridges, 137, 250
Lander, Frederick W., 118
Landsat, 48
Lane, Joseph, 328
Langley, Samuel Pierpont, 4, 5, 274
Lassen, Peter, 44

Latter-Day Saints. *See* Mormons
Law, John, 334
Lawson, Alfred, 13
Lawson, Harry, 77
Lemoyne, Jean-Baptiste, 334
Leach, James B., 211
League of American Wheelmen, 77, 213, 274–276, 433
League of Nations, 301
Leavenworth & Pike's Peak Express Company, 276–277
Ledyard, John, 278
Lee, Robert E., 416
Lee Highway, 277
Lehigh & Hudson River, 43
Lehigh Valley (LV), 42, 43
Lehman, William, 389
Leiper, Thomas, 277
Leland, Henry M., 62
Lenoir, Joseph E., 62
León, Alonso de, Jr., 108
Leonardo da Vinci, 234
Less-than-truckload freight (LTL), 524
Less-than-carload (LCL) freight, 249, 250, 521
Lesseps, Ferdinand de, 383
Lewis, Meriwether, 165, 278–279, 333
Lewis and Clark Trail, 118, 277–279
Leyden, Robert, 400
Liberty engine, 5–6
Liberty Ships, 308
Licensing, 208
Lilienthal, Otto, 4
Lincoln, Abraham, 64, 66, 129, 375, 398, 399, 402
Lincoln, Robert Todd, 402
Lincoln Highway, 188, 279–280
Lincoln Highway Association, 188, 279, 280
Lincoln Town Car, 67
Lindbergh, Charles A., 281–282
List, Friedrich, 39
Livingston, Robert, 166, 208, 319
Livingston, William A., 177
Livingston, Fargo & Company, 37, 177
Lockheed, 8, 14, 47, 302, 313, 314
Locks, canal, 112
Locomotives, 81, 283–289
   electric, 284–285
   steam, 286–288
Loewy, Raymond, 225, 289
Lomonosov, Mikhail, 234
Long Island Airways (LIA), 516
Long Island Railroad (LIRR), 253, 289–291, 390
Long Island Speedway, 68

Lorenzo, Frank, 20, 29, 84, 138, 139, 168, 291–292, 534
Louisa Railroad, 120
Louisiana Purchase, 277
Louisville & Nashville Railroad (L&N), 177, 292–293
Lovell, James A., 54, 55, 56, 57, 83
Lowe, Thaddeus S. C., 22, 23, 293–294
Lowe Observatory, 293
Lucius D. Clay Committee, 36
Luna I, 46

McAdam, John L., 295, 430, 516, 567
Macadamized roads and other surfaces, 295
McAdoo, William G., 39, 184, 296, 421, 533
McAuliffe, S. Christa, 58
McCallum, Daniel Craig, 296–297
McCallum, David C., 416, 417
McCallum Inflexible Arch Truss, 91
McClellan, George B., 328
McConway & Torley Corporation, 266
McCoy, Elijah, 297
McCoy, Joseph G., 126
McDivitt, James A., 54, 56
MacDonald, Thomas H., 297–298, 357
MacDonald, Thomas M., 95, 178
McDonnell F-4 Phantom, 8
Machinists Union, 28
McIntyre, Duncan, 110
Mack, Jack, 96, 519
McKay, Donald, 133
McKay, Thomas, 44
McKeen, William Riley, Jr., 283, 298
McKeen Motor Car Company, 298
McKinley, William, 398, 399
Mackintosh, Charles, 507
McLean Trucking Co. v. U.S., 298
MacMillan, Kirkpatrick, 77
McNamara, Robert, 198
McNary-Watres Air Mail Act, 28, 298
Macready, John, 10
McReynolds, James C., 312
Madison, James, 82, 132, 227, 228, 277, 378, 431, 567
Magellan, 48
Mail contractor, 107
Mail routes, 85
Maine Central Railroad (MEC), 299
Maine Turnpike, 180
Majors, Alexander, 276, 299–300
Malaria, 214
Mallet steam engines, 287, 530
Man in Space, 50
Manifest Destiny, 300–301, 324
Manly, Charles, 4, 274

Mann, James R., 301
Manned space travel, 50–58
Mann-Elkins Act of 1910, 258, 301–302, 348, 393
Mansfield, Josephine, 190
Marcy, Randolph B., 374
Marietta, 302
Mariner, 46, 48
Market Demand Act of 1932, 360
Marshall, John, 119, 147, 208, 265, 335
Martin, Glenn Luther, 7, 8, 302–304, 517
Masery, Alfred, 519
Mason, George W., 304
Massachusetts Institute of Technology, 155
Massanet, Damián, 108
Master Car Builders Association, 266
Masterson, Bat, 150
Maury, Matthew Fountaine, 134
Maxi-Stack car, 254
Maxwell, Lucien, 94, 128, 129, 157, 368
Maxwell-Briscoe Company, 94, 157
Mayflower, 26
Maysville Road Veto, 305, 339, 378, 432, 567
Mazda, 66
Means, James, 4
Mears, Otto, 305–306
Mechanics Union, 292
Mechanization and Modernization (M&M) Agreement, 90, 137
Melan, Joseph, 94
Mercer, Charles Fenton, 120
Merchant marine, 306–310
Merchant Marine Acts, 307, 308, 310–312
Merchant Ship Sales Act of 1946, 309
Mercury, 46, 52
Mercury, 64, 66, 129
Meridian Highway, 312
Miami and Erie Canal, 114, 312
Michaux, Pierre, 77
Michelin brothers, 77
Michigan Central, 37, 297
Michigan Public Utilities Commission et al. v. Duke Cartage Company, 204, 312–313
Middlesex Canal, 112, 113, 313, 566
Military Air Transport Service (MATS), 313–314, 517
Military Airlift Command (MAC), 314
Military aviation, 5–9
Military Railroad Act of 1862, 296, 416
Military Transportation Act of 1904, 116, 314
Miller, Arjay, 198
Miller Platform, 403
Milwaukee Road, 270, 285, 314–315
Minivans, 67

Mir, 57
Mississippi Central Railroad, 248
Mississippi River, 164
Missouri Compromise, 130, 374
Missouri Pacific Railroad (MoPAC), 214, 216, 316–317
Missouri-Kansas-Texas Railroad, 315–316
Mitchell, Edgar D., 56
Mitchell, William "Billy," 5, 6, 24, 302, 317–318
Mobile & Ohio, 226
Mohawk & Hudson Railroad (M&H), 343
Molson, John, 567
Monarch Sleeping Car Company, 403
Monon Route, 293
Monoplane fighter, 6
Monroe, James, 101, 228
Montalvo, Ordoñez de, 105
Montana Trail, 318–319
Monterey Bay, 106
Montgolfier, Etienne, 21
Montgolfier, Joseph Michel, 21
Moore, William, 213, 434
Morat, Alexander, 22
Morey, Samuel, 319–320
Morgan, John Pierpont, 94, 230, 315, 320–322, 354, 541
Morley, W. R., 150
Mormon Trail, 117, 118, 232, 322–326
Mormon War, 103
Mormons, 103, 322–326
Morris Canal, 114, 567
Morse, Samuel F. B., 73, 505
Morton, J. Sterling, 357
Morton, Levi P., 315
Motor Carrier Act of 1935, 169, 224, 256, 326–327, 515, 524
Motor Carrier Act of 1980, 260, 327, 328, 524
Motor Carrier Act of 1991, 254, 327–328
Motor Carrier Safety Bureau, 151, 185
Motor Trend, 67
Motorcycles, 77–80
Motoring clubs, 68
Motorized bicycle, 79
Mount Vernon Memorial Parkway, 116
Mule trains, 200
Mules, 203
Mullan, John, 329
Mullan Road, 328–330
Municipal Planning Organizations (MPOs), 255
Munn v. Illinois, 99, 218, 330–331, 341, 528
Murphy, Joseph, 201
Murphy's wagons, 201
Mustang, 64, 66, 198

Myers, Mary H., 23

N. L. & G. Griswold, 133
Nader, Ralph, 65, 333
Named highways, 279–280, 312, 338, 364, 371, 392
Nash, Charles, 63, 64, 304
Nash-Kelvinator, 304
Nast, Thomas, 190
Natchez Trace, 165, 333–336, 566
Natchez-Under-The-Hill, 165
National Academy of Engineering, 97
National Advisory Committee for Aeronautics (NACA), 14, 336
National Aeronautics and Space Administration (NASA), 18, 46, 48, 53, 336, 337
National Air Pilots Association, 12
National Air Races (1929), 163
National Airlines, 28
National Environmental Policy Act, 181
National Good Roads Association (NGRA), 213
National Good Roads League, 276
National Good Roads Train, 213
National Highway Commission, 26
National Highway Institute, 181
National Highway Research, 36
National Highway Safety Bureau, 151, 185
National Highway Traffic Safety Administration, 151
National Highways Association, 280
National Industrial Recovery Act of 1933 (NIRA), 171, 233–234, 337–338, 349, 360
National Labor Relations Act, 393
National Labor Relations Board, 28, 256, 405
National League for Good Roads, 276, 434
National Master Freight Agreement (NMFA), 256
National Old Trails Highway, 338
National Park Service, 27
National Rail Passenger Act of 1971, 338
National Railroad Passenger Corporation (NRPC), 40, 338, 405, 422
National Recovery Act, 28
National Recovery Administration (NRA), 45, 170, 326, 507
  trucking codes, 348–350
National Road, 144, 186, 207, 305, 338–340, 431, 527, 566
National Transcontinental, 110
National Transportation Safety Board (NTSB), 184, 340–341
National Weather Service, 24
Natural Gas Policy Act of 1978, 393

Nebbia v. New York, 341
Nelson, Knute, 273
Nemacolin's Trail, 89, 142, 565
Neuhart, David E., 341–342
New Haven Railroad, 84, 250, 251, 290, 320
New Orleans Conditions, 342–343
New Panama Canal Company, 232
New York Air, 138, 291
New York Barge Canal System, 173, 343
New York Central Securities Co. v. U.S., 343
New York Central System (NYC), 30, 37, 121, 157, 175, 215, 229, 250, 251, 252, 283, 285, 343–345, 387, 391, 540
New York City Quarantine Commission, 395
New York, Lake Erie & Western Railroad, 215
New York, New Haven and Hartford Railroad, 3, 387
New York Throughway, 180
New York Times, 217
New York Transportation Authority, 290
New York World, 217
Niagara Bridge, 93
Nichols, Ruth, 162
Nickel Plate, 43
Ninety-Nines, 163
Nissan (Datsun), 65–66
Nixon, Richard, 340, 400, 427
Niza, Marcos de, 209
NLRB v. Jones and Laughlin Steel Corporation, 405
Nobles, William H., 44
Nolan, Philip, 109
Noonan, Fred, 161
Norfolk & Western Railway (N&W), 175, 345–346
Norfolk Southern Railroad System, 43, 121, 136, 346
North American, 8, 9
North River of Clermont, 206
The North River Steamboat, 166
Northeast Rail Services Act of 1981, 136, 346, 423
Northern American Free Trade Agreement, 96
Northern Illinois Toll Highway, 180
Northern Pacific Railway (NP), 95, 123, 141, 175, 221, 270, 320, 321, 322, 346–347, 347, 372, 542–543
Northern Securities Company, 221, 231, 240, 322, 347
Northern Securities Company v. U.S., 270, 347–348
Northway, 63
Northwest Airlines, 17, 20, 348
Northwest Passage, 106
Norvell, Mrs. Lipscomb, 109

NRA, 326
NRA Trucking Codes, 348–350
NYC. *See* New York Central System.
Nyrop, Donald W., 348

Oakland, 63
Object lesson roads, 351
Ocean liners, 351–356
Ocean Mail Act, 310
Office of Public Road Inquiry (OPRI), 154, 356, 434
Office of Public Roads (OPR), 356–357
Office of Public Roads and Rural Engineering (OPRRE), 357
Office of Road Inquiry (ORI), 27, 213, 340, 351, 357–358, 434
Ogden, Aaron, 208
Ogden, Peter Skene, 101, 318
O'Hare Field, 17
Ohio and Erie Canal, 114, 358
Ohio Enabling Act of 1803, 431
Ohio State Roads Commission, 154
Ohio Turnpike, 180
Oil cup for locomotives, 297
Oil industry, 358–362
Oil Pollution Act of 1990, 362
Oklahoma Condition, 342
Old Spanish Trail, 103, 362–364, 566
Old Spanish Trail Highway, 364
Oldfield, Barney, 68
Olds, Ransom E., 365
Olds, Robert, 163
Oldsmobile, 62, 63, 64, 66, 94, 129, 365
Omnibus Reconciliation Act of 1981, 41, 366
Oñate, Juan de, 362
Orbiting Astronomical Observatories, 47
Order of Railway Conductors (ORC), 408–409
Oregon Trail, 117, 118, 366–369
Oregon Treaty, 278
Organization of Petroleum Exporting Countries (OPEC), 369–370
O'Sullivan, John L., 300
Otto, Nikolaus, 62
Overland Mail Company, 107, 505
Overland Route, 86
Overland Telegraph Company, 506
Overman, A. H., 78
Oxen, 202
Ozark Airlines, 513

Pacific Aero Products Company, 81
Pacific Great Eastern Railway (PGE), 75, 95
Pacific Highway, 371
Pacific Mail Steamship Company, 107, 371

Pacific Motor Transport, 251
Pacific Railroad Act of 1862, 140, 153, 267, 371–372, 417
Pacific Railroad Survey, 372–377
Pacific Telegraph Company, 506
Pacific Union Express Company, 377
Pacific Wagon Road Office, 377–379
Packard Motor Company, 7, 62, 63, 64, 189, 304
Page, Logan Waller, 27, 357, 379, 434
Paine, Thomas, 92
Palmer, Aaron H., 383
Palmer, William J., 150, 151
Pan American Airways (PAA), 16, 17, 20, 149, 379–380
Pan American Congress, 297
Pan American Highway, 179, 380–382
Panama Canal, 112, 212, 214, 233, 307, 382–386
Panama Canal Act of 1912, 386
Panama Canal Company, 233
Panama Railway, 232
Parcel post, 38
Parke, John G., 375
Parker, James S., 185
Parsons, Levi, 315
Pattie, James Ohio, 209–210
Pattman, Wright, 388
Patullo, Thomas "Duff," 30
Paul R. Tregurtha, 220
Paw Paw Tunnel, 120
Peck's Shipyard at Cleveland, 219
Pecqueur, Onésiphore, 62
Pedraja, René de la, 309
Peik v. Chicago & Northwestern Railroad Company, 218
Pell, Claiborne, 386–387
Pell Plan, 386–387
Pembina Carts, 201
Penn Central Railroad, 45, 135, 259
Penn Central Transportation Company (PC), 135, 387–388, 391
Pennsylvania Fiscal Agency, 140
Pennsylvania Main Line Canal, 114, 388
Pennsylvania Railroad (PRR), 3, 74, 112, 121, 141, 156, 174, 175, 214, 229, 250, 266, 285, 289, 290, 387, 390–391
Pennsylvania Society for the Promotion of Internal Improvements, 388
People's Express, 138, 291, 292
PepsiCo, 38
Pere Marquette Railroad, 170
Perlman, Alfred E., 345
Pershing, John, 5
Pescara, Pateras, 234

Philadelphia & Reading Railroad, 42, 73
Philadelphia Wagon Road, 392
Piccard, Jeannette, 24
Pierce, Franklin, 104, 324, 328
Pierce-Arrow, 62
Piggyback, 249
Pike's Peak Ocean-to-Ocean Highway, 392
Pinto, 65
Pioneer, 46, 47
Pipeline cases, 393
Pipelines, 392–394
Piper, William, 11
Piper Aircraft Corporation, 10, 11
Planetary science, 46
Plank roads, 394–395
Plant, Henry B., 3–4
Platt, Thomas C., 395–396, 532
Plumb, Glenn, 513
Plummer, Henry, 319
Plymouth, 64, 129
Pocock, George, 62
Pogie Bogie, 253
Poli, Robert, 400
Polk, James K., 131, 300
Pomeroy and Company Express, 177–178
Pontiac, 63, 64, 66, 129
Pony Express, 103, 116, 241, 396, 505–506
Pope, Albert A., 78
Pope, John, 375
Popular Sovereignty, 374
Porsche, Ferdinand, 65
Port and Tanker Safety Act of 1978, 362, 397
Porter, David Dixon, 105
Porter, Peter B., 171
Portolá, Juan, 106
Ports and Waterways Safety Act of 1972, 397
Post Office Appropriation Acts, 397
Potomac Company, 113, 119
Potomac River basin, 119
Potomac River Company, 398
Potter, I. B., 213
Powderly, Clarence V., 407
Powers, Francis Gary, 47
Praeger, Otto, 12
Pratt, Thomas, 91, 93
Pratt & Whitney, 14, 18
Presidential trains, 398–400
Prest-O-Lite Company, 188
Prince, Frederick H., 170
Proclamation of 1763, 222
Professional Air Traffic Controllers
    Organization (PATCO), 19, 400–401
*Progress and Feasibility of Toll Roads and Their
    Relationship to the Federal-Aid Program*, 179
Prudential, 38

Pruyn, John V. L., 343
Pryor, Nathaniel, 279
Public Roads Administration (PRA), 32, 95,
    185, 401, 520
Public transportation, 71
Public Works Administration, 6
Pullman, George Mortimer, 148, 399,
    402–403
Pullman Car Company, 81, 402, 409
Putnam, George P., 161

Quimby, Harriet, 5, 161

R. J. Hackett, 219
Racing, 68
Radial engines, 14
Radial-powered fighters, 7
Radio Corporation of America, 47, 48
Rail Diesel Cars (RDCs), 298
Rail Passenger Service Act of 1970, 40, 405,
    422
Railroad Labor Act, 28, 405
Railroad Operations Modular Processing
    System (ROMPS), 509
Railroad Retirement Act of 1934, 405
*Railroad Retirement Board v. Alton Railroad
    Company*, 405
Railroad Revitalization and Regulatory
    Reform Act of 1976, 135, 406, 423
Railroad Unification Act of 1931, 406–407
Railroad unions, 407–411
Railroad War Board, 411–412
Railroads
    before and during the Civil War, 412–417
    from Appomattox to deregulation,
        417–424
Rails and crossties, 424–425
Rail-Trailer, 251
Railway Accounting Officers Association, 45
Railway Express Agency (REA), 39, 252
Railway Labor Conference (RLC), 410
Railway Labor Executives Association
    (RLEA), 410
Railway Treasury Officers Association, 45
Rambler, 304
Ramón, Diego, 108
Ramsey, David, 166
Ramsey, James, 165
Randolph, Asa Philip, 410, 425–426
Ranger, 46
Reading Company, 42
Reading Railroad, 42, 93, 320
Reagan, Ronald, 19, 41, 49, 136, 401
Realco, 252
Red Cloud, 87, 88, 89

Reed-Bullwinkle Act of 1948, 259, 422, 426
Regional Rail Reorganization (3-R) Act of 1973, 135, 423, 426–427, 534
Registration, 70
Rehabilitation Act of 1973, 98
Reitsch, Hanna, 235
Relay, 48
Rentschler, Frederick, 82
Reo Car Company, 62, 94, 157, 365, 518
Reorganization Act of 1920, 6
Reorganization Act of 1939, 129
Report on Manufactures, 227
Reuther, Walter Philip, 427–428
Ribbicoff, Abraham, 333
Richmond & Petersburg Railroad, 60
Richmond-Petersburg Turnpike, 180
Rickenbacker, Eddie, 167
Ride, Sally Kristen, 57, 428–429
Riding clothes, 78
Rio Grande Railroad. *See* Denver & Rio Grande Western
Ripley, William Z., 185, 429, 514
Ripley Report, 421, 429
River travel. *See* Early river travel
The Road and Handbook, 275
Road maps, 69
Roads and highways
    colonial times to WWI, 429–437
    since WWI, 437–446
Robber barons, 215
Robert E. Lee, 248
Robert Stephenson & Company, 286
Roberts, Nathan S., 120, 172, 446
Robertson, Eugene, 22
Robertson, James, 334
Robinson v. Baldwin, 273, 307, 446–447
Rochester Telephone Corporation v. U.S., 447
Rock, Michael J., 400
Rock Island Lines, 270, 447–448
Rockefeller, John D., 191, 197, 214, 315, 359, 448–449
Roebling, John A., 93, 389
Rogers, Ted V., 349
Rolls-Royce Merlins, 7
Romney, George W., 63, 64, 304, 450
Roosa, Stuart A., 56
Roosevelt, Eleanor, 163
Roosevelt, Franklin Delano, 28, 30, 129, 155, 170, 233–234, 244, 259, 301, 308, 336, 337, 349, 398, 399
Roosevelt, Nicholas J., 450–451, 567
Roosevelt, Theodore, 4, 5, 212, 230, 233, 274, 322, 383, 385, 396, 398
Route 66, 451
Royal roads, 105

Rumsey, James, 191, 451–452, 566
Rush-Bagot Agreement of 1817, 218, 278
Rusk, Thomas J., 211, 374
Russell, William Hepburn, 116, 276, 396, 456–457, 545
Russell, Majors & Waddell Company, 116, 128, 276, 299, 396, 453–456, 506, 545
Ryan, Gene, 251, 252

Saavedra, Alvaro de, 383
SABRE (Semi-Automated Business Research Environment), 35, 139
Safety Appliance Act of 1893, 134, 266, 420, 459–460
Sagan, Carl, 58
Sage, Russell, 141, 153, 214, 216, 460
St. Clair, Arthur, 143
St. Lawrence Seaway, 460–463
St. Lawrence Seaway Development Corporation, 151
St. Louis & Southwestern Railroad (SL&SW), 214, 463
St. Louis Bridge, 93
St. Louis-San Francisco Railway, 95, 463–464
St. Mary's Falls Canal, 115
St. Paul & Pacific Railroad, 220
Saltillo, 107
Santa Anna, António López de, 109
Santa Fe Railway (AT&SF), 150, 230–232, 252, 284, 288, 372, 464–467
Santa Fe Trail, 467–470, 567
Santee Canal, 112, 470, 566
Saratoga, 6
SatCom, 48
Satellite Business Systems (SBS), 48
Satellites, 48
Saturn, 67
Sault Ste. Marie Canal, 115, 470
Saunders, Wallace, 267
Sawyers Wagon Road, 470–471
Scandinavian Airlines System (SAS), 20
Schechter Poultry Corp. v. U.S., 338
Schirra, Walter M., Jr., 53, 54, 55, 56
Schuyler, Philip, 171
Schuylkill River Bridge, 93
Schwabacher cases, 422, 471
Schweikart, Russell L., 56
Schwinn, Ignaz, 79
Scott, David R., 54, 56
Scott, Levi, 43, 44
Scott, Thomas A., 141, 471–472
Scott, Walter, 147
Seaboard Air Line Railroad (SAL), 60, 142, 177, 472

Seaboard Coast Line Industries, 177
Seaboard Coast Line Railroad, 60, 472
Seatrain, 137
Sebastián Vicaíno, 106
Second Bank of the United States, 82
Seibert, Leonard G., 402
Selden, George B., 62
Semi-Automated Business Research
    Environment (SABRE), 35, 139
Serra, Junípero, 106
Settles, Carolyn, 61
Seventy Years on the Frontier, 299
Seward, William H., 30
Shenandoah Valley, 537
Shepard, Alan B., 53, 56
Sheridan, Philip H., 88
Sherman, William T., 88
Sherman Antitrust Act of 1890, 73, 130, 347,
    472–473
Shipping Act of 1916, 307, 311, 473
Shipping Act of 1984, 310, 473–474
Shopping centers or malls, 70
Shreve, Henry Miller, 165, 166, 175, 204,
    474–475, 567
Sieberling, Charles A., 188–189
Siebert, T. Lawrence, 267
Siemans, Wilhelm, 285
Sigma, 53
Signal Corps, 5
Sikorsky, Igor, 16, 82, 236–237, 517
Silverton, Gladstone, and Northerly, 305
Silverton Northern, 305–306
Silverton Railroad, 305
Simmons, Vera, 24
Simpson, J. H., 103
Siskiyou Trail, 475–477
Six, Robert, 138
Sixteen Hour Act, 409
Sky science, 46
Skylab, 57
Slayton, Donald K., 53, 55, 57, 477–478
Slidell, W. H., 374
Sloan, Alfred P., Jr., 64, 158, 478
Sloanism, 129, 478
Smeed, E. C., 416
Smith, Adam, 39
Smith, Al, 398
Smith, Cyrus R., 34, 35, 139
Smith, Jedediah, 101, 117, 118, 363, 567
Smith, Joseph, 322
Smith, Junius, 352
Smith, S. S., 22
Smith, William Sooy, 93
Smith v. Cahoon, 204
Smithsonian Institution, 4

Smoky Hill Trail, 478–479
Smyth v. Ames, 331
Snook, Neta, 162
Social Security Act, 405
Socialist Party, 148
Society of Automobile Engineers (SAE), 63
Society of Friends (Quakers), 222
Soo Line, 315, 479
Sorenson, Charles, 271
South Carolina Canal and Railroad
    Company, 286
South Pass, 479–480
Southeastern Express Company, 39
Southern Express, 3–4, 4, 38, 39
Southern Pacific (SP), 151, 230, 245, 251,
    252, 253, 259, 267, 269, 298, 320, 372,
    480–482, 530
Southern Railroad, 342, 343, 346
Southern Railway System, 321, 482–483
Southwest Airlines, 20
Southwest Division of Varney Speed Lines,
    138
Soviet Union, 46
Soyuz, 55
Space Transportation System, 57
Spanish Trail, 483
Spaulding, Albert G., 78
Spencer, Hamilton, 532
Spine cars, 253
The Spirit of St. Louis, 282
Spitzer, Lyman, Jr., 48
Spoils system in American politics, 132
Spokane, Portland & Seattle Railroad, 95
Spooner Act of 1903, 483–484
Spotswood, Alexander, 221
Sprague, Frank, 510–511
Sproles et al. v. Binford, 484
Sputnik, 50, 52
Squatter Sovereignty, 374
Stagecoaches and other horse-drawn
    conveyances, 484–491, 567
Staggers Rail Act of 1980, 136, 250, 253,
    260, 423, 491–492
Standard Oil, 197, 359, 360, 362, 394
Standard Transportation Code (STC), 509
Stanford, Leland, 142, 268, 418, 492
Stanley, 62
Starrucca Viaduct, 92
State aid, 186
Statute labor, 492–493
Steam locomotives, 286–288
Steamboats, 175, 191, 204, 493–496
    in Civil War, 496–498
    racing of, 498
Steel, 76

Steel bridge, 93
Steinbeck, John, 71
Stemmatographer, 157
Stephenson et al. v. Binford, 498–499
Steven, Elisha, 102
Stevens, Isaac I., 328, 329, 376
Stevens, John, Jr., 499–500
Stevens, John F., 221, 286, 384, 412, 499, 566
Stevens, Robert L., 413, 424–425
Stevens, Thomas, 276
Stewardesses, 15.
Stillwell, Arthur Edward, 500
Stinson Trimotors, 149
Stockton, Robert F., 414
Stokes, Ned, 190
Stone, Roy, 27, 351, 357, 433, 500–501
Stone v. Wisconsin, 218
Strategic Air Command, 8
Strategic Defense Initiative (SDI), 49, 50
Strobridge, J. H., 142
Stuart, Robert, 117
Stubbs, Lewis, 280
Studebaker, 63–65, 128, 201, 304, 501–502
Stutz, Wilbur, 161
Sublette, Milton, 366–367
Submarines, 205
Suburbs, 70
Subways, 512
Super Bus, 99
Super C, 252
Supercoaches, 225
Supersonic Transport (SST), 9, 18
Surface Transportation Assistance Act of 1978, 502
Surface Transportation Assistance Act of 1982, 502–503
Survey of the Roads of the United States of America, 566
Surveyor, 46
Suspension bridges, 92, 93
Suzuki, 80
Swearengin, John E., 362
Sweigert, John L., Jr., 56
Symington, William, 165, 503
Syncom, 48

Trails, 424
Taft, William Howard, 341, 398
Talleyrand-Périgord, Charles Maurice de, 279
Tanana Valley Railroad, 34
Taney, Roger B., 119
Tank Vessel Act of 1936, 397
Taurus/Mercury Sable, 67

Taxes, 186
Taylor, Frederick, 195
Teamsters, 202, 204
Teamsters National Union, 255
Tejas Indians, 108
Telegraph, 73, 505–506
TeleRail Automated Information Network (TRAIN), 509
Telestar, 48
Television and Infrared Observation Satellite (TIROS), 47
Tennessee Gas, 393
Tereshkova, Valentina, 53
Texas & New Orleans Railway v. Brotherhood of Railway and Steamship Clerks, 405
Texas & Pacific (T&P), 153, 214, 216, 245, 316
Texas Eastern, 393
Texas International, 291
Théson, Jean, 62
Thomas, Philip E., 73
Thomas Viaduct, 92
Thompson, Jacob, 211, 377
Thomson, John E., 390
Thomson, Robert, 77
Thornton, Charles "Tex," 197
Thornton, Henry W., 110
Thunderbird, 64, 198
Thurman, J. Strom, 399
Tigrett, Isaac B. "Ike," 226
Tinkam, Abiel W., 328
Tire and rubber industry, 506–508
Tobin, Dan, 256
Toll bridges, 565
Toll roads, 187
Tompkins, Daniel B., 171
Tonquin, 117
TOFC. *See* Trailer-on-flatcar.
TOPICS (Traffic Operations Program to Increase Capacity and Safety), 181
Torpedo bombers, 7
Torpedoes, 205
Town, Ithiel, 91
Town Truss, 91
Toyota, 65
Track indicator, 157
Traffic lanes and signals, 69
Traffic Operations Program to Increase Capacity and Safety (TOPICS), 181
Trailer Train (TTX), 252
Trailer-on-flatcar (TOFC or piggyback), 249–253, 256, 521
Train control, 508–510
Trains in cities, 510–512
Trans Alaska Pipeline System (TAPS), 394

Trans West Airlines (TWA), 242–243
Trans World Airlines (TWA), 14, 17, 20, 242–243, 512–513
Transamerica, 252
Transbus, 98
Transcontinental highway, 188, 189
Transportation Act of 1920, 39, 131, 170, 185, 257, 258, 421, 513–514
Transportation Act of 1940, 45, 258, 421
Transportation Act of 1958, 156, 259, 422, 515
Treaty of Ghent, 130
Treaty of Greenville, 143, 218
Treaty of Versailles, 307
Trésaguet, Jean Pierre Marie, 295, 430, 516
Trestle, 91
Trimotor, 13
Trippe, Juan, 15, 16, 379–380, 516–518
Tropical diseases, 213
Trout, Bobbi, 162
Trucking, 204, 250, 518–527
Truffaut, Jules, 77
Truman, Harry, 155, 399, 408
Truman, Henry, 155
Trump, Donald, 140
Truss-and-arch bridges, 91
Tsolkovsky, Konstatine, 50
Turnpikes, 527
Twain, Mark, 325
Twentieth Century Limited train, 344–345
Twin Coach's Model 40, 96
Two Percent Fund, 431, 527
Two-wheeled carts, 201
TTX. *See* Trailer Train.
Tyler, John, 101
Typhoid fever, 214
Tyson and Brothers—United Theater Ticket Offices, Inc. v. Blanton, 527–528

Unidentified flying objects (UFOs), 56–57
Uniform Relocation Assistance and Real Property Acquisitions Policy Act, 529
Union Canal, 114
Union Car Company, 403
Union Pacific Railroad (UP), 96, 111, 118, 122, 123, 140, 153, 216, 230, 239–240, 283, 287–288, 321, 325, 341, 342, 347, 372, 418, 529–531
Union Pacific/Southern Pacific's Pacific Fruit Express Company, 74
United Aircraft Transportation Corporation, 82
United Airlines (UAL), 14, 20, 531–532
United Nations (UN), 76
United Parcel Service (UPS), 137, 252, 327

U.S. Army Corps of Engineers, 378
U.S. Army Signal Corps, 155
U.S. Coast Guard, 151, 397
U.S. Department of Agriculture, 10, 356
U.S. Department of Commerce, 129, 401
U.S. Department of the Army, 57, 148, 155
U.S. Department of the Navy, 148
U.S. Department of Transportation (DOT), 27, 33, 36, 80, 95, 97, 136, 151–152, 184, 185, 341, 401, 406, 511, 534
United States Express Company, 37, 38, 532–533
U.S. Filter, 299
U.S. Forest Service, 27, 178, 179
U.S. Highway 1, 85
U.S. House Committee on Merchant Marine and Fisheries, 310
U.S. Maritime Commission, 311
United States Motor Corporation, 94
U.S. Navy, 5
U.S. Postal Service, 3, 38, 40, 41, 99, 137
United States Railroad Administration (USRA), 184, 410, 421, 426, 533–534
United States Railway Association, 135–136, 534
U.S. Rubber Company, 507
U.S. Shipping Board, 307
U.S.-Soviet mission to Mars, 58
United States Steel Corporation, 76, 320
U.S. v. E.C. Knight Co., 331
U.S. Weather Bureau, 47
Universal Machine Language Equipment Register (UMLER), 509
Unmanned space probes, 45–50
Unsafe at Any Speed, 65, 333
Unsinkable Molly Brown, 54
Urban Mass Transit Act of 1964, 97
Urban Mass Transit Administration, 151
Urban Mass Transportation Act, 98
Urban Mass Transportation Administration, 97
USAir, 20, 534–535
Utah War, 325

V-8 engines, 66, 195
Valley Turnpike, 537
Van Allen, James, 45
Van Buren, Martin, 40, 132, 537–539
Van Horne, William C., 110, 111
Van Pool, 252
Van Rensselaer, Morris, 171
Van Rensselaer, Stephen, 171, 172, 343
Vanderbilt, Cornelius, 156, 190, 215, 216, 353, 403, 539–540
Vanderbilt, William H., 68, 407, 540–541, 545

Index

Vans, 71
Vermont Railway (VTR), 541–542
Verne, Jules, 50
Vertical omnirange (VOR), 183
VIA Rail Canada, Incorporated
Vidal, Eugene L., 11
Viking, 48
Villa, Franciso "Pancho," 5
Villard, Henry, 542–543
Virginia Central, 120
Virginian Railway, 288
Volkswagen, 65, 304
Von Braun, Werner, 53
Von Sauerbronn, Drais, 77
Vought-Sikorsky, 6
Voyager, 48

Wabash and Erie Canal, 43, 114, 214, 216, 545
Waddell, William Bradford, 276, 545
Wagner, Webster, 545–546
Wagner Drawing Room Car Company, 403
Wagner-Connery Act, 405
Wagner-Crosser Act, 405
Wagon Box Fight, 202
Wagon roads, 75
Waite, Morrison R., 330
Walker, Joseph, 101, 102
Wallace, Henry, 399
War Emergency Pipelines, Inc., 393
War Labor Board, 410
War Productions Board, 393
Ward, W. E., 94
Warren, Edward, 21
Warren Bridge Company, 119
Washington, George, 89, 119, 142, 194, 227
Washington Agreement, 342
Washington Disarmament Conference of 1922, 6
Washington's Road, 546
WASP bill, 163
Watered stock, 156, 215, 216
Watson, Elkanah, 171
Wayne, Henry C., 104, 105
Wayne, "Mad Anthony," 143
Weather satellites, 47
Webb, William, 133
Weber, John H., 101
Webster-Ashburton treaty, 278
Welland Canal, 567
Wells, Henry, 177, 546
Wells Fargo & Company, 3, 4, 37, 38, 39, 177, 319, 377, 547–549
Wells Fargo Express Company, 175
West, Benjamin, 205

West Virginia Central, 214
Westar, 48
Western Air Express, 15
Western Engineer, 166
Western Express, 177
Western Inland Lock Navigation Company, 171
Western Maryland, 214
Western Pacific Railroad (WP), 269, 549–550
Western Union, 217
Westinghouse, George, 550–551
Weston, William, 172
Weston-Mott, 63
Wheeling & Lake Erie, 214
Wheeling Bridge, 93
The Wheelman, 275
Whipple, Amiel, 375–376
Whipple, Squire, 93
Whiskey Rebellion, 143
White, Canvass, 172, 551
White, Edward H., 54, 55
White Brothers Trucks, 552
White Pass & Yukon Railroad, 552
White Star Line, 353–354
Whitman, Marcus, 367, 368
Whitney, Asa, 328, 373
Whitney, Silas, 277
Wickman, Carl E., 224
Wilderness Road, 552–554, 566
Wilkie, Wendell, 273, 296, 301, 307, 336, 398, 399, 533
Will Rogers Highway, 554–556
Willamette Valley, 74
Willard, Daniel, 74
Willys, John North, 64, 556
Willys-Overland, 63, 64, 128
Wilmot Proviso, 101
Wilson, Woodrow, 130, 184, 228, 258
Winona & St. Paul Railroad Company v. Blake, 218
Winton Motor Company, 62, 284, 518
Wise, John, 22
Wolf, Connie, 24
Wolff Packing Co. v. Court of Industrial Relations, 528
Wolfskill, William, 364
Women's Air Force Service Pilots (WASPs), 163
Women's Auxiliary Ferry Squadron (WAFS), 163
Women's Flying Training Detachment (WFTD), 163
Wood, Zachary Taylor, 125
Wooden bridges, 91

Wooden railways, 277
Woodruff, Theodore T., 556–557
Woodward, Absolam, 128
Workers' conditions on the rails, 134
Works Progress Administration (WPA), 32
Wortham, Louis J., 109
Wright, Benjamin, 120, 172, 265, 557
Wright, Orville, 4–5, 78, 144, 274, 557–558
Wright, Wilbur, 4–5, 78, 144, 274, 557–558
Wulfson, Jay, 541
Wyeth, Nathaniel, 366, 367

X-Planes, 559

Yamaha, 80
Yamamoto, Isoroku, 7
Yankee Clipper, 16

Yellow Coach, 96, 97
Yellow fever, 213–214
Yellowstone, 166
Yellowstone Trail Highway, 561
Yorktown, 6
Young, Brigham, 103, 299, 322, 323
Young, Ewing, 210
Young, John W., 54
Young, Robert E., 345
Yount, George, 364
Yugo, 65

Zahm, Albert F., 336
Zane, Ebenezer, 143, 144, 563
Zane's Trace, 144, 563
Zeppelins, 24
Zuñiga, Alvaro Manrique de, 107